A TOOL FOR TRAVELERS AND STUDENTS

Recent years have brought a tremendous upsurge of interest in everything Italian, including the country, its people, its music and art, its literature—and its *language*. Without question, Italian is one of the most beautiful and expressive languages in the world.

However, until now there has never been available in this country an Italian-English, English-Italian dictionary thoroughly designed to teach American students how the language is pronounced. The WORLD-WIDE ITALIAN DICTIONARY is the *first* to meet this need. The pronunciation is supplied for every one of the 18,000 Italian words here included. And a clear set of rules is provided for pronouncing any word in the language just from seeing it spelled.

Included in both languages are many scientific and general words of recent origin that have never appeared in any Italian-English dictionary. Completely up-to-date, this guide contains abundant translations of idioms, and when entry words have two or more distinct meanings, subject labels (in parentheses) guide the user to the particular translation that fits the meaning.

Asterisks identify irregular Italian verbs, for which the complete conjugations are listed at the front of the book. Hundreds of the more common personal names in both languages are conveniently assembled and translated in separate lists. A conversational guide at the end of the book, with six illustrated pages of traffic information (including road signs), and sections of practical and statistical information (including conversion tables), will prove invaluable to student and traveler alike.

In addition to all of the extras, this dictionary has all the usual features of a good foreign dictionary, including gender identification. Look through it thoroughly and learn of its riches—only then can you get all the benefits it is capable of providing.

WORLD-WIDE

DICTIONARY

ITALIAN

Italian-English *English-Italian*

(AMERICAN ENGLISH)

Compiled by VITTORE E. BOCCHETTA
Former Professor of Humanities, Verona, Italy
Former Lecturer in Italian, University of Chicago
Candidate for Ph.D., University of Chicago

with a

TRAVELER'S CONVERSATION GUIDE

Containing hundreds of expressions and items of information useful to tourists, students, and businessmen

FAWCETT PREMIER • NEW YORK

EDITORS
Richard J. Wiezell, M.A.
Jean Rich, M.S.

A Fawcett Premier Book
Published by Ballantine Books

Library of Congress Catalog Card Number: 65-12915

ISBN 0-449-30036-6

This edition published by arrangement with Follett Publishing Company

Manufactured in the United States of America

First Fawcett Premier Edition: June 1967
First Ballantine Books Edition: January 1984
Second Printing: August 1986

A DICTIONARY OF FIRSTS

Recent years have brought a tremendous upsurge of interest in everything Italian, including the country, its people, its music and art, its literature—and its LANGUAGE. A growing number of Americans proudly claim Italian as their favorite foreign tongue. And with good reason! For it is, without question, one of the most beautiful and expressive languages in the world.

However, the means of acquiring a good speaking acquaintance with this language have not kept pace with the increasing demand. Outside the universities there have been few opportunities for oral instruction, and until now there has never been available in this country an Italian-English, English-Italian dictionary thoroughly designed to teach American students how the language is pronounced. The FOLLETT WORLD-WIDE ITALIAN DICTIONARY is the *first* to meet this need. The pronunciation is supplied for every one of the 18,000 Italian words here included. And a clear set of rules is provided for pronouncing any word in the language just from seeing it spelled.

But pronunciation is only one of the *firsts* which users of this work will enjoy. Included in both languages are many scientific and general words of recent origin that have never before appeared in any Italian-English dictionary. The knowledge of Italian here conveyed is completely up to date.

When entry words have two or more distinct meanings, subject labels (in parentheses) guide the user to the particular translation that fits the meaning. This feature guarantees the appropriate word for every occasion, thereby avoiding the embarrassment that comes from using the wrong word to translate a given meaning.

All entries of Italian irregular verbs are identified by means of asterisks. These asterisks signify that complete conjugations for such verbs are supplied in alphabetical order in the Italian grammar section on pages 25 to 33.

Hundreds of the more common personal names in both languages are conveniently assembled and translated in separate lists on pages 230 to 236 and 436 to 441.

Translations and pronunciations are provided at the end of the book for hundreds of conversational questions and expressions in both English and Italian. This section will prove useful to travelers and students alike.

For motorists and others who may be interested, five pages of traffic information are included, much of it in the form of pictures for quick recognition.

In addition to these *firsts*, this dictionary has all the usual features common to other good foreign language dictionaries, such as gender indication for all noun entries on the Italian side of the work. On the English side, all noun equivalents in Italian are also indicated as to gender, with the exception of masculine nouns ending in **-o** and feminine nouns ending in **-a, -sione, -tione,** and **-zione.**

The vocabulary includes just about every word in both languages that American users will have need of.

Especially helpful are the translations of abundant idioms, each entered under its appropriate key word.

The last three pages contain the sort of special statistical information that travelers sooner or later feel an interest in but seldom find conveniently at hand when wanted.

The compiler and publisher of this dictionary have spared no pains or expense in their effort to make it the best of its kind. It is hoped, therefore, that purchasers will begin their use of it by thoroughly acquainting themselves with its many features. Only by so doing will they get from it all the benefits that it is capable of providing.

THE PUBLISHER

CONTENTS

Italian-English **Page**

English-Italian **Page**

PRONUNCIATION KEY

Symbols	*English Sounds*
	Vowels
â	*a*rm, f*a*ther
ā	b*a*by, g*a*te
e	b*e*t, m*e*n
ē	b*e*, h*e*
ō	g*o*, sp*o*ke
ô	g*o*ne, n*o*rth
ū	bl*ue*, t*oo*
	Consonants
b	*b*a*b*y, tu*b*
ch	*ch*ild, cat*ch*
d	*d*a*d*, su*dd*en
f	*f*at, a*f*ter
g	*g*ate, ba*g*
j	*j*et, a*j*ar
k	*k*itten, ta*k*e
l	*l*ate, *l*i*l*y
m	*m*et, da*m*p
n	*n*ot, se*n*d
p	*p*at, sto*p*
r	ve*r*y (with a trill)
s	*s*at, la*s*t
sh	*sh*op, di*sh*
t	*t*ell, *t*as*t*e
v	*v*ery, gi*v*e
w	*w*e, q*u*ack
y	*y*es, *y*ou
z	*z*ero, ro*s*e

GUIDE TO ITALIAN PRONUNCIATION

Beginning students of Italian will find the pronunciations in this dictionary very helpful in learning to speak the language. Not only are all the main entries accurately pronounced throughout, but complete Italian pronunciations are provided for all the various inflected endings of regular verbs and for hundreds of conversational phrases. With such help readily available at the flip of a page, acquiring a good speaking acquaintance with this new language is almost as simple as learning to pronounce the unfamiliar words we sometimes encounter in our native language.

But it won't always be convenient to consult a FOLLETT WORLD-WIDE ITALIAN DICTIONARY every time one wants the pronunciation of an Italian word. Sooner or later the serious student will need a sufficient mastery of the language to enable him to pronounce any word from seeing it spelled. Fortunately, such a mastery is not hard to acquire.

Italian is one of the easiest new languages for Americans to learn to speak. It has only 21 letters, one of which is always silent. It has only 26 sounds, all but one of which are completely familiar to English-speaking students. But like American English, the language is pronounced somewhat differently in different parts of the country. In most parts of Italy it is correct to give the letters *e* and *o* only one sound apiece, regardless of stress or position. But in Central Italy (which includes Florence and Rome) each of these letters has two different sounds, depending, first, on whether it is stressed or unstressed and, second, on where it occurs in the word. Because of these regional variations, it is impossible to provide pronunciations or rules that are wholly accurate for such widely scattered places as Milan, Venice, Florence, Rome, Naples and Palermo.

Nevertheless, American visitors to Italy will have little difficulty with regional differences once they become sufficiently familiar with the pronunciations and guide rules provided in this dictionary.

The first rule of good Italian pronunciation is to utter every syllable of every word clearly and distinctly. More use is made of the lips, tongue, and lower jaw than is customary in English speech. Vowel sounds, even when they are unstressed, are always pure and full-rounded—never slurred. Consonants (except *h*) are always plainly audible—never dropped (as the *t* in lis*t*en and the *b* in clim*b*).

Stress and Accent

There are no rules that will enable anyone unfamiliar with the language to tell where the stress falls in Italian words. It usually falls on the next-to-last syllable. *Examples*: **anno** (ân'nō), **madre** (mâ'drā), **economia** (ā·kō·nō·mē'â), **esitare** (ā·zē·tâ'rā). But in many words the stress falls on other syllables. *Examples*: **edile** (e'dē·lā), **piccolo** (pēk'kō·lō), **perchè** (pār·kā').

In the inflection of verbs the stress often changes position from form to form. *Examples*: **esitare** (ā·zē·tâ'rā), **esito** (e'zē·tō), **esitano** (e'zē·tâ·nō), **esiterò** (ā·zē·tā·rō').

When the stress falls on the last vowel of a word, the vowel is written or printed with an accent mark, thus: **ò**. This accent is part of the spelling and must always appear in writing and printing. *Examples*: **più** (pyū) **perchè** (pār·kā'), **civiltà** (chē·vēl·tâ').

Some one-syllable words are written with accent marks to distinguish them from words similar in spelling and sound but different in meaning. *Examples*: **di** (meaning *of*) and **dì** (meaning *day*), **se** (meaning *if*) and **sè** (meaning *oneself*).

The Italian Alphabet and Its Sounds

Asterisks (*) refer to the explanatory notes on the following pages.

Italian Letter	*English Sound*	*Phonetic Symbol*	*Italian Word*	*Phonetic Respelling*
a	father	â	**capra**	kâ'prâ
b	baby	b	**basta**	bâ'stâ
c*	car	k	**cava**	kâ'vâ
	child	ch	**cine**	chē'nā
d	dim	d	**donna**	dōn'nâ
e*	they	ā	**mente**	mān'tā
	bet	e	**fegato**	fe'gâ·tō
f	fat	f	**fede**	fā'dā
g*	gate	g	**gamba**	gâm'bâ
	gentle	j	**gente**	jān'tā
h	(silent)	(none)	**hanno**	ân'nō
i*	police	ē	**di**	dē
	yes	y	**dieci**	dyā'chē
l	lap	l	**lana**	lâ'nâ
m	met	m	**meno**	mā'nō
n	not	n	**nano**	nâ'nō
o*	spoken	ō	**piccolo**	pēk'kō·lō
	gone	ô	**gomito**	gô'mē·tō
p	pat	p	**pasta**	pâ'stâ
q	quack	k	**quando**	kwân'dō
r*	(see below)	r	**caro**	kâ'rō
s*	sat	s	**sala**	sâ'lâ
	rose	z	**rosa**	rō'zâ
t	taste	t	**tardi**	târ'dē
u*	too	ū	**uno**	ū'nō
	quit	w	**uomo**	wō'mō
v	valve	v	**vivo**	vē'vō
z, zz*	lets	ts	**razza**	râ'tsâ
	adz	dz	**mezzo**	mā'dzō

Combined Letters

ch	chorus	k	**chiaro**	kyâ'rō
ci*	chart	ch	**ciao**	châ'ō
	cheese	chē	**ciclo**	chē'klō
gh	ghost	g	**ghiro**	gē'rō
gi*	digest	j	**giorno**	jōr'nō
	gee	jē	**giglio**	jē'lyō
gli*	million	ly	**foglia**	fô'lyâ
	will ye	lyē	**egli**	ā'lyē
gn	onion	ny	**bagno**	bâ'nyō
qu	quack	kw	**questo**	kwā'stō
sc*	shine	sh	**scena**	shā'nâ
	scar	sk	**scusa**	skū'zâ
sch	scheme	sk	**schema**	skā'mâ
sci*	shop	sh	**scialle**	shâl'lā
	she	shē	**sci**	shē

**Explanation of the Sounds*

c has the sound of *k* when it is followed by the letters a, o, u, h, l, or r. *Examples*: **caro** (kâ'rō), **corpo** (kōr'pō), **cuore** (kwō'rā), **che** (kā), **classe** (klâs'sā), **credo** (krā'dō).

has the sound of *ch* when it is followed by e or i. *Examples*: **cena** (chā'nâ), **cine** (chē'nā), **cielo** (chā'lō), **ciao** (châ'ō). (See the two sounds of **ci** below.)

e has the sound of *e* in b*e*t when it occurs with stress:

1) in the third-from-last (or fourth-from-last) syllable of a word. *Examples*: **iberico** (ē·be'rē·kō), **medico** (me'dē·kō).
2) in the next-to-last syllable when the last syllable is spelled with two vowels. *Examples*: **sedia** (se'dyâ), **secchio** (sek'kyō).

has the sound of *ey* in *they* (*a* in b*a*by) in all other situations, both stressed and unstressed. *Examples*: **cine** (chē'nā), **quel** (kwāl), **temere** (tā·mā'rā), **genovese** (jā·nō·vā'zā), **gentilmente** (jān·tēl·mān'tā).

g has the sound of *g* in *g*ate when followed by a, o, u, h, l, or r. *Examples*: **gamba** (gâm'bâ), **gola** (gō'lâ), **gusto** (gū'stō), **ghiro** (gē'rō), **globo** (glō'bō), **grande** (grân'dā). *Exception*: **gl** has the sound of *ly* in certain words. See below.

has the sound of *g* in *g*entle (*j* in *j*et) when followed by e or i. *Examples*: **gente** (jān'tā), **gigante** (jē·gân'tā), **giallo** (jâl'lō). See the two sounds of **gi** below.

i has the sound of *i* in police (*e* in b*e*) when it is the only vowel in a syllable or follows another vowel in the same syllable. *Examples*: **di** (dē), **Dio** (dē'ō), **idea** (ē·dā'â), **difficile** (dēf·fē'chē·lā), **eroico** (ā·rô'ē·kō), **eroicamente** (ā·rōē·kâ·mān'tā).

has the sound of *y* in *y*et when it is unstressed and is followed by another vowel. *Examples*: **dieci** (dyā'chē), **più** (pyū), **bestia** (be'styâ). *Exception*: **i** is silent before a, e, o, and u when it follows c or g: **ciao** (châ'ō), **giocare** (jō·kâ'rā).

o has the sound of *o* in g*o*ne when it occurs with stress:

1) in the third-from-last (or fourth-from-last) syllable of a word. *Examples*: **povero** (pô'vā·rō), **geografo** (jā·ô'grâ·fō).
2) in the next-to-last syllable when the last syllable is spelled with two vowels. *Examples*: **goccia** (gô'châ), **gloria** (glô'ryâ).

has the sound of *o* in g*o* in all other situations, both stressed and unstressed. *Examples*: **piccolo** (pēk'kō·lō), **nove** (nō'vā), **orbo** (ōr'bō), **opporre** (ōp·pōr'rā).

r is unlike any sound natural to English. It is produced by rapidly vibrating the tip of the tongue against the base of the upper front teeth. *Examples*: **caro** (kâ'rō), **rosa** (rō'zâ), **tardi** (târ'dē).

s has the sound *s* in ro*s*e (*z* in *z*ero):

1) between vowels. *Examples*: **rosa** (rō'zâ), **contesa** (kōn·tā'zâ).
2) before b, d, g, l, m, n, r, or v. *Examples*: **sguardo** (zgwâr'dō), **slavo** (zlâ'vō), **mutismo** (mū·tē'zmō), **svolta** (zvōl'tâ).

has the sound *s* in *s*at in all other situations; *Examples*: **sano** (sâ'nō), **scala** (skâ'lâ), **scansia** (skân·sē'â), **stesso** (stās'sō), **gres** (grās).

u has the sound of *oo* in t*oo* when it is the only vowel sound in a syllable or follows another vowel in the same syllable. *Examples*: **uno** (ū'nō), **tutto** (tūt'tō), **più** (pyū), **rauco** (râ'ū·kō), **raucedine** (râū·che'dē·nā).

has the sound of *w* in *w*ay when followed by a vowel in the same syllable. *Examples*: **nuovo** (nwō'vō), **guerra** (gwār'râ), **quel** (kwāl), **cuore** (kwō'rā).

z, zz usually has the sound of *dz* in *adz*:

1) at the start of words. *Examples*: **zampa** (dzâm'pâ), **zio** (dzē'ō), **zuppa** (dzūp'pâ).
2) in all verbs ending in **-izzare,** including all their inflected forms: **-izzante,**

-izzato, etc. *Examples*: **scandalizzare** (skân·dâ·lē·dzâ'rā), **fertilizzante** (fār·tē·lē·dzân'tā).

usually has the sound of *ts* in le*ts* when it occurs elsewhere. *Examples*: **azionare** (â·tsyō·nâ'rā), **ambizioso** (âm·bē·tsyō'zō), **altezza** (âl·tā'tsâ), **alleanza** (âl·lā·ân'-tsâ).

Exceptions: there are too many exceptions, however, to account for them all. Certain words may be pronounced either *dz* or *ts* within the same region.

ci has the sound of *ch* in *ch*art when it is followed by a, e, o, or u. *Examples*: **ciao** (châ'ō), **provincia** (prō·vēn'châ), **ciò** (chō), **ciuco** (chū'kō), **sufficiente** (sūf·fē·chān'tā).

has the sound of *chee* in *chee*se when it is not followed in the same syllable by another vowel. *Examples*: **ci** (chē), **dieci** (dyā'chē), **ciclo** (chē'klō).

gi has the sound of *g* in gentle (*j* in *j*ug) when it is followed in the same syllable by a, o, or u. *Examples*: **già** (jâ), **grigio** (grē'jō), **giubba** (jūb'bâ).

has the same sound of *gee* (*jee* in *jee*p) when it is not followed in the same syllable by another vowel. *Examples*: **dogi** (dō'jē), **geologia** (jā·ō·lō·jē'â).

gl has the sound of *gl* in *gl*ad when followed by a, e, o, or u. *Examples*: **glaciale** (glâ·châ'lā), **gleba** (glā'bâ), **globo** (glō'bō).

gli has the sound of *lli* in mi*lli*on when it is followed in the same syllable by another vowel (a, e, o, u). *Examples*: **foglia** (fô'lyâ), **biglietto** (bē·lyāt'tō), **figlio** (fē'lyō).

has the sound of *l ye* in wi*ll ye* when it occurs at the end of a word. *Examples*: **gli** (lyē), **egli** (ā'lyē).

has the sound of *glee* when it is followed in the same word by a consonant. *Examples*: **glicogeno** (glē·kô'jā·nō), **negligenza** (nā·glē·jān'tsâ).

sc has the sound of *sh* in *sh*ine before e or i. *Examples*: **scena** (shā'nâ), **scimmia** (shēm'myâ).

has the sound of *sc* in *sc*ar in all other cases. *Examples*: **scusa** (skū'zâ), **schema** (skā'mâ), **scritto** (skrēt'tō).

sci has the sound of *sh* in *sh*op when it is followed by another vowel. *Examples*: **scialle** (shâl'lā), **scienza** (shān'tsâ), **sciocco** (shōk'kō), **sciupare** (shū·pâ'rā).

has the sound of *she* when it is not followed in the same syllable by another vowel. *Examples*: **sci** (shē), **scibile** (shē'bē·lā), **trascinare** (trâ·shē·nâ'rā).

Diphthongs

When two vowels occur together in words, they are usually pronounced as one syllable. Such one-syllable combinations are known as *diphthongs*. Some well-known English examples are *oi* in *boil* and *ou* in *house*. Diphthongs are frequent occurrences in Italian, and it is therefore important to know how to pronounce them.

The five vowels occur in just about every possible combination. But the more common diphthongs combine a *strong* vowel with a *weak* one. Strong vowels (**a, e,** and **o**) are so called because they usually *sound* stronger (louder) than weak vowels (**i** and **u**) when combined. *Examples:* **mai** (mâ'ē), **causa** (kâ'ū·zâ), **poi** (pō'ē), **Europa** (āū·rō'pâ), **piace** (pyâ'chā), **dieci** (dyā'chē), **Pasqua** (pâ'skwâ), **uomo** (wō'mō).

When the two weak vowels (**i, u**) combine to form a diphthong, it is usually the **u** that is stressed. *Examples:* **piuma** (pyū'mâ), **più** (pyū). Where the **i** is stressed, **u** has the sound of w. *Examples:* **guida** (gwē'dâ), **qui** (kwē).

The combination of two strong vowels (**a, e, o**) results, not in a diphthong, but in two syllables. *Examples:* **paese** (pâ·ā'zā), **poeta** (pō·ā'tâ), **ciaō** (châ'ō), **boa** (bō'â), **eroe** (ā·rō'ā), **poeticamente** (pō·ā·tē·kâ·mān'tā).

Two syllables also result when **i** and **u** carry the stress in combination with **a, e,** or **o**. *Examples:* **zio** (dzē'ō), **siano** (sē'â·nō), **Aida** (â·ē'dâ) **eroina** (ā·rō·ē'nâ), **due** (dū'ā), **tuo** (tū'ō).

Syllable Division

Both in speaking and writing, Italian words divide into syllables according to the following simple rules:

1) a single consonant always belongs with the vowel which follows it. *Examples:* **rosa** (rō'zâ), **capitolo** (kâ·pē'tō·lō).

2) When **l, m, n,** and **r** are followed by other consonants, these four letters belong with the preceding vowels. *Examples:* **alto** (âl'tō), **lento** (lān'tō), **corpo** (kōr'pō).

3) All double consonants are separated. *Examples*: **accollare** (âk·kōl·lâ'rā), **passato** (pâs·sâ'tō), **correre** (kôr'rā·rā).

4) When **s** is followed by a consonant (or consonants) other than s, it is never separated from what follows. *Examples:* **basta** (bâ'stâ), **questo** (kwā'stō), **destro** (dā'strō), **lasciare** (lâ·shâ'rā).

5) Any consonant followed by **l** or **r** belongs in the syllable that follows it. *Examples:* **ciclo** (chē'klō), **madre** (mâ'drā).

A BRIEF GUIDE TO ITALIAN GRAMMAR

GENDER OF NOUNS AND ADJECTIVES

1 The Noun

Nouns in Italian are either masculine or feminine, the gender having been determined by custom and usage. Those ending in **-o** are usually masculine, and those ending in **-a, -sione, -tione,** and **-zione** are usually feminine.

Examples:

il libro the book
la coperta the cover
la tensione the tension
la questione the question
la rivoluzione the revolution

Nouns referring to people usually have a masculine and a feminine form, often contrary to English. Masculine nouns ending in **-o** customarily change the **-o** to **-a** for the feminine form. Those ending in **-e** usually change the **-e** to **-a**; others have no special feminine form, the difference being shown by the feminine article. Some change **-ore** to **-oressa** or **-rice.** Those masculine nouns ending in **-a** usually have no special form for the feminine, the difference being shown by the gender of the article; a few change the **-a** to **-essa.**

Examples:

ladro male thief — **ladra** woman thief
signore gentleman — **signora** lady
il cantante the male singer — **la cantante** the female singer
professore male professor — **professoressa** lady professor
pittore male painter — **pittrice** woman painter
il socialista the man socialist — **la socialista** the woman socialist
poeta male poet — **poetessa** woman poet

As in English, some nouns are completely different in the feminine form.

Examples:

uomo man — **donna** woman
marito husband — **moglie** wife
genero son-in-law — **nuora** daughter-in-law
fratello brother — **sorella** sister

2 The Adjective

Contrary to English usage, in Italian the adjective always takes the gender of the noun it modifies. Masculine adjectives that end in **-o** change the **-o** to **-a** for the feminine form; masculine adjectives that end in **-e** are unchanged in the feminine.

Examples:

lo studente serioso	**la studentessa seriosa**
l'uomo gentile	**la donna gentile**

NUMBER OF NOUNS AND ADJECTIVES

1 The Noun

Masculine singular forms ending in **-o** and **-a** change the **-o** or **-a** to **-i** to form the plural.

Examples:

ragazzo boy	**ragazzi** boys
soldato soldier	**soldati** soldiers
artista male artist	**artisti** male artists

Feminine singular forms ending in **-a** change the **-a** to **-e** to form the plural.

Examples:

donna woman	**donne** women
ragazza girl	**ragazze** girls
artista woman artist	**artiste** woman artists

Masculine and feminine singular forms ending in **-e** change the **-e** to **-i** to form the plural.

Examples:

il cantante the male singer	**i cantanti** the male singers
la cantante the woman singer	**le cantanti** the woman singers
l'origine the origin	**le origini** the origins
il pittore the male painter	**i pittori** the male painters
la pittrice the woman painter	**le pittrici** the woman painters

Masculine and feminine singular forms of one syllable, those in which the last vowel is accented, and those ending in **-i**, do not change in the plural.

Examples:

il re the king	**i re** the kings
la virtù the virtue	**le virtù** the virtues
la civiltà the civilization	**le civiltà** the civilizations
l'analisi the analysis	**le analisi** the analyses

Feminine singular forms that end in **-cia** and **-gia** preceded by a consonant, and in which the **i** is not stressed, change **-cia** and **-gia** to **-ce** and **-ge** respectively. Otherwise, the general rule of change from **-a** to **-e** applies.

Examples:

guancia cheek	**guance** cheeks
mancia tip	**mance** tips
farmacia drug store	**farmacie** drug stores
valigia suitcase	**valigie** suitcases
camicia shirt	**camicie** shirts

Masculine and feminine singular forms ending in **-co, -go, -ca,** and **-ga** generally change to **-chi, -ghi, -che,** and **-ghe,** inserting the **h** to maintain the hard sound of **c** and **g.** There are some common words which are exceptions, however.

Examples:

tacco heel	**tacchi** heels
lago lake	**laghi** lakes
monaca nun	**monache** nuns
spiga ear of corn	**spighe** ears of corn
amico friend	**amici** friends
greco Greek	**greci** Greeks

As in English, in Italian some plural forms are entirely different.

Examples:

bue ox	**buoi** oxen
uomo man	**uomini** men
dio god	**dei** gods

Some masculine singular forms become feminine in the plural by changing **-o** to **-a.** Such nouns often have a regular plural which has a figurative meaning.

Examples:

l'uovo the egg	**le uova** the eggs
il dito the finger	**le dita** the fingers
il braccio the arm	**le braccia** the arms (human)
	i bracci the arms (of the sea)

2 The Adjective

Masculine singular forms ending in **-o** change **-o** to **-i** to form the plural.

Examples:

il libro giallo the yellow book	**i libri gialli** the yellow books
il cappello rosso the red hat	**i cappelli rossi** the red hats

Feminine singular forms ending in **-a** change **-a** to **-e** to form the plural.

Example:

la camicia rossa the red shirt	**le camicie rosse** the red shirts

Masculine and feminine singular forms ending in **-e** change the **-e** to **-i** to form the plural.

Examples:

una signora gentile a kind woman	**delle signore gentili** some kind women
un signore gentile a kind man	**dei signori gentili** some kind men

The use of **h** to retain the hard sound of **c** and **g** is the same as for the plural of nouns.

Example:

un libro bianco a white book	**dei libri bianchi** some white books

ARTICLES

1 The Definite Article "the"

	Singular	Plural
Masculine:	**il lo l'**	**i gli**
Feminine:	**la l'**	**le**

The eight forms of the definite article are used as follows:

MASCULINE SINGULAR

- **il** before nouns beginning with any consonant *except* s followed by another consonant, or **z**

    Examples: **il maestro** **il padre** **il salone**

- **lo** before nouns beginning with s followed by another consonant, or **z**

    Examples: **lo sbaglio** **lo zucchero** **lo zio**

- **l'** before nouns beginning with any vowel

    Examples: **l'amico** **l'uovo** **l'occhio**

FEMININE SINGULAR

- **la** before nouns beginning with any consonant

    Examples: **la parola** **la donna** **la spazzola**

- **l'** before nouns beginning with any vowel

    Examples: **l'amica** **l'ostrica** **l'uva**

MASCULINE PLURAL

- **i** before nouns beginning with any consonant *except* s followed by another consonant, or **z**

    Examples: **i maestri** **i padri** **i saloni**

- **gli** before nouns beginning with any vowel, s followed by another consonant, or **z**

    Examples: **gli amici** **gli sbagli** **gli zii**

FEMININE PLURAL

- **le** before all nouns

    Examples: **le parole** **le donne** **le amiche**

2 The Indefinite Article "a" or "an"

Masculine:	**un**	**uno**
Feminine:	**una**	**un'**

The four forms of the indefinite article are used as follows:

MASCULINE

- **un** before nouns beginning with any vowel or consonant except s followed by another consonant, or **z**

    Examples: **un uomo** **un cavallo** **un tavolo**

- **uno** before nouns beginning with s followed by another consonant, or **z**

    Examples: **uno sbaglio** **uno sfogo** **uno zio**

FEMININE

- **una** before nouns beginning with any consonant

Examples: **una donna** **una stanza** **una tazza**

- **un'** before nouns beginning with any vowel

Examples: **un'amica** **un'estasi** **un'unità**

3 The Combined Preposition

	a	da	di	in	su	con
il	**al**	**dal**	**del**	**nel**	**sul**	**col**
lo	**allo**	**dallo**	**dello**	**nello**	**sullo**	
l'	**all'**	**dall'**	**dell'**	**nell'**	**sull'**	
la	**alla**	**dalla**	**della**	**nella**	**sulla**	
i	**ai**	**dai**	**dei**	**nei**	**sui**	**coi**
gli	**agli**	**dagli**	**degli**	**negli**	**sugli**	
le	**alle**	**dalle**	**delle**	**nelle**	**sulle**	

The various forms of the definite article combine with the prepositions **a, da, di, in, su,** and **con** as shown above. Those forms not given for **con** exist, but are considered obsolete.

Examples:

del padre of the father
dalla madre from the mother
nello sguardo in the glance
sul libro in the book
nel paese in the village
col ragazzo with the boy

dei padri of the fathers
dalle madri from the mothers
negli sguardi in the glances
sui libri in the books
nei paesi in the villages
coi ragazzi with the boys

In Italian, the combined prepositions formed with **di** are often used to indicate the partitive quality of the following noun. In English translation, this same idea is usually rendered by the words *some* or *any*.

Examples:

dei libri some books
del denaro some money
dello zucchero some sugar

dell'antipasto some hors d'oeuvres
degli sbagli some mistakes
della frutta some fruit

PRONOUNS

1 The Subject Pronouns

	Singular
I	**io**
you (*familiar*)	**tu**
he	**lui, egli**
she	**lei, ella**
you (*formal*)	**Lei**

	Plural
we	**noi**
you (*familiar*)	**voi**
they (*m*)	**loro, essi**
they (*f*)	**loro, esse**
you (*formal*)	**Loro**

The subject pronouns are used much less than in English, since the verb ending is usually enough to clarify the subject. They are used when stress on the subject is indicated. The forms **egli, ella, essi,** and **esse** are literary. In conversation the alternatives are always used.

Examples:

Io dico che non è vero!	I say it isn't so!
Ci sono andato io, non lui	I'm the one who's been there, not he.
Noi americani viaggiamo assai.	We Americans travel quite a bit.
Lei è molto gentile.	You're very kind.

2 The Object Pronouns

Singular

	direct	indirect	preposition
me	**mi**	**mi (me)**	**me**
you *(fam)*	**ti**	**ti (te)**	**te**
him, it *(m)*	**lo**	**gli (glie)**	**lui**
her, it *(f)*	**la**	**le (glie)**	**lei**
you *(for m)*	**La**	**Le (Glie)**	**Lei**
you *(for f)*	**La**	**Le (Glie)**	**Lei**

Plural

	direct	indirect	preposition
us	**ci**	**ci (ce)**	**noi**
you *(fam)*	**vi**	**vi (ve)**	**voi**
them *(m)*	**li**	**loro**	**loro**
them *(f)*	**le**	**loro**	**loro**
you *(for m)*	**Li**	**Loro**	**Loro**
you *(for f)*	**Le**	**Loro**	**Loro**

The pronouns precede all indicative and subjunctive forms of the verb and all formal commands (those using **Lei** or **Loro**). They follow and are attached to the present participle, the infinitive, and all familiar commands. (However, the pronouns may also *precede* negative familiar commands, at the speaker's option.) The forms **loro** and **Loro** are exceptions to the foregoing: they always follow *all* forms of the verb and are never attached to them. The indirect object pronouns precede the direct when used in combination. When pronouns are attached, the final **e** of the infinitive is dropped.

Examples:

Mi scrive ogni settimana.	He writes me every week.
Ti dico la verità.	I'm telling you *(fam)* the truth.
Non posso dirti il perchè.	I can't tell you the reason.
Mi dica subito.	Tell me at once. *(for)*
Dimmi pure.	Go right ahead and tell me. *(fam)*
Ci ha visto ieri sera.	He saw us yesterday evening.
È stato fatto per noi.	It was done for us.
Sono andato da lei.	I went over to her place.
Non la vedo più.	I don't see her any longer.
Non La vedo quasi mai.	I almost never see you *(for)*.
Manderò loro il libro stasera.	I'll send them the book tonight.
Scriverò Loro una lettera subito.	I'll write you *(for)* at once.
Non farlo adesso.	Don't do it now. *(fam)*
Non la scrivere adesso.	Don't write it now. *(fam)*
Faccia pure.	Go right ahead and do it. *(for)*
Non lo faccia oggi.	Don't do it today.
Non posso descriverlo.	I can't describe it.

The indirect forms **mi, ti, ci,** and **vi** change to **me, te, ce,** and **ve,** respectively, when used in combination with other pronouns. The indirect forms **gli** and **le** change to **glie** when combined with other pronouns and are fused with them. The indirect form **Le** changes to **Glie** when combined with other pronouns and also fuses with them.

Examples:

Adesso Glielo faccio io.	I'll do it for you this time. (*for*)
Non posso dirtelo.	I can't tell it to you. (*fam*)
Me lo racconti dopo.	Tell me about it later. (*for*)
Te l'ho detto tante volte.	I've told you about it so many times.
Ce lo dirai tu.	You'll tell us about it.
Non posso spiegarglielo.	I can't explain it to him.

The prepositional forms of the pronoun are often used as substitutes for the direct and indirect forms, whenever the speaker wishes to stress or emphasize the pronoun. In such cases, the prepositional forms normally follow the verb.

Examples:

Ho visto lui, non lei.	I saw *him*, not *her*.
Riguarda noi, non te.	It's *our* concern, not *yours*.
Scrive a noi, non a te.	He's writing *us*, not *you*.

ADVERBS

Most adverbs are derived from the corresponding adjective by adding the suffix **-mente** to the feminine form of the adjective.

Examples:

Adjective	*Adverb*
rapido quick	**rapidamente** quickly
garbato polite	**garbatamente** politely

In the case of invariable adjectives ending in **e**, the **e** is dropped before adding **-mente** in adjectives ending in **-le** or **-re** preceded by a vowel. Otherwise, **-mente** is added *without* dropping the final **e**.

Examples:

Adjective	*Adverb*
generale general	**generalmente** generally
cortese courteous	**cortesemente** courteously

NEGATION

Italian does not make use of any auxiliary verb, such as the English *do*, to form negative statements. The adverb **non** is regularly placed before the conjugated verb to convey the negative idea. The double negative is common when the negative adjective or pronoun follows the verb. If they precede, the adverb **non** is no longer used.

Examples:

Mi dispiace, ma non so dirtelo.	I'm sorry, but I can't tell you.
Non è partito ancora.	He hasn't left yet.
Nessuno lo sa.	No one knows.
Non ha scritto a nessuno.	He has written no one.
Non vedo nessuno.	I don't see anyone.

QUESTIONS

As in the case of negative statements, there is no Italian form which corresponds to the English auxiliary *do*. Questions are regularly formed by the inversion of subject and verb, as in English questions formed with the verb *to be*.

Examples:

È italiano Lei?	Are you Italian?
Gliel'ha detto lui?	Did he tell him?
È tornata la sua sorella?	Has his sister returned?

CONJUGATION OF VERBS

1 Regular Verbs

All regular verbs entered in the dictionary conform to one of the following basic patterns.

In the regular conjugations below, the verb forms are given in the following order: first, second, and third person singular; followed by first, second, and third person plural.

–ARE VERBS *Example:* **amare** (â·mâ'rā) to love

PRESENT PARTICIPLE **amando** (â·mân'dō)
PAST PARTICIPLE **amato** (â·mâ'tō)
PRESENT **amo** (â'mō), **ami** (â'mē), **ama** (â'mâ), **amiamo** (â·myâ'mō), **amate** (â·mâ'tā), **amano** (â'mâ·nō)
FUTURE **amerò** (â·mā·rō'), **amerai** (â·mā·râ'ē), **amerà** (â·mā·râ'), **ameremo** (â·mā·rā'mō), **amerete** (â·mā·rā'tā), **ameranno** (â·mā·rân'nō)
CONDITIONAL **amerei** (â·mā·rā'ē), **ameresti** (â·mā·rā'stē), **amerebbe** (â·mā·rāb'bā), **ameremmo** (â·mā·rām'mō), **amereste** (â·mā·rā'stā), **amerebbero** (â·mā·reb'bā·rō)
PRESENT SUBJUNCTIVE **ami** (â'mē), **ami** (â'mē), **ami** (â'mē), **amiamo** (â·myâ'mō), **amiate** (â·myâ'tā), **amino** (â'mē·nō)
IMPERFECT **amavo** (â·mâ'vō), **amavi** (â·mâ'vē), **amava** (â·mâ'vâ), **amavamo** (â·mâ·vâ'mō), **amavate** (â·mâ·vâ'tā), **amavano** (â·mâ'vâ·nō)
PAST DEFINITE **amai** (â·mâ'ē), **amasti** (â·mâ'stē), **amò** (â·mō'), **amammo** (â·mâm'mō), **amaste** (â·mâ'stā), **amarono** (â·mâ'rō·nō)
PAST SUBJUNCTIVE **amassi** (â·mâs'sē), **amassi** (â·mâs'sē), **amasse** (â·mâs'sā), **amassimo** (â·mâs'sē·mō), **amaste** (â·mâ'stā), **amassero** (â·mâs'sā·rō)

–ERE VERBS *Example:* **credere** (kre'dā·rā) to believe

PRESENT PARTICIPLE **credendo** (krā·dān'dō)
PAST PARTICIPLE **creduto** (krā·dū'tō)
PRESENT **credo** (krā'dō), **credi** (krā'dē), **crede** (krā'dā), **crediamo** (krā·dyâ'mō), **credete** (krā·dā'tā), **credono** (kre'dō·nō)
FUTURE **crederò** (krā·dā·rō'), **crederai** (krā·dā·râ'ē), **crederà** (krā·dā·râ'), **crederemo** (krā·dā·rā'mō), **crederete** (krā·dā·rā'tā), **crederanno** (krā·dā·rân'nō)
CONDITIONAL **crederei** (krā·dā·rā'ē), **crederesti** (krā·dā·rā'stē), **crederebbe** (krā·dā·rāb'bā), **crederemmo** (krā·dā·rām'mō), **credereste** (krā·dā·rā'stā), **crederebbero** (krā·dā·reb'bā·rō)
PRESENT SUBJUNCTIVE **creda** (krā'dâ), **creda** (krā'dâ), **creda** (krā'dâ), **crediamo** (krā·dyâ'mō), **crediate** (krā·dyâ'tā), **credano** (kre'dâ·nō)
IMPEFECT **credevo** (krā·dā'vō), **credevi** (krā·dā'vē), **credeva** (krā·dā'vâ), **credevamo** (krā·dā·vâ'mō), **credevate** (krā·dā·vâ'tā), **credevano** (krā·de'vâ·nō)
PAST DEFINITE **credei** (krā·dā'ē), **credesti** (krā·dā'stē), **credè** (krā·dā'), **credemmo** (krā·dām'mō), **credeste** (krā·dā'stā), **crederono** (krā·de'rō·nō)
PAST SUBJUNCTIVE **credessi** (krā·dās'sē), **credessi** (krā·dās'sē), **credesse** (krā·dās'sā), **credessimo** (krā·des'sē·mō), **credeste** (krā·dā'stā), **credessero** (krā·des'sā·rō)

–IRE VERBS (ISC) *Example:* **capire** (kâ·pē'rā) to understand

PRESENT PARTICIPLE **capendo** (kâ·pān'dō)
PAST PARTICIPLE **capito** (kâ·pē'tō)
PRESENT **capisco** (kâ·pē'skō), **capisci** (kâ·pē'shē), **capisce** (kâ·pē'shā), **capiamo** (kâ·pyâ'mō), **capite** (kâ·pē'tā), **capiscono** (kâ·pē'skō·nō)

FUTURE **capirò** (kâ·pē·rō′), **capirai** (kâ·pē·râ′ē), **capirà** (kâ.pē·râ′), **capiremo** (kâ·pē·rā′mō), **capirete** (kâ·pē·rā′tā), **capiranno** (kâ·pē·rân′nō)
CONDITIONAL **capirei** (kâ·pē·rā′ē), **capiresti** (kâ·pē·rā′stē), **capirebbe** (kâ·pē·rāb′bā), **capiremmo** (kâ·pē·rām′mō), **capireste** (kâ·pē·rā′stā), **capirebbero** (kâ·pē·reb′bā·rō)
PRESENT SUBJUNCTIVE **capisca** ((kâ·pē′skâ), **capisca** (kâ·pē′skâ), **capisca** (kâ·pē′skâ), **capiamo** (kâ·pyâ′mō), **capiate** (kâ·pyâ′tā), **capiscano** (kâ·pē′skâ·nō)
IMPERFECT **capivo** (kâ·pē′vō), **capivi** (kâ·pē′vē), **capiva** (kâ·pē′vâ), **capivamo** (kâ·pē·rā′mō), **capirete** (kâ·pē·rā′tā), **capiranno** (kâ·pē·rân′nō)
PAST DEFINITE **capii** (kâ·pē′ē), **capisti** (kâ·pē′stē), **capì** (kâ·pē′), **capimmo** (kâ·pēm′-mō) **capiste** (kâ·pē′stā), **capirono** (kâ·pē′rō·nō)
PAST SUBJUNCTIVE **capissi** (kâ·pēs′sē), **capissi** (kâ·pēs′sē), **capisse** (kâ·pēs′sā), **capissimo** (kâ·pēs′sē·mō), **capiste** (kâ·pē′stā), **capissero** (kâ·pēs′sā·rō)

–IRE VERBS *Example:* **dormire** (dōr·mē′rā) to sleep

PRESENT PARTICIPLE **dormendo** (dōr·mān′dō)
PAST PARTICIPLE **dormito** (dōr·mē′tō)
PRESENT **dormo** (dōr′mō), **dormi** (dōr′mē), **dorme** (dōr′mā), **dormiamo** (dōr·myâ′mō), **dormite** (dōr·mē′tā), **dormono** (dôr′mō·nō)
FUTURE **dormirò** (dōr·mē·rō′), **dormirai** (dōr·mē·râ′ē), **dormirà** (dōr·mē·râ′), **dormiremo** (dōr·mē·rā′mō), **dormirete** (dōr·mē.rā′tā), **dormiranno** (dōr·mē·rân′nō)
CONDITIONAL **dormirei** (dōr·mē·rā′ē), **dormiresti** (dōr·mē·rā′stē), **dormirebbe** (dōr·mē·rāb′bā), **dormiremmo** (dōr·mē·rām′mō), **dormireste** (dōr·mē·rā′stā), **dormirebbero** (dōr·mē·reb′bā·rō)
PRESENT SUBJUNCTIVE **dorma** (dōr′mâ), **dorma** (dōr′mâ), **dorma** (dōr′mâ), **dormiamo** (dōr·myâ′mō), **dormiate** (dōr·myâ′tā), **dormano** (dôr′mâ·nō)
IMPERFECT **dormivo** (dōr·mē′vō), **dormivi** (dōr·mē′vē), **dormiva** (dōr·mē′vâ), **dormivamo** (dōr·mē·vâ′mō), **dormivate** (dōr·mē·vâ′tā), **dormivano** (dōr·mē′vâ·nō)
PAST DEFINITE **dormii** (dōr·mē′ē), **dormisti** (dōr·mē′stē), **dormì** (dōr·mē′), **dormimmo** (dōr·mēm′mō), **dormiste** (dōr·mē′stā), **dormirono** (dōr·mē′rō·nō)
PAST SUBJUNCTIVE **dormissi** (dōr·mēs′sē), **dormissi** (dōr·mēs′sē), **dormisse** (dōr·mēs′-sā), **dormissimo** (dōr·mēs′sē·mō), **dormiste** (dōr·mē′stā), **dormissero** (dōr·mēs′sā·rō)

VERB USAGE

The present tense in Italian is sometimes used in cases where the future is called for in English, when the future is immediate.

Examples:

Vado subito.	I'll go at once.
Partiamo stasera.	We'll leave this evening.

The imperfect tense is used in Italian instead of the past definite or the compound past when repeated or habitual action is implied in the past. The modal *used to* is often used in English to convey the same idea. The imperfect is also used when indefinite time is implied in the past.

Examples:

Andavo alla spiaggia ogni fine di settimana.	I used to go to the beach every weekend.
Andavamo in città ogni domenica.	We went to town every Sunday.
Eravamo lì nel pomeriggio.	We were there in the afternoon.

The compound past **(passato prossimo)** or present perfect, is used for a single action in the past, or when definite time limits are indicated.

Examples:

Sono andati a Fiesole ieri sera.	They went to Fiesole last night.
Siamo rimasti a Volterra per tre giorni.	We stayed in Volterra for three days.

The past definite is also used for a single action in the past, or when definite time limits are indicated. It is a more formal tense and is found in writing more often than conversation. It is also used in combination with the compound past to clarify the time element of actions in the past.

Examples:

Dante scrisse la Divina Commedia, capolavoro del medioevo italiano.	Dante wrote *The Divine Comedy*, a masterpiece of the Italian Middle Ages.
Le ho dato il libro che comprai l'altro ieri.	I gave her the book that I bought the day before yesterday.

2 Auxiliary Verbs avere and essere

As in English, the verb **avere** *(to have)* is used to form the compound tenses, *but not exclusively*. Many verbs of motion, all reflexive and reciprocal verb forms, verbs that imply change in condition, and verbs in the passive voice are conjugated with the verb **essere** *(to be)*. The Italian equivalent of our present perfect, using the auxiliary in the present tense with the past participle, is often used with the idea of the simple past in English. The past participle always agrees with the subject when the verb **essere** is used; it never does when **avere** is used.

Examples:

L'ho fatto io ieri l'altro.	I did it the day before yesterday.
La mia sorella non è ancora partita.	My sister hasn't left yet.
La lettera è stata scritta da me.	The letter was written by me.
È stato visto dappertutto.	He has been seen everywhere.
Si è fatta male.	She hurt herself.
Si sono parlati per mezz'ora.	They talked to one another for a half-hour.
Ci siamo visti in città.	We saw each other in town.
Non ho mai sentito una cosa simile.	I've never heard anything like that before.

In the conjugations below, the verb forms are given in the following order: first, second, and third person singular; followed by first, second, and third person plural.

avere (â·vā'rā) to have

PRESENT PARTICIPLE **avendo** (â·vān'dō)

PAST PARTICIPLE **avuto** (â·vū'tō)

PRESENT **ho** (ō), **hai** (â'ē), **ha** (â), **abbiamo** (âb·byâ'mō), **avete** (â·vā'tā), **hanno** (ân'nō)

FUTURE **avrò** (â·vrō'), **avrai** (â·vrâ'ē), **avrà** (â·vrâ'), **avremo** (â·vrā'mō), **avrete** (â·vrā'tā), **avranno** (â·vrân'nō)

CONDITIONAL **avrei** (â·vrā'ē), **avresti** (â·vrā'stē), **avrebbe** (â·vrāb'bā), **avremmo** (â·vrām'mō), **avreste** (â·vrā'stā), **avrebbero** (â·vreb'bā·rō)

PRESENT SUBJUNCTIVE **abbia** (âb'byâ), **abbia** (âb'byâ), **abbia** (âb'byâ), **abbiamo** (âb·byâ'mō), **abbiate** (âb·byâ'tā), **abbiano** (âb·byâ'nō)

IMPERFECT **avevo** (â·vā'vō), **avevi** (â·vā'vē), **aveva** (â·vā'vâ), **avevamo** (â·vā·vâ'mō), **avevate** (â·vā·vâ'tā), **avevano** (â·ve'vâ·nō)

PAST DEFINITE **ebbi** (āb'bē), **avesti** (â·vā'stē), **ebbe** (āb'bā), **avemmo** (â·vām'mō), **aveste** (â·vā'stā), **ebbero** (eb'bā·rō)

PAST SUBJUNCTIVE **avessi** (â·vās'sē), **avessi** (â·vās'sē), **avesse** (â·vās'sā), **avessimo** (â·ves'sē·mō), **aveste** (â·vā'stā), **avessero** (â·ves'sā·rō)

essere (es'sā·rā) to be

PRESENT PARTICIPLE **essendo** (ās·sān'dō)

PAST PARTICIPLE **stato** (stâ'tō)

PRESENT **sono** (sō'nō), **sei** (sā'ē), **è** (ā), **siamo** (syâ'mō), **siete** (syā'tā), **sono** (sō'nō)
FUTURE **sarò** (sâ·rō'), **sarai** (sâ·râ'ē), **sarà** (sâ·râ'), **saremo** (sâ·rā'mō), **sarete** (sâ·rā'tā), **saranno** (sâ·rân'nō)
CONDITIONAL **sarei** (sâ·rā'ē), **saresti** (sâ·rā'stē), **sarebbe** (sâ·rāb'bā), **saremmo** (sâ·rām'mō), **sareste** (sâ·rā'stā), **sarebbero** (sâ·reb'bā·rō)
PRESENT SUBJUNCTIVE **sia** (sē'â), **sia** (sē'â), **sia** (sē'â), **siamo** (syâ'mō), **siate** (syâ'tā), **siano** (sē'â·nō)
IMPERFECT **ero** (ā'rō), **eri** (ā'rē), **era** (ā'râ), **eravamo** (ā·râ·vâ'mō), **eravate** (ā·râ·vâ'tā), **erano** (e'râ·nō)
PAST DEFINITE **fui** (fū'ē), **fosti** (fō'stē), **fu** (fū), **fummo** (fūm'mō), **foste** (fō'stā), **furono** (fū'rō·nō)
PAST SUBJUNCTIVE **fossi** (fōs'sē), **fossi** (fōs'sē), **fosse** (fōs'sā), **fossimo** (fôs'sē·mō), **foste** (fō'stā), **fossero** (fôs'sā·rō)

3 Irregular Verbs

The following list contains all the irregular verbs entered in this dictionary. For those verbs whose conjugation is identical to a root verb, the user is referred to that verb (for example, **rimettere** see **mettere**).

In the conjugations offered below, only those tenses containing one or more irregular forms are given. Other tenses are formed on the model of the regular verbs given previously.

The present subjunctive is not given when the regular subjunctive endings are used with the stem of the first person singular of the present indicative (for example, **dica, dica, dica, diciamo, diciate, dicano** from **dico**).

It will be noted that many of the verbs given below show an irregularity only in the past participle and in the past definite. As stated previously, the past participle always agrees with the subject when the verb **essere** is used, and never does so with forms of the verb **avere**. However, when the verb **avere** is employed, the past participle *always* agrees with third-person direct object pronouns, singular or plural. The past participle may or may not agree in gender and number with first- and second-person direct object pronouns, noun objects, or preceding relative pronouns, at the speaker's option.

Space does not permit including the pronunciation of inflected forms of irregular verbs. But comparison with the pronunciations already given for the inflected forms of regular verbs plus the rules of pronunciation set forth on pages 10-14, should enable the reader to supply his own pronunciation for the words listed here.

The verb forms are given in the following order: first, second, and third person singular; followed by first, second, and third person plural.

accadere to happen, see **cadere**
accendere to ignite
PAST PARTICIPLE **acceso**
PAST DEFINITE **accesi, accendesti, accese, accendemmo, accendeste, accesero**
accludere to enclose
PAST PARTICIPLE **accluso**
PAST DEFINITE **acclusi, accludesti, accluse, accludemmo, accludeste, acclusero**
accogliere to receive, see **cogliere**
accorgersi to perceive
PAST PARTICIPLE **accorto**
PAST DEFINITE **accorsi, accorgesti, accorse, accorgemmo, accorgeste, accorsero**
accorrere to run up, see **correre**
addurre to allege
PRESENT PARTICIPLE **adducendo**
PAST PARTICIPLE **addotto**
PRESENT **adduco, adduci, adduce, adduciamo, adducete, adducono**
IMPERFECT **adducevo, adducevi, adduceva, adducevamo, adducevate, adducevano**
PAST DEFINITE **addussi, adducesti, addusse, adducemmo, adduceste, addussero**
PAST SUBJUNCTIVE **adducessi, adducessi, adducese, adducessimo, adduceste, adducessero**
adempiere to fulfill, see **compiere**
affliggere to afflict
PAST PARTICIPLE **afflitto**
PAST DEFINITE **afflissi, affliggesti, afflisse, affliggemmo, affliggeste, afflissero**
aggiungere to add, see **giungere**
ammettere to admit, see **mettere**
andare to go
PRESENT **vado, vai, va, andiamo, andate, vanno**
FUTURE **andrò, andrai, andrà, andremo, andrete, andranno**
CONDITIONAL **andrei, andresti, andrebbe, andremmo, andreste, andrebbero**
PRESENT SUBJUNCTIVE **vada, vada, vada,**

andiamo, andiate, vadano
apparire to appear
PAST PARTICIPLE **apparso**
PRESENT **appaio, appari, appare, appariamo, apparite, appaiono**
PAST DEFINITE **apparsi, apparisti, apparse, apparimmo, appariste, apparsero**
appartenere to belong, see **tenere**
appendere to hang up, see **pendere**
apprendere to learn, see **prendere**
aprire to open
PAST PARTICIPLE **aperto**
PAST DEFINITE **apersi, apristi, aperse, aprimmo, apriste, apersero**
ardere to burn
PAST PARTICIPLE **arso**
PAST DEFINITE **arsi, ardesti, arse, ardemmo, ardeste, arsero**
arrendersi to surrender, see **rendere**
ascendere to ascend, see **scendere**
ascrivere to ascribe, see **scrivere**
assistere to attend
PAST PARTICIPLE **assistito**
assolvere to absolve, see **solvere**
assumere to assume
PAST PARTICIPLE **assunto**
PAST DEFINITE **assunsi, assumesti, assunse, assumemmo, assumeste, assunsero**
astrarre to abstract, see **trarre**
attendere to wait for, see **tendere**
attenere to maintain, see **tenere**
attingere to reach, see **tingere**
attrarre to attract, see **trarre**
avvenire to happen, see **venire**
avvincere to bind, see **vincere**
avvolgere to roll up, see **volgere**

benedire to bless, see **dire**
benvolere to like, see **volere**
bere to drink
PRESENT PARTICIPLE **bevendo**
PAST PARTICIPLE **bevuto**
PRESENT **bevo, bevi, beve, beviamo, bevete, bevono**
FUTURE **berrò, berrai, berrà, berremo, berrete, berranno**
CONDITIONAL **berrei, berresti, berrebbe, berremmo, berreste, berrebero**
IMPERFECT **bevevo, bevevi, beveva, bevevamo, bevevate, bevevano**
PAST DEFINITE **bevvi, bevesti, bevve, bevemmo, beveste, bevvero**
PAST SUBJUNCTIVE **bevessi, bevessi, bevesse, bevessimo, beveste, bevessero**

cadere to fall
FUTURE **cadrò, cadrai, cadrà, cadremo, cadrete, cadranno**
CONDITIONAL **cadrei, cadresti, cadrebbe, cadremmo, cadreste, cadrebbero**
PAST DEFINITE **caddi, cadesti, cadde, cademmo, cadeste, caddero**
capovolgere to upset, see **volgere**
chiedere to request
PAST PARTICIPLE **chiesto**
PAST DEFINITE **chiesi, chiedesti, chiese, chiedemmo, chiedeste, chiesero**
chiudere to close
PAST PARTICIPLE **chiuso**
PAST DEFINITE **chiusi, chiudesti, chiuse, chiudemmo, chiudeste, chiusero**
cingere to encircle
PAST PARTICIPLE **cinto**
PAST DEFINITE **cinsi, cingesti, cinse, cingemmo, cingeste, cinsero**
circoncidere to circumcise, see **decidere**
circonvenire to circumvent, see **venire**
cogliere to gather
PAST PARTICIPLE **colto**
PRESENT **colgo, cogli, coglie, cogliamo, cogliete, colgono**
PAST DEFINITE **colsi, cogliesti, colse, cogliemmo, coglieste, colsero**
coinvolgere to involve, see **volgere**
commuovere to move, see **muovere**
comparire to appear, see **apparire**
compiangere to regret, see **piangere**
compiere or **compire** to accomplish
PRESENT PARTICIPLE **compiendo**
PAST PARTICIPLE **compiuto** or **compito**
PRESENT **compio, compi, compie, compiamo, compite, compiono**
FUTURE **compirò, compirai, compirà, compiremo, compirete, compiranno**
CONDITIONAL **compirei, compiresti, compirebbe, compiremmo, compireste, compirebbero**
PRESENT SUBJUNCTIVE **compia, compia, compia, compiamo, compiate, compiano**
IMPERFECT **compivo, compivi, compiva, compivamo, compivate, compivano**
PAST DEFINITE **compii, compisti, compì, compimmo, compiste, compirono**
PAST SUBJUNCTIVE **compissi, compissi, compisse, compissimo, compiste, compissero**
comporre to compose, see **porre**
comprendere to understand, see **prendere**
comprimere to squeeze
PAST PARTICIPLE **compresso**
PAST DEFINITE **compressi, comprimesti, compresse, comprimemmo, comprimeste, compressero**
compromettere to risk, see **mettere**
concludere to conclude, see **accludere**
concorrere to compete, see **correre**
condividere to share in, see **dividere**
condolersi to sympathize, see **dolere**
condurre to conduct, see **addurre**
confarsi to suit, see **fare**
confondere to confuse, see **fondere**
congiungere to connect, see **giungere**
connettere to connect
PAST PARTICIPLE **connesso**
PAST DEFINITE **connessi, connettesti, connesse, connettemmo, connetteste, connessero**
conoscere to know
PAST DEFINITE **conobbi, conoscesti, conobbe, conoscemmo, conosceste, conobbero**
consistere to consist
PAST PARTICIPLE **consistito**

contendere to contest, see **tendere**
contenere to contain, see **tenere**
contorcere to contort, see **torcere**
contraddire to contradict, see **dire**
contraffare to counterfeit, see **fare**
contrarre to contract, see **trarre**
convergere to converge
PAST PARTICIPLE **converso**
PAST DEFINITE **conversi, convergesti, converse, convergemmo, convergeste, conversero**
convincere to convince, see **vincere**
convivere to cohabit, see **vivere**
coprire to cover
PAST PARTICIPLE **coperto**
correre to run
PAST PARTICIPLE **corso**
PAST DEFINITE **corsi, corresti, corse, corremmo, correste, corsero**
corrispondere to correspond, see **rispondere**
corrodere to corrode, see **rodere**
corrompere to corrupt, see **rompere**
cospargere to sprinkle, see **spargere**
crescere to grow
PAST DEFINITE **crebbi, crescesti, crebbe, crescemmo, cresceste, crebbero**
crocifiggere to crucify, see **figgere**
cuocere to cook
PRESENT PARTICIPLE **cocendo**
PAST PARTICIPLE **cotto**
PRESENT **cuocio, cuoci, cuoce, cociamo, cocete, cuociono**
FUTURE **cocerò, cocerai, cocerà, coceremo, cocerete, coceranno**
CONDITIONAL **cocerei, coceresti, cocerebbe, coceremmo, cocereste, cocerebbero**
PRESENT SUBJUNCTIVE **cuocia, cuocia, cuocia, cociamo, cociate, cuociano**
IMPERFECT **cocevo, cocevi, coceva, cocevamo, cocevate, cocevano**
PAST DEFINITE **cossi, cocesti, cosse, cocemmo, coceste, cossero**
PAST SUBJUNCTIVE **cocessi, cocessi, cocesse, cocessimo, coceste, cocessero**

dare to give
PRESENT **do, dai, dà, diamo, date, danno**
FUTURE **darò, darai, darà, daremo, darete, daranno**
CONDITIONAL **darei, daresti, darebbe, daremmo, dareste, darebbero**
PRESENT SUBJUNCTIVE **dia, dia, dia, diamo, diate, diano**
PAST DEFINITE **diedi, desti, diede, demmo, deste, diedero**
PAST SUBJUNCTIVE **dessi, dessi, desse, dessimo, deste, dessero**
decadere to decay, see **cadere**
decidere to decide
PAST PARTICIPLE **deciso**
PAST DEFINITE **decisi, decidesti, decise, decidemmo, decideste, decisero**
decomporre to decompose, see **porre**
decorrere to elapse, see **correre**
decrescere to decrease, see **crescere**
dedurre to deduce, see **addurre**
deflettere to deflect
PAST PARTICIPLE **deflesso**
PAST DEFINITE **deflessi, deflettesti, deflesse, deflettemmo, defletteste, deflessero**
deludere to delude
PAST PARTICIPLE **deluso**
PAST DEFINITE **delusi, deludesti, deluse, deludemmo, deludeste, delusero**
deporre to deposit, see **porre**
descrivere to describe, see **scrivere**
desistere to desist, see **esistere**
desumere to infer, see **assumere**
detenere to detain, see **tenere**
detrarre to detract, see **trarre**
devolvere to devolve, see **volvere**
difendere to defend
PAST PARTICIPLE **difeso**
PAST DEFINITE **difesi, difendesti, difese, difendemmo, difendeste, difesero**
dimettere to dismiss, see **mettere**
dipendere to depend, see **pendere**
dipingere to paint
PAST PARTICIPLE **dipinto**
PAST DEFINITE **dipinsi, dipingesti, dipinse, dipingemmo, dipingeste, dipinsero**
dire to say
PRESENT PARTICIPLE **dicendo**
PAST PARTICIPLE **detto**
PRESENT **dico, dici, dice, diciamo, dite, dicono**
IMPERFECT **dicevo, dicevi, diceva, dicevamo, dicevate, dicevano**
PAST DEFINITE **dissi, dicesti, disse, dicemmo, diceste, dissero**
PAST SUBJUNCTIVE **dicessi, dicessi, dicesse, dicessimo, diceste, dicessero**
dirigere to direct
PAST PARTICIPLE **diretto**
PAST DEFINITE **diressi, dirigesti, diresse, dirigemmo, dirigeste, diressero**
dischiudere to disclose, see **chiudere**
disciogliere to untie, see **sciogliere**
disconoscere to ignore, see **conoscere**
discorrere to discourse, see **correre**
discutere to discuss
PAST PARTICIPLE **discusso**
PAST DEFINITE **discussi, discutesti, discusse, discutemmo, discuteste, discussero**
disdire to deny, see **dire**
disfare to undo, see **fare**
disgiungere to detach, see **giungere**
disperdere to disperse, see **perdere**
dispiacere to displease, see **piacere**
disporre to dispose, see **porre**
dissolvere to dissolve, see **solvere**
dissuadere to dissuade
PAST PARTICIPLE **dissuaso**
PAST DEFINITE **dissuasi, dissuadesti, dissuase, dissuademmo, dissuadeste, dissuasero**
distendere to stretch, see **tendere**
distinguere to distinguish
PAST PARTICIPLE **distinto**
PAST DEFINITE **distinsi, distinguesti, distinse, distinguemmo, distingueste, di-**

stinsero
distogliere to divert, see **togliere**
distrarre to distract, see **trarre**
distruggere to destroy
PAST PARTICIPLE **distrutto**
PAST DEFINITE **distrussi, distruggesti, distrusse, distruggemmo, distruggeste, distrussero**
divellere to uproot
PAST PARTICIPLE **divelso**
PAST DEFINITE **divelsi, divellesti, divelse, divellemmo, divelleste, divelsero**
divenire to become, see **venire**
dividere to divide
PAST PARTICIPLE **diviso**
PAST DEFINITE **divisi, dividesti, divise, dividemmo, divideste, divisero**
dolere to pain
PRESENT **dolgo, duoli, duole, dogliamo, dolete, dolgono**
FUTURE **dorrò, dorrai, dorrà, dorremo, dorrete, dorrano**
CONDITIONAL **dorrei, dorresti, dorrebbe, dorremmo, dorreste, dorrebbero**
PRESENT SUBJUNCTIVE **dolga, dolga, dolga, dogliamo, dogliate, dolgano**
PAST DEFINITE **dolsi, dolesti, dolse, dolemmo, doleste, dolsero**
dovere to owe
PRESENT **devo, devi, deve, dobbiamo, dovete, devono**
FUTURE **dovrò, dovrai, dovrà, dovremo, dovrete, dovranno**
CONDITIONAL **dovrei, dovresti, dovrebbe, dovremmo, dovreste, dovrebbero**
PRESENT SUBJUNCTIVE **deva, deva, deva, dobbiamo, dobbiate, devano**

eccellere to excel
PAST PARTICIPLE **eccelso**
PAST DEFINITE **eccelsi, eccellesti, eccelse, eccellemmo, eccelleste, eccelsero**
eleggere to elect
PAST PARTICIPLE **eletto**
PAST DEFINITE **elessi, eleggesti, elesse, eleggemmo, eleggeste, elessero**
elidere to elide
PAST PARTICIPLE **eliso**
PAST DEFINITE **elisi, elidesti, elise, elidemmo, elideste, elisero**
eludere to elude, see **deludere**
emergere to emerge
PAST PARTICIPLE **emerso**
PAST DEFINITE **emersi, emergesti, emerse, emergemmo, emergeste, emersero**
emettere to emit, see **mettere**
empire to fill
PRESENT PARTICIPLE **empiendo**
PRESENT **empio, empi, empie, empiamo, empite, empiono**
PRESENT SUBJUNCTIVE **empia, empia, empia, empiamo, empiate, empiano**
erigere to erect
PAST PARTICIPLE **eretto**
PAST DEFINITE **eressi, erigesti, eresse, erigemmo, erigeste, eressero**
erompere to erupt, see **rompere**
escludere to exclude, see **accludere**
esigere to exact
PAST PARTICIPLE **esatto**
esistere to exist, see **assistere**
espandere to expand, see **spandere**
espellere to expel
PAST PARTICIPLE **espulso**
PAST DEFINITE **espulsi, espellesti, espulse, espellemmo, espelleste, espulsero**
esplodere to explode
PAST PARTICIPLE **esploso**
PAST DEFINITE **esplosi, esplodesti, esplose, esplodemmo, esplodeste, esplosero**
esporre to expose, see **porre**
esprimere to express, see **comprimere**
estendere to extend, see **tendere**
estinguere to extinguish, see **distinguere**
estollere to extol
PAST PARTICIPLE **estolto**
PAST DEFINITE **estolsi, estollesti, estolse, estollemmo, estolleste, estolsero**
estorcere to extort, see **torcere**
estrarre to extract, see **trarre**
estromettere to oust, see **mettere**
evadere to escape
PAST PARTICIPLE **evaso**
PAST DEFINITE **evasi, evadesti, evase, evademmo, evadeste, evasero**

fare to make
PRESENT PARTICIPLE **facendo**
PAST PARTICIPLE **fatto**
PRESENT **faccio, fai, fa, facciamo, fate, fanno**
FUTURE **farò, farai, farà, faremo, farete, faranno**
CONDITIONAL **farei, faresti, farebbe, faremmo, fareste, farebbero**
PRESENT SUBJUNCTIVE **faccia, faccia, faccia, facciamo, facciate, facciano**
IMPERFECT **facevo, facevi, faceva, facevamo, facevate, facevano**
PAST DEFINITE **feci, facesti, fece, facemmo, faceste, fecero**
PAST SUBJUNCTIVE **facessi, facessi, facesse, facessimo, faceste, facessero**
fendere to split
PAST PARTICIPLE **fesso**
figgere to fix
PAST PARTICIPLE **fitto**
PAST DEFINITE **fissi, figgesti, fisse, figgemmo, figgeste, fissero**
fingere to feign
PAST PARTICIPLE **finto**
PAST DEFINITE **finsi, fingesti, finse, fingemmo, fingeste, finsero**
flettere to flex
PAST PARTICIPLE **flesso**
PAST DEFINITE **flessi, flettesti, flesse, flettemmo, fletteste, flessero**
fondere to cast
PAST PARTICIPLE **fuso**
PAST DEFINITE **fusi, fondesti, fuse, fondemmo, fondeste, fusero**
fraintendere to misunderstand, see **tendere**

frangere to break
PAST PARTICIPLE **franto**
PAST DEFINITE **fransi, frangesti, franse, frangemmo, frangeste, fransero**
frapporre to insert, see **porre**
friggere to fry
PAST PARTICIPLE **fritto**
PAST DEFINITE **frissi, friggesti, frisse, friggemmo, friggeste, frissero**

genuflettersi to genuflect, see **flettere**
giacere to lie
PRESENT **giaccio, giaci, giace, giacciamo, giacete, giacciono**
PRESENT SUBJUNCTIVE **giaccia, giaccia, giaccia, giacciamo, giacciate, giacciano**
PAST DEFINITE **giacqui, giacesti, giacque, giacemmo, giaceste, giacquero**
giungere to arrive
PAST PARTICIPLE **giunto**
PAST DEFINITE **giunsi, giungesti, giunse, giungemmo, giungeste, giunsero**

illudere to deceive, see **deludere**
immergere to immerse, see **emergere**
immettere to infuse, see **mettere**
imporre to impose, see **porre**
imprimere to print, see **comprimere**
includere to include, see **accludere**
incorrere to incur, see **correre**
indire to notify, see **dire**
indisporre to upset, see **porre**
indulgere to gratify
PAST PARTICIPLE **indulto**
PAST DEFINITE **indulsi, indulgesti, indulse, indulgemmo, indulgeste, indulsero**
indurre to induce, see **addurre**
infliggere to inflict
PAST PARTICIPLE **inflitto**
PAST DEFINITE **inflissi, infliggesti, inflisse, infliggemmo, infliggeste, inflissero**
infondere to infuse, see **fondere**
frammettere to interpose, see **mettere**
infrangere to violate, see **frangere**
ingiungere to enjoin, see **giungere**
insistere to insist
PAST PARTICIPLE **insistito**
intendere to intend, see **tendere**
intercorrere to elapse, see **correre**
interdire to forbid, see **dire**
interporre to interpose, see **porre**
interrompere to interrupt, see **rompere**
intervenire to intervene, see **venire**
intingere to dip, see **tingere**
intraprendere to undertake, see **prendere**
intrattenere to entertain, see **tenere**
introdurre to insert, see **addurre**
intromettersi to interfere, see **mettere**
invadere to invade, see **evadere**
involgere to involve, see **volgere**
irrompere to break out, see **rompere**
iscrivere to enroll, see **scrivere**

ledere to injure
PAST PARTICIPLE **leso**
PAST DEFINITE **lesi, ledesti, lese, ledemmo, ledeste, lesero**
leggere to read
PAST PARTICIPLE **letto**
PAST DEFINITE **lessi, leggesti, lesse, leggemmo, leggeste, lessero**

malintendere to misunderstand, see **tendere**
mantenere to maintain, see **tenere**
mettere to put
PAST PARTICIPLE **messo**
PAST DEFINITE **misi, mettesti, mise, mettemmo, metteste, misero**
mordere to bite
PAST PARTICIPLE **morso**
PAST DEFINITE **morsi, mordesti, morse, mordemmo, mordeste, morsero**
morire to die
PAST PARTICIPLE **morto**
PRESENT **muoio, muori, muore, moriamo, morite, muoiono**
FUTURE **morrò, morrai, morrà, morremo, morrete, morranno**
CONDITIONAL **morrei, morresti, morrebbe, morremmo, morreste, morrebbero**
PRESENT SUBJUNCTIVE **muoia, muoia, muoia, moriamo, moriate, muoiano**
mungere to milk
PAST PARTICIPLE **munto**
PAST DEFINITE **munsi, mungesti, munse, mungemmo, mungeste, munsero**
muovere to move
PAST PARTICIPLE **mosso**
PAST DEFINITE **mossi, movesti, mosse, movemmo, moveste, mossero**

nascere to be born
PAST PARTICIPLE **nato**
PAST DEFINITE **nacqui, nascesti, nacque, nascemmo, nasceste, nacquero**
nascondere to hide
PAST PARTICIPLE **nascosto**
PAST DEFINITE **nascosi, nascondesti, nascose, nascondemmo, nascondeste, nascosero**
nuocere to harm
PAST PARTICIPLE **nociuto**
PRESENT **nuoccio, nuoci, nuoce, nociamo, nocete, nuocciono**
PRESENT SUBJUNCTIVE **noccia, noccia, noccia, nociamo, nociate, nocciano**
PAST DEFINITE **nocqui, nocesti, nocque, nocemmo, noceste, nocquero**

occorrere to be necessary, see **correre**
offendere to offend
PAST PARTICIPLE **offeso**
PAST DEFINITE **offesi, offendesti, offese, offendemmo, offendeste, offesero**
offrire to offer
PAST PARTICIPLE **offerto**
omettere to omit, see **mettere**
opporre to oppose, see **porre**

opprimere to oppress, see **comprimere**
ottenere to obtain, see **tenere**

parere to appear
PAST PARTICIPLE **parso**
PRESENT **paio, pari, pare, pariamo, parete, paiono**
FUTURE **parrò, parrai, parrà, parremo, parrete, parranno**
CONDITIONAL **parrei, parresti, parrebbe, parremmo, parreste, parrebbero**
PRESENT SUBJUNCTIVE **paia, paia, paia, pariamo, pariate, paiano**
PAST DEFINITE **parvi, paresti, parve, paremmo, pareste, parvero**
pendere to hang
PAST PARTICIPLE **peso**
PAST DEFINITE **pesi, pendesti, pese, pendemmo, pendeste, pesero**
percorrere to travel across, see **correre**
percuotere to strike
PRESENT PARTICIPLE **percotendo**
PAST PARTICIPLE **percosso**
PRESENT **percuoto, percuoti, percuote, percotiamo, percotete, percuotono**
FUTURE **percoterò, percoterai, percoterà, percoteremo, percoterete, percoteranno**
CONDITIONAL **percoterei, percoteresti, percoterebbe, percoteremmo, percotereste, percoterebbero**
PRESENT SUBJUNCTIVE **percuota, percuota, percuota, percotiamo, percotiate, percuotano**
IMPERFECT **percotevo, percotevi, percoteva, percotevamo, percotevate, percotevano**
PAST DEFINITE **percossi, percotesti, percosse, percotemmo, percoteste, percossero**
PAST SUBJUNCTIVE **percotessi, percotessi, percotesse, percotessimo, percoteste, percotessero**
perdere to lose
PAST PARTICIPLE **perso**
PAST DEFINITE **persi, perdesti, perse, perdemmo, perdeste, persero**
permanere to stay
PAST PARTICIPLE **permaso**
PRESENT **permango, permani, permane, permaniamo, permanete, permangono**
FUTURE **permarrò, permarrà, permarremo, permarrete, permarranno**
CONDITIONAL **permarrei, permarresti, permarrebbe, permarremmo, permarreste, permarrebbero**
PRESENT SUBJUNCTIVE **permanga, permanga, permanga, permaniamo, permaniate, permangano**
PAST DEFINITE **permasi, permanesti, permase, permanemmo, permaneste, permasero**
permettere to permit, see **mettere**
persistere to persist
PAST PARTICIPLE **persistito**
persuadere to persuade
PAST PARTICIPLE **persuaso**
PAST DEFINITE **persuasi, persuadesti, persuase, persuademmo, persuadeste, persuasero**
pervenire to achieve, see **venire**
piacere to please
PRESENT **piaccio, piaci, piace, piacciamo, piacete, piacciono**
PRESENT SUBJUNCTIVE **piaccia, piaccia, piaccia, piacciamo, piacciate, piacciano**
PAST DEFINITE **piacqui, piacesti, piacque, piacemmo, piaceste, piacquero**
piangere to cry
PAST PARTICIPLE **pianto**
PAST DEFINITE **piansi, piangesti, pianse, piangemmo, piangeste, piansero**
piovere to rain
PAST DEFINITE **piovvi, piovesti, piovve, piovemmo, pioveste, piovvero**
porgere to hand over
PAST PARTICIPLE **porto**
PAST DEFINITE **porsi, porgesti, porse, porgemmo, porgeste, porsero**
porre to place
PRESENT PARTICIPLE **ponendo**
PAST PARTICIPLE **posto**
PRESENT **pongo, poni, pone, poniamo, ponete, pongono**
FUTURE **porrò, porrai, porrà, porremo, porrete, porranno**
CONDITIONAL **porrei, porresti, porrebbe, porremmo, porreste, porrebbero**
PRESENT SUBJUNCTIVE **ponga, ponga, ponga, poniamo, poniate, pongano**
IMPERFECT **ponevo, ponevi, poneva, ponevamo, ponevate, ponevano**
PAST DEFINITE **posi, ponesti, pose, ponemmo, poneste, posero**
PAST SUBJUNCTIVE **ponessi, ponessi, ponesse, ponessimo, poneste, ponessero**
posporre to postpone, see **porre**
possedere to own, see **sedere**
potere to be able
PRESENT **posso, puoi, può, possiamo, potete, possono**
FUTURE **potrò, potrai, potrà, potremo, potrete, potranno**
CONDITIONAL **potrei, potresti, potrebbe, potremmo, potreste, potrebbero**
predire to foretell, see **dire**
predisporre to predispose, see **porre**
prefiggere to prefix, see **figgere**
premettere to premise, see **mettere**
prendere to take
PAST PARTICIPLE **preso**
PAST DEFINITE **presi, prendesti, prese, prendemmo, prendeste, presero**
prescindere to disregard
PAST PARTICIPLE **prescisso**
PAST DEFINITE **prescissi, prescindesti, prescisse, prescindemmo, prescindeste, prescissero**
prescrivere to prescribe, see **scrivere**
presiedere to preside, see **sedere**
presumere to presume
PAST PARTICIPLE **presunto**
PAST DEFINITE **presunsi, presumesti, presunse, presummemo, presumeste, presunsero**

presuppore to imply, see **porre**
pretendere to claim, see **tendere**
prevalere to prevail, see **valere**
prevedere to foresee, see **vedere**
prevenire to warn, see **venire**
produrre to produce, see **addurre**
profondere to squander, see **fondere**
promettere to promise, see **mettere**
promuovere to promote, see **muovere**
propendere to incline, see **pendere**
proporre to propose, see **porre**
prorompere to break out, see **rompere**
prosciogliere to free, see **sciogliere**
proscrivere to banish, see **scrivere**
proteggere to protect
PAST PARTICIPLE **protetto**
PAST DEFINITE **protessi, proteggesti, protesse, proteggemmo, proteggeste, protessero**
protrarre to prolong, see **trarre**
povenire to originate, see **venire**
provvedere to provide, see **vedere**
pungere to sting
PAST PARTICIPLE **punto**
PAST DEFINITE **punsi, pungesti, punse, pungemmo, pungeste, punsero**
putrefare to rot, see **fare**

racchiudere to lock in, see **chiudere**
raccogliere to collect, see **cogliere**
radere to shave
PAST PARTICIPLE **raso**
PAST DEFINITE **rasi, radesti, rase, rademmo, radeste, rasero**
raggiungere to reach, see **giungere**
rarefare to rarefy, see **fare**
ravvedersi to repent, see **vedere**
recidere to cut off
PAST PARTICIPLE **reciso**
PAST DEFINITE **recisi, recidesti, recise, recidemmo, recideste, recisero**
redigere to edit
PAST PARTICIPLE **redatto**
PAST DEFINITE **redassi, redigesti, redasse, redigemmo, redigeste, redassero**
redimere to redeem
PAST PARTICIPLE **redento**
PAST DEFINITE **redensi, redimesti, redense, redimemmo, redimeste, redensero**
reggere to uphold
PAST PARTICIPLE **retto**
PAST DEFINITE **ressi, reggesti, resse, reggemmo, reggeste, ressero**
rendere to render
PAST PARTICIPLE **reso**
PAST DEFINITE **resi, rendesti, rese, rendemmo, rendeste, resero**
reprimere to repress, see **comprimere**
resistere to resist
PAST PARTICIPLE **resistito**
respingere to repel, see **spingere**
restringere to restrict, see **stringere**
richiedere to request, see **chiedere**
riconoscere to recognize, see **conoscere**
ricorrere to appeal, see **correre**
ridere to laugh
PAST PARTICIPLE **riso**
PAST DEFINITE **risi, ridesti, rise, ridemmo, rideste, risero**
ridurre to reduce, see **addurre**
riempire to fill, see **empire**
rifare to redo, see **fare**
riflettere to reflect, see **flettere**
rimanere to remain
PAST PARTICIPLE **rimasto**
PRESENT **rimango, rimani, rimane, rimaniamo, rimanete, rimangono**
FUTURE **rimarrò, rimarrai, rimarrà, rimarremo, rimarrete, rimarranno**
CONDITIONAL **rimarrei, rimarresti, rimarrebbe, rimarremmo, rimarreste, rimarrebbero**
PRESENT SUBJUNCTIVE **rimanga, rimanga, rimanga, rimaniamo, rimaniate, rimangano**
PAST DEFINITE **rimasi, rimanesti, rimase, rimanemmo, rimaneste, rimasero**
rimettere to replace, see **mettere**
rimpiangere to regret, see **piangere**
rinchiudere to enclose, see **chiudere**
rincrescere to cause regret, see **crescere**
rinvenire to find, see **venire**
riporre to put back, see **porre**
riprodurre to reproduce, see **addurre**
riscuotere to cash, see **scuotere**
risiedere to reside, see **sedere**
risolvere to resolve, see **solvere**
rispondere to answer
PAST PARTICIPLE **risposto**
PAST DEFINITE **risposi, rispondesti, rispose, rispondemmo, rispondeste, risposero**
ritenere to hold, see **tenere**
ritorcere to twist, see **torcere**
riuscire to succeed, see **uscire**
rivedere to revise, see **vedere**
rivolgersi to apply, see **volgere**
rodere to gnaw
PAST PARTICIPLE **roso**
PAST DEFINITE **rosi, rodesti, rose, rodemmo, rodeste, rosero**
rompere to break
PAST PARTICIPLE **rotto**
PAST DEFINITE **ruppi, rompesti, ruppe, rompemmo, rompeste, ruppero**

salire to go up
PRESENT **salgo, sali, sale, saliamo, salite, salgono**
PRESENT SUBJUNCTIVE **salga, salga, salga, saliamo, saliate, salgano**
sapere to know
PRESENT **so, sai, sa, sappiamo, sapete, sanno**
FUTURE **saprò saprai, saprà, sapremo, saprete, sapranno**
CONDITIONAL **saprei, sapresti, saprebbe, sapremmo, sapreste, saprebbero**
PRESENT SUBJUNCTIVE **sappia, sappia, sappia, sappiamo, sappiate, sappiano**
PAST DEFINITE **seppi, sapesti, seppe, sapemmo, sapeste, seppero**
scadere to fall due, see **cadere**
scegliere to choose

PAST PARTICIPLE **scelto**
PRESENT **scelgo, scegli, sceglie, scegliamo, scegliete, scelgono**
PRESENT SUBJUNCTIVE **scelga, scelga, scelga, scegliamo, scegliate, scelgano**
scendere to go down
PAST PARTICIPLE **sceso**
PAST DEFINITE **scesi, scendesti, scese, scendemmo, scendeste, scesero**
scindere to split
PAST PARTICIPLE **scisso**
PAST DEFINITE **scissi, scindesti, scisse, scindemmo, scindeste, scissero**
sciogliere to untie
PAST PARTICIPLE **sciolto**
PRESENT **sciolgo, sciogli, sciolgie, sciogliamo, sciogliete, sciolgono**
PRESENT SUBJUNCTIVE **sciolga, sciolga, sciolga, sciogliamo, sciogliate, sciolgano**
PAST DEFINITE **sciolsi, sciogllesti, sciolse, sciogliemmo, scioglieste, sciolsero**
scommettere to bet, see **mettere**
scomparire to disappear, see **apparire**
scomporre to upset, see **porre**
sconfiggere to defeat, see **figgere**
scoprire to uncover, see **coprire**
scorgere to perceive, see **accorgersi**
scorrere to scan, see **correre**
scrivere to write
PAST PARTICIPLE **scritto**
PAST DEFINITE **scrissi, scrivesti, scrisse, scrivemmo, scriveste, scrissero**
scuotere to shake
PAST PARTICIPLE **scosso**
PAST DEFINITE **scossi, scotesti, scosse, scotemmo, scoteste, scossero**
sedere to sit
PRESENT **siedo, siedi, siede, sediamo, sedete, siedono**
PRESENT SUBJUNCTIVE **sieda, sieda, sieda, sediamo, sediate, siedano**
sedurre to seduce, see **addurre**
smettere to stop, see **mettere**
soccorrere to help, see **correre**
soddisfare to satisfy, see **fare**
soffriggere to brown, see **friggere**
soffrire to suffer, see **offrire**
soggiungere to reply, see **giungere**
solere to be used to
PAST PARTICIPLE **solito**
PRESENT **soglio, suoli, suole, sogliamo, solete, sogliono**
PRESENT SUBJUNCTIVE **soglia, soglia, soglia, sogliamo, sogliate, sogliano**
solvere to solve
PAST PARTICIPLE **solto**
sommergere to submerge, see **immergere**
sopprimere to suppress, see **comprimere**
sopraffare to overpower, see **fare**
sopraggiungere to overtake, see **giungere**
sopravvivere to survive, see **vivere**
sorgere to rise
PAST PARTICIPLE **sorto**
PAST DEFINITE **sorsi, sorgesti, sorse, sorgemmo, sorgeste, sorsero**
sorprendere to surprise, see **prendere**
sorreggere to support, see **reggere**
sorridere to smile, see **ridere**
sospendere to suspend, see **pendere**
sostenere to uphold, see **tenere**
sottomettere to subjugate, see **mettere**
sottoporre to submit, see **porre**
sottoscrivere to subscribe, see **scrivere**
sottrarre to subtract, see **trarre**
spargere to scatter
PAST PARTICIPLE **sparso**
PAST DEFINITE **sparsi, spargesti, sparse, spargemmo, spargeste, sparsero**
spegnere to extinguish
PAST PARTICIPLE **spento**
PRESENT **spengo, spegni, spegne, spegniamo, spegnete, spengono**
PRESENT SUBJUNCTIVE **spenga, spenga, spenga, spegniamo, spegniate, spengano**
PAST DEFINITE **spensi, spegnesti, spense, spegnemmo, spegneste, spensero**
spendere to spend
PAST PARTICIPLE **speso**
PAST DEFINITE **spesi, spendesti, spese, spendemmo, spendeste, spesero**
spingere to push
PAST PARTICIPLE **spinto**
PAST DEFINITE **spinsi, spingesti, spinse, spingemmo, spingeste, spinsero**
stare to be
PRESENT **sto, stai, sta, stiamo, state, stanno**
FUTURE **starò, starai, starà, staremo, starete, staranno**
CONDITIONAL **starei, staresti, starebbe, staremmo, stareste, starebbero**
PRESENT SUBJUNCTIVE **stia, stia, stia, stiamo, stiate, stiano**
PAST DEFINITE **stetti, stesti, stette, stemmo, steste, stettero**
PAST SUBJUNCTIVE **stessi, stessi, stesse, stessimo, steste, stessero**
stendere to stretch, see **tendere**
storcere to twist, see **torcere**
strafare to overdo, see **fare**
stringere to squeeze
PAST PARTICIPLE **stretto**
PAST DEFINITE **strinsi, stringesti, strinse, stringemmo, stringeste, strinsero**
succedere to happen
PAST PARTICIPLE **successo**
PAST DEFINITE **successi, succedesti, successe, succedemmo, succedeste, successero**
supporre to suppose, see **porre**
svolgere to unroll, see **volgere**

tacere to keep quiet
PRESENT **taccio, taci, tace, tacciamo, tacete, tacciono**
PRESENT SUBJUNCTIVE **taccia, taccia, taccia, tacciamo, tacciate, tacciano**
PAST DEFINITE **tacqui, tacesti, tacque, tacemmo, taceste, tacquero**
tendere to tend
PAST PARTICIPLE **teso**
PAST DEFINITE **tesi, tendesti, tese, tendemmo, tendeste, tesero**
tenere to hold
PRESENT **tengo, tieni, tiene, teniamo,**

tenete, tengono
FUTURE **terrò, terrai, terrà, terremo, terrete, terranno**
CONDITIONAL **terrei, terresti, terrebbe, terremmo, terreste, terrebbero**
PRESENT SUBJUNCTIVE **tenga, tenga, tenga, teniamo, teniate, tengano**
PAST DEFINITE **tenni, tenesti, tenne, tenemmo, teneste, tennero**
tergere to wipe
PAST PARTICIPLE **terso**
PAST DEFINITE **tersi, tergesti, terse, tergemmo, tergeste, tersero**
tingere to dye
PAST PARTICIPLE **tinto**
PAST DEFINITE **tinsi, tingesti, tinse, tingemmo, tingeste, tinsero**
togliere to take away
PAST PARTICIPLE **tolto**
PRESENT **tolgo, togli, toglie, togliamo, togliete, tolgono**
PRESENT SUBJUNCTIVE **tolga, tolga, tolga, togliamo, togliate, tolgano**
PAST DEFINITE **tolsi, togliesti, tolse, togliemmo, toglieste, tolsero**
torcere to twist
PAST PARTICIPLE **torto**
PAST DEFINITE **torsi, torcesti, torse, torcemmo, torceste, torsero**
tradurre to translate, see **addurre**
transigere to compromise, see **esigere**
trarre to take in
PRESENT PARTICIPLE **traendo**
PAST PARTICIPLE **tratto**
PRESENT **traggo, trai, trae, traiamo, traete, traggono**
FUTURE **trarrò, trarrai, trarrà, trarremo, trarrete, trarranno**
CONDITIONAL **trarrei, trarresti, trarrebbe, trarremmo, trarreste, trarrebbero**
PRESENT SUBJUNCTIVE **tragga, tragga, tragga, traiamo, traiate, traggano**
IMPERFECT **traevo, traevi, traeva, traevamo, traevate, traevano**
PAST DEFINITE **trassi, traesti, trasse, traemmo, traeste, trassero**
PAST SUBJUNCTIVE **traessi, traessi, traesse, traessimo, traeste, traessero**
trascendere to transcend, see **scendere**
trascorrere to elapse, see **correre**
trasmettere to transmit, see **mettere**
trattenere to withhold, see **tenere**
travolgere to overcome, see **volgere**

uccidere to kill
PAST PARTICIPLE **ucciso**
PAST DEFINITE **uccisi, uccidesti, uccise, uccidemmo, uccideste, uccisero**
udire to hear
PRESENT **odo, odi, ode, udiamo, udite, odono**
PRESENT SUBJUNCTIVE **oda, oda, oda, udiamo, udiate, odano**
ungere to grease
PAST PARTICIPLE **unto**
PAST DEFINITE **unsi, ungesti, unse, ungemmo, ungeste, unsero**
uscire to exit
PRESENT **esco, esci, esce, usciamo, uscite, escono**
PRESENT SUBJUNCTIVE **esca, esca, esca, usciamo, usciate, escano**

valere to be worth
PAST PARTICIPLE **valso**
PRESENT **valgo, vali, vale, valiamo, valete, valgono**
FUTURE **varrò, varrai, varrà, varremo, varrete, varranno**
CONDITIONAL **varrei, varresti, varrebbe, varremmo, varreste, varrebbero**
PRESENT SUBJUNCTIVE **valga, valga, valga, valiamo, valiate, valgano**
PAST DEFINITE **valsi, valesti, valse, valemmo, valeste, valsero**
vedere to see
PAST PARTICIPLE **visto**
FUTURE **vedrò, vedrai, vedrà, vedremo, vedrete, vedranno**
CONDITIONAL **vedrei, vedresti, vedrebbe, vedremmo, vedreste, vedrebbero**
PAST DEFINITE **vidi, vedesti, vide, vedemmo, vedeste, videro**
venire to come
PRESENT PARTICIPLE **venuto**
PRESENT **vengo, vieni, viene, veniamo, venite, vengono**
FUTURE **verrò, verrai, verrà, verremo, verrete, verranno**
CONDITIONAL **verrei, verresti, verrebbe, verremmo, verreste, verrebbero**
PRESENT SUBJUNCTIVE **venga, venga, venga, veniamo, veniate, vengano**
PAST DEFINITE **venni, venisti, venne, venimmo, veniste, vennero**
vincere to win
PAST PARTICIPLE **vinto**
PAST DEFINITE **vinsi, vincesti, vinse, vincemmo, vinceste, vinsero**
vivere to live
PAST PARTICIPLE **vissuto**
FUTURE **vivrò, vivrai, vivrà, vivremo, vivrete, vivranno**
CONDITIONAL **vivrei, vivresti, vivrebbe, vivremmo, vivreste, vivrebbero**
PAST DEFINITE **vissi, vivesti, visse, vivemmo, viveste, vissero**
volere to want
PRESENT **voglio, vuoi, vuole, vogliamo, volete, vogliono**
FUTURE **vorrò, vorrai, vorrà, vorremo, vorrete, vorranno**
CONDITIONAL **vorrei, vorresti, vorrebbe, vorremmo, vorreste, vorrebbero**
PRESENT SUBJUNCTIVE **voglia, voglia, voglia, vogliamo, vogliate, vogliano**
PAST DEFINITE **volli, volesti, volle, volemmo, voleste, vollero**
volgere to turn
PAST PARTICIPLE **volto**
PAST DEFINITE **volsi, volgesti, volse, volgemmo, volgeste, volsero**

ABBREVIATIONS

a	adjective	*interj*	interjection
adv	adverb	*lit*	literature
aesp	aerospace	*m*	masculine
agr	agriculture	*math*	mathematics
anat	anatomy	*mech*	mechanics
arch	architecture	*med*	medicine
art	article	*mil*	military
ast	astronomy	*min*	mineralogy
auto	automobile	*mus*	music
avi	aviation	*n*	noun
biol	biology	*naut*	nautical
bot	botany	*phot*	photography
chem	chemistry	*phys*	physics
coll	colloquial	*pl*	plural
com	commerce	*pol*	politics
comp	compound	*prep*	preposition
conj	conjunction	*print*	printing
dent	dentistry	*pron*	pronoun
eccl	ecclesiastic	*rad*	radio
elec	electricity	*rail*	railway
f	feminine	*sl*	slang
fam	familiar	*theat*	theatre
fig	figuratively	*TV*	television
for	formal	*vi*	verb intransitive
geog	geography	*vt*	verb transitive
geol	geology	*vt&i*	verb transitive and intransitive
gram	grammar	*zool*	zoology

* An asterisk following an Italian entry indicates that it is one of the irregular verbs for which conjugation is supplied in the grammar section, pages 25 to 33.

Italian-English

A

a (â) *prep* to, at, in, until
abate (â·bâ'tā) *m* abbot
abbacchiamento (âb·bâk·kyâ·mān'tō) *m* dejection, depression
abbacchiare (âb·bâk·kyâ'rā) *vt* to deject, depress
abbacchiarsi (âb·bâk·kyâr'sē) *vr* to lose one's courage; to become dejected
abbacchiato (âb·bâk·kyâ'tō) *a* dejected, dispirited, depressed
abbacchio (âb·bâk'kyō) *m* lamb
abbacinamento (âb·bâ·chē·nâ·mān'tō) *m* dazzling; bewilderment
abbacinare (âb·bâ·chē·nâ'rā) *vt* to dazzle, blind
abbaco (âb'bâ·kō) *m* abacus
abbadessa (âb·bâ·dās'sâ) *f* abbess
abbadia (âb·bâ·dē'â) *f* abbey
abbagliamento (âb·bâ·lyâ·mān'tō) *m* mistake, confusion
abbagliante (âb·bâ·lyân'tā) *a* dazzling; — *m* (*auto*) high-beam headlight
abbagliare (âb·bâ·lyâ'rā) *vt* to dazzle; to confuse, bewilder
abbaglio (âb·bâ'lyō) *m* dazzling, bewilderment; mistake
abbaiamento (âb·bâ·yâ·mān'tō) *m* barking
abbaiare (âb·bâ·yâ'rā) *vi* to bark
abbaiatore (âb·bâ·yâ·tō'rā) *m* muckraker
abbaino (âb·bâ·ē'nō) *m* dormer; attic window
abbandonamento (âb·bân·dō·nâ·mān'tō) *m* abandonment; surrender
abbandonare (âb·bân·dō·nâ'rā) *vt* to abandon; to fail
abbandonarsi (âb·bân·dō·nâr'sē) *vr* to indulge oneself; to lose one's spirits
abbandonatamente (âb·bân·dō·nâ·tâ·mān'tā) *adv* carelessly; passionately
abbandonato (âb·bân·dō·nâ'tō) *a* abandoned, deserted
abbandono (âb·bân·dō'nō) *m* abandonment; recklessness
abbarbagliamento (âb·bâr·bâ·lyâ·mān'tō) *m* dazzling; dizziness
abbarbagliare (âb·bâr·bâ·lyâ'rā) *vt* to dazzle; to deceive, bewilder
abbarbicare (âb·bâr·bē·kâ'rā) *vi* to take root; to become established
abbarbicato (âb·bâr·bē·kâ'tō) *a* rooted; settled
abbarcare (âb·bâr·kâ'rā) *vt* to heap, pile up
abbassamento (âb·bâs·sâ·mān'tō) *m* abatement; reduction
abbassare (âb·bâs·sâ'rā) *vt* to lower; to cut off, reduce
abbassarsi (âb·bâs·sâr'sē) *vr* to stoop, bow down; to humble oneself; to debase oneself
abbasso (âb·bâs'sō) *adv* down; low; —! *interj* down with!
abbastanza (âb·bâ·stân'tsâ) *adv* enough; quite
abbattere (âb·bât'tā·rā) *vt* to knock down; to shoot down; to fell; to deject
abbattersi (âb·bât'tār·sē) *vr* to be dejected; to lose one's spirits; to be demolished
abbattimento (âb·bât·tē·mān'tō) *m* demolition; cutting down; dejection
abbattuto (âb·bât·tū'tō) *a* demolished; dejected
abbazia (âb·bâ·tsē'â) *f* abbey
abbecedario (âb·bā·chā·dâ'ryō) *m* primer, first reader
abbellimento (âb·bāl·lē·mān'tō) *m* embellishment, beautifying
abbellire (âb·bāl·lē'rā) *vt* to embellish, beautify
abbeverare (âb·bā·vā·râ'rā) *vt* to water (*livestock*)
abbigliamento (âb·bē·lyâ·mān'tō) *m* wearing apparel; **industria dell'—** clothing industry
abbigliare (âb·bē·lyâ'rā) *vt* to dress; to adorn; to clothe
abbigliarsi (âb·bē·lyâr'sē) *vr* to get dressed; to attire oneself
abbinare (âb·bē·nâ'rā) *vt* to couple, join
abbindolare (âb·bēn·dō·lâ'rā) *vt* to cheat, deceive, defraud

abboccamento (âb·bōk·kâ·mān'tō) *m* interview
abboccare (âb·bōk·kâ'rā) *vt* to bite *(fish)*; — **all'amo** to take the bait
abboccarsi (âb·bōk·kâr'sē) *vr* to confer with; to converse in private
abboccato (âb·bōk·kâ'tō) *a* sweetish; palatable
abbonamento (âb·bō·nâ·mān'tō) *m* subscription
abbonare (âb·bō·nâ'rā) *vt* to give a discount to
abbonarsi (âb·bō·nâr'sē) *vr* to subscribe; to take a subscription
abbondanza (âb·bōn·dân'tsâ) *f* abundance, wealth
abbondare (âb·bōn·dâ'rā) *vi* to abound; to teem
abbondevole (âb·bōn·de'vō·lā) *a* abundant, plentiful
abbondevolezza (âb·bōn·dā·vō·lā'tsâ) *f* abundance, plenty
abbondevolmente (âb·bōn·dā·vōl·mān'tā) *adv* abundantly; in large numbers
abbottonare (âb·bōt·tō·nâ'rā) *vt* to button
abbottonato (âb·bōt·tō·nâ'tō) *a* buttoned
abbozzare (âb·bō·tsâ'rā) *vt* to delineate; to sketch; to outline, rough in
abbracciare (âb·brâ·châ'rā) *vt* to hug, embrace
abbraccio (âb·brâ'chō) *m* embrace, hug
abbreviare (âb·brā·vyâ'rā) *vt* to abbreviate; to curtail
abbreviatura (âb·brā·vyâ·tū'râ) *f* abbreviation, shortening
abbronzare (âb·brōn·dzâ'rā) *vt* to bronze; to tan
abbronzato (âb·brōn·dzâ'tō) *a* suntanned
abbronzatura (âb·brōn·dzâ·tū'râ) *f* sunburn; bronzing; tanning
abbrunare (âb·brū·nâ'rā), **abbrunire** (âb·brū·nē'rā) *vt* to brown; to tan
abbrunarsi (âb·brū·nâr'sē), **abbrunirsi** (âb·brū·nēr'sē) *vr* to become sunburned; to wear mourning
abbrunato (âb·brū·nâ'tō), **abbrunito** (âb·brū·nē'tō) *a* browned; dark; tanned
abbrustolire (âb·brū·stō·lē'rā) *vt* to roast; to broil; to toast
abbrutimento (âb·brū·tē·mān'tō) *m* brutality
abbrutire (âb·brū·tē'rā) *vt* to brutalize
abbrutirsi (âb·brū·tēr'sē) *vr* to become brutal
abbrutito (âb·brū·tē'tō) *a* brutalized
abbuono (âb·bwō'nō) *m* allowance
abdicare (âb·dē·kâ'rā) *vi* to abdicate
abdicato (âb·dē·kâ'tō) *a* abdicated
abdicazione (âb·dē·kâ·tsyō'nā) *f* abdication
aberrazione (â·bār·râ·tsyō'nā) *f* aberration
abete (â·bā'tā) *m* fir tree
abietto (âb·byāt'tō) *a* despicable, low, mean
abigeato (â·bē·jā·â'tō) *m* rustling, cattle theft
abile (â'bē·lā) *a* able, skillful
abilità (â·bē·lē·tâ') *f* ability, aptitude
abilitazione (â·bē·lē·tâ·tsyō'nā) *f* certificate of competence
abilmente (â·bēl·mān'tā) *adv* ably
abisso (â·bēs'sō) *m* abyss, chasm
abitabile (â·bē·tâ'bē·lā) *a* habitable
abitacolo (â·bē·tâ'kō·lō) *m* (*avi*) cockpit
abitante (â·bē·tân'tā) *m* inhabitant
abitare (â·bē·tâ'rā) *vt&i* to live in, inhabit
abitazione (â·bē·tâ·tsyō'nā) *f* residence, home
abito (â'bē·tō) *m* suit (*clothing*)
abituale (â·bē·twâ'lā) *a* habitual, accustomed
abitualmente (â·bē·twâl·mān'tā) *adv* usually, customarily
abituare (â·bē·twâ'ra) *vt* to accustom
abituarsi (â·bē·twâr'sē) *vr* to accustom oneself; to grow used to
abituato (â·bē·twâ'tō) *a* used to, in the habit of
abitudine (â·bē·tū'dē·nā) *f* custom; usage
abluzione (â·blū·tsyō'nā) *f* ablution
abolire (â·bō·lē'rā) *vt* to abolish; to do away with
abolizione (ā·bō·lē·tsyō'nā) *f* abolition
abominabile (â·bō·mē·nâ'bē·lā) *a* abominable, loathsome
abominare (â·bō·mē·nâ'rā) *vt* to abominate, loathe
abominazione (â·bō·mē·nâ·tsyō'nā) *f* abomination
abominevole (â·bō·mē·ne'vō·lā) *a* abominable
aborrire (â·bōr·rē'rā) *vt* to abhor; to detest
abortire (â·bōr·tē'rā) *vi* to miscarry; to come to nothing, fall short
aborto (â·bōr'tō) *m* miscarriage; abortion; falling short
abrasione (â·brâ·zyō'nā) *f* abrasion
abrogare (â·brō·gâ'rā) *vt* to abrogate
abside (âb'zē·dā) *f* apse
abusare (â·bū·zâ'rā) *vi* to take advantage of; to abuse; to impose on
abusato (â·bū·zâ'tō) *a* abused; misused
abusivamente (â·bū·zē·vâ·mān'tā) *adv* unjustly
abusivo (â·bū·zē'vō) *a* abusive; unjust
abuso (â·bū'zō) *m* abuse; imposition
accademia (âk·kâ·de'myâ) *f* academy
accademico (âk·kâ·de'mē·kō) *a* academic; scholastic
accademista (âk·kâ·dā·mē'stâ) *m&f* academy member
accadere * (âk·kâ·dā'rā) *vi* to happen
accalappiare (âk·kâ·lâp·pyâ'rā) *vt* to inveigle, entrap; to hoodwink
accalappiacani (âk·kâ·lâp·pyâ·kâ'nē) *m* dogcatcher
accalorarsi (âk·kâ·lō·râr'sē) *vr* to become excited; to be aroused
accampamento (âk·kâm·pâ·mān'tō) *m* encampment, camp
accampare (âk·kâm·pâ'rā) *vi* to encamp; to state, contend
accanire (âk·kâ·nē'rā) *vt* to irritate; to vex

accanirsi (âk·kâ·nēr'sē) *vr* to be persistent
accanito (âk·kâ·nē'to) *a* furious; obstinate
accanto (âk·kân'tō) *adv&prep* near, by, beside
accapparrare (âk·kâp·pâr·râ'rā) *vt (com)* to corner; to hoard
accappatoio (âk·kâp·pâ·tô'yō) *m* bathrobe
accapigliarsi (âk·kâ·pē·lyâr'sē) *vr* to come to blows; to scuffle, grapple
accapponare (âk·kâp·pō·nâ'rā) *vt* to castrate; — **la pelle** *(fig)* to cause goose pimples
accarezzare (âk·kâ·rā·tsâ'rā) *vt* to caress, pet
accasciamento (âk·kâ·shâ·mān'tō) *m* depression; fatigue
accasciare (âk·kâ·shâ'rā) *vt* to depress
accasciarsi (âk·kâ·shâr'sē) *vr* to become depressed
accattone (âk·kât·tō'nā) *m* mendicant, beggar
accecare (â·chā·kâ'rā) *vt* to blind; to bewilder
accedere (â·che'dā·rā) *vi* to approach; to consent to, accept
accelerare (â·chā·lā·râ'rā) *vt* to speed up, accelerate
accelerato (â·chā·lā·râ'tō) *a* accelerated; — *m* local train; **–re** (â·chā·lā·râ·tō'rā) *m (auto)* accelerator pedal
accelerazione (â·chā·lā·râ·tsyō'nā) *f* acceleration; *(auto)* pickup
accendere * (â·chen'dā·rā) *vt* to light; to illuminate; to motivate, stir
accendersi * (â·chen'dār·sē) *vr* to catch fire; to burn
accendisigari (â·chān·dē·sē'gâ·rē) *m* cigarette lighter
accennare (â·chān·nâ'rā) *vt&i* to hint; to point out; to treat, deal with
accensione (â·chān·syō'nā) *f (auto)* ignition
accento (â·chān'tō) *m* accent
accerchiare (â·chār·kyâ'rā) *vt* to surround; to ring
accertare (â·chār·tâ'rā) *vt* to make sure of; to verify
acceso (â·chā'zō) *a* lighted, lit, on
accessibile (â·chās·sē'bē·lā) *a* approachable
accesso (â·chās'sō) *m* access; spasm, fit
accessorio (â·chās·sô'ryō) *a* accessory; — *m* fixture; equipment
accetta (â·chāt'tâ) *f* hatchet
accettabile (â·chāt·tâ'bē·lā) *a* acceptable, agreeable
accettare (â·chāt·tâ'rā) *vt* to accept
accettazione (â·chāt·tâ·tsyō'nā) *f* acceptance, agreement
accettevole (â·chāt·te'vō·lā) *a* pleasant; acceptable
accettevolmente (â·chāt·tā·vōl·mān'tā) *adv* acceptably
accezione (â·chā·tsyō'nā) *f* accepted meaning of a word; accepted expression
acchiappare (âk·kyâp·pâ'rā) *vt* to catch; to snare
acchito (âk·kē'tō) *m* lead, leading off
acciacchi (â·châk'kē) *mpl* infirmities; weaknesses
acciaio (â·châ'yō) *m* steel
accidentale (â·chē·dān·tâ'lā) *a* accidental; casual, happenstance
accidentalmente (â·chē·dān·tâl·mān'tā) *adv* accidentally
accidentato (â·chē·dān·tâ'tō) *a* uneven
accidente (â·chē·dān'tā) *m* apoplectic stroke; accident
accidia (â·chē'dyâ) *f* indolence; laziness
accigliarsi (â·chē·lyâr'sē) *vr* to knit one's brows; to scowl
accigliato (â·chē·lyâ'tō) *a* frowning; unhappy
accingersi (â·chēn'jār·sē) *vr* to get ready
accinto (â·chēn'tō) *a* ready, prepared
acciottolato (â·chōt·tō·lâ'tō) *m* cobblestone pavement
acciuffare (â·chūf·fâ'rā) *vt* to catch; to grasp, grab
acciuga (ā·chū'gâ) *f* anchovy
acclamare (âk·klâ·mâ'rā) *vt* to acclaim
acclamazione (âk·klâ·mâ·tsyō'nā) *f* acclamation
acclimatazione (âk·klē·mâ·tâ·tsyō'nā) *f* acclimatation
acclimatarsi (âk·klē·mâ·târ'sē) *vr* to grow acclimated; to get used to
accludere * (âk·klū'dā·rā) *vt* to enclose, attach
accluso (âk·klū'zō) *a* enclosed, attached
accogliere * (âk·kô'lyā·rā) *vt* to welcome; to receive
accoglienza (âk·kō·lyān'tsâ) *f* welcome; reception
accoglimento (âk·kō·lyē·mān'tō) *m* reception; assemblage
accollare (âk·kōl·lâ'rā) *vt* to shoulder; to join
accollarsi (âk·kōl·lâr'sē) *vr* to take charge of; to assume
accollato (âk·kōl·lâ'tō) *a* high-necked
accoltellare (âk·kōl·tāl·lâ'rā) *vt* to stab with a knife
accomandare (âk·kō·mân·dâ'rā) *vt* to give into custody; to commend, hand over
accomandatario (âk·kō·mân·dâ·tâ'ryō) *m (com)* general partner
accomandita (âk·kō·mân·dē'tâ) *f* limited partnership
accomiatarsi (âk·kō·myâ·târ'sē) *vr* to take one's leave; to say good-bye; to part
accomodamento (âk·kō·mō·dâ·mān'tō) *m* adjustment, settlement; repair
accomodare (âk·kō·mō·dâ'rā) *vt* to adjust; to repair
accomodarsi (âk·kō·mō·dâr'sē) *vr* to sit down, be seated
accomodato (âk·kō·mō·dâ'tō) *a* adjusted; repaired
accomodatura (âk·kō·mō·dâ·tū'râ) *f* adjusting; fixing, repairing
accompagnare (âk·kōm·pâ·nyâ'rā) *vt* to accompany, go with

accompagnatore (âk·kōm·pâ·nyâ·tō·rā) *m* escort; *(mus)* accompanist
acconciare (âk·kōn·châ'rā) *vt* to ready; to adapt
acconciatura (âk·kōn·châ·tū'râ) *f* hairdo
acconsentimento (âk·kōn·sān·tē·mān'tō) *m* consent, agreement
acconsentire (âk·kōn·sān·tē'rā) *vi* to consent, agree
accontentare (âk·kōn·tān·tâ'rā) *vt* to please; to make happy
acconto (âk·kōn'tō) *m* *(com)* account; deposit
accoppare (âk·kōp·pâ'rā) *vt* to kill; to beat to death
accoppiamento (âk·kōp·pyâ·mān'tō) *m* coupling
accoppiare (âk·kōp·pyâ'rā) *vt* to match; to unite
accorciare (âk·kōr·châ'rā) *vt* to make shorter, abbreviate
accordare (âk·kōr·dâ'rā) *vt* to grant; *(mus)* to tune; to permit
accordo (âk·kōr'dō) *m* agreement, consensus; **d'—!** agreed!
accorgersi * (âk·kôr'jār·sē) *vr* to notice, observe
accorgimento (âk·kōr·jē·mān'tō) *m* shrewdness; circumspection; prudence
accorrere * (âk·kôr'rā·rā) *vi* to run; to rush up
accortamente (âk·kōr·tâ·mān'tā) *adv* shrewdly, cunningly
accorto (âk·kōr'tō) *a* shrewd, circumspect
accostamento (âk·kōs·tâ·mān'tō) *m* approach, access
accostare (âk·kō·stâ'rā) *vt* to approach, draw near
accreditare (âk·krā·dē·tâ'rā) *vt* *(com)* to extend credit to, credit
accreditarsi (âk·krā·dē·târ'sē) *vr* to gain esteem, be credited
accreditato (âk·krā·dē·tâ'tō) *a* accredited; authorized; estimable, worthy
accrescere * (âk·kre'shā·rā) *vt* to increase
accudire (âk·kū·dē'rā) *vi* to care for
accumulare (âk·kū·mū·lâ'rā) *vt* to accumulate
accumulatore (âk·kū·mū·lâ·tō'rā) *m* *(elec)* battery
accumulazione (âk·kū·mū·lâ·tsyō'nā) *f* accumulation
accuratamente (âk·kū·râ·tâ·mān'tā) *adv* accurately, exactly
accurato (âk·kū·râ'tō) *a* accurate, precise
accuratezza (âk·kū·râ·tā'tsâ) *f* accuracy
accusa (âk·kū'zâ) *f* accusation; **atto d'—** indictment; **capo d'—** count of an indictment **–re** (âk·kū·zâ'rā) *vt* to accuse, indict; **–to** (âk·kū·zâ'tō) *a* accused; **–to** *m* defendant
acerbo (â·châr'bō) *a* not ripe; sour
acerrimo (â·cher'rē·mō) *a* very fierce
acetico (â·che'tē·kō) *a* acetic
aceto (â·chā'tō) *m* vinegar; **–liera** (â·chā·tō·lyā'râ) *f* set of cruets for oil and vinegar
acidità (â·chē·dē·tâ') *f* acidity
acido (â'chē·dō) *a&m* acid
acino (â'chē·nō) *m* grape; grapeseed
acqua (âk'kwâ) *f* water; **— ossigenata** hydrogen peroxide; **— potabile** drinking water; **— di Colonia** cologne, toilet water; **–forte** (âk·kwâ·fōr'tā) *f* etching; **–io** (âk·kwâ'yō) *m* sink; **–piano** (âk·kwâ·plâ'nō) *m* aquaplane; **–rio** (âk·kwâ'ryō) *m* aquarium; **–vite** (âk·kwâ·vē'tā) *f* brandy; **–zzone** (âk·kwâ·tsō'nā) *m* shower of rain
acquattarsi (âk·kwât·târ'sē) *vr* to crouch; to hide
acquerello (âk·kwā·rāl'lō) *m* water color
acquirente (âk·kwē·rān'tā) *m&f* purchaser, customer
acquisire (âk·kwē·zē'rā) *vt* to acquire
acquistare (âk·kwē·stâ'rā) *vt* to buy
acquitrino (âk·kwē·trē'nō) *m* swamp, marsh
acre (â'krā) *a* acrid, sharp
acrobata (â·krô'bâ·tâ) *m&f* acrobat
acromatico (â·krō·mâ'tē·kō) *a* achromatic
acuire (â·kwē'rā) *vt* to whet, sharpen
aculeo (â·kū'lā·o) *m* sting; goad, spur; stimulus
acume (â·kū'mā) *m* sharpness, insight; subtlety
acustica (â·kū'stē·kâ) *f* acoustics
acutezza (â·kū·tā'tsâ) *f* acuteness
acuto (â·kū'tō) *a* sharp
adagiare (â·dâ·jâ'rā) *vt* to lay; to put
adagio (â·dâ'jō) *adv* slowly; easily
adattabile (â·dât·tâ'bē·lā) *a* applicable
adattabilità (â·dât·tâ·bē·lē·tâ') *f* suitability, aptitude
adattamento (â·dât·tâ·mān'tō) *m* adaptation; adjustment
adattare (â·dât·tâ'rā) *vt* to adapt
adatto (â·dât'tō) *a* fitting, suitable, fit
addebitare (âd·dā·bē·tâ'rā) *vt* to debit
addebito (âd·de'bē·tō) *m* debit
addentare (âd·dān·tâ'rā) *vt* to bite
addestrare (âd·dā·strâ'rā) *vt* to drill; to instruct; to prepare
addetto (âd·dā'tō) *m* attendant; **— d'ambasciata** attaché
addio (âd·dē'ō) *interj&m* good-bye
addirittura (âd·dē·rēt·tū'râ) *adv* absolutely, altogether
additamento (âd·dē·tâ·mān'tō) *m* indication, designation
additare (âd·dē·tâ'rā) *vt* to indicate, show
addizionale (âd·dē·tsyō·nâ'lā) *a* additional
addizionare (âd·dē·tsyō·nâ'rā) *vt* to add
addizionatrice (âd·dē·tsyō·nâ·trē'chā) *f* adding machine
addizione (âd·dē·tsyō'nā) *f* *(math)* addition
addolcimento (âd·dōl·chē·mān'tō) *m* softening; mitigation
addolcire (âd·dōl·chē'rā) *vt* to sweeten; to soften
addolcitore (âd·dōl·chē·tō'rā) *m* water softener
addolorare (âd·dō·lō·râ'rā) *vt* to afflict, grieve; to sadden

addolorarsi (âd·dō·lō·râr'sē) *vr* to grieve; to be saddened
addolorato (âd·dō·lō·râ'tō) *a* saddened
addome (âd·dō'mā) *m* abdomen, belly
addormentare (âd·dōr·mān·tâ'rā) *vt* to put to sleep
addormentarsi (âd·dōr·mān·târ'sē) *vr* to fall asleep
addosso (âd·dōs'sō) *prep&adv* on; on one's back
addurre * (âd·dūr'rā) *vt* to adduce
adeguatamente (â·dā·gwâ·tâ·mān'tā) *adv* equally; adequately
adeguato (â·dā·gwâ'tō) *a* adequate
adempiere * (â·dem'pyā·rā) *vt* to accomplish; to perform
adempimento (â·dām·pē·mān'tō) *m* execution, accomplishment; performance
aderente (â·dā·rān'tā) *m* follower; — *a* tight-fitting
aderire (â·dā·rē'rā) *vi* to join; to consent; to adhere
adesione (â·dā·zyō'nā) *f* adherence
adesivo (â·dā·zē'vō) *a* adhesive
adesso (â·dās'sō) *adv* now, at the present time
adiacente (â·dyâ·chān'tā) *a* adjacent, contiguous
adiacenza (â·dyâ·chān'tsâ) *f* contiguity
adipe (â'dē·pā) *m* grease, fat
adiposo (â·dē·pō'zō) *a* adipose, fatty
adirare (â·dē·râ'rā) *vt* to anger
adirarsi (â·dē·râr'sē) *vr* to get angry
adirato (â·dē·râ'tō) *a* angry
adocchiare (â·dōk·kyâ'rā) *vt* to behold; to eye, ogle
adocchiato (â·dōk·kyâ'tō) *a* beheld; eyed
adolescente (â·dō·lā·shān'tā) *mf&a* adolescent; — *m&f* teenager
adolescenza (â·dō·lā·shān'tsâ) *f* adolescence
adombramento (â·dōm·brâ·mān'tō) *m* offense; shade; resentment
adombrare (â·dōm·brâ'rā) *vt* to shade
adombrarsi (â·dōm·brâr'sē) *vr* to get hurt; to become suspicious
adoperabile (â·dō·pā·râ'bē·lā) *a* employable; usable
adoperare (â·dō·pā·râ'rā) *vt* to use
adorabile (â·dō·râ'bē·lā) *a* adorable
adorare (â·dō·râ'rā) *vt* to adore, worship
adoratore (â·dō·râ·tō'rā) *m* adorer, worshiper
adornare (â·dōr·nâ'rā) *vt* to adorn
adorno (â·dōr'nō) *a* adorned; — *m* ornament
adottare (â·dōt·tâ'rā) *vt* to adopt; to make use of
adottato (â·dōt·tâ'tō) *a* adopted; used
adottivo (â·dōt·tē'vō) *a* adoptive; adopted
adozione (â·dō·tsyō'nā) *f* adoption
adulare (â·dū·lâ'rā) *vt* to flatter
adulatore (â·dū·lâ·tō'rā) *m* flatterer
adulazione (â·dū·lâ·tsyō'nā) *f* flattery
adulterare (â·dūl·tā·râ'rā) *vt* to adulterate; to represent falsely
adulterio (â·dūl·te'ryō) *m* adultery
adultero (â·dūl'tā·rō) *m* adulterer; — *a* adulterous
adulto (â·dūl'tō) *a&m* adult
adunare (â·dū·nâ'rā) *vt* to convene, gather
adunata (â·dū·nâ'tâ) *f* rally, meeting, gathering
aereo (â·e'rā·ō) *a* air; — *m* airplane; **in** — by plane
aerodinamico (â·ā·rō·dē·nâ'mē·kō) *a* streamlined
aerodromo (â·ā·rô'drō·mō) *m* airport
aerofaro (â·ā·rō·fâ'rō) *m* aerial beacon
aerogramma (â·ā·rō·grâm'mâ) *m* air letter
aerolito (â·ā·rô'·lē·tō) *m (ast)* aerolite
aerometro (â·ā·rô'mā·trō) *m* aerometer
aeronauta (â·ā·rō·nâ'ū·tâ) *m&f* aeronaut, airman
aeronautica (â·ā·rō·nâ'ū·tē·kâ) *f* aeronautics; — **militare** air force
aeroplano (â·ā·rō·plâ'nō) *m* airplane
aeroporto (â·ā·rō·pōr'tō) *m* airport
aerosilurante (â·ā·rō·sē·lū·rân'tā) *m* torpedo plane
aerospazio (â·ā·rō·spâ'tsyō) *m* aerospace
aerostatica (â·ā·rō·stâ'tē·kâ) *f* aerostatics
aerostazione (â·ā·rō·stâ·tsyō'nā) *f* air terminal
aerostiere (â·ā·rō·styā'rā) *m* balloonist
aerotermo (â·ā·rō·tār'mō) *m* unit heater
aerotrasportato (â·ā·rō·trâ·spōr·tâ'tō) *a* transported by airplane, airborne
afa (â'fâ) *f* closeness, sultry weather
afelio (â·fe'lyō) *m (ast)* aphelion
affabile (âf·fâ'bē·lā) *a* affable, civil, pleasant
affabilità (âf·fâ·bē·lē·tâ') *f* affability, pleasantness
affabilmente (âf·fâ·bēl·mān'tā) *adv* affably, pleasantly
affaccendato (âf·fâ·chān·dâ'tō) *a* busy, occupied
affacciarsi (âf·fâ·châr'sē) *vr* to show oneself, appear; to lean out
affamare (âf·fâ·mâ'rā) *vt* to famish
affamato (âf·fâ·mâ'tō) *a* starved, famished
affannare (âf·fân·nâ'rā) *vt* to bother, worry
affannarsi (âf·fân·nâr'sē) *vr* to bustle, be anxious; to go to a lot of trouble
affannato (âf·fân·nâ'tō) *a* anxious; upset
affanno (âf·fân'nō) *m* affliction; trouble
affannosamente (âf·fân·nō·zâ·mān'tā) *adv* asthmatically; anxiously
affare (âf·fâ'rā) *m* affair; business; transaction
affarista (âf·fâ·rē'stâ) *m (com)* speculator; go-getter
affascinante (âf·fâ·shē·nân'tā) *a* fascinating, charming
affaticare (âf·fâ·tē·kâ'rā) *vt* to fatigue
affatto (âf·fât'tō) *adv* completely; **non** — not at all
affermare (âf·fār·mâ'rā) *vt* to affirm; to certify
affermarsi (âf·fār·mâr'sē) *vr* to succeed; to make a good showing
afferrare (âf·fār·râ'rā) *vt* to grab; to conceive of, comprehend
affettare (âf·fāt·tâ'rā) *vt* to slice; to af-

fect, make a show of
affettato (âf·fāt·tâ'tō) *a* sliced; affected
affetto (âf·fāt'tō) *m* affection
affettivo (âf·fāt·tē'vō) *a* emotional
affettuoso (âf·fāt·twō'zō) *a* affectionate
affettuosamente (âf·fāt·twō·zâ·mān'tā) *adv* affectionately
affettuosità (âf·fāt·twō·zē·tâ') *f* fondness
affezionare (âf·fā·tsyō·nâ'rā) *vt* to make fond; to endear oneself to
affezionarsi (âf·fā·tsyō·nâr'sē) *vr* to grow fond of, become attached to
affezionato (âf·fā·tsyō·nâ'tō) *a* fond; affectionate; attached
affidare (âf·fē·dâ'rā) *vt* to commit, trust; to give to one's keeping
affidarsi (âr·fē·dâr'sē) *vr* to have confidence; to depend on
affilare (âf·fē·lâ'rā) *vt* to sharpen
affinchè (âf·fēn·kā') *conj* so that; in order that; in order to
affine (âf·fē'nā) *a* related
affinità (âf·fē·nē·tâ') *f* affinity
affissione (âf·fēs·syō'nā) *f* posting; **proibita l'—** post no bills
affisso (âf·fēs'sō) *m* poster; **vietati gli affissi** post no bills
affittare (âf·fēt·tâ'rā) *vt* to rent
affitto (âf·fēt'tō) *m* rent
affliggere * âf·flēj'jā·rā) *vt* to afflict; to upset, bother
afflitto (âf·flēt'tō) *a* afflicted; sad
afflizione (âf·flē·tsyō'nā) *f* affliction; grief
affogare (âf·fō·gâ'rā) *vt&i* to drown; to overwhelm
affogato (âf·fō·gâ'tō) *a* drowned; (*egg*) poached
affondamento (âf·fōn·dâ·mān'tō) *m* sinking; submerging
affondare (âf·fōn·dâ'rā) *vt* to sink
affrancatura (âf·frân·kâ·tū'râ) *f* postage
affresco (âf·frā'skō) *m* fresco
affrettare (âf·frāt·tâ'rā) *vt* to hurry, speed up
affrettato (âf·frāt·tâ'tō) *a* hasty; in a hurry
affrontare (âf·frōn·tâ'rā) *vt* to defy; to face; to insult
affronto (âf·frōn'tō) *m* affront, insult
affumicare (âf·fū·mē·kâ'rā) *vt* to cure, smoke
affumicato (âf·fū·mē·kâ'tō) *a* smoked, cured
affusolato (âf·fū·zō·lâ'tō) *a* slender; tapering
afoso (â·fō'zō) *a* sultry; excessively hot
Africa (â'frē·kâ) *f* Africa
africano (â·frē·kâ'nō) *a* African
agenda (â·jān'dâ) *f* notebook
agente (â·jān'tā) *m* agent; **— di cambio** stockbroker; **— di polizia** policeman; **— investigativo** detective; **— delle tasse** tax collector
agenzia (â·jān·tsē'â) *f* agency; **— di collocamento** employment agency; **— di trasporti** freight company; **— di viaggi** travel agency
agevolazione (â·jā·vō·lâ·tsyō'nā) *f* facility; ease; (*com*) easy terms
aggeggio (âj·je'jō) *m* gadget
aggettivo (âj·jāt·tē'vō) *m* adjective
aggiornamento (âj·jōr·nâ·mān'tō) *m* updating
aggiornare (aj·jōr·nâ'rā) *vt* to adjourn; to update; — *vi* to dawn
aggiornato (âj·jōr·nâ'tō) *a* up-to-date
aggiramento (âj·jē·râ·mān'tō) *m* circumvention; fraud
aggirare (âj·jē·râ'rā) *vt* to surround; to turn around; to take in, defraud
aggirarsi (âj·jē·râr'sē) *vr* to ramble; to roam; to tramp
aggiratore (âj·jē·râ·tō'rā) *m* rambler; deceiver, swindler
aggiungere * (âj·jūn'jā·rā) *vt* to add; to rejoin
aggiunta (âj·jūn'tâ) *f* addition
aggiunto (âj·jūn'tō) *a* added
aggiustaggio (âj·jū·stâj'jō) *m* (*mech*) adjustment, alignment
aggiustare (âj·jū·stâ'rā) *vt* to fix; to adjust
aggiustatore (âj·jū·stâ·tō'rā) *m* (*mech*) fitter
aggrappare (âg·grâp·pâ'rā) *vt* to grapple; to grab hold of
aggrapparsi (âg·grâp·pâr'sē) *vr* to cling to tightly
aggravamento (âg·grâ·vâ·mān'tō) *m* surcharge; aggravation
aggravante (âg·grâ·vân'tā) *a* aggravating
aggravare (âg·grâ·vâ'rā) *vt* to make worse, worsen
aggravarsi (âg·grâ·vâr'sē) *vr* to get worse, worsen
aggravio (âg·grâ'vyō) *m* injury; burden, charge
aggredire (âg·grā·dē'rā) *vt* to attack
aggregare (âg·grā·gâ'rā) *vt* to aggregate, mass together
aggregarsi (âg·grā·gâr'sē) *vr* to join, become a member
aggregato (âg·grā·gâ'tō) *a* aggregated; — *m* aggregation, assembly
aggressione (âg·grās·syō'nā) *f* aggression
aggressivo (âg·grās·sē'vō) *a* aggressive
aggressore (âg·grās·sō'rā) *m* aggressor
aggrottare (âg·grōt·tâ'rā) *vt* to pucker; (*agr*) to embank; **— le ciglia** to frown
agguantare (âg·gwân·tâ'rā) *vt* to catch hold of, clasp
agiatamente (â·jâ·tâ·mān'tā) *adv* comfortably, easily
agiatezza (â·jâ·tā'tsâ) *f* welfare, wellbeing
agiato (â·jâ'tō) *a* well off; wealthy
agilità (â·jē·lē·tâ') *f* agility; quickness
agire (â·jē'rā) *vi* to act; to behave
agitare (â·jē·tâ'rā) *vt* to shake; to upset
agitarsi (â·jē·târ'sē) *vr* to get excited
agitatore (â·jē·tâ·tō'rā) *m* agitator; ringleader
agitazione (â·jē·tâ·tsyō'nā) *f* agitation, excitement
agli (â'lyē) *prep* to the
aglio (â'lyō) *m* garlic
agnello (â·nyāl'lō) *m* lamb

ago (â'gō) *m* needle
agonia (â·gō·nē'â) *f* agony
agosto (â·gō'stō) *m* August
agricolo (â·grē'kō·lō) *a* agricultural
agricoltore (â·grē·kōl·tō'rā) *m* farmer
agricultura (â·grē·kūl·tū'râ) *f* farming
agrifoglio (â·grē·fô'lyō) *m* holly
agrimensore (â·grē·mān·sō'rā) *m* surveyor
agrumeto (â·grū·mā'tō) *m* citrus grove
agrumi (â·grū'mē) *mpl* citrus fruit
ai (â'ē) *prep* to the
aia (â'yâ) *f* threshing area; governess, tutor
aiuola (â·ywō'lâ) *f* flower bed
aiutante (â·yū·tân'tā) *m* helper, aid
aiutare (â·yū·tâ'rā) *vt* to help, be of assistance to
aiuto (â·yū'tō) *m* help
al (âl), **allo** (âl'lō), **alla** (âl'lâ), **all'** (âll) *prep* to the, on the; with; in the manner of
ala (â'lâ) *f* wing; **–to** (â·lâ'tō) *a* winged
alare (â·lâ'rā) *m* andiron
alba (âl'bâ) *f* dawn
Albania (âl·bâ·nē'â) *f* Albania
albanese (âl·bâ·nā'zā) *a&m* Albanian
albatro (âl'bâ·trō) *m (bot)* arbutus; *(zool)* albatross
albeggiare (âl·bāj·jâ'rā) *vi* to break (*day*); to dawn
albergatore (âl·bār·gâ·tō'rā) *m* hotel manager; hotelman
albergo (âl·bār'gō) *m* hotel; **— diurno** public bathing and washing facilities
albero (âl'bā·rō) *m* tree
albicocca (âl·bē·kōk'kâ) *f* apricot
albume (âl·bū'mā) *m* albumen
alcali (âl'kâ·lē) *m* alkali; **–no** (âl·kâ·lē'nō) *a* alkaline
alcole (âl·kō'lā), **alcool** (āl'kō·ōl) *m* alcohol
alcuno (âl·kū'nō) *a&pron* some, any, none, no
alesatore (â·lā·zâ·tō'rā) *m* ream, bore
alettone (â·lāt·tō'nā) *m* (*avi*) aileron
alga (âl'gâ) *f* seaweed
algebra (âl'jā·brâ) *f* algebra
algebrico (âl·je'brē·kō) *a* algebraic
aliante (â·lyân'tā) *m* (*avi*) glider
alice (â·lē'chā) *f* anchovy
alienare (â·lyā·nâ'rā) *vi* to alienate; to make over
alienato (â·lyā·nâ'tō) *a* alienated; **— mentale** lunatic, madman
alimentare (â·lē·mān·tâ'rā) *a* alimentary; **paste alimentari** spaghetti; **generi alimentari** groceries
alimentarista (â·lē·mān·tâ·rē'stâ) *m* grocer
alimentazione (â·lē·mān·tâ·tsyō'nā) *f* feeding; (*mech*) stoking
alimento (â·lē·mān'tō) *m* nourishment
aliscafo (â·lē·skâ'fō) *m* hydrofoil speedboat
alito (â'lē·tō) *m* breath; breeze
allacciamento (âl·lâ·châ·mān'tō) *m* lacing; *(elec)* connection, link
allacciare (âl·lâ·châ'rā) *vt* to lace
allargare (âl·lâr·gâ'rā) *vt* to broaden; to extend
allarme (âl·lâr'mā) *m* alarm
allattare (âl·lât·tâ'rā) *vt* to nurse; breastfeed
alleanza (âl·lā·ân'tsâ) *f* alliance
alleato (âl·lā·â'tō) *a* allied
allegato (âl·lā·gâ'tō) *a* enclosed; **—** *m* enclosure, attachment
alleggerire (âl·lāj·jā·rē'rā) *vt* to lighten; to make easier
alleggerirsi (âl·lāj·jā·rēr'sē) *vr* to relieve oneself; (*fig*) to undress
alleggerito (âl·lāj·jā·rē'tō) *a* lightened, alleviated
allegoria (âl·lā·gō·rē'â) *f* allegory
allegria (âl·lā·grē'â) *f* gaiety, happiness
allegro (âl·lā'grō) *a* cheerful, gay
allenamento (âl·lā·nâ·mān'tō) *m* training, workout, exercise
allenatore (âl·lā·nâ·tō'rā) *m* trainer, coach
allevare (âl·lā·vâ'rā) *vt* to breed; to raise, educate
alleviare (âl·lā·vyâ'rā) *vt* to alleviate
allibratore (âl·lē·brâ·tō'rā) *m* bookie, bookmaker
allievo (âl·lyā'vō) *m* pupil
allineare (âl·lē·nā·â'rā) *vt* to form into ranks; to line up
allinearsi (âl·lē·nā·âr'sē) *vr* to align oneself; to get in line
allodola (âl·lô'dō·lâ) *f* skylark
allogeno (âl·lô'jā·nō) *m* alien
alloggiare (âl·lōj·jâ'rā) *vt* to house, lodge; **—** *vi* to stay, be accommodated
alloggio (âl·lôj'jō) *m* lodging
allontanamento (âl·lōn·tâ·nâ·mān'tō) *m* distance; remoteness
allontanare (âl·lōn·tâ·nâ'rā) *vt* to keep away; to take away
allora (âl·lō'râ) *adv* then
alloro (âl·lō'rō) *m* laurel; **foglie d'—** bay leaves
allume (âl·lū'mā) *m* alum
alluminio (âl·lū·mē'nyō) *m* aluminum
allungamento (âl·lūn·gâ·mān'tō) *m* lengthening, prolonging
allungare (âl·lūn·gâ'rā) *vt* to lengthen; to prolong
allusione (âl·lū·zyō'nā) *f* allusion
alluvionato (âl·lū·vyō·nâ'tō) *m* flood victim; **—** *a* flooded
alluvione (âl·lū·vyō'nā) *f* flood
almanacco (âl·mâ·nâk'kō) *m* almanac
almeno (âl·mā'nō) *adv* at least
alone (â·lō'nā) *m* halo
Alpi (âl'pē) *fpl*
alpinista (âl·pē·nē'stâ) *m&f* mountain climber
alquanto (âl·kwân'tō) *adv* somewhat; a bit
alt! (âlt) *interj* stop!
altalena (âl·tâ·lā'nâ) *f* swing
altamente (âl·tâ·mān'tā) *adv* highly; nobly
altare (âl·tâ'rā) *m* altar
alterare (âl·tā·râ'rā) *vt* to alter; to distort
alterazione (âl·tā·râ·tsyō'nā) *f* alteration;

distortion
alternare (âl·tär·nâ'rā) *vt* to alternate
alternarsi (âl·tär·nâr'sē) *vr* to follow each other; to take turns
alternativa (âl·tär·nâ·tē'vâ) *f* alternative
alternato (âl·tär·nâ'tō) *a* alternating; **corrente alternata** alternating current
alternatore (âl·tär·nâ·tō'rā) *m* (*elec*) alternator
altezza (âl·tā'tsâ) *f* height; loftiness
altigiano (âl·tē·jâ'nō) *m* mountaineer
altimetro (âl·tē'mâ·trō) *m* altimeter
altipiano (âl·tē·pyâ'nō) *m* plateau
alto (âl'tō) *a* high; tall; loud; **–forno** (âl·tō·fōr'nō) *m* blast furnace; **–locato** (âl·tō·lō·kâ'tō) *a* prominent; **–mare** (âl·tō·mâ'rā) *m* high sea; **–parlante** (âl·tō·pâr·lân'tā) *m* loudspeaker
altrimenti (âl·trē·mān'tē) *adv* otherwise, if not
altro (âl'trō) *a* other; **un** — another
altrove (âl·trō'vā) *adv* elsewhere, somewhere else
altrui (âl·trū'ē) *pron* another's, others', of others
alunno (â·lūn'nō) *m* pupil, scholar
alveare (âl·vā·â'rā) *m* beehive
alzare (âl·tsâ'rā) *vt* to lift, raise
alzarsi (âl·tsâr'sē) *vr* to get up, arise
amabile (â·mâ'bē·lā) *a* amiable, friendly
amabilità (â·mâ·bē·lē·tâ') *f* amiability, friendliness
amabilmente (â·mâ·bēl·mān'tā) *adv* kindly, friendly
amante (â·mân'tā) *a* fond; — *f&m* mistress; lover
amare (â·mâ'rā) *vt* to love
amaretto (â·mâ·rāt'tō) *m* macaroon
amareggiare (â·mâ·rāj·jâ'rā) *vt* to embitter
amarezza (â·mâ·rā'tsâ) *f* bitterness; resentfulness
amaro (â·mâ'rō) *a* bitter; — *m* bitters
ambasciata (âm·bâ·shâ'tâ) *f* embassy
ambasciatore (âm·bâ·shâ·tō'rā) *m* ambassador
ambedue (âm·bā·dū'ā) *a&pron* both
ambiente (âm·byān'tā) *m* atmosphere, environment
ambiguamente (âm·bē·gwâ·mān'tā) *adv* ambiguously, vaguely
ambiguità (âm·bē·gwē·tâ') *f* ambiguity, vagueness
ambiguo (âm·bē'gwō) *a* ambiguous, vague
ambizione (âm·bē·tsyō'nā) *f* ambition, heart's desire
ambizioso (âm·bē·tsyō'zō) *a* ambitious; covetous
ambo (âm'bō) *a&pron* both
ambra (âm'brâ) *f* amber
ambulanza (âm·bū·lân'tsâ) *f* ambulance
ambulatorio (âm·bū·lâ·tô'ryō) *m* dispensary
ameno (â·mā'nō) *a* cheerful, gay
America (â·me'rē·kâ) *f* America
americanata (â·mā·rē·kâ·nâ'tâ) *f* something spectacular; eccentric and exaggerated action
americano (â·mā·rē·kâ'nō) *m* American
amianto (â·myân'tō) *m* asbestos
amica (â·mē'kâ) *f* girl friend; sweetheart
amichevole (â·mē·ke'vō·lā) *a* friendly
amicizia (â·mē·chē'tsyâ) *f* friendship; **fare** — to become friendly, establish a friendship
amico (â·mē'kō) *m* friend
amido (â'mē·dō) *m* starch
ammaccare (âm·mâk·kâ'rā) *vt* to bruise
ammaccato (âm·mâk·kâ'tō) *a* battered; bruised
ammaccatura (âm·mâk·kâ·tū'râ) *f* bruise; knob; lump; hammer mark; contusion
ammainare (âm·mâē·nâ'rā) *vt* to lower; to haul down (*sails*)
ammalarsi (âm·mâ·lâr'sē) *vi* to become ill, get sick
ammalato (âm·mâ·lâ'tō) *a* ill, sick; — *m* patient
ammannire (âm·mân·nē'rā) *vt* to prime, prepare
ammanco (âm·mân'kō) *m* deficit, shortage
ammansare (âm·mân·sâ'rā), **ammansire** (âm·mân·sē'rā) *vt* to tame; to calm; to pacify
ammassare (âm·mâs·sâ'rā) *vt* to amass; to heap; to gather
ammasso (âm·mâs'sō) *m* heap; mass
ammattire (âm·mât·tē'rā) *vi* to go mad, lose one's mind
ammattito (âm·mât·tē'tō) *a* mad, insane
ammazzare (âm·mâ·tsâ'rā) *vt* to kill, do away with
ammenda (âm·mān'dâ) *f* fine
ammettere * (âm·met'tā·rā) *vt* to admit
amministrare (âm·mē·nē·strâ'rā) *vt* to administer
amministrativamente (âm·mē·nē·strâ·tē·vâ·mān'tā) *adv* administratively
amministrativo (âm·mē·nē·strâ·tē'vō) *a* administrative
amministrato (âm·mē·nē·strâ'tō) *a* administered
amministratore (âm·mē·nē·strâ·tō'rā) *m* administrator, manager
amministrazione (âm·mē·nē·strâ·tsyō'nā) *f* administration; business office
ammirabile (âm·mē·râ'bē·lā) *a* admirable
ammiraglio (âm·mē·râ'lyō) *m* admiral
ammirare (âm·mē·râ'rā) *vt* to admire; to think highly of
ammirativo (âm·mē·râ·tē'vō) *a* admirable
ammiratore (âm·mē·râ·tō'rā) *m* admirer
ammirazione (âm·mē·râ·tsyō'nā) *f* admiration
ammissibile (âm·mēs·sē'bē·lā) *a* admissible
ammissibilità (âm·mēs·sē·bē·lē·tâ') *f* admissibility
ammissione (âm·mēs·syō'nā) *f* admission
ammobiliato (âm·mō·bē·lyâ'tō) *a* furnished
ammogliare (âm·mō·lyâ'rā) *vt* to give in marriage; to marry

ammogliarsi (âm·mō·lyâr'sē) *vr* to get married; to marry
ammogliato (âm·mō·lyâ'tō) *a* married; — *m* married man
ammoniaca (âm·mō·nē'â·kâ) *f* ammonia
ammonire (âm·mō·nē'rā) *vt* to warn
ammonito (âm·mō·nē'tō) *a* admonished; under surveillance
ammonizione (âm·mō·nē·tsyō'nā) *f* admonition
ammontare (âm·mōn·tâ'rā) *vi* to amount; to cost; — *m* amount
ammorbidire (âm·mōr·bē·dē'rā) *vt* to make soft; to make supple
ammortamento (âm·mōr·tâ·mān'tō) *m* amortization
ammortizzare (âm·mōr·tē·dzâ'rā) *vt* to amortize; to break, deflect; to deaden, cushion
ammortizzatore (âm·mōr·tē·dzâ·tō'rā) *m* (*auto*) shock absorber
ammucchiare (âm·mūk·kyâ'rā) *vt* to pile up, amass, collect
ammuffire (âm·mūf·fē'rā) *vi* to get musty
ammuffito (âm·mūf·fē'tō) *a* moldy
ammutinarsi (âm·mū·tē·nâr'sē) *vr* to mutiny; to rebel
amnistia (âm·nē·stē'â) *f* amnesty
amo (â'mō) *m* fishhook
amore (â·mō'rā) *m* love; **–ggiare** (â·mō·rāj·jâ'rā) *vt&i* to make love; to flirt **–vole** (â·mō·re'vō·lā) *a* loving; lovely; affectionate; **–volmente** (â·mō·rā·vōl·mān'tā) *adv* kindly; lovably
amorosamente (â·mō·rō·zâ·mān'tā) *adv* with love, lovingly
amoroso (â·mō·rō'zō) *a* amorous; fond; — *m* lover, suitor
amper (âm·pār') *m* (*elec*) ampere; **–aggio** (âm·pā·râj'jō) *m* amperage; **–ometro** (âm·pā·rô'mā·trō) *m* ammeter
ampiezza (âm·pyā'tsâ) *f* largeness; amplitude
ampio (âm'pyō) *a* abundant; ample
amplesso (âm·plās'sō) *m* hug, embrace
ampliare (âm·plyâ'rā) *vt* to amplify, extend
amplificare (âm·plē·fē·kâ'rā) *vt* to amplify; to enrich
amplificatore (âm·plē·fē·kâ·tō'rā) *m* amplifier
amplificazione (âm·plē·fē·kâ·tsyō'nā) *f* amplification
amputare (âm·pū·tâ'rā) *vt* to amputate
anabbagliante (â·nâb·bâ·lyân'tā) *a* antiglare
anagrafe (â·nâ'grâ·fā) *f* vital statistics; **ufficio d'** — bureau of records
analfabeta (â·nâl·fâ·bā'tâ) *a* illiterate
analisi (â·nâ'lē·zē) *f* analysis
analitico (â·nâ·lē'tē·kō) *a* analytical, analytic
analizzare (â·nâ·lē·dzâ'rā) *vt* to analyse; to break down, decompose
analizzatore (â·nâ·lē·dzâ·tō'rā) *m* analyst; (*TV*) scanning disk
ananasso (â·nâ·nâs'sō) *m* pineapple
anarchia (â·nâr·kē'â) *f* anarchy
anarchico (â·nâr'kē·kō) *m* anarchist
anatomia (â·nâ·tō·mē'â) *f* anatomy
anatra (â'nâ·trâ) *f* duck
anca (ân'kâ) *f* hip
anche (ân'kā) *adv* too, as well, also
ancora (ân'kō·râ) *f* anchor; **–ggio** (ân·kō·râj'jō) *m* anchorage, anchoring; **–re** (ân·kō·râ'rā) *vt* to anchor, cast anchor; **–rsi** (ân·kō·râr'sē) *vr* to anchor; lay anchor
ancora (ân·kō'râ) *adv* still, yet, as yet
andare * ân·dâ'râ) *vi* to go; — **a piedi** to walk; — **in macchina** to drive; to ride
andata (ân·dâ'tâ) *f* going; **biglietto di — semplice** one-way ticket; **biglietto di — e ritorno** round-trip ticket
aneddoto (â·ned'dō·tō) *m* anecdote
anello (ân·nāl'lō) *m* ring
anemografo (â·nā·mô'grâ·fō) *m* anemograph
anemometro (â·nā·mô'mā·trō) *m* anemometer
anemoscopio (â·nā·mō·skô'pyō) *m* anemoscope
aneroide (â·nā·rô'ē·dā) *m* aneroid
anestesia (â·nā·stā·zē'â) *f* anesthesia
anestesista (â·nā·stā·zē'stâ) *m* anesthetist
anestetico (â·nā·ste'tē·kō) *a&m* anesthetic
anestizzante (â·nā·stē·dzân'tā) *m* anesthetic
anestizzare (â·nā·stē·dzâ'rā) *vt* to anesthetize
anestizzato (â·nā·stē·dzâ'tō) *a* anesthetized
aneto (â·nā'tō) *m* (*bot*) dill
anfibio (ân·fē'byō) *a* amphibious; — *m* amphibian; — (*mil*) duck, amphibious truck
anfiteatro (ân·fē·tā·â'trō) *m* amphitheater
anfora (ân'fō·râ) *f* vase
angelo (ân'jā·lō) *m* angel
angheria (ân·gā·rē'â) *f* imposition; annoyance
angolo (ân'gō·lō) *m* corner
angoscia (ân·gô'shâ) *f* anguish, torment
anguilla (ân·gwēl'lâ) *f* eel
anguria (ân·gū'ryâ) *f* watermelon
anima (â'nē·mâ) *f* soul; **–le** (â·nē·mâ'lā) *m* animal, beast; **–le** *a* bestial, beastly; stupid
animare (â·nē·mâ'rā) *vt* to animate; to encourage
animarsi (â·nē·mâr'sē) *vi* to take courage
animazione (â·nē·mâ·tsyō'na) *f* animation
animella (â·nē·māl'lâ) *f* sweetbread
animosità (â·nē·mō·zē·tâ') *f* animosity
animoso (â·nē·mō'zō) *a* bold; malevolent, evil
anione (â·nyō'nā) *m* (*phys*) anion
annacquare (ân·nâk·kwâ'rā) *vt* to water; to add water to, dilute
annaffiare (ân·nâf·fyâ'rā) *vt* to water, sprinkle
annegare (ân·nā·gâ'rā) *vt* to drown
annerire (ân·nā·rē'rā) *vt&i* to blacken;

to get black
annessione (ân·nās·syō'nā) *f* annexation
annientare (ân·nyān·tâ'rā) *vt* to annihilate; to wipe out
anniversario (ân·nē·vār·sâ'ryō) *m* anniversary
anno (ân'nō) *m* year; — **bisestile** leap year
annodare (ân·nō·dâ'rā) *vt* to tie; to knot
annoiare (ân·nō·yâ'rā) *vt* to bore; to tire out
annoiarsi (ân·nō·yâr'sē) *vi* to get bored; to be worn-out
annoiato (ân·nō·yâ'tō) *a* bored; weary
annotare (ân·nō·tâ'rā) *vt* to annotate; to footnote
annotazione (ân·nō·tâ·tsyō'nā) *f* annotation; note
annuale (ân·nwâ'lā), **annuo** (ân'nwō) *a* yearly, annual
annuario (ân·nwâ'ryō) *m* yearbook; directory
annullamento (ân·nūl·lâ·mān'tō) *m* annulment
annullare (ân·nūl·lâ'rā) *vt* to annul
annunziare (ân·nūn·tsyâ'rā) *vt* to announce; to publicize
annunziatore (ân·nūn·tsyâ·tō'rā) *m* announcer
annunzio (ân·nūn'tsyō) *m* announcement; — **pubblicitario** advertisement
ano (â'nō) *m* anus
anodico (â·nô'dē·kō) *a* anodic
anodino (â·nô'dē·nō) *a* anodyne
anodo (â'nō·dō) *m* (*elec*) anode
anonimo (â·nô'nē·mō) *a* anonymous
anormale (â·nōr·mâ'lā) *a* abnormal
anormalità (â·nōr·mâ·lē·tâ') *f* abnormality
ansia (ân'syâ), **ansietà** (ân·syā·tâ') *f* anxiety
ansiosamente (ân·syō·zâ·mān'tā) *adv* anxiously
ansioso (ân·syō'zō) *a* anxious
antartico (ân·târ'tē·kō) *m&a* antarctic
antenato (ân·tā·nâ'tō) *m* ancestor; predecessor
antenna (ân·tān'nâ) *f* antenna
antecessore (ân·tā·chās·sō'rā) *m* predecessor
anteprima (ân·tā·prē'mâ) *f* preview
anteriore (ân·tā·ryō'rā) *a* previous; front
anteriorità (ân·tā·ryō·rē·tâ') *f* priority
anteriormente (ân·tā·ryōr·mān'tā) *adv* previously, before
antiacido (ân·tyâ'chē·dō) *m&a* antacid
anticamente (ân·tē·kâ·mān'tā) *adv* formerly; in days of yore
anticamera (ân·tē·kâ'mā·râ) *f* waiting room
antichità (ân·tē·kē·tâ') *f* antiquity
anticipare (ân·tē·chē·pâ'rā) *vt* to advance; to anticipate
anticipatamente (ân·tē·chē·pâ·tâ·mān'tā) *adv* in advance
anticipato (ân·tē·chē·pâ'tō) *a* in advance; **pagamento** — advance payment
anticipo (ân·tē'chē·pō) *m* advance
anticlericale (ân·tē·klā·rē·kâ'lā) anticlerical
antico (ân·tē'kō) *a* ancient
anticongelante (ân·tē·kōn·jā·lân·tā) *m* (*auto*) antifreeze
antidetonante (ân·tē·dā·tō·nân'tā) *a* antiknock
antidoto (ân·tē'dō·tō) *m* antidote
antifrizione (ân·tē·frē·tsyō'nā) *f* antifriction
antiincendio (ân·tē·ēn·chen'dyō) *a* fireproofing
antimagnetico (ân·tē·mâ·nye'tē·kō) *a* antimagnetic
antimeridiano (ân·tē·mā·rē·dyâ'nō) *a* forenoon, morning
antimonio (ân·tē·mô'nyō) *m* (*chem*) antimony
antipasto (ân·tē·pâ'stō) *m* hors d'oeuvres, appetizers
antipatia (ân·tē·pâ·tē'â) *f* dislike
antipatico (ân·tē·pâ'tē·kō) *a* disagreeable
antiquariato (ân·tē·kwâ·ryâ'tō) *m* secondhand book business
antiquario (ân·tē·kwâ'ryō) *m* antique dealer
antiquato (ân·tē·kwâ'tō) antiquated
antisemita (ân·tē·sā·mē'tâ) *a* anti-semitic
antisettico (ân·tē·set'tē·kō) *a* antiseptic
antologia (ân·tō·lō·jē'â) *f* anthology
antracene (ân·trâ·chā'nā) *m* (*chem*) anthracene
antracite (ân·trâ·chē'tā) *m* anthracite
anzi (ân'tsē) *adv* rather, instead
anzianità (ân·tsyâ·nē·tâ') *f* seniority
anziano (ân·tsyâ'nō) *a* elder; elderly
anzichè (ân·tsē·kā') *conj* rather than, in place of
anzitutto (ân·tsē·tūt'tō) *adv* above all
ape (â'pā) *f* bee
aperitivo (â·pā·rē·tē'vō) *m* aperitif
apertamente (â·pār·tâ·mān'tā) *adv* openly, publicly
aperto (â·pār'tō) *a* open
apertura (â·pār·tū'râ) *f* opening, aperture, hole
apoplessia (â·pō·plās·sē'â) *f* stroke
apostolo (â·pô'stō·lō) *m* apostle
appaiare (âp·pâ·yâ'rā) *vt* to match, find a mate for
appaltatore (âp·pâl·tâ·tō'rā) *m* contractor
appalto (âp·pâl'tō) *m* contract; bid
appannato (âp·pân·nâ'tō) *a* dim; dull
apparecchiare (âp·pâ·rāk·kyâ'rā) *vt* to prepare; — **la tavola** to set the table
apparecchiatura (âp·pâ·rāk·kyâ·tū'râ) *f* equipment
apparecchio (âp·pâ·rek'kyō) *m* apparatus; telephone; radio; plane
apparente (âp·pâ·rēn'tā) *a* apparent; **-mente** (âp·pâ·rān·tā·mān'tā) *adv* apparently, seemingly
apparenza (āp·pâ·rān'tsâ) *f* appearance
apparire * (âp·pâ·rē'rā) *vi* to appear
apparizione (âp·pâ·rē·tsyō'nā) *f* apparition, vision
appartamento (âp·pâr·tâ·mān'tō) *m* apartment

appartenere * (âp·pâr·tā·nā'rā) *vi* to belong; to be in one's field
appassire (âp·pâs·sē'rā) *vt&i* to dry; to wither
appassito (âp·pâs·sē'tō) *a* faded
appellarsi (âp·pāl·lâr'sē) *vi* to appeal
appello (âp·pāl'lō) *m* appeal; roll call; **corte d'** — court of appeals, appellate court
appena (âp·pā'nâ) *adv* hardly; as soon as; just as
appendere * (âp·pen'dā·rā) *vt* to hang
appendice (âp·pān·dē'chā) *f* appendix; **romanzo d'**— serial novel
appendicite (âp·pān·dē·chē'tā) *f* appendicitis
appetito (âp·pā·tē'tō) *m* appetite; **buon** —! enjoy your dinner!
appetitoso (âp·pā·tē·tō'zō) *a* appetizing, delicious
appiccicare (âp·pē·chē·kâ'rā) *vt* to stick; to glue together
applaudire (âp·plâū·dē'rā) *vt* to applaud
applauso (âp·plâ'ū·zō) *m* applause
applicare (âp·plē·kâ'rā) *vt* to apply; to place
applicazione (âp·plē·kâ·tsyō'nā) *f* application; appliance
appoggiare (âp·pōj·jâ'rā) *vt* to support
appoggiarsi (âp·pōj·jâr'sē) *vr* to lean against
appoggio (âp·pôj'jō) *m* support, backing
apporto (āp·pōr'tō) *m* contribution
appositamente (âp·pō·zē·tâ·mān'tā) *adv* on purpose
apprendere * (âp·pren'dā·rā) *vt* to learn
apprendista (âp·prān·dē'stâ) *m* apprentice
appresso (âp·prās'sō) *adv* later; next; nearby
apprezzare (âp·prā·tsâ'rā) *vt* to appreciate; to value
approdare (âp·prō·dâ'rā) *vi* to land
approdo (âp·prō'dō) *m* landing
approfittare (âp·prōf·fēt·tâ'rā) *vi* to make the most of, profit by
approfittarsi (âp·prōf·fēt·târ'sē) *vr* to draw profit from, avail oneself of, take advantage of
appropriare (âp·prō·pryâ'rā) *vt* to adjust; to suit; to appropriate
appropriarsi (âp·prō·pryâr'sē) *vi* to steal, make off with
appropriato (âp·prō·pryâ'tō) *a* proper, fitting
appropriazione (âp·prō·pryâ·tsyō'nā) *f* appropriation; — **indebita** embezzlement
approssimativo (âp·prōs·sē·mâ·tē'vō) *a* approximate
approssimato (âp·prōs·sē·mâ'tō) *a* approached
approssimazione (âp·prōs·sē·mâ·tsyō'nā) *f* approximation
approvabile (âp·prô·vâ'bē·lā) *a* commendable
approvare (âp·prō·vâ'rā) *vt* to approve, commend
approvazione (âp·prō·vâ·tsyō'nā) *f* approval; commendation
appuntamento (âp·pūn·tâ·mān'tō) *m* appointment, date
appuntare (âp·pūn·tâ'rā) *vt* to sharpen; to pin on; to note
appunto (âp·pūn'tō) *m* remark; note; **per l'**— *adv* exactly, precisely
aprile (â·prē'lā) *m* April; **pesce d'**— April fool
apripista (â·prē·pē'stâ) *m* bulldozer
aprire * (â·prē'rā) *vt* to open; to split
aprirsi * (â·prēr'sē) *vi* to burst; to split open
apriscatole (â·prē·skâ'tō·lā) *m* can opener
aquila (â'kwē·lâ) *f* eagle
aquilino (â·kwē·lē'nō) *a* hooked, aquiline
aquilone (â·kwē·lō'nā) *m* kite
arabo (â'râ·bō) *m* Arab; — *a* Arabian
arachide (â·râ'kē·dā) *f* peanut
aragosta (â·râ·gō'stâ) *f* lobster
araldica (â·râl'dē·kâ) *f* heraldry
aranceto (â·rân·chā'tō) *m* orange grove
arancia (â·rân'châ) *f* orange; **–ta** (â·rân·châ'tâ) *f* orangeade
aratro (â'râ·trō) *m* plow
arazzo (â·râ'tsō) *m* tapestry
arbitro (âr'bē·trō) *m* judge; referee
arcangelo (âr·kân'jā·lō) *m* archangel
architetto (âr·kē·tāt'tō) *m* architect
architettura (âr·kē·tāt·tū'râ) *f* architecture
archiviare (âr·kē·vyâ'rā) *vt* to file; to put on file
archivio (âr·kē'vyō) *m* file; archives
arcivescovo (âr·chē·ve'skō·vō) *m* archbishop
arco (âr'kō) *m* arch; **strumenti ad** — string instruments; **tiro con l'**— archery; **–baleno** (âr·kō·bâ·lā'nō) *m* rainbow
ardente (âr·dān'tā) *a* burning; passionate
ardere * (âr'dā·rā) *vt&i* to burn
ardesia (âr·de'zyâ) *f* slate
ardito (âr·dē'tō) *a* bold, intrepid
area (â'rā·â) *f* area, zone
arena (â·rā'nâ) *f* arena; sand
arenoso (â·rā·nō'zō) *a* sandy
argano (âr'gâ·nō) *m* winch; capstan
argentato (âr·jān·tâ'tō) *a* silver-plated
argenteria (âr·jān·tā·rē'â) *f* silverware
argento (âr·jān'tō) *m* silver
argilla (âr·jēl'lâ) *f* clay
argine (âr'jē·nā) *m* embankment; barricade
argo (âr'gō) *m* argon
argomento (âr·gō·mān'tō) *m* argument subject; reason; indication
argutamente (âr·gū·tâ·mān'tā) *adv* shrewdly, artfully; wittily
arguto (âr·gū'tō) *a* witty, sharp
arguzia (âr·gū'tsyâ) *f* wit, humor; guile
aria (â'ryâ) *f* air; appearance
arido (â'rē·dō) *a* arid; dull, insipid
ariete (â·ryā'tā) *m* (*zool*) ram; (*mil*) battering ram
aringa (â·rēn'gâ) *f* herring
arioso (â·ryō'zō) *a* airy, light
aristocratico (â·rē·stō·krâ'tē·kō) *a* aris-

tocratic; patrician; noble
aristocrazia (â·rē·stō·krâ·tsē'â) *f* aristocracy, nobility
aritmetica (â·rēt·me'tē·kâ) *f* arithmetic
arlecchino (âr·lāk·kē'nō) *m* buffoon, jester
arma (âr'mâ) *f* armament, arm
armadietto (âr·mâ·dyāt'tō) *m* small cabinet; — **per medicinali** medicine chest
armadio (âr·mâ'dyō) *m* wardrobe; — **a muro** closet
armamentario (âr·mâ·mān·tâ'ryō) *m* outfit; — **chirurgico** surgical instruments
armamento (âr·mâ·mān'tō) *m* (*mil*) armament; ship's rigging; (*mech*) assembly
armare (âr·mâ'rā) *vt* to arm; to put together, assemble
armata (âr·mâ'tâ) *f* fleet; **corpo d'—** army corps
armato (âr·mâ'tō) *a* armed; **–re** (âr·mâ·tō'rā) *m* shipowner
armatura (âr·mâ·tū'râ) *f* armor; (*elec*) armature; framework
arme (âr'mā) *f* weapon; **–ria** (âr·mā·rē'â) *f* armory
armistizio (âr·mē·stē'tsyō) *m* armistice
armonia (âr·mō·nē'â) *f* harmony
armonica (âr·mô'nē·kâ) *f* harmonica
armonioso (âr·mō·nyō'zō) *a* harmonious, melodious
armonizzare (âr·mō·nē·dzâ'rā) *vt&i* to harmonize
arnese (âr·nā'zā) *m* tool; **cattivo** — rogue
arnione (âr·nyō'nā) *m* kidney
aroma (â·rō'mâ) *m* flavor, aroma; **–tico** (â·rō·mâ'tē·kō) *a* flavorful, aromatic
arpa (âr'pâ) *f* harp
arpia (âr·pē'â) *f* (*fig*) shrew, scold
arrabbiarsi (âr·râb·byâr'sē) *vr* to get angry
arrampicarsi (âr·râm·pē·kâr'sē) *vr* to climb
arrecare (âr·rā·kâ'rā) *vt* to cause, bring about, give
arredamento (âr·rā·dâ·mān'tō) *m* furnishings
arredare (âr·rā·dâ'rā) *vt* to furnish
arredatore (âr·rā·dâ·tō'rā) *m* interior decorator
arredo (âr·rā'dō) *m* outfit; (*eccl*) vestments
arrembare (âr·rām·bâ'rā) *vt* to board, get aboard (*forcibly*)
arrendevole (âr·rān·de'vō·lā) *a* limber, flexible; (*fig*) tractable; **–zza** (âr·rān·dā·vō·lā'tsâ) *f* litheness; willing obedience; pliancy
arrendersi * (âr·ren'dār·sē) *vr* to give oneself up, surrender, yield
arrestare (âr·rā·stâ'rā) *vt* to arrest
arresto (ār·rā'stō) *m* arrest; failure; — **alla dogana** customs stop
arretrare (âr·rā·trâ'rā) *vt&i* to withdraw; — *vi* to fall back
arretrato (âr·rā·trâ'tō) *m* arrears; — *a* backward; delinquent; **numero** — back issue
arricchimento (âr·rēk·kē·mān'tō) *m* enrichment; embellishment
arricchire (âr·rēk·kē'rā) *vt* to enrich; (*fig*) to enhance, point up
arricchirsi (âr·rēk·kēr'sē) *vr* to get rich, become rich
arricchito (âr·rēk·kē'tō) *a* enriched; — *m* parvenu; — **di guerra** war profiteer
arricciare (âr·rē·châ'rā) *vt* to curl; — **il naso** to turn up one's nose
arringa (âr·rēn'gâ) *f* harangue; (*law*) plea
arrischiare (âr·rē·skyâ'rā) *vt* to risk
arrischiato (âr·rē·skyâ'tō) *a* risky
arrivare (âr·rē·vâ'rā) *vt* to arrive; to succeed in
arrivato (âr·rē·vâ'tō) *a* arrived; successful; — *m* success
arrivederci (âr·rē·vā·dār'chē) *inter* goodbye, so long, see you later
arrivista (âr·rē·vē'stâ) *m* (*coll*) social climber
arrivo (âr·rē'vō) *m* arrival
arrogante (âr·rō·gân'tā) *a* overbearing; supercilious; **–mente** (âr·rō·gân·tā·mān'tā) *adv* domineeringly, haughtily
arroganza (âr·rō·gân'tsâ) *f* arrogance; insolence
arrossire (âr·rōs·sē'rā) *vi* to blush
arrostire (âr·rō·stē'rā) *vt* to roast
arrostito (âr·rō·stē'tō) *a* roasted
arrosto (âr·rō'stō) *m* roast
arrotare (âr·rō·tâ'rā) *vt* to sharpen, hone; to smooth out
arrotino (âr·rō·tē'nō) *m* knife sharpener
arrotolare (âr·rō·tō·lâ'rā) *vt* to roll
arrotondare (âr·rō·tōn·dâ'rā) vt to make round; to round off (*a figure*)
arroventare (âr·rō·vān·tâ'rā) *vt* to make red-hot
arroventato (âr·rō·vān·tâ'tō) *a* red-hot
arruffare (âr·rūf·fâ'rā) *vt* to ruffle; to tangle; to make disorderly
arrugginirsi (âr·rūj·jē·nēr'sē) *vr* to rust
arrugginito (âr·rūj·jē·nē'tō) *a* rusty
arruvidire (âr·rū·vē·dē'rā) *vt* to roughen, make rough
arsella (âr·sāl'lâ) *f* mussel
arsenico (âr·se'nē·kō) *m* arsenic
arso (âr'sō) *a* burnt, burned
arte (âr'tā) *f* art; — **sacra** religious art; **–fatto** (âr·tā·fât'tō) *a* adulterated; **–fice** (âr·te'fē·chā) *m* skilful craftsman; (*fig*) author, perpetrator
arteria (âr·te'ryâ) *f* artery
artico (âr'tē·kō) *a&m* arctic
articolazione (âr·tē·kō·lâ·tsyō'nā) *f* articulation; joint
articolo (âr·tē'kō·lō) *m* article
artificiale (âr·tē·fē·châ'lā) *a* artificial
artificialmente (âr·tē·fē·châl·mān'tā) *adv* artificially
artificio (âr·tē·fē'chō) *m* ingenuity; device; trick, wile; **fuochi d'—** fireworks; **–so** (âr·tē·fē·chō'zō) *a* sly, cunning, tricky
artigianato (âr·tē·jâ·nâ'tō) *m* arts and crafts
artigiano (âr·tē·jâ'nō) *m* craftsman
artiglieria (âr·tē·lyā·rē'â) *f* artillery

artiglio (âr·tē'lyō) *m* claw
artista (âr·tē'stâ) *m&f* artist; — **di canto** singer; — **drammatico** actor
artistico (âr·tē'stē·kō) *a* artistic; tasteful
arto (âr'tō) *m* limb
artrite (âr·trē'tā) *f* arthritis
arzillo âr·dzēl'lō) *a* sprightly, active
asbesto (â·zbā'stō) *m* asbestos
ascella (â·shāl'lâ) *f* armpit
ascendente (â·shān·dān'tā) *a* ascending, upward; — *m* (*astr*) ascendant; forebear; power, influence
ascendere * (â·schen'dā·rā) *vt&i* to go up, climb; to rise
Ascensione (â·shān·syō'nā) *f* Ascension
ascensionista (â·shān·syō·nē'stâ) *m* mountain climber
ascensore (â·shān·sō'rā) *m* elevator
ascensorista (â·shān·sō·rē'stâ) *m* elevator operator
ascesa (â·shā'zâ) *f* ascent; climb
ascesso (â·shās'sō) *m* abscess
ascia (â'shâ) *f* ax
asciugacapelli (â·shū·gâ·kâ·pāl'lē) *m* hair dryer
asciugamano (â·shū·gâ·mâ'nō) *m* hand towel
asciugante (â·shū·gân'tā) *a* drying, absorbent; **carta** — blotting paper
asciugare (â·shū·gâ'rā) *vt* to wipe, dry off; to absorb
asciugato (â·shū·gâ'tō) *a* dried; wiped up
asciugatoio (â·shū·gâ·tô'yō) *m* towel
asciutto (â·shūt'tō) *a* dry; hard, merciless
ascoltare (â·skōl·tâ'rā) *vt* to listen to; to pay attention
ascoltatore (â·skōl·tâ·tō'rā) *m* listener
ascolto (â·skōl'tō) *m* listening; attention; **prestare** — to listen, pay attention
ascrivere * (â·skrē'vā·rā) *vt* to attribute; to impute; to assign
asettico (â·set'tē·kō) *a* aseptic, antiseptic
asfalto (â·sfâl'tō) *m* asphalt
asfissia (â·sfēs'syâ) *f* asphyxia; **–re** (â·sfēs·syâ'rā) *vt* to asphyxiate
Asia (â'zyâ) *f* Asia
asiatico (â·zyâ'tē·kō) *m&a* Asiatic
asilo (â·zē'lō) *m* asylum; — **infantile** kindergarten; — **notturno** welfare center
asimmetria (â·sēm·mā·trē'â) *f* asymmetry
asimmetrico (â·sēm·me'trē·kō) *a* asymmetrical
asino (â'zē·nō) *m* donkey, ass
asma (â'zmâ) *f* asthma
asola (ä'zō·lä) *f* buttonhole
asparago (â·spâ'râ·gō) *m* asparagus
aspettare (â·spāt·tâ'rā) *vt* to wait for, await
aspettarsi (â·spāt·târ'sē) *vr* to expect; to count on
aspettativa (ā·spāt·tâ·tē'vâ) *f* expectancy, anticipation; leave of absence
aspetto (â·spāt'tō) *m* appearance; **sala d'**— waiting room
aspirante (â·spē·rân'tā) *m* applicant
aspirapolvere (â·spē·râ·pôl'vā·rā) *m* vacuum cleaner
aspirare (â·spē·râ'rā) *vt* to aspire to; to inhale
aspirativo (â·spē·râ·tē'vō) *a* aspirate, to be aspirated
aspirato (â·spē·râ'tō) *a* sought after; aspired to; (*gram*) aspirated; **–re** (â·spē·râ·tō'rā) *m* vacuum cleaner
aspirazione (â·spē·râ·tsyō'nā) *f* desire, aim; inhalation
aspirina (â·spē·rē'nâ) *f* aspirin
aspo (â'spō) *m* reel
asportare (â·spōr·tâ'rā) *vt* to take out, remove
asprezza (â·sprā'tsâ) *f* curtness, asperity; acidity, tart taste
aspro (â'sprō) *a* sour; harsh
assaggiare (âs·sâj·jâ'rā) *vt* to taste
assai (âs·sâ'ē) *adv* enough; much
assale (âs·sâ'lā) *m* axle (*auto*)
assalire (âs·sâ·lē'rā) *vt* to attack
assalitore (âs·sâ·lē·tō'rā) *m* aggressor; attacker
assaltare (âs·sâl·tâ'rā) *vt* to assault, assail
assalto (âs·sâl'tō) *m* assault, aggression
assassinare (âs·sâs·sē·nâ'rā) *vt* to murder; to assassinate
assassinio (âs·sâs·sē'nyō) *m* murder
assassino (âs·sâs·sē'nō) *m* murderer
asse (âs'sā) *m* axis; axle; wooden board
assediare (âs·sā·dyâ'rā) *vt* to lay siege to
assediato (âs·sā·dyâ'tō) *a* beset, attacked
assediante (âs·sā·dyân'tā) *m* besieger; — *a* besieging
assedio (âs·se'dyō) *m* siege
assegnamento (âs·sā·nyâ·mān'tō) *m* reliance; assignment
assegnare (âs·sā·nyâ'rā) *vt* to grant, award; to designate
assegno (âs·sā'nyō) *m* check; — **per viaggiatori** traveler's check
assemblea (âs·sām·blā'â) *f* assembly, gathering
assembramento (âs·sām·brâ·mān'tō) *m* concourse, assemblage, crowd
assennatezza (âs·sān·nâ·tā'tsâ) *f* sagacity; common sense, prudence
assennato (âs·sān·nâ'tō) *a* judicious; wise
assentarsi (âs·sān·târ'sē) *vr* to absent oneself; not to be present
assente (âs·sān'tā) *a* absent; missing
assenza (âs·sān'tsâ) *f* absence
asserire (âs·sā·rē'rā) *vt* to assert; to claim
asserzione (âs·sār·tsyō'nā) *f* declaration, affirmation
assestamento (âs·sā·stâ·mān'tō) *m* settlement, adjustment
assestare (âs·sā·stâ'rā) *vt* to put in order, arrange; to balance; — **un colpo** to deliver a blow
assetato (âs·sā·tâ'tō) *a* thirsty
assiale (âs·syâ'lā) *a* axial
assicurare (âs·sē·kū·râ'rā) *vt* to insure; to make certain of
assicurarsi (âs·sē·kū·râr'sē) *vr* to make sure, be certain
assicurata (âs·sē·kū·râ'tâ) *f* insured letter

assicurazione (âs·sē·kū·râ·tsyō'nā) *f* insurance; — **sulla vita** life insurance; — **per la responsabilità civile** liability insurance
assiduamente (âs·sē·dwâ·mān'tā) *adv* perseveringly
assiduo (âs·sē'dwō) *a* diligent
assieme (âs·syā'mā) *adv* together
assillare (âs·sēl·lâ'rā) *vt* to incite, goad; to urge, spur on; — *vi* to be riled up; to be upset
assillo (âs·sēl'lō) *m* urge, impulse; tormenting thought; bête noire, bugbear
assimilare (âs·sē·mē·lâ'rā) *vt* to assimilate, digest; (*fig*) to take in, grasp
assimilarsi (âs·sē·mē·lâr'sē) *vr* to be assimilated; to become like
assimilazione (âs·sē·mē·lâ·tsyō'nā) *f* assimilation
assistente (âs·sē·stān·tā) *m* assistant; — **sociale** social worker
assistenza (âs·sē·stān'tsâ) *f* assistance; — **sociale** social work
assistenziale (âs·sē·stān·tsyâ'lā) *a* charitable; **opere assistenziali** social welfare
assistenziario (âs·sē·stān·tsyâ'ryō) *m* welfare department
assistere * (âs·sē'stā·rā) *vt* to assist; — *vi* to be present
assistiti (âs·sē·stē'tē) *mpl* welfare cases, relief recipients
asso (âs'sō) *m* ace
associare (âs·sō·châ'rā) *vt* to associate
associarsi (âs·sō·châr'sē) *vi* to associate; to be associated; to join
associazione (âs·sō·châ·tsyō'nā) *f* association; — **a delinquere** crime syndicate
assodare (âs·sō·dâ'rā) *vt* to make solid; to make sure of
assolto (âs·sōl'tō) *a* acquitted
assolutamente (âs·sō·lū·tâ·mān'tā) *adv* absolutely
assoluto (âs·sō·lū'tō) *a&m* absolute; positive
assoluzione (âs·sō·lū·tsyō'nā) *f* absolution; acquittal
assolvere * (âs·sôl'vā·rā) *vt* to absolve; to perform (*task*)
assomigliare (âs·sō·mē·lyâ'rā) *vi* to resemble
assonante (âs·sō·nân'tā) *a* assonant
assonanza (âs·sō·nân'tsâ) *f* assonance
assorbente (âs·sōr·bān'tā) *a* absorbent
assorbire (âs·sōr·bē'rā) *vt* to absorb; to engulf
assordire (âs·sōr·dē'rā) *vt* to deafen; to stun; — *vi* to become deaf
assortimento (âs·sōr·tē·mān'tō) *adv* assortment, line; variety
assortire (âs·sōr·tē'rā) *vt* to sort; to furnish, provide
attingere * (ât·tēn'jā·rā) *vt* to draw, come by, obtain; to arrive at
attinico (ât·tē'nē·kō) *a* actinic
attirare (ât·tē'râ'rā) *vt* to attract, call; to appeal to
attitudine (ât·tē·tū'dē·nā) *f* aptitude, talent, natural ability
attivamente (ât·tē·vâ·mān'tā) *adv* actively
attività (ât·tē·vē·tâ') *f* activity
attivo (ât·tē'vō) *a* active; animated
attizzare (ât·tē·tsâ'rā) *vt* to stir, poke (*fire*); to instigate; to egg on
attizzatoio (ât·tē·tsâ·tô'yō) *m* poker
atto (ât'tō) *m* act; action; deed; — **di nascita** birth certificate; — **di morte** death certificate
attonito *a* (ât·tô'nē·tō) *a* astonished
attorcigliare (ât·tōr·chē·lyâ'rā) *vt* to wind around, twist about
attorcigliarsi (ât·tōr·chē·lyâr'sē) *vr* to twist around, twine about
attore (ât·tō'rā) *m* actor; plaintiff (*law*)
attorno (ât·tōr'nō) *adv* around, all about
attraccare (ât·trâk·kâ'rā) *vt* to dock at, come alongside
attraente (ât·trâ·ān'tā) *a* attractive, charming
attrarre * (ât·trâr'rā) *vt* to attract; to appeal to
attrattiva (ât·trât·tē'vâ) *f* charm, appeal
attrattivo (ât·trât·tē'vō) *a* attractive, appealing
attraversamento (ât·trâ·vār·sâ·mān'tō) *m* crossing; — **pedonale** crosswalk
attraversare (ât·trâ·vār·sâ'rā) *vt* to cross, go across
attraverso (ât·trâ·vār'sō) *adv* across, to the other side of
attrazione (ât·trâ·tsyō'nā) *f* attraction; appeal
attrezzare (ât·trā·tsâ'rā) *vt* to equip, provide
attrezzatura (ât·trā·tsâ·tū'râ) *f* equipment
attrezzi (ât·trā'tsē) *mpl* tools; **borsa degli** — tool kit
attribuire (ât·trē·bwē'rā) *vt* to attribute, lay; to regard, consider
attributo (ât·trē·bū'tō) *m* attribute
attrice (ât·trē'chā) *f* actrice
attrito (ât·trē'tō) *m* attrition
attuale (ât·twâ'lā) *a* actual; contemporary
attualità (ât·twâ·lē·tâ') *f* current events
attualmente (ât·twâl·mān'tā) *adv* now, at the present time
attuare (ât·twâ'rā) *vt* to actuate; to accomplish, execute; to implement
attutire (ât·tū·tē'rā) *vt* to deaden, muffle; to alleviate
attutirsi (ât·tū·tēr'sē) *vr* to be muffled; to be alleviated
audace (âū·dâ'chā) *a* bold, daring
audacia (âū·dâ'châ) *f* daring, boldness, audacity
audiofrequenza (âū·dyō·frā·kwān'tsâ) *f* (*rad*) audiofrequency
auditorio (âū·dē·tô'ryō) *m* auditorium; television studio
audizione (âū·dē·tsyō'nā) *f* hearing, audition
augurare (âū·gū·râ'rā) *vt* to wish; to hope for
augurio (âū·gū'ryō) *m* wish; omen
aula (â'ū·lâ) *f* hall; schoolroom
aumentare (âū·mān·tâ'rā) *vt* to increase;

to broaden
aumento (âū·mān'tō) *m* raise, increase; broadening
aureo (â'ū·rā·ō) *a* golden
aureomicina (âū·rā·ō·mē·chē'nâ) *f* aureomycin
auricolare (âū·rē·kō·lâ'rā) *a* auricular
aurora (âū·rō'râ) *f* daybreak, dawn
ausiliario (âū·zē·lyâ'ryō) *m* auxiliary
ausilio (âū·zē'lyō) *m* assistance, aid
auspici (âū·spē'chē) *mpl* auspices
auspicio (âū·spē'chō) *m* omen
austerità (âū·stā·rē·tâ') *f* austerity
austero (âū·stā'rō) *a* sober, austere; plain
austriaco (âū·strē'â·kō) *a&m* Austrian
autarchia (âū·târ·kē'â) *f* self-sufficiency
autenticare (âū·tān·tē·kâ'rā) *vt* to notarize; to authenticate
autentico (âū·ten'tē·kō) *a* authentic, real
autista (âū·tē'stâ) *m* driver
auto (â'ū·tō) *m* car; **–accensione** (âū·tō·â·chān·syō'nā) *f* autoignition; **–adescante** (âū·tō·â·dā·skân'tā) *a* (*mech*) self-starting; **–biografia** (âū·tō·byō·grâ·fē'â) *f* autobiography; **–blinda** (âū·tō·blēn'dâ) *f* armored car; **–bus** (âū·tō·būs') *m* bus; **–campeggio** (âū·tō·kâm·pej'jō) *m* camping in a trailer; **–carro** (âū·tō·kâr'rō) *m* truck; **–cisterna** (âū·tō·chē·stār'nâ) *f* tank truck; **–clave** (âū·tō·klâ'vā) *f* autoclave; (*med*) sterilizer; **–corriera** (âū·tō·kōr·ryā'râ) *f* intercity bus; **–crazia** (âū·tō·krâ·tsē'â) *f* autocracy; **–decisione** (âū·tō·dā·chē·zyō'nā) *f* self-determination; **–dromo** (âū·tō·drō'mō) *m* motordrome; **–fficina** (âū·tōf·fē·chē'nâ) *f* auto repair shop; **–genesi** (âū·tō·je'nā·zē) *f* abiogenesis; spontaneous generation; **–geno** (âū·tô'jā·nō) autogenic;
assortito (âs·sōr·tē'tō) *a* assorted; various
assumere * (âs·sū'mā·rā) *vt* to assume; to employ; to fulfill
Assunzione (âs·sūn·tsyō'nā) *f* Assumption
assurdità (âs·sūr·dē·tâ') *f* absurdity; nonsense
assurdo (âs·sūr'dō) *a* absurd, ridiculous
asta (â'stâ) *f* pole; **vendita all'—** auction sale
astemio (â·ste'myō) *m* teetotaler; — *a* abstemious
astenersi (â·stā·nār'sē) *vr* to abstain
astensione (â·stān·syō'nā) *f* abstention
asterisco (â·stā·rē'skō) *m* asterisk
astio (â'styō) *m* grudge
astracan (â·strâ'kân) *m* astrakhan; **pelliccia d'—** astrakhan fur
astrale (â·strâ'lā) *a* astral
astrarre * (â·strâr'rā) *vt&i* to abstract; to set apart, highlight
astrarsi * (â·strâr'sē) *vr* to wander off
astrattismo (â·strât·tē'zmō) *m* abstract art
astro (â'strō) *m* star; **–fisica** (â·strō·fē'zē·kâ) *f* astrophysics; **–fotometrico** (â·strō·fō·tō·me'trē·kō) *a* astrophotometric; **–logia** (â·strō·lō·jē'â) *f* astrology; **–logo** (â·strô'lō·gō) *m* astrologer; **–metria** (â·strō·mā·trē'â) *f* astrometry; **–nauta** (â·strō·nâ'ū·tâ) *m* astronaut; **–nautica** (â·strō·nâ'ū·tē·kâ) *f* space travel, astronautics; **–nave** (â·strō·nâ'vā) *f* spaceship; **–nomia** (â·strō·nō·mē'â) *f* astronomy; **–nomico** (â·strō·nô'mē·kō) *a* astronomical; **–nomo** (â·strô'nō·mō) *m* astronomer
astuccio (â·stū'chō) *m* case, box
astuto (â·stū'tō) *a* shrewd, clever
astuzia (â·stū'tsyâ) *f* craftiness, asstuteness; ruse
ateismo (â·tā·ē'zmō) *m* atheism
ateo (â'tā·ō) *m* atheist
atlante (â·tlân'tā) *m* atlas
atlantico (â·tlân'tē·kō) *a* Atlantic
atleta (â·tlā'tâ) m athlete
atletica (â·tle'tē·kâ) *f* athletics, sports
atmosfera (â·tmō·sfā'râ) *f* atmosphere
atomico (â·tô'mē·kō) *a* atomic; **energia atomica** atomic energy
atomizzare (â·tō·mē·dzâ'rā) *vt* to annihilate; to destroy
atomo (â'tō·mō) *m* atom; **scissione dell'—** atomic fission
atrio (â'tryō) *m* hall
atroce (â·trō'chā) *a* frightful, atrocious
atrocità (â·trō·chē·tâ') *f* atrocity
atrofia (â·trō·fē'â) *f* atrophy
attaccamento (ât·tâk·kâ·mān'tō) *m* devotion, love
attaccapanni (ât·tâk·kâ·pân'nē) *m* coat hanger
attaccare (ât·tâk·kâ'rā) vt to attack; to attach; to sew; to stick
attacco (ât·tâk'kō) *m* attack
attecchire (ât·tāk·kē'rā) *vt* to stick, take hold
atteggiamento (ât·tāj·jâ·mān'tō) *m* attitude
atteggiare (ât·tāj·jâ'rā) *vt* to adapt, make conform; to cause to comply
atteggiarsi (ât·tāj·jâr'sē) *vr* to take an attitude, take a position
attempato (ât·tām·pâ'tō) *a* grown old, elderly
attendarsi (ât·tān·dâr'sē) *vr* to camp out, pitch camp
attendente (ât·tān·dān'tā) *m* orderly
attendere * (ât·ten'dā·rā) *vt* to wait for, anticipate
attendibile (ât·tān·dē'bē·lā) *a* reliable
attendibilità (ât·tān·dē·bē·lē·tâ') *f* trustworthiness; assurance
attenere * (ât·tā·nā'rā) *vi* to belong to
attenersi * (ât·tā·nār'sē) *vr* to conform to; to stick to; — **alle istruzioni** to follow instructions
attentamente (ât·tān·tâ·mān'tā) *adv* carefully
attentare (ât·tān·tâ'rā) *vi* to attempt
attentato (ât·tān·tâ'tō) *m* attempt
attento (ât·tān'tō) *a* careful; **attenti a** beware of; watch out for; **attenti ai treni** railroad crossing
attenuare (ât·tā·nwâ'rā) *vt* to lessen; to diminish
attenzione (ât·tān·tsyō'nā) *f* attention; **—! lavori in corso!** caution! road under

repair!; — **agli animali** beware of animals; **fare** — to be careful
atterraggio (ât·tär·râj'jō) *m* (*avi*) landing; — **di fortuna** emergency landing; — **cieco** blind landing; — **strumentale** instrument landing; **carrello di** — landing gear
atterrare (ât·tär·râ'rā) *vi* to land; — *vt* to fell; to knock to the ground
atterrire (ât·tär·rē'rā) *vt* to frighten
attesa (ât·tā'zâ) *f* waiting
attestare (ât·tā·stâ'rā) *vt* to testify to; to declare
attestato (ât·tā·stâ'tō) *m* testimonial
attiguo (ât·tē'gwō) *a* adjoining, next
attillato (ât·tēl·lâ'tō) *a* close-fitting; dressed up; coquettish
attimo (ât'tē·mō) *m* instant
autogenetic; **–giro** (âū·tō·jē'rō) *m* gyroplane; autogyro; **–grafo** (âū·tô'grâ·fō) *m* autograph; **–lesione** (âū·tō·lā·zyō'nā) *f* self-inflicted wound; **–lettiga** (âū·tō·lāt·tē'gâ) *f* ambulance; **–linea** (âū·tō·lē'nā·â) *f* bus line; **–ma** (âū·tō'mâ) *m* robot, automation; **–matico** (âū·tō·mâ'tē·kō) *a* automatic; **–mazione** (âū·tō·mâ·tsyō'nā) *f* automation; **–mezzo** (âū·tō·mā'dzō) *m* motor vehicle; **–mobile** (âū·tō·mô'bē·lā) *m* automobile; **–mobilismo** (âū·tō·mō·bē·lē'zmō) *m* motoring; **–mobilista** (âū·tō·mō·bē·lē'stâ) *m* driver; **–motrice** (âū·tō·mō·trē'chā) *f* self-propelled railroad car; **–nomia** (âū·tō·nō·mē'â) *f* self-government; (*avi*) cruising range; **–parcheggio** (âū·tō·pâr·kej'jō) *m* parking lot; **–pompa** (âū·tō·pōm'pâ) *f* fire engine; **–psia** (âū·tō·psē'â) *f* autopsy; **–pubblica** (âū·tō·pūb'blē·kâ) *f* taxi, taxicab; **–pullman** (âū·tō·pūl'mân) *m* luxury bus; **–raduno** (âū·tō·râ·dū'nō) *m* automobile meet; **–re** (âū·tō'rā) *m* author; **–rimessa** (âū·tō·rē·mās'sâ) *f* garage; **–rità** (âū·tō·rē·tâ') *f* authority; **–rizzare** (âū·tō·rē·dzâ'rā) *vt* to authorize; **–rizzazione** (âū·tō·rē·dzâ·tsyō'nā) *f* authorization; **–scafo** (âū·tō·skâ'fō) *m* motor boat; **–scatto** (âū·tō·skât'tō) *m* (*phot*) automatic release; **–stello** (âū·tō·stāl'lō) *m* motel; **–stop** (âū·tō·stōp') *m* hitchhiking; **–stoppista** (âū·tō·stōp·pē'stâ) *m&f* hitchhiker; **–strada** (âū·tō·strâ'dâ) *f* superhighway, expressway, turnpike; **–suggestione** (âū·tō·sūj·jā·styō'nā) *f* autosuggestion; **–tipia** (âū·tō·tē·pē'â) *f* autotype, facsimile; **–trasporto** (âū·tō·trâ·spōr'tō) *m* trucking; **–treno** (âū·tō·trā'nō) *m* trailer truck; **–veicolo** (âū·tō·vā·ē'kō·lō) *m* motor vehicle; **–vettura** (âū·tō·vāt·tū'râ) *f* passenger car
autunno (âū·tūn'nō) *m* fall, autumn
avallare (â·vâl·lâ'rā) *vt* to guarantee
avambraccio (â·vâm·brâ'chō) *m* forearm
Avana (â·vâ'nâ) *f* Havana; **a–** *m* Havana cigar
avanguardia (â·vân·gwâr'dyâ) *f* vanguard
avanguardista (â·vân·gwâr·dē'stâ) *m* scout
avanscoperta (â·vân·skō·pār'tâ) *f* (*mil*) scouting
avanti (â·vân'tē) *adv* ahead; come in!; **–eri** (â·vân·tyā'rē) *adv* day before yesterday
avanzamento (â·vân·tsâ·mān'tō) *m* progression; promotion
avanzare (â·vân·tsâ'rā) *vt* to advance; — *vi* to be left over
avanzata (â·vân·tsâ'tâ) *f* advance
avanzato (â·vân·tsâ'tō) *a* advanced; **cibo** — leftover food; **notte avanzata** late at night; **età avanzata** great age, old age
avanzo (â·vân'tsō) *m* leftover
avaro (â·vâ'rō) *a* stingy; — *m* miser
avena (â·vā'nâ) *f* oats
avere * (â·vā'rā) *vt* to have
avi (â'vē) *mpl* ancestors
aviatore (â·vyâ·tō'rā) *m* aviator
aviatrice (â·vyâ·trē'chā) *f* aviatrix
aviazione (â·vyâ·tsyō'nā) *f* aviation
avidità (â·vē·dē·tâ') *f* great eagerness; greed
avido (â'vē·dō) *a* avid, anxious
aviere (â·vyā'rā) *m* aviator
aviogetto (â·vyō·jāt'tō) *m* jet plane
aviolinea (â·vyō·lē'nā·â) *f* air line
avioraduno (â·vyō·râ·dū'nō) *m* air meet
aviorimessa (â·vyō·rē·mās'sâ) *f* hangar
avitaminosi (â·vē·tâ·mē·nō'zē) *f* avitaminosis
avo (â'vō) *m* grandfather
avorio (â·vô'ryō) *m* ivory
avvallamento (âv·vâl·lâ·mān'tō) *m* valley; hollow
avvallare (âv·vâl·lâ'rā) *vt* to hollow out; to level (*land*)
avvallarsi (âv·vâl·lâr'sē) *vr* to sink; (*fig*) to give up, admit defeat
avvalorare (âv·vâ·lō·râ'rā) *vt* to increase the value of; to strengthen
avvalorarsi (âv·vâ·lō·râr'sē) *vr* to increase in value; to make oneself valuable; to become stronger
avvantaggiamento (âv·vân·tâj·jâ·mān'tō) *m* advantage, benefit; improvement
avvantaggiare (âv·vân·tâj·jâ'rā) *vt* to improve; to benefit
avvantaggiarsi (âv·vân·tâj·jâr'sē) *vr* to get profit from; to take advantage of
avvedutezza (âv·vā·dū·tā'tsâ) *f* prudence; keenness; astuteness
avveduto (âv·vā·dū'tō) *a* wary; prudent; shrewd
avvelenare (âv·vā·lā·nâ'rā) *vt* to poison
avvelenatore (âv·vā·lā·nâ·tō'rā) *m* poisoner
avvenenza (âv·vā·nān'tsâ) *f* charm; prettiness
avvenimento (âv·vā·nē·mān'tō) *m* event, happening
avvenire * (âv·vā·nē'rā) *vi* to happen; — *m* future
avventare (âv·vān·tâ'rā) *vt* to hazard; to rush at; to fling
avventarsi (âv·vān·târ'sē) *vr* to pounce; to rush upon
avventato (âv·vān·tâ'tō) *a* rash, heedless
avventore (âv·vān·tō'rā) *m* customer

avventura (âv·vān·tū'râ) *f* adventure; **–re** (âv·vān·tū·râ'rā) *vt* to venture; **–rsi** (âv·vān·tū·râr'sē) *vr* to venture, dare; **–to** (âv·vān·tū·râ'tō) *a* fortunate, lucky
avventuriere (âv·vān·tū·ryā'rā) *m* adventurer
avverbio (âv·ver'byō) *m* adverb
avversario (âv·vār·sâ'ryō) *m* adversary; enemy
avversione (âv·vār·syō'nā) *f* dislike
avversità (âv·vār·sē·tâ') *f* adversity
avvertenza (âv·vār·tān'tsâ) *f* notice, warning; foreword, preface
avvertimento (âv·vār·tē·mān'tō) *m* warning
avvertire (âv·vār·tē'rā) *vt* to notify; to warn; to sense, notice
avvezzare (âv·vā·tsâ'rā) *vt* to accustom
avviamento (âv·vyâ·mān'tō) *m* introduction to a subject; (*auto*) starter; **scuola d'— commerciale** business school, commercial college
avviare (âv·vyâ'rā) *vt* to start, activate
avviarsi (âv·vyâr'sē) *vr* to set out; to advance, proceed
avvicendamento (âv·vē·chān·dâ·mān'tō) rotation; alternation
avvicinamento (âv·vē·chē·nâ·mān'tō) *m* approach, drawing near
avvicinare (âv·vē·chē·nâ'rā) *vt* to bring closer
avvicinarsi (âv·vē·chē·nâr'sē) *vr* to get closer, draw nearer
avvilimento (âv·vē·lē·mān'tō) *m* dejection; debasement
avvilire (âv·vē·lē'rā) *vt* to mortify; to deject; to debase
avvilirsi (âv·vē·lēr'sē) *vr* to lose heart; to debase oneself
avviluppare (âv·vē·lūp·pâ'rā) *vt* to enfold; to wrap
avvilupparsi (âv·vē·lūp·pâr'sē) *vr* to wrap up, bundle up; to become involved
avvinazzato (âv·vē·nâ·tsâ'tō) *a* tipsy
avvincere * (âv·vēn'chā·rā) *vt* to truss up; to bind; to fascinate
avvincersi * (âv·vēn'chār·sē) *vr* to hug each other; to become obligated, obligate oneself
avvinto (âv·vēn'tō) *a* tied, bound; (*fig*) fascinated
avvisare (âv·vē·zâ'rā) *vt* to inform, advise
avviso (âv·vē'zō) *m* notice, advice
avvitamento (âv·vē·tâ·mān'tō) *m* (*avi*) spin; screwing
avvitare (âv·vē·tâ'rā) *vt* to screw
avvivare (âv·vē·vâ'rā) *vt* to animate; to make vivacious
avvizzire (âv·vē·tsē'rā) *vi* to wither
avvocato (âv·vō·kâ'tō) *m* lawyer
avvocatura (âv·vō·kâ·tū'râ) *f* practice of law
avvolgere * (âv·vôl'jā·rā) *vt* to wrap up; to envolve, mix up
avvolgimento (âv·vōl·jē·mān'tō) *m* winding; hoodwinking
avvoltoio (âv·vōl·tô'yō) *m* vulture
azienda (â·tsyān'dâ) *f* business, firm; **— di soggiorno** municipal tourist bureau; **–le** (â·tsyān·dâ'lā) *a* pertaining to business, business
azionare (â·tsyō·nâ'rā) *vt* to operate; to activate
azione (â·tsyō'nā) *f* action; share
azionista (â·tsyō·nē'stâ) *m* stockholder
azoto (â·dzō'tō) *m* nitrogen
azzannare (â·dzân·nâ'rā) *vt* to gore, tusk
azzardare (â·dzâr·dâ'rā) *vt* to risk
azzardo (â·dzâr'dō) *m* risk; **giuoco d'—** gambling
azzeccare (â·dzāk·kâ'rā) *vt* to guess
azzimo (â'dzē·mō) *a* unleavened
azzuffarsi (â·dzūf·fâr'sē) *vr* to come to blows, fight
azzurro (â·dzūr'rō) *a* blue; **–gnolo** (â·dzūr·rô'nyō·lō) *a* bluish

B

babbeo (bâb·bā'ō) *m* idiot, simpleton
babbo (bâb·bō) *m* dad
babordo (bâ·bōr'dō) *m* (*naut*) port
bacato (bâ·kâ'tō) *a* rotten; worm-eaten
bacca (bâk'kâ) *f* berry
baccalà (bâk·kâ·lâ') *m* codfish, cod
baccano (bâk·kâ'nō) *m* noise, racket
baccello (bâ·chāl'lō) *m* (*bot*) pod
bacchetta (bâk·kāt'tâ) *f* (*mus*) baton
baciare (bâ·châ'rā) *vt* to kiss
bacile (bâ·chē'lā) *m* basin
bacinella (bâ·chē·nāl'lâ) *f* shallow bowl; (*phot*) tray
bacio (bâ'chō) *m* kiss
baco (bâ'kō) *m* caterpillar; **— da seta** silkworm
badare (bâ·dâ'rā) *vi* to mind; to be careful
badessa (bâ·dās'sâ) *f* abbess
badia (bâ·dē'â) *f* abbey
badile (bâ·dē'lā) *m* shovel
baffi (bâf'fē) *mpl* mustache
bagagliaio (bâ·gâ·lyâ'yō) *m* baggage car
bagaglio (bâ·gâ'lyō) *m* baggage; **deposito bagagli** checkroom; **ufficio bagagli** baggage room
bagarino (bâ·gâ·rē'nō) *m* scalper on the stock market; ticket scalper
bagattella (bâ·gât·tāl'lâ) *f* bagatelle, trifle
baggianata (bâj·jä·nä'tä) *f* foolishness, nonsense
bagliore (bâ·lyō'rā) *m* gleam, dazzle; beam, ray
bagnante (bâ·nyân'tā) *m&f* bather
bagnare (bâ·nyâ'rā) *vt* to wet; to dampen
bagnarola (bâ·nyâ·rō'lâ) *f* bathtub
bagnarsi (bâ·nyâr'sē) *vr* to get wet; to bathe; **vietato —** no swimming
bagnasciuga (bâ·nyâ·shū'gâ) *f* shoreline
bagnino (bâ·nyē'nō) *m* lifeguard
bagno (bâ'nyō) *m* bath; **costume da —** bathing suit; **stanza da —** bathroom;

vasca **da** — bathtub; **–maria** (bâ·nyō·mâ·rē'â) *m* bain-marie
baia (bâ'yâ) *f* bay, harbor
baio (bâ'yō) *m* bay (*horse*)
baionetta (bâ·yō·nāt'tâ) *f* bayonet
baita (bâ'ē·tâ) *f* mountain hut
balaustra (bâ·lâ·ū'strâ), **balaustrata** (bâ·lâū·strâ'tâ) *f* railing
balbettare (bâl·bāt·tâ'rā) *vt* to stammer; to speak haltingly
balbuziente (bâl·bū·tsyān'tā) *m* stammerer
balcone (bâl·kō'nā) *m* balcony
baldacchino (bâl·dâk·kē'nō) *m* canopy
baldoria (bâl·dô'ryâ) *f* revelry, wassail
balena (bâ·lā'nâ) *f* whale
balenare (bâ·lā·nâ'rā) *vi* to flash; to lightning; (*fig*) to cross the mind
balenio (bâ·lā·nē'ō) *m* flashing, dazzling
baleno (bâ·lā'nō) *m* lightning flash; **in un** — in a flash, instantly
balestra (bâ·lā'strâ) *f* leaf spring
balestre (bâ·lā'strā) *fpl* auto springs
balia (bâ·lyâ) *f* wet nurse
balistico (bâ·lē'stē·kō) *a* ballistic
balla (bâl'lâ) *f* bale
ballare (bâl·lâ'rā) *vt&i* to dance
ballatoio (bâl·lâ·tô'yō) *m* balcony, gallery
ballerina (bâl·lā·rē'nâ) *f* dancer
balletto (bâl·lāt'tō) *m* ballet
ballo (bâl'lō) *m* ball, dance
balneare (bâl·nā·â'râ) *a* bathing; **stazione** — bathing resort
balocco (bâ·lōk'kō) *m* toy
balordo (bâ·lōr'dō) *a* silly; mentally slow
balordaggine (bâ·lōr·dâj'jē·nā) *f* silliness; foolish conduct; mental deficiency
balsamo (bâl'sâ·mō) *m* balsam
balsamico (bâl·sâ'mē·kō) *a* balmy; like balsam
baluardo (bâ·lwâr'dō) *m* bulwark
balza (bâl'tsâ) *f* cliff; wide ruffle
balzano (bâl·tsâ'nō) *a* strange, unpredictable; white-footed (*horse*)
balzare (bâl·tsâ'rā) *vi* to jump, leap; — **dal letto** to jump out of bed; — **in piedi** to jump to one's feet
bambagia (bâm·bâ'jâ) *f* cotton batting
bambinaia (bâm·bē·nâ'yâ) *f* nursemaid; — **a ore** baby-sitter
bambinesco (bâm·bē·nā'skō) *a* childish
bambino (bâm·bē'nō) *m* baby; child
bambola (bâm'bō·lâ) *f* doll
banca (bân'kâ) *f* bank; **–rella** (bân·kâ·rāl'lâ) *f* street stall; pushcart; **–rio** (bân·kâ'ryō) *a* banking; **–rotta** (bân·kâ·rōt'tâ) *f* bankruptcy
banchetto (bân·kāt'tō) *m* banquet
banchiere (bân·kyā'rā) *m* banker
banchina (bân·kē'nâ) *f* pier; platform
banco (bân'kō) *m* counter; bench; bank; **–nota** (ban·kō·nō'tâ) *f* banknote, bill
banda (bân'dâ) *f* band; gang
bandiera (bân·dyā'râ) *f* flag
bandito (bân·dē'tō) *m* bandit
banditore (bân·dē·tō'rā) *m* auctioneer
bando (bân'dō) *m* exile; banishment; (*pol*) proclamation
bandoliera (bân·dō·lyā'râ) *f* (*mil*) shoulder belt
bandolo (bân'dō·lō) *m* last of a skein; — **di un problema** clue for solving a problem
bar (bâr) *m* bar; café
bara (bâ'râ) *f* casket; bier
baracca (bâ·râk'kâ) *f* hut; barrack; **piantare — e burattini** to give it up as a bad job, give it up as a lost cause
barare (bâ·râ'rā) *vi* to cheat in a game
baratro (bâ'râ·trō) *m* crevice; abyss; gulf
barattare (bâ·rât·tâ'rā) *vt* (*com*) to trade on; to exchange, barter
baratto (bâ·rât'tō) *m* board of trade; bartering
barattolo (bâ·rât'tō·lō) *m* can; jar; tin
barba (bâr'bâ) *f* beard; **che —!** what a nuisance! **fare la** — to shave
barbabietola (bâr·bâ·bye'tō·lâ) *f* beet
barbagianni (bâr·bâ·jân'nē) *m* owl; (*fig*) simpleton
barbaro (bâr'bâ·rō) *a* barbarous
barberia (bâr·bā·rē'â) *f* barbershop
barbetta (bâr·bāt'tâ) *f* goatee
barbiere (bâr·byā'rā) *m* barber
barbiturico (bâr·bē·tū'rē·kō) *m* barbiturate
barbone (bâr·bō'nā) *m* (*coll*) hobo; long-bearded man
barboso (bâr·bō'zō) *a* boring
barbuto (bâr·bū'tō) *a* bearded
barca (bâr'kâ) *f* boat; **–iuolo** (bâr·kâ·ywō'lō) *m* boatman
barcollare (bâr·kōl·lâ'rā) *vi* to reel, stagger
barella (bâ·rāl'lâ) *f* stretcher; **–re** (bâ·rāl·lâ'rā) *vt* to transport by stretcher; — *vi* to stagger
baricentro (bâ·rē·chān'trō) *m* center of gravity
barile (bâ·rē'lā) *m* barrel, cask
baritono (bâ·rē'tō·nō) *m* baritone
baro (bâ'rō) *m* cardsharp; cheat
baroccio (bâ·rô'chō) *m* handcart
barometro (bâ·rô'mā·trō) *m* barometer
barone (bâ·rō'nā) *m* baron
baronessa (bâ·rō·nās'sâ) *f* baroness
barra (bâr'râ) *f* bar; (*naut*) tiller
barricata (bâr·rē·kâ'tâ) *f* barricade
barriera (bâr·ryā'râ) *f* barrier; — **doganale** customs station
baruffa (bâ·rūf'fâ) *f* fight, brawl
barzelletta (bâr·dzāl·lāt'tâ) *f* joke; witty story
basalto (bâ·zâl'tō) *m* (*min*) basalt
basare (bâ·zâ'rā) *vt* to base
base (bâ'zā) *f* base; basis
basetta (bâ·zāt'tâ) *f* sideburn
basilica (bâ·zē'lē·kâ) *f* basilica
basilico (bâ·zē'lē·kō) *m* (*bot*) basil
bassifondi (bâs·sē·fōn'dē) *mpl* scum of society, underworld
basso (bâs'sō) *m* bass; — *a* low; mean
bassorilievo (bâs·sō·rē·lyā'vō) *m* bas-relief
bassotto (bâs·sōt'tō) *m* basset (*dog*)
basta! (bâ'stâ) *interj* that's enough!; **–re** (bâ·stâ'rā) *vt* to suffice, be sufficient

bastardo (bâ·stâr'dō) *m&a* hybrid; bastard
bastimento (bâ·stē·mān'tō) *m* ship, boat
bastione (bâ·styō'nā) *m* rampart; fortification
basto (bâ'stō) *m* packsaddle
bastonare (bâ·stō·nâ'rā) *vt* to beat, club
bastone (bâ·stō'nā) *m* club; cane; spade (*cards*)
batosta (bâ·tō'stâ) *f* blow, calamity
battaglia (bât·tâ'lyâ) *f* battle
battaglione (bât·tâ·lyō'nā) *m* battalion
battelliere (bât·tāl·lyā'rā) *m* boatman
battello (bât·tāl'lō) *m* boat, small craft
battere (bât'tā·rā) *vt&i* to strike; to hit; to beat; to defeat; — **alla porta** to knock at the door; — **bandiera** (*fig*) to fly a flag; —**d'occhi** to blink one's eyes; — **di piedi** to stamp one's feet; — **il nemico** to defeat the enemy; — **il tacco** (*fig*) to abscond; to take to one's heels; — **le mani** to applaud, clap
batteria (bât·tā·rē'â) *f* battery; (*mus*) percussion instruments; — **da cucina** cooking utensils
batteriologia (bât·tā·ryō·lō·jē'â) *f* bacteriology
batteriologo (bât·tā·ryô'lō·gō) *f* bacteriologist
batterista (bât·tā·rē'stâ) *m* drummer
battersi (bât'tār·sē) *vr* to hit oneself; to beat each other up; to fight, battle; **battersela** to flee, take flight
battesimo (bât·te'zē·mō) *m* baptism; **nome di** — Christian name
battezzare (bât·tā·dzâ'rā) *vt* to christen; to baptize
batticuore (bât·tē·kwō'rā) *m* heartbeat
battistero (bât·tē·stā'rō) *m* baptistry
battistrada (bât·tē·strâ'dâ) *m* scout; tread (*tire*)
battuta (bât·tū'tâ) *f* beat; stroke; cue; (*mus*) bar
batuffolo (bâ·tūf'fō·lō) *m* wad
baule (bâ·ū'lā) *m* trunk
bauxite (bâūk·sē'tā) *f* (*min*) bauxite
bava (bâ'vâ) *f* foam (*mouth*); slobber; silk floss; **-glino** (bâ·vâ·lyē'nō) *m* bib
bavaglio (bâ·vâ'lyō) *m* gag
bavero (bâ'vā·rō) *m* coat collar
bazza (bâ'dzâ) f prominent chin; (*fig*) good fortune; windfall; trick (*cards*)
bazzicare (bâ·tsē·kâ'rā) *vt* to frequent
bazzotto (bâ·dzōt'tō) *a* soft-boiled
beatificare (bā·â·tē·fē·kâ'rā) *vt* (*eccl*) to beatify
beatificazione (bā·â·tē·fē·kâ·tsyō'nā) *f* beatification
beatitudine (bā·â·tē·tū'dē·nā) *f* exalted happiness, beautitude; bliss; **Sua B–** His Holiness
beato (bā·â'tō) *a* blessed; lucky
beccaccia (bāk·kâ'châ) *f* woodcock
beccaio (bāk·kâ'yō) *m* butcher
beccamorto (bāk·kâ·mōr'tō) *m* gravedigger; (*fig*) unpleasantness
beccare (bāk·kâ'rā) *vt* to peck
beccarsi (bāk·kâr'sē) *vi* to peck each other; (*fig*) to get; — **un raffreddore** to catch a cold
beccheggio (bāk·kej'jō) *m* pitching (*ship*)
becchino (bāk·kē'nō) *m* gravedigger
becco (bāk'kō) *m* beak; burner; he-goat; cuckold
befana (bā·fâ'nâ) *f* Epiphany; Italian counterpart of Santa Claus
beffa (bāf'fâ) *f* mockery, derision; **-rdo** (bāf·fâr'dō) *m* derider; **-rdo** *a* mocking; **-re** (bāf·fâ'rā) *vt* to mock, poke fun at; **-rsi** (bāf·fâr'sē) *vr* to hold up to ridicule, make fun of
belare (bā·lâ'rā) *vi* to bleat
belga (bāl'gâ) *m&a* Belgian
belladonna (bāl·lâ·dōn'nâ) *f* (*bot*) belladonna
belletto (bāl·lāt'tō) *m* rouge
bellezza (bāl·lā'tsâ) *f* beauty; **concorso di** — beauty contest; **istituto di** —, **salone di** — beauty parlor, beauty shop
bellico (bel'lē·kō) *a* having to do with war; **materiale** — military supplies; **-so** (bāl·lē·kō'zō) *a* pugnacious; bellicose; quarrelsome
belligerante (bāl·lē·jā·rân'tā) *m&a* belligerent
bellimbusto (bāl·lēm·bū'stō) *m* fop, dandy
bellino (bāl·lē'nō) *a* cute; pretty; darling
bello (bāl'lō) *a* beautiful; handsome; lovely; fine; wonderful
beltà (bāl·tâ') *f* beauty; loveliness; handsomeness
belva (bāl'vâ) *f* wild beast; (*fig*) savage person
belvedere (bāl·vā·dā'rā) *m* observation car; belvedere
benaccetto (bān·nâ·chāt'tō) *a* welcome; well-received
benallevato (bā·nâl·lā·vâ'tō) *a* well-bred
benalzato! (bā·nâl·tsâ'tō) *a* (*coll*) good morning!
benamato (bā·nâ·mâ'tō) *a* beloved
benarrivato (bā·nâr·rē·vâ'tō) *a* welcome, pleasant
benaugurato (bā·nâū·gū·râ'tō) *a* auspicious; well-received
benavventurato (bā·nâv·vān·tū·râ'tō) *a* lucky, fortunate
bencreato (bān·krā·â'tō) *a* well-bred; well-born
benda (bān'dâ) *f* bandage; **-re** (bān·dâ'rā) *vt* to bandage; to swathe
bene (bā'nā) *adv* well; O.K. (*coll*); — *m* good; love; **beni immobili** real estate
benedettino (bā·nā·dāt·tē'nō) *m&a* Benedictine
benedetto (bā·nā·dāt'tō) *a* blessed, holy
benedire * (bā·nā·dē'rā) *vt* to bless
benedizione (bā·nā·dē·tsyō'nā) *f* benediction
beneducato (bā·nā·dū·kâ'tō) *a* well brought up, well-mannered
benefattore (bā·nā·fât·tō'rā) *m* benefactor
beneficare (bā·nā·fē·kâ'rā) *vt* to benefit
beneficato (bā·nā·fē·kâ'tō) *a* benefited
beneficenza (bā·nā·fē·chān'tsâ) *f* charity
beneficiario (bā·nā·fē·châ'ryō) *m* beneficiary; — *a* beneficial
beneficiata (bā·nā·fē·châ'tâ) *f* benefit per-

formance
beneficio (bā·nā·fē'chō) *m* benefit
benefico (bā·ne'fē·kō) *a* altruistic, beneficent
benemerenza (bā·nā·mā·rān'tsâ) *f* merit, worth; good turn, favor
benemerito (bā·nā·me'rē·tō) *a* deserving
beneplacito (bā·nā·plâ'chē·tō) *m* approbation; consent
benessere (bā·nes'sā·rā) *m* well-being
benestante (bā·nā·stân'tā) *a* well-to-do
benevolo (bā·ne'vō·lō) *a* kind, gentle, benevolent
benfatto (bān·fât'tō) *a* handsome, well built (*person*)
beniamino (bān·yâ·mē'nō) *m* favorite
benigno (bā·nē'nyō) *a* benign
benino (bā·nē'nō) *adv* pretty well
beninteso (bā·nēn·tā'zō) *adv* of course, certainly; — *conj* provided; with the understanding that
benissimo (bā·nēs'sē·mō), **benone** (bā·nō'nā) *adv&a* very well; swell
benpensante (bān·pān·sân'tā) *a* sensible; judicious; — *m* a judicious, moderate person
benservito (bān·sār·vē'tō) *m* reference; **dare il** — (*fig*) to discharge, fire
bensì (bān·sē') *adv* indeed, of course
bentornato (bān·tōr·nâ'tō) *m* welcome; —! *interj* welcome back!
benvenuto (bān·vā·nū'tō) *m&a* welcome
benvisto (bān·vē'stō) *a* liked; welcome
benvolere * (bān·vō·lā'rā) *vt* to like very much; — *m* attachment, affection, love
benzina (bān·dzē'nâ) *f* gasoline; — **per l'accenditore** lighter fuel
bere * (bā'rā) *vt* to drink; to absorb
berlina (bār·lē'nâ) *f* (*auto*) sedan
berlinetta (bār·lē·nāt'tâ) *f* (*auto*) two-door sedan
bernoccolo (bār·nôk'kō·lō) *m* bump; knock; swelling
berretto (bār·rāt'tō) *m* cap
bersaglio (bār·sâ'lyō) *m* target
bertuccia (bār·tū'châ) *f* monkey; ape
bestemmia (bā·stem'myâ) *f* blasphemy, swear word; **–re** (bā·stām·myâ'rā) *vt* to curse
bestia (be'styâ) *f* animal; — *a* stupid; **–le** (bā·styâ'lā) *a* brutal, beastly; **–lità** (bā·styâ·lē·tâ') *f* bestiality; absurdity; **–me** (bā·styâ'mā) *m* cattle
betatrone (bā·tâ·trō'nā) *m* betatron
betoniera (bā·tō·nyā'râ) *f* concrete mixer
bettola (bet'tō·lâ) *f* saloon; tavern
bevanda (bā·vân'dâ) *f* beverage
biacca (byâk'kâ) *f* white lead
biada (byâ'dâ) *f* fodder
biancastro (byân·kâ'strō) *a* whitish
biancheria (byân·kā·rē'â) *f* linen; — **intima** lingerie
bianco (byân'kō) *a* white; **–segno** (byân·kō·sā'nyō) *m* blank check; **–spino** (byân·kō·spē'nō) *m* hawthorn
biasimare (byâ·zē·mâ'rā) *vt* to reprove; to criticize; to blame
biasimo (byâ'zē·mō) *m* blame
biasimevole (byâ·zē·me'vō·lā) *a* blameworthy, reproachable
Bibbia (Bēb'byâ) *f* Bible
biberone (bē·bā·rō'nā) *m* nursing bottle
bibita (bē'bē·tâ) *f* drink; — **gasata** soft drink
bibliografia (bē·blyō·grâ·fē'â) *f* bibliography
biblioteca (bē·blyō·tā'kâ) *f* library; — **di prestito** lending library; — **pubblica** public library; **–rio** (bē·blyō·tā·kâ'ryō) *m* librarian
bicarbonato (bē·kâr·bō·nâ'tō) *m* bicarbonate
bicchiere (bēk·kyā'rā) *m* drinking glass, tumbler
bicicletta (bē·chē·klāt'tâ) *f* bicycle
bicimotore (bē·chē·mō·tō'rā) *m* motorbike
bidello (bē·dāl'lō) *m* janitor, custodian
bidone (bē·dō'nā) *m* drum; large can; (*fig*) swindle
bieco (byā'kō) *a* angry (*look*); sinister; evil; squinting
biella (byāl'lâ) *f* connecting rod
biennale (byān·nâ'lā) *a* biennial
bietola (bye'tō·lâ) *f* beet
bifolco (bē·fōl'kō) *m* peasant; farm laborer
biforcazione (bē·fōr·kâ·tsyō'nā) *f* junction, fork
biga (bē'gâ) *f* chariot
bigamia (bē·gâ·mē'â) *f* bigamy
bigamo (bē'gâ·mō) *a* bigamous; — *m* bigamist
bigio (bē'jō) *a* gray; dull
bigiotteria (bē·jōt·tā·rē'â) *f* costume jewelry
bigliettaio (bē·lyāt·tâ'yō) *m* ticket seller; conductor
bigletteria (bē·lyāt·tā·rē'â) *f* ticket office
biglietto (bē·lyāt'tō) *m* ticket; — **da visita** calling card
bigodino (bē·gō·dē'nō) *m* hair curler
bilancia (bē·lân'châ) *f* scales; **–re** (bē·lân·châ'rā) *vt* to counterbalance; **–re** *vi* to balance; **–rsi** (bē·lân·châr'sē) *vi* to be in balance; to weigh one alternative against another; to evaluate one's possibilities
bilanciere (bē·lân·chā'rā) *m* pendulum; scale; beam (*scale*); balance wheel (*watch*)
bilancio (bē·lân'chō) *m* budget; balance sheet
bile (bē'lā) *f* bile
bilia (bē'lyâ) *f* billiard ball; table pocket; **–rdo** (bē·lyâr'dō) *m* billiards
bilico (bē'lē·kō) *m* balance
bilingue (bē·lēn'gwā) *a* bilingual
bilione (bē·lyō'nā) *m* billion
bimbo (bēm'bō) *m* baby; child
bimetallico (bē·mā·tâl'lē·kō) *a* bimetallic
bimotore (bē·mō·tō'rā) *m* twin-engine plane
binario (bē·nâ'ryō) *m* track, rails
binoccolo (bē·nôk'kō·lō) *m* binoculars
biochimica (byō·kē'mē·kâ) *f* biochemis-

try
biografia (byō·grâ·fē'â) *f* biography
biologia (byō·lō·jē'â) *f* biology
biologo (byô'lō·gō) *m* biologist
biondo (byōn'dō) *a* blond, fair
biossido (byôs'sē·dō) *m* dioxide
bipede (bē'pā·dā) *m&a* biped
biplano (bē·plâ'nō) *m* biplane
bipolare (bē·pō·lâ'rā) *a* bipolar
biposto (bē·pō'stō) *a* two-seat
birbante (bēr·bân'tā) *m* rascal
biricchino (bē·rēk·kē'nō) *m* prankster, mischief (*person*)
birillo (bē·rēl'lō) *m* bowling pin
birmano (bēr·mâ'nō) *m&a* Burmese
biro (bē'rō) *m* ballpoint pen
birra (bēr'râ) *f* beer
birreria (bēr·rā·rē'â) *f* beer garden; bar, saloon
bisavolo (bē·zâ'vō·lō) great-grandfather
bisbigliare (bē·zbē·lyā'rā) *vt* to whisper
biscazziere (bē·skâ·tsyā'rā) *m* gambling house operator
biscia (bē'shâ) *f* water snake, garter snake
biscotto (bē·skōt'tō) *m* cracker; cookie
bisestile (bē·zā·stē'lā) *a* bissextile; **anno** — leap year
bisettrice (bē·zāt·trē'chā) *f* bisector
bisognare (bē·zō·nyâ'rā) *vi* to be needed, be wanting
bisogno (bē·zō'nyō) *m* need, necessity; **–so** (bē·zō·nyō'zō) *a* needy; destitute
bisso (bēs'sō) *m* fine linen
bistecca (bē·stāk'kâ) *f* beefsteak; — **ai ferri** broiled steak
bisticciarsi (bē·stē·châr'sē) *vi* to quarrel, wrangle, argue
bistrattare (bē·strât·tâ'rā) *vt* to abuse; to mistreat
bisturì (bē·stū·rē') *m* surgeon's knife, scalpel
bitume (bē·tū'mā) *m* bitumen
bituminoso (bē·tū·mē·nō'zō) *a* bituminous
bivalente (bē·vâ·lān'tā) *a* bivalent
bivalenza (bē·vâ·lān'tsâ) *f* bivalence
bivio (bē'vyō) *m* junction, fork
bizza (bē'dzâ) *f* brief anger; whim; **fare le bizze** to be in a foul mood; **–rria** (bē·dzâr·rē'â) *f* oddness; whimsy; **–rro** (bē·dzâr'rō) *a* bizarre, fantastic; **cavallo –rro** spirited horse
blandire (blân·dē'rā) *vt* to blandish; to fondle
blando (blân'dō) *a* soft; weak
blasone (blâ·zō'nā) *m* escutcheon
blatta (blât'tâ) *f* cockroach
bleso (blā'zō) *m* lisper; — *a* lisping
blinda (blēn'dâ) *f* armor; **–to** (blēn·dâ'tō) *a* armored; **carro –to** armored car
bloccare (blōk·kâ'rā) *vt* to block; — **i freni** to jam the brakes
blocco (blōk'kō) *m* block; blockade
blu (blū') *a* blue
bluffare (blūf·fâ'rā) *vt* to bluff, deceive
blusa (blū'zâ) *f* blouse
boa (bō'â) *f* buoy; (*zool*) boa
bobina (bō·bē'nâ) *f* coil; spool
bocca (bōk'kâ) *f* mouth; **in — al lupo!** good luck to you!; **–le** (bōk·kâ'lā) *m* pitcher; **–porto** (bōk·kâ·pōr'tō) *m* (*naut*) hatch
bocce (bō'chā) *fpl* game of bowling
boccetta (bō·chāt'tâ) *f* small bottle, flask
bocchino (bōk·kē'nō) *m* cigarette holder
boccia (bô'châ) *f* carafe; flower bud; bowling ball
bocciare (bō·châ'rā) *vt* to flunk
bocciodromo (bō·chō·drō'mō) *m* bowling alley
bocciuolo (bō·chwō'lō) *m* bud
boccone (bōk·kō'nā) *m* bite, mouthful
bocconi (bōk·kō'nē) *adv* flat on one's face; **cadere** — to fall flat on one's face
boia (bô'yâ) *m* executioner
boicottare (bōē·kōt·tâ'rā) *vt* to boycott
bolla (bōl'lâ) *f* bubble; blister
bollare (bōl·lâ'rā) *vt* to stamp
bollente (bōl·lān'tā) *a* boiling
bolletta (bōl·lāt'tâ) *f* bill; — **del gas** gas bill; **essere in** — to be flat broke (*coll*)
bollettino (bōl·lāt·tē'nō) *m* bulletin; — **meteorologico** weather bulletin
bollire (bōl·lē'rā) *vt* to boil
bollito (bōl·lē'tō) *a* boiled; — *m* boiled beef; **–re** (bōl·lē·tō'rā) *m* kettle; boiler
bollitura (bōl·lē·tū'râ) *f* boiling
bollo (bōl'lō) *m* stamp; **carta da** — official paper; **marca da** — revenue stamp
bomba (bōm'bâ) *f* bomb; — **atomica** atomic bomb; — **all'idrogeno** H-bomb; **–rdamento** (bōm·bâr·dâ·mān'tō) *m* bombing; (*phys*) bombardment; **–rdare** (bōm·bâr·dâ'rā) *vt* to bomb, shell; to bombard; **–rdiere** (bōm·bâr·dyā'rā) *m* bombardier; bomber (*plane*)
bombetta (bōm·bāt'tâ) *f* derby, bowler (*hat*)
bombola (bôm'bō·lâ) *f* cylinder; glass tank
bonario (bō·nâ'ryō) *a* gentle, meek, kind, good-natured
bonifica (bō·nē'fē·kâ) *f* land reclamation
bonsenso (bōn·sān'sō) *m* common sense
bontà (bōn·tâ') *f* goodness
borace (bō·râ'chā) *m* borax
borbottare (bōr·bōt·tâ'rā) *vt* to mutter
bordata (bōr·dâ'tâ) *f* (*naut*) broadside; tack
bordeggiare (bōr·dāj·jâ'rā) *vi* to veer; (*naut*) to tack
bordello (bōr·dāl'lō) *m* brothel; racket
borderò (bōr·dā·rō') *m* list; note
bordo (bōr'dō) *m* edge; board; **a** — on board
borghese (bōr·gā'zā) *a* middle-class, bourgeois; **abito** — civilian clothes
borgo (bōr'gō) *m* suburb; village; **–mastro** (bōr·gō·mâ'strō) *m* mayor
boria (bô'ryâ) *f* arrogance, vainglory
borico (bô'rē·kō) *a* boric
borraccia (bōr·râ'châ) *f* canteen, bottle, water bottle
borsa (bōr'sâ) *f* handbag; briefcase; scholarship, fellowship; stock exchange; — **di gomma per acqua calda** hot-water bottle; — **di ghiaccio** ice bag; **–iolo** (bōr·sâ·yō'lō) *m* pickpocket; **–nerista**

(bōr·sâ·nā·rē'stâ) *m* black marketeer
borsellino (bōr·sāl·lē'nō) *m* purse
borsetta (bōr·sāt'tâ) *f* handbag
borsista (bōr·sē'stâ) *m* stockbroker
boscaglia (bō·skâ'lyâ) *f* wood, forest
boscaiolo (bō·skâ·yō'lō) *m* woodsman
boschetto (bō·skāt'tō) *m* grove, thicket
bosco (bō'skō) *m* woods; **–so** (bō·skō'zō) *a* woody
bossolo (bôs'sō·lō) *m* cartridge case (*gun*)
botanico (bō·tâ'nē·kō) *a* botanical
botta (bōt'tâ) *f* blow; misfortune
botte (bôt'tā) *f* cask
bottega (bōt·tā'gâ) *f* store, shop
botteghino (bōt·tā·gē'nō) *m* box office
bottiglia (bōt·tē'lyâ) *f* bottle
bottiglieria (bōt·tē·lyā·rē'â) *f* store where bottled wine is sold; wineshop
bottino (bōt·tē'nō) *m* loot
bottone (bōt·tō'nā) *m* button
bove (bō'vā) *m* ox
bovini (bō·vē'nē) *mpl* cattle
bovino (bō·vē'nō) *a* bovine
bozza (bō'tsâ) *f* printer's proof, galley; sketch
bozzetto (bō·tsāt'tō) *m* draft; sketch
braccialetto (brâ·châ·lāt'tō) *m* bracelet
bracciante (brâ·chân'tā) *m* laborer
braccio (brâ'chō) *m* arm
bracciuolo (brâ·chwō'lō) *m* arm (*chair*)
bracco (brâk'kō) *m* setter (*dog*)
brace (brâ'chā) *f* embers
braciere (brâ·chyā'rā) *m* brazier
braciuola (brâ·chwō'lâ) *f* chop, cutlet
brado (brâ'dō) *a* untamed (*animal*)
brama (brâ'mâ) *f* desire; greed; **–re** (brâ·mâ'rā) *vt* to covet; to wish for
bramoso (brâ·mō'zō) *a* yearning, greedy, desirous
branca (brân'kâ) *f* branch, speciality; claw
branco (brân'kō) *m* flock; crowd; herd
brancolare (brân·kō·lâ'rā) *vi* to grope one's way
branda (brân'dâ) *f* cot
brandire (brân·dē'rā) *vt* to brandish
brando (brân'dô) *m* sword
brano (brâ'nō) *m* passage, selection (*literature*)
bravamente (brâ·vâ·mān'tā) *adv* bravely, courageously
bravare (brâ·vâ'rā) *vt&i* to menace; to brag
bravata (brâ·vâ'tâ) *f* bravado
bravo (brâ'vō) *a* skillful; —! *interj* well done! fine!
bravura (brâ·vū'râ) *f* ability, skill; courage
breccia (bre'châ) *f* gap; breach; breccia
brefotrofio (brā·fō·trô'fyō) *m* foundling home
bretelle (brā·tāl'lā) *fpl* suspenders
breve (brā'vā) *a* brief; **in** — in brief; **–mente** (brā·vā·mān'tā) *adv* briefly
brevettare (brā·vāt·tâ'rā) *vt* to patent
brevetto (brā·vāt'tō) *m* patent
brezza (brā'tsâ) *f* breeze
bricco (brēk'kō) *m* kettle; pot; — **del caffè** coffee pot; — **del tè** teapot
briccone (brēk·kō'nā) *m* scoundrel
briciola (brē'chō·lâ) *f* crumb
bridgista (brēd'jē'stâ) *m* bridge player
briga (brē'gâ) *f* care, worry; exertion
brigadiere (brē·gâ·dyā'rā) *m* brigadier; police sergeant
brigante (brē·gân'tā) *m* highwayman; brigand
brigantino (brē·gân·tē'nō) *m* (*naut*) brigantine
brigantaggio (brē·gân·tâj'jō) *m* robbery, banditry
brigare (brē·gâ'rā) *vt&i* to intrigue; to strive; to solicit, petition
brigata (brē·gâ'tâ) *f* (*coll*) gang, crew; (*mil*) brigade
briglia (brē'lyâ) *f* bridle
brillamento (brēl·lâ·mān'tō) *m* brilliance
brillante (brēl·lân'tā) *a* brilliant; — *m* diamond
brillantina (brēl·lân·tē'nâ) *f* brilliantine
brillare (brēl·lâ'rā) *vi* to shine; to glisten
brillo (brēl'lō) *a* tipsy
brina (brē'nâ) *f* frost
brindare (brēn·dâ'rā) *vi* to drink a toast
brindisi (brēn'dē·zē) *m* toast
brio (brē'ō) *m* vivacity; cheerfulness; spirit; **–sità** (bryō·zē·tâ') *f* vivacity; **–so** (bryō'zō) *a* lively; cheerful
britannico (brē·tân'nē·kō) *a* British
brivido (brē'vē·dō) *m* chill; thrill
brizzolato (brē·tsō·lâ'tō) *a* grey-haired, grizzled
brocca (brōk'kâ) *f* pitcher
broccolo (brôk'kō·lō) *m* broccoli
brodo (brō'dō) *m* broth
brogliaccio (brō·lyâ'chō) *m* scratch pad
bromatologia (brō·mâ·tō·lō·jē'â) *f* dietetics
bromuro (brō·mū'rō) *m* bromide
bronchi (brōn'kē) *mpl* bronchi (*anat*); **–te** (brōn·kē'tā) *f* bronchitis
broncio (brôn'chō) *m* pouting
brontolare (brōn·tō·lâ'rā) *vi* to grumble; to complain
bronzina (brōn·dzē'nâ) *f* (*mech*) bushing
bronzo (brōn'dzō) *m* bronze
brossura (brōs·sū'râ) *f* paperback book
brucare (brū·kâ'rā) *vt* to browse
bruciare (brū·châ'rā) *vt* to burn
bruciato (brū·châ'tō) *a* burnt, burned
bruciatura (brū·châ·tū'râ) *f* scorch, burn; burning
bruciore (brū·chō'rā) *m* burning, smarting; — **di stomaco** heartburn
bruco (brū'kō) *m* caterpillar
brullo (brūl'lō) *a* bare, naked; forsaken, abandoned
bruma (brū'mâ) *f* fog
bruna (brū'nâ), **brunetta** (brū·nāt'tâ) *f* brunette
brunire (brū·nē'rā) *vt* to brown; to burnish
brunito (brū·nē'tō) *a* browned; burnished
brunitura (brū·nē·tū'râ) *f* browning; burnishing
bruno (brū'nō) *a* brown; dark
brusco (brū'skō) *a* rude, brusque, sharp; (*fig*) unexpected, sudden; sour, sharp (*taste*); **una brusca decisione** a quick decision; **con le brusche** brusquely

bruscolo (brū'skō·lō) *m* cinder
brutale (brū·tâ'lâ) *a* brutal
brutalità (brū·tâ·lē·tâ') *f* brutality
bruto (brū'tō) *m&a* brute
bruttezza (brū·tā'tsâ) *f* ugliness; unpleasantness
brutto (brūt'tō) *a* ugly; unvarnished, plain
buca (bū'kâ) *f* hole, perforation; — **delle lettere** mail drop; **–re** (bū·kâ'rā) *vt* to puncture; to make a hole in
bucatini (bū·kâ·tē'nē) *mpl* medium-size macaroni
bucato (bū·kâ'tō) *m* laundry, wash
buccia (bū'châ) *f* skin, rind
buccina (bū·chē'nâ) *f* bugle
buco (bū'kō) *m* hole
budello (bū·dāl'lō) *m* intestine
budino (bū·dē'nō) *m* pudding
bue (bū'ā) *m* ox; **carne di** — beef
bufalo (bū'fâ·lō) *m* buffalo
bufera (bū·fā'râ) *f* storm; tempest; hurricane
buffo (būf'fō) *a* comic, funny, droll; —, **–ne** (būf·fō'nā) *m* buffoon, jester, clown
bugia (bū·jē'â) *f* falsehood; **–rdo** (bū·jâr'dō) *m* liar; **–rdo** *a* false
bugigattolo (bū·jē·gât'tō·lō) *m* cubbyhole
bugno (bū'nyō) *m* beehive
buio (bū'yō) *m* darkness; — *a* dark
bullo (būl'lō) *m (coll)* hoodlum
bullone (būl·lō'nā) *m* bolt
buono (bwō'nō) *a* good; — *m* bond; **Buon Capo d'Anno** Happy New Year; **Buon Natale** Merry Christmas; **Buona Pasqua** Happy Easter; **Buona sera** Good evening; **Buona notte** Good night; **Buon viaggio** Have a pleasant journey
buonaccordo (bwō·nâk·kōr'dō) *m* harmony; (*mus*) harpsichord
buonanima (bwō·nâ'nē·mâ) *a* recently deceased
buonanno! (bwō·nân'nō) *m* Happy New Year!
buonappetito! (bwō·nâp·pā·tē'tō) *m* enjoy your meal!
buonavoglia (bwō·nâ·vô'lyâ) *f* willingness, good will; **di** — willingly
buondì (bwōn·dē'), **buongiorno** (bwōn·jōr'nō) *m* good day, good morning
buongustaio (bwōn·gū·stâ'yō) *m* gourmet, gastronome, epicure
buongusto (bwōn·gū'stō) *m* good taste, discernment
buonsenso (bwōn·sān'sō) *m* common sense, sense
buontempo (bwōn·tām'pō) *m* good weather
burattino (bū·rât·tē'nō) *m* puppet
burbero (būr'bā·rō) *a* rough, surly
burla (būr'lâ) *f* practical joke; **–re** (būr·lâ'rā) *vt&i* to poke fun at, to jest; to fool; **–rsi** (būr·lâr'sē) *vr* to ridicule, laugh at
burocrazia (bū·rō·krâ·tsē'â) *f* bureaucracy
burrasca (būr·râ'skâ) *f* storm
burrato (būr·râ'tō) *a* buttered
burro (būr'rō) *m* butter
burrone (būr·rō'nā) *m* ravine
busecca (bū·zāk'kâ) *f* tripe
bussare (būs·sâ'rā) *vi* to knock
bussola (būs'sō·lâ) *f* compass; inner door
busta (bū'stâ) *f* envelope
bustina (bū·stē'nâ) *f* little envelope; (*mil*) overseas cap
busto (bū'stō) *m* bust; corset
buttare (būt·tâ'rā) *vt* to throw
buttero (būt'tā·rō) *m* pockmark; cowboy

C

cabala (kâ'bâ·lâ) *f* cabala, occultism; cabal
cabalista (kâ·bâ·lē'stâ) *m* cabalist
cabalistico (kâ·bâ·lē'stē·kō) *a* cabalistic
cabina (kā·bē'nâ) *f* cabin; cockpit; — **rimorchio** house trailer; — **telefonica** telephone booth
cablografare (kâ·blō·grâ·fâ'rā) *vi* to cable, send a cablegram
cablogramma (kâ·blō·grâm'mâ) *m* cablegram
cabotaggio (kâ·bōt·tâj'jō) *m* (*naut*) coastal trade; limited trade
cacao (kâ·kâ'ō) *m* cocoa
caccia (kâ'châ) *f* hunting; — *m* fighter plane; **–gione** (kâ·châ·jō'nā) *f* game, venison; **–re** (kâ·châ'rā) *vt* to chase; to pursue; to banish; **–tore** (kâ·châ·tō'rā) *m* hunter; **–torpediniera** (kâ·châ·tōr·pā·dē·nyā'râ) *f* (*naut*) destroyer; **–vite** (kâ·châ·vē'tā) *m* screwdriver
cacio (kâ'chō) *m* cheese
cacofonia (kâ·kō·fō·nē'â) *f* cacophony
cacografia (kâ·kō·grâ·fē'â) *f* cacography, poor handwriting
cacto (kâk'tō) *m* cactus
cadauno (kâ·dâ·ū'nō) *pron* each one, every
cadavere (kâ·dâ'vā·rā) *m* corpse, body, cadaver
cadenza (kâ·dān'tsâ) *f* cadence, rhythm; **–to** (kâ·dān·tsâ'tō) *a* rhythmical
cadere * (kâ·dā'rā) *vi* to fall
cadetto (kâ·dāt'tō) *m* cadet
caduco (kâ·dū'kô) *a* perishable; transitory
caffè (kâf·fā') *m* coffee; café; coffee-house; — **concerto** theater-restaurant; — **in polvere,** — **solubile** instant coffee
caffeina (kâf·fā·ē'nâ) *f* caffeine
caffelatte (kâf·fā·lât'tā) *m* coffee with milk
caffettiera (kâf·fā·tyā'râ) *f* coffeepot; jalopy
cafone (kâ·fō'nā) *m* yokel
cagionare (kâ·jō·nâ'rā) *vt* to cause, be the reason for
cagione (kâ·jō'nā) *f* cause
cagionevole (kâ·jō·nē'vō·lā) *a* sickly, infirm; weak
cagna (kâ'nyâ) *f* bitch; **–ra** (kâ·nyâ'râ) *f* barking; commotion, racket
cagnolino (kâ·nyō·lē'nō) *m* puppy

cala (kâ'lâ) *f* (*naut*) bay; creek
calabrese (kâ·lâ·brā'zā) *mf&a* Calabrian
calafatare (kâ·lâ·fâ·tâ'rā) *vt* (*naut*) to caulk
calamaio (kâ·lâ·mâ'yō) *m* inkwell
calamaro (kâ·lâ·mâ'rō) *m* squid
calamita (kâ·lâ·mē'tâ) *f* magnet
calamità (kâ·lâ·mē·tâ') *f* calamity, disaster
calamitoso (kâ·lâ·mē·tō'zō) *a* calamitous, disastrous
calapranzi (kâ·lâ·prân'dzē) *m* dumb-waiter
calare (kâ·lâ'rā) *vt* to lower; — *vi* to pounce upon
calca (kâl'kâ) *f* crowd
calcare (kâl·kâ'rā) *vt* to tread; to press; (*fig*) to lay stress upon
calcare (kâl·kâ'rā) *a* calcarious; — *m* limestone
calcagno (kâl·kâ'nyō) *m* heel
calce (kâl'chā) *f* lime, quicklime; **–struzzo** (kâl·chā·strū'tsō) *m* concrete
calciatore (kâl·châ·tō'rā) *m* soccer player
calcina (kâl·chē'nâ) *f* mortar, lime; **–ccio** (kâl·chē·nâ'chō) *m* fragment of mortar, piece of concrete
calcinare (kâl·chē·nâ'rā) *vt* to render (*fat*); to put lime on
calcio (kâl'chō) *m* kick; soccer; calcium
calcista (kâl·chē'stâ) *m* soccer player
calco (kâl'kō) *m* plaster cast
calcolare (kâl·kō·lâ'rā) *vt* to figure, compute
calcolatore (kâl·kō·lâ·tō'rā) *m* computer
calcolatrice (kâl·kō·lâ·trē'chā) *f* calculating machine
calcolo (kâl'kō·lō) *m* calculation; calculus; (*med*) stone
caldaia (kâl·dâ'yâ) *f* boiler
caldarrosta (kâl·dâr·rō'stâ) *f* roast chestnut
calderaio (kâl·dā·râ'yō) *m* coppersmith
caldo (kâl'dō) *m* heat; — *a* warm; hot; **sentir** — to be warm, feel hot
calendario (kâ·lān·dâ'ryō) *m* calendar
calesse (kâ·lās'sā) *m* buggy, carriage
calibro (kâ'lē·brō) *m* gauge
calice (kâ'lē·chā) *f* chalice
caligine (kâ·lē'jē·nā) *f* fog; smog; mist; (*fig*) ignorance
callifugo (kâl·lē·fū'gō) *m* corn pad
calligrafia (kâl·lē·grâ·fē'â) *f* penmanship
callo (kâl'lō) *m* corn (*foot*)
calma (kâl'mâ) *f* calm; **—!** Don't get excited!; **–nte** (kâl·mân'tā) *m* sedative; **–re** (kâl·mâ'rā) *vt* to calm down
calmiere (kâl·myā'rā) *m* price-control authority
calmo (kâl'mō) *a* calm
calo (kâ'lō) *m* descent; diminishing; reduction
calore (kâ·lō'rā) *m* heat
caloria (kâ·lō·rē'â) *f* calorie
calorifero (kâ·lō·rē'fā·rō) *m* heater
caloroso (kâ·lō·rō'zō) *a* warm
caloscia (kâ·lô'shâ) *f* overshoe, rubber
calotta (kâ·lōt'tâ) *f* scull cap; (*anat*) skull
calpestare (kâl·pā·stâ'rā) *vt* to trample, step on
calunnia (kâ·lūn'nyâ) *f* calumny; **–re** (kâ·lūn·nyâ'rā) *vt* to defame; **–tore** (kâ·lūn·nyâ·tō'rā) *m* defamer
Calvario (kâl·vâ'ryō) *m* Calvary
Calvinismo (kâl·vē·nē'zmō) *m* Calvinism
calvinista (kâl·vē·nē'stâ) *m* Calvinist
calvizie (kâl·vē'tsyā) *f* baldness
calvo (kâl'vō) *a* bald
calza (kâl'tsâ) *f* sock; stocking
calzare (kâl·tsâ'rā) *vt* to wear; — *vi* to fit
calzatoio (kâl·tsâ·tô'yō) *m* shoehorn
calzatura (kâl·tsâ·tū'râ) *f* footwear
calzaturificio (kâl·tsâ·tū·rē·fē'chō) *m* shoe factory
calzino (kâl·tsē'nō) *m* anklet, sock
calzolaio (kâl·tsō·lâ'yō) *m* cobbler, shoemaker; shoe dealer
calzoni (kâl·tsō'nē) *mpl* trousers
camaleonte (kâ·mâ·lā·ōn'tā) *m* (*zool*) chameleon
camarilla (kâ·mâ·rēl'lâ) *f* gang, clique
cambiabile (kâm·byâ'bē·lā) *a* changeable, fickle
cambiale (kâm·byâ'lā) *f* promissory note
cambiamento (kâm·byâ·mān'tō) *m* change; mutation
cambiare (kâm·byâ'rā) *vt* to change
cambiato (kâm·byâ'tō) *a* changed
cambiavalute (kâm·byâ·vâ·lū'tā) *m* foreign money changer
cambio (kâm'byō) *m* change; — **di velocità** gearshift; **corso del** — exchange rate; **leva di** — gear shift
cambusa (kâm·bū'zâ) *f* (*naut*) galley; storage room
camera (kâ'mā·râ) *f* bedroom; — **ardente** mortuary chapel; — **d'aria** inner tube; — **di commercio** chamber of commerce
camerata (kâ·mā·râ'tâ) *m* comrade
cameriera (kâ·mā·ryā'râ) *f* waitress; maid
cameriere (kâ·mā·ryā'rā) *m* waiter; steward
camerino (kâ·mā·rē'nō) *m* closet; (*theat*) dressing room
camice (kâ'mē·chā) *m* smock
camiceria (kâ·mē·chā·rē'â) *f* shirt shop
camicetta (kâ·mē·chāt'tâ) *f* blouse
camicia (kâ·mē'châ) *f* shirt; — **da notte** nightgown; **–io** (kâ·mē·châ'yō) *m* shirtmaker
camiciotto (kâ·mē·chōt'tō) *m* overalls; coverall
camiciuola (kâ·mē·chwō'lâ) *f* bodice; vest
caminetto (kâ·mē·nāt'tō) *m* fireplace, hearth
camino (kâ·mē'nō) *m* fireplace, chimney
camionale (kâ·myō·nâ'lā) *f* highway
camioncino (kâ·myōn·chē'nō) *m* pick-up truck
camione (kâ·myō'nā) *m* motor truck; **–tta** (kâ·myō·nāt'tâ) *f* jeep
camionista (kâ·myō·nē'stâ) *m* truck driver
cammello (kâm·māl'lō) *m* camel
cammeo (kâm·mā'ō) *m* cameo
camminare (kâm·mē·nâ'rā) *vi* to walk; to

stroll
camminata (kâm·mē·nâ'tâ) *f* walk
cammino (kâm·mē'nō) *m* walk; way
camomilla (kâ·mō·mēl'lâ) *f* camomile
camorra (kâ·mōr'râ) *f* secret criminal gang; racket, extortion
camorrista (kâ·mōr·rē'stâ) *m* racketeer, gangster
camoscio (kâ·mô'shō) *m* chamois
campagna (kâm·pâ'nyâ) *f* country, rural areas; campaign
campagnuolo (kâm·pâ·nywō'lō) *m* peasant; — *a* rustic
campale (kâm·pâ'lā) *a* hard (*fig*); **battaglia** — pitched battle; **giornata** — hard day
campana (kâm·pâ'nâ) *f* bell; **–io** (kâm·pâ·nâ'yō), **–ro** (kâm·pâ·nâ'rō) *m* bellman
campanello (kâm·pâ·nāl'lō) *m* small bell; doorbell
campanile (kâm·pâ·nē'lā) *m* belfry
campanilismo (kâm·pâ·nē·lē'zmō) *m* sectionalism
campanilista (kâm·pâ·nē·lē'stâ) *m* sectionalist
campare (kâm·pâ'rā) *vi* to manage to get along, stick it out; **si campa** we get by
campata (kâm·pâ'tâ) *f* (*arch*) bay; bridge span
campeggiare (kâm·pāj·jâ'rā) *vi* to camp
campeggio (kâm·pej'jō) *m* camping
campestre (kâm·pā'strā) *a* rural, country
Campidoglio (kâm·pē·dô'lyō) *m* Capitol
campionario (kâm·pyō·nâ'ryō) *m* sample case
campionato (kâm·pyō·nâ'tō) *m* championship
campione (kâm·pyō·nā) *m* champion; sample
campo (kâm'pō) *m* field; — **di tennis** tennis court; — **sportivo** stadium; **–santo** (kâm·pō·sân'tō) *m* cemetery
camuffare (kâ·mūf·fâ'rā) *vt* to camouflage
camuso (kâ·mū'zō) *a* flat; **dal naso** — snub-nosed
canadese (kâ·nâ·dā'zā) *m&a* Canadian
canaglia (kâ·nâ'lyâ) *f* rabble, mob
canale (kâ·nâ'lā) *m* canal; channel
canapa (kâ'nâ·pâ) *f* hemp
canapè (kâ·nâ·pā') *m* sofa
canapo (kâ'nâ·pō) *m* cable, rope; towline
canarino (kâ·nâ·rē'nō) *m* canary
canavaccio (kâ·nâ·vâ'chō) *m* canvass; (*lit*) plot
cancellare (kân·chāl·lâ'rā) *vt* to cancel; to erase
cancellata (kân·chāl·lâ'tâ) *f* fence, railing
cancellatura (kân·chāl·lâ·tū'râ) *f* erasure, taking out
cancellazione (kân·chāl·lâ·tsyō'nā) *f* cancelling, annulment
cancelleria (kân·chāl·lā·rē'â) *f* chancellery; chancery; **oggetti di** — stationery
cancelliere (kân·chāl·lyā'rā) *m* chancellor; court clerk
cancello (kân·chāl'lō) *m* gate
canceroso (kân·chā·rō'zō) *a* cancerous
cancrena (kân·krā'nâ) *f* gangrene
cancro (kân'krō) *m* cancer
candeggina (kân·dāj·jē'nâ) *f* bleach
candela (kân·dā'lâ) *f* candle; spark plug; **–bro** (kân·dā·lâ'brō) *m* candelabrum
candeliere (kân·dā·lyā'rā) *m* candlestick
candelora (kân·dā·lō'râ) *f* Candlemas
candente (kân·dān'tā) *a* glowing, incandescent
candidato (kân·dē·dâ'tō) *m* candidate
candidatura (kân·dē·dâ·tū'râ) *f* candidacy
candidezza (kân·dē·dā'tsâ) *f*, **candore** (kân·dō'rā) *m* dazzling whiteness; (*fig*) candor, innocence
candido (kân'dē·dō) *a* white; (*fig*) candid; artless
candito (kân·dē'tō) *a* candied
cane (kâ'nā) *m* dog; — **da caccia** hunting dog; — **da fermo** setter; — **da guardia** watch dog; — **da presa** retriever; — **da punta** pointer; — **poliziotto** police dog; — **randagio** stray dog
canestra (kâ·nā'strâ) *f*, **canestro** (kâ·nā'strō) *m* basket; **palla** — basketball
canfora (kân'fō·râ) *f* camphor
canicola (kâ·nē'kō·lâ) *f* dog days; (*ast*) Dog Star; **–re** (kâ·nē·kō·lâ'rā) *a* sultry (*weather*)
canile (kâ·nē'lā) *m* doghouse
canino (kâ·nē'nō) *m* puppy, whelp; — *a* canine; **dente** — eyetooth; **tosse canina** whooping cough
canizie (kâ·nē'tsyā) *f* hoariness, gray hairs
canna (kân'nâ) *f* cane; reed; organ pipe; gun barrel
cannella (kân·nāl'lâ) *f* cinnamon
cannello (kân·nāl'lō) *m* tube; welding torch; blowpipe; — **della pipa** pipe stem; **–ni** (kân·nāl·lō'nē) *mpl* large macaroni
cannibale (kân·nē'bâ·lā) *m* cannibal
cannocchiale (kân·nōk·kyâ'lā) *m* binoculars
cannolo (kân·nō'lō) *m* cylindrical pastry filled with sweet cream
cannonata (kân·nō·nâ'tâ) *f* cannon shot; (*sl*) smash hit
cannone (kân·nō'nā) *m* cannon; clever person; big shot; **–ggiamento** (kân·nō·nāj·jâ·mān'tō) *m* gun shot; bombardment; **–ggiare** (kân·nō·nāj·jâ'rā) *vt* to bombard (*cannon*); to cannonade
cannoniera (kân·nō·nyā'râ) *f* gunboat
cannoniere (kân·nō·nyā'rā) *m* gunner
cannuccia (kân·nū'châ) *f* pipe stem; — **da bere** drink
canoa (kâ·nō'â) *f* canoe
canone (kâ'nō·nā) *m* canon; rent; — **della radio** annual fee paid by owners of radio sets
canonica (kâ·nô'nē·kâ) *f* rectory
canonico (kâ·nô'nē·kō) *m* canon; — *a* canonical; **diritto** — canon law
canonizzare (kâ·nō·nē·dzâ'rā) *vt* to canonize
canoro (kâ·nō'rō) *a* melodious; musical
canottaggio (kâ·nōt·tâj'jō) *m* rowing

canottiera (kâ·nōt·tyā'râ) *f* T-shirt; straw hat
canottiere (kâ·nōt·tyā'rā) *m* rower, oarsman
canotto (kâ·nōt'tō) *m* canoe; shell
cantante (kân·tân'tā) *m&f* singer
cantare (kân·tâ'rā) *vt&i* to sing
cantero (kân'tā·rō) *m* chamber pot
cantico (kân'tē·kō) *m* canticle
cantiere (kân·tyā'rā) *m* shipyard; construction yard
cantilena (kân·tē·lā'nâ) *f* singsong
cantina (kân·tē'nâ) *f* cellar
cantiniere (kân·tē·nyā'rā) *m* butler; wine steward
canto (kân'tō) *m* song; singing; corner; canto
cantonata (kân·tō·nâ'tâ) *f* corner; angle; (*fig*) stupid mistake
cantone (kân·tō'nā) *m* corner; Swiss canton; (*arch*) corner stone
cantuccio (kân·tū'chō) *m* nook
canuto (kâ·nū'tō) *a* hoary
canzonare (kân·tsō·nâ'rā) *vt* to jeer, to poke fun at
canzone (kân·tsō'nā) *f* song; **–tta** (kan·tsō·nāt'tâ) *f* chanson, ballad; **–ttista** (kân·tsō·nāt·tē'stâ) *m&f* balladeer, singer of chansons
canzoniere (kân·tsō·nyā'rā) *m* songbook
caos (kâ'ōs) *m* chaos
capace (kâ·pâ'chā) *a* ample; able
capacità (kâ·pâ·chē·tâ') *f* capacity
capanna (kâ·pân'nâ) *f* cottage
capannone (kâ·pân·nō'nā) *m* shed
caparbio (kâ·pâr'byō) *a* stubborn
caparra (kâ·pâr'râ) *f* earnest money
capeggiare (kâ·pāj·jâ'rā) *vt* to head, lead
capellini (kâ·pāl·lē'nē) *mpl* very thin spaghetti
capello (kâ·pāl'lō) *m* hair
capelluto (kâ·pāl·lū'tō) *a* hairy; **cuoio —** scalp
capestro (kâ·pā'strō) *m* halter; gallows
capezzale (kâ·pā·tsâ'lā) *m* bolster; **al — di** at the bedside of
capezzolo (kâ·pe'tsō·lō) *m* teat, nipple
capillare (kâ·pēl·lâ'rā) *a* capillary; **vasi capillari** capillaries
capire (kâ·pē'rā) *vt* to understand, comprehend
capitale (kâ·pē·tâ'lā) *a&m* capital
capitalista (kâ·pē·tâ·lē'stâ) *m* capitalist
capitalizzare (kâ·pē·tâ·lē·dzâ'rā) *vt* to capitalize on
capitano (kâ·pē·tâ'nō) *m* captain
capitare (kâ·pē·tâ'rā) *vi* to arrive; to reach; to happen unexpectedly; to be by chance
capitello (kâ·pē·tāl'lō) *m* (*arch*) capital
capitolare (kâ·pē·tō·lâ'rā) *vi* to surrender, capitulate
capitolazione (kâ·pē·tō·lâ·tsyō'nā) *f* surrender, capitulation
capitolo (kâ·pē'tō·lō) *m* chapter
capitombolo (kâ·pē·tôm'bō·lō) *m* tumble, cropper
capo (kâ'pō) *m* head; **–banda** (kâ·pō·bân'dâ) *m* ringleader; (*mus*) bandmaster; **–caccia** (kâ·pō·kâ'châ) *m* master of the hounds (*hunt*); **–cchia** (kâ·pôk'·kyâ) *f* head (*nail, pin*); **–ccia** (kâ·pô'·châ) *m* family head; foreman; boss; **–chino** (kâ·pō·kē'nō) *adv* with bowed head; **–chino** *a* nodding; **–comico** (kâ·pō·kô'mē·kō) *m* leading comedian; actor-manager; **–cronista** (kâ·pō·krō·nē'stâ) *m* city editor; **–cuoco** (kâ·pō·kwō'kō) *m* chef; **–danno** (kâ·pō·dân'nō) *m* New Year's Day; **–fabbrica** (kâ·pō·fâb'brē·kâ) *m* foreman; **–fila** (kâ·pō·fē'lâ) *m* first in line; **–fitto** (kâ·pō·fēt'tō) *adv* headlong; **–giro** (kâ·pō·jē'rō) *m* dizziness; **–lavoro** (kâ·pō·lâ·vō'rō) *m* masterpiece; **–linea** (kâ·pō·lē'nā·â) *m* transportation terminal; **–lino** (kâ·pō·lē'nō) *m* little head; **far –lino** to peep out; **–lista** (kâ·pō·lē'stâ) *m* head of list; **–luogo** (kâ·pō·lwō'gō) *m* chief city; **–mastro** (kâ·pō·mâ'strō) *m* contractor; foreman (*building*); **–posto** (kâ·pō·pō'stō) *m* corporal of the guard; **–rale** (kâ·pō·râ'lā) *m* corporal; **–rione** (kâ·pō·ryō'nā) *m* chief; ward alderman; **–sala** (kâ·pō·sâ'lâ) *m* maître d'hôtel; master of ceremonies; **–saldo** (kâ·pō·sâl'dō) *m* stronghold; main point; key position; **–scuola** (kâ·pō·skwō'lâ) *m* founder of a literary movement; **–sezione** (kâ·pō·sā·tsyō'nā) *m* section head, department manager; **–squadra** (kâ·pō·skwâ'drâ) *m* group leader; foreman; **–stazione** (kâ·pō·stâ·tsyō'nā) *m* station master; **–stipite** (kâ·pō·stē'pē·tā) *m* family founder; (*arch*) column shaft; **–tare** (kâ·pō·tâ'rā) *vi* to capsize; **–treno** (kâ·pō·trā'nō) *m* train conductor; **–verso** (kâ·pō·vār'sō) paragraph; **–volgere** * (kâ·pō·vôl'jā·rā) *vt* to turn over; **–volto** (kâ·pō·vōl'tō) *a* upside down; capsized
cappa (kâp'pâ) *f* topcoat; cape; k (*alphabet*)
cappare (kâp·pâ'rā) *vt* to pick out, select
cappella (kâp·pāl'lâ) *f* chapel; **–no** (kâp·pāl·lâ'nō) *m* chaplain
cappellaio (kâp·pāl·lâ'yō) *m* hatter
cappelleria (kâp·pāl·lā·rē'â) *f* hat store
cappelliera (kâp·pāl·lyā'râ) *f* hat box
cappello (kâp·pāl'lō) *m* hat
capperi (kâp'pā·rē) *mpl* (*bot*) capers
cappone (kâp·pō'nā) *m* capon
cappotta (kâp·pōt'tâ) *f* convertible car top
cappotto (kâp·pōt'tō) *m* overcoat; slam (*bridge game*)
cappuccino (kâp·pū·chē'nō) *m* Capuchin; demitasse with whipped cream
cappuccio (kâp·pū'chō) *m* hood
capra (kâ'prâ) *f* nanny goat; **–io** (kâ·prâ'·yō) *m* goatherd
capretto (kâ·prāt'tō) *m* kid
capriata (kâ·pryâ'tâ) *f* truss; scaffolding
capriccio (kâ·prē'chō) *m* whim
capriola (kâ·pryō'lâ) *f* somersault
capro (kâ'prō) *m* billy goat; **— espiatorio** (*fig*) scapegoat

capsula (kâ'psū·lâ) *f* capsule
carabina (kâ·râ·bē'nâ) *f* carbine
carabiniere (kâ·râ·bē·nyā'rā) *m* national policeman in Italy
caracollare (kâ·râ·cōl·lâ'rā) *vt&i* to wheel about, prance on horseback; to caracole
caraffa (kâ·râf'fâ) *f* carafe, decanter
caramella (kâ·râ·māl'lâ) *f* caramel candy; monocle; **–io** (kâ·râ·māl·lâ'yō) *m* confectioner
carato (kâ·râ'tō) *m* carat
carattere (kâ·rât'tā·rā) *m* character; type
caratterista (kâ·rât·tā·rē'stâ) *m* character actor
caratteristica (kâ·rât·tā·rē'stē·kâ) *f* peculiarity; trait
caratteristico (kâ·rât·tā·rē'stē·kō) *a* characteristic
caratterizzare (kâ·rât·tā·rē·dzâ'rā) *vt* to characterize
carbonaia (kâr·bō·nâ'yâ) *f* coal pit; (*naut*) bunker; coaler (*ship*)
carbonaio (kâr·bō·nâ'yō) *m* coal dealer; charcoal burner; coalman
carbonaro (kâr·bō·nâ'rō) *m* (*pol*) Carbonaro
carbonchio (kâr·bôn'kyō) *m* (*med*) carbuncle
carbone (kâr·bō'nā) *m* charcoal; coal; carbon
carboniera (kâr·bō·nyā'râ) *f* (*naut*) collier, coal barge
carbonizzare (kâr·bō·nē·dzâ'rā) *vt* to char, carbonize
carborundum (kâr·bō·rūn'dūm) *m* carborundum
carburante (kâr·bū·rân'tā) *m* fuel
carburatore (kâr·bū·râ·tō'rā) *m* carburetor
carburo (kâr·bū'rō) *m* carbide
carcassa (kâr·kâs'sâ) *f* carcass; (*naut*) derelict
carcere (kâr'chā·rā) *m* jail
carceriere (kâr·chā·ryā'rā) *m* jailer
carciofo (kâr·chō'fō) *m* artichoke
carda (kâr'dâ) *f* carding machine; **–re** (kâr·dâ'rā) *vt* to comb out, card (*fibers*)
cardanico (kâr·dâ'nē·kō) *a* universal; **giunto —** (*mech*) universal joint
cardellino (kâr·dāl·lē'nō) *m* goldfinch
cardinale (kâr·dē·nâ'lā) *m&a* cardinal
cardine (kâr'dē·nā) *m* hinge
cardiologo (kâr·dyô'lō·gō) *m* cardiologist, heart specialist
cardo (kâr'dō) *m* thistle
carena (kâ·rā'nâ) *f* (*naut*) keel; **–re** (kâ·rā·nâ'rā) *vt* (*naut*) to careen; (*avi*) to fair
carestia (kâ·rā·stē'â) *f* famine
carezza (kâ·rā'tsâ) *f* caress; **–re** (kâ·rā·tsâ'rā) *vt* to caress; to coax, wheedle
carezzevole (kâ·rā·tse'vō·lā) *a* caressing; cajoling
cariato (kâ·ryâ'tō) *a* carious, decayed
carica (kâ'rē·kâ) *f* office; charge; **–re** (kâ·rē·kâ'rā) *vt* to load; to wind a clock; to charge with; **–to** (kâ·rē·kâ'tō) *a* enriched; loaded
caricatura (kâ·rē·kâ·tū'râ) *f* caricature
carico (kâ'rē·kō) *m* load, burden
carie (kâ'ryā) *f* decay; cavity (*tooth*)
carità (kâ·rē·tâ') *f* charity; mercy; **per —!** for goodness' sake!
caritatevole (kâ·rē·tâ·te'vō·lā), **caritativo** ((kâ·rē·tâ·tē'vō) *a* charitable
carlinga (kâr·lēn'gâ) *f* cockpit; fuselage
carminio (kâr·mē'nyō) *m* carmine; (*coll*) lipstick
carnagione (kâr·nâ·jō'nā) *f* complexion
carnale (kâr·nâ'lā) *a* carnal, sensual; corporeal
carne (kâr'nā) *f* meat; flesh; **–fice** (kâr·ne'fē·chā) *m* hangman; **–vale** (kâr·nā·vâ'lā) *m* carnival; pre-Lenten period
carnivoro (kâr·nē'vō·rō) *a* carnivorous
caro (kâ'rō) *a* dear; expensive
carogna (kâ·rō'nyâ) *f* carrion; (*fig*) cad
carosello (kâ·rō·zāl'lō) *m* merry-go-round
carota (kâ·rō'tâ) *f* carrot
carovana (kâ·rō·vâ'nâ) *f* convoy; caravan
carpentiere (kâr·pān·tyā'rā) *m* carpenter
carreggiata (kâr·rāj·jâ'tâ) *f* roadbed; lane
carrettiere (kâr·rāt·tyā'rā) *m* carter
carriaggio (kâr·ryâj'jō) *m* cartage
carriera (kâr·ryā'râ) *f* career
carrista (kâr·rē'stâ) *m* driver of military tank
carro (kâr'rō) *m* car, wagon, truck; **— armato** tank; **— funebre** hearse; **–zza** (kâr·rō'tsâ) *f* carriage, coach; **–zzabile** (kâr·rō·tsâ'bē·lā) *a* passable (*road*); **–zzella** (kân·rō·tsāl'lâ) *f* baby carriage; **–zzeria** (kâr·rō·tsā·rē'â) *f* (*auto*) body; **–zziere** (kâr·rō·tsyā'rā) *m* (*auto*) body maker; **–zzino** (kâr·rō·tsē'nō) *m* sulky
carrucola (kâr·rū'kō·lâ) *f* pulley
carta (kâr'tâ) *f* paper; card; map; **— carbone, — copiativa** carbon paper; **— da bollo** official paper; **— da parati** wall paper; **— da scrivere** writing paper **— di tornasole** litmus paper; **— d'identità** identity card; **— eliografica** heliographic paper; **— geografica** map; **— gommata** gummed paper; **— igienica** toilet paper; **— incatramata** tarred paper; **— intestata** letterhead; **— milimetrata** squared paper; **— moschicida** fly paper; **— oleata** oilpaper; **— ondulata** corrugated paper; **— pergamena** parchment paper; **— smerigliata** sandpaper; **— sugante** blotting paper; **— velina** tissue paper; **— vetrata** sandpaper; glass paper; **aver — bianca** to have carte blanche; **–ceo** (kâr·tâ·chā'ō) *a* paper, papery; **–pecora** (kâr·tâ·pe'kō·râ) *f* vellum, parchment; **–pesta** (kâr·tâ·pā'stâ) *f* papier-mâché; **carte da giuoco** playing cards
carteggio (kâr·tej'jō) *m* documents; correspondence
cartella (kâr·tāl'lâ) *f* folder; schoolbag; portfolio
cartelliera (kâr·tāl·lyā'râ) *f* filing cabinet
cartello (kâr·tāl'lō) *m* sign; placard; **–ne** (kâr·tāl·lō'na) *m* poster
cartiera (kâr·tyā'râ) *f* paper mill
cartilagine (kâr·tē·lâ'jē·nā) *f* cartilage

cartoccio (kâr·tô'chō) paper bag; paper cornucopia
cartolaio (kâr·tō·lâ'yō) *m* stationer
cartoleria (kâr·tō·lā·rē'â) *f* stationery store
cartolina (kâr·tō·lē'nâ) *f* postcard; — **illustrata** picture postcard; — **postale** postal card, postcard
cartoncino (kâr·tōn·chē'nō) *m* thin cardboard
cartone (kâr·tō'nā) *m* cardboard; — **animato** animated cartoon
cartuccia (kâr·tū'châ) *f* cartridge
casa (kâ'zâ) *f* house; home; firm; — **colonica** farmhouse; — **communale** town hall; — **di ricovero** poorhouse; — **di salute** sanitarium; private hospital; — **di tolleranza** brothel; — **editrice** publishing company; — **signorile** mansion; **partita in** — (*sport*) home game
casacca (kâ·zâk'kâ) *f* jacket
casaccio (kâ·zâ'chō) *m* nasty business; **a** — carelessly; at random
casale (kâ·zâ'lā) *m* hamlet
casalingo (kâ·zâ·lēn'gō) *a* homemade; homey, cozy; **oggetti casalinghi** household appliances
casamento (kâ·zâ·mān'tō) *m* apartment house
casato (kâ·zâ'tō) *m* birth; lineage; family name
cascame (kâ·skâ'mā) *m* waste
cascare (kâ·skâ'rā) *vi* to fall, tumble
cascata (kâ·skâ'tâ) *f* waterfall
cascina (kâ·shē'nâ) *f* dairy farm
casco (kâ'skō) *m* helmet
caseificio (kâ·zāē·fē'chō) *m* cheese factory
caseina (kâ·zā·ē'nâ) *f* casein
casella (kâ·zāl'lâ) *f* pigeonhole, compartment; — **postale** post-office box
caserma (kâ·zār'mâ) *f* barracks; — **dei pompieri** firehouse
casetta (kâ·zāt'tâ) *f* cottage
casimiro (kâ·zē·mē'rō) *m* cashmere
casino (kâ·zē'nō) *m* casino; clubhouse; (*coll*) brothel
caso (kâ'zō) *m* case; chance; — **a parte** particular case; **far** — **a** to pay attention to; **in** — **che** in case; **in** — **contrario** otherwise, on the contrary; **in tal** — under such circumstances; **puta** — **che** supposing that; **a** — by chance; **mero** — mere chance; **non fa il** — it doesn't matter
casolare (kâ·zō·lâ'rā) *m* hovel
caspita! (kâ'spē·tâ) *interj* heavens!
cassa (kâs'sâ) *f* box; crate; cash; cashier's counter; — **cranica** cranium; — **da morto** casket; — **dell'orologio** watch case; — **di risparmio** savings bank; — **toracica** chest; **avanzo di** — cash on hand; **gran** — (*mus*) bass drum; **–forte** (kâs·sâ·fōr'tā) *f* safe; **–panca** (kâs·sâ·pân'kâ) wooden bench, seat
cassata (kâs·sâ'tâ) *f* cream cake tart; — **siciliana** ice cream; sherbert
casseruola (kâs·sā·rūō'lâ) *f* saucepan
cassetta (kâs·sāt'tâ) *f* box; — **di sicurezza** safe-deposit box; — **postale** mailbox
cassetto (kâs·sāt'tō) *m* drawer; **–ne** (kâs·sāt·tō'nā) *m* chest of drawers
cassiere (kâs·syā'rā) *m* cashier; teller
casta (kâ'stâ) *f* caste
castagna (kâ·stâ'nyâ) *f* chestnut
castagno (kâ·stâ'nyō) *m* chestnut tree; chestnut color
castello (kâ·stāl'lō) *m* castle
castigare (kâ·stē·gâ'rā) *vt* to punish
castigo (kâ·stē'gō) *m* punishment
castità (kâ·stē·tâ') *f* chastity
casto (kâ'stō) *a* chaste
castoro (kâ·stō'rō) *m* beaver
castrare (kâ·strâ'rā) *vt* to emasculate, castrate
castrato (kâ·strâ'tō) *a* castrated; — *m* eunuch
castroneria (kâ·strō·nā·rē'â) *f* absurdity; gross error
casuale (kâ·zwâ'lā) *a* by chance; casual
casualità (kâ·zwâ·lē·tâ') *f* happenstance, chance; fortuitousness
catacomba (kâ·tâ·kōm'bâ) *f* catacomb
catafalco (kâ·tâ·fâl'kō) *m* catafalque; scaffold
catalessi (kâ·tâ·lās'sē) *f* trance, catalepsy
catalogo (kâ·tâ'lō·gō) *m* catalog
catapecchia (kâ·tâ·pek'kyâ) *f* slum dwelling
cataplasma (kâ·tâ·plâ'zmâ) *m* poultice
catarifrangente (kâ·tâ·rē·frân·jān'tā) *m* reflector
catarro (kâ·târ'rō) *m* catarrh
catasta (kâ·tâ'stâ) *f* heap, mound
catasto (kâ·tâ'stō) *m* real estate register
catastrofe (kâ·tâ'strō·fā) *f* catastrophe
catechismo (kâ·tā·kē'zmō) *m* catechism
categoria (kâ·tā·gō·rē'â) *f* category
catena (kâ·tā'nâ) *f* chain; **–ccio** (kâ·tā·nâ'chō) *m* bolt
cateratta (kâ·tā·rât'tâ) *f* cataract
catinella (kâ·tē·nāl'lâ) *f* washbowl
catino (kâ·tē'nō) *m* basin
catrame (kâ·trâ'mā) *m* tar
cattedra (kât'tā·drâ) *f* chair, professorship
cattedrale (kât·tā·drâ'lā) *f* cathedral
cattivo (kât·tē'vō) *a* bad; poor, badly done
cattolicismo (kât·tō·lē·chē'zmō), **cattolicesimo** (kât·tō·lē·che'zē·mō) *m* Catholicism
cattolico (kât·tô'lē·kō) *m&a* Catholic
cattura (kât·tū'râ) *f* capture; **mandato di** — warrant for arrest; **–re** (kât·tū·râ'rā) *vt* to seize, capture; **–to** (kât·tū·râ'tō) *a* seized, captured
caucciù (kâū·chū') *m* rubber
causa (kâ'ū·zâ) *f* cause; lawsuit; **a** — **di** because of; **far** — to sue, bring action; **–re** (kâū·zâ'rā) *vt* to cause; to effect, produce
caustico (kâ'ū·stē·kō) *a* caustic; trenchant
cautela (kâū·tā'lâ) *f* caution
cauterio (kâū·te'ryō) *m* (*med*) cauterizing
cauto (kâ'ū·tō) *a* careful; cautious
cauzione (kâū·tsyō'nā) *f* guarantee; bail

cava (kâ'vâ) *f* quarry
cavalcare (kâ·vâl·kâ'rā) *vi* to ride horseback; — *vt* to straddle
cavalcavia (kâ·vâl·kâ·vē'â) *m* overpass
cavaliere (kâ·vâ·lyā'rā) *m* horseman; rider; knight; dancing partner
cavalla (kâ·vâl'lâ) *f* mare
cavalleresco (kâ·vâl·lā·rā'skō) *a* chivalrous
cavalleria (kâ·vâl·lā·rē'â) *f* cavalry; chivalry
cavalletta (kâ·vâl·lāt'tâ) *f* grasshopper
cavalletto (kâ·vâl·lāt'tō) *m* easel
cavallo (kâ·vâl'lō) *m* horse; (*chess*) knight
cavallone (kâ·vâl·lō'nā) *m* large wave, comber
cavare (kâ·vâ'rā) *vt* to take out; to get, obtain
cavatappi (kâ·vâ·tâp'pē), **cavaturaccioli** (kâ·vâ·tū·râ'chō·lē) *m* corkscrew
cavatina (kâ·vâ·tē'nâ) *f* (*mus*) cavatina; sustained air, lilting melody
caverna (kâ·vār'nâ) *f* grotto; cave
cavernoso (kâ·vār·nō'zō) *a* deep; deep-set (*eyes*)
cavezza (kâ·vā'tsâ) *f* halter (*horse*)
cavia (kâ'vyâ) *f* guinea pig
caviale (kâ·vyâ'lā) *m* caviar
caviglia (kâ·vē'lyâ) *f* ankle
cavillare (kâ·vēl·lâ'rā) *vi* to cavil, find fault
cavillo (kâ·vēl'lō) *m* cavil, unnecessary faultfinding; **–so** (kâ·vēl·lō'zō) *a* captious, faultfinding
cavità (kâ·vē·tâ') *f* hole; cavity
cavo (kâ'vō) *m* cable; — *a* hollow
cavolfiore (kâ·vōl·fyō'rā) *m* cauliflower
cavolo (kâ'vō·lō) *m* cabbage
cazzotto (kâ·tsōt'tō) *m* punch, blow
cazzuola (kâ·tswō'lâ) *f* trowel
ce (chā) *pron* to us, us; — *adv* here, there
cece (chā'chā) *m* chick-pea
cecità (chā·chē·tâ') *f* blindness; (*fig*) heedlessness, foolishness
ceco (chā'kō) *m&a* Czech
cedere (che'dā·rā) *vt&i* to yield, give in; to fall down, collapse
cedevole (chā·de'vō·lā) *a* yielding; (*fig*) docil
cedimento (chā·dē·mān'tō) *m* yielding, ceding; settling, subsidence
cedola (che'dō·lâ) *f* coupon
cedro (chā'drō) *m* cedar; citron
ceduo (che'dwō) *a* ready for clearing; **bosco** — cordwood
ceffo (chāf'fō) *m* muzzle; snout; **brutto** — rascally face; **–ne** (chāf·fō'nā) *m* slap, smack
celare (chā·lâ'rā) *vt* to hide; to cover up, dissemble
celata (chā·lâ'tâ) *f* ambush; visor (*helmet*)
celebrare (chā·lā·brâ'rā) *vt* to celebrate; to extole
celebrazione (chā·lā·brâ·tsyō'nā) *f* celebration
celebre (che'la·brā) *a* famous; illustrious
celebrità (chā·lā·brē·tâ') *m* celebrity
celere (che'lā·rā) *a* quick; — *f* police riot squad
celerimetro (chā·lā·rē'mā·trō) *m* speedometer
celeste (chā·lā'stā) *a* celestial; blue
celia (che'lyâ) *f* joke, lark
celibe (che'lē·bā) *a* single; — *m* bachelor
cella (chāl'lâ) *f* cell; cellar; cave
cellofane (chāl·lō·fâ'nā) *f* cellophane
cellula (chel'lū·lâ) *f* cell; **–re** (chāl·lū·lâ'rā) *a* cellular; **–re** *m* jail; patrol wagon
celluloide (chāl·lū·lô'ē·dā) *f* celluloid
cembalo (chem'bâ·lō) *m* harpsichord; tambourine
cemento (chā·mān'tō) *m* cement, concrete; — **armato** reinforced concrete
cena (chā'nâ) *f* supper; **–re** (chā·nâ'rā) *vi* to have supper
cenciaiuolo (chān·châ·ywō'lō) *m* rag picker
cencio (chen'chō) *m* rag; **–so** (chān·chō'zō) *a* ragged
cenere (che'nā·rā) *f* ash
cenno (chān'nō) *m* hint; indication
censimento (chān·sē·mān'tō) *m* census
censo (chān'sō) *m* census; **–re** (chān·sō'rā) *m* critic, censor
censura (chān·sū'râ) *f* censorship; **–re** (chān·sū·râ'rā) *vt* to censure; to blame; to criticize
centauro (chān·tâ'ū·rō) *m* centaur
centellinare (chān·tāl·lē·nâ'rā) *vt* to sip on, drink in sips
centenario (chān·tā·nâ'ryō) *m&a* centennial
centesimo (chān·te'zē·mō) *m* centime; hundredth part
centigrado (chān·tē'grâ·dō) *m* centigrade
centimetro (chān·tē'mā·trō) *m* centimeter
centina (chen'tē·nâ) *f* truing; (*arch*) fantail; (*avi*) rib
centinaio (chān·tē·nâ'yō) *m* hundred; **a centinaia** by hundreds
cento (chān'tō) *a* hundred; **–mila** (chān·tō·mē'lâ) *a* hundred thousand
centrale (chān·trâ'lā) *a* central; — *f* central office; — **elettrica** power plant
centralinista (chān·trâ·lē·nē'stâ) *m&f* switchboard operator
centralino (chān·trâ·lē'nō) *m* telephone switchboard
centrare (chān·trâ'rā) *vt* to center; to hit dead center
centrifugo (chān·trē'fū·gō) *a* centrifugal
centripeto (chān·trē'pā·tō) *a* centripetal
centro (chān'trō) *m* center; centerpiece; downtown
centuplicare (chān·tū·plē·kâ'rā) to multiply by one hundred
centuria (chān·tū'ryâ) *f* century
ceppo (chāp'pō) *m* log
cera (chā'râ) *f* wax; mien; **–lacca** (chā·râ·lâk'kâ) *f* sealing wax
ceramica (chā·râ'mē·kâ) *f* ceramics; pottery
cerata (chā·râ'tâ) *f* oilskin, oilcloth
cerbiatto (chār·byât'tō) *m* young deer, fawn

cerbottana (chār·bōt·tâ'nâ) peashooter; blowpipe
cerca (chār'kâ) *f* search; **–re** (chār·kâ'rā) *vt&i* to seek; to try, make an attempt
cerchio (cher'kyō) *m* circle; loop; **–ne** (chār·kyō'nā) *m* rim *(wheel)*
cereale (chā·rā·â'lā) *m* cereal
cerebrale (chā·rā·brâ'lā) *a* cerebral; — *m* intellectual
cereo (che'rā·ō) *a* waxy; wan, pale
cerfoglio (chār·fô'lyō) *m* chervil
cerimonia (chā·rē·mô'nyâ) *f* ceremony; **–le** (chā·rē·mō·nyâ'lā) *m* protocol
cerimoniere (chā·rē·mō·nyā'rā) *m* master of ceremonies
cerimonioso (chā·rē·mō·nyō'zō) *a* formal; ceremonious
cerino (chā·rē'nō) *m* wax match
cerniera (chār·nyā'râ) *f* hinge; — **lampo** zipper
cero (chā'rō) *m* taper, candle
cerotto (chā·rōt'tō) *m* plaster
certamente (chār·tâ·mān'tā) *adv* surely, of course
certezza (chār·tā'tsâ) *f* certainty
certificato (chār·tē·fē·kâ'tō) *m* certificate; — **medico** health certificate
certo (chār'tō) *a* certain, sure; — *adv* certainly
certosa (chār·tō'zâ) *f* charterhouse
certosino (chār·tō·zē'nō) *m* Carthusian monk
ceruleo (chā·rū'lā·ō) *a* cerulean
cerume (chā·rū'mā) *m* cerumen, wax in the ear
cerusico (chā·rū'zē·kō) *m* surgeon
cervello (chār·vāl'lō) *m* brain
cervo (chār'vō) *m* deer; — **volante** kite
cerziorare (chār·tsyō·râ'rā) *vt* to assure; to ascertain
cesellare (chā·zāl·lâ'rā) *vt* to chisel; to engrave
cesellatore (chā·zāl·lâ·tō'rā) *m* carver; engraver
cesello (chā·zāl'lō) *m* chisel
cesoia (chā·zô'yâ) *f* scissors
cespite (che'spē·tā) *m* source of one's income
cespuglio (chā·spū'lyō) *m* thicket; shrubbery
cessare (chās·sâ'rā) *vt* to cease, stop
cesso (chās'sō) *m* toilet
cesta (chā'stâ) *f* basket
cestinare (chā·stē·nâ'rā) *vt* to reject; to discard
cestino (chā·stē'nō) *m* small basket; — **da viaggio** lunch basket
cesura (chā·zū'râ) *f* caesura
ceto (chā'tō) *m* class; order; rank
cetra (chā'trâ) *f* cithern; harp; lyre
cetriuolo (chā·trywō'lō) *m* cucumber; (*fig*) fool
che (kā) *conj* than, that; — *pron* what, which, who
chè (kā) *conj* because
chellerina (kāl·lā·rē'nâ) *f* waitress
cheppia (kep'pyâ) *f* shad
cherubino (kā·rū·bē'nō) *m* cherub
chi (kē) *pron* who, that, whom
chiacchiera (kyâk'kyā·râ) *f* gossip; **–re** (kyâ·kyā·râ'rā) *vi* to chat; **–ta** (kyâ·kyā·râ'tâ) *f* tittle-tattle, prattle
chiacchierone (kyâ·kyā·rō'nā) *m* prattler; gossip; windbag
chiamare (kyâ·mâ'rā) *vt* to call; to call upon
chiamata (kyâ·mâ'tâ) *f* call
chiara (kyâ'râ) *f* egg white
chiaramente (kyâ·râ·mān'tā) *adv* clearly, obviously
chiarezza (kyâ·rā'tsâ) *f* plainness; clearness
chiarificazione (kyâ·rē·fē·kâ·tsyō'nā) *f* clarification
chiarimento (kyâ·rē·mān'tō) *m* explanation
chiarire (kyâ·rē'rā) *vt* to clear up; to clarify
chiaro (kyâ'rō) *a* clear; light; **–re** (kyâ·rō'rā) *m* glimmer; **–scuro** (kyâ·rō·skū'rō) *m* interplay of light and shadow; chiaroscuro; **–veggente** (kyâ·rō·vāj·jān'tā) *a* clearsighted; **–veggente** *m&f* clairvoyant
chiasso (kyâs'sō) *m* noise; **–so** (kyâs·sō'zō) *a* noisy; loud
chiatta (kyât'tâ) *f* barge
chiave (kyâ'vā) *f* key; — **inglese** monkey wrench
chiazza (kyâ'tsâ) *f* stain, spot; scar; mottling; **–to** (kyâ·tsâ'tō) *a* mottled, speckled, spotted
chiavica (kyâ'vē·kâ) *f* sewer
chiavistello (kyâ·vē·stāl'lō) *m* door bolt
chicca (kēk'kâ) *f* candy
chicchera (kēk'kā·râ) *f* demitasse
chicchessia (kē·kās·sē'â) *pron* anybody, whoever
chicco (kēk'kō) *m* bean; grain
chiedere * (kye'dā·rā) *vt* to ask; to implore
chiesa (kyā'zâ) *f* church
chiesto (kyā'stō) *a* asked, requested, sought
chifel (kē'fāl) *m* crescent-shaped roll
chiglia (kē'lyâ) *f* keel
chilo (kē'lō) *m* kilogram; **–ciclo** (kē·lō·chē'klō) *m* kilocycle; **–gramma** (kē·lō·grâm'mâ) *m* kilogram; **–metro** (kē·lô'mā·trō) *m* kilometer; **–watt** (kē·lō·vât') *m* kilowatt
chimera (kē·mā'râ) *f* chimera
chimica (kē'mē·kâ) *f* chemistry
chimico (kē'mē·kō) *m* chemist; — *a* chemical
chimo (kē'mō) *m* chyme
chimono (kē·mō'nō) *m* kimono
china (kē'nâ) *f* slope; **–re** (kē·nâ'rā) *vt* to bow; to bend; **–rsi** (kē·nâr'sē) *vi* to bow down; to bend oneself; to stoop; (*fig*) to submit oneself
chincaglie (kēn·kâ'lyā) *fpl* trinkets
chineseria (kē·nā·zā·rē'â) *f* chinoiserie; red tape
chinino (kē·nē'nō) *m* quinine
chino (kē'nō) *a* inclined, bent
chioccia (kyō'châ) *f* brooding hen; **–re** (kyō·châ'rā) *vi* to cluck, to cackle

chiocciola (kyô'chō·lâ) *f* snail
chiodo (kyō'dō) *m* nail; — **di garofano** clove
chioma (kyō'mâ) *f* hair, head of hair; (*animal*) mane
chiosa (kyō'zâ) *f* annotation; comment
chiosco (kyō'skō) *m* newsstand; stand
chiostro (kyō'strō) *m* cloister
chiotto (kyōt'tō) *a* still, silent
chiromante (kē·rō·mân'tā) *m&f* palmist
chiromanzia (kē·rō·mân·tsē'â) *f* chiromancy, palmistry
chirurgia (kē·rūr·jē'â) *f* surgery
chirurgico (kē·rūr'jē·kō) *a* surgical
chirurgo (kē·rūr'gō) *m* surgeon
chissà (kēs·sâ') *interj* heaven only knows, who knows
chitarra (kē·târ'râ) *f* guitar
chiudere * (kyū'dā·rā) *vt* to close; — **a chiave** to lock
chiunque (kyūn'kwā) *pron* anybody, whoever
chiusa (kyū'zâ) *f* lock (*canal*); dam
chiuso (kyū'zō) *a* closed, shut
chiusura (kyū·zū'râ) *f* closing; — **lampo** zipper
ci (chē) *pron* us, to us; — *adv* here, there
ciabatta (châ·bât'tâ) *f* old shoe; slipper; **–re** (châ·bât·tâ'rā) *vi* to move with a shuffle
ciabattino (châ·bât·tē'nō) *m* cobbler
ciabattone (châ·bât·tō'nā) *m* fumbler
cialda (châl'dâ) *f* waffle
cialtrone (châl·trō'nā) *m* scoundrel
ciambella (châm·bāl'lâ) *f* ring-shaped cake; doughnut
ciamberlano (châm·bār·lâ'nō) *m* chamberlain
cianfrusaglia (chân·frū·zâ'lyâ) *f* trifle
cianidrico (châ·nē'drē·kō) *a* hydrocyanic, prussic
cianina (châ·nē'nâ) *f* cyanin
cianogeno (châ·nô'jā·nō) *m* cyanogen
cianotico (châ·nô'tē·kō) *a* cyanic; blue in color
cianotipia (châ·nō·tē·pē'â) *f* blueprint
cianuro (châ·nū'rō) *m* cyanide
ciao (châ'ō) *interj* hello, good-bye
ciaramella (châ·râ·māl'lâ) *f* bagpipe
ciarlare (châr·lâ'rā) *vi* to chatter
ciarlatano (châr·lâ·tâ'nō) *m* charlatan
ciascuno (châ·skū'nō) *a* each, every; — *pron* each one, every one
cibare (chē·bâ'rā) *vt* to nourish; to feed
cibaria (chē·bâ'ryâ) *f* foodstuff
cibo (chē'bō) *m* food
cicala (chē·kâ'lâ) *f* cicada
cicalino (chē·kâ·lē'nō) *m* electric buzzer
cicatrice (chē·kâ·trē'chā) *f* scar
cicca (chēk'kâ) *f* butt; stump
ciccia (chē'châ) *f* flesh, meat; *(coll)* fat
ciccioli (chē'chō·lē) *mpl* fatty scraps of meat
ciccione (chē·chō'nā) *m* fleshy individual; fat person
cicerone (chē·châ·rō'nā) *m* cicerone, guide
cicisbeo (chē·chē·zbā'ō) *m* gallant; gigolo; ladies' man
ciclamino (chē·klâ·mē'nō) *m* cyclamen
ciclismo (chē·klē'zmō) *m* cycling
ciclista (chē·klē'stâ) *m&f* cyclist
ciclo (chē'klō) *m* cycle
ciclomotore (chē·klō·mō·tō'rā) *m* motorbike
ciclone (chē·klō'nā) *m* tornado, cyclone
ciclope (chē·klō'pā) *m* cyclops
ciclopico (chē·klô'pē·kō) *a* enormous, cyclopean
ciclopista (chē·klō·pē'stâ) *f* bicycle path
ciclostile (chē·klō·stē'lā) *m* mimeograph
ciclotrone (chē·klō·trō'nā) *m (phys)* cyclotron
cicogna (chē·kō'nyâ) *f* stork
cicoria (chē·kô'ryâ) *f* chicory
ciecamente (chā·kâ·mān'tā) *adv* blindly; *(fig)* inconsiderately
cieco (chā'kō) *a* blind
cielo (chā'lō) *m* sky, heaven
cifra (chē'frâ) *f* figure, amount; **–rio** (chē·frâ'ryō) *m* code
ciglio (chē'lyō) *m* eyelash; edge
cigno (chē'nyō) *m* swan
cignone (chē·nyō'nā) *m* chignon
cigolare (chē·gō·lâ'rā) *vi* to squeak
cilecca (chē·lāk'kâ) *f* misfiring; jamming; **far** — to misfire
cilicio (chē·lē'chō) *m* sackcloth
ciliegia (chē·lye'jâ) *f* cherry
cilindrata (chē·lēn·drâ'tâ) *f (auto)* displacement of a cylinder
cilindro (chē·lēn'drō) *m* cylinder
cima (chē'mâ) *f* peak; summit
cimare (chē·mâ'rā) *vt* to shear *(fabric);* to lop off, trim
cimasa (chē·mâ'zâ) *f (arch)* cyma, curved molding
cimelio (chē·me'lyō) *m* ancient remains
cimentare (chē·mān·tâ'rā) *vt* to attempt, try; to risk
cimentarsi (chē·mān·târ'sē) *vi* to incur a risk; to test one's ability
cimice (chē'mē·chā) *f* bedbug
cimiero (chē·myā'rō) *m* crest *(helmet)*
ciminiera (chē·mē·nyā'râ) *f* smokestack
cimitero (chē·mē·tā'rō) *m* cemetery
cimosa (chē·mō'zâ) *f* selvage *(fabric)*
cimurro (chē·mūr'rō) *m* glanders *(horse)*; distemper *(dog)*
Cina (chē'nâ) *f* China
cinabro (chē·nâ'brō) *m* cinnabar
cincin (chēn·chēn') *interj* Here's to you!; To your health!
cine (chē'nā) *m* movie, movies, movie theater; **–asta** (chē·nā·â'stâ) *m* film star; movie fan; **–città** (chē·nā·chēt·tâ') *f* movie studio; **–ma** (chē'nā·mâ) *m* movie, movies; **–mateatro** (chē·nā·mâ·tā·â'trō) *m* movie theater; **–matografaio** (chē·nā·mâ·tō·grâ·fâ'yō) *m* motion picture man; **–matografare** (chē·nā·mâ·tō·grâ·fâ'rā) *vt* to film; **–matografia** (chē·nā·mâ·tō·grâ·fē'â) *f* filmmaking; **–matografo** (chē·nā·mâ·tô'grâ·fō) *m* motion picture theater; **–presa** (chē·nā·prā'zâ) *f* movie shot; **–scopio** (chē·nā·skô'pyō) *m* TV picture tube, kinescope; **–scrittore** (chē·nā·skrēt·tō'-

rā) *m* motion picture writer; **–teca** (chē·nā·tā'kâ) *f* film library
cinese (chē·nā'zā) *a&m* Chinese
cinetica (chē·ne'tē·kâ) *f* kinetics
cingere * (chēn'jā·rā) *vt* to gird; to encompass
cinghia (chēn'gyâ) *f* belt
cinghiale (chēn·gyâ'lā) *m* wild boar
cinguettare (chēn·gwāt·tâ'rā) *vi* to chirp; to chatter; to twitter
cinguettio (chēn·gwāt·tē'ō) *m* chirping
cinico (chē'nē·kō) *a* cynical
ciniglia (chē·nē'lyâ) *f* chenille
cinodromo (che·nô'drō·mō) *m* dog track
cinofilo (chē·nô'fē·lō) *m* dog lover
cinquanta (chēn·kwân'tâ) *a* fifty
cinquantenario (chēn·kwân·tā·nâ'ryō) *m* fiftieth anniversary
cinquantesimo (chēn·kwân·te'zē·mō) *a* fiftieth
cinquantina (chēn·kwân·tē'nâ) *f* about fifty
cinque (chēn'kwā) *a* five
cinquecento (chēn·kwā·chān'tō) *a* five hundred; **il C–** the sixteenth century
cinquennio (chēn·kwen'nyō) *m* five-year period
cinta (chēn'tâ) *f* fence, enclosure
cintura (chēn·tū'râ) *f* belt; girdle
cinturino (chēn·tū·rē'nō) *m* belt; **— per orologio** wristwatch band
ciò (chō') *pron* this, that, it
ciocca (chōk'kâ) *f* cluster; lock
cioccolata (chōk·kō·lâ'tâ) *f* chocolate
cioccolatino (chōk·kō·lâ·tē'nō) *m* chocolate candy
ciocia (chō'châ) *f* sandal worn in the area of Rome; **–ro** (chō·châ'rō) *m* Roman peasant
cioè (chō·ā') *conj* that is, namely
ciondolare (chōn·dō·lâ'rā) *vt* to dangle, swing
ciondolo (chôn'dō·lō) *m* locket
ciotola (chô'tō·lā) *f* cup, bowl
ciottolo (chôt'tō·lō) *m* cobblestone; pebble
cipiglio (chē·pē'lyō) *m* scowl, frown
cipolla (chē·pōl'lâ) *f* onion
cipresso (chē·prās'sō) *m* cypress
cipria (chē'pryâ) *f* face powder
circa (chēr'kâ) *adv* about; almost; circa
circo (chēr'kō) *m* circus
circolare (chēr·kō·la'rā) *a&f* circular; — *f* circular letter; — *vi* to circulate, move around
circolazione (chēr·kō·lâ·tsyō'nā) *f* circulation; traffic; **— vietata** do not enter; **documento di —** registration card
circolo (chēr'kō·lō) *m* circle; club
circoncidere * (chēr·kōn·chē'dā·rā) *vt* to circumcise
circoncisione (chēr·kōn·chē·zyō'nā) *f* circumcision
circondare (chēr·kōn·dâ'rā) *vt* to surround
circondario (chēr·kōn·dâ'ryō) *m* provincial district
circonferenza (chēr·kōn·fā·rān'tsâ) *f* circumference
circonflesso (chēr·kōn·flās'sō) *a* circumflex
circonlocuzione (chēr·kōn·lō·cū·tsyō'nā) *f* circumlocution; evasion
circonvallazione (chēr·kōn·vâl·lâ·tsyō'nā) *f* belt highway; belt bus line; bypass
circonvenire * (chēr·kōn·vā·nē'rā) *vt* to circumvent; to baffle
circoscritto (chēr·kō·skrēt'tō) *a* circumscribed, limited
circostanza (chēr·kō·stân'tsâ) *f* circumstance
circuire (chēr·kwē'rā) *vt* to surround, enclose; (*fig*) to entrap; to go around, bypass
circuitare (chēr·kwē·tâ'rā) *vi* (*avi*) to circle before landing
circuito (chēr·kwē'tō) *m* circuit; **corto —** short circuit
cirro (chēr'rō) *m* lock (*hair*); (*bot*) cirrus, tendril; cirrus cloud; (*med*) scirrhus
cispa (chē'spâ) *f* bleariness; discharge of rheum from the eye
cisposo (chē·spō'zō) *a* bleary-eyed
cisterna (chē·stār'nâ) *f* cistern, tank; **acqua di —** rain water; **nave —** tanker (*naut*)
cistifellea (chē·stē·fel'lā·â) *f* gall bladder
citare (chē·tâ'rā) *vt* to cite, mention; to sue
citazione (chē·tâ·tsyō'nā) *f* subpoena; summons; quotation, citation
citofono (chē·tô'fō·nō) *m* intercom
citrato (chē·trâ'tō) *m* citrate; **— di magnesio** magnesium; **— di magnesia** effervescent antacid
citroniera (chē·trō·nyā'râ) *f* hothouse
citrullo (chē·trūl'lō) *m* nincompoop
città (chēt·tâ') *f* city; **— giardino** garden city
cittadina (chēt·tâ·dē'nâ) *f* town; **–nza** (chēt·tâ·dē·nân'tsâ) *f* citizenship
cittadino (chēt·tâ·dē'nō) *m* citizen; — *a* civic
ciuco (chū'kō) *m* jackass
ciuffo (chūf'fō) *m* lock, tuft
ciurma (chūr'mâ) *f* ship's crew; mob; hands; **–glia** (chūr·mâ'lyâ) *f* rabble, mob; **–re** (chūr·mâ'rā) *vt* to swindle, trick, cheat; to charm
civetta (chē·vāt'tâ) *f* screechowl; (*fig*) flirt, coquette; **–re** (chē·vāt·tâ'rā) *vi* to flirt
civetteria (chē·vāt·tā·rē'â) *f* coquetry
civettuolo (chē·vāt·twō'lō) *a* saucy, coquettish
civile (chē·vē'lā) *a&m* civilian; — *a* civilized; civil
civilista (chē·vē·lē'stâ) *m* civil lawyer
civilizzare (chē·vē·lē·dzâ'rā) *vt* to civilize
civilizzato (chē·vē·lē·dzâ'tō) *a* civilized; **–re** (chē·vē·lē·dzâ·tō'rā) *a* civilizing
civilmente (chē·vēl·mān'tā) *adv* politely, civilly
civiltà (chē·vēl·tâ') *f* civilization; politeness
civismo (chē·vē'zmō) *m* civic pride, civic duty
clackson (klâk'sōn) *m* (*auto*) horn

clamoroso (klâ·mō·rō'zō) *a* sensational
clandestino (klân·dā·stē'nō) *a* underhand, clandestine
clarinetto (klâ·rē·nāt'tō) *m* clarinet
classe (klâs'sā) *f* class
classicista (klâs·sē·chē'stâ) *m* classical scholar
classico (klâs'sē·kō) *a* classic; classical
classifica (klâs·sē'fē·kâ) *f* rating, grading; **–re** (klâs·sē·fē·kâ'rā) *vt* to classify; **–tore** (klâs·sē·fē·kâ·tō'rā) *m* folder; **–zione** (klâs·sē·fē·kâ·tsyō'nā) *f* classification
classismo (klâs·sē'zmō) *m* class consciousness
clausola (klâ'ū·zō·lâ) *f* clause
claustrale (klâū·strâ'lā) *a* cloistered, solitary
claustro (klâ'ū·strō) *m* cloister
clausura (klâū·zū'râ) *f* seclusion, cloistering
clava (klâ'vâ) *f* club
clavicembalo (klâ·vē·chem'bâ·lō) *m* harpsichord
clavicola (klâ·vē'kō·lâ) *f* collarbone
clemente (klā·mān'tā) *a* mild, merciful, clement
clemenza (klā·mān'tsâ) *f* clemency
cleptomania (klāp·tō·mâ·nē'â) *f* kleptomania
clericale (klā·rē·kâ'lā) *a* clerical, pertaining to the clergy
clero (klā'rō) *m* clergy
clessidra (klās·sē'drâ) *f* water clock, clepsydra
cliente (kyān'tā) *m&f* customer, client; **–la** (klyān·tā'lâ) *f* patronage; clients, customers
clima (klē'mâ) *m* climate; **–tico** (klē·mâ'tē·kō) *a* climatic; **stazione climatica** health resort, spa
clinica (klē'nē·kâ) *f* clinic, hospital
clinico (klē'nē·kō) *a* clinical
clistere (klē·stā'rā) *m* enema
cloaca (klō·â'kâ) *f* drain; sewer
clorato (klō·râ'tō) *m* chlorate
cloro (klō'rō) *m* chlorine; **–filla** (klō·rō·fēl'lâ) *f* chlorophyl; **–formio** (klō·rō·fôr'myō) *m* chloroform
cloruro (klō·rū'rō) *m* chloride
coabitare (kō·â·bē·tâ'rā) *vi* to cohabit
coadiuvare (kō·â·dyū·vâ'rā) *vt* to aid, assist, help; — *vi* to cooperate, to collaborate
coagulare (kō·â·gū·lâ'rā) *vt* to coagulate
coagulo (kō·â'gū·lō) *m* coagulum, clot (*blood*), curd (*milk*)
coalizione (kō·â·lē·tsyō'nā) *f* coalition
coalizzarsi (kō·â·lē·dzâr'sē) *vi* to form a coalition
coartare (kō·âr·tâ'rā) *vt* to force, coerce
coassiale (kō·âs·syâ'lā) *a* coaxial
cobalto (kō·bâl'tō) *m* cobalt
cocainomane (kō·kâē·nô'mâ·nā) *m* cocaine addict
coccarda (kōk·kâr'dâ) *f* cockade, rosette
cocchiere (kōk·kyā'rā) *m* coachman
cocchio (kôk'kyō) *m* carriage, coach; chariot
cocciniglia (kō·chē·nē'lyâ) *f* cochineal, red dye
coccio (kô'chō) *m* pottery fragment
cocciuto (kō·chū'tō) *a* stubborn
cocco (kōk'kō) *m* coconut; (*fig*) darling
coccodrillo (kōk·kō·drēl'lō) *m* crocodile
cocomero (kō·kô'mā·rō) *m* watermelon
coda (kō'dâ) *f* tail; **far** — to stand in line
codardia (kō·dâr·dē'â) *f* cowardice
codardo (kō·dâr'dō) *a* cowardly; — *m* coward
codesto (kō·dā'stō) *a&pron* that
codice (kô'dē·chā) *m* code; — **della strada** traffic regulations; — **penale** criminal law code
coefficiente (kō·āf·fē·chān'tā) *m* coefficient
coerente (kō·ā·rān'tā) a consistent
coesione (kō·ā·zyō'nā) *f* cohesion
coesistenza (kō·ā·zē·stān'tsâ) *f* coexistence
coesore (kō·ā·zō'rā) *m* (*elec*) coherer
coetaneo (kō·ā·tâ'nā·ō) *a* coetaneous, contemporary, coeval
cofano (kô'fâ·nō) *m* (*auto*) hood; coffer
coffa (kōf'fâ) *f* (*naut*) crow's nest, top, foretop
cogliere * (kô'lyā·rā) *vt* to pick; to take hold of
cognata (kō·nyâ'tâ) *f* sister-in-law
cognato (kō·nyâ'tō) *m* brother-in-law
cognizione (kō·nyē·tsyō'nā) *f* knowledge; recognition
cognome (kō·nyō'mā) *m* family name, last name
coibente (kōē·bān'tā) *m* (*phys*) non-conducting, insulating material
coincidenza (kōēn·chē·dān'tsâ) *f* coincidence; connection, transfer
coincidere (kōēn·chē'dā·rā) *vi* to coincide
coinvolgere * (kōēn·vôl'jā·rā) *vt* to involve; to implicate
coito (kô'ē·tō) *m* coition
col (kōl) *prep* with the
colà (kō·lâ') *adv* there
colabrodo (kō·lâ·brō'dō) *m* strainer
colare (kō·lâ'rā) *vt* to strain
colata (kō·lâ'tâ) *f* metal casting
colazione (kō·lâ·tsyō'nā) *f* lunch; breakfast; **prima** — breakfast
colei (kō·lā'ē) *pron* she
colera (kō·lā'râ) *f* cholera
colesterina (kō·lā·stā·rē'nâ) *f* cholesterol
colibrì (kō·lē·brē') *m* hummingbird
colica (kô'lē·kâ) *f* colic
colla (kōl'lâ) *f* glue
collaborare (kōl·lâ·bō·râ'rā) *vi* to contribute; to collaborate
collaborazione (kōl·lâ·bō·râ·tsyō'nā) *f* collaboration
collaborazionista (kōl·lâ·bō·râ·tsyō·nē'stâ) *m* collaborationist
collana (kōl·lâ'nâ) *f* necklace; collection; series of related books
collare (kōl·lâ'rā) *m* collar
collasso (kōl·lâs'sō) *m* collapse; — **cardiaco** heart attack
collaterale (kōl·lâ·tā·râ'lā) *a&m* collateral

collaudare (kōl·lâū·dâ'rā) *vt* to test
collaudo (kōl·lâ'ū·dō) *m* testing
colle (kôl'lā) *m* hill
collega (kōl·lā'gâ) *m* colleague; **–mento** (kōl·lā·gâ·mān'tō) *m* liaison; relationship
collegiale (kōl·lā·jâ'lā) *m* student at a boarding school
collegio (kōl·le'jō) *m* academy; boarding school
collera (kôl'lā·râ) *f* rage; anger
colletta (kōl·lāt'tâ) *f* collection
collettivismo (kōl·lāt·tē·vē'zmō) *m* collectivism
collettività (kōl·lāt·tē·vē·tâ') *f* community
collettivo (kōl·lāt·tē'vō) *a* collective
colletto (kōl·lāt'tō) *m* collar; — **floscio** soft collar
collettore (kōl·lāt·tō'rā) *m* (*mech*) exhaust manifold; (*elect*) commutator; main sewer; — *a* collecting
collezione (kōl·lā·tsyō'nā) *f* collection
collezionista (kōl·lā·tsyō·nē'stâ) *m* collector
collimare (kōl·lē·mâ'rā) *vi* to agree, be in accord, jibe; to coincide
collina (kōl·lē'nâ) *f* hill
collisione (kōl·lē·zyō'nā) *f* collision
collo (kōl'lō) *m* neck; parcel
collocamento (kōl·lō·kâ·mān'tō) *m* employment; situation
collocare (kōl·lō·kâ'rā) *vt* to place; to situate
collocarsi (kōl·lō·kâr'sē) *vr* to place oneself, range, take a position
collocazione (kōl·lō·kâ·tsyō'nā) *f* placement, placing
collodio (kōl·lô'dyō) *m* (*chem*) collodion
colloidale (kōl·lōē·dâ'lā) *a* (*chem*) colloidal
colloquio (kōl·lô'kwēō) *m* interview, talk
collusione (kōl·lū·zyō'nā) *f* collusion
colluttazione (kōl·lūt·tâ·tsyō'nā) *f* brawl, fight
colmare (kōl·mâ'rā) *vt* to fill
colmo (kōl'mō) *a* full; — *m* height, upper reaches
colombaia (kō·lōm·bâ'yâ) *f* dove cote
Colombia (kō·lôm'byâ) *f* Colombia; **–no** (kō·lōm'byâ'nō) *m&a* Colombian
colombo (kō·lōm'bō) *m* pigeon
colonia (kō·lô'nyâ) *f* colony; — **estiva** summer camp; **–li** (kō·lō·nyâ'lē) *mpl* spices
colonizzare (kō·lō·nē·dzâ'rā) *vt* to colonize
colonna (kō·lōn'nâ) *f* column; **–to** (kō·lōn·nâ'tō) *m* colonnade
colonnello (kō·lōn·nāl'lō) *m* colonel
colono (kō·lô'nō) *m* tenant farmer; sharecropper
colorante (kō·lō·rân'tā) *a* coloring
colore (kō·lō'rā) *m* color; paint
colorire (kō·lō·rē'rā) *vt* to color, paint
colorito (kō·lō·rē'tō) *m* complexion, coloring
colossale (kō·lōs·sâ'lā) *a* colossal
Colosseo (kō·lōs·sā'ō) *m* Colosseum
colosso (kō·lōs'sō) *m* giant, colossus
colpa (kōl'pâ) *f* fault
colpevole (kōl·pe'vō·lā) *a* guilty
colpire (kōl·pē'rā) *vt* to hit
colpo (kōl'pō) *m* blow
coltellata (kōl·tāl·lâ'tâ) *f* knife wound
coltelleria (kōl·tāl·lā·rē'â) *f* cutlery
coltello (kōl·tāl'lō) *m* knife
coltivare (kōl·tē·vâ'rā) *vt* to cultivate
coltivatore (kōl·tē·vâ·tō'rā) *m* cultivator; farmer; grower
coltivazione (kōl·tē·vâ·tsyō'nā) *f* cultivation
colto (kōl'tō) *a* educated, cultivated
coltre (kōl'trā) *f* blanket
coltrone (kōl·trō'nā) *m* quilt
coltura (kōl·tū'râ), **cultura** (kūl·tū'râ) *f* culture
colubro (kō·lū'brō) *m* snake, serpent
colui (kō·lū'ē) *pron* he, the one who, he who
comandamento (kō·mân·dâ·mān'tō) *m* commandment
comandante (kō·mân·dân'tā) *m* commander; captain of a ship
comandare (kō·mân·dâ'rā) *vt* to command
comando (kō·mân'dō) *m* command
comare (kō·mâ'rā) *f* crony; housewife; godmother
combaciare (kōm·bâ·châ'rā) *vi* to tally, jibe, agree
combattente (kōm·bât·tān'tā) *m* combatant; **ex** — veteran
combattere (kōm·bât'tā·rā) *vt&i* to fight; to struggle against
combattimento (kōm·bât·tē·mān'tō) *m* fight, struggle
combinare (kōm·bē·nâ'rā) *vt* to arrange; to bring together
combinazione (kōm·bē·nâ·tsyō'nā) *m* combination; coincidence; **per** — by chance
combriccola (kōm·brēk'kō·lâ) *f* clique, ring, gang
combustibile (kōm·bū·stē'bē·lā) *m* fuel
come (kō'mā) *prep&conj* as, like; — *adv* how; — **mai?** how in the world?
cometa (kō·mā'tâ) *f* comet
comico (kô'mē·kō) *a* funny; — *m* comedian
comignolo (kō·mē'nyō·lō) *m* chimney top; gable
cominciare (kō·mēn·châ'rā) *vt&i* to begin
comitato (kō·mē·tâ'tō) *m* committee
comitiva (kō·mē·tē'vâ) *f* party; **viaggio in** — conducted tour
comizio (kō·mē'tsyō) *m* meeting, rally
comma (kōm'mâ) *m* paragraph; (*gram*) clause between commas; comma
commedia (kōm·me'dyâ) *f* comedy
commediografo (kōm·mā·dyô'grâ·fō) *m* playwright
commemorare (kōm·mā·mō·râ'rā) *vt* to commemorate, celebrate
commenda (kōm·mān'dâ) *f* allowance; order of knighthood; **–tore** (kōm·mān·dâ·tō'rā) *m* commander; knight commander
commensale (kōm·mān·sâ'lā) *m* table

companion
commentare (kōm·mān·tâ'rā) *vt* to comment on; to footnote
commentatore (kōm·mān·tâ·tō'rā) *m* commentator
commento (kōm·mān'tō) *m* comment; annotation
commerciale (kōm·mār·châ'lā) *a* commercial
commercialista (kōm·mār·châ·lē'stâ) *m* business lawyer
commerciante (kōm·mār·chân'tā) *m* merchant, businessman
commerciare (kōm·mār·châ'rā) *vi* to be in business; — *vt* to deal in
commercio (kōm·mer'chō) *m* commerce; — **librario** book business
commessa (kōm·mās'sâ) *f* order; salesgirl
commesso (kōm·mās'sō) *m* clerk; — **viaggiatore** traveling salesman
commestibile (kōm·mā·stē'bē·lā) *m* foodstuff
commettere (kōm·met'tā·rā) *vt* to perpetrate; to commit
commiato (kōm·myâ'tō) *m* leave; departure
commilitone (kōm·mē·lē·tō'nā) *m* fellow soldier; companion; comrade
commissariato (kōm·mēs·sâ·ryâ'tō) *m* commissariat; — **di polizia** police station
commissario (kōm·mēs·sâ'ryō) *m* commissioner; — **di bordo** purser; — **di pubblica sicurezza** local chief of police
commissionare (kōm·mēs·syō·nâ'rā) *vt* to order, place an order for
commissionario (kōm·mēs·syō·nâ'ryō) *m* sales agent; commission salesman
commissione (kōm·mēs·syō'nā) *f* commission; committee; order
commisto (kōm·mē'stō) *a* mixed
commosso (kōm·mōs'sō) *a* moved; saddened
commovente (kōm·mō·vān'tā) *a* moving, touching; saddening
commozione (kōm·mō·tsyō'nā) *f* emotion; commotion
commuovere * (kōm·mwô'vā·rā) *vt* to move; to cause to feel sympathy for
commutare (kōm·mū·tâ'rā) *vt* to commute, set aside
commutatore (kōm·mū·tâ·tō'rā) *m* (*elec*) switch
comò (kō·mō') *m* chest of drawers
comodino (kō·mō·dē'nō) *m* bedside table
comodità (kō·mō·dē·tâ') *f* comfort; convenience
comodo (kô'mō·dō) *a* comfortable; convenient
compagnia (kōm·pâ·nyē'â) *f* company
compagno (kōm·pâ'nyō) *m* companion
companatico (kōm·pâ·nâ'tē·kō) *m* food eaten with bread
comparare (kōm·pâ·râ'rā) *vt* to compare
comparativo (kōm·pâ·râ·tē'vō) *a&m* comparative
comparazione (kom·pâ·râ·tsyō'nā) *f* comparison, likening
compare (kōm·pâ'rā) *m* godfather; buddy (*coll*)
comparire * (kōm·pâ·rē'rā) *vi* to appear; to make one's appearance
comparsa (kôm·pâr'sâ) *f* (*theat*) extra
compartimento (kōm·pâr·tē·mān'tō) *m* compartment
compartire (kōm·pâr·tē'rā) *vt* to share, divide, partition
compassione (kōm·pâs·syō'nā) *f* sympathy; **—vole** (kōm·pâs·syō·ne'vō·lā) *a* pitiful, piteous, woeful; sympathizing, pitying
compasso (kōm·pâs'sō) *m* compass
compatibile (kōm·pâ·tē'bē·lā) *a* consistent; compatible
compatibilità (kōm·pâ·tē·bē·lē·tâ') *f* consistency; compatibility
compatire (kōm·pâ·tē'rā) *vt* to pity
compatto (kōm·pât'tō) *a* compact
compendiare (kōm·pān·dyâ'rā) *vt* to resume, summarize, make a compendium of
compendio (kōm·pen'dyō) *m* summary
compenetrare (kōm·pā·nā·trâ'rā) *vt* to penetrate, pervade
compenetrarsi (kōm·pā·nā·trâr'sē) *vr* to become diffused; to penetrate thoroughly
compensare (kōm·pān·sâ'rā) *vt* to reward
compensato (kōm·pān·sâ'tō) *a* compensated; — *m* plywood
compenso (kōm·pān'sō) *m* reward
competente (kōm·pā·tān'tā) *a* qualified, competent; — *m* expert
competenza (kōm·pā·tān'tsâ) *f* competence
competizione (kōm·pā·tē·tsyō'nā) *f* contest, competition
compiacente (kōm·pyâ·chān'tā) *a* indulgent, complaisant, obliging
compiangere * (kōm·pyân'jā·rā) *vt* to pity
compilare (kōm·pē·lâ'rā) *vt* to compile
compire * (kōm·pē'rā), **compiere** (kôm'pyā·rā) *vt* to complete, do, carry out
compito (kôm'pē·tō) *m* school work; duty; task
compiuto (kōm·pyū'tō) *a* completed, finished, accomplished
compleanno (kōm·plā·ân'nō) *m* birthday
complessivamente (kōm·plās·sē·vâ·mān'tā) *adv* inclusively, on the whole, totally
complessivo (kōm·plās·sē'vō) *a* inclusive, encompassing; complete
complesso (kōm·plās'sō) *a&m* complex; — *m* organization, outfit
completare (kōm·plā·tâ'rā) *vt* to complete, fulfill
completo (kōm·plā'tō) *a* complete; full; — *m* man's suit of clothing
complicare (kōm·plē·kâ'rā) *vt* to complicate; to confuse
complicato (kōm·plē·kâ'tō) *a* complicated
complicazione (kōm·plē·kâ·tsyō'nā) *f* complication
complice (kôm'plē·chā) *m&f* accomplice
complimentare (kōm·plē·mān·tâ'rā) *vt* to compliment, congratulate
complimenti (kōm·plē·mān'tē) *mpl* re-

gards; congratulations; **fare i —** to compliment; to be ceremonious; to congratulate
complimento (kōm·plē·mān'tō) *m* compliment
complottare (kōm·plōt·tâ'rā) *vt&i* to plot
componente (kōm·pō·nān'tā) *m* component part
componimento (kōm·pō·nē·mān'tō) *m* composition; structure
comporre * (kōm·pōr'rā) *vt* to compose; to construct; to write up
comportamento (kōm·pōr·tâ·mān'tō) *m* behavior
comportarsi (kōm·pōr·târ'sē) *vr* to behave
compositoio (kōm·pō·zē·tô'yō) *m* (*print*) composing stick
compositore (kōm·pō·zē·tō'rā) *m* composer; typesetter
composizione (kōm·pō·zē·tsyō'nā) *f* composition; typesetting
composta (kōm·pō'stâ) *f* compote
compostezza (kōm·pō·stā'tsâ) *f* composure, self-possession, self-assurance
compostiera (kōm·pō·styā'râ) *f* compote (*dish*)
composto (kōm·pō'stō) *a* composed; compound; — *m* compound
compra (kōm'prâ) *f* purchase; **— vendita terreni** real estate agency; **–re** (kōm·prâ'rā) *vt* to purchase, buy; **–tore** (kōm·prâ·tō'rā) *m* buyer
comprendere * (kōm·pren'dā·rā) *vt* to understand; to contain, include
comprensorio (kōm·prān·sô'ryō) *m* reclamation area
compreso (kōm·prā'zō) *a* included, including; understood
compressa (kōm·prās'sâ) *f* tablet; pad
compressione (kōm·prās·syō'nā) *f* compression
compressore (kōm·prās·sō'rā) *m* compressor; **— stradale** steam roller
comprimere * (kōm·prē'mā·rā) *vt* to press, squeeze; to compress; to repress (*feeling*)
compromesso (kōm·prō·mās'sō) *a* involved; compromised; — *m* compromise
compromettere * (kōm·prō·met'tā·rā) *vt* to compromise; to involve
comproprietario (kōm·prō·pryā·tâ'ryō) *m* co-owner, joint owner
comprovare (kōm·prō·vâ'rā) *vt* to evidence, prove
compulsare (kōm·pūl·sâ'rā) *vt* to consult, have reference to
compunto (kōm·pūn'tō) *a* contrite; ashamed; afflicted; demure
computare (kōm·pū·tâ'rā) *vt* to compute
computista (kōm·pū·tē'stâ) *m* accountant
computisteria (kōm·pū·tē·stā·rē'â) *f* bookkeeping
computo (kôm'pū·tō) *m* computation, calculation
comunale (kō·mū·nâ'lā) *a* municipal; **palazzo —** city hall
comune (kō·mū'nā) *a* common; — *m* municipality; **–lla** (kō·mū·nāl'lâ) *f* gang, clique; **–mente** (kō·mū·nā·mān'tā) *adv* usually, commonly
comunicare (kō·mū·nē·kâ'rā) *vt* to communicate with; — *vi* to be connected
comunicato (kō·mū·nē·kâ'tō) *m* communiqué
comunicazione (kō·mū·nē·kâ·tsyō'nā) *f* communication; telephone connection
comunione (kō·mū·nyō'nā) *f* Communion; communion
comunismo (kō·mū·nē'zmō) *m* Communism
comunista (kō·mū·nē'stâ) *m&a* Communist
comunità (kō·mū·nē·tâ') *f* community
comunque (kō·mūn'kwā) *adv* however
con (kōn) *prep* with
conato (kō·nâ'tō) *m* impulse; effort; attempt
conca (kōn'kâ) *f* vase; basin; tub; (*geog*) valley; lock (*canal*)
concatenare (kōn·kâ·tā·nâ'rā) *vt* to join; to link, unite
concatenazione (kōn·kâ·tā·nâ·tsyō'nā) *f* linking, connection, union
concavo (kôn'kâ·vō) *a* concave
concedere (kōn·che'dā·rā) *vt* to grant
concentramento (kōn·chān·trâ·mān'tō) *m* concentration
concentrare (kōn·chān·trâ'rā) *vt* to concentrate
concentrato (kōn·chān·trâ'tō) *m* concentrate; — *a* concentrated
concentrazione (kōn·chān·trâ·tsyō'nā) *f* concentration
concentrico (kōn·chen'trē·kō) *a* concentric
concepire (kōn·chā·pē'rā) *vt* to conceive; to originate
conceria (kōn·chā·rē'â) *f* tannery
concertista (kōn·chār·tē'stâ) *m&f* concert artist
concerto (kōn·chār'tō) *m* concert; agreement, accord
concessionario (kōn·chās·syō·nâ'ryō) *m* sole agent; distributor; dealer
concessione (kōn·chās·syō'nā) *f* concession; dealership
concetto (kōn·chāt'tō) *m* concept, idea
concezione (kōn·chā·tsyō'nā) *f* conception
conchiglia (kōn·kē'lyâ) *f* shell
concia (kôn'châ) *f* tanning; tannery; **–re** (kōn·châ'rā) *vt* to tan; to fix
conciliare (kōn·chē·lyâ'rā) *vt* to reconcile, conciliate
conciliarsi (kōn·chē·lyâr'sē) *vr* to agree with; to gain one's esteem, win one over
conciliazione (kōn·chē·lyâ·tsyō'nā) *f* conciliation, reconciliation
concilio (kōn·chē'lyō) *m* council
concimare (kōn·chē·mâ'rā) *vt* to fertilize; to manure
concime (kōn·chē'mā) *m* manure
conciso (kōn·chē'zō) *a* concise
concistoro (kōn·chē·stō'rō) *m* concistory
concitato (kōn·chē·tâ'tō) *a* excited, aroused
concittadino (kōn·chēt·tâ·dē'nō) *m* fellow citizen, countryman

concludere * (kōn·klū'dā·rā) *vt&i* to conclude; to come to a decision
conclusione (kōn·klū·zyō'nā) *f* conclusion
concordanza (kōn·kōr·dân'tsâ) *f* accord, agreement; concordance
concordare (kōn·kōr·dâ'rā) *vt* to cause to agree; to bring into harmony
concordato (kōn·kōr·dâ'tō) *a* arranged, agreed upon; — *m* agreement; concordate
concordia (kōn·kôr'dyâ) *f* harmony, peace; mutual consent, concord
concorrente (kōn·kōr·rān'tā) *m* competitor
concorrenza (kōn·kōr·rān'tsâ) *f* competition
concorrere * (kōn·kôr'rā·rā) *vi* to compete
concorso (kōn·kōr'sō) *m* attendance; contest
concreto (kōn·krā'tō) *a* concrete, actual
concubina (kōn·kū·bē'nâ) *f* concubine; **–to** (kōn·kū·bē·nâ'tō) *m* concubinage
concupiscente (kōn·kū·pē·shān'tā) *a* concupiscent
concupiscenza (kōn·kū·pē·shān'tsâ) *f* lust, concupiscence
concussione (kōn·kūs·syō'nā) *f* extortion; concussion
condanna (kōn·dân'nâ) *f* condemnation; sentence; **–re** (kōn·dân·nâ'rā) *vt* to sentence; **–to** (kōn·dân·nâ'tō) *m* convict
condensare (kōn·dān·sâ'rā) *vt* to condense; to abridge
condensatore (kōn·dān·sâ·tō'rā) *m* condenser
condimento (kōn·dē·mān'tō) *m* seasoning
condire (kōn·dē'rā) *vt* to season
condividere * (kōn·dē·vē'dā·rā) *vt* to share
condizionale (kōn·dē·tsyō·nâ'lā) *a* conditional; **condanna —** suspended sentence; — *m* (*gram*) conditional mood
condizionare (kōn·dē·tsyō·nâ'rā) *vt* to condition; to prepare, ready
condizionato (kōn·dē·tsyō·nâ'tō) *a* conditioned; **aria condizionata** air conditioning; **–re** (kōn·dē·tsyō·nâ·tō'rā) *m* air conditioner
condizione (kōn·dē·tsyō'nā) *f* condition, term
condoglianza (kōn·dō·lyân'tsâ) *f* sympathy, condolence
condolersi * (kōn·dō·lār'sē) *vr* to sympathize with, condole with
condonare (kōn·dō·nâ'rā) *vt* to pardon, forgive, condone
condonato (kōn·dō·nâ'tō) *a* pardoned, condoned
condono (kōn·dō'nō) *m* pardon, forgiveness
condotta (kōn·dōt'tâ) *f* behavior; management
condottiero (kōn·dōt·tyā'rō) *m* leader, condottiere, mercenary soldier
condotto (kon·dōt'tō) *m* pipeline; — *a* led
conducente (kōn·dū·chān'tā) *a* leading; — *m* conductor; driver
conducibilità (kōn·dū·chē·bē·lē·tâ') *f* (*phys*) conductivity
condurre * (kōn·dūr'rā) *vt* to take, escort
conduttività (kōn·dūt·tē·vē·tâ') *f* (*phys*) conductivity
conduttore (kōn·dūt·tō'rā) *m* driver; train conductor; operator
confabulare (kōn·fâ·bū·lâ'rā) *vi* to talk, chat
confacente (kōn·fâ·chān'tā) *a* proper, suitable; agreeable to; becoming
confarsi * (kōn·fâr'sē) *vr* to fit; to agree; to suit; to content oneself
confederare (kōn·fā·dā·râ'rā) *vt* to confederate
confederato (kōn·fā·dā·râ'tō) *a* confederated; — *m* confederate
confederazione (kōn·fā·dā·râ·tsyō'nā) *f* confederacy, confederation
conferenza (kōn·fā·rān'tsâ) *f* lecture; **— al vertice** summit conference; **— stampa** press conference
conferenziere (kōn·fā·rān·tsyā'rā) *m* lecturer
conferire (kōn·fā·rē'rā) *vt&i* to confer
conferma (kōn·fār'mâ) *f* confirmation; **–re** (kōn·fār·mâ'rā) *vt* to confirm
confessare (kōn·fās·sâ'rā) *vt* to confess
confessionale (kōn·fās·syō·nâ'lā) *m&a* confessional
confessione (kōn·fās·syō'nā) *f* confession
confessore (kōn·fās·sō'rā) *m* confessor
confettiera (kōn·fāt·tyā'râ) *f* candy box
confettiere (kōn·fāt·tyā'rā) *m* confectioner
confetto (kōn·fāt'tō) *m* piece of candy
confettura (kōn·fāt·tū'râ) *f* marmalade
confezionare (kōn·fā·tsyō·nâ'rā) *vt* to manufacture; to draw up; to outline
confezione (kōn·fā·tsyō'nā) *f* ready-to-wear manufacture
conficcare (kōn·fēk·kâ'rā) *vt* to nail in, drive in; to embed
conficcarsi (kōn·fēk·kâr'sē) *vr* to be embedded, be thrust in
confidare (kōn·fē·dâ'rā) *vt&i* to trust; to confide in; to be on familiar terms with
confidenza (kōn·fē·dān'tsâ) *f* familiarity; confidence
confidenziale (kōn·fē·dān·tsyâ'lā) *a* confidential
configurare (kōn·fē·gū·râ'rā) *vt* to shape, outline; (*fig*) to idealize
configurazione (kōn·fē·gū·râ·tsyō'nā) *f* configuration, contour
confinare (kōn·fē·nâ'rā) *vt* to intern; — *vi* to border
confine (kōn·fē'nā) *m* border
confino (kōn·fē'nō) *m* internment
confiscare (kōn·fē·skâ'rā) *vt* to confiscate
conflitto (kōn·flēt'tō) *m* conflict
confluente (kōn·flūān'tā) *m* confluent, tributary
confondere * (kōn·fôn'dā·rā) *vt* to confuse; to mistake
conformare (kōn·fōr·mâ'rā) *vt* to conform

conformarsi (kōn·fōr·mâr'sē) *vr* to content oneself; to adapt oneself, accustom oneself
conforme (kōn·fōr'mā) *adv* in conformity; — *a* conforming
conformista (kōn·fōr·mē'stâ) *m* conformist
conformità (kōn·fōr·mē·tâ) *f* conformity
confortabile (kōn·fōr·tâ'bē·lā) *a* consolable
confortare (kōn·fōr·tâ'rā) *vt* to comfort, solace
confortevole (kōn·fōr·te'vō·lā) *a* comfortable
conforto (kōn·fōr'tō) *m* comfort
confraternità (kōn·frâ·tār·nē·tâ') *f* brotherhood; fraternity
confrontare (kōn·frōn·tâ'rā) *vt* to compare; to relate
confronto (kōn·frōn'tō) *m* comparison; (*law*) confrontation
confusione (kōn·fū·zyō'nā) *f* confusion
confuso (kōn·fū'zō) *a* confused
confutare (kōn·fū·tâ'rā) *vt* to refute; to deny
confutazione (kōn·fū·tâ·tsyō'nā) *f* refutation, confutation
congedare (kōn·jā·dâ'rā) *vt* to dismiss
congedo (kōn·jā'dō) *m* discharge; leave
congegno (kōn·jā'nyō) *m* device
congelare (kōn·jā·lâ'rā) *vt* to freeze
congelato (kōn·jā·lâ'tō) *a* frozen
congenito (kōn·je'nē·tō) *a* congenital
congestione (kōn·jā·styō'nā) *f* congestion; traffic jam
congettura (kōn·jāt·tū'râ) *f* supposition
congiungere * (kōn·jūn'jā·rā) *vt* to join, unite
congiuntivo (kōn·jūn·tē'vō) *m* subjunctive
congiunto (kōn·jūn'tō) *m* relative
congiuntura (kōn·jūn·tū'râ) *f* trade outlook, market conditions; emergency
congiunzione (kōn·jūn·tsyō'nā) *f* conjunction
congiura (kōn·jū'râ) *f* plot; **–re** (kōn·jū·râ'rā) *vt&i* to plot; to conjure; **–to** (kōn·jū·râ'tō) *a* plotted; conjured
conglomerato (kōn·glō·mā·râ'tō) *m* concrete; conglomerate
congratulare (kōn·grâ·tū·lâ'rā) *vt* to congratulate
congratulazione (kōn·grâ·tū·lâ·tsyō'nā) *f* congratulation
congrega (kôn'grā·gâ) *f* congregation; **–re** (kōn·grā·gâ'rā) *vt* to congregate; **–zione** (kōn·grā·gâ·tsyō'nā) *f* congregation
congressista (kōn·grās·sē'stâ) *m* member of a convention; congressman
congresso (kōn·grās'sō) *m* congress; convention, meeting
congruente (kōn·grūān'tā) *a* congruent
congruenza (kōn·grūān'tsâ) *f* congruence; consistency
congruo (kôn'grūō) *a* congruous
conguaglio (kōn·gwâ'lyō) *m* balance
coniare (kō·nyâ'rā) *vt* to coin
conico (kô'nē·kō) *a* conic
coniglio (kō·nē'lyō) *m* rabbit
conio (kô'nyō) *m* coinage
coniugare (kō·nyū·gâ'rā) *vt* to conjugate
coniugazione (kō·nyū·gâ·tsyō'nā) *f* conjugation
coniuge (kô'nyū·jā) *m* spouse
coniugi (kô'nyū·jē) *mpl* husband and wife, couple
connaturale (kōn·nâ·tū·râ'lā) *a* connatural, inborn
connazionale (kōn·nā·tsyō·nâ'lā) *m* compatriot
connessione (kōn·nās·syō'nā) *f* connection
connettere * (kōn·net'tā·rā) *vt* to connect
connivenza (kōn·nē·vān'tsâ) *f* connivance
connubio (kōn·nū'byō) *m* marriage, match; blend, union
cono (kō'nō) *m* cone; — **gelato** ice cream cone
conoscente (kō·nō·shān'tā) *m&f* acquaintance
conoscenza (kō·nō·shān'tsâ) *f* knowledge; acquaintance
conoscere * (kō·nô'shā·rā) *vt* to know; to be aware of
conoscitore (kō·nō·shē·tō'rā) *m* connoisseur
conosciuto (kō·nō·shū'tō) *a* known
conquista (kōn·kwē'stâ) *f* conquest; **–re** (kōn·kwē·stâ'rā) *vt* to conquer; **–tore** (kōn·kwē·stâ·tō'rā) *m* conqueror; (*coll*) ladies' man
consacrare (kōn·sâ·krâ'rā) *vt* to consecrate
consacrazione (kōn·sâ·krâ·tysō'nā) *f* consecration
consanguineo (kōn·sân·gwē' nā·ō) *a* akin; consanguineous
consanguinità (kōn·sân·gwē·nē·tâ') *f* consanguinity
consapevole (kōn·sâ·pe'vō·lā) *a* aware, knowing; informed
conscio (kôn'shō) *a* conscious
consecutivo (kōn·sā·kū·tē'vō) *a* successive, consecutive; following
consegna (kōn·sā'nyâ) *f* assignment; delivery; **–re** (kōn·sā·nyâ'rā) *vt* to deliver; **–tario** (kōn·sā·nyâ·tâ'ryō) *m* consignee
conseguente (kōn·sā·gwān'tā) *a* ensuing, resulting, consequent; **–mente** (kōn·sā·gwān·tā·mān'tā) *adv* consequently, as a result
conseguenza (kōn·sā·gwān'tsâ) *f* consequence
conseguire (kōn·sā·gwē'rā) *vt* to attain
consenso (kōn·sān'sō) *m* consent
consentimento (kōn·sān·tē·mān'tō) *m* consent
consentire (kōn·sān·tē'rā) *vi* to consent
conserva (kōn·sār'vâ) *f* preserve; — **di pomodoro** tomato paste; **in** — canned; **conserve alimentari** canned foods; **–re** *vt* (kōn·sār·vâ'rā) to conserve; **–tivo** (kōn·sār·vâ·tē'vō) *a* conservative; **–tore** (kōn·sār·vâ·tō'rā) *a* conservative; (*coll*) traditionalist; **–torio** (kōn·sār·vâ·tô'ryō) *m* conservatory of music; finishing

school; **-zione** (kōn·sār·vâ·tsyō'nā) *f* preservation, conservation
consesso (kōn·sās'sō) *m* meeting, assembly
considerare (kōn·sē·dā·râ'rā) *vt* to consider
considerazione (kōn·sē·dā·râ·tsyō'nā) *f* consideration
considerevole (kōn·sē·dā·re'vō·lā) *a* considerable
consigliare (kōn·sē·lyâ'rā) *vt* to advise
consigliere (kōn·sē·lyā'rā) *m* adviser; — **delegato** member of board of directors
consiglio (kōn·sē'lyō) *m* advice; council
consistente (kōn·sē·stān'tā) *a* solid, strong; consisting of
consistenza (kōn·sē·stān'tsâ) *f* solidity, firmness; consistency
consistere * (kōn·sē'stā·rā) *vi* to consist, be composed
consociazione (kōn·sō·châ·tsyō'nā) *f* association
consocio (kōn·sô'chō) *m* partner
consolare (kōn·sō·lâ'rā) *vt* to console; — *a* consular
consolato (kōn·sō·lâ'tō) *m* consulate; — *a* consoled
consolazione (kōn·sō·lâ·tsyō'nā) *f* consolation
console (kôn'sō·lā) *m* consul
consolidare (kōn·sō·lē·dâ'rā) *vt* to strengthen; to consolidate
consolidarsi (kōn·sō·lē·dâr'sē) *vr* to become firm; to strengthen oneself; to be consolidated; to take root
consolidato (kōn·sō·lē·dâ'tō) *m* funded debt
consonante (kōn·sō·nân'tā) *f* consonant
consorte (kōn·sōr'tā) *m&f* spouse
consorzio (kōn·sôr'tsyō) *m* combine, syndicate; — **agrario** farmers' cooperative
consueto (kōn·swā'tō) *a* customary, habitual, usual; — *m* custom, habit, wont
consuetudine (kōn·swā·tū'dē·nā) *f* custom
consulente (kōn·sū·lān'tā) *a&m* consultant
consultare (kōn·sūl·tâ'rā) *vt* to consult
consultivo (kōn·sūl·tē'vō) *a* advisory
consulto (kōn·sūl'tō) *m* consultation; **-re** (kōn·sūl·tō'rā) *m* adviser, counsellor
consumare (kōn·sū·mâ'rā) *vt* to consume; to use up
consumato (kōn·sū·mâ'tō) *m* consommé; — *a* used up; accomplished, finished
consumazione (kōn·sū·mâ·tsyō'nā) *f* consummation; drinks; meal
consumo (kōn·sū'mō) *m* consumption
consunto (kōn·sūn'tō) *a* consumptive
consunzione (kōn·sūn·tsyō'nā) *f* consumption
contabile (kōn·tâ'bē·lā) *m* accountant; bookkeeper
contabilità (kōn·tâ·bē·lē·tâ') *f* auditing; bookkeeping
contachilometro (kōn·tâ·kē·lô'mā·trō) *m* speedometer
contadino (kōn·tâ·dē'nō) *m* peasant; farm hand
contagio (kōn·tâ'jō) *m* contagion; **-so** (kōn·tâ·jō'zō) *a* contagious
contagiri (kōn·tâ·jē'rē) *m (mech)* revolutions indicator, speedometer
contagocce (kōn·tâ·gō'chā) *m* medicine dropper
contaminare (kōn·tâ·mē·nâ'rā) *vt* to infect
contaminazione (kōn·tâ·mē·nâ·tsyō'nā) *f* contamination
contante (kōn·tân'tā) *a&m* cash
contare (kōn·tâ'rā) *vt* to count; to expect; to depend on
contatore (kōn·tâ·tō'rā) *m* meter
contatto (kōn·tât'tō) *m* contact
conte (kōn'tā) *m* count; **-a** (kōn·tā'â) *f* county; earldom; **-ssa** (kōn·tās'sâ) *f* countess
conteggiare (kōn·tāj·jâ'rā) *vt* to figure
conteggio (kōn·tej'jō) *m* count; — **alla rovescia** (*aesp*) countdown
contegno (kōn·tā'nyō) *m* behavior, deportment; aloofness
contemplare (kōn·tām·plâ'rā) *vt* to contemplate; to view
contemplativo (kōn·tām·plâ·tē'vō) *a* contemplative
contemplazione (kōn·tām·plâ·tsyō'nā) *f* contemplation
contemporaneo (kōn·tām·pō·râ'nā·ō) *a* contemporary
contendere * (kōn·ten'dā·rā) *vi* to contend
contenente (kōn·tā·nān'tā) *a* containing
contenere * (kōn·tā·nā'rā) *vt* to contain; to encompass
contentare (kōn·tān·tâ'rā) *vt* to please; to satisfy
contentezza (kōn·tān·tā'tsâ) *f* joy
contento (kōn·tān'tō) *a* glad; satisfied
contenuto (kōn·tā·nū'tō) *m* contents
contenzione (kōn·tān·tsyō'nā) *f* debate; contention
contenzioso (kōn·tān·tsyō'zō) *a* contentious, quarrelsome
contesa (kōn·tā'zâ) *f* contest; contention
conteso (kōn·tā'zō) *a* opposed; contested
contestare (kōn·tā·stâ'rā) *vt* to object; to contest
contestazione (kōn·tā·stâ·tsyō'nā) *f* objection; dispute; opposition; contention
contesto (kōn·tā'stō) *m* context; compound; structure; texture; — *a* formed; interwoven
contiguo (kōn·tē'gwō) *a* adjoining
continente (kōn·tē·nān'tā) *m* continent; — *a* temperate, continent
continenza (kōn·tē·nān'tsâ) *f* continence
contingentare (kōn·tēn·jān·tâ'rā) *vt* to ration
contingente (kōn·tēn·jān'tā) *a&m* contingent
contingenza (kōn·tēn·jān'tsâ) *f* contingence
continuamente (kōn·tē·nwâ·mān'tā) *adv* always, continually
continuamento (kōn·tē·nwâ·mān'tō) *m* continuation; prolongation
continuare (kōn·tē·nwâ'rā) *vt&i* to con-

tinue; to prolong
continuato (kōn·tē·nwâ'tō) *a* continued
continuazione (kōn·tē·nwâ·tsyō'nā) *f* continuation
continuità (kōn·tē·nwē·tâ') *f* continuity
continuo (kōn·tē'nwō) *a* continuous
conto (kōn'tō) *m* count; account; bill
contorcere * (kōn·tôr'chā·rā) *vt* to twist
contorno (kōn·tōr'nō) *m* side dish; contour; outline
contorsione (kōn·tōr·syō'nā) *f* contortion
contorto (kōn·tōr'tō) *a* twisted, contorted
contrabbandiere (kōn·trâb·bân·dyā'rā) *m* smuggler
contrabbando (kōn·trâb·bân'dō) *m* smuggling
contrabbasso (kōn·trâb·bâs'sō) *m* contrabass
contraccambiare (kōn·trâk·kâm·byâ'rā) *vt* to reciprocate; to exchange; to return
contraccolpo (kōn·trâk·kōl'pō) *m* counterblow; repercussion; retaliation
contrada (kōn·trâ'dâ) *f* district, region; country road
contradetto (kōn·trâd·dāt'tō) *a* contradicted
contraddire * (kōn·trâd·dē'rā) *vt* to contradict, gainsay
contraddizione (kōn·trâd·dē·tsyō'nā) *f* contradiction
contraente (kōn·trâ·ān'tā) *a* contracting; — *m* contractor
contraereo (kōn·trâ·e'rā·ō) *a* antiaircraft
contraffare * (kōn·trâf·fâ'rā) *vt* to counterfeit; to impersonate
contraffatto (kōn·trâf·fât'tō) *a* false; **–re** (kōn·trâf·fât·tō'rā) *m* counterfeiter
contraffazione (kōn·trâf·fâ·tsyō'nā) *f* forgery
contrafforte (kōn·trâf·fōr'tā) *m* *(arch)* buttress, pier
contralto (kōn·trâl'tō) *m* contralto
contrammiraglio (kōn·trâm·mē·râ'lyō) *m* rear admiral
contrappeso (kōn·trâp·pā'zō) *m* counterpoise, counterweight
contrappunto (kōn·trâp·pūn'tō) *m* counterpoint
contrariamente (kōn·trâ·ryâ·mān'tā) *adv* contrarily
contrariare (kōn·trâ·ryâ'rā) *vt* to contradict; to oppose, counteract
contrarietà (kōn·trâ·ryā·tâ') *f* adversity
contrario (kōn·trâ'ryō) *a* contrary
contrarre * (kōn·trâr'rā) *vt* to contract
contrassegno (kōn·trâs·sā'nyō) *m* sign, token
contrastante (kōn·trâ·stân'tā) *a* contrasting; — *m&f* contestant
contrastare (kōn·trâ·stâ'rā) *vt* to contrast
contrasto (kōn·trâ'stō) *m* contrast
contrattare (kōn·trât·tâ'rā) *vt&i* to bargain; to contract; to deal
contrattempo (kōn·trât·tām'pō) *m* mishap; misfortune
contratto (kōn·trât'tō) *m* contract; — *a* contracted
contravvenzione (kōn·trâv·vān·tsyō'nā) *f* violation
contrazione (kōn·trâ·tsyō'nā) *f* contraction
contribuente (kōn·trē·bwān'tā) *m* taxpayer
contribuire (kōn·trē·bwē'rā) *vt* to contribute
contributo (kōn·trē·bū'tō) *m* contribution
contrito (kōn·trē'tō) *a* contrite
contrizione (kōn·trē·tsyō'nā) *f* contrition
contro (kōn'trō) *prep* against
controcurva (kōn·trō·kūr'vā) *f* S-curve
controfigura (kōn·trō·fē·gū'râ) *f* stand-in; substitute
controllare (kōn·trōl·lâ'rā) *vt* to verify, check
controllo (kōn·trōl'lō) *m* control, check; **–re** (kōn·trōl·lō'rā) *m* train conductor; auditor; ticket collector
contromarca (kōn·trō·mâr'kâ) *f* check, ticket stub
contromarcia (cōn·trō·mâr'châ) *f* reverse *(auto)*
controproducente (kōn·trō·prō·dū·chān'tā) *a* self-defeating
controrivoluzione (kōn·trō·rē·vō·lū·tsyō'nā) *f* counterrevolution
controversia (kōn·trō·ver'syâ) *f* controversy
contumacia (kōn·tū·mâ'châ) *f* default
contumelia (kōn·tū·me'lyâ) *f* contumely, outrage, insult
conturbante (kōn·tūr·bân'tā) *a* glamorous; disturbing
conturbare (kōn·tūr·bâ'rā) *vt* to disturb; to upset
contusione (kōn·tū·zyō'nā) *f* bruise
contuttochè (kōn·tūt·tō·kā') *conj* although, though, despite the fact that
contuttociò (kōn·tūt·tō·chō') *adv* however, nevertheless
convalescente (kōn·vâ·lā·shān'tā) *m&f* convalescent
convalescenza (kōn·vâ·lā·shān'tsâ) *f* recovery, convalescence
convalescenziario (kōn·vâ·lā·shān·tsyâ'ryō) *m* convalescent home, sanitarium
convalidare (kōn·vâ·lē·dâ'rā) *vt* to validate; to prove
convegno (kōn·vā'nyō) *m* meeting, convention
convenevoli (kōn·vā·ne'vō·lē) *mpl* amenities, pleasantries
conveniente (kōn·vā·nyān'tā) *a* convenient; appropriate; profitable
convenienza (kōn·vā·nyān'tsâ) *f* convenience
convenire * (kōn·vā·nē'rā) *vi* to agree; to be proper
convento (kōn·vān'tō) *m* monastery; convent
convenuto (kōn·vā·nū'tō) *m* defendant
convenzione (kōn·vān·tsyō'nā) *f* convention
convergere * (kōn·ver'jā·rā) *vi* to converge
conversare (kōn·vār·sâ'rā) *vi* to converse
conversazione (kōn·vār·sâ·tsyō'nā) *f* conversation
conversione (kōn·vār·syō'nā) *f* conversion

converso (kōn·vār'sō) *m* lay brother
convertire (kōn·vār·tē'rā) *vt* to convert
convertito (kōn·vār·tē'tō) *m* convert
convesso (kōn·vās'sō) *a* convex
convincente (kōn·vēn·chān'tā) *a* convincing
convincere * (kōn·vēn'chā·rā) *vt* to convince; to satisfy
convinzione (kōn·vēn·tsyō'nā) *f* conviction
convitare (kōn·vē·tâ'rā) *vt* to invite
convitato (kōn·vē·tâ'tō) *m* guest; — *a* invited
convito (kōn·vē'tō) *m* feast; banquet
convitto (kōn·vēt'tō) *m* academy, boarding school, private school; **–re** (kōn·vēt·tō'rā) *m* student at a boarding school
convivente (kōn·vē·vān'tā) *m* cohabitant
convivenza (kōn·vē·vān'tsâ) *f* cohabitation
convivere * (kōn·vē'vā·rā) *vi* to cohabit
convocare (kōn·vō·kâ'rā) *vt* to convoke; to bring into play
convogliare (kōn·vō·lyâ'rā) *vt* to convey; to convoy
convoglio (kōn·vô'lyō) *m* convoy
convulsione (kōn·vūl·syō'nā) *f* convulsion
cooperare (kō·ō·pā·râ'rā) *vi* to cooperate
cooperativa (kō·ō·pā·râ·tē'vâ) *f* cooperative
coordinare (kō·ōr·dē·nâ'rā) *vt* to coordinate
copale (kō·pâ'lā) *f* patent leather; lacquer
coperchio (kō·per'kyō) *m* top, lid
coperta (kō·pār'tâ) *f* blanket; *(naut)* deck; **sopra** — on deck
copertina (kō·pār·tē'nâ) *f* book jacket, dust jacket
coperto (kō·pār'tō) *m* cover; cover charge; **–ne** (kō·pār·tō'nā) *m* tire; tarpaulin
copertura (kō·pār·tū'râ) *f* coverage
copia (kô'pyâ) *f* copy; print; **–lettere** (kō·pyâ·let'tā·rā) *f* automatic typewriting unit; **–re** (kō·pyâ'rā) *vt* to copy; **–tivo** (kō·pyâ·tē'vō) *a* copying; **–tore** (kō·pyâ·tō'rā) *m* imitator
copione (kō·pyō'nā) *m* script
copiosità (kō·pyō·zē·tâ') *f* plentifulness, abundance, copiousness
copioso (kō·pyō'zō) *a* plentiful, abundant, copious
copista (kō·pē'stâ) *m* copyist
copisteria (kō·pē·stā·rē'â) *f* letter service
coppa (kōp'pâ) *f* cup; bowl
coppia (kôp'pyâ) *f* couple, pair
copribusto (kō·prē·bū'stō) *m* bodice
copricapo (kō·prē·kâ'pō) *m* headgear
coprifuoco (kō·prē·fwō'kō) *m* curfew
copriletto (kō·prē·lāt'tō) *m* bedspread
coprire * (kō·prē'rā) *vt* to cover
copula (kô'pū·lâ) *f* conjunction; copulation; *(gram)* copula, conjunction; **–re** (kō·pū·lâ'rā) *vt* to copulate
coraggio (kō·râj'jō) *m* courage; **–so** (kō·râj·jō'zō) *a* brave
corale (kō·râ'lā) *a* choral
corallo (kō·râl'lō) *m* coral
coramella (kō·râ·māl'lâ) *f* razor strop
coratella (kō·râ·tāl'lâ) *f* pluck
corazza (kō·râ'tsâ) *f* armor; **–ta** (kō·râ·tsâ'tâ) *f* battleship
corazziere (kō·râ·tsyā'rā) *m (mil)* cuirassier
corbellare (kōr·bāl·lâ'rā) *vt* to make fun of; to tease
corbelleria (kōr·bāl·lā·rē'â) *f* nonsense
corbello (kōr·bāl'lō) *m* basket
corbezzoli! (kōr·be'tsō·lē) *interj* gosh!
corda (kōr'dâ) *f* rope; string
cordiale (kōr·dyâ'lā) *a&m* cordial
cordialità (kōr·dyâ·lē·tâ') *f* cordiality; regards
cordicella (kōr·dē·chāl'lâ) *f* string, lace
cordigliera (kōr·dē·lyā'râ) *f (geog)* cordillera
cordoglio (kōr·dô'lyō) *m* sorrow
cordoncino (kōr·dōn·chē'nō) *m* string, lace
cordone (kōr·dō'nā) *m* cordon
coreografia (kō·rā·ō·grâ·fē'â) *f* choreography
coreografo (kō·rā·ô'grâ·fō) *m* choreographer
coriaceo (kō·ryâ'chā·ō) *a* leathery; *(fig)* tough
coriandoli (kō·ryân'dō·lē) *mpl* confetti
coricare (kō·rē·kâ'rā) *vt* to put to bed
coricarsi (kō·rē·kâr'sē) *vr* to go to bed
corifeo (kō·rē·fā'ō) *m* coryphaeus
corindone (kō·rēn·dō'nā) *m (min)* corundum
corinzio (kō·rēn'tsyō) *a* Corinthian
corista (kō·rē'stâ) *m* chorister; diapason
corna (kōr'nâ) *fpl* horns
cornacchia (kōr·nâk'kyâ) *f* crow
cornamusa (kōr·nâ·mū'zâ) *f* bagpipe
cornata (kōr·nâ'tâ) *f* butt, ram
cornea (kôr'nā·â) *f (anat)* cornea
corneo (kôr'nā·ō) *a* horny, corneous
cornetta (kōr·nāt'tâ) *f (mus)* cornet
cornice (kōr·nē'chā) *f* frame
cornicione (kōr·nē·chō'nā) *m* eaves, cornice; entablature
corniolo (kōr·nyō'lō) *m (bot)* dogwood
corno (kōr'nō) *m* horn
cornucopia (kōr·nū·kô'pyâ) *f* horn of plenty, cornucopia
cornuto (kōr·nū'tō) *a* horned; — *m* cuckold
coro (kō'rō) *m* choir, chorus
corollario (kō·rōl·lâ'ryō) *m* corollary
corona (kō·rō'nâ) *f* crown
coronario (kō·rō·nâ'ryō) *a* coronary
corpacciuto (kōr·pâ·chū'tō) *a* stout, fleshy
corpo (kōr'pō) *m* body, undershirt; **–rale** (kōr·pō·râ'lā) *a* bodily, corporeal; **–ralmente** (kōr·pō·râl·mān'tā) *adv* bodily, corporally; **–ratura** (kōr·pō·râ·tū'râ) *f* physique, build; **–razione** (kōr·pō·râ·tsyō'nā) *f* guild; corporation
corpulento (kōr·pū·lān'tō) *a* stout, corpulent
corpuscolo (kōr·pū'skō·lō) *m* corpuscle
corredare (kōr·rā·dâ'rā) *vt* to equip, provide, furnish
corredo (kōr·rā'dō) *m* trousseau; outfit
correggia (kōr·rej'jâ) *f* girdle; leather

belt
correggere (kōr·rej'jā·rā) *vt* to correct
correlativo (kōr·rā·lâ·tē'vō) *a* correlative
corrente (kōr·rān'tā) *f* stream; current; — *a* running; — **alternata** alternating current; — **continua** direct current; **al** — up-to-date
correo (kōr·rā'ō) *m* accomplice
correre * (kôr'rā·rā) *vi* to run
corretto (kōr·rāt'tō) *a* correct; **–re** (kōr·rāt·tō'rā) *m* corrector; *(print)* proofreader
correzionale (kōr·rā·tsyō·nâ'lā) *m* reformatory
correzione (kōr·rā·tsyō'nā) *f* correction
corridoio (kōr·rē·dô'yō) *m* corridor
corridore (kōr·rē·dō'rā) *m* runner
corriera (kōr·ryā'râ) *f* intercity bus
corriere (kōr·ryā'rā) *m* messenger, courier; mail
corrispettivo (kōr·rē·spāt·tē'vō) *m* recompense; — *a* corresponding
corrispondente (kōr·rē·spōn·dān'tā) *m* correspondent
corrispondenza (kōr·rē·spōn·dān'tsâ) *f* correspondence
corrispondere * (kōr·rē·spôn'dā·rā) *vi* to correspond
corrodere * (kōr·rô'dā·rā) *vt* to corrode; to waste
corrompere * (kôr·rôm'pā·rā) *vt* to bribe, corrupt
corrosione (kōr·rō·zyō'nā) *f* corrosion
corrosivo (kōr·rō·zē'vō) *a* corrosive
corroso (kōr·rō'zō) *a* corroded
corrotto (kōr·rōt'tō) *a* corrupted
corrugare (kōr·rū·gâ'rā) *vt* to corrugate
corruzione (kōr·rū·tsyō'nā) *f* corruption
corsa (kōr'sâ) *f* race; fare; stroke
corsaro (kōr·sâ'rō) *m* pirate, corsair
corseggiare (kōr·sāj·jâ'rā) *vi* to pirate
corsetto (kōr·sāt'tō) *m* corset
corsia (kōr·sē'â) *f* lane; ward
corsivo (kōr·sē'vō) *m* italics
corso (kōr'sō) *m* course; main street; Corsican
corte (kōr'tā) *f* court; courtship; courtyard; **–ggiare** (kōr·tāj·jâ'rā) *vt* to court; **–ggiatore** (kōr·tāj·jâ·tō'rā) *m* suitor; wooer
corteo (kōr·tā'ō) *m* parade, procession
cortese (kōr·tā'zā) *a* polite, courteous; **–mente** (kōr·tā·zā·mān'tā) *adv* courteously, politely, kindly
cortesia (kōr·tā·zē'â) *f* politeness, courtesy
cortigiana (kōr·tē·jâ'nâ) *f* courtesan
cortigiano (kōr·tē·jâ'nō) *m* courtier; *(fig)* flatterer
cortile (kōr·tē'lā) *m* courtyard
cortina (kōr·tē'nâ) *f* curtain; — **di acciaio** iron curtain; — **di fumo** smoke screen; **–ggio** (kōr·tē·nâj'jō) *m* curtains, drapes; *(mil)* barrage
corto (kōr'tō) *a* short; — **circuito** short circuit; — **di vista** shortsighted; **–metraggio** (kōr·tō·mā·trâj'jō) *m* short subject *(movies)*
corvetta (kōr·vāt'tâ) *f (naut)* corvette
corvino (kōr·vē'nō) *a* crowlike; raven, jet black, corvine
corvo (kōr'vō) *m* crow
cosa (kō'zâ) *f* thing; matter; **che —?** what?
coscia (kô'shâ) *f* thigh
coscienza (kō·shān'tsâ) *f* conscience; consciousness
coscio (kô'shō), **cosciotto** (kô·shōt'tō) *m* leg; — **d'agnello** leg of lamb
coscritto (kō·skrēt'tō) *m* draftee
coscrizione (kō·skrē·tsyō'nā) *f (mil)* draft
così (kō·zē') *adv* thus, so, in this way
cosmetico (kō·zme'tē·kō) *m&a* cosmetic
cosmico (kô'zmē·kō) *a* cosmic
cosmo (kō'zmō) *m* cosmos; **–grafia** (kō·zmō·grâ·fē'â) *f* cosmography; **–logia** (kō·zmō·lō·jē'â) *f* cosmology; **–polita** (kō·zmō·pō·lē'tâ) *a&m* cosmopolitan
cospargere * (kō·spâr'jā·rā) *vt* to sprinkle, to bedew; to strew
cospetto (kō·spāt'tō) *m* view; presence; sight
cospicuo (kō·spē'kwō) *a* conspicuous; in evidence
cospirare (kō·spē·râ'rā) *vi* to plot, conspire
cospiratore (kō·spē·râ·tō'rā) *m* conspirator
cospirazione (kō·spē·râ·tsyō'nā) *f* plot, conspiracy
costa (kō'stâ) *f* coast; rib; slope; side
costà (kō·stâ') *adv* over there, there
costanza (kō·stân'tsâ) *f* constancy; faithfulness
costare (kō·stâ'rā) *vi* to cost
costata (kō·stâ'tâ) *f* chop *(meat)*
costatare (kō·stâ·tâ'rā) *vt* to ascertain
costei (kō·stā'ē) *pron* she, that girl, that woman
costellazione (kō·stāl·lâ·tsyō'nā) *f* constellation
costernare (kō·stār·nâ'rā) *vt* to consternate; to upset
costernarsi (kō·stār·nâr'sē) *vi* to be dismayed
costernazione (kō·stār·nâ·tsyō'nā) *f* dismay
costiero (kō·styā'rō) *a* coastal
costipazione (kō·stē·pâ·tsyō'nā) *f* constipation; cold
costituire (kō·stē·twē'rā) *vt* to constitute; to set up
costituirsi (kō·stē·twēr'sē) *vr* to give oneself up, surrender; to be composed of
costituzione (kō·stē·tū·tsyō'nā) *f* constitution
costo (kō'stō) *m* cost
costola (kô'stō·lâ) *f* rib
costoletta (kō·stō·lāt'tâ) *f* cutlet, chop
costoro (kō·stō'rō) *pron* these; those
costoso (kō·stō'zō) *a* costly, expensive
costringere * (kō·strēn'jā·rā) *vt* to compel, make
costruire (kō·strūē'rā) *vt* to construct
costruttore ((kō·strūt·tō'rā) *m* builder
costruzione (kō·strū·tsyō'nā) *f* construction
costui (kō·stū'ē) *pron* he, that fellow, that man

costumatezza (kō·stū·mâ·tā'tsâ) *f* politeness
costumato (kō·stū·mâ'tō) *a* well-bred
costume (kō·stū'mā) *m* custom; costume; habit
costumista (kō·stū·mē'stâ) *m* (*theat*) costumer
costura (kō·stū'râ) *f* seam
cotale (kō·tâ'lā) *pron* such a one, such
cotanto (kō·tân'tō) *a* as much; — *adv* so much
cote (kō'tā) *f* hone
cotechino (kō·tā·kē'nō) *m* pork sausage
cotenna (kō·tān'nâ) *f* rind; pigskin
cotesto (kō·tā'stō), **codesto** (kō·dā'stō) *a* that: — *pron* that one by you
cotogna (kō·tō'nyâ) *f* quince; **–ta** (kō·tō·nyâ'tâ) *f* quince jam
cotone (kō·tō'nā) *m* cotton; — **idrofilo** absorbent cotton
cotoniere (kō·tō·nyā'rā) *m* cotton merchant
cotonificio (kō·tō·nē·fē'chō) *m* cotton mill
cotonina (kō·tō·nē'nâ) *f* calico
cottimo (kôt'tē·mō) *m* piecework
cotto (kōt'tō) *a* cooked; **ben** — well done; **poco** — rare
cottura (kōt·tū'râ) *f* cooking
cova (kō'vâ) *f* brooding, brood; **–re** (kō·vâ'rā) *vt* to hatch, brood; **–ta** (kō·vâ'tâ) *f* covey, brood; hatch
covo (kō'vō) *m* hole, den; lair
covone (kō·vō'nā) *m* sheaf
cozza (kō'tsâ) *f* mussel
cozzare (kō·tsâ'rā) *vt&i* to bump, bump into
cozzo (kō'tsō) *m* shock; collision; butt; clash; (*fig*) conflict, contrast
crac (krâk) *m* (*com*) crash, failure
crampo (krâm'pō) *m* cramp
cranio (krâ'nyō) *m* skull
crapula (krâ'pū·lâ) *f* intemperance in food and drink
crapulone (krâ·pū·lō'nā) *m* reveller; guzzler; debauchee
crasso (krâs'sō) *a* coarse, crass, gross; **ignoranza crassa** gross ignorance
cratere (krâ·tā'rā) *m* crater
crauti (krâ'ū·tē) *mpl* sauerkraut
cravatta (krâ·vât'tâ) *f* necktie
creanza (krā·ân'tsâ) *f* education; breeding; politeness
creare (krā·â'rā) *vt* to create; to bring up
creatore (krā·â·tō'rā) *m* creator
creatura (krā·â·tū'râ) *f* creature
creazione (krā·â·tsyō'nā) *f* creation
credente (krā·dān'tā) *m&f* believer
credenza (krā·dān'tsâ) *f* belief; cupboard; credit
credere (kre'dā·rā) *vi&t* to believe; to think
credibile (krā·dē'bē·lā) *a* credible
credibilità (krā·dē·bē·lē·tâ') *f* credibility
credito (kre'dē·tō) *m* credit; **–re** (krā·dē·tō'rā) *m* creditor
credo (krā'dō) *m* creed, belief
credulo (kre'dū·lō) *a* gullible
crema (krā'mâ) *f* cream; — **da scarpe** shoe polish; — **per la pelle** cold cream
cremagliera (krā·mâ·lyā'râ) *f* rack; **ferrovia a** — cog railway
crematoio (krā·mâ·tô'yō) *m* crematory
cremazione (krā·mâ·tsyō'nā) *f* cremation
cremeria (krā·mā·rē'â) *f* icecream parlor
cremisi (kre'mē·zē) *m* crimson
Cremlino (krām·lē'nō) *m* Kremlin
cremore (krā·mō'rā) *m* essence; — **tartaro** cream of tartar
crepa (krā'pâ) *f* crack
crepare (krā·pâ'rā) *vi* (*coll*) to die; to split open, crack open
crepitare (krā·pē·tâ'rā) *vi* to crackle
crepuscolo (krā·pū'skō·lō) *m* twilight
crescere * (kre'shā·rā) *vt* to grow
crescione (krā·shō'nā) *m* watercress
cresima (kre'zē·mâ) *f* (*eccl*) confirmation; **–re** (krā·zē·mâ'rā) *vt* to confirm
crespo (krā'spō) *m* crepe; — *a* curly, crisp, woolly
cresta (krā'stâ) *f* crest; comb of a cock
creta (krā'tâ) *f* clay; **–ceo** (krā·tâ'chā·ō) *a* chalky, claylike
cretino (krā·tē'nō) *m* moron, idiot
cricco (krēk'kō) *m* jack
criminale (krē·mē·nâ'lā) *m* criminal
criminalista (krē·mē·nâ·lē'stâ) *m* criminal lawyer; criminologist
criminalità (krē·mē·ná·lē·tâ') *f* criminality
crimine (krē'mē·nā) *m* crime
crine (krē'nā) *m* horsehair
criniera (krē·nyā'râ) *f* mane
cripta (krēp'tâ) *f* crypt
crisi (krē'zē) *f* crisis
cristalleria (krē·stâl·lā·rē'â) *f* crystalware
cristallizzare (krē·stâl·lē·dzâ'rā) *vt* to crystallize
cristallizzato (krē·stâl·lē·dzâ'tō) *a* crystallized
cristallizzazione (krē·stâl·lē·dzâ·tsyō'nā) *f* crystallization
cristallo (krē·stâl'lō) *m* crystal, glass
cristianesimo (krē·styâ·ne'zē·mō) *m* Christianity
cristiano (krē·styâ'nō) *m* Christian
Cristo (krē'stō) *m* Christ
criterio (krē·te'ryō) *m* criterion
critica (krē'tē·kâ) *f* criticism; **–re** (krē·tē·kâ'rā) *vt* to criticize, find fault with
critico (krē'tē·kō) *a* critical; — *m* critic
crivellare (krē·vāl·lâ'rā) *vt* to riddle; to sift
crivello (krē·vāl'lō) *m* riddle; sieve
croccante (krōk·kân'tā) *a* crisp
crocchetta (krōk·kāt'tâ) *f* croquette
croce (krō'chā) *f* cross; **–rossina** (krō·chā·rōs·sē'nâ) *f* Red Cross nurse; **–via** (krō·chā·vē'â) *f* intersection
crociata (krō·châ'tâ) *f* crusade
crociera (krō·chā'râ) *f* cruise
crocifiggere * (krō·chē·fēj'jā·rā) *vt* to crucify
crocifissione (krō·chē·fēs·syō'nā) *f* crucifixion
crocifisso (krō·chē·fēs'sō) *m* crucifix
crogiuolo (krō·jwō'lō) *m* melting pot
crollare (krōl·lâ'rā) *vi* to fall in, collapse;

— *vt* to shrug, shake
crollo (krōl'lō) *m* crash, collapse
cromatico (krō·mâ'tē·kō) *a* chromatic
cromo (krō'mō) *m* chromium
cromotelevisore (krō·mō·tā·lā·vē·zō'rā) *m* color television set
cronaca (krô'nâ·kâ) *f* news; chronicle
cronico (krô'nē·kō) *a* chronic
cronista (krō·nē'stâ) *m* reporter
cronologico (krō·nō·lô'jē·kō) *a* chronological
cronometrista (krō·nō·mā·trē'stâ) *m* timekeeper
cronometro (krō·nô'mā·trō) *m* stop watch
crosta (krō'stâ) *f* crust; **–ceo** (krō·stâ'chā·ō) *m* shellfish; **–ta** (krō·stâ'tâ) *f* pie
crostino (krō·stē'nō) *m* toast; canapé
crucciare (krū·châ'rā) *vt* to irritate; to worry
crucciarsi (krū·châr'sē) *vr* to get irritated; to get vexed
cruccio (krū'chō) *m* grief; anger, vexation; worry
cruciale (krū·châ'lā) *a* crucial; critical; decisive
cruciare (krū·châ'rā) *vt* to torment, grieve
cruciverba (krū·chē·vār'bâ) *m* crossword puzzle
crudele (krū·dā'lā) *a* cruel
crudeltà (krū·dāl·tâ') *f* cruelty
crudezza (krū·dā'tsâ) *f* rawness; crudeness; coarseness; (*fig*) rudeness
crudo (krū'dō) *a* raw; cruel
cruento (krūān'tō) *a* bloody; dreadful
crumiro (krū·mē'rō) *m* scab; strikebreaker
cruna (krū'nâ) *f* eye of a needle
crusca (krū'skâ) *f* bran
cruscotto (krū·skōt'tō) *m* dashboard
cubico (kū'bē·kō) *a* cubic
cubismo (kū·bē'zmō) *m* cubism
cubito (kū'bē·tō) *m* elbow; cubit (*measure*)
cubo (kū'bō) *m* cube
cuccagna (kūk·kâ'nyâ) *f* land of plenty; **albero di** — greased pole
cuccetta (kū·chāt'tâ) *f* berth
cucchiaiata (kūk·kyâ·yâ'tâ) *f* spoonful
cucchiaino (kūk·kyâ·ē'nō) *m* teaspoon
cucchiaio (kūk·kyâ'yō) *m* spoon; — **da tavola** tablespoon
cuccia (kū'châ) *f* doghouse; dog bed
cucciolo (kū·chō'lō) *m* puppy
cucco (kūk'kō) *m* pet, favorite; **vecchio** — stupid old man
cuccù (kū·kū'), **cuculo** (kū'kū·lō) *m* cuckoo
cuccuma (kūk'kū·mâ) *f* kettle
cucina (kū·chē'nâ) *f* kitchen; range; cuisine; **libro di** — cookbook; **–re** (kū·chē·nâ'rā) *vt&i* to cook
cuciniere (kū·chē·nyā'rā) *m* cook
cucinino (kū·chē·nē'nō) *m* kitchenette
cucire (kū·chē'rā) *vt* to sew; **macchina da cucire** sewing machine
cucitura (kū·chē·tū'râ) *f* sewing
cuffia (kūf'fyâ) *f* baby cap; hood; bathing cap; headphone
cugina (kū·jē'nâ) *f*, **cugino** (kū·jē'nō) *m* cousin
cui (kū'ē) *pron* whom, to whom
culatta (kū·lât'tâ) *f* breech (*gun barrel*); rump, seat
culla (kūl'lâ) *f* cradle; **–re** (kūl·lâ'rā) *vt* to rock, lull
culo (kū'lō) *m* bottom (*bottle*); arse; rump
culto (kūl'tō) *m* worship
cultura (kūl·tū'râ) *f* culture
cumulativo (kū·mū·lâ·tē'vō) *a* cumulative
cumulo (kū'mū·lō) *m* heap
cuna (kū'nâ) *f* cradle
cuneo (kū'nā·ō) *m* wedge
cunetta (kū·nāt'tâ) *f* ditch
cuoca (kwō'kâ) *f* woman cook
cuocere * (kwô'chā·rā) *vt* to cook
cuoco (kwō'kō) *m* cook; **capo** — chef
cuoio (kwô'yō) *m* leather
cuore (kwō'rā) *m* heart
cupidigia (kū·pē·dē'jâ) *f* greed
cupido (kū'pē·dō) *a* greedy, covetous, eager
cupo (kū'pō) *a* dark; deep
cupola (kū'pō·lâ) *f* cupola, dome
cupone (kū·pō'nā) *m* coupon
cura (kū'râ) *f* care, treatment; **–re** (kū·râ'rā) *vt* to treat; to edit; **–to** (kū·râ'tō) *m* curate; pastor; **–to** *a* cured; **–tore** (kū·râ·tō'rā) *m* (*law*) receiver
curia (kū'ryâ) *f* (*eccl*) curia; — **vescovile** bishop's court
curiosare (kū·ryō·zâ'rā) *vi* to pry, look around
curiosità (kū·ryō·zē·tâ') *f* curiosity; place of interest, tourist attraction
curioso (kū·ryō'zō) *a* curious
curva (kūr'vâ) *f* curve; — **e controcurva** double curve; — **stretta** sharp turn; **–re** (kūr·vâ'rā) *vt* to curve; to bend; **–rsi** (kūr·vâr'sē) *vr* to stoop, bow down **–tura** (kūr·vâ·tū'râ) *f* bending, curvature
curvo (kūr'vō) *a* curved, stooped
cuscinetto (kū·shē·nāt'tō) *m* pincushion; **stato** — buffer state; — **a sfere** ball bearing
cuscino (kū·shē'nō) *m* pillow
cuspide (kū'spē·dā) *f* point; peak
custode (kū·stō'dā) *m&f* caretaker
custodia (kū·stô'dyâ) *f* care; custody; keeping
custodire (kū·stō·dē'rā) *vt* to keep; to take care of, look after
cutaneo (kū·tâ'nā·ō) *a* cutaneous, of the skin
cute (kū'tā) *f* skin (*human*)
cuticola (kū·tē'kō·lâ) *f* cuticle

D

da (dâ) *prep* from, by, at; as
dabbenaggine (dâb·bā·nâj'jē·nā) *f* simplicity; simplemindedness
dabbene (dâb·bā'nā) *a* naive, simple

daccapo (dâk·kâ'pō) *adv* once more, over again
dacchè (dâk·kā') *conj* since
dadi (dâ'dē) *mpl* dice
dado (dâ'dō) *m* die; cube; nut
daga (dâ'gâ) *f* dagger
dagherrotipo (dâ·gār·rô'tē·pō) *m* daguerrotype
dagli (dâ'lyē), **dai** (dâ'ē), **dalla** (dâl'lâ), **dalle** (dâl'lā), **dallo** (dâl'lō) *prep* from the; by the; at the
daino (dâ·ē'nō) *m* deer, buck; **pelle di —** buckskin
dalia (dâ'lyâ) *f* dahlia
daltonico (dâl·tô'nē·kō) *a* color-blind
daltonismo (dâl·tō·nē'zmō) *m* color blindness, daltonism
dama (dâ'mâ) *f* lady; checkers; **— di compagnia** lady-in-waiting
damascare (dâ·mâ·skâ'rā) *vt* to damask
damascato (dâ·mâ·skâ'tō) *a* damasked
damascatura (dâ·mâ·skâ·tū'râ) *f* damasking
damaschinare (dâ·mâ·skē·nâ'rā) *vt* to damascene
damasco (dâ·mâ'skō) *m* damask
damerino (dâ·mā·rē'nō) *m* fop, dandy
damigella (dâ·mē·jāl'lâ) *f* young maiden; **— d'onore** bridesmaid
damigiana (dâ·mē·jâ'nâ) *f* demijohn
damma (dâm'mâ) *f* doe, deer
danaro (dâ·nâ'rō) *m* money; **–so** (dâ·nâ·rō'zō) *a* moneyed, rich, well-to-do
danese (dâ·nā'zā) *a* Danish
Danimarca (dâ·nē·mâr'kâ) *f* Denmark
dannabile (dân·nâ'bē·lā) *a* blameworthy; damnable
dannare (dân·nâ'rā) *vt* to condemn, damn; to harrass; to lay the blame on
dannato (dân·nâ'tō) *a* damned; blamed
dannazione (dân·nâ·tsyō'nā) *f* damnation
danneggiare (dân·nāj·jâ'rā) *vt* to damage
danneggiato (dân·nāj·jâ'tō) *a* damaged; **—** *m* victim
danno (dân'nō) *m* damage; **–so** (dân·nō'zō) *a* harmful
dante (dân'tā) *m* buck; **pelle di —** buckskin
dantesco (dân·tā'skō) *a* Dantesque, in the style of Dante
danza (dân'tsâ) *f* dance; **–nte** (dân·tsân'tā) *a* dancing
dappertutto (dâp·pār·tūt'tō) *adv* everywhere
dappocaggine (dâp·pō·kâj'jē·nā) *f* worthlessness; ineptness
dappoco (dâp·pō'kō) *a* worthless; inept
dappresso (dâp·prās'sō) *adv* close by, near, near at hand
dapprima (dâp·prē'mâ) *adv* first, at first
dardeggiare (dâr·dāj·jâ'rā) *vt* to dart; to shoot out
dardo (dâr'dō) *m* arrow; dart
dare * (dâ'rā) *vt* to give; **—** *vi* to look on; **—** *m* (*com*) debit; **— e avere** debits and credits; **passare al —** to transfer to the debit side of the ledger
darsena (dâr'sā·nâ) *f* (*naut*) basin, wet dock
darsi * (dâr'sē) *vr* to be a devotee of; to surrender; to addict oneself; **— agli affari** to go into business; **— all'alcool** to become an alcoholic; **— alla fuga** to flee; **darsela a gambe** to take to one's heels; **— al mare** to sail; **— d'attorno, — da fare** to work painstakingly; **— la briga di** to go to the trouble of; **— il caso** to be necessary; **— pace** to become resigned; **— per vinto** to give in; **può —** maybe, perhaps
data (dâ'tâ) *f* date; **–re** (dâ·tâ'rā) *vt* to date
datario (dâ·tâ'ryō) *m* (*eccl*) datary
dati (dâ'tē) *mpl* data, facts
dativo (dâ·tē'vō) *m* (*gram*) dative
dato (dâ'tō) *m* element; factor; indication; hint; **—** *a* established; given; indicated; devoted to; addicted; **— che** since, seeing that, in view of the fact that
datore (dâ·tō'rā) *m* giver; **— di lavoro** boss; patron
dattero (dât'tā·rō) *m* date; date palm
dattilografare (dât·tē·lō·grâ·fâ'rā) *vt* to type, typewrite
dattilografia (dât·tē·lō·grâ·fē'â) *f* typing
dattilografo (dât·tē·lô'grâ·fō) *m*, **dattilografa** (dât·tē·lô'grâ·fâ) *f* typist
dattiloscopia (dât·tē·lō·skō·pē'â) *f* verification of finger prints
dattiloscritto (dât·tē·lō·skrēt'tō) *a* typed, typewritten
dattorno (dât·tōr'nō) *adv* around; **levarsi —** to get rid of; **qui —** around here, in this area
davanti (dâ·vân'tē) *adv* in front, before
davanzale (dâ·vân·tsâ'lā) *m* window sill
davvero (dâv·vā'rō) *adv* really, indeed, in all earnestness
daziario (dâ·tsyâ'ryō) *a* concerning customs, customs; **cinta daziaria** series of toll gates; customs; **tariffa daziaria** customs duty
daziere (dâ·tsyā'rā) *m* customs official
dazio (dâ'tsyō) *m* duty, excise, tax
dea (dā'â) *f* goddess
deambulare (dā·âm·bū·lâ'rā) *vi* to walk about, stroll around
debellamento (dā·bāl·lâ·mān'tō) *m* defeat, overthrow
debellare (dā·bāl·lâ'rā) *vt* to defeat; to subdue; to conquer
debellatore (dā·bāl·lâ·tō'rā) *m* conqueror
debilitante (dā·bē·lē·tân'tā) *a* weakening, debilitating
debilitare (dā·bē·lē·tâ'rā) *vt* to weaken
debilitazione (dā·bē·lē·tâ·tsyō'nā) *f* weakening, debilitation
debitamente (dā·bē·tâ·mān'tā) *adv* properly, correctly
debito (de'bē·tō) *m* debt; **— ipotecario** mortgage; **essere pieno di debiti** to be up to one's neck in debts; **farsi — di** to make a special point of; **mettere a —, scrivere a —** to debit; **uscire di —** to pay one's debts; **—** *a* proper, due; **a tempo —** in good time; **— modo** proper way; **–re** (dā·bē·tō'rā) *m* debtor
debole (de'bō'lā) *a* weak; **–zza** (dā·bō'lā'-

tsâ) *f* weakness
deboscíato (dā·bō·shâ'tō) *a* debauched
debraiare (dā·brâ·yâ'rā) *vt* (*auto*) to declutch, release the clutch of
debuttante (dā·būt·tân'tā) *m&f* (*theat*) actor or actress making his first stage appearance
debuttare (dā·būt·tâ'rā) *vi* to make one's debut
debutto (dā·būt'tō) *m* debut
decade (de'kâ·dā) *f* decade; group of ten
decadente (dā·kâ·dān'tā) *a* decadent, declining
decadenza (dā·kâ·dān'tsâ) *f* decline, decadence
decadere * (dā·kâ·dā'rā) *vi* to decay; — **da una carica** to end a term in office; to lose one's office
decaduto (dā·kâ·dū'tō) *a* deposed; declining; impoverished
decaedro (dā·kâ·ā'drō) *m* (*geom*) decahedron
decagono (dā·kâ'gō·nō) *m* (*geom*) decagon
decagrammo (dā·kâ·grâm'mō) *m* decagram
decalcare (dā·kâl·kâ'rā) *vt* to trace, make a tracing of
decalco (dā·kâl'kō) *m* tracing; **–mania** (dā·kâl·kō·mâ·nē'â) *f* decalcomania, transfer
decalitro (dā·kâ'lē·trō) *m* ten liters
decalogo (dā·kâ'lō·gō) *m* decalogue
decampare (dā·kâm·pâ'rā) *vi* to decamp
decano (dā·kâ'nō) *m* dean
decantare (dā·kân·tâ'rā) *vt* to extol; to decant (*alcohol*)
decantazione (dā·kân·tâ·tsyō'nā) *f* decanting; water purification
decapitare (dā·kâ·pē·tâ'rā) *vt* to behead
decapitazione (dā·kâ·pē·tâ·tsyō'nā) *f* beheading, decapitation
decappotabile (dā·kâp·pōt·tâ'bē·lā) *a* convertible
decarburare (dā·kâr·bū·râ'rā) *vt* to decarbonize
decation (dā·kât·lōn') *m* decathlon
decedere (dā·che'dā·rā) *vi* to die, pass on
deceduto (dā·chā·dū'tō) *a* dead, passed on
decennale (dā·chān·nâ'lā) *m* decennium
decenne (dā·chān'nā) *a* decennial, ten years old
decennio (dā·chen'nyō) *m* decade
decente (dā·chān'tā) *a* proper, decent
decentrare (dā·chān·trâ'rā) *vt* to decentralize
decenza (dā·chān'tsâ) *f* decency
decesso (dā·chās'sō) *m* death, demise
decidere * (dā·chē'dā·rā) *vt* to decide
decidersi * (dā·chē'dār·sē) *vr* to arrive at a decision, make up one's mind
deciduo (dā·chē'dwō) *a* deciduous
decifrabile (dā·chē·frâ'bē·lā) *a* decipherable
decifrare (dā·chē·frâ'rā) *vt* to decode
decifrazione (dā·chē·frâ·tsyō'nā) *f* deciphering; decoding; explanation
decima (de'chē·mâ) *f* tithe; **–le** (dā·chē·mâ'lā) *a* decimal; **–re** (dā·chē·mâ'rā) *vt* to decimate, ravage
decimazione (dā·chē·mâ·tsyō'nā) *f* decimation
decimetro (dā·chē'mā·trō) *m* decimeter
decimo (de'chē·mō) *m* tithe, tenth part; — *a* tenth; **–primo** (dā·chē·mō·prē'mō) *a* eleventh; **–secondo** (dā·chē·mō·sā·kōn'dō) *a* twelfth; **–terzo** (dā·chē·mō·tār'tsō) *a* thirteenth
decina (dā·chē'nâ) *f* about ten
decisamente (dā·chē·zâ·mān'tā) *adv* positively, definitely, decidedly
decisione (dā·chē·zyō'nā) *f* decision
decisivamente (dā·chē·zē·vâ·mān'tā) *adv* conclusively, finally, decisively
decisivo (dā·chē·zē'vō) *a* conclusive, final, decisive
deciso (dā·chē'zō) *a* decided, resolved, settled
declamare (dā·klâ·mâ'rā) *vt&i* to declaim, orate
declamazione (dā·klâ·mâ·tsyō'nā) *f* declaiming, harangue
declassare (dā·klâs·sâ'rā) *vt* to downgrade
declinare (dā·klē·nâ'rā) *vt&i* to decline
declinazione (dā·klē·nâ·tsyō'nā) *f* declination
declive (dā·klē'vā) *a* sloping, declining
declivio (dā·klē'vyō) *m* declivity, slope, hillside
decollaggio (dā·kōl·lâj'jō), **decollo** (dā·kōl'lō) *m* (*avi*) take-off
decollare (dā·kōl·lâ'rā) *vi* (*avi*) to take off
decolorante (dā·kō·lō·rân'tā) *m* decolorizer; bleach
decolorare (dā·kō·lō·râ'rā) *vt* to bleach; to decolorize
decolorazione (dā·kō·lō·râ·tsyō'nā) *f* bleaching
decomporre * (dā·kōm·pōr'rā) *vt* to take apart; (*math*) to factor; to decay
decomporsi * (dā·kōm·pōr'sē) *vr* to putrefy, become decomposed
decomposizione (dā·kōm·pō·zē·tsyō'nā) *f* putrefaction, decomposition
decomposto (dā·kōm·pō'stō) *a* decomposed, rotten
decompressione (dā·kōm·prās·syō'nā) *f* decompression
decorare (dā·kō·râ'rā) *vt* to decorate
decorativo (dā·kō·râ·tē'vō) *a* decorative
decorato (dā·kō·râ'tō) *a* decorated; — *m* medal winner; **–re** (dā·kō·râ·tō'rā) *m* decorator
decorazione (dā·kō·râ·tsyō'nā) *f* decoration
decoro (dā·kō'rō) *m* decorum; decency; **–samente** (dā·kō·rō·zâ·mān'tā) *adv* decently; decorously; **–so** (dā·kō·rō'zō) *a* proper; decorous
decorrenza (dā·kōr·rān'tsâ) *f* beginning; coming into force; end of a period
decorrere * (dā·kôr'rā·rā) *vi* to go by, elapse; to accrue; **a — da** from, starting with
decorso (dā·kōr'sō) *m* development, course; lapse, period — **d'una malattia** the course of an illness; — *a* elapsed, gone by

decotto (dā·kōt'tō) *m* extract; decoction
decrepito (dā·krē'pē·tō) *a* ailing, decrepit
decrescente (dā·krā·shān'tā) *a* decreasing
decrescere * (dā·kre'shā·rā) *vi* to lessen; to decrease, diminish
decretare (dā·krā·tâ'rā) *vt* to decree; to stipulate
decreto (dā·krā'tō) *m* decree
decuplicare (dā·kū·plē·kâ'rā) *vt* to multiply by ten
decuplicazione (dā·kū·plē·kâ·tsyō'nā) *f* tenfold increase
decuplo (de'kū·plō) *a* ten times larger, multiplied by ten
decurtare (dā·kūr·tâ'rā) *vt* to cut down, curtail
dedalo (de'dâ·lō) *m* labyrinth, maze
dedica (de'dē·kâ) *f* dedication; **–re** (dā·dē·kâ'rā) *vt* to dedicate; **–rsi** (dā·dē·kâr'sē) *vr* to devote oneself, dedicate oneself; **–toria** (dā·dē·kâ·tô'ryâ) *f* dedication; **–torio** (dā·dē·kâ·tô'ryō) *a* dedicatory; **–zione** (dā·dē·kâ·tsyō'nā) *f* dedication, devotion
dedito (de'dē·tō) *a* dedicated; devoted; addicted
dedizione (dā·dē·tsyō'nā) *f* abnegation; submission
dedotto (dā·dōt'tō) *a* deducted; deduced, derived
dedurre * (dā·dūr'rā) *vt* to deduct, deduce, reason
deduttivo (dā·dūt·tē'vō) *a* deductive
deduzione (dā·dū·tsyō'nā) *f* deduction, reasoning
defalcamento (dā·fâl·kâ·mān'tō) *m* defection; default; curtailment
defalcare (dā·fâl·kâ'rā) *vt* to deduct; to curtail
defalcazione (dā·fâl·kâ·tsyō'nā) *f* defalcation; abatement
defecare (dā·fā·kâ'rā) *vt&i* to defecate; to empty *(bowels)*; *(chem)* to purify *(a liquid)*
defecazione (dā·fā·kâ·tsyō'nā) *f* bowel movement, defecation; excrement
defenestrare (dā·fā·nā·strâ'rā) *vt* to oust, turn out
deferente (dā·fā·rān'tā) *a* deferential
deferenza (dā·fā·rān'tsâ) *f* respect, deference; consideration; compliance
deferimento (dā·fā·rē·mān'tō) *m* deferment; regard, deference
deferire (dā·fā·rē'rā) *vt&i* to defer; — **all'autorità** to denounce; to submit for legal action
defezionare (dā·fā·tsyō·nâ'rā) *vi* to defect; — *vt* to betray
defezione (dā·fā·tsyō'nā) *f* defection; betrayal
deficiente (dā·fē·chān'tā) *a* feeble-minded
deficienza (dā·fē·chān'tsâ) *f* lack, insufficience, deficiency
deficit (de'fē·chēt) *m* deficit
definibile (dā·fē·nē'bē·lā) *a* definable
definire (dā·fē·nē'rā) *vt* to define; to limit
definitivamente (dā·fē·nē·tē·vâ·mān'tā) *adv* definitely, absolutely; once and for all
definitivo (dā·fē·nē·tē'vō) *a* conclusive, definitive
definizione (dā·fē·nē·tsyō'nā) *f* definition; limitation
deflazione (dā·flâ·tsyō'nā) *f* deflation
deflettere * (dā·flet'tā·rā) *vi* to deflect
deflettore (dā·flāt·tō'rā) *m (avi)* deflector
deflorare (dā·flō·râ'rā) *vt* to rape, ravish; to deflower
deflorazione (dā·flō·râ·tsyō'nā) *f* rape, violation
deformare (dā·fōr·mâ'rā) *vt* to deform
deformazione (dā·fōr·mâ·tsyō'nā) *f* deformation
deforme (dā·fōr'mā) *a* deformed; ugly
deformità (dā·fōr·mē·tâ') *f* deformity
defraudare (dā·frâū·dâ'rā) *vt* to defraud; to deceive
defraudazione (dā·frâū·dâ·tsyō'nā) *f* deceit, defrauding
defunto (dā·fūn'tō) *a* dead; late
degenerare (dā·jā·nā·râ'rā) *vi* to degenerate
degenerato (dā·jā·nā·râ'tō) *a&m* degenerate
degente (dā·jān'tā) *a* sick in bed; — *m* bed patient
degenza (dā·jān'tsâ) *f* period of illness; hospital stay; **certificato di** — medical certificate of illness
deglutire (dā·glū·tē'rā) *vt* to swallow
deglutizione (dā·glū·tē·tsyō'nā) *f* swallowing
degnamente (dā·nyâ·mān'tā) *adv* properly, worthily; adequately
degnare (dā·nyâ'rā) *vt* to grant, authorize
degnarsi (dā·nyâr·sē) *vr* to deign, see fit
degnazione (dā·nyâ·tsyō'nā) *f* compliance; authorization; condescension; authorization
degno (dā'nyō) *a* worthy; adequate
degradare (dā·grâ·dâ'rā) *vt* to degrade
degradazione (dā·grâ·dâ·tsyō'nā) *f* debasement, degradation
degrassaggio (dā·grâs·sâj'jō) *m* greasing
degustare (dā·gū·stâ'rā) *vt* to taste; to make a sampling of
degustazione (dā·gū·stâ·tsyō'nā) *f* tasting
deificare (dāē·fē·kâ'rā) *vt* to idolize, deify
deificazione (dāē·fē·kâ·tsyō'nā) *f* deification
delatore (dā·lâ·tō'rā) *m* informer
delazione (dā·lâ·tsyō'nā) *f* secret accusal; informing
delebile (dā·le'bē·lā) *a* removable, delible
delega (de'lā·gâ) *f* power of attorney; **–re** (dā·lā·gâ'rā) *vt* to delegate; **–to** (dā·lā·gâ'tō) *m* delegate; director; **–zione** (dā·lā·gâ·tsyō'nā) *f* commission; delegation
delibera (dā·lē'bā·râ) *f* deliberation; auction sale; **–re** (dā·lē·bā·râ'rā) *vt&i* to deliberate; **–tamente** (dā·lē·bā·râ·tâ·mān'tā) *adv* on purpose, deliberately; **–to** (dā·lē·bā·râ'tō) *a* resolved; **–to** *m* resolution
delicatamente (dā·lē·kâ·tâ·mān'tā) *adv* sensitively, delicately
delicatezza (dā·lē·kâ·tā'tsâ) *f* delicacy; tact

delicato (dā·lē·kâ'tō) *a* delicate; tactful
delinquente (dā·lēn·kwān'tā) *a&m* criminal
delinquenza (dā·lēn·kwān'tsâ) *f* crime
delinquere (dā·lēn'kwā·rā) *vi (law)* to commit a crime; **associazione a —** partnership in crime
delirare (dā·lē·râ'rā) *vi* to be delirious
delirio (dā·lē'ryō) *m* delirium
delitto (dā·lēt'tō) *m* crime
delizia (dā·lē'tsyâ) *f* great joy, delight; tastiness
delizioso (dā·lē·tsyō'zō) *a* delightful; delicious; exquisite
delucidazione (dā·lū·chē·dâ·tsyō'nā) *f* explanation, elucidation
deludere * (dā·lū'dā·rā) *vt* to disappoint; to avoid
delusione (dā·lū·zyō'nā) *f* disappointment
deluso (dā·lū'zō) *a* tricked; disappointed
demagogia (dā·mâ·gō·jē'â) *f* demagoguery
demagogico (dā·mâ·gô'jē·kō) *a* demagogic
demagogo (dā·mâ·gō'gō) *m* demagogue
demaniale (dā·mâ·nyâ'lā) *a* owned by the government
demanio (dā·mâ'nyō) *m* public property; government property
demarcazione (dā·mâr·kâ·tsyō'nā) *f* demarcation
demente (dā·mān'tā) *a* demented
demenza (dā·mān'tsâ) *f* madness, insanity
demilitarizzare (dā·mē·lē·tâ·rē·dzâ'rā) *vt* to demilitarize
democratico (dā·mō·krâ'tē·kō) *a* democratic
democrazia (dā·mō·krâ·tsē'â) *f* democracy
democristiano (dā·mō·krē·styâ'nō) *a&m* Christian Democrat
demodossologia (dā·mō·dōs·sō·lō·jē'â) *f* study of public opinion
demografico (dā·mō·grâ'fē·kō) *a* demographic
demolire (dā·mō·lē'rā) *vt* to wreck, knock down
demolizione (dā·mō·lē·tsyō'nā) *f* demolition
demone (de'mō·nā), **demonio** (dā·mô'nyō) *m* demon
demonietto (dā·mō·nyāt'tō) *m* little devil, imp
demoralizzare (dā·mō·râ·lē·dzâ'rā) *vt* to demoralize; to cause to lose heart
demoralizzazione (dā·mō·râ·lē·dzâ·tsyō'nā) *f* demoralization, losing heart
denaro (dā·nâ'rō) *m* money; **— contante** cash; **denari** diamonds *(cards)*
denaturante (dā·nâ·tū·rân'tā) *m* denaturant
denaturare (dā·nâ·tū·râ'rā) *vt* to denature
denaturato (dā·nâ·tū·râ'tō) *a* denatured; **alcool —** denatured alcohol
denicotinizzare (dā·nē·kō·tē·nē·dzâ'rā) *vt* to denicotinize
denigrare (dā·nē·grâ'rā) *vt* to defame, cast aspersions on
denigratore (dā·nē·grâ'tō'rā) *m* slanderer
denigrazione (dā·nē·grâ·tsyō'nā) *f* detraction; defamation, slander
denominare (dā·nō·mē·nâ'rā) *vt* to name
denominativo (dā·nō·mē·nâ·tē'vō) *a* denominative
denominatore (dā·nō·mē·nâ·tō'rā) *m (math)* denominator
denominazione (dā·nō·mē·nâ·tsyō'nā) *f* title, denomination
denotare (dā·nō·tâ'rā) *vt* to signify, mean
densità (dān·sē·tâ') *f* density
denso (dān'sō) *a* dense
dentale (dān·tâ'lā), **dentario** (dān·tâ'ryō) *a* dental
dentaruolo (dān·tâ·rūō'lō) *m* pacifier
dentata (dān·tâ'tâ) *f* bite; bite mark
dentato (dān·tâ'tō) *a* notched; toothed; cogged; *(bot)* dentate
dentatura (dān·tâ·tū'râ) *f* set of teeth, denture
dente (dān'tā) *m* tooth; **— canino** eye tooth; **— d'elefante** tusk; **— del giudizio** wisdom tooth; **— per —** tit for tat; **otturare un —** to fill a tooth; **denti d'ingranaggio** cogs *(gear)*; **dai denti lunghi** *(fig)* greedy; **mal di denti** toothache; **mettere i denti** to cut one's teeth; **mostrare i denti** *(fig)* to show one's teeth *(fig)*; **non è pane per i tuoi denti** *(fig)* it's not your cup of tea; it's out of your field
dentellare (dān·tāl·lâ'rā) *vt* to indent, tooth; to make notches in
dentellatura (dān·tāl·lâ·tū'râ) *f* notching; toothing
dentello (dān·tāl'lō) *m (mech)* notch, tooth; *(arch)* dentil
dentiera (dān·tyā'râ) *f* denture, plate
dentifricio (dān·tē·frē'chō) *m* dentrifice
dentista (dān·tē'stâ) *m* dentist
dentro (dān'trō) *adv* inside, within
denudare (dā·nū·dâ'rā) *vt* to lay bare, denude
denudarsi (dā·nū·dâr'sē) *vr* to strip oneself; to undress
denuncia (dā·nūn'châ), **denunzia** (dā·nūn'tsyâ) *f* report; complaint, censuring
denunciare (dā·nūn·châ'rā), **denunziare** (dā·nūn·tsyâ'rā) *vt* to denounce; to report
denutrito (dā·nū·trē'tō) *a* undernourished
denutrizione (dā·nū·trē·tsyō'nā) *f* undernourishment, inadequate diet
deodorante (dā·ō·dō·rân'tā) *a&m* deodorant; antiperspirant
deossidante (dā·ōs·sē·dân'tā) *a (chem)* deoxidizer
deossidazione (dā·os·sē·dâ·tsyō'nā) *f* deoxygenation
deperibile (dā·pā·rē'bē·lā) *a* perishable
deperimento (dā·pā·rē·mān'tō) *m* decay; wasting away; decline; **— nervoso** nervous exhaustion
depilare (dā·pē·lâ'rā) *vt* to depilate
depilatorio (dā·pē·lâ'tô'ryō) *m* depilatory
depilazione (dā·pē·lâ·tsyō'nā) *f* hair removal

deplorare (dā·plō·râ'rā) *vt* to deplore
deplorevole (dā·plō·re'vō·lā) *a* deplorable
depolarizzare (dā·pō·lâ·rē·dzâ'rā) *vt* *(elec)* to depolarize
deponente (dā·pō·nān'tā) *m* *(law)* witness; — *a&m* deponent
deporre * (dā·pōr'rā) *vt* to lay down; — *vi* to testify, give testimony
deportare (dā·pōr·tâ'rā) *vt* to deport
deportazione (dā·pōr·tâ·tsyō'nā) *f* deportation
depositante (dā·pō·zē·tân'tā) *m* depositor
depositario (dā·pō·zē·tâ'ryō) *m* depository
deposito (dā·pô'zē·tō) *m* deposit; — **bagagli** baggage room; — **di colli a mano** checkroom
deposizione (dā·pō·zē·tsyō'nā) *f* deposition; declaration
depravare (dā·prâ·vâ'rā) *vt* to corrupt, deprave
depravato (dā·prâ·vâ'tō) *a* depraved
depravazione (dā·prâ·vâ·tsyō'nā) *f* corruption, depravation
deprecare (dā·prā·kâ'rā) *vt* to deprecate; to disapprove of
depressione (dā·prās·syō'nā) *f* depression
depresso (dā·prās'sō) *a* dejected, saddened
deprezzamento (dā·prā·tsâ·mān'tō) *m* depreciation, drop in value
deprezzare (dā·prā·tsâ'rā) *vt* to disparage
deprimente (dā·prē·mān'tā) *a* depressing
depurare (dā·pū·râ'rā) *vt* to purify
depuratore (dā·pū·râ·tō'rā) *m* cleaner; — **d'acqua** water softener; — **d'aria** air cleaner; air filter
deputato (dā·pū·tâ'tō) *m* deputy; delegate
deputazione (dā·pū·tâ·tsyō'nā) *f* committee; delegation, authorized commission
deragliamento (dā·râ·lyâ·mān'tō) *m* derailment
deragliare (dā·râ·lyâ'rā) *vi* to derail
derapare (dā·râ·pâ'rā) *vi* to skid, careen
derapata (dā·râ·pâ'tâ) *f* *(avi)* skidding
derelitto (dā·rā·lēt'tō) *m* derelict, waif; **ospizio dei derelitti** home for lost children; — *a* abandoned, forsaken *(children)*
deretano (dā·rā·tâ'nō) *m* buttocks, derriere
deridere (dā·rē'dā·rā) *vt* to deride
derisione (dā·rē·zyō'nā) *f* ridicule
deriva (dā·rē'vâ) *f* drift; **–re** (dā·rē·vâ'rā) *vi* to derive; **–zione** (dā·rē·vâ·tsyō'nā) *f* derivation; telephone extension
derma (dār'mâ) *f* *(anat)* skin; dermis; **–tite** (dār·mâ·tē'tā) *f* *(med)* dermatitis; **–tologia** (dār·mâ·tō·lō·jē'â) *f* *(med)* dermatology
dermoide (dār·mô'ē·dā) *f* imitation leather, leatherette
deroga (de'rō·gâ) *f* noncompliance; **–re** (dā·rō·gâ'rā) *vi* to fail to comply; to depart from; **–toria** (dā·rō·gâ·tô'ryâ) *f* *(law)* conditional clause
derrata (dār·râ'tâ) *f* foodstuff
derubare (dā·rū·bâ'rā) *vt* to rob
desco (dā'skō) *m* table; table ready for dinner
descrittivamente (dā·skrēt·tē·vâ·mān'tā) *adv* descriptively
descrittivo (dā·skrēt·tē'vō) *a* descriptive
descrivere * (dā·skrē'vā·rā) *vt* to describe
descrizione (dā·skrē·tsyō'nā) *f* description
desensibilizzatore (dā·sān·sē·bē·lē·dzâ·tō'rā) *m* *(phot)* desensitizer
deserto (dā·zār'tō) *m* desert; — *a* abandoned, deserted
desiderabile (dā·zē·dā·râ'bē·lā) *a* desirable
desiderare (dā·zē·dā·râ'rā) *vt* to wish
desiderio (dā·zē·de'ryō) *m* desire, wish
desideroso (dā·zē·dā·rō'zō) *a* anxious
designare (dā·zē·nyâ'rā) *vt* to designate
designazione (dā·zē·nyâ·tsyō'nā) *f* nomination, designation
desinare (dā·zē·nâ'rā) *m* dinner, supper; — *vi* to dine; **dopo** — after dinner
desinenza (dā·zē·nān'tsâ) *f* ending, suffix
desistere * (dā·zē'stā·rā) *vi* to desist; to refrain
desolante (dā·zō·lân'tā) *a* grievous, trying *(fig)*; distressing; discouraging
desolatamente (dā·zō·lâ·tâ·mān'tā) *adv* desolately
desolato (dā·zō·lâ'tō) *a* dejected, desolate; **–re** (dā·zō·lâ·tō'rā) *m* destroyer, desolator
desolazione (dā·zō·lâ·tsyō'nā) *f* grief, anguish, distress; desolation; ruin
despota (de'spō·tâ) *m* despot
desquamazione (dā·skwâ·mâ·tsyō'nā) *f* scaling *(fish)*
destare (dā·stâ'rā) *vt* to awaken; to arouse, stir up
destarsi (dā·stâr'sē) *vr* to wake up, arise
destinare (dā·stē·nâ'rā) *vt* to destine, decree; to appoint; to address, send
destinatario (dā·stē·nâ·tâ'ryō) *m* addressee
destinato (dā·stē·nâ'tō) *a* intended; ordained, destined; — **a perire** doomed to perish; — **a New York** appointed to New York
destinazione (dā·stē·nâ·tsyō'nā) *f* destination
destino (dā·stē'nō) *m* fate; destination
destituire (dā·stē·twē'rā) *vt* to remove, turn out of office
destituzione (dā·stē·tū·tsyō'nā) *f* removal
desto (dā'stō) *a* wide awake *(fig)*; fast, sharp, lively
destra (dā'strâ) *f* right hand; **a** — to the right
destramente (dā·strâ·mān'tā) *adv* cleverly, dexterously
destreggiare (dā·strāj·jâ'rā) *vi*, **destreggiarsi** (dā·strāj·jâr'sē) *vr* to devise, contrive, manage smartly; to strive; to manipulate
destrezza (dā·strā'tsâ) *f* dexterity
destriero (dā·stryā'rō) *m* steed, war-horse
destro (dā'strō) *a* clever; — *m* chance; righthand side; **–rso** (dā·strōr'sō) *a* righthanded; clockwise
destrosio (dā·strô'zyō) *m* dextrose
desumere * (dā·zū'mā·rā) *vt* to deduce
desumibile (dā·zū·mē'bē·lā) *a* deducible;

inferential
desunto (dā·zūn'tō) *a* deduced, inferred; derived
detenere * (dā·tā·nā'rā) *vt* to keep; to hold under arrest; to detain; to retain; — **un incarico** to hold a job, occupy a post
detentore (dā·tān·tō'rā) *m* holder; possessor
detenuto (dā·tā·nū'tō) *a* detained; — *m* prisoner, convict
detenzione (dā·tān·tsyō'nā) *f* detention
detergente (dā·tār·jān'tā) *a&m* detergent
detergere (dā·ter'jā·rā) *vt* to clean
deteriorabile (dā·tā·ryō·râ'bē·lā) *a* susceptible to deterioration
deterioramento (dā·tā·ryō·râ·mān'tō) *m* deterioration
deteriorare (dā·tā·ryō·râ'rā) *vt&i* to deteriorate, spoil
deteriorato (dā·tā·ryō·râ'tō) *a* deteriorated; damaged, wasted, spoiled
determinante (dā·tār·mē·nân'tā) *a* determining; **causa** — determining factor
determinare (dā·tār·mē·nâ'rā) *vt* to establish; to cause; to resolve, decide
determinarsi (dā·tār·mē·nâr'sē) *vr* to resolve, make up one's mind
determinatamente (dā·tār·mē·nâ·tâ·mān'tā) *adv* determinedly
determinatezza (dā·tār'mē·nâ·tā'tsâ) *f* resoluteness, firmness *(spirit)*; determination
determinativo (dā·tār·mē·nâ·tē'vō) *a* determining, decisive; clinching *(coll)*
determinato (dā·tār·mē·nâ'tō) *a* determined, fixed
determinismo (dā·tār·mē·nē'zmō) *m* determinism
detersivo (dā·tār·sē'vō) *m* detergent
detestabile (dā·tā·stâ'bē·lā) *a* hateful, detestable
detestare (dā·tā·stâ'rā) *vt* to detest, hate
detettore (dā·tāt·tō'rā) *m* detector
detonazione (dā·tō·nâ·tsyō'nā) *f* detonation
detrarre * (dā·trâr'rā) *vt* to deduct; to detract from
detrattore (dā·trât·tō'rā) *m* detractor
detrimento (dā·trē·mān'tō) *m* detriment, harm
detrito (dā·trē'tō) *m* debris; rubbish
detronizzare (dā·trō·nē·dzâ'rā) *vt* to dethrone
detta (dāt'tâ) *f* opinion; word; **a — di tutti** according to general opinion; **a — tua** according to you; **–fono** (dāt·tâ'fō·nō) *m* dictaphone; **–re** (dāt·tâ'rā) *vt* to dictate; **–to** (dāt·tâ'tō) *m* dictation; **–tura** (dāt·tâ·tū'râ) *f* dictation *(act)*; **scrivere sotto –tura** to write from dictation
dettagliante (dāt·tâ·lyân'tā) *m* retailer
dettagliare (dāt·tâ·lyâ'rā) *vt* to retail; to detail, relate in detail
dettagliatamente (dāt·tâ·lyâ·tâ·mān'tā) *adv* detailedly, in detail
dettaglio (dāt·tâ'lyō) *m* specific, detail; retail sale
detto (dāt'tō) *m* expression; saying, proverb, maxim; motto; witticism; **secondo il** — as the saying goes; **detti memorabili** memorable words, **i detti di Cristo** Christ's words; — *a* said, called, named; — **fatto** no sooner said than done; **Alessandro — il Grande** Alexander the Great; **è presto** — it is easy to say
deturpare (dā·tūr·pâ'rā) *vt* to disfigure; to spoil; to deface
deturpazione (dā·tūr·pâ·tsyō'nā) *f* disfigurement
devastare (dā·vâ·stâ'rā) *vt* to devastate, ruin
devastazione (dā·vâ·stâ·tsyō'nā) *f* ruin, waste, havoc, devastation
deviare (dā·vyâ'rā) *vi* to deviate; to detour, switch
deviatore (dā·vyâ·tō'rā) *m* switchman
deviazione (dā·vyâ·tsyō'nā) *f* detour
deviazionista (dā·vyâ·tsyō·nē'stâ) *m* deviationist; deviate
devitalizzare (dā·vē·tâ·lē·dzâ'rā) *vt* to devitalize
devoluto (dā·vō·lū'tō) *a* transmitted, delivered over, transferred
devoluzione (dā·vō·lū·tsyō'nā) *f* transmission, transfer, devolution
devolvere * (dā·vôl'vā·rā) *vt* to transfer, devolve; to appropriate
devolversi * (dā·vôl'vār·sē) *vr* to be transferred, devolve; to be assigned; to turn
devotissimo (dā·vō·tēs'sē·mō) *a* very devoted; highly devout; very sincerely
devoto (dā·vō'tō) *a* devout, pious; devoted, attached; destined; — *m* devout person
devozione (dā·vō·tsyō'nā) *f* devotion; **fare le proprie devozioni** to do one's devotions
di (dē) *prep* of, about, from, any, by, at, some, with
dì (dē) *m* day; **a — 10 di dicembre** on the 10th of December; **al — d'oggi** nowadays; **buon** — good day; **mezzodì** midday; **sul fare del** — at dawn
diabete (dyâ·bā'tā) *m* diabetes
diabolicamente (dyâ·bō·lē·kâ·mān'tā) *adv* devilishly, diabolically
diabolico (dyâ·bô'lē·kō) *a* devilish, diabolic
diacono (dyâ'kō·nō) *m (eccl)* deacon
diadema (dyâ·dā'mâ) *m* tiara
diafano (dyâ'fâ·nō) *a* transparent
diaframma (dyâ·frâm'mâ) *m* diaphragm
diagnosi (dyâ'nyō·zē) *f* diagnosis
diagnosticare (dyâ·nyō·stē·kâ'rā) *vt* to diagnose
diagnostico (dyâ·nyô'stē·kō) *a* diagnostic; — *m* diagnostician
diagonale (dyâ·gō·nâ'lā) *a* diagonal
diagramma (dyâ·grâm'mâ) *m* diagram
dialettale (dyâ·lāt·tâ'lā) *a* dialectical
dialettica (dyâ·let'tē·kâ) *f* dialectics
dialetto (dyâ·lāt'tō) *m* dialect
dialogo (dyâ'lō·gō) *m* dialogue
diamante (dyâ·mân'tā) *m* diamond
diamantifero (dyâ·mân·tē'fâ·rō) *a* diamond-bearing
diamantino (dyâ·mân·tē'nō) *a* adamant, rigid

diametro (dyâ'mā·trō) *m* diameter
diamine! (dyâ'mē·nā) *interj* good heavens!
diana (dyâ'nâ) *f* morning star; *(mil)* **suonar la** — to sound reveille
diapason (dyâ'pâ·zōn) *m* tuning fork
diapositiva (dyâ·pō·zē·tē'vâ) *f* slide; color transparency
diaria (dyâ'ryâ) *f* travelling allowance
diario (dyâ'ryō) *m* diary; — *a* daily
diarrea (dyâr·rā'â) *f* diarrhea
diavoleria (dyâ·vō·lā·rē'â) *f* mischief, deviltry
diavoletto (dyâ·vō·lāt'tō) *m* little devil, imp, mischief
diavolo (dyâ'vō·lō) *m* devil; —! *interj* heck! what the heck!
dibattere (dē·bât'tā·rā) *vt* to discuss, debate
dibattersi (dē·bât'tār·sē) *vr* to struggle; to contest; to flounder
dibattimento (dē·bât·tē·mān'tō) *m* debate
dibattuto (dē·bât·tū'tō) *a* discussed, debated; controversial; contested; **questione dibattuta** controversial issue
dicastero (dē·kâ·stā'rō) *m* government department; department of a Cabinet member
dicembre (dē·chām'brā) *m* December
diceria (dē·chā·rē'â) *f* rumor, gossip
dichiarare (dē·kyâ·râ'rā) *vt* to declare
dichiarazione (dē·kyâ·râ·tsyō'nā) *f* declaration; — **giurata** affidavit
diciannove (dē·chân·nō'vā) *a* nineteen; **–simo** (dē·chân·nō·ve'zē·mō) *a* nineteenth
diciassette (dē·châs·sāt'tā) *a* seventeen; **–simo** (dē·châs·sāt·te'zē·mō) *a* seventeenth
diciottesimo (dē·chōt·te'zē·mô) *a* eighteenth
diciotto (dē·chōt'tō) *a* eighteen
dicitore (dē·chē·tō'rā) *m* speaker, lecturer
dicitura (dē·chē·tū'râ) *f* phrasing, wording; style; delivery; pronunciation; **con la seguente** — worded as follows; **una bella** — a good delivery *(speech)*
dicotiledone (dē·kō·tē·le'dō·nā) *m (bot)* dicotyledon
didascalia (dē·dâ·skâ·lē'â) *f* caption; stage directions
didattico (dē·dât'tē·kô) *a* educational
dieci (dyā'chē) *a* ten; **–mila** (dyā·chē·mē'lâ) *a* ten thousand; **–millesimo** (dyā·chē·mēl·le'zē·mō) *a* ten thousandth; **–na** (dyā·chē'nâ) *f* about ten; half a score
diesis (dyā'zēs) *m (mus)* sharp
dieta (dyā'tâ) *f* diet
dietetica (dyā·te'tē·kâ) *f* dietetics
dietetico (dyā·te'tē·kō) *a* dietetic
dietro (dyā'trō) *prep&adv* behind, after; — **accettazione** *(com)* on agreement, upon acceptance; — **front!** *(mil)* about face!; — **le quinte** *(fig)* behind the scene; — **le spalle** behind one's back; — **ricevuta** against receipt; — **richiesta** upon request; — **sborso di** on payment of; **andar** — to follow behind; **per di** — from behind; **tener** — to follow; to agree
difatti (dē·fât'tē) *adv* really, in fact
difendere * (dē·fen'dā·rā) *vt* to defend; to uphold
difensore (dē·fān·sō'rā) *m* defender
difesa (dē·fā'zâ) *f* defense; — **legittima** self defense; **prendere la — di** to take the side of; to go to the defense of; **senza** — defenseless
difeso (dē·fā'zō) *a* sheltered; protected, defended
difetto (dē·fāt'tō) *m* fault, flaw; **–so** (dē·fāt·tō'zō) *a* faulty; fallible
diffamare (dēf·fâ·mâ'rā) *vt* to defame
diffamazione (dēf·fâ·mâ·tsyō'nā) *f* defamation
differente (dēf·fā·rān'tā) *a* different
differenziale (dēf·fā·rān·tsyâ'lā) *a&m* differential
differire (dēf·fā·rē'rā) *vi* to delay, put off
difficile (dēf·fē'chē·lā) *a* difficult
difficilmente (dēf·fē·chēl·mān'tā) *adv* with difficulty; barely; hardly possible
difficoltà (dēf·fē·kōl·tâ') *f* difficulty
diffida (dēf·fē'dâ) *f* warning; notice; **–re** (dēf·fē·dâ'rā) *vt* to enjoin, warn; **–re** *vi* to distrust
diffidente (dēf·fē·dān'tā) *a* distrustful
diffidenza (dēf·fē·dān'tsâ) *f* suspicion, diffidence
diffondere (dēf·fôn'dā·rā) *vt* to spread
diffusamente (dēf·fū·zâ·mān'tā) *adv* abundantly
diffusione (dēf·fū·zyō'nā) *f* diffusion
diffuso (dēf·fū'zō) *a* widespread, rife
difterite (dēf·tā·rē'tā) *f* diphtheria
diga (dē'gâ) *f* dam
digeribile (dē·jā·rē'bē·lā) *a* digestible
digerire (dē·jā·rē'rā) *vt* to digest
digerito (dē·jā·rē'tō) *a* digested
digestione (dē·jā·styō'nā) *f* digestion
digestivo (dē·jā·stē'vō) *a* digestive
digesto (dē·jā'stō) *m (law)* digest
digiunare (dē·jū·nâ'rā) *vi* to fast
digiuno (dē·jū'nō) *m* fast
dignità (dē·nyē·tâ') *f* dignity
dignitario (dē·nyē·tâ'ryō) *m* dignitary
dignitosamente (dē·nyē·tō·zâ·mān'tā) *adv* with dignity, properly.
dignitoso (dē·nyē·tō'zō) *a* dignified
digressione (dē·grās·syō'nā) *f* digression
digrignare (dē·grē·nyâ'rā) *vi* to grind one's teeth, gnash one's teeth
dilagare (dē·lâ·gâ'rā) *vi* to overflow, run over
dilaniare (dē·lâ·nyâ'rā) *vt* to lacerate, tear
dilapidare (dē·lâ·pē·dâ'rā) *vt* to squander, spend foolishly
dilapidato (dē·lâ·pē·dâ'tō) *a* squandered, spent recklessly
dilatare (dē·lâ·tâ'rā) *vt* to dilate
dilatazione (dē·lâ·tâ·tsyō'nā) *f* expansion; dilation
dilazionare (dē·lâ·tsyō·nâ'rā) *vt* to delay
dilazione (dē·lâ·tsyō'nā) *f* respite, delay
dileguare (dē·lā·gwâ'rā) *vt* to disperse, scatter; to route, set to route
dilemma (dē·lām'mâ) *m* dilemma
dilettante (dē·lāt·tân'tā) *m&a* amateur

dilettevole (dē·lāt·te'vō·lā) *a* delightful, charming
diletto (dē·lāt'tō) *m* delight; — *a* beloved
diligente (dē·lē·jān'tā) *a* diligent
diligenza (dē·lē·jān'tsâ) *f* diligence
diluire (dē·lwē'rā) *vt* to dilute
diluvio (dē·lū'vyō) *m* deluge
dimagrare (dē·mâ·grâ'rā), **dimagrire** (dē·mâ·grē'rā) *vi* to reduce, lose weight
dimensione (dē·mān·syō'nā) *f* dimension
dimenticanza (dē·mān·tē·kân'tsâ) *f* oversight; absentmindedness
dimenticare (dē·mān·tē·kâ'rā) *vt* to forget
dimesso (dē·mās'sō) *a* humble; dismissed
dimettere * (dē·met'tā·rā) *vt* to dismiss; to stop, give up
dimettersi * (dē·met'tār·sē) *vr* to resign
diminuire (dē·mē·nwē'rā) *vt&i* to decrease, abate, lessen
diminutivo (dē·mē·nū·tē'vō) *a&m* diminutive
diminuzione (dē·mē·nū·tysō'nā) *f* decrease
dimissionare (dē·mēs·syō·nâ'rā) *vt* to discharge, dismiss; — *vi* to resign
dimissionario (dē·mēs·syō·nâ'ryō) *a* resigning
dimissione (dē·mēs·syō'nā) *f* resignation
dimora (dē·mō'râ) *f* residence; **–re** (dē·mō·râ'rā) *vt* to stay, dwell, live; to delay
dimostrare (dē·mō·strâ'rā) *vt* to demonstrate; to evidence, show
dimostrazione (dē·mō·strâ·tsyō'nā) *f* evidence, demonstration
dinamica (dē·nâ'mē·kâ) *f* dynamics
dinamico (dē·nâ'mē·kō) *a* dynamic
dinamite (dē·nâ·mē'tā) *f* dynamite
dinamo (dē'nâ·mō) *f* generator; dynamo
dinanzi (dē·nân'tsē) *prep&adv* before
dinastia (dē·nâ·stē'â) *f* dynasty
dindo (dēn'dō), **dindio** (dēn'dyō) *m* turkey
dinoccolato (dē·nōk·kō·lâ'tō) *a* awkward; slouchy; sloppy
dinosauro (dē·nō·sâ'ū·rō) *m* dinosaur
dintorni (dēn·tōr'nē) *mpl* environs
Dio (dē'ō) *m* God, Almighty, Lord
dio (dē'ō) *m* deity, god
diocesi (dyô'chā·zē) *f* diocese
diodo (dyō'dō) *m* diode
dipanare (dē·pâ·nâ'rā) *vt* to unravel; to clear up, solve
dipartimento (dē·pâr·tē·mān'tō) *m* department
dipendente (dē·pān·dān'tā) *a&m* dependent
dipendenza (dē·pān·dān'tsâ) *f* dependence
dipendere * (dē·pen'dā·rā) *vi* to depend
dipingere * (dē·pēn'jā·rā) *vt* to paint; to describe, depict
dipinto (dē·pēn'tō) *a* painted; — *m* painting, picture
diploma (dē·plō'mâ) *m* diploma; **–re** (dē·plō·mâ'rā) *vt* to confer a diploma; **–rsi** (dē·plō·mâr'sē) *vr* to obtain a diploma, be graduated; **–tica** (dē·plō·mâ'tē·kâ) *f* art of diplomacy; **–ticamente** (dē·plō·mâ·tē·kâ·mān'tā) *adv* diplomatically; **–tico** (dē·plō·mâ'tē·kō) *a* diplomatic; **–tico** *m* diplomat; **–to** (dē·plō·mâ'tō) *m* graduate; **–zia** (dē·plō·mâ·tsē'â) *f* diplomacy
diporto (dē·pōr'tō) *m* pleasure
diramare (dē·râ·mâ'rā) *vt* to send out, circulate
diramarsi (dē·râ·mâr'sē) *vr* to ramify, branch out
diramazione (dē·râ·mâ·tsyō'nā) *f* ramification, branching out
dire * (dē'rā) *vt* to say; to tell; — **pane al pane** *(fig)* to call a spade a spade *(fig)*; **a — il vero** to tell the truth; **aver a che — con qualcuno** to quarrel with somebody; **che cosa vuol —?** what does it mean?; **come si suol —** as the saying goes; **lasciar —** to let people talk; **mandare a —** to send word; **per così —** as it were, so to speak; **si dice** it is said; **vale a —** that is to say; **voler —** to mean to say; **al — di tutti** according to public opinion; **l'arte del —** public speaking; **oltre ogni —** beyond description
direttamente (dē·rāt·tâ·mān'tā) *adv* directly
direttissimo (dē·rāt·tēs'sē·mō) *m* through train; — *a* very direct
direttiva (dē·rāt·tē'vâ) *f* directive; policy; direction
diretto (dē·rāt'tō) *a* direct; — *m* fast train
direttore (dē·rāt·tō'rā) *m*, **direttrice** (dē·rāt·trē'chā) *f* director, manager
direzione (dē·rā·tsyō'nā) *f* direction, management; board of directors
dirigente (dē·rē·jān'tā) *a&m* executive
dirigere * (dē·rē'jā·rā) *vt* to manage, run; *(mus)* to conduct
dirigersi * (dē·rē'jār·sē) *vr* to apply
dirigibile (dē·rē·jē'bē·lā) *m* dirigible
dirigismo (dē·rē·jē'zmō) *m* planned economy
dirimpetto (dē·rēm·pāt'tō) *adv&prep* opposite
diritto (dē·rēt'tō) *m* right; law; — *a* straight; — **canonico** canon law; — **d'autore** copyright; **a buon —** with good reason, justifiedly; **maggior —** all the more reason; **sempre —** straight ahead; **a — o a rovescio** by fair means or foul
diroccato (dē·rōk·kâ'tō) *a* in ruins
dirottamente (dē·rōt·tâ·mān'tā) *adv* excessviely, extremely, torrentially; **piangere —** to shed floods of tears
dirottare (dē·rōt·tâ'rā) *vt* to detour
dirotto (dē·rōt'tō) *a* pouring; torrential; **pioggia dirotta** downpour; **a —** freely, without restraint; **piove a —** it's raining cats and dogs
dirozzare (dē·rō·dzâ'rā) *vt* to educate; to polish; to refine
dirupo (dē·rū'pō) *m* precipice; ravine
disabbigliare (dē·zâb·bē·lyâ'rā) *vt* to undress
disabitato (dē·zâ·bē·tâ'tō) *a* deserted
disaccordo (dē·zâk·kōr'dō) *m* disaccord, disagreement
disadatto (dē·zâ·dât'tō) *a* maladjusted; not suitable
disadorno (dē·zâ·dōr'nō) *a* bare, plain,

unadorned; **stile** — terse style
disagevole (dē·zâ·je'vō·lā) *a* uneasy; hard, difficult; uncomfortable, rough
disagio (dē·zâ'jō) *m* discomfort; anxiety, disquiet
disanimare (dē·zâ·nē·mâ'rā) *vt* to dispirit, discourage
disanimato (dē·zâ·nē·mâ'tō) *a* dispirited, discouraged
disapprovare (dē·zâp·prō·vâ'rā) *vt* to disapprove of
disappunto (dē·zâp·pūn'tō) *m* disappointment
disarcionare (dē·zâr·chō·nâ'rā) *vt* to unsaddle; to unhorse
disarmamento (dē·zâr·mâ·mān'tō) **disarmo** (dē·zâr'mō) *m* disarmament
disarmare (dē·zâr·mâ'rā) *vt* to dismantle; to disarm; *(naut)* to unrig; *(fig)* to subdue, quiet
disarmonico (dē·zâr·mô'nē·kō) *a* discordant
disarticolare (dē·zâr·tē·kō·lâ'rā) *vt* to disjoint, throw out of joint
disarticolarsi (dē·zâr·tē·kō·lâr'sē) *vr* to get dislocated, be thrown out of joint
disastrato (dē·zâ·strâ'tō) *m* victim
disastro (dē·zâ'strō) *m* disaster
disastroso (dē·zâ·strō'zō) *a* catastrophic
disattento (dē·zât·tān'tō) *a* careless
disattenzione (dē·zât·tān·tsyō'nā) *f* carelessness, negligence, lack of attention
disavanzo (dē·zâ·vân'tsō) *m* deficit
disavventura (dē·zâv·vān·tū'râ) *f* bad luck, mishap, misfortune
disavvezzare (dē·zâv·vā·tsâ'rā) *vt* to dissuade; to help break the habit of; to disaccustom, wean away from
disavvezzato (dē·zâv·vā·tsâ'tō) *a* unaccustomed, not used
disboscamento (dē·zbō·skâ·mān'tō) *m* deforestation
disboscare (dē·zbō·skâ'rā) *vt* to deforest
disbrigare (dē·zbrē·gâ'rā) *vt* to disentangle, disengage; to expedite, dispatch
disbrigarsi (dē·zbrē·gâr'sē) *vr* to hurry; to get rid of; to acquit oneself
disbrigo (dē·zbrē'gō) *m* dispatch; carrying through, completion
discapito (dē·skâ'pē·tō) *m* loss, damage; spoilage
discendente (dē·shān·dān'tā) *m* descendant; — *a* descending
discendenza (dē·shān·dān'tsâ) *f* extraction, lineage; origin, descent
discepolo (dē·she'pō·lō) *m* disciple
discernare (dē·shār'nā·rā) *vt* to discern
discernimento (dē·shār·nē·mān'tō) *m* discernment; **aver** — to have good sense, have good judgment
discesa (dē·shā'zâ) *f* descent; — **dei prezzi** decline in prices; — **in picchiata** *(avi)* nose dive; — **rapida** steep grade; **la** — **dei barbari** the barbarian invasion of Italy; **forte** — steep descent; **in** — downhill, going down
dischiudere * (dē·skyū'dā·rā) *vt* to disclose, reveal
dischiuso (dē·skyū'zō) *a* disclosed; open, above board
discinto (dē·shēn'tō) *a* undressed; messy; unprepared
disciogliere * (dē·shô'lyā·rā) *vt* to loosen; to untie, unbind; to release; to melt
disciolto (dē·shōl'tō) *a* loose; dissolved; melted
disciplina (dē·shē·plē'nâ) *f* discipline; **-re** (dē·shē·plē·nâ'rā) *vt* to discipline; **-tamente** (dē·shē·plē·nâ·tâ·mān'tā) *adv* with discipline; **-to** (dē·shē·plē·nâ'tō) *a* disciplined, well-trained
disco (dē'skō) *m* record; *(sports)* disc, quoit; *(rail)* signal; — **combinatore** telephone dial; — **sul ghiaccio** ice hockey; — **volante** flying saucer; **-teca** (dē·skō·tā'kâ) *f* record library
discolorare (dē·skō·lō·râ'rā) *vt* to discolor
discolpare (dē·skōl·pâ'rā) *vt* to justify, vindicate
discolparsi (dē·skōl·pâr'sē) *vr* to vindicate oneself, clear oneself
disconoscere * (dē·skō·nô'shā·rā) *vt* to disavow; to show ingratitude for
discordanza (dē·skōr·dân'tsâ) *f* disagreement, discordance; *(mus)* discord
discorde (dē·skōr'dā) *a* discordant, not agreed; dissonant
discordia (dē·skôr'dyâ) *f* dissension
discorrere * (dē·skôr'rā·rā) *vi* to talk
discorsa (dē·skōr'sâ) *f* tiresome talk
discorso (dē·skōr'sō) *m* talk, speech
discosto (dē·skō'stō) *adv&a* distant, far away; detached
discreditare (dē·skrâ·dē·tâ'rā) *vt* to discredit
discredito (dē·skre'dē·tō) *m* discredit
discrepanza (dē·skrā·pân'tsâ) *f* discrepancy, variance
discretamente (dē·skrā·tâ·mān'tā) *adv* discreetly, fairly, tolerably
discretezza (dē·skrā·tā'tsâ) *f* moderation, discretion; prudence
discreto (dē·skrā'tō) *a* fair; discreet
discrezione (dē·skrā·tsyō'nā) *f* discretion
discriminare (dē·skrē·mē·nâ'rā) *vt* to discriminate between, choose among
discriminazione (dē·skrē·mē·nâ·tsyō'nā) *f* discrimination, taste
discussione (dē·skūs·syō'nā) *f* argument; debate; discussion
discutere * (dē·skū'tā·rā) *vt* to discuss; to argue
discutibile (dē·skū·tē'bē·lā) *a* debatable
disdegnare (dē·zdā·nyâ'rā) *vt* to disdain
disdegno (dē·zdā'nyō) *m* disdain
disdetta (dē·zdāt'tâ) *f* mishap, bad luck
disdire * (dē·zdē'rā) *vt* to cancel; to deny; — **la camera** to check out of a hotel
disdoro (dē·zdō'rō) *m* dishonor
disegnare (dē·zā·nyâ'rā) *vt* to draw
disegnatore (dē·zā·nyâ·tō'rā) *m* draftsman, designer
disegno (dē·zā'nyō) *m* drawing, design; — **di legge** parliamentary bill; **punta da** — thumbtack
diseredare (dē·zā·rā·dâ'rā) *vt* to disinherit
disertare (dē·zār·tâ'ra) *vt* to desert

diserzione (dē·zār·tsyō'nā) *f* desertion
disfare * (dē·sfâ'rā) *vt* to undo, untie; to disassemble
disfarsi * (dē·sfâr'sē) *vr* to dispose of; to be dissolved; — **di qualcuno** to get rid of someone, shake someone
disfatta (dē·sfât'tâ) *f* defeat
disfattista (dē·sfât·tē'stâ) *m* defeatist
disfida (dē·sfē'dâ) *f* defiance; challenge
disfunzione (dē·sfūn·tsyō'nā) *f (med)* disorder, malfunction; derangement
disgelo (dē·zjā'lō) *m* thawing
disgiungere * (dē·zjūn'jā·rā) *vt* to detach, disjoin
disgiuntivo (dē·zjūn·tē'vō) *a (gram)* disjunctive
disgrazia (dē·zgrâ'tsyâ) *f* accident; misfortune; **cadere in** — to fall into disfavor; **per** — unfortunately; **–tamente** (dē·zgrâ·tsyâ·tâ·mān'tā) *adv* unfortunately, unhappily; **–to** (dē·zgrâ·tsyâ'tō) *a* unfortunate; **–to** *m* ruffian
disguido (dē·zgwē'dō) *m* error in mail delivery, misrouting
disgustare (dē·zgū·stâ'rā) *vt* to disgust
disgustarsi (dē·zgū·stâr'sē) *vr* to feel disgust; to fall out, quarrel
disgusto (dē·zgū'stō) *m* disgust; disliking
disillusione (dē·zēl·lū·zyō'nā) *f* rude awakening; disappointment
disimpegnare (dē·zēm·pā·nyâ'rā) *vt* to free, disentangle; to carry out, discharge
disincagliare (dē·zēn·kâ·lyâ'rā) *vt (naut)* to refloat
disincantato (dē·zēn·kân·tâ'tō) *a* disenchanted; disappointed
disinfestante (dē·zēn·fā·stân'tā) *m* exterminator
disinfestare (dē·zēn·fā·stâ'rā) *vt* to exterminate; to fumigate
disinfettante (dē·zēn·fāt·tân'tā) *a&m* disinfectant
disinfettare (dē·zēn·fāt·tâ'rā) *vt* to disinfect
disinfezione (dē·zēn·fā·tsyō'nā) *f* disinfection
disingannare (dē·zēn·gân·nâ'rā) *vt* to disillusion, disenchant; to give the true picture
disinganno (dē·zēn·gân'nō) *m* disenchantment, rude awakening
disinnestare (dē·zēn·nā·stâ'rā) *vt* to disconnect, separate
disintegrare (dē·zēn·tā·grâ'rā) *vt* to split
disintegrazione (dē·zēn·tā·grâ·tsyō'nā) *f* fission, splitting
disinteressato (dē·zēn·tā·rās·sâ'tō) *a* impartial
disinvolto (dē·zēn·vōl'tō) *a* nonchalant
disinvoltura (dē·zēn·vōl·tū'râ) *f* nonchalance; ease of manner
dislivello (dē·zlē·vāl'lō) *m* unevenness; gradient; drop
dislocamento (dē·zlō·kâ·mān'tō) *m* displacement
disobbediente (dē·zōb·bā·dyān'tā) *a* disobedient
disobbedire (dē·zōb·bā·dē'rā) *vt* to disobey
disobbligante (dē·zōb·blē·gân'tā) *a* rude
disobbligarsi (dē·zōb·blē·gâr'sē) *vi* to return a favor
disoccupare (dē·zōk·kū·pâ'rā) *vt* to terminate one's employment; to idle, put out of work
disoccuparsi (dē·zōk·kū·pâr'sē) *vr* to give up one's job; to curtail one's commitments
disoccupato (dē·zōk·kū·pâ'tō) *a* unemployed
disoccupazione (dē·zōk·kū·pâ·tsyō'nā) *f* unemployment
disonestà (dē·zō·nā·stâ') *f* dishonesty
disonesto (dē·zō·nā'stō) *a* dishonest
disonorante (dē·zō·nō·rân'tā) *a* dishonoring
disonorare (dē·zō·nō·râ'rā) *vt* to dishonor
disonorato (dē·zō·nō·râ'tō) *a* without honor
disonore (dē·zō·nō'rā) *m* disgrace, shame; **–vole** (dē·zō·nō·re'vō·lā) *a* dishonorable
disopra (dē·sō'prâ) *adv* above, upstairs; — *m* top, upperside; **al** — above, up above; **al — di ogni sospetto** above suspicion; **il piano** — upstairs, the floor above
disordinare (dē·zōr·dē·nâ'rā) *vt* to disarrange, disorder; — *vi* to exceed
disordinatamente (dē·zōr·dē·nâ·tâ·mān'tā) *adv* disorderly; inordinately
disordinato (dē·zōr·dē·nâ'tō) *a* untidy, messy
disordine (dē·zôr'dē·nā) *m* disorder
disorganizzato (dē·zōr·gâ·nē·dzâ'tō) *a* disorganized
disorganizzazione (dē·zōr·gâ·nē·dzâ·tsyō'nā) *f* disorganization
disorientamento (dē·zō·ryān·tâ·mān'tō) *m* bewilderment
disorientare (dē·zō·ryān·tâ'rā) *vt* to bewilder, disorient
disorientarsi (dē·zō·ryān·târ'sē) *vr* to lose one's way
disorientato (dē·zō·ryān·tâ'tō) *a* bewildered; **essere** — to have lost one's bearings
disossato (dē·zōs·sâ'tō) *a* boned, without bones
disotto (dē·sōt'tō) *adv* below, downstairs; — *m* bottom, under side; **al — di** below, beneath; — *a* lower; **il piano** — downstairs, the lower floor; **la parte** — the lower part
dispaccio (dē·spâ'chō) *m* dispatch; — **telegrafico** telegraph message
disparatamente (dē·spâ·râ·tâ·mān'tā) *adv* disparately; unevenly
dispari (dē'spâ·rē) *a* odd, uneven
disparte (dē·spâr·tā) *adv* aside, apart; **in** — to one side; separately
dispensa (dē·spān'sâ) *f* pantry; section; dispensation; **–re** (dē·spān·sâ'rā) *vt* to dispense; **–rio** (dē·spān·sâ'ryō) *m* dispensary; **–to** (dē·spān·sâ'tō) *a* dispensed; distributed; exonerated; **–to dal servizio** exempted from service; **–to dal-**

la posta distributed by mail
dispepsia (dē·spā·psē'â) *f* dyspepsia
disperare (dē·spā·râ'rā) *vi* to despair; **far** — to drive to despair; to be the death of *(fig)*
disperarsi (dē·spā·râr'sē) *vr* to give up hope
disperatamente (dē·spā·râ·tâ·mān'tā) *adv* desperately
disperato (dē·spā·râ'tō) *a* hopeless; useless; — *m* penniless man
disperazione (dē·spā·râ·tsyō'nā) *f* despair; uselessness
disperdere * (dē·sper'dā·rā) *vt* to disperse
dispersione (dē·spār·syō'nā) *f* dispersal
disperso (dē·spār'sō) *a* missing
dispetto (dē·spāt'tō) *m* spite; **a — di** despite, in spite of; **far** — to annoy, vex; to spite; **–samente** (dē·spāt·tō·zâ·mān'tā) *adv* maliciously; **–so** (dē·spāt·tō'zō) *a* malicious, spiteful
dispiacente (dē·spyâ·chān'tā) *a* unpleasant; sorry
dispiacere (dē·spyâ·chā'rā) *m* sorrow; regret; — * *vi* to be displeasing, displease; to inconvenience; **mi dispiace** I am sorry; **se non ti dispiace** if you please
dispiaceri (dē·spyâ·chā'rē) *mpl* troubles *(fig)*; **aver** — to be in trouble
disponibile (dē·spō·nē'bē·lā) *a* available
disponibilità (dē·spō·nē·bē·lē·tâ') *f* availability
disporre * (dē·spōr'rā) *vt* to arrange; to dispose of; to order; — **di mezzi** to have means at one's disposal; — **le cose in modo da** to arrange matters so that; **poter — di** to be able to dispose of; **l'uomo propone e Dio dispone** man proposes, God disposes
disporsi * (dē·spōr'sē) *vr* to place oneself; to be prepared; to be ready for; — **a uscire** to be ready to leave
dispositivo (dē·spō·zē·tē'vō) *m* device; — **di segnalazione** indicator
disposizione (dē·spō·zē·tsyō'nā) *f* disposal; arrangement; order; **a** — available; on hand; at one's service; **d'accordo alla** — in accordance with the rules; — **per la musica** talent for music
disposto (dē·spō'stō) *a* inclined; prepared
dispotico (dē·spô'tē·kō) *a* despotic
dispotismo (dē·spō·tē'zmō) *m* despotism
dispregiativo (dē·sprā·jâ·tē'vō) *a* disparaging; *(gram)* pejorative
disprezzabile (dē·sprā·tsâ'bē·lā) *a* despicable
disprezzare (dē·sprā·tsâ'rā) *vt* to despise
disprezzo (dē·sprā'tsō) *m* contempt
disputa (dē'spū·tâ) *f* dispute, quarrel; **–re** (dē·spū·tâ'rā) *vt&i* to contend; to argue
disquisizione (dē·skwē·zē·tsyō'nā) *f* dissertation
dissanguare (dēs·sân·gwâ'rā) *vt* to bleed; to draw blood from
dissapore (dēs·sâ·pō'rā) *m* disappointment; disagreement, difference
dissecare (dēs·sā·kâ'ra) *vt* to dissect
disseminare (dēs·sā·mē·nâ'rā) *vt* to spread, disseminate
disseminato (dēs·sā·mē·nâ'tō) *a* strewn; covered; disseminated; — **di fiori** covered with flowers; — **di pietre** strewn with stones
dissenso (dēs·sān'sō) *m* dissent, dissension
dissenteria (dēs·sān·tā·rē'â) *f* dysentery
dissentire (dēs·sān·tē'rā) *vi* to disagree, be in disagreement
disseppellire (dēs·sāp·pāl·lē'rā) *vt* to exhume, disinter; *(fig)* to revive
dissertazione (dēs·sār·tâ·tsyō'nā) *f* dissertation
disservizio (dēs·sār·vē'tsyō) *m* poor service
dissesto (dēs·sā'stō) *m* failure; trouble
dissetare (dēs·sā·tâ'rā) *vt* to quench one's thirst
dissezione (dēs·sā·tsyō'nā) *f* dissection
dissidente (dēs·sē·dān'tā) *m* dissenter
dissidio (dēs·sē'dyō) *m* disagreement
dissimile (dēs·sē'mē·lā) *a* dissimilar
dissimulare (des·sē·mū·lâ'rā) *vt* to dissimulate, hide, feign
dissimularsi (dēs·sē·mū·lâr'sē) *vr* to disguise oneself; to be hidden
dissimulatamente (dēs·sē·mū·lâ·tâ·mān'tā) *adv* deceptively; deceitfully
dissimulazione (dēs·sē·mū·lâ·tsyō'nā) *f* dissimulation; deceit, trickery
dissipare (dēs·sē·pâ'rā) *vt* to dispel; to waste; to squander; — **gli averi** to squander one's patrimony; — **i sospetti** to remove one's suspicions; to cast off one's doubts
dissiparsi (dēs·sē·pâr'sē) *vr* to vanish, disappear
dissociazione (dēs·sō·châ·tsyō'nā) *f* dissassociation
dissodare (dēs·sō·dâ'rā) *vt* to clear *(land)*; to break up *(soil)*
dissoluto (dēs·sō·lū'tō) *a* dissolute
dissoluzione (dēs·sō·lū·tsyō'nā) *f* dissolution
dissolvere * (dēs·sôl'vā·rā) *vt* to dissolve; to dispel
dissonanza (dēs·sō·nân'tsâ) *f* dissonance
dissotterrare (dēs·sōt·tār·râ'rā) *vt* to disinter
dissuadere * (dēs·swâ·dā'rā) *vt* to dissuade
dissuasione (dēs·swâ·zyō'nā) *f* dissuasion
distaccamento (dē·stâk·kâ·mān'tō) *m* detachment
distaccare (dē·stâk·kâ'rā) *vt* to detach
distacco (dē·stâk'kō) *m* aloofness; distance; separation; parting; difference; — **doloroso** painful parting; — **notevole** considerable distance; **il — fra i due** the difference between the two
distante (dē·stân'tā) *a* distant, far
distanza (dē·stân'tsâ) *f* distance
distanziare (dē·stân·tsyâ'rā) *vt* to leave behind; to keep at a distance
distare (dē·stâ'rā) *vi* to be distant
distendere * (dē·sten'dā·rā) *vt* to stretch out, extend
distensione (dē·stān·syō'nā) *f* relaxation
distesa (dē·stā'zâ) *f* expanse; **–mente** (dē·stā·zâ·mān'tā) *adv* at length, extensively

disteso (dē·stā'zō) *a* stretched out; **lungo** — at full length; **per** — in detail
distillare (dē·stēl·lâ'rā) *vt* to distill
distillarsi (dē·stēl·lâr'sē) *vr* to be distilled, be extracted; — **il cervello** to rack one's brain
distilleria (dē·stēl·lā·rē'â) *f* distillery
distinguere * (dē·stēn'gwā·rā) *vt* to distinguish
distinguersi * (dē·stēn'gwār·sē) *vr* to stand out, be preeminent
distinta (dē·stēn'tâ) *f* list; itemized invoice; price list; **–mente** (dē·stēn·tâ·mān'tā) *adv* distinctly
distintivo (dē·stēn·tē'vō) *m* badge; — *a* distinctive
distinto (dē·stēn'tō) *a* distinct; distinguished; **modo** — different way; refined manners; **famiglia distinta** eminent family; **nascita distinta** aristocratic birth; **pronuncia distinta** clear pronunciation
distinzione (dē·stēn·tsyō'nā) *f* distinction; **senza** — indiscriminately
distogliere * (dē·stô'lyā·rā) *vt* to distract, divert, deter; to dissuade; to draw away
distorsione (dē·stōr·syō'nā) *f* sprain
distrarre * (dē·strâr'rā) *vt* to distract; to entertain, amuse, divert; — **fondi** to misappropriate funds
distrarsi * (dē·strâr'sē) *vr* to become distracted, divert one's attention; to relax
distrattamente (dē·strât·tâ·mān'tā) *adv* absentmindedly, inattentively, heedlessly
distratto (dē·strât'tō) *a* absent-minded, inattentive
distrazione (dē·strâ·tsyō'nā) *f* distraction; relaxation; misappropriation; amusement
distretto (dē·strāt'tō) *m* district
distrettuale (dē·strāt·twâ'lā) *a* of a district; **giudice** — district judge
distribuire (dē·strē·bwē'rā) *vt* to distribute
distributore (dē·strē·bū·tō'rā) *m* distributor
distribuzione (dē·strē·bū·tsyō'nā) *f* distribution
districare (dē·strē·kâ'rā) to disentangle; to extricate
districato (dē·strē·kâ'tō) *a* disentangled; extricated
distrofia (dē·strō·fē'â) *f* dystrophy
distruggere * (dē·strūj'jā·rā) *vt* to destroy
distrutto (dē·strūt'tō) *a* destroyed; **–re** (dē·strūt·tō'rā) *m* destroyer
distruzione (dē·strū·tsyō'nā) *f* destruction
disturbare (dē·stūr·bâ'rā) *vt* to disturb
disturbarsi (dē·stūr·bâr'sē) *vr* to bother, take the trouble
disturbo (dē·stūr'bō) *m* trouble
disubbidiente (dē·zūb·bē·dyān'tā) *a* disobedient
disubbidienza (dē·zūb·bē·dyān'tsâ) disobedience
disubbidire (dē·zūb·bē·dē'rā) *vt&i* to disobey, disregard; to be heedless of
disuguaglianza (dē·zū·gwâ·lyân'tsâ) *f* unevenness; inequality; difference, disparity
disuguagliare (dē·zū·gwâ·lyâ'rā) *vt* to make unequal
disuguale (dē·zū·gwâ'lā) *a* unequal; uneven
disunione (dē·zū·nyō'nā) *f* disunity, discord
disunire (dē·zū·nē'rā) *vt* to disunite
disunirsi (dē·zū·nēr'sē) *vr* to become disunified, split up
disunito (dē·zū·nē'tō) *a* disunited
disusato (dē·zū·zâ'tō) *a* obsolete
disuso (dē·zū'zō) *m* disuse, obsolescence
disutile (dē·zū'tē·lā) *a* harmful; useless
disviare (dē·zvyâ'rā) *vt* to mislead, lead astray
disviarsi (dē·zvyâr'sē) *vr* to go astray, lose one's bearings
disvio (dē·zvē'ō) *m* straying; misrouting
dita (dē'tâ) *fpl* fingers; **mordersi le** — to regret something bitterly
ditale (dē·tâ'lā) *m* thimble
ditali (dē·tâ'lē) *mpl* elbow macaroni
dito (dē'tō) *m* finger; toe; — **alluce** big toe; — **annulare** ring finger; — **indice** forefinger, index finger; — **medio** middle finger; — **mignolo** little finger — **pollice** thumb; **a un — della tragedia** on the brink of tragedy; **il — di Dio** *(fig)* the hand of God; **legarsela al** — to bear a grudge; to make a point of remembering; **mostrare a** — to point at; **un — di vino** a drop of wine
ditta (dēt'tâ) *f* firm, concern
dittatore (dēt·tâ·tō'rā) *m* dictator
dittatoriale (dēt·tâ·tō·ryâ'lā) *a* dictatorial
dittatura (dēt·tâ·tū'râ) *f* dictatorship
dittongo (dēt·tōn'gō) *m* diphthong
diuretico (dyū·re'tē·kō) *a&m* diuretic
diurnista (dyūr·nē'stâ) *m* temporary employee; worker paid by the day; dayworker
diurno (dyūr'nō) *a* daily; **albergo** — public baths; **lavoro** — work paid by the day; daywork; **scuola diurna** day school
diuturno (dyū·tūr'nō) *a* continual; eternal
diva (dē'vâ) *f (theat)* star
divagare (dē·vâ·gâ'rā) *vi* to roam, ramble
divagazione (dē·vâ·gâ·tsyō'nā) *f* deviation; diversion
divano (dē·vâ'nō) *m* sofa, couch
divario (dē·vâ'ryō) *m* difference, discrepancy
divampare (dē·vâm·pâ'rā) *vi* to burst into flames; *(fig)* to break out; to flare up
divaricare (dē·vâ·rē·kâ'rā) *vt* to spread apart; to stretch out, extend
divellere * (dē·vel'lā·rā) *vt* to uproot
divenire * (dē·vā·nē'rā), **diventare** (dē·vān·tâ'rā) *vi* to become, get; — **amici** to become friends; — **pallido** to turn pale; — **ricco** to grow wealthy; — **vecchio** to grow old; **far — matto** to drive mad
diverbio (dē·ver'byō) *m* argument, quarrel
divergenza (dē·vār·jān'tsâ) *f* disagreement, difference of opinion
diversamente (dē·vār·sâ·mān'tā) *adv* in a different way, differently
diversità (dē·vār·sē·tâ') *f* variety, unlike-

ness; diversity
diversivo (dē·vār·sē′vō) *m* pastime
diverso (dē·vār′sō) *a* different; diverse
divertente (dē·vār·tān′tā) *a* amusing
divertimento (dē·vār·tē·mān′tō) *m* fun, recreation; **buon —!** have fun!
divertire (dē·vār·tē′rā) *vt* to amuse; to give pleasure to
divertirsi (dē·vār·tēr′sē) *vr* to have a good time, enjoy oneself
divetta (dē·vāt′tâ) *f* (*theat*) starlet
dividendo (dē·vē·dān′dō) *m* dividend
dividere * (dē·vē′dā·rā) *vt* to divide; to share; to take part in
divieto (dē·vyā′tō) *m* prohibition; **— di fumare** no smoking; **— di parcheggio,** **— di posteggio** no parking; **— di passaggio** do not enter; **— di segnalazione acustica** horn blowing forbidden; **— di sorpasso** no passing; **— di sosta** no parking; **— di svolta a destra** no right turn; **— di svolta a sinistra** no left turn; **— di svolta a destra o a sinistra** no turns; **— di transito** no thoroughfare
divinamente (dē·vē·nâ·mān′tā) *adv* exquisitely, divinely, beautifully
divinatorio (dē·vē·nâ·tô′ryō) *a* forecasting, predicting; divining
divinazione (dē·vē·nâ·tsyō′nā) *f* divining
divinità (dē·vē·nē·tâ′) *f* divinity
divinizzare (dē·vē·nē·dzâ′rā) *vt* to deify
divino (dē·vē′nō) *a* divine
divisa (dē·vē′zâ) *f* uniform; currency, bills
divisare (dē·vē·zâ′rā) *vt* to plan, design, devise
divisibile (dē vē zē′bē lā) *a* divisible
divisione (dē·vē·zyō′nā) *f* division
divismo (dē·vē′zmō) *m* filmdom, movie world; worship of movie stars
divisore (dē·vē·zō′rā) *m* divisor
divisorio (dē·vē·zô′ryō) *a* dividing; **muro —** partition
divo (dē·vō) *m* (*theat*) star
divorare (dē·vō·râ′rā) *vt* to devour
divorato (dē·vō·râ′tō) *a* devoured; wasted; **— dalla febbre** wasted by fever; **–re** (dē·vō·râ·tō′rā) *m* big eater; **–re di ricchezze** squanderer, wastrel
divorziare (dē·vōr·tsyâ′rā) *vi* to get a divorce
divorzio (dē·vôr′tsyō) *m* divorce; **chiedere il —** to ask for a divorce
divulgare (dē·vūl·gâ′rā) *vt* to divulge, disclose
divulgazione (dē·vūl·gâ·tsyō′nā) *f* divulgation, spreading; **opera di —** popular literary work
dizionario (dē·tsyō·nâ′ryō) *m* dictionary
dizione (dē·tsyō′nā) *f* diction
do (dō) *m* (*mus*) do
doccia (dô′châ) *f* shower, shower bath
docente (dō·chān′tā) *m* teacher; **libero —** guest professor
docenza (dō·chān′tsâ) *f* teaching profession
docile (dô′chē·lā) *a* docile, tame
docilità (dō·chē·lē·tâ′) *f* tameness, docility
docilmente (dō·chēl·mān′tā) *adv* submissively, mildly
documentare (dō·kū·mān·tâ′rā) *vt* to document, prove
documentario (dō·kū·mān·tâ′ryō) *m* documentary film
documenti (dō·kū·mān′tē) *mpl* papers
documento (dō·kū·mān′tō) *m* document
dodicenne (dō·dē·chān′nā) *a* twelve years old
dodicesimo (dō·dē·che′zē·mō) *a* twelfth
dodici (dô′dē·chē) *a* twelve
doga (dō′gâ) *f* stave; **–re** (dō·gâ′rā) *vt* to put the staves on (*barrel*)
dogale (dō·gâ′lā) *a* of the doge
dogana (dō·gâ′nâ) *f* duty, customs; **–le** (dō·gâ·nâ′lā) *a* customs, concerning customs
doganiere (dō·gâ·nyā′rā) *m* customs official
dogaressa (dō·gâ·rās′sâ) doge's wife
dogato (dō·gâ′tō) *m* office of the doge
doge (dō′jā) *m* doge
doglia (dô′lyâ) *f* labor pains; birth pains
dogma (dōg′mâ) *m* dogma; **–tico** (dōg·mâ′tē·kō) *a* dogmatic; **–tizzare** (dōg·mâ·tē·dzâ′rā) *vt* to dogmatize
dolce (dōl′chā) *a* sweet; soft; mild; (*mus*) dolce; (*gram*) soft; **—** *m* candy; **— ricordo** pleasant memory; **acqua —** fresh water; soft water; **carattere —** mild temper; **carbone —** charcoal; **clima —** mild climate; **–mente** (dōl·chā·mān′tā) *adv* softly; **–ria** (dōl·chā·rē′â) *f* candy store; **–zza** (dōl·chā′tsâ) *f* sweetness; **— mia!** sweetheart!
dolciastro (dōl·châ′strō) *a* sweetish
dolciumi (dōl·chū′mē) *mpl* candies
dolente (dō·lān′tā) *a* sorry
dolere * (dō·lā′rā) *vi* to hurt, ache; to cause sorrow; to make grieve
dolicocefalo (dō·lē·kō·che′fâ·lō) dolichocephalous
dollaro (dôl′lâ·rō) *m* dollar
dolo (dō′lō) *m* fraud; **–so** (dō·lō′zō) *a* deceitful, fraudulent; **incendio –so** arson
dolore (dō·lō′rā) *m* sorrow; pain; **— di denti** toothache; **— di stomaco** stomachache; **— di testa** headache
dolorosamente (dō·lō·rō·zâ·mān′tā) *adv* painfully; unfortunately
doloroso (dō·lō·rō′zō) *a* sad; painful; unfortunate
domanda (dō·mân′dâ) *f* question; application; request; **–re** (dō·mân·dâ′rā) *vt* to ask; to inquire about; **-rsi** (dō·mân·dâr′sē) *vr* to wonder, question
domani (dō·mâ′nē) *m&adv* tomorrow; **dopo–** (dō·pō·dō·mâ′nē), **— l'altro** day after tomorrow; **— otto** week from tomorrow; **pensare a —** to think of the future; **un — non lontano** the near future
domare (dō·mâ′rā) *vt* to tame; **— una sommossa** to suppress a rebellion; **— un cavallo** to break a horse; **— un incendio** to get a fire under control
domato (dō·mâ′tō) *a* subdued; quenched; broken; tamed; **–re** (dō·mâ·tō′rā) *m* tamer, trainer

domattina (dō·mât·tē'nâ) *adv* tomorrow morning
domenica (dō·me'nē·kâ) *f* Sunday; **–le** (dō·mā·nē·kâ'lā) *a* Sunday, concerning Sunday
domenicano (dō·mā·nē·kâ'nō) *a&m* Dominican
domestica (dō·me'stē·kâ) *f* housemaid; **–re** (dō·mā·stē·kâ'rā) *vt* to tame
domestichezza (dō·mā·stē·kā'tsâ) *f* familiarity
domestico (dō·me'stē·kō) *m* servant; — *a* domestic
domicilio (dō·mē·chē'lyō) *m* home address; residence
dominante (dō·mē·nân'tā) *a* prevailing; outstanding; dominant
dominare (dō·mē·nâ'rā) *vt&i* to dominate
dominatore (dō·mē·nâ·tō'rā) *m* ruler; — *a* ruling, dominant
dominazione (dō·mē·nâ·tsyō'nā) *f* domination
dominio (dō·mē'nyō) *m* control, power
domino (dô'mē·nō) *m* domino
donare (dō·nâ'rā) *vt* to donate
donatore (dō·nâ·tō'rā) *m* donor; — **di sangue** blood donor
donazione (dō·nâ·tsyō'nā) *f* donation
donde (dōn'dā) *adv* from where; as a result, consequently
dondolare (dōn·dō·lâ'rā) *vt* to rock, sway
dondolo (dôn'dō·lō) *m* toy; swaying; **sedia a** — rocking chair
donna (dōn'nâ) *f* woman; queen (*cards*); — **di servizio** housemaid; **–ccia** (dōn·nâ'châ) *f* woman of easy virtue; ill-tempered woman; **–iuolo** (dōn·nâ·ywō'lō) *m* ladies' man
dono (dō'nō) *m* gift
donzella (dōn·dzāl'lâ) *f* maid, maiden
dopo (dō'pō) *prep* after; *adv* later; **–guerra** (dō·pō·gwār'râ) *m* postwar period; **–pranzo** (dō·pō·prân'dzō) *m* afternoon; — **si vedrà** we'll see later on; **il giorno** — the next day; **poco** — shortly afterwards
doppiaggio (dōp·pyâj'jō) *m* film dubbing
doppiamente (dōp·pyâ·mān'tā) *adv* doubly
doppiare (dōp·pyâ'rā) *vt* (*naut*) to double, sail around; to dub (*movies*)
doppietta dōp·pyāt'tâ) *f* double-barreled shotgun
doppio (dôp'pyō) *a* double; two-faced; **–ne** (dōp·pyō'nā) *m* copy, duplicate
dorare (dō·râ'rā) *vt* to gild
dorato (dō·râ'tō) *a* gilded, gilt
dorico (dô'rē·kō) *a* Doric; Dorian
dormiglione (dōr·mē·lyō'nā) *m* sleepyhead; lazybones
dormire (dōr·mē'rā) *vi* to sleep; **chi dorme non piglia pesci** (*fig*) the early bird catches the worm
dormitina (dōr·mē·tē'nâ) *f* nap, short sleep
dormitorio (dōr·mē·tô'ryō) *m* dormitory
dormiveglia (dōr·mē·ve'lyâ) *m* doze; fitful sleep
dorsale (dōr·sâ'lā) *a* dorsal
dorso (dōr'sō) *m* back
dosaggio (dō·zâj'jō) *m* dosage
dosare (dō·zâ'rā) *vt* to dose
dose (dō'zā) *f* dose
dosso (dōs'sō) *m* back; **togliersi di** — to get rid of; to take off
dotare (dō·tâ'rā) *vt* to endow; to furnish, provide
dotazione (dō·tâ·tsyō'nā) *f* endowment; donation
dote (dō'tā) *f* dowry; talent; quality
dotto (dōt'tō) *a* learned; **–re** (dōt·tō'rā) *m* doctor; scholar; **–ressa** (dōt·tō·rās'sâ) *f* woman doctor
dottrina (dōt·trē'nâ) *f* doctrine; — **cristiana** catechism
dove (dō'vā) *adv* where; **il** — the place; **per ogni** — everywhere
dovere (dō·vā'rā) *m* duty; **avere il** — **di** to have the duty of, be obliged; **farsi un** — **di** to make a point of, consider it one's duty to; **prima il** —, **dopo il piacere** work before pleasure; **stare a** — to behave properly; — * *vt&i* to owe; to have to; to be obliged to; to feel it one's duty to; to be due
doveroso (dō·vā·rō'zō) *a* right; dutiful; legitimate
dovunque (dō·vūn'kwā) *adv* wherever
dovuto (dō·vū'tō) *a* right, just, proper; due; rightful; **a tempo** — in due time; **in modo** — in the proper way; **in dovuta considerazione** in just consideration
dozzina (dō·dzē'nâ) *f* dozen; board; **–le** (dō·dzē·nâ'lā) *a* common, cheap; **–nte** (dō·dzē·nân'tā) *m* boarder, lodger
draga (drâ'gâ) *f* dredge; **–ggio** (drâ·gâj'jō) *m* dredging; **–mine** (drâ·gâ·mē'nā) *m* minesweeper; **–re** (drâ·gâ'rā) *vt* to dredge
drago (drâ'gō) *m* dragon
dramma (drâm'mâ) *m* drama; **–tica** (drâm·mâ'tē·kâ) *f* dramatic art, dramatics; **–tico** (drâm·mâ'tē·kō) *a* dramatic; **–tizzare** (drâm·mâ·tē·dzâ'rā) *vt* to dramatize; **–turgo** (drâm·mâ·tūr'gō) *m* playwright
drappeggio (drâp·pej'jō) *m* drapery
drappello (drâp·pāl'lō) *m* platoon
drappo (drâp'pō) *m* cloth; drapery; — **funebre** pall
drastico (drâ'stē·kō) *a* drastic
drenaggio (drā·nâj'jō) *m* drainage
drenare (drā·nâ'rā) *vt* to drain
dribblare (drēb·blâ'rā) *vt* to dribble (*sport*)
dritto (drēt'tō) *a* straight; honest
drizzare (drē·tsâ'rā) *vt* to straighten
droga (drō'gâ) *f* drug; spice; **–re** (drō·gâ'rā) *vt* to drug, dope; to spice
drogheria (drō·gā·rē'â) *f* grocery store
droghiere (drō·gyā'rā) *m* grocer
dromedario (drō·mā·dâ'ryō) *m* dromedary
dualismo (dwâ·lē'zmō) *m* dualism; duality
dualista (dwâ·lē'stâ) *m&f* dualist
dualità (dwâ·lē·tâ') *f* duality, dualism
dubbio (dūb'byō) *m* doubt; —, **–so** (dūb·byō'zō) *a* doubtful, dubious

dubitabile (dū·bē·tâ'bē·lā) *a* questionable, open to doubt
dubitare (dū·bē·tâ'rā) *vi* to doubt
duca (dū'kâ) *m* duke; **–le** (dū·kâ'lā) *a* ducal
duce (dū'chā) *m* captain; leader, chief
duchessa (dū·kās'sâ) *f* duchess
due (dū'ā) *a* two; — **volte** twice; **tutt'e** — both; **uno dei** — one or the other, one of the two
duecento (dwā·chān'tō) *a* two hundred; **il D–** the thirteenth century
duellante (dwāl·lān'tā) *m* duelist
duellare (dwāl·lâ'rā) *vi* to duel, fight a duel
duemila (dwā·mē'lâ) *a* two thousand
duetto (dwāt'tō) *m* duet
duna (dū'nâ) *f* dune
dunque (dūn'kwā) *adv* so, therefore
duodeno (dwō·dā'nō) *m* duodenum
duo (dū'ō) *m* (*mus*) duo, duet; **–decimo** (dwō·de'chē·mō) *a* twelfth
duolo (dwō'lō) *m* suffering, grief
duomo (dwō'mō) *m* cathedral
duplex (dū'plāks) *m* telephone party line
duplicare (dū·plē·kâ'rā) *vt* to duplicate
duplicato (dū·plē·kâ'tō) *m* duplicate
duplice (dū'plē·chā) *a* double, twofold; **in — copia** in duplicate
duplicità (dū·plē·chē·tâ') *f* duplicity, falseness
durabile (dū·râ'bē·lā) *a* durable
duramente (dū·râ·mān'tā) *adv* hard; harshly; bitterly; sharply; roughly; cruelly
durante (dū·rân'tā) *prep* during; — *a* lasting
durare (dū·râ'rā) *vt* to endure; — *vi* to last
durata (dū·râ'tâ) *f* duration
duraturo (dū·râ·tū'rō), **durevole** (dū·re'vō·lā) *a* durable, lasting
durevolezza (dū·rā·vō·lā'tsâ) *f* durability
durevolmente (dū·rā·vōl·mān'tā) *adv* lastingly, durably
durezza (dū·rā'tsâ) *f* hardness, harshness
duro (dū'rō) *a* hard, tough; stale; **–ne** (dū·rō'nā) *a* stupid; **–ne** *m* callous
duttile (dūt'tē·lā) *a* ductile, plastic; yielding
duttilità (dūt·tē·lē·tâ') *f* plasticity; pliability

E

e (ā) *conj* and; well then? and so?
ebanista (ā·bâ·nē'stâ) *m* cabinet maker
ebano (e'bâ·nō) *m* ebony
ebbene (āb·bā'nā) *adv* well then
ebbrezza (āb·brā'tsâ) *f* intoxication; (*fig*) rapture
ebbro (āb'brō) *a* drunk; — **d'amore** mad with love; — **di gioia** exultant with joy
ebdomadario (āb·dō·mâ·dâ'ryō) *a&m* weekly
ebete (e'bā·tā) *a* stupid, obtuse
ebetismo (ā·bā·tē'zmō) *m* stupidity, dullness
ebollizione (ā·bōl·lē·tsyō'nā) *f* boiling; (*fig*) enthusiasm, excitement
ebraico (ā·brâ'ē·kō) *a&m* Hebrew
ebreo (ā·brā'ō) *a* Jewish; — *m* Jew
ecatombe (ā·kâ·tōm'bā) *f* massacre, slaughter
eccedenza (ā·chā·dān'tsâ) *f* excess; surplus
eccedere (ā·che'dā·rā) *vt&i* to exceed; to exaggerate, carry too far
eccellente (ā·chāl·lān'tā) *a* excellent; **–mente** (ā·chāl·lān·tā·mān'tā) *adv* very well, excellently
eccellenza (ā·chāl·lān'tsâ) *f* excellence; **Vostra Eccelenza** Your Excellency
eccellere * (ā·chel'lā·rā) *vt* to excel; to outshine
eccentricamente (ā·chān·trē·kâ·mān'tā) *adv* eccentrically
eccentricità (ā·chān·trē·chē·tâ') *f* eccentricity
eccentrico (ā·chen'trē·kō) *a&m* eccentric
eccepibile (ā·chā·pē'bē·lā) *a* questionable, objectionable
eccepire (ā·chā·pē'rā) *vt* to take exception to, object to
eccessivamente (ā·chās·sē·vâ·mān'tā) *adv* excessively, overly
eccessività (ā·chās·sē·vē·tâ') *f* excessiveness; overstatement
eccessivo (ā·chās·sē'vō) *a* excessive, overdone
eccesso (ā·chās'sō) *m* excess
eccetera (ā·che'tā·râ) *m* and so forth
eccetto (ā·chāt'tō) *prep* except; but; **tutti — uno** all but one
eccettuare (ā·chāt·twâ'rā) *vt* to except
eccettuato (ā·chāt·twâ'tō) *a* excepted; omitted, left out
eccezionale (ā·chā·tsyō·nâ'lā) *a* exceptional
eccezione (ā·chā·tsyō'nā) *f* exception
eccidio (ā·chē'dyō) *m* massacre
eccitabile (ā·chē·tâ'bē·lā) *a* excitable, emotional
eccitamento (ā·chē·tâ·mān'tō) *m* excitement; fervor
eccitante (ā·chē·tân'tā) *m* stimulant; — *a* stimulating, moving
eccitare (ā·chē·tâ'rā) *vt* to excite, stir; to arouse, move
eccitativo (ā·chē·tâ·tē'vō) *a* moving, rousing
eccitato (ā·chē·tâ'tō) *a* excited; **–re** (ā·chē·tâ·tō'rā) *m* arouser; **–re** *a* exciting
eccitazione (ā·chē·tâ·tsyō'nā) *f* excitement, arousing, stimulation
ecclesiastico (āk·klā·zyâ'stē·kō) *a* ecclesiastical; — *m* clergyman
ecco (āk'kō) *adv* here; **—!** *interj* look!; **–mi qua!** Here I am!; — **fatto** that's done; — **tutto** that's all
eccome (āk·kō'mā) *adv* and how, how in the world
echeggiante (ā·kāj·jân'tā) *a* resounding,

reverberating
echeggiare (ā·kāj·jâ'rā) *vi* to echo; to reverberate
eclettico (ā·klet'tē·kō) *a&m* eclectic
eclissare (ā·klēs·sâ'rā) *vt* to eclipse
eclissarsi (ā·klēs·sâr'sē) *vr* to abscond, disappear
eclissi (ā·klēs'sē) *m* eclipse
eclittica (ā·klēt'tē·kâ) *f* ecliptic
eco (ā'kō) *m* echo; — **della stampa** service providing newspaper clippings; **fare — alle parole di** to mouth the words of; **farsi — della diceria** to repeat a rumor
economato (ā·kō·nō·mâ'tō) *m* stewardship; administration
economia (ā·kō·nō·mē'â) *f* economy; — **planificata** controlled economy; — **politica** political economy; political economics
economicamente (ā·kō·nō·mē·kâ·mān'tā) *adv* economically
economico (ā·kō·nô'mē·kō) *a* economical; cheap
economista (ā·kō·nō·mē'stâ) *m* economist
economizzare (ā·kō·nō·mē·dzâ'rā) *vt* to economize; to husband
economizzatore (ā·kō·nō·mē·dzâ·tō'rā) *m* economizer; saver
economo (ā·kô'nō·mō) *m* administrator; steward; — *a* saving, thrifty
ecumenico (ā·kū·me'nē·kō) *a* ecumenical
eczema (āk·dzā'mâ) *m* eczema
ed (ād) *conj* and
edema (ā·dā'mâ) *m (med)* edema
edera (e'dā·râ) *f* ivy
edicola (ā·dē'kō·lâ) *f* newsstand
edicolista (ā·dē·kō·lē'stâ) *m* newsstand operator
edificare (ā·dē·fē·kâ'rā) *vt* to build; to edify, educate
edificante (ā·dē·fē·kân'tā) *a* educative, edifying
edificio (ā·dē·fē'chō) *m* building
edile (e'dē·lā) *a* building; — *m* building contractor
edilizia (ā·dē·lē'tsyâ) *f* construction; building industry
edilizio (ā·dē·lē'tsyō) *a* building
edito (e'dē·tō) *a* published; edited
editore (ā·dē·tō'rā) *m* publisher; editor; — *a* publishing; **casa editrice** publishing house
editoriale (ā·dē·tō·ryâ'lā) *m* editorial
editto (ā·dēt'tō) *m* edict
edizione (ā·dē·tsyō'nā) *f* edition; — **esaurita** edition out of print
edonista (ā·dō·nē'stâ) *mf&a* hedonist
edotto (ā·dōt'tō) *a* notified, informed
educare (ā·dū·kâ'rā) *vt* to educate, teach
educatamente (ā·dū·kâ·tâ·mān'tā) *adv* politely, in a well-bred manner
educativo (ā·dū·kâ·tē'vō) *a* educational
educato (ā·dū·kâ'tō) *a* well-mannered, polite
educatore (ā·dū·kâ·tō'rā) *m* educator
educazione (ā·dū·kâ·tsyō'nā) *f* good manners; education; **senza** — rowdy, ill-mannered
effeminatamente (āf·fā·mē·nâ·tâ·mān'tā) *adv* effeminately
effeminatezza (āf·fā·mē·nâ·tā'tsâ) *f* effeminacy
efferatamente (āf·fā·râ·tâ·mān'tā) *adv* brutally
efferatezza (āf·fā·râ·tā'tsâ) *f* ferociousness; barbarism
efferato (āf·fā·râ'tō) *a* savage, ferocious
effervescente (āf·fār·vā·shān'tā) *a* effervescent
effervescenza (āf·fār·vā'shān'tsâ) *f* effervescence; (*fig*) agitation, excitement
effetti (āf·fāt'tē) *mpl* possessions, effects; bills
effettista (āf·fāt·tē'stâ) *m* sensationalist
effettivamente (āf·fāt·tē·vâ·mān'tā) *adv* really, as a matter of fact
effettivo (āf·fāt·tē'vō) *a* actual, true; present, current
effetto (āf·fāt'tō) *m* effect; (*mech*) action; (*com*) bill; **a quest'** — to this purpose; **far l'** — **di** to seem; to give the appearance of; **in** — really, truly; in fact
effettuabile (āf·fāt·twâ'bē·lā) *a* feasible
effettuare (āf·fāt·twâ'rā) *vt* to fulfill, complete
effettuazione (āf·fāt·twâ·tsyō'nā) *f* completion, fulfillment, carrying out
efficace (āf·fē·kâ'chā) *a* effective; **–mente** (āf·fē·kâ·chā·mān'tā) *adv* efficiently, effectively
efficacia (āf·fē·kâ'châ) *f* efficacy, effect
efficiente (āf·fē·chyān'tā) *a* efficient; **–mente** (āf·fē·chyān·tā·mān'tā) *adv* efficiently, effectively
efficienza (āf·fē·chyān'tsâ) *f* efficiency **essere in** — to be in good working order
effige (āf·fē'jā) *f* effigy
effimero (āf·fē'mā·rō) *a* short-lived
efflusso (āf·flūs'sō) *m* outflow
effrazione (āf·frâ·tsyō'nā) *f* housebreaking
effusione (āf·fū·zyō'nā) *f* effusion; (*fig*) warmheartedness
effuso (āf·fū'zō) *a* given out; diffused; distributed
egemonia (ā·jā·mō·nē'â) *f* hegemony
egida (e'jē·dâ) *f* auspices, sponsorship
Egitto (ā·jēt'tō) *m* Egypt
egiziano (ā·jē·tsyâ'nō) *a&m* Egyptian
egli (ā'lyē) *pron* he
egloga (e'glō·gâ) *f* eglogue
egoismo (ā·gō·ē'zmō) *m* egoism
egoista (ā·gō·ē'stâ) *m* egoist
egoisticamente (ā·gōē·stē·kâ·mān'tā) *adv* selfishly
egoistico (ā·gō·ē'stē·kō) *a* selfish
egotismo (ā·gō·tē'zmō) *m* egotism
egotista (ā·gō·tē'stâ) *m* egotist
egregiamente (ā·grā·jâ·mān'tā) *adv* excellently
egregio (ā·gre'jō) *a* distinguished
egresso (ā·grās'sō) *m* way out, exit
egretta (ā·grāt'tâ) *f* egret
eguaglianza (ā·gwâ·lyân'tsâ) *f* equality
eguagliare (ā·gwâ·lyâ'rā) *vt* to equalize; to make even
eguale (ā·gwâ'lā) *a* equal; **rendere** — to

level; to smooth out
eiaculare (ā·yâ·kū·lâ'rā) *vt* to ejaculate
eiaculazione (ā·yâ·kū·lâ·tsyō'nā) *f* ejaculation
eiettore (ā·yāt·tō'rā) *m* (*mech*) release, ejector
eiezione (ā·yā·tsyō'nā) *f* ejection, release
elaborare (ā·lâ·bō·râ'rā) *vt* to work out in detail; to elaborate
elaborato (ā·lâ·bō·râ'tō) *a* carefully done; detailed
elaborazione (ā·lâ·bō·râ·tsyō'nā) *f* elaboration; refinement
elargire (ā·lâr·jē'rā) *vt* to lavish, expend profusely
elargizione (ā·lâr·jē·tsyō'nā) *f* lavish donation; munificence
elasticamente (ā·lâ·stē·kâ·mān'tā) *adv* resiliently, bouyantly
elasticità (ā·lâ·stē·chē·tâ') *f* elasticity; bouyancy
elastico (ā·lâ'stē·kō) *m* rubber band; spring; — *a* elastic; bouyant, adaptable
elefante (ā·lā·fân'tā) *m* elephant; **–essa** (ā·lā·fân·tās'sâ) *f* female elephant
elegante (ā·lā·gân'tā) *a* smart, elegant; **–mente** (ā·lā·gân·tā·mān'tā) *adv* smartly, elegantly
elegantone (ā·lā·gân·tō'nā) *a* overly elegant; chic
eleganza (ā·lā·gân'tsâ) *f* elegance
eleggere * (ā·lej'jā·rā) *vt* to elect; to select
eleggibile (ā·lāj·jē'bē·lā) *a* eligible
eleggibilità (ā·lāj·jē·bē·lē·tâ') *f* qualification, eligibility
elegia (ā·lā·jē'â) *f* elegy
elementale (ā·lā·mān·tâ'lā) *a* elemental
elementare (ā·lā·mān·tâ'rā) *a* elementary
elemento (ā·lā·mān'tō) *m* element; component
elemosina (ā·lā·mô'zē·nâ) *f* charity; **–re** (ā·lā·mō·zē·nâ'rā) *vt&i* to solicit alms, beg; to entreat
elencare (ā·lān·kâ'rā) *vt* to list
elenco (ā·lān'kō) *m* list; — **telefonico** telephone book
elettivo (ā·lāt·tē'vō) *a* elective
eletto (ā·lāt'tō) *a* elected; chosen
elettorale (ā·lāt·tō·râ'lā) *a* electoral; **scheda** — ballot; **urna** — ballot box
elettorato (ā·lāt·tō·râ'tō) *m* right to vote, suffrage
elettore (ā·lāt·tō'rā) *m* voter
elettricamente (ā·lāt·trē·kâ·mān'tā) *adv* electrically, with electricity
elettricista (ā·lāt·trē·chē'stâ) *m* electrician
elettricità (ā·lāt·trē·chē·tâ') *f* electricity
elettrico (ā·let'trē·kō) *a* electrical, electric
elettrificare (ā·lāt·trē·fē·kâ'rā) *vt* to electrify; to charge with a current
elettrificazione (ā·lāt·trē·fē·kâ·tsyō'nā) *f* electrification
elettrizzare (ā·lāt·trē·dzâ'rā) *vt* to thrill, to excite, electrify
elettro (ā·lāt'trō) *m* yellow amber; **–biologia** (ā·lāt·trō·byō·lō·jē'â) *f* electrobiology; **–calamita** (ā·lāt·trō·kâ·lâ·mē'tâ) *f* electromagnet; **–cardiogramma** (ā·lāt·trō·kâr·dyō·grâm'mâ) *m* electrocardiogram; **–cuzione** (ā·lāt·trō·kū·tsyō'nā) *f* electrocution; **–dinamica** (ā·lāt·trō·dē·nâ'mē·kâ) *f* electrodynamics; **–do** (ā·lāt·trō'dō) *m* electrode; **–domestico** (ā·lāt·trō·dō·me'stē·kō) *m* electrical appliance; **–dotto** (ā·lāt·trō·dōt'tō) *m* power plant; **–lisi** (ā·lāt·trō·lē'zē) *f* electrolysis; **–lito** (ā·lāt·trō·lē'tō) *m* electrolyte; **–metallurgia** (ā·lāt·trō·mā·tâl·lūr·jē'â) *f* electrometallurgy; **–metro** (ā·lāt·trô'mā·trō) *m* electrometer; **–motore** (ā·lāt·trō·mō·tō'rā) *m&a* electromotor; **–motrice** (ā·lāt·trō·mō·trē'chā) *f* electrified railroad car; **–ne** (ā·lāt·trō'nā) *m* electron; **–nica** (ā·lāt·trô'nē·kâ) *f* electronics; **–nico** (ā·lāt·trô'nē·kō) *a* electronic; **–scopio** (ā·lāt·trō·skô'pyō) *m* electroscope; **–squasso** (ā·lāt·trō·skwâs'sō) *m* electric shock; jolt of electricity; **–statica** (ā·lāt·trō·stâ'tē·kâ) *f* electrostatics; **–statico** (ā·lāt·trō·stâ'tē·kō) *a* electrostatic; **–tecnica** (ā·lāt·trō·tek'nē·kâ) *f* electrical engineering; **–tecnico** (ā·lāt·trō·tek'nē·kō) *a* electric; **–terapia** (ā·lāt·trō·tā·râ·pē'â) *f* electrotherapy; **–termica** (ā·lāt·trō·ter'mē·kâ) *f* electrothermics; **–termico** (ā·lāt·trō·ter'mē·kō) *a* electrothermic; **–tipia** (ā·lāt·trō·tē·pē'â) *f* electrotype; **–treno** (ā·lāt·trō·trā'nō) *m* electrified train
elevare (ā·lā·vâ'rā) *vt* to raise; to hoist
elevarsi (ā·lā·vâr'sē) *vr* to raise oneself; to stand out, tower above
elevatamente (ā·lā·vâ·tâ·mān'tā) *adv* highly, loftily
elevatezza (ā·lā·vâ·tā'tsâ) *f* loftiness, highness; nobility
elevato (ā·lā·vâ'tō) *a* high, raised
elevatore (ā·lā·vâ·tō'rā) *m* elevator
elevazione (ā·lā·vâ·tsyō'nā) *f* elevation
elezione (ā·lā·tsyō'nā) *f* election; appointment; choice; option
elfo (āl'fō) *m* elf
elica (e'lē·kâ) *f* propeller; (*naut*) screw
elicottero (ā·lē·kôt'tā·rō) *m* helicopter
elidere * (ā·lē'dā·rā) *vt* to cancel out; to elide; to suppress
eliminare (ā·lē·mē·nâ'rā) *vt* to eliminate; to delete; to exclude; to obviate
eliminarsi (ā·lē·mē·nâr'sē) *vr* to be eliminated; to be obviated
eliminatoria (ā·lē·mē·nâ·tô'ryâ) *f* (*sport*) heat
eliminatorio (ā·lē·mē·nâ·tô'ryō) *a* eleminating; deleting
eliminazione (ā·lē·mē·nâ·tsyō'nā) *f* elimination, removal; exclusion; suppression
ella (āl'lâ) *pron* she
ellisse (āl·lēs'sā) *f* ellipse
ellissoide (āl·lēs·sô'ē·dā) *m&a* ellipsoid
ellissi (āl·lēs'sē) *f* ellipsis
ellittico (āl·lēt'tē·kō) *a* elliptical
ellenico (āl·le'nē·kō) *m&a* Hellenic
elmetto (āl·māt'tō) (*mil*) helmet
elmo (āl'mō) *m* helmet
elocuzione (ā·lō·kū·tsyō'nā) *f* elocution; oratorical style

elogiare (ā·lō·jâ'rā) *vt* to praise, commend
elogiabile (ā·lō·jâ'bē·lā) *a* commendable, praiseworthy
elogiatore (ā·lō·jâ·tō'rā) *m* eulogist
elogio (ā·lô'jō) *m* praise
eloquente (ā·lō·kwān'tā) *a* eloquent; golden-tongued; **–mente** (ā·lō·kwān·tā·mān'tā) *adv* forcefully, eloquently
eloquenza (ā·lō·kwān'tsâ) *f* eloquence
elsa (āl'sâ) *f* hilt
elucubrare (ā·lū·kū·brâ'rā) *vt* to muse, mull over
elucubrazione (ā·lū·kū·brâ·tsyō'nā) *f* musing, thoughtful consideration
eludere * (ā·lū'dā·rā) *vt* to elude, evade; to avoid
elusione (ā·lū·zyō'nā) *f* evasion, avoidance
elusivo (ā·lū·zē'vō) elusive, evasive
emaciato (ā·mâ·châ'tō) *a* emaciated
emanare (ā·mâ·nâ'rā) *vt&i* to emanate from, spring from, originate; to publicize
emanazione (ā·mâ·nâ·tsyō'nā) *f* issue, issuing; promulgation
emancipare (ā·mân·chē·pâ'rā) *vt* to free, liberate
emancipazione (ā·mân·chē·pâ·tsyō'nā) *f* liberation, emancipation
emarginare (ā·mâr·jē·nâ'rā) *vt* to note on the margin; to make marginal notes on
emarginato (ā·mâr·jē·nâ'tō) *a* annotated; foot-noted
emblema (ām·blā'mâ) *m* emblem, sign
embolia (ām·bō·lē'â) *f* embolism
embolo (em'bō·lō) *m* embolus, blood clot
embrice (em'brē·chā) *m* roofing tile
embriologia (ām·bryō·lō·jē'â) *f* embryology
embriologo (ām·bryô'lō·gō) *m* embryologist
embrionale (ām·bryō·nâ'lā) *a* embryonic; inchoate
embrione (ām·bryō'nā) *m* embryo
emendamento (ā·mān·dâ·mān'tō) *m* amendment
emendare (ā·mān·dâ'rā) *vt* to amend
emendarsi (ā·mān·dâr'sē) *vr* to correct oneself, reform
emergenza (ā·mār·jān'tsâ) *f* emergency
emergere * (ā·mēr'jā·rā) *vi* to distinguish oneself; to out, become public
emerso (ā·mār'sō) *a* emerged
emerito (ā·me'rē·tō) *a* emeritus; eminent
emeroteca (ā·mā·rō·tā'kâ) *f* periodical room
emesso (ā·mās'sō) *a* emitted, issued
emettere * (ā·met'tā·rā) *vt* to emit; — **un grido** to cry out
emicrania (ā·mē·krâ'nyâ) *f* migraine headache
emigrante (ā·mē·grân'tā) *a&m* emigrant
emigrare (ā·mē·grâ'rā) *vi* to emigrate
emigrato (ā·mē·grâ'tō) *m* emigrant
emigrazione (ā·mē·grâ·tsyō'nā) *f* emigration
eminente (ā·mē·nān'tā) *a* eminent, well-known; **–mente** (ā·mē·nān·tā·mān'tā) *adv* eminently; highly, greatly
eminenza (ā·mē·nān'tsâ) *f* eminence
emisfero (ā·mē·sfā'rō) *m* hemisphere
emissario (ā·mēs·sâ'ryō) *m* emissary
emissione (ā·mēs·syō'nā) *f* emission; broadcast
emittente (ā·mēt·tān'tā) *m* broadcaster; broadcasting station; — *a* broadcasting; issuing
emofilia (ā·mō·fē·lē'â) *f* hemophilia
emoglobina (ā·mō·glō·bē'nâ) *f* hemoglobin
emolliente (ā·mōl·lyān'tā) *a&m* emollient
emolumento (ā·mō·lū·mān'tō) *m* fee; wages
emorragia (ā·mōr·râ·jē'â) *f* hemorrhage
emorroidi (ā·mōr·rô'ē·dē) *fpl* hemorrhoids
emostatico (ā·mō·stâ'tē·kō) *m&a* hemostatic
emoteca (ā·mō·tā'kâ) *f* blood bank
emotivo (ā·mō·tē'vō) *a* excitable
emozionale (ā·mō·tsyō·nâ'lā) *a* emotional, excitable
emozionante (ā·mō·tsyō·nân'tā) *adv* touching, thrilling
emozione (ā·mō·tsyō'nā) *f* emotion; suspense
empietà (ām·pyā·tâ') *f* impiety
empio (em'pyō) *a* impious; cruel
empire * (ām·pē'rā) *vt* to fill; to fill in, close up
empiricamente (ām·pē·rē·kâ·mān'tā) *adv* empirically, experimentally
empirico (ām·pē'rē·kō) *a* empirical
emporio (ām·pô'ryō) *m* bazaar; market place; department store
emù (ā·mū') *m (zool)* emu
emulare (ā·mū·lâ'rā) *vt* to emulate; to rival
emulazione (ā·mū·lâ·tsyō'nā) *f* emulation
emulsione (ā·mūl·syō'nā) *f* emulsion
encefalite (ān·chā·fâ·lē'tā) *f* encephalitis
enciclica (ān·chē'klē·kâ) *f* encyclical
enciclopedia (ān·chē·klō·pā·dē'â) *f* encyclopedia
enciclopedico (ān·chē·klō·pe'dē·kō) *a* encyclopedic
encomiabile (ān·kō·myâ'bē·lā) *a* laudable, worthy of commendation
encomiare (ān·kō·myâ'rā) *vt* to commend, praise
encomio (ān·kô'myō) *m* praise
endemico (ān·de'mē·kō) *a* endemic
endivia (ān·dē'vyâ) *f* endive
endocardo (ān·dō·kâr'dō) *m* endocardium
endocrino (ān·dô'krē·nō) *a* endocrine; **–logia** (ān·dō·krē·nō·lō·jē'â) *f* endocrinology
endogeno (ān·dô'jā·nō) *a* endogenous
endogetto (ān·dō·jāt'tō) *m* rocket
endovenoso (ān·dō·vā·nō'zō) *a* intravenous
energetico (ā·nār·je'tē·kō) *m* tonic
energia (ā·nār·jē'â) *f* power; energy; determination
energicamente (ā·nār·jē·kâ·mān'tā) *adv* energetically, forcefully

energico (ā·ner'jē·kō) *a* vigorous, resolute
energumeno (ā·nār·gū'mā·nō) *m* demoniac
enfasi (en'fâ·zē) *f* stress, emphasis
enfaticamente (ān·fâ·tē·kâ·mān'tā) *adv* emphatically
enigma (ā·nēg'mâ) *f* puzzle, riddle
enigmista (ā·nēg·mē'stâ) *m* puzzler
enigmistico (ā·nēg·mē'stē·kō) *a* puzzling
enimmistica (ān·nēm·mē'stē·kâ) *m* brainteaser
enologo (ā·nô'lō·gō) *m* wine-making expert; expert in wines
enorme (ā·nōr'mā) *a* enormous
enormità (ā·nōr·mē·tâ') *f* hugeness; enormity
ente (ān'tā) *m* being; agency; institution; — **morale** *(law)* body corporate; *(com)* corporation
enteroclisma (ān·tā·rō·klē'zmâ) *m* enema
entità (ān·tē·tâ') *f* entity; significance, import
entomologia (ān·tō·mō·lō·jē'â) *f* entomology
entrambi (ān·trâm'bē) *pron* both
entrante (ān·trân'tā) *a* next, coming
entrare (ān·trâ'rā) *vi* to enter; — **in particolari** to go into details; — **in possesso di** to take possession of
entrata (ān·trâ'tâ) *f* entrance; *(com)* income, asset; — **libera** free admission; — **in vigore** *(law)* enforcement; — **pubblica** government revenue
entro (ān'trō) *prep* within
entusiasmare (ān·tū·zyâ·zmâ'rā) *vt* to enthuse; to awaken the interest of
entusiasmarsi (ān·tū·zyâ·zmâr'sē) *vr* to become enthusiastic; to be inspired
entusiasmo (ān·tū·zyâ'zmō) *m* enthusiasm
entusiasta (ān·tū·zyâ'stâ) *a* enthusiastic
enumerare (ā·nū·mā·râ'rā) *vt* to enumerate
enunciare (ā·nūn·châ'rā) *vt* to enunciate
enunciato (ā·nūn·châ'tō) *a* enunciated
enunciazione (ā·nūn·châ·tsyō'nā) *f* enunciation
epa (ā'pâ) *f* belly
epatite (ā·pâ·tē'tā) *f* hepatitis
epicentro (ā·pē·chān'trō) *m* focal point; epicenter
epiciclo (ā·pē·chē'klō) *m* epicycle
epico (e'pē·kō) *a* epic
epicureo (ā·pē·kū·rā'ō) *a&m* epicurean
epidemia (ā·pē·dā·mē'â) *f* epidemic
epidermide (ā·pē·der'mē·dā) *f* epidermis
Epifania (ā·pē·fâ·nē'â) *f* Epiphany
epiglottide (ā·pē·glôt'tē·dā) *f* epiglottis
epigrafe (ā·pē'grâ·fā) *f* dedication, preface
epigramma (ā·pē·grâm'mâ) *m* epigram
epilessia (ā·pē·lās·sē'â) *f* epilepsy
epilettico (ā·pē·let'tē·kō) *a* epileptic
epilogo (ā·pē'lō·gō) *m* epilogue
episcopale (ā·pē·skō·pâ'lā) *a* episcopal
episodio (ā·pē·zô'dyō) *m* episode
epistolario (ā·pē·stō·lâ'ryō) *m* exchange of letters; correspondence
epitaffio (ā·pē·tâf'fyō) *m* epitaph
epitelio (ā·pē·te'lyō) *m* epithelium
epiteto (ā·pē'tā·tō) *m* epithet
epoca (e'pō·kâ) *f* epoch, age
epopea (ā·pō·pā'â) *f* epic poem, saga
eppure (āp·pū'rā) *conj* yet, nonetheless, nevertheless
epurare (ā·pū·râ'rā) *vt* to purge
epurazione (ā·pū·râ·tsyō'nā) *f* purge, purification
equamente (ā·kwâ·mān'tā) *adv* fairly, justly
equanime (ā·kwâ'nē·mā) *a* just, fair; calm, composed
equanimità (ā·kwâ·nē·mē·tâ') *f* justness; composure
equatore (ā·kwâ·tō'rā) *m* equator
equatoriale (ā·kwâ·tō·ryâ'lā) *a* equatorial
equazione (ā·kwâ·tsyō'nā) *f* equation
equestre (ā·kwā'strā) *a* equestrian
equidistante (ā·kwē·dē·stân'tā) *a* equidistant
equilibrato (ā·kwē·lē·brâ'tō) *a* sensible, stable
equilibrio (ā·kwē·lē'bryō) *m* balance; stability
equilibrismo (ā·kwē·lē·brē'zmō) *m* acrobatics
equilibrista (ā·kwē·lē·brē'stâ) *m* tightrope walker
equinozio (ā·kwē·nô'tsyō) *m* equinox
equipaggiare (ā·kwē·pâj·jâ'rā) *vt* to equip
equipaggio (ā·kwē·pâj'jō) *m* crew
equità (ā·kwē·tâ') *f* equity; fairness
equitazione (ā·kwē·tâ·tsyō'nā) *f* horsemanship
equivalente (ā·kwē·vâ·lān'tā) *a&m* equivalent
equivoco (ā·kwē'vō·kō) *m* misunderstanding; — *a* equivocal, unclear
equo (e'kwō) *a* fair; equitable
era (ā'râ) *f* era
erario (ā·râ'ryō) *m* treasury
erba (ār'bâ) *f* grass; herb; **in** — immature; inexperienced; latent
erbaccia (ār·bâ'châ) *f* weed
erbaggio (ār·bâj'jō) *m* vegetable
erbivendolo (ār·bē·ven'dō·lō) *m* vegetable dealer
erbivoro (ār·bē'vō·rō) *a* herbivorous
erede (ā·rā'dā) *m* heir
ereditiera (ā·rā·dē·tyā'râ) *f* heiress
eredità (ā·rā·dē·tâ') *f* inheritance; **lasciare in** — to bequeath, leave in one's will
ereditario (ā·rā·dē·tâ'ryō) *a* hereditary
ereditato (ā·rā·dē·tâ'tō) *a* inherited
eremita (ā·rā·mē'tâ) *m* hermit
eremo (ā·rā'mō) *m* hermitage
eresia (ā·rā·zē'â) *f* heresy
eretico (ā·re'tē·kō) *a&m* heretic
eretto (ā·rāt'tō) *a* erect
erezione (ā·rā·tsyō'nā) *f* erection
ergastolano (ār·gâ·stō·lâ'nō) *m* prisoner convicted for life
ergastolo (ār·gâ'stō·lō) *m* penitentiary; life sentence; life imprisonment
erica (e'rē·kâ) *f* heather
erigere * (ā·rē'jā·rā) *vt* to erect; to build; to found; to institute

ermellino (ār·māl·lē'nō) *m* ermine
ermetico (ār·me'tē·kō) *a* hermetic
ernia (er'nyâ) *f* rupture, hernia
eroe (ā·rō'ā) *m* hero
eroina (ā·rō·ē'nâ) *f* heroine; *(med)* heroin
eroicamente (ā·rōē·kâ·mān'tā) *adv* heroically
eroico (ā·rô'ē·kō) *a* heroic
eroismo (ā·rō·ē'zmō) *m* heroism
erogare (ā·rō·gâ'rā) *vt* to give, distribute, deal out
erogatore (ā·rō·gâ·tō'rā) *m* distributor; — *a* distributing
erogazione (ā·rō·gâ·tsyō'nā) *f* distribution; donation
erompere * (ā·rôm'pā·rā) *vi* to break out
erosione (ā·rō·zyō'nā) *f* erosion
erotico (ā·rô'tē·kō) *a* erotic
erpete (er'pā·tā) *m (med)* shingles
erpice (er'pē·chā) *m* harrow, cultivator
errare (ār·râ'rā) *vi* to err; to make a mistake; to wander
errabondo (ār·râ·bōn'dō) *a* rambling, wandering
errante (ār·rân'tā) *a* errant; wandering; roaming; **cavaliere** — knight errant
errata corrige (ār·râ'tâ kôr'rē·jā) *(print)* errata
errato (ār·râ'tō) *a* wrong, mistaken
erroneo (ār·rô'nā·ō) *a* wrong, mistaken
errore (ār·rō'rā) *m* mistake
erta (ār'tâ) *f* ascent; slope
erto (ār'tō) *a* steep
erudire (ā·rū·dē'rā) *vt* to educate, teach
erudirsi (ā·rū·dēr'sē) *vr* to educate oneself
erudito (ā·rū·dē'tō) *a* learned; — *m* scholar
erudizione (ā·rū·dē·tsyō'nā) *f* erudition
eruttare (ā·rūt·tâ'rā) *vi* to belch
eruttazione (ā·rūt·tâ·tsyō'nā) *f* belching
eruzione (ā·rū·tsyō'nā) *f* eruption; *(med)* inflammation, rash
esacerbare (ā·zâ·chār·bâ'rā) *vt* to aggravate; to exasperate
esacerbarsi (ā·zâ·chār·bâr'sē) *vr* to be exasperated; to be at one's wit's end
esaedro (ā·zâ·ā'drō) *m* hexahedron
esagono (ā·zâ'gō·nō) *m* hexagon
esagonale (ā·zâ·gō·nâ'lā) *a* hexagonal
esagerare (ā·zâ·jā·râ'rā) *vt* to exaggerate; — *vi* to go too far
esageratamente (ā·zâ·jā·râ·tâ·mān'tâ) *adv* exaggeratedly
esagerato (ā·zâ·jā·râ'tō) *a* exaggerated
esagerazione (ā·zâ·jā·râ·tsyō'nā) *f* exaggeration
esalare (ā·zâ·lâ'rā) *vt&i* to exhale
esalante (ā·zâ·lân'tā) *a* exhaling
esaltare (ā·zâl·tâ'rā) *vt* to extol, praise highly
esaltarsi (ā·zâl·târ'sē) *vr* to sing one's own praises; to become overly enthusiastic
esaltato (ā·zâl·tâ'tō) *a* fanatical; — *m* fanatic
esaltazione (ā·zâl·tâ·tsyō'nā) *f* exaltation; excess enthusiasm
esame (ā·zâ'mā) *f* examination
esaminando (ā·zâ·mē·nân'dō) *m* candidate for an academic degree
esaminare (ā·zâ·mē·nâ'rā) *vt* to examine; to put to the test
esangue (ā·zân'gwā) *a* bloodless
esanime (ā·zâ'nē·mā) *a* lifeless
esasperare (ā·zâ·spā·râ'rā) *vt* to exasperate
esasperarsi (ā·zâ·spā·râr'sē) *vr* to become irritated
esasperato (ā·zâ·spā·râ'tō) *a* exasperated, irritated
esasperazione (ā·zâ·spā·râ·tsyô'nā) *f* exasperation, irritation
esattezza (ā·zât·tā'tsâ) *f* exactness, precision, care
esatto (ā·zât'tō) *a* exact, correct
esattore (ā·zât·tō'rā) *m* revenue agent, tax collector
esattoria (ā·zât·tō·rē'â) *f* internal revenue office
esaudimento (ā·zâū·dē·mān'tō) *m* agreement; granting
esaudire (ā·zâū·dē'rā) *vt* to grant; to agree to
esaudito (ā·zâū·dē'tō) *a* granted; complied with
esauriente (ā·zâū·ryān'tā) *a* exhaustive, complete
esaurimento (ā·zâū·rē·mān'tō) *m* exhaustion; breakdown
esaurire (ā·zâū·rē'rā) *vt* to exhaust; *(com)* to sell out
esaurirsi (ā·zâū·rēr'sē) *vr* to overwork oneself; to become exhausted
esaurito (ā·zâū·rē'tō) *a* sold out; out of print
esausto (ā·zâ'ū·stō) *a* exhausted
esautorare (a·zâū·tō·râ'rā) *vt* to discredit, cast aspersions on
esazione (ā·zâ·tsyō'nā) *f* tax collection
esca (ā'skâ) *f* bait; *(fig)* temptation
escandescenza (ā·skân·dā·shān'tsâ) *f* fit of anger, outburst of rage
escavatore (ā·skâ·vâ·tō'rā) *m* excavator
escavazione (ā·skâ·vâ·tsyō'nā) *f* excavation
esclamare (ā·sklâ·mâ'rā) *vi* to exclaim
esclamativo (ā·sklâ·mâ·tē'vō) *a* exclamatory
esclamazione (ā·sklâ·mâ·tsyō'nā) *f* exclamation
escludere * (ā·sklū'dā·rā) *vt* to exclude; to rule out
esclusione (ā·sklū·zyō'nā) *f* exclusion
esclusiva (ā·sklū·zē'vâ) *f* exclusive right; sole dealership
esclusivo (ā·sklū·zē'vō) *a* exclusive
escluso (ā·sklū'zō) *a* excluded; expected
escomiare (ā·skō·myâ'rā) *vt* to dismiss
escremento (ā·skrā·mān'tō) *m* excrement
escrescenza (ā·skrā·shān'tsâ) *f* outgrowth
escursione (ā·skūr·syō'nā) *f* excursion
escursionista (ā·skūr·syō·nē'stâ) *m&f* member of a tour
escussione (ā·skūs·syō'nā) *f* examination of witnesses
esecrare (ā·zā·krâ'rā) *vt* to detest, have a loathing for

esecutivo (ā·zā·kū·tē'vō) *a* executive; — *m* executive board, board of directors
esecutore (ā·zā·kū·tō'rā) *m (law)* executor; executioner; performer; *(pol)* enactor
esecuzione (ā·zā·kū·tsyō'nā) *f* execution; performance; *(pol)* enactment
esedra (ā·zā'drâ) *f* outdoor bench
eseguire (ā·zā·gwē'rā) *vt* to execute; to perform; to accomplish; to fulfill; — **un progetto** to carry out a plan; — **un pagamento** to make a payment
esempio (ā·zem'pyō) *m* example; sample, demonstration; instance
esemplare (ā·zām·plâ'rā) *m* copy, pattern; — *a* exemplary
esentare (ā·zān·tâ'rā) *vt* to exempt
esente (ā·zān'tā) *a* exempt, free
esenzione (ā·zān·tsyō'nā) *f* exemption
esequie (ā·ze'kwēā) *fpl* funeral services
esercente (ā·zār·chān'tā) *a* practicing; — *m* dealer; shopkeeper, merchant; tradesman
esercire (ā·zār·chē'rā) *vt* to operate, carry on *(business)*
esercitare (ā·zār·chē·tâ'rā) *vt* to exercize; to exert; to practice, make use of
esercitarsi (ā·zār·chē·târ'sē) *vr* to practice; *(sport)* to train, work out
esercitato (ā·zār·chē·tâ'tō) *a* trained; experienced
esercitazione (ā·zār·chē·tâ·tsyō'nā) *f* exercise
esercito (ā·zer'chē·tō) *m* army
esercito (ā·zār·chē'tō) *a* operated, managed; carried on
esercizio (ā·zār·chē'tsyō) *m* drill; exercize; business
esibire (ā·zē·bē'rā) *vt* to show, display; to sport, make a show of
esibirsi (ā·zē·bēr'sē) *vr* to show oneself; to volunteer; *(theat)* to play a part
esibitore (ā·zē·bē·tō'rā) *m*, **esibitrice** (ā·zē·bē·trē'chā) *f* exhibitor
esibizione (ā·zē·bē·tsyō'nā) *f* exhibit, display
esibizionismo (ā·zē·bē·tsyō·nē'zmō) *m* exhibitionism; show, pomp
esibizionista (ā·zē·bē·tsyō·nē'stâ) *m* show-off *(coll)*
esigente (ā·zē·jān'tā) *a* demanding
esigenza (ā·zē·jān'tsâ) *f* exigency; requirement
esigere * (ā·zē'jā·rā) *vt* to collect; to demand, exact, require
esigibile (ā·zē·jē'bē·lā) *a* collectible
esiguo (ā·zē'gwō) *a* meager
esile (e'zē·lā) *a* slender, slight
esilità (ā·zē·lē·tâ') *f* slenderness, slightness
esiliare (ā·zē·lyâ'rā) *vt* to exile
esiliarsi (ā·zē·lyâr'sē) *vr* to seclude oneself
esiliato (ā·zē·lyâ'tō) *a* exiled; — *m* exile *(person)*
esilio (ā·zē'lyō) *m* exile
esimere (ā·zē'mā·rā) *vt* to exempt, release; to dispense with, do away with
esimersi (ā·zē'mār·sē) *vr* to evade; to avoid; to shirk, to get out of doing; to be able to help, refrain from
esistente (ā·zē·stān'tā) *a* existent; existing, living; extant
esistenza (ā·zē·stān'tsâ) *f* existence
esistere * (ā·zē'stā·rā) *vi* to exist, live
esitabile ā·zē·tâ'bē·lā) *a* marketable
esitante (ā·zē·tân'tā) *a* hesitant, hesitating
esitare (ā·zē·tâ'rā) *vt* to hesitate
esitazione (ā·zē·tâ·tsyō'nā) *f* hesitation
esito (e'zē·tō) *m* success; outcome, upshot; *(com)* sale
esiziale (ā·zē·tsyâ'lā) *a* fatal, deadly
esodo (e'zō·dō) *m* exodus; flight
esofago (ā·zô'fâ·gō) *m* esophagus
esoftalmico (ā·zōf·tâl'mē·kō) *a (med)* exophthalmic
esonerare (ā·zō·nā·râ'rā) *vt* to exonerate, clear
esonero (ā·zô'nā·rō) *m* exoneration; exemption
esorbitante (ā·zōr·bē·tân'tā) *a* exorbitant
esorbitare (ā·zōr·bē·tâ'rā) *vi* to exceed
esorcismo (ā·zōr·chē'zmō) *m* exorcism
esorcizzare (ā·zōr·chē·dzâ'rā) *vt* to exorcise
esordire (ā·zōr·dē'rā) *vi* to start, begin
esordio (ā·zôr'dyō) *m* debut; beginning
esoso (ā·zō'zō) *a* hateful; stingy; greedy
esotico (ā·zô'tē·kō) *a* exotic
espandere * (ā·spân'dā·rā) *vt* to spread; to expand, enlarge
espansione (ā·spân·syō'nā) *f* expansion
espansionismo (ā·spân·syō·nē'zmō) *m (pol)* expansionism
espansività (ā·spân·sē·vē·tâ') *f* expansiveness
espansivo (ā·spân·sē'vō) *a* demonstrative; expansive
espatriare (ā·spâ·tryâ'rā) *vt* to exile, banish
espatrio (ā·spâ'tryō) *m* expatriation
espediente (ā·spā·dyān'tā) *m* expedient
espellere * (ā·spel'lā·rā) *vt* to expel; to shoot out, eject
esperienza (ā·spā·ryān'tsā) *f* experiment; experience
esperimentare (ā·spā·rē·mān·tâ'rā) *vt* to experience, undergo; to test, put to the test
esperimentato (ā·spā·rē·mān·tâ'tō) *a* experienced, skillful; proven, tested
esperimentatore (ā·spā·rē·mān·tâ·tō'rā) *m* tester, experimenter
esperimento (ā·spā·rē·mān'tō) *m* experiment
espertamente (ā·spār·tâ·mān'tā) *adv* skillfully
esperto (ā·spār'tō) *a* skilled; — *m* expert
espettorare (ā·spāt·tō·râ'rā) *vt* to expectorate
espiare (ā·spyâ'rā) *vt* to expiate
espiatorio (ā·spyâ·tô'ryō) *a* expiatory, serving as an atonement; **capro** — whipping boy, scapegoat
espiazione (ā·sypâ·tsyō'nā) *f* expiation
espirare (ā·spē·râ'rā) *vt* to expire
espirazione (ā·spē·râ·tsyō'nā) *f* expiration

espletare (ā·splā·tâ'rā) *vt* to complete, fulfill; to execute, perform
esplicare (ā·splē·kâ'rā) *vt* to explain in detail; to detail
esplicito (ā·splē'chē·tō) *a* explicit
esplodere * (ā·splô'dā·rā) *vt&i* to explode
esplorare (ā·splō·râ'rā) *vt* to explore
esploratore (ā·splō·râ·tō'rā) *m* explorer; **giovane —** boy scout
esplorazione (ā·splō·râ·tsyō'nā) *f* exploration; *(mil)* reconnaissance
esplosione (ā·splō·zyō'nā) *f* explosion
esplosivo (ā·splō·zē'vō) *a&m* explosive
esploso (ā·splō'zō) exploded
esponente (ā·spō·nān'tā) *a&m* exponent
esporre * (ā·spōr'rā) *vt* to display, exhibit, show; to open, expose
esportare (ā·spōr·tâ'rā) *vt* to export
esportatore (ā·spōr·tâ·tō'rā) *m*, **esportatrice** (ā·spōr·tâ·trē'chā) *f* exporter
esportazione (ā·spōr·tâ·tsyō'nā) *f* export, exporting
esposimetro (ā·spō·zē'mā·trō) *m* exposure meter
espositore (ā·spō·zē·tō'rā) *m*, **espositrice** (ā·spō·zē·trē'chā) *f* exhibitor
esposizione (ā·spō·zē·tsyō'nā) *f* exposition, exhibit; show, demonstration
esposto (ā·spō'stō) *a* displayed; **—** *m* report
espressamente (ā·sprās·sâ·mān'tā) *adv* purposely; on purpose
espressione (ā·sprās·syō'nā) *f* expression
espressività (ā·sprās·sē·vē·tâ') *f* expressiveness
espressivo (ā·sprās·sē'vō) *a* clear, meaningful
espresso (ā·sprās'sō) *m* special delivery
esprimere * (ā·sprē'mā·rā) *vt* to express
esprimersi * (ā·sprē'mār·sē) *vr* to express oneself
espropriare (ā·sprō·pryâ'rā) *vt* to take over, expropriate; to evict
espropriazione (ā·sprō·pryâ·tsyō'nā) *f* expropriation; eviction
espugnare (ā·spū·nyâ'rā) *vt* to conquer; to storm, overrun
espulsione (ā·spūl·syō'nā) *f* expulsion
espulso (ā·spūl'sō) *a* expelled; **-re** (ā·spūl·sō'rā) *m (mech)* ejector, release
essa (âs'sâ) *pron* she
esse (âs'sā) *pron fpl* they
essenza (âs·sān'tsâ) *f* essence
essenziale (âs·sān·tsyâ'lā) *a* essential
essenzialmente (âs·sān·tsyâl·mān'tā) *adv* essentially
essere * (es'sā·rā) *vi* to be, exist; to become; to happen; to stand; **— di** to belong to; **— in grado di** to be able to
essicare (âs·sē·kâ'rā) *vt* to dry up
essicarsi (âs·sē·kâr'sē) *vr* to become dry, dry up
essicativo (âs·sē·kâ·tē'vō) *a* drying, dehydrating
essicazione (âs·sē·kâ·tsyō'nā) *f* drying, dehydrating
esso (âs'sō) *pron* he
essi (âs'sē) *pron mpl* they
essudare (âs·sū·dâ'rā) *vt&i* to exude
essudazione (âs·sū·dâ·tsyō'nā) *f* exudation
est (âst) *m* east; East; Orient; **dell'—** eastern; Oriental
estasi (e'stâ·zē) *f* ecstasy; great enthusiam
estasiare (ā·stâ·zyâ'rā) *vt* to enrapture; to enthuse
estasiarsi (ā·stâ·zyâr'sē) *vr* to become enthusiastic; to gush
estasiato (ā·stâ·zyâ'tō) *a* enraptured; highly enthused
estatico (ā·stâ'tē·kō) *a* ecstatic
estate (ā·stâ'tā) *f* summer
estendere * (ā·sten'dā·rā) *vt* to extend; to reach out
estendersi * (ā·sten'dār·sē) *vr* to expand; to stretch oneself
estensamente (ā·stān·sâ·mān'tā) *adv* extensively; fully
estensione (ā·stān·syō'nā) *f* extension
estensivo (ā·stān·sē'vō) *a* extensive
estenuante (ā·stā·nwân'tā) *a* oppressive, exhausting
esteriore (ā·stā·ryō'rā) *a* external; **—** *m* exterior; outer surface
esteriorità (ā·stā·ryō·rē·tâ') *f* external appearances
esternamente (ā·stār·nâ·mān'tā) *adv* externally, outwardly
esterno (ā·stār'nō) *a* external; **—** *m* outside; **alunno —** day pupil
estero (e'stā·sō) *a* foreign; **all'—** abroad, overseas
esterrefatto (ā·stār·rā·fât'tō) *a* frightened, horrified
esteso (ā·stā'zō) *a* extensive; far-reaching
esteta (ā·stā'tâ) *m* aesthete
estetica (ā·ste'tē·kā) *f* aesthetics
estetista (ā·stā·tē'stâ) *m* beautician
estimare (ā·stē·mâ'rā) *vt* to estimate
estimativo (ā·stē·mâ·tē'vō) *a* estimated; approximate
estimatore (ā·stē·mâ·tō'rā) *m* appraiser, estimator
estimazione (ā·stē·mâ·tsyō'nā) *f* estimation; appraisal
estimo (e'stē·mō) *m* survey; appraisal
estinguere * (ā·stēn·gwā·rā) *vt* to extinguish; **— il conto** to pay the bill
estinguersi * (ā·stēn'gwār·sē) *vr* to be extinguished, die out
estinto (ā·stēn'tō) *a* extinct; dead; **-re** (ā·stēn·tō'rā) *m* fire extinguisher
estinzione (ā·stēn·tsyō'nā) *f* extinction
estivo (ā·stē'vō) *a* summer; **scuola estiva** summer school
estollere * (ā·stôl'lā·rā) *vt* to extol, praise
estorcere * (ā·stôr'chā·rā) *vt* to extort
estorsione (ā·stōr·syō'nā) *f* extortion
estradare (ā·strâ·dâ'rā) *vt* to extradite
estradizione (ā·strâ·dē·tsyō'nā) *f* extradition
estraneo (ā·strâ'nā·ō) *m* stranger; alien; **—** *a* extraneous
estrarre * (ā·strâr'rā) *vt* to extract; to pull out, draw out
estratto (ā·strât'tō) *m* extract; **—** *a* drawn out, extracted; **-re** (ā·strât·tō'rā) *m* extractor

estrazione (ā·strâ·tsyō'nā) *f* extraction
estremista (ā·strā·mē'stâ) *m* extremist
estremità (ā·strā·mē·tâ') *f* extremity; **da una — all'altra** from one end to the other
estremo (ā·strā'mō) *a&m* extreme
estro (ā'strō) *m* imagination, fancy; inspiration; **–so** (ā·strō'zō) *a* whimsical
estromettere * (ā·strō·met'tā·rā) *vt* to oust
estuario (ā·stwâ'ryō) *m* estuary, mouth
esuberante (ā·zū·bā·rân'tā) *a* exuberant; **–mente** (ā·zū·bā·rân·tā·mān'tā) *adv* exuberantly
esuberanza (ā·zū·bā·rân'tsâ) *f* exuberance; plenty
esulare (ā·zū·lâ'rā) *vi* to go into exile
esule (e'zū·lā) *m* refugee, exile
esultante (ā·zūl·tân'tā) *a* exultant, jubilant
esultanza (ā·zūl·tân'tsâ) *f* exultation
esultare (ā·zūl·tâ'rā) *vi* to exult
esumare (ā·zū·mâ'rā) *vt* to exhume
età (ā·tâ') *f* age
etano (ā·tâ'nō) *m* ethane
etere (e'tā·rā) *m* ether
etereo (ā·te'rā·ō) *a* ethereal
eternamente (ā·tār·nâ·mān'tā) *adv* eternally
eternare (ā·tār·nâ'rā) *vt* to perpetuate
eternit (e'tār·nēt) *m* building material of asbestos and cement
eternità (ā·tār·nē·tâ') *f* eternity
eterno (ā·tār'nō) *a* eternal; **in —** forever
eterodina (ā·tā·rō·dē'nâ) *f* heterodyne
eterodosso (ā·tā·rō·dōs'sō) *a* unorthodox
eterogeneo (ā·tā·rō·je'nā·ō) *a* heterogeneous
etica (e'tē·kâ) *f* ethics
eticamente (ā·tē·kâ·mān'tā) *adv* ethically
etichetta (ā·tē·kāt'tâ) *f* label; etiquette; **senza —** unceremoniously
etico (e'tē·kō) *a* ethical; *(med)* consumptive
etile (ā·tē'lā) *m (chem)* ethyl; **–ne** (ā·tē·lā'nā) *m* ethylene
etimologia (ā·tē·mō·lō·jē'â) *f* etymology
etimologico (ā·tē·mō·lō'jē·kō) *a* etymological
Etiopia (ā·tyô'pyâ) *f* Ethiopia
etnico (et'nē·kō) *a* ethnic
etnologia (āt·nō·lō·jē'â) *f* ethnology
etnologo (āt·nô'lō·gō) *m* ethnologist
etrusco (ā·trū'skō) *a&m* Etruscan
ettagono (āt·tâ'gō·nō) *m* heptagon
ettaro (et'tâ·rō) *m* hectare
ettogrammo (āt·tō·grâm'mō) *m* hectogram, 100 grams
ettolitro (āt·tô'lē·trō) *m* hectoliter
ettowatt (āt·tō'vât) *m* 100 watts
eucaristia (āū·kâ·rē·stē'â) *f* Eucharist
eucaristico (āū·kâ·rē'stē·kō) *a* Eucharistic
eufemismo (āū·fā·mē'zmō) *m* euphemism
eufonia (āū·fō·nē'â) *f* euphony
eugenetica (āū·jā·ne'tē·kâ) *f* eugenics
eunuco (āū·nū'kō) *m* eunuch
Europa (āū·rō'pâ) *f* Europe
europeo (āū·rō·pā'ō) *a&m* European
eutanasia (āū·tâ·nâ'zyâ) *f* euthanasia
evacuare (ā·vâ·kwâ'rā) *vt* to evacuate
evadere * (ā·vâ'dā·rā) *vt&i* to escape; to flee; to settle *(obligation)*; to fill *(an order)*
evanescente (ā·vâ·nā·shān'tā) *a* evanescent, ephemeral
evangelista (ā·vân·jā·lē'stâ) *m* evangelist
evangelizzare (ā·vân·jā·lē·dzâ'rā) *vt&i* to evangelize
evaporare (ā·vâ·pō·râ'rā) *vt&i* to evaporate
evaporazione (ā·vâ·pō·râ·tsyō'nā) *f* evaporation
evasione (ā·vâ·zyō'nā) *f* evasion
evasivamente (ā·vâ·zē·vâ·mān'tā) *adv* evasively
evaso (ā·vâ'zō) *m* fugitive
evenienza (ā·vā·nyān'tsâ) *f* occurrence; emergency; eventuality; **per ogni —** just in case
evento (ā·vān'tō) *m* event
eventuale (ā·vān·twâ'lā) *a* possible; eventual
eventualmente (ā·vān·twâl·mān'tā) *adv* later on; possibly
eventualità (ā·vān·twâ·lē·tâ') *f* possibility; need, necessity
evidente (ā·vē·dān'tā) *a* evident, obvious
evidentemente (ā·vē·dān·tā·mān'tā) *adv* clearly, obviously
evidenza (ā·vē·dān'tsâ) *f* evidence; **arrendersi all' — dei fatti** to be convinced of the truth of the evidence
evirare (ā·vē·râ'rā) *vt* to emasculate; to weaken
evirato (ā·vē·râ'tō) *a* emasculated
evitare (ā·vē·tâ'rā) *vt* to avoid; to get around, get out of
evitabile (ā·vē·tâ'bē·lā) *a* preventable, avoidable
evo (ā'vō) *m* age; **— medio** Middle Ages; **— moderno** present day, present
evocare (ā·vō·kâ'rā) *vt* to call upon, evoke; to bring to mind
evocazione (ā·vō·kâ·tsyō'nā) *f* evoking; remembrance
evolutista (ā·vō·lū·tē'stâ) *m* evolutionist
evolutivo (ā·vō·lū·tē'vō) *a* evolutive, evolutionary
evolto (ā·vōl'tō) *a* evolved; civilized
evoluzione (ā·vō·lū·tsyō'nā) *f* evolution
evolvere (ā·vôl'vā·rā) *vt* to evolve, develop
evolversi (ā·vôl'vār·sē) *vr* to develop
ex (āks) *prefix* late, past, former

F

fa (fâ) *adv* ago; **tempo —** some time ago; **— m** *(mus)* F, fa; **— diesis** F sharp
fabbisogno (fâb·bē·zō'nyō) *m* needs, necessary items
fabbrica (fâb'brē·kâ) *f* factory; building; **marca di —** trademark

fabbricare (fâb·brē·kâ'rā) *vt* to manufacture, fabricate; to construct
fabbricato (fâb·brē·kâ'tō) *m* building; — *a* built, made manufactured
fabbricatore (fâb·brē·kâ·tō'rā) *m* manufacturer, builder
fabbricazione (fâb·brē·kâ·tsyō'nā) *f* manufacture
faccenda (fâ·chān'dâ) *f* business, affair; chore, task
faccendiere (fâ·chān·dyā'rā) *m* meddler
faccetta (fâ·chāt'tâ) *f* facet
facchinata (fâk·kē·nâ'tâ) *f* toil, drudgery; foul language
facchino (fâk·kē'nō) *m* porter
faccia (fâ'châ) *f* face; front; **cambiar** — to change completely; — **tosta** effrontery; nerve *(sl)* **–le** (fâ·châ'lā) *a* facial; **–ta** (fâ·châ'tâ) *f* façade
face (fâ'chā) *f* flame, torch
faceto (fâ·chā'tō) *a* witty, humorous
facezia (fâ·che'tsyâ) *f* joke; note of humor
fachiro (fâ·kē'rō) *m* fakir
facile (fâ'chē·lā) *a* easy; inclined
facilità (fâ·chē·lē·tâ') *f* ease, facility
facilitare (fâ·chē·lē·tâ'rā) *vt* to facilitate, make easy
facilitazione (fâ·chē·lē·tâ·tsyō'nā) *f* *(com)* easy credit terms; making easy
facilmente (fâ·chēl·mān'tā) *adv* easily; more than likely
facilone (fâ·chē·lō'nā) *m* easy-going person; person easy to get along with
facinoroso (fâ·chē·nō·rō'zō) *a* wicked; lawless
facoltà (fâ·kōl·tâ') *f* faculty; power; means
facoltativo (fâ·kōl·tâ·tē'vō) *a* optional
facoltoso (fâ·kōl·tō'zō) *a* well-to-do, with means
facondia (fâ·kôn'dyâ) *f* eloquence
facondo (fâ·kōn'dō) *a* talkative; eloquent
fagiano (fâ·jâ'nō) *m* pheasant
fagiolini (fâ·jō·lē'nē) *mpl* string beans
fagiuolo (fâ·jwō'lō) *m* bean; **andare a** — *(coll)* to be fine with, please
fagotto (fâ·gōt'tō) *m* bundle; *(mus)* bassoon
faina (fâ·ē'nâ) *f* *(zool)* marten
falange (fâ·lân'jā) *f* phalanx
falce (fâl'chā) *f* scythe; **–tto** (fâl·chāt'tō) *m* sickle
falciare (fâl·châ'rā) *vt* to mow
falciatore (fâl·châ·tō'rā) *m* harvester
falciatrice (fâl·châ·trē'chā) *f* mechanical harvester
falco (fâl'kō) *m* hawk; **–ne** (fâl·kō'nā) *m* falcon
falda (fâl'dâ) *f* brim *(hat)*; flap; bottom *(coat)*; — **di monte** foot of a mountain; — **di neve** snowflake
falegname (fâ·lā·nyâ'mā) *m* carpenter; **–ria** (fâ·lā·nyâ·mā·rē'â) *f* carpentry
falena (fâ·lā'nâ) *f* moth
falla (fâl'lâ) *f* leak; weaving fault
fallace (fâl·lâ'chā) *a* fallacious
fallacia (fâl·lâ'châ) *f* fallacy
fallibile (fâl·lē'bē·lā) *a* fallible
fallibilità (fâl·lē·bē·lē·tâ') *f* fallibility
fallimentare (fâl·lē·mān·tâ'rā) *a* ruinous; causing bankruptcy; **procedura** — bankruptcy proceedings
fallimento (fâl·lē·mān'tō) *m* failure; *(com)* bankruptcy
fallire (fâl·lē'rā) *vi* to fail; *(com)* to go bankrupt
fallito (fâl·lē'tō) *a* failed; bankrupt
fallo (fâl'lō) *m* fault, error
falò (fâ·lō') *m* bonfire
falsamente (fâl·sâ·mān'tā) *adv* falsely
falsare (fâl·sâ'rā) *vt* to forge; to distort, falsify
falsariga (fâl·sâ·rē'gâ) *f* example, sample
falsario (fâl·sâ'ryō) *m* counterfeiter
falsificare (fâl·sē·fē·kâ'rā) *vt* to falsify; to counterfeit
falsificatore (fâl·sē·fē·kâ·tō'rā) *m* forger
falsificazione (fâl·sē·fē·kâ·tsyō'nā) *f* forgery; counterfeiting
falsità (fâl·sē·tâ') *f* falsehood
falso (fâl'sō) *a* false; forged
fama (fâ'mâ) *f* fame
fame (fâ'mā) *f* hunger; **aver** — to be hungry; **–lico** (fâ'me'lē·kō) *a* starving; famished
famigerato (fâ·mē·jā·râ'tō) *a* notorious; of ill repute, with a bad reputation
famiglia (fâ·mē'lyâ) *f* family
familiare (fâ·mē·lyâ'rā) *a* familiar; colloquial; — *m* relative; servant
familiarità (fâ·mē·lyâ·rē·tâ') *f* familiarity
familiarizzarsi (fâ·mē·lyâ·rē·dzâr'sē) *vr* to become familiar
famosamente (fâ·mō·zâ·mān'tā) *adv* famously
famoso (fâ·mō'zō) *a* famous; notorious
fanale (fâ·nâ'lē) *m* lamp; *(auto)* headlight
fanaticamente (fâ·nâ·tē·kâ·mān'tā) *adv* fanatically
fanatico (fâ·nâ'tē·kō) *a* fanatical; — *m* fanatic
fanatismo (fâ·nâ·tē'zmō) *m* bigotry
fanciulla (fân·chūl'lâ) *f* girl
fanciullaggine (fân·chūl·lâj'jē·nā) *f* puerility, childishness
fanciullescamente (fân·chūl·lā·skâ·mān'tā) *adv* childishly
fanciullezza (fân·chūl·lā'tsâ) *f* childhood
fanciullo (fân·chūl'lō) *m* boy
fandonia (fân·dô'nyâ) *f* humbug, tall tale
fanfara (fân·fâ'râ) *f* brass band
fanfaronata (fân·fâ·rō·nâ'tâ) *f* bravado, blustering manner
fanfarone (fân·fâ·rō'nā) *m* braggart
fanghiglia (fân·gē'lyâ) *f* slush, mire
fango (fân'gō) *m* mud; **–so** (fân·gō'zō) *a* muddy
fannullone (fân·nūl·lō'nā) *m* loafer, idler
fantascienza (fân·tâ·shyān'tsâ) *f* science fiction
fantasia (fân·tâ·zē'â) *f* fancy; fiction
fantasioso (fân·tâ·zyō'zō) *a* fanciful, whimsical
fantasma (fân·tâ'zmâ) *m* phantom
fantasticamente (fân·tâ·stē·kâ·mān'tā) *adv* fantastically
fantasticare (fân·tâ·stē·kâ'rā) *vi* to day-

dream; to engage in flights of fancy
fantasticheria (fân·tâ·stē·kā·rē'â) *f* reverie, daydreaming
fante (fân'tā) *m* infantryman; jack (*cards*); **–ria** (fân·tā·rē'â) *f* infantry
fantino (fân·tē'nō) *m* jockey
fantoccio (fân·tô'chō) *m* puppet; figurehead
fantomatico (fân·tō·mâ'tē·kō) *a* ghostly
farabutto (fâ·râ·būt'tō) *m* crook; (*coll*) rogue, cad
farad (fâ'râd) *m* farad
faraglione (fâ·râ·lyō'nā) *m* cliff
farcire (fâr·chē'rā) *vt* to stuff
farcito (fâr·chē'tō) *a* stuffed
fardello (fâr·dāl'lō) *m* bundle; burden; **far —** to leave, make one's departure
fare * (fâ'rā) *vt* to make; to do; **— caldo** to be warm; **— coraggio** to encourage; **— fiasco** to fail; **— finta** to feign; **— freddo** to be cold; **— fronte a** to face; **— il maestro** to teach; **— le carte** to deal the cards; **— male** to injure; **— onore** to honor; **— paura** to scare; **— sapere** to inform; **— silenzio** to be silent; **— tardi** to be late; **— una domanda** to question; **— una parte** to play a part; **— uno scherzo** to play a trick; **— vedere** to show; **— visita** to visit; **fa lo stesso** it makes no difference
faretra (fâ·rā'trâ) *f* quiver
farfalla (fâr·fâl'lâ) *f* butterfly; (*mech*) throttle
farina (fâ·rē'nâ) *f* flour; **–ceo** *a* (fâ·rē·nâ'chā·ō) farinaceous
farinoso (fâ·rē·nō'zō) *a* floury
faringe (fâ·rēn'jā) *f* pharynx
fariseo (fâ·rē·zā'ō) *a* hypocrite
farmaceutica (fâr·mâ·che'ū·tē·kâ) *f* pharmaceutics
farmaceutico (fâr·mâ·che'ū·tē·kō) *a* pharmaceutical
farmacia (fâr·mâ·chē'â)*f* drugstore
farmacista (fâr·mâ·chē'stâ) *m* druggist
farmaco (fâr'mâ·kō) *m* medicine
faro (fâ'rō) *m* headlight; lighthouse; **— di atterraggio** (*avi*) landing light
farragine (fâr·râ'jē·nā) *f* hodgepodge, potpourri
farsa (fâr'sâ) *f* farce
farsi * (fâr'sē) *vr* to become; to be done; **— capire** to make oneself understood; **— la barba** to shave; **— male** to hurt oneself
fascia (fâ'shâ) *f* strip; bandage; **–re** (fâ·shâ'rā) *vt* to bandage
fasciatura (fâ·shâ·tū'râ) *f* bandaging
fascicolo (fâ·shē'kō·lō) *m* pamphlet
fascino (fâ'shē·nō) *m* charm, glamour
fascio (fâ'shō) *m* bundle
fascismo (fâ·shē'zmō) *m* Fascism
fascista (fâ·shē'stâ) *m&a* Fascist
fase (fâ'zā) *f* phase; period; era
fastidio (fâ·stē'dyō) *m* trouble; **–samente** (fâ·stē·dyō·zâ·mān'tā) *adv* with difficulty; **–so** (fâ·stē·dyō'zō) *a* annoying; tiresome
fasto (fâ'stō) *m* display, pomp; **–samente** (fâ·stō·zâ·mān'tā) *adv* pompously; **–so** (fâ·stō'zō) *a* pompous
fata (fâ'tâ) *f* fairy
fatale (fâ·tâ'lā) *a* fatal; inevitable
fatalista (fâ·tâ·lē'stâ) *m* fatalist
fatalità (fâ·tâ·lē·tâ') *f* destiny, fate
fatica (fâ·tē'kâ) *f* effort, toil; fatigue; **–re** (fâ·tē·kâ'rā) *vi* to work hard
faticosamente (fâ·tē·kō·zâ·mān'tā) *adv* laboriously, with great effort
faticoso (fâ·tē·kō'zō) *a* fatiguing
fato (fâ'tō) *m* fortune; destiny
fatta (fât'tâ) *f* sort; action; **–ccio** (fât·tâ'chō) *m* crime, evildoing
fattezze (fât·tā'tsā) *fpl* features (*face*); outline
fattibile (fât·tē'bē·lā) *a* feasible
fatto (fât'tō) *m* fact; deed; **—** *a* done; made; **badare al — suo** to mind one's own business; **cogliere sul —** to catch in the act; **giorno —** broad daylight; **in — di** regarding, as concerns
fattore (fât·tō'rā) *m* factor; farmer; maker
fattoria (fât·tō·rē'â) *f* farm
fattorino (fât·tō·rē'nō) *m* messenger; bus conductor; mailman
fattura (fât·tū'râ) *f* (*com*) invoice; **–re** (fât·tū·râ'rā) *vt* to invoice
fatuamente (fâ·twâ·mān'tā) *adv* foolishly
fatuità (fâ·twē·tâ') *f* foolishness
fatuo (fâ'twō) *a* silly, foolish
fausto (fâ'ū·stō) *a* lucky; happy
fautore (fâū·tō'rā) *m* patron, supporter
fava (fâ'vâ) *f* broad bean
favilla (fâ·vēl'lâ) *f* spark
favo (fâ'vō) *m* (*med*) carbuncle; honeycomb
favola (fâ'vō·lâ) *f* fable
favolosamente (fâ·vō·lō·zâ·mān'tā) *adv* fabulously; incredibly
favore (fâ·vō'rā) *m* favor; **fare un —** to do a favor; **giorni di —** (*com*) days of grace; **–ggiare** (fâ·vō·rāj·jâ'rā) *vt* to support, favor; **–ggiamento** (fâ·vō·rāj·jâ·mān'tō) *m* support, backing; **–vole** (fâ·vō·re'vō·lā) *a* favorable; **tempo –vole** opportune time
favorire (fâ·vō·rē'rā) *vt* to aid; to oblige
favoritismo (fâ·vō·rē·tē'zmō) *m* partiality
favorito (fâ·vō·rē'tō) *a* favorite; favored
fazione (fâ·tsyō'nā) *f* faction; political party
faziosamente (fâ·tsyō·zâ·mān'tā) *adv* contentiously; in an argumentive way
fazioso (fâ·tsyō'zō) *a* dissentive; argumentive
fazzoletto (fâ·tsō·lāt'tō) *m* handkerchief
febbraio (fāb·brâ'yō) *m* February
febbre (fāb'brā) *f* fever; **aver —** to run a fever; **— da cavallo** high fever
febbrile (fāb·brē'lā) *a* feverish; agitated
fecale (fā·kâ'lā) *a* fecal
feccia (fā'châ) *f* scum
fecola (fe'kō·lâ) *f* starch
fecondare (fā·kōn'dâ·rā) *vt* to pollinate; to fertilize
fecondativo (fā·kōn·dâ·tē'vō) *a* creative
fecondo (fā·kōn'dō) *a* fertile
fede (fā'dā) *f* faith; wedding ring; certificate; **— di nascita** birth certificate; **de-**

gno di — trustworthy; **far** — to bear witness; **prestar** — to give credence to; **romper** — to break one's word
fedele (fā·dā'lā) *a* faithful
fedelmente (fā·dāl·mān'tā) *adv* loyally; exactly
fedeltà (fā·dāl·tâ') *f* faithfulness; exactness
federa (fe'dā·râ) *f* pillowcase
federale (fā·dā·râ'lā) *a* federal
federare (fā·dā·râ'rā) *vt* to federate
federazione (fā·dā·râ·tsyō'nā) *f* federation
fedina (fā·dē'nâ) *f* police record
fegataccio (fā·gâ·tâ'chō) *m* madcap, daredevil
fegato (fe'gâ·tō) *m* liver; (*sl*) courage; **aver** — to be brave; **–so** (fā·gâ·tō'zō) (*med*) bilious; cross, testy
felce (fāl'chā) *f* fern
felice (fā·lē'chā) *a* happy; **–mente** (fā·lē·chā·mān'tā) *adv* happily; safely
felicità (fā·lē·chē·tâ') *f* happiness
felicitare (fā·lē·chē·tâ'rā) *vt* to congratulate; to bless; to make happy
felicitazione (fā·lē·chē·tâ·tsyō'nā) *f* congratulation
felino (fā·lē'nō) *a* feline
fellone (fāl·lō'nā) *a* ruthless
fellonia (fāl·lō·nē'â) *f* felony; treason
felpato (fāl·pâ'tō) *a* soft, carpet-like
feltro (fāl'trō) *m* felt
femmina (fem'mē·nâ) *f* woman; female
femminile (fām·mē·nē'lā) *a* feminine
femore (fe'mō·rā) *m* thighbone
fendere * (fen'dā·rā) *vt* to split, cleave
fenditura (fān·dē·tū'râ) *f* cleft, split, opening
fenico (fe'nē·kō) *a* carbolic
fenolo (fā·nō'lō) *m* phenol
fermentare (fār·mān·tâ'rā) *vt* to ferment; to foment
fermentazione (fār·mān·tâ·tsyō'nā) *f* fermentation; fomenting
fermento (fār·mān'tō) *m* ferment; agitation, foment
feroce (fā·rō'chā) *a* ferocious; wild; **–mente** (fā·rō·chā·mān'tā) *adv* savagely, fiercely
ferragosto (fār·râ·gō'stō) *m* Assumption Day
ferramenta (fār·râ·mān'tâ) *fpl* hardware
ferravecchio (fār·râ·vek'kyō) *m* scrap iron dealer
ferreo (fer'rā·ō) *a* iron; strong
ferri (fār'rē) *mpl* tools; **cuocere ai** — to grill (*food*)
ferriera (fâr·ryā'râ) *f* steel mill, iron works
ferro (fār'rō) *m* iron; (*fig*) sword; — **da calze** knitting needle; — **da stiro** flatiron; **–via** (fār·rō·vē'â) *f* railroad; **-viario** (fār·rō·vyâ'ryō) *a* railroad; **–viere** (fār·rō·vyā'rā) *m* railroad man
fertile (fer'tē·lā) *a* fertile
fertilità (fār·tē·lē·tâ') *f* fertility
fertilizzante (fār·tē·lē·dzân'tā) *m* fertilizer
fertilizzare (fār·tē·lē·dzâ'rā) *vt* to fertilize
fertilizzazione (fār·tē·lē·dzâ·tsyō'nā) *f* fertilization
fertilmente (fār·tēl·mān'tā) *adv* fruitfully
fervente (fār·vān'tā) *a* fervent; **–mente** (fār·vān·tā·mān'tā) *adv* fervently
fervore (fār·vō'rā) *m* zeal, fervor
fesso (fās'sō) *a* cleft, cracked open
fessura (fās·sū'râ) *f* crack, crevice
festa (fā'stâ) *f* feast; party; holiday; **far — a** to welcome; to fete
festeggiamento (fā·stāj·jâ·mān'tō) *m* rejoicing
festeggiare (fā·stāj·jâ'rā) *vt* to celebrate; to rejoice over
festino (fā·stē'nō) *m* banquet
festività (fā·stē·vē·tâ') *f* festivity; celebration
festivo (fā·stē'vō) *a* festive; **giorno** — holiday
fetale (fā·tâ'lā) *a* fetal
feto (fā'tō) *m* fetus
fetente (fā·tān'tā) *a* stinking
fetido fe'tē·dō) *a* malodorous
fetore (fā·tō'rā) *m* stench
fetta (fāt'tâ) *f* slice; rasher
fettuccia (fāt·tū'châ) *f* ribbon
fettuccine (fāt·tū·chē'nā) *fpl* noodles
feudale (fāū·dâ'lā) *a* feudal
feudalismo (fāū·dâ·lē'zmō) *m* feudalism
fiaba (fyâ'bâ) *f* fable
fiacca (fyâk'kâ) *f* laziness; weakness; **batter** — (*coll*) to be sluggish; **–re** (fyâk·kâ'rā) *vt* to tire; to break down
fiacchere (fyâk'kā·rā) *m* carriage
fiacco (fyâk'kō) *a* weary; sluggish; lazy
fiaccola (fyâk'kō·lâ) *f* torch; **–ta** (fyâk·kō·lâ'tâ) *f* torchlight parade
fiacre (fyâ'krā) *m* hansom, carriage
fiala (fyâ'lâ) *f* vial
fiamma (fyâm'mâ) *f* flame; **–nte** (fyâm·mân'tā) *a* flaming; **–nte nuovo** brand-new
fiammifero (fyâm·mē'fā·rō) *m* match (*light*)
fiammingo (fyâm·mēn'gō) *m&a* Flemish
fiancheggiare (fyân·kāj·jâ'rā) *vt* to border on; (*fig*) to help, support; (*mil*) to flank
fianco (fyân'kō) *m* hip; flank; side; **di** — sideways; on one side; — **destro!** right turn!; — **sinistro!** left turn!
fiaschetteria (fyâ·skāt·tā·rē'â) *f* wine shop
fiasco (fyâ'skō) *m* flask; fiasco
fiatare (fyâ·tâ'rā) *vi* to breathe; (*fig*) to tell in secret
fiato (fyâ'tō) *m* breath
fibbia (fēb'byâ) *f* buckle
fibra (fē'brâ) *f* fiber; (*fig*) character, moral fiber
fibroso (fē·brō'zō) *a* fibrous
ficcanaso (fēk·kâ·nâ'zō) *m* busybody; intruder
fico (fē'kō) *m* fig; **non valere un** — to be absolutely worthless
fidanzamento (fē·dân·tsâ·mān'tō) *m* engagement
fidanzarsi (fē·dân·tsâr'sē) *vr* to get engaged
fidanzata (fē·dân·tsâ'tâ) *f* fiancée

fidanzato (fē·dân·tsâ'tō) *m* fiancé; — *a* engaged
fidare (fē·dâ'rā) *vt* to trust, have confidence in
fidarsi (fē·dâr'sē) *vr* to rely upon; to confide in; to dare
fidatamente (fē·dâ·tâ·mān'tā) *adv* trustingly
fidato (fē·dâ'tō) *a* faithful; devoted
fido (fē'dō) *m* faithful; devoted; — *m* (*com*) credit
fiducia (fē·dū'châ) *f* trust, confidence
fiduciario (fē·dū·châ'ryō) *m* trustee
fiduciosamente (fē·dū·chō·zâ·mān'tā) *adv* confidently, trustfully
fiducioso (fē·dū·chō'zō) *a* confident; hopeful
fiele (fyā'lā) *m* gall; (*fig*) grudge
fienile (fyā·nē'lā) *m* hayloft
fieno (fyā'nō) *m* hay; **febbre del** — hay fever
fiera (fyā'râ) *f* fair; — **di beneficenza** charity bazaar
fiera (fyā'râ) *f* wild animal
fieramente (fyā·râ·mān'tā) *adv* fiercely
fierezza (fyā·rā'tsâ) *f* fierceness; pride
fiero (fyā'rō) *a* proud; violent
fievole (fye'vō·lā) *a* feeble, weak
fievolmente (fyā·vōl·mān'tā) *adv* feebly, weakly
fifa (fē'fâ) *f* cowardice; fear
fifone (fē·fō'nā) *m* coward; softie (*coll*)
figgere * (fēj'jā·rā) *vt* to drive in, stick in
figlia (fē'lyâ) *f* daughter
figliastra (fē·lyâ'strâ) *f* step-daughter
figliastro (fē·lyâ'strō) *m* step-son
figlio (fē'lyō) *m* son; **–ccia** (fē·lyô'châ) *f* goddaughter; foster daughter; **–ccio** (fē·lyô'chō) *m* godson; godchild; foster son
figliuola (fē·lywō'lâ) *f* daughter
figliuoli (fē·lywō'lē) *mpl* children
figliuolo (fē·lywō'lō) *m* son
figura (fē·gū'râ) *f* figure; picture; appearance; face card; **far la — di** to seem to be; **–bile** (fē·gū·râ'bē·lā) *a* imaginable
figurare (fē·gū·râ'rā) *vt* (*math*) to figure; — *vi* to appear; to look well
figurarsi (fē·gū·râr'sē) *vr* to imagine, suppose
figurina (fē·gū·rē'nâ) *f* figurine
figurinista (fē·gū·rē·nē'stâ) *m* fashion designer
figurino (fē·gū·rē'nō) *m* fashion plate; pattern
figuro (fē·gū'rō) *m* rascal
fila (fē'lâ) *f* row; line; suite; **di** — one after the other
filaccia (fē·lâ'châ) *f* raveling
filamento (fē·lâ·mān'tō) *m* filament
filantropia (fē·lân·trō·pē'â) *f* philanthropy
filantropo (fē·lân'trō·pō) *m* philanthropist
filare (fē·lâ'rā) *vt&i* to spin; to run; to woo; — **diritto** to go straight ahead; to behave properly; **far — qualcuno** (*fig*) to make someone toe the mark
filarmonico (fē·lâr·mô'nē·kō) *a* philharmonic
filastrocca (fē·lâ·strōk'kâ) *f* hodgepodge, rigmarole
filatelista (fē·lâ·tā·lē'stâ) *m&f* stamp collector, philatelist
filato (fē·lâ'tō) *a* spun; — *m* yarn
filatura (fē·lâ·tū'râ) *f* spinning
filetto (fē·lāt'tō) *m* thread (*screw*); fillet
fili (fē'lē) *mpl* electric wiring; — **ad alta tensione** high-tension wires
filiale (fē·lyâ'lā) *a* filial; — *f* (*com*) branch, regional office
filibustiere (fē·lē·bū·styā'rā) *m* filibuster, freebooter
film (fēlm) *m* movie film
filo (fe'lō) *m* thread; wire; clue; cutting edge; — **d'erba** blade of grass; — **di voce** thin voice; **per — e per segno** exactly; in detail; **–bus** *m* trolley bus; **–ne** *m* vein; long loaf of bread; **–via** *f* trolley line
filodrammatico (fē·lō·drâm·mâ'tē·kō) *m* (*theat*) amateur performer
filologo (fē·lô'lō·gō) *m* philologist
filosofia (fē·lō·zō·fē'â) *f* philosophy
filosofico (fē·lō·zô'fē·kō) *a* philosophic
filosofo (fē·lô'zō·fō) *m* philosopher
filtrare (fēl·trâ'rā) *vt&i* to filter
filtro (fēl'trō) *m* filter
finale (fē·nâ'lā) *a* final; *m* — finale; finish
finalista (fē·nâ·lē'stâ) *m* finalist
finalità (fē·nâ·lē·tâ') *f* end; purpose
finalmente (fē·nâl·mān'tā) *adv* at last; in the long run
finanche (fē·nân'kā) *adv* even; too
finanza (fē·nân'tsâ) *f* finance; **guardia di** — revenue official
finanziamento (fē·nân·tsyâ·mān'tō) *m* financing, financial backing
finanziare (fē·nân·tsyâ'rā) *vt* to finance
finanziario (fē·nân·tsyâ'ryō) *a* financial
finanziatore (fē·nân·tsyâ·tō'rā) *m* backer; angel (*sl*)
finanziere (fē·nân·tsyā'rā) *m* financier
finca (fēn'kâ) *f* (*print*) column
finchè (fēn·kā') *conj* while; until
fine (fē'nā) *m* end, reason; — *f* close; limit; result; — *a* thin; refined; **–zza** (fē·nā'tsâ) *f* finesse; refinement
finestra (fē·nā'strâ) *f* window
fingere * (fēn'jā·rā) *vt* to pretend, feign; to counterfeit
fingersi * (fēn'jār·sē) *vr* to pretend to be; to act
finimento (fē·nē·mān'tō) *m* accomplishment; completion; ornament; harness (*horse*)
finire (fē·nē'rā) *vt* to finish, end; — **male** to come to grief, come to a bad end
finito (fē·nē'tō) *a* finished; perfect; accomplished; finite
Finlandia (fēn·lân'dyâ) *f* Finland
finlandese (fēn·lân·dā'zā) *a* Finnish
fino (fē'nō) *a* shrewd; thin, fine; **udito** — keen ear; — *prep* until; — **a** up to; — **là** up to that point; — **a che** until
finocchio (fē·nôk'kyō) *m* fennel
finora (fē·nō'râ) *adv* up to now, previously
finta (fēn'tâ) *f* pretense; **far – di** to feign, pretend

finto (fēn'tō) *a* false, artificial
finzione (fēn·tsyō'nā) *f* pretense; humbug
fioccare (fyōk·kâ'rā) *vi* to fall in flakes, snow
fiocco (fyōk'kō) *m* tassel; flake
fionda (fyōn'dâ) *f* sling
fiore (fyō'rā) *m* flower; club (*card*) **— di** cream of, best of
fiorentino (fyō·rān·tē'nō) *a&m* Florentine
fioretto (fyō·rāt'tō) *m* foil (*fencing*)
fiorancio (fyō·rân'chō) *m* marigold
fioraio (fyō·râ·yō) *m* florist
fiorire (fyō·rē'rā) *vi* to bloom, flower; (*fig*) to prosper, thrive
fiorista (fyō·rē'stâ) *m* florist, nurseryman
fiorito (fyō·rē'tō) *a* blooming, flowering
fiotto (fyōt'tō) *m* gush; stream; (*naut*) wave
Firenze (fē·rān'tsā) *f* Florence
firma (fēr'mâ) *f* signature; **–re** (fēr·mâ'rā) *vt* to sign; **–tario** (fēr·mâ·tâ'ryō) *m* signer
firmamento (fēr·mâ·mān'tō) *m* firmament
fisarmonica (fē·zâr·mô'nē·kâ) *f* accordion
fisarmonicista (fē·zâr·mō·nē·chē'stâ) *m* accordion player
fischiare (fē·skyâ'rā) *vt&i* to whistle; to hiss
fischio (fē'skyō) *m* whistle; hiss
fiscale (fē·skâ'lā) *a* fiscal; **avvocato —** public prosecutor
fisco (fē'skō) *m* treasury
fisica (fē'zē·kâ) *f* physics
fisico (fē'zē·kō) *a* physical, bodily; **—** *m* physique; physicist
fisiologia (fē·zyō·lō·jē'â) *f* physiology
fisionomia (fē·zyō·nō·mē'â) *f* physiognomy
fisima (fē'zē·mâ) *f* whim
fissare (fēs·sâ'rā) *vt* to fasten, fix; to stare at; to decide, determine; **— un posto** to reserve a seat
fissarsi (fēs·sâr'sē) *vr* to establish oneself; to settle down
fissazione (fēs·sâ·tsyō'nā) *f* fixation; obsession
fissile (fēs'sē·lā) *a* fissionable
fissione (fēs·syō'nā) *f* fission
fisso (fēs'sō) *a* fixed; **—** *adv* steadily
fistola (fē'stō·lâ) *f* (*med*) fistula
fitta (fēt'tâ) *f* pang, sharp pain
fittabile (fēt·tâ'bē·lā) *m* lessee, tenant farmer
fittamente (fēt·tâ·mān'tā) *adv* thickly, densely; frequently
fittizio (fēt·tē'tsyō) *a* fictitious
fitto (fēt'tō) *m* rent, income; lease
fitto (fēt'tō) *a* dense, thick; **notte fitta** pitch dark; **a capo fitto** headlong
fiumana (fyū·mâ'nâ) *f* stream; **una — di gente** (*fig*) a crowd of people
fiume (fyū'mā) *m* river; **un — di parole** (*fig*) a flood of words
fiutare (fyū·tâ'rā) *vt* to smell; to scent; (*fig*) to foresee
fiuto (fyū'tō) *m* scent; (*fig*) talent, flair; acute perception
flaccido (flâ'chē·dō) *a* spineless; flabby, soft
flacone (flâ·kō'nā) *m* flacon, vial
flagellare (flâ·jāl·lâ'rā) *vt* to whip, scourge
flagellazione (flâ·jāl·lâ·tsyō'nā) *f* whipping
flagello (flâ·jāl'lō) *m* scourge; utter ruin
flagrante (flâ·grân'tā) *a* evident; **in —** in the act
flagranza (flâ·grân'tsâ) *f* flagrancy; **colto in —** surprised red-handed
flanella (flâ·nāl'lâ) *f* flannel
flangia (flân'jâ) *f* flange
flautista (flâū·tē'stâ) *m* flutist
flauto (flâ'ū·tō) *m* flute
flebile (fle'bē·lā) *a* mournful, wailing
flebilmente (flā·bēl·mān'tā) *adv* mournfully, plaintively; weakly
flebite (flā·bē'tā) *f* (*med*) phlebitis
flemma (flām'mâ) *f* calmness; **–ticamente** (flām·mâ·tē·kâ·mān'tā) *adv* calmly, coolly
flemmone (flām·mō'nā) *m* (*med*) phlegm
flessibile (flās·sē'bē·lā) *a* flexible
flessibilità (flās·sē·bē·lē·tâ') *f* flexibility
flessibilmente (flās·sē·bēl·mān'tā) *adv* flexibility
flessione (flās·syō'nā) *f* bend; (*gram*) inflection
flessuoso (flās·swō'zō) *a* sinuous; bending
flettere * (flet'tā·rā) *vt* to flex; to bend
flirtare (flēr·tâ'rā) *vi* to flirt
florido (flô'rē·dō) *a* florid
florilegio (flô·rē·le'jō) *m* anthology, collection
floscio (flô'shō) *a* limp, flabby
flotta (flōt'tâ) *f* (*naut*) fleet; **–nte** (flōt·tân'tā) *a* floating
flottiglia (flōt·tē'lyâ) *f* flotilla
fluente (flūān'tā) *a* flowing; fluent
fluidamente (flūē·dâ·mān'tā) *adv* fluently; smoothly
fluidezza (flūē·dā'tsâ) *f* fluency
fluido (flū'ē·dō) *m&a* fluid
fluorescente (flūō·rā·shān'tā) *a* flourescent
fluorescenza (flūō·rā·shān'tsâ) *f* fluorescence
fluoridrico (flūō·rē'drē·kō) *a* hydrofluoric
fluoro (flūō'rō) *m* fluorine
fluoruro (flūō·rū'rō) *m* fluorine
flusso (flūs'sō) *m* flux
flutto (flūt'tō) *m* (*naut*) wave
fluttuante (flūt·twân'tā) *a* floating; fluctuating
fluttuare (flūt·twâ'rā) *vi* to fluctuate; to swing
fluttuazione (flūt·twâ·tsyō'nā) *f* fluctuation
fobia (fō·bē'â) *f* phobia; aversion
foca (fō'kâ) *f* seal
focaccia (fō·kâ'châ) *f* cake; **rendere pan per —** (*fig*) to give blow for blow
foce (fō'chā) *f* river mouth
fochista (fō·kē'stâ) *m* fireman
focolare (fō·kō·lâ'rā) *m* fireplace; home
focoso (fō·kō'zō) *a* fiery, impetuous
fodera (fô'dā·râ) *f* lining; **–re** (fō·dā·râ'rā) *vt* to line

foga (fō'gâ) *f* élan, ardor
foggia (fôj'jâ) *f* shape; manner; **a — di** like; **alla — di** after the fashion of; **–re** (fôj·jâ'rā) *vt* to shape
foglia (fô'lyâ) *f* leaf; **mangiare la —** to take a hint; to catch on; **–me** (fō·lyâ'mā) *m* foliage
foglietto (fō·lyāt'tō) *m* small leaf of paper; **— volante** handbill
foglio (fô'lyō) *m* sheet; (*print*) folio, page number; **–lina** (fō·lyō·lē'nâ) *f* leaflet
fogna (fō'nyâ) *f* sewer; **–tura** (fō·nyâ·tū'râ) *f* drainage system, sewers
folata (fō·lâ'tâ) *f* gust, puff (*wind*); sudden flight of birds
folgorante (fōl·gō·rân'tā) *a* shining; flashing; burning
folgorare (fōl·gō·râ'rā) *vt&i* to flash; to strike (*lightning*); to burn
folgorato (fōl·gō·râ'tō) *a* struck by lightning; electrocuted
folgore (fôl'gō·rā) *f* thunderbolt
folla (fōl'lâ) *f* mob, crowd
folle (fōl'lā) *a* insane, mad; (*mech*) unfastened; **in —** (*mech*) in neutral; **–mente** (fōl·lā·mān'tā) *adv* madly, foolishly
follia (fōl·lē'â) *f* folly; insanity
folto (fōl'tō) *a* thick, dense
fomentare (fō·mān·tâ'rā) *vt* to foment; to incite
fomentatore (fō·mān·tâ·tō'rā) *m* agitator, inciter
fomento (fō·mān'tō) *m* agitation, forment
fonda (fōn'dâ) *f* holster; **alla —** at anchor; **–ccio** (fōn·dâ'chō) *m* remnant; sediment; **–co** (fôn'dâ·kō) *m* warehouse; **–le** (fōn·dâ'lā) *m* (*theat*) backdrop; seabed; **–mentale** (fōn·dâ·mān·tâ'lā) *a* fundamental; **–mentalmente** (fōn·dâ·mān·tâl·mān'tā) *adv* fundamentally; **–mento** (fōn·dâ·mān'tō) *m* principle, basis; **–re** (fōn·dâ'rā) *vt* to found; to base; **–tezza** (fōn·dâ·tā'tsâ) *f* base, basis; **–tore** (fōn·dâ·tō'rā) *m* founder; **–zione** (fōn·dâ·tsyō'nâ) *f* foundation
fondente (fōn·dān'tā) *a* melting; fusing; **—** *m* fondant
fondere * (fôn'dā·rā) *vt&i* to melt; to fuse
fonderia (fōn·dā·rē'â) *f* foundry
fondersi (fôn'dār·sē) *vr* to melt; to dissolve
fondina (fōn·dē'nâ) *f* holster; *(coll)* soup plate
fonditore (fōn·dē·tō'rā) *m* smelter
fonditura (fōn·dē·tū'râ) *f* smelting
fondo (fōn'dō) *m* fund; bottom; property, land; **— di magazzino** stock on hand; **—dei pantaloni** seat of the pants; **articolo di —** (*press*) editorial; feature article; **dar —** (*naut*) to anchor; **gara di —** endurance test; **in — alla strada** at the end of the street; **—** *a* deep
fonetica (fō·ne'tē·kâ) *f* phonetics
fonetico (fō·ne'tē·kō) *a* phonetic
fonico (fô'nē·kō) *a* phonic
fonogeno (fō·nô'jā·nō) *m* (*rad*) pickup
fonografico (fō·nō·grâ'fē·kō) *a* phonographic; **disco —** phonograph record
fonografo (fō·nô'grâ·fō) *m* phonograph
fontana (fōn·tâ'nâ) *f* fountain
fonte (fōn'tā) *f* spring (*water*); font; origin
foraggio (fō·râj'jō) *m* fodder
forare (fō·râ'rā) *vt* to pierce; to drill *(hole)*; to punch *(ticket)*
foratrice (fō·râ·trē'chā) *f (mech)* drill
foratura (fō·râ·tū'râ) *f* puncture; flat tire
forbici (fôr'bē·chē) *fpl* scissors
forbire (fōr·bē'rā) *vt* to furbish, polish
forbito (fōr·bē'tō) *a* elegant; polished
forca (fōr'kâ) *f* gallows; pitchfork; **far la — a** to be untrue to; to treat someone shabbily; to do someone dirt (*sl*); **–iuolo** (fōr·kâ·ywō'lō) *m* (*pol*) reactionary
forcella (fōr·chāl'lâ) *f* hairpin; tree fork; bicycle fork
forchetta (fōr·kāt'tâ) *f* fork (*table*)
forchettone (fōr·kāt·tō'nā) *m* carving fork
forcina (fōr·chē'nâ) *f* hairpin
forcipe (fôr'chē·pā) *m* forceps
forense (fō·rān'sā) *a* forensic
foresta (fō·rā'stâ) *f* forest; **una — di capelli** *(fig)* a mop of hair
forestale (fō·rā·stâ'lā) *a* forest; **guardia —** forest ranger
forestiero (fō·rā·styā'rō) *m* foreigner; stranger; **—** *a* foreign
forfora (fôr'fō·râ) *f* dandruff
forgia (fôr'jâ) *f* forge; **–re** (fōr·jâ'rā) *vt* to forge, shape
forma (fōr'mâ) *f* form; way; **–le** (fōr·mâ'lā) *a* formal; usual; **–lità** (fōr·mâ·lē·tâ') *f* formality; **–lizzare** (fōr·mâ·lē·dzâ'rā) *vt* to shock, astonish; **–lizzarsi** (fōr·mâ·lē·dzâr'sē) *vr* to be astonished, be shocked; to be offended; **–lmente** (fōr·mâl·mān'tā) *adv* with formality; **–re** (fōr·mâ'rā) *vt* to form; **–rsi** (fōr·mâr'sē) *vr* to mature, develop; **–tivo** (fōr·mâ·tē'vō) *a* formative; **–to** (fōr·mâ'tō) *m* format; size; **–to** *a* formed; shaped; molded; **–tore** (fōr·mâ·tō'rā) *m*, **–trice** (fōr·mâ·trē'chā) *f* modeler; creator; educator; **–zione** (fōr·mâ·tsyō'nâ) *f* formation; forming
formaggio (fōr·mâj'jō) *m* cheese
formaldeide (fōr·mâl·de'ē·dā) *f* formaldehyde
formica (fōr·mē'kâ) *f* ant; **–io** (fōr·mē·kâ'yō) *m* ant hill; *(fig)* swarm
formico (fôr'mē·kō) *a (chem)* formic; **acido —** formic acid; **–lante** (fōr·mē·kō·lân'tā) *a* swarming; **–lare** (fōr·mē·kō·lâ'rā) *vi* to swarm; **–lio** (fōr·mē·kō·lē'ō) *n* tingling sensation, prickling
formidabile (fōr·mē·dâ'bē·lā) *a* formidable
formidabilmente (fōr·mē·dâ·bēl·mān'tā) *adv* dreadfully; formidably
formoso (fōr·mō'zō) *a* shapely; buxom
formula (fôr'mū·lâ) *f* formula; **–re** (fōr·mū·lâ'rā) *vt* to formulate; to express, couch
fornace (fōr·nâ'chā) *f* furnace; oast
fornaio (fōr·nâ'yō) *m* baker
fornello (fōr·nāl'lō) *m* kitchen range,

stove
fornire (fōr·nē'rā) *vt* to supply
fornitore (fōr·nē·tō'rā) *m* caterer; supplier
fornitura (fōr·nē·tū'râ) *f* supplies; equipment
forno (fōr'nō) *m* bakery; oven; *(theat)* empty house; **al** — baked; **alto** — blast furnace; — **crematorio** crematory
foro (fō'rō) *m* hole; forum; *(law)* bar
forse (fōr'sā) *adv* perhaps; — *m* doubt
forsennato (fōr·sān·nâ'tō) *a* crazy; — *m* madman
forte (fōr'tā) *a* strong; loud; — *adv* strongly; loudly; — **guadagno** large profit; — **pioggia** heavy rain; **dar man** — to uphold; **–zza** (fōr·tā'tsâ) *f* fortress
fortificare (fōr·tē·fē·kâ'rā) *vt* to fortify
fortificarsi (fōr·tē·fē·kâr'sē) *vr* to be fortified; to become strengthened
fortuitamente (fōr·twē·tâ·mān'tā) *adv* by chance
fortuito (fōr·tū'ē·tō) *a* casual; accidental; **caso** — coincidence
fortuna (fōr·tū'nâ) *f* luck; fortune; success; **atterraggio di** — (avi) forced landing; **–le** (fōr·tū·nâ'lā) *m* storm; tempest; **–tamente** (fōr·tū·nâ·tâ·mān'tā) *adv* fortunately; luckily; **–to** (fōr·tū·nâ'tō) *a* lucky; fortunate; successful; happy
fortunosamente (fōr·tū·nō·zâ·mān'tā) *adv* tempestuously
fortunoso (fōr·tū·nō'zō) *a* stormy; risky, dangerous
foruncolo (fō·rūn'kō·lō) *m (med)* boil
forviare (fōr·vyâ'rā) *vt* to lead astray
forza (fōr'tsâ) *f* force, power; strength; — **motrice** driving power; **a viva** — with might and main; **a** — **di** by dint of; **farsi** — to gather courage; **–re** (fōr·tsâ'rā) *vt* to compel, force; **–re una serratura** to pick a lock; **–re un blocco** to run a blockade; **–tamente** (fōr·tsâ·tâ·mān'tā) *adv* necessarily; **–to** (fōr·tsâ'tō) *a* forced; **–to** *m* convict; **lavoro –to** forced labor
forziere (fōr·tsyā'rā) *m* strongbox
forzosamente (fōr·tsō·zâ·mān'tā) *adv* forcibly
forzoso (fōr·tsō'zō) *a* forced
foscamente (fō·skâ·mān'tā) *adv* darkly; gloomily; obscurely
foschia (fō·skē'â) *f* mist; fog
fosco (fō'skō) *a* dark; gloomy, dull
fosfato (fō·sfâ'tō) *m* phosphate
fosforescente (fō·sfō·rā·shān'tā) *a* phosphorescent
fosforo (fô'sfō·rō) *m* phosphorus
fossa (fōs'sâ) *f* ditch; grave; moat; **–to** (fōs·sâ'tō) *m* ditch
fossetta (fōs·sāt'tâ) *f* dimple
fossile (fôs'sē·lā) *m&a* fossil
fossilizzare (fōs·sē·lē·dzâ'rā) *vt* to fossilize
fotocalcografia (fō·tō·kâl·kō·grâ·fē'â) *f* photogravure
fotocellula (fō·tō·chel'lū·lâ) *f* photoelectric cell
fotochimica (fō·tō·kē'mē·kâ) *f* photochemistry
fotocollografia (fō·tō·kōl·lō·grâ·fē'â) *f* colortype
fotoelettrico (fō·tō·ā·let'trē·kō) *a* photoelectric
fotogenico (fō·tō·je'nē·kō) *a* photogenic
fotografare (fō·tō·grâ·fâ'rā) *vt* to photograph
fotografia (fō·tō·grâ·fē'â) *f* photograph; — **istantanea** *f* snapshot
fotografico (fō·tō·grâ'fē·kō) *a* photographic
fotografo (fō·tô'grâ·fō) *m* photographer
fotoincisione (fō·tō·ēn·chē·zyō'nā) *f* photoengraving
fotometro (fō·tô'mā·trō) *m* light meter
fotone (fō·tō'nā) *m* photon
fotoritocco (fō·tō·rē·tōk'kō) *m (photo)* retouching
fotosfera (fō·tō·sfā'râ) *f* photosphere
fototerapia (fō·tō·tā·râ·pē'â) *f* phototherapy
fra (frâ) *prep* among; between; within, in *(time)*; — **di noi** between us; — **me e me** to myself; — **poco** soon
frac (frâk) *m* frock coat; *(sl)* tails
fracassare (frâ·kâs·sâ'rā) *vt* to smash, break up
fracassarsi (frâ·kâs·sâr'sē) *vr* to smash, shatter; to crash
fracasso (frâ·kâs'sō) *m* racket, uproar
fradicio (frâ'dē·chō) *a* rotten; soaked; **ubriaco** — dead drunk
fradiciume (frâ·dē·chū'mā) *m* rottenness
fragile (frâ'jē·lā) *a* frail, fragile; brittle
fragilità (frâ·jē·lē·tâ') *f* brittleness; weakness
fragola (frâ'gō·lâ) *f* strawberry
fragore (frâ·gō'rā) *m* loud noise; rumble; clang
fragorosamente (frâ·gō·rō·zâ·mān'tā) *adv* noisily, loudly
fragoroso (frâ·gō·rō'zō) *a* noisy, loud
fragrante (frâ·grân'tā) *a* fragrant
fragranza (frâ·grân'tsâ) *f* fragrance
fraintendere * (frâēn·ten'dā·rā) *vt* to misunderstand; to understand in part
frainteso (frâēn·tā'zō) *a* misunderstood
frammentario (frâm·mān·tâ'ryō) *a* fragmentary; — *m* fragment
frana (frâ'nâ) *f* landslide
francamente (frân·kâ·mān'tā) *adv* frankly, openly
francatura (frân·kâ·tū'râ) *f* postage
francese (frân·chā'zā) *a* French; — *m* Frenchman
franchezza (frân·kā'tsâ) *f* frankness
franchigia (frân·kē'jâ) *f* franchise; — **postale** free postage
franco (frân'kō) *a* frank, candid; — **a bordo** *(com)* F.O.B. free on board; — **di porto** *(com)* postpaid; **essere** — **con** to be frank with; **farla franca** to go scot-free; **–bollo** (frân·kō·bōl'lō) *m* postage stamp; **–tiratore** (frân·kō·tē·râ·tō'rā) *m* sniper; guerilla
frangente (frân·jān'tā) *m* bad situation, tight spot; *(naut)* breaker; reef

frangere * (frân'jā·rā) *vt* to crush; to dash to pieces
frangia (frân'jâ) *f* fringe
frantumare (frân·tū·mâ'rā) *vt* to shatter; to sliver
frantumi (frân·tū'mē) *mpl* splinters; small pieces; slivers; **andare in** — to break into small pieces
frapporre * (frâp·pōr'rā) *vt* to interpose
frapporsi * (frâp·pōr'sē) *vr* to interfere; to step between
frapposizione (frâ·pō·zē·tsyō'nā) *f* interference
frasca (frâ'skâ) *f* *(bot)* branch; frivolous person; frivolity; **saltar di palo in** — *(coll)* to ramble, speak disjointedly
frase (frâ'zā) *f* sentence; phrase; **–ggiare** (frâ·zāj·jâ'rā) *vt&i* to phrase; **–ologia** (frâ·zā·ō·lō·jē'â) *f* phraseology
frassino (frâs'sē·nō) *m* ash *(tree)*
frastagliamento (frâ·stâ·lyâ·mān'tō) *m* indentation; notching
frastagliare (frâ·stâ·lyâ'rā) *vt* to notch; to indent
frastagliato (frâ·stâ·lyâ'tō) *a* jagged; indented
frastornare (frâ·stōr·nâ'rā) *vt* to disturb, upset
frastuono (frâ·stwō'nō) *m* uproar; din
frate (frâ'tā) *m* friar; **–llanza** (frâ·tāl·lân'tsâ) *f* brotherhood; **–ellastro** (frâ·tāl·lâ'strō) *m* half-brother; **–llo** (frâ·tāl'lō) *m* brother; **–rnamente** (frâ·tār·nâ·mān'tā) *adv* fraternally; **–rnità** (frâ·tār·nē·tâ') *f* fraternity, brotherhood; **–rnizzare** (frâ·tār·nē·dzâ'rā) *vi* to fraternize; **–rno** (frâ·tār'nō) *a* fraternal
fratricida (frâ·trē·chē'dâ) *m* fratricide *(person)*
fratta (frât'tâ) *f* hedge, bush
frattaglie (frât·tâ'lyā) *fpl* giblets
frattanto (frât·tân'tō) *adv* meanwhile
frattempo (frât·tām'pō) *m* meantime; interval
frattura (frât·tū'râ) *f* fracture; **–re** (frât·tū·râ'rā) *vt* to break, fracture
fraudolentemente (frâū·dō·lān·tā·mān'tā) *adv* deceitfully; fraudulently
fraudolento (frâū·dō·lān'tō) *a* deceitful; fraudulent
frazionamento (frâ·tsyō·nâ·mān'tō) *m* division; separation
frazionare (frâ·tsyō·nâ'rā) *vt* to divide, separate; *(chem)* to fractionate
frazionario (frâ·tsyō·nâ'ryō) *a* fragmentary
frazione (frâ·tsyō'nā) *f* fraction; *(fig)* whistle-stop, one-horse town
freccia (fre'châ) *f* arrow; indicating needle; **–ta** (frā·châ'tâ) *(fig)* bitter word; gibe, taunt
freddamente (frād·dâ·mān'tā) *adv* coolly, coldly
freddezza (frād·dā'tsâ) *f* coolness; coldness
freddo (frād'dō) *a&m* cold; **aver** — *(person)* to be cold; **far** — *(weather)* to be cold; **sentir** — to feel cold; **–loso** (frād·dō·lō'zō) *a* cold-blooded, susceptible to the cold
freddura (frād·dū'râ) *f* pun; witticism
fregare (frā·gâ'rā) *vt* to rub; *(coll)* to swindle
fregarsene (frā·gâr'sā·nā) *vr* *(coll)* not to give a hang
fregatura (frā·gâ·tū'râ) *f* rubbing; *(coll)* swindle, deceit
fregiare (frā·jâ'rā) *vt* to decorate
fregiarsi (frā·jâr'sē) *vr* to deck oneself out
fregio (fre'jō) *m* adornment
frego (frā'gō) *m* cancellation; striking out
fremente (frā·mān'tā) *a* quivering; shuddering
fremere (fre'mā·rā) *vi* to fume, fret; to tremble
fremito (fre'mē·tō) *m* thrill; quiver
frenare (frā·nâ'rā) *vt* to check, restrain; *(mech)* to brake
frenarsi (frā·nâr'sē) *vr* to restrain oneself; to keep one's temper
frenatore (frā·nâ·tō'rā) *m* brakeman
frenesia (frā·nā·zē'â) *f* frenzy, flurry
freneticamente (frā·nā·tē·kâ·mān'tā) *adv* frantically
frenetico (frā·ne'tē·kō) *a* frantic; **applauso** — loud cheers
freno (frā'nō) *m* brake; restraint; **senza** — unrestrained
frenologia (frā·nō·lō·jē'â) *f* phrenology
frequentare (frā·kwān·tâ'rā) *vt* to frequent; to attend
frequente (frā·kwān'tā) *a* frequent; **–mente** *adv* frequently
frequenza (frā·kwān'tsâ) *f* frequency; attendance; **modulazione di** — frequency modulation
fresa (frā'zâ) *f* *(mech)* cutter; milling machine
frescamente (frā·skâ·mān'tā) *adv* freshly; coolly; recently
freschezza (frā·skā'tsâ) *f* freshness; coolness *(weather)*
fresco (frā'skō) *a* fresh, new; — *m* cool weather; **al** — outdoors
fretta (frāt'tâ) *f* hurry, haste; **in** — **e furia** hurriedly
frettolosamente (frāt·tō·lō·zâ·mān'tā) *adv* swiftly
friabile (fryâ'bē·lā) *a* brittle; friable
friabilità (fryâ·bē·lē·tâ') *f* brittleness; friability
friggere * (frēj'jā·rā) *vt* to fry
frigorifero (frē·gō·rē'fā·rō) *m* refrigerator
frittata (frēt·tâ'tâ) *f* omelet; **fare una** — *(fig)* to mess things up, botch a job
frittella (frēt tāl'lâ) *f* fritter
fritto (frēt'tō) *a* fried; **essere** — *(fig)* to be done for; to be worn out; — **e rifritto** *(fig)* trite
frivolamente (frē·vō·lâ·mān'tā) *adv* frivolously
frivoleggiare (frē·vō·lāj·jâ'rā) *vi* to trifle; to fritter away one's time
frivolezza (frē·vō·lā'tsâ) *f* frivolity
frivolo (frē'vō·lō) *a* frivolous
frizione (frē·tsyō'nā) *f* massage; *(auto)* clutch; friction
frizzante (frē·tsân'tā) *a* racy; piquant

frizzo (frē'tsō) *m* witticism; witty remark
frodare (frō·dâ'rā) *vt* to defraud; to hoax
frodatore (frō·dâ·tō'rā) *m* defrauder
frodo (frō'dō) *m* smuggling; **cacciatore di —** poacher
frollare (frōl·lâ'rā) *vt&i* to tenderize *(meat)*; to make soft, fluff up
frollo (frōl'lō) *a* fluffy, soft
frondoso (frōn·dō'zō) *a* leafy
frontale (frōn·tâ'lā) *a* frontal
fronte (frōn'tā) *f* forehead; **–ggiare** (frōn·tāj·jâ'rā) *vt* to confront; **–spizio** (frōn·tā·spē'tsyō) *m* title page; **— a —** face to face; **far — al pericolo** to face danger; **far — alle spese** to meet expenses; **mettere di — a** to confront with; **di — a** in front of, facing
frontiera (frōn·tyā'râ) *f* border, frontier
fronzolo (frôn'dzō·lō) *m* ribbon; *(fig)* trifle
frotta (frōt'tâ) *f* crowd, flock
frottola (frôt'tō·lâ) *f* fib; nonsense
frugare (frū·gâ'rā) *vt* to search through carefully, comb through
fruire (frūē'rā) *vt* to enjoy the use of
frullare (frūl·lâ'rā) *vt* to beat up, whisk; **—** *vi* to flutter; **— per il capo** *(fig)* to get into one's head
frumento (frū·mān'tō) *m* wheat; **–ne** (frū·mān·tō'nā) *m* maize
frusciare (frū·shâ'rā) *vi* to rustle
fruscio (frū·shē'ō) *m* rustle
frusta (frū'stâ) *f* whip
frustare (frū·stâ'rā) *vt* to scourge
frustata (frū·stâ'tâ) *f* lash; whipping
frustino (frū·stē'nō) *m* horsewhip
frutta (frūt'tâ) *f* fruit
fucina (fū·chē'nâ) *f* forge
fuco (fū'kō) *m (zool)* drone
fuga (fū'gâ) *f* fleeing, flight; *(mus)* fugue; **–ce** (fū·gâ'chā) *a* transient, fleeting; **–cemente** (fū·gâ·chā·mān'tā) *adv* fleetingly; **–re** (fū·gâ'rā) *vt* to frighten away, put to flight
fuggiasco (fūj·jâ'skō) *m* fugitive
fuggibile (fūj·jē'bē·lā) *a* avoidable
fuggifuggi (fūj·jē·fūj'jē) *m (coll)* panic, stampede
fuggire (fūj·jē'rā) *vi* to flee, escape; **—** *vt* to avoid; to shrink from
fuggitivo (fūj·jē·tē'vō) *m&a* fugitive
fulcro (fūl'krō) *m* fulcrum
fulgido (fūl'jē·dō) *a* bright, shining
fuliggine (fū·lēj'jē·nā) *f* soot
fulminare (fūl·mē·nâ'rā) *vt* to strike down
fulmine (fūl'mē·nā) *m* lightning; thunderbolt; **–ità** (fūl·mē·nāē·tâ') *f* extreme rapidity; **–o** (fūl·mē'nā·ō) *a* extremely fast
fulvo (fūl'vō) *a* tawny, tan
fumaiolo (fū·mâ·yō'lō) *m* funnel; smokestack
fumare (fū·mâ'rā) *vt&i* to smoke; **vietato —** no smoking
fumata (fū·mâ'tâ) *f* smoke
fumetto (fū·māt'tō) *m* comic strip
fumigare (fū·mē·gâ'rā) *vi* to fumigate
fumigazione (fū·mē·gâ·tsyō'nā) *f* fumigation
fumista (fū·mē'stâ) *m* heating technician
fumo (fū'mō) *m* smoke; *(fig)* humbug; **mandare in —** *(fig)* to reduce to nothing; **vendere —** *(fig)* to humbug; **–so** (fū·mō'zō) *a* smoky
fumogeno (fū·mô'jā·nō) *a* producing smoke; **cortina fumogena** smokescreen
fune (fū'nā) *f* cable; rope
funebre (fū'nā·brā) *a* funerial, mournful
funebri (fū'nā·brē) *fpl* funeral; **impresario di pompe —** funeral director, undertaker
funestare (fū·nā·stâ'rā) *vt* to ruin, wreck; to cast a pall over, sadden
fungo (fūn'gō) *m* fungus; mushroom
funicolare (fū·nē·kō·lâ'rā) *f* cable railway
funzionale (fūn·tsyō·nâ'lā) *a* functional
funzionare (fūn·tsyō·nâ'rā) *vi* to function
funzionario (fūn·tsyō·nâ'ryō) *m* official
funzione (fūn·tsyō'nā) *f* function
fuoco (fwō'kō) *m* fire; **fuochi d'artificio** fireworks; **a —** *(phot)* in focus
fuorchè (fwōr·kā') *prep* except, with the exception of; **—** *conj* unless
fuori (fwō'rē) *prep* outside of; **—** *adv* outside, out; **— casa** not at home; **— di sè** beside oneself; **— di tempo** badly timed; **— d'uso** obsolete; **— giuoco** *(sport)* offside; **— servizio** off duty; **— strada** astray; mistaken; **lasciar —** to omit; **tutti fuori tu** all except you; **— legge** outlaw; **— serie** *a* custom-built
fuoruscito (fwō·rū·shē'tō) *m* exile
fuorviare (fwōr·vyâ'rā) *vt* to mislead, lose
fuorviarsi (fwōr·vyâr'sē) *vr* to become lost
furberia (fūr·bā·rē'â) *f* cunning, artfulness; craftiness
furbesco (fūr·bā'skō) *a* artful, crafty
furbo (fūr'bō) *a* crafty, sly; clever
furente (fū·rān'tā) *a* furious; **— d'ira** infuriated
furetto (fū·rāt'tō) *m (zool)* ferret
furfante (fūr·fân'tā) *m* rogue; villain
furgone (fūr·gō'nā) *m* van; wagon
furia (fū'ryâ) *f* rage, fury; **aver —** to be in a great hurry; **a — di** by force of
furiosamente (fū·ryō·zâ·mān'tā) *adv* furiously; violently
furioso (fū·ryō'zō) *a* furious
furore (fū·rō'râ) *m* fury, wrath; *(fig)* enthusiasm; **–ggiare** (fū·rō·rāj·jâ'rā) *vi* to be highly successful; to be the rage
furtivamente (fūr·tē·vâ·mān'tā) *adv* furtively, on the sly
furtivo (fūr·tē'vō) *a* furtive, sly
furto (fūr'tō) *m* theft; **— con scasso** burglary
fusibile (fū·zē'bē·lā) *m* fuse
fusione (fū·zyo'nā) *f* fusion; *(com)* merger
fuso (fū'zō) *m* spindle; **–liera** (fū·zō·lyā'râ) *f (avi)* fuselage; **— orario** time zone; **diritto come un —** straight as a ramrod; **fare le fusa** to purr
fuso (fū'zō) *a* fused; melted
fustigare (fū·stē·gâ'rā) *vt* to flog
fustigazione (fū·stē·gâ·tsyō'nā) *f* flogging

fusto (fū'stō) *m (bot, anat)* trunk; mannequin; cask
futile (fū'tē·lā) *a* futile, useless; frivolous
futilità (fū·tē·lē·tâ') *f* futility, uselessness
futurista (fū·tū·rē'stâ) *m* futurist
futuro (fū·tū'rō) *a&m* future

G

gabbanella (gâb·bâ·nāl'lâ) *f* smock
gabbare (gâb·bâ'rā) *vt* to mock; to trick
gabbarsi (gâb·bâr'sē) *vr* to make sport of
gabella (gâ·bāl'lâ) *f* duty, excise tax; **–re** (gâ·bāl·lâ'rā) *vt* to charge; to tax; to pretend to be, pass oneself off as
gabbia (gâb'byâ) *f* cage; crate; **mettere in —** *(fig)* to put into prison
gabbiano (gâb·byâ'nō) *m* seagull
gabinetto (gâ·bē·nāt'tō) *m (pol)* cabinet; office; washroom; **— di decenza** toilet; **— di lettura** reading room
gaffa (gâf'fâ) *f (coll)* blunder
gagà (gâ·gâ') *m (sl)* dandy, dude
gaggia (gâj·jē'â) *f* acacia
gagliardetto (gâ·lyâr·dāt'tō) *m* pennant
gagliardo (gâ·lyâr'dō) *a* vigorous; stouthearted
gaglioffo (gâ·lyōf'fō) *m* loafer, lout
gaiamente (gâ·yâ·mān'tā) *adv* gaily, brightly
gaiezza (gâ·yā'tsâ) *f* gaiety; vividness
gaio (gâ'yō) *a* merry, gay; bright
gala (gâ'lâ) *f* festivity; **pranzo di —** formal dinner
galante (gâ·lân'tā) *a* polite; courteous; **—** *m* gallant; **donna —** call girl; **avventura —** love affair; **–ria** (gâ·lân·tā·rē'â) *f* politeness; courtesy
galantuomo (gâ·lân·twō'mō) *m* honest man; gentleman
galateo (gâ·lâ·tā'ō) *m* etiquette
galeotto (gâ·lā·ōt'tō) *m* convict; rascal; galley slave
galera (gâ·lā'râ) *f* jail; *(naut)* galley; **vita da —** wretched life
galla (gâl'lâ) *f* blister; **a —** afloat
galleggiante (gâl·lāj·jân'tā) *a* floating **—** *m (naut)* float
galleria (gâl·lā·rē'â) *f* gallery; tunnel
galletto (gâl·lāt'tō) *m* spring chicken
gallina (gâl·lē'nâ) *f* hen, chicken; **–ccio** (gâl·lē·nâ'chō) *m* turkey
gallo (gâl'lō) *m* rooster
gallone (gâl·lō'nā) *m* stripe, chevron; braid; gallon
galoppare (gâ·lōp·pâ'rā) *vi* to gallop
galoppatoio (gâ·lōp·pâ·tô'yō) *m* bridle path
galoppino (gâ·lōp·pē'nō) *m* errand boy; *(pol)* solicitor
galoppo (gâ·lōp'pō) *m* gallop
galvani (gâl·vâ'nē) *mpl (print)* electrotype
galvanizzare (gâl·vâ·nē·dzâ'rā) *vt* to galvanize
galvanoplastica (gâl·vâ·nō·plâ'stē·kâ) *f* electroplating
gamba (gâm'bâ) *f* leg; **andare a gambe levate** fall headlong; **darsela a gambe** to take to one's heels; **essere in —** to be smart; **fare il passo secondo la —** *(fig)* to cut the coat according to the cloth; **–le** (gâm·bâ'lā) *m* legging
gamberetto (gâm·bā·rāt'tō) *m* shrimp
gambero (gâm'bā·rō) *m* spiny lobster
gambo (gâm'bō) *m* stem
gamella (gâ·māl'lâ) *f* mess kit
gamma (gâm'mâ) *f* range, gamut; *(mus)* scale
ganascia (gâ·nâ'shâ) *f (anat)* jaw
gancio (gân'chō) *m* hook; clasp
ganghero (gân'gā·rō) *m* hinge; **uscir dai gangheri** to fly off the handle
ganglio (gân'glyō) *m* ganglion
gara (gâ'râ) *f* contest, match; competition; **andare a —** to compete
garagista (gâ·râ·jē'stâ) *m* garageman, automobile mechanic
garante (gâ·rân'tā) *m* guarantor
garantire (gâ·rân·tē'rā) *vt* to guarantee, vouch for
garanzia (gâ·rân·tsē'â) *f* guaranty, security
garbare (gâr·bâ'rā) *vi* to please
garbatamente (gâr·bâ·tâ·mān'tā) *adv* politely
garbatezza (gâr·bâ·tā'tsâ) *f* kindness; courtesy
garbato (gâr·bâ'tō) *a* polite
garbo (gâr'bō) *m* politeness; **con —** graciously; **mal —** rudeness; **senza —** clumsy, awkward
garbuglio (gâr·bū'lyō) *m* confusion; mess
gareggiare (gâ·rāj·jâ'rā) *vi* to compete
gargarismo (gâr·gâ·rē'zmō) *m* gargle, gargling
garguglia (gâr·gū'lyâ) *f* gargoyle
garofano (gâ·rô'fâ·nō) *m* carnation
garrese (gâr·rā'zā) *m* withers *(horse)*
garretto (gâr·rāt'tō) *m* fetlock *(horse)*; *(anat)* ankle
garrulo (gâr'rū·lō) *a* garrulous
garza (gâr'dzâ) *f* gauze
gas (gâs) *m* gas; **–odotto** (gâ·zō·dōt'tō) *m* gasline; **–olio** (gâ·zô'lyō) *m* fuel oil; **–sare** (gâs·sâ'rā) *vt* to charge *(liquid)*; **–sato** (gâs·sâ'tō) *a* charged; **–ista** (gâ·zē'stâ) *m* gasman; **–osa** (gâ·zō'zâ) *f* soft drink; **–oso** (gâ·zō'zō) *a* gaseous, fizzy
gastrico (gâ'strē·kō) *a* gastric
gastrite (gâ·strē'tā) *f (med)* gastritis
gatta (gât'tâ) *f* female cat; **— ci cova** *(coll)* there is something brewing; **avere una — da pelare** *(fig)* to be in trouble; **–buia** (gât·tâ·bū'yâ) *f* jail; **–morta** (gât·tâ·mōr'tâ) *f* hypocrite
gattino (gât·tē'nō) *m* kitten
gatto (gât'tō) *m* tomcat; **essere in quattro gatti** to be few in number
gattò (gât·tō') *m* French pastry
gaudente (gâū·dān'tā) *a* epicurean; cheerful; **—** *m* bon vivant
gaudio (gâ'ū·dyō) *m* joy; **mal comune**

mezzo — trouble shared is trouble halved
gavazzare (gâ·vâ·tsâ'rā) *vi* to wassail, revel
gavitello (gâ·vē·tāl'lō) *m* buoy
gazzarra (gâ·dzâr'râ) *f* racket, uproar
gazzella (gâ·dzāl'lâ) *f* gazelle
gazzettino (gâ·dzāt·tē'nō) *m* bulletin; *(fig)* gossip
gelare (jā·lâ'rā) *vt&i* to freeze
gelarsi (jā·lâr'sē) *vr* to be frozen, freeze
gelateria (jā·lâ·tā·rē'â) *f* ice cream shop
gelatiere (jā·lâ·tyā'rā) *m* ice cream seller
gelatina (jā·lâ·tē'nâ) *f* gelatin
gelatinoso (jā·lâ·tē·nō'zō) *a* gelatinous
gelato (jā·lâ'tō) *m* ice cream; — *a* frozen
gelidamente (jā·lē·dâ·mān'tā) *adv* icily
gelido (je'lē·dō) *a* icy; freezing
gelo (jā'lō) *m* frost; *(fig)* chilly manner; **–ne** (jā·lō'nā) *m* chilblain
gelosamente (jā·lō·zâ·mān'tā) *adv* jealously
gelosia (jā·lō·zē'â) *f* jealousy; jalousie, venetian blind
geloso (jā·lō'zō) *a* jealous, showing envy
gelsomino (jāl·sō·mē'nō) *m* jasmine
gemello (jā·māl'lō) *a&m* twin; **bottoni gemelli** cuff links
gemere (je'mā·rā) *vi* to groan, moan
gemito (je'mē·tō) *m* lament, groan
geminare (jā·mē·nâ'rā) *vt* to pair, couple
geminazione (jā·mē·nâ·tsyō'nā) *f* gemination, pairing
gemma (jām'mâ) *f* gem; bud; **–zione** (jām·mâ·tsyō'nā) *f (bot)* budding
gemmato (jām·mâ'tō) *a* studded with gems
gendarme (jān·dâr'mā) *m* policeman; **–ria** (jān·dâr·mā·rē'â) *f* police force
genealogia (jā·nā·â·lō·jē'â) *f* genealogy
genealogico (jā·nā·â·lô'jē·kō) *a* genealogical; **albero** — family tree
generale (jā·nā·râ'lā) *a&m* general; **tenersi sulle generali** to be vague
generalità (jā·nā·râ·lē·tâ') *f* generality; — *fpl* personal data
generalizzare (jā·nā·râ·lē·dzâ'rā) *vt&i* to generalize
generalmente (jā·nā·râl·mān'tā) *adv* generally, as a rule
generare (jā·nā·râ'rā) *vt* to generate, bring forth
generatore (jā·nā·râ·tō'rā) *m* generator
generazione (jā·nā·râ·tsyō'nā) *f* generation
genere (je'nā·rā) *m* kind; genus; *(gram)* gender; **generi di prima necessità** primary needs of life; **generi alimentari** groceries; **il — tragico** *(lit)* tragedy, tragic genre
generico (jā·ne'rē·kō) *a* generic; indefinite
genero (je'nā·rō) *m* son-in-law
generosamente (jā·nā·rō·zâ·mān'tā) *adv* generously
generosità (jā·nā·rō·zē·tâ') *f* generosity
generoso (jā·nā·rō'zō) *a* generous
genesi (je'nā·zē) *f* genesis; origin
genetica (jā·ne'tē·kâ) *f* genetics
gengiva (jān·jē'vâ) *f (dent)* gum
gengivite (jân·jē·vē'tā) *f* gingivitis
geniale (jā·nyâ'lā) *a* genial, pleasant; talented
genialità (jā·nyâ·lē·tâ') *f* geniality; ingeniousness
genialmente (jā·nyâl·mān'tā) *adv* genially; ingeniously
genio (je'nyō) *m* genius, talent; *(mil)* engineer; — **civile** public works administration; **andare a** — to be to one's liking
genitale (jā·nē·tâ'lā) *a&m* genital
genitivo (jā·nē·tē'vō) *m* genitive
genitore (jā·nē·tō'rā) *m*, **genitrice** (jā·nē·trē'chā) *f* parent
genitura (jā·nē·tū'râ) *f* procreation
gennaio (jān·nâ'yō) *m* January
Genova (je'nō·vâ) *f* Genoa
genovese (jā·nō·vā'zā) *a&m* Genovese
gentaglia (jān·tâ'lyâ) *f* mob, rabble
gente (jān'tā) *f* people; — **di mare** seamen; **diritto delle genti** international law
gentildonna (jān·tēl·dōn'nâ) *f* lady
gentile (jān·tē'lā) *a* polite; kind; **–zza** (jān·tē·lā'tsâ) *f* kindness
gentilizio (jān·tē·lē'tsyō) *a* noble; **stemma gentilizia** coat of arms
gentilmente (jān·tēl·mān'tā) *adv* kindly; courteously
gentiluomo (jān·tē·lwō'mō) *m* gentleman
genuflessione (jā·nū·flās·syō'nā) *f* genuflection
genuflesso (jā·nū·flās'sō) *a* knelt in prayer
genuflettersi * (jā·nū·flet'tār·sē) *vr* to genuflect
genuinità (jā·nwē·nē·tâ') *f* genuineness
genuino (jā·nwē'nō) *a* genuine
geofisica (jā·ō·fē'zē·kâ) *f* geophysics
geografia (jā·ō·grâ·fē'â) *f* geography
geografico (jā·ō·grâ'fē·kō) *a* geographical
geografo (jā·ô'grâ·fō) *m* geographer
geologia (jā·ō·lō·jē'â) *f* geology
geologico (jā·ō·lô'jē·kō) *a* geological
geologo (jā·ô'lō·gō) *m* geologist
geometria (jā·ō·mā·trē'â) *f* geometry
geometrico (jā·ō·me'trē·kō) *a* geometrical
geranio (jā·râ'nyō) *m* geranium
gerarca (jā·râr'kâ) *m* leader, head
gerarchia (jā·râr·kē'â) *f* hierarchy
gerente (jā·rān'tā) *m* director, manager
gerenza (jā·rān'tsâ) *f* board of directors, management
gergo (jār'gō) *m* slang
Germania (jār·mâ'nyâ) *f* Germany
germano (jār·mâ'nō) *a* germane; — *m* full brother; mallard duck; **cugino** — first cousin
germe (jār'mā) *m* germ, sprout, shoot; *(fig)* root, cause
germinare (jār·mē·nâ'rā) *vt&i* to germinate
germinazione (jār·mē·nâ·tsyō'nā) *f* germination
germogliare (jār·mō·lyâ'rā) *vt&i* to sprout, shoot up
germoglio (jār·mô'lyō) *m* shoot, bud
geroglifico (jā·rō·glē'fē·kō) *m&a* hieroglyphic

gerontocomio (jā·rōn·tō·kô'myō) *m* old people's home
gerontoiatria (jā·rōn·tō·yâ·trē'â) *f* geriatrics
gerundio (jā·rūn'dyō) *m* gerund
Gerusalemme (jā·rū·zâ·lām'mā) *f* Jerusalem
gessaio (jās·sâ'yō) *m* plasterer; maker of plaster statues
gessare (jās·sâ'rā) *vt* to plaster
gessatura (jās·sâ·tū'râ) *f* plastering
gesso (jās·sō) *m* chalk; plaster of Paris; **–so** (jās·sō'zō) *a* chalk-like, chalky
gesta (jā'stâ) *fpl* achievements; feats of derring-do
gestante (jā·stân'tā) *f* pregnant woman
gestazione (jā·stâ·tsyō'nā) *f* pregnancy; question
gesticolare (jā·stē·kō·lâ'rā) *vi* to gesticulate
gesticolazione (jā·stē·kō·lâ·tsyō'nā) *f* gesticulation, gesturing
gestione (jā·styō'nā) *f* administering, managing
gestire (jā·stē'rā) *vt (com)* to operate; to gesture
gesto (jā'stō) *m* gesture; **–re** (jā·stō'rā) *m* manager; operator
Gesù (jā·zū') *m* Jesus
gesuita (jā·zwē'tâ) *m* Jesuit
gettare (jāt·tâ'rā) *vt* to throw, cast; — *vi (bot)* to bud, shoot up; **— a terra** to knock down; **— l'ancora** *(naut)* to cast anchor; **— le fondamenta** to lay the foundation; **— la moneta** to toss a coin; **— via il denaro** to waste one's money, throw away one's money
gettarsi (jāt·târ'sē) *vr* to cast oneself, dash oneself; to spring forward
gettata (jāt·tâ'tâ) *f* rough cast
gettatore (jāt·tâ·tō'rā) *m* caster, molder
gettito (jet'tē·tō) *m* yield, output
getto (jāt'tō) *m* throw; jet, spout; **a — continuo** uninterruptedly; **opera di —** inspired work; **–ne** (jāt·tō'nā) *m* token
gheriglio (gā·rē'lyō) *m* center, kernel
gherminella (gār·mē·nāl'lâ) *f* trickery; mischief
ghermire (gār·mē'rā) *vt* to snatch, grab; to hold tightly
gherone (gā·rō'nā) *m* gore *(clothing)*
ghetta (gāt'tâ) *f* spat *(clothing)*
ghiacciaia (gyâ·châ'yâ) *f* refrigerator; ice box
ghiacciaio (gyâ·châ'yō) *m* glacier
ghiacciare (gyâ·châ'rā) *vt* to ice over; to freeze
ghiacciarsi (gyâ·châr'sē) *vr* to freeze, become frozen
ghiacciata (gyâ·châ'tâ) *f* cool drink
ghiacciato (gyâ·châ'tō) *a* iced, ice-cold; frozen
ghiaccio (gyâ'chō) *m* ice; **rompere il —** to break the ice *(fig)*
ghiacciuolo (gyâ·chwō'lō) *m* icicle
ghiaia (gyâ'yâ) *f* gravel
ghianda (gyân'dâ) *f* acorn; **–ia** (gyân·dâ'yâ) *f* jay
ghiera (gyā'râ) *f* ferrule
ghigliottina (gē·lyōt·tē'nâ) *f* guillotine **–re** (gē·lyōt·tē·nâ'rā) *vt* to guillotine
ghignare (gē·nyâ'rā) *vi* to sneer, leer
ghigno (gē'nyō) *m* smirk, sneer
ghiotta (gyōt'tâ) *f* drip pan
ghiotto (gyōt'tō) *a* gluttonous; tasty; **–ne** (gyōt·tō'nā) *m* glutton; gourmand; **–neria** (gyōt·tō·nā·rē'â) *f* delicacy; gluttony
ghiribizzo (gē·rē·bē'tsō) *m* whim
ghirigoro (gē·rē·gō'rō) *m* spiral design
ghirlanda (gēr·lân'dâ) *f* wreath, garland
ghiro (gē'rō) *m* dormouse; **dormire come un —** to sleep like a top
ghisa (gē'zâ) *f* cast iron
già (jâ) *adv* formerly, already; **G–!** *adv* Right! Of course!
giacchè (jâk·kā') *conj* now that; since, in view of the fact that
giacchetta (jâk·kāt'tâ) *f* jacket, coat
giacente (jâ·chān'tā) *a* lying down; in abeyance
giacere * (jâ'chā·rā) *vi* to lie, lie at rest
giacimento (jâ·chē·mān'tō) *m (min)* deposit, layer
giacinto (jâ·chēn'tō) *m* hyacinth
giaculatoria (jâ·kū·lâ·tô'ryâ) *f* short prayer
giada (jâ'dâ) *m (min)* jade
giaggiolo (jâj·jō'lō) *m (bot)* iris
giaguaro (jâ·gwâ'rō) *m* jaguar
giallastro (jâl·lâ'strō) *a* yellowish
giallo (jâl'lō) *a* yellow; **— d'uovo** yolk; **romanzo —** mystery novel; **–gnolo** (jâl·lô'nyō·lō) *a* yellowish
Giamaica (jâ·mâ'ē·kâ) Jamaica
giammai (jâm·mâ'ē) *adv* never
gianduiotto (jân·dū·yōt'tō) *m* chocolate candy
giannizzero (jan·nē'tsā·rō) *m (fig)* underling, hireling
Giappone (jâp·pō'nā) *m* Japan; **–se** (jâ·pō·nā'zā) *m&a* Japanese
giara (jâ'râ) *f* jug
giardinaggio (jâr·dē·nâj'jō) *m* gardening
giardinetta (jâr·dē·nāt'tâ) *f* station wagon
giardiniera (jâr·dē·nyā'râ) *f* vegetable soup; jardiniere; woman gardener; **maestra —** kindergarten teacher
giardiniere (jâr·dē·nyā'rā) *m* gardener
giardino (jâr·dē'nō) *m* garden; **— d'infanzia** kindergarten; **— publico** public park; **— zoologico** zoo
giarrettiera (jâr·rāt·tyā'râ) *f* garter
giavazzo (jâ·vâ'tsō) *m (min)* jet
gigante (jē·gân'tā) *a&m* giant; **far passi da —** *(fig)* to make great progress; **–ggiare** (jē·gân·tāj·jâ'rā) *vi* to tower; **–sco** (jē·gân·tā'skō) *a* gigantic
gigione (jē·jō'nā) *m (sl)* ham actor
giglio (jē'lyō) *m* lily
gilè (jē·lā') *m* vest
ginecologia (jē·nā·kō·lō·jē'â) *f* gynecology
ginecologo (jē·nā·kô'lō·gō) *m* gynecologist
ginepraio (jē·nā·prâ'yō) *m* confused situation; **cacciarsi in un —** to be in a mess
ginepro (jē·nā'prō) *m* juniper
Ginevra (jē·nā'vrâ) *f* Geneva

gingillare (jēn·jēl·lâ'rā) *vi* to dawdle
gingillarsi (jēn·jēl·lâr'sē) *vr* to toy with, trifle
gingillo (jēn·jēl'lō) *m* knicknack, trinket; — **fantasia** costume jewelry
ginnasiale (jēn·nâ·zyâ'lā) *a* high-school; **licenza** — high-school diploma
ginnasio (jēn·nâ'zyō) *m* high school
ginnasta (jēn·nâ'stâ) *m* gymnast, athlete
ginnastica (jēn·nâ'stē·kâ) *f* gymnastics
ginnastico (jēn·nâ'stē·kō) *a* athletic, gymnastic
ginocchio (jē·nôk'kyō) *m* knee; **–ni** (jē·nōk·kyō'nē) *adv* kneeling, knelt
giocare (jō·kâ'rā) *vt&i* to play; to bet; to make a fool of; to deceive; — **d'azzardo** to gamble
giocatore (jō·kâ·tō'rā) *m* player; — **di borsa** stockbroker
giocattolo (jō·kât'tō·lō) *m* toy
giochetto (jō·kāt'tō) *m* trick
giocoforza (jō·kō·fōr'tsâ) *f* necessity, essential
giocoliere (jō·kō·lyā'rā) *m* juggler
giocondità (jō·kōn·dē·tâ') *f* gaiety
giocondo (jō·kōn'dō) *a* gay
giocosamente (jō·kō·zâ·mān'tā) *adv* jokingly
giocoso (jō·kō'zō) *a* facetious, humorous
giogaia (jō·gâ'yâ) *f* mountain range
giogo (jō'gō) *m* yoke
gioia (jô'yâ) *f* joy, delight; jewel; **fuoco di** — bonfire
gioielleria (jō·yāl·lā·rē'â) *f* jewelry store; jewelry
gioielliere (jō·yāl·lyā'rā) *m* jeweler
gioiello (jō·yāl'lō) *m* gem
gioiosamente (jō·yō·zâ·mān'tā) *adv* joyfully
gioioso (jō·yō'zō) *a* joyful
gioire (jō·ē'rā) *vi* to rejoice
giornalaio (jōr·nâ·lâ'yō) *m* newsboy; newspaper dealer
giornale (jōr·nâ'lā) *m* newspaper; — **di bordo** logbook; — **settimanale** weekly; — **radio** newscast
giornaliero (jōr·nâ·lyā'rō) *a* daily; — *m* day laborer
giornalismo (jōr·nâ·lē'zmō) *m* journalism
giornalista (jōr·nâ·lē'stâ) *m* newspaperman, journalist
giornalmente (jōr·nâl·mān'tā) *adv* daily, every day
giornata (jōr·nâ'tâ) *f* day; **vivere alla** — to live from hand to mouth; **–ccia** (jōr·nâ·tâ'châ) bad day
giorno (jōr'nō) *m* day;— **feriale** weekday; — **festivo** holiday; **di** — in the daytime; **allo spuntar del** — at daybreak; **al cader del** — at sunset; **ai nostri giorni** in our time; **al** — **d'oggi** nowadays; **metter a** — to bring up-to-date; **essere a** — to be conversant with
giostra (jō'strâ) *f* merry-go-round; tournament; **–re** (jō·strâ'rā) *vi* to joust
giovamento (jō·vâ·mān'tō) *m* aid; advantage
giovane (jô'vâ·nā), **giovine** (jô'vē·nā) *a* young; — *m* youth; **–tto** (jō·vâ·nāt'tō) boy; **–tta** (jō·vâ·nāt'tâ) *f* girl
giovanile (jō·vâ·nē'lā) *a* juvenile; youthful
giovanotto (jō·vâ·nōt'tō) *m* young man
giovare (jō·vâ'rā) *vi* to be of help; to avail
giovarsi (jō·vâr'sē) *vr* to profit by; to avail oneself of; — **a vicenda** to aid each other
giovenca (jō·vān'kâ) *f* heifer
gioventù (jō·vān·tū') *f* youth
giovevole (jō·ve'vō·lā) *a* advantageous; profitable
giovevolmente (jō·vā·vōl·mān'tā) *adv* profitably
giovinastro (jō·vē·nâ'strō) *m* scamp
giovinezza (jō·vē·nā'tsâ) *f* youth
giraffa (jē·râf'fâ) *f* giraffe
girare (jē·râ'rā) *vt* to turn, spin, revolve; *(movies)* to film; *(com)* to endorse; — **un pericolo** to avoid a danger; — **l'occhio intorno** to glance around; — **al largo** to keep aloof
giracapo (jē·râ·kâ'pō) *m* vertigo
giradischi (jē·râ·dē'skē) *m* record player
giramento (jē·râ·mān'tō) *m* turning; **aver** — **di testa** to be dizzy
giramondo (jē·râ·mōn'dō) *m* adventurer; world traveler
girandola (jē·rân'dō·lâ) *f* pinwheel
girante (jē·rân'tā) *m* *(com)* endorser; — *a* revolving, turning
girarrosto (jē·râr·rō'stō) *m* rotisserie
girarsi (jē·râr'sē) *vr* to turn about; — **sui tacchi** to turn on one's heels
girasole (jē·râ·sō'lā) *m* sunflower
girata (jē·râ'tâ) *f* turn; *(com)* endorsement; **–rio** (jē·râ·tâ'ryō) *m* endorsee
giratorio (jē·râ·tô'ryō) *a* revolving, spinning
giravolta (jē·râ·vōl'tâ) *f* twirl, pirouette; *(fig)* about-face
giretto (jē·rāt'tō) *m* short walk
girevole (jē·re'vō·lā) *a* whirling, revolving
girino (jē·rē'nō) *m* tadpole
giro (jē'rō) *m* turn; walk; **fare un** — to take a walk; **prendere in** — to make fun of; **a** — **di posta** by return mail; **mettere in** — **notizie** to spread rumors; **mettersi in** — to form a circle; — **d'affari** *(com)* turnover; **cambiali in** — *(com)* outstanding bills; **–pilota** (jē·rō·pē·lō'tâ) *m* automatic pilot; **–scopio** (jē·rō·skô'pyō) *m* gyroscope; **–stato** (jē·rō·stâ'tō) *m* gyrostat; **–vagare** (jē·rō·vâ·gâ'rā) *vi* to loaf, idle; **–vago** (jē·rô'vâ·gō) *m* peddler; vagrant; **–vago** *a* roaming
gita (jē'tâ) *f* trip, outing; — **in comitiva** conducted tour
gitana (jē·tâ'nâ) *f* gypsy
giù (jū) *adv* downstairs; down, below; **essere** — **di morale** *(coll)* to have the blues, be discouraged; **su per** — approximately; **non mi va** — *(fig)* I can't believe it
giubba (jūb'bâ) *f* jacket
giubilante (jū·bē·lân'tā) *a* exultant, jubi-

lant

giubilare (jū·bē·lâ'rā) *vi* to exult, be overjoyed

giubileo (jū·bē·lā'ō) *m* jubilee, celebration

giubilo (jū'bē·lō) *m* jubilation

giudaismo (jū·dâ·ē'zmō) *m* Judaism

giudeo (jū·dā'ō) *m* Jew; — *a* Jewish

giudicare (jū·dē·kâ'rā) *vt&i* to judge, pass judgment; to believe

giudicato (jū·dē·kâ'tō) *a* judged; — *m* sentence *(law)*

giudice (jū'dē·chā) *m* judge; — **istruttore** coroner; — **di pace,** — **conciliatore** justice of the peace

giudiziale (jū·dē·tsyâ'lā) *a* judicial

giudizialmente (jū·dē·tsyâl·mān'tā) *adv* judicially

giudiziario (jū·dē·tsyâ'ryō) *a* judicial, court

giudizio (jū·dē'tsyō) *m* wisdom, judgment; **formare un** — to form an opinion; **dente del** — wisdom tooth; **a mio** — in my opinion; **aver** — to be wise; **senza** — careless, rash; **metter** — to become wise; to grow up emotionally; **citare in** — to sue; **comparire in** — to appear in court

giudiziosamente (jū·dē·tsyō·zâ·mān'tā) *adv* judiciously, wisely

giugno (jū'nyō) *m* June

giugulare (jū·gū·lâ'rā) *a (anat)* jugular; — *vt* to strangle

giulebbe (jū·lāb'bā) *m* julep

giulivo (jū·lē'vō) *a* happy, joyful

giullare (jūl·lâ'rā) *m* clown, jester

giumenta (jū·mān'tâ) *f* mare

giunchiglia (jūn·kē'lyâ) *f* jonquil

giunco (jūn'kō) *m (bot)* rush

giungere * (jūn'jā·rā) *vt&i* to arrive, reach; to connect

giungla (jūn'glâ) *f* jungle

giunta (jūn'tâ) *f* board, commission; **per** — besides

giunto (jūn'tō) *a* arrived; joined; — *m (mech)* joint; — **cardanico** universal joint

giuntura (jūn·tū'râ) *f* articulation; joint

giuoco (jwō'kō) *m* game; *(mech)* play; — **d'azzardo** gambling; — **di prestigio;** sleight of hand; — **di parole** pun; **farsi** — **di** to make a fool of

giuramento (jū·râ·man'tō) *m* oath *(law)*

giurare (jū·râ'rā) *vt* to swear *(oath)*

giurato (jū·râ'tō) *a* sworn; — *m* juror

giuria (jū·rē'â) *f* jury

giureconsulto (jū·rā·kōn·sūl'tō) *m* law expert, jurist

giuridicamente (jū·rē·dē·kâ·mān'tā) *adv* legally, juridically

giurisdizione (jū·rē·dzē·tsyō'nā) *f* jurisdiction

giurisprudenza (jū·rē·sprū·dān'tsâ) *f* law, jurisprudence

giurista (jū·rē'stâ) *m* jurist

giusta (jū'stâ) *prep* in accordance with

giustamente (jū·stâ·mān'tā) *adv* correctly; justly; precisely

giustificabile (jū·stē·fē·kâ'bē·lā) *a* justifiable

giustificare (jū·stē·fē·kâ'rā) *vt* to justify

giustificarsi (jū·stē·fē·kâr'sē) *vr* to justify one's actions; to explain oneself

giustificativo (jū·stē·fē·kâ·tē'vō) *m* statement; **documento** — voucher

giustificazione (jū·stē·fē·kâ·tsyō'nā) *f* explanation; justification

giustizia (jū·stē'tsyâ) *f* justice; **con** — equitably; **farsi** — **da sè** to take the law into one's own hands; **render** — to be fair, to do justice to; **–re** (jū·stē·tsyâ'rā) *vt* to execute; **–to** (jū·stē·tsyâ'tō) *a* put to death

giustiziere (jū·stē·tsyā'rā) *m* executioner

giusto (jū'stō) *a* just; correct; — *adv* right; exactly; — **mezzo** golden mean

glabro (glâ'brō) *a* hairless

glaciale (glâ·châ'lā) *a* icy, ice; glacial

gladiatore (glâ·dyâ·tō'rā) *m* gladiator

gladiolo (glâ·dyō'lō) *m* gladiola

glandola (glân'dō·lâ) *f* gland

glandolare (glân·dō·lâ'rā) *a* glandular

glaucoma (glâū·kō'mâ) *f* glaucoma

gleba (glā'bâ) *f* earth; **servo della** — serf; proletarian

gli (lyē) *art mpl* the; — *pron* to him, to it

glicerina (glē·chā·rē'nâ) *f* glycerine

glicerofosfato (glē·chā·rō·fō·sfâ'tō) *m* glycerophosphate

glicogeno (glē·kô'jā·nō) *m* glycogen

globale (glō·bâ'lā) *a* global; overall; lump *(payment)*

globalmente (glō·bâl·mān'tā) *adv* in the aggregate

globo (glō'bō) *m* globe

globulo (glô'bū·lō) *m* globule; corpuscle

gloria (glô'ryâ) *f* glory; *(eccl)* aureole

gloriarsi (glō·ryâr'sē) *vr* to pride oneself on

glorificare (glō·rē·fē·kâ'rā) *vt* to glorify; to worship

glorificazione (glō·rē·fē·kâ·tsyō'nā) *f* glorification, worship

gloriosamente (glō·ryō·zâ·mān'tā) *adv* magnificently; gloriously

glossare (glōs·sâ'rā) *vt* to gloss

glossario (glōs·sâ'ryō) *m* glossary

glottide (glôt'tē·dā) *f* glottis

glutine (glū'tē·nā) *m* gluten

glutinoso (glū·tē·nō'zō) *a* glutinous

gnocco (nyōk'kō) *m* dumpling

gnomo (nyō'mō) *m* goblin, gnome

gnorri (nyōr'rē) *m* ignorance; **fare lo** — to turn a deaf ear; to pretend ignorance

gobba (gōb'bâ) *f* hump

gobbo (gōb'bō) *m* hunchback

goccia (gô'châ) *f* drop; **assomigliarsi come due gocce d'acqua** to be like two peas in a pod

gocciolare (gō·chō·lâ'rā) *vi* to drip

gocciolio (gō·chō·lē'ō) *m* trickle; dripping

godere * (gō·dā'rā) *vt&i* to enjoy; to rejoice; **godersi la vita** to enjoy life; **godersela** to enjoy oneself; — **credito** to have a good credit rating

godimento (gō·dē·mān'tō) *m* enjoyment; possession

goffaggine (gōf·fâj'jē·nā) *f* awkwardness;

gaucheness
goffo (gōf'fō) *a* clumsy; gauche
gogna (gō'nyâ) *f* pillory; **mettere alla** — to expose to public ridicule
gol (gōl) *m* goal *(sport)*
gola (gō'lâ) *f* throat; gorge; gluttony; groove; **far** — to tempt; to make one's mouth water; **aver l'acqua alla** — to be in dire straits
goletta (gō·lāt'tâ) *f* schooner
golfo (gōl'fō) *m* gulf; pullover, sweater
Golgota (gôl'gō·tâ) *m* Golgotha
goliardo (gō·lyâr'dō) *m* university student
golosamente (gō·lō·zâ·mān'tā) *adv* greedily, gluttonously
golosità (gō·lō·zē·tâ') *f* gluttony
goloso (gō·lō'zō) *a* gluttonous; — *n* glutton
gomena (gô'mā·nâ) *f* hawser, cable
gomitata (gō·mē·tâ'tâ) *f* nudge, shove with one's elbow
gomito (gô'mē·tō) *m* elbow; **alzare il** — *(fig)* to drink heavily; **alzare troppo il** — to drink too much
gomma (gōm'mâ) *f* rubber; eraser; innertube; tire; — **lacca** shellac; — **liquida** mucilage; — **piuma** foam rubber; **-to** (gōm·mâ'tō) *a* gummed
gommoso (gōm·mō'zō) *a* gummy, sticky
gommosità (gōm·mō·zē·tâ') *f* stickiness, gumminess
gondola (gôn'dō·lâ) *f* gondola
gondoliere (gōn·dō·lyā'rā) *m* gondolier
gonfiamento (gōn·fyâ·mān'tō) *m* swelling; *(fig)* exaggeration
gonfiare (gōn·fyâ'rā) *vt* to inflate, swell; to exaggerate
gonfiarsi (gōn·fyâr'sē) *vr* to swell up, swell
gonfiatura (gōn·fyâ·tū'râ) *f* puffiness; *(fig)* overstatement
gonfio (gôn'fyō) *a* swollen
gonfiore (gōn·fyō'rā) *m* swelling
gongolante (gōn·gō·lân'tā) *a* elated
gongolare (gōn·gō·lâ'rā) *vi* to rejoice
goniometria (gō·nyō·mā·trē'â) *f* goniometry
goniometro (gō·nyô'mā·trō) *m* protractor
gonna (gōn'nâ) *f* skirt
gonnella (gōn·nāl'lâ) *f* petticoat, slip; skirt
gonorrea (gō·nōr·rā'â) *f* gonorrhea
gonzo (gōn'dzō) *m* fool
gora (gō'râ) *f* pond; canal, ditch
gorgheggiare (gōr·gāj·jâ'rā) *vi* to warble
gorgo (gōr'gō) *m* whirlpool
gorgogliare (gōr·gō·lyâ'rā) *vi* to gurgle
gorgoglio (gōr·gō·lyē'ō) *m* gurgle
gorilla (gō·rēl'lâ) *m* gorilla
gota (gō'tâ) *f* cheek
gotico (gô'tē·kō) *a* Gothic
gotta (gōt'tâ) *f* gout
governante (gō·vār·nân'tā) *m* ruler; — *f* governess; housekeeper
governare (gō·vār·nâ'rā) *vt* to rule, govern
governarsi (gō·vār·nâr'sē) *vr* to control oneself; to govern oneself
governativo (gō·vār·nâ·tē'vō) *a* governmental; **impiegato** — government employee
governatore (gō·vār·nâ·tō'rā) *m* governor
governo (gō·vār'nō) *m* government, administration; control, steering
gozzo (gō'dzō) *m* crop *(bird)*; goiter
gozzoviglia (gō·dzō·vē'lyâ) *f* excessive drinking, debauchery
gozzovigliare (gō·dzō·vē·lyâ'rā) *vi* to debauch; to revel; to eat and drink excessively
gracidare (grâ·chē·dâ'rā) *vi* to croak; to cluck
gracile (grâ'chē·lā) *a* delicate; slender
gracilità (grâ·chē·lē·tâ') *f* slimness; feebleness
gracilmente (grâ·chēl·mān'tā) *adv* gracefully
gradatamente (grâ·dâ·tâ·mān'tā) *adv* gradually
gradevole (grâ·de'vō·lā) *a* pleasant, nice
gradevolezza (grâ·dā·vō·lā'tsâ) *f* agreeableness
gradevolmente (grâ·dā·vōl·mān'tā) *adv* pleasantly, agreeably
gradimento (grâ·dē·mān'tō) *m* approval, liking
gradinata (grâ·dē·nâ'tâ) *f* stairway; tier *(seats)*
gradino (grâ·dē'nō) *m* step *(stair)*
gradire (grâ·dē'rā) *vt* to accept; to like; to appreciate
gradito (grâ·dē'tō) *a* pleasant; welcome
grado (grâ'dō) *m* liking; grade, degree, rank; **mettere in** — **di** to enable to; **essere in** — **di** to be able to; **di buon** — willingly; **di proprio** — of one's own accord
graduale (grâ·dwâ'lā) *a* gradual
gradualmente (grâ·dwâl·mān'tā) *adv* gradually
graduare (grâ·dwâ'rā) *vt* to graduate, adjust
graduato (grâ·dwâ'tō) *a* graduated; graduate; — *m* non-commissioned officer
graduatoria (grâ·dwâ·tô'ryâ) *f* classification
graduazione (grâ·dwâ·tsyō'nā) *f* graduation
graffiare (grâf·fyâ'rā) *vt* to scratch
graffiatura (grâf·fyâ·tū'râ) *f* scratch
graffio (grâf'fyō) *m* scratch
grafia (grâ·fē'â) *f* spelling; handwriting
graficamente (grâ·fē·kâ·mān'tā) *adv* graphically
grafico (grâ'fē·kō) *a* graphic; — *m* graph; blue print
grafite (grâ·fē'tā) *f* graphite
grafologia (grâ·fō·lō·jē'â) *f* graphology
grafologo (grâ·fô'lō·gō) *m* graphologist
gramaglie (grâ·mâ·lyā) *fpl* mourning
grammatica (grâm·mâ'tē·kâ) *f* grammar
grammaticale (grâm·mâ·tē·kâ'lā) *a* grammatical
grammaticalmente (grâm·mâ·tē·kâl·mān'tā) *adv* grammatically
grammatico (grâm·mâ'tē·kō) *m* grammarian
grammo (grâm'mō) *m* gram
grammofono (grâm·mô'fō·nō) *m* phonograph

gramo (grâ'mō) *a* miserable, wretched
grana (grâ'nâ) *f* grain; *(sl)* trouble, difficulty; **formaggio** — Parmesan cheese
granaglie (grâ·nâ'lyā) *fpl* cereals
granaio (grâ·nâ'yō) *m* barn; granary
granata (grâ·nâ'tâ) *f* grenade; broom
granatina (grâ·nâ·tē'nâ) *f* grenadine
granato (grâ·nâ'tō) *m* pomegranate; garnet
grancassa (grân·kâs'sâ) *f* bass drum; **suonare la** — to broadcast loudly
granchio (grân'kyō) *m* crab; **prendere un** — to make a gross error
grandangolare (grân·dân·gō·lâ'rā) *a* *(phot)* wide-angle
grande (grân'dā) *a* great; big, large; tall; — *m* great man; **in** — wholesale; — **conoscenza di** vast knowledge of; **fare il** — to put on airs; **fare le cose in** — to do things on a large scale; **farsi** — to grow up
grandeggiare (grân·dāj·jâ'rā) *vi* to tower over; to act in a haughty manner
grandemente (grân·dā·mān'tā) *adv* greatly; very much
grandezza (grân·dā'tsâ) *f* greatness; grandeur; largeness
grandinare (grân·dē·nâ'rā) *vi* to hail *(weather)*
grandinata (grân·dē·nâ'tâ) *f* hailstorm
grandiosamente (grân·dyō·zâ·mān'tā) *adv* majestically; pompously
grandiosità (grân·dyō·zē·tâ') *f* grandeur
grandioso (grân·dyō'zō) *a* majestic; pompous
granduca (grân·dū'kâ) *m* grand duke
granduchessa (grân·dū·kās'sâ) *f* grand duchess
granello (grâ·nāl'lō) *m* grain; speck
granfia (grân'fyâ) *f* claw
granita (grâ·nē'tâ) *f* sherbet
granitico (grâ·nē'tē·kō) *a* granite; *(fig)* adamant, unyielding
granito (grâ·nē'tō) *m* granite
grano (grâ'nō) *m* grain *(cereal)*; wheat — **d'uva** grape; — **di rosario** rosary bead; — **di caffè** coffee bean
granulare (grâ·nū·lâ'rā) *a* granular; — *vt* to granulate
granulato (grâ·nū·lâ'tō) *a* granulated
granulo (grâ'nū·lō) *m* granule
granuloso (grâ·nū·lō'zō) *a* granular
grappa (grâp'pâ) *f* clamp; brandy
grappolo (grâp'pō·lō) *m* cluster
grascia (grâ'shâ) *f* lard
grassamente (grâs·sâ·mān'tā) *adv* plentifully; *(fig)* lasciviously
grassatore (grâs·sâ·tō'rā) *m* bandit, highwayman
grassazione (grâs·sâ·tsyō'nā) *m* holdup
grassetto (grâs·sāt'tō) *m* bold-faced type
grassezza (grâs·sā'tsâ) *f* fatness; *(fig)* licentiousness
grasso (grâs'sō) *a* fat, stout; productive; gross; greasy; — *m* fat, grease; **martedì** — Shrove Tuesday, Mardi Gras; **grasse risate** peals of laughter
grassoccio (grâs·sô'chō) *a* chubby, plump
grassume (grâs·sū'mā) *m* fatness; grease; smut
grata (grâ'tâ) *f* grate
gratamente (grâ·tâ·mān'tā) *adv* gratefully
gratella (grâ·tāl'lâ) *f* grill
graticcio (grâ·tē'chō) *m* basketry; trellis work
gratificare (grâ·tē·fē·kâ'rā) *vt* to reward; to gratify; to tip
gratificazione (grâ·tē·fē·kâ·tsyō'nā) *f* bonus, tip; reward, satisfaction
gratis (grâ'tēs) *adv* gratis, free
grato (grâ'tō) *a* grateful; pleasing
grattacapo (grât·tâ·kâ'pō) *m* worry, trouble
grattacielo (grât·tâ·chā'lō) *m* skyscraper
grattamento (grât·tâ·mān'tō) *m* rubbing; scraping, scratching
grattare (grât·tâ'rā) *vt&i* to scratch; to grate; *(sl)* to steal
grattato (grât·tâ'tō) *a* grated
grattugia (grât·tū'jâ) *f* grater; **-re** (grât·tū·jâ'rā) *vt* to grate
gratuitamente (grâ·twē·tâ·mān'tā) *adv* gratis, gratuitously
gratuito (grâ·twē'tō) *a* free, gratis; unmotivated; — **patrocinio** free legal aid
gravabile (grâ·vâ'bē·lâ) *a* dutiable; liable
gravame (grâ·vâ'mā) *m* taxation; lien; mortgage; burden
gravato (grâ·vâ'tō) *a* burdened; loaded; — **d'assegno** C.O.D., cash on delivery; — **di lavoro** overworked
grave (grâ'vā) *a* serious, grave; dangerous; — **negligenza** gross negligence; **essere** — to be seriously ill; — **d'anni** aged
gravemente (grâ·vā·mān'tā) *adv* gravely; dangerously; solemnly
gravezza (grâ·vā'tsâ) *f* seriousness, gravity
gravida (grâ'vē·dâ) *a* pregnant
gravidanza (grâ·vē·dân'tsâ) *f* pregnancy
gravido (grâ'vē·dō) *a* full; heavy; **panino** — sandwich
gravina (grâ·vē'nâ) *f* pickax
gravità (grâ·vē·tâ') *f* seriousness; importance; gravity; weight
gravitare (grâ·vē·tâ'rā) *vi* to gravitate
gravitazionale (grâ·vē·tâ·tsyō·nâ'lā) gravitational
gravitazione (grâ·vē·tâ·tsyō'nā) *f* gravitation
gravosità (grâ·vō·zē·tâ') *f* heftiness, weight; bother
gravoso (grâ·vō'zō) *a* burdensome
grazia (grâ'tsyâ) *f* grace; pardon; attractiveness; **far la** — to pardon; to grant a favor; to answer a prayer; **anno di** — A.D., year of Our Lord; **colpo di** — death blow; **in** — **di** on behalf of; **senza** — awkward; **troppa** — excess of a good thing
graziare (grâ·tsyâ'rā) *vt* to pardon, reprieve
grazie! (grâ'tsyā) *interj* thank you!, thanks!
grazioso (grâ·tsyō'zō) *a* pretty, charming
graziosamente (grâ·tsyō·zâ·mān'tā) *adv* gracefully
grecale (grā·kâ'lā) *m* northeast wind
Grecia (gre'châ) *f* Greece

greco (grā'kō) *a&m* Greek
gregario (grā·gâ'ryō) *m* follower; — *a* sociable
gregge (grāj'jā) *m* herd
grembiale (grām·byâ'lā) *m* apron
grembo (grām'bō) *m* bosom; lap *(anat)*
gremire (grā·mē'rā) *vt* to fill; to crowd
gremito (grā·mē'tō) *a* full, packed; overcrowded
greppia (grep'pyâ) *f* crib, manger; livelihood
greppo (grāp'pō) *m* cliff
gres (grās) *m* sandstone
grettamente (grāt·tâ·mān'tā) *adv* avariciously; meanly
grettezza (grāt·tā'tsâ) *f* pettiness; avarice
gretto (grāt'tō) *a* miserly
greve (grā'vā) *a* oppressive, irksome
grezzo (grā'dzō) *a* raw; coarse
gridare (grē·dâ'rā) *vi* to cry, scream
grido (grē'dō) *m* cry, shout; **di** — famous, well-known
grifagno (grē·fâ'nyō) *a* rapacious
griffa (grēf'fâ) *f* jaw *(mech)*
grifo (grē'fō) *m* snout
grigiastro (grē·jâ'strō) *a* grayish
grigio (grē'jō) *a* gray
griglia (grē'lyâ) *f* grill; grate; grid *(rad)*
grilletto (grēl·lāt'tō) *m* trigger
grillo (grēl'lō) *m* *(zool)* cricket; *(coll)* whim, caprice
grinfia (grēn'fyâ) *f* claw
grinta (grēn'tâ) *f* stern look; sulky expression
grinza (grēn'dzâ) *f* wrinkle; **non fare una** — to be perfect, be without a flaw
grippaggio (grēp·pâj'jō) *m* jamming *(mech)*
grippare (grēp·pâ'rā) *vi* to jam *(mech)*
grippe (grēp'pā) *m* influenza
grissino (grēs·sē'nō) *m* bread stick
gronda (grōn'dâ) *f* eaves; **–ia** (grōn·dâ'yâ) *f* gutter; **–re** (grōn·dâ'rā) *vi* to drip; to pour out; **–nte** (grōn·dân'tā) *a* streaming; dripping
groppa (grōp'pâ) *f* back, croup *(horse)*; **avere molti anni sulla** — *(fig)* to be very old; **in** — on one's back
groppone (grōp·pō'nā) *m* back; **piegare il** — to yield; to be submissive
grossa (grōs'sâ) *f* gross
grossezza (grōs·sā'tsâ) *f* bigness; thickness; uncouthness
grossista (grōs·sē'stâ) *m* wholesaler
grosso (grōs'sō) *a* big; thick; large; **pezzo** — big shot; **sbagliarsi di** — to be completely wrong; **farle grosse** to act ridiculously; **in modo** — roughly speaking; **fare la voce grossa** to threaten; **mare** — rough sea
grossolanità (grōs·sō·lâ·nē·tâ') *f* vulgarity; lack of refinement; uncouthness
grossolano (grōs·sō·lâ'nō) *a* coarse; common, vulgar
grotta (grōt'tâ) *f* grotto, cavern
grottesco (grōt·tā'skō) *a* grotesque
groviglio (grō·vē'lyō) *m* knot; snare; entanglement; *(fig)* mess
gru (grū) *f* crane
gruccia (grū'châ) *f* crutch; *(coll)* coat hanger
grufolare (grū·fō·lâ'rā) *vi* to root; to rummage
grugnire (grū·nyē'rā) *vi* to grunt
grugnito (grū·nyē'tō) *m* grunt
grugno (grū'nyō) *m* snout, muzzle; **fare il** — *(coll)* to sulk; **un brutto** — *(coll)* a homely face
grullagine (grūl·lâ'jē·nā) *f* foolishness
grullo (grūl'lō) *m* simpleton; — *a* foolish
grumo (grū'mō) *m* clot; **–so** (grū·mō'zō) *a* clotted
grumolo (grū'mō·lō) *m* core
gruppo (grūp'pō) *m* group; flock
gruviera (grū·vyā'râ) *f* Gruyère
gruzzolo (grū'tsō·lō) *m* savings, nest egg
guadagnare (gwâ·dâ·nyâ'rā) *vt* to earn, gain; to win; — **un porto** to reach a port; **—il tempo perduto** to make up time
guadagnarsi (gwâ·dâ·nyâr'sē) *vr* to earn for oneself; — **un raffreddore** to catch cold
guadagno (gwâ·dâ'nyō) *m* earnings, profit
guadare (gwâ·dâ'rā) *vt* to ford
guado (gwâ'dō) *m* ford
guaina (gwâ'ē·nâ) *f* scabbard, sheath
guaio (gwâ'yō) *m* misfortune; trouble; breakdown *(mech)*
guaire (gwâ·ē'rā) *vi* to yelp, whine
gualcire (gwâl·chē'rā) *vt* to crumple, rumple
gualcito (gwâl·chē'tō) *a* crumpled
guancia (gwân'châ) *f* cheek; **–le** (gwân·châ'lā) *m* pillow
guantaio (gwân·tâ'yō) *m* glovemaker
guanteria (gwân·tā·rē'â) *f* glove shop
guanto (gwân'tō) *m* glove; **trattare coi guanti** to handle with care
guantone (gwân·tō'nā) *m* boxing glove
guardaboschi (gwâr·dâ·bō'skē) *m* forester
guardacaccia (gwâr·dâ·kâ'châ) *m* gamekeeper
guardacosta (gwâr·dâ·kō'stâ) *m* coastguard
guardamano (gwâr·dâ·mâ'nō) *m* handrail
guardaportone (gwâr·dâ·pōr·tō'nā) *m* doorman
guardare (gwâr·dâ'rā) *vt* to look at; to consider; to guard; — **il letto** *(fig)* to stay in bed; — **per il sottile** to be very squeamish
guardaroba (gwâr·dâ·rō'bâ) *f* cloakroom; wardrobe
guardarsi (gwâr·dâr'sē) *vr* to be careful of; to abstain from; to look at one another
guardata (gwâr·dâ'tâ) *f* look; **–ccia** (gwâr·dâ·tâ'châ) *f* scowling look
guardia (gwâr'dyâ) *f* guard; watchman; policeman; — **del corpo** bodyguard; — **forestale** forest ranger; — **doganale** customs agent
guardiamarina (gwâr·dyâ·mâ·rē'nâ) *m* ensign
guardiano (gwâr·dyâ'nō) *m* watchman
guardingo (gwâr·dēn'gō) *a* cautious
guaribile (gwâ·rē'bē·lā) *a* curable
guarigione (gwâ·rē·jō'nā) *f* recovery, cure

guarire (gwâ·rē'rā) *vi* to recover one's health; — *vt* to cure, heal
guaritore (gwâ·rē·tō'rā) *m* healer
guarnigione (gwâr·nē·jō'nā) *f* garrison
guarnire (gwâr·nē'rā) *vt* to garnish, trim; to fortify *(mil)*
guarnizione (gwâr·nē·tsyō'nā) *f* trimming; garnish; gasket, packing *(mech)*
guasconata (gwâ·skō·nâ'tâ) *f* bragging
guastafeste (gwâ·stâ·fā'stā) *m* killjoy, wet blanket
guastamestieri (gwâ·stâ·mā·styā'rē) *m* strikebreaker; bungler
guastare (gwâ·stâ'rā) *vt* to spoil, ruin
guastarsi (gwâ·stâr'sē) *vr* to go bad, spoil
guastatore (gwâ·stâ·tō'rā) *m* destroyer, despoiler
guasto (gwâ'stō) *a* out of order; spoiled; — *m* damage; — **al motore** breakdown, engine trouble
guatare (gwâ·tâ'rā) *vt* to look askance at; to ogle
guazza (gwâ'tsâ) *f* dew
guazzabuglio (gwâ·tsâ·bū'lyō) *m* hodgepodge; potpourri
guazzo (gwâ'tsō) *m* slush
guercio (gwer'chō) *a* squint-eyed; one-eyed
guerra (gwār'râ) *f* war; **ministero della** — war department
guerrafondaio (gwār·râ·fōn·dâ'yō) *m* warmonger
guerreggiare (gwār·rāj·jâ'rā) *vt&i* to fight; to war against; to wage war
guerresco (gwār·rā'skō) *a* martial
guerriglia (gwār·rē'lyâ) *f* guerrilla war
gufo (gū'fō) *m* screech owl
guglia (gū'lyâ) *f* spire
Guiana (gū·yâ'nâ) *f* Guiana
guida (gwē'dâ) *f* guide; guidance; leadership; drive *(auto)*; — **telefonica** telephone book; **–re** (gwē·dâ'rā) *vt* to guide, conduct, lead; to drive; **–tore** (gwē·dâ·tō'rā) *m* driver, motorist
guiderdone (gwē·dār·dō'nā) *m* reward
guidoslitta (gwē·dō·zlēt'tâ) *f* bobsled
guinzaglio (gwēn·tsâ'lyō) *m* leash
guisa (gwē'zâ) *f* way; manner; **a** — **di** as, like; **in tal** — in such a manner; **in ogni** — in every way; **di** — **che** so that
guizzare (gwē·tsâ'rā) *vi* to dart; to flash *(light)*
guscio (gū'shō) *m* pod; shell; **restar nel proprio** — to be unsociable, be withdrawn
gustare (gū·stâ'rā) *vt* to taste; — *vi* to like, enjoy
gustevole (gū·ste'vō·lā) *a* tasty
gusto (gū'stō) *m* taste, flavor; gusto
gustosamente (gū·stō·zâ·mān'tā) *adv* tastefully; agreeably
gustoso (gū·stō'zō) *a* tasty; savory; amusing
gutturale (gūt·tū·râ'lā) *a* guttural
gutturalmente (gūt·tū·râl·mān'tā) *adv* gutturally

I

i (ē) *art mpl* the
iarda (yâr'dâ) *f* yard *(measure)*
iato (yâ'tō) *m* hiatus; gap
iattanza (yât·tân'tsâ) *f* bragging
iattura (yât·tū'râ) *f* misfortune
iberico (ē·be'rē·kō) *a&m* Iberian
ibernazione (ē·bār·nâ·tsyō'nā) *f* hibernation
ibridazione (ē·brē·dâ·tsyō'nā) *f* hybridization
ibrido (ē'brē·dō) *m&a* hybrid
icona (ē·kō'nâ) *f* icon
iconoclastico (ē·kō·nō·klâ'stē·kō) *a* iconoclastic
Iddio (ēd·dē'ō) *m* God, Lord
idea (ē·dā'â) *f* idea, opinion; **–le** (ē·dā·â'lā) *n&a* ideal; **–lismo** (ē·dā·â·lē'zmō) *m* idealism; **–lista** (ē·dā·â·lē'stâ) *m* idealist; **–lizzare** (ē·dā·â·lē·dzâ'rā) *vt* to idealize; **–lizzazione** (ē·dā·â·lē·dzâ·tsyō'nā) *f* idealization; **–lmente** (ē·dā·âl·mān'tā) *adv* ideally; **–re** (ē·dā·â'rā) *vt* to conceive, plan; **–tore** (ē·dā·â·tō'rā) *m* inventor, creator; **–zione** (ē·dā·â·tsyō'nā) *f* ideation
idem (ē'dām) *adv* idem
identicamente (ē·dān·tē·kâ·mān'tā) *adv* exactly, identically
identico (ē·den'tē·kō) *a* identical
identificare (ē·dān·tē·fē·kâ'rā) *vt* to identify
identificarsi (ē·dān·tē·fē·kâr'sē) *vr* to identify onself; to feel drawn toward
identificazione (ē·dān·tē·fē·kâ·tsyō'nā) *f* identification
identità (ē·dān·tē·tâ') *f* identity; **carta d'** — identification card
ideologia (ē·dā·ō·lō·jē'â) *f* ideology
ideologico (ē·dā·ō·lô'jē·kō) *a* ideological
idillio (ē·dēl'lyō) *m* romance, idyl
idioma (ē·dyō'mâ) *m* vernacular; language
idiomatico (ē·dyō·mâ'tē·kō) *a* idiomatic; **espressione idiomatica** idiom
idiosincrasia (ē·dyō·sēn·krâ·zē'â) *f* allergy; repugnance; aversion; peculiarity
idiota (ē·dyō'tâ) *a* idiotic — *m* idiot
idiotismo (ē·dyō·tē'zmō) *m* idiocy; idiom, expression
idolatrare (ē·dō·lâ·trâ'rā) *vt* to idolize
idolo (ē'dō·lō) *m* idol
idoneamente (ē·dō·nā·â·mān'tā) *adv* conveniently
idoneità (ē·dō·nāē·tâ') *f* fitness, aptness
idoneo (ē·dô'nā·ō) *a* qualified; fit
idrante (ē·drân'tā) *m* hydrant
idrato (ē·drâ'tō) *m* hydrate; — **di carbone** carbohydrate
idraulica (ē·drâ'ū·lē·kâ) *f* hydraulics
idraulico (ē·drâ'ū·lē·kō) *a* hydraulic; — *m* plumber
idrocarburo (ē·drō·kâr·bū'rō) *m* hydrocarbon
idrodinamica (ē·drō·dē·nâ'mē·kâ) *f* hydrodynamics

idroelettrico (ē·drō·ā·let'trē·kō) *a* hydroelectric
idrofilo (ē·drô'fē·lō) *a* absorbent; **cotone** — absorbent cotton
idrofobia (ē·drō·fō·bē'â) *f* hydrophobia
idrofobo (ē·drô'fō·bō) *a* hydrophobic
idrografia (ē·drō·grâ·fē'â) *f* hydrography
idrografo (ē·drô'grâ·fō) *m* hydrographer
idrogeno (ē·drô'jā·nō) *m* hydrogen
idrolisi (ē·drō·lē'zē) *f* hydrolysis
idrometria (ē·drō·mā·trē'â) *f* hydrometry
idrometro (ē·drô'mā·trō) *m* water gauge
idropico (ē·drô'pē·kō) *a* dropsical
idropisia (ē·drō·pē·zē'â) *f* dropsy
idroplano (ē·drō·plâ'nō) *m* hydroplane
idroponica (ē·drō·pô'nē·kâ) *f* hydroponics
idroscalo (ē·drō·skâ'lō) *m* seaplane station
idroscì (ē·drō·shē') *m* water ski
idrosilurante (ē·drō·sē·lū·rân'tā) *m* torpedoplane
idrostatica (ē·drō·stâ'tē·kâ) *f* hydrostatics
idrovia (ē·drō·vē'â) *f* waterway
iena (yā'nâ) *f* hyena
ieri (yā'rē) *adv* yesterday; — **l'altro** the day before yesterday; — **sera** yesterday evening
iettatura (yā·tâ·tū'râ) *f* evil eye; **portare** — to bring misfortune; **avere la** — to be unlucky
igiene (ē·jā'nā) *f* hygienics, hygiene
igienico (ē·je'nē·kō) *a* hygenic; **carta igienica** toilet paper, bathroom tissue
ignaro (ē·nyâ'rō) *a* unaware, lacking information
ignavia (ē·nyâ'vyâ) *f* indolence
ignifugo (ē·nyē'fū·gō) *a* fire-resistant
ignizione (ē·nyē·tsyō'nā) *f* ignition
ignobile (ē·nyô'bē·lā) *a* base, ignoble
ignobilmente (ē·nyō·bēl·mān'tā) *adv* ignobly
ignominia (ē·nyō·mē'nyâ) *f* disgrace
ignominiosamente (ē·nyō·mē·nyō·zâ·mān'tā) *adv* shamefully, dishonorably
ignominioso (ē·nyō·mē·nyō'zō) *a* shameful; dishonorable
ignorante (ē·nyō·rân'tā) *a* ignorant; — *m* ignoramus
ignoranza (ē·nyō·rân'tsâ) *f* ignorance
ignorare (ē·nyō·râ'rā) *vt* to be ignorant, be unaware; to lack information; to ignore
ignorato (ē·nyō·râ'tō) *a* disregarded; unknown
ignoto (ē·nyō'tō) *a* unknown
ignudo (ē·nyū'dō) *a* stripped, nude
il (ēl) *art m* the
ilare (ē·lâ'rā) *a* cheerful
ilarità (ē·lâ·rē·tâ') *f* hilarity; merriment; **scoppio d'** — burst of laughter; **destare** — to provoke laughter
illanguidimento (ēl·lân·gwē·dē·mān'tō) *m* listlessness; languishing
illanguidire (ēl·lân·gwē·dē'rā) *vt&i* to weaken; to become languid
illazione (ēl·lâ·tsyō'nā) *f* inference, deduction
illecitamente (ēl·lā·chē·tâ·mān'tā) *adv* illicitly
illecito (ēl·le'chē·tō) *a* illicit
illegale (ēl·lā·gâ'lā) *a* illegal
illegalità (ēl·lā·gâ·lē·tâ') *f* illegality
illegalmente (ēl·lā·gâl·mān'tā) *adv* illegally
illeggibile (ēl·lāj·jē'bē·lā) *a* illegible
illegittimo (ēl·lā·jēt'tē·mō) *a* illegitimate
illeso (ēl·lā'zō) *a* unharmed
illetterato (ēl·lāt·tā·râ'tō) *a* illiterate
illibato (ēl·lē·bâ'tō) *a* pure, innocent
illimitatamente (ēl·lē·mē·tâ·tâ·mān'tā) *adv* without bounds, unlimitedly
illimitato (ēl·lē·mē·tâ'tō) *a* unlimited
illividire (ēl·lē·vē·dē'rā) *vt* to make livid; — *vi* to become livid
illividito (ēl·lē·vē·dē'tō) *a* livid
illogico (ēl·lô'jē·kō) *a* illogical
illudere * (ēl·lū'dā·rā) *vt* to deceive
illuminante (ēl·lū·mē·nân'tā) *a* lighting up; illuminating
illuminare (ēl·lū·mē·nâ'rā) *vt* to light up; to enlighten
illuminarsi (ēl·lū·mē·nâr'sē) *vr* to grow bright
illuminato (ēl·lū·mē·nâ'tō) *a* lighted; enlightened
illuminazione (ēl·lū·mē·nâ·tsyō'nā) *f* lighting; illumination; enlightenment
illusione (ēl·lū·zyō'nā) *f* illusion; **farsi illusioni** to build dream castles; **vivere di illusioni** to live in a dream world
illusionista (ēl·lū·zyō·nē'stâ) *m* magician
illuso (ēl·lū'zō) *a* deluded — *m* daydreamer
illusorio (ēl·lū·zô'ryō) *a* fallacious; unreal
illustrare (ēl·lū·strâ'rā) *vt* to illustrate; to make famous; to explain
illustrativo (ēl·lū·strâ·tē'vō) *a* illustrative
illustratore (ēl·lū·strâ·tō'rā) *m* illustrator
illustrazione (ēl·lū·strâ·tsyō'nā) *f* illustration; explanation; glory
illustre (ēl·lū'·strā) *a* illustrious
imbaldanzire (ēm·bâl·dân·tsē'rā) *vt* to make bold; — *vi* to become bold
imballaggio (ēm·bâl·lâj'jō) *m* packing
imballare (ēm·bâl·lâ'rā) *vt* to pack; *(mech)* to race
imballatore (ēm·bâl·lâ·tō'rā) *m* packer
imballatrice (ēm·bâl·lâ·trē'chā) *f* packing machine; baling machine
imballo (ēm·bâl'lō) *m* packing; *(mech)* racing
imbalsamare (ēm·bâl·sâ·mâ'rā) *vt* to embalm; to stuff
imbambolato (ēm·bâm·bō·lâ'tō) *a* listless; sleepy
imbandierare (ēm·bân·dyā·râ'rā) *vt* to decorate with flags
imbandierato (ēm·bân·dyā·râ'tō) *a* decorated with flags
imbandigione (ēm·bân·dē·jō'nā) *f* banquet preparations
imbandire (ēm·bân·dē'rā) *vt* to set *(table)*; to ready, prepare; to serve; — **un pranzo** to serve a feast
imbarazzante (ēm·bâ·râ·tsân'tā) *a* embar-

rassing; puzzling; obstructing
imbarazzare (ēm·bâ·râ·tsâ'rā) *vt* to embarrass; to perplex; to obstruct
imbarazzarsi (ēm·bâ·râ·tsâr'sē) *vr* to become confused, grow embarrassed; *(coll)* to interfere with
imbarazzato (ēm·bâ·râ·tsâ'tō) *a* embarrassed; bewildered
imbarazzo (ēm·bâ·râ'tsō) *m* embarrassment; constipation; financial difficulties; **essere d'** — to be in the way; **trovarsi in imbarazzi** to find oneself in a difficult situation; **levarsi d'** — to get out of trouble; — **di stomaco** indigestion
imbarcadero (ēm·bâr·kâ·dā'rō) *m* pier
imbarcare (ēm·bâr·kâ'rā) *vt* to take on board; to ship
imbarcarsi (ēm·bâr·kâr'sē) *vr* to go aboard, board; to sail; — **in un'impresa difficile** to embark on a difficult task
imbarcatoio (ēm·bâr·kâ·tô'yō) *m* wharf
imbarcazione (ēm·bâr·kâ·tsyō'nā) *f* boat, ship
imbarco (ēm·bâr'kō) *m* loading pier; embarkation; shipping
imbardare (ēm·bâr·dâ'rā) *vi* to yaw *(avi)*
imbarilare (ēm·bâ·rē·lâ'rā) *vt* to put into barrels
imbastardire (ēm·bâ·stâr·dē'rā) *vt* to corrupt; to debase
imbastardirsi (ēm·bâ·stâr·dēr'sē) *vr* to degenerate
imbastardito (ēm·bâ·stâr·dē'tō) *a* degenerate; corrupted
imbastire (ēm·bâ·stē'rā) *vt* to baste; — **un discorso** to prepare a speech
imbattersi (ēm·bât'tār·sē) *vr* to run across
imbattibile (ēm·bât·tē'bē·lā) *a* unbeatable
imbattuto (ēm·bât·tū'tō) *a* unsurpassed; unbeaten
imbavagliare (ēm·bâ·vâ·lyâ'rā) *vt* to gag
imbeccare (ēm·bāk·kâ'rā) *vt* *(fig)* to coach, prompt
imbeccata (ēm·bāk·kâ'tâ) *f* cue, prompting
imbecillaggine (ēm·bā·chēl·lâj'jē·nā) *f* imbecility, foolishness
imbecille (ēm·bā·chēl'lā) *m* imbecile, simpleton
imbelle (ēm·bāl'lā) *a* cowardly, fainthearted; unwarlike
imbellettarsi (ēm·bāl·lāt·târ'sē) *vr* to put on make-up
imbellire (ēm·bāl·lē'rā) *vt* to beautify; to ornament; — *vi* to become more handsome; to grow more beautiful
imberbe (ēm·bār'bā) *a* beardless; young
imbestialire (ēm·bā·styâ·lē'rā) *vt* to brutalize
imbestialirsi (ēm·bā·styâ·lēr'sē) *vr* to become brutal; to get furious
imbevere (ēm·be'vā·rā) *vt* to drench; to absorb
imbeversi (ēm·be'vār·sē) *vr* to become soaked; — **di** to be imbued with, to absorb, to assimilate
imbevuto (ēm·bā·vū'tō) *a* drenched; imbued
imbiancamento (ēm·byân·kâ·mān'tō) *m* whitewashing; bleaching; turning white *(hair)*
imbiancare (ēm·byân·kâ'rā) *vt* to whitewash; to whiten
imbiancato (ēm·byân·kâ'tō) *a* whitened
imbiancatura (ēm·byân·kâ·tū'râ) *f* whitewash; bleach
imbianchino (ēm·byân·kē'nō) *m* house painter
imbizzarrirsi (ēm·bē·dzâr·rēr'sē) *vr* to become enraged; to frisk *(animals)*
imboccare (ēm·bōk·kâ'rā) *vt* to feed; to enter; — *vi* to fit in *(mech)*
imbocco (ēm·bōk'kō) *m* aperture; entrance; mouth
imboscare (ēm·bō·skâ'rā) *vt* to ambush; to conceal
imboscarsi (ēm·bō·skâr'sē) *vr* to lie in ambush; *(fig)* to shirk
imboscata (ēm·bō·skâ'tâ) *f* ambush
imboscato (ēm·bō·skâ'tō) *m* slacker
imbottigliamento (ēm·bōt·tē·lyâ·mān'tō) *m* bottling; *(fig)* blockade
imbottita (ēm·bōt·tē'tâ) *f* quilt
imbottito (ēm·bōt·tē'tō) *a* padded, stuffed
imbottitura (ēm·bōt·tē·tū'râ) *f* quilting; padding
imbracciatura (ēm·brâ·châ·tū'râ) *f* rifle sling
imbrattare (ēm·brât·tâ'rā) *vt* to soil, stain
imbrattatele (ēm·brât·tâ·tā'lā) *m* dauber; bad painter
imbrigliare (ēm·brē·lyâ'rā) *vt* to bridle; to check
imbroccare (ēm·brōk·kâ'rā) *vt* to hit; to guess right
imbrogliare (ēm·brō·lyâ'rā) *vt* to cheat; to confuse
imbrogliarsi (ēm·brō·lyâr'sē) *vr* to become confused; to meddle with
imbroglio (ēm·brô'lyō) *m* fraud; mess
imbroglione (ēm·brō·lyō'nā) *m* crook; swindler
imbronciarsi (ēm·brōn·châr'sē) *vr* to pout; to grow dark *(sky)*
imbrunire (ēm·brū·nē'rā) *vi* to get dark; to turn brown
imbruttire (ēm·brūt·tē'rā) *vt* to disfigure; to make homely
imbucare (ēm·bū·kâ'rā) *vt* to mail; to put in the mailbox
imburrare (ēm·būr·râ'rā) *vt* to butter
imburrato (ēm·būr·râ'tō) *a* buttered
imbuto (ēm·bū'tō) *m* funnel
imene (ē·mā'nā) *m* hymen
imitare (ē·mē·tâ'rā) *vt* to imitate
imitato (ē·mē·tâ'tō) *a* imitated
imitatore (ē·mē·tâ·tō'rā) *m* imitator, mimic
imitazione (ē·mē·tâ·tsyō'nā) *f* imitation
immacolato (ēm·mâ·kō·lâ'tō) *a* immaculate; **l'Immacolata** the Virgin Mary
immagazzinaggio (ēm·mâ·gâ·dzē·nâj'jō) *m* storage, storing
immagazzinare (ēm·mâ·gâ·dzē·nâ'rā) *vt* to store; to lay by
immaginabile (ēm·mâ·jē·nâ'bē·lā) *a* imaginable

immaginare (ēm·mâ·jē·nâ'rā) *vt* to imagine
immaginario (ēm·mâ·jē·nâ'ryō) *a* imaginary
immaginativa (ēm·mâ·jē·nâ·tē'vâ) *f* imagination
immaginativo (ēm·mâ·jē·nâ·tē'vō) *a* imaginative
immaginazione (ēm·mâ·jē·nâ·tsyō'nā) *f* imagination
immagine (ēm·mâ'jē·nā) *f* image
immancabile (ēm·mân·kâ'bē·lā) *a* sure; unfailing
immancabilmente (ēm·mân·kâ·bēl·mān'tā) *adv* without fail; certainly
immane (ēm·mâ'nā) *a* enormous
immanente (ēm·mâ·nān'tā) *a* inherent
immantinente (ēm·mân·tē·nān'tā) *adv* immediately, at once
immateriale (ēm·mâ·tā·ryâ'lā) *a* immaterial
immatricolarsi (ēm·mâ·trē·kō·lâr'sē) *vr* to register, matriculate *(school)*
immaturità (ēm·mâ·tū·rē·tâ') *f* immaturity
immaturo (ēm·mâ·tū'rō) *a* immature, not ripe
immediatamente (ēm·mā·dyâ·tâ·mān'tā) *adv* immediately
immediato (ēm·mā·dyâ'tō) *a* immediate
immemorabile (ēm·mā·mō·râ'bē·lā) *a* immemorial
immemore (ēm·me'mō·rā) *a* forgetful
immensamente (ēm·mān·sâ·mān'tā) *adv* immensely
immensità (ēm·mān·sē·tâ') *f* immensity
immenso (ēm·mān'sō) *a* immense
immergere * (ēm·mer'jā·rā) *vt* to dip, immerse
immergersi * (ēm·mer'jār·sē) *vr* to plunge, dive into
immeritato (ēm·mā·rē·tâ'tō) *a* undeserved
immeritevole (ēm·mā·rē·te'vō·lā) *a* unworthy
immeritevolmente (ēm·mā·rē·tā·vōl·mān'tā) *adv* undeservingly
immersione (ēm·mār·syō'nā) *f* immersion **linea d'** — waterline
immerso (ēm·mār'sō) *a* immersed
immettere * (ēm·met'tā·rā) *vt* to bring in; *(fig)* to infuse, inspire
immettersi * (ēm·met'tār·sē) *vr* to enter into; to penetrate
immigrante (ēm·mē·grân'tā) *a&m* immigrant
immigrare (ēm·mē·grâ'rā) *vi* to immigrate
immigrato (ēm·mē·grâ'tō) *a* immigrant
immigrazione (ēm·mē·grâ·tsyō'nā) *f* immigration
imminente (ēm·mē·nān'tā) *a* impending
imminenza (ēm·mē·nān'tsâ) *f* imminence
immischiare (ēm·mē·skyâ'rā) *vt* to entangle; to implicate
immischiarsi (ēm·mē·skyâr'sē) *vr* to interfere, meddle
immiserire (ēm·mē·zā·rē'rā) *vt* to impoverish
immiserirsi (ēm·mē·zā·rēr'sē) to become destitute
immissario (ēm·mēs·sâ'ryō) *a* tributary *(river)*
immobile (ēm·mô'bē·lā) *a* motionless; immovable; — *m* property
immobili (ēm·mô'bē·lē) *mpl* property, real estate
immobiliare (ēm·mō·bē·lyâ'rā) *a* pertaining to real estate; **credito** — real estate mortgage
immobilità (ēm·mō·bē·lē·tâ') *f* immobility; stability
immobilizzare (ēm·mō·bē·lē·dzâ'rā) *vt* to immobilize; to freeze *(capital)*
immolare (ēm·mō·lâ'rā) *vt* to sacrifice, offer up
immolarsi (ēm·mō·lâr'sē) *vr* to sacrifice oneself
immolazione (ēm·mō·lâ·tsyō'nā) *f* sacrifice, immolation
immondizia (ēm·mōn·dē'tsyâ) *f* filth; garbage
immondo (ēm·mōn'dō) *a* filthy, impure
immorale (ēm·mō·râ'lā) *a* immoral
immoralità (ēm·mō·râ·lē·tâ') *f* immorality
immoralmente (ēm·mō·râl·mān'tā) *adv* immorally
immortalare (ēm·mōr·tâ·lâ'rā) *vt* to immortalize
immortale (ēm·mōr·tâ'lā) *a* immortal, everlasting
immortalità (ēm·mōr·tâ·lē·tâ') *f* immortality
immoto (ēm·mō'tō) *a* motionless
immune (ēm·mū'nā) *a* immune; exempt; unhurt
immunità (ēm·mū·nē·tâ') *f* immunity
immunizzare (ēm·mū·nē·dzâ'rā) *vt* to immunize
immunizzazione (ēm·mū·nē·dzâ·tsyō'nā) *f* immunization
immutabile (ēm·mū·tâ'bē·lā) *a* immutable
immutabilità (ēm·mū·tâ·bē·lē·tâ') *f* constancy
immutato (ēm·mū·tâ'tō) *a* unchanged, unvaried
imo (ē'mō) *a* lowest; — *m* bottom
impaccare (ēm·pâk·kâ'rā) *vt* to pack, make a package of
impacchettare (ēm·pâk·kāt·tâ'rā) *vt* to put in a package; to pack
impacciare (ēm·pâ·châ'rā) *vt* to trouble; to impede, hinder
impacciato (ēm·pâ·châ'tō) *a* embarrassed, ill at ease
impaccio (ēm·pâ'chō) *m* embarrassment; trouble; hindrance; **levarsi d'**— to get out of a difficult situation
impacco (ēm·pâk'kō) *m (med)* compress
impadronirsi (ēm·pâ·drō·nēr'sē) *vr* to get possession, seize; to become master
impagabile (ēm·pâ·gâ'bē·lā) *a* irreplaceable; priceless
impaginare (ēm·pâ·jē·nâ'rā) *vt* to make into pages, paginate
impaginazione (ēm·pâ·jē·nâ·tsyō'nā) *f*

numbering of pages, pagination
impagliare (ēm·pâ·lyâ'rā) *vt* to stuff; to cover with straw
impalare (ēm·pâ·lâ'rā) *vt* to impale
impalato (ēm·pâ·lâ'tō) *a* stiff; impaled
impalcatura (ēm·pâl·kâ·tū'râ) *f* scaffolding
impallidire (ēm·pâl·lē·dē'rā) *vi* to turn pale
impalpabile (ēm·pâl·pâ'bē·lā) *a* intangible; inappreciable
impanare (ēm·pâ·nâ'rā) *vt* to bread; to thread *(mech)*
impantanarsi (ēm·pân·tâ·nâr'sē) *vr* to bog down; to get stuck in the mud; to wallow; *(fig)* to get mixed up in
impaperarsi (ēm·pâ·pā·râr'sē) *vr* to fluff a line *(theat)*; to mispronounce; to stammer
impappinarsi (ēm·pâp·pē·nâr'sē) *vr* to get flustered
imparagonabile (ēm·pâ·râ·gō·nâ'bē·lā) *a* incomparable, peerless
imparare (ēm·pâ·râ'rā) *vt* to learn; — **a memoria** to memorize
impareggiabile (ēm·pâ·rāj·jâ'bē·lā) *a* incomparable
imparentarsi (ēm·pâ·rān·târ'sē) *vr* to marry into
imparentato (ēm·pâ·rān·tâ'tō) *a* related
impari (ēm·pâ'rē) *a* odd, uneven; inadequate
impartire (ēm·pâr·tē'rā) *vt* to give, bestow
imparziale (ēm·pâr·tsyâ'lā) *a* impartial
imparzialità (ēm·pâr·tsyâ·lē·tâ') *f* impartiality
imparzialmente (ēm·pâr·tsyâl·mān'tā) *adv* impartially
impassibile (ēm·pâs·sē'bē·lā) *a* impassive; unfeeling, insensible
impassibilità (ēm·pâs·sē·bē·lē·tâ') *f* aloofness, impassiveness
impassibilmente (ēm·pâs·sē·bēl·mān'tā) *adv* impassively, aloofly
impastare (ēm·pâ·stâ'rā) *vt* to knead; to paste
impasticciare (ēm·pâ·stē·châ'rā) *vt* to make a mess of; to soil
impasto (ēm·pâ'stō) *m* mixture
impattare (ēm·pât·tâ'rā) *vi* to be quits; to tie the score
impavidamente (ēm·pâ·vē·dâ·mān'tā) *adv* undauntedly
impavido (ēm·pâ'vē·dō) *a* brave, fearless
impaurire (ēm·pâū·rē'rā) *vt* to frighten
impaurirsi (ēm·pâū·rēr'sē) *vr* to become frightened; to be intimidated
impazientare (ēm·pâ·tsyān·tâ'rā) *vt* to bore; to annoy; to irritate
impazientarsi (ēm·pâ·tsyān·târ'sē) *vr* to get impatient
impazientemente (ēm·pâ·tsyān·tā·mān'tā) *adv* impatiently
impazienza (ēm·pâ·tsyān'tsâ) *f* impatience
impazzata (ēm·pâ·tsâ'tâ) *f* folly, madness; **all'—** rashly; madly
impazzito (ēm·pâ·tsē'tō) *a* demented
impazzire (ēm·pâ·tsē'rā) *vi* to go mad
impeccabile (ēm·pāk·kâ'bē·lā) *a* impeccable
impeccabilità (ēm·pāk·kâ·bē·lē·tâ') *f* impeccability, flawlessness
impeccabilmente (ēm·pāk·kâ·bēl·mān'tā) *adv* impeccably, faultlessly
impedenza (ēm·pā·dān'tsâ) *f (elec)* impedance
impedimento (ēm·pā·dē·mān'tō) *m* impediment; obstacle, hindrance
impedire (ēm·pā·dē'rā) *vt* to prevent; to impede; — **la circolazione** to block traffic
impegnare (ēm·pā·nyâ'rā) *vt* to pawn; to hire; to pledge
impegnarsi (ēm·pā·nyâr'sē) *vr* to involve oneself; to give one's services
impegnativo (ēm·pā·nyâ·tē'vō) *a* binding, obliging
impegnato (ēm·pā·nyâ'tō) *a* involved; occupied; pawned
impegno (ēm·pā'nyō) *m* pledge; obligation
impegolarsi (ēm·pā·gō·lâr'sē) *vr* to become involved, get mixed up
impellente (ēm·pāl·lān'tā) *a* urgent
impellicciato (ēm·pāl·lē·châ'tō) *a* dressed in furs; furred; veneered *(furniture)*
impenetrabile (ēm·pā·nā·trâ'bē·lā) *a* impenetrable; — **all'aria** airtight
impenetrabilmente (ēm·pā·nā·trâ·bēl·mān'tā) *adv* impenetrably
impenitente (ēm·pā·nē·tān'tā) *a* unrepenting
impennarsi (ēm·pān·nâr'sē) *vr (fig)* to get angry; to rise up on its hind legs
impennato (ēm·pān·nâ'tō) *a* rearing, prancing *(horse)*
impensabile (ēm·pān·sâ'bē·lā) *a* unthinkable
impensato (ēm·pān·sâ'tō) *a* unexpected
impensierire (ēm·pān·syā·rē'rā) *vt* to cause alarm; to worry
impensierirsi (ēm·pān·syā·rēr'sē) *vr* to grow anxious, become uneasy
imperante (ēm·pā·rân'tā) *a* reigning, prevailing
imperativo (ēm·pā·râ·tē'vō) *a* imperative; — *m* imperative *(gram)*
imperatore (ēm·pā·râ·tō'rā) *m* emperor
impercettibile (ēm·pār·chāt·tē'bē·lā) *a* unnoticeable
imperdonabile (ēm·pār·dō·nâ'bē·lā) *a* unpardonable
imperfetto (ēm·pār·fāt'tō) *a* defective; — *m* imperfect *(gram)*
imperfezione (ēm·pār·fā·tsyō'nā) *f* imperfection
imperiale (ēm·pā·ryâ'lā) *a* imperial
imperialismo (ēm·pā·ryâ·lē'zmō) *m* imperialism
imperialista (ēm·pā·ryâ·lē'stâ) *m* imperialist
imperiosamente (ēm·pā·ryō·zâ·mān'tā) *adv* dictatorially
imperioso (ēm·pā·ryō'zō) *a* peremptory; arrogant
imperituro (ēm·pā·rē·tū'rō) *a* undying
imperizia (ēm·pā·rē'tsyâ) *f* awkwardness;

lack of skill
impermalirsi (ēm·pār·mâ·lēr'sē) *vr* to resent; to take offense
impermeabile (ēm·pār·mā·â'bē·lā) *a* waterproof; — *m* raincoat
imperniare (ēm·pār·nyâ'rā) *vt* to pivot; to base; to found
impero (ēm·pā'rō) *m* empire
imperseveranza (ēm·pār·sā·vā·rân'tsâ) *f* inconstancy
impersonare (ēm·pār·sō·nâ'rā) *vt* to impersonate
imperterrito (ēm·pār·ter'rē·tō) *a* fearless, intrepid
impertinente (ēm·pār·tē·nān'tā) *a* impertinent, saucy, fresh
impertinenza (ēm·pār·tē·nān'tsâ) *f* impudence, impertinence
imperturbabile (ēm·pār·tūr·bâ'bē·lā) *a* imperturbable, calm, serene
imperturbabilità (ēm·pār·tūr·bâ·bē·lē·tâ') *f* calmness, serenity
imperturbabilmente (ēm·pār·tūr·bâ·bēl·mān'tā) *adv* imperturbably, calmly
imperversare (ēm·pār·vār·sâ'rā) *vi* to storm, rage *(weather)*; to become furious, rampage
impervio (ēm·per'vyō) *a* impervious
impetigine (ēm·pā·tē'jē·nā) *f (med)* impetigo
impeto (ēm'pā·tō) *m* impetus; **di primo —** impulsively; at first; **fare — su** to attack; **pieno d'—** vigorous
impettito (ēm·pāt·tē'tō) *a* stiff; erect; **camminare —** to strut
impetuosamente (ēm·pā·twō·zâ·mān'tā) *adv* impulsively; violently
impetuosità (ēm·pā·twō·zē·tâ') *f* impetuousness; fervor
impetuoso (ēm·pā·twō'zō) *a* impetuous
impiantare (ēm·pyân·tâ'rā) *vt* to plant; to set up; to establish
impiantito (ēm·pyân·tē'tō) *m* flooring
impianto (ēm·pyân'tō) *m* installation, establishment; plant *(com)*; **spese d'—** initial expenses
impiastro (ēm·pyâ'strō) *m* poultice; *(fig)* bore
impiccagione (ēm·pēk·kâ·jō'nā) *f* hanging *(person)*
impiccare (ēm·pēk·kâ'rā) *vt* to hang *(person)*
impiccato (ēm·pēk·kâ'tō) *a&m* hanged
impicciarsi (ēm·pē·châr'sē) *vr* to meddle, become involved
impiccio (ēm·pē'chō) *m* trouble; obstacle
impiccolire (ēm·pēk·kō·lē'rā) *vt* to diminish, reduce
impiccolirsi (ēm·pēk·kō·lēr'sē) *vr* to diminish, grow smaller
impiegare (ēm·pyā·gâ'rā) *vt* to employ; to use; *(com)* to invest
impiegarsi (ēm·pyā·gâr'sē) *vr* to be hired; to find a job
impiegato (ēm·pyā·gâ'tō) *m* employee; clerk; — *a* employed
impiego (ēm·pyā'gō) *m* employment, job; use; investment
impigliarsi (ēm·pē·lyâr'sē) *vr* to get entangled; to be caught in
impinguare (ēm·pēn·gwâ'rā) *vt* to fatten
impiombare (ēm·pyōm·bâ'rā) *vt* to cover with lead; to fill *(tooth)*
impiparsi (ēm·pē·pâr'sē) *vr* not to give a hang; to be totally unconcerned
implacabile (ēm·plâ·kâ'bē·lā) *a* unrelenting; implacable
implacabilità (ēm·plâ·kâ·bē·lē·tâ') *f* implacability
implacabilmente (ēm·plâ·kâ·bēl·mān'tā) *adv* unrelentingly, implacably
implicare (ēm·plē·kâ'rā) *vt* to involve; to imply
implicitamente (ēm·plē·chē·tâ·mān'tā) *adv* implicity
implicito (ēm·plē'chē·tō) *a* implicit
implorare (ēm·plō·râ'rā) *vt* to implore
implorazione (ēm·plō·râ·tsyō'nā) *f* imploring, entreaty
implume (ēm·plū'mā) *a* without feathers
impolverare (ēm·pōl·vā·râ'rā) *vt* to cover with dust, make dusty
impolverarsi (ēm·pōl·vā·râr'sē) *vr* to get dusty
imponente (ēm·pō·nān'tā) *a* imposing
imponenza (ēm·pō·nān'tsâ) *f* impressiveness, grandeur
imponibile (ēm·pō·nē'bē·lā) *a* taxable
impopolare (ēm·pō·pō·lâ'rā) *a* unpopular
impopolarità (ēm·pō·pō·lâ·rē·tâ') *f* unpopularity
imporre * (ēm·pōr'rā) *vt* to impose; to inflict
imporsi * (ēm·pōr'sē) *vr* to impose upon; to intrude oneself
importante (ēm·pōr·tân'tā) *a* important
importanza (ēm·pōr·tân'tsâ) *f* importance; **darsi —** to give oneself airs; to throw one's weight around
importare (ēm·pōr·tâ'rā) *vt* to import; — *vi* to matter, be of concern
importatore (ēm·pōr·tâ·tō'rā) *m* importer
importazione (ēm·pōr·tâ·tsyō'nā) *f* importation, import
importo (ēm·pōr'tō) *m* cost, amount
importunare (ēm·pōr·tū·nâ'rā) *vt* to importune; to bother
importuno (ēm·pōr·tū·nō) *a* inopportune; annoying; troublesome
imposizione (ēm·pō·zē·tsyō'nā) *f* imposition
impossessarsi (ēm·pōs·sās·sâr'sē) *vr* to get possession of
impossibile (ēm·pōs·sē'bē·lā) *a* impossible
impossibilità (ēm·pōs·sē·bē·lē·tâ') *f* impossibility
imposta (ēm·pō'stâ) *f* tax; shutter
impostazione (ēm·pō·stâ·tsyō'nā) *f* basis, foundation; attitude, manner
impostare (ēm·pō·stâ'rā) *vt* to mail; to place
impostore (ēm·pō·stō'rā) *m* impostor
impostura (ēm·pō·stū'râ) *f* imposture; deception; swindle
impotente (ēm·pō·tān'tā) *a* impotent; powerless
impotenza (ēm·pō·tān'tsâ) *f* impotence

impoverire (ēm·pō·vā·rē'rā) *vt* to impoverish
impraticabile (ēm·prâ·tē·kâ'bē·lā) *a* impassable; not feasible; impracticable; impractical
imprecare (ēm·prā·kâ'rā) *vi* to curse
imprecazione (ēm·prā·kâ·tsyō'nā) *f* curse, imprecation
imprecisabile (ēm·prā·chē·zâ'bē·lā) *a* undeterminable
imprecisione (ēm·prā·chē·zyō'nā) *f* inaccuracy; lack of precision
impreciso (ēm·prā·chē'zō) *a* vague
impregnare (ēm·prā·nyâ'rā) *vt* to impregnate
imprendere (ēm·pren'dā·rā) *vt* to undertake; to start
imprendibile (ēm·prān·dē'bē·lā) *a* untakeable; unassailable; impregnable
imprenditore (ēm·prān·dē·tō'rā) *m* contractor
impreparato (ēm·prā·pâ·râ'tō) *a* unprepared
impreparazione (ēm·prā·pâ·râ·tsyō'nā) *f* lack of preparation
impresa (ēm·prā'zâ) *f* undertaking; exploit; *(com)* firm; *(theat)* management
impresario (ēm·prā·zâ'ryō) *m* contractor; *(theat)* impresario; **— di pompe funebri** mortician
imprescindibile (ēm·prā·shēn·dē'bē·lā) *a* unavoidable; indispensable
impressionabile (ēm·prās·syō·nâ'bē·lā) *a* sensitive, impressionable
impressionare (ēm·prās·syō·nâ'rā) *vt* to stir; to impress
impressionarsi (ēm·prās·syō·nâr'sē) *vr* to be deeply stirred
impressione (ēm·prās·syō'nā) *f* impression
impressionismo (ēm·prās·syō·nē'zmō) *m* impressionism
impressionista (ēm·prās·syō·nē'stâ) *m* impressionist
impresso (ēm·prās'sō) *a* pressed; imprinted, engraved
impressore (ēm·prās·sō'rā) *m* pressman *(print)*
imprevedibile (ēm·prā·vā·dē'bē·lā) *a* unforeseeable
imprevidente (ēm·prā·vē·dān'tā) *a* improvident
imprevisto (ēm·prā·vē'stō) *a* unforeseen
imprigionamento (ēm·prē·jō·nâ·mān'tō) *m* confinement, imprisonment
imprigionare (ēm·prē·jō·nâ'rā) *vt* to imprison
imprimere * (ēm·prē'mā·rā) *vt* to impress; to print; to engrave
improbabile (ēm·prō·bâ'bē·lā) *a* improbable
improbabilità (ēm·prō·bâ·bē·lē·tâ') *f* improbability
improbabilmente (ēm·prō·bâ·bēl·mān'tā) *adv* improbably
improbo (ēm'prō·bō) *a* dishonest; wicked; *(fig)* hard, difficult
impronta (ēm·prōn'tâ) *f* print; mark; **— digitale** fingerprint
improperio (ēm·prō·pe'ryō) *m* abuse, insult, impropriety
impropriamente (ēm·prō·pryâ·mān'tā) *adv* improperly
improprietà (ēm·prō·pryā·tâ') *f* impropriety
improprio (ēm·prô'pryō) *a* improper, unbecoming
improrogabile (ēm·prō·rō·gâ'bē·lā) *a* not postponable, not deferrable
improrogabilmente (ēm·prō·rō·gâ·bēl·mān'tā) *adv* without delay, without postponement
improvvido (ēm·prôv'vē·dō) *a* improvident
improvvisamente (ēm·prōv·vē·zâ·mān'tā) *adv* suddenly; unexpectedly
improvvisare (ēm·prōv·vē·zâ'rā) *vi* to improvise; to extemporize; to ad-lib
improvvisazione (ēm·prōv·vē·zâ·tsyō'nā) *f* extemporization, improvisation
improvviso (ēm·prōv·vē'zō) *a* unforeseen; sudden; **all' —** suddenly
imprudente (ēm·prū·dān'tā) *a* imprudent
imprudentemente (ēm·prū·dān·tā·mān'tā) *adv* rashly
imprudenza (ēm·prū·dān'tsâ) *f* imprudence
impudente (ēm·pū·dān'tā) *a* impudent
impudenza (ēm·pū·dān'tsâ) *f* impudence, brazenness
impudicamente (ēm·pū·dē·kâ·mān'tā) *adv* immodestly, shamelessly
impudicizia (ēm·pū·dē·chē'tsyâ) *f* shamelessness, immodesty
impugnabile (ēm·pū·nyâ'bē·lā) *a* questionable; impugnable
impugnare (ēm·pū·nyâ'rā) *vt* to contest; to grip
impugnatura (ēm·pū·nyâ·tū'râ) *f* grip *(hand)*; hilt
impulsivo (ēm·pūl·sē'vō) *a* impulsive
impulso (ēm·pūl'sō) *m* impulse; **dare — a** to set in motion, put into operation
impunemente (ēm·pū·nā·mān'tā) *adv* with impunity
impunità (ēm·pū·nē·tâ') *f* impunity
impuntarsi (ēm·pūn·târ'sē) *vr* to be stubborn
impuntigliarsi (ēm·pūn·tē·lyâr'sē) *vr* to be obstinate; to get it into one's head
impuramente (ēm·pū·râ·mān'tā) *adv* impurely
impurità (ēm·pū·rē·tâ') *f* impurity
impuro (ēm·pū'rō) *a* impure
imputare (ēm·pū·tâ'rā) *vt* to blame, accuse; *(law)* to indict
imputato (ēm·pū·tâ'tō) *m* *(law)* defendant; **—** *a* accused
imputazione (ēm·pū·tâ·tsyō'nā) *f* accusation
imputridire (ēm·pū·trē·dē'rā) *vi* to rot
in (ēn) *prep* in; at; by; to; into
inabile (ē·nâ'bē·lā) *a* unable; unfit
inabilità (ē·nâ·bē·lē·tâ') *f* inability
inabissare (ē·nâ·bēs·sâ'rā) *vt* to engulf; to sink
inabissarsi (ē·nâ·bēs·sâr'sē) *vr* to be submerged, sink
inaccessibile (ē·nâ·chās·sē'bē·lā) *a* inac-

cessible
inaccettabile (ēn·nâ·chāt·tâ'bē·lā) *a* unacceptable
inacidire (ē·nâ·chē·dē'rā) *vt&i* to sour
inadattabile (ē·nâ·dât·tâ'bē·lā) *a* unadaptable
inadeguato (ē·nâ·dā·gwâ'tō) *a* inadequate
inadempiuto (ē·nâ·dām·pyū'tō) *a* uncompleted; unfulfilled
inadoprabile (ē·nâ·dō·prâ'bē·lā) *a* unusable
inalare (ē·nâ·lâ'rā) *vt* to inhale
inalatore (ē·nâ·lâ·tō'rā) *m* inhaler *(med)*
inalazione (ē·nâ·lâ·tsyō'nā) *f* inhalation
inalberare (ē·nâl·bā·râ'rā) *vt* to hoist
inalienabile (ē·nâ·lyā·nâ'bē·lā) *a* inalienable
inalienare (ē·nâ·lyā·nâ'rā) *vt* to estrange, alienate
inalterabile (ē·nâl·tā·râ'bē·lā) *a* unalterable
inalterato (ē·nâl·tā·râ'tō) *a* unaltered, unchanged
inamidare (ē·nâ·mē·dâ'rā) *vt* to starch
inammissibile (ē·nâm·mēs·sē'bē·lā) *a* inadmissible
inamovibile (ē·nâ·mō·vē'bē·lā) *a* irremovable
inane (ē·nâ'nā) *a* vapid; inane
inanimato (ē·nâ·nē·mâ'tō) *a* inanimate
inanizione (ē·nâ·nē·tsyō'nā) *f* exhaustion; emptiness, vapidness
inappetenza (ē·nâp·pā·tān'tsâ) *f* lack of appetite
inapplicabile (ē·nâp·plē·kâ'bē·lā) *a* inapplicable
inapprezzabile (ē·nâp·prā·tsâ'bē·lā) *a* imperceptible; invaluable
inaridire (ē·nâ·rē·dē'rā) *vt* to dry up
inaridirsi (ē·nâ·rē·dēr'sē) *vr* to become sere, grow arid
inarrivabile (ē·nâr·rē·vâ'bē·lā) *a* unsurpassable; unattainable
inarticolato (ē·nâr·tē·kō·lâ'tō) *a* inarticulate
inaspettatamente (ē·nâ·spāt·tâ·tâ·mān'tā) *adv* unexpectedly
inaspettato (ē·nâ·spāt·tâ'tō) *a* unexpected
inasprimento (ē·nâ·sprē·mān'tō) *m* aggravation; embitterment; harshness
inasprire (ē·nâ·sprē'rā) *vt* to embitter
inasprirsi (ē·nâ·sprēr'sē) *vr* to become exasperated; to grow embittered
inattivo (ē·nât·tē'vō) *a* inactive
inaudito (ē·nâū·dē'tō) *a* unprecedented; unheard-of
inaugurale (ē·nâū·gū·râ'lā) *a* inaugural
inaugurare (ē·nâū·gū·râ'rā) *vt* to inaugurate
inaugurazione (ē·nâū·gū·râ·tsyō'nā) *f* inauguration
incagliare (ēn·kâ·lyâ'rā) *vi* to be stranded; to be brought to a halt; — *vt* to jam; to obstruct, bring to a halt
incagliarsi (ēn·kâ·lyâr'sē) *vr* to be hindered; to run aground
incaglio (ēn·kâ'lyō) *m* deterrent; *(fig)* deadlock
incalcolabile (ēn·kâl·kō·lâ'bē·lā) *a* incalculable, uncountable
incallire (ēn·kâl·lē'rā) *vi* to become callous; to get hard
incalzante (ēn·kâl·tsân'tā) *a* in pursuit, chasing
incalzare (ēn·kâl·tsâ'rā) *vt* to press, harass; to pursue
incamerare (ēn·kâ·mā·râ'rā) *vt* to appropriate; to annex
incamminare (ēn·kâm·mē·nâ'rā) *vt* to set in motion; to give a start to
incamminarsi (ēn·kâm·mē·nâr'sē) *vr* to start out; to set out for
incanalare (ēn·kâ·nâ·lâ'rā) *vt* to channel
incancellabile (ēn·kân·chāl·lâ'bē·lā) *a* unforgettable; indelible, irradicable
incandescente (ēn·kân·dā·shān'tā) *a* incandescent
incantare (ēn·kân·tâ'rā) *vt* to charm
incantatore (ēn·kân·tâ·tō'rā) *m* enchanter, charmer
incantesimo (ēn·kân·te'zē·mō) *m* charm; enchantment; magic, sorcery
incantevole (ēn·kân·te'vō·lā) *a* enchanting
incanto (ēn·kân'tō) *m* magic; charm; auction sale
incapace (ēn·kâ·pâ'chā) *a* incapable
incapacità (ēn·kâ·pâ·chē·tâ') *f* incapacity, inability
incappare (ēn·kâp·pâ'rā) *vi* to run into, come upon
incappucciare (ēn·kâp·pū·châ'rā) *vt* to hood; to bundle up
incarcerare (ēn·kâr·chā·râ'rā) *vt* to imprison
incarcerazione (ēn·kâr·chā·râ·tsyō'nā) *f* incarceration, imprisonment
incaricare (ēn·kâ·rē·kâ'rā) *vt* to entrust
incaricarsi (ēn·kâ·rē·kâr'sē) *vr* to take upon oneself
incaricato (ēn·kâ·rē·kâ'tō) *a* entrusted, charged; — *m* agent; — **d'affari** chargé d'affaires
incarico (ēn·kâ'rē·kō) *m* appointment; duty; task
incartare (ēn·kâr·tâ'rā) *vt* to wrap in paper
incassare (ēn·kâs·sâ'rā) *vt* to cash; to collect; to case
incasso (ēn·kâs'sō) *m* collection, take
incastonare (ēn·kâ·stō·nâ'rā) *vt* to set *(gems)*
incastrare (ēn·kâ·strâ'rā) *vt* to insert, fit in
incastrarsi (ēn·kâ·strâr'sē) *vr* to be embedded; to fit in
incastro (ēn·kâ'strō) *m* recess *(arch)*; groove, joint; — **a coda di rondine** dovetailing
incatenare (ēn·kâ·tā·nâ'rā) *vt* to chain; *(fig)* to fascinate
incatramare (ēn·kâ·trâ·mâ'rā) *vt* to tar
incautamente (ēn·kâū·tâ·mān'tā) *adv* rashly, carelessly
incauto (ēn·kâ'ū·tō) *a* incautious, rash
incavato (ēn·kâ·vâ'tō) *a* hollow
incavo (ēn·kâ'vō) *m* hole; hollow
incendiare (ēn·chān·dyâ'rā) *vt* to put fire

to
incendiario (ēn·chān·dyâ'ryō) *m* arsonist
incendiarsi (ēn·chān·dyâr'sē) *vr* to catch fire
incendio (ēn·chen'dyō) *m* fire; — **doloso** arson
incenerire (ēn·chā·nā·rē'rā) *vt* to incinerate
incensamento (ēn·chān·sâ·mān'tō) *m (fig)* flattery; incensing
incensare (ēn·chān·sâ'rā) *vt* to incense; *(fig)* to flatter
incenso (ēn·chān'sō) *m* incense; *(fig)* flattery
incensurabile (ēn·chān·sū·râ'bē·lā) *a* above criticism
incensurato (ēn·chān·sū·râ'tō) *a* uncensured
incentivo (ēn·chān·tē'vō) *m* incentive
incepparsi (ēn·chāp·pâr'sē) *vr* to jam, become obstructed
incerare (ēn·chā·râ'rā) *vt* to wax *(surface)*
incerata (ēn·chā·râ'tâ) *f* oilskin
incertezza (ēn·chār·tā'tsâ) *f* uncertainty; indecision; **tenere nell'—**; to keep in suspense; — **del tempo** unsettled weather
incerto (ēn·chār'tō) *a* dubious, uncertain; irresolute; **luce incerta** dim light; — *m* uncertainty; gratuity, perquisite
incerti (ēn·chār'tē) *mpl* perquisites
incessante (ēn·chās·sân'tā) *a* incessant; **–mente** (ēn·chās·sân·tā·mān'tā) *adv* incessantly
incetta (ēn·chāt'tâ) *f* cornering *(goods)*; buying up
incettare (ēn·chāt·tâ'rā) *vt* to buy up; to corner *(goods)*
inchiesta (ēn·kyā'stâ) *f* investigation; inquiry; inquest
inchinare (ēn·kē·nâ'rā) *vt* to bend; — *vi* to bow
inchinarsi (ēn·kē·nâr'sē) *vr* to lower oneself; to bow to
inchino (ēn·kē'nō) *m* bow
inchiodare (ēn·kyō·dâ'rā) *vt* to rivet; to nail; — **al letto** *(fig)* to confine to bed
inchiostro (ēn·kyō'strō) *m* ink
inciampare (ēn·châm·pâ'rā) *vi* to stumble, trip
inciampo (ēn·châm'pō) *m* obstacle, hindrance; *(fig)* difficulty
incidentalmente (ēn·chē·dān·tâl·mān'tā) *adv.* accidentally; incidentally
incidente (ēn·chē·dān'tā) *m* accident; incident; — **automobilistico** automobile accident
incidere * (ēn·chē'dā·rā) *vt* to engrave; to record; to cut into; — **una canzone** to record a song; — **all'acquaforte** to etch
incinta (ēn·chēn'tâ) *a* pregnant
incipriare (ēn·chē·pryâ'rā) *vt* to powder
incipriarsi (ēn·chē·pryâr'sē) *vr* to powder oneself; to put on powder
incisione (ēn·chē·zyō'nā) *f* engraving, etching; incision
incisivo (ēn·chē·zē'vō) *a* incisive; — *m* incisor
incisore (ēn·chē·zō'rā) *m* engraver
incitamento (ēn·chē·tâ·mān'tō) *m* incitement
incitare (ēn·chē·tâ'rā) *vt* to incite
incivile (ēn·chē·vē'lā) *a* uncivilized; ill-mannered, discourteous
incivilirsi (ēn·chē·vē·lēr'sē) *vr* to become civilized
inclemente (ēn·klā·mān'tā) *a* inclement
inclinare (ēn·klē·nâ'rā) *vt&i* to bend; to incline; to be inclined
inclinarsi (ēn·klē·nâr'sē) *vr* to incline toward; to lean
inclinazione (ēn·klē·nâ·tsyō'nā) *f* inclination
incline (ēn·klē'nā) *a* apt to; inclined
includere * (ēn·klū'dā·rā) *vt* to include
inclusione (ēn·klū·zyō'nā) *f* inclusion
incluso (ēn·klū'zō) *a* included
incoerente (ēn·kō·ā·rān'tā) *a* incoherent; inconsistent
incognita (ēn·kô'nyē·tâ) *f* unknown quantity
incognito (ēn·kô'nyē·tō) *a* unknown; **in** — incognito
incollare (ēn·kōl·lâ'rā) *vt* to glue, paste
incollerito (ēn·kōl·lā·rē'tō) *a* angry
incollerirsi (ēn·kōl·lā·rēr'sē) *vr* to get angry
incolore (ēn·kō·lō'rā) *a* colorless
incolpabilità (ēn·kōl·pâ·bē·lē·tâ') *f* innocence
incolpare (ēn·kōl·pâ'rā) *vt* to blame
incolto (ēn·kōl'tō) *a* uncouth; uncultivated
incolume (ēn·kô'lū·mā) *a* uninjured, safe and sound
incolumità (ēn·kō·lū·mē·tâ') *f* safety
incombenza (ēn·kōm·bān'tsâ) *f* task; errand
incombere (ēn·kôm'bā·rā) *vi* to be incumbent; to impend
incombustibile (ēn·kōm·bū·stē'bē·lā) *a* fireproof; incombustible
incominciare (ēn·kō·mēn·châ'rā) *vt&i* to begin, start
incommestibile (ēn·kōm·mā·stē'bē·lā) *a* inedible
incomodare (ēn·kō·mō·dâ'rā) *vt* to disturb
incomodarsi (ēn·kō·mō·dâr'sē) *vr* to take the trouble, trouble oneself
incomodità (ēn·kō·mō·dē·tâ') *f* annoyance; trouble; discomfort
incomodo (ēn·kô'mō·dō) *m* trouble; — *a* bothersome; uncomfortable
incomparabile (ēn·kōm·pâ·râ'bē·lā) *a* incomparable
incompatibile (ēn·kōm·pâ·tē'bē·lā) *a* inconsistent; incompatible
incompatibilità (ēn·kōm·pâ·tē·bē·lē·tâ') *f* inconsistency; incompatibility
incompetente (ēn·kōm·pā·tān'tā) *a* incompetent
incompleto (ēn·kōm·plā'tō) *a* incomplete
incomprensibile (ēn·kōm·prān·sē'bē·lā) *a* incomprehensible
incomprensione (ēn·kōm·prān·syō'nā) *f* incomprehension, misunderstanding
incompreso (ēn·kōm·prā'zō) *a* unappre-

ciated; misunderstood
inconcepibile (ēn·kōn·chā·pē'bē·lā) *a* inconceivable
incondizionatamente (ēn·kōn·dē·tsyō·nâ·tâ·mān'tā) *f* unreservedly, unconditionally
incondizionato (ēn·kōn·dē·tsyō·nâ'tō) *a* unconditional
inconfessabile (ēn·kōn·fās·sâ'bē·lā) *a* unmentionable
inconfondibile (ēn·kōn·fōn·dē'bē·lā) *a* unmistakable
inconfutabile (ēn·kōn·fū·tâ'bē·lā) *a* irrefutable
incongruente (ēn·kōn·grūān'tā) *a* incongruous
incongruenza (ēn·kōn·grūān'tsâ) *f* incongruity
inconsapevole (ēn·kōn·sâ·pe'vō·lā) *a* unaware; unconscious; unknowing
inconsapevolmente (ēn·kōn·sâ·pā·vōl·mān'tā) unwittingly, unknowingly
inconsiderato (ēn·kōn·sē·dā·râ'tō) *a* inconsiderate; rash
inconsistente (ēn·kōn·sē·stān'tā) *a* unfounded; inconsistent
inconsolabile (ēn·kōn·sō·lâ'bē·lā) *a* inconsolable
inconsueto (ēn·kōn·swā'tō) *a* unusual
incontaminato (ēn·kōn·tâ·mē·nâ'tō) *a* stainless; uncontaminated
incontentabile (ēn·kōn·tān·tâ'bē·lā) *a* exacting; impossible to please; never satisfied
incontrare (ēn·kōn·trâ'rā) *vt* to meet; — **favore** to be successful
incontrarsi (ēn·kōn·trâr'sē) *vr* to meet, get together
incontro (ēn·kōn'trō) *m* meeting; match *(sport)*; — *prep* towards, to; **andare — a qualcuno** to go to meet someone; **andare — a spese** to incure expenses; **andare — al pericolo** to face danger
inconveniente (ēn·kōn·vā·nyān'tā) *m* inconvenience; — *a* inconvenient; unbecoming
incoraggiamento (ēn·kō·râj·jâ·mān'tō) *m* encouragement; **per —** by way of encouragement
incoraggiante (ēn·kō·râj·jân'tā) *a* encouraging
incoraggiare (ēn·kō·râj·jâ'rā) *vt* to encourage
incoraggiarsi (ēn·kō·râj·jâr'sē) *vr* to take heart, muster one's courage
incoronare (ēn·kō·rō·nâ'rā) *vt* to crown
incoronazione (ēn·kō·rō·nâ·tsyō'nā) *f* coronation
incorporare (ēn·kōr·pō·râ'rā) *vt* to annex; to incorporate
incorporarsi (ēn·kōr·pō·râr'sē) *vr* to be incorporated
incorreggibile (ēn·kōr·rāj·jē'bē·lā) *a* incorregible
incorrere * (ēn·kôr'rā·rā) *vi* to incur
incorrettamente (ēn·kōr·rāt·tâ·mān'tā) *adv* incorrectly
incorrettezza (ēn·kōr·rāt·tā'tsâ) *f* incorrectness
incorruttibile (ēn·kōr·rūt·tē'bē·lā) *a* incorruptible
incosciente (ēn·kō·shān'tā) *a* unconscious; irresponsible
incoscienza (ēn·kō·shān'tsâ) *f* unconsciousness; lack of responsibility
incostante (ēn·kō·stân'tā) *a* changeable; fickle, inconstant
incostituzionale (ēn·kō·stē·tū·tsyō·nâ'lā) *a* unconstitutional
incredibile (ēn·krā·dē'bē·lā) *a* incredible
incrementare (en·krā·mān·tâ'rā) *vt* to increase
incremento (ēn·krā·mān'tō) *m* increase, increment; **dare — a** to favour; to foster
increscioso (ēn·krā·shō'zō) *a* unpleasant, regrettable
incriminare (ēn·krē·mē·nâ'rā) *vt* to impeach; to incriminate
incriminazione (ēn·krē·mē·nâ·tsyō'nā) *f* impeachement; accusation
incrinatura (ēn·krē·nâ·tū'râ) *f* flaw; crack
incrociare (ēn·krō·châ'rā) *vt* to cross; — **le braccia** to fold one's arms
incrociato (ēn·krō·châ'tō) *a* crossed; **parole incrociate** crossword puzzle
incrociatore (ēn·krō·châ·tō'rā) *m (naut)* cruiser
incrocio (ēn·krô'chō) *m* crossing; junction
incrostare (ēn·krō·stâ'rā) *vt* to encrust
incrostarsi (ēn·krō·stâr'sē) *vr* to become encrusted
incubatrice (ēn·kū·bâ·trē'chā) *f* incubator
incubazione (ēn·kū·bâ·tsyō'nā) *f* incubation
incubo (ēn'kū·bō) *m* nightmare
incudine (ēn·kū'dē·nā) *f* anvil
inculcare (ēn·kūl·kâ'rā) *vt* to impress; to inculcate
incurabile (ēn·kū·râ'bē·lā) *a* incurable
incurante (ēn·kū·rân'tā) *a* negligent, heedless, careless
incuranza (ēn·kū·rân'tsâ) *f* inaccuracy; carelessness
incuriosire (ēn·kū·ryō·zē'rā) *vt* to make curious
incuriosirsi (ēn·kū·ryō·zēr'sē) *vr* to become curious
incursionare (ēn·kūr·syō·nâ'rā) *vt* to raid; to make inroads upon
incursione (ēn·kūr·syō'nā) *f* inroad; raid
incutere * (ēn·kū'tā·rā) *vt* to command; to inspire
indaffarato (ēn·dâf·fâ·râ'tō) *a* very busy
indagare (ēn·dâ·gâ'rā) *vt* to investigate
indagine (ēn·dâ'jē·nā) *f* investigation; poll; research
indebitamente (ēn·dā·bē·tâ·mān'tā) *adv* unduly; improperly
indebitarsi (ēn·dā·bē·târ'sē) *vr* to get into debt
indebito (ēn·de'bē·tō) *a* undue; unbecoming; **appropriazione indebita** embezzlement
indebolimento (ēn·dā·bō·lē·mān'tō) *m* weakening
indebolire (ēn·dā·bō·lē'rā) *vt&i* to

weaken
indebolirsi (ēn·dā·bō·lēr'sē) *vr* to become weak
indecente (ēn·dā·chān'tā) *a* indecent
indecenza (ēn·dā·chān'tsâ) *f* indecency; **e un'—** it's a shame
indecisione (ēn·nā·chē·zyō'nā) *f* indecision; hesitation
indeciso (ēn·dā·chē'zō) *a* not decided; irresolute
indecoroso (ēn·dā·kō·rō'zō) *a* indecorous
indefesso (ēn·dā·fās'sō) *a* tireless
indefinibile (ēn·dā·fē·nē'bē·lā) *a* hard to define; indescribable
indefinito (ēn·dā·fē·nē'tō) *a* indefinite
indegnamente (ēn·dā·nyâ·mān'tā) *adv* unworthily
indegnità (ēn·dā·nyē·tâ') *f* indignity; unworthiness
indegno (ēn·dā'nyō) *a* unworthy
indelebile (ēn·dā·le'bē·lā) *a* indelible
indelicatezza (ēn·dā·lē·kâ·tā'tsâ) *f* indelicacy
indelicato (ēn·dā·lē·kâ'tō) *a* indelicate
indemagliabile (ēn·dā·mâ·lyâ'bē·lā) *a* runproof
indemoniato (ēn·dā·mō·nyâ'tō) *a* possessed, demonic
indennità (ēn·dān·nē·tâ') *f* indemnity
indennizzare (ēn·dān·nē·dzâ'rā) *vt* to compensate for; to indemnify
indennizzo (ēn·dān·nē'dzō) *m* compensation; indemnity
indescrivibile (ēn·dā·skrē·vē'bē·lā) *a* indescribable
indeterminato (ēn·dā·tār·mē·nâ'tō) *a* indeterminate, indefinite
indetto (ēn·dāt'tō) *a* established; fixed; announced
India (ēn'dyâ) *f* India
indiano (ēn·dyâ'nō) *a* Indian; **in fila indiana** in single file; **far l'—** to feign ignorance
indiavolato (ēn·dyâ·vō·lâ'tō) *a* difficult; furious; devilish
indicante (ēn·dē·kân'tā) *a* indicative of, indicating
indicare (ēn·dē·kâ'rā) *vt* to indicate; to point at; to mean
indicativo (ēn·dē·kâ·tē'vō) *a* indicative
indicato (ēn·dē·kâ'tō) *a* suitable, right
indicatore (ēn·dē·kâ·tō'rā) *m* indicator; sign; directory
indicazione (ēn·dē·kâ·tsyō'nā) *f* indication; information
indice (ēn'dē·chā) *m* index; sign *(fig)*
indicibile (ēn·dē·chē'bē·lā) *a* hard to express; unutterable
indietreggiare (ēn·dyā·trāj·jâ'rā) *vi* to draw back; to fall back; to back up
indietro (ēn·dyā'trō) *adv* behind, back; **voltarsi —** to turn round; **all'—** backwards; **essere —** to run slow *(watch)*
indifferente (ēn·dēf·fā·rān'tā) *a* indifferent
indifferenza (ēn·dēf·fā·rān'tsâ) *f* indifference; coldness
indigeno (ēn·dē'jā·nō) *a&m* native
indigente (ēn·dē·jān'tā) *a* indigent, destitute
indigeribile (ēn·dē·jā·rē'bē·lā) *a* indigestible
indigestione (ēn·dē·jā·styō'nā) *f* indigestion; **fare —** to eat too much
indigesto (ēn·dē·jā'stō) *a* indigestible; unpleasant, tiresome
indignare (ēn·dē·nyâ'rā) *vt* to make indignant; to anger
indignarsi (ēn·dē·nyâr'sē) *vr* to become indignant; to get angry
indignazione (ēn·dē·nyâ·tsyō'nā) *f* indignation
indimenticabile (ēn·dē·mān·tē·kâ'bē·lā) *adv* unforgettable
indipendente (ēn·dè·pān·dān'tā) *a* independent
indipendentemente (ēn·dē·pān·dān·tā·mān'tā) *adv* independently
indipendenza (ēn·dē·pān·dān'tsâ) *f* independence
indire * (ēn·dē'rā) *vt* to order; to notify; **— una riunione** to call a meeting
indirettamente (ēn·dē·rāt·tâ·mān'tā) *adv* indirectly
indiretto (ēn·dē·rāt'tō) *a* indirect
indirizzare (ēn·dē·rē·tsâ'rā) *vt* to direct; to address *(mail)*
indirizzario (ēn·dē·rē·tsâ'ryō) *m* mailing list
indirizzarsi (ēn·dē·rē·tsâr'sē) *vr* to apply oneself to; to go toward
indirizzo (ēn·dē·rē'tsō) *m* address *(mail)*; course, direction
indisciplina (ēn·dē·shē·plē'nâ) *f* unruliness, lack of discipline
indisciplinato (ēn·dē·shē·plē·nâ'tō) *a* unruly, lacking in discipline
indiscretamente (ēn·dē·skrā·tâ·mān'tā) *adv* indiscreetly
indiscreto (ēn·dē·skrā'tō) *a* indiscreet
indiscrezione (ēn·dē·skrā·tsyō'nā) *f* indiscretion
indiscusso (ēn·dē·skūs'sō) *a* undisputed; undiscussed
indispensabile (ēn·dē·spān·sâ'bē·lā) *a* indispensable; necessary; **—** *m* necessity
indispensabilmente (ēn·dē·spān·sâ·bēl·mān'tā) *adv* indispensably, necessarily
indispettire (ēn·dē·spāt·tē'rā) *vt* to irritate; to annoy
indispettirsi (ēn·dē·spāt·tēr'sē) *vr* to get irritated, become vexed
indisporre * (ēn·dē·spōr'rā) *vt* to disincline; to upset
indisposizione (ēn·dē·spō·zē·tsyō'nā) *f* indisposition
indisposto (ēn·dē·spō'stō) *a* indisposed
indissolubile (ēn·dēs·sō·lū'bē·lā) *a* indissoluble; permanent
indistintamente (ēn·dē·stēn·tâ·mān'tā) *adv* dimly; indistinctly
indistinto (ēn·dē·stēn'tō) *a* vague, indistinct
indistruttibile (ēn·dē·strūt·tē'bē·lā) *a* indestructible
indivia (ēn·dē'vyâ) *f* endive, chicory
individuale (ēn·dē·vē·dwâ'lā) *a* individ-

ual
individualista (ēn·dē·vē·dwâ·lē'stâ) *m* individualist
individualità (ēn·dē·vē·dwâ·lē·tâ') *f* individuality
individualizzare (ēn·dē·vē·dwâ·lē·dzâ'-rā) *vt* to specify
individuare (ēn·dē·vē·dwâ'rā) *vt* to identify; to specify; to single out
individuo (ēn·dē·vē'dwō) *m* individual; person, fellow
indivisibile (ēn·dē·vē·zē'bē·lā) *a* indivisible
indiviso (ēn·dē·vē'zō) *a* undivided, whole
indiziare (ēn·dē·tsyâ'rā) *vt* to suspect
indiziario (ēn·dē·tsyâ'ryō) *a* circumstantial
indizio (ēn·dē'tsyō) *m* circumstance; clue; indication
Indocina (ēn·dō·chē'nâ) *f* Indochina
indoeuropeo (ēn·dō·āū·rō·pā'ō) *a* Indo-European
indole (ēn'dō·lā) *f* disposition, character; **uomo di buona** — good-natured man
indolente (ēn·dō·lān'tā) *a* indolent, lazy
indolenza (ēn·dō·lān'tsâ) *f* laziness, indolence
indolenzito (ēn·dō·lān·tsē'tō) *a* numb
indomabile (ēn·dō·mâ'bē·lā) *a* indomitable; untamable; unconquerable
indomani (ēn·dō·mâ'nē) *m* next day
indorare (ēn·dō·râ'rā) *vt* to gild
indorato (ēn·dō·râ'tō) *a* gilded; browned
indossare (ēn·dōs·sâ'rā) *vt* to wear; to put on, don
indossatrice (ēn·dōs·sâ·trē'chā) *f* model, mannequin
indosso (ēn·dōs'sō) *adv* on (*oneself*)
indotto (ēn·dōt'tō) *a* induced; **corrente indotta** induced current; — *m* (*elec*) armature, rotor; induction coil
indovinare (ēn·dō·vē·nâ'rā) *vt&i* to guess; to foresee; to hit the mark
indovinato (ēn·dō·vē·nâ'tō) *a* guessed; well done; fine
indovinello (ēn·dō·vē·nāl'lō) *m* riddle, puzzle
indovino (ēn·dō·vē'nō) *m* fortuneteller
indubbiamente (ēn·dūb·byâ·mān'tā) *adv* certainly, undoubtedly
indubbio (ēn·dūb'byō) *a* undoubted, sure; undisputed
indubitabile (ēn·dū·bē·tâ'bē·lā) *a* indubitable, doubtless
indugiare (ēn·dū·jâ'rā) *vi* to delay; to hesitate
indugio (ēn·dū'jō) *m* delay; **rompere gl'indugi** to come to a decision
indulgente (ēn·dūl·jān'tā) *a* indulgent
indulgenza (ēn·dūl·jān'tsâ) *f* indulgence
indulgere * (ēn·dūl'jā·rā) *vi* to indulge in; to be indulgent; — *vt* to allow; to grant; to gratify
indumento (ēn·dū·mān'tō) *m* garment
indurire (ēn·dū·rē'rā) *vt&i* to harden; to inure
indurirsi (ēn·dū·rēr'sē) *vr* to become inured; to become hardened
indurre * (ēn·dūr'rā) *vt* to induce
indursi * (ēn·dūr'sē) *vt* to make up one's mind; to decide; to bring upon oneself
industria (ēn·dū'stryâ) *f* industry
industriale (ēn·dū·stryâ'lā) *m* industrialist; — *a* industrial; **stabilimento** — factory
industrializzare (ēn·dū·stryâ·lē·dzâ'rā) *vt* to industrialize
industrialmente (ēn·dū·stryâl·mān'tā) *adv* industrially
industriarsi (ēn·dū·stryâr'sē) *vr* to strive; to do one's utmost
industriosamente (ēn·dū·stryō·zâ·mān'tā) *adv* industriously
induttanza (ēn·dūt·tân'tsâ) *f* (*elec*) inductance
induttivo (ēn·dūt·tē'vō) *a* inductive
induttore (ēn·dūt·tō'rā) *m* (*elec*) inductor
induzione (ēn·dū·tsyō'nā) *f* induction
inebriare (ē·nā·bryâ'rā) *vt* to intoxicate, make drunk
inebriarsi (ē·nā·bryâr'sē) *vr* to go into raptures; to get drunk
inedia (ē·ne'dyâ) *f* starvation
inedito (ē·ne'dē·tō) *a* unpublished
ineducato (ē·nā·dū·kâ'tō) *a* ill-bred, rude
ineffabile (ē·nāf·fâ'bē·lā) *a* ineffable
inefficace (ē·nāf·fē·kâ'chā) *a* ineffectual, inefficacious
ineguaglianza (ē·nā·gwâ·lyân'tsâ) *f* inequality
ineguale (ē·nā·gwâ'lā) *a* uneven, unequal
ineluttabile (ē·nā·lūt·tâ'bē·lā) *a* inevitable
inerente (ē·nā·rān'tā) *a* inherent; concerning, with relation to; incidental
inerme (ē·nār'mā) *a* unarmed
inerpicarsi (ē·nār·pē·kâr'sē) *vr* to clamber
inerte (ē·nār'tā) *a* inert; inactive
inerzia (ē·ner'tsyâ) *f* inertia; inertness
inesatto (ē·nā·zât'tō) *a* inaccurate; inexact
inesauribile (ē·nā·zâū·rē'bē·lā) *a* inexhaustible
inesistente (ē·nā·zē·stān'tā) *a* nonexistant
inesorabile (ē·nā·zō·râ'bē·lā) *a* inexorable, relentless
inesorabilmente (ē·nā·zō·râ·bēl·mān'tā) *adv* inexorably
inesperto (ē·nā·spār'tō) *a* inexperienced, lacking in experience
inesplicabile (ē·nā·splē·kâ'bē·lā) *a* inexplicable
inesplorato (ē·nā·splō·râ'tō) *a* unexplored
inesploso (ē·nā·splō'zō) *a* unexploded
inestimabile (ē·nā·stē·mâ'bē·lā) *adv* invaluable, inestimable
inettitudine (ē·nāt·tē·tū'dē·nā) *f* ineptitude, incapacity, unfitness
inetto (ē·nāt'tō) *a* inept, unfit
inevaso (ē·nā·vâ'zō) *a* outstanding, pending
inevitabile (ē·nā·vē·tâ'bē·lā) *a* inevitable
inevitabilmente (ē·nā·vē·tâ·bēl·mān'tā) *adv* inevitably, unavoidably
inezia (ē·ne'tsyâ) *f* trifle
infallibile (ēn·fâl·lē'bē·lā) *a* infallible

infame (ēn·fâ'mā) *a* infamous, outrageous
infamia (ēn·fâ'myâ) *f* infamy, ignominy
infangare (ēn·fân·gâ'rā) *vt* to spatter with mud; to defame
infangarsi (ēn·fân·gâr'sē) *vr* to get muddy
infantile (ēn·fân·tē'lā) *a* infantile; **asilo —** kindergarten; **capriccio —** childish whim
infanzia (ēn·fân'tsyâ) *f* childhood; infancy
infarcire (ēn·fâr·chē'rā) *vt* to stuff; (*fig*) to cram
infarinare (ēn·fâ·rē·nâ'rā) *vt* to flour
infarinarsi (ēn·fâ·rē·nâr'sē) *vr* (*coll*) to powder oneself; (*fig*) to get a smattering of, dabble in
infarinatura (ēn·fâ·rē·nâ·tū'râ) *f* (*fig*) smattering; dabbling
infastidire (ēn·fâ·stē·dē'rā) *vt* to annoy, bother
infastidirsi (ēn·fâ·stē·dēr'sē) *vr* to be annoyed; to get bored
infaticabile (ēn·fâ·tē·kâ'bē·lā) *a* tireless
infatti (ēn·fât'tē) *adv* indeed, in fact
infatuazione (ēn·fâ·twâ·tsyō'nā) *f* infatuation
infausto (ēn·fâ'ū·stō) *a* unlucky; inauspicious
infedele (ēn·fā·dā'lā) *a* unfaithful; infidel
infedeltà (ēn·fā·dāl·tâ') *f* unfaithfulness; infidelity
infelice (ēn·fā·lē'chā) *a* unhappy
infelicità (ēn·fā·lē·chē·tâ') *f* unhappiness
inferiore (ēn·fā·ryō'rā) *a* inferior; lower
inferiorità (ēn·fā·ryō·rē·tâ') *f* inferiority
inferire (ēn·fā·rē'rā) *vt&i* to infer, deduce; — *vt* to inflict
infermeria (ēn·fār·mā·rē'â) *f* infirmary
infermiera (ēn·fār·myā'râ) *f* nurse
infermiere (ēn·fār·myā'rā) *m* male nurse
infermità (ēn·fār·mē·tâ') *f* infirmity
infermo (ēn·fār'mō) *a* ill, sick
infernale (ēn·fār·nâ'lā) *a* hellish
inferno (ēn·fār'nō) *m* hell
inferriata (ēn·fār·ryâ'tâ) *f* metal grating
infervorato (ēn·fār·vō·râ'tō) *a* fervent
infestare (ēn·fā·stâ'rā) *vt* to infest
infesto (ēn·fā'stō) *a* harmful
infettare (ēn·fāt·tâ'rā) *vt* to infect
infettarsi (ēn·fāt·târ'sē) *vr* to be infected
infettivo (ēn·fāt·tē'vō) *a* infectious
infetto (ēn·fāt'tō) *a* infected
infezione (ēn·fā·tsyō'nā) *f* infection
infiammabile (ēn·fyâm·mâ'bē·lā) *a* combustible, inflammable
infiammarsi (ēn·fyâm·mâr'sē) *vr* (*med*) to become inflamed; (*fig*) to become excited
infiammazione (ēn·fyâm·mâ·tsyō'nā) *f* inflammation
infido (ēn'fē·dō) *a* untrustworthy
infierire (ēn·fyā·rē'rā) *vi* to rage; to be merciless
infilare (ēn·fē·lâ'rā) *vt* to thread; to slip into, put on; to string
infiltrarsi (ēn·fēl·trâr'sē) *vr* to penetrate, infiltrate
infiltrazione (ēn·fēl·trâ·tsyō'nā) *f* infiltration, penetration
infimo (ēn'fē·mō) *a* lowest
infine (ēn·fē'nā) *adv* after all; at last
infingardo (ēn·fēn·gâr'dō) *a* lazy
infinità (ēn·fē·nē·tâ') *f* infinity; **un'— di gente** a crowd of people
infinitamente (ēn·fē·nē·tâ·mān'tā) *adv* infinitely
infinito (ēn·fē·nē'tō) *a&m* infinite; (*gram*) infinitive
infinocchiare (ēn·fē·nōk·kyâ'rā) *vt* to hoodwink; to fool
infischiarsi (ēn·fē·skyâr'sē) *vr* not to care a bit; to treat lightly
inflazione (ēn·flâ·tsyō'nā) *f* inflation
inflessibile (ēn·flās·sē'bē·lā) *a* inflexible, rigid
inflessibilmente (ēn·flās·sē·bēl·mān'tā) *adv* inflexibly, rigidly
infliggere * (ēn·flēj'jā·rā) *vt* to inflict
influente (ēn·flūān'tā) *a* prominent, influential
influenza (ēn·flūān'tsâ) *f* influence; (*med*) influenza
influenzare (ēn·flūan·tsâ'rā) *vt* to influence; to bias
influire (ēn·flūē'rā) *vi* to affect; to exert influence on
influsso (ēn·flūs'sō) *m* influence; influx
infocato (ēn·fō·kâ'tō) *a* inflamed; angry; red-hot
infondatezza (ēn·fōn·dâ·tā'tsâ) *f* lack of support
infondato (ēn·fōn·dâ'tō) *a* groundless
infondere * (ēn·fôn'dā·rā) *vt* to infuse; **— coraggio a** to give courage to
informare (ēn·fōr·mâ'rā) *vt* to inform; to acquaint
informarsi (ēn·fōr·mâr'sē) *vr* to inquire; to obtain information
informatore (ēn·fōr·mâ·tō'rā) *m* informant; informer
informazione (ēn·fōr·mâ·tsyō'nā) *f* information; inquiry; investigation; **servizio —** intelligence agency
informe (ēn·fōr'mā) *a* shapeless
informicolamento (ēn·fōr·mē·kō·lâ·mān'tō) *m* tingling sensation
infornare (ēn·fōr·nâ'rā) *vt* to place in the oven
infornata (ēn·fōr·nâ'tâ) *f* ovenful; batch
infortunio (ēn·fōr·tū'nyō) *m* accident
infossare (ēn·fōs·sâ'rā) *vt* to bury; to dig
infossato (ēn·fōs·sâ'tō) *a* fallen in, sunken; **occhi infossati** hollow eyes
infradiciare (ēn·frâ·dē·châ'rā) *vt* to soak; to drench
infradiciarsi (ēn·frâ·dē·châr'sē) *vr* to get soaked; to be drenched
inframmettere * (ēn·frâm·met'tā·rā) *vt* to interpose
inframmettersi * (ēn·frâm·met'tār·sē) *vr* to intervene; to interfere; to meddle
infrangere * (ēn·frân'jā·rā) *vt* to shatter, break; to violate
infrangersi * (ēn·frân'jār·sē) *vr* to break up; to be smashed; to shatter
infrangibile (ēn·frân·jē'bē·lā) *a* unbreakable; **vetro —** safety glass
infrazione (ēn·frâ·tsyō'nā) *f* infraction
infreddatura (ēn·frād·dâ·tū'râ) *f* cold

(*med*)
infruttifero (ēn·frūt·tē'fā·rō) *a* unprofitable, unfruitful; **capitale** -- capital not bearing interest
infuori (ēn·fwō'rē) *adv* out; outwards; **all'** — **di** except
infuriarse (ēn·fū·ryâr'sē) *vr* to lose one's temper
ingaggiare (ēn·gâj·jâ'rā) *vt* to enlist, hire; (*mech*) to start
ingannare (ēn·gân·nâ'rā) *vt* to deceive; — **il tempo** to while away the time
ingannarsi (ēn·gân·nâr'sē) *vr* to deceive oneself; to be mistaken
inganno (ēn·gân'nō) *m* deception, trick; fraud; stratagem
ingegnarsi (ēn·jā·nyâr'sē) *vr* to strive, try; to do everything possible
ingegnere (ēn·jā·nyā'rā) *m* engineer; — **elettrotecnico** electrical engineer
ingegneria (ēn·jā·nyā·rē'â) *f* engineering
ingegnosamente (ēn·jā·nyō·zâ·mān'tā) *adv* ingeniously
ingegnoso (ēn·jā·nyō'zō) *a* clever, witty
ingelosire (ēn·jā·lō·zē'rā) *vt* to make jealous, make envious
ingelosirsi (ēn·jā·lō·zēr'sē) *vr* to become jealous
ingenio (ēn·je'nyō) *m* brains, talent; wits
ingente (ēn·jān'tā) *a* huge
ingenuamente (ēn·jā·nwâ·mān'tā) *adv* innocently, ingenuously
ingenuità (ēn·jā·nwē·tâ') *f* ingenuousness
ingenuo (ēn·je'nwō) *a* naive
ingerenza (ēn·jā·rān'tsâ) *f* interference
ingerire (ēn·jā·rē'rā) *vt* to swallow
ingerirsi (ēn·jā·rēr'sē) *vr* to meddle
inghiottire (ēn·gyōt·tē'rā) *vt* to swallow; to engulf (*fig*)
ingiallire (ēn·jâl·lē'rā) *vt&i* to yellow, turn yellow
inginocchiarsi (ēn·jē·nōk·kyâr'sē) *vr* to kneel down, fall to one's knees
inginocchiatoio (ēn·jē·nōk·kyâ·tô'yō) *m* prie-dieu
ingiungere * (ēn·jūn'jā·rā) *vt* to command; to enjoin
ingiunzione (ēn·jūn·tsyō'nā) *f* injunction
ingiuria (ēn·jū'ryâ) *f* insult; abuse
ingiuriare (ēn·jū·ryâ'rā) *vt* to abuse; to insult
ingiuriosamente (ēn·jū·ryō·zâ·mān'tā) *adv* offensively; insultingly
ingiurioso (ēn·jū·ryō'zō) *a* outrageous; insulting; offending
ingiustamente (ēn·jū·stâ·mān'tā) *adv* unfairly, unjustly
ingiustificabile (ēn·jū·stē·fē·kâ'bē·lā) *a* unjustifiable
ingiustizia (ēn·jū·stē'tsyâ) *f* injustice
ingiusto (ēn·jū'stō) *a* unjust, unfair
inglese (ēn·glā'zā) *a&m* English
ingoiare (ēn·gō·yâ'rā) *vt* to swallow; to down
ingombrante (ēn·gōm·brân'tā) *a* bulky, encumbering
ingombrare (ēn·gōm·brâ'rā) *vt* to clutter; to encumber; (*rail*) to block (*tracks*)
ingombrarsi (ēn·gōm·brâr'sē) *vr* to become obstructed; to block up
ingombro (ēn·gōm'brō) *m* obstruction; impediment; — *a* encumbered; **essere d'— a qualcuno** to be in someone's way
ingordigia (ēn·gōr·dē'jâ) *f* greed, greediness; avarice
ingordo (ēn·gōr'dō) *a* gluttonous
ingorgare (ēn·gōr·gâ'rā) *vt* to bar the way; to obstruct; to choke up
ingorgo (ēn·gōr'gō) *m* obstruction; traffic jam; (*med*) engorgement
ingranaggio (ēn·grâ·nâj'jō) *m* gearing, gears; works; **ingranaggi d'orologio** cogwheels of a clock
ingranare (ēn·grâ·nâ'rā) *vt* (*auto*) to throw into gear; to engage; (*mech*) to mesh
ingrandimento (ēn·grân·dē·mān'tō) *m* enlargement; amplification; **lente d'—** magnifying glass
ingrandire (ēn·grân·dē'rā) *vt* to enlarge; to increase
ingrandirsi (ēn·grân·dēr'sē) *vr* to increase; to grow larger
ingrassaggio (ēn·grâs·sâj'jō) *m* greasing, lubrication
ingrassare (ēn·grâs·sâ'rā) *vt* to fatten; to grease; — *vi* to get fat
ingrassarsi (ēn·grâs·sâr'sē) *vr* (*fig*) to take pleasure in; to get fat; to become larger; to increase
ingrassatore (ēn·grâs·sâ·tō'rā) *m* greaser; grease gun
ingratitudine (ēn·grâ·tē·tū'dē·nā) *f* ingratitude
ingrato (ēn·grâ'tō) *a* ungrateful; hard, unpleasant; sterile, unproductive (*soil*)
ingresso (ēn·grās'sō) *m* entrance; — **libero** free admission; **vietato l'—** no admittance
ingrossamento (ēn·grōs·sâ·mān'tō) *m* swelling; increase; thickening
ingrossare (ēn·grōs·sâ'rā) *vt* to increase, swell; to make bigger
ingrossarsi (ēn·grōs·sâr'sē) *vr* to increase; to become bigger; to swell; to grow rough (*sea*)
ingrosso (ēn·grōs·sō) **all'—** wholesale; approximately
inguaiare (ēn·gwâ·yâ'rā) *vt* to get into trouble; to cause trouble
inguaiarsi (ēn·gwâ·yâr'sē) *vr* to get oneself into trouble
inguantarsi (ēn·gwân·târ'sē) *vr* to put on one's gloves
inguaribile (ēn·gwâ·rē'bē·lā) *a* incurable
inguine (ēn'gwē·nā) *m* (*anat*) groin
inibire (ē·nē·bē'rā) *vt* to inhibit
inibizione (ē·nē·bē·tsyō'nā) *f* inhibition
iniettare (ē·nyāt·tâ'rā) *vt* to inject
iniettore (ē·nyāt·tō'rā) *m* injector; jet
iniezione (ē·nyā·tsyō'nā) *f* injection
inimicizia (ē·nē·mē·chē'tsyâ) *f* enmity
ininterrottamente (ē·nēn·tār·rōt·tâ·mān'tā) *adv* uninterruptedly
ininterrotto (ē·nēn·tār·rōt'tō) *a* uninterrupted
iniquità (ē·nē·kwē·tâ') *f* iniquity; injustice

iniziale (ē·nē·tsyâ'lā) *a&f* initial
iniziare (ē·nē·tsyâ'rā) *vt* to start; to initiate; to commence
iniziarsi (ē·nē·tsyâr'sē) *vr* to begin, commence
iniziativa (ē·nē·tsyâ·tē'vâ) *f* initiative
inizio (ē·nē'tsyō) *m* beginning
innamorare (ēn·nâ·mō·râ'rā) *vt* to captivate, charm; to make fall in love
innamorarsi (ēn·nâ·mō·râr'sē) *vr* to become enamored; to fall in love
innamorato (ēn·nâ·mō·râ'tō) *a* in love; — *m* sweetheart, lover
innanzi (ēn·nân'tsē) *prep* before; — **tutto** above all, first
innato (ēn·nâ'tō) *a* innate
innegabile (ēn·nā·gâ'bē·lā) *a* undeniable
innestare (ēn·nā·stâ'rā) *vt* to graft; (*mech*) to throw into gear; to inoculate
innesto (ēn·nā'stō) *m* inoculation; graft; — **del vaccino** vaccination
inno (ēn'nō) *m* hymn; anthem
innocente (ēn·nō·chān'tā) *a* innocent; guiltless; simple
innocentemente (ēn·nō·chān·tā·mān'tā) *adv* innocently
innocenza (ēn·nō·chān'tsâ) *f* innocence; simplicity
innocuo (ēn·nô'kwō) *a* harmless
innovazione (ēn·nō·vâ·tsyō'nā) *f* innovation, change
inoculare (ē·nō·kū·lâ'rā) *vt* to inoculate
inoculazione (ē·nō·kū·lâ·tsyō'nā) *f* inoculation
inodoro (ē·nō·dō'rō) *a* odorless
inoffensivo (ē·nōf·fān·sē'vō) *a* harmless, inoffensive
inoltrare (ē·nōl·trâ'rā) *vt* to forward
inoltrarsi (ē·nōl·trâr'sē) *vr* to penetrate; to advance
inoltrato (ē·nōl·trâ'tō) *a* advanced; forwarded; **in inverno** — late in winter
inoltre (ē·nōl'trā) *adv* besides; furthermore
inoltro (ē·nōl'trō) *m* forwarding
inondare (ē·nōn·dâ'rā) *vt* to flood
inondazione (ē·nōn·dâ·tsyō'nā) *f* flooding; inundation
inoperoso (ē·nō·pā·rō'zō) *a* idle, indolent; inactive
inopportuno (ē·nōp·pōr·tū'nō) *a* awkward, inopportune; badly timed
inorganico (ē·nōr·gâ'nē·kō) *a* inorganic
inorgoglirsi (ē·nōr·gō·lyēr'sē) *vr* to swell with pride
inorridire (ē·nōr·rē·dē'rā) *vt* to instill horror in; to frighten; to terrify; — *vi* to be terrified; to become horror-struck; to be filled with fear
inospitabile (ē·nō·spē·tâ'bē·lā) *a* inhospitable, forbidding
inosservato (ē·nōs·sār·vâ'tō) *a* unobserved
inossidabile (ē·nōs·sē·dâ'bē·lā) *a* stainless (*metal*)
inquietante (ēn·kwēā·tân'tā) *a* alarming
inquietare (ēn·kwēā·tâ'rā) *vt* to make nervous; to worry; to upset
inquietarsi (ēn·kwēā·târ'sē) *vr* to become alarmed; to grow uneasy
inquieto (ēn·kwēā'tō) *a* restless; upset; apprehensive
inquietudine (ēn·kwēā·tū'dē·nā) *f* apprehension, nervousness
inquilino (ēn·kwē·lē'nō) *m* tenant
inquisizione (ēn·kwē·zē·tsyō'nā) *f* inquisition
insabbiare (ēn·sâb·byâ'rā) *vt* to sand, fill with sand; (*fig*) to pigeonhole
insabbiarsi (ēn·sâb·byâr'sē) *vr* to get stuck in the sand; (*coll*) to be hindered, be delayed; to be handicapped
insaccare (ēn·sâk·kâ'rā) *vt* to put in a sack; to bag
insaccato (ēn·sâk·kâ'tō) *a* in a sack; bagged; **carne insaccata** sausage
insalata (ēn·sâ·lâ'tâ) *f* salad
insalatiera (ēn·sâ·lâ·tyā'râ) *f* salad bowl
insalubre (ēn·sâ·lū'brā) *a* insalubrious, unhealthful
insanabile (ēn·sâ·nâ'bē·lā) *a* incurable
insanguinare (ēn·sân·gwē·nâ'rā) *vt* to stain with blood
insaponare (ēn·sâ·pō·nâ'rā) *vt* to lather; to soap
insaponarsi (ēn·sâ·pō·nâr'sē) *vr* to lather oneself; to soap oneself
insaponata (ēn·sâ·pō·nâ'tâ) *f* lathering; soaping
insapore (ēn·sâ·pō'rā) *a* tasteless, insipid
insaputa (ēn·sâ·pū'tâ) **all'— di** unknown to, without one's knowledge
insaziabile (ēn·sâ·tsyâ'bē·lā) *a* unappeasable, insatiable, implacable
inscenare (ēn·shā·nâ'rā) *vt* to promote; to stage
inségna (ēn·sā'nyâ) *f* flag; sign, indication
insegnamento (ēn·sā·nyâ·mān'tō) *m* teaching; tuition; education
insegnante (ēn·sā·nyân'tā) *m&f* teacher
insegnare (ēn·sā·nyâ'rā) *vt* to teach
inseguimento (ēn·sā·gwē·mān'tō) *m* chase, pursuit
inseguire (ēn·sā·gwē'rā) *vt* to pursue, chase
insellare (ēn·sāl·lâ'rā) *vt* to saddle
insenatura (ēn·sā·nâ·tū'râ) *f* harbor, inlet
insensibile (ēn·sān·sē'bē·lā) *a* insensible; hardhearted, insensitive
insensibilità (ēn·sān·sē·bē·lē·tâ') *f* indifference, insensitivity; insensibility
inseparabile (ēn·sā·pâ·râ'bē·lā) *a* inseparable; inextricable
inseparabilmente (ēn·sā·pâ·râ·bēl·mān'tā) *adv* inseparably; inextricably
inserire (ēn·sā·rē'rā) *vt* to insert
inserirsi (ēn·sā·rēr'sē) *vr* to be contained in, form part of
inservibile (ēn·sār·vē'bē·lā) *a* useless
inserviente (ēn·sār·vyān'tā) *m* attendant
inserzione (ēn·sār·tsyō'nā) *f* advertisement; insertion
inserzionista (ēn·sār·tsyō·nē'stâ) *m* advertiser
insetticida (ēn·sāt·tē·chē'dâ) *m* insecticide
insetto (ēn·sāt'tō) *m* insect
insidia (ēn·sē'dyâ) *f* trap, snare; peril; **–re**

(ēn·sē·dyâ'rā) *vt* to tempt; to trap
insidiosamente (ēn·sē·dyō·zâ·mān'tā) *adv* insidiously
insidioso (ēn·sē·dyō'zō) *a* insidious
insieme (ēn·syā'mā) *adv* together; — *m* ensemble, whole; **mettere una fortuna —** to amass a fortune; **mettere —** (*mech*) to assemble
insigne (ēn·sē'nyā) *a* famous, notable; notorious
insignificante (ēn·sē·nyē·fē·kân'tā) *a* insignificant, inconsequential; lacking in meaning
insindacabile (en·sēn·dâ·kâ'bē·lā) *a* unobjectionable; irreproachable; undisputable
insinuante (ēn·sē·nwân'tā) *a* insinuating, winning
insinuare (ēn·sē·nwâ'rā) *vt* to insinuate, suggest; to introduce, instill
insinuarsi (ēn·sē·nwâr'sē) *vr* to creep into, enter stealthily
insipido (ēn·sē'pē·dō) *a* tasteless; uninteresting
insistente (ēn·sē·stān'tā) *a* insistent
insistere * (ēn·sē'stā·rā) *vi* to insist
insoddisfatto (ēn·sōd·dē·sfât'tō) *a* dissatisfied; displeased
insofferenza (ēn·sōf·fā·rān'tsâ) *f* impatience; intolerance
insolazione (ēn·sō·lâ·tsyō'nā) *f* sunstroke
insolente (ēn·sō·lān'tā) *a* insolent, impudent
insolenza (ēn·sō·lān'tsâ) *f* sauciness; insolence, impudence
insolitamente (ēn·sō·lē·tâ·mān'tā) *adv* seldom, infrequently
insolito (ēn·sô'lē·tō) *a* unusual, rare
insolubile (ēn·sō·lū'bē·lā) *a* insolvable; insoluble
insolvente (ēn·sōl·vān'tā) *a* insolvent
insolvibile (ēn·sōl·vē'bē·lā) *a* insolvent; insoluble; uncollectible
insomma (ēn·sōm'mâ) *adv* in conclusion; briefly; after all
insonne (ēn·sōn'nā) *a* sleepless
insonnia (ēn·sôn'nyâ) *f* insomnia
insopportabile (ēn·sōp·pōr·tâ'bē·lā) *adv* unbearable
insormontabile (ēn·sōr·mōn·tâ'bē·lā) *adv* insurmountable, insuperable
insospettabile (ēn·sō·spāt·tâ'bē·lā) *a* above suspicion; not suspect
insostenibile (ēn·sō·stā·nē'bē·lā) *a* indefensible, untenable; insufferable
instabile (ēn·stâ'bē·lā) *a* unsure, unsteady, insecure
installare (ēn·stâl·lâ'rā) *vt* to install; to set up
installarsi (ēn·stâl·lâr'sē) *vr* to get settled
installazione (ēn·stâl·lâ·tsyō'nā) *f* installation
instancabile (ēn·stân·kâ'bē·lā) *a* indefatigable, unwearying
instancabilmente (ēn·stân·kâ·bēl·mān'tā) *adv* untiringly
instaurare (ēn·stâū·râ'rā) *vt* to establish; to institute
instaurazione (ēn·stâū·râ·tsyō'nā) *f* establishing, installation
insù (ēn·sū') *adv* upward, up; **naso all'—** pug nose
insubordinazione (ēn·sū·bōr·dē·nâ·tsyō'nā) *f* insubordination
insuccesso (ēn·sū·chās'sō) *m* failure
insudiciare (ēn·sū·dē·châ'rā) *vt* to tarnish; to soil
insudiciarsi (ēn·sū·dē·châr'sē) *vr* to get dirty; to become tarnished
insufficiente (ēn·sūf·fē·chān'tā) *a* insufficient
insufficienza (ēn·sūf·fē·chān'tsâ) *f* insufficiency; **— di prove** lack of sufficient evidence
insulina (ēn·sū·lē'nâ) *f* insulin
insulso (ēn·sūl'sō) *a* vapid, stupid, empty
insultare (ēn·sūl·tâ'rā) *vt* to insult; to vilify
insulto (ēn·sūl'tō) *m* insult; (*med*) attack, stroke
insuperabile (ēn·sū·pā·râ'bē·lā) *a* unsurmountable
insuperbirsi (ēn·sū·pār·bēr'sē) *vr* to fill with pride; to become arrogant
insurrezionale (ēn·sūr·rā·tsyō·nâ'lā) *a* insurgent, insurrectionary
insurrezione (ēn·sūr·rā·tsyō'nā) *f* uprising, insurrection
intaccare (ēn·tâk·kâ'rā) *vt* to notch; to indent; to damage; to eat away
intagliare (ēn·tâ·lyâ'rā) *vt* to carve; to sculpt
intagliato (ēn·tâ·lyâ'tō) *a* carved
intagliatore (ēn·tâ·lyâ·tō'rā) *m* engraver; sculptor
intaglio (ēn·tâ'lyō) *m* carving; intaglio
intangibile (ēn·tân·jē'bē·lā) *a* intangible; impalpable
intanto (ēn·tân'tō) *adv* meanwhile; **— che** until; while
intarsiare (ēn·târ·syâ'rā) *vt* to veneer; to inlay
intarsio (ēn·târ'syō) *m* veneering; inlaid work
intasato (ēn·tâ·zâ'tō) *a* stopped up; clogged
intatto (ēn·tât'tō) *a* intact
integrale (ēn·tā·grâ'lā) *a* whole; integral; **pane —** wholewheat bread
integrare (ēn·tā·grâ'rā) *vt* to integrate
integrazione (ēn·tā·grâ·tsyō'nā) *f* integration
integrità (ēn·tā·grē·tâ') *f* integrity
intelaiare (ēn·tā·lâ·yâ'rā) *vt* to frame
intelaiatura (ēn·tā·lâ·yâ·tū'râ) *f* frame; chassis (*auto*)
intelletto (ēn·tāl·lāt'tō) *m* intellect; judgment
intellettuale (ēn·tāl·lāt·twâ'lā) *a&m* intellectual
intelligente (ēn·tāl·lē·jān'tā) *a* intelligent; skillful
intelligentemente (ēn·tāl·lē·jān·tā·mān'tā) *adv* skillfully; intelligently
intelligenza (ēn·tāl·lē·jān'tsâ) *f* intelligence
intemerato (ēn·tā·mā·râ'tō) *a* spotless, pure, honorable

intemperante (ēn·tām·pā·rân'tā) *a* intemperate; immoderate
intemperanza (ēn·tām·pā·rân'tsâ) *f* intemperance; immoderation
intemperie (ēn·tām·pe'ryā) *fpl* bad weather, unpleasant weather
intempestivamente (ēn·tām·pā·stē·vâ·mān'tā) *adv* out of turn; at the wrong time
intempestivo (ēn·tām·pā·stē'vō) *a* badly timed, inopportune
intendente (ēn·tān·dān'tā) *m* superintendent, head
intendenza (ēn·tān·dān'tsâ) *f* superintendency; — **di finanza** excise office
intendere * (ēn·ten'dā·rā) *vt* to understand; to plan, intend; **darla ad** — to lead one to believe
intendersi * (ēn·ten'dār·sē) *vr* to be well versed in, know a great deal about; to come to terms; **intendersela** to be in agreement; to get along well with one another
intendimento (ēn·tān·dē·mān'tō) *m* understanding; aim, purpose
intenditore (ēn·tān·dē·tō'rā) *m* connoisseur
intenerire (ēn·tā·nā·rē'rā) *vt* to move, stir (*emotions*); to soften
intenerirsi (ēn·tā·nā·rēr'sē) *vr* to be moved to pity, feel compassion; to become tender
intensamente (ēn·tān·sâ·mān'tā) *adv* deeply, intensely
intensificare (ēn·tān·sē·fē·kâ'rā) *vt* to intensify; to heighten; to redouble
intensità (ēn·tān·sē·tâ') *f* intensity
intensivo (ēn·tān·sē'vō) *a* intensive
intenso (ēn·tān'sō) *a* intense
intentare (ēn·tān·tâ'rā) *vt* (*law*) to bring (*action*), file (*suit*)
intento (ēn·tān'tō) *m* aim; — *a* intent, concentrated
intenzionale (ēn·tān·tsyō·nâ'lā) *a* deliberate
intenzionalmente (ēn·tān·tsyō·nâl·mān'·tā) *adv* intentionally
intenzionato (ēn·tān·tsyō·nâ'tō) *a* inclined, predisposed
intenzione (ēn·tān·tsyō'nā) *f* intention; **aver l'** — **di fare** to mean to do; **aver buone intenzioni** to mean well
interamente (ēn·tā·râ·mān'tā) *adv* entirely
interasse (ēn·tā·râs'sā) *m* (*auto*) wheelbase
intercalare (ēn·tār·kâ·lâ'rā) *vt* to insert
intercedere (ēn·tār·che'dā·rā) *vi* to intercede; to intervene
intercessione (ēn·tār·chās·syō'nā) *f* intercession
intercettare (ēn·tār·chāt·tâ'rā) *vt* to intercept; to tap (*telephone*)
intercezione (ēn·tār·chā·tsyō'nā) *f* interception; intervention
intercomunicante (ēn·tār·kō·mū·nē·kân'tā) *a* connecting, linking
intercorrere * (ēn·tār·kôr'rā·rā) *vi* to elapse; to come between
intercostale (ēn·tār·kō·stâ'lā) *a* (*anat*) intercostal
intercutaneo (ēn·tār·kū·tâ'nā·ō) *a* subcutaneous
interdetto (ēn·tār·dāt'tō) *a* forbidden, prohibited
interdire * (ēn·tār·dē'rā) *vt* to forbid; to disqualify
interdizione (ēn·tār·dē·tsyō'nā) *f* loss of civil rights; restraint; interdiction
interessamento (ēn·tā·rās·sâ·mān'tō) *m* interest, care
interessante (ēn·tā·rās·sân'tā) *a* interesting
interessare (ēn·tā·rās·sâ'rā) *vt&i* to interest; to concern; to be important; — **qualcuno in un affare** to form a business partnership with someone
interessarsi (ēn·tā·rās·sâr'sē) *vr* to take an interest in; to attend to
interessato (ēn·tā·rās·sâ'tō) *a* interested; partial; having an interest
interesse (ēn·tā·rās'sā) *m* interest
interessenza (ēn·tā·rās·sān'tsâ) *f* (*com*) percentage, commission
interferenza (ēn·tār·fā·rān'tsâ) *f* interference; meddling
interferire (ēn·tār·fā·rē'rā) *vi* to interfere
interiezione (ēn·tā·ryā·tsyō'nā) *f* interjection
interim (ēn'tā·rēm) *m* interim; meanwhile
interinale (ēn·tā·rē·nâ'lā) *a* provisional, temporary
interiora (ēn·tā·ryō'râ) *fpl* intestines
interiore (ēn·tā·ryō'rā) *a&m* interior
interlocutore (ēn·tār·lō·kū·tō'rā) *m* questioner; speaker
interloquire (ēn·tār·lō·kwē'rā) *vi* to break in (*conversation*); to intrude, interfere
interludio (ēn·tār·lū'dyō) *m* interlude
intermediario (ēn·tār·mā·dyâ'ryō) *m* intermediary, middleman
intermezzo (ēn·tār·mā'dzō) *m* intermezzo, intermission; interval
interminabile (ēn·tār·mē·nâ'bē·lā) *a* endless
intermittente (ēn·tār·mēt·tān'tā) *a* intermittent, recurrent
internamente (ēn·tār·nâ·mān'tā) *adv* internally, within
internare (ēn·tār·nâ'rā) *vt* to confine, intern
internazionale (ēn·tār·nâ·tsyō·nâ'lā) *a* international
internazionalista (ēn·tār·nâ·tsyō·nâ·lē'·stâ) *m* internationalist
interno (ēn·tār'nō) *a* internal; **commercio** — domestic trade; — *m* interior; **Ministro dell'**— Secretary of the Interior
intero (ēn·tā'rō) *m* total, whole; — *a* complete, entire
interporre * (ēn·tār·pōr'rā) *vt* to interpose; to interject
interporsi * (ēn·tār·pōr'sē) *vr* to intercede; to mediate
interposizione (ēn·tār·pō·zē·tsyō'nā) *f* intervention
interpretare (ēn·tār·prā·tâ'rā) *vt* to interpret; to construe

interpretazione (ēn·tār·prā·tâ·tsyō'nā) *f* version, account; interpretation; **— erronea** misinterpretation
interprete (ēn·ter'prā·tā) *m&f* interpreter; actor, actress
interrogante (ēn·tār·rō·gân'tā) *a* questioning
interrogare (ēn·tār·rō·gâ'rā) *vt* to question; query; to consult
interrogativo (ēn·tār·rō·gâ·tē'vō) *a* interrogative; **punto —** question mark
interrogatorio (ēn·tār·rō·gâ·tô'ryō) *m* questioning; cross-examination
interrompere * (ēn·tār·rôm'pā·rā) *vt* to interrupt; *(elec)* to disconnect, turn off
interrompersi * (ēn·tār·rôm'pār·sē) *vr* to stop; to interrupt oneself
interrotto (ēn·tār·rōt'tō) *a* interrupted; discontinued
interruttore (ēn·tār·rūt·tō'rā) *m* interrupter; switch *(elec)*
interruzione (ēn·tār·rū·tsyō'nā) *f* interruption; **senza —** uninterruptedly, continuously
interurbano (ēn·tā·rūr·bâ'nō) *a* long-distance
intervallo (ēn·tār·vâl'lō) *m* break; interval
intervenire * (ēn·tār·vā·nē'rā) *vi* to intervene; to take part in, participate in
intervento (ēn·tār·vān'tō) *m* intervention; attendance
intervista (ēn·tār·vē'stâ) *f* interview; **–re** (ēn·tār·vē·stâ'rā) *vt* to interview
intesa (ēn·tā'zâ) *f* understanding, agreement
inteso (ēn·tā'zō) *a* heard; understood; **non darsi per —** not to give a rap; to turn a deaf ear
intestato (ēn·tā·stâ'tō) *a* headed; *(com)* registered; *(law)* intestate; **carta intestata** letterhead
intestazione (ēn·tā·stâ·tsyō'nā) *f* headline, heading
intestino (ēn·tā·stē'nō) *m* intestine; **—** *a* domestic; internal
intimamente (ēn·tē·mâ·mān'tā) *adv* intimately, closely
intimare (ēn·tē·mâ'rā) *vt* to summon; to intimate
intimazione (ēn·tē·mâ·tsyō'nā) *f* injunction, order
intimidazione (ēn·tē·mē·dâ·tsyō'nā) *f* intimidation; threat
intimità (ēn·tē·mē·tâ') *f* intimacy; confidence
intimo (ēn'tē·mō) *a* intimate; private
intingere * (ēn·tēn'jā·rā) *vt&i* to dip
intingolo (ēn·tēn'gō·lō) *m* gravy, sauce
intirizzire (ēn·tē·rē·tsē'rā) *vt* to freeze, benumb
intitolare (ēn·tē·tō·lâ'rā) *vt* to dedicate; to name
intitolato (ēn·tē·tō·lâ'tō) *a* entitled, named
intollerabile (ēn·tōl·lā·râ'bē·lā) *a* unbearable; insufferable
intollerante (ēn·tōl·lā·rân'tā) *a* intolerant
intolleranza (ēn·tōl·lā·rân'tsâ) *f* intolerance
intonaco (ēn·tô'nâ·kō) *m* plaster
intonazione (ēn·tō·nâ·tsyō'nā) *f* intonation
intontire (ēn·tōn·tē'rā) *vt* to daze, stun
intontirsi (ēn·tōn·tēr'sē) *vr* to be dazed; to be stunned
intontito (ēn·tōn·tē'tō) *a* stunned; dazed
intoppo (ēn·tōp'pō) *m* obstacle; *(fig)* difficulty
intorbidire (ēn·tōr·bē·dē'rā) *vt* to muddy; to confuse
intorbidirsi (ēn·tōr·bē·dēr'sē) *vr* to grow muddy; to become confused
intorno (ēn·tōr'nō) *adv* around
intossicare (ēn·tōs·sē·kâ'rā) *vt* to poison
intossicazione (ēn·tōs·sē·kâ·tsyō'nā) *f* poisoning; **— da cibi** ptomaine poisoning
intraducibile (ēn·trâ·dū·chē'bē·lā) *a* untranslatable
intralciare (ēn·trâl·châ'rā) *vt* to obstruct
intralcio (ēn·trâl'chō) *m* obstacle, obstruction
intrallazzo (ēn·trâl·lâ'tsō) *m* *(sl)* racket, black market
intransigente (ēn·trân·sē·jān'tā) *a* uncompromising, hard
intransigenza (ēn·trân·sē·jān'tsâ) *f* severity, intransigence
intransitivo (ēn·trân·sē·tē'vō) *a* *(gram)* intransitive
intraprendente (ēn·trâ·prān·dān'tā) *a* resourceful; enterprising, industrious
intraprendenza (ēn·trâ·prān·dān'tsâ) *f* initiative, enterprise, industry
intraprendere * (ēn·trâ·pren'dā·rā) *vt* to undertake; to take on
intrattabile (ēn·trât·tâ'bē·lā) *a* hard; intractable, unruly
intrattenere * (ēn·trât·tā·nā'rā) *vt* to entertain
intrattenersi * (ēn·trât·tā·nār'sē) *vr* to dwell on; to linger; to pause
intrattenimento (ēn·trât·tā·nē·mān'tō) *m* entertainment
intrattenitrice (ēn·trât·tā·nē·trē'chā) *f* B-girl
intravenoso (ēn·trâ·vā·nō'zō) *a* intravenous
intreccio (ēn·tre'chō) *m* story, plot
intrepido (ēn·tre'pē·dō) *a* brave, intrepid
intrigante (ēn·trē·gân'tā) *a* scheming, tricky
intrigare (ēn·trē·gâ'rā) *vt* to plot; to scheme
intrigarsi (ēn·trē·gâr'sē) *vr* to meddle
intrigo (ēn·trē'gō) *m* plot, intrigue, scheme
intrinseco (ēn·trēn'sā·kō) *a* intrinsic
intriso (ēn·trē'zō) *a* sodden, soaked; **—** *m* mixture
introdotto (ēn·trō·dōt'tō) *a* shown in, admitted *(entry)*; introduced
introdurre * (ēn·trō·dūr'rā) *vt* to insert; to show in; to introduce
introduzione (ēn·trō·dū·tsyō'nā) *f* introduction
introitare (ēn·trōē·tâ'rā) *vt* to collect; to

cash
introito (ēn·trô'ē·tō) *m* receipts; income; *(eccl)* introit
intromettersi * (ēn·trō·met'tār·sē) *vt* to interfere with, meddle in; to arbitrate
introspezione (ēn·trō·spā·tsyō'nā) *f* introspection, self-examination
intruso (ēn·trū'zō) *m* intruder
intuire (ēn·twē'rā) *vi* to guess; to sense; to intuit
intuito (ēn·tū'ē·tō) *m* intuition; insight
intuizione (ēn·twē·tsyō'nā) *f* intuition; intuitiveness
inumano (ē·nū·mâ'nō) *a* inhuman; brutal
inumidire (ē·nū·mē·dē'rā) *vt* to moisten, dampen
inumidirsi (ē·nū·mē·dēr'sē) *vr* to become moist, dampen
inusitato (ē·nū·zē·tâ'tō) *a* unusual, strange; obsolete
inutile (ē·nū'tē·lā) *a* useless
inutilità (ē·nū·tē·lē·tâ') *f* uselessness; futility
inutilmente (ē·nū·tēl·mān'tā) *adv* uselessly; in vain
invadente (ēn·vâ·dān'tā) *a* aggressive, pushy; invading
invadenza (ēn·vâ·dān'tsâ) *f* aggressiveness, pushiness; interference
invadere * (ēn·vâ'dā·rā) *vt* to invade
invalidità (ēn·vâ·lē·dē·tâ') *f* invalidity
invalido (ēn·vâ'lē·dō) *a&m* invalid; — **di guerra** disabled war veteran
invano (ēn·vâ'nō) *adv* in vain, vainly, to no avail
invariabile (ēn·vâ·ryâ'bē·lā) *a* invariable; unvarying
invasione (ēn·vâ·zyō'nā) *f* invasion; incursion
invasore (ēn·vâ·zō'rā) *m* invader
invecchiare (ēn·vāk·kyâ'rā) *vt* to age, make old; — *vi* to become old, age
invece (ēn·vā'chā) *adv* on the contrary; rather, instead
inventare (ēn·vān·tâ'rā) *vt* to invent, create; to discover
inventario (ēn·vān·tâ'ryō) *f* inventory
inventiva (ēn·vān·tē'vâ) *f* inventiveness
inventivo (ēn·vān·tē'vō) *a* inventive, creative
inventore (ēn·vān·tō'rā) *m* inventor
invenzione (ēn·vān·tsyō'nā) *f* invention; **brevetto d'—** patent
invernale (ēn·vār·nâ'lā) *a* winter
inverno (ēn·vār'nō) *m* winter
invero (ēn·vā'rō) *adv* really, indeed
inverosimile (ēn·vā·rō·sē'mē·lā) *a* unlikely; hard to believe; implausible
inversamente (ēn·vār·sâ·mān'tā) *adv* inversely
inversione (ēn·vār·syō'nā) *f* reverse; reversal; inversion
inverso (ēn·vār'sō) *a* inverted, inverse; **senso** — opposite direction; — *adv* toward; **all'—** backwards; **all'inversa** badly, wrong
invertibile (ēn·vār·tē'bē·lā) *a* reversible
invertire (ēn·vār·tē'rā) *vt* to reverse; to invert
investigare (ēn·vā·stē·gâ'rā) *vt* to investigate; to research
investigatore (ēn·vā·stē·gâ·tō'rā) *m* investigator; — **privato** private investigator, detective
investigazione (ēn·vā·stē·gâ·tsyō'nā) *f* research; investigation; scrutiny
investimento (ēn·vā·stē·mān'tō) *m (com)* investment; collision, smashup
investire (ēn·vā·stē'rā) *vt* to invest; to run over; to smash into; to assail
investirsi (ēn·vā·stēr'sē) *vr* to collide with, crash into; *(naut)* to run aground; to take a deep interest; to go into thoroughly
invetriata (ēn·vā·tryâ'tâ) *f* skylight; glass door
invettiva (ēn·vāt·tē'vâ) *f* invective, vituperation
invidia (ēn·vē'dyâ) *n* jealousy, envy; **-bile** (ēn·vē·dyâ'bē·lā) *a* enviable
invincibile (ēn·vēn·chē'bē·lā) *a* invincible
invio (ēn·vē'ō) *m* shipment; remittance
invitante (ēn·vē·tân'tā) *a* inviting
invitare (ēn·vē·tâ'rā) *vt* to invite
invitato (ēn·vē·tâ'tō) *a* invited; — *m* guest
invito (ēn·vē'tō) *m* invitation
invocare (ēn·vō·kâ'rā) *vt* to invoke; to call upon
invocazione (ēn·vō·kâ·tsyō'nā) *f* appeal; invocation
involgere * (ēn·vôl'jā·rā) *vt* to involve; to envelop
involontariamente (ēn·vō·lōn·tâ·ryâ·mān'tā) *adv* involuntarily; unintentionally
involtini (ēn·vōl·tē'nē) *mpl* meat rolls
involto (ēn·vōl'tō) *m* package; — *a* wrapped
involucro (ēn·vô'lū·krō) *m* wrapper; cover; envelope
inzuccherare (ēn·dzūk·kā·râ'rā) *vt* to sweeten, put sugar in; *(fig)* to wheedle
inzuppare (en·dzūp·pâ'rā) *vt* to soak; to dunk
inzupparsi (ēn·dzūp·pâr'sē) *vr* to get drenched, get soaked to the skin
io (ē'ō) *pron* I; — **stesso** I myself
iodio (yô'dyō) *m* iodine
iosa (yō'sâ) *adv* **a** — in great quantity, in abundance
iperbole (ē·per'bō·lā) *f* hyperbole; *(geom)* hyperbola
iperbolico (ē·pār·bô'lē·kō) *a* hyperbolic, given to hyperbole
ipersonico (ē·pār·sô'nē·kō) *a* hypersonic
ipnosi (ēp·nō'zē) *f* hypnosis; trance
ipnotismo (ēp·nō·tē'zmō) *m* hypnotism
ipnotizzare (ēp·nō·tē·dzâ'rā) *vt* to hypnotize
ipocrisia (ē·pō·krē·zē'â) *f* hypocrisy
ipocrita (ē·pô'krē·tâ) *m* hypocrite
ipoteca (ē·pō·tā'kâ) *f* mortgage
ipotenusa (ē·pō·tā·nū'zâ) *f* hypotenuse
ipotesi (ē·pô'tā·zē) *f* hypothesis; assumption
ippica (ēp'pē·kâ) *f* horse racing
ippico (ēp'pē·kō) *a* relating to horses

ippodromo (ēp·pô′drō·mō) *m* racetrack
ippopotamo (ēp·pō·pô′tâ·mō) *m* hippopotamus
ira (ē′râ) *f* anger, wrath
iracheno (ē·râ·kā′nō) *a&m* Iraqi
Irak, Iraq (ē′râk) *m* Iraq
iranico (ē·râ′nē·kō) *a&m* Iranian
irascibile (ē·râ·shē′bē·lā) *a* irascible, short-tempered
irato (ē·râ′tō) *a* angry, wrathful
iride (ē′rē·dā) *f* iris; rainbow
Irlanda (ēr·lân′dâ) *f* Ireland
irlandese (ēr·lân·dā′zā) *a&m* Irish; — *m* Irishman
ironia (ē·rō·nē′â) *f* irony
ironico (ē·rô′nē·kō) *a* ironic; sarcastic
irradiare (ēr·râ·dyâ′rā) *vt* to radiate; to irradiate
irradiarsi (ēr·râ·dyâr′sē) *vr* to shine, radiate
irradiazione (ēr·râ·dyâ·tsyō′nā) *f* irradiation, shining
irragionevole (ēr·râ·jō·ne′vō·lā) *a* unreasonable; unfair
irreale (ēr·rā·â′lā) *a* unreal
irrealtà (ēr·rā·âl·tâ′) *f* unreality
irregolare (ēr·rā·gō·lâ′rā) *a* irregular; uneven
irregolarità (ēr·rā·gō·lâ·rē·tâ′) *f* irregularity; nonconformity; disorder
irremovibile (ēr·rā·mō·vē′bē·lā) *a* irremovable; steadfast, firm
irreparabile (ēr·rā·pâ·râ′bē·lā) *a* irreparable; beyond repair
irreperibile (ēr·rā·pā·rē′bē·lā) *a* elusive; impossible to find
irreprensibile (ēr·rā·prān·sē′bē·lā) *a* irreproachable; blameless, faultless
irrequieto (ēr·rā·kwēā′tō) *a* restless; uneasy
irresistibile (ēr·rā·zē·stē′bē·lā) *a* irresistible
irresponsabile (ēr·rā·spōn·sâ′bē·lā) *a* heedless; irresponsible
irrevocabile (ēr·rā·vō·kâ′bē·lā) *a* irrevocable; unchangeable
irriconoscibile (ēr·rē·kō·nō·shē′bē·lā) *a* unrecognizable
irrigare (ēr·rē·gâ′rā) *vt* to irrigate
irrigazione (ēr·rē·gâ·tsyō′nā) *f* irrigation, watering
irrigidire (ēr·rē·jē·dē′rā) *vt&i* to stiffen; to tighten
irrigidirsi (ēr·rē·jē·dēr′sē) *vr* to become rigid; to harden; to become obdurate; to be unyielding in one's attitude
irrisorio (ēr·rē·zô′ryō) *a* trifling, paltry; ridiculous
irritabile (ēr·rē·tâ′bē·lā) *a* irritable
irritabilità (ēr·rē·tâ·bē·lē·tâ′) *f* irritability
irritante (ēr·rē·tân′tā) *a* irritating, chafing
irritare (ēr·rē·tâ′rā) *vt* to irritate, aggravate, chafe; to rub the wrong way
irritarsi (ēr·rē·târ′sē) *vr* to get angry, become irritated; to fret
irritazione (ēr·rē·tâ·tsyō′nā) *f* irritation; exasperation
irrompere * (ēr·rôm′pā·rā) *vi* to overflow; to break out
irruente (ēr·rūān′tā) *a* rash, impetuous
irruzione (ēr·rū·tsyō′nā) *f* irruption; incursion; overflowing
iscrivere * (ē·skrē′vā·rā) *vt* to enroll; to register
iscriversi * (ē·skrē′vār·sē) *vr* to enroll; to join; to register
iscrizione (ē·skrē·tsyō′nā) *f* registration; enlistment; membership; **domanda d'—** application; **modulo d'—** entry blank; **tassa d'—** entry fee, registration fee
Islanda (ē·zlân′dâ) *f* Iceland
isola (ē′zō·lâ) *f* island
isolamento (ē·zō·lâ·mān′tō) *m* isolation; *(elec)* insulation
isolano (ē·zō·lâ′nō) *m* islander; — *a* island
isolante (ē·zō·lân′tā) *m* insulator; — *a* insulating
isolare (ē·zō·lâ′rā) *vt* to seclude; to isolate; to keep apart; *(elec)* to insulate
isolarsi (ē·zō·lâr′sē) *vr* to live in seclusion; to isolate oneself
isolatamente (ē·zō·lâ·tâ·mān′tā) *adv* isolatedly; separately
isolato (ē·zō·lâ′tō) *a* isolated; insulating; — *m* city block
isolatore (ē·zō·lâ·tō′rā) *m (elec)* insulator
isolazionismo (ē·zō·lâ·tsyō·nē′zmō) *m* isolationism
isolazionista (ē·zō·lâ·tsyō·nē′stâ) *m* isolationist
isoscele (ē·sô′shā·lā) *a (geom)* isosceles
isotopo (ē·zô′tō·pō) *m* isotope
ispanico (ē·spâ′nē·kō) *a* Hispanic
ispettore (ē·spāt·tō′rā) *m* inspector; examiner
ispezionare (ē·spā·tsyō·nâ′rā) *vt* to inspect; to examine
ispezione (ē·spā·tsyō′nā) *f* inspection; examination
ispirare (ē·spē·râ′rā) *vt* to inspire; to enthuse
ispirarsi (ē·spē·râr′sē) *vr* to become inspired; to draw inspiration
ispirazione (ē·spē·râ·tsyō′nā) *f* inspiration; enthusiasm
Israele (ē·zrâ·ā′lā) *m* Israel
israelita (ē·zrâ·ā·lē′tâ) *a* Jewish; — *m&f* Jew
istantanea (ē·stân·tâ′nā·â) *f* snapshot
istantaneamente (ē·stân·tâ·nā·â·mān′tā) *adv* at once, immediately; momentarily
istantaneo (ē·stân·tâ′nā·ō) *a* instantaneous; momentary
istante (ē·stân′tā) *m* instant; — *a* urgent, pressing; **sull'—** immediately; on the spot
istanza (ē·stân′tsâ) *f* petition; plea
isterismo (ē·stā·rē′zmō) *m* hysteria
istigazione (ē·stē·gâ·tsyō′nā) *f* instigation; incitement
istintivamente (ē·stēn·tē·vâ·mān′tā) *adv* instinctively
istinto (ē·stēn′tō) *m* instinct
istituire (ē·stē·twē′rā) *vt* to establish; to institute
istituto (ē·stē·tū′tō) *m* institute, institution

istmo (ēst'mō) *m* isthmus
istrice (ē'strē·chā) *m* porcupine
istruire (ē·strūē'rā) *vt* to teach, educate, instruct
istruirsi (ē·strūēr'sē) *vr* to learn; to become proficient
istruito (ē·strūē'tō) *a* educated
istruttivo (ē·strūt·tē'vō) *a* educational; instructive
istruttore (ē·strūt·tō'rā) *m* instructor
istruttoria (ē·strūt·tô'ryâ) *f* inquest
istruzione (ē·strū·tsyō'nā) *f* instruction; education
istupidirsi (ē·stū·pē·dēr'sē) *vr* to grow stupid; to become stupified
Italia (ē·tâ'lyâ) *f* Italy; — **meridionale** Southern Italy; — **settentrionale** Northern Italy
italianista (ē·tâ·lyâ·nē'stâ) *m* Italian scholar, Italianist
italianità (ē·tâ·lyâ·nē·tâ') *f* Italian characteristics, Italian feeling
italianizzare (ē·tâ·lyâ·nē·dzâ'rā) *vt* to italianize
italiano (ē·tâ·lyâ'nō) *m&a* Italian
itinerario (ē·tē·nā·râ'ryō) *m* itinerary
itterizia (ēt·tā·rē'tsyâ) *f (med)* jaundice
ittiologia (ēt·tyō·lō·jē'â) *f* ichthyology
Iugoslavia (yū·gō·slâ'vyâ) *f* Yugoslavia
iugoslavo (yū·gō·slâ'vō) *m&a* Yugoslav
iuta (yū'tâ) *f* jute
ivi (ē'vē) *adv* there

L

la (lâ) *art f* the; — *pron* her; it; you
là (lâ) *adv* there; **al di** — beyond; on the other side
labaro (lâ'bâ·rō) *m* flag; standard
labbra (lâb'brâ) *fpl* lips
labbro (lâb'brō) *m* lip; rim
labile (lâ'bē·lā) *a* shaky; feeble; fleeting, ephemeral
labirinto (lâ·bē·rēn'tō) *m* labyrinth
laboratorio (lâ·bō·râ·tô'ryō) *m* laboratory; workshop
laborioso (lâ·bō·ryō'zō) *a* industrious; difficult; painstaking
laburismo (lâ·bū·rē'zmō) *m* labor movement; labor party
laburista (lâ·bū·rē'stâ) *a (pol)* labor; — *m* laborite
lacca (lâk'kâ) *f* lacquer; nail polish
lacchè (lâk·kā') *m* flunky; lackey
laccio (lâ'chō) *m* string; noose; snare; — **da scarpe** shoelace
lacerante (lâ·chā·rân'tā) *a* rending, piercing
lacerare (lâ·chā·râ'rā) *vt* to tear; to rip
lacerazione (lâ·chā·râ·tsyō'nā) *f* laceration; rip; tear
laconico (lâ·kô'nē·kō) *a* succinct, concise
lacrima (lâ'krē·mâ), **lagrima** (lâ'grē·mâ) *f* tear
lacrimare (lâ·krē·mâ'rā) *vi* to weep; to water *(eyes)*; *(fig)* to trickle
lacrimogeno (lâ·krē·mô'jā·nō) *a* tear-producing; **gas** — teargas
lacuna (lâ·kū'nâ) *f* blank, gap
ladro (lâ'drō) *m* thief
ladrone (lâ·drō'nā) *m* highwayman
ladruncolo (lâ·drūn'kō·lō) *m* petty thief
laggiù (lâj·jū') *adv* down there
lagnanza (lâ·nyân'tsâ) *f* complaint; criticism
lagnarsi (lâ·nyâr'sē) *vr* to complain
laico (lâ'ē·kō) *m* layman; — *a* laic, lay
lama (lâ'mâ) *f* blade, cutting edge; — *m* lama; *(zool)* llama
lambiccare (lâm·bēk·kâ'rā) *vt* to distill; **lambiccarsi il cervello** to rack one's brains
lambire (lâm·bē'rā) *vt* to touch lightly; to skim over; to lap
lamentare (lâ·mān·tâ'rā) *vt* to regret; to complain about
lamentarsi (lâ·mān·târ'sē) *vr* to complain, grumble
lamentela (lâ·mān·tā'lâ) *f* complaint
lamento (lâ·mān'tō) *m* moan; complaining; **–so** (lâ·mān·tō'zō) *a* sorrowful
lamiera (lâ·myā'râ) *f* sheet *(metal)*; — **di ferro** sheet iron
laminatoio (lâ·mē·nâ·tô'yō) *m* rolling mill
lampada (lâm'pâ·dâ) *f* lamp
lampadario (lâm·pâ·dâ'ryō) *m* chandelier
lampadina (lâm·pâ·dē'nâ) *f* light bulb; — **tascabile** flashlight
lampante (lâm·pân'tā) *a* clear; obvious; flashing
lampeggiare (lâm·pāj·jâ·rā) *vi* to lightning; to flash
lampeggiatore (lâm·pāj·jâ·tō'rā) *m (auto)* directional light
lampeggio (lâm·pej'jō) *m* flashing; lightning
lampione (lâm·pyō'nā) *m* lamppost; street light
lampo (lâm'pō) *m* lightning flash; **chiusura** — zipper; **guerra** — blitzkrieg
lampone (lâm·pō'nā) *m* raspberry
lana (lâ'nâ) *f* wool; — **di acciaio** steel wool; **buona** — rascal
lancetta (lân·chāt'tâ) *f* watch hand; clock hand
lancia (lân'châ) *f* spear; launch
lanciafiamme (lân·châ·fyâm'mā) *m* flamethrower
lanciarazzo (lân·châ·râ'tsō) *m* bazooka
lanciare (lân·châ'rā) *vt* to hurl, throw; to launch
lanciarsi (lân·châr'sē) *vr* to hurl oneself, fling oneself; to leap
lanciatore (lân·châ·tō'rā) *m* baseball pitcher
lancinante (lân·chē·nân'tā) *a* excruciating; **dolore** — piercing pain
lancio (lân'chō) *m* throw; leap; — **del disco** discus throw; — **del peso** shotput; — **del martello** hammer throw; **pista di** — *(avi)* runway
languido (lân'gwē·dō) *a* languorous; logy

languire (lân·gwē'rā) *vi* to languish
languore (lân·gwō'rā) *m* languor; sluggishness
laniero (lâ·nyā'rō) *a* woolen
lanificio (lâ·nē·fē'chō) *m* woolen mill
lanterna (lân·tār'nâ) *f* lantern
lanugine (lâ·nū'jē·nā) *f* down; soft hair; fuzz
lapide (lâ'pē·dā) *f* stone slab; tombstone
lapis (lâ'pēs) *m* pencil; — **per le labbra** lipstick; — **per le ciglia** eyebrow pencil
lardo (lâr'dō) *m* lard; bacon
larghezza (lâr·gā'tsâ) *f* breadth, width
largo (lâr'gō) *a* broad, wide; — *m* width; **farsi** — to push one's way through; **prendere il** — *(fig)* to sneak away; **di manica larga** placid, easygoing
laringite (lâ·rēn·jē'tā) *f* laryngitis
larvato (lâr·vâ'tō) *a* disguised, concealed
lasagna (lâ·zâ'nyâ) *f* large noodle
lasagnone (lâ·zâ·nyō'nā) *m (fig)* foolish fellow, dolt
lasciapassare (lâ·shâ·pâs·sâ'rā) *m* permit, authorization
lasciare (lâ·shâ'rā) *vt* to leave; to let; to stop; — **cadere** to drop
lasciarsi (lâ·shâr'sē) *vr* to allow oneself; to part
lascito (lâ'shē·tō) *m* legacy
lascivo (lâ·shē'vō) *a* lascivious
lassativo (lâs·sâ·tē'vō) *a&m* laxative
lassù (lâs·sū') *adv* up there
lastra (lâ'strâ) *f* plate, slab
lastrico (lâ'strē·kō) *m* flagstone; pavement
lastrone (lâ·strō'nā) *m* large slab
latente (lâ·tān'tā) *a* latent; quiescent
laterale (lâ·tā·râ'lā) *a* lateral
laterizi (lâ·tā·rē'tsē) *mpl* tiles, bricks
latifondista (lâ·tē·fōn·dē'stâ) *m* owner of a landed estate; big landowner
latifondo (lâ·tē·fōn'dō) *m* large landed estate
latino (lâ·tē'nō) *m&a* Latin
latitante (lâ·tē·tân'tā) *a&m* fugitive
latitudine (lâ·tē·tū'dē·nā) *f* latitude
lato (lâ'tō) *m* side; — *a* broad
latore (lâ·tō'rā) *m* bearer
latrare (lâ·trâ'rā) *vi* to howl; to bark
latrina (lâ·trē'nâ) *f* latrine, toilet
latta (lât'tâ) *f* tin; tinplate; tin can
lattaio (lât·tâ'yō) *m* milkman
lattante (lât·tân'tā) *a* unweaned; — *m* suckling
latte (lât'tā) *m* milk; — **condensato** condensed milk; — **scremato** skimmed milk; **fratello di** — foster brother
latteria (lât·tā·rē'â) *f* dairy; dairy farm
latticini (lât·tē·chē'nē) *mpl* dairy products
lattico (lât'tē·kō) *a* lactic; **acido** — lactic acid
lattoniere (lât·tō·nyā'rā) *m* tinman, tinsmith
lattuga (lât·tū'gâ) *f* lettuce
laurea (lâ'ū·rā·â) *f* academic degree
laurearsi (lâu·rā·âr'sē) *vr* to take one's degree; to be graduated
lauro (lâ'ū·rō) *m* laurel; **foglie di** — bay leaves
lauto (lâ'ū·tō) *a* sumptuous; magnificent
lava (lâ'vâ) *f* lava
lavabiancheria (lâ·vâ·byân·kā·rē'â) *f* washing machine
lavabile (lâ·vâ'bē·lā) *a* washable
lavabo (lâ·vâ'bō) *m* washbowl, washbasin
lavaggio (lâ·vâj'jō) *m* washing; — **del cervello** brainwashing
lavagna (lâ·vâ'nyâ) *f* blackboard
lavamano (lâ·vâ·mâ'nō) *m* washstand
lavanda (lâ·vân'dâ) *f (bot)* lavender
lavandaia (lâ·vân·dâ'yâ) *f* washwoman, laundress
lavandaio (lâ·vân·dâ'yō) *m* laundryman
lavanderia (lâ·vân·dā·rē'â) *f* laundry
lavandino (lâ·vân·dē'nō) *m* sink; washstand
lavapiatti (lâ·vâ·pyât'tē) *m* dishwasher
lavare (lâ·vâ'rā) *vt* to wash; — **a secco** to dry-clean
lavarsi (lâ·vâr'sē) *vr* to wash oneself; to wash up; — **le mani** *(fig)* to wash one's hands
lavata (lâ·vâ'tâ) *f* wash; — **di capo** scolding; severe reproof
lavativo (lâ·vâ·tē'vō) *m* enema; *(fig)* bore
lavina (lâ·vē'nâ) *f* landslide
lavorante (lâ·vō·rân'tā) *m* worker
lavorare (lâ·vō·râ'rā) *vt&i* to work; — **la terra** to work the soil
lavorativo (lâ·vō·râ·tē'vō) *a* working; **giorno** — workday
lavorato (lâ·vō·râ'tō) *a* worked; processed; wrought
lavoratore (lâ·vō·râ·tō'rā) *m* workman; — *a* working
lavoratrice (lâ·vō·râ·trē'chā) *f* workwoman
lavorazione (lâ·vō·râ·tsyō'nā) *f* workmanship; processing; working
lavoro (lâ·vō'rō) *m* work; **lavori stradali** road under construction; **camera del** — trade union
lazzaretto (lâ·dzâ·rāt'tō) *m* isolation hospital, lazaretto
lazzarone (lâ·dzâ·rō'nā) *m* beggar; bum; *(sl)* rascal
le (lā) *art fpl* the; — *pron* them; to her; to it
leale (lā·â'lā) *a* sincere, true; loyal
lealtà (lā·âl·tâ') *f* loyalty; fairness
lebbra (lāb'brâ) *f* leprosy
lebbroso (lāb·brō'zō) *a* leprous; — *m* leper
leccapiedi (lāk·kâ·pyā'dē) *m* toady, flatterer
leccare (lāk·kâ'rā) *vt* to lick; *(fig)* to flatter
leccornia (lāk·kôr'nyâ) *f (food)* delicacy
lecito (le'chē·tō) *a* permissible; legal
ledere * (le'dā·rā) *vt* to injure, hurt
lega (lā'gâ) *f* league; union; alloy
legaccio (lā·gâ'chō) *m* string; shoelace; garter
legale (lā·gâ'lā) *a* statutory; legal; **per via** — through legal means; — *m* lawyer
legalizzare (lā·gâ·lē·dzâ'rā) *vt* to legalize; to notarize

legame (lā·gâ'mā) *m* tie; bond
legare (lā·gâ'rā) *vt* to tie; to bind; to bequeath
legarsi (lā·gâr'sē) *vr* to bind oneself; **legarsela al dito** *(fig)* to hold a grudge
legato (lā·gâ'tō) *a* tied; bound; — *m* envoy; ambassador; *(law)* legacy
legatore (lā·gâ·tō'rā) *m* bookbinder
legatura (lā·gâ·tū'râ) *f* binding; *(mus)* slur
legazione (lā·gâ·tsyō'nā) *f* legation
legge (lāj'jā) *f* law; **di** — of necessity; **proposta di** — *(pol)* bill
leggenda (lāj·jān'dâ) *f* legend; caption
leggere * (lej'jā·rā) *vt* to read
leggerezza (lāj·jā·rā'tsâ) *f* levity; lightness; thoughtlessness
leggermente (lāj·jār·mān'tā) *adv* lightly; easily
leggero (lāj·jā'rō) *a* light *(weight)*; nimble; inconsiderate; easy
leggiadro (lāj·jâ'drō) *a* lovely; graceful
leggibile (lāj·jē'bē·lā) *a* legible
leggio (lāj·jē'ō) *m* *(eccl)* lectern; reading desk
leghista (lā·gē'stâ) *m* club member; union member
legislativo (lā·jē·zlâ·tē'vō) *a* legislative, lawmaking
legislatore (lā·jē·zlâ·tō'rā) *m* legislator, lawmaker
legislatura (lā·jē·zlâ·tū'râ) *f* legislature
legislazione (lā·jē·zlâ·tsyō'nā) *f* legislation, lawmaking
legittima (lā·jēt'tē·mâ) *f* *(law)* legitim
legittimo (lā·jēt'tē·mō) *a* lawful, legal; legitimate
legna (lā'nyâ) *f* firewood; brushwood
legnaiolo (lā·nyâ·yō'lō) *m* woodcutter
legname (lā·nyâ'mā) *m* lumber; **deposito** — lumberyard
legnata (lā·nyâ'tā) *f* beating, thrashing
legno (lā'nyō) *m* wood; timber; **testa di** — *(fig)* blockhead, dunce; — **compensato** plywood
legume (lā·gū'mā) *m* legume; vegetable
lei (lā'ē) *pron* you *(for)*; she; her
lembo (lām'bō) *m* flap; edge; **all'estremo — della terra** to the ends of the earth
lemme lemme (lām'mā lām'mā) *adv* slowly
lendine (len'dē·nā) *m* nit
lenire (lā·nē'rā) *vt* to soothe, calm; to allay
lenone (lā·nō'nā) *m* procurer, pimp; white slaver
lentamente (lān·tā·mān'tā) *adv* slowly; gradually
lente (lān'tā) *f* lens; — **d'ingrandimento** magnifying glass
lentezza (lān·tā'tsâ) *f* slothfulness; slowness
lenti (lān'tē) *fpl* eyeglasses
lenticchia (lān·tēk'kyâ) *f* lentil
lentiggine (lān·tēj'jē·nā) *f* freckle
lento (lān'tō) *a* slow; loose, slack; — *adv* slowly
lenza (lān'tsâ) *f* fishing line, line for angling
lenzuola (lān·tswō'lâ) *fpl* bedsheets
lenzuolo (lān·tswō'lō) *m* bedsheet
leone (lā·ō'nā) *m* lion
leonessa (lā·ō·nās'sâ) *f* lioness
leopardo (lā·ō·pâr'dō) *m* leopard
lepre (lā'prā) *f* hare
lesina (le'zē·nâ) *f* awl; parsimony
lesinare (lā·zē·nâ'rā) *vi* to be stingy; to be very sparing
lesione (lā·zyō'nā) *f* lesion; wound
leso (lā'zō) *a* hurt; damaged
lessare (lās·sâ'rā) *vt* to boil
lesso (lās'sō) *m* boiled beef
lestofante (lā·stō·fân'tā) *m* swindler; shyster
letamaio (lā·tâ·mâ'yō) *m* manure pile
letame (lā·tâ'mā) *m* manure
letizia (lā·tē'tsyâ) *f* joy, gaiety
lettera (let'tā·rā) *f* letter; **alla** — literally
letteralmente (lāt·tā·râl·mān'tā) *adv* literally
letterario (lāt·tā·râ'ryō) *a* literary; **proprietà letteraria** copyright
letterato (lāt·tā·râ'tō) *m* man of letters, man of learning; — *a* learned
letteratura (lāt·tā·râ·tū'râ) *f* literature
lettiga (lāt·tē'gâ) *f* *(med)* stretcher
lettino (lāt·tē'nō) *m* small bed; cot
letto (lāt'tō) *m* bed; — **da campeggio** camp bed; — **a sacco** sleeping bag; **figli del primo** — children of the first marriage
lettura (lāt·tū'râ) *f* reading
leva (lā'vâ) *f* lever; *(mil)* draft
levante (lā·vân'tā) *m* Levant; East
levare (lā·vâ'rā) *vt* to remove, take out; to lift; — **il campo** to break camp; — **il bollore** to bring to a boil; — **il tacco** to decamp; — **l'ancora** to weigh anchor; — **la seduta** to adjourn the meeting
levarsi (lā·vâr'sē) *vr* to get off; to get up; to rise; — **il pane dalla bocca** *(fig)* to make great sacrifices; — **del sole** sunrise
levata (lā·vâ'tâ) *f* rising; removal; — **delle lettere** mail collection
levatrice (lā·vâ·trē'chā) *f* midwife
levigato (lā·vē·gâ'tō) *a* smooth, smoothed
levriere (lā·vryā'rā) *m* greyhound
lezione (lā·tsyō'nā) *f* lesson; class
li (lē) *pron* them
lì (lē) *adv* there
Libano (lē'bâ·nō) *m* Lebanon
libbra (lēb'brâ) *f* pound *(weight)*
libellula (lē·bel'lū·lâ) *f* dragonfly
liberale (lē·bā·râ'lā) *a* generous, free; liberal
liberamente (lē·bā·râ·mān'tā) *adv* freely; openly
liberare (lē·bā·râ'rā) *vt* to free, set free
liberarsi (lē·bā·râr'sē) *vr* to rid oneself; to free oneself
liberato (lē·bā·râ'tō) *a* liberated, freed, set free
liberatore (lē·bā·râ·tō'rā) *m* liberator
liberazione (lē·bā·râ·tsyō'nā) *f* liberation, setting free, freeing
liberismo (lē·bā·rē'zmō) *m* free trade
liberista (lē·bā·rē'stâ) *m* free trader
libero (lē'bā·rō) *a* free; vacant; unhampered; **a piede** — out on bail; **all'aria libera** outdoors; — **arbitrio** free

will; **verso** — free verse
libertà (lē·bār·tâ') *f* freedom, liberty; lack of restraint
libertario (lē·bār·tâ'ryō) *m&a* libertarian
libertinaggio (lē·bār·tē·nâj'jō) *m* libertinism, licentiousness
libertino (lē·bār·tē'nō) *m* libertine, rake
libidine (lē·bē'dē·nā) *f* lust
libraio (lē·brâ'yō) *m* bookdealer
libreria (lē·brā·rē'â) *f* bookstore; bookcase
librettista (lē·brāt·tē'stâ) *m* librettist
libretto (lē·brāt'tō) *m* booklet; libretto
libro (lē'brō) *m* book; — **di bordo** *(naut)* log; — **mastro** *(com)* ledger
licenza (lē·chān'tsâ) *f* license; leave; authorization
licenziare (lē·chān·tsyâ'rā) *vt* to dismiss, fire; to authorize
licenziarsi (lē·chān·tsyâr'sē) *vr* to resign; to take one's degree
licenzioso (lē·chān·tsyō'zō) *a* licentious, debauched
liceo (lē·chā'ō) *m* high school; — **scientifico** technical school
licitazione (lē·chē·tâ·tsyō'nā) *f* bid; auction sale
lido (lē'dō) *m* beach, shore
lietamente (lyā·tâ·mān'tā) *adv* happily, gleefully
lieto (lyā'tō) *a* glad, happy
lieve (lyā'vā) *a* light *(weight)*; simple, easy
lievemente (lyā·vā·mān'tā) *adv* lightly; softly
lievito (lye'vē·tō) *m* yeast
ligure (lē·gū'rā) *m&a* Ligurian
lilla (lēl'lâ) *f* lilac; — *m* lilac color
lima (lē'mâ) *f* file
limare (lē·mâ'rā) *vt* to file
limatura (lē·mâ·tū'râ) *f* filings
limetta (lē·māt'tâ) *f* lime *(fruit)*
limitare (lē·mē·tâ'rā) *vt* to limit, check
limitarsi (lē·mē·târ'sē) *vr* to confine oneself, limit oneself
limitatamente (lē·mē·tâ·tâ·mān'tā) *adv* in a limited way, limitedly
limitazione (lē·mē·tâ·tsyō'nā) *f* limitation, check
limite (lē'mē·tā) *m* limit; — **massimo di velocità** speed limit
limonata (lē·mō·nâ'tâ) *f* lemonade
limone (lē·mō'nā) *m* lemon
limoso (lē·mō'zō) *a* slimy, muddy, miry
limpido (lēm'pē·dō) *a* clear, limpid
lince (lēn'chā) *f* lynx
linciaggio (lēn·châj'jō) *m* lynching
linciare (lēn·châ'rā) *vt* to lynch
lindo (lēn'dō) *a* neat; orderly
linea (lē'nā·â) *f* line; figure; — **tranviaria** streetcar line; — **automobilistica** bus line
lineetta (lē·nā·āt'tâ) *f* dash; hyphen
lingotto (lēn·gōt'tō) *m* ingot
lingua (lēn'gwâ) *f* language; tongue; **conoscere una — correntemente** to speak a language fluently; **in — povera** in plain words
linguista (lēn·gwē'stâ) *m* linguist
linguistica (lēn·gwē'stē·kâ) *f* linguistics
lino (lē'nō) *m* linen; flax
linoleum (lē·nô'lāūm) *m* linoleum
linosa (lē·nō'zâ) *f* linseed
linotipia (lē·nō·tē·pē'â) *f* linotype composition
linotipista (lē·nō·tē·pē'stâ) *m&f* linotype operator
liocorno (lyō·kōr'nō) *m* unicorn
Lipsia (lē'psyâ) *f* Leipzig
liquefare (lē·kwā·fâ'rā) *vt&i* to melt
liquefazione (lē·kwā·fâ·tsyō'nā) *f* melting
liquidare (lē·kwē·dâ'rā) *vt* to liquidate
liquidazione (lē·kwē·dâ·tsyō'nā) *f* liquidation; clearance sale
liquido (lē'kwē·dō) *a&m* liquid; **denaro —** cash
liquirizia (lē·kwē·rē'tsyâ) *f* licorice
liquore (lē·kwō'rā) *m* liquor; liqueur
liquoroso (lē·kwō·rō'zō) *a* highly alcoholic
lira (lē'râ) *f* lira; lyre
lirico (lē'rē·kō) *a* lyrical
Lisbona (lē·zbō'nâ) *f* Lisbon
lisca (lē'skâ) *f* fishbone
lisciare (lē·shâ'rā) *vt* to smooth; to flatter
lisciarsi (lē·shâr'sē) *vr* to dress carefully; to groom oneself; to preen
liscio (lē'shō) *a* smooth; straight *(drink)*
liscivia (lē·shē'vyâ) *f* lye
lista (lē'stâ) *f* list; bill of fare; — **dei vini** wine list
listino (lē·stē'nō) *m* bulletin; price list
litania (lē·tâ·nē'â) *f* litany; *(fig)* long list
lite (lē'tā) *f* argument, row; lawsuit
litigare (lē·tē·gâ'rā) *vt* to argue, dispute, contend; — *vi* to quarrel
litigio (lē·tē'jō) *m* lawsuit; quarrel, dispute
litografia (lē·tō·grâ·fē'â) *f* lithography
litorale (lē·tō·râ'lā) *a* coastal; — *m* coastline
litro (lē'trō) *m* liter; **un quarto di —** a half-pint
Lituania (lē·twâ'nyâ) *f* Lithuania
lituano (lē·twâ'nō) *a&m* Lithuanian
liturgia (lē·tūr·jē'â) *f* liturgy
liutaio (lyū·tâ'yō) *m* stringed-instrument maker
liuto (lyū'tō) *m* lute
livellare (lē·vāl·lâ'rā) *vt* to level; to make uniform
livellazione (lē·vāl·lâ·tsyō'nā) *f* levelling; standardization
livello (lē·vāl'lō) *m* level; **passaggio a —** railroad crossing; **sul — del mare** above sea level; — **delle acque** water level; waterline
livido (lē'vē·dō) *a* livid; pale; *(fig)* jealous; — *m* contusion, bruise
lo (lō) *art m* the; — *pron* it, him
lobbia (lôb'byâ) *f* fedora
lobo (lō'bō) *m (anat)* lobe
locale (lō·kâ'lā) *a* local; — *m* room; place; — **di lusso** high-class establishment
località (lō·kâ·lē·tâ') *f* position; town
localizzare (lō·kâ·lē·dzâ'rā) *vt* to localize; to find, locate
locanda (lō·kân'dâ) *f* inn
locandiere (lō·kân·dyā'rā), *m* **locandiera**

(lō·kân·dyā'râ) *f* innkeeper
locandina (lō·kân·dē'nâ) *f (theat)* handbill
locare (lō·kâ'rā) *vt* to rent; **locasi** for rent
locatario (lō·kâ·tâ'ryō) *m* tenant
locativo (lō·kâ·tē'vō) *a (gram)* locative
locatore (lō·kâ·tō'rā) *m* lessor
locazione (lō·kâ·tsyō'nā) *f* rent; lease
locomotiva (lō·kō·mō·tē'vâ) *f* engine, locomotive
locomozione (lō·kō·mō·tsyō'nā) *m* locomotion
locusta (lō·kū'stâ) *f* locust
lodare (lō·dâ'rā) *vt* to praise; to extol
lodarsi (lō·dâr'sē) *vr* to praise oneself; to swell with pride
lode (lō'dā) *f* praise
lodevole (lō·de'vō·lā) *a* laudable
logaritmo (lō·gâ·rēt'mō) *m* logarithm
loggia (lôj'jâ) *f (theat)* box, loge; balcony
loggione (lōj·jō'nā) *m (theat)* gallery
logorare (lō·gō·râ'rā) *vt* to wear out
logorarsi (lō·gō·râr'sē) *vr* to wear oneself out; to become worn out
logorio (lō·gō·rē'ō) *m* waste; wear
logoro (lô'gō·rō) *a* worn-out
lombaggine (lōm·bâj'jē·nā) *f* lumbago
Lombardia (lōm·bâr·dē'â) *f* Lombardy
lombata (lōm·bâ'tâ) *f* loin *(meat)*
lombo (lōm'bō) *m* sirloin; loin
Londra (lōn'drâ) *f* London
lontananza (lōn·tâ·nân'tsâ) *f* time away, absence; distance
lontano (lōn·tâ'nō) *a* distant; absent; — *adv* far, a long way
lontra (lōn'trâ) *f* otter
loquace (lō·kwâ'chā) *a* talkative
lordare (lōr·dâ'rā) *vt* to dirty; to foul
lordo (lōr'dō) *a* dirty, filthy; *(com)* gross
loro (lō'rō) *pron* they, them, to them; you, to you; yours; theirs; — *a* your; their
losco (lō'skō) *a* one-eyed; shady, sinister
lotta (lōt'tâ) *f* struggle; wrestling; — **libera** catch-as-catch-can wrestling; **partita di** — wrestling match
lottare (lōt·tâ'rā) *vi* to struggle; to wrestle
lottatore (lōt·tâ·tō'rā) *m* fighter; wrestler; struggler
lotteria (lōt·tā·rē'â) *f* lottery
lottizzare (lōt·tē·dzâ'rā) *vt* to parcel out; to allot
lotto (lōt'tō) *m* lottery; parcel, plot *(land)*
lozione (lō·tsyō'nā) *f* lotion; — **per la barba** shaving lotion; — **per gli occhi** eyewash
lubrificante (lū·brē·fē·kân'tā) *a* lubricating; — *m* lubricant
lubrificare (lū·brē·fē·kâ'rā) *vt* to lubricate
lubrificazione (lū·brē·fē·kâ·tsyō'nā) *f* lubrication
lucchetto (lūk·kāt'tō) *m* padlock
luccicare (lū·chē·kâ'rā) *vi* to gleam; to shimmer
luccichio (lū·chē·kē'ō) *m* glimmer
luccio (lū'chō) *m* pike *(fish)*
lucciola (lū'chō·lâ) *f* firefly
luce (lū'chā) *f* light; — **di arresto** stoplight; — **di posizione** parking light; **filtro** — light filter
lucente (lū·chān'tā) *a* luminous, shining; sparkling; gleaming
lucernario (lū·chār·nâ'ryō) *m* skylight
lucertola (lū·cher'tō·lâ) *f* lizard
lucidare (lū·chē·dâ'rā) *vt* to polish, shine; to trace *(drawing)*
lucidatrice (lū·chē·dâ·trē'chā) *f* floor polisher
lucidità (lū·chē·dē·tâ') *f* lucidity; — **di mente** clearness of mind
lucido (lū'chē·dō) *a* shining; lucid; — *m* polish; — **per le scarpe** shoe polish
lucignolo (lū·chē'nyō·lō) *m* wick
lucro (lū'krō) *m* profit
luglio (lū'lyō) *m* July
lui (lū'ē) *pron* he; him
lumaca (lū·mâ'kâ) *f* snail; **a passo di** — at a snail's pace
lume (lū'mā) *m* light; lamp *(fig)* understanding; **a — di naso** at first glance; roughly speaking
luminoso (lū·mē·nō'zō) *a* shining, bright
luna (lū'nâ) *f* moon; — **di miele** honeymoon; **al chiaro di** — by moonlight; **avere la** — to be in an ugly mood
lunario (lū·nâ'ryō) *m* almanac; **sbarcare il** — *(fig)* to make both ends meet
lunatico (lū·nâ'tē·kō) *a* moody, capricious; lunatical
lunedì (lū·nā·dē') *m* Monday
lungamente (lūn·gâ·mān'tā) *adv* lengthily, at length
lunghezza (lūn·gā'tsâ) *f* length
lungimirante (lūn·jē·mē·rân'tā) *a* far-sighted
lungo (lūn'gō) *a* long; thin; — *prep* beside, along; **a — andare** in the long run; — **disteso** headlong; **tirare in** — to put off, delay
lungomare (lūn·gō·mâ'rā) *m* boardwalk; street by the sea
luogo (lwō'gō) *m* place; spot; **aver** — to take place; to happen; **in — di** instead of
lupo (lū'pō) *m* wolf; **In bocca al —!** Good luck to you! — **di mare** veteran seaman
lurido (lū'rē·dō) *a* filthy, lewd, lurid
lusinga (lū·zēn'gâ) *f* flattery
lusingare (lū·zēn·gâ'rā) *vt* to cajole; to flatter
lusingarsi (lū·zēn·gâr'sē) *vr* to trust, hope; to feel confident; to flatter
lusinghiero (lū·zēn·gyā'rō) *a* flattering; promising
lussazione (lūs·sâ·tsyō'nā) *f (med)* dislocation
lusso (lūs'sō) *m* luxury
lussuoso (lūs·swō'zō) *a* deluxe, magnificent
lussureggiante (lūs·sū·rāj·jân'tā) *a* luxuriant; overabundant
lustrare (lū·strâ'rā) *vt* to shine; to clean; to polish
lustrascarpe (lū·strâ·scâr'pā) *m* bootblack, shoeblack; shoeshine boy
lustro (lū'strō) *m* luster; — *a* bright, shining; polished

lutto (lūt'tō) *m* mourning; — **pesante** deep sorrow

luttuoso (lūt·twō'zō) *a* sorrowful, mournful; saddening

M

ma (mâ) *conj* but
macabro (mâ·kâ'brō) *a* macabre; eerie
maccheroni (mâk·kā·rō'nē) *mpl* macaroni
macchia (mâk'kyâ) *f* stain; blemish; thicket
macchiare (mâk·kyâ'rā) *vt* to dirty; to stain
macchiarsi (mâk·kyâr'sē) *vr* to ruin one's reputation; to get dirty
macchietta (mâk·kyāt'tâ) *f* eccentric; odd character
macchiettista (mâk·kyāt·tē'stâ) *m* mimic
macchina (mâk'kē·nâ) *f* machine; automobile; engine; — **fotografica** camera; — **da cucire** sewing machine; — **da scrivere** typewriter
macchinalmente (mâk·kē·nâl·mān'tā) *adv* mechanically; automatically
macchinario (mâk·kē·nâ'ryō) *m* machinery; works, working parts
macchinazione (mâk·kē·nâ·tsyō'nā) *f* intrigue; conspiracy
macchinetta (mâk·kē·nāt'tâ) *f* little machine; — **per i capelli** hair clippers; — **del caffè** coffeepot
macchinista (mâk·kē·nē'stâ) *m* machinist; engineer; stoker; stagehand
macchinosamente (mâk·kē·nō·zâ·mān'tā) *adv* heavily; complicatedly
macedonia (mâ·chā·dô'nyâ) *m* fruit salad
macellaio (mâ·chāl·lâ'yō) *m* butcher
macellare (mâ·chāl·lâ'rā) *vt* to butcher
macellazione (mâ·chāl·lâ·tsyō'nā) *f* slaughtering, butchering
macelleria (mâ·chāl·lā·rē'â) *f* butcher shop
macello (mâ·chāl'lō) *m* slaughterhouse; *(fig)* slaughter, massacre
macerare (mâ·chā·râ'rā) *vt* to steep, macerate
maceria (mâ·che'ryâ) *f* ruins, debris
macero (mâ'chā·rō) *a* macerated
macigno (mâ·chē'nyō) *m* boulder, large rock
macilento (mâ·chē·lān'tō) *a* cadaverous, emaciated
macina (mâ'chē·nâ) *f* millstone
macinacaffè (mâ·chē·nâ·kâf·fā') *m* coffee mill
macinapepe (mâ·chē·nâ·pā'pā) *m* pepper mill
macinare (mâ·chē·nâ'rā) *vt* to grind; to pulverize
macinato (mâ·chē·nâ'tō) *a* ground; milled; — *m* flour; ground grain
macinino (mâ·chē·nē'nō) *m* small mill; *(coll)* old car; *(sl)* jalopy
macrocosmo (mâ·krō·kō'zmō) *m* macrocosm
madornale (mâ·dōr·nâ'lā) *a* huge, behemoth
madre (mâ'drā) *f* mother
madreperla (mâ·drā·pār'lâ) *f* mother-of-pearl, nacre
madrigna (mâ·drē'nyâ) *f* stepmother
madrina (mâ·drē'nâ) *f* godmother; foster mother
maestà (mâ·ā·stâ') *f* majesty, stateliness
maestosamente (mâ·ā·stō·zâ·mān'tā) *adv* majestically; regally
maestra (mâ·ā'strâ) *f* teacher
maestranza (mâ·ā·strân'tsâ) *f* workmen
maestria (mâ·ā·strē'â) *f* proficiency; dexterity
maestro (mâ·ā'strō) *m* teacher; master; — *a* main; masterful; **strada maestra** highway; main road; **vento** — northwest wind
magari (mâ·gâ'rē) *adv* perhaps, maybe; – ! *interj* God grant!, if only!
magazzinaggio (mâ·gâ·dzē·nâj'jō) *m* storage
magazziniere (mâ·gâ·dzē·nyā'rā) *m* warehouseman
magazzino (mâ·gâ·dzē'nō) *m* warehouse; depot; store
maggio (mâj'jō) *m* May
maggiorana (mâj·jō·râ'nâ) *f* marjoram
maggioranza (mâj·jō·rân'tsâ) *f* majority
maggiorare (mâj·jō·râ'rā) *vt* to raise; to increase
maggiorato (mâj·jō·râ'tō) *a* raised; increased
maggiorazione (mâj·jō·râ·tsyō'nā) *f* increase
maggiordomo (mâj·jōr·dō'mō) *m* majordomo
maggiore (mâj·jō'rā) *a* greater; elder; larger; — *m (mil)* major
maggiorenne (mâj·jō·rān'nā) *a* of age
maggiormente (mâj·jōr·mān'tā) *adv* greatly; all the more
magia (mâ·jē'â) *f* magic; witchcraft
magistrale (mâ·jē·strâ'lā) *a* dextrous; skillful; masterful; **istituto** — teachers college; **scuola** — normal school; **con tono** — in a commanding voice
magistralmente (mâ·jē·strâl·mān'tā) *adv* adroitly; masterfully
magistrato (mâ·jē·strâ'tō) *m* judge
magistratura (mâ·jē·strâ·tū'râ) *f* judiciary, bench
maglia (mâ'lyâ) *f* mesh; undershirt; **lavorare a** — to knit
maglieria (mâ·lyā·rē'â) *f* knitted goods; hosiery
maglietta (mâ·lyāt'tâ) *f* undershirt
maglione (mâ·lyō'nā) *m* sweater
magnanimità (mâ·nyâ·nē·mē·tâ') *f* magnanimity; largess
magnanimo (mâ·nyâ'nē·mō) *a* generous, liberal
magnano (mâ·nyâ'nō) *m* locksmith
magnate (mâ·nyâ'tā) *m* patron; magnate
magnesia (mâ·nye'zyâ) *f* magnesia
magnesio (mâ·nye'zyō) *m* magnesium
magnete (mâ·nyā'tā) *m* magneto; magnet
magnetico (mâ·nye'tē·kō) *a* magnetic
magnetofono (mâ·nyā·tō·fō'nō) *m* tape

recorder
magnificamente (mâ·nyē·fē·kâ·mān'tā) *adv* magnificently, splendidly
magnificenza (mâ·nyē·fē·chān'tsâ) *f* pomp; magnificence
magnifico (mâ·nyē'fē·kō) *a* magnificent
mago (mâ'gō) *m* magician
magrezza (mâ·grā'tsâ) *f* skinniness; scantiness
magro (mâ'grō) *a* lean, thin; — *m* Lenten abstinence
mai (mâ'ē) *adv* ever, never; **non si sa —** one never can tell; **caso —** if, just in case; **come —?** how in the world?, how ever?; — **più** never again
maiale (mâ·yâ'lā) *m* swine; **carne di —** pork; **grasso di —** lard
maialetto (mâ·yâ·lāt'tō) *m* suckling pig
maiolica (mâ·yô'lē·kâ) *f* majolica
maionesa (mâ·yō·nā'zâ) *f* mayonnaise
maiuscola (mâ·yū'skō·lâ) *f* capital letter
maiuscolo (mâ·yū'skō·lō) *a* capital; large, gross
mal (mâl) *m* pain; sickness; **— di mare** seasickness; **— d'aereo** airsickness; **— di denti** toothache; **— di pancia** stomachache; **— di testa** headache
malafede (mâ·lâ·fā'dā) *f* bad faith
malaffare (mâ·lâf·fâ'rā) *m* dissolute living; **donna di —** woman of easy virtue
malagiato (mâ·lâ·jâ'tō) *a* ill at ease; badly off
malagrazia (mâ·lâ·grâ'tsyâ) *f* rudeness; disfavor
malalingua (mâ·lâ·lēn'gwâ) *f* gossip; slanderer
malamente (mâ·lâ·mān'tā) *adv* badly
malandato (mâ·lân·dâ'tō) *a* in poor condition; worn-out
malandrino (mâ·lân·drē'nō) *m* ruffian, tough; gangster
malanimo (mâ·lâ'nē·mō) *m* spitefulness; ill will, malice
malanno (mâ·lân'nō) *m* calamity; sickness
malapena (mâ·lâ·pā'nâ) *adv* hardly; scarcely; just
malaria (mâ·lâ'ryâ) *f (med)* malaria
malato (mâ·lâ'tō) *a* sick; — *m* patient
malattia (mâ·lât·tē'â) *f* disease, illness
malaugurio (mâ·lâū·gū'ryō) *m* bad omen, bad sign
malavita (mâ·lâ·vē'tā) *f* underworld
malcaduco (mâl·kâ·dū'kō) *m (med)* epilepsy
malcapitato (mâl·kâ·pē·tâ'tō) *a* unlucky, unfortunate
malcauto (mâl·kâ'ū·tō) *a* unwary, rash; heedless
malcerto (mâl·chār'tō) *a* uncertain, dubious
malconcio (mâl·kôn'chō) *a* bruised, beaten; ill-used, mistreated
malcontento (mâl·kōn·tān'tō) *a* discontented; dissatisfied; — *m* dissatisfaction; malcontent
malcostume (mâl·kō·stū'mā) *m* dissipation; bad habit; immorality
maldestro (mâl·dā'strō) *a* gauche; unskillful; coarse
maldicente (mâl·dē·chān'tā) *a* slanderous; gossipy; — *n* slanderer; gossip (*person*)
maldicenza (mâl·dē·chān'tsâ) *f* slander; gossip (*act*)
male (mâ'lā) *m* evil; disease; pain; misfortune; — *adv* badly; **far —** to hurt; to harm; **farsi —** to hurt oneself; to injure oneself; **niente di —** everything's all right
maledetto (mâ·lā·dāt'tō) *a* damned, cursed
maledire (mâ·lā·dē'rā) *vt* to curse
maledizione (mâ·lā·dē·tsyō'nā) *f* curse, malediction; (*fig*) bad luck
maleducato (mâ·lā·dū·kâ'tō) *a* ill-bred; unmannerly
maleficio (mâ·lā·fē'chō) *m* sorcery; spell, enchantment
malefico (mâ·le'fē·kō) *a* evil; harmful; ruinous
maleodorante (mâ·lā·ō·dō·rân'tā) *a* smelly, malodorous
maleolente (mâ·lā·ō·lān'tā) *a* evil-smelling; foul-smelling
malerba (mâ·lār'bâ) *f* weed
malessere (mâ·les'sā·rā) *m* uneasiness; indisposition; discomfort
malfatto (mâl·fât'tō) *m* misdeed; evil act; — *a* misshapen; poorly made
malfattore (mâl·fât·tō'rā) *m* criminal
malgarbo (mâl·gâr'bō) *m* lack of grace; rudeness; awkwardness
malgrado (mâl·grâ'dō) *prep* despite, notwithstanding; **a mio —** against my will; **— ciò** however, nevertheless
malgusto (mâl·gū'stō) *m* poor taste
malia (mâ·lē'â) *f* fascination, charm
maliarda (mâ·lyâr'dâ) *f* enchantress
maligno (mâ·lē'nyō) *a* malignant; wicked: evil-minded
malinconia (mâ·lēn·kō·nē'â) *f* melancholy; unhappiness; depression
malinconico (mâ·lēn·kô'nē·kō) *a* melancholy
malincuore (mâ·lēn·kwō'rā) *adv* unwillingly
malintendere * (mâ·lēn·ten'dā'rā) *vt* to misunderstand
malinteso (mâ·lēn·tā'zō) *m* misunderstanding
malizia (mâ·lē'tsyâ) *f* malice; cunning
maliziosamente (mâ·lē·tsyō·zâ·mān'tā) *adv* maliciously, evilly
malizioso (mâ·lē·tsyō'zō) *a* malicious; roguish; tricky
malleabile (mâl·la·â'bē·lā) *a* pliable, yielding
malleolo (mâl·le'ō·lō) *m* anklebone
malmenare (mâl·mā·nâ'rā) *vt* to manhandle; to mishandle; to mistreat
malo (mâ'lō) *a* bad; evil; **mala voglia** ill will; **mala riuscita** failure
malocchio (mâ·lôk'kyō) *m* evil eye
malore (mâ·lō'rā) *m* indisposition, sickness; sudden collapse
malsano (mâl·sâ'nō) *a* unhealthy
maltempo (mâl·tām'pō) *m* bad weather
maltrattare (mâl·trât·tâ'rā) *vt* to mistreat,

treat badly
malumore (mâ·lū·mō'rā) *m* bad humor; bad mood
malvagio (mâl·vâ'jō) *a* wicked
malvagità (mâl·vâ·jē·tâ') *f* evil, wickedness
malversazione (mâl·vār·sâ·tsyō'nā) *f* embezzlement, defalcation
malvisto (mâl·vē'stō) *a* unpopular; disliked; not well-thought-of
malvivente (mâl·vē·vān'tā) *m* gangster; scoundrel
malvolentieri (mâl·vō·lān·tyā'rē) *adv* unwillingly; against one's will
malvolere (mâl·vō·lā'rā) *m* malevolence
mamma (mâm'mâ) *f* mother
mammalucco (mâm·mâ·lūk'kō) *m* (*sl*) nitwit, dope
mammella (mâm·māl'lâ) *f* breast; udder; teat
mammifero (mâm·mē'fā·rō) *m* mammal
mammola (mâm'mō·lâ) *f* (*bot*) violet
manata (mâ·nâ'tâ) *f* handful; slap
mancante (mân·kân'tā) *a* missing; short
mancanza (mân·kân'tsâ) *f* want; lack; fault; **in — di** in the absence of; **in — di meglio** for want of something better; **sentire la — di** to miss
mancare (mân·kâ'râ) *vi* to be lacking; to be at fault; to be missing; — *vt* to miss; to fall short of; — **alla parola** to break one's word; **Non ci mancherebbe altro!** That's the last straw!
mancia (mân'châ) *f* tip
manciata (mân·châ'tâ) *f* handful
mancino (mân·chē'nō) *a* left-handed; **colpo** — shady deal; dishonest action
Manciuria (mân·chū'ryâ) *f* Manchuria
manco (mân'kō) *adv* not even; — *a* left
mandamento (mân·dâ·mān'tō) *m* local jurisdiction
mandare (mân·dâ'rā) *vt* to send; — **via** to dismiss; — **a gambe all'aria** to knock head over heels; (*fig*) to upset; to put an end to; — **a picco** (*naut*) to sink; — **ad effetto** to carry out; accomplish; — **per le lunghe** to delay, put off; — **giù** to swallow; (*fig*) to stomach, brook
mandarino (mân·dâ·rē'nō) *m* (*bot*) tangerine
mandatario (mân·dâ·tâ'ryō) (*pol*) mandatary; (*law*) abettor, accomplice; (*com*) agent
mandato (mân·dâ'tō) *m* mandate; warrant
mandibola (mân·dē'bō·lâ) *m* (*anat*) jaw
mandolinista (mân·dō·lē·nē'stâ) *m* mandolin player
mandolino (mân·dō·lē'nō) *m* mandolin
mandorla (mân'dōr·lâ) *f* almond
mandorlato (mân·dōr·lâ'tō) *m* almond cake
mandorlo (mân'dōr·lō) *m* almond tree
mandria (mân'dryâ) *f* large group, drove; herd; flock
maneggiare (mâ·nāj·jâ'rā) *vt* to handle; to manipulate
maneggiarsi (mâ·nāj·jâr'sē) *vr* to manage; to get along
manesco (mâ·nā'skō) *a* quarrelsome
manette (mâ·nāt'tā) *fpl* handcuffs
manganello (mân·gâ·nāl'lō) *m* billy, club
mangiare (mân·jâ'rā) *vt* to eat; to corrode; (*fig*) to squander; to take (*chess*)
mangiatoia (mân·jâ·tô'yâ) *f* manger; crib
mangiatore (mân·jâ·tō'rā) *m* big eater
mangime (mân·jē'mā) *m* chicken feed; fodder
mania (mâ·nē'â) *f* mania; pet project, special interest
maniaco (mâ·nē'â·kō) *a* fanatic; — *m* maniac
manica (mâ'nē·kâ) *f* sleeve; gang; **un altro paio di maniche** a horse of a different color; **di — larga** lenient, indulgent; **la M—** the English channel
manicaretto (mâ·nē·kâ·rāt'tō) *m* tidbit, delicacy
manichino (mâ·nē·kē'nō) *m* mannequin, dummy
manico (mâ'nē·kō) *m* handle
manicomio (mâ·nē·kô'myō) *m* mental hospital, mental institution
manicotto (mâ·nē·kōt'tō) *m* muff; large stuffed macaroni
maniera (mâ·nyā'râ) *f* manner, way; **in nessuna** — by no means; **in ogni** — anyhow; **bella** — fine manner; **in una — o nell'altra** one way or another; **di — che** so that; **in che — ?** by what means?, how?
manifattura (mâ·nē·fât·tū'râ) *f* manufacture; production
manifatturare (mâ·nē·fât·tū·râ'rā) *vt* to manufacture; to produce
manifatturiero (mâ·nē·fât·tū·ryā'rō) *a* manufacturing
manifestare (mâ·nē·fā·stâ'rā) *vt* to manifest; to evince, evidence
manifestarsi (mâ·nē·fā·stâr'sē) *vr* to declare oneself; to show oneself
manifestazione (mâ·nē·fā·stâ·tsyō'nā) *f* display; manifestation; show
manifestino (mâ·nē·fā·stē'nō) *m* handbill
manifesto (mâ·nē·fā'stō) *m* poster; waybill; manifest; — *a* obvious; evident
maniglia (mâ·nē'lyâ) *f* handle, knob
manipolare (mâ·nē·pō·lâ'rā) *vt* to manipulate
maniscalco (mâ·nē·skâl'kō) *m* blacksmith
mannaia (mân·nâ'yâ) *f* axe
mano (mâ'nō) *f* hand; coat of paint; **venire alle mani** to come to blows; **chiedere la** — to ask in marriage; **a — a —** little by little; **alla** — easy to get along with, tractable; **far man bassa** to rob; **–dopera** (mâ·nō·dô'pā·râ) *f* labor, work with the hands; **–pola** (mâ·nô'pō·lâ) *f* handgrip, handle; handlebar
manovella (mâ·nō·vāl'lâ) *f* handle; crank
manovrare (mâ·nō·vrâ'rā) *vt* to operate; to maneuver; to switch
manovratore (mâ·nō·vrâ·tō'rā) *m* motorman; driver
manrovescio (mân·rō·ve'shō) *m* backhanded blow; backhand
mansione (mân·syō'nā) *f* task; duty

mansueto (mân·swā'tō) *a* tame; meek
mantello (mân·tāl'lō) *m* cloak; wrap; coat (*animal*)
mantenere * (mân·tā·nā'rā) *vt* to keep; — **la destra** to keep to the right
mantenersi * (mân·tā·nār'sē) *vr* to maintain oneself; to keep
mantenimento (mân·tā·nē·mān'tō) *m* support; maintenance
mantice (mân'tē·chā) *m* bellows
manuale (mâ·nwâ'lā) *m* handbook; — *a* manual, done by hand
manubrio (mâ·nū'bryō) *m* handlebar; dumbbell
manutenzione (mâ·nū·tān·tsyō'nā) *f* upkeep; servicing
manzo (mân'dzō) *m* beef
mappamondo (mâp·pâ·mōn'dō) *m* globe; map of the world
marachella (mâ·râ·kāl'lâ) *f* trick; fraud
maramaldo (mâ·râ·mâl'dō) *m* coward
marasma (mâ·râ'zmâ) *m* (*fig*) chaos
marca (mâr'kâ) *f* brand; make; trademark; mark
marcare (mâr·kâ'rā) *vt* to mark
marchesa (mâr·kā'zâ) *f* marquise
marchese (mâr·kā'zā) *m* marquis
marchiano (mâr·kyâ'nō) *a* gross, enormous
marchio (mâr'kyō) *m* brand; stamp
marcia (mâr'châ) *f* gear, speed; march; pus
marciapiede (mâr·châ·pyā'dā) *m* sidewalk; platform (*railroad station*)
marciare (mâr·châ'rā) *vi* to march; to function, work
marciatram (mâr·châ·trâm') *f* streetcar platform
marcio (mâr'chō) *a* rotten; — *m* rot
marcire (mâr·chē'rā) *vi* to rot
marciume (mâr·chū'mā) *m* rottenness
marconigramma (mâr·kō·nē·grâm'mâ) *m* radiogram
marconista (mâr·kō·nē'stâ) *m* wireless operator
mare (mâ'rā) *m* sea; (*fig*) huge amount
marea (mâ·rā'â) *f* tide
maremoto (mâ·rā·mō'tō) *m* tidal wave
maresciallo (mâ·rā·shâl'lō) *m* marshal; warrant officer
margarina (mâr·gâ·rē'nâ) *f* margarine
margherita (mâr·gā·rē'tâ) *f* (*bot*) daisy
margine (mâr'jē·nā) *m* edge; margin
marina (mâ·rē'nâ) *f* shore; navy; seascape; — **mercantile** merchant marine
marinaio (mâ·rē·nâ'yō) *m* sailor; marine
marinare (mâ·rē·nâ'rā) *vt* to marinate; to pickle; — **la scuola** to play hooky
marionetta (mâ·ryō·nāt'tâ) *f* marionette
maritare (mâ·rē·tâ'rā) *vt* to marry, join in marriage
maritarsi (mâ·rē·târ'sē) *vr* to get married
marito (mâ·rē'tō) *m* husband
marittimo (mâ·rēt'tē·mō) *m* seaman; — *a* maritime
mariuolo (mâ·rywō'lō) *m* swindler, thief
marmaglia (mâr·mâ'lyâ) *f* rabble; mob
marmellata (mâr·māl·lâ'tâ) *f* jam, preserve
marmitta (mâr·mēt'tâ) *f* large pot, kettle
marmo (mâr'mō) *m* marble
marmocchio (mâr·môk'kyō) *m* brat, spoiled child
marmotta (mâr·mōt'tâ) *f* (*zool*) marmot
maroso (mâ·rō'zō) *m* billow, wave, breaker
marrone (mâr·rō'nā) *m* chestnut; — *a* chestnut (*color*)
marsina (mâr·sē'nâ) *f* dress coat; tails (*coll*)
marsupiale (mâr·sū·pyâ'lā) *m&a* marsupial
martedì (mâr·tā·dē') *m* Tuesday
martellare (mâr·tāl·lâ'rā) *vt* to hammer; — *vi* to pulse, throb
martellista (mâr·tāl·lē'stâ) *m* (*sport*) hammer thrower
martello (mâr·tāl'lō) *m* hammer
martire (mâr'tē·rā) *m* martyr
martirio (mâr·tē'ryō) *m* martyrdom
martirizzare (mâr·tē·rē·dzâ'rā) *vt* to martyr
martirizzarsi (mâr·tē·rē·dzâr'sē) *vr* to martyr oneself
martora (mâr'tō·râ) *f* (*zool*) marten
marzapane (mâr·dzâ·pâ'nā) *f* marzipan
marziale (mâr·tsyâ'lā) *a* martial; war
marziano (mâr·tsyâ'nō) *a&m* Martian
marzo (mâr'tsō) *m* March
mascalzone (mâ·skâl·tsō'nā) *m* cad, scoundrel
mascella (mâ·shāl'lâ) *f* jaw
maschera (mâ'skā·râ) *f* mask; (*theat*) usher; (*fencing*) face guard
mascherare (mâ·skā·râ'rā) *vt* to mask; to hide, conceal
mascherarsi (mâ·skā·râr'sē) *vr* to masquerade; to wear a mask
maschietta (mâ·skyāt'tâ) *f* tomboy; **capelli alla** — bobbed hair
maschile (mâ·skē'lā) *m* masculine; male
maschio (mâ'skyō) *a&m* male; — *a* manly
masnada (mâ·znâ'dâ) *f* gang of toughs
massa (mâs'sâ) *f* mass
massacrare (mâs·sâ·krâ'rā) *vt* to massacre
massacro (mâs·sâ'krō) *m* massacre
massaggiare (mâs·sâj·jâ'rā) *vt* to massage
massaggiatore (mâs·sâj·jâ·tō'rā) *m* masseur
massaggiatrice (mâs·sâj·jâ·trē'chā) *f* masseuse
massaggio (mâs·sâj'jō) *m* massage
massaia (mâs·sâ'yâ) *f* housewife
masseria (mâs·sā·rē'â) *f* farm; herd
masserizie (mâs·sā·rē'tsyā) *fpl* utensils; household goods
massicciata (mâs·sē·châ'tâ) *f* roadbed
massiccio (mâs·sē'chō) *a* huge, bulky
massima (mâs'sē·mâ) *f* rule; maxim
massimamente (mâs·sē·mâ·mān'tā) *adv* most of all; especially
massimo (mâs'sē·mō) *a* greatest; best; utmost; — *m* maximum
masso (mâs'sō) *m* large rock; boulder
massone (mâs·sō'nā) *m* Freemason
massoneria (mâs·sō·nā·rē'â) *f* Freemasonry

mastello (mâ·stāl'lō) *m* tub
masticare (mâ·stē·kâ'rā) *vt* to chew; (*fig*) to meditate; to grumble about
masticazione (mâ·stē·kâ·tsyō'nā) *f* chewing, mastication
mastice (mâ'stē·chā) *m* rubber cement
mastino (mâ·stē'nō) *m* mastiff
mastodonte (mâ·stō·dōn'tā) *m* mastodon
mastro (mâ'strō) *m* master; *(com)* ledger
matassa (mâ·tâs'sâ) *f* skein
matematica (mâ·tā·mâ'tē·kâ) *f* mathematics
matematico (mâ·tā·mâ'tē·kō) *a* mathematical; — *m* mathematician
materasso (mâ·tā·râs'sō) *m* mattress
materia (mâ·te'ryâ) *f* matter, substance; (*med*) pus
materiale (mâ·tā·ryâ'lā) *a&m* material
materialista (mâ·tā·ryâ·lē'stâ) *m* materialist
materializzare (mâ·tā·ryâ·lē·dzâ'rā) *vt* to materialize
materialmente (mâ·tā·ryâl·mān'tā) *adv* materially
maternità (mâ·tār·nē·tâ') *f* maternity
materno (mâ·tār'nō) *a* maternal
matita (mâ·tē'tâ) *f* pencil
matricola (mâ·trē'kō·lâ) *f* freshman; register; registration
matricolazione (mâ·trē·kō·lâ·tsyō'nā) *f* matriculation
matrigna (mâ·trē'nyâ) *f* stepmother
matrimoniale (mâ·trē·mō·nyâ'lā) *a* wedding, matrimonial; **anello** — wedding ring; **letto** — double bed
matrimonio (mâ·trē·mô'nyō) *m* marriage
mattacchione (mât·tâk·kyō'nā) *m* wit, joker
mattarello (mât·tâ·rāl'lō) *m* rolling pin
mattatoio (mât·tâ·tô'yō) *m* slaughterhouse, abattoir
mattina (mât·tē'nâ) *f* morning
mattinata (mât·tē·nâ'tâ) *f* morning hours; matinee; whole morning long
mattino (mât·tē'nō) *m* early morning
matto (mât'tō) *a* crazy; insane; — *m* maniac; **scacco** — (*chess*) checkmate
mattonato (mât·tō·nâ'tō) *m* tile floor
mattone (mât·tō'nā) *m* brick; dull book; boring article; tiresome person
mattonella (mât·tō·nāl'lâ) *f* floor tile
mattutino (mât·tū·tē'nō) *a* early; morning; — *m* (*eccl*) Matins
maturare (mâ·tū·râ'rā) *vt&i* to ripen; to fall due, come due
maturazione (mât·tū·râ·tsyō'nā) *f* ripening; (*com*) maturity
maturità (mâ·tū·rē·tâ') *f* maturity; **esame di** — final exam before graduation
maturo (mâ·tū'rō) *a* mature, ripe
mausoleo (mâū·zō·lā'ō) *m* mausoleum
mazza (mâ'tsâ) *f* club; cane; (*sport*) bat
mazzo (mâ'tsō) *m* bunch; deck *(cards)*; classification
me (mā) *pron* me
meccanica (māk·kâ'nē·kâ) *f* mechanics
meccanico (māk·kâ'nē·kō) *a* mechanical; — *m* mechanic
meccanismo (māk·kâ·nē'zmō) *m* mechanism; working parts, works
meccanizzare (māk·kâ·nē·dzâ'rā) *vt* to mechanize; to automate
meccanizzazione (māk·kâ·nē·dzâ·tsyō'nā) *f* mechanization; automation
mecenate (mā·chā·nâ'tā) *m* patron
meco (mā'kō) *pron* with me
medaglia (mā·dâ'lyâ) *f* medal
medaglione (mā·dâ·lyō'nā) *m* medallion
medesimo (mā·de'zē·mō) *a* same
media (me'dyâ) *f* average; **in** — on the average
mediano (mā·dyâ'nō) *m* football halfback; — *a* mean
mediante (mā·dyân'tā) *prep* by means of, with, by
mediatore (mā·dyâ·tō'rā) *m (com)* stockbroker; mediator
medicamento (mā·dē·kâ·mān'tō) *m* medicine; medication
medicare (mā·dē·kâ'rā) *vt* to medicate; to dress; to treat
medicarsi (mā·dē·kâr'sē) *vr* to treat oneself, doctor oneself; to take medication
medicastro (mā·dē·kâ'strō) *m* quack, charlatan
medicazione (mā·dē·kâ·tsyō'nā) *f* (*med*) dressing; medication; treatment
medicina (mā·dē·chē'nâ) *f* medication, medicine; remedy
medicinali (mā·dē·chē·nâ'lē) *mpl* drugs
medico (me'dē·kō) *m* doctor; physician; — **chirurgo** physician and surgeon; — **condotto** town doctor
medio (me'dyō) *a* average; middle; — *m* average, mean
mediocre (mā·dyō'krā) *a* mediocre, ordinary
mediocrità (mā·dyō·krē·tâ') *f* mediocrity; lack of distinction
medioevale (mā·dyō·ā·vâ'lā) *a* Medieval
medioevo (mā·dyō·ā'vō) *m* Middle Ages
meditare (mā·dē·tâ'rā) *vt&i* to meditate; to mull over; to deliberate
meditazione (mā·dē·tâ·tsyō'nā) *f* meditation; deliberation
Mediterraneo (mā·dē·tār·râ'nā·ō) *m&a* Mediterranean
megafono (mā·gâ'fō·nō) *m* megaphone
megalomane (mā·gâ·lô'mâ·nā) *m&a* megalomaniac
megaton (me'gâ·tōn) *m* megaton
meglio (me'lyō) *a&adv* better; **il** — the best
mela (mā'lâ) *f* apple
melacotogna (mā·lâ·kō·tō'nyâ) *f* quince
melagrana (mā·lâ·grâ'nâ) *f* pomegranate
melanzana (mā·lân·dzâ'nâ) *f* eggplant
melassa (mā·lâs'sâ) *f* molasses
melenso (mā·lān'sō) *a* retarded; silly
mellifluo (māl·lē'flūō) *a* (*speech*) honeyed, flattering
melma (māl'mâ) *f* mire
melo (mā'lō) *m* apple tree
melodia (mā·lō·dē'â) *f* melody
melodioso (mā·lō·dyō'zō) *a* melodious
melodramma (mā·lō·drâm'mâ) *m* melodrama
melograno (mā·lō·grâ'nō) *m* pomegranate

tree
melone (mā·lō'nā) *m* melon, cantaloupe; **— d'inverno** honeydew melon
membra (māmˈbrâ) *fpl* (*anat*) limbs
membrana (mām·brâ'nâ) *f* membrane
membro (mām'brō) *m* member; (*anat*) limb
memorabile (mā·mō·râ'bē·lā) *a* notable; memorable
memoria (mā·mô'ryâ) *f* memory; memento; remembrance; **imparare a —** to memorize
memoriale (mā·mō·ryâ'lā) *m* memorial
memorie (mā·mô'ryā) *fpl* memoirs
mena (mā'nâ) *f* intrigue; plot
menare (mā·nâ'rā) *vt* to lead, guide; to wag (*tail*); **— le mani** to come to blows; **— per le lunghe** to postpone, put off; **— il can per l'aia** (*coll*) to beat around the bush; **— vanto** to brag, boast
mendicante (mān·dē·kân'tā) *m* beggar; **—** *a* begging; beggarly
mendicare (mān·dē·kâ'rā) *vt&i* to beg; to entreat
mendicità (mān·dē·chē·tâ') *f* begging; mendicancy; **ricovero di —** poorhouse; poor farm
meneghino (mā·nā·gē'nō) *a&m* Milanese
menestrello (mā·nā·strāl'lō) *m* minstrel
meningite (mā·nēn·jē'tā) *f* meningitis
meno (mā'nō) *m prep* less; **—** *adv* save, excepting; less; **il —** the least; **a — che** except that; only; **a — che non** unless; **fare a —** to do without; **— male** so much the better; it's a good thing
menomamente (mā·nō·mâ·mān'tā) *adv* not in the least, by no means, not at all
menomare (mā·nō·mâ'rā) *vt* to belittle; to prejudice, have an adverse affect on; to decrease
menomazione (mā·nō·mâ·tsyō'nā) *f* impairment; decrease
mensa (mān'sâ) *f* table; (*mil*) mess
mensile (mān·sē'lā) *a* monthly; **—** *m* salary
mensilità (mān·sē·lē·tâ') *f* monthly installment
mensilmente (mān·sēl·mān'tā) *adv* monthly, every month
mensola (men'sō·lâ) *f* console table; bracket
menta (mān'tâ) *f* mint
mentale (mān·tâ'lā) *a* mental, cerebral
mentalità (mān·tâ·lē·tâ') *f* mentality, mind
mentalmente (mān·tâl·mān'tā) *adv* mentally
mente (mān'tā) *m* mind
mentire (mān·tē'rā) *vi* to lie; **—** *vt* to misrepresent, falsify
mentitore (mān·tē·tō·rā) *m* liar; falsifier
mento (mān'tō) *m* chin
mentolo (mān·tō'lō) *m* menthol
mentre (mān'trā) *conj* while
menzionare (mān·tsyō·nâ'rā) *vt* to mention; to cite
menzione (mān·tsyō'nā) *f* mention; citing
menzogna (mān·dzō'nyâ) *f* lie; misrepresentation
menzognero (mān·dzō·nyā'rō) *m* liar; **—** *a* lying, false
meramente (mā·râ·mān'tā) *adv* simply, merely
meraviglia (mā·râ·vē'lyâ) *f* wonder; astonishment
meravigliare (mā·râ·vē·lyâ'rā) *vt* to astonish
meravigliarsi (mā·râ·vē·lyâr'sē) *vr* to wonder; to be surprised
meravigliosamente (mā·râ·vē·lyō·zâ·mān'tā) *adv* wonderfully, splendidly
meraviglioso (mā·râ·vē·lyō'zō) *a* wonderful, splendid
mercante (mār·kân'tā) *m* merchant; dealer; **fare orecchie da —** (*fig*) to turn a deaf ear; to ignore someone completely
mercanteggiare (mār·kân·tāj·jâ'rā) *vt* to haggle over, bargain over
mercantile (mār·kân·tē'lā) *a* mercantile; commercial
mercanzia (mār·kân·tsē'â) *f* merchandise
mercatino (mār·kâ·tē'nō) *m* market vendor; marketeer
mercato (mār·kâ'tō) *m* market; **— nero** black market; **a buon —** cheap
merce (mār'chā) *f* merchandise
mercede (mār·chā'dā) *f* pay; wages; reward
mercenario (mār·chā·nâ'ryō) *m&a* mercenary
merceria (mār·chā·rē'â) *f* notions store
mercoledì (mār·kō·lā·dē') *m* Wednesday
mercurio (mār·kū'ryō) *m* mercury, quicksilver
merda (mār'dâ) *f* filth; feces; dung
merenda (mā·rān'dâ) *f* afternoon snack; **— all'aperto** picnic
meridiana (mā·rē·dyâ'nâ) *f* sundial; meridian line
meridiano (mā·rē·dyâ'nō) *m&a* meridian
meridionale (mā·rē·dyō·nâ'lā) *a* southern; **—** *m* Southerner
meridione (mā·rē·dyō'nā) *m* south; **il M—** Southern Italy
meringa (mā·rēn'gâ) *f* meringue
meritare (mā·rē·tâ'rā) *vt* to deserve, be worthy of
meritarsi (mā·rē·târ'sē) *vr* to merit, deserve; to have a right to
meritatamente (mā·rē·tâ·tâ·mān'tā) *adv* deservedly; with just cause
meritevole (mā·rē·te'vō·lā) *a* worthy
merito (me'rē·tō) *m* merit; reward; value; **in — a** with reference to; **entrare in — a** to go fully into the matter of
merletto (mār·lāt'tō) *m* lace
merlo (mār'lō) *m* blackbird
merluzzo (mār·lū'tsō) *m* codfish; **olio di fegato di —** cod-liver oil
mero (mā'rō) *a* mere; absolute
meschino (mā·skē'nō) *a* unfortunate, destitute; stingy
mescita (me'shē·tâ) *f* bar; wine shop
mescolanza (mā·skō·lân'tsâ) *f* hodgepodge; mixture
mescolare (mā·skō·lâ'rā) *vt* to mix
mescolarsi (mā·skō·lâr'sē) *vr* to meddle;

to get involved; to participate
mese (mā'zā) *m* month
messa (mās'sâ) *f* Mass; placement; positioning; — **cantata** High Mass; — **in piega** finger wave; — **in scena** staging, mise-en-scène; — **a fuoco** (*photo*) focus; — **in vigore** putting into effect, enforcement
messaggero (mās·sâj·jā'rō) *m* messenger
messaggio (mās·sâj'jō) *m* message
messicano (mās·sē·kâ'nō) *a&m* Mexican
Messico (mes'sē·kō) *m* Mexico
messo (mās'sō) *m* messenger; — *a* placed, laid
mesticheria (mā·stē·kā·rē'â) *f* paint store
mestiere (mā·styā'rā) *m* trade; profession; business
mestizia (mā·stē'tsyâ) *f* sadness, sorrow
mesto (mā'stō) *a* unhappy, sad; melancholy
mestola (me'stō·lâ) *f* ladle
mestruo (me'strūō) *m* menses
meta (mā'tâ) *f* goal, ambition; target (*fig*)
metà (mā·tâ') *f* half
metafora (mā·tâ'fō·râ) *f* metaphor
metaforicamente (mā·tâ·fō·rē·kâ·mān'tā) *adv* metaphorically
metallico (mā·tâl'lē·kō) *a* metallic
metallurgico (mā·tâl·lūr'jē·kō) *m* metallurgical worker; — *a* metallurgical
metano (mā·tâ'nō) *m* natural gas; methane
metanodotto (mā·tâ·nō·dōt'tō) *m* gas pipeline
meteorologia (mā·tā·ō·rō·lō·jē'a) *f* meteorology
meteorologico (mā·tā·ō·rō·lô'jē·kō) *a* meteorological; **bollettino** — weather report
meticcio (mā·tē'chō) *m&a* half-breed; mongrel
meticoloso (mā·tē·kō·lō'zō) *a* overly exact; finicky; meticulous
metodico (mā·tô'dē·kō) *a* methodical
metodo (me'tō·dō) *m* method
metraggio (mā·trâj'jō) *m* measurement in meters; yardage
metrico (me'trē·kō) *a* metric; **sistema — decimale** metric system
metro (mā'trō) *m* meter; yardstick
metropoli (mā·trô'pō·lē) *f* metropolis
metropolitana (mā·trō·pō·lē·tâ'nâ) *f* subway (*train*)
metropolitano (mā·trō·pō·lē·tâ'nō) *a* metropolitan; — *m* policeman
mettere * (met'tā·rā) *vt* to put, set, place; — **al corrente** to inform, acquaint; to bring up to date; — **in atto** to accomplish, bring about; — **in dubbio** to put in doubt; — **in marcia** to start; to put into operation; — **in opera** to bring into play, make use of; — **in salvo** to rescue; — **i punti sugli i** (*fig*) to dot one's i's
mettersi * (met'tār·sē) *vr* to put on; to dress in; to place oneself; — **in cammino** to start off, set out; — **in mezzo** to interfere; — **d'accordo** to come to an agreement
mezzadro (mā·dzâ'drō) *m* sharecropper
mezzaluna (mā·dzâ·lū'nâ) *f* halfmoon
mezzanino (mā·dzâ·nē'nō) *m* mezzanine
mezzano (mā·dzâ'nō) *m* pander, pimp; — *a* middle
mezzanotte (mā·dzâ·nōt'tā) *f* midnight
mezzo (mā'dzō) *adj&adv* half; — *m* half; means; **per — di** by means of; **togliersi di** — to get out of the way
mezzogiorno (mā·dzō·jōr'nō) *m* south; noon
mezzotermine (mā·dzō·ter'mē·nā) *m* compromise; modus vivendi
mi (mē) *pron* me; to me
miagolare (myâ·gō·lâ'rā) *vi* to mew
mica (mē'kâ) *adv* not in the least; not at all; — *f* crumb; mica
miccia (mē'châ) *f* fuse (*explosive*)
micidiale (mē·chē·dyâ'lā) *a* fatal; deadly
micio (mē'chō) *m* tomcat
microbo (mē'krō·bō) *m* microbe
microcamera (mē·krō·kâ'mā·râ) *f* pocket camera
microcosmo (mē·krō·kō'zmō) *m* microcosm
microfilm (mē·krō·fēlm') *m* microfilm
microfono (mē·krô'fō·nō) *m* microphone
microfotografia (mē·krō·fō·tō·grâ·fē'â) *f* microphotograph, microprint
microlettore (mē·krō·lāt·tō'rā) *m* microfilm viewer
micromotore (mē·krō·mō·tō'rā) *m* bicycle motor
microscopio (mē·krō·skô'pyō) *m* microscope
microsolco (mē·krō·sōl'kō) *a* microgroove; **disco** — long-playing record
midolla (mē·dōl'lâ) *f* crumb
midollo (mē·dōl'lō) *m* (*anat*) marrow; — **spinale** spinal cord
miei (myā'ē) *pron* mine; — *a* my
miele (myā'lā) *m* honey
mietere (mye'tā·rā) *vt* to harvest; to mow
mietitore (myā·tē·tō'rā) *m* reaper, harvester
mietitrice (myā·tē·trē'chā) *f* harvester; (*mech*) reaper, reaping machine
migliaio (mē·lyâ'yō) *m* thousand
miglio (mē'lyō) *m* mile; millet
miglioramento (mē·lyō·râ·mān'tō) *m* improvement; bettering
migliorare (mē·lyō·râ'rā) *vt&i* to improve; to better
migliorarsi (mē·lyō·râr'sē) *vr* to improve oneself; to grow better
migliore (mē·lyō'rā) *a* better; superior; **il** — the best
miglioria (mē·lyō·rē'â) *f* improvement
mignolo (mē'nyō·lō) *m* little finger; little toe
Milano (mē·lâ'nō) *f* Milan
miliardo (mē·lyâr'dō) *m* billion
milionario (mē·lyō·nâ'ryō) *m* millionaire
milione (mē·lyō'nā) *m* million
militante (mē·lē·tân'tā) *a* aggressive, militant
militare (mē·lē·tâ'rā) *a* military; — *m* serviceman; — *vi* to militate
militarismo (mē·lē·tâ·rē'zmō) *m* militarism

militarmente (mē·lē·târ·mān'tā) *adv* by armed force; militarily
milite (mē'lē·tā) *m* soldier; — **ignoto** unknown soldier; — **della polizia stradale** highway patrolman
millantatore (mēl·lân·tâ·tō'rā) *m* braggart
mille (mēl'lā) *a* thousand
millenario (mēl·lā·nâ'ryō) *a* millenial
millennio (mēl·len'nyō) *m* millennium
millesimo (mēl·le'zē·mō) *a* thousandth
millimetro (mēl·lē'mā·trō) *m* millimeter
milza (mēl'tsâ) *f* spleen
mimica (mē'mē·kâ) *f* mimicry
mimetizzare (mē·mā·tē·dzâ'rā) *vt* to camouflage
mimo (mē'mō) *m* mimic; pantomime dancer
mina (mē'nâ) *f* mine
minaccia (mē·nâ'châ) *f* threat
minacciare (mē·nâ·châ'rā) *vt* to threaten
minaccioso (mē·nâ·chō'zō) *a* menacing
minare (mē·nâ'rā) *vt* to mine; to weaken, undermine
minareto (mē·nâ·rā'tō) *m* minaret
minatore (mē·nâ·tō'rā) *m* miner
minerale (mē·nā·râ'lā) *m&a* mineral
mineralogia (mē·nā·râ·lō·jē'â) *f* mineralogy
minerario (mē·nā·râ'ryō) *a* mining
minestra (mē·nā'strâ) *f* soup
minestrone (mē·nā·strō'nā) *m* vegetable soup; (*fig*) potpourri, hodgepodge
mingherlino (mēn·gār·lē'nō) *a* thin; lithe, svelte
miniatura (mē·nyâ·tū'râ) *f* miniature
miniera (mē·nyā'râ) *f* mine; — **di ferro** iron mine
minimamente (mē·nē·mâ·mān'tā) *adv* by no means; not in the least
minimizzare (mē·nē·mē·dzâ'rā) *vt* to minimize; to belittle
minimo (mē'nē·mō) *m* minimum; — *a* least, lowest, smallest; cheapest; slightest
minio (mē'nyō) *m* red lead
ministero (mē·nē·stā'rō) *m* ministry, department; **M– degli Esteri** State Department; **pubblico** — public prosecutor, prosecuting attorney, district attorney
ministro (mē·nē'strō) *m* minister; secretary, cabinet member
minoranza (mē·nō·rân'tsâ) *f* minority
minorativo (mē·nō·râ·tē'vō) *a* lessening, diminishing
minorato (mē·nō·râ'tō) *a* disabled, handicapped
minorazione (mē·nō·râ·tsyō'nā) *f* diminishing, reduction; handicap
minore (mē·nō'rā) *a* less; minor; younger
minorenne (mē·nō·rān'nā) *m&a* minor
minuscola (mē·nū'skō·lâ) *f* small letter, lowercase letter
minuscolo (mē·nū'skō·lō) *a* tiny, minute
minuta (mē·nū'tâ) *f* rough copy; draft
minutante (mē·nū·tân'tā) *m* retailer
minuteria (mē·nū·tā·rē'â) *f* nicknack
minuto (mē·nū'tō) *m* minute; — *a* small; **al** — at retail
minuziosamente (mē·nū·tsyō·zâ·mān'tā) *adv* minutely, in detail
minuzioso (mē·nū·tsyō'zō) *a* detailed; accurate; complete
mio (mē'ō) *pron* mine; — *a* my
miope (mē'ō·pā) *a* shortsighted; nearsighted
mira (mē'râ) *f* aim; sight; target
mirabilmente (mē·râ·bēl·mān'tā) *adv* wonderfully; admirably
miracolo (mē·râ'kō·lō) *m* miracle
miracolosamente (mē·râ·kō·lō·zâ·mān'tā) *adv* miraculously; astoundingly
miracoloso (mē·râ·kō·lō'zō) *a* miraculous; astounding
miraggio (mē·râj'jō) *m* mirage, vision
mirare (mē·râ'rā) *vt* to look at; — *vi* to aim
mirarsi (mē·râr'sē) *vr* to gaze at oneself; — **intorno** to look around; to be on the qui vive
miriade (mē·rē'â·dā) *f* great number
mirino (mē·rē'nō) *m* gunsight; (*photo*) viewfinder
mirra (mēr'râ) *f* myrrh
mirto (mēr'tō) *m* myrtle
misantropo (mē·zân'trō·pō) *m* misanthrope; — *a* misanthropic
miscela (mē·shā'lâ) *f* blending; mixture
mischia (mē'skyâ) *f* fight, fray
mischiare (mē·skyâ'rā) *vt* to jumble; to mix up
mischiarsi (mē·skyâr'sē) *vr* to interfere; to meddle
miscredente (mē·skrā·dān'tā) *a* unbelieving; — *m* unbeliever
miscuglio (mē·skū'lyō) *m* blending, mix
miserabile (mē·zā·râ'bē·lā) *a* contemptible; miserable; vile
miserabilmente (mē·zā·râ·bēl·mān'tā) *adv* badly; wretchedly
miseria (mē·ze'ryâ) *f* want; poverty; (*fig*) bagatelle, trifle
misericordia (mē·zā·rē·kôr'dyâ) *f* pity; mercy
misfatto (mē·sfât'tō) *m* wrongdoing, offense
missile (mēs·sē'lā) *m* missile; — **balistico** ballistic missile; — **guidato** guided missile
missionario (mē·syō·nâ'ryō) *m* missionary
missione (mēs·syō'nā) *f* mission
misterioso (mē·stā·ryō'zō) *a* mysterious, arcane
mistero (mē·stā'rō) *m* mystery
misticismo (mē·stē·chē'zmō) *m* mysticism
mistificare (mē·stē·fē·kâ'rā) *vt* to adulterate; to deceive, hoodwink
mistificazione (mē·stē·fē·kâ·tsyō'nā) *f* hoax, deceit, trick
misto (mē'stō) *a* mixed; **scuola mista** coeducational school
misura (mē·zū'râ) *f* measure; criterion, yardstick
misurare (mē·zū·râ'rā) *vt* to measure; to evaluate
misurarsi (mē·zū·râr'sē) *vr* to evaluate oneself; to vie, compete; to try on (*clothing*)

misurato (mē·zū·râ'tō) *a* measured; cautious
mite (mē'tā) *a* temperate; mellow, gentle
mitigare (mē·tē·gâ'rā) *vt* to mitigate; to ease
mitigarsi (mē·tē·gâr'sē) *vr* to abate, subside
mito (mē'tō) *m* myth
mitra (mē'trâ) *f* miter; submachine gun
mitragliatrice (mē·trâ·lyâ·trē'chā) *f* machine gun
mittente (mēt·tān'tā) *m* sender; — *a* sending
mobile (mô'bē·lā) *m* piece of furniture; — *f* riot squad; — *a* mobile; shifting; undependable, flighty; **sabbie mobili** quicksand
mobilia (mō·bē'lyâ) *f* furniture
mobiliare (mō·bē·lyâ'rā) *a* personal; movable; **proprietà** — personal property
mobiliere (mō·bē·lyā'rā) *m* furniture manufacturer; furniture dealer
mobilità (mō·bē·lē·tâ') *f* mobility; flightiness; fickleness
mobilitare (mō·bē·lē·tâ'rā) *vt* to marshal; to mobilize
mobilitazione (mō·bē·lē·tâ·tsyō'nā) *f* mobilization; marshaling
mocassino (mō·kâs·sē'nō) *m* mocassin
moccioso (mō·chō'zō) *m* brat; nasty individual
moda (mō'dā) *f* fashion; **di** — fashionable, **fuori di** — out of style; **ultima** — latest style
modalità (mō·dâ·lē·tâ') *f* form, characteristic
modello (mō·dāl'lō) *m* sample; pattern; model
moderare (mō·dā·râ'rā) *vt* to moderate; to relax, cool
moderarsi (mō·dā·râr'sē) *vr* to hold oneself back; to control oneself, keep oneself under control
moderato (mō·dā·râ'tō) *a* moderate; temperate
moderazione (mō·dā·râ·tsyō'nā) *f* moderation
modernamente (mō·dār·nâ·mān'tā) *adv* modernly; in the latest style; fashionably
modernizzare (mō·dār·nē·dzâ'rā) *vt* to modernize; to update
moderno (mō·dār'nō) *a* modern; current
modestamente (mō·dā·stâ·mān'tā) *adv* modestly; unassumingly
modestia (mō·de'styâ) *f* modesty; reserve; unassumingness
modesto (mō·dā'stō) *a* modest; reserved
modifica (mō·dē'fē·kâ) *f* alteration; **–re** (mō·dē·fē·kâ'rā) *vt* to change, alter, modify
modificazione (mō·dē·fē·kâ·tsyō'nā) *f* revision; change; modification
modista (mō·dē'stâ) *f* milliner
modisteria (mō·dē·stā·rē'â) *f* millinery shop; millinery
modo (mō'dō) *m* way; manner; habit; **in ogni** — anyhow; in any event; **oltre** — extremely; excessively; **fare a** — **suo** to get one's own way; to do as one pleases; **in** — **da** so as to; **in nessun** — by no means; **per** — **di dire** as it were, so to speak
modulazione (mō·dū·lâ·tsyō'nā) *f* modulation; intonation
modulo (mô'dū·lō) *m* blank, form
moffetta (mōf·fāt'tâ) *f* skunk
mogano (mô'gâ·nō) *m* mahogany
moglie (mô'lyā) *f* wife
mola (mō'lâ) *f* grindstone
molare (mō·lâ'rā) *vt* to grind; — *a&m* molar
mole (mō'lā) *f* bulk, mass; greater part
molecola (mō·le'kō·lâ) *f* molecule
molestare (mō·lā·stâ'rā) *vt* to bother; to annoy; to trouble
molestia (mō·le'styâ) *f* nuisance; trouble; bother; annoyance
molla (mōl'lâ) *f* spring
mollare (mōl·lâ'rā) *vt* to loosen; — *vi* to yield
molle (mōl'lā) *a* soft; tender; effeminate, weak
molle (mōl'lā) *fpl* tongs
mollette (mōl·lāt'tā) *fpl* small tongs; paper clips; — **per la biancheria** clothespins
mollettiere (mōl·lāt·tyā'rā) *fpl* leggings
mollezza (mōl·lā'tsâ) *f* effeminacy; softness; weakness
mollica (mōl·lē'kâ) *f* bread crumb
mollusco (mōl·lū'skō) *m* shellfish, mollusk
molo (mō'lō) *m* pier
molteplice (mōl·te'plē·chā) *a* multiple, manifold
moltiplicare (mōl·tē·plē·kâ'rā) *vt* to multiply
moltiplicatore (mōl·tē·plē·kâ·tō'rā) *m* multiplier
moltiplicazione (mōl·tē·plē·kâ·tsyō'nā) *f* multiplication
moltissimo (mōl·tēs'sē·mō) *a&adv* very much, a great deal
moltitudine (mōl·tē·tū'dē·nā) *f* throng, multitude
molto (mōl'tō) *a* much; — *adv* very
momentaneamente (mō·mān·tâ·nā·â·mān'tā) *adv* temporarily; for the moment; at any moment
momentaneo (mō·mān·tâ'nā·ō) *a* ephemeral; transitory
momento (mō·mān'tō) *m* moment
monaca (mô'nâ·kâ) *f* nun
monaco (mô'nâ·kō) *m* friar; monk
Monaco (mô'nā·kō) *m* Monaco; — **di Baviera** Munich
monarca (mō·nâr'kâ) *m* monarch
monarchia (mō·nâr·kē'â) *f* monarchy
monarchico (mō·nâr'kē·kō) *a* monarchical; — *m (pol)* monarchist
monastero (mō·nâ'stā'rō) *m* monastery; cloister; convent
moncherino (mōn·kā·rē'nō) *m* stump
mondanità (mōn·dâ·nē·tâ') *f* mundanity, worldliness
mondano (mōn·dâ'nō) *a* worldly; **vita**

mondana society life; high society
mondezzaio (mōn·dā·tsâ'yō) *m* garbage dump
mondiale (mōn·dyâ'lā) *a* world-wide; world
mondo (mōn'dō) *m* world; **un — di gente** a very large crowd; **da che — è —** since the dawn of time; **andare all'altro —** to die, pass on; **caschi il —!** come what may!; **venire al —** to be born; **—** *a* pure, spotless
monello (mō·nāl'lō) *m* urchin; street arab
moneta (mō·nā'tâ) *f* money; coin
mongolo (môn'gō·lō) *m&a* Mongolian, Mongol
monile (mō·nē'lā) *m* necklace
monocolo (mō·nô'kō·lō) *m* monocle
monofase (mō·nō·fâ'zā) *a* (*elec*) single-phase
monolito (mō·nō·lē'tō) *m* monolith
monologo (mō·nô'lō·gō) *m* monologue
monopattino (mō·nō·pât·tē'nō) *m* scooter
monopolizzare (mō·nō·pō·lē·dzâ'rā) *vt* to monopolize; to corner
monopolio (mō·nō·pô'lyō) *m* monopoly
monotonia (mō·nō·tō·nē'â) *f* tedium, monotony
monotono (mō·nô'tō·nō) *a* tiresome; monotonous
montacarico (mōn·tâ·kâ'rē·kō) *m* freight elevator
montaggio (mōn·tâj'jō) *m* montage; (*mech*) assemblage; editing (*movies*)
montagna (mōn·tâ'nyâ) *f* mountain
montagnoso (mōn·tâ·nyō'zō) *a* mountainous
montanaro (mōn·tâ·nâ'rō) *m* mountaineer; **—** *a* mountain
montante (mōn·tân'tā) *m* uppercut (*boxing*); **—** *f* amount; (*avi*) strut
montare (mōn·tâ'rā) *vt* to climb up; (*mech*) to assemble; to praise, boost; **—** *vi* to ascend, go up
montarsi (mōn·târ'sē) *vr* to make a scene; to get upset
montatura (mōn·tâ·tū'râ) *f* ballyhoo; publicity buildup; publicity stunt
montavivande (mōn·tâ·vē·vân'dā) *m* dumbwaiter
monte (mōn'tā) *m* mountain; lots, large quantity; **— di pietà** pawnshop; **andare a —** to amount to nothing; to fall through; **mandare a —** to ruin, upset, foil
montone (mōn·tō'nā) *m* mutton; ram
montuoso (mōn·twō'zō) *a* mountainous
monumento (mō·nū·mān'tō) *m* monument
mora (mō'râ) *f* blackberry; delay
morale (mō·râ'lā) *a* moral; **—** *f* morals; **—** *m* morale, spirits
moralità (mō·râ·lē·tâ') *f* moral character; morality
moratoria (mō·râ·tô'ryâ) *f* moratorium; suspension
morbidezza (mōr·bē·dā'tsâ) *f* softness; weakness
morbido (môr'bē·dō) *a* soft; weak; effete
morbillo (mōr·bēl'lō) *m* measles
mordace (mōr·dâ'chā) *a* biting, sarcastic, trenchant
mordere * (môr'dā·rā) *vt* to bite; to eat away
morente (mō·rān'tā) *a* fading away; dying
moretta (mō·rāt'tâ) *f* brunette
morfina (mōr·fē'nâ) *f* morphine
moribondo (mō·rē·bōn'dō) *a* dying
morigerato (mō·rē·jā·râ'tō) *a* wellbred; mannerly
morire * (mō·rē'rā) *vi* to die; to fade away; to pass away
mormorare (mōr·mō·râ'rā) *vi&t* to murmur; to grumble; to rustle
mormorio (mōr·mō·rē'ō) *m* murmur; rustling
moro (mō'rō) *m* Negro; Moor; blackberry bush
moroso (mō·rō'zō) *a* in arrears, late
morsa (mōr'sâ) *f* vise
morsetto (mōr·sāt'tō) *m* clamp
morso (mōr'sō) *m* bite; sting; morsel
mortaio (mōr·tâ'yō) *m* mortar
mortale (mōr·tâ'lā) *a&m* mortal
morte (mōr'tā) *f* death
mortella (mōr·tāl'lâ) *f* myrtle; **— di palude** cranberry
mortificare (mōr·tē·fē·kâ'rā) *vt* to mortify; to humble, shame
mortificarsi (mōr·tē·fē·kâr'sē) *vr* to humiliate oneself; to be ashamed
mortificazione (mōr·tē·fē·kâ·tsyō'nā) *f* mortification; shame
morto ((mōr'tō) *a* dead; **capitale —** (*com*) dormant capital; **binario —** (*rail*) siding; **giorno dei morti** All Souls' Day
mosaico (mō·zâ'ē·kō) *m* mosaic
mosca (mō'skâ) *f* fly; **— bianca** (*fig*) oddity, rarity; exception
Mosca (mō'skâ) *f* Moscow
moscerino (mō·shā·rē'nō) *m* gnat
moschea (mō·skā'â) *f* mosque
moschetto (mō·skāt'tō) *m* rifle, musket
moscone (mō·skō'nā) *m* bluebottle fly; (*fig*) hanger-on
moscovita (mō·skō·vē'tâ) *m&a* Muscovite
mossa (mōs'sâ) *f* move, movement; gesture; impetus; **— di corpo** bowel movement
mossiere (mōs·syā'rā) *m* starter (*race*)
mosso (mōs'sō) *a* moved; removed; **mare —** rough sea
mostarda (mō·stâr'dâ) *f* mustard
mosto (mō'stō) *m* fermenting grape juice; new wine
mostra (mō'strâ) *f* show, exhibit; **far — di** to pretend; to feign; to make a great show of; **far — di sè** to make oneself conspicuous
mostrare (mō·strâ'rā) *vt* to show; to evidence
mostrarsi (mō·strâr'sē) *vr* to appear, seem; to turn out, prove
mostro (mō'strō) *m* monster
mostruoso (mō·strūō'zō) *a* monstrous
mota (mō'tâ) *f* slime, mire; mud
motivare (mō·tē·vâ'rā) *vt* to motivate; to account for; to justify

motivazione (mō·tē·vâ·tsyō'nā) *f* motivation; motive
motivo (mō·tē'vō) *m* motive; motif; reason, cause; (*mus*) theme
moto (mō'tō) *m* motion: uprising; **–aratura** (mō·tō·â·râ·tū'râ) *f* mechanized farming; **–cicletta** (mō·tō·chē·klāt'tâ) *f* motorcycle; **–ciclista** (mō·tō·chē·klē'stâ) *m* motorcyclist; **–dromo** (mō·tō·drō'mō) *m* motordrome; **–furgoncino** (mō·tō·fūr·gōn·chē'nō) *m* motorcycle truck; **–leggiera** (mō·tō·lāj·jā'râ) *f* motorbike; motor scooter; **–nave** (mō·tō·nâ'vā) *f* motor ship; **–peschereccio** (mō·tō·pā·skā·rā'chō) *m* motorized fishing boat; **–re** (mō·tō'rā) *m* motor; **–re** *a* driving, propelling; forcing; **forza motrice** driving force; **–retta** (mō·tō·rāt'tâ) *f* motor scooter; **–rino** (mō·tō·rē'nō) *m* small motor; (*auto*) self-starter; **–rista** (mō·to·rē'stâ) *m* motorman; driver; mechanic; machinist; **–rizzare** (mō·tō·rē·dzâ'rā) *vt* to motorize; **–scafo** (mō·tō·skâ'fō) *m* motorboat; **–vedetta** (mō·tō·vā·dāt'tâ) *f* police motorboat; **–veicolo** (mō·tō·vā·ē'kō·lō) *m* motor vehicle; **–zattera** (mō·tō·tsât'tā·râ) *f* (*mil*) landing craft
motto (mōt'tō) *m* motto; — **di spirito** witticism
movente (mō·vān'tā) *m* motive, reason; — *a* moving
movimento (mō·vē·mān'tō) *m* movement; hustle; gesture; — **ferroviario** railway traffic; — **d'affari** (*com*) turnover
mozione (mō·tsyō'nā) *f* (*pol*) motion, resolution
mozzafiato (mō·tsâ·fyâ'tō) *a* breathtaking; thrilling
mozzare (mō·tsâ'rā) *vt* to cut, sever
mozzicone (mō·tsē·kō'nā) *m* cigar stub; stump
mozzo (mō'tsō) *m* (*naut*) cabin boy; hub (*wheel*); — *a* severed
mucca (mūk'kâ) *f* cow
mucchio (mūk'kyō) *m* pile; (*coll*) lot, great deal
mucosa (mū·kō'zâ) *f* mucous membrane
muffa (mūf'fâ) *f* mould
muffola (mūf'fō·lâ) *f* kiln
mugghiare (mūg·gyâ'rā), **muggire** (mūj·jē'rā) *vi* to bellow; to low; to roar; to howl
mughetto (mū·gāt'tō) *m* lily of the valley
mugnaio (mū·nyâ'yō) *m* miller
mugolare (mū·gō·lâ'rā) *vi* to whine
mulatto (mū·lât'tō) *m* mulatto
mulinello (mū·lē·nāl'lō) *m* whirlwind; whirlpool; windlass; whirl
mulino (mū·lē'nō) *m* mill
mulo (mū'lō) *m* mule
multa (mūl'tâ) *f* fine; **–re** (mūl·tâ'rā) *vt* to fine; to penalize
mummia (mūm'myâ) *f* mummy
mungere * (mūn'jā·rā) *vt* to milk; (*fig*) to sweat, fleece
municipale (mū·nē·chē·pâ'lā) *a* municipal
municipalità (mū·nē·chē·pâ·lē·tâ') *f* municipal authority
municipio (mū·nē·chē'pyō) *m* city hall; town hall
munificenza (mū·nē·fē·chān'tsâ) *f* liberality, largess
munifico (mū·nē'fē·kō) *a* generous; munificent
munire (mū·nē'rā) *vt* to fortify; to provide
munirsi (mū·nēr'sē) *vr* to prepare oneself; to get ready
munizione (mū·nē·tsyō'nā) *f* ammunition
muovere * (mwô'vā·rā) *vt* to cause; to move; to stir up; — **una domanda** to ask a question
muoversi * (mwô'vār·sē) *vr* to move; to stir; to shake
mura (mū'râ) *fpl* city walls
muraglione (mū·râ·lyō'nā) *m* bulwark; high wall
murare (mū·râ'rā) *vt* to wall; to close up
muratore (mū·râ·tō'rā) *m* bricklayer; mason
muratura (mū·râ·tū'râ) *f* masonry
muro (mū'rō) *m* wall; impediment
muschio (mū'skyō) *m* moss
muscolo (mū'skō·lō) *m* muscle
muscoloso (mū·skō·lō'zō) *a* muscular; sinewy
museo (mū·zā'ō) *m* museum
museruola (mū·zā·rūō'lâ) *f* muzzle; nose (*animal*)
musica (mū'zē·kâ) *f* music
musicale (mū·zē·kâ'lā) *a* musical
musicante (mū·zē·kân'tā) *m* professional musician
musicista (mū·zē·chē'stâ) *m* musician
muso (mū'zō) *m* muzzle; nose (*animal*)
mussolina (mūs·sō·lē'nâ) *f* muslin
musulmano (mū·zūl·mâ'nō) *m&a* Muslim, Moslem
mutabile (mū·tâ'bē·lā) *a* capricious, changeable; mutable
mutamento (mū·tâ·mān'tō) *m* variation; change; mutation
mutande (mū·tân'dā) *fpl* underpants, drawers
mutandine (mū·tân·dē'nā) *fpl* panties; shorts; briefs: — **da bagno** swimming trunks
mutare (mū·tâ'rā) *vt* to change; to mutate
mutevole (mū·te'vō·lā) *a* changeable
mutilato (mū·tē·lâ'tō) *a* maimed; — *m* cripple; — **della guerra** disabled war veteran
mutismo (mū·tē'zmō) *m* muteness; uncommunicativeness
muto (mū'tō) *a* mute; **cinema** — silent film
mutria (mū'tryâ) *f* haughtiness; nerve, cheek, gall
mutuamente (mū·twâ·mān'tā) *adv* mutually
mutuo (mū'twō) *a* mutual; — *m* loan

N

nacchere (nâk'kā·rā) *fpl* castanets
nafta (nâf'tâ) *f* naphtha; fuel oil
naftalina (nâf·tâ·lē'nâ) *f* napthaline
naia (nâ'yâ) *f* cobra
nailon (nâ'ē·lōn) *m* nylon
nano (nâ'nō) *a&m* dwarf
napoletano (nâ·pō·lā·tâ'nō) *a&m* Neapolitan
Napoli (nâ'pō·lē) *f* Naples
narcotico (nâr·kô'tē·kō) *a&m* narcotic
narcotizzare (nâr·kō·tē·dzâ'rā) *vt* to anesthetize; to drug
narice (nâ·rē'chā) *f* nostril
narrare (nâr·râ'rā) *vt* to relate, tell
narratore (nâr·râ·tō'rā) *m* storyteller; narrator
narrazione (nâr·râ·tsyō'nā) *f* telling, narration; narrative, account
nasale (nâ·zâ'lā) *a* nasal
nascere * (nâ'shā·rā) *vt* to be born; to spring up; to originate
nascita (nâ'shē·tâ) *f* birth; provenance
nascondere * (nâ·skôn'dā·rā) *vt* to hide; to cover, disguise
nascondersi * (nâ·skôn'dār·sē) *vr* to keep out of sight, conceal oneself
nascondiglio (nâ·skōn·dē'lyō) *m* cache; hiding place
nascostamente (nâ·skō·stâ·mān'tā) *adv* stealthily; secretly; underhandedly
nascosto (nâ·skō'stō) *a* hidden; underhanded, sly
nasello (nâ·zāl'lō) *m* door latch
naso (nâ'zō) *m* nose; **— a —** face to face; **restare con un palmo di —** (*fig*) to be disappointed; to be taken aback
nastro (nâ'strō) *m* tape; ribbon; **— isolante** friction tape; **— trasportatore** conveyor belt; **sega a —** band saw
Natale (nâ·tâ'lā) *m* Christmas, Yule; **vigilia di —** Christmas Eve; **Buon — !** Merry Christmas!
natale (nâ·tâ'lā) *a* native; **—** *m* birth; ancestry
natalità (nâ·tâ·lē·tâ') *f* birthrate
natalizio (nâ·tâ·lē'tsyō) *m* birthday; **—** *a* natal
natante (nâ·tân'tā) *a* afloat, floating; **—** *m* watercraft
natica (nâ'tē·kâ) *f* buttock
nativo (nâ·tē'vō) *a&m* native
nato (nâ'tō) *a* born; sprung up, originated
natura (nâ·tū'râ) *f* nature; type; **— morta** (*art*) still life
naturale (nâ·tū·râ'lā) *a* natural; **di grandezza —** life-size
naturalezza (nâ·tū·râ·lā'tsâ) *f* artlessness; naturalness; **con —** naively; simply
naturalismo (nâ·tū·râ·lē'zmō) *m* naturalism
naturalista (nâ·tū·râ·lē'stâ) *m* naturalist
naturalizzare (nâ·tū·râ·lē·dzâ'rā) *vt* to naturalize; to grant citizenship to
naturalizzarsi (nâ·tū·râ·lē·dzâr'sē) *vr* to become naturalized; to become a citizen
naturalizzazione (nâ·tū·râ·lē·dzâ·tsyō'nā) *f* naturalization
naturalmente (nâ·tū·râl·mān'tā) *adv* of course
naturismo (nâ·tū·rē'zmō) *m* nudism
naufragare (nâū·frâ·gâ'rā) *vi* to be shipwrecked; to fail, be spoiled; **far —** to shipwreck, cast away; to ruin, spoil, upset
naufragio (nâū·frâ'jō) *m* shipwreck; (*fig*) failure; ruining, upsetting
naufrago (nâ'ū·frâ·gō) *m* cast away, shipwrecked; ruined, upset; **—** *m* shipwreck victim, castaway; **— della vita** (*fig*) pariah, outcast
nausea (nâ'ū·zā·â) *f* nausea; **far — a** to repulse, disgust
nauseante (nâū·zā·ân'tā) *a* disgusting, loathsome
nautica (nâ'ū·tē·kâ) *f* science of navigation, navigation
nautico (nâ'ū·tē·kō) *a* nautical
navale (nâ·vâ'lā) *a* naval
navata (nâ·vâ'tâ) *f* (*arch*) nave, aisle
nave (nâ'vā) *f* boat; ship
navetta (nâ·vāt'tâ) *f* shuttle; **fare la —** to ply back and forth
navicella (nâ·vē·chāl'lâ) *f* (*avi*) nacelle; small vessel
navigabile (nâ·vē·gâ'bē·lā) *a* navigable
navigante (nâ·vē·gân'tā) *m* sailor; **—** *a* sailing
navigare (nâ·vē·gâ'rā) *vt* to sail; to navigate
navigato (nâ·vē·gâ'tō) *a* (*fig*) sly, experienced, knowing
navigazione (nâ·vē·gâ·tsyō'nā) *f* navigation
nazionale (nâ·tsyō·nâ'lā) *a&m* national
nazionalismo (nâ·tsyō·nâ·lē'zmō) *m* nationalism
nazionalista (nâ·tsyō·nâ·lē'stâ) *m* nationalist
nazionalità (nâ·tsyō·nâ·lē·tâ') *f* nationality
nazionalizzare (nâ·tsyō·nâ·lē·dzâ'rā) *vt* to nationalize
nazione (nâ·tsyō'nā) *f* nation
ne (nā) *pron* some, any; of him, of it, of her; from there
nè (nā) *conj* neither, nor; **— . . . —** neither . . . nor
neanche (nā·ân'kā) *adv* not even, even; **—** *conj* neither; **— per sogno** by no means; I shouldn't dream of it
nebbia (neb'byâ) *f* fog
nebbioso (nāb·byō'zō) *a* hazy, foggy
nebulizzare (nā·bū·lē·dzâ'rā) *vt* to nebulize, atomize
nebulizzatore (nā·bū·lē·dzâ·tō'rā) *m* aerosol bomb; atomizer
nebulosa (nā·bū·lō'zâ) *f* (*astr*) nebula
nebuloso (nā·bū·lō'zō) *a* cloudy; nebulous, indistinct
necessariamente (nā·chās·sâ·ryâ·man'tā) *adv* by necessity, necessarily
necessario (nā·chās·sâ'ryō) *a* necessary

necessità (nā·chās·sē·tâ′) *f* poverty; necessity
necessitare (nā·chās·sē·tâ′rā) *vt* to compel; to need, be in need of; to necessitate; — *vi* to be needed, be necessary
necrologia (nā·krō·lō·jē′â) *f* obit, death notice; eulogy
necrologio (nā·krō·lô′jō) *m* obituary
necrosi (nā·krō′zē) *f* gangrene, necrosis
nefando (nā·fân′dō) *a* wicked, infamous
nefasto (nā·fâ′stō) *a* ill-fated, ill-starred; unfavorable
nefrite (nā·frē′tā) *f* nephritis
negare (nā·gâ′rā) *vt* to deny; to gainsay; to negate
negativa (nā·gâ·tē′vâ) *f* negative; denial
negativamente (nā·gâ·tē·vâ·mān′tā) *adv* negatively
negazione (nā·gâ·tsyō′nā) *f* denial; negation; contradiction
negli (nā′lyē) *prep* in the
negligente (nā·glē·jān′tā) *a* lax, heedless, negligent
negligentemente (nā·glē·jān·tā·mān′tā) *adv* negligently, heedlessly
negligenza (nā·glē·jān′tsâ) *f* laxity, negligence
negoziante (nā·gō·tsyân′tā) *m* storekeeper; merchant; dealer
negoziare (nā·gō·tsyâ′rā) *vt&i* (*com*) to do business; to negotiate
negoziato (nā·gō·tsyâ′tō) *m* negotiation; deal
negozio (nā·gô′tsyō) *m* store, shop
negra (nā′grâ) *f* Negro woman
negriero (nā·gryā′rō) *m* slave dealer; — *a* slave
negro (nā′grō) *m* Negro
negromante (nā·grō·mân′tā) *m* sorcerer
nei (nā′ē), **nel** (nāl), **nella** (nāl′lâ), **nelle** (nāl′lā), **negli** (nā′lyē) *prep* in the
nemico (nā·mē′kō) *m* enemy; — *a* enemy; hostile
nemmeno (nām·mā′nō) *adv* not even, even; — *conj* neither
neo (nā′ō) *m* mole (*growth*); (*fig*) imperfection, flaw
neon (nā′ōn) *m* neon; **luci al** — neon lights
neonato (nā·ō·nâ′tō) *a* newborn
nepotismo (nā·pō·tē′zmō) *m* partiality; nepotism
neppure (nāp·pū′rā) *adv* not even, even; — *conj* neither
nerastro (nā·râ′strō) *a* somewhat black, blackish
nerbata (nār·bâ′tâ) *f* flogging, whipping
nerbo (nār′bō) *m* thong; sinew; whip; **il — del partito** the backbone of the party
nerboruto (nār·bō·rū′tō) *a* sinewy, muscular
neretto (nā·rāt′tō) *m* (*print*) boldface type
nero (nā′rō) *a* black
nervo (nār′vō) *m* nerve; (*arch*) rib
nervosismo (nār·vō·zē′zmō) *m* nervousness; nervous condition
nervoso (nār·vō′zō) *a* nervous
nespola (ne′spō·lâ) *f* medlar; (*coll*) blow; beating
nessuno (nās·sū′nō) *a* any, no; — *pron* nobody, none, no one, anyone
nettare (nāt·tâ′rā) *vt* to clean
nettare (net′tâ·rā) *m* nectar
nettezza (nāt·tā′tsâ) *f* tidiness; cleanness
netto (nāt′tō) *a* clean; distinct; (*com*) net; — **di spese** free of charge
neurologia (nāū·rō·lō·jē′â) *f* neurology
neurologo (nāū·rô′lō·gō) *m* neurologist
neutrale (nāū·trâ′lā) *a* neutral; imparital; undecided
neutralità (nāū·trâ·lē·tâ′) *f* neutrality
neutralizzare (nāū·trâ·lē·dzâ′rā) *vt* to neutralize
neutralizzazione (nāū·trâ·lē·dzâ·tsyō′nā) *f* neutralization
neutralmente (nāū·trâl·mān′tā) *adv* neutrally
neutro (ne′ū·trō) *a* neutral; — *m* neuter
neutrone (nāū·trō′nā) *m* neutron
neve (nā′vā) *f* snow
nevicare (nā·vē·kâ′rā) *vi* to snow
nevicata (nā·vē·kâ′tâ) *f* snowfall
nevischio (nā·vē′skyō) *m* fine snow; sleet
nevoso (nā·vō′zō) *a* snow-capped; snowy
nevralgia (nā·vrâl·jē′â) *f* neuralgia
nevrastenico (nā·vrâ·ste′nē·kō) *a&m* neurasthenic
nevrotico (nā·vrô′tē·kō) *a&m* neurotic
nevvero (nāv·vā′rō) *interj* isn't that right?; don't you think?; aren't they?; isn't it?
nicchia (nēk′kyâ) *f* niche; cranny, nook
nichel (nē′kāl) *m* nickel
nichelare (nē·kā·lâ′rā) *vt* to nickel; to nickel-plate
nichelato (nē·kā·lâ′tō) *a* nickel-plated
nicotina (nē·kō·tē′nâ) *f* nicotine
nidiata (nē·dyâ′tâ) *f* brood, nest
nidificare (nē·dē·fē·kâ′rā) *vi* to build one's nest
nido (nē′dō) *m* nest
niente (nyān′tā) *m* nothing, nothingness; — *adv* not at all; — *a* no; **far finta di —** to close one's eyes to a situation; to feign indifference; — **affatto** not at all; — **altro?** anything else?; — **di nuovo?** is there any news?; **non fa** — it doesn't matter; don't worry about it; — **meno della verità** nothing less than the truth
nientemeno (nyān·tā·mā′nō) *adv* nevertheless; —! *interj* well really!; you don't say!
nimbo (nēm′bō) *m* halo; rain cloud
ninfa (nēn′fâ) *f* nymph; (*zool*) chrysalis
ninnananna (nēn·nâ·nân′nâ) *f* cradlesong, lullaby
ninnolo (nēn′nō·lō) *m* trinket
nipote (nē·pō′tā) *m&f* nephew; niece; grandson; granddaughter
nipponico (nēp·pô′nē·kō) *a* Japanese
nitidamente (nē·tē·dâ·mān′tā) *adv* limpidly; obviously
nitidezza (nē·tē·dā′tsâ) *f* brightness; clearness; brilliance
nitido (nē′tē·dō) *a* clear, distinct; brilliant, bright
nitrico (nē′trē·kō) *a* nitric
nitrito (nē·trē′tō) *m* winny, neigh
nitrocellulosa (nē·trō·chāl·lū·lō′zâ) *f* guncotton

tête-à-tête, privately; **dare nell'—** to attract attention; **a — e croce** roughly speaking; **costare un —** to be extremely costly
occhiolino (ōk·kyō·lē'nō) *m* wink; **fare l '—** to wink
occidentale (ō·chē·dān·tâ'lā) *a* western; Occidental
occidente (ō·chē·dān'tā) *m* west; Occident, West
occorrente (ōk·kōr·rān'tā) *a* necessary; — *m* necessity, requisite
occorrenza (ōk·kōr·rān'tsâ) *f* circumstance; necessity; **all'—** in case of emergency; if necessary
occorrere * (ōk·kôr'rā·rā) *vi* to happen; to be necessary; to be fitting
occultare (ōk·kūl·tâ'rā) *vt* to keep secret; to secrete, hide
occulto (ōk·kūl'tō) *a* mysterious; esoteric; hidden; occult
occupare (ōk·kū·pâ'rā) *vt* to take possession of; to occupy
occuparsi (ōk·kū·pâr'sē) *vr* to engage in; to interest oneself in
occupato (ōk·kū·pâ'tō) *a* taken; busy; occupied
occupazione (ōk·kū·pâ·tsyō'nā) *f* work, job; occupation
oceano (ō·che'â·nō) *m* ocean
oculare (ō·kū·lâ'rā) *a* ocular; **testimonio —** eyewitness
oculato (ō·kū·lâ'tō) *a* cautious, wary
oculista (ō·kū·lē'stâ) *m* oculist
od (ōd) *conj* or
odiare (ō·dyâ'rā) *vt* to hate
odiernamente (ō·dyār·nâ·mān'tā) *adv* nowadays, currently, presently
odierno (ō·dyār'nō) *a* of today, current, present
odio (ô'dyō) *m* hatred
odiosamente (ō·dyō·zâ·mān'tā) *adv* hatefully; disgustingly
odioso (ō·dyō'zō) *a* odious; hateful
Odissea (ō·dēs·sā'â) *f* Odyssey; (*fig*) ups and downs of life
odontoiatria (ō·dōn·tō·yâ·trē'â) *f* dentistry, odontology
odorare (ō·dō·râ'rā) *vt&i* to smell
odorato (ō·dō·râ'tō) *m* sense of smell
odore (ō·dō'rā) *m* scent, smell
odoroso (ō·dō·rō'zō) *a* sweet-scented, fragrant
offendere * (ōf·fen'dā·rā) *vt* to offend
offendersi * (ōf·fen'dār·sē) *vr* to feel hurt, take offense; to be irritated; to be piqued
offensiva (ōf·fān·sē'vâ) *f* offensive; onslaught
offensivo (ōf·fān·sē'vō) *a* insulting
offensore (ōf·fān·sō'rā) *m* offender
offerente (ōf·fā·rān'tā) *m* bidder
offerta (ōf·fār'tâ) *f* offer; bid
offesa (ōf·fā'zâ) *f* insult; offense
officina (ōf·fē·chē'nâ) *f* shop; plant; **capo —** foreman
officioso (ōf·fē·chō'zō) *a* polite; obliging; unofficial; semiofficial
offrire * (ōf·frē'rā) *vt* to afford, present; to offer
offrirsi * (ōf·frēr'sē) *vr* to present oneself; volunteer
offuscare (ōf·fū·skâ'rā) *vt* to darken; to obscure, eclipse
offuscarsi (ōf·fū·skâr'sē) *vr* to darken; to get dim; to decline
oggetto (ōj·jāt'tō) *m* object; purpose
oggi (ōj'jē) *m&adv* today
oggidì (ōj·jē·dē') *adv* nowadays, at present
ogni (ō'nyē) *a* each, every; **— tanto** now and then, from time to time; **in — luogo** everywhere; **in — modo** in any case; anyhow
Ognissanti (ō·nyēs·sân'tē) *m* All Saints' Day
ognuno (ō·nyū'nō) *pron* each one; everyone
Olanda (ō·lân'dâ) *f* Holland
olandese (ō·lân·dā'zā) *a* Dutch
oleandro (ō·lā·ân'drō) *m* oleander
oleificio (ō·lāē·fē'chō) *m* oil mill
oleodotto (ō·lā·ō·dōt'tō) *m* oil pipeline
oleografia (ō·lā·ō·grâ·fē'â) *f* oleograph
oleoso (ō·lā·ō'zō) *a* oily
olezzante (ō·lā·tsân'tā) *a* fragrant, sweet-scented
olezzare (ō·lā·tsâ'rā) *vi* to smell sweet
olfatto (ōl·fât'tō) *m* sense of smell
oliare (ō·lyâ'rā) *vt* to lubricate, oil
oliatore (ō·lyâ·tō'rā) *m* oilcan; oiler
oliera (ō·lyā'râ) *f* set of cruets for oil and vinegar
oligarchia (ō·lē·gâr·kē'â) *f* oligarchy
olimpiadi (ō·lēm·pē'â·dē) *fpl* Olympic games
olimpico (ō·lēm'pē·kō) *a* Olympic; Olympian; **giuochi olimpici** Olympic games
olimpionico (ō·lēm·pyô'nē·kō) *m* Olympic champion
olio (ô'lyō) *m* oil; **— d'oliva** olive oil; **— di fegato di merluzzo** codliver oil; **— di ricino** castor oil; **— lubrificante** lubricating oil
oliva (ō·lē'vâ) *f* olive
olivastro (ō·lē·vâ'strō) *a* olive (*color*)
oliveto (ō·lē·vā'tō) *m* olive grove
olivo (ō·lē'vō) *m* olive tree
olmo (ōl'mō) *m* elm
oltraggiare (ōl·trâj·jâ'rā) *vt* to ravage; to insult; to outrage
oltraggio (ōl·trâj'jō) *m* insult; outrage; **— al pudore** obscenity; **— alla giustizia** contempt of court
oltraggioso (ōl·trâj·jō'zō) *a* insulting; outrageous
oltranza (ōl·trân'tsâ) *f* extreme, uttermost, utmost; excess; **ad —** out and out; to the bitter end; **guerra ad —** war to the death
oltranzista (ōl·trân·tsē'stâ) *m* diehard; extremist; radical
oltre (ōl'trā) *prep* past, beyond; — *adv* further, farther; ahead; on; **— un mese** over a month; **— a ciò** besides, moreover; in addition to that; **-chè** (ōl·trā·kā') *conj* aside from the fact that; **-mare** (ōl·trā·mâ'rā) *m* ultramarine, deep

blue; **–mare** *adv* overseas; **–modo** (ōl·trā·mō'dō) *adv* exceedingly; **–passare** (ōl·trā·pâs·sâ'rā) *vt* to exceed; to overtake; **–passare i limiti** to go too far; to go overboard (*fig*); **–tomba** (ōl·trā·tōm'bâ) *f* afterlife, next world
omaccione (ō·mâ·chō'nā) *m* big fellow
omaggi (ō·mâj'jē) *mpl* respects
omaggiare (ō·mâj·jâ'rā) *vt* to present; to pay one's respects to
omaggio (ō·mâj'jō) *m* compliment; gift; homage; **— di** compliments of
ombelico (ōm·bā·lē'kō) *m* navel
ombra (ōm'brâ) *f* shadow; resentment, umbrage; shade
ombreggiare (ōm·brāj·jâ'rā) *vt* to shade; to cast a shadow on
ombreggiatura (ōm·brāj·jâ·tū'râ) *f* shading, shade
ombrellino (ōm·brāl·lē'nō) *m* parasol
ombrello (ōm·brāl'lō) *m* umbrella
ombrellone (ōm·brāl·lō'nā) *m* beach umbrella
ombroso (ōm·brō'zō) *a* shady; easily offended; skittish
omeopatia (ō·mā·ō·pâ·tē'â) *f* homeopathy
omero (ô'mā·rō) *m* shoulder; humerus
omertà (ō·mār·tâ') *f* code of silence among criminals
omesso (ō·mās'sō) *a* omitted
omettere * (ō·met'tā·rā) *vt* to omit; to disregard
ometto (ō·māt'tō) *m* little man; (*coll*) coat hanger
omicida (ō·mē·chē'dâ) *m* murderer
omicidio (ō·mē·chē'dyō) *m* homicide; **— premeditato** premeditated murder; **— colposo** manslaughter; **tentato —** attempted murder
omino (ō·mē'nō) *m* little fellow
omissione (ō·mēs·syō'nā) *f* omission; mistake; disregard
omnibus (ôm'nē·būs) *m* local train; bus
omogeneità (ō·mō·jā·nāē·tâ') *f* uniformity; homogeneity
omogeneo (ō·mō·je'nā·ō) *a* homogeneous; correspondent
omogenizzato (ō·mō·jā·nē·dzâ'tō) *a* homogenized
omologare (ō·mō·lō·gâ'rā) *vt* to probate; to ratify
omologia (ō·mō·lō·jē'â) *f* homology; approval, ratification
omonimo (ō·mô'nē·mō) *m* homonym
omosessuale (ō·mō·sās·swâ'lā) *m&a* homosexual
oncia (ôn'châ) *f* ounce
onda (ōn'dâ) *f* wave; **andare in —** (*rad*) to go on the air
ondata (ōn·dâ'tâ) *f* breaker, surf; wave; outbreak; **— di freddo** cold wave
onde (ōn'dā) *adv* from where; through where; consequently; **—** *pron* whose; of which; with which; by which; of whom; with whom; **—** *conj* so that, in order that
ondeggiare (ōn·dāj·jâ'rā) *vt* to wave; to waver
ondina (ōn·dē'nâ) *f* siren, water nymph, undine
ondulare (ōn·dū·lâ'rā) *vt&i* to undulate, wave; **— i capelli** to wave one's hair
ondulato (ōn·dū·lâ'tō) *a* wavy; **cartone —** corrugated board
ondulazione (ōn·dū·lâ·tsyō'nā) *f* waving; **— permanente** permanent wave
onere (ô'nā·rā) *m* burden
oneroso (ō·nā·rō'zō) *a* burdensome
onestà (ō·nā·stâ') *f* integrity; honesty
onesto (ō·nā'stō) *a* fair; true; honest; straightforward, upstanding
onnipotente (ōn·nē·pō·tān'tā) *a* almighty, omnipotent
onnivoro (ōn·nē'vō·rō) *a* omnivorous
onomastico (ō·nō·mâ'stē·kō) *m* name day
onorabilità (ō·nō·râ·bē·lē·tâ') *f* honor; good name
onoranza (ō·nō·rân'tsâ) *f* tribute, honor; esteem, regard
onorare (ō·nō·râ'rā) *vt* to honor; to regard, esteem
onorario (ō·nō·râ'ryō) *a* honorary; **—** *m* fee
onorarsi (ō·nō·râr'sē) *vr* to take pride; to have the honor
onore (ō·nō'rā) *m* honor; acclaim; **serata d' —** benefit performance; **fare — ai propri impegni** to keep one's commitments
onorevole (ō·nō·re'vō·lā) *a* honorable; esteemed
onorevolmente (ō·nō·rā·vōl·mān'tā) *adv* honorably; with distinction
onorificenza (ō·nō·rē·fē·chān'tsâ) *f* decoration
onta (ōn'tâ) *f* disgrace; dishonor
ontano (ōn·tâ'nō) *m* alder
ontologia (ōn·tō·lō·jē'â) *f* ontology
ONU (ō'nū) *f* United Nations
opaco (ō·pâ'kō) *a* opaque; lackluster
opera (ô'pā·râ) *f* work; opera
operaio (ō·pā·râ'yō) *m* workman
operare (ō·pā·râ'rā) *vt* to work, operate; to cause; **—** *vi* to function, perform
operatore (ō·pā·râ·tō'rā) *m* operator; cameraman
operatorio (ō·pā·râ·tô'ryō) *a* (*med*) operable
operazione (ō·pā·râ·tsyō'nā) *f* transaction; operation
operetta (ō·pā·rāt'tâ) *f* musical comedy
operosità (ō·pā·rō·zē·tâ') *f* industry, diligence
operoso (ō·pā·rō'zō) *a* industrious, diligent
opificio (ō·pē·fē'chō) *m* plant, factory
opinare (ō·pē·nâ'rā) *vi* to suppose; to opine; to consider
opinione (ō·pē·nyō'nā) *f* opinion, idea
oppio (ôp'pyō) *m* opium
opponente (ōp·pō·nān'tā) *m* opponent; **—** *a* adverse; opposing
opporre * (ōp·pōr'rā) *vt* to oppose
opporsi * (ōp·pōr'sē) *vr* to withstand; to be opposed
opportunamente (ōp·pōr·tū·nâ·mān'tā) *adv* opportunely; at the right time

opportunista (ōp·pōr·tū·nē'stâ) *m* opportunist
opportunità (ōp·pōr·tū·nē·tâ') *f* opportunity; timeliness
opportuno (ōp·pōr·tū'nō) *a* opportune; **considerare** — to think advisable; **a tempo** — at the right time
oppositore (ōp·pō·zē·tō'rā) *m* antagonist; opponent
opposizione (ōp·pō·zē·tsyō'nā) *f* opposition
opposto (ōp·pō'stō) *a&m* opposed; opposite; contrary
oppressione (ōp·prās·syō'nā) *f* oppression
oppressore (ōp·prās·sō'rā) *m* oppressor
opprimente (ōp·prē·mān'tā) *a* oppressing, oppressive
opprimere * (ōp·prē'mā·rā) *vt* to oppress; to lord it over; to bully
oppugnare (ōp·pū·nyâ'rā) *vt* to confute; to refute
oppure (ōp·pū'rā) *conj* or else, or
optare (ōp·tâ'rā) *vi* to choose, make a choice, opt
optometria (ōp·tō·mā·trē'â) *f* optometry
opulento (ō·pū·lān'tō) *a* well-to-do, affluent
opulenza (ō·pū·lān'tsâ) *f* affluence
opuscolo (ō·pū'skō·lō) *m* pamphlet, leaflet
ora (ō'râ) *f* time; hour; — **di punta** rush hour; — *adv* now; **che — è?** What time is it?; **di buon'—** early in the morning; — **legale** daylight saving time
orafo (ō'râ·fō) *m* goldsmith
orale (ō·râ'lā) *a* oral
oralmente (ō·râl·mān'tā) *adv* verbally, orally
orare (ō·râ'rā) *vi* to pray
orario (ō·râ'ryō) *m* timetable; — *a* hourly; — **di visita** visiting hours; **segnale** — (*rad*) time signal
oratore (ō·râ·tō'rā) *m* public speaker, orator
oratoria (ō·rā·tô'ryâ) *f* public speaking, oratory
oratorio (ō·râ·tô'ryō) *m* private chapel; (*mus*) oratorio; — *a* oratorical
orazione (ō·râ·tsyō'nā) *f* prayer; public discourse, oration
orbene (ōr·bā'nā) *adv* well; so; well now
orbita (ôr'bē·tâ) *f* orbit
orbo (ōr'bō) *a* blind; (*fig*) lacking
orchestra (ōr·kā'strâ) *f* orchestra
orchestrale (ōr·kā·strâ'lā) *m* orchestra member; — *a* orchestral
orchestrare (ōr·kā·strâ'rā) *vt* to score, orchestrate
orchestrazione (ōr·kā·strâ·tsyō'nā) *f* orchestration
orchidea (ōr·kē·dā'â) *f* orchid
orco (ōr'kō) *m* ogre
orda (ōr'dâ) *f* horde, swarm, throng
ordigno (ōr·dē'nyō) *m* device; implement; tool, instrument
ordinale (ōr·dē·nâ'lā) *a* ordinal (*number*)
ordinamento (ōr·dē·nâ·mān'tō) *m* arrangement, placement; ordinance
ordinanza (ōr·dē·nân'tsâ) *f* order; writ; (*mil*) ordinance
ordinare (ōr·dē·nâ'rā) *vt* to order; (*eccl*) to ordain; to set up, place
ordinariamente (ōr·dē·nâ·ryâ·mān'tā) *adv* usually, commonly; routinely
ordinario (ōr·dē·nâ'ryō) *a* ordinary; common; coarse; regular; — *m* professor
ordinarsi (ōr·dē·nâr'sē) *vr* to get organized; to put one's house in order (*fig*)
ordinatamente (ōr·dē·nâ·tâ·mān'tā) *adv* orderly; methodically; neatly
ordinato (ōr·dē·nâ'tō) *a* put in order, tidied; orderly; ordered; methodical
ordinazione (ōr·dē·nâ·tsyō'nā) *f* order; ordination; (*med*) prescription
ordine (ôr'dē·nā) *m* order, decree
ordire (ōr·dē'rā) *vt* to scheme, plot
ordito (ōr·dē'tō) *m* warp (*weaving*); scheming; network
orecchino (ō·rāk·kē'nō) *m* earring
orecchio (ō·rek'kyō) *m* ear
orecchioni (ō·rāk·kyō'nē) *mpl* mumps
orefice (ō·re'fē·chā) *m* goldsmith; jeweler
oreficeria (ō·rā·fē·chā·rē'â) *f* jewelry store; jewelry
orfanello (ōr·fâ·nāl'lō) *f* orphan boy
orfano (ôr'fâ·nō) *m&a* orphan
orfanotrofio (ōr·fâ·nō·trō'fyō) *m* orphanage
organetto (ōr·gâ·nāt'tō) *m* accordion; — **di Barberia** hurdy-gurdy
organico (ōr·gâ'nē·kō) *a* organic; — *m* staff, personnel
organismo (ōr·gâ·nē'zmō) *m* organism
organista (ōr·gâ·nē'stâ) *m&f* organist
organizzare (ōr·gâ·nē·dzâ'rā) *vt* to set up, organize; to constitute
organizzatore (ōr·gâ·nē·dzâ·tō'rā) *m* organizer
organizzazione (ōr·gâ·nē·dzâ·tsyō'nā) *f* organization, setup; makeup
organo (ôr'gâ·nō) *m* organ
orgia (ôr'jâ) *f* orgy
orgoglio (ōr·gô'lyō) *m* pride; boastfulness
orgogliosamente (ōr·gō·lyō·zâ·mān'tā) *adv* haughtily; with pride
orgoglioso (ōr·gō·lyō'zō) *a* proud; swelled with pride
orientale (ō·ryān·tâ'lā) *a* eastern; Oriental; — *m* Oriental
orientamento (ō·ryān·tâ·mān'tō) *m* bearings; orientation
orientare (ō·ryān·tâ'rā) *vt* to orient
orientarsi (ō·ryān·târ'sē) *vr* to get one's bearings; to adapt oneself, get used to
orientazione (ō·ryān·tâ·tsyō'nā) *f* orientation; bearings, position
oriente (ō·ryān'tā) *m* East, Orient; east
origano (ō·rē'gâ·nō) *m* oregano, marjoram
originale (ō·rē·jē·nâ'lā) *a* original; strange, unusual; — *m&f* eccentric person; — *m* original
originalità (ō·rē·jē·nâ·lē·tâ') *f* originality; strangeness
originalmente (ō·rē·jē·nâl·mān'tā) *adv* originally; strangely
originare (ō·rē·jē·nâ'rā) *vt&i* to originate; to spring from

originariamente (ō·rē·jē·nâ·ryâ·mān'tā) *adv* originally; at first
originario (ō·rē·jē·nâ'ryō) *a* of a specified origin; — **italiano** of Italian extraction
origine (ō·rē'jē·nā) *f* source; font; origin
orina (ō·rē'nâ) *f* urine
orinare (ō·rē·nâ'rā) *vi* to urinate
orinatoio (ō·rē·nâ·tô'yō) *m* urinal
oriundo (ō·ryūn'dō) *a* of a specified descent; from a specified country; — **svedese** of Swedish descent
orizzontale (ō·rē·dzōn·tâ'lā) *a* horizontal
orizzontalmente (ō·rē·dzōn·tâl·mān'tā) *adv* horizontally
orizzontarsi (ō·rē·dzōn·târ'sē) *vr* to get one's bearings; to grow used to
orizzonte (ō·rē·dzōn'tā) *m* horizon
orlare (ōr·lâ'rā) *vt* to hem
orlatura (ōr·lâ·tū'râ) *f* hem; hemming
orlo (ōr'lō) *m* edge; brim; hem; verge
orma (ōr'mâ) *f* footstep; track
ormai (ōr·mâ'ē) *adv* by now; from now on
orme (ōr'mā) *fpl* trail; spoor
ormeggiare (ōr·māj·jâ'rā) *vt* to tie up, dock, moor
ormeggiarsi (ōr·māj·jâr'sē) *vr* to lie at anchor
ormeggio (ōr·mej'jō) *m* mooring, docking
ormone (ōr·mō'nā) *m* hormone
ornamentale (ōr·nâ·mān'tâ'lā) *a* decorative
ornamento (ōr·nâ·mān'tō) *m* ornament; adornment
ornare (ōr·nâ'rā) *vt* to ornament; to adorn
ornato (ōr·nâ'tō) *m* design; ornamental motif; — *a* adorned; ornamented
ornitologo (ōr·nē·tô'lō·gō) *m* ornithologist
ornitorinco (ōr·nē·tō·rēn'kō) *m* duckbill, platypus
oro (ō'rō) *m* gold; riches
orologeria (ō·rō·lō·jā·rē'â) *f* watchmaker's shop
orologiaio (ō·rō·lō·jâ'yō) *m* watchmaker
orologio (ō·rō·lô'jō) *m* clock; watch; — **da polso** wristwatch
oroscopo (ō·rô'skō·pō) *m* horoscope
orpello (ōr·pāl'lō) *m* tinsel; gold foil
orrendamente (ōr·rān·dâ·mān'tā) *adv* dreadfully, frightfully
orrendo (ōr·rān'dō) *a* horrible, horrifying
orribile (ōr·rē'bē·lā) *a* horrible, terrible
orribilmente (ōr·rē·bēl·mān'tā) *adv* horribly, frightfully
orrido (ôr'rē·dō) *a* horrid, horrible; — *m* cliff, precipice
orripilante (ōr·rē·pē·lân'tā) *a* thrilling; hair-raising
orrore (ōr·rō'rā) *m* fright, horror
orsa (ōr'sâ) *f* female bear
orsacchiotto (ōr·sâ·kyōt'tō) *m* bear cub
orso (ōr'sō) *m* bear
orsù (ōr·sū') *interj* come on now, well then
ortaggi (ōr·tâj'jē) *mpl* vegetables
ortica (ōr·tē'kâ) *f* nettle; (*fig*) prod, goad
orticaria (ōr·tē·kâ'ryâ) *f* (*med*) nettle rash
orticolo (ōr·tē'kō·lō) *a* horticultural
orticultore (ōr·tē·kūl·tō'rā) *m* truck farmer
orticultura (ōr·tē·kūl·tū'râ) *f* truck farming
orto (ōr'tō) *m* orchard; truck farm; — **botanico** botanical garden
ortofrutticoli (ōr·tō·frūt·tē'kō·lē) *mpl* farm produce
ortografia (ōr·tō·grâ·fē'â) *f* spelling
ortolano (ōr·tō·lâ'nō) *m* truck farmer; vegetable dealer
ortopedico (ōr·tō·pe'dē·kō) *a* orthopedic; — *m* orthopedist
orzaiolo (ōr·dzâ·yō'lō) *m* (*med*) sty
orzare (ōr·dzâ'rā) *vi* (*naut*) to luff
orzo (ōr'dzō) *m* barley
osare (ō·zâ'rā) *vt&i* to dare
oscenità (ō·shā·nē·tâ') *f* obscenity, lewdness
osceno (ō·shā'nō) *a* obscene, lewd
oscillare (ō·shēl·lâ'rā) *vi* to sway, swing; to delay, hesitate
oscillazione (ō·shēl·lâ·tsyō'nā) *f* oscillation, swaying; hesitation
oscuramente (ō·skū·râ·mān'tā) *adv* dimly, obscurely
oscuramento (ō·skū·râ·mān'tō) *m* blackout; darkening
oscurare (ō·skū·râ'rā) *vt* to darken
oscurarsi (ō·skū·râr'sē) *vr* to become dim; to get dark
oscurità (ō·skū·rē·tâ') *f* obscurity; dark; darkness
oscuro (ō·skū'rō) *a* obscure; unknown; dim, dark; uncertain
ospedale (ō·spā·dâ'lā) *m* hospital
ospitale (ō·spē·tâ'lā) *m* hospitable
ospitalità (ō·spē·tâ·lē·tâ') *f* hospitality
ospitalmente (ō·spē·tâl·mān'tā) *adv* hospitably
ospitare (ō·spē·tâ'rā) *vt* to entertain; to accommodate; to fete
ospite (ô'spē·tā) *m* host; guest; boarder; — *f* hostess
ospizio (ō·spē'tsyō) *m* poorhouse; orphanage; old people's home
ossa (ōs'sâ) *fpl* bones
ossario (ōs·sâ'ryō) *m* charnel
ossatura (ōs·sâ·tū'râ) *f* skeleton; framework, structure; build, physique
osseo (ôs'sā·ō) *a* bony
ossequi (ōs·se'kwē) *mpl* respects, greetings, best regards
ossequio (ōs·se'kwēō) *m* respect, homage
ossequiosamente (ōs·sā·kwēō·zâ·mān'tā) *adv* respectfully
ossequioso (ōs·sā·kwēō'zō) *a* deferential, respectful
osservanza (ōs·sār·vân'tsâ) *f* observance; **con** — respectfully yours
osservare (ōs·sār·vâ'rā) *vt* to observe; to follow, comply with
osservatorio (ōs·sār·vâ·tô'ryō) *m* observatory
osservazione (ōs·sār·vâ·tsyō'nā) *f* observation; remark
ossessionare (ōs·sās·syō·nâ'rā) *vt* to obsess, preoccupy
ossessionato (ōs·sās·syō·nâ'tō) *a* possessed, obsessed

ossessione (ōs·sās·syō'nā) *f* obsession; fear
ossia (ōs·sē'â) *conj* or, in other words, that is to say
ossidare (ōs·sē·dâ'rā) *vt* to oxidize
ossido (ôs'sē·dō) *m* oxide
ossigenare (ōs·sē·jā·nâ'rā) *vt* to oxygenate; to bleach *(hair)*
ossigeno (ōs·sē'jā·nō) *m* oxygen
osso (ōs'sō) *m* bone; **— buco** bone marrow
ostacolare (ō·stâ·kō·lâ'rā) *vt* to impede; to hinder
ostacolista (ō·stâ·kō·lē'stâ) *m (sport)* hurdler
ostacolo (ō·stâ'kō·lō) *m* obstacle; handicap; bar; *(sport)* hurdle
ostaggio (ō·stâj'jō) *m* hostage
ostante (ō·stân'tā) *a* hindering; impeding; **ciò non —** nevertheless, however
oste (ō'stā) *m* host; innkeeper
ostello (ō·stāl'lō) *m* hostel; **— della gioventù** youth hostel
ostensibilmente (ō·stān·sē·bēl·mān'tā) *adv* ostensibly, visibly
ostensivamente (ō·stān·sē·vâ·mān'tā) *adv* visibly, apparently
ostensorio (ō·stān·sô'ryō) *m (eccl)* monstrance
ostentare (ō·stān·tâ'rā) *vt* to show off; to brag about
ostentazione (ō·stān·tâ·tsyō'nā) *f* display; affectation; brag, bragging
osteria (ō·stā·rē'â) *f* tavern
ostessa (ō·stās'sâ) *f* hostess; airline stewardess; landlady
ostetrica (ō·ste'trē·kâ) *f* midwife
ostetricia (ō·stā·trē'châ) *f* obstetrics
ostetrico (ō·ste'trē·kō) *m* obstetrician
ostia (ô'styâ) *f* wafer; *(eccl)* Host
ostico (ô'stē·kō) *a* unpleasant; hard
ostile (ō·stē'lā) *a* hostile
ostilità (ō·stē·lē·tâ') *f* hostility, enmity
ostilmente (ō·stēl·mān'tā) *adv* inimically
ostinarsi (ō·stē·nâr'sē) *vr* to stick to; to persist in; to be obstinate
ostinato (ō·stē·nâ'tō) *a* obstinate
ostinazione (ō·stē·nâ·tsyō'nā) *f* obstinacy
ostracismo (ō·strâ·chē'zmō) *m* ostracism; avoidance
ostracizzare (ō·strâ·chē·dzâ'rā) *vt* to ostracize; to avoid
ostrica (ô'strē·kâ) *f* oyster
ostruire (ō·strūē'rā) *vt* to obstruct; to impede
ostruzionismo (ō·strū·tsyō·nē'zmō) *m* obstructionism
otite (ō·tē'tā) *f* otitis
otre (ō'trā) *m* wineskin
ottaedro (ōt·tâ·ā'drō) *m* octahedron
ottagono (ōt·tâ'gō·nō) *m* octagon
ottano (ōt·tâ'nō) *m* octane
ottanta (ōt·tân'tâ) *a* eighty
ottantesimo (ōt·tân·te'zē·mō) *a* eightieth
ottantina (ōt·tân·tē'nâ) *f* about eighty
ottava (ōt·tâ'vâ) *f* octave
ottavino (ōt·tâ·vē'nō) *m* piccolo
ottavo (ōt·tâ'vō) *a* eighth; **—** *n (mus)* octave; *(print)* octavo
ottemperare (ōt·tām·pā·râ'rā) *vi* to comply
ottemperanza (ōt·tām·pā·rân'tsâ) *f* compliance, obedience
ottenere * (ōt·tā·nā'rā) *vt* to obtain; to get
ottica (ôt'tē·kâ) *f* optics
ottico (ôt'tē·kō) *m* optician; **—** *a* optical
ottimamente (ōt·tē·mâ·mān'tā) *adv* very well; fine; excellently
ottimismo (ōt·tē·mē'zmō) *m* optimism
ottimista (ōt·tē·mē'stâ) *m&f* optimist
ottimo (ôt'tē·mō) *a* excellent; fine
otto (ōt'tō) *m* eight; **oggi a —** a week from today
ottobre (ōt·tō'brā) *m* October
ottocento (ōt·tō·chān'tō) *a* eight hundred; **l'O-** the nineteenth century
ottomana (ōt·tō·mâ'nâ) *f* sofa, ottoman
ottone (ōt·tō'nā) *m* brass
ottuagenario (ōt·twâ·jā·nâ'ryō) *a&m* octogenarian
otturare (ōt·tū·râ'rā) *vt* to fill in; to plug up
otturatore (ōt·tū·râ·tō'rā) *m (photo)* shutter
otturazione (ōt·tū·râ·tsyō'nā) *f* filling; obstruction
ottuso (ōt·tū'zō) *a* obtuse, dull
ovaia (ō·vâ'yâ) *f* ovary
ovale (ō·vā'lā) *a* oval
ovatrice (ō·vâ·trē'chā) *f* incubator
ovatta (ō·vât'tâ) *f* wadding
ovazione (ō·vā·tsyō'nā) *f* ovation
ove (ō'vā) *conj* whereas; **—** *adv* where, wherein
ovest (ō'vāst) *m* west
ovile (ō·vē'lā) *m* sheepfold
ovini (ō·vē'nē) *mpl* sheep
ovino (ō·vē'nō) *a* sheep, ovine
ovunque (ō·vūn'kwā) *adv* everywhere
ovvero (ōv·vā'rō) *conj* or; or otherwise
ovviare (ō·vyâ'rā) *vt* to avoid; to obviate
ovvio (ôv'vyō) *a* clear, obvious
oziare (ō·tsyâ'rā) *vi* to laze; to idle
ozio (ô'tsyō) *m* idleness
oziosamente (ō·tsyō·zâ·mān'tā) *adv* idly; lazily
ozioso (ō·tsyō'zō) *a* lazy; idle
ozono (ō·dzō'nō) *m* ozone

P

pacatamente (pâ·kâ·tâ·mān'tā) *adv* calmly, peacefully
pacatezza (pâ·kâ·tā'tsâ) *f* calmness; quiet
pacato (pâ·kâ'tō) *a* calm, quiet
pacchetto (pâk·kāt'tō) *m* package, parcel
pacchia (pâk'kyâ) *f* good things of life; cakes and ale *(fig)*
pacchianata (pâk·kyâ·nâ'tâ) *f* vulgarity
pacchiano pâk·kyâ'nō) *a* common, cheap
pacco (pâk'kō) *m* package, parcel; **— postale** parcel post
paccotiglia (pâk·kō·tē'lyâ) *f* inferior merchandise, rubbish
pace (pâ'chā) *f* peace; **lasciare in —** to

leave alone
pachiderma (pâ·kē·dār'mâ) *m* pachyderm
paciere (pâ·chā'rā) *m* peacemaker
pacificamente (pâ·chē·fē·kâ·mān'tā) *adv* peacefully
pacificare (pâ·chē·fē·kâ'rā) *vt* to pacify; to assuage, quiet
pacificarsi (pâ·chē·fē·kâr'sē) *vr* to be reconciled; to settle one's differences
pacifico (pâ·chē'fē·kō) *a* peaceful; pacific; quiet; **Oceano P–** Pacific Ocean
pacifismo (pâ·chē·fē'zmō) *m* pacifism
pacioccone (pâ·chōk·kō'nā) *m*, **paciocсona** (pâ·chōk·kō'nâ) *f* fat, easygoing person
padella (pâ·dāl'lâ) *f* frying pan; bedpan
padiglione (pâ·dē·lyō'nā) *m* pavilion; exhibition hall
Padova (pâ'dō·vâ) *f* Padua
padovano (pâ·dō·vâ'nō) *m&f* Paduan
padre (pâ'drā) *m* father
padrigno (pâ·drē'nyō) *m* stepfather
padrino (pâ·drē'nō) *m* godfather, foster father
padrona (pâ·drō'nâ) *f* lady, mistress (*household*); landlady; proprietress
padronanza (pâ·drō·nân'tsâ) *f* mastery; composure; **— di una lingua** command of a language
padrone (pâ·drō'nā) *m* master; employer; landlord; proprietor; owner
padroneggiare (pâ·drō·nāj·jâ'rā) *vt* to control; to domineer
padroneggiarsi (pâ·drō·nāj·jâr'sē) *vr* to exhibit self-control
paesaggio (pâ·ā·zâj'jō) *m* scenery; landscape
paesano (pâ·ā·zâ'nō) *m* fellow townsman; peasant
paese (pâ·ā'zā) *m* country; town; village
paesista (pâ·ā·zē'stâ) *m* landscape painter
paffuto (pâf·fū'tō) *a* chubby, plump
paga (pâ'gâ) *f* wage, pay
pagaia (pâ·gâ'yâ) *f* paddle (*canoe*)
pagamento (pâ·gâ·mān'tō) *m* payment; **— alla consegna** COD, collect on delivery
paganesimo (pâ·gâ·ne'zē·mō) *m* paganism
pagano (pâ·gâ'nō) *a&m* heathen
pagare (pâ·gâ'rā) *vt* to pay, pay for
pagella (pâ·jāl'lâ) *f* report card
paggio (pâj'jō) *m* valet, page
pagina (pâ'jē·nâ) *f* page (*book*)
paglia (pâ'lyâ) *f* straw
pagliaccio (pâ·lyâ'chō) *m* clown; jester
pagliaio (pâ·lyâ'yō) *m* haystack
paglierino (pâ·lyā·rē'nō) *a* yellowish
paglietta (pâ·lyāt'tâ) *f* straw hat
pagnotta (pâ·nyōt'tâ) *f* loaf of bread; (*fig*) daily bread, daily wages
pago (pâ'gō) *a* satisfied
paio (pâ'yō) *m* couple; pair; two; **un altro — di maniche** (*fig*) a horse of a different color; a different matter
pala (pâ'lâ) *f* shovel; blade (*propeller*)
palanca (pâ·lân'kâ) *f* stake; (*coll*) money
palata (pâ·lâ'tâ) *f* shovelful
palato (pâ·lâ'tō) *m* palate
palazzo (pâ·lâ'tsō) *m* palace; large apartment building; **— di giustizia** court house
palco (pâl'kō) *m* (*theat*) box
palcoscenico (pâl·kō·she'nē·kō) *m* stage
paleolitico (pâ·lā·ō·lē'tē·kō) *a* paleolithic
paleontologia (pâ·lā·ōn·tō·lō·jē'â) *f* paleontology
palesare (pâ·lā·zâ'rā) *vt* to disclose, reveal
palesarsi (pâ·lā·zâr'sē) *vr* to prove oneself to be; to turn out to be
palese (pâ·lā'zā) *a* obvious, apparent
palesemente (pâ·lā·zā·mān'tā) *adv* obviously, apparently
Palestina (pâ·lā·stē'nâ) *f* Palestine
palestra (pâ·lā'strâ) *f* gymnasium
paletta (pâ·lāt'tâ) *f* palette; blade (*fan*); small shovel
paletto (pâ·lāt'tō) *m* bolt, bar; small post
palio (pâ'lyō) *m* prize, race; **mettere in —** to raffle off
palizzata (pâ·lē·tsâ'tâ) *f* palisade
palla (pâl'lâ) *f* ball; **— salutare** medicine ball; **— soffice a basi** softball; **cogliere la — al balzo** (*fig*) to take advantage of an opportunity; **–base** (pâl·lâ·bâ'zā) *f* baseball; **–canestro** (pâl·lâ·kâ·nā'strō) *m* basketball; **–corda** (pâl·lâ·kōr'dâ) *f* tennis; **–maglio** (pâl·lâ·mâ'lyō) *f* croquet; **–nuoto** (pâl·lâ·nwō'tō) *f* water polo; **–tavola** (pâl·lâ·tâ'vō·lâ) *f* table tennis; **–volo** (pâl·lâ·vō'lō) *f* volley ball
palliare (pâl·lyâ'rā) *vt* to veil; to disguise
palliativo (pâl·lyâ·tē'vō) *a* palliative
pallidamente (pâl·lē·dâ·mān'tā) *adv* faintly; wanly
pallidezza (pâl·lē·dā'tsâ) *f* wanness; paleness
pallido (pâl'lē·dō) *a* pale
pallina (pâl·lē'nâ) *f* marble (*toy*); small ball
pallini (pâl·lē'nē) *mpl* buckshot
pallonaio (pâl·lō·nâ'yō) *m* balloon man
palloncino (pâl·lōn·chē'nō) *m* toy balloon; Chinese lantern
pallone (pâl·lō'nā) *m* balloon; football; **— americano** bubble gum; **— gonfiato** (*fig*) pretentious nobody, windbag (*coll*)
pallore (pâl·lō'rā) *m* paleness
pallottola (pâl·lōt'tō·lâ) *f* bullet
pallottolaia (pâl·lōt·tō·lâ'yâ) *f* bowling alley; bowling green
pallottoliere (pâl·lōt·tō·lyā'rā) *m* abacus
pallovale (pâl·lō·vâ'lā) *f* rugby
palma (pâl'mâ) *f* palm
palmare (pâl·mâ'rā) *a* evident, obvious
palmeto (pâl·mā'tō) *m* palm grove
palmipede (pâl·mē'pā·dā) *m* webfooted
palmo (pâl'mō) *m* span; palm (*hand*)
palo (pâ'lō) *m* pole; stick; post
palombaro (pâ·lōm·bâ'rō) *m* deep-sea diver
palombo (pâ·lōm'bō) *m* dove
palpare (pâl·pâ'rā) *vt* to feel, touch; to palpate
palpebra (pâl'pā·brâ) *f* eyelid
palpitante (pâl·pē·tân'tā) *a* throbbing; exciting
palpitare (pâl·pē·tâ'rā) *vi* to palpitate,

throb
palpitazione (pâl·pē·tâ·tsyō'nā) *f* palpitation
palpito (pâl'pē·tō) *m* throb
paltò (pâl·tō') *m* overcoat
palude (pâ·lū'dā) *f* swamp
panama (pâ'nâ·mâ) *m* Panama hat
panare (pâ·nâ'rā) *vt* to bread; to crumb
panca (pân'kâ) *f* bench
pancetta (pân·chāt'tâ) *f* bacon; protruding stomach, potbelly
panchina (pân·kē'nâ) *f* (*rail*) platform; garden seat
pancia (pân'châ) *f* belly
panciera (pân·chā'râ) *f* abdominal belt; girdle
panciotto (pân·chōt'tō) *m* vest
pandemonio (pân·dā·mô'nyō) *m* pandemonium; din
pandorato (pân·dō·râ'tō) *m* French toast
pane (pâ'nā) *m* bread
panetteria (pâ·nāt·tā·rē'â) *f* bakery
panettiere (pâ·nāt·tyā'rā) *m* baker
panettone (pâ·nāt·tō'nā) *m* raisin bread
panfilo (pân'fē·lō) *m* yacht
pania (pâ'nyâ) *f* birdlime
panico (pâ'nē·kō) *m* panic
paniere (pâ·nyā'rā) *m* basket
panificare (pâ·nē·fē·kâ'rā) *vt* to make into bread
panificazione (pâ·nē·fē·kâ·tsyō'nā) *f* baking of bread
panificio (pâ·nē·fē'chō) *m* wholesale bakery
panino (pâ·nē'nō) *m* roll; — **imbottito** sandwich
panna (pân'nâ) *f* cream; (*auto*) engine trouble; flat tire; — **montata** whipped cream
pannello (pân·nāl'lō) *m* panel
panno (pân'nō) *m* cloth
pannocchia (pân·nôk'kyâ) *f* (*bot*) spike; corncob
pannolino (pân·nō·lē'nō) *m* diaper; sanitary napkin
panorama (pâ·nō·râ'mâ) *m* view, panorama
pantaloni (pân·tâ·lō'nē) *mpl* pants, trousers
pantano (pân·tâ'nō) *m* quagmire, swamp
pantera (pân·tā'râ) *f* panther
pantofola (pân·tô'fō·lâ) *f* slipper
pantostato (pân·tō·stâ'tō) *m* toast
panzana (pân·dzâ'nâ) *f* tall tale, yarn
Papa (pâ'pâ) *m* (*eccl*) Pope
papà (pâ·pâ') *m* father, papa
papale (pâ·pâ'lā) *a* papal
papalina (pâ·pâ·lē'nâ) *f* skullcap
papato (pâ·pâ'tō) *m* papacy
papavero (pâ·pâ'vā·rō) *m* poppy; (*fig*) important person
papera (pâ'pā·râ) *f* goose; (*theat*) muffing a line
papero (pâ'pā·rō) *m* gander
pappa (pâp'pâ) *f* pap
pappagallo (pâp·pâ·gâl'lō) *m* parrot
pappagorgia (pâp·pâ·gôr'jâ) *f* double chin
para (pâ'râ) *f* latex; crepe rubber
parabola (pâ·râ'bō·lâ) *f* parable; (*math*) parabola
parabrezza (pâ·râ·brā'tsâ) *m* windshield
paracadute (pâ·râ·kâ·dū'tā) *m* parachute
paracadutista (pâ·râ·kâ·dū·tē'stâ) *m* paratrooper
paracalli (pâ·râ·kâl'lē) *m* corn pad
paracarro (pâ·râ·kâr'rō) *m* highway guard post; guard rail
paracolpi (pâ·râ·kōl'pē) *m* (*auto*) fender
paracqua (pâ·râk'kwâ) *m* umbrella
paradisiaco (pâ·râ·dē·zē'â·kō) *a* heavenly
paradiso (pâ·râ·dē'zō) *m* heaven, empyrean, paradise
paradosso (pâ·râ·dōs'sō) *m* paradox
parafango (pâ·râ·fân'gō) *m* (*auto*) fender
parafare (pâ·râ·fâ'rā) *vt* to initial
paraffina (pâ·râf·fē'nâ) *f* paraffin
parafrasare (pâ·râ·frâ·zâ'rā) *vt* to paraphrase; to restate
parafulmine (pâ·râ·fūl'mē·nā) *m* lightning rod
parafuoco (pâ·râ·fwō'kō) *m* fire screen
paraggi (pâ·râj'jē) *mpl* surroundings; environs
paragonabile (pâ·râ·gō·nâ'bē·lā) *a* comparable
paragonare (pâ·râ·gō·nâ'rā) *vt* to compare
paragone (pâ·râ·gō'nā) *m* comparison; **pietra di** — standard, guage
paragrafo (pâ·râ'grâ·fō) *m* paragraph
paralisi (pâ·râ'lē·zē) *f* paralytic stroke; paralysis
paralizzare (pâ·râ·lē·dzâ'rā) *vt* to paralyze
paralizzarsi (pâ·râ·lē·dzâr'sē) *vr* to become paralyzed
parallela (pâ·râl·lā'lâ) *f* parallel
parallelo (pâ·râl·lā'lō) *a* parallel
paralume (pâ·râ·lū'mā) *m* lamp shade
paranco (pâ·rân'kō) *m* (*mech*) tackle
paraocchi (pâ·râ·ōk'kē) *mpl* goggles
parapetto (pâ·râ·pāt'tō) *m* rampart; parapet
parapiglia (pâ·râ·pē'lyâ) *m* hurry-scurry, turmoil
parapioggia (pâ·râ·pyôj'jâ) *m* umbrella
parare (pâ·râ'rā) *vt* to parry; to adorn
pararsi (pâ·râr'sē) *vr* to take shelter; to dress up
parasole (pâ·râ·sō'lā) *m* parasol
parassita (pâ·râs·sē'tâ) *m* parasite
parastatale (pâ·râ·stâ·tâ'lā) *a* government-recognized
parata (pâ·râ'tâ) *f* parry; parade
parato (pâ·râ'tō) *m* tapestry; **carta da parati** wallpaper
paraurti (pâ·râ·ūr'tē) *m* (*auto*) bumper
parcamente (pâr·kâ·mān'tā) *adv* frugally; parsimoniously
parcella (pâr·chāl'lâ) *f* bill; lawyer's fee
parcheggiare (pâr·kāj·jâ'rā) *vt* to park
parcheggio (pâr·kej'jō) *m* parking lot; parking; — **avanti** parking ahead
parchimetro (pâr·kē'mā·trō) *m* parking meter
parco (pâr'kō) *m* park

parco (pâr'kō) *a* frugal
parecchio (pâ·rek'kyō) *a* enough; some; — *adv* much
pareggiare (pâ·rāj·jâ'rā) *vt* (*com*) to balance; to equalize
pareggiarsi (pâ·rāj·jâr'sē) *vi* to be an equal match; to match oneself
pareggio (pâ·rej'jō) *m* balance; tie, even score
parente (pâ·rān'tā) *m&f* relative
parentela (pâ·rān·tā'lâ) *f* relationship, relation
parentesi (pâ·ren'tā·zē) *f* parenthesis; **fra** — in brackets; (*fig*) by the way
parere (pâ·rā'rā) *m* opinion; — * *vi* to appear, seem
parete (pâ·rā'tā) *f* wall (*interior*)
pari (pâ'rē) *a* even, equal
Parigi (pâ·rē'jē) *f* Paris
parigino (pâ·rē·jē'nō) *m&a* Parisian
pariglia (pâ·rē'lyâ) *f* pair; **rendere la** — (*coll*) to retaliate in kind; to give blow for blow
parità (pâ·rē·tâ') *f* parity
parlamentare (pâr·lâ·mān·tâ'rā) *a* parliamentary; — *m* member of a parliament; — *vi* to confer
parlamento (pâr·lâ·mān'tō) *a* parley; parliament
parlantina (pâr·lân·tē'nâ) *f* glibness; talkativeness
parlare (pâr·lâ'rā) *vt* to talk, speak
parlata (pâr·lâ'tâ) *f* accent; way of speaking, speech
parlato (pâr·lâ'tō) *a* spoken; **cinema** — sound movie
parmigiano (pâr·mē·jâ'nō) *a&m* Parmesan
parodia (pâ·rō·dē'â) *f* parody
parola (pâ·rō'lâ) *f* word; parole
parolaccia (pâ·rō·lâ'châ) *f* indecent expression; abusive word
paroliere (pâ·rō·lyā'rā) *m* lyricist
parolina (pâ·rō·lē'nâ) *f* term of endearment; affectionate word
parossismo (pâ·rōs·sē'zmō) *m* paroxysm
parrocchia (pâr·rôk'kyâ) *f* parish
parrocchiale (pâr·rōk·kyâ'lā) *a* parochial
parrocchiano (pâr·rōk·kyâ'nō) *m* parishioner
parroco (pâr'rō·kō) *m* pastor; priest
parrucca (pâr·rūk'kâ) *f* wig
parrucchiere (pâr·rūk·kyā'rā) *m* barber; hairdresser
parsimonia (pâr·sē·mô'nyâ) *f* parsimony; thriftiness
parte (pâr'tā) *f* part; share; role
partecipare (pâr·tā·chē·pâ'rā) *vt* to announce; — *vi* to participate
partecipazione (pâr·tā·chē·pâ·tsyō'nā) *f* participation; announcement
partecipe (pâr·te'chē·pā) *a* sharing; participating
parteggiare (pâr·tāj·jâ'rā) *vi* to take sides, side; to be partial
partenza (pâr·tān'tsâ) *f* leave-taking, departure
participio (pâr·tē·chē'pyō) *m* participle
particola (pâr·tē'kō·lâ) *f* (*eccl*) Host; particle
particolare (pâr·tē·kō·lâ'rā) *a* particular; — *m* detail
particolarità (pâr·tē·kō·lâ·rē·tâ') *f* peculiarity; characteristic
particolarmente (pâr·tē·kō·lâr·mān'tā) *adv* particularly, specially
partigiano (pâr·tē·jâ'nō) *m&a* partisan
partita (pâr·tē'tâ) *f* game, match; (*com*) lot; — **doppia** (*com*) double entry
partito (pâr·tē'tō) *m* political party; match (*in marriage*)
partitura (pâr·tē·tū'râ) *f* (*mus*) score
partizione (pâr·tē·tsyō'nā) *f* division
parto (pâr'tō) *m* childbirth; (*fig*) fruit, result
partoriente (pâr·tō·ryān'tā) *a* in childbirth
partorire (pâr·tō·rē'rā) *vt* to give birth to, be delivered of; — *vi* to give birth
parvenza (pâr·vān'tsâ) *f* appearance, sham
parziale (pâr·tsyâ'lā) *a* partial
parzialità (pâr·tsyâ·lē·tâ') *f* bias
parzialmente (pâr·tsyâl·mān'tā) *adv* in part; in a biased manner
pascolare (pâ·skō·lâ'rā) *vt&i* to browse; to graze; to pasture
pascolo (pâ'skō·lō) *m* pasture
Pasqua (pâ'skwâ) *f* Easter
passabile (pâs·sâ'bē·lā) *a* bearable; passable
passaggio (pâs·sâj'jō) *m* passage; (*auto*) lift; ride; — **a livello** railroad crossing; — **a livello con barriera** guarded crossing; — **a strisce** marked crosswalk
passamaneria (pâs·sâ·mâ·nā·rē'â) *f* dry goods store; ribbon manufacture
passamano (pâs·sâ·mâ'nō) *m* ribbon; braid; passing from hand to hand
passamontagna (pâs·sâ·mōn·tâ'nyâ) *m* winter cap
passante (pâs·sân'tā) *m* pedestrian; passerby
passaporto (pâs·sâ·pōr'tō) *m* passport
passare (pâs·sâ'rā) *vt&i* to pass; to surpass; to spend (*time*); **passarla liscia** to go scot-free; to escape uninjured; — **la vita** to spend one's life; — **oltre** to progress, go ahead; to go beyond
passatempo (pâs·sâ·tām'pō) *m* pastime
passato (pâs·sâ'tō) *a&m* past
passeggero (pâs·sāj·jā'rō) *m* passenger; — *a* temporary, transitory
passeggiare (pâs·sāj·jâ'rā) *vi* to take a walk; to go for a drive
passeggiata (pâs·sāj·jâ'tâ) *f* walk; drive
passeggio (pâs·sej'jō) *m* walkway; promenade, walk
passerella (pâs·sā·rāl'lâ) *f* gangway
passero (pâs'sā·rō) *m* sparrow
passibile (pâs·sē'bē·lā) *a* liable
passionale (pâs·syō·nâ'lā) *a* vehement; ardent
passione (pâs·syō'nā) *f* passion; love
passivamente (pâs·sē·vâ·mān'tā) *adv* passively
passività (pâs·sē·vē·tâ') *fpl* (*com*) liabilities; — *f* passiveness
passivo (pâs·sē'vō) *a* passive; — *m* liability

passo (pâs'sō) *m* pace, step; passage (*book*); (*geog*) straits; **al —** slow; slowly; **— carrabile** driveway
pasta (pâ'stâ) *f* spaghetti; paste, dough; pastry; **— dentifricia** toothpaste; **— frolla** puff pastry; **–io** (pâ·stâ'yō) *m* spaghetti maker; spaghetti dealer
pastello (pâ·stāl'lō) *m* pastel; pastel drawing
pastetta (pâ·stāt'tâ) *f* batter (*food*)
pasticca (pâ·stēk'kâ) *f* (*med*) tablet; **— per la tosse** cough drop
pasticcere (pâ·stē·chā'rā) *m* pastry cook
pasticceria (pâ·stē·chā·rē'â) *f* pastry shop
pasticcino (pâ·stē·chē'nō) *m* cake; cookie
pasticcio (pâ·stē'chō) *m* pie; (*fig*) jumble; trouble; bungling
pasticcione (pâ·stē·chō'nā) *m* bungler
pastificio (pâ·stē·fē'chō) *m* spaghetti factory
pastiglia (pâ·stē'lyâ) *f* (*med*) tablet
pastinaca (pâ·stē·nâ'kâ) *f* parsnip
pasto (pâ'stō) *m* meal; **vino da —** table wine
pastoia (pâ·stô'yā) *f* hobble, fetter
pastore (pâ·stō'rā) *m* shepherd; pastor
pastorizia (pâ·stō·rē'tsyâ) *f* stock raising
pastorizzato (pâ·stō·rē·dzâ'tō) *a* pasteurized
pastoso (pâ·stō'zō) *a* pasty; mellow
pastrano (pâ·strâ'nō) *m* heavy overcoat, greatcoat
patata (pâ·tâ'tā) *f* potato
patatine (pâ·tâ·tē'nā) *fpl* little potatoes; **— fritte** potato chips
patema (pâ·tā'mâ) *m* anxiety; anguish
patentare (pâ·tān·tâ'rā) *vt* to grant a license to; to award a degree to
patente (pâ·tān'tā) *a* patent, clear; **—** *f* license; patent; **— di guida** driver's license
paternale (pâ·tār·nâ'lā) *f* rebuke, reprimand; **—** *a* paternal
paternità (pâ·tār·nē·tâ') *f* paternity
paterno (pâ·tār'nō) *a* paternal, fatherly
paternostro (pâ·tār·nō'strō) *m* the Lord's Prayer
patetico (pâ·te'tē·kō) *a* pathetic; sentimental
patibolare (pâ·tē·bō·lâ'rā) *a* criminal, guilty; **faccia —** hangdog appearance
patibolo (pâ·tē'bō·lō) *m* gallows
patimento (pâ·tē·mān'tō) *m* sorrow, anguish; pain
patina (pâ'tē·nâ) *f* patina; (*med*) furring; **–re** (pâ·tē·nâ'rā) *vt* to varnish; to daub
patire (pâ·tē'rā) *vt&i* to suffer; to tolerate; to undergo; **— la fame** to be starving
patito (pâ·tē'tō) *a* emaciated; lean
patologia (pâ·tō·lō·jē'â) *f* pathology
patologo (pâ·tô'lō·gō) *m* pathologist
patria (pâ'tryâ) *f* one's own country; one's native land
patricidio (pâ·trē·chē'dyō) *m* patricide
patrigno (pâ·trē'nyō) *m* stepfather
patrimonio (pâ·trē·mô'nyō) *m* estate; fortune; inheritance
patriotta (pâ·tryōt'tâ) *m&f* patriot
patriottico (pâ·tryôt'tē·kō) *a* patriotic
patrizio (pâ·trē'tsyō) *a* aristocratic; patrician
patrocinare (pâ·trō·chē·nâ'rā) *vt* to sponsor; to defend; to protect
patrocinatore (pâ·trō·chē·nâ·tō'rā) *m* protector; (*law*) counsel for the defense; (*com*) sponsor
patrocinio (pâ·trō·chē'nyō) *m* legal assistance; patronage; sponsorship; protection
patronato (pâ·trō·nâ'tō) *m* charitable organization; patronage; **— scolastico** agency to assist school children
patrono (pâ·trō'nō) *m* patron; protector; **santo —** patron saint
patteggiare (pât·tāj·jâ'rā) *vt&i* to bargain; to reach an agreement
pattinaggio (pât·tē·nâj'jō) *m* skating; **— artistico** figure skating
pattinare (pât·tē·nâ'rā) *vi* to skate
pattinatore (pât·tē·nâ·tō'rā) *m*, **pattinatrice** (pât·tē·nâ·trē'chā) *f* skater
pattino (pât'tē·nō) *m* skate; (*avi*) skid; sled runner; **— a rotelle** roller skate; **— da ghiaccio** ice skate
patto (pât'tō) *m* agreement, pact; **a — che** providing, on condition that; **a nessun —** by no means; under no circumstances
pattuglia (pât·tū'lyâ) *f* patrol
pattuire (pât·twē'rā) *vt&i* to bargain; to agree on
pattuito (pât·twē'tō) *a* agreed upon
pattume (pât·tū'mā) *m* garbage, rubbish
pattumiera (pât·tū·myā'râ) *f* garbage can
pauperismo (pâū·pā·rē'zmō) *m* pauperism; extreme poverty
paura (pâ·ū'râ) *f* fear; **aver —** to be afraid; **far —** to fill with dread, frighten
paurosamente (pâū·rō·zâ·mān'tā) *adv* fearfully, filled with dread
pauroso (pâū·rō'zō) *a* frightened; timid
pausa (pâ'ū·zâ) *f* pause; interval
pavese (pâ·vā'zā) *m* banner, standard
pavimentazione (pâ·vē·mān·tâ·tsyō'nā) *f* pavement; flooring
pavimento (pâ·vē·mān'tō) *m* floor; pavement
pavone (pâ·vō'nā) *m* peacock
pavoneggiarsi (pâ·vō·nāj·jâr'sē) *vr* to strut; to prance
pazientare (pâ·tsyān·tâ'rā) *vi* to be patient; to be long-suffering
paziente (pâ·tsyān'tā) *am&f* patient; **–mente** (pâ·tsyān·tā·mān'tā) *adv* patiently
pazienza (pâ·tsyān'tsâ) *f* patience; long-suffering
pazzamente (pâ·tsâ·mān'tā) *adv* rashly; madly
pazzesco (pâ·tsā'skō) *a* crazy, reckless, foolish
pazzia (pâ·tsē'â) *f* madness; rashness
pazzo (pâ'tsō) *a* insane, demented
pecca (pāk'kâ) *f* flaw; **–minoso** (pâk·kâ·mē·nō'zō) *a* sinful; **–re** (pāk·kâ'rā) *vi* to sin; to fall short, be inadequate; **–tore** (pāk·kâ·tō'rā) *m* sinner, transgressor
peccato (pāk·kâ'tō) *m* sin; shame, pity, bad luck; **che —!** what a shame!

pece (pā'chā) *f* pitch; — **liquida** tar
pecora (pe'kō · râ) *f* sheep; (*fig*) servile individual; **-io** (pā · kō · râ'yō) *m* shepherd
peculato (pā · kū · lâ'tō) *m* embezzlement
peculio (pā · kū'lyō) *m* nest egg, savings
pedaggio (pā · dâj'jō) *m* toll, fee
pedalare (pā · dâ · lâ'rā) *vt&i* to pedal
pedale (pā · dâ'lā) *m* pedal
pedana (pā · dâ'nâ) *f* platform; mat *(sport)*
pedante (pā · dân'tā) *a* pedantic; — *m* pedant
pedata (pā · dâ'tâ) *f* kick; footprint
pedestre (pā · dā'strā) *a* pedestrian, unimaginative, commonplace
pediatra (pā · dyâ'trâ) *m* pediatrician
pediatria (pā · dyâ · trē'â) *f* pediatrics
pedicure (pā · dē · kū'rā) *m&f* chiropodist
pediluvio (pā · dē · lū'vyō) *m* footbath
pedina (pā · dē'nâ) *f* (*chess*) man, pawn
pedinare (pā · dē · nâ'rā) *vt* to shadow, tail
pedone (pā · dō'nā) *m* pedestrian; (*chess*) pawn, man
peggio (pej'jō) *adv* worse; **il** — the worst
peggioramento (pāj · jō · râ · mān'tō) *m* aggravation; worsening
peggiorare (pāj · jō · râ'rā) *vi* to get worse; to worsen
peggiore (pāj · jō'rā) *a* worse; **il** — the worst
pegno (pā'nyō) *m* forfeit; pledge; **in — d'amore** as a token of love
pelame (pā · lâ'mā) *m* plumage; coat of hair (*animal*)
pelare (pā · lâ'rā) *vt* to peel, skin; to fleece, swindle
pelarsi (pā · lâr'sē) *vr* to lose its leaves (*tree*); to grow bald
pellaio (pāl · lâ'yō) *m* leather dealer; tanner
pellame (pāl · lâ'mā) *m* pelts
pelle (pāl'lā) *f* skin; rind; hide; **lasciarci la** — (*fig*) to die
pellegrinaggio (pāl · lā · grē · nâj'jō) *m* pilgrimage
pellegrino (pāl · lā · grē'nō) *m* pilgrim; — *a* wandering
pelletterie (pāl · lāt · tā · rē'ā) *fpl* leather goods
pellicceria (pāl · lē · chā · rē'â) *f* fur store
pelliccia (pāl · lē'châ) *f* fur; fur coat
pellicciaio (pāl · lē · châ'yō) *m* furrier
pellicola (pāl · lē'kō · lâ) *f* film
pellirossa (pāl · lē · rōs'sâ) *m* North American Indian, redskin
pelo (pā'lō) *m* fur (*animal*); hair; **contro** — against the grain; **aver il — sul cuore** to be unscrupulous; **montare a** — to ride bareback; **non aver peli sulla lingua** to be frank; **-so** (pā · lō'zō) *a* hairy; **carità pelosa** selfish kindness
peltro (pāl'trō) *m* pewter
peluria (pā · lū'ryâ) *f* fuzz, down
pena (pā'nâ) *f* punishment; trouble; — **capitale** capital punishment; **a mala** — hardly; **non vale la** — it isn't worthwhile; **fare** — to move to pity; to be a shame; **-le** (pā · nâ'lā) *a* penal; **-lista** (pā · nâ · lē'stâ) *m* criminal lawyer
pendente (pān · dān'tā) *a* leaning; in abeyance; — *m* pendant
pendere * (pen'dā · rā) *vi* to hang; to be unsettled
pendio (pān · dē'ō) *m* grade, slope
pendola (pen'dō · lâ) *f* pendulum clock
pendolo (pen'dō · lō) *m* pendulum
pene (pā'nā) *m* penis
penetrante (pā · nā · trân'tā) *a* penetrating; pervading
penetrare (pā · nā · trâ'rā) *vi* to penetrate, enter
penetrazione (pā · nā · trâ · tsyō'nā) *f* keenness; penetration
penna (pān'nâ) *f* pen; feather; — **a sfera** ballpoint pen; — **stilografica** fountain pen
pennacchio (pān · nâk'kyō) *m* plume, panache
pennellare (pān · nāl · lâ'rā) *vt&i* to paint
pennello (pān · nāl'lō) *m* brush; — **da barba** shaving brush
pennino (pān · nē'nō) *m* nib; pen point
pennone (pān · nō'nā) *m* pennant
pennuto (pān · nū'tō) *a* feathered
penombra pā · nōm'brâ) *f* dim light
penosamente (pā · nō · zâ · mān'tā) *adv* distressingly; painfully
penoso (pā · nō'zō) *a* painful
pensare (pān · sâ'rā) *vt&i* to think; to intend
pensata (pān · sâ'tâ) *f* thought
pensatore (pān · sâ · tō'rā) *m* thinker; **libero** — free thinker
pensiero (pān · syā'rō) *m* thought; **-so** (pān · syā · rō'zō) *a* thoughtful; serious
pensile (pān · sē'lā) *a* hanging; **giardino** — roof garden
pensilina (pān · sē · lē'nâ) *f* marquee; shelter
pensionante (pān · syō · nân'tā) *m* boarder
pensione (pān · syō'nā) *f* pension; boarding house; **mezza** — room with breakfast and one other meal; **in** — retired
pensosamente (pān · sō · zâ · mān'tā) *adv* pensively
pentagono (pān · tâ'gō · nō) *m* pentagon
Pentecoste (pān · tā · kō'stā) *f* Pentecost; Whitsunday
pentimento (pān · tē · mān'tō) *m* repentance
pentirsi (pān · tēr'sē) *vr* to change one's mind; to have a change of heart; to repent, regret
pentola (pen'tō · lâ) *f* pot; — **a pressione** pressure cooker
penultimo (pā · nūl'tē · mō) *m&a* next to last
penuria (pā · nū'ryâ) *f* need, penury
penzolare (pān · tsō · lâ'rā) *vi* to hang down; to swing
penzoloni (pān · tsō · lō'nē) *adv* swinging, dangling
pepaiola (pā · pâ · yō'lâ) *f* pepper shaker, pepper mill
pepato (pā · pâ'tō) *a* peppery: (*fig*) expensive; **pan** — gingerbread
pepe (pā'pā) *m* pepper
peperita (pā · pā · rē'tâ) *f* peppermint
peperone (pā · pā · rō'nā) *m* (*bot*) pepper; chili

pepita (pā·pē'tâ) *f* nugget
per (pār) *prep* for; through; in order to; on account of; by means of; — **favore** if you please; — **lo meno** at least; — **piacere** please; — **quanto** however; — **così dire** in a manner of speaking, so to speak; — **l'appunto** exactly; — **ora** for now
pera (pā'râ) *f* pear
perbene (pār·bā'nā) *a* nice; refined; respectable; **persona** — decent person, well-bred person; — *adv* nicely, carefully
percalle (pār·kâl'lā) *m* percale
percentuale (pār·chān·twâ'lā) *f* percentage
percepibile (pār·chā·pē'bē·lā) *a* perceptible
percepire (pār·chā·pē'rā) *vt* to conceive; to gain, secure; to collect; to descry, make out
percettività (pār·chāt·tē·vē·tâ') *f* perceptiveness
percettore (pār·chāt·tō'rā) *m* collector
percezione (pār·chā·tsyō'nā) *f* perception; collecting
perchè (pār·kā') *conj* why; because
perciò (pār·chō') *conj* therefore
percorrere * (pār·kôr'rā·rā) *vt* to run over, travel across
percorso (pār·kōr'sō) *m* route; trip, run; — **filoviario** trolleybus route; **durante il** — on the way
percossa (pār·kōs'sâ) *f* blow, shock
percuotere * (pār·kwō'tā·rā) *vt* to strike; to shock; to hit
percussore (pār·kūs·sō'rā) *m* firing pin
perdere * (per'dā·rā) *vt* to lose; to waste; to miss; — **il treno** to miss the train
perdersi * (per'dār·sē) *vr* to be spoiled; to vanish; to get lost, be lost; to miscarry
perdita (per'dē·tâ) *f* loss
perdizione (pār·dē·tsyō'nā) *f* perdition; ruin
perdonare (pār·dō·nâ'rā) *vt* to forgive
perdono (pār·dō'nō) *m* forgiveness; pardon
perdutamente (pār·dū·tâ·mān'tā) *adv* desperately; head over heels, deeply
perduto (pār·dū'tō) *a* lost
perenne (pā·rān'nā) *a* perennial; eternal
perennemente (pā·rān·nā·mān'tā) *adv* eternally
perennità (pā·rān·nē·tâ') *f* eternity
perentoriamente (pā·rān·tō·ryâ·mān'tā) *adv* peremptorily, imperiously
perentorio (pā·rān·tô'ryō) *a* without delay; decisive
perequazione (pā·rā·kwâ·tsyō'nā) *f* equalization; standardization
perfettamente (pār·fāt·tâ·mān'tā) *a* perfectly, flawlessly
perfetto (pār·fāt'tō) *a* perfect, flawless
perfezionamento (pār·fā·tsyō·nâ·mān'tō) *m* improvement; perfection; **corso di** — postgraduate course
perfezionare (pār·fā·tsyō·nâ'rā) *vt* to perfect; to complete
perfezionarsi (pār·fā·tsyō·nâr'sē) *vr* to improve oneself; to achieve perfection; to learn perfectly
perfezione (par·fā·tsyō'nā) *f* perfection
perfidia (pār·fē'dyâ) *f* perfidy
perfido (per'fē·dō) *a* perfidious
perfino (pār·fē'nō) *adv* even, the very
perforare (pār·fō·râ'rā) *vt* to perforate, pierce
perforatrice (pār·fō'râ·trē'chā) *f* (*mech*) drill
perforazione (pār·fō·râ·tsyō'nā) *f* perforation
pergamena (pār·gâ·mā'nâ) *f* parchment
pergolato (pār·gō·lâ'tō) *m* arbor; pergola
pericolante (pā·rē·kō·lân'tā) *a* shaky, unsound, rickety
pericolo (pā·rē'kō·lō) *m* danger
pericolosamente (pā·rē·kō·lō·zâ·mān'tā) *adv* dangerously
pericoloso (pā·rē·kō·lō'zō) *a* dangerous
periferia (pā·rē·fā·rē'â) *f* periphery; suburbs
perimetro (pā·rē'mā·trō) *m* perimeter
periodicamente (pā·ryō·dē·kâ·mān'tā) *adv* periodically
periodico (pā·ryō'dē·kō) *a&m* periodical
periodo (pā·rē'ō·dō) *m* period
peripezia (pā·rē·pā·tsē'â) *f* ups and downs, vicissitudes
perire (pā·rē'rā) *vi* to perish
periscopio (pā·rē·skô'pyō) *m* periscope
perito (pā·rē'tō) *a* perished; expert; — *m* expert
perizia (pā·rē'tsyâ) *f* survey, examination; skill; **–re** (pā·rē·tsyâ'rā) *vt* to estimate
perla (pār'lâ) *f* pearl
perlustrare (pār·lū·strâ'rā) *vt* (*mil*) to scout
permaloso (pār·mâ·lō'zō) *a* hypersensitive; ill-tempered
permanente (pār·mâ·nān'tā) *a* permanent; — *f* permanent wave; — *m* railroad pass
permanentemente (pār·mâ·nān·tā·mān'tā) *adv* permanently
permanenza (pār·mâ·nān'tsâ) *f* stay
permanere * (pār·mâ·nā'rā) *vi* to remain; to stay
permeabile (pār·mā·â'bē·lā) *a* penetrable; permeable
permesso (pār·mās'sō) *m* permit; excuse me, pardon me; — *a* permitted, allowed; **È** — ? May I?
permettere * (pār·met'tā·rā) *vt* to tolerate; to authorize, permit
permettersi (pār·met'tār·sē) *vr* to allow oneself to; to take the liberty of
permuta (pār·mū'tâ) *f* trade-in; exchange; **–re** (pār·mū·tâ'rā) *vt* to turn in; to trade in; to trade, swap
pernice (pār·nē'chā) *f* partridge
perniciosamente (pār·nē·chō·zâ·mān'tā) *adv* perniciously
pernicioso (pār·nē·chō'zō) *a* extremely harmful; fatal
perno (pār'nō) *m* turning point; pivot
pernottare (pār·nōt·tâ'rā) *vi* to spend the night

pero (pā'rō) *m* pear tree
però (pā·rō') *conj* but, however; consequently
perorare (pā·rō·râ'rā) *vt&i* to defend; to plead *(a case)*
perpendicolare (pār·pān·dē·kō·lâ'rā) *a&f* perpendicular
perpetuamente (pār·pā·twâ·mān'tā) *adv* perpetually
perpetuare (pār·pā·twâ'rā) *vt* to perpetuate
perpetuarsi (pār·pā·twâr'sē) *vr* to be perpetuated
perpetuo (pār·pe'twō) *a* perpetual
perplessità (pār·plās·sē·tâ') *f* perplexity
perplesso (pār·plās'sō) *a* perplexed
perquisire (pār·kwē·zē'rā) *vt* to search, make an official search of
perquisizione (pār·kwē·zē·tsyō'nā) *f* investigation; police search
persecuzione (pār·sā·kū·tsyō'nā) *f* persecution
perseguitare (pār·sā·gwē·tâ'rā) *vt* to persecute
perseverante (pār·sā·vā·rân'tā) *a* unrelenting
perseveranza (pār·sā·vā·rân'tsâ) *f* perseverance
perseverare (pār·sā·vā·râ'rā) *vi* to persist, persevere
persiana (pār·syâ'nâ) *f* shutter — **avvolgibile** venetian blind
persico (per'sē·kō) *a&m* Persian; **pesce —** perch *(fish)*
persistenza (pār·sē·stān'tsâ) *f* perseverance; pertinacity; stick-to-itiveness
persistere * (pār·sē'stā·rā) *vi* to persist
perso (pār'sō) *a* lost
persona (pār·sō'nâ) *f* person; **–ggio** (pār·sō·nâj'jō) *m* person of note; *(theat)* character; **–le** (pār·sō·nâ'lā) *m* personnel; staff; **–le** *f* one-man show; **–le** *a* personal
personalità (pār·sō·nâ·lē·tâ') *f* personality
personalmente (pār·sō·nâl·mān'tā) *adv* in person
personificare (pār·sō·nē·fē·kâ'rā) *vt* to embody; to symbolize; to impersonate
personificazione (pār·sō·nē·fē·kâ·tsyō'nā) *f* embodiment, personification; symbol
perspicace (pār·spē·kâ'chā) *a* penetrating, shrewd
perspicacia (pār·spē·kâ'châ) *f* shrewdness, penetration
persuadere * (pār·swâ·dā'rā) *vt* to persuade; to win over
persuadersi * (pār·swâ·dār'sē) *vr* to be convinced; to be persuaded; to be won over
persuasione (pār·swâ·zyō'nā) *f* persuasion
persuasivo (pār·swâ·zē'vō) *a* persuasive
pertanto (pār·tân'tō) *adv* therefore, as a result, for that reason
pertica (per'tē·kâ) *f* pole
pertinacia (pār·tē·nâ'châ) *f* pertinacity
pertinenza (pār·tē·nān'tsâ) *f* competence
pertosse (pār·tōs'sā) *f* whooping cough
perturbare (pār·tūr·bâ'rā) *vt* to disturb, upset
perturbazione (pār·tūr·bâ·tsyō'nā) *f* upsetting, disturbance
Perù (pā·rū') *m* Peru; **valere un —** *(coll)* to be extremely valuable
peruviano (pā·rū·vyâ'nō) *a* Peruvian
pervenire * (pār·vā·nē'rā) *vi* to reach, arrive; to achieve
perversione (pār·vār·syō'nā) *f* perversion
perversità (pār·vār·sē·tâ') *f* depravity; perversity
perverso (pār·vār'sō) *a* perverse; wicked
pervertire (pār·vār·tē'rā) *vt* to pervert
pervertirsi (pār·vār·tēr'sē) *vr* to degenerate: to become perverted
pesa (pā'zâ) *f* scale; **–ggio** (pā·zâj'jō) *m* weighing; **–nte** (pā·zân'tā) *a* heavy; boring; hard *(work)*; **–ntemente** (pā·zân·tā·mān'tā) *adv* heavily; **–ntezza** (pā·zân·tā'tsâ) *f* heaviness; **–ntezza allo stomaco** indigestion; **–re** (pā·zâ'rā) *(fig)* to consider; to influence; to weigh; **–rsi** (pā·zâr'sē) *vr* to weigh oneself
pesca (pā'skâ) *f* peach; fishing; bazaar; raffle; **–ggio** (pā·skâj'jō) *m* *(naut)* draft; **–re** (pā·skâ'rā) *vt&i* to fish; **–re nel torbido** *(fig)* to fish in troubled waters; **–tore** (pā·skâ·tō'rā) *m* fisherman
pesce (pā'shā) *m* fish; **— d'aprile** April Fool joke; **–cane** (pā·shā·kâ'nā) *m* shark; *(coll)* profiteer; **–spada** (pā·shā·spâ'dâ) *m* swordfish
peschereccio (pā·skā·re'chō) *a* concerning fishing, fishing; **—** *m* fishing boat
pescheria (pā·skā·rē'â) *f* fish market
pescivendolo (pā·shē·ven'dō·lō) *m* fish dealer
pesco (pā'skō) *m* peach tree
pesista (pā·zē'stâ) *m* *(sport)* weightlifter
peso (pā'zō) *m* weight; **— gallo** bantamweight; **— leggero** lightweight; **— lordo** gross weight; **— massimo** heavyweight; **— medio** middleweight; **— mosca** flyweight; **— piuma** featherweight
pessimamante (pās·sē·mâ·mān'tā) *adv* very badly
pessimismo (pās·sē·mē'zmō) *m* pessimism
pessimista (pās·sē·mē'stâ) *m* pessimist
pessimo (pes'sē·mō) *a* worst; very bad
pestaggio (pā·stâj'jō) *m* beating, drubbing
pestare (pā·stâ'rā) *vt* to pound; to trample
peste (pā'stā) *f* plague
pestello (pā·stāl'lō) *m* pestle
pestifero (pā·stē'fā·rō) *a* bothersome; *(coll)* harmful
pestilenza (pā·stē·lān'tsâ) *f* plague, pestilence; *(fig)* stench
pesto (pā'stō) *a* pounded; **occhio —** black eye; **buio —** black, extremely dark; **carta pesta** papier mâché
petalo (pe'tâ·lō) *m* petal
petardo (pā·târ'dō) *m* firecracker
petente (pā·tān'tā) *n* petitioner
petizione (pā·tē·tsyō'nā) *f* petition
petonciano (pā·tōn·châ'nō) *m* eggplant
petroliera (pā·trō·lyā'râ) *f* tanker
petrolio (pā·trô'lyō) *m* oil; kerosene; petroleum

pettegolezzo (pāt·tā·gō·lā'tsō) *m* gossip, idle chatter
pettegolo (pāt·te'gō·lō) *a* gossipy; — *m* gossip
pettinare (pāt·tē·nâ'rā) *vt* to comb
pettinarsi (pāt·tē·nâr'sē) *vr* to comb one's hair
pettinatore (pāt·tē·nâ·tō'rā) *m,* **pettinatrice** (pāt·tē·nâ·trē'chā) *f* hairdresser
pettinatura (pāt·tē·nâ·tū'râ) *f* hairdo
pettine (pet'tē·nā) *m* comb; **tutti i nodi vengono al** — *(coll)* murder will out; it will all come out in the wash
pettiniera (pāt·tē·nyā'râ) *f* dressing table; comb case
pettirosso (pāt·tē·rōs'sō) *m* robin
petto (pāt'tō) *m* breast; chest; **a due petti** double-breasted; — **a** — vis-à-vis; **prendere di** — to face squarely; **prendersela a** — to throw oneself into something heart and soul; to be deeply hurt
petulante (pā·tū·lân'tā) *a* saucy; nervy *(sl)*; peevish
pezza (pā'tsâ) *f* patch; bolt of cloth
pezzente (pā·tsān'tā) *m* miser; beggar
pezzettino (pā·tsāt·tē'nō) *m* little bit
pezzo (pā'tsō) *m* piece; story; — **di ricambio** spare part; — **grosso** important person; big shot *(sl)*; **un** — **d'uomo** a well-built man
piacente (pyâ·chān'tā) *a* attractive, pleasing
piacere (pyâ·chā'rā) *m* favor; pleasure; — * *vi* to please; to like; **Molto** — **! P— di conoscerla!** I am glad to know you!, Very happy to meet you!; **per** — please
piacevole (pyâ·che'vō·lā) *a* pleasant, pleasing, gracious
piacevolmente (pyâ·chā·vōl·mān'tā) *adv* graciously, pleasantly
piacimento (pyâ·chē·mān'tō) *m* liking, pleasure
piaga (pyâ'gâ) *f* sore; *(fig)* catastrophe; **mettere il dito sulla** — *(fig)* to hit the nail on the head; to find the rub; **–re** (pyâ·gâ'rā) *vt* to cause a sore, form a sore; to wound; **–rsi** (pyâ·gâr'sē) *vr* to ulcerate
piagnucolare (pyâ·nyū·kō·lâ'rā) *vi* to whine
pialla (pyâl'lâ) *f* plane *(tool)*; **–re** (pyâl·lâ'rā) *vt* to plane
piallatrice (pyâl·lâ·trē'chā) *f* planer *(machine)*
pianamente (pyâ·nâ·mān'tā) *adv* in a smooth way; clearly; softly; simply
pianale (pyâ·nâ'lā) *m (rail)* flatcar
pianella (pyâ·nāl'lâ) *f* slipper, mule; tile
pianerottolo (pyâ·nā·rôt'tō·lō) *m* landing *(stairway)*
pianeta (pyâ·nā'tâ) *m* planet; — *f (eccl)* chasuble
piangere * (pyân'jā·rā) *vi&t* to cry; to mourn; to weep
pianificare (pyâ·nē·fē·kâ'rā) *vt* to plan; to outline
pianificato (pyâ·nē·fē·kâ'tō) *a* planned; outlined
pianificazione (pyâ·nē·fē·kâ·tsyō'nā) *f* planning; outline
pianino (pyâ·nē'nō) *m* barrel organ, hurdy-gurdy; — *adv* slowly; gently
pianista (pyâ·nē'stâ) *m* pianist
piano (pyâ'nō) *m* plan, project; story, floor; *(mus)* piano; — **regolatore** city planning; — *a* flat; level; plain, clear; — *adv* slowly; softly; quietly; **primo** — *(photo)* close-up
pianoforte (pyâ·nō·fōr'tā) *m* piano; — **a coda** grand piano; — **verticale** upright piano
pianta (pyân'tâ) *f* plant; map; sole of foot; **–gione** (pyân·tâ·jō'nā) *f* planting; plantation; **–re** (pyân·tâ'rā) *vt* to plant; to jilt; to cast aside; **–re in asso** to leave in the lurch; **–re chiodi** *(fig)* to incur debts; **–rsi** (pyân·târ'sē) *vr* to take a stance; to settle, establish oneself; **Piantala!** *(coll)* Stop it!; **–tore** (pyân·tâ·tō'rā) *m* planter
pianto (pyân'tō) *m* crying, weeping; — *a* rued; mourned
piantonare (pyân·tō·nâ'rā) *vt* to watch over; to guard
piantone (pyân·tō'nā) *m (mil)* sentinel, orderly; *(bot)* shoot
pianura (pyâ·nū'râ) *f* plain
piastra (pyâ'strâ) *f* sheet, plate
piastrella (pyâ·strāl'lâ) *f* tile
piattaforma (pyât·tâ·fōr'mâ) *f* platform
piattino (pyât·tē'nō) *m* saucer
piatto (pyât'tō) *m* dish; plate; *(mus)* cymbal; — *a* flat; dull
piattola (pyât'tō·lâ) *f* roach; beetle; thumbtack; *(fig)* bore, tiresome person
piazza (pyâ'tsâ) *f* square; market place; **letto a due piazze** double bed; **prezzo di** — market price; **far** — **pulita** to make a clean sweep; — **d'armi** *(mil)* drill field; **–le** (pyâ·tsâ'lā) *m* large open square; **–re** (pyâ·tsâ'rā) *vt* to sell; *(sport)* to place; **–rsi** (pyâ·tsâr'sē) *vr (sport)* to place
piazzista (pyâ·tsē'stâ) *m* traveling salesman; agent; dealer
picca (pēk'kâ) *f* ruffled pride; lance; pick; *(cards)* spade; **per** — *(fig)* out of spite; **–rsi** (pēk·kâr'sē) *vr* to be offended; **–nte** (pēk·kân'tā) *a* sharp; racy
picchè (pēk·kā') *m* piqué
picchetto (pēk·kāt'tō) *m* picket
picchiare (pēk·kyâ'rā) *vt* to hit, beat
picchiarsi (pēk·kyâr'sē) *vr* to beat one another; to scuffle, fight
picchiata (pēk·kyâ'tâ) *f* beating; *(avi)* dive
picchio (pēk'kyō) *m* knock; woodpecker
piccineria (pē·chē·nā·rē'â) *f* pettiness, narrowness
piccino (pē·chē'nō) *m* child; — *a* small; petty, narrow; cheap; narrow-minded; unimportant
piccionaia (pē·chō·nâ'yâ) *f* dovecote; *(theat)* upper gallery
piccione (pē·chō'nā) *m* dove; pigeon
picciuolo (pē·chwō'lō) *m* stem
picco (pēk'kō) *m* peak; **andare a** — to go to the bottom, sink
piccolezza (pēk·kō·lā'tsâ) *f* trifle; small-

ness; unimportance
piccolo (pēk'kō·lō) *a* small, little; — *m* little fellow
piccone (pēk·kō'nā) *m* pick
piccoso (pēk·kō'zō) *a* touchy, hypersensitive
piccozza (pēk·kō'tsâ) *f* pickax
pidocchio (pē·dôk'kyō) *m* louse; *(coll)* stingy person, miser; **–so** (pē·dōk·kyō'zō) *a* lousy; *(coll)* stingy, miserly
piede (pyā'dā) *m* foot; **stare in piedi** to stand; **a piedi** on foot
piedistallo (pyā·dē·stâl'lō) *m* pedestal
piega (pyā'gâ) *f* fold; crease; pleat; **–mento** (pyā·gâ·mān'tō) *m* bending; pleating, creasing; *(mil)* retreat; **–re** (pyā·gâ'rā) *vt* to fold; to bend; to yield; **–rsi** (pyā·gâr'sē) *vr* to submit; to bend
pieghevole (pyā·ge'vō·lā) *a* folding, pliable; — *m* folder
pieghevolmente (pyā·gā·vōl·mān'tā) *adv* flexibly
Piemonte (pyā·mōn'tā) *m* Piedmont
piemontese (pyā·mōn·tā'zā) *a&m* Piedmontese
piena (pyā'nâ) *f* flood; mob
pienamente (pyâ·nâ·mān'tā) *adv* absolutely; entirely; quite
pienezza (pyā·nā'tsâ) *f* fullness; plenty
pieno (pyā'nō) *a* full; — *m* fullness; climax; **fare il** — to fill the gas tank; **in piena notte** in the dead of night; **in — giorno** in broad daylight; **–ne** (pyā·nō'nā) *m* huge crowd; *(theat)* full house
pietà (pyā·tâ') *f* piety; pity; mercy; *(art)* Pietà; **Monte di P–** pawnshop
pietanza (pyā·tân'tsâ) *f* dish, course
pietosamente (pyā·tō·zâ·mān'tā) *adv* mercifully; charitably; pitifully
pietoso (pyā·tō'zō) *a* pitiful; pitiable; merciful
pietra (pyā'trâ) *f* stone; **metterci una — sopra** *(fig)* to let bygones be bygones
pietrificare (pyā·trē·fē·kâ'rā) *vt* to petrify, turn to stone
pietrisco (pyā·trē'skō) *m* gravel
pievano (pyā·vâ'nō) *m* rural parish priest
pieve (pyā'vā) *f* rural parish
piffero (pēf'fā·rō) *m (mus)* fife
pigiama (pē·jâ'mâ) *m* pajamas
pigiare (pē·jâ'rā) *vt* to crush; to press
pigiarsi (pē·jâr'sē) *vr* to crowd together; to mill around
pigione (pē·jō'nā) *f* rent
pigliare (pē·lyâ'rā) *vt* to take; — **a sinistra** to turn to the left; — **fuoco** to catch fire
pigliarsi (pē·lyâr'sē) *vr* to catch, take; — **a pugni** to come to blows; — **la sbornia** to get drunk; — **un raffreddore** to catch cold
pigmeo (pēg·mā'ō) *m* pygmy
pigna (pē'nyâ) *f* pine cone
pignatta (pē·nyât'tâ) *f* pot *(cooking)*
pignolo (pē·nyō'lō) *a* faultfinding; fussy; pedantic
pignolo (pē·nyō'lō) *m* pine nut
pignoramento (pē·nyō·râ·mān'tō) *m* distraint; attachment, legal seizure
pignorare (pē·nyō·râ'rā) *vt* to distrain; to attach; to seize legally
pigolare (pē·gō·lâ'rā) *vi* to chirp
pigolio (pē·gō·lē'ō) *m* chirping; chirp
pigramente (pē·grâ·mān'tā) *adv* lazily
pigrizia (pē·grē'tsyâ) *f* laziness
pigro (pē'grō) *a* lazy
pila (pē'lâ) *f* pile; battery; baptismal font
pilastro (pē·lâ'strō) *m* pillar
pillacchera (pēl·lâk'kā·râ) *f* mud splash
pillola (pēl'lō·lâ) *f* pill
pillotare (pēl·lōt·tâ'rā) *vt* to baste *(meat)*; *(fig)* to lambaste
pilota (pē·lō'tâ) *m* pilot; **–ggio** (pē·lō·tâj'jō) *m* piloting; **corso di –ggio** aviation course; **–re** (pē·lō·tâ'rā) *vt* to drive; to fly
pinacoteca (pē·nâ·kō·tā'kâ) *f* art gallery; art museum
pineta (pē·nā'tâ) *f* pine wood
pingue (pēn'gwā) *a* lucrative; fat; rich
pinguino (pēn·gwē'nō) *m* penguin
pinna (pēn'nâ) *f* fin
pino (pē'nō) *m* pine tree
pinze (pēn'tsā) *fpl* pliers; pincers; **–tte** (pēn·tsāt'tā) *fpl* tweezers
pio (pē'ō) *a* pious, charitable
pioggia (pyôj'jâ) *f* rain
piombare (pyōm·bâ'rā) *vt* to seal; to fall upon; *(dent)* to fill
piombino (pyōm·bē'nō) *m* plumb, plumb line
piombo (pyōm'bō) *m* plummet; lead; **procedere con i piedi di —** *(fig)* to proceed with great caution
pioniere (pyō·nyā'rā) *m* pioneer
pioppo (pyōp'pō) *m* poplar
piorrea (pyōr·rā'â) *f* pyorrhea
piovere * (pyô'vā·rā) *vi* to rain
piovigginare (pyō·vēj·jē·nâ'rā) *vi* to drizzle
piovigginoso (pyō·vēj·jē·nō'zō) *a* drizzling
piovoso (pyō·vō'zō) *a* rainy
pipa (pē'pâ) *f* pipe
pipistrello (pē·pē·strāl'lō) *m (zool)* bat
pira (pē'râ) *f* pyre
piramide (pē·râ'mē·dā) *f* pyramid
pirata (pē·râ'tâ) *m* pirate
piroga (pē·rō'gâ) *f* canoe
pirometro (pē·rô'mā·trō) *m* pyrometer
piroscafo (pē·rô'skâ·fō) *m* steamship
pirotecnica (pē·rō·tek'nē·kâ) *f* fireworks
pisciare (pē·shâ'rā) *vi* to urinate
piscina (pē·shē'nâ) *f* swimming pool
piscio (pē'shō) *m* urine
pisello (pē·zāl'lō) *m* pea
pisolino (pē·zō·lē'nō) *m* doze, nap; catnap; **fare un —** to catnap
pista (pē'stâ) *f* track; racetrack; — **di decollaggio** runway; — **d'atterraggio** landing strip; — **d'involo** runway; — **da ballo** dance floor; **seguire la — di** to track; to shadow
pistacchio (pē·stâk'kyō) *m* pistachio
pistola (pē·stō'lâ) *f* pistol; gun
pistone (pē·stō'nā) *m* piston
pitone (pē·tō'nā) *m* python
pitonessa (pē·tō·nās'sâ) *f* prophetess

pittima (pēt'tē·mâ) *f* hairsplitter, pedant
pittore (pēt·tō'rā) *m*, **pittrice** (pēt·trē'chā) *f* painter
pittoresco (pēt·tō·rā'skō) *a* picturesque
pittura (pēt·tū'râ) *f* painting; paint; **–re** (pēt·tū·râ'rā) *vt* to paint
più (pyū) *adv* more; — *prep* plus; — **presto** sooner; more quickly; — **volte** several times; **sempre** — more and more; **mai** — never again; **in** — in addition; **tutt'al** — at most; **per lo** — generally, for the most part; **per di** — besides, moreover; **a** — **non posso** as much as I could
piuma (pyū'mâ) *f* feather
piumino (pyū·mē'nō) *m* powder puff; feather duster
piuolo (pywō'lō) *m* peg
piuttosto (pyūt·tō'stō) *adv* rather, instead
pizza (pē'tsâ) *f* pizza, Neapolitan open meat and cheese pie
pizzardone (pē·tsâr·dō'nā) *m (coll)* policeman; cop *(sl)*
pizzicagnolo (pē·tsē·kâ'nyō·lō) *m* grocer
pizzicare (pē·tsē·kâ'rā) *vt* to nip; to pinch; *(mus)* to pluck
pizzicheria (pē·tsē·kā·rē'â) *f* delicatessen; grocery
pizzico (pē'tsē·kō) *m* smarting, tingling; tiny bit, pinch; **–tto** (pē·tsē·kōt'tō) *m* pinch
pizzo (pē'tsō) *m* lace
placare (plâ·kâ'rā) *vt* to appease, placate
placarsi (plâ·kâr'sē) *vr* to subside; to be placated
placca (plâk'kâ) *f* metal badge; **–re** (plâk·kâ'rā) *vt* to plate; **–to** (plâk·kâ'tō) *a* plated; **–tura** (plâk·kâ·tū'râ) *f* plating
placidamente (plâ·chē·dâ·mān'tā) *adv* tranquilly, placidly
placido (plâ'chē·dō) *a* placid
plafone (plâ·fō'nā) *m* ceiling
plaga (plâ'gâ) *f* country, locality
plagiario (plâ·jâ'ryō) *m* plagiarist
plagio (plâ'jō) *m* plagiarism
planare (plâ·nâ'rā) *vi* to glide, volplane
plancia (plân'châ) *f (naut)* bridge
plantigrado (plân·tē'grâ·dō) *a&m* plantigrade
plasma (plâ'zmâ) *f* plasma; **–re** (plâ·zmâ'rā) *vt* to mould, shape
plastico (plâ'stē·kō) *a* plastic
platano (plâ'tâ·nō) *m (bot)* sycamore
platea (plâ·tā'â) *f (theat)* orchestra pit
platino (plâ'tē·nō) *m* platinum
plausibile (plâū·zē'bē·lā) *a* reasonable; likely; plausible
plebe (plā'bā) *f* populace; mob; **–o** (plā·bā'ō) *a* plebeian
plebiscitario (plā·bē·shē·tâ'ryō) *a* unanimous
plebiscito (plā·bē·shē'tō) *m* plebiscite
plenario (plā·nâ'ryō) *a* plenary
plenilunio (plā·nē·lū'nyō) *m* moonlight; full moon
plenipotenziario (plā·nē·pō·tān·tsyâ'ryō) *a* plenipotentiary
pletora (ple'tō·râ) *f* excess, plethora
plettro (plāt'trō) *m* plectrum
pleurite (plāū·rē'tā) *f* pleurisy
plico (plē'kō) *m* envelope
plotone (plō·tō'nā) *m* platoon; — **d'esecuzione** firing squad
plumbeo (plūm'bā·ō) *a* leaden; dull
plurale (plū·râ'lā) *m&a* plural
plutocrate (plū·tō·krâ'tā) *m* plutocrat
plutocrazia (plū·tō·krâ·tsē'â) *f* plutocracy
plutonio (plū·tô'nyō) *m (min)* plutonium
pluviale (plū·vyâ'lā) *a* rain
pluviometro (plū·vyô'mā·trō) *m* rain guage
pneumatico (pnāū·mâ'tē·kō) *a* pneumatic, air; — *m* inner tube; tire
po' (pō) *a&adv* little
poco (pō'kō) *a&adv* little; **fra** — soon, in a short while; **a** — **a** — gradually, little by little
podagra (pō·dâ'grâ) *f* gout
podere (pō·dā'rā) *m* farm
poderosamente (pō·dā·rō·zâ·mān'tā) *adv* powerfully
poderoso (pō·dā·rō'zō) *a* ponderous; powerful
podestà (pō·dā·stâ') *m* mayor; — *f* authority, power
podio (pô'dyō) *m* podium; dais
podista (pō·dē'stâ) *m* foot racer
poema (pō·ā'mâ) *m* long poem; epopee
poesia (pō·ā·zē'â) *f* poetry; short poem
poeta (pō·ā'tâ) *m*, **poetessa** (pō·ā·tās'sâ) *f* poet
poggiacapo (pōj·jâ·kâ'pō) *m* headrest
poggiapiedi (pōj·jâ·pyā'dē) *m* footstool
poggiare (pōj·jâ'rā) *vt&i* to rest; to place; to lean on; — **a sinistra** to keep to the left
poggiarsi (pōj·jâr'sē) *vr* to lean on
poggiolo (pōj·jō'lō) *m* balcony
poi (pō'ē) *adv* then; later; afterwards
poichè (pōē·kā') *conj* after; when; since; as; for
polacco (pō·lâk'kō) *a&m* Polish; — *m* Pole
polemica (pō·le'mē·kâ) *f* controversy; polemic
polemico (pō·le'mē·kō) *a* controversial; polemical
polemizzare (pō·lā·mē·dzâ'rā) *vi* to argue
polenta (pō·lān'tâ) *f* cornmeal mush
policlinico (pō·lē·klē'nē·kō) *m* general hospital; medical center
poligamia (pō·lē·gâ·mē'â) *f* poligamy
poliglotta ((pō·lē·glōt'tâ) *a&m* polyglot
poligono (pō·lē'gō·nō) *m* target range
poliomielite (po·lyō·myā·lē'tā) *f* infantile paralysis, poliomyelitis
polipo (pô'lē·pō) *m* polyp
politeama (pō·lē·tā·â'mâ) *m* theater
politecnico (pō·lē·tek'nē·kō) *m* engineering school; polytechnical institute
politica (pō·lē'tē·kâ) *f* policy, regulation; politics; **–nte** (pō·lē·tē·kân'tā) *m* political dabbler, small-time politician
politico (pō·lē'tē·kō) *a* political; — *m* statesman; politician; **–ne** (pō·lē·tē·kō'nā) *m* schemer; cunning person
polizia (pō·lē·tsē'â) *f* police; **agente di** —

police officer; — **stradale** highway patrol; traffic police; — **dei costumi** vice squad
poliziesco (pō·lē·tsyā'skō) *a* police; **romanzo** — detective story
poliziotto (pō·lē·tsyōt'tō) *m* policeman; — **in borghese** plainclothesman
polizza (pô'lē·dzâ) *f* insurance policy; pawn ticket; certificate; — **di carico** bill of lading
pollaio (pōl·lâ'yō) *m* hencoop
pollame (pōl·lâ'mā) *m* poultry
pollastra (pōl·lâ'strâ) *f*, **pollastro** (pōl·lâ'strō) *m* spring chicken
polleria (pōl·lā·rē'â) *f* poultry store
pollice (pôl'lē·chā) *m* thumb; big toe; inch
polline (pôl'lē·nā) *m* pollen
pollivendolo (pōl·lē·ven'dō·lō) *m* poultry dealer
pollo (pōl'lō) *m* chicken
polmone (pōl·mō'nā) *m* lung; — **d'acciaio** iron lung
polmonite (pōl·mō·nē'tā) *f* pneumonia
polo (pō'lō) *m* (*geog, phys*) pole; polo
Polonia (pō·lô'nyâ) *f* Poland
polonio (pō·lô'nyō) *m* (*min*) polonium
polpa (pōl'pâ) *f* pulp; flesh (*animal*); **–ccio** (pōl·pâ'chō) *m* (*anat*) calf; **–strello** (pōl·pâ·strāl'lō) *m* tip of the finger
polpetta (pōl·pāt'tâ) *f* meat ball; croquette
polpettone (pōl·pāt·tō'nā) *m* hash; hodgepodge; meat loaf
polpo (pōl'pō) *m* octopus
polsino (pōl·sē'nō) *m* cuff
polso (pōl'sō) *m* wrist; pulse; (*fig*) energy, strength
poltiglia (pōl·tē'lyâ) *f* mash; slush, mud
poltrona (pōl·trō'nâ) *f* easy chair; (*theat*) orchestra seat
poltronaggine (pōl·trō·nâj'jē·nā) *f* laziness; lassitude
poltrone (pōl·trō'nā) *a* lazy; — *m* loafer; **–ria** (pōl·trō·nā·rē'â) *f* laziness
polvere (pôl'vā·rā) *f* powder; dust
polveriera (pōl·vā·ryā'rā) *f* powder magazine
polverizzare (pōl·vā·rē·dzâ'rā) *vt* to pulverize
polverizzatore (pōl·vā·rē·dzâ·tō'rā) *m* atomizer
polverone (pōl·vā·rō'nā) *m* dust cloud
polveroso (pōl·vā·rō'zō) *a* dusty
pomata (pō·mâ'tâ) *f* pomade
pomello (pō·māl'lō) *m* cheekbone
pomeridiano (pō·mā·rē·dyâ'nō) *a* P.M.; afternoon
pomeriggio (pō·mā·rēj'jō) *m* afternoon
pomice (pô'mē·chā) *f* pumice
pomiciare (pō·mē·châ'rā) *vt* to polish with pumice; to flatter; to softsoap (*coll*)
pomodoro (pō·mō·dō'rō) *m* tomato
pompa (pōm'pâ) *f* pomp; parade; pump; — **da incendio** fire engine; **–re** (pōm·pâ'rā) *vt* to pump; (*fig*) to praise; **pompe funebri** funeral; **impresario di pompe funebri** funeral director, undertaker
pompelmo (pōm·pāl'mō) *m* grapefruit
pompiere (pōm·pyā'rā) *m* fireman
pomposamente (pōm·pō·zâ·mān'tā) *adv* pompously, ostentatiously
pomposo (pōm·pō'zō) *a* pompous, swelled
ponderare (pōn·dā·râ'rā) *vt&i* to ponder; to ruminate (*fig*)
ponderato (pōn·dā·râ'tō) *a* considered; pondered
ponderoso (pōn·dā·rō'zō) *a* ponderous; weighty
ponente (pō·nān'tā) *m* West; west; west wind
ponte (pōn'tā) *m* bridge; (*naut*) deck; — **levatoio** drawbridge; — **stretto** narrow bridge; — **passeggiata** promenade deck; — **aereo** airlift
pontefice (pōn·te'fē·chā) *m* pontiff; Pope
pontificio (pōn·tē·fē'chō) *a* papal, pontifical
pontile (pōn·tē'lā) *m* pier, dock
pontone (pōn·tō'nā) *m* pontoon
popolano (pō·pō·lâ'nō) *m* commoner; — *a* of the masses, popular
popolare (pō·pō·lâ'rā) *a* popular; low-priced; — *vt* to people
popolarità (pō·pō·lâ·rē·tâ') *f* popularity, celebrity
popolarizzare (pō·pō·lâ·rē·dzâ'rā) *vt* to popularize
popolarsi (pō·pō·lâr'sē) *vr* to crowd, get crowded; to become populated
popolazione (pō·pō·lâ·tsyō'nā) *f* population
popolo (pô'pō·lō) *m* people
popone (pō·pō'nā) *m* cantaloupe; melon
poppa (pōp'pâ) *f* (*anat*) breast; (*naut*) stern; **–re** (pōp·pâ'rā) *vt&i* to nurse; **–toio** (pōp·pâ·tô'yō) *m* rubber nipple; nursing bottle
porcellana (pōr·chāl·lâ'nâ) *f* porcelain; china
porcellino (pōr·chāl·lē'nō) *m* suckling pig
porcheria (pōr·kā·rē'â) *f* dirt, trash; monkey business (*sl*)
porchetta (pōr·kāt'tâ) *f* roast duckling, pig
porcile (pōr·chē'lā) *m* pigsty, pigpen
porcino (pōr·chē'nō) *a* porcine
porco (pōr'kō) *m* pig, hog; pork
porgere * (pôr'jā·rā) *vt* to hand over; to offer; to give
porgersi * (pôr'jār·sē) *vr* to come forward, volunteer one's services
poro (pō'rō) *m* pore; **–oso** (pō·rō'zō) *a* porous
porre * (pōr'rā) *vt* to place, put
porro (pōr'rō) *m* leek; (*med*) wart
porta (pōr'tâ) *f* door; gate
portaaerei (pōr·tâ·â·e'rāē) *f* aircraft carrier
portabagagli (pōr·tâ·bâ·gâ'lyē) *m* redcap, porter; (*auto*) trunk; (*rail*) rack
portabastoni (pōr·tâ·bâ·stō'nē) *m* golf caddie
portacarte (pōr·tâ·kâr'tā) *m* file folder
portacenere (pōr·tâ·che'nā·rā) *m* ashtray
portacipria (pōr·tâ·chē'pryâ) *m* compact
portafiori (pōr·tâ·fyō'rē) *m* flower stand
portafogli (pōr·tâ·fō'lyē) *m* wallet
portafoglio (pōr·tâ·fô'lyō) *m* portfolio

portafortuna (pōr·tâ·fōr·tū'nâ) *m* charm; amulet
portagioielli (pōr·tâ·jō·yāl'lē) *m* jewelry case
portalampada (pōr·tâ·lâm'pâ·dâ) *f* lamp socket
portale (pōr·tâ'lā) *m* door; portal
portalettere (pōr·tâ·let'tā·rā) *m* mailman
portamento (pōr·tâ·mān'tō) *m* behavior, bearing
portamonete (pōr·tâ·mō·nā'tā) *m* purse
portantina (pōr·tân·tē'nâ) *f* sedan chair
portaordine (pōr·tâ·ôr'dē·nā) *m* messenger
portapenne (pōr·tâ·pān'nā) *m* penholder
portare (pōr·tâ'rā) *vt* to take, bring, carry; to wear
portaritratti (pōr·tâ·rē·trât'tē) *m* picture frame
portarsi (pōr·târ'sē) *vr* to behave, demean oneself
portasapone (pōr·tâ·sâ·pō'nā) *m* soap dish
portasigarette (pōr·tâ·sē·gâ·rāt'tā) *m* cigarette case
portasigari (pōr·tâ·sē'gâ·rē) *m* cigar case
portata (pōr·tâ'tâ) *f* course (*meal*); reach; range; **a — di mano** within reach
portatile (pōr·tâ'tē·lā) *a* portable
portatore (pōr·tâ·tō'rā) *m* bearer
portauovo (pōr·tâ·wō'vō) *m* eggcup
portavoce (pōr·tâ·vō'chā) *m* speaking tube; megaphone; spokesman
portellino (pōr·tāl·lē'nō) *m* porthole
portento (pōr·tān'tō) *m* miracle; marvel; **–samente** (pōr·tān·tō·zâ·mān'tā) *adv* marvelously, prodigiously; **–so** (pōr·tān·tō'zō) *a* wonderful, portentous
portico (pôr'tē·kō) *m* porch; portico
portiera (pōr·tyā'râ) *f* door curtain, portiere; door (*auto*)
portiere (pōr·tyā'rā) *m* doorman; (*sport*) goalkeeper
portinaia (pōr·tē·nâ'yâ) *f* woman doorkeeper
portinaio (pōr·tē·nâ'yō) *m* janitor; doorman
portineria (pōr·tē·nā·rē'â) *f* doorman's quarters
porto (pōr'tō) *m* port; postage; shipping charge; **— assegnato** COD; **franco di —** postpaid; **— d'armi** gun license
Portogallo (pōr·tō·gâl'lō) *m* Portugal
portoghese (pōr·tō·gā'zā) *a&m* Portuguese
portone (pōr·tō'nā) *m* gate; main door
portuale (pōr·twâ'lā) *m* dockhand; — *a* port
porzione (pōr·tsyō'nā) *f* share; portion; serving
posa (pō'zâ) *f* pose; pause; (*photo*) exposure; **senza —** continuously; **–mine** (pō·zâ·mē'nā) *m* minelayer; **–piano** (pō·zâ·pyâ'nō) *m* slowpoke; "handle with care" (*label*); **–re** (pō·zâ'rā) *vt* to lay; to rest; to pose; **–rsi** (pō·zâr'sē) *vr* to come to rest; to place oneself; to alight; **–ta** (pō·zâ'tâ) *f* cover (*knife, fork, spoon*); **–mente** (pō·zâ·tâ·mān'tā) *adv* calmly, sedately; **–tezza** (pō·zâ·tā'tsâ) *f* gravity, composure, sedateness; **–to** (pō·zâ'tō) *a* laid; staid, quiet
posbellico (pō·zbel'lē·kō) *a* postwar
poscia (pô'shâ) *adv* afterwards, subsequently
poscritto (pō·skrēt'tō) *m* postscript, PS
posdatato (pō·zdâ·tâ'tō) *a* postdated
positiva (pō·zē·tē'vâ) *f* (*photo*) positive
positivamente (pō·zē·tē·vâ·mān'tā) *adv* positively
positivo (pō·zē·tē'vō) *a* positive; matter-of-fact, factual
posizione (pō·zē·tsyō'nā) *f* position; status
posporre * (pō·spōr'rā) *vt* to postpone, delay
possedere * (pōs·sā·dā'rā) *vt* to have; to own
possedimento (pōs·sā·dē·mān'tō) *m* property, holdings; possession; colony
possesso (pōs·sās'sō) *m* possession; **–re** (pōs·sās·sō'rā) *m* owner
possibile (pōs·sē'bē·lā) *a* possible; workable
possibilità (pōs·sē·bē·lē·tâ') *f* possibility, occasion
possibilmente (pōs·sē·bēl·mān'tā) *adv* possibly, perhaps
possidente (pōs·sē·dān'tā) *m* property owner; possessor
posta (pō'stâ) *f* mail; post office; stake; **— aerea** air mail; **fermo in —** general delivery; **a —** purposely; **stare alla —** to watch; **–le** (pō·stâ'lā) *a* postal; **casella –le** post-office box; **cassetta –le** mailbox; **cassa –le** postal savings; **vaglia –le** money order
posteggiare (pō·stāj·jâ'rā) *vt* to park
posteggio (pō·stej'jō) *m* parking; parking lot; place to park; **— per auto pubbliche** taxi stand
postelegrafico (pō·stā·lā·grâ'fē·kō) *m* postal telegraph office employee
postergare (pō·stār·gâ'rā) *vt* to procrastinate; to postpone, delay
posteri (pô'stā·rē) *mpl* posterity
posteriore (pō·stā·ryō'rā) *a* rear; posterior; later
posteriormente (pō·stā·ryōr·mān'tā) *adv* later, subsequently; posteriorly
posticcio (pō·stē'chō) *a* fake, false; artificial
posticipare (pō·stē·chē·pâ'rā) *vt* to postpone
posticipatamente (pō·stē·chē·pâ·tâ·mān'tā) *adv* afterward, after the event; too late
posticipazione (pō·stē·chē·pâ·tsyō'nā) *f* postponement
postilla (pō·stēl'lâ) *f* footnote
postino (pō·stē'nō) *m* mailman
posto (pō'stō) *m* place; seat; site; job; — *a* placed; **— che** supposing that
postribolo (pō·strē'bō·lō) *m* brothel
postulante (pō·stū·lân'tā) *m* applicant; candidate
postulare (pō·stū·lâ'rā) *vt* to make application for; to request

postumo (pô'stū·mō) *a* posthumous; — *m* aftermath
potabile (pō·tâ'bē·lā) *a* drinkable
potare (pō·tâ'rā) *vt* to prune; to lop off
potassa (pō·tâs'sâ) *f* potash
potassio (pō·tâs'syō) *m* potassium
potentato (pō·tān·tâ'tō) *m* potentate
potente (pō·tān'tā) *a* powerful; **–mente** (pō·tān·tā·mān'tā) *adv* vigorously
potenza (pō·tān'tsâ) *f* power, dominion
potenzialmente (pō·tān·tsyâl·mān'tā) *adv* potentially
potere (pō·tā'rā) *m* power; — * *vi* to be able; **può essere** it may be, perhaps; **non può essere** it can't be true; **non ne posso più** I can't take it any longer
potestà (pō·tā·stâ') *f* power; authority; **la P– divina** the Almighty
poveraccio (pō·vā·râ'chō) *m* poor wretch, poor fellow
poveramente (pō·vā·râ·mān'tā) *adv* miserably; poorly
povero (pō'vā·rō) *a* poor; unlucky
povertà (pō·vār·tâ') *f* poverty, lack
pozione (pō·tsyō'nā) *f* potion
pozzanghera (pō·tsân'gā·râ) *f* puddle
pozzo (pō'tsō) *m* well; **un — di sapienza** (*fig*) a fountain of knowledge
Praga (prâ'gâ) *f* Prague
prammatica (prâm·mâ'tē·kâ) *f* custom, way; **di —** required
pranzare (prân·dzâ'rā) *vi* to dine
pranzo (prân'dzō) *m* dinner
prassi (prâs'sē) *f* procedure; practice, praxis
prateria (prâ·tā·rē'â) *f* prairie
pratica (prâ'tē·kâ) *f* practice; experience; file, papers; **–mente** (prâ·tē·kâ·mān'tā) *adv* practically; **–re** (prâ·tē·kâ'rā) *vt&i* to practice; to associate with
praticità (prâ·tē·chē·tâ') *f* usefulness; practicability
pratico (prâ'tē·kō) *a* experienced; practical; — *m* expert
prato (prâ'tō) *m* meadow
preaccennato (prā·â·chān·nâ'tō) *a* aforementioned
preambolo (prā·âm'bō·lō) *m* preamble
preavvisare (prā·âv·vē·zâ'rā) *vt* to preinform, advise in advance
preavviso (prā·âv·vē'zō) *m* notice; warning
prebellico (prā·bel'lē·kō) *a* prewar
precario (prā·kâ'ryō) *a* precarious, risky
precauzione (prā·kâū·tsyō'nā) *f* precaution
precedente (prā·chā·dān'tā) *a* previous; — *m* precedent; **–mente** (prā·chā·dān·tā·mān'tā) *adv* previously
precedenti (prā·chā·dān'tē) *mpl* background
precedenza (prā·chā·dān'tsâ) *f* precedence; **diritto di —** right of way
precedere (prā·che'dā·rā) *vi* to precede; to outstrip
precetto (prā·chāt'tō) *m* maxim; rule; — **pasquale** (*eccl*) Easter duty; **–re** (prā·chāt·tō'rā) *m* tutor
precipitare (prā·chē·pē·tâ'rā) *vt&i* to fall, crash; to precipitate; to collapse
precipitarsi (prā·chē·pē·târ'sē) *vr* to dash; to hurl oneself
precipitatamente (prā·chē·pē·tâ·tâ·mān'tā) *adv* rashly, headlong
precipitazione (prā·chē·pē·tâ·tsyō'nā) *f* rashness; precipitation
precipitosamente (prā·chē·pē·tō·zâ·mān'tā) *adv* precipitously; hastily
precipizio (prā·chē·pē'tsyō) *m* cliff, precipice
precipuo (prā·chē'pwō) *a* chief, main, head
precisamente (prā·chē·zâ·mān'tā) *adv* exactly, just
precisare (prā·chē·zâ'rā) *vt* to specify; to make clear; to point up, underline
precisione (prā·chē·zyō'nā) *f* accuracy, precision
preciso (prā·chē'zō) *a* exact; precise; accurate
preclaro (prā·klâ'rō) *a* prominent, famous
precoce (prā·kō'chā) *a* precocious; **–mente** (prā·kō·chā·mān'tā) *adv* precociously; prematurely
precursore (prā·kūr·sō'rā) *m* forerunner
preda (prā'dâ) *f* prey; **–re** (prā·dâ'rā) *vt* to prey upon; to rob
predecessore (prā·dā·chās·sō'rā) *m* forerunner
predellino (prā·dāl·lē'nō) *m* step; (*auto*) running board; baby's high chair
predestinare (prā·dā·stē·nâ'rā) *m* forerunner, predecessor
predestinazione (prā·dā·stē·nâ·tsyō'nā) *f* predestination
predetto (prā·dāt'tō) *a* aforementioned
predica (pre'dē·kâ) *f* sermon; **–re** (prā·dē·kâ'rā) *vt* to preach; to lecture; to reprove; **–tore** (prā·dē·kâ·tō'rā) *m* preacher
prediletto (prā·dē·lāt'tō) *a&m* favorite, pet
predire * (prā·dē'rā) *vt* to foretell
predisporre * (prā·dē·spōr'rā) *vt* to predispose; to arrange in advance
predisposizione (prā·dē·spō·zē·tsyō'nā) *f* prearrangement; tendency
predisposto (prā·dē·spō'stō) *a* favorable; predisposed
predominare (prā·dō·mē·nâ'rā) *vt&i* to dominate; to hold sway
predominio (prā·dō·mē'nyō) *m* supremacy, predominance
predone (prā·dō'nā) *m* robber
prefazione (prā·fâ·tsyō'nā) *f* preface
prefabbricato (prā·fâb·brē·kâ'tō) *a* prefabricated
preferenza (prā·fā·rān'tsâ) *f* partiality, preference
preferenziale (prā·fā·rān·tsyâ'lā) *a* preferential; **azioni preferenziali** (*com*) preferred stock
preferibile (prā·fā·rē'bē·lā) *a* preferable
preferibilmente (prā·fā·rē·bēl·mān'tā) *adv* preferably, rather
preferire (prā·fā·rē'ra) *vt* to prefer
preferito (prā·fā·rē'tō) *a* preferred; favorite

prefetto (prā·fāt'tō) *m* prefect, provincial governor
prefettura (prā·fāt·tū'râ) *f* prefecture, office of provincial governor
prefiggere * (prā·fēj'jā·rā) *vi* to predetermine; to arrange in advance; (*gram*) to prefix
prefiggersi * (prā·fēj'jār·sē) *vr* to aim, intend; to make up one's mind to
prefisso (prā·fēs'sō) *m* prefix; — *a* intended, arranged beforehand
pregare (prā·gâ'rā) *vt* to beg; to pray; to supplicate
pregevole (prā·je'vō·lā) *a* valuable
preghiera (prā·gyā'râ) *f* request; supplication; prayer
pregiare (prā·jâ'rā) *vt* to esteem; to prize; to appreciate
pregiarsi (prā·jâr'sē) *vr* to have the honor to; to be pleased to
pregiato (prā·jâ'tō) *a* valued, esteemed
pregio (pre'jō) *m* merit; value
pregiudicare (prā·jū·dē·kâ'rā) *vt* to prejudge; to prejudice
pregiudicarsi (prā·jū·dē·kâr'sē) *vr* to ruin one's chances; to damage one's reputation
pregiudicato (prā·jū·dē·kâ'tō) *m* ex-convict
pregiudizio (prā·jū·dē'tsyō) *m* prejudice
prego! (prā'gō) *interj* Please! You're welcome! Don't mention it! Not at all!
pregustare (prā·gū·stâ'rā) *vt* to look forward to, anticipate; to foretaste
preistorico (prāē·stô'rē·kō) *a* prehistoric
prelevamento (prā·lā·vâ·mān'tō) *m* (*com*) draft; withdrawal
prelevare (prā·lā·vâ'rā) *vt* to pick up; to withdraw
prelibato (prā·lē·bâ'tō) *a* delicious; superb
preliminare (prā·lē·mē·nâ'rā) *a&m* preliminary
prematuro (prā·mâ·tū'rō) *a* premature
premeditare (prā·mā·dē·tâ'rā) *vt* to premeditate; to plan in advance
premeditato (prā·mā·dē·tâ'tō) *a* intentional; premeditated
premeditazione (prā·mā·dē·tâ·tsyō'nā) *f* premeditation; advance planning
premere (pre'mā·rā) *vt* to press, squeeze; (*fig*) to urge; — *vi* to be urgent; to be of great importance
premessa (prā·mās'sâ) *f* premise
premettere * (prā·met'tā·rā) *vt* to lay down in advance; to give preference to; to premise; to prefix
premiare (prā·myâ'rā) *vt* to reward
premiato (prā·myâ'tō) *m* prize winner; — *a* rewarded
premiazione (prā·myâ·tsyō'nā) *f* prize distribution, awarding of prizes
preminenza (prā·mē·nān'tsâ) *f* preeminence
premio (pre'myō) *m* reward; prize; (*com*) premium
premunire (prā·mū·nē'rā) *vt* to forewarn; to arm in advance; to caution
premunirsi (prā·mū·nēr'sē) *vr* to guard against; to protect oneself against
premura (prā·mū'râ) *f* care; haste; concern
premuroso (prā·mū·rō'zō) *a* eager to help; obliging
prendere * (pren'dā·rā) *vt* to take; to catch, seize; to turn; — **a sinistra** to make a left turn; — **una malattia** to catch a disease; — **quota** (*avi*) to gain altitude; (*fig*) to catch on, gain in favor; — **terra** (*naut&avi*) to land; — **il mare** to put out to sea; — **a noleggio** to hire; — **di mira** to stare at
prendersi * (pren'dār·sē) *vr* to become entangled; to be taken; – **a pugni** to come to blows; — **la libertà di** to take the liberty of; **prendersela** to take it wrong; to have one's feelings hurt
prendisole (prān·dē·sō'lā) *m* sunsuit
prenotare (prā·nō·tâ'rā) *vt* to reserve; to engage; to subscribe to; to book
prenotarsi (prā·nō·târ'sē) *vr* to take out a subscription; to make a reservation
prenotazione (prā·nō·tâ·tsyō'nā) *f* reservation; subscription
preoccupare (prā·ōk·kū·pâ'rā) *vt* to worry, bother; to annoy
preoccuparsi (prā·ōk·kū·pâr'sē) *vr* to worry; to be preoccupied
preoccupato (prā·ōk·kū·pâ'tō) *a* upset, worried, bothered
preoccupazione (prā·ōk·kū·pâ·tsyō'nā) *f* worry, bother; annoyance
preparare (prā·pâ·râ'rā) *vt* to prepare, ready
prepararsi (prā·pâ·râr'sē) *vr* to ready oneself; to prepare oneself
preparato (prā·pâ·râ'tō) *a* prepared; — *m* (*med*) preparation
preponderante (prā·pōn·dā·rân'tā) *a* predominant
preposizione (prā·pō·zē·tsyō'nā) *f* preposition
prepotente (prā·pō·tān'tā) *a* tyrannical; arrogant; overbearing; — *m* bully; tyrant
prepotenza (prā·pō·tān'tsâ) *f* domineering manner; abuse of power; arrogance
prerogativa (prā·rō·gâ·tē'vâ) *f* privilege; prerogative
presa (prā'zâ) *f* seizure; grasp; influence; (*elec*) outlet; plug; (*photo*) shot; **macchina da** — movie camera
presagio (prā·zâ'jō) *m* foreboding, omen
presagire (prā·zâ·jē'rā) *vt&i* to forebode; to be a forewarning
presbite (pre'zbē·tā) *a* farsighted
prescindere * (prā·shēn'dā·rā) *vt* to disregard; to depart from
prescrivere * (prā·skrē'vā·rā) *vt* to prescribe
prescrizione (prā·skrē·tsyō'nā) *f* prescription
presentare (prā·zān·tâ'rā) *vt* to present; to introduce
presentarsi (prā·zān·târ'sē) *vr* to appear, come into view; to introduce oneself, present oneself
presentatore (prā·zān·tâ·tō'rā) *m* master

of ceremonies
presentazione (prā·zān·tâ·tsyō'nā) *f* presentation
presente (prā·zān'tā) *a&m* present
presentimento (prā·zān·tē·mān'tō) *m* foreboding, feeling
presenza (prā·zān'tsâ) *f* presence
presenziare (prā·zān·tsyâ'rā) *vt&i* to attend; to witness; to take part; to intervene
presepio (prā·ze'pyō) *m* crib, manger, crèche
preservare (prā·zār·vâ'rā) *vt* to maintain, keep; to save
preservativo (prā·zār·vâ·tē'vō) *a* preservative; — *m* prophylactic
preservazione (prā·zār·vâ·tsyō'nā) *f* preservation
preside (pre'zē·dā) *m* presiding officer; principal of a secondary school; dean; **–nte** (prā·zē·dān'tā) *m*, **–ntessa** (prā·zē·dān·tās'sâ) *f* president; **–nza** (prā·zē·dān'tsâ) *f* president's office; presidency; **–nziale** (prā·zē·dān·tsyâ'lā) *a* presidential
presidiare (prā·zē·dyâ'rā) *vt* to garrison; (*mil*) to defend
presidio (prā·zē'dyō) *m* garrison
presiedere * (prā·sye'dā·rā) *vi* to preside
preso (prā'zō) *a* captured; taken
pressa (prās'sâ) *f* press; crowd
pressante (prās·sân'tā) *a* momentous, of great concern
pressappoco (prās·sâp·pō'kō) *adv* approximately; almost
pressi (prās'sē) *mpl* neighborhood, environment
pressione (prās·syō'nā) *f* pressure
presso (prās'sō) *adv* near; — *prep* in care of; — **a poco** just about; **–chè** (prās·sō·kā') *adv* nearly, almost
prestabilire (prā·stâ·bē·lē'rā) *vt* to preestablish; to fix in advance
prestanome (prā·stâ·nō'mā) *m* (*coll*) figurehead; dupe, cat's-paw
prestare (prā·stâ'rā) *vt* to impute; to lend; — **fede** to trust; — **ascolto** to listen, pay attention; — **giuramento** to take an oath; — **obbedienza** to obey; — **attenzione** to pay attention, be attentive
prestarsi (prā·stâr'sē) *vr* to volunteer one's services; to adapt oneself; to lend itself
prestazione (prā·stâ·tsyō'nā) *f* service, favor
prestigiatore (prā·stē·jâ·tō'rā) *m* juggler
prestigio (prā·stē'jō) *m* prestige; **giuoco di** — sleight of hand, legerdemain
prestissimo (prā·stēs'sē·mō) *a* very early; very quickly
prestito (pre'stē·tō) *m* loan; **dare in** — to lend
presto (prā'stō) *adv* soon; quickly; early; **si fa — a dire** it's very easy to say
presumere * (prā·zū'mā·rā) *vi* to presume; to boast
presunto (prā·zūn'tō) *a* alleged; presumed
presuntuoso (prā·zūn·twō'zō) *a* conceited
presunzione (prā·zūn·tsyō'nā) *f* conceit
presupporre * (prā·sūp·pōr'rā) *vt* to imply; to presuppose
prete (prā'tā) *m* priest
pretendente (prā·tān·dān'tā) *m* suitor; pretender
pretendere * (prā·ten'dā·rā) *vt&i* to claim, pretend; to charge; to demand
preterintenzionale (prā·tā·rēn·tān·tsyō·nâ'lā) *a* involuntary, unintentional
pretesa (prā·tā'zâ) *f* pretense; claim; pretension; demand
pretesto (prā·tā'stō) *m* pretext
pretore (prā·tō'rā) *m* municipal judge
prettamente (prāt·tâ·mān'tā) *adv* merely; clearly
pretto (prāt'tō) *a* pure; mere
pretura (prā·tū'râ) *f* district court
prevalente (prā·vâ·lān'tā) *a* prevalent; prevailing
prevalenza (prā·vâ·lān'tsâ) *f* prevalence
prevalere * (prā·vâ·lā'rā) *vi* to prevail
prevalersi * (prā·vâ·lār'sē) *vr* to avail oneself of; to make use of
prevaricazione (prā·vâ·rē·kâ·tsyō'nā) *f* graft; collusion; malfeasance
prevedere * (prā·vā·dā'rā) *vt* to forecast; to anticipate; to foresee
prevedibile (prā·vā·dē'bē·lā) *a* foreseeable
preveggenza (prā·vāj·jān'tsâ) *f* foresight
prevenire * (prā·vā·nē'rā) *vt* to warn; to precede; to prevent
preventivare (prā·vān·tē·vâ'rā) *vt* to estimate
preventivato (prā·vān·tē·vâ'tō) *a* estimated
preventivo (prā·vān·tē'vō) *m* estimated budget; — *a* preventive
prevenuto (prā·vā·nū'tō) *a* forewarned; disposed; — *m* defendant
prevenzione (prā·vān·tsyō'nā) *f* prevention; bias; precaution
previamente (prā·vyâ·mān'tā) *adv* formerly
previdente (prā·vē·dān'tā) *a* provident
previdenza (prā·vē·dān'tsâ) *f* providence; prudence; — **sociale** social security
previsione (prā·vē·zyō'nā) *f* forecast
prezioso (prā·tsyō'zō) *a* precious
prezzemolo (prā·tse'mō·lō) *m* parsley
prezzo (prā'tsō) *m* price; — **fisso** set price; **pranzo a — fisso** table d'hôte
prezzolato (prā·tsō·lâ'tō) *a* bribed; hired
prigione (prē·jō'nā) *f* prison
prigionia (prē·jō·nē'â) *f* imprisonment
prigioniero (prē·jō·nyā'rō) *m* prisoner
prima (prē'mâ) *adv* before; at first; — *f* première; **quanto** —, — **possibile** as soon as possible; **–rio** (prē·mâ'ryō) *a* primary; **–rio** *m* hospital head of staff; **–tista** (prē·mâ·tē'stâ) *m* record holder; **–to** (prē·mâ'tō) *m* supremacy; (*sport*) record
primavera (prē·mâ·vā'râ) *f* spring
primeggiare (prē·māj·jâ'rā) *vi* to excel; to stand out
primitivo (prē·mē·tē'vō) *a&m* primitive
primizia (prē·mē'tsyâ) *f* early fruit
primo (prē'mō) *a&m* first; **–genito** (prē·mō·ge'nē·tō) *a* firstborn

primula (prē'mū·lâ) *f* primrose
principale (prēn·chē·pâ'lā) *a* principal; primary; — *m* boss; employer
principalmente (prēn·chē·pâl·mān'tā) *adv* primarily; essentially; mainly
principe (prēn'chē·pā) *m* prince; **–sco** (prēn·chē·pā'skō) *a* princely; **–ssa** (prēn·chē·pās'sâ) *f* princess
principiante (prēn·chē·pyân'tā) *m&f* beginner; — *a* beginning, elementary
principiare (prēn·chē·pyâ'rā) *vt&i* to begin, start out
principio (prēn·chē'pyō) *m* beginning, start; precept
priore (pryō'rā) *m* prior
priorità (pryō·rē·tâ') *f* priority
prisma (prē'zmâ) *m* prism
privare (prē·vâ'rā) *vt* to deprive
privarsi (prē·vâr'sē) *vr* to do without, get along without; to abstain from
privatamente (prē·vâ·tâ·mān'tā) *adv* privately, in private
privatista (prē·vâ·tē'stâ) *m* student in a private school
privativa (prē·vâ·tē'vâ) *f* exclusive right; monopoly; patent; — **dei tabacchi** tobacco shop
privato (prē·vâ'tō) *a&m* private
privazione (prē·vâ·tsyō'nā) *f* suffering; privation
privilegio (prē·vē·le'jō) *m* privilege
privo (prē'vō) *a* deprived, wanting
pro (prō) *m* advantage, profit
probabile (prō·bâ'bē·lā) *a* probable; believable
probabilità (prō·bâ·bē·lē·tâ') *f* probability
probabilmente (prō·bâ·bēl·mān'tā) *adv* probably
problema (prō·blā'mâ) *m* problem; difficulty; **–tico** (prō·blā·mâ'tē·kō) *a* questionable; difficult
probo (prō'bō) *a* honest, upright
proboscide (prō·bô'shē·dā) *f* proboscis; trunk (*elephant*)
procaccia (prō·kâ'châ) *m* rural mailman; **–re** (prō·kâ'châ·rā) *vt* to obtain; to procure; **–rsi** (prō·kâ·châr'sē) *vr* to secure; to earn for oneself
procace (prō·kâ'chā) *a* forward; coquettish; shapely, provocative
procedente (prō·chā·dān'tā) *a* proceeding
procedere (prō·che'dā·rā) *vi* to proceed; (*law*) to prosecute; — *m* conduct
procedimenti (prō·chā·dē·mān'tē) *mpl* transactions, proceedings
procedimento (pro·chā·dē·mān'tō) *m* method; procedure
procedura (prō·chā·dū'râ) *f* procedure
processare (prō·chās·sâ'rā) *vt* to try, prosecute
processione (prō·chās·syō'nā) *f* procession
processo (prō·chās'sō) *m* trial; lawsuit; process; — **verbale** official record, minutes of a meeting
processuale (prō·chās·swâ'lā) *a* (*law*) trial
procinto (prō·chēn'tō) *m* preparations; **essere in — di** to be about to
proclama (prō·klâ'mâ) *m* proclamation; **–re** (prō·klâ·mâ'rā) *vt* to proclaim
proclamazione (prō·klâ·mâ·tsyō'nā) *f* proclamation
proclive (prō·klē'vā) *a* disposed, inclined, amenable
procrastinare (prō·krâ·stē·nâ'rā) *vi* to procrastinate; to temporize
procreare (prō·krā·â'rā) *vt* to procreate; to give birth to
procura (prō·kū'râ) *f* power of attorney; proxy
procurare (prō·kū·râ'rā) *vt* to secure; to try; to supply
procurarsi (prō·kū·râr'sē) *vr* to secure; to obtain for oneself
procuratore (prō·kū·râ·tō'rā) *m* prosecutor; administrator; attorney
proda (prō'dâ) *f* bank, shore; (*naut*) prow
prode (prō'dā) *a* brave; — *m* hero; **–zza** (prō·dā'tsâ) *f* valor, bravery
prodigare (prō·dē·gâ'rā) *vt* to lavish, give in profusion
prodigarsi (prō·dē·gâr'sē) *vr* to devote oneself; to spare no pains, do one's best
prodigio (prō·dē'jō) *m* marvel; prodigy **–samente** (prō·dē·jō·zâ·mān'tā) *adv* prodigiously
prodigo (prô'dē·gō) *m* spendthrift; — *a* prodigal; lavish
proditorio (prō·dē·tô'ryō) *a* sneaky, treacherous
prodotto (prō·dōt'tō) *m* product; child (*fig*) — *a* produced
prodromo (prô'drō·mō) *m* symptom, sign
produrre * (prō·dūr'rā) *vt* to produce
prodursi * (prō·dūr'sē) *vr* to happen, take place
produttivo (prō·dūt·tē'vō) *a* fruitful, productive
produttore (prō·dūt·tō'rā) *m* producer
produzione (prō·dū·tsyō'nā) *f* production
profanare (prō·fâ·nâ'rā) *vt* to desecrate, profane
profanazione (prō·fâ·nâ·tsyō'nā) *f* desecration, profaning
profano (prō·fâ'nō) *m* layman; outsider; — *a* worldly, secular, profane; unskilled
proferire (prō·fā·rē'rā) *vt* to utter
proferirsi (prō·fā·rēr'sē) *vr* to offer one's assistance, volunteer one's aid
professare (prō·fās·sâ'rā) *vt&i* to profess
professarsi (prō·fās·sâr'sē) *vr* to profess oneself to be; to declare oneself
professione (pro·fās·syō'nā) *f* profession
professionista (prō·fās·syō·nē'stâ) *m&f* professional
professore (prō·fās·sō'rā) *m*, **professoressa** (prō·fās·sō·rās'sâ) *f* professor
profeta (prō·fā'tâ) *m* prophet
profetico (prō·fe'tē·kō) *a* prophetic
profetizzare (prō·fā·tē·dzâ'rā) *vt* to foretell; to prophesy
profezia (prō·fā·tsē'â) *f* prophecy
proficuo (prō·fē'kwō) *a* profitable, fruitful
profilare (prō·fē·lâ'rā) *vt* to outline
profilarsi (prō·fē·lâr'sē) *vr* to be evident,

stand out
profilassi (prō·fē·lâs'sē) *f* prevention; (*med*) prophylaxis
profilo (prō·fē'lō) *m* profile; side view
profittare (prō·fēt·tâ'rā) *vi* to profit; to derive benefit
profitto (prō·fēt'tō) *m* advantage, profit
profondamente (prō·fōn·dâ·mān'tā) *adv* deeply
profondere * (prō·fôn'dā·rā) *vt* to squander, throw away
profondersi * (prō·fôn'dār·sē) *vr* to be lavish; to show munificence
profondità (prō·fōn·dē·tâ') *f* depth
profondo (prō·fōn'dō) *a* profound, deep
profugo (prô'fū·gō) *m* refugee
profumare (prō·fū·mâ'rā) *vt* to scent, perfume
profumarsi (prō·fū·mâr'sē) *vr* to wear perfume; to put on perfume
profumatamente (prō·fū·mâ·tâ·mān'tā) *adv* dearly; munificently
profumeria (prō·fū·mā·rē'â) *f* perfume shop, perfumery
profumo (prō·fū'mō) *m* scent, perfume
profusione (prō·fū·zyō'nā) *f* profusion; great number
progenitore (prō·jā·nē·tō'rā) *m*, **progenitrice** (prō·jā·nē·trē'chā) *f* ancestor
progettare (prō·jāt·tâ'rā) *vt* to plan; to design
progettista (prō·jāt·tē'stâ) *m* designer; planner
progetto (prō·jāt'tō) *m* plan; design
programma (prō·grâm'mâ) *m* program; **— di viaggio** itinerary; **–re** (prō·grâm·mâ'rā) *vt* to schedule; **–zione** (prō·grâm·mâ·tsyō'nā) *f* theater bill; programming
progredire (prō·grā·dē'rā) *vi* to make progress; to advance
progresso (prō·grās'sō) *m* progress
proibire (prōē·bē'rā) *vt* to forbid
proibito (prōē·bē'tō) *a* forbidden; **è — fumare** no smoking
proibizione (prōē·bē·tsyō'nā) *f* prohibition
proiettare (prō·yāt·tâ'rā) *vt* to project; to show (*movie*)
proiettile (prō·yet'tē·lā) *m* bullet; missile
proiettore (prō·yāt·tō'rā) *m* projector; searchlight
proiezione (prō·yā·tsyō'nā) *f* projection; showing (*movie*)
prole (prō'lā) *f* offspring; issue
proletario (prō·lā·tâ'ryō) *a&m* proletarian
prolificare (prō·lē·fē·kâ'rā) *vi* to spread, multiply
prolifico (prō·lē'fē·kō) *a* fruitful; inventive, creative
prolisso (prō·lēs'sō) *a* verbose; long-winded; pedantic
prologo (prô'lō·gō) *m* introduction; prologue
prolungamento (prō·lūn·gâ·mān'tō) *m* lengthening, prolongation
prolungare (prō·lūn·gâ'rā) *vt* to extend; to stretch out
prolungarsi (prō·lūn·gâr'sē) *vr* to continue, extend
promemoria (prō·mā·mô'ryâ) *m* memorandum, note
promessa (prō·mās'sâ) *f* promise
promesso (prō·mās'sō) *a* promised; betrothed, engaged
promettente (prō·māt·tān'tā) *a* hopeful, promising
promettere * (prō·met'tā·rā) *vt* to promise
promiscuo (prō·mē'skwō) *a* mixed; promiscuous; **scuola promiscua** coeducational school; **matrimonio —** mixed marriage
promontorio (prō·mōn·tô'ryō) *m* promontory
promosso (prō·mōs'sō) *a* passed (*student*); promoted
promozione (prō·mō·tsyō'nā) *f* promotion; advancement
promulgare (pro·mūl·gâ'rā) *vt* to issue; to proclaim, promulgate
promuovere * (prō·mwô'vā·rā) *vt* to promote; to pass (*students*)
pronipote (prō·nē·pō'tā) *m&f* grandnephew, grandniece
pronipoti (prō·nē·pō'tē) *mpl* descendants
pronome (prō·nō'mā) *m* pronoun
pronostico (prō·nô'stē·kō) *m* omen, forecast; prediction
prontamente (prōn·tâ·mān'tā) *adv* readily; quickly
prontezza (prōn·tā'tsâ) *f* promptness
pronto (prōn'tō) *a* ready; hello (*telephone*); **— soccorso** first aid
pronunzia (prō·nūn'tsyâ) *f* pronunciation; **–re** (prō·nūn·tsyâ'rā) *vt* to pronounce; to utter; **–rsi** (prō·nūn·tsyâr'sē) *vr* to declare oneself, avow oneself
propaganda (prō·pâ·gân'dâ) *f* propaganda; advertisement; advertising; **a titolo di —** for advertising purposes
propagandista (prō·pâ·gân·dē'stâ) *m* propagandist; canvasser
propagare (prō·pâ·gâ'rā) *vt* to spread; to distribute
propagarsi (prō·pâ·gâr'sē) *vr* to extend; to propagate; to spread
propalare (prō·pâ·lâ'rā) *vt* to divulge
propendere * (prō·pen'dā·rā) *vi* to lean; to incline
propensione (prō·pān·syō'nā) *f* propensity, inclination; native ability
propenso (prō·pān'sō) *a* inclined, amenable
propinquo (prō·pēn'kwō) *a* related; similar; near
propiziamente (prō·pē·tsyâ·mān'tā) *adv* propitiously
propizio (prō·pē'tsyō) *a* favorable
proponimento (prō·pō·nē·mān'tō) *m* intent, resolution
proporre * (prō·pōr'rā) *vt* to propose; to suggest
proporsi * (prō·pōr'sē) *vr* to volunteer oneself; to resolve, mean
proporzionato (prō·pōr·tsyō·nâ'tō) *a* proportionate
proporzione (prō·pōr·tsyō'nā) *f* propor-

tion

proposito (prō·pô'zē·tō) *m* determination; purpose; reason; **a** — by the way

proposizione (prō·pō·zē·tsyō'nā) *f* proposition, proposal

proposta ((prō·pō'stâ) *f* proposal

propriamente (prō·pyrâ·mān'tā) *adv* appropriately, properly

proprietà (prō·pryā·tâ') *f* property; decorum

proprietario (prō·pryā·tâ'ryō) *m* proprietor

proprio (prô'pryō) *a* one's own; proper; exact; — *adv* just; really; **lavorare in** — to be in business for oneself

propugnare (prō·pū·nyâ'rā) *vt* to advocate, be in favor of; to rally around

propulsione (prō·pūl·syō'nā) *f* propulsion; — **a reazione** jet propulsion

propulsore (prō·pūl·sō'rā) *m* propeller

prora (prō'râ) *f* (*naut*) bow

proroga (prô'rō·gâ) *f* deferment; postponement; **–re** (prō·rō·gâ'rā) *vt* to put off; to defer; (*com*) to extend

prorompere * (prō·rôm'pā·rā) *vi* to break out; — **in pianto** to burst into tears

prosa (prō'zâ) *f* prose; **teatro di** — legitimate theater; **–ico** (prō·zâ'ē·kō) *a* prosaic; hackneyed, trite

prosciogliere * (prō·shô'lyā·rā) *vt* to free, liberate; to absolve

prosciugamento (prō·shū·gâ·mān'tō) *m* draining

prosciugare (prō·shū·gâ'rā) *vt* to drain; to dry

prosciutto (prō·shūt'tō) *m* ham

proscrivere * (prō·skrē'vā·rā) *vt* to banish, outlaw

proscrizione (prō·skrē·tsyō'nā) *f* banishment, proscription

proseguimento (prō·sā·gwē·mān'tō) *m* resuming; continuation

proseguire (prō·sā·gwē'rā) *vt&i* to continue; to resume, make a fresh start; — **diritto** to keep going straight ahead

prosopopea (prō·zō·pō·pā'â) *f* pose, self-importance, affectation

prosperare (prō·spā·râ'rā) *vi* to thrive; to do well

prosperità (prō·spā·rē·tâ') *f* prosperity

prosperosamente (prō·spā·rō·zâ·mān'tā) *adv* prosperously

prosperoso (prō·spā·rō'zō) *a* prosperous; thriving; plump

prospettare (prō·spāt·tâ'rā) *vt* to describe; to outline, lay out

prospettiva (prō·spāt·tē'vâ) *f* project; prospective; prospect

prospetto (prō·spāt'tō) *m* prospect; plan; prospectus

prospiciente (prō·spē·chān'tā) *a* facing; looking over, opening on

prossimamente (prōs·sē·mâ·mān'tā) *adv* in the near future, soon, shortly

prossimità (prōs·sē·mē·tâ') *f* proximity

prossimo (prôs'sē·mō) *a* next; — *m* fellowman; neighbor

prostituta (prō·stē·tū'tâ) *f* prostitute

prostrazione (prō·strâ·tsyō'nā) *f* prostration; depression (*mental*)

protagonista (prō·tâ·gō·nē'stâ) *m&f* protagonist

proteggere * (prō·tej'jā·rā) *vt* to protect

protervo (prō·tār'vō) *a* stubborn

protesta (prō·tā'stâ) *f* protest; protestation; **–nte** (prō·tā·stân'tā) *m&a* Protestant; **–re** (prō·tā·stâ'rā) *vt&i* to protest

protetto (prō·tāt'tō) *m* favorite; protégé; **–rato** (prō·tāt·tō·râ'tō) *m* protectorate; **–re** (prō·tât·tō'rā) *m* protector

protezione (prō·tā·tsyō'nā) *f* protection; aegis

protocollare (prō·tō·kōl·lâ'rā) *vt* to file; to enter on the record

protocollo (prō·tō·kōl'lō) *m* protocol; file, record

prototipo (prō·tō·tē'pō) *m* prototype

protozoo (prō·tō·dzō'ō) *m* protozoan

protrarre * (prō·trâr'rā) *vt* to drag out, prolong

protuberanza (prō·tū·bā·rân'tsâ) *f* protuberance

prova (prō'vâ) *f* test; proof; (*theat*) rehearsal; (*law*) evidence, testimony; **–re** (prō·vâ'rā) *vt&i* to prove; to try; to experience; **–rsi** (prō·vâr'sē) *vr* to make an attempt

proveniente (prō·vā·nyān'tā) *a* arising, originating

provenienza (prō·vā·nyān'tsâ) *f* origin, font

provenire * (prō·vā·nē'rā) *vi* to originate, come from

provento (prō·vān'tō) *m* profit, income

proverbiale (prō·vār·byâ'lā) *a* notorious; proverbial; **essere** — to be a byword

proverbio (prō·ver'byō) *m* proverb

provetta (prō·vāt'tâ) *f* test tube

provetto (prō·vāt'tō) *a* skillful, able

provincia (prō·vēn'châ) *f* province; **–le** (prō·vēn·châ'lā) *a* provincial; insular (*fig*)

provino (prō·vē'nō) *m* test tube; screen test

provocante (prō·vō·kân'tā) *a* provoking; seductive

provocare (prō·vō·kâ'rā) *vt* to provoke, create

provocativo (prō·vō·kâ·tē'vō) *a* provocative

provocatore (prō·vo·kâ·tō'rā) *m* instigator; — *a* provocative

provocazione (prō·vō·kâ·tsyō'nā) *f* provocation

provolone (prō·vō·lō'nā) *m* hard cheese made from goat's milk

provvedere * (prōv·vā·dā'rā) *vt&i* to provide; to supply

provvedersi * (prōv·vā·dār'sē) *vr* to furnish oneself with; to lay in

provvedimento (prōv·vā·dē·mān'tō) *m* measure, precaution; (*pol*) ordinance

provveditore (prōv·vā·dē·tō'rā) *m* (*com*) supplier; superintendent; — **agli studi** superintendent of schools

provvidenza (prōv·vē·dān'tsâ) *f* providence

provvidenziale (prōv·vē·dān·tsyâ'lā) *a*

providential
provvido (prôv'vē·dō) *a* provident
provvigione (prōv·vē·jō'nā) *f* provision; (*com*) commission
provvisoriamente (prōv·vē·zō·ryâ·mān'tā) *adv* temporarily
provvisorio (prōv·vē·zô'ryō) *a* provisional, temporary
provvista (prōv·vē'stâ) *f* stock, supplies, provisions
prozia (prō·dzē'â) *f* great-aunt
prozio (prō·dzē'ō) *m* great-uncle
prua (prū'â) *f* (*naut*) bow, prow
prudente (prū·dān'tā) *a* prudent; **–mente** (prū·dān·tā·mān'tā) *adv* prudently
prudenza (prū·dān'tsâ) *f* prudence; husbandry
prudenziale (prū·dān·tsyâ'lā) *a* precautionary; prudent
prudere (prū'dā·rā) *vi* to itch
prugna (prū'nyâ) *f* plum; **— secca** prune
pruno (prū'nō) *m* bramble
prurito (prū·rē'tō) *m* itching, itch
Prussia (prūs'syâ) *f* Prussia
pseudonimo (psāū·dô'nē·mō) *m* pseudonym; pen name
psicanalisi (psē·kâ·nâ'lē·zē) *f* psychoanalysis
psichiatra (psē·kyâ'trâ) *m* psychiatrist
psichiatria (psē·kyâ·trē'â) *f* psychiatry
psichico (psē'kē·kō) *a* psychic
psicologo (psē·kô'lō·gō) *m* psychologist
psicopatico (psē·kō·pâ'tē·kō) *m* psychopath; — *a* psychopathic
psicosi (psē·kō'zē) *f* psychosis
pubblicamente (pūb·blē·kâ·mān'tā) *adv* publicly, in public
pubblicare (pūb·blē·kâ'rā) *vt* to publish; to publicize, make public
pubblicazione (pūb·blē·kâ·tsyō'nā) *f* publication
pubblicista (pūb·blē·chē'stâ) *m* press agent
pubblicità (pūb·blē·chē·tâ') *f* advertising; publicity
pubblicitario (pūb·blē·chē·tâ'ryō) *a* advertising
pubblico (pūb'blē·kō) *m&a* public; audience
pubertà (pū·bār·tâ') *f* puberty
pudicizia (pū·dē·chē'tsyâ) *f* chastity; bashfulness; modesty
pudico (pū'dē·kō) *a* modest; decent
pudore (pū·dō'rā) *m* modesty; decency
puerile (pwā·rē'lā) *a* childish
puerilità (pwā·rē·lē·tâ') *f* childishness
puerizia (pwā·rē'·tsyâ) *f* childhood
pugilato (pū·jē·lâ'tō) *m* boxing, prizefighting
pugilista (pū·jē·lē'stâ) *m* prizefighter, boxer
pugilistica (pū·jē·lē'stē·kâ) *f* boxing
pugilistico (pū·jē·lē'stē·kō) *a* boxing
pugnalare (pū·nyâ·lâ'rā) *vt* to stab
pugnalata (pū·nyâ·lâ'tâ) *f* stab
pugnale (pū·nyâ'lā) *m* dagger
pugno (pū'nyō) *m* fist; handful
pulce (pūl'chā) *f* flea; **mettere una — nell'orecchio** to put a bee in one's bonnet
pulcino (pūl·chē'nō) *m* chick
puledra (pū·lā'drâ) *f* filly
puledro (pū·lā'drō) *m* colt
puleggia (pū·lej'jâ) *f* pulley
pulire (pū·lē'rā) *vt* to clean; to polish
pulirsi (pū·lēr'sē) *vr* to clean up; to tidy up; **— il naso** to blow one's nose; **— la bocca** to wipe one's lips
pulito (pū·lē'tō) *a* clean; polished
pulitura (pū·lē·tū'râ) *f* cleaning; **— a secco** dry cleaning
pulizia (pū·lē·tsē'â) *f* cleanliness; cleaning
pullulare (pūl·lū·lâ'rā) *vi* to swarm, teem
pulpito (pūl'pē·tō) *m* pulpit; **Senti da che — viene la predica!** *(coll)* Just look who's talking! You're a fine one!
pulsante (pūl·sân'tā) *m* push button
pulsare (pūl·sâ'rā) *vi* to throb, pulsate
pulsazione (pūl·sâ·tsyō'nā) *f* pulsation; vibration
pungente (pūn·jān'tā) *a* piercing, sharp, caustic
pungere * (pūn'jā·rā) *vt* to sting; to irritate; to hurt the feelings of; to arouse, provoke, spur on
pungersi * (pūn'jār·sē) *vr* to prick oneself; to take offense
pungiglione (pūn·jē·lyō'nā) *m* insect sting; stimulus, goad
pungolo (pūn'gō·lō) *m* goad
punire (pū·nē'·rā) *vt* to punish
punitivo (pū·nē·tē'vō) *a* punitive
punizione (pū·nē·tsyō'nā) *f* punishment
punta (pūn'tâ) *f* tip; point; **ora di —** rush hour; **fare la — alla matita** to sharpen one's pencil; **–re** (pūn·tâ'rā) *vt* to aim, point; to stake, wager; — *vi* to bet; **–ta** (pūn·tâ'tâ) *f* installment; issue *(magazine)*
punteggiare (pūn·tāj·jâ'rā) *vt&i* to punctuate; to dot
punteggiatura (pūn·tāj·jâ·tū'râ) *f* dotting; punctuation
punteggio (pūn·tej'jō) *m (sport)* score
puntellare (pūn·tāl·lâ'rā) *vt* to prop, support; to shore up
puntello (pūn·tāl'lō) *m* stay, prop
punteruolo (pūn·tā·rūō'lō) *m* awl, punch
puntiglio (pūn·tē'lyō) *m* false pride; point of honor; spite; **–so** (pūn·tē·lyō'zō) *a* stubborn; punctilious
puntina (pūn·tē'nâ) *f* thumbtack
puntino (pūn·tē'nō) *m* dot; **a —** *(coll)* just right, perfectly; **cuocere a —** to cook just right
punto (pūn'tō) *m* point; period; dot; mark *(school)*; — *a* pricked; — *adv* by no means; **— e virgola** semicolon; **due punti** colon; **— esclamativo** exclamation point; **— interrogativo** question mark; **giungere a buon —** to arrive at the right moment
puntuale (pūn·twâ'lā) *a* punctual; careful
puntualità (pūn·twâ·lē·tâ') *f* punctuality
puntualmente (pūn·twâl·mān'tā) *adv* punctually; precisely, carefully
puntuazione (pūn·twâ·tsyō'nā) *f* punctu-

ation
puntura (pūn·tū'râ) *f* sting; *(med)* injection; — **di zanzara** mosquito bite
punzecchiare (pūn·dzāk·kyâ'rā) *vt* to tease; to prick; to spur
punzone (pūn·tsō'nā) *m* punch
pupa (pū'pâ) *f (coll)* baby, little girl; doll; **–zzo** (pū·pâ'tsō) *m* puppet, marionette
pupilla (pū·pēl'lâ) *f* pupil of the eye
pupillo (pū·pēl'lō) *m* ward, charge
pupo (pū'pō) *m (coll)* baby, little boy
puramente (pū·râ·mān'tā) *adv* merely, simply
purchè (pūr·kā') *conj* provided
pure (pū'rā) *adv* also, too; yet, still, even; by all means
purè (pū·rā') *m* thick soup; — **di patate** mashed potatoes
purezza (pū·rā'tsâ) *f* purity
purga (pūr'gâ) *f* purging, purge; **–nte** (pūr·gân'tā) *m* laxative, purge, physic; **–re** (pūr·gâ'rā) *vt* to purify; to purge; to expurgate
purgatorio (pūr·gâ·tô'ryō) *m* Purgatory
purificare (pū·rē·fē·kâ'rā) *vt* to purify
puritano (pū·rē·tâ'nō) *m&a* puritan
puro (pū'rō) *a* pure; genuine; mere, plain; **–sangue** (pū·rō·sân'gwā) *m* thoroughbred
purtroppo (pūr·trōp'pō) *adv* unfortunately
purulento (pū·rū·lān'tō) *a* purulent
pus (pūs) *m* pus
pusillanime (pū·zēl·lâ'nē·mā) *a* pusillanimous, cowardly
pustola (pū'stō·lâ) *f (med)* boil, pustule
putativo (pū·tâ·tē'vō) *a* reputed; supposed, putative
putiferio (pū·tē·fe'ryō) *m* racket, uproar, row
putredine (pū·tre'dē·nā) *f* rottenness
putrefare * (pū·trā·fâ'rā) *vi* to rot
putrefarsi * (pū·trā·fār'sē) *vr* to putrify; to decompose
putrefazione (pū·trā·fâ·tsyō'nā) *f* putrefaction
putrido (pū'trē·dō) *a* rotten, putrid
puttana (pūt·tâ'nâ) *f* whore, prostitute
puzza (pū'tsâ) *f* stench, foul odor; **–re** (pū·tsâ'rā) *vi* to stink, have an unpleasant smell
puzzo (pū'tsō) *m* stench, stink
puzzola (pū'tsō·lâ) *f* polecat, skunk
puzzolente (pū·tsō·lān'tā) *a* stinking, foul-smelling

Q

qua (kwâ') *adv* here; — **e là** here and there
quaderno (kwâ·dār'nō) *m* notebook
quadrangolo (kwâ·drân'gō·lō) *m* quadrangle
quadrante (kwâ·drân'tā) *m* quadrant; face *(clock)*; dial *(watch)*
quadrare (kwâ·drâ'rā) *vt&i* to fit; to make square; to please, be to one's liking; to adjust; *(com)* to balance
quadrato (kwâ·drâ'tō) *a* squared; — *m* square; ring *(sport)*
quadrettato (kwâ·drāt·tâ'tō) *a* checkered
quadretto (kwâ·drāt'tō) *m* small square; check
quadri (kwâ'drē) *mpl (cards)* diamonds
quadrifoglio (kwâ·drē·fô'lyō) *m* four-leaf clover
quadriglia (kwâ·drē'lyâ) *f* quadrille
quadrilatero (kwâ·drē·lâ'tā·rō) *a&m* quadrilateral
quadrimotore (kwâ·drē·mō·tō'rā) *m* four-engine plane
quadro (kwâ'drō) *m* painting; picture; — *a* square; — **commutatore** *(elec)* switchboard
quadrupede (kwâ·drū'pā·dā) *m&a* quadruped
quadruplicare (kwâ·drū·plē·kâ'rā) *vt* to quadruple
quadruplo (kwâ'drū·plō) *m* quadruple
quaggiù (kwâj·jū') *adv* down here; on earth
quaglia (kwâ'lyâ) *f (zool)* quail
quagliare (kwâ·lyâ'rā) *vt&i* to curdle; to coagulate
qualche (kwâl'kā) *a* some, any
qualcosa (kwâl·kō'zâ) *pron* something, anything
qualcuno (kwâl·kū'nō) *pron* someone, anyone
quale (kwâ'lā) *a&pron* what, which
qualifica (kwâ·lē'fē·kâ) *f* qualification; requisite; **–re** (kwâ·lē·fē·kâ'rā) *vt* to qualify
qualità (kwâ·lē·tâ') *f* quality; type
qualora (kwâ·lō'râ) *adv* just in case; whenever; if and when
qualsiasi (kwâl·sē'â·sē) *a&pron* whatever, any
qualunque (kwâ·lūn'kwā) *a* any, whatever
qualvolta (kwâl·vōl'tâ) *adv* whenever; in the event that; **ogni** — whenever
quando (kwân'dō) *adv* when; whenever
quanti (kwân'tē) *a&pron* how many
quantico (kwân'tē·kō), **quantistico** (kwân·tē'stē·kō) *a (math)* quantic
quantità (kwân·tē·tâ') *f* quantity
quantitativo (kwân·tē·tâ·tē'vō) *m* quantity, sum, amount
quanto (kwân'tō) *a&pron* as much, how much; — **a** as to, as concerns
quantunque (kwân·tūn'kwā) *conj* although, even though
quaranta (kwâ·rân'tâ) *a* forty; **–mila** (kwâ·rân·tâ·mē'lâ) *a* forty thousand
quarantenne (kwâ·rân·tān'nā) *a* forty years old
quarantesimo (kwâ·rân·te'zē·mō) *a* fortieth
quaresima (kwâ·re'zē·mâ) *f* Lent; **–le** (kwâ·rā·zē·mâ'lā) *a* Lenten
quartetto (kwâr·tāt'tō) *m* quartet
quartiere (kwâr·tyā'rā) *m* area, district; quarter; apartment
quarto (kwâr·tō) *a* fourth; — *m* quarter
quarzo (kwâr'tsō) *m* quartz

quasi (kwâ'sē) *adv* almost
quassù (kwâs·sū') *adv* up here; here above
quatto (kwât'tō) *a* squat; crouched, huddled; cowed
quattordicenne (kwât·tōr·dē·chān'nā) *a* fourteen years old
quattordicesimo (kwât·tōr·dē·che'zē·mō) *a* fourteenth
quattordici (kwât·tôr'dē·chē) *a* fourteen
quattrino (kwât·trē'nō) *m* cent; money
quattro (kwât'trō) *a* four; **fare — passi** to go for a walk; **dirgliene —** to give someone a piece of one's mind; to tell someone off; **in – e quattr'otto** in a hurry, quickly; **farsi in —** to do one's best; **a quattr'occhi** privately, secretly
quattrocento (kwât·trō·chān'tō) *a* four hundred; **il Q–** the fifteenth century
quegli (kwā'lyē) *a* those; — *pron* he
quei (kwā'ē) *a* those
quel (kwāl) *a&pron* that
quelli (kwāl'lē) *pron* those
quello (kwāl'lō) *a&pron* that
quercia (kwer'châ) *f* oak
querela (kwā·rā'lâ) *f* legal action; complaint; **–re** (kwā·rā·lâ'rā) *vt* to sue
quesito (kwā·zē'tō) *m* question, query
questi (kwā'stē) *a&pron* these
questionamento (kwā·styō·nâ·mān'tō) *m* quarrel, altercation
questionare (kwā·styô·nâ'rā) *vi* to argue; to altercate
questionario (kwā·styō·nâ'ryō) *m* questionaire
questione (kwā·styō'nā) *f* argument; problem, matter
questo (kwā'stō) *a&pron* this, the latter
questore (kwā·stō'rā) *m* provincial chief of police
questua (kwe'stwâ) *f* collection for charity
questura (kwā·stū'râ) *f* police headquarters
questurino (kwā·stū·rē'nō) *m* policeman
qui (kwē) *adv* here
quiescenza (kwēā·shān'tsâ) *f* retirement; quiescence
quietanza (kwēā·tân'tsâ) *f* receipt; **–re** (kwēā·tân·tsâ'rā) *vt* to receipt
quietare (kwēā·tâ'rā) *vt* to calm, quiet down; to silence
quietarsi (kwēā·târ'sē) *vr* to become quiet; to grow silent
quiete (kwēā'tā) *f* peace and quiet; silence
quieto (kwēā'tō) *a* quiet; peaceful; shy, retiring
quindi (kwēn'dē) *adv* therefore; afterwards; as a result
quindicenne (kwēn·dē·chān'nā) *a* fifteen years old
quindicesimo (kwēn·dē·che'zē·mō) *a* fifteenth
quindici (kwēn'dē·chē) *a* fifteen; **–mila** (kwēn·dē·chē·mē'lâ) *a* fifteen thousand; **–na** (kwēn·dē·chē'nâ) *f* about fifteen; two weeks
quinquagenario (kwēn·kwâ·jā·nâ'ryō) *a* fifty years old
quintale (kwēn·tâ'lā) *m* quintal
quintessenza (kwēn·tās·sān'tsâ) *f* quintessence
quintetto (kwēn·tāt'tō) *m* quintet
quinto (kwēn'tō) *a* fifth
quintuplicare (kwēn·tū·plē·kâ'rā) *vt* to quintuple
quisquilia (kwē·skwē'lyâ) *f* trifle; bagatelle
quota (kwō'tâ) *f* share; quota; installment; *(avi)* height; **–re** (kwō·tâ'rā) *vt* to quote; to assess; **–zione** (kwō·tâ·tsyō'nā) *f* quotation; **prendere —** *(avi)* to gain altitude, climb; **volare a bassa —** to fly at a low altitude
quotidianamente (kwō·tē·dyâ·nâ·mān'tā) *adv* every day, daily
quotidiano (kwō·tē·dyâ'nō) *a* daily; — *m* daily newspaper
quotizzare (kwō·tē·dzâ'rā) *vt* to assess, evaluate
quotizzazione (kwō·tē·dzâ·tsyō'nā) *f* assessment, evaluation
quoto (kwō'tō), **quoziente** (kwō·tsyān'tā) *m* quotient

R

rabarbaro (râ·bâr'bâ·rō) *m* rhubarb
rabberciare (râb·bār·châ'rā) *vt* to patch
rabbia (râb'byâ) *f* anger, rage; hydrophobia
rabbino (râb·bē'nō) *m* rabbi
rabbiosamente (râb·byō·zâ·mān'tā) *adv* furiously; rabidly
rabbioso (râb·byō'zō) *a* furious, angry; rabid
rabbrividire (râb·brē·vē·dē'rā) *vi* to shiver, shake
rabbuffare (râb·būf·fâ'rā) *vt* to scold; to ruffle, upset
rabbuffarsi (râb·būf·fâr'sē) *vr* to become disturbed; to get upset
rabbuffo (râb·būf'fō) *m* reprimand, scolding
rabdomante (râb·dō·mân'tā) *m* water witch, dowser
raccappezzarsi (râk·kâp·pā·tsâr'sē) *vr* to figure out, understand
raccapricciante (râk·kâ·prē·chân'tā) *a* frightful, horrifying
raccapriccio (râk·kâ·prē'chō) *m* horror
raccattare (râk·kât·tâ'rā) *vt* to pick up, gather
racchetta (râk·kāt'tâ) *f* tennis racket; snowshoe
racchiudere * (râk·kyū'dā·rā) *vt* to contain; to lock in
raccogliere * (râk·kô'lyā·rā) *vt* to gather, collect; to marshal; to accept
raccogliersi * (râk·kô'lyār·sē) *fr* to reflect, ponder; to assemble, gather together; to concentrate one's mind
raccoglimento (râk·kō·lyē·mān'tō) *m* self-absorption; gathering; mental concentration

raccolta (râk·kōl'tâ) *f* collection; harvest
raccoltamente (râk·kōl·tâ·mān'tā) *adv* pensively, musingly
raccolto (râk·kōl'tō) *m* harvest, crop; — *a* gathered; quiet
raccomandare (râk·kō·mân·dâ'rā) *vt* to recommend; to register
raccomandarsi (râk·kō·mân·dâr'sē) *vr* to urge, entreat; to remind
raccomandata (râk·kō·mân·dâ'tâ) *f* registered letter
raccomandazione (râk·kō·mân·dâ·tsyō'nā) *f* recommendation; registry *(letter)*
raccomodare (râk·kō·mō·dâ'rā) *vt* to repair; to set right
raccontare (râk·kōn·tâ'rā) *vt* to relate, tell
racconto (râk·kōn'tō) *m* story; account
raccordo (râk·kōr'dō) *m* junction; connection
rachitico (râ·kē'tē·kō) *a* rickety
racimolare (râ·chē·mō·lâ'rā) *vt* to scrape together; to gather at random
rada (râ'dâ) *f (naut)* roadstead
radar (râ'dâr) *m* radar; **–ista** (râ·dâ·rē'stâ) *m* radarman
raddolcire (râd·dōl·chē'rā) *vt* to sweeten; to make mild
raddolcirsi (râd·dōl·chēr'sē) *vr* to become mild; to get sweet; *(fig)* to be soothed
raddoppiare (râd·dōp·pyâ'rā) *vt* to double
raddoppio (râd·dôp'pyō) *m* doubling
raddrizzare (râd·drē·tsâ'rā) *vt* to make straight
raddrizzarsi (râd·drē·tsâr'sē) *vr* to right; to straighten up
raddrizzatore (râd·drē·dzâ·tō'rā) *m (elec)* rectifier, converter
radere * (râ'dā·rā) *vt* to shave; to raze
radersi * (râ'dār·sē) *vr* to shave, shave oneself
radiare (râ·dyâ'rā) *vt* to expel; to cross out, delete; — *vi* to beam; to radiate
radiatore (râ·dyâ·tō'rā) *m* radiator
radicalmente (râ·dē·kâl·mān'tā) *adv* radically; completely
radicarsi (râ·dē·kâr'sē) *vr* to take root; to take hold
radicchio (râ·dēk'kyō) *m* wild chicory
radice (râ·dē'chā) *f* root
radio (râ'dyō) *f* radio; — *m (min)* radium; — **stazione** radio station; **–amatore** (râ·dyō·â·mâ·tō'rā) *m* ham *(sl)*; **–attività** (râ·dyō·ât·tē·vē·tâ') *f* radioactivity; **–auditore** (râ·dyō·âū·dē·tō'rā) *m* radio listener; **–comandato** (râ·dyō·kō·mân·dâ'tō) *a* radiocontrolled; **–comando** (râ·dyō·kō·mân'dō) *m* remote control; radio control; **–commentatore** (râ·dyō·kōm·mān·tâ·tō'rā) *m* radio commentator; **–cronista** (râ·dyō·krō·nē'stâ) *m* newscaster; **–diffusione** (râ·dyō·dēf·fū·zyō'nā) *f* broadcasting; **–faro** (râ·dyō·fâ'rō) *m* radio beacon; **–fonico** (râ·dyō·fô'nē·kō) *a* radio; **trasmissione radiofonica** broadcast; **–frequenza** (râ·dyō·frā·kwān'tsâ) *f* radio frequency; **–goniometro** (râ·dyō·gō·nyô'mā·trō) *m* direction finder; **–grafia** (râ·dyō·grâ·fē'â) *f* X ray; **–gramma** (râ·dyō·grâm'mâ) *m* radiogram; **–localizzatore** (râ·dyō·lō·kâ·lē·dzâ·tō'rā) *m* radar; **–logia** (râ·dyō·lō·jē'â) *f* radiology; **–logo** (râ·dyô'lō·gō) *m* radiologist; **–scopia** (râ·dyō·skō·pē'â) *f* radioscopy; **–so** (râ·dyō'zō) *a* bright, radiant; **–telefono** (râ·dyō·tā·le'fō·nō) *m* radiotelephone; **–telegrafia** (râ·dyō·tā·lā·grâ·fē'â) *f* radiotelegraphy; **– telegrafista** (râ·dyō·tā·lā·grâ·fē'stâ) *m* wireless operator; **–telegramma** (râ·dyō·tā·lā·grâm'mâ) *m* radiotelegram; **–terapia** (râ·dyō·tā·râ·pē'â) *f* radiotherapy; **–trasmissione** (râ·dyō·trâ·zmēs·syō'nā) *f* broadcast; **-trasmittente** (râ·dyō·trâ·zmēt·tān'tā) *a* broadcasting
rado (râ'dō) *a* thin; rare; **di** — seldom
radunare (râ·dū·nâ'rā) *vt* to collect, gather
radunarsi (râ·dū·nâr'sē) *vr* to assemble, meet
raduno (râ·dū'nō) *m* rally; meeting, assembly
radura (râ·dū'râ) *f* clearing, glade
rafano (râ'fâ·nō) *m* horseradish
raffermo (râf·fār'mō) *a* stale
raffica (râf'fē·kâ) *f* gust; shower
raffigurare (râf·fē·gū·râ'rā) *vt* to symbolize; to recognize; to represent
raffigurarsi (râf·fē·gū·râr'sē) *vr* to imagine
raffigurazione (râf·fē·gū·râ·tsyō'nā) *f* recognition; representation
raffinamento (râf·fē·nâ·mān'tō) *m* thinning, refining
raffinare (râf·fē·nâ'rā) *vt* to refine
raffinarsi (râf·fē·nâr'sē) *vr* to become refined
raffinatezza (râf·fē·nâ·tā'tsâ) *f* refinement
raffinato (râf·fē·nâ'tō) *a* refined; cultured; *(fig)* sly, clever
raffineria (râf·fē·nā·rē'â) *f* refinery
rafforzare (râf·fōr·tsâ'rā) *vt* to reinforce
rafforzarsi (râf·fōr·tsâr'sē) *vr* to be strengthened, become stronger
raffreddamento (râf·frād·dâ·mān'tō) *m* cooling; — **ad acqua** *(mech)* water cooling
raffreddare (râf·frād·dâ'rā) *vt* to cool
raffreddarsi (râf·frād·dâr'sē) *vr* to get cold; to catch a cold
raffreddato (râf·frād·dâ'tō) *a* cooled; **essere** — to have a cold
raffreddore (râf·frād·do'rā) *m* cold
raffronto (râf·frōn'tō) *m* comparison
raganella (râ·gâ·nāl'lâ) *f* rattle
ragazza (râ·gâ'tsâ) *f* girl; **nome di** — maiden name
ragazzata (râ·gâ·tsâ'tâ) *f* boyish prank
ragazzo (râ·gâ'tsō) *m* boy
raggiante (râj·jân'tā) *a* beaming, radiant
raggio (râj'jō) *m* ray; spoke; *(geom)* radius
raggirare (râj·jē·râ'rā) *vt* to swindle
raggirarsi (râj·jē·râr'sē) *vr* to turn about; to ramble
raggiro (rāj·jē'rō) *m* trick; subterfuge
raggiungere * (râj·jūn'jā·rā) *vt* to reach
raggiungersi * (râj·jūn'jār·sē) *vr* to meet

again; to rejoin
raggomitolare (râg·gō·mē·tō·lâ'rā) *vt* to coil; to roll up
raggomitolarsi (râg·gō·mē·tō·lâr'sē) *vr* to coil up; to roll oneself up
raggranellare (râg·grâ·nāl·lâ'rā) *vt* to scrape together
raggrinzire (râg·grēn·dzē'rā) *vt&i* to become wrinkled; to wrinkle
raggrinzirsi (râg·grēn·dzēr'sē) *vr* to become wrinkled
raggrinzito (râg·grēn·dzē'tō) *a* wrinkled
raggruppare (râg·grūp·pâ'rā) *vt* to collect; to group; to regroup
raggrupparsi (râg·grūp·pâr'sē) *vr* to cluster; to form a group
raggruzzolare (râg·grū·tsō·lâ'rā) *vt* to put together, save up
ragguaglio (râg·gwâ'lyō) *m* report; comparison
ragguardevole (râg·gwâr·de'vō·lā) *a* prominent
ragionamento (râ·jō·nâ·mān'tō) *m* argument
ragionare (râ·jō·nâ'rā) *vi* to reason; to talk
ragione (râ·jō'nā) *f* reason; motive; — **sociale** trade name; **aver** — to be right; **rendersi** — to understand; to account for; **dar** — **di** to explain about; **in** — **di 10 km all'ora** at the rate of 10 kilometers an hour; **–ria** (râ·jō·nā·rē'â) *f* accounting, bookkeeping; **–vole** (râ·jō·ne'vō·lā) *a* reasonable; **–volmente** (râ·jō·nā·vōl·mān'tā) *adv* reasonably
ragioniere (râ·jō·nyā'rā) *m* accountant
ragliare (râ·lyâ'rā) *vi* to bray
ragnatela (râ·nyâ·tā'lâ) *f* spider web
ragno (râ'nyō) *m* spider
rallegramenti (râl·lā·grâ·mān'tē) *mpl* congratulations
rallegramento (râl·lā·grâ·mān'tō) *m* rejoicing
rallegrare (râl·lā·grâ'rā) *vt* to cheer, make glad
rallegrarsi (râl·lā·grâr'sē) *vr* to be glad; — **con** to congratulate; to be glad for
rallentamento (râl·lān·tâ·mān'tō) *m* relaxing; slowing
rallentare (râl·lān·tâ'rā) *vt* to slow down
rallentarsi (râl·lān·târ'sē) *vr* to slow down; to become slack; *(mech)* to get loose
ramaiolo (râ·mâ·yō'lō) *m* ladle
ramanzina (râ·mân·dzē'nâ) *f* scolding
rame (râ'mā) *m* copper
ramificare (râ·mē·fē·kâ'rā) *vi* to branch; to ramify
ramificazione (râ·mē·fē·kâ·tsyō'nā) *f* branching; ramification
rammaricare (râm·mâ·rē·kâ'rā) *vt* to vex; to sadden; to mortify
rammaricarsi (râm·mâ·rē·kâr'sē) *vr* to complain; to regret; to grieve
rammarico (râm·mâ'rē·kō) *m* regret
rammendare (râm·mān·dâ'rā) *vt* to mend; to repair; to darn
rammendo (râm·mān'dō) *m* darning, mending
rammentare (râm·mān·tâ'rā) *vt* to remind; to recall
rammentarsi (râm·mān·târ'sē) *vr* to remember, recollect
rammollire (râm·mōl·lē'rā) *vt* to soften; to pacify
rammollirsi (râm·mōl·lēr'sē) *vr* to become effeminate; to grow senile; to become soft
rammollito (râm·mōl·lē'tō) *a* soft; senile; effeminate
ramo (râ'mō) *m* branch; line
ramolaccio (râ·mō·lâ'chō) *m* radish
ramoscello (râ·mō·shāl'lō) *m* twig
rampa (râm'pâ) *f* rail; ramp
rampicante (râm·pē·kân'tā) *a* climbing; — *m (bot)* creeper
rampino (râm·pē'nō) *m* hook
rampogna (râm·pō'nyâ) *f* rebuke
rampollo (râm·pōl'lō) *m* scion, offspring; *(coll)* child
rampone (râm·pō'nā) *m* harpoon
rana (râ'nâ) *f* frog
rancidezza (rān·chē·dā'tsâ) *f* rancidity
rancido (rân'chē·dō) *a* rancid; rank
rancore (rân·kō'rā) *m* grudge; malice
randagio (rân·dâ'jō) *a* stray
randello (rân·dāl'lō) *m* club, cudgel
rango (rân'gō) *m* rank, station
rannicchiarsi (rân·nēk·kyâr'sē) *vr* to crouch
rannuvolarsi (rân·nū·vō·lâr'sē) *vr* to cloud over; to darken
rantolare (rân·tō·lâ'rā) *vi* to have a rattle in one's throat
rantolo (rân'tō·lō) *m* death rattle; rattle
rapa (râ'pâ) *f* turnip; **testa di** — ignoramus
rapace (râ·pâ'chā) *a* greedy; plundering; — *m* bird of prey
rapare (râ·pâ'rā) *vt* to shave; to crop
rapida (râ'pē·dâ) *f* rapids
rapidamente (râ·pē·dâ·mān'tā) *adv* rapidly
rapidità (râ·pē·dē·tâ') *f* rapidity
rapido (râ'pē·dō) *a* quick; — *m* express train
rapimento (râ·pē·mān'tō) *m* abduction
rapina (râ·pē'nâ) *f* robbery; holdup; **–tore** (râ·pē·nâ·tō'rā) *m* holdup man
rapire (râ·pē'rā) *vt* to kidnap; to ravish
rapitore (râ·pē·tō'rā) *m* kidnapper; rapist
rappacificare (râp·pâ·chē·fē·kâ'rā) *vt* to reconcile; to pacify
rappacificarsi (râp·pâ·chē·fē·kâr'sē) *vr* to become reconciled
rappacificazione (râp·pâ·chē·fē·kâ·tsyō'nā) *f* reconciliation
rappezzare (râp·pā·tsâ'rā) *vt* to patch up
rappezzo (râp·pā'tsō) *m* patch
rapportare (râp·pōr·tâ'rā) *vt* to relate, report
rapporto (râp·pōr'tō) *m* reference; relationship; intercourse; statement; ratio; report; **rapporti sessuali** sexual relations; **in** — **a** in relation to; **in** — **di due a quattro** in the ratio of two to four; **sotto tutti i rapporti** in every respect
rappresaglia (râp·prā·zâ'lyâ) *f* retaliation

rappresentante (râp·prā·zān·tân'tā) *m* representative; agent
rappresentanza (râp·prā·zān·tân'tsâ) *f* agency; representation
rappresentare (râp·prā·zān·tâ'rā) *vt* to represent; to act as agent for; *(theat)* to perform
rappresentazione (râp·prā·zān·tâ·tsyō'nā) *f* representation; *(theat)* performance
raramente (râ·râ·mān'tā) *adv* infrequently; rarely
rarefare * (râ·rā·fâ'rā) *vt* to rarefy
rarefazione (râ·rā·fâ·tsyō'nā) *f* rarefaction
raro (râ'rō) *a* unusual, strange; rare; hard to come by
rasare (râ·zâ'rā) *vt* to shave
raschiare (râ·skyâ'rā) *vt* to scrape
rasentare (râ·zān·tâ'rā) *vt* to brush; to touch lightly, shave
rasente (râ·zān'tā) *prep* very near, close to
raso (râ'zō) *m* satin
raso (râ'zō) *a* shaved; cut close; **—io** (râ·zō'yō) *m* razor
raspa (râ'spâ) *f* rasp; **—re** (râ·spâ'rā) *vt* to scrape, rasp; to paw
rassegna (râs·sā'nyâ) *f* review; **—re** (râs·sā·nyâ'rā) *vt* to resign; **—rsi** (râs·sā·nyâr'sē) *vr* to resign oneself; **—zione** (râs·sā·nyâ·tsyō'nā) *f* resignation
rasserenare (râs·sā·rā·nâ'rā) *vt* to calm, clear up
rasserenarsi (râs·sā·rā·nâr'sē) *vr* to calm down; *(weather)* to clear up; *(sky)* to brighten
rassettare (râs·sāt·tâ'rā) *vt* to tidy up; to repair
rassicurare (râs·sē·kū·râ'rā) *vt* to reassure
rassicurarsi (râs·sē·kū·râr'sē) *vr* to make sure; to reassure oneself
rassomiglianza (râs·sō·mē·lyân'tsâ) *f* resemblance
rassomigliare (râs·sō·mē·lyâ'rā) *vi* to resemble, look like
rastrellamento (râ·strāl·lâ·mān'tō) *m* raking; *(mil)* mop up
rastrellare (râ·strāl·lâ'rā) *vt* to rake; *(mil)* to mop up
rastrello (râ·strāl'lō) *m* rake *(tool)*
rata (râ'tâ) *f* installment
rateale (râ·tā·â'lā) *a* by installments; **pagamento —** partial payment
ratealmente (râ·tā·âl·mān'tā) *adv* in installments
ratifica (râ·tē'fē·kâ) *f* ratification; **—re** (râ·tē·fē·kâ'rā) *vt* to ratify
ratto (rât'tō) *m* abduction; rape; rat
rattoppare (rât·tōp·pâ'rā) *vt* to patch
rattoppo (rât·tōp'pō) *m* patch
rattrappirsi (rât·trâp·pēr'sē) *vr* to become contracted
rattristare (rât·trē·stâ'rā) *vt* to grieve, sadden
rattristarsi (rât·trē·stâr'sē) *vr* to be sorry; to become sad
raucedine (râū·che'dē·nā) *f* hoarseness
rauco (râ'ū·kō) *a* hoarse
ravanello (râ·vâ·nāl'lō) *m* radish
ravvedersi * (rāv·vā·dār'sē) *vr* to repent
ravvedimento (râv·vā·dē·mān'tō) *m* reformation; repentance
ravviare (râv·vyâ'rā) *vt* to fix up
ravviarsi (râv·vyâr'sē) *vr* to primp; to tidy up; **— i capelli** to comb one's hair
ravvisare (râv·vē·zâ'rā) *vt* to recognize
ravvivare (râv·vē·vâ'rā) *vt* to revive
ravvolgimento (râv·vōl·jē·mān'tō) *m* winding; rolling up
raziocinio (râ·tsyō·chē'nyō) *m* reason; sense; reasoning
razionale (râ·tsyō·nâ'lā) *a* rational
razionare (râ·tsyō·nâ'rā) *vt* to ration
razione (râ·tsyō'nā) *f* ration
razza (râ'tsâ) *f* race; kind; **di — pura** thoroughbred
razzia (râ·tsē'â) *f* raid
razzismo (râ·tsē'zmō) *m* racialism; racism
razzo (râ'tsō) *m* rocket; **motore a —** jet engine; **— interplanetario** spaceship
re (rā) *m* king; *(mus)* re
reagire (rā·â·jē'rā) *vi* to react
reale (rā·â'lā) *a* royal; real
realizzare (rā·â·lē·dzâ'rā) *vt* to realize; *(com)* to make a profit of; to achieve, attain; to collect
realizzarsi (rā·â·lē·dzâr'sē) *vr* to come true; to happen
realizzazione (rā·â·lē·dzâ·tsyō'nā) *f* achievement; execution; collection
realmente (rā·âl·mān'tā) *adv* really
reato (rā·â'tō) *m* crime; **corpo del —** evidence
reattore (rā·ât·tō'rā) *m* reactor; inductor; *(avi)* jet plane
reazionario (rā·â·tsyō·nâ'ryō) *a* reactionary
reazione (rā·â·tsyō'nā) *f* reaction; **— a catena** chain reaction; **propulsione a —** jet propulsion
recapitare (rā·kâ·pē·tâ'rā) *vt* to deliver
recapito (rā·kâ'pē·tō) *m* delivery address
recare (rā·kâ'rā) *vt* to bring; to take
recarsi (rā·kâr'sē) *vr* to go to; to have recourse to
recensione (rā·chān·syō'nā) *f* book review
recensionista (rā·chān·syō·nē'stâ) *f* book reviewer
recensire (rā·chān·sē'rā) *vt* to review
recente (rā·chān'tā) *a* recent; **—mente** (rā·chān·tā·mān'tā) *adv* recently
recessione (rā·chās·syō'nā) *f* recession
recidere * (rā·chē'dā·rā) *vt* to cut off
recidivo (rā·chē·dē'vō) *m* repeater; habitual offender
recinto (rā·chēn'tō) *m* enclosure
recipiente (rā·chē·pyān'tā) *m* container
reciprocamente (rā·chē·prō·kâ·mān'tā) *adv* reciprocally
reciproco (rā·chē'prō·kō) *a* mutual
reciso (rā·chē'zō) *a* cut off; curt
recita (re'chē·tâ) *f* performance, recital
recitare (rā·chē·tâ'rā) *vt* to recite; *(theat)* to perform, act; **— a soggetto** *(theat)* to improvise
reclamare (rā·klâ·mâ'rā) *vt* to claim, de-

mand; — *vi* to complain; to file a complaint
reclame (rā·klâ'mā) *f* advertisement
reclamo (rā·klâ'mō) *m* claim, complaint
recluso (rā·klū'zō) *m* convict, recluse; **–rio** (rā·klū·zô'ryō) *m* penitentiary
recluta (re'klū·tâ) *f* recruit; selectee; **–mento** (rā·klū·tâ·mān'tō) *m* recruiting
recondito (rā·kôn'dē·tō) *a* hidden
redarguire (rā·dâr·gwē'rā) *vt* to scold; to censure
redattore (rā·dât·tō'rā) *m* editor
redazione (rā·dâ·tsyō'nā) *f* editorial staff; editing
redditizio (rād·dē·tē'tsyō) *a* profitable
reddito (red'dē·tō) *m* income
redentore (rā·dān·tō'rā) *m* redeemer; **il R–** the Saviour
redenzione (rā·dān·tsyō'nā) *f* redemption
redigere * (rā·dē'jā·rā) *vt* to draw up, draft; to edit
redimere * (rā·dē'mā·rā) *vt* to redeem
redimersi * (rā·dē'mār·sē) *vr* to redeem oneself
redine (re'dē·nā) *f* rein; bridle
redivivo (rā·dē·vē'vō) *a* come back to life; another of the same type, second
reduce (re'dū·chā) *m* veteran; — *a* returning
refe (rā'fā) *m* thread
referenza (rā·fā·rān'tsâ) *f* reference
refettorio (rā·fât·tô'ryō) *m* refectory; *(mil)* mess hall
refezione (rā·fā·tsyō'nā) *f* light meal, snack
refrattario (rā·frât·tâ'ryō) *a* intractable; unruly
refrigerare (rā·frē·jā·râ'rā) *vt* to refrigerate; to refresh, restore
refrigerio (rā·frē·je'ryō) *m* relief; refreshment
refurtiva (rā·fūr·tē'vâ) *f* stolen property, stolen goods
regalare (rā·gâ·lâ'rā) *vt* to present; to make a gift of
regalo (rā·gâ'lō) *m* gift, present
reggente (rāj·jān'tā) *m&f* regent
reggere * (rej'jā·rā) *vt&i* to uphold; to support; to rule
reggersi * (rej'jār·sē) *vr* to stand, endure; to control oneself
reggia (rej'jâ) *f* palace, royal residence
reggicalze (rāj·jē·kâl'tsā) *m* garter belt
reggimento (rāj·jē·mān'tō) *m* regiment
reggipetto (rāj·jē·pāt'tō), **reggiseno** (rāj·jē·sā'nō) *m* brassiere
regia (rā·jē'â *f* directing *(movie, play)*; *(theat)* producing; — **dei tabacchi** tobacco monopoly
regime (rā·jē'mā) *m* regime; diet
regina (rā·jē'nâ) queen
regio (re'jō) *a* royal, regal
regione (rā·jō'nā) *f* district; region
regista (rā·jē'stâ) *m* director *(movie, play)*; *(theat)* producer
registrare (rā·jē·strâ'rā) *vt* to register; to record
registratore (rā·jē·strâ·tō'rā) *m* recorder; register; — **di cassa** cash register; — **a nastro** tape recorder
registrazione (rā·jē·strâ·tsyō'nā) *f* registration; recording
registro (rā·jē'strō) *m* register; record
regnare (rā·nyâ'rā) *vi* to reign, rule
regno (rā'nyō) *m* kingdom; rule
regola (re'gō·lâ) *f* rule; **–mento** (rā·gō·lâ·mān'tō) *m* regulation; **–re** (rā·gō·lâ'rā) *a* regular; **–re** *vt* to adjust; **–rizzare** (rā·gō·lâ·rē·dzâ'rā) *vt* to remedy; to straighten; to make regular; **–rmente** (rā·gō·lâr·mān'tā) *adv* regularly; **–rsi** (rā·gō·lâr'sē) *vr* to act, behave; **–tezza** (rā·go·lâ·tā'tsâ) *f* order; moderation; **–tore** (rā·gō·lâ·tō'rā) *m* regulator; **–tore** *a* regulating
regolo (re'gō·lō) *m* ruler; — **calcolatore** slide rule
regresso (rā·grās'sō) *m* regression
reincarnazione (rāēn·kâr·nâ·tsyō'nā) *f* reincarnation
reintegrare (rāēn·tā·grâ'rā) *vt* to reinstate
reintegrazione (rāēn·tā·grâ·tsyō'nā) *f* reinstatement
relativamente (rā·lâ·tē·vâ·mān'tā) *adv* relatively
relativo (rā·lâ·tē'vō) *a* relative; related
relatore (rā·lâ·tō'rā) *m* reporter
relazione (rā·lâ·tsyō'nā) *f* relation, connection; account, report
relegare (rā·lā·gâ'rā) *vt* to relegate; to confine, enclose
religione (rā·lē·jō'nā) *f* religion
religiosamente (rā·lē·jō·zâ·mān'tā) *adv* religiously
religioso (rā·lē·jō'zō) *a* religious
reliquia (rā·lē'kwēâ) *f* relic
relitto (rā·lēt'tō) *m* wreck, remains
remare (rā·mâ'rā) *vi* to row
rematore (rā·mâ·tō'rā) *m* oarsman
reminiscenza (rā·mē·nē·shān'tsâ) *f* reminiscence, memory
remissivo (rā·mēs·sē'vō) *a* obedient; humble; docile
remo (rā'mō) *m* oar
remoto (rā·mō'tō) *a* secluded; remote; **passato** — *(gram)* past definite
rendere * (ren'dā·rā) *vt* to render; to yield; to make; to return
rendersi * (ren'dār·sē) *vr* to become; — **necessario** to become necessary; — **conto di** to realize; to take note of, notice
rendiconto (rān·dē·kōn'tō) *m* report; statement
rendita (ren'dē·tâ) *f* income, return
rene (rā'nā) *m* kidney
renitente (rā·nē·tān'tā) *a* unwilling; opposed; **—alla leva** *(mil)* draft dodger
renna (rān'nâ) *f* reindeer
reo (rā'ō) *m&a* accused; convict; — *a* guilty
reostato (rā·ō'stâ·tō) *m* *(elec)* rheostat
reparto (rā·pâr'tō) *m* department; *(mil)* detachment
repentaglio (rā·pān·tâ'lyō) *m* danger, risk
repente (rā·pān'tā) *a* sudden
repentino (rā·pān·tē'nō) *a* unexpected,

sudden
reperibile (rā·pā·rē'bē·lā) *a* to be found; available
reperto (rā·pār'tō) *m (law)* findings, evidence; (*med*) report
repertorio (rā·pār·tô'ryō) *m* repertory
replica (re'plē·kâ) *f* reply; retort; repetition
repressione (rā·prās·syō'nā) *f* repression
reprimere * (rā·prē'mā·rā) *vt* to repress, stifle; to hold back
reprimersi * (rā·prē'mār·sē) to restrain oneself, control oneself
reprobo (re'prō·bō) *a* depraved
repubblica (rā·pūb'blē·kâ) *f* republic
repulsione (rā·pūl·syō'nā) *f* repulsion
repulsivo (rā·pūl·sē'vō) *a* repellent; repulsive
reputare (rā·pū·tâ'rā) *vt* to deem, think
reputarsi (rā·pū·târ'sē) *vr* to regard oneself, think oneself
reputazione (rā·pū·tâ·tsyō'nā) *f* reputation
requie (re'kwēā) *f* rest; peace; requiem; **senza** — unceasingly
requisire (rā·kwē·zē'rā) *vt* to requisition, request
requisito (rā·kwē·zē'tō) *m* requirement
requisizione (rā·kwē·zē·tsyō'nā) *f* requisition
resa (rā'zâ) *f* surrender; return; yield
residente (rā·zē·dān'tā) *a&m* resident
residenza (rā·zē·dān'tsâ) *f* residence
residuo (rā·zē'dwō) *m* remainder; residue
resina (re'zē·nâ) *f* rosin; resin
resipola (rā·zē'pō·lâ) *f* erysipelas
resistente (rā·sē·stān'tā) *a* strong; fast *(color)*; resistant
resistenza (rā·zē·stān'tsâ) *f* resistance
resistere * (rā·zē'stā·rā) *vi* to resist, oppose; to endure, withstand
resoconto (rā·zō·kōn'tō) *m* account, report
respingere * (rā·spēn'jā·rā) *vt* to reject; to repel; — **al mittente** to return to the sender
respinto (rā·spēn'tō) *a* rejected; refused; returned to the sender
respirare (rā·spē·râ'rā) *vi* to breathe
respirazione (rā·spē·râ·tsyō'nā) *f* respiration
respiro (rā·spē'rō) *m* breath; respite; delay; **esalare l'ultimo** — to breath one's last; to die
responsabile (rā·spōn·sâ'bē·lā) *a* answerable; liable; responsible
responsabilità (rā·spōn·sâ·bē·lē·tâ') *f* responsibility; — **civile** personal liability
ressa (rās'sâ) *f* crowd, mob
restare (rā·stâ'rā) *vi* to stay, remain
restaurare (rā·stâū·râ'rā) *vt* to restore
restaurazione (rā·stâū·râ·tsyō'nā) *f* restoration
restauro (rā·stâ'ū·rō) *m* repair; restoration
restio (rā·stē'ō) *a* reluctant; obstinate
restituire (rā·stē·twē'rā) *vt* to return, bring back
restituzione (rā·stē·tū·tsyō'nā) *f* restitution
resto (rā'stō) *m* remainder; change
restringere * (rā·strēn'jā·rā) *vt* to tighten; to restrict; to cut down
restringersi * (rā·strēn'jār·sē) *vr* to shrink, contract; to restrain oneself, limit oneself
restrizione (rā·strē·tsyō'nā) *f* restriction; — **mentale** mental reservation; **senza** — unreservedly
resurrezione (rā·zūr·rā·tsyō'nā) *f* resurrection
resuscitare (rā·zū·shē·tâ'rā) *vt&i* to resuscitate; to revive
retata (rā·tâ'tâ) *f* haul; netful; police raid
rete (rā'tā) *f* net; network; *(soccer)* goal; — **metallica** wire mesh; — **ferroviaria** railway system
reticella (rā·tē·chāl'lâ) *f* hairnet; baggage rack
reticente (rā·tē·chān'tā) *a* reticent; reluctant
reticolato (rā·tē·kō·lâ'tō) *m* barbed wire
retina (re'tē·nâ) *f (anat)* retina
retribuire (rā·trē·bwē'rā) *vt* to reward
retribuzione (rā·trē·bū·tsyō'nā) *f* compensation
retrobottega (rā·trō·bōt·tā'gâ) *f* back room of a store
retrocarica (rā·trō·kâ'rē·kâ) *f* (*mil*) breechloading; **a** — breechloading; **fucile a** — breechloader
retrocedere (rā·trō·che'dā·rā) *vi* to go back, recede; — *vt* to demote
retrocessione (rā·trō·chās·syō'nā) *f* demotion; recession
retrogrado (rā·trô'grâ·dō) *m* reactionary; — *a* backward, retrograde
retroguardia (rā·trō·gwâr'dyâ) *f* (*mil*) rearguard
retromarcia (rā·trō·mâr'châ) *f* (*auto*) reverse gear; backing up
retroscena (rā·trō·shā'nâ) *f* (*theat*) backstage
retta (rāt'tâ) *f* charges; fee; **dar** — to pay attention
rettangolo (rāt·tân'gō·lō) *m* rectangle
rettificare (rāt·tē·fē·kâ'rā) *vt* to rectify, set right
rettificazione (rāt·tē·fē·kâ·tsyô'nā) *f* rectification
rettile (ret'tē·lā) *m* reptile
rettilineo (rāt·tē·lē'nā·ō) *a* rectilinear; — *m* straight line
rettitudine (rāt·tō·tū'dē·nā) *f* honesty
retto (rāt'tō) *a* straight; honest
rettore (rāt·tō'rā) *m* director; rector; — **magnifico** university president
reuma (re'ū·mâ) *m* rheumatism
reverendo (rā·vā·rān'dō) *a* reverend; — *m* ecclesiastic
revisionare (rā·vē·zyō·nâ'rā) *vt* to revise; (*mech*) to overhaul; (*com*) to audit
revisione (rā·vē·zyō'nā) *f* audit; (*mech*) overhauling
revisore (rā·vē·zō'rā) *m* reviser; auditor; — **di bozze** proofreader
revoca (re'vō·kâ) *f* revocation; **–re** (rā·vō·kâ'rā) *vt* to revoke

revolver (rā·vōl'vār) *m* revolver, pistol; **–ata** (rā·vōl·vā·râ'tâ) *f* pistol shot
riabilitare (ryâ·bē·lē·tâ'rā) *vt* to rehabilitate; to reform
riabilitazione (ryâ·bē·lē·tâ·tsyō'nā) *f* rehabilitation; reformation
rialzare (ryâl·tsâ'rā) *vt* to raise
rialzarsi (ryâl·tsâr'sē) *vr* to get up again; to rise
rianimare (ryâ·nē·mâ'rā) *vt* to cheer up; to reanimate
rianimarsi (ryâ·nē·mâr'sē) *vr* to take heart; to cheer up
riassunto (ryâs·sūn'tō) *m* recapitulation; summary
riattaccare (ryât·tâk·kâ'rā) *vt* to start again; to reattach; **— il ricevitore** to hang up the receiver
riattivare (ryât·tē·vâ'rā) *vt* to reactivate
ribalta (rē·bâl'tâ) *f* (*theat*) stage apron; **luci della —** footlights
ribassare (rē·bâs·sâ'rā) *vt* to reduce; to lower; to cut (*prices*); to curtail
ribasso (rē·bâs'sō) *m* reduction, cut; curtailment
ribattere (rē·bât'tā·rā) *vt* to repel; to hit again; — *vi* to retort
ribellarsi (rē·bāl·lâr'sē) *vr* to rebel; to rise in revolt
ribelle (rē·bāl'lā) *m&a* rebel
ribellione (rē·bāl·lyō'nā) *f* rebellion
ribrezzo (rē·brā'tsō) *m* nausea; disgust
ricaduta (rē·kâ·dū'tâ) *f* relapse
ricalcare (rē·kâl·kâ'rā) *vt* to trample; to retrace; to trace (*drawing*)
ricamare (rē·kâ·mâ'rā) *vt* to embroider
ricambiare (rē·kâm·byâ'rā) *vt* to reciprocate
ricambio (rē·kâm'byō) *m* exchange, interchange; metabolism; **pezzo di —** spare part
ricamo (rē·kâ'mō) *m* embroidery
ricapitolazione (rē·kâ·pē·tō·lâ·tsyō'nā) *f* recapitulation
ricattatore (rē·kât·tâ·tō'rā) *m* blackmailer
ricatto (rē·kât'tō) *m* blackmail
ricavare (rē·kâ·vâ'rā) *vt* to derive; to get out, obtain
ricavato (rē·kâ·vâ'tō) *m* proceeds
riccamente (rēk·kâ·mān'tā) *adv* richly
ricchezza (rēk·kā'tsâ) *f* wealth
riccio (rē'chō) *m* curl of hair; — *a* curly
ricco (rēk'kō) *a* rich
ricerca (rē·chār'kâ) *f* search; **–re** *vt* (rē·chār·kâ'rā) *vt* to search; to research; **–tezza** (rē·chār·kâ·tā'tsâ) *f* affectation; **–to** (rē·chār·kâ'tō) *a* wanted; popular; affected
ricetta (rē·chāt'tâ) *f* prescription, recipe
ricettatore (rē·chāt·tâ·tō'rā) *m* fence, receiver of stolen goods
ricevente (rē·chā·vān'tā) *m* receiver, recipient
ricevere (rē·che'vā·rā) *vt&i* to receive
ricevimento (rē·chā·vē·mān'tō) *m* reception, receipt
ricevitore (rē·chā·vē·tō'rā) *m* receiver
ricevuta (rē·chā·vū'tâ) *f* receipt
richiamare (rē·kyâ·mâ'rā) *vt* to call back; to rebuke; to recall
richiamarsi (rē·kyâ·mâr'sē) *vr* to have recourse to, resort to
richiamo (rē·kyâ'mō) *m* reproof; recall
richiedente (rē·kyā·dān'tā) *m* applicant
richiedere * (rē·kye'dā·rā) *vt* to request; to require; to apply for; to send for
richiesta (rē·kyā'stâ) *f* demand
ricino (rē'chē·nō) *m* castor-oil plant; **olio di —** castor oil
ricognizione (rē·kō·nyē·tsyō'nā) *f* military reconnaissance
ricolmo (rē·kōl'mō) *a* brimful, chock-full
ricompensa (rē·kōm·pān'sâ) *f* reward
riconoscenza (rē·kō·nō·shān'tsâ) *f* gratitude
riconoscere * (rē·kō·nô'shā·rā) *vt* to recognize
riconoscimento (rē·kō·nō·shē·mān'tō) *m* identification; recognition
ricordare (rē·kōr·dâ'rā) *vt&i* to remember, recall
ricordarsi (rē·kōr·dâr'sē) *vr* to remember, recall
ricordo (rē·kōr'dō) *m* souvenir; memory; recollection
ricorrere * (rē·kôr'rā·rā) *vi* to appeal; to recur; to take recourse
ricorso (rē·kōr'sō) *m* appeal
ricostituente (rē·kō·stē·twān'tā) *m* tonic; restorative
ricoverare (rē·kō·vā·râ'rā) *vt* to shelter, give refuge to
ricoverarsi (rē·kō·vā·râr'sē) *vr* to take refuge, seek shelter
ricovero (rē·kô'vā·rō) *m* refuge; shelter
ricreazione (rē·krā·â·tsyō'nā) *f* rest; recreation
ricuperare (rē·kū·pā·râ'rā) *vt* to regain; to salvage
ricupero (rē·kū'pā·rō) *m* salvage; recovery
ricusare (rē·kū·zâ'rā) *vt* to reject, refuse; to spurn
ridda (rēd'dâ) *f* confusion
ridere * (rē'dā·rā) *vi* to laugh
ridersi * (rē'dār·sē) *vr* to make fun of
ridicolo (rē·dē'kō·lō) *a* ridiculous; funny
ridotto (rē·dōt'tō) *m* (*theat*) lobby, foyer; — *a* reduced
ridurre * (rē·dūr'rā) *vt* to reduce
ridursi * (rē·dūr'sē) *vr* to be reduced; to sink, be degraded
riduzione (rē·dū·tsyō'nā) *f* reduction; adaptation; (*mus*) arrangement
riecheggiare (ryā·kāj·jâ'rā) *vi* to resound
riempire * (ryām·pē'rā) *vt* to fill
rievocare (ryā·vō·kâ'rā) *vt* to recall; to bring to mind
rifare * (rē·fâ'rā) *vt* to do again; redo
rifarsi * (rē·fâr'sē) *vr* to get even; to begin; to recoup; to become once more
riferire (rē·fā·rē'rā) *vt* to refer; to report
riferirsi (rē·fā·rēr'sē) *vr* to refer to; to concern, deal with
riffa (rēf'fâ) *f* raffle; lottery
rifiutare (rē·fyū·tâ'rā) *vt&i* to refuse; to deny

rifiutarsi (rē·fyū·târ'sē) *vr* to decline; to refuse
rifiuto (rē·fyū'tō) *m* refusal; rubbish; garbage; *(cards)* revoking
riflessione (rē·flās·syō'nā) *f* reflection
riflessivo (rē·flās·sē'vō) *a* thoughtful; meditative; (*gram*) reflexive
riflettere * (rē·flet'tā·rā) *vt* to reflect
riflettore (rē·flāt·tō'rā) *m* searchlight; reflector
riflusso (rē·flūs'sō) *m* reflux, ebb
riforma (rē·fōr'mā) *f* reform; reformation
riformatorio (rē·fōr·mâ·tô'ryō) *m* reformatory
rifornimento (rē·fōr·nē·mān'tō) *m* supply
rifornire (rē·fōr·nē'rā) *vt* to supply
rifornirsi (rē·fōr·nēr'sē) *vr* to supply oneself with, lay in a supply
rifrazione (rē·frâ·tsyō'nā) *f* refraction
rifugiarsi (rē·fū·jâr'sē) *vr* to take shelter
rifugio (rē·fū'jō) *m* shelter
riga (rē'gâ) *f* line; ruler (*measure*); (*mus*) staff
rigattiere (rē·gât·tyā'rā) *m* junkman
rigenerazione (rē·jā·nā·râ·tsyō'nā) *f* regeneration
rigidamente (rē·jē·dâ·mān'tā) *adv* severely; rigidly
rigido (rē'jē·dō) *a* stiff; severe
rigore (rē·gō'rā) *m* severity; rigor
rigoroso (rē·gō·rō'zō) *a* strict; severe
riguardo (rē·gwâr'dō) *m* respect; consideration; viewpoint
rigurgitare (rē·gūr·jē·tâ'rā) *vi* to overflow; to regurgitate
rilasciare (rē·lâ·shâ'rā) *vt* to release
rilascio (rē·lâ'shō) *m* release
rilassamento (rē·lâs·sâ·mān'tō) *m* slackening, relaxation
rilassarsi (rē·lâs·sâr'sē) *vr* to slacken
rilassato (rē·lâs·sâ'tō) *a* slack; loose
rilegare (rē·lā·gâ'rā) *vt* to retie; to bind (*book*); to refasten
rilevare (rē·lā·vâ'rā) *vt* to point out; to relieve
rilievo (rē·lyā'vō) *m* relief
riluttanza (rē·lūt·tân'tsâ) *f* reluctance
rima (rē'mâ) *f* rhyme
rimandare (rē·mân·dâ'rā) *vt* to send back; to put off; to postpone
rimanenza (rē·mâ·nān'tsâ) *f* remainder
rimanere * (rē·mâ·nā'rā) *vi* to remain
rimarchevole (rē·mâr·ke'vō·lā) *a* remarkable, extraordinary
rimarginare (rē·mâr·jē·nâ'rā) *vt* to heal
rimarginarsi (rē·mâr·jē·nâr'sē) *vr* to heal up
rimasuglio (rē·mâ·zū'lyō) *m* leavings; residue
rimbalzare (rēm·bâl·tsâ'rā) *vi* to bounce
rimbambito (rēm·bâm·bē'tō) *a* senile; silly
rimboccare (rēm·bōk·kâ'rā) *vt* to tuck up
rimbombo (rēm·bōm'bō) *m* roar, boom
rimborsare (rēm·bōr·sâ'rā) *vt* to refund
rimborso (rēm·bōr'sō) *m* refund
rimediare (rē·mā·dyâ'rā) *vt* to remedy
rimedio (rē·me'dyō) *m* remedy
rimenata (rē·mā·nâ'tâ) *f* upbraiding, talking-to
rimessa (rē·mās'sâ) *f* remittance; hangar; garage
rimettere * (rē·met'tā·rā) *vt* to put back, replace; to postpone; to remit
rimettersi * (rē·met'tār·sē) *vr* to get better; to resume; to put on again; (*weather*) to improve
rimodernare (rē·mō·dār·nâ'rā) *vt* to modernize
rimorchiare (rē·mōr·kyâ'rā) *vt* to tow; to tug
rimorchiatore (rē·mōr·kyâ·tō'rā) *m* tugboat
rimorchio (rē·môr'kyō) *m* (*auto*) trailer
rimorso (rē·mōr'sō) *m* remorse
rimostranza (rē·mō·strân'tsâ) *f* remonstrance
rimpatriare (rēm·pâ·tryâ'rā) *vt* to repatriate
rimpiangere * (rēm·pyân'jā·rā) *vt* to regret; to feel sorry about
rimpianto (rēm·pyân'tō) *m* regret; — *a* regretted
rimproverare (rēm·prō·vā·râ'rā) *vt* to reproach
rimproverarsi (rēm·prō·vā·râr'sē) *vr* to regret; to blame oneself
rimprovero (rēm·prô'vā·rō) *m* scolding
rimunerare (rē·mū·nā·râ'rā) *vt* to reward
rimunerazione (rē·mū·nā·râ·tsyō'nā) *f* repayment; reward
rinascimento (rē·nâ·shē·mān'tō) *m* Renaissance; rebirth
rincalzo (rēn·kâl'tsō) *m* support; reinforcement
rincaro (rēn·kâ'rō) *m* rising costs; increasing prices
rinchiudere * (rēn·kyū'dā·rā) *vt* to shut in; to enclose
rinchiudersi * (rēn·kyū'dār·sē) *vr* to shut oneself up
rincrescere * (rēn·kre'shā·rā) *vi* to cause regret; to cause sorrow; **mi rincresce** I am sorry
rinforzare (rēn·fōr·tsâ'rā) *vt* to reinforce; to support, prop
rinforzarsi (rēn·fōr·tsâr'sē) *vr* to grow stronger
rinforzo (rēn·fōr'tsō) *m* reinforcement
rinfrescarsi (rēn·frā·skâr'sē) *vr* to cool off; to refresh oneself
rinfresco (rēn·frā'skō) *m* refreshment
rinfusa (rēn·fū'zâ) *f* **alla** — pell-mell, confusedly; (*com*) in bulk
ringhiare (rēn·gyâ'rā) *vi* to growl, snarl
ringhiera (rēn·gyā'râ) *f* banister, balcony
ringraziamento (rēn·grâ·tsyâ·mān'tō) *m* thanks
ringraziare (rēn·grâ·tsyâ'rā) *vt* to thank
rinnegare (rēn·nā·gâ'rā) *vt* to disown; to repudiate
rinnegato (rēn·nā·gâ'tō) *m* renegade
rinnovare (rēn·nō·vâ'rā) *vt* to renew
rinnovo (rēn·nō'vō) *m* renewal
rinoceronte (rē·nō·chā·rōn'tā) *m* rhinoceros
rinomato (rē·nō·mâ'tō) *a* renowned, known

rintocco (rēn·tōk'kō) *m* toll, knell
rintracciare (rēn·trâ·châ'rā) *vt* to trace
rinunzia (rē·nūn'tsyâ) *f* renunciation; **–re** (rē·nūn·tsyâ'rā) *vt&i* to renounce
rinvenire * (rēn·vā·nē'rā) *vt* to find; to rediscover; — *vi* to recover one's senses
rinvio (rēn·vē'ō) *m* adjournment; postponement
rionale (ryō·nâ'lā) *a* neighborhood
rione (ryō'nā) *m* district, section, neighborhood
riparare (rē·pâ·râ'rā) *vt* to repair
ripararsi (rē·pâ·râr'sē) *vr* to take shelter
riparazione (rē·pâ·râ·tsyō'nā) *f* repair; amends
ripartizione (rē·pâr·tē·tsyō'nā) *f* allotment; distribution
ripasso (rē·pâs'sō) *m* review; repetition
ripercussione (rē·pār·kūs·syō'nā) *f* repercussion
ripetere (rē·pe'tā·rā) *vt* to repeat; to rehearse
ripetitore (rē·pā·tē·tō'rā) *m* coach; — **televisivo** television relay
ripetizione (rē·pā·tē·tsyō'nā) *f* repetition; **fucile a** — repeater rifle
ripetutamente (rē·pā·tū·tâ·mān'tā) *adv* repeatedly
ripiano (rē·pyâ'nō) *m* shelf; ledge
ripido (rē'pē·dō) *a* steep
ripiego (rē·pyā'gō) *m* expedient
ripieno (rē·pyā'nō) *a* stuffed, crammed
riporre * (rē·pōr'rā) *vt* to put back, replace
riportare (rē·pōr·tâ'rā) *vt* to bring back; to receive; to carry over
riposarsi (rē·pō·zâr'sē) *vr* to rest
riposo (rē·pō'zō) *m* rest
ripostiglio (rē·pō·stē'lyō) *m* closet; locker
ripresa (rē·prā'zâ) *f* capture; resumption; retrieving; (*sport*) round
riprodurre * (rē·prō·dūr'rā) *vt* to reproduce
riprodursi * (rē·prō·dūr'sē) *vr* to recur; to reproduce, be reproduced
riproduzione (rē·prō·dū·tsyō'nā) *f* reproduction
ripugnante (rē·pū·nyân'tā) *a* repulsive, loathsome
ripugnare (rē·pū·nyâ'rā) *vi* to disgust; to be repugnant to
risacca (rē·zâk'kâ) *f* surf
risalto (rē·zâl'tō) *m* prominence; evidence
risaputo (rē·sâ·pū'tō) *a* well-known, widely known
risarcimento (rē·zâr·chē·mān'tō) *m* reparation; indemnification
risarcire (rē·zâr·chē'rā) *vt* to indemnify
risata (rē·zâ'tâ) *f* laugh, peal of laughter
riscaldamento (rē·skâl·dâ·mān'tō) *m* heating, warming
riscaldare (rē·skâl·dâ'rā) *vt* to heat; to excite
riscaldarsi (rē·skâl·dâr'sē) *vr* to warm up; to become excited
riscaldo (rē·skâl'dō) *m* inflammation
riscattare (rē·skât·tâ'rā) *vt* to redeem
riscattarsi (rē·skât·târ'sē) *vr* to get revenge, get even
rischiarare (rē·skyâ·râ'rā) *vt* to light up; to make clear
rischiare (rē·skyâ'rā) *vt* to risk
rischio (rē'skyō) *m* risk
risciacquare (rē·shâk'kwâ·rā) *vt* to rinse, wash out
riscontro (rē·skōn'trō) *m* reply; verification
riscossa (rē·skōs'sâ) *f* revenge; rebellion; rescue
riscossione (rē·skōs'syō'nā) *f* collection
riscuotere * (rē·skwô'tā·rā) *vt* to cash; to collect
risentimento (rē·zān·tē·mān'tō) *m* resentment
risentito (rē·zān·tē'tō) *a* resentful
riserva (rē·zār'vâ) *f* reserve; **–re** (rē·zār·vâ'rā) *vt* to reserve; to set aside; **–to** (rē·zār·vâ'tō) *a* reserved; confidential
risiedere * (rē·zye'dā·rā) *vi* to reside
risipola (rē·zē'pō·lâ) *f* erysipelas
risma (rē'zmâ) *f* ream (*paper*); kind
riso (rē'zō) *m* laugh; rice
risolto (rē·zōl'tō) *a* settled, resolved
risoluto (rē·zō·lū'tō) *a* resolute
risoluzione (rē·zō·lū·tsyō'nā) *f* resolution; solution
risolvere * (rē·zôl'vā·rā) *vt&i* to resolve; to solve
risolversi * (rē·zôl'vār·sē) *vr* to end in, come to; to decide
risonanza (rē·sō·nân'tsâ) *f* resonance
risorgimento (rē·sōr·jē·mān'tō) *m* revival, renaissance
risorsa (rē·zōr'sâ) *f* resource
risparmiare (rē·spâr·myâ'rā) *vt* to save
risparmio (rē·spâr'myō) *m* saving
rispecchiare (rē·spāk·kyâ'rā) *vt* to reflect, mirror
rispettabile (rē·spāt·tâ'bē·lā) *a* decent; considerable
rispettare (rē·spāt·tâ'rā) *vt* to respect
rispettivamente (rē·spāt·tē·vâ·mān'tā) *adv* respectively
rispettivo (rē·spāt·tē'vō) *a* one's own; particular, respective
rispetto (rē·spāt'tō) *m* respect; **–so** (rē·spāt·tō'zō) *a* respectful
rispondere * (rē·spôn'dā·rā) *vt&i* to answer, reply
risposta (rē·spō'stâ) *f* answer
rissa (rēs'sâ) *f* brawl
ristampa (rē·stâm'pâ) *f* reprint
ristorante (rē·stō·rân'tā) *m* restaurant; **vettura** — dining car
ristrettezza (rē·strāt·tā'tsâ) *f* restriction; narrowness; — **economica** financial difficulties
risultare (rē·zūl·tâ'rā) *vi* to result, end
risultato (rē·zūl·tâ'tō) *m* result
risveglio (rē·zve'lyō) *m* revival; awakening
risvolta (rē·zvōl'tâ) *f* lapel, cuff
ritaglio (rē·tâ'lyō) *m* clipping; — **di tempo** free moment
ritardare (rē·târ·dâ'rā) *vt&i* to delay
ritardo (rē·târ'dō) *m* delay; postponement
ritegno (rē·tā'nyō) *m* restraint
ritenere * (rē·tā·nā'rā) *vt* to hold

ritenersi * (rē·tā·nār'sē) *vr* to think oneself; to refrain from
ritirare (rē·tē·râ'rā) *vt* to withdraw, take back
ritirarsi (rē·tē·râr'sē) *vr* to shrink (*materials*); to retreat; to retire
ritirata (rē·tē·râ'tâ) *f* water closet; bathroom, lavatory; retreat
ritiro (rē·tē'rō) *m* retirement; withdrawal
ritmo (rēt'mō) *m* cadence, rhythm
rito (rē'tō) *m* rite
ritoccare (rē·tōk·kâ'rā) *vt* to retouch
ritocco (rē·tōk'kō) *m* retouching; finishing touch
ritorcere * (rē·tôr'chā·rā) *vt* to twist; to retort
ritorcersi * (rē·tôr'chār·sē) *vr* to get twisted
ritornare (rē·tōr·nâ'rā) *vt&i* to return, go back
ritornello (rē·tōr·nāl'lō) *m* refrain; (*coll*) boring repetition, same old thing
ritorno (rē·tōr'nō) *m* return; **di andata e —** round-trip
ritrattare (rē·trât·tâ'rā) *vt* to retract; to paint a portrait of
ritrattazione (rē·trât·tâ·tsyō'nā) *f* withdrawal, retraction
ritratto (rē·trât'tō) *m* portrait
ritrovare (rē·trō·vâ'rā) *vt* to meet again, meet; to find again
ritrovarsi (rē·trō·vâr'sē) *vr* to meet, meet again; to rendezvous
ritrovato (rē·trō·vâ'tō) *m* finding; expedient
ritrovo (rē·trō'vō) *m* meeting place; **— notturno** night club
ritto (rēt'tō) *a* upright; straight; erect; **—** *adv* straight ahead; directly
rituale (rē·twâ'lā) *a* customary; ritual
riunione (ryū·nyō'nā) *f* reunion; meeting
riunire (ryū·nē'rā) *vt* to assemble; to draw together
riunirsi (ryū·nēr'sē) *vr* to get together; to reunite
riuscire * (ryū·shē'rā) *vt* to succeed in; to go out again; **— negli esami** to pass one's exams; **non —** to fail
riuscita (ryū·shē'tâ) *f* outcome; success; **cattiva —** failure
riva (rē'vâ) *f* shore, bank
rivale (rē·vâ'lā) *a&m* rival
rivedere * (rē·vā·dā'rā) *vt* to see again; to revise, go over; **arrivederla** good-bye, I'll be seeing you
rivelare (rē·vā·lâ'rā) *vt* to reveal, uncover
rivelarsi (rē·vā·lâr'sē) *vr* to show oneself to be, prove oneself
rivelatore (rē·vā·lâ·tō'rā) *m* revealer; (*rad*) detector
rivelazione (rē·vā·lâ·tsyō'nā) *f* revelation, uncovering
rivendicazione (rē·vān·dē·kâ·tsyō'nā) *f* vindication, vengeance
rivendita (rē·ven'dē·tâ) *f* shop; retail selling; **— di sale e tabacchi** tobacco shop, tobacconist
rivenditore (rē·vān·dē·tō'rā) *m* retailer, retail merchant
riverenza (rē·vā·rān'tsâ) *f* reverence; bow
rivestimento (rē·vā·stē·mān'tō) *m* lining, covering, coating
riviera (rē·vyā'râ) *f* shore, seashore
rivincita (rē·vēn'chē·tâ) *f* revenge; (*sport*) return match
rivista (rē·vē'stâ) *f* review, parade; magazine; musical comedy
rivolgersi * (rē·vôl'jār·sē) *vr* to apply to; to have recourse to, turn to
rivolta (rē·vōl'tâ) *f* revolt
rivoltella (re·vōl·tāl'lâ) *f* revolver
rivoluzione (rē·vō·lū·tsyō'nā) *f* revolution
roba (rō'bâ) *f* things; stuff; belongings, possessions
robivecchio (rō·bē·vek'kyō) *m* junkman
robusto (rō·bū'stō) *m* robust; sturdy, sinewy
rocca (rōk'kâ) *f* rock; fortress
rocchetto (rōk·kāt'tō) *m* spool; reel
roccia (rô'châ) *f* cliff; rock; precipice
rodere * (rô'dā·rā) *vt* to gnaw; to corrode away
rodersi * (rô'dār·sē) *vr* to be worried; to be upset; **— le unghie** to bite one's nails
roditore (rō·dē·tō'rā) *m* rodent
rogna (rō'nyâ) *f* (*med*) mange; scab
rognone (rō·nyō'nā) *m* kidney
Roma (rō'mâ) *f* Rome
romano (rō·mâ'nō) *a&m* Roman
romantico (rō·mân'tē·kō) *a* romantic
romanziere (rō·mân·dzyā'rā) *m* novelist
romanzo (rō·mân'dzō) *m* novel; **—** *a* Romance
rombo (rōm'bō) *m* roar, thunder; (*math*) rhombus; turbot (*fish*)
rompere * (rôm'pā·rā) *vt* to break; to shatter
rompersi * (rôm'pār·sē) *vr* to get shattered; to break
rompighiaccio (rōm·pē·gyâ'chō) *m* (*naut*) icebreaker
rompiscatole (rōm·pē·skâ'tō·lā) *m* pest, bore, nuisance
ronda (rōn'dâ) *f* rounds, patrol, watch
rondella (rōn·dāl'lâ) *f* (*mech*) washer
rondine (rôn'dē·nā) *f* swallow (*bird*)
rondone (rōn·dō'nā) *m* swift (*bird*)
ronzare (rōn·dzâ'rā) *vi* to whir; to buzz; to flirt
ronzino (rōn·dzē'nō) *m* nag, jade (*horse*)
ronzio (rōn·dzē'ō) *m* buzzing, whirring
rosa (rō'zâ) *f* rose; **— dei venti** rose compass; **all'acqua di —** (*fig*) quasi; so-called
rosario (rō·zâ'ryō) *m* rosary
rosicante (rō·zē·kân'tā) *a&m* rodent
rosicchiare (rō·zēk·kyâ'rā) *vt* to nibble at, nibble; to eat away gradually
rosmarino (rō·zmâ·rē'nō) *m* rosemary
rosolare (rō·zō·lâ'rā) *vt* to brown
rosolia (rō·zō·lē'â) *f* German measles
rosolio (rō·zô'lyō) *m* cordial, liqueur
rospo (rō'spō) *m* (*zool*) toad; **ingoiare un —** (*fig*) to swallow a bitter pill
rossetto (rōs·sāt'tō) *m* rouge; **— per le labbra** lipstick
rosso (rōs'sō) *a* red; **-re** (rōs·sō'rā) *m*

blush; (*fig*) shame
rosticceria (rō·stē·chā·rē'â) *f* rotisserie
rotaia (rō·tâ'yâ) *f* rail
rotante (rō·tân'tā) *a* rotating
rotativa (rō·tâ·tē'vâ) *f* rotary press
rotella (rō·tāl'lâ) *f* caster; (*anat*) knee cap; **pattini a rotelle** roller skates
rotocalco (rō·tō·kâl'kō) *m* rotogravure
rotolare (rō·tō·lâ'rā) *vt&i* to roll up, roll
rotolarsi (rō·tō·lâr'sē) *vr* to wallow; to roll around
rotondamente (rō·tōn·dâ·mān'tā) *adv* roundly; (*coll*) frankly
rotondo (rō·tōn'dō) *a* round
rotta (rōt'tâ) *f* route; **a — di collo** (*fig*) headlong; from bad to worse
rottame (rōt·tâ'mā) *m* wreckage
rottami (rōt·tâ'mē) *mpl* ruins; rubbish
rotto (rōt'tō) *a* broken
rottura (rōt·tū'râ) *f* break; breach
rovente (rō·vān'tā) *a* red-hot
rovesciare (rō·vā·shâ'rā) *vt* to ruin, overturn, upset
rovesciarsi (rō·vā·shâr'sē) *vr* to capsize; to be upset
rovescio (rō·ve'shō) *m* reverse; **a —** inside out; upside down
rovina (rō·vē'nâ) *f* ruin; **–re** (rō·vē·nâ'rā) *vt* to ruin; **–rsi** (rō·vē·nâr'sē) to ruin oneself, become ruined; **–to** (rō·vē·nâ'tō) *a* ruined
rovistare (rō·vē·stâ'rā) *vt&i* to rummage through, sift through
rozzamente (rō·dzâ·mān'tā) *adv* awkwardly; roughly
rozzo (rō'dzō) *a* course, rough, awkward
rubare (rū·bâ'rā) *vt* to steal
rubinetto (rū·bē·nāt'tō) *m* faucet, tap
rubino (rū·bē'nō) *m* ruby
rubrica (rū'brē·kâ) *f* newspaper column; address book; directory
rudemente (rū·dā·mān'tā) *adv* coarsely, rudely
rudere (rū'dā·rā) *m* ruin
rudimentale (rū·dē·mān·tâ'lā) *a* rudimentary
rudimento (rū·dē·mān'tō) *m* rudiment
ruffiano (rūf·fyâ'nō) *m* pander; go-between
ruga (rū'gâ) *f* wrinkle
ruggine (rūj'jē·nā) *f* rust; grudge, bad blood
ruggire (rūj·jē'rā) *vi* to roar
ruggito (rūj·jē'tō) *m* roar
rullio (rūl·lē'ō) *m* rolling, roll
rullo (rūl'lō) *m* roller; cylinder
Rumania (rū·mâ·nē'â) *f* Romania
rumeno (rū·mā'nō) *a&m* Romanian
ruminante (rū·mē·nân'tā) *a&m* ruminant
rumore (rū·mō'rā) *m* noise; loudness
rumorosamente (rū·mō·rō·zâ·mān'tā) *adv* noisily, loudly
rumoroso (rū·mō·rō'zō) *a* noisy, loud
ruolo (rūō'lō) *m* list; (*theat*) role
ruota (rūō'tâ) *f* wheel
rupe (rū'pā) *f* cliff, precipice
rurale (rū·râ'lā) *a* rural
ruscello (rū·shāl'lō) *m* brook, rivulet
russare (rūs·sâ'rā) *vi* to snore
Russia (rūs'syâ) *f* Russia
russo (rūs'sō) *a&m* Russian
rustico (rū'stē·kō) *a* rustic, country
ruttare (rūt·tâ'rā) *vi* to belch
rutto (rūt'tō) *m* belch
ruvidamente (rū·vē·dâ·mān'tā) *adv* coarsely
ruvidezza (rū·vē·dā'tsâ) *f* roughness
ruvido (rū'vē·dō) *a* coarse; rough
ruzzolare (rū·tsō·lâ'rā) *vt* to knock down, topple; **—** *vi* to tumble down, topple over
ruzzolone (rū·tsō·lō'nā) *m* fall, tumble

S

sabato (sâ'bâ·tō) *m* Saturday
sabbia (sâb'byâ) *f* sand
sabbbioso (sâb·byō'zō) *a* sandy
sabotaggio (sâ·bō·tâj'jō) *m* sabotage
sabotare (sâ·bō·tâ'rā) *vt* to sabotage
saccarina (sâk·kâ·rē'nâ) *f* saccharine
saccente (sâ·chān'tā) *m* smart aleck; dilettante; **—** *a* knowing, apparently wise
saccheggiare (sâk·kāj·jâ'rā) *vt* to plunder, sack
saccheggio (sâk·kej'jō) *m* pillage, sacking
sac[illegible] (sâk'kō) *m* bag; **— a pelo** sleeping [illegible]g; **— da montagna** knapsack
saccoccia (sâk·kô'châ) *f* pocket
sacerdote (sâ·chār·dō'tā) *m* priest; **–ssa** (sâ·chār·dō·tās'sâ) *f* priestess
sacerdozio (sâ·chār·dô'tzyō) *m* priesthood
sacramento (sâ·krâ·mān'tō) *m* sacrament
sacrario (sâ·krâ'ryō) *m* sanctuary
sacrificare (sâ·krē·fē·kâ'rā) *vt* to sacrifice
sacrificarsi (sâ·krē·fē·kâr'sē) *vr* to sacrifice oneself; to make great sacrifices
sacrificio (sâ·krē·fē'chō) *m* sacrifice
sacrilegio (sâ·krē·le'jō) *m* sacrilege
sacro (sâ'krō) *a* holy; sacred
sadismo (sâ·dē'zmō) *m* sadism
saetta (sâ·āt'tâ) *f* arrow; lightning flash
sagace (sâ·gâ'chā) *a* sagacious, wise
saggezza (sâj·jā'tsâ) *f* prudence, wisdom
saggiare (sâj·jâ'rā) *vt* to taste
saggio (sâj'jō) *m* wise man, savant; essay; sample; **—** *a* wise
sagoma (sâ'gō·mâ) *f* outline; shape; mold; **–re** (sâ·gō·mâ'rā) *vt* to form, mold
sagra (sâ'grâ) *f* festival; **–to** (sâ·grâ'tō) *m* church square
sagrestano (sâ·grā·stâ'nō) *m* sexton
sagrestia (sâ·grā·stē'â) *f* sacristy
saio (sâ'yō) *m* (*eccl*) frock, habit
sala (sâ'lâ) *f* room; **— d'aspetto** waiting room; **— da ballo** dance hall; **— da pranzo** dining room
salace (sâ·lâ'chā) *a* salacious, racy
salame (sâ·lâ'mā) *m* salami
salamoia (sâ·lâ·mô'yâ) *f* pickle, brine
salare (sâ·lâ'rā) *vt* to salt, put salt on
salario (sâ·lâ'ryō) *m* salary, wages

salatino (sâ·lâ·tē'nō) *m* salted cracker
salato (sâ·lâ'tō) *a* salted; (*fig*) very expensive, dear
saldamente (sâl·dâ·mān'tā) *adv* solidly, firmly
saldare (sâl·dâ'rā) *vt* to weld; to solder; (*com*) to balance, settle; — **un conto** to pay a bill
saldatura (sâl·dâ·tū'râ) *f* welding, soldering; — **ossidrica** oxyhydrogen welding
saldo (sâl'dō) *m* (*com*) balance; — *a* steadfast, dependable
sale (sâ'lā) *m* salt; (*fig*) wit
salgemma (sâl·jām'mâ) *m* rock salt
salice (sâ'lē·chā) *m* willow
salina (sâ·lē'nâ) *f* saltworks; salt marsh
salire * (sâ·lē'rā) *vt&i* to go up, climb, rise
saliscendi (sâ·lē·shān'dē) *m* latch; going up and down, up-and-down movement
salita (sâ·lē'tâ) *f* rise, climb
saliva (sâ·lē'vâ) *f* saliva
salma (sâl'mâ) *f* body, corpse
salmo (sâl'mō) *m* psalm
salmone (sâl·mō'nā) *m* salmon
salnitro (sâl·nē'trō) *m* niter, saltpeter
salone (sâ·lō'nā) *m* salon, hall
salotto (sâ·lōt'tō) *m* living room
salsa (sâl'sâ) *f* sauce; **–manteria** (sâl·sâ·mân·tā·rē'â) *f* delicatessen
salsedine (sâl·se'dē·nā) *f* saltiness
salsiccia (sâl·sē'châ) *f* sausage
salso (sâl'sō) *a* salty, briny
saltare (sâl·tâ'rā) *vt&i* to jump; to skip
saltellare (sâl·tāl·lâ'rā) *vi* to skip, hop, jump about
saltimbanco (sâl·tēm·bân'kō) *m* mountebank; acrobat
salto (sâl'tō) *m* jump, bound; precipice
saltuariamente (sâl·twâ·ryâ·mān'tā) *adv* fitfully; desultorily
salubre (sâ'lū·brā) *a* wholesome, healthful
salumeria (sâ·lū·mā·rē'â) *f* delicatessen
salumi (sâ·lū'mē) *mpl* salted products
salutare (sâ·lū·tâ'rā) *vt* to greet; to salute; — *a* healthy
salute (sâ·lū'tā) *f* health; salvation; well-being; **S–!** *interj* To your health!; **casa di** — nursing home
saluto (sâ·lū'tō) *m* greeting; **saluti cordiali** cordially yours
salvacondotto (sâl·vâ·kōn·dōt'tō) *m* safe-conduct
salvadanaio (sâl·vâ·dâ·nâ'yō) *m* piggy bank
salvagente (sâl·vâ·jān'tā) *m* life belt
salvaguardia (sâl·vâ·gwâr'dyâ) *f* safeguard
salvare (sâl·vâ'rā) *vt* to save, rescue
salvarsi (sâl·vâr'sē) *vr* to take shelter; to save oneself
salvataggio (sâl·vâ·tâj'jō) *m* rescue; **barca da** — lifeboat
salvezza (sâl·vā'tsâ) *f* safety; salvation
salvia (sâl'vyâ) *f* (*bot*) sage
salvietta (sâl·vyāt'tâ) *f* napkin
salvo (sâl'vō) *a* safe; — *adv&prep* except; — *m* safekeeping
sanatoria (sâ·nâ·tô'ryâ) *f* indemnity; sanction
sanatorio (sâ·nâ·tô'ryō) *m* sanatorium
sancire (sân·chē'rā) *vt* to decree; to authorize, sanction
sandalino (sân·dâ·lē'nō) *m* light kayak
sandalo (sân'dâ·lō) *m* sandal
sanforizzare (sân·fō·rē·dzâ'rā) *vt* to sanforize
sangue (sân'gwā) *m* blood; **al** — rare
sanguinare (sân·gwē·nâ'rā) *vi* to bleed
sanguinario (sân·gwē·nâ'ryō) *a* sanguinary
sanguinoso (sân·gwē·nō'zō) *a* bloody
sanguisuga (sân·gwē·sū'gâ) *f* (*fig*) bloodsucker; (*zool*) leech
sanitario (sâ·nē·tâ'ryō) *a* sanitary; **ufficio** — health officer
sano (sâ'nō) *a* sane; wholesome; — **e salvo** safe and sound
santamente (sân·tâ·mān'tā) *adv* piously
santificare (sân·tē·fē·kâ'rā) *vt* to sanctify; to canonize
santità (sân·tē·tâ') *f* holiness
santo (sân'tō) *a* holy; — *m* saint; **–la** (sân'tō·lâ) *f* godmother; **–lo** (sân'tō·lō) *m* godfather
santuario (sân·twâ'ryō) *m* shrine
sanzione (sân·tsyō'nā) *f* sanction
sapere * (sâ·pā'rā) *vt&i* to know; to taste of; to smell of; — *m* erudition, learning
sapido (sâ'pē·dō) *a* tasty, delectable, delicious
sapiente (sâ·pyān'tā) *a* learned; — *m&f* scholar; **–mente** (sâ·pyān·tā·mān'tā) *adv* wisely, learnedly
sapientone (sâ·pyān·tō'nā) *m* wiseacre, smart aleck; dabbler, dilettante
sapienza (sâ·pyān'tsâ) *f* wisdom
saponata (sâ·pō·nâ'tâ) *f* lather; soapy water
sapone (sâ·pō'nā) *m* soap; — **da bucato** laundry soap; — **da barba** shaving stick; shaving cream; **–tta** (sâ·pō·nāt'tâ) *f* cake of soap
saponiera (sâ·pō·nyā'râ) *f* soap dish
sapore (sâ·pō'rā) *m* taste, savor
saporito (sâ·pō·rē'tō) *a* tasty, delectable
sarcasmo (sâr·kâ'zmō) *m* sarcasm
sarcastico (sâr·kâ'stē·kō) *a* sarcastic
sarda (sâr·dâ), **sardella** (sâr·dāl'lâ), **sardina** (sâr·dē'nâ) *f* sardine
Sardegna (sâr·dā'nyâ) *f* Sardinia
sardo (sâr'dō) *a&m* Sardinian
sardonico (sâr·dô'nē·kō) *a* scornful, sardonic
sarta (sâr'tâ) *f* dressmaker, seamstress
sarto (sâr'tō) *m* tailor; **–ria** (sâr·tō·rē'â) *f* tailor shop
sasso (sâs'sō) *m* stone
sassofonista (sâs·sō·fō·nē'stâ) *m* saxophone player
sassofono (sâs·sô'fō·nō) *m* saxophone
satellite (sâ·tel'lē·tā) *m* satellite
satira (sâ'tē·râ) *f* satire
satiro (sâ'tē·rō) *m* satyr
saturazione (sâ·tū·râ·tsyō'nā) *f* saturation
saturnismo (sâ·tūr·nē'zmō) *m* lead poisoning
saturo (sâ'tū·rō) *a* saturated

savio (sâ'vyō) *a* wise; well-behaved
saziare (sâ·tsyâ'rā) *vt* to sate; to satisfy completely
saziarsi (sâ·tsyâr'sē) *vr* to tire of; to become sated
sazietà (sâ·tsyā·tâ') *f* surfeit, satiety
sazio (sâ'tsyō) *a* full, satiated
sbadataggine (zbâ·dâ·tâj'jē·nā) *f* carelessness
sbadatamente (zbâ·dâ·tâ·mān'tā) *adv* carelessly
sbadato (zbâ·dâ'tō) *a* careless
sbadigliare (zbâ·dē·lyâ'rā) *vi* to yawn
sbadiglio (zbâ·dē'lyō) *m* yawn
sbagliare (zbâ·lyâ'rā) *vi* to make a mistake, commit an error; — *vt* to miss; to misjudge
sbagliato (zbâ·lyâ'tō) *a* wrong, mistaken
sbaglio (zbâ'lyō) *m* mistake; error
sballare (zbâl·lâ'rā) *vt* to unpack; **sballarle grosse** *(fig)* to talk big; to tell tall tales
sballato (zbâl·lâ'tō) *a* false; *(fig)* unbalanced; foolish
sbalordimento (zbâ·lōr·dē·mān'tō) *m* amazement, astonishment
sbalordire (zbâ·lōr·dē'rā) *vt* to astound
sbalordirsi (zbâ·lōr·dēr'sē) *vr* to be astounded, be amazed
sbalorditivo (zbâ·lōr·dē·tē'vō) *a* amazing, astounding
sbalzare (zbâl·tsâ'rā) *vt* to overthrow; to discharge, to dismiss
sbalzo (zbâl'tsō) *m* leap; jump; **a —** in bas-relief
sbandamento (zbân·dâ·mān'tō) *m* dispersing; disbanding; *(auto)* skidding; *(naut)* listing
sbandare (zbân·dâ'rā) *vi* to swerve; to go out of control; — *vt* to break up, scatter
sbandarsi (zbân·dâr'sē) *vr* to disband; *(auto)* to skid; *(naut)* to heel, tip
sbaragliare (zbâ·râ·lyâ'rā) *vt* to rout, scatter, set to flight
sbaraglio (zbâ·râ'lyō) *m* hubbub; rout; dispersion; *(fig)* jeopardy; **gettarsi allo —** to jeopardize oneself, put oneself in a dangerous position
sbarazzare (zbâ·râ·tsâ'rā) *vt* to rid; to clear; to disencumber, extricate
sbarazzarsi (zbâ·râ·tsâr'sē) *vr* to dispose of; to get rid of
sbarazzino (zbâ·râ·tsē'nō) *m* urchin, scamp, mischief
sbarbare (zbâr·bâ'rā) *vt* to shave
sbarbarsi (zbâr·bâr'sē) *vr* to shave
sbarbatello (zbâr·bâ·tāl'lō) *m* stripling, young lad
sbarcare (zbâr·kâ'rā) *vt&i* to land; **— il lunario** to make both ends meet
sbarco (zbâr'kō) *m* landing; disembarkation
sbarra (zbâr'râ) *f* lever; crowbar; *(print)* dash; *(naut)* tiller; **–mento** (zbâr·râ·mān'tō) *m* barrier; barrage; **–re** (zbâr·râ'rā) *vt* to bar
sbattere (zbât'tā·rā) *vt* to slam, bang; to stamp; to beat *(eggs)*; **— gli occhi** to blink one's eyes
sbellicarsi (zbāl·lē·kâr'sē) *vr* **— dalle risa** to split one's sides with laughter
sberleffo (zbār·lāf'fō) *m* grimace; scar
sbiadire (zbyâ·dē'rā) *vi* to fade, fade out
sbieco (sbyā'kō) *a* oblique; awry; **di —** askance; askew
sbigottito (zbē·gōt·tē'tō) *a* dismayed
sbilanciare (zbē·lân·châ'rā) *vt&i* to unbalance; *(fig)* to derange
sbilanciarsi (zbē·lân·châr'sē) *vr* to lose one's balance; *(fig)* to live beyond one's income
sbirciare (zbēr·châ'rā) *vt&i* to eye, ogle, glance at, peer at
sbirro (zbēr'rō) *m* stool pigeon *(coll)*
sbizzarrirsi (zbē·dzâr·rēr'sē) *vr* to follow one's whims
sboccare (zbōk·kâ'rā) *vi* to flow into
sboccato (zbōk·kâ'tō) *a* foulmouthed
sbocciare (zbō·châ'rā) *vi* to bloom
sbocco (zbōk'kō) *m* outlet
sbollire (zbōl·lē'rā) *vi* to stop boiling; *(fig)* to calm down
sbornia (zbôr'nyâ) *f* intoxication
sborsare (zbōr·sâ'rā) *vt* to pay out, lay out
sbottonare (zbōt·tō·nâ'rā) *vt* to unbutton
sbottonarsi (zbōt·tō·nâr'sē) *vi* to open up; *(fig)* to speak freely
sbraitare (zbrâē·tâ'rā) *vi* to shout; to shriek
sbranare (zbrâ·nâ'rā) *vt* to rip to shreds
sbrigare (zbrē·gâ'rā) *vt* to finish off; to hurry up
sbrigarsi (zbrē·gâr'sē) *vr* to rush, hurry up
sbrigativamente (zbrē·gâ·tē·vâ·mān'tā) *adv* promptly, rapidly
sbrigliato (zbrē·lyâ'tō) *a* unbridled, untrammeled
sbrinatore (zbrē·nâ·tō'rā) *m* defroster
sbrogliare (zbrō·lyâ'rā) *vt* to unravel; to untangle; to clear away
sbrogliarsi (zbrō·lyâr'sē) *vr* to rid oneself of; to untangle oneself
sbronzo (zbrōn'dzō) *a (sl)* drunk
sbucare (zbū·kâ'rā) *vi* to come out
sbucciare (zbū·châ'rā) *vt* to peel
sbuffare (zbūf·fâ'rā) *vi* to pant; to puff
scabbia (skâb'byâ) *f* scabies; mange
scabroso (skâ·brō'zō) *a* rugged; hard; complicated
scacchi (skâk'kē) *mpl* chess; **a —** checkered
scacchiera (skâk·kyā'râ) *f* chessboard
scacciare (skâ·châ'rā) *vt* to drive out, eject; to disperse, scatter
scacco (skâk'kō) *m* square; chessboard; **subire uno —** to suffer a defeat; **— matto** checkmate
scadente (skâ·dān'tā) *a* of poor quality, inferior
scadenza (skâ·dān'tsâ) *f* expiration
scadere * (skâ·dā'rā) *vi* to fall due
scaduto (skâ·dū'tō) *a* expired, run out
scafandro (skâ·fân'drō) *m* deep-sea diving
scaffale (skâf·fâ'lā) *m* shelf
scafo (skâ'fō) *m* hull of a ship
scaglia (skâ'lyâ) *f* scale *(fish)*; flake; shell *(tortoise)*; spangle; chip
scagliare (skâ·lyâ'rā) *vt* to hurl

scagliarsi (skâ·lyâr'sē) *vr* to hurl oneself at, rush at
scagliola (skâ·lyō'lâ) *f* plaster of Paris
scala (skâ'lâ) *f* stairs, ladder; **–re** (skâ·lâ'rā) *vt* to scale down, reduce; to climb, ascend; **–re** *a* graduated
scalcinato (skâl·chē·nâ'tō) *a (fig)* seedy, shabby; run-down
scaldabagno (skâl·dâ·bâ'nyō) *m* water heater
scaldare (skâl·dâ'rā) *vt* to warm up, heat
scaldarsi (skâl·dâr'sē) *vr* to warm up; to get roiled up
scalea (skâ·lā'â) *f* stairway
scalfittura (skâl·fēt·tū'râ) *f* scratch, scrape
scalinata (skâ·lē·nâ'tâ) *f* stairway
scalino (skâ·lē'nō) *m* step
scalmanato (skâl·mâ·nâ'tō) *a* excited, upset
scalo (skâ'lō) *m* port of call; — **merci** freight yard; **senza** — nonstop
scalogna (skâ·lō'nyâ) *f* jinx, whammy
scalpello (skâl·pāl'lō) *m* chisel; *(med)* scalpel
scaltrezza (skâl·trā'tsâ) *f* sharpness, artfulness
scaltro (skâl'trō) *a* shrewd
scalzo (skâl'tsō) *a* barefooted
scambiare (skâm·byâ'rā) *vt* to take for, exchange
scambio (skâm'byō) *m* exchange; *(com)* trade
scampagnata (skâm·pâ·nyâ'tâ) *f* picnic
scampare (skâm·pâ'rā) *vt&i* to avoid; to escape; to get out of
scampo (skâm'pō) *m* escape; prawn
scampolo (skâm'pō·lō) *m* remnant; mill end
scanalatura (skâ·nâ·lâ·tū'râ) *f* rabbet *(carpentry)*; channeling
scandaglio (skân·dâ'lyō) *m (naut)* sounding; sounding line
scandalistico (skân·dâ·lē'stē·kō) *a* sensational
scandalizzare (skân·dâ·lē·dzâ'rā) *vt* to scandalize
scandalizzarsi (skân·dâ·lē·dzâr'sē) *vr* to be scandalized
scandalo (skân'dâ·lō) *m* scandal; **pietra dello** — stumbling block; **–so** (skân·dâ·lō'zō) *a* shocking; libelous
Scandinavia (skân·dē·nâ'vyâ) *f* Scandinavia
scandinavo (skân·dē'nâ·vō) *a* Scandinavian
scannare (skân·nâ'rā) *vt* to butcher
scansafatiche (skân·sâ·fâ·tē'kā) *m* loafer, ne'er-do-well
scansare (skân·sâ'rā) *vt* to dodge; to shun; to avoid
scansarsi (skân·sâr'sē) *vr* to dodge; to step aside, get out of the way
scansia (skân·sē'â) *f* shelf; bookcase
scanso (skân'sō) *m* avoidance; **a — di malintesi** in order to avoid misunderstandings
scantinato (skân·tē·nâ'tō) *m* basement
scanzonato (skân·tsō·nâ'tō) *a* free and easy, devil-may-care; frisky
scapaccione (skâ·pâ·chō'nā) *m* cuff, slap
scapestrato (skâ·pā·strâ'tō) *m* rake; — *a* dissolute
scapigliato (skâ·pē·lyâ'tō) *a* disheveled
scapito (skâ'pē·tō) *m* detriment
scapola (skâ'pō·lâ) *f* shoulder blade; scapula
scapolo (skâ'pō·lō) *m* bachelor
scappamento (skâp·pâ·mān'tō) *m* gas escape; *(mech)* exhaust
scappare (skâp·pâ'rā) *vi* to flee; to escape; **lasciarsi — l'occasione** to miss one's chance; **lasciarsi — la parola** to let a word slip, forget oneself
scappata (skâp·pâ'tâ) *f* escapade; excursion
scappatoia (skâp·pâ·tô'yâ) *f* means of escaping; loophole
scarabocchiare (skâ·râ·bōk·kyâ'rā) *vt&i* to scrawl
scarabocchio (skâ·râ·bôk'kyō) *m* blot; scribble, scrawl
scarafaggio (skâ·râ·fâj'jō) *m* bug; cockroach
scaramuccia (skâ·râ·mū'châ) *f* skirmish
scaraventare (skâ·râ·vān·tâ'rā) *vt* to hurl, throw
scaraventarsi (skâ·râ·vān·târ'sē) *vr* to throw oneself
scarcerare (skâr·chā·râ'rā) *vt* to release from prison
scaricare (skâ·rē·kâ'rā) *vt* to unload; to discharge
scaricarsi (skâ·rē·kâr'sē) *vr* to run down *(timepiece)*; to relieve oneself; to empty into
scaricatore (skâ·rē·kâ·tō'rā) *m* stevedore
scarico (skâ'rē·kō) *m* discharge; — *a* discharged; not loaded; **turbo di** — exhaust pipe; **a — di coscienza** in order to relieve one's mind, to ease one's conscience
scarlattina (skâr·lât·tē'nâ) *f* scarlet fever
scarno (skâr'nō) *a* emaciated
scarola (skâ·rō'lâ) *f* escarole
scarpa (skâr'pâ) *f* shoe
scarseggiare (skâr·sāj·jâ'rā) *vi* to be scarce; to be short in supply
scarsità (skâr·sē·tâ') *f* scarcity, dearth
scarso (skâr'sō) *a* scarce, short
scarto (skâr'tō) *m* rejected goods; dodge, side movement
scassinare (skâs·sē·nâ'rā) *vt* to break into
scassinatore (skâs·sē·nâ·tō'rā) *m* burglar
scasso (skâs'sō) *m* housebreaking; burglary
scatenare (skâ·tā·nâ'rā) *vt* to unchain; *(fig)* to cause
scatenarsi (skâ·tā·nâr'sē) *vr* to break loose; *(fig)* to fly into a rage
scatola (skâ'tō·lâ) *f* box; **in** — canned; **–me** (skâ·tō·lâ'mā) *m* canned goods
scattare (skât·tâ'rā) *vi* to spring up; *(photo)* to click *(shutter)*
scatto (skât'tō) *m* outburst; click; spring lock
scaturire (skâ·tū·rē'rā) *vi* to spring, gush up
scavare (skâ·vâ'rā) *vt* to dig up, uncover

scavatrice (skâ·vâ·trē'chā) *f* excavating machine
scavo (skâ'vō) *m* excavation
scegliere * (she'lyā·rā) *vt* to choose
scelleratezza (shāl·lā·râ·tā'tsâ) *f* wickedness, evil
scellerato (shāl·lā·râ'tō) *a* wicked; — *m* miscreant
scelta (shāl'tâ) *f* choice, selection
scelto (shāl'tō) *a* chosen; choice, select
scemenza (shā·mān'tsâ) *f* foolishness
scemo (shā'mō) *a* foolish; stupid; — *m* fool
scempiaggine (shām·pyâj'jē·nā) *f* foolishness
scempio (shem'pyō) *m* devastation; confusion; massacre, slaughter
scena (shā'nâ) *f* scene; stage; **–rio** (shā·nâ'ryō) *m* scenario; *(theat)* set; **–rista** (shā·nâ·rē'stâ) *m* scriptwriter; **–ta** (shā·nâ'tâ) *f* row, scene
scendere * (shen'dā·rā) *vi* to get down, go down, come down
sceneggiatore (shā·nāj·jâ·tō'rā) *m* scenarist, movie writer; TV writer
scenografia (shā·nō·grâ·fē'â) *f* scene painting; scenography
scenografo (shā·nô'grâ·fō) *m* scene painter
scervellarsi (shār·vāl·lâr'sē) *vr* to cudgel one's brains, ponder deeply
scettro (shāt'trō) *m* scepter
scheda (skā'dâ) *f* index card; ballot; **–re** (skā·dâ'rā) *vt* to classify; **–rio** (skā·dâ'ryō) *m* card file
schedina (skā·dē'nâ) *f* index card; — **del totocalcio** football pool ticket
scheggia (skej'jâ) *f* chip; splinter
scheletro (ske'lā·trō) *m* skeleton
schema (skā'mâ) *m* outline, sketch; plan, blueprint
schematicamente (skā·mâ·tē·kâ·mān'tā) *adv* schematically
scherma (skār'mâ) *f* fencing
schermitore (skār·mē·tō'rā) *m* fencer
schermo (skār'mō) *m* screen *(TV, movies)*; defense, protection
schernire (skār·nē'rā) *vt* to mock, make fun of
scherno (skār'nō) *m* ridicule; contempt; sneering
scherzare (skār·tsâ'rā) *vi* to joke; to trifle
scherzo (skār'tsō) *m* joke; trick *(mischief)*; **–so** (skār·tsō'zō) *a* playful; **–samente** (skār·tsō·zâ·mān'tā) *adv* jokingly, playfully
schiaccianoci (skyâ·châ·nō'chē) *m* nutcracker
schiacciante (skyâ·chân'tā) *a* overwhelming, decisive
schiacciare (skyâ·châ'rā) *vt* to crush; to put down, quell
schiacciarsi (skyâ·châr'sē) *vr* to be crushed; to be squashed; to be suppressed
schiaffo (skyâf'fō) *m* slap
schiamazzare (skyâ·mâ·tsâ'rā) *vi* to howl, clamor; to squawk
schiamazzo (skyâ·mâ'tsō) *m* howling; shouting; clamor
schianto (skyân'tō) *m* clap, crash; noise; *(fig)* pang; **di** — suddenly
schiarire (skyâ·rē'rā) *vt* to clear up; — *vi* to fade
schiarirsi (skyâ·rēr'sē) *vr* to grow light; to become clear, lighten
schiavista (skyâ·vē'stâ) *m* slave trader; **stato** — slave state
schiavitù (skyâ·vē·tū') *f* slavery
schiavo (skyâ'vō) *m&a* slave
schiena (skyā'nâ) *f* *(anat)* back; **–le** (skyā·nâ'lā) *m* back *(chair)*
schiera (skyā'râ) *f* band, group; *(mil)* rank; **–rsi** (skyā·râr'sē) *vr* *(mil)* to draw up
schiettamente (skyāt·tâ·mān'tā) *adv* straightforwardly, frankly
schiettezza (skyāt·tā'tsâ) *f* openness; frankness
schietto (skyāt'tō) *a* sincere, frank
schifare (skē·fâ'rā) *vt* to loathe
schifiltoso (skē·fēl·tō'zō) *a* fastidious
schifo (skē'fō) *m* disgust; **fare** — **a** to make sick, be repugnant to; **–so** (skē·fō'zō) *a* disgusting
schioppo (skyōp'pō) *m* shotgun
schiuma (skyū'mâ) *f* froth, foam
schizzare (skē·tsâ'rā) *vt&i* to splash; to sketch
schizzinoso (skē·tsē·nō'zō) *a* snooty *(coll)*; fastidious; hypercritical
schizzo (skē'tsō) *m* sketch; splash; squirt
sci (shē) *m* ski; — **nautico** water ski; **fare il** — **nautico** to water ski
scia (shē'â) *f* wake; track
sciabola (shâ'bō·lâ) *f* saber
sciacquare (shâk·kwâ'rā) *vt* to rinse
sciacquarsi (shâk·kwâr'sē) *vr* to rinse out one's mouth
sciagura (shâ·gū'râ) *f* misfortune; accident; adversity; **–to** (shâ·gū·râ'tō) *m* wretch; **–to** *a* unhappy; unfortunate
scialacquare (shâ·lâk·kwâ'rā) *vt* to squander
scialbo (shâl'bō) *a* pallid, drab; vague
scialle (shâl'lā) *m* shawl
scialuppa (shâ·lūp'pâ) *f* launch
sciamare (shâ·mâ'rā) *vi* to swarm; to crowd together
sciame (shâ'mā) *m* swarm
sciampagna (shâm·pâ'nyâ) *f* champagne
sciampagnino (shâm·pâ·nyē'nō) *m* soft drink
sciampagnone (shâm·pâ·nyō'nā) *m* playboy
sciancato (shân·kâ'tō) *m* cripple; — *a* lame, crippled
sciare (shâ'rā) *vi* to ski
sciarada (shâ·râ'dâ) *f* charade
sciarpa (shâr'pâ) *f* scarf, muffler; sash
sciatore (shâ·tō'rā) *m* skier
sciatto (shât'tō) *a* slovenly, untidy, unkempt
scibile (shē'bē·lā) *m* knowledge, information
scientificamente (shān·tē·fē·kâ·mān'tā) *adv* scientifically
scientifico (shān·tē'fē·kō) *a* scientific
scienza (shān'tsâ) *f* science
scienziato (shān·tsyâ'tō) *m* scientist

scilinguagnolo (shē·lēn·gwâ'nyō·lō) *m* *(anat)* tongue ligament; *(coll)* **aver lo — sciolto** to have a gift for gab; to be a great talker
scimmia (shēm'myâ) *f* monkey, ape
scimmiottare (shēm·myōt·tâ'rā) *vt&i* to imitate; to mimic; to parody
scimunito (shē·mū·nē'tō) *a* foolish, moronic; — *m* moron, fool
scindere * (shēn'dā·rā) *vt* to split
scintilla (shēn·tēl'lâ) *f* sparkle; **–nte** (shēn·tēl·lân'tā) *a* sparkling; **–re** (shēn·tēl·lâ'rā) *vi* to sparkle
scioccamente (shōk·kâ·mān'tā) *adv* foolishly, nonsensically
sciocchezza (shōk·kā'tsâ) *f* nonsense; trifle
sciocco (shōk'kō) *a* foolish, silly; nonsensical
sciogliere * (shô'lyā·rā) *vt* to unite; to solve; to free; — **la lingua** to become talkative; — **un voto** to fulfill a vow; — **un dubbio** to settle a doubt; — **un contratto** to annul a contract
sciogliersi * (shô'lyār·sē) *vr* to dissolve, melt; to get loose
scioglilingua (shō·lyē·lēn'gwâ) *m* tongue-twister
sciolto (shōl'tō) *a* loose; unrestrained; free
scioperante (shō·pā·rân'tā) *m* striker *(labor)*; — *a* striking
scioperare (shō·pā·râ'rā) *vi* to go on strike
scioperato (shō·pā·râ'tō) *a&m* ne'er-do-well
sciopero (shô'pā·rō) *m* strike
sciovia (shō·vē'â) *f* ski lift
sciovinismo (shō·vē·nē'zmō) *m* chauvinism
scipito (shē·pē'tō) *a* dull; tasteless
scirocco (shē·rōk'kō) *m* hot, dry wind; sirocco
sciroppo (shē·rōp'pō) *m* syrup
scissione (shēs·syō'nā) *f* fission; split
sciupare (shū·pâ'rā) *vt* to spoil; to waste
sciuparsi (shū·pâr'sē) *vr* to spoil, get spoiled
sciupone (shū·pō'nā) *m* squanderer, spendthrift, wastrel
scivolare (shē·vō·lâ'rā) *vi* to slide; to slip
scivolone (shē·vō·lō'nā) *m* slip *(footing)*
scocciante (skō·chân'tā) *a* tiresome, annoying
scocciare (skō·châ'rā) *vt* *(coll)* to bother, annoy; to shell *(nut)*; to break *(egg)*
scocciarsi (skō·châr'sē) *vr* to become bored; to be annoyed
scodella (skō·dāl'lâ) *f* soup plate; bowl: **–re** (skō·dāl·lâ'rā) *vt* to dish up, serve
scodinzolare (skō·dēn·tsō·lâ'rā) *vi* to wag its tail
scogliera (skō·lyā'râ) *f* cliff
scoglio (skô'lyō) *m* rock; *(fig)* problem
scoiattolo (skō·yât'tō·lō) *m* squirrel
scolare (skō·lâ'rā) *vt&i* to drain
scolaresca (skō·lâ·rā'skâ) *f* school children
scolastico (skō·lâ'stē·kō) *a* scholastic; **anno** — school year
scolaro (skō·lâ'rō) *m* pupil
scollacciato (skōl·lâ·châ'tō) *a* low-necked, décolleté; suggestive, risqué
scollatura (skōl·lâ·tū'râ) *f* ungluing; decolletage
scolo (skō'lō) *m* drainpipe; drain; drainage; *(sl)* gonorrhea
scolorina (skō·lō·rē'nâ) *f* ink eradicator
scolorire (skō·lō·rē'rā) *vi* to fade
scolorirsi (skō·lō·rēr'sē) *vr* to get pale; to lose one's color
scolorito (skō·lō·rē'tō) *a* discolored
scolpire (skōl·pē'rā) *vt* to sculpture, sculpt
scombro (skōm'brō) *m* mackerel
scombussolare (skōm·būs·sō·lâ'rā) *vt* to upset; to confuse, disorganize
scommessa (skōm·mās'sâ) *f* wager, bet
scommettere * (skōm·met'tā·rā) *vt* to bet
scomodare (skō·mō·dâ'rā) *vt* to disturb; to put out
scomodarsi (skō·mō·dâr'sē) *vr* to disturb oneself; to put oneself out
scomodo (skô'mō·dō) *a* uncomfortable, inconvenient; — *m* discomfort
scomparire * (skōm·pâ·rē'rā) *vi* to disappear
scomparsa (skōm·pâr'sâ) *f* disappearance
scompartimento (skōm·pâr·tē·mān'tō) *m* compartment; section
scompigliare (skōm·pē·lyâ'rā) *vt* to disarrange, upset; to disorganize
scompiglio (skōm·pē'lyō) *m* to-do *(coll)*; bustle; disorder
scomporre * (skōm·pōr'rā) *vt* to take apart; *(fig)* to ruffle, upset; *(math)* to resolve
scomporsi * (skōm·pōr'sē) *vr* to get mad, lose one's temper; to become decomposed, decompose
scomunica (skō·mū'nē·kâ) *f* excommunication
sconcertare (skōn·chār·tâ'rā) *vt* to baffle, disconcert, upset
sconcertante (skōn·chār·tân'tā) *a* baffling, upsetting
sconcezza (skōn·chā'tsâ) *f* immodesty; obscenity
sconcio (skôn'chō) *a* indecent; — *m* shame; indecency
sconclusionato (skōn·klū·zyō·nâ'tō) *a* disjointed; rambling; meaningless
sconfiggere * (skōn·fēj'jā·rā) *vt* to defeat
sconfinato (skōn·fē·nâ'tō) *a* limitless, boundless
sconfitta (skōn·fēt'tâ) *f* defeat
sconforto (skōn·fōr'tō) *m* discomfort, distress; depression
scongiurare (skōn·jū·râ'rā) *vt* to implore; to plead
scongiuro (skōn·jū'rō) *m* plea; exorcism
sconnesso (skōn·nās'sō) *a* disconnected
sconosciuto (skō·nō·shū'tō) *a* unknown; — *m* stranger
sconquassare (skōn·kwâs·sâ'rā) *vt* to wreck; to smash
sconquasso (skōn·kwâs'sō) *m* ruin; smash
sconsigliare (skōn·sē·lyâ'rā) *vt* to discourage; to convince against
sconsolato (skōn·sō·lâ'tō) *a* disconsolate, grieving
scontare (skōn·tâ'rā) *vt* to pay for, do

penance for; *(com)* to discount
scontento (skōn·tān'tō) *a* dissatisfied; — *m* discontent
sconto (skōn'tō) *m* discount; allowance
scontrino (skōn·trē'nō) *m* check, ticket
scontro (skōn'trō) *m* crash, collision; *(sport)* bout, match
scontroso (skōn·trō'zō) *a* touchy, hypersensitive
sconvolgere (skōn·vôl'jā·rā) *vt* to throw into disorder; to upset, turn over
sconvolto (skōn·vōl'tō) *a* troubled, upset
scopa (skō'pâ) *f* broom; **–re** (skō·pâ'rā) *vt&i* to sweep
scoperta (skō·pār'tâ) *f* discovery
scoperto (skō·pār'tō) *a* uncovered; bare
scopo (skō'pō) *m* purpose, aim, objective
scoppiare (skōp·pyâ'rā) *vi* to burst; to break out; — **dall'invidia** to turn green with envy; — **in pianto** to burst into tears
scoppio (skôp'pyō) *m* explosion; **motore a** — internal combustion engine
scoprire * (skō·prē'rā) *vt* to discover; to uncover
scoprirsi * (skō·prēr'sē) *vr* to make one's purpose known; *(coll)* to tip one's hat
scoraggiamento (skō·râj·jâ·mān'tō) *m* discouragement, dejection
scoraggiare (skō·râj·jâ'rā) *vt* to discourage, deject
scoraggiarsi (skō·râj·jâr'sē) *vr* to lose heart, become downhearted
scorciatoia (skōr·châ·tô'yâ) *f* shortcut
scordare (skōr·dâ'rā) *vt* to put out of tune; to forget
scordarsi (skōr·dâr'sē) *vr* to forget; to get out of tune
scorgere * (skôr'jā·rā) *vt* to perceive, observe, see
scoria (skô'ryâ) *f* scum; dross
scorno (skōr'nō) *m* disgrace, shame
scorpacciata (skōr·pâ·châ'tâ) *f* bellyful
scorrere * (skôr'rā·rā) *vt* to scan; — *vi* to pass, go by *(time)*; to flow by, run by
scorrettamente (skōr·rāt·tâ·mān'tā) *adv* unsuitably, incorrectly
scorrettezza (skōr·rāt·tā'tsâ) *f* misbehavior; faultiness
scorretto (skōr·rāt'tō) *a* incorrect, faulty
scorrevole (skōr·re'vō·lā) *a* sliding; fluent
scorrimento (skōr·rē·mān'tō) *m* sliding; **porta a** — sliding door
scorso (skōr'sō) *a* last; past
scorsoio (skōr·sô'yō) *a* slipping, running; **nodo** — slipknot
scorta (skōr'tâ) *f* escort; stock, reserve supply
scortese (skōr·tā'zā) *a* rude, ill-mannered
scorticare (skōr·tē·kâ'rā) *vt* to skin; *(fig)* to fleece
scorza (skōr'tsâ) *f* bark; *(fig)* outer surface
scosceso (skō·shā'zō) *a* sheer, steep
scossa (skōs'sâ) *f* shake; shock; **a scosse** in an irregular way, by fits and starts
scostare (skō·stâ'rā) *vt* to remove, take away
scostarsi (skō·stâr'sē) *vr* to step aside; to move away
scostumato (skō·stū·mâ'tō) *a* dissolute; ill-mannered
scotennare (skō·tān·nâ'rā) *vt* to scalp; to skin
scottare (skōt·tâ'rā) *vt&i* to burn; to sting; to scald; to be very hot
scottarsi (skōt·târ'sē) *vr* to get burned; to scald oneself
scottatura (skōt·tâ·tū'râ) *f* burn
Scozia (skô'tsyâ) *f* Scotland
scozzese (skō·tsā'zā) *a* Scotch; — *m* Scot
screditato (skrā·dē·tâ'tō) *a* discredited, disreputed
scremato (skrā·mâ'tō) *a* skimmed
screpolato (skrā·pō·lâ'tō) *a* chapped; cracked, split
screzio (skre'tsyō) *m* spat, difference
scribacchiare (skrē·bâk·kyâ'rā) *vt* to scribble
scricchiolare (skrēk·kyō·lâ'rā) *vi* to creak; to rasp
scricchiolio (skrēk·kyō·lē'ō) *m* rasping; creaking
scrigno (skrē'nyō) *m* jewel case; cashbox
scriteriato (skrē·tā·ryâ'tō) *a* foolish, rash, unwise
scritta (skrēt'tâ) *f* sign; caption; inscription
scritto (skrēt'tō) *a* written; — *m* writing; **–io** (skrēt·tô'yō) *m* desk; **–re** (skrēt·tō'rā) *m*, **scrittrice** (skrēt·trē'chā) *f* writer
scrittura (skrēt·tū'râ) *f* handwriting; *(law)* deed; *(theat)* booking; *(com)* entry; **la Sacra** — the Holy Scriptures; **avere bella** — to have a good handwriting; **–re** (skrēt·tū·râ'rā) *vt (theat)* to book, engage
scrivania (skrē·vâ·nē'â) *f* writing desk
scrivano (skrē·vâ'nō) *m* clerk; transcriber
scrivere * (skrē'vā·rā) *vt&i* to write, write up
scroccare (skrōk·kâ'rā) *vt* to live at another's expense; to sponge *(coll)*
scroccone (skrōk·kō'nā) *m* parasite; sponger *(coll)*
scrofa (skrō'fâ) *f* sow
scroscio (skrô'shō) *m* burst; shower *(rain)*; **piovere a** — to rain cats and dogs *(coll)*
scrupolo (skrū'pō·lō) *m* scruple; **–samente** (skrū·pō·lō·zâ·mān'tā) *adv* scrupulously
scrutatore (skrū·tâ·tō'rā) *m* investigator
scrutinio (skrū·tē'nyō) *m* grade average *(school)*; scrutiny, careful examination
scucire (skū·chē'rā) *vt* to rip, unstitch
scucito (skū·chē'tō) *a* ripped, unsewed
scucitura (skū·chē·tū'râ) *f* ripped seam
scuderia (skū·dā·rē'â) *f* stable
scudiscio (skū·dē'shō) *m* whip, lash
scudo (skū'dō) *m* shield; escutcheon; *(fig)* protection, aegis
sculacciare (skū·lâ·châ'rā) *vt* to spank
sculacciatura (skū·lâ·châ·tū'râ) *f* spanking
sculaccione (skū·lâ·chō'nā) *m* spanking
scultore (skūl·tō'rā) *m* sculptor
scultura (skūl·tū'râ) *f* sculpture
scuola (skwō'lâ) *f* school; — **professionale** vocational school

scuotere * (skwô'tā·rā) *vt* to shake
scuotersi * (skwô'tār·sē) *vr* to bestir oneself; to rouse oneself
scure (skū'rā) *f* hatchet, ax
scuro (skū'rō) *a* dark; swarthy; — *m* obscurity; shading *(art)*
scusa (skū'zâ) *f* excuse; apology; justification; — **magra** poor excuse; **–re** (skū·zâ'rā) *vt* to excuse; to justify
scusarsi (skū·zâr'sē) *vr* to justify oneself; to excuse oneself
sdebitarsi (zdā·bē·târ'sē) *vr* to meet one's obligations; to return a favor
sdegno (zdā'nyō) *m* indignation; **–samente** (zdā·nyō·zâ·mān'tā) *adv* scornfully; haughtily; **–so** (zdā·nyō'zō) *a* haughty, disdainful
sdentato (zdān·tâ'tō) *a* toothless
sdoganare (zdō·gâ·nâ'rā) *vt* to clear through customs
sdolcinato (zdōl·chē·nâ'tō) *a* affected, cloying
sdraiarsi (zdrâ·yâr'sē) *vi* to stretch out; to lie extended
sdraio (zdrâ'yō) *a* reclining, stretched out; **sedia a** — deck chair
sdrucciolare (zdrū·chō·lâ'rā) *vi* to slip
sdrucciolevole (zdrū·chō·le'vō·lā) *a* slippery, slick
sdrucito (zdrū·chē'tō) *a* ripped, torn
se (sā) *conj* if; — **mai** if at all
sè (sā) *pron* herself, himself; itself; oneself; themselves
sebbene (sāb·bā'nā) *conj* although, despite the fact that
seccante (sāk·kân'tā) *a* boresome, tiring
seccare (sāk·kâ'rā) *vt&i* to bother, annoy; to dry; to sere
seccarsi (sāk·kâr'sē) *vr* to wither; *(coll)* to be bored
seccatore (sāk·kâ·tō'rā) *m* pest, bore
seccatura (sāk·kâ·tū'râ) *f* nuisance
secchia (sek'kyâ) *f*, **secchio** (sek'kyō) *m* pail
secco (sāk'kō) *a* dry; sharp, cold
secessione (sā·chās·syō'nā) *f* secession
secolare (sā·kō·lâ'rā) *m* layman; — *a* worldly, secular
secolo (se'kō·lō) *m* century
secondo (sā·kōn'dō) *m&a* second; — *prep* according to
secrezione (sā·krā·tsyō'nā) *f* secretion
sedano (se'dâ·nō) *m* celery
sedare (sā·dâ'rā) *vt* to quell; to appease
sedativo (sā·dâ·tē'vō) *m&a* sedative
sede (sā'dā) *f* see *(eccl)*; main office, home office
sedentario (sā·dān·tâ'ryō) *a* sedentary
sedere * (sā·dā'rā) *vi* to sit; — *m* rump
sedersi * (sā·dār'sē) *vr* to seat oneself
sedia (se'dyâ) *f* chair; — **a rotelle** wheel chair; — **a sdraio** deck chair, chaise longue
sedicenne (sā·dē·chān'nā) *a* sixteen years old
sedicente (sā·dē·chān'tā) *a* self-styled
sedicesimo (sā·dē·che'zē·mō) *a* sixteenth
sedici (se'dē·chē) *a* sixteen
sedile (sā·dē'lā) *m* seat
sedizione (sā·dē·tsyō'nā) *f* mutiny; sedition
seducente (sā·dū·chān'tā) *a* seductive; glamorous, attractive
sedurre * (sā·dūr'rā) *vt* to seduce; to entrance
seduta (sā·dū'tâ) *f* meeting
seduzione (sā·dū·tsyō'nā) *f* seduction; attraction, glamour
sega (sā'gâ) *f* saw; **–re** (sā·gâ'rā) to saw; **–tura** (sā·gâ·tū'râ) *f* sawdust
segale (sā·gâ'lā) *f* rye
segaligno (sā·gâ·lē'nyō) *a* slim, wiry
segnalare (sā·nyâ·lâ'rā) *vt* to indicate, point out
segnalarsi (sā·nyâ·lâr'sē) *vr* to distinguish oneself; to become well known
segnalazione (sā·nyâ·lâ·tsyō'nā) *f* signal; indication
segnale (sā·nyâ'lā) *m* signal; — **acustico** auto horn
segnalibro (sā·nyâ·lē'brō) *m* bookmark
segnare (sā·nyâ'rā) *vt* to mark; to note, point to
segno (sā'nyō) *m* sign; token; **cogliere il** — to hit the mark; **in — d'affetto** as a token of affection; **per filo e per** — with all the details, completely
segregare (sā·grā·gâ'rā) *vt* to segregate; to keep isolated
segregarsi (sā·grā·gâr'sē) *vr* to isolate oneself; to live in seclusion
segregazione (sā·grā·gâ·tsyō'nā) *f* segregation; solitary confinement *(prison)*
segretaria (sā·grā·tâ'ryâ) *f*, **segretario** (sā·grā·tâ'ryō) *m* secretary
segreteria (sā·grā·tā·rē'â) *f* secretariat; central office
segretezza (sā·grā·tā'tsâ) *f* secrecy, privacy
segreto (sā·grā'tō) *m* privacy, secret; — *a* private, secret
seguace (sā·gwâ'chā) *m* follower
seguente (sā·gwān'tā) *a* following, coming
segugio (sā·gū'jō) *m* bloodhound
seguire (sā·gwē'rā) *vt* to follow; to continue; **far** — to forward *(mail)*
seguito (se'gwē·tō) *m* continuation; following; party; retinue
sei (sā'ē) *a* six
seicento (sāē·chān'tō) *a* six hundred; **il S–** the seventeenth century
seimila (sāē·mē'lâ) *a* six thousand
selettore (sā·lāt·tō'rā) *m* selector
selezionare (sā·lā·tsyō·nâ'rā) *vt* to select; to make a selection of
selezione (sā·lā·tsyō'nā) *f* selection; digest
sella (sāl'lâ) *f* saddle
selvaggina (sāl·vâj·jē'nâ) *f* game
selvaggio (sāl·vâj'jō) *a&m* savage
selvatico (sāl·vâ'tē·kō) *a* wild
selz (sālts) *f* soda water; seltzer
semaforo (sā·mâ'fō·rō) *m* traffic light
sembrare (sām·brâ'râ) *vt&i* to seem; to appear to be
seme (sā'mā) *m* seed; cause, origin
semestre (sā·mā'strā) *m* six months; semester

semina (se′mē·nâ) *f* seed; sowing; **–re** (sā·mē·nâ′rā) *vt* to sow; **–tore** (sā·mē·nâ·tō′rā) *m* sower; **–trice** (sā·mē·nâ·trē′chā) *f* mechanical seeder
semita (sā·mē′tâ) *m* Semite
semola (se′mō·lâ) *f* fine flour; bran; freckle; **pan di** — white bread
semolino (sā·mō·lē′nō) *m* semolina
semovente (sā·mō·vān′tā) *a* self-propelled
semplice (sem′plē·chā) *a* simple; plain; easy; **–mente** (sām·plē·chā·mān′tā) *adv* plainly, obviously; easily
semplicione (sām·plē·chō′nā), **sempliciotto** (sām·plē·chōt′tō) *m* simpleton
semplicità (sām·plē·chē·tâ′) *f* simplicity; ease
sempre (sām′prā) *adv* ever; always; **–chè** (sām·prā·kā′) *conj* with the condition that; **–verde** (sām·prā·vār′dā) *m&a* evergreen
senape (se′nâ·pā) *f* mustard
senato (sā·nâ′tō) *m* senate; **–re** (sā·nâ·tō′rā) *m* senator
senilità (sā·nē·lē·tâ′) *f* senility
senno (sān′nō) *m* wisdom; common sense
seno (sā′nō) *m* breast; bay; *(math)* sine
senonchè (sā·nōn·kā′) *adv* otherwise, if not; — *conj* except for the fact that; unless
sensale (sān·sâ′lā) *m* middleman; broker; agent
sensato (sān·sâ′tō) *a* sensible, reasonable; wise; rational
sensazionale (sān·sā·tsyō·nâ′lā) *a* sensational; moving, stirring
sensazione (sān·sâ·tsyō′nā) *f* sensation
sensibile (sān·sē′bē·lā) *a* sensitive
sensibilità (sān·sē·bē·lē·tâ′) *f* sensitivity; susceptibility
senso (sān′sō) *m* sense; meaning; direction; way; — **unico** one way; — **vietato** do not enter *(street)*; **buon** — common sense; **in** — **contrario** in the opposite way; to the contrary
sensuale (sān·swâ′lā) *a* sensual
sentenza (sān·tān′tsâ) *f* sentence; verdict
sentiero (sān·tyā′rō) *m* path, trail
sentimentale (sān·tē·mān·tâ′lā) *a* sentimental; romantic
sentimento (sān·tē·mān′tō) *m* feeling; viewpoint
sentinella (sān·tē·nāl′lâ) *f* sentinel
sentire (sān·tē′rā) *vt* to hear; to feel
sentirsi (sān·tēr′sē) *vr* to feel
sentitamente (sān·tē·tâ·mān′tā) *adv* sincerely, cordially, deeply
sentore (sān·tō′rā) *m* feeling, premonition, forewarning
senza (sān′tsâ) *prep* without
senzatetto (sān·tsâ·tāt′tō) *m* homeless person
separare (sā·pâ·râ′rā) *vt* to separate
separarsi (sā·pâ·râr′sē) *vr* to part, diverge
separazione (sā·pâ·râ·tsyō′nā) *f* separation
sepolcro (sā·pōl′krō) *m* tomb; burial vault
sepolto (sā·pōl′tō) *a* buried
sepoltura (sā·pōl·tū′râ) *f* burial
seppellire (sāp·pāl·lē′rā) *vt* to bury
sequenza (sā·kwān′tsâ) *f* sequence
sequestrare (sā·kwā·strâ′rā) *vt* to attach, seize; to seclude, keep hidden
sequestro (sā·kwā′strō) *m* attachment, confiscating; — **giudiziale** distraint; — **di stipendio** attachment of salary
sera (sā′râ) *f* evening; **verso** — at dusk; **di** — at night; **–le** (sā·râ′lā) *a* evening; **–ta** (sā·râ′tâ) *f* evening; *(theat)* evening performance
serbare (sār·bâ′rā) *vt* to keep, reserve
serbarsi (sār·bâr′sē) *vr* to keep for oneself; to take care of
serbatoio (sār·bâ·tô′yō) *m* tank; cistern, storage tank
serenata (sā·rā·nâ′tâ) *f* serenade
serenità (sā·rā·nē·tâ′) *f* calm; serenity
sereno (sā·rā′nō) *a* serene; clear, cloudless; — *m* cloudless sky
sergente (sār·jān′tā) *m* sargeant
seriamente (sā·ryâ·mān′tā) *adv* solemnly; seriously
serie (se′ryā) *f* series; **fuori** — custom-built; **produzione in** — **massa** mass production
serietà (sā·ryā·tâ′) *f* seriousness
serio (se′ryō) *a* serious; responsible; **sul** — seriously, earnestly
sermone (sār·mō′nā) *m* sermon
sermoneggiare (sār·mō·nāj·jâ′rā) *vi* to harangue, lecture
serpe (sār′pā) *m* snake; **–ggiare** (sār·pāj·jâ′rā) *vi* to wander, meander; **–ntino** (sār·pān·tē′nō) *a* snaky; **–ntino** *m* coil
serpente (sār·pān′tā) *m* snake, serpent
serra (sār′râ) *f* hothouse; **–glio** (sār·râ′lyō) *m* menagerie; **–nda** (sār·rân′dâ) *f* rolling shutter; **–re** (sār·râ′rā) *vt* to lock; to close; to squeeze; to close up *(ranks)*; **–ta** (sār·râ′tâ) *f* lockout; **–tura** (sār·râ·tū′râ) *f* lock; **–tura di sicurezza** safety lock
serva (sār′vâ) *f* maid
servilismo (sār·vē·lē′zmō) *m* fawning; servility
servire (sār·vē′rā) *vt&i* to serve
servirsi (sār·vēr′sē) *vr* to make use of; to help oneself *(food)*
servitore (sār·vē·tō′rā) *m* servant
servitù (sār·vē·tū′) *f* servitude; bondage; servants of a home as a group
servizievole (sār·vē·tsye′vō·lā) *a* convenient; serviceable; helpful
servizio (sār·vē′tsyō) *m* service; **mezzo** — part-time service; **donna di** — maid
servo (sār′vō) *m* servant; — *a* servile; **–freno** (sār·vō·frā′nō) *m* hydraulic brake booster; **–sterzo** (sār·vō·stār′tsō) *m* hydraulic steering
sessagenario (sās·sâ·jā·nâ′ryō) *a&m* sexagenarian
sessagesima (sās·sâ·je′zē·mâ) *f* *(eccl)* Sexagesima
sessanta (sās·sân′tâ) *a* sixty
sessantesimo (sās·sân·te′zē·mō) *a* sixtieth
sessione (sās·syō′nā) *f* meeting; session
sesso (sās′sō) *m* sex
sessuale (sās·swâ′lā) *a* sexual
sestetto (sā·stāt′tō) *m* sextet

sesto (sā'stō) *a* sixth
seta (sā'tâ) *f* silk
setaccio (sā·tâ'chō) *m* sieve; crib
sete (sā'tā) *f* thirst; **aver —** to be thirsty
setificio (sā·tē·fē'chō) *m* silk mill
setola (se'tō·lâ) *f* bristle
setta (sāt'tâ) *f* sect
settanta (sāt·tân'tâ) *a* seventy
settantesimo (sāt·tân·te'zē·mō) *a* seventieth
sette (sāt'tā) *a* seven
settecento (sāt·tā·chān'tō) *a* seven hundred; **il S—** the eighteenth century
settemila (sāt·tā·mē'lâ) *a* seven thousand
settembre (sāt·tām'brā) *m* September
settennale (sāt·tān·nâ'lā) *a* septennial
settentrionale (sāt·tān·tryō·nâ'lā) *a* northern
settentrione (sāt·tān·tryō'nā) *m* north
settenne (sāt·tān'nā) *a* seven years old
settimana (sāt·tē·mâ'nâ) *f* week; **–le** (sāt·tē·mâ·nâ'lā) *a&m* weekly
settimo (set'tē·mō) *a* seventh
settore (sāt·tō'rā) *m* department, field, area
settuagenario (sāt·twâ·jā·nâ'ryō) *a&m* septuagenarian
severamente (sā·vā·râ·mān'tā) *adv* severely; with austerity
severità (sā·vā·rē·tâ') *f* strictness, severity
severo (sā·vā'rō) *a* strict; severe
seviziare (sā·vē·tsyâ'rā) *vt* to torture; to mistreat, treat badly
sezione (sā·tsyō'nā) *f* section
sfaccendato (sfâ·chān·dâ'tō) *m* loafer, ne'er-do-well; — *a* lazy, idle
sfacciataggine (sfâ·châ·tâj'jē·nā) *f* impudence
sfacciatamente (sfâ·châ·tâ·mān'tā) *adv* impudently
sfacciato (sfâ·châ'tō) *a* brazen; impudent
sfacelo (sfâ·chā'lō) *m* collapse, ruin
sfamare (sfâ·mâ'rā) *vt* to feed; to satisfy one's hunger
sfarzo (sfâr'tsō) *m* pomp
sfasciarsi (sfâ·shâr'sē) *vr* to be smashed up; to collapse; to come apart
sfavillante (sfâ·vēl·lân'tā) *a* scintillating, sparkling
sfavorevole (sfâ·vō·re'vō·lā) *a* unfavorable
sfavorevolmente (sfâ·vō·rā·vōl·mān'tā) *adv* unfavorably
sfegatato (sfā·gâ·tâ'tō) *a* passionate; — *m* hothead
sfera (sfā'râ) *f* sphere; **penna a —** ballpoint pen
sferrare (sfār·râ'rā) *vt* to release; **— uno schiaffo** to slap violently; **— un attacco** *(mil)* to launch an attack
sfiatato (sfyâ·tâ'tō) *a* breathless
sfibrante (sfē·brân'tā) *a* weakening, enervating
sfida (sfē'dâ) *f* defiance; challenge; **–re** (sfē·dâ'ra) *vt* to challenge
sfiducia (sfē·dū'châ) *f* distrust
sfigurato (sfē·gū·râ'tō) *a* disfigured
sfilata (sfē·lâ'tâ) *f* parade; fashion show; procession
sfinge (sfēn'jā) *f* sphinx
sfinimento (sfē·nē·mān'tō) *m* breakdown; faint; exhaustion
sfinirsi (sfē·nēr'sē) *vr* to become run-down
sfinito (sfē·nē'tō) *a* exhausted, run-down
sfiorare (sfyō·râ'rā) *vt* to brush, graze; to go over quickly, scan hurriedly
sfiorire (sfyō·rē'rā) *vi* to wither
sfociare (sfō·châ'rā) *vi* to flow into
sfoderare (sfō·dā·râ'rā) *vt* to unsheath; *(fig)* to vaunt, make a great display of
sfogare (sfō·gâ'rā) *vt* to vent, unleash
sfogarsi (sfō·gâr'sē) *vr* to give vent to one's emotions, vent one's wrath
sfoggio (sfôj'jō) *m* ostentation, parade
sfogliatella (sfō·lyâ·tāl'lâ) *f* puff pastry
sfogo (sfō'gō) *m* vent; relief; *(med)* rash; **dar — a** to give free rein to
sfollagente (sfōl·lâ·jān'tā) *m* billy, night stick
sfollare (sfōl·lâ'rā) *vt* to evacuate; — *vi* to disperse
sfollato (sfōl·lâ'tō) *m* evacuee
sfondare (sfōn·dâ'rā) *vt* to succeed in; to achieve; to break through, break open; to make it *(coll)*
sfondo (sfōn'dō) *m* background
sformato (sfōr·mâ'tō) *a* deformed
sfornare (sfōr·nâ'rā) *vt* to take out of the oven
sfornito (sfōr·nē'tō) *a* devoid; lacking; destitute
sfortuna (sfōr·tū'nâ) *f* bad luck; **–tamente** (sfōr·tū·nâ·tâ·mān'tā) *adv* unluckily; **–to** (sfōr·tū·nâ'tō) *a* unlucky
sforzare (sfōr·tsâ'rā) *vt* to force, make
sforzarsi (sfōr·tsâr'sē) *vr* to strive; to do one's best
sforzo (sfōr'tsō) *m* effort, attempt
sfracellare (sfrâ·chāl·lâ'rā) *vt* to smash, crash
sfracellarsi (sfrâ·chāl·lâr'sē) *vr* to be smashed, dash to pieces
sfrattare (sfrât·tâ'rā) *vt* to evict; to expel, oust
sfratto (sfrât'tō) *m* eviction
sfregio (sfre'jō) *m* scar; gash; *(fig)* insult
sfrenato (sfrā·nâ'tō) *a* dissolute; unrestrained, untrammeled
sfrontato (sfrōn·tâ'tō) *a* brazen
sfruttamento (sfrūt·tâ·mān'tō) *m* exploitation; depletion
sfruttare (sfrūt·tâ'rā) *vt* to deplete; to exploit
sfruttatore (sfrūt·tā·tō'rā) *m* exploiter; **— di donne** pimp, pander
sfuggire (sfūj·jē'rā) *vi* to escape; — *vt* to avoid, evade
sfuggita (sfūj·jē'tâ) *f* **di —** in passing; incidentally, by the way
sfumare (sfū·mâ'rā) *vi* to vanish, disappear; — *vt* *(art)* to shade; *(mus)* to diminish
sfumatura (sfū·mâ·tū'râ) *f* nuance, shade
sfuriata (sfū·ryâ'tâ) *f* tirade, fit of rage
sfuso (sfū'zō) *a* *(com)* in bulk
sgabello (zgâ·bāl'lō) *m* stool
sgambettare (zgâm·bāt·tâ'rā) *vi* to trip along; to toddle

sgambetto (zgâm·bāt'tō) *m* caper, gambol; **fare lo — a** (*fig*) to oust
sganciare (zgân·châ'rā) *vt* to unfasten; to unhook; (*avi*) to drop (*bombs*)
sgangheratamente (zgân·gā·râ·tâ·mān'tā) *adv* grossly, immoderately; **ridere —** to guffaw
sgangherato (zgân·gā·râ'tō) *a* rickety; rude, gross
sgarbato (zgâr·bâ'tō) *a* rude
sgarbo (zgâr'bō) *m* discourtesy, impoliteness
sgelare (zjā·lâ'rā) *vi* to melt, thaw
sgelo (zjā'lō) *m* thaw
sgobbare (zgōb·bâ'rā) *vt* to work doggedly
sgobbone (zgōb·bō'nā) *m* (*coll*) hard worker; grind (*coll*)
sgocciolare (zgō·chō·lâ'rā) *vi* to drip
sgomberare (zgōm·bā·râ'rā), **sgombrare** (zgōm·brâ'rā) *vt* to clear out; to leave, depart from
sgombero (zgôm'bā·rō), **sgombro** (zgōm'-brō) *m* clearance, removal; — *a* clear, free; empty
sgomentare (zgō·mān·tâ'rā) *vt* to upset; to dismay; to frighten
sgomentarsi (zgō·mān·târ'sē) *vr* to lose heart; to become frightened
sgomento (zgō·mān'tō) *m* panic; fear
sgonfiare (zgōn·fyâ'rā) *vt* to deflate
sgonfiarsi (zgōn·fyâr'sē) *vr* to deflate, be deflated; (*med*) to go down (*swelling*)
sgorbio (zgôr'byō) *m* blot; daub; scrawl; stain
sgozzare (zgō·dzâ'rā) *vt* to slaughter; to slit the throat of
sgradevole (zgrâ·de'vō·lā) *a* disagreeable, displeasing
sgradevolmente (zgrâ·dā·vōl·mān'tā) *adv* unpleasantly
sgradito (zgrâ·dē'tō) *a* unwelcome, badly received, unpleasant
sgrammaticato (zgrâm·mâ·tē·kâ'tō) *a* ungrammatical
sgranare (zgrâ·nâ'rā) *vt* to shell, husk; **— gli occhi** (*fig*) to open one's eyes wide
sgranchire (zgrân·kē'rā) *vt* to stretch out, extend
sgranchirsi (zgrân·kēr'sē) *vr* to stretch oneself; **— le gambe** to stretch one's legs; (*fig*) to go for a short walk
sgravare (zgrâ·vâ'rā) *vt* to ease; to unload
sgravarsi (zgrâ·vâr'sē) *vr* to relieve oneself; (*med*) to be delivered; to litter (*animals*); **— la coscienza** (*fig*) to assuage one's conscience
sgraziato (zgrâ·tsyâ'tō) *a* awkward
sgridare (zgrē·dâ'rā) *vt* to reprimand, scold
sgridata (zgrē·dâ'tâ) *f* scolding
sguaiatamente (zgwâ·yâ·tâ·mān'tā) *adv* uncouthly, coarsely
sguaiato (zgwâ·yâ'tō) *a* vulgar, low
sguainare (zgwâē·nâ'rā) *vt* to uncover, unsheathe
squalcito (zgwâl·chē'tō) *a* crumpled, rumpled
sgualdrina (zgwâl·drē'nâ) *f* prostitute
sguardo (zgwâr'dō) *m* glance, look
sguattero (zgwât'tā·rō) *m* dishwasher
sgusciare (zgū·shâ'rā) *vt* to shell; to remove the husk from; — *vi* to slip away unnoticed, make off unobserved
sì (sē) *adv* yes
si (sē) *pron* one, oneself; himself, herself; we, ourselves; each other, themselves
sia (sē'â) *conj* either; or; whether
sicario (sē·kâ'ryō) *m* hired assassin, mercenary
sicchè (sēk·kā') *conj* so that, in order that
siccità (sē·chē·tâ') *f* drought
siccome (sēk·kō'mā) *conj* since, in view of the fact that
Sicilia (sē·chē'lyâ) *f* Sicily
siciliano (sē·chē·lyâ'nō) *a&m* Sicilian
sicuramente (sē·kū·râ·mān'tā) *adv* safely, surely
sicurezza (sē·kū·rā'tsâ) *f* assurance; safety; security; **consiglio di —** security council; **pubblica —** police; **uscita di —** emergency door
sicuro (sē·kū'rō) *a* safe; reliable, sure; — *m* safety; **andare sul —** to play safe; — *adv* surely; **di —** certainly, surely
siderurgico (sē·dā·rūr'jē·kō) *a* iron and steel; **stabilimento —** steel mill
siepe (syā'pā) *f* hedge
siero (syā'rō) *m* serum
sifilide (sē·fē'lē·dā) *f* (*med*) syphilis
sifilitico (sē·fē·lē'tē·kō) *a* (*med*) syphilitic
sigaraio (sē·gâ·râ'yō) *m* cigar maker; cigar dealer
sigaretta (sē·gâ·rāt'tâ) *f* cigarette; **sigarette sfuse** cigarettes sold individually
sigaretto (sē·gâ·rāt'tō) *m* cigarillo, small cigar
sigaro (sē'gâ·rō) *m* cigar
sigillare (sē·jēl·lâ'rā) *vt* to seal
sigillo (sē·jēl'lō) *m* seal
sigla (sē'glâ) *f* monogram; initials; **–re** (sē·glâ'rā) *vt* to initial
significare (sē·nyē·fē·kâ'rā) *vt* to mean
significativamente (sē·nyē·fē·kâ·tē·vâ·mān'tā) *adv* meaningfully; significantly
significativo (sē·nyē·fē·kâ·tē'vō) *a* significant, meaningful
significato (sē·nyē·fē·kâ'tō) *m* meaning, importance
signora (sē·nyō'râ) *f* lady; mistress, Mrs.; madam
signore (sē·nyō'rā) *m* gentleman; lord; Mister, Mr.
signorile (sē·nyō·rē'lā) *a* refined, dignified
signorina (sē·nyō·rē'nâ) *f* young lady; Miss
silenziatore (sē·lān·tsyâ·tō'rā) *m* muffler
silenzio (sē·len'tsyō) *m* silence; **–samente** (sē·lān·tsyō·zâ·mān'tā) *adv* noiselessly; silently; **–so** (sē·lān·tsyō'zō) *a* silent
silice (sē'lē·chā) *f* flint, silica
silicio (sē'lē·chō) *m* silicon
sillaba (sēl'lâ·bâ) *f* syllable; **–re** (sēl·lâ·bâ'rā) *vt* to spell out; to syllable; to syllabify; **–rio** (sēl·lâ·bâ'ryō) *m* primer; speller
silo (sē'lō) *m* silo

silografia (sē·lō·grâ·fē'â) *f* wood engraving
siluetta (sē·lūāt'tâ) *f* silhouette
silurante (sē·lū·rân'tā) *f* torpedo boat, destroyer; **aereo** — (*avi*) torpedo-carrying airplane
silurare (sē·lū·râ'rā) *vt* to torpedo; (*fig*) to dismiss, fire
siluro (sē·lū'rō) *m* torpedo
silvestre (sēl·vā'strā) *a* wild; sylvan; rustic
simbolizzare (sēm·bō·lē·dzâ'rā) *vt&i* to represent; to symbolize
simbolo (sēm'bō·lō) *m* symbol
simile (sē'mē·lā) *a* alike, similar; like
simpatia (sēm·pâ·tē'â) *f* sympathy; liking
simpatico (sēm·pâ'tē·kō) *a* nice; likable
simpatizzante (sēm·pâ·tē·dzân'tā) *a* friendly; pleasant; — *m* advocate
simpatizzare (sēm·pâ·tē·dzâ'rā) *vt&i* to be favorable to; to hit it off with, get along well with
simulare (sē·mū·lâ'rā) *vt&i* to simulate, pretend
simulatore (sē·mū·lâ·tō'rā) *m*, **simulatrice** (sē·mū·lâ·trē'chā) *f* pretender; liar
simulazione (sē·mū·lâ·tsyō'nā) *f* pretense; lying
simultaneamente (sē·mūl·tâ·nā·â·mān'-tā) *adv* simultaneously
simultaneo (sē·mūl·tâ'nā·ō) *a* simultaneous
sinagoga (sē·nâ·gō'gâ) *f* synagogue
sinceramente (sēn·chā·râ·mān'tā) *adv* really; sincerely; with conviction; truthfully speaking
sincerarsi (sēn·chā·râr'sē) *vr* to be convinced; to make sure; to be certain
sincerità (sēn·chā·rē·tâ') *f* honesty; sincerity; conviction
sincero (sēn·chā'rō) *a* sincere, frank, honest
sincronizzare (sēn·krō·nē·dzâ'rā) *vt&i* to synchronize
sindacabile (sēn·dâ·kâ'bē·lā) *a* blameworthy, faulty; controllable; subject to verification
sindacale (sēn·dâ·kâ'lā) *a* pertaining to a trade union, trade-union; syndical
sindacalista (sēn·dâ·kâ·lē'stâ) *m* trade unionist
sindacare (sēn·dâ·kâ'rā) *vt* to verify; to control; to find fault with, blame
sindacato (sēn·dâ·kâ'tō) *m* trade union; syndicate
sindaco (sēn'dâ·kō) *m* mayor; auditor
sinfonia (sēn·fō·nē'â) *f* symphony
singhiozzare (sēn·gyō·tsâ'rā) *vi* to sob
singhiozzo (sēn·gyō'tsō) *m* sob; hiccup
singolare (sēn·gō·lâ'rā) *a* peculiar; odd; strange; (*gram*) singular
sinistra (sē·nē'strâ) *f* left; left hand; **–to** (sē·nē·strâ'tō) *m* accident victim
sinistro (sē·nē'strō) *a* left; sinister, eerie; — *m* accident
sino (sē'nō) *prep* as far as; till; up to; until; **–ra** (sē·nō'râ) *adv* hitherto, as yet, till now
sintetico (sēn·te'tē·kō) *a* synthetic
sintomo (sēn'tō·mō) *m* symptom
sintonizzare (sēn·tō·nē·dzâ'rā) *vt* (*rad*) to tune in
sipario (sē·pâ'ryō) *m* (*theat*) curtain
sirena (sē·rā'nâ) *f* siren
siringa (sē·rēn'gâ) *f* syringe
sistema (sē·stā'mâ) *m* method; system; procedure; **–re** (sē·stā·mâ'rā) *vt* to arrange, organize, set up; **–rsi** (sē·stā·mâr'sē) *vr* to settle, get settled; **–zione** (sē·stā·mâ·tsyō'nā) *f* settlement; arranging; organization
situazione (sē·twâ·tsyō'nā) *f* situation
slacciare (zlâ·châ'rā) *vt* to untie; to undo
slacciarsi (zlâ·châr'sē) *vr* to undo one's buttons; to come undone, become unfastened
slanciare (zlân·châ'rā) *vt* to throw, hurl; to give rise to; to spur on, incite
slanciarsi (zlân·châr'sē) *vr* to throw oneself, rush; to become slender
slanciato (zlân·châ'tō) *a* slim, slender; thrown; incited, spurred on
slancio (zlân'chō) *m* dash; impulse; goad, motivation; **prendere lo** — to start off, rush off; to begin hurriedly; — **di generosità** impulse of generosity; **pieno di** — full of energy, full of vigor
slavo (zlâ'vō) *a* Slavonic, Slavic; — *m* Slav
sleale (zlā·â'lā) *a* disloyal
slegare (zlā·gâ'rā) *vt* to untie
slegarsi (zlā·gâr'sē) *vr* to get loose; to become undone
slegato (zlā·gâ'tō) *a* untied; loose
slitta (zlēt'tâ) *f* sled; toboggan; **–re** (zlēt·tâ'rā) *vi* to skid; to slide
slogare (zlō·gâ'rā) *vt* to sprain; to dislocate
slogarsi (zlō·gâr'sē) *vr* to be dislocated; to be sprained; — **una caviglia** to dislocate one's ankle
slogatura (zlō·gâ·tū'râ) *f* dislocation; sprain
sloggiare (zlōj·jâ'rā) *vt* to evict; to oust; to dislodge
smacchiare (zmâk·kyâ'rā) *vt* to clean; to take out the stains on
smacco (zmâk'kō) *m* disgrace; affront
smagliatura (zmâ·lyâ·tū'râ) *f* ravel; run in one's stocking
smaltare (zmâl·tâ'rā) *vt* to glaze; to enamel
smaltire (zmâl·tē'rā) *vt* to free oneself of, get rid of; to digest; (*com*) to sell out; — **la sbornia** to sleep off a drunk
smalto (zmâl'tō) *m* enamel; — **per le unghie** nail polish
smania (zmâ'nyâ) *f* frenzy, mania; urge; delirium
smarrimento (zmâr·rē·mān'tō) *m* miscarriage of justice; loss, losing; perturbation
smarrire (zmâr·rē'rā) *vt* to lose; to bewilder
smarrirsi (zmâr·rēr'sē) *vr* to become lost
smarrito (zmâr·rē'tō) *a* lost
smemorato (zmā·mō·râ'tō) *a* forgetful; absent-minded
smentire (zmān·tē'rā) *vt* to deny; to give

the lie to; to discredit
smentita (zmān·tē'tâ) *f* disapproval; denial; refutation
smeraldo (zmā·râl'dō) *m* emerald
smerigliato (zmā·rē·lyâ'tō) *a* emery; **vetro —** ground glass
smeriglio (zmā·rē'lyō) *m* emery
smettere * (zmet'tā·rā) *vt&i* to stop, put a stop to
smidollato (zmē·dōl·lâ'tō) *a* pithless, feeble, spineless
smilzo (zmēl'tsō) *a* slender, thin
smistamento (zmē·stâ·mān'tō) *m* assortment, distribution; (*rail*) switching
smisurato (zmē·zū·râ'tō) *a* limitless, immeasurable
smobiliato (zmō·bē·lyâ'tō) *a* unfurnished
smobilitazione (zmō·bē·lē·tâ·tsyō'nā) *f* demobilization
smodatamente (zmō·dâ·tâ·mān'tā) *adv* excessively, immoderately
smoderato (zmō·dā·râ'tō) *a* intemperate, immoderate; overdone
smoking (zmō'kēn) *m* tuxedo
smontare (zmōn·tâ'rā) *vt* to dismantle, take apart; — *vi* to get off
smorfia (zmôr'fyâ) *f* grimace
smorzare (zmōr·tsâ'rā) *vt* to quench; to put out (*light*); to deaden (*sound*); to tone down
smorzarsi (zmōr·tsâr'sē) *vr* to die away, fade away; to go off, go out (*light*)
smunto (zmūn'tō) *a* wan, gaunt, pale
snaturato (znâ·tū·râ'tō) *a* pitiless, unfeeling; unnatural, twisted
snello (znāl'lō) *a* slender; quick, spry
snervante (znār·vân'tā) *a* very tiring, enervating
snobismo (znō·bē'zmō) *m* snobbery
snodato (znō·dâ'tō) *a* articulate, expressive; plastic, adaptable
snudare (znū·dâ'rā) *vt* to bare; to uncover, expose
soave (sō·â'vā) *a* soft; sweet; **–mente** (sō·â·vā·mān'tā) *adv* gently, softly
sobborgo (sōb·bōr'gō) *m* suburb
sobillare (sō·bēl·lâ'rā) *vt* to stir up; to foment
sobillatore (sō·bēl·lâ·tō'rā) *m* instigator
sobrietà (sō·bryā·tâ') *f* moderation, soberness
socchiuso (sōk·kyū'zō) *a* ajar
soccorrere * (sōk·kôr'rā·rā) *vt* to help; — *vi* to take place
soccorso (sōk·kōr'sō) *m* help; **pronto —** first aid
sociale (sō·châ'lā) *a* social
socialismo (sō·châ·lē'zmō) *m* socialism
socialista (sō·châ·lē'stâ) *m&a* socialist
soddisfacente (sōd·dē·sfâ·chān'tā) *a* sufficient, satisfactory
soddisfare * (sōd·dē·sfâ'rā) *vt* to satisfy, content
soddisfarsi * (sōd·dē·sfâr'sē) *vr* to be satisfied, be contented
soddisfatto (sōd·dē·sfât'tō) *a* satisfied, contented
soddisfazione (sōd·dē·sfâ·tsyō'nā) *f* satisfaction, contentment
sodo (sō'dō) *a* solid, hard; stable; **uovo —** hard-boiled egg
sofferenza (sōf·fā·rān'tsâ) *f* pain, suffering
soffiare (sōf·fyâ'rā) *vt&i* to puff; to blow
soffice (sôf'fē·chā) *a* soft
soffietto (sōf·fyāt'tō) *m* bellows; (*fig*) publicity, advertisement
soffio (sôf'fyō) *m* puff; breath of air
soffitta (sōf·fēt'tâ) *f* attic
soffitto (sōf·fēt'tō) *m* ceiling
soffocare (sōf·fō·kâ'rā) *vt&i* to choke
soffriggere * (sōf·frēj'jā·rā) *vt* to fry lightly, brown
soffrire * (sōf·frē'rā) *vi&t* to suffer; to undergo; to endure, bear
sofisticato (sō·fē·stē·kâ'tō) *a* adulterated; sophisticated
sofisticheria (sō·fē·stē·kā·rē'â) *f* cavil, quibbling
soggetto (sōj·jāt'tō) *m* theme, subject; — *a* under the control of, subject to
soggezione (sōj·jā·tsyō'nā) *f* awe; discomfort
soggiorno (sōj·jōr'nō) *m* residence, stay; **sala di —** living room
soggiungere * (sōj·jūn'jā·rā) *vt&i* to reply; to add, attach
soglia (sô'lyâ) *f* threshold
sogliola (sô'lyō·lâ) *f* sole (*fish*)
sognare (sō·nyâ'rā) *vt&i* to dream
sognatore (sō·nyâ·tō'rā) *m* daydreamer; dreamer
sogno (sō'nyō) *m* dream
solaio (sō·lâ'yō) *m* loft
solamente (sō·lâ·mān'tā) *adv* only
solcare (sōl·kâ'rā) *vt* to furrow, plow
solco (sōl'kō) *m* furrow
soldato (sōl·dâ'tō) *m* soldier
soldo (sōl'dō) *m* penny; wages; **non aver un —** to be penniless
sole (sō'lā) *m* sun
soleggiato (sō·lāj·jâ'tō) *a* bright, sunny
solenne (sō·lān'nā) *a* downright; serious, solemn
solere * (sō·lā'rā) *vi* to be in the habit of, have the custom of, be used to
solerte (sō·lār'tā) *a* industrious
solerzia (sō·ler'tsyâ) *f* diligence, zeal
soletta (sō·lāt'tâ) *f* insole
solfatara (sōl·fâ·tâ'râ) *f* sulphur mine
solforico (sōl·fô'rē·kō) *a* sulphuric; **acido —** sulphuric acid
solforoso (sōl·fō·rō'zō) *a* sulphurous
solfuro (sōl·fū'rō) *m* sulphide
solidarietà (sō·lē·dâ·ryā·tâ') *f* solidarity
solidezza (sō·lē·dā'tsâ) *f* soundness, firmness
solidità (sō·lē·dē·tâ') *f* solidity, firmness
solido (sô'lē·dō) *a&m* solid; reliable, firm
solitario (sō·lē·tâ'ryō) *a* lonely; — *m* hermit; solitaire (*gem, cards*)
solito (sô'lē·tō) *a* usual; customary; **al —** as usual; **il — ritornello** the same old thing; **essere — di** to be accustomed to; **di —** usually, customarily
solitudine (sō·lē·tū'dē·nā) *f* loneliness
sollecitare (sōl·lā·chē·tâ'rā) *vt* to urge, request; to plead with

sollecitazione (sōl·lā·chē·tâ·tsyō'nā) *f* plea; urging, request
sollecito (sōl·le'chē·tō) *a* prompt
sollecitudine (sōl·lā·chē·tū'dē·nā) *f* promptness; concern
solleone (sōl·lā·ō'nā) *m* sultry weather
solleticare (sōl·lā·tē·kâ'rā) *vt* to tickle; to excite; — **la fantasia** to stir one's imagination; — **l'appetito** to whet one's appetite
solletico (sōl·le'tē·kō) *m* tickling; **fare il** — to tickle
sollevare (sōl·lā·vâ'rā) *vt* to lift; to relieve
sollevarsi (sōl·lā·vâr'sē) *vr* to revolt; to rise; (*avi*) to take off
sollevazione (sōl·lā·vâ·tsyō'nā) *f* uprising, revolt
solo (sō'lō) *m* (*mus*) solo; — *a* alone; lonely; **a** — solo; **una sola persona** one person only; **da** — by oneself; **da** — **a** — privately, in private; — *adv* only; **non** — not only
solstizio (sōl·stē'tsyō) *m* solstice
solubile (sō·lū'bē·lā) *a* soluble
soluzione (sō·lū·tsyō'nā) *f* solution (*liquid*)
solvente (sōl·vān'tā) *a&m* solvent
solvere * (sôl'vā·rā) *vt* to solve; to dissolve
solvibile (sōl·vē'bē·lā) *a* sound, able to pay, solvent
soma (sō'mâ) *f* load, weight; **–ro** (sō·mâ'rō) *m* donkey, jackass
somatico (sō·mâ'tē·kō) *a* physical, somatic
somigliante (sō·mē·lyân'tā) *a* resembling; alike
somiglianza (sō·mē·lyân'tsâ) *f* resemblance
somigliare (sō·mē·lyâ'rā) *vi* to resemble; — **come due gocce d'acqua** to be like two peas in a pod
somma (sōm'mâ) *f* sum, amount; (*math*) adding; **–re** (sōm·mâ'rā) *vt&i* to add; to amount to, come to; **–rio** (sōm·mâ'ryō) *m* summary
sommergere * (sōm·mer'jā·rā) *vt* to sink; to flood; to submerge; to inundate; (*fig*) to overcome, upset
sommergersi * (sōm·mer'jār·sē) *vr* to be swamped, be inundated; to dive; to sink
sommergibile (sōm·mār·jē'bē·lā) *m* submarine
sommerso (sōm·mār'sō) *a* submerged, inundated, sunken
sommessamente (sōm·mās·sâ·mān'tā) *adv* submissively; in a low voice; in a subdued tone
somministrare (sōm·mē·nē·strâ'rā) *vt* to supply; to administer; — **una medicina** to give a medicine
sommissione (sōm·mēs·syō'nā) *f* submission
sommo (sōm'mō) *a* highest; — *m* top
sommossa (sōm·mōs'sâ) *f* uprising
sommozzatore (sōm·mō·tsâ·tō'rā) *m* frogman
sonaglio (sō·nâ'lyō) *m* rattle; harness bell; **serpente a sonagli** rattlesnake
sonda (sōn'dâ) *f* (*med*) probe; sounding line; **–ggio** (sōn·dâj'jō) *m* sounding; poll, concensus
sonico (sô'nē·kō) *a* sonic; **barriera sonica** sound barrier
sonnambulo (sōn·nâm'bū·lō) *m* sleepwalker
sonnellino (sōn·nāl·lē'nō) *m* nap
sonnifero (sōn·nē'fā·rō) *m* narcotic; sleeping pill; — *a* sleep-inducing
sonno (sōn'nō) *m* sleep; **aver** — to be sleepy; **–lenza** (sōn·nō·lān'tsâ) *f* drowsiness
sonoro (sō·nō'rō) *a* resonant, resounding; **onde sonore** sound waves
sontuosamente (sōn·twō·zâ·mān'tā) *adv* sumptuously, splendidly
sontuoso (sōn·twō'zō) *a* splendid, sumptuous
sopore (sō·pō'rā) *m* sleepiness, torpor
soppiatto (sōp·pyât'tō) *m* **di** — stealthily, on the sly
sopportabile ((sōp·pōr·tâ'bē·lā) *a* tolerable, bearable
sopportare (sōp·pōr·tâ'rā) *vt&i* to bear, stand, abide
sopportazione (sōp·pōr·tâ·tsyō'nā) *f* fortitude, restraint, tolerance
soppressione (sōp·prās·syō'nā) *f* abolition; suppression
sopprimere * (sōp·prē'mą·rā) to suppress; to abolish
sopra (sō'prâ) *prep* over, above; — *adv* upstairs; up above; **–bito** (sō·prâ'bē·tō) *m* overcoat; **–ccennato** (sō·prâ·chān·nâ'tō) *a* aforesaid, previously mentioned; **–cciglio** (sō·prâ·chē'lyō) *m* eyebrow; **–ccoperta** (sō·prâk·kō·pār'tâ) *f* bedspread; book jacket; **–ddetto** (sō·prâd·dāt'tō) *a* above mentioned; **–ffare** * (sō·prâf·fâ'rā) *vt* to overpower; **–ffazione** (sō·prâf·fâ·tsyō'nā) *f* overwhelming, oppression; **–ggiungere** * (sō·prâj·jūn'jā·rā) *vt&i* to occur; to overtake; **–luogo** (sō·prâ·lwō'gō) *m* on-the-spot investigation; **–mmobile** (sō·prâm·mō'bē·lā) *m* knick-knack; **–nnome** (sō·prân·nō'mā) *m* nickname; surname; **–nnumero** (sō·prân·nū'mā·rō) *m* surplus; **in –nnumero** in excess; **–no** (sō·prâ'nō) *m&a* soprano; **–scarpe** (sō·prâ·skâr'pā) *fpl* overshoes; **–ssalto** (sō·prâs·sâl'tō) *m* jolt, start; **di** — **ssalto** with a start; suddenly; **–ssedere** (sō·prâs·sā·dā'rā) *vi* to preside; to defer, wait; **–ttassa** (sō·prât·tâs'sâ) *f* surtax; **–ttutto** (sō·prât·tūt'tō) *adv* above all; **–vvalutare** (sō·prâv·vâ·lū·tâ'rā) *vt* to overestimate; **–vvento** (sō·prâv·vān'tō) *m* advantage, whip hand; **–vvivere** * (sō·prâv·vē'vā·rā) *vi* to survive; **–vvivere a** to outlive
sopruso (sō·prū'zō) *m* abuse, imposition; assault
soqquadro (sōk·kwâ'drō) *m* ado, confusion
sorbetto (sōr·bāt'tō) *m* sherbet; ice cream
sorbire (sōr·bē'rā) *vt* to sip; to drink slowly

sorbirsi (sōr·bēr'sē) *vr* to swallow; to submit to; — **una predica** (*fig*) to have to endure a scolding
sorcio (sôr'chō) *m* mouse
sordità (sōr·dē·tâ') *f* deafness
sordo (sōr'dō) *a&m* deaf; **–muto** (sōr·dō·mū'tō) *a&m* deaf-mute
sorella (sō·rāl'lâ) *f* sister; **–stra** (sō·rāl·lâ'strâ) *f* stepsister; halfsister
sorgente (sōr·jān'tā) *f* spring; source; — *a* rising, ascendant
sorgere * (sôr'jā·rā) *vi* to rise; to ascend; to be due to, be the result of
sormontare (sōr·mōn·tâ'rā) *vt* to overcome, surmount
sornione (sōr·nyō'nā) *a* wily, sly
sorpassare (sōr·pâs·sâ'rā) *vt* to pass; to exceed
sorpassarsi (sōr·pâs·sâr'sē) *vr* to outdo oneself
sorpassato (sōr·pâs·sâ'tō) *a* obsolete, passé
sorpasso (sōr·pâs'sō) *m* passing (*auto*); **divieto di** — no passing
sorprendente (sōr·prān·dān'tā) *a* astounding, amazing
sorprendere * (sōr·pren'dā·rā) *vt* to surprise; to take by surprise; — **la buona fede di** to deceive
sorpresa (sōr·prā'zâ) *f* surprise
sorreggere * (sōr·rej'jā·rā) *vt* to bolster, hold up, support
sorridere * (sōr·rē'dā·rā) *vi* to smile
sorriso (sōr·rē'zō) *m* smile
sorso (sōr'sō) *m* sip
sorta (sōr'tâ) *f* type, sort
sorte (sōr'tā) *f* luck; lot; fate; doom; **–ggiare** (sōr·tāj·jâ'rā) *vt* to draw by lot
sortilegio (sōr·tē·le'jō) *m* necromancy, witchcraft
sorvegliante (sōr·vā·lyân'tā) *m* watchman
sorveglianza (sōr·vā·lyân'tsâ) *f* surveillance, watch
sorvegliare (sōr·vā·lyâ'rā) *vt* to watch over, keep watch over
sosia (sô'zyâ) *m* double, counterpart
sospendere * (sō·spen'dā·rā) *vt* to suspend; to hold in abeyance
sospensione (sō·spān·syō'nā) *f* discontinuing, suspension
sospettare (sō·spāt·tâ'rā) *vt* to suspect; to suppose
sospetto (sō·spāt'tō) *m* suspicion; supposition; **–samente** (sō·spāt·tō·zâ·mān'tā) *adv* suspiciously; **–so** (sō·spāt·tō'zō) *a* suspicious; cautious, fearful
sospirare (sō·spē·râ'rā) *vt&i* to sigh; to yearn for
sospiro (sō·spē'rō) *m* sigh
sossopra (sōs·sō'prâ) *adv* upside down; topsy-turvy
sosta (sō'stâ) *f* stop; — **vietata** no parking; — **regolamentata** limited parking; **senza** — persistently, unremittingly
sostanza (sō·stân'tsâ) *f* substance
sostanzioso (sō·stân·tsyō'zō) *a* nutritive; substantial
sostare (sō·stâ'rā) *vi* to stop; to pause; to park
sostegno (sō·stā'nyō) *m* support
sostenere * (sō·stā·nā'rā) *vt* to support; to uphold; to hold; to back up
sostenitore (sō·stā·nē·tō'rā) *m* supporter
sostentamento (sō·stān·tâ·mān'tō) *m* maintenance, support
sostituire (sō·stē·twē'rā) *vt* to substitute; to act in the stead of
sostituto (sō·stē·tū'tō) *a* substitute
sostituzione (sō·stē·tū·tsyō'nā) *f* substitution
sottaceti (sōt·tâ·chā'tē) *mpl* pickles
sottana (sōt·tâ'nâ) *f* petticoat; skirt; cassock
sotterfugio (sōt·tār·fū'jō) *m* subterfuge
sotterraneo (sōt·tār·râ'nā·ō) *a* underground; — *m* basement
sotterrare (sōt·tār·râ'rā) *vt* to bury
sottigliezza (sōt·tē·lyâ'tsâ) *f* subtlety; (*fig*) insight; tenuousness
sottile (sōt·tē'lā) *a* thin; subtle, crafty
sottinteso (sōt·tēn·tā'zō) *a* understood, implied; — *m* implication
sotto (sōt'tō) *prep* under, below, — *adv* down, down below; **–bicchiere** (sōt·tō·bēk·kyā'rā) *m* coaster; **–coperta** (sōt·tō·kō·pār'tâ) *adv* below deck; **–coperta** *f* (*naut*) lower decks; **–fascia** (sōt·tō·fâ'shâ) *m* printed matter; **–gola** (sōt·tō·gō'lâ) *f* chin strap; **–lineare** (sōt·tō·lē·nā·â'rā) *vt* to underline; to stress, point up; **–mano** (sōt·tō·mâ'nō) *adv* at hand; on hand; **di –mano** stealthily, underhandedly; **–marino** (sōt·tō·mâ·rē'nō) *m* submarine; **–messo** (sōt·tō·mās'sō) *a* docile, submissive; **–mettere** * (sōt·tō·met'tā·rā) *vt* to conquer, subjugate; to submit; **–mettersi** * (sōt·tō·met'tār·sē) *vr* to cede, surrender; **–missione** (sōt·tō·mēs·syō'nā) *f* self-abasement; subdual; submission; **–passaggio** (sōt·tō·pâs·sâj'jō) *m* underpass; **–porre** * (sōt·tō·pōr'rā) *vt* to submit; **–porsi** * (sōt·tō·pōr'sē) *vr* to submit to; to undergo; **–scrivere** * (sōt·tō·skrē'vā·rā) *vt&i* to sign; to subscribe to; **–scriversi** * (sōt·tō·skrē'vār·sē) *vr* to subscribe to; to approve; **–segretario** (sōt·tō·sā·grā·tâ'ryō) *m* undersecretary; **–sopra** (sōt·tō·sō'prâ) *adv* in confusion; upside down; **–suolo** (sōt·tō·swō'lō) *m* subsoil; **–valutare** (sōt·tō·vâ·lū·tâ'rā) *vt* to underestimate; **–veste** (sōt·tō·vā'stā) *f* underwear; man's vest; **–voce** (sōt·tō·vō'chā) *adv* softly; in a low voice
sottrare * (sōt·trâr'rā) *vt* to deduct, subtract
sottrarsi * (sōt·trâr'sē) *vr* to escape, elude, avoid
sottrazione (sōt·trâ·tsyō'nā) *f* subtraction, deduction
sottufficiale (sōt·tūf·fē·châ'lā) *m* non-commissioned officer
sovente (sō·vān'tā) *adv* often, with frequency
sovrano (sō·vrâ'nō) *a&m* sovereign
sovrumano (sō·vrū·mâ'nō) *a* superhuman
sovvenzionare (sōv·vān·tsyō·nâ'rā) *vt* to

subsidize, provide financial backing for
sovvenzione (sōv·vān·tsyō'nā) *f* subsidy; scholarship
sovversivo (sōv·vār·sē'vō) *a* subversive
sozzo (sō'tsō) *a* filthy
spaccalegna (spâk·kâ·lā'nyâ) *m* wood cutter
spaccare (spâk·kâ'rā) *vt* to split
spaccarsi (spâk·kâr'sē) *vr* to cleave, split, crack open
spaccato (spâk·kâ'tō) *m* cross section
spacciare (spâ·châ'rā) *vt* to spread, circulate; to sell; to palm off
spacciarsi (spâ·châr'sē) *vr* to masquerade as; to pass for
spacciatore (spâ·châ·tō'rā) *m* peddler
spaccone (spâk·kō'nā) *m* braggart
spada (spâ'dâ) *f* sword
spaesato (spâ·ā·zâ'tō) *a* out of one's natural environment; ill at ease
Spagna (spâ'nyâ) *f* Spain
spagnolo (spâ·nyō'lō) *a* Spanish; — *m* Spaniard
spago (spâ'gō) *m* twine, string
spaiato (spâ·yâ'tō) *a* unmatched, mateless, odd
spalancare (spâ·lân·kâ'rā) *vt* to open wide, throw open
spalare (spâ·lâ'rā) *vt* to shovel
spalla (spâl'lâ) *f* shoulder
spalleggiare (spâl·lāj·jâ'rā) *vt* to back; to endorse
spalliera (spâl·lyā'râ) *f* chair back
spallina (spâl·lē'nâ) *f* epaulet
spalmare (spâl·mâ'rā) *vt* to spread with; to cover with
sparadrappo (spâ·râ·drâp'pō) *m* adhesive plaster; adhesive tape
sparare (spâ·râ'rā) *vt&i* to shoot
sparatoia (spâ·râ·tô'yâ) *f* shooting
sparecchiare (spâ·rāk·kyâ'rā) *vt* to remove, clear away; to clear *(table)*
spargere * (spâr'jā·rā) *vt* to scatter; to shed, drop
spargimento (spâr·jē·mān'tō) *m* spilling; scattering; — **di sangue** bloodshed
sparire (spâ·rē'rā) *vi* to disappear
sparlare (spâr·lâ'rā) *vi* to slander
sparo (spâ'rō) *m* shot
spartito (spâr·tē'tō) *m (mus)* score
spartitraffico (spâr·tē·trâf'fē·kō) *m* safety island
spartizione (spâr·tē·tsyō'nā) *f* distribution, apportionment
spasimante (spâ·zē·mân'tā) *a* lovelorn; — *m* lover, swain
spasimo (spâ'zē·mō) *m* pang; *(med)* spasm
spasmodico (spâ·zmô'dē·kō) *a* spasmodic; *(med)* spastic
spassionatamente (spâs·syō·nâ·tâ·mān'tā) *adv* fairly; without emotion
spasso (spâs'sō) *m* relaxation; **andare a** — to take a walk; **–so** (spâs·sō'zō) *a* funny, amusing
spauracchio (spâū·râk'kyō) *m* bugbear; scarecrow
spavalderia (spâ·vâl·dā·rē'â) *f* haughtiness
spaventapasseri (spâ·vān·tâ·pâs'sā·rē) *m* scarecrow
spaventare (spâ·vān·tâ'rā) *vt* to frighten
spaventarsi (spâ·vān·târ'sē) *vr* to be frightened, be aghast, be terrified
spaventevole (spâ·vān·te'vō·lā) *a* dreadful, horrifying
spaventosamente (spâ·vān·tō·zâ·mān'tā) *adv* awfully; frightfully
spavento (spâ·vān'tō) *m* scare; fright; **–so** (spâ·vān·tō'zō) *a* awful
spaziale (spâ·tsyâ'lā) *a* spatial
spazientirsi (spâ·tsyān·tēr'sē) *vr* to lose one's patience
spazio (spâ'tsyō) *m* room, space; **–so** (spâ·tsyō'zō) *a* roomy
spazzacamino (spâ·tsâ·kâ·mē'nō) *m* chimney sweep
spazzamine (spâ·tsâ·mē'nā) *m (naut)* mine sweeper
spazzaneve (spâ·tsâ·nā'vā) *m* snowplow
spazzare (spâ·tsâ'rā) *vt* to sweep
spazzatura (spâ·tsâ·tū'râ) *f* sweepings
spazzino (spâ·tsē'nō) *m* street cleaner
spazzola (spâ'tsō·lâ) *f* brush; **–re** (spâ·tsō·lâ'rā) *vt* to brush
spazzolino (spâ·tsō·lē'nō) *m* small brush; — **da denti** toothbrush
specchiarsi (spāk·kyâr'sē) *vr* to look at one's reflection; to be mirrored, be reflected
specchiera (spāk·kyā'râ) *f* dressing table; mirror
specchio (spek'kyō) *m* mirror; — **retrovisivo** *(auto)* rearview mirror
speciale (spā·châ'lā) *a* special; unusual
specialista (spā·châ·lē'stâ) *m* specialist
specialità (spā·châ·lē·tâ') *f* specialty
specie (spe'chā) *f* kind, species; — *adv* especially, above all
specificare (spā·chē·fē·kâ'rā) *vt* to specify, detail
specifico (spā·chē'fē·kō) *a* specific, detailed; — *m* specific, particular
speculazione (spā·kū·lâ·tsyō'nā) *f* speculation
spedire (spā·dē'rā) *vt* to ship; to mail; to send
spedizione (spā·dē·tsyō'nā) *f* shipment; expedition; — **di bagaglio** forwarding of luggage
spedizioniere (spā·dē·tsyō·nyā'rā) *m* forwarding agent
spegnere * (spe'nyā·rā) *vt* to put out; to quench; to extinguish; — **la radio** to turn off the radio
spegnersi * (spe'nyār·sē) *vr* to disappear; to die out
spelonca (spā·lōn'kâ) *f* den, cavern
spendere * (spen'dā·rā) *vt&i* to spend; to make use of
spensierato (spān·syā·râ'tō) *a* carefree, troublefree
speranza (spā·rân'tsâ) *f* hope
sperare (spā·râ'rā) *vt&i* to hope; to intend, plan
sperduto (spār·dū'tō) *a* lost, led astray
spergiuro (spār·jū'rō) *m* perjurer; perjury
sperimentare (spā·rē·mān·tâ'rā) *vt* to experiment with, try out, put to the test

sperma (spār'mâ) *m* sperm
sperone (spā·rō'nā) *m (naut)* ram; *(arch)* abutment
spesa (spā'zâ) *f* expense; **fare le spese** to shop
spesso (spās'sō) *adv* often; — *a* frequent; thick, heavy; **-re** (spās·sō'rā) *m* thickness
spettacolare (spāt·tâ·kō·lâ'rā) *a* spectacular
spettacolo (spāt·tâ'kō·lō) *m* show; — **continuo** continuous performance; **-so** (spāt·tâ·kō·lō'zō) *a* striking, unusual
spettanza (spāt·tân'tsâ) *f* concern; due, right
spettare (spāt·tâ'rā) *vi* to be one's turn; to belong to; to be one's business; to be one's duty
spettatore (spāt·tâ·tō'rā) *m* spectator
spettinare (spāt·tē·nâ'rā) *vt* to tousle one's hair; to ruin one's hairdo
spezie (spe'tsyā) *fpl* spices
spezzare (spā·tsâ'rā) *vt* to break
spezzarsi (spā·tsâr'sē) *vr* to be broken; to break, shatter
spezzatino (spā·tsâ·tē'nō) *m* stew
spia (spē'â) *f* spy
spiacevole (spyâ·che'vō·lā) *a* unpleasant
spiaggia (spyâj'jâ) *f* beach, strand
spiare (spyâ'rā) *vt* to spy on
spiccare (spēk·kâ'rā) *vt* to detach; — *vi* to stand out
spiccarsi (spēk·kâr'sē) *vr* to be outstanding; to become detached; to isolate oneself
spicchio (spēk'kyō) *m* garlic clove; segment of fruit, slice of fruit
spicciarsi (spē·châr'sē) *vr* to hurry up, rush
spicciativo (spē·châ·tē'vō) *a* efficient; prompt, quick
spiccioli (spē'chō·lē) *mpl* small change
spiedo (spyā'dō) *m* spit *(cooking)*
spiegamento (spyā·gâ·mān'tō) *m* spreading out; *(mil)* deployment
spiegare (spyā·gâ'rā) *vt* to explain
spiegarsi (spyā·gâr'sē) *vr* to explain oneself, make oneself understood; **Mi spiego?** Do I make myself clear?
spiegazione (spyā·gâ·tsyō'nā) *f* explanation
spietato (spyā·tâ'tō) *a* relentless; without pity
spiga (spē'gâ) *f (bot)* ear
spilla (spēl'lâ) *f* brooch; tie-pin
spillo (spēl'lō) *m* pin; — **di sicurezza** safety pin
spilorcio (spē·lôr'chō) *a* stingy; — *m* miser
spilungone (spē·lūn·gō'nā) *m* lanky fellow; *(fig)* lamppost; — *a* tall and thin
spina (spē'nâ) *f* thorn; spine; fish bone; *(elec)* plug
spinacio (spē·nâ'chō) *m* spinach
spingere * (spēn'jā·rā) *vt* to push; — **all'eccesso** to go too far, carry things to extremes
spinoso (spē·nō'zō) *a* thorny; ticklish, delicate
spinta (spēn'tâ) *f* shove; push; *(fig)* impetus
spinterogeno (spēn·tā·rô'jā·nō) *m (auto)* distributor
spinto (spēn'tō) *a* daring, suggestive; immoderate; **-ne** (spēn·tō'nā) *m* violent shove
spionaggio (spyō·nâj'jō) *m* espionage
spioncino (spyōn·chē'nō) *m* peephole
spiraglio (spē·râ'lyō) *m* fissure; vent; hole; *(fig)* gleam, glimmering, ray of hope
spirale (spē·râ'lā) *f&a* spiral; **a** — in spiral fashion
spirare (spē·râ'rā) *vt&i* to expire, die; to fall due; to infuse, inspire
spiritismo (spē·rē·tē'zmō) *m* spirit rapping; spiritualism
spirito (spē'rē·tō) *m* wit; spirit; ghost; alcohol; — **denaturato** denatured alcohol; **prontezza di** — ready wit; **povero di** — narrow-minded; **S— Santo** Holy Ghost; **-so** (spē·rē·tō'zō) *a* witty, humorous
spirituale (spē·rē·twâ'lā) *a* spiritual
splendere (splen'dā·rā) *vi* to shine; to gleam, glisten
splendidamente (splān·dē·dâ·mān'tā) *adv* magnificently, stupendously
splendido (splen'dē·dō) *a* glorious; sumptuous, magnificent
splendore (splān·dō'rā) *m* magnificence; radiance; splendor
spoglia (spô'lyâ) *f* skin, hide; loot; — **mortale** mortal remains; **-re** (spō·lyâ'rā) *vt* to strip; *(fig)* to examine minutely; **-rello** (spō·lyâ·rāl'lō) *m* strip tease; **-rsi** (spō·lyâr'sē) *vr* to undress; **-toio** (spō·lyâ·tô'yō) *m* dressing room; locker room
spola (spō'lâ) *f* shuttle; **fare la** — *(fig)* to ply, go back and forth
spolverare (spōl·vā·râ'rā) *vt* to dust off
sponda (spōn'dâ) *f* shore
spontaneo (spōn·tâ'nā·ō) *a* spontaneous
sporadicamente (spō·râ·dē·kâ·mān'tā) *adv* sporadically
sporcaccione (spōr·kâ·chō'nā) *m* filthy person, swine
sporcare (spōr·kâ'rā) *vt* to dirty, soil
sporco (spōr'kō) *a* unclean, filthy, dirty
sport (spōrt) *m* sport
sporta (spōr'tâ) *f* shopping bag
sportello (spōr·tāl'lō) *m* ticket window
sportivo (spōr·tē'vō) *a* sporting; — *m* sportsman
sposa (spō'zâ) *f* wife, bride; **-lizio** (spō·zâ·lē'tsyō) *m* wedding; **-re** (spō·zâ'rā) *vt* to marry; **-rsi** (spō·zâr'sē) *vr* to get married; **-to** (spō·zâ'tō) *a* married
sposo (spō'zō) *m* husband, bridegroom
sposi (spō'zē) *mpl* bride and groom, wedding couple
spostare (spō·stâ'rā) *vt* to move; to change
spostarsi (spō·stâr'sē) *vr* to change one's place; to move to another seat
spostato (spō·stâ'tō) *m* misfit; — *a* maladjusted
sprazzo (sprâ'tsō) *m* flash, gleam; — **d'intelligenza** glimmer of understanding
sprecare (sprā·kâ'rā) *vt* to waste

spreco (sprā'kō) *m* waste; **–ne** (sprā·kō'nā) *m* waster, spendthrift
spregio (spre'jō) *m* despising; disrespect; scorn
spregiudicato (sprā·jū·dē·kâ'tō) *a* impartial; broadminded; unprejudiced
spremere (spre'mā·rā) *vt* to squeeze; to wring out
spremilimoni (sprā·mē·lē·mō'nē) *m* lemon squeezer
spremuta (sprā·mū'tâ) *f* fruit juice; — **di arancia** orange juice
sprezzante (sprā·tsân'tā) *a* contemptuous, despising
sproloquio (sprō·lô'kwyō) *m* long-winded talk, very wordy speech
spronare (sprō·nâ'rā) *vt* to stimulate, rouse; to spur on; *(naut)* to ram
sproporzionato (sprō·pōr·tsyō·nâ'tō) *a* out of proportion
sproposito (sprō·pô'zē·tō) *m* nonsense; error; faux pas; **fare uno** — to make a blunder; **parlare a** — to get off the subject; **costare uno** — to cost a fortune
spropriazione (sprō·pryâ·tsyō'nā) *f* expropriation
sprovvisto (sprōv·vē'stō) *a* deficient in; unprovided for; **alla sprovvista** unexpectedly, by surprise
spruzzare (sprū·tsâ'rā) *vt* to spatter; to sprinkle
spruzzatore (sprū·tsâ·tō'rā) *m* sprayer
spudoratezza (spū·dō·râ·tā'tsâ) *f* brazenness; lack of decorum
spudorato (spū·dō·râ'tō) *a* shameless; insolent
spugna (spū'nyâ) *f* sponge
spulciare (spūl·châ'rā) *vt* to deflea; *(fig)* to scrutinize, inspect minutely
spuma (spū'mâ) *f* froth, foam; **–nte** (spū·mân'tā) *a* sparkling, foaming; **–nte** *m* champagne, sparkling wine
spuntare (spūn·tâ'rā) *vt* to blunt; to break the point of; *(com)* to check off; to unfasten; — *vi* to show up; to rise; to peep out; to cut *(teeth)*; **spuntarcela** to win out, overcome all difficulties; **lo — del giorno** daybreak, dawn
spuntarsi (spūn·târ'sē) *vr* to become blunt; to lose its point *(pencil)*
spuntino (spūn·tē'nō) *m* snack
sputacchiera (spū·tâk·kyā'râ) *f* cuspidor
sputare (spū·tâ'rā) *vt&i* to spit, expectorate
sputo (spū'tō) *m* saliva, spit
squadra (skwâ'drâ) *f* team; square; *(avi)* squadron; — **mobile** riot squad
squagliare (skwâ·lyâ'rā) *vt* to melt
squagliarsi (skwâ·lyâr'sē) *vr* to take French leave; to vanish, disappear
squalificare (skwâ·lē·fē·kâ'rā) *vt* to disqualify
squallido (skwâl'lē·dō) *a* bleak, miserable
squallore (skwâl·lō'rā) *m* dismalness, gloominess; squalor, misery
squalo (skwâ'lō) *m* shark
squama (skwâ'mâ) *f* scale *(fish, reptile)*; flake of paint
squarciare (skwâr·châ'rā) *vt* to tear apart, rip apart
squarciarsi (skwâr·châr'sē) *vr* to rip in two, tear apart, be torn up
squarcio (skwâr'chō) *m*; tear, rip; gash, cut
squattrinato (skwât·trē·nâ'tō) *a* penniless, broke
squilibrato (skwē·lē·brâ'to) *a* deranged; mentally unbalanced; — *m* madcap; hare-brained individual
squillo (skwēl'lō) *m* ring; blare, blast; peal of bells
squisitezza (skwē·zē·tā'tsâ) *f* exquisiteness; deliciousness
squisito (skwē·zē'tō) *a* delicious; exquisite
squoiare (skwō·yâ'rā) *vt* to skin
sradicare (zrâ·dē·kâ'rā) *vt* to abolish; to pull out by the roots; to eradicate
sregolatezza (zrā·gō·lâ·tā'tsâ) *f* debauchery, dissipation; confusion
stabile (stâ'bē·lā) *m* building; piece of real estate; — *a* stable, constant
stabilimento (stā·bē·lē·mān'tō) *m* establishment
stabilire (stâ·bē·lē'rā) *vt* to establish, found; to lay down
stabilirsi (stâ·bē·lēr'sē) *vr* to settle, take up residence
stabilità (stâ·bē·lē·tâ') *f* steadiness
staccare (stâk·kâ'rā) *vt* to detach, separate
staccarsi (stâk·kâr'sē) *vr (avi)* to take off; to come loose; to stand out, be outstanding
staccio (stâ'chō) *m* sieve
stadio (stâ'dyō) *m* stadium; phase, level
staffa (stâf'fâ) *f* stirrup; **perdere le staffe** *(fig)* to lose one's temper
staffetta (stâf·fāt'tâ) *f* courier; messenger; **corsa a** — relay race
staffilata (stâf·fē·lâ'tâ) *f* whipping; lash; *(fig)* taunt
staffile (stâf·fē'lā) *m* whip
stagione (stâ·jō'nā) *f* season
stagno (stâ'nyō) *m* tin; — *a* watertight; airtight; **–la** (stâ·nyō'lâ) *f* tinfoil
stagno (stâ'nyō) *m* pond
stalla (stâl'lâ) *f* stable, stall
stallone (stâl·lō'nā) *m* stallion
stamani (stâ·mâ'nē) *adv* this morning
stamattina (stâ·mât·tē'nâ) *adv* this morning
stampa (stâm'pâ) *f* press; printing; **–re** (stâm·pâ'rā) *vt* to print
stampe (stâm'pā) *fpl* printed matter
stampella (stâm·pāl'lâ) *f* crutch; coat hanger
stamperia (stâm·pā·rē'â) *f* printing office
stampiglia (stâm·pē'lyâ) *f (mech)* stamp
stampino (stâm·pē'nō) *m* stencil
stampo (stâm'pō) *m* sort; stamp, mould
stancare (stân·kâ'rā) *vt* to tire
stancarsi (stân·kâr'sē) *vr* to grow tired
stanchezza (stân·kā'tsâ) *f* fatigue; exhaustion
stanco (stân'kō) *a* tired, worn-out
stanga (stân'gâ) *f* bar; shaft
stanotte (stâ·nōt'tā) *adv* last night; tonight
stantio (stân·tē'ō) *a* insipid, stale, inane

stantuffo (stân·tūf'fō) *m* plunger; piston
stanza (stân'tsâ) *f* room
stanziamento (stân·tsyâ·mān'tō) *m* appropriation, grant
stanziare (stân·tsyâ'rā) *vt* to appropriate, allocate
stare * (stâ'rā) *vi* to be; to stand; to remain; — **in piedi** to stand; — **fermo** to stand still; — **per** to be about to
starnutire (stâr·nū·tē'rā) *vi* to sneeze
starnuto (stâr·nū'tō) *m* sneeze
stasera (stâ·sā'râ) *f* tonight
statale (stâ·tâ'lā) *a* governmental
statistica (stâ·tē'stē·kâ) *f* statistics
stato (stâ'tō) *m* condition, state
statua (stâ'twâ) *f* statue
statunitense (stâ·tū·nē·tān'sā) *a* American, of the United States.
statura (stâ·tū'râ) *f* stature
statuto (stâ·tū'tō) *m* constitution; by-law; *(law)* statute
stavolta (stâ·vōl'tâ) *adv* this time, on this occasion
stazionare (stâ·tsyō·nâ'rā) *vi* to park; to stay, remain
stazione (stâ·tsyō'nā) *f* station; — **climatica** health resort; — **di villeggiatura** summer resort
stazza (stâ'tsâ) *f (naut)* displacement
stecca (stāk'kâ) *f* stick; spoke; billiard cue; plectrum; carton of cigarettes; *(mus)* false note; umbrella rib
stecchino (stāk·kē'nō) *m* toothpick
stecconata (stāk·kō·nâ'tâ) *f* fence
stella (stāl·lâ) *f* star; *(fig)* destiny; asterisk; — **filante** shooting star; streamer
stelo (stā'lō) *m (bot)* stem
stemma (stām'mâ) *m* coat of arms
stemperare (stām·pā·râ'rā) *vt* to dilute; to melt
stendere * (sten'dā·rā) *vt* to stretch; to spread; to compose, draft *(document)*
stendersi * (sten'dār·sē) *vr* to relax; to reach; to stretch out
stenodattilografo (stā·nō·dât·tē·lô'grâ·fō) *m* stenographer
stento (stān'tō) *m* struggle; suffering; lack; **a** — with difficulty; hardly
steppa (stāp'pâ) *f* steppe, prairie
sterco (stār'kō) *m* dung
sterile (ste'rē·lā) *a* sterile; of no avail, useless
sterilità (stā·rē·lē·tâ') *f* sterility
sterilizzare (stā·rē·lē·dzâ'rā) *vt* to sterilize
sterminare (stār·mē·nâ'rā) *vt* to exterminate
sterminato (stār·mē·nâ'tō) *a* immense; limitless
sterminio (stār·mē'nyō) *m* enormity; extermination
sterpo (stār'pō) *m* underbrush; brambles
sterratore (stār·râ·tō'rā) *m* ditchdigger
sterzare (stār·tsâ'rā) *vt&i* to swerve; to steer
sterzo (stār'tsō) *m (auto)* steering mechanism
stesso (stās'sō) *a* same, very same; **fa lo** — it's immaterial, it makes no difference
stia (stē'â) *f* hencoop
stilare (stē·lâ'rā) *vt* to draw up *(document)*
stile (stē'lā) *m* style; stylus
stilografica (stē·lō·grâ'fē·kâ) *f* fountain pen
stima (stē'mâ) *f* esteem; opinion; *(com)* estimate; **–re** (stē·mâ'rā) *vt* to esteem; to consider, deem; *(com)* to estimate; **–rsi** (stē·mâr'sē) to consider oneself, deem oneself
stimolare (stē·mō·lâ'rā) *vt* to stimulate; to urge
stimolo (stē'mō·lō) *m* stimulus; urging
stinco (stēn'kō) *m* shin
stipendio (stē·pen'dyō) *m* salary
stipite (stē'pē·tā) *m* jamb; stalk, stem; lineage
stipo (stē'pō) *m* cabinet
stipulare (stē·pū·lâ'rā) *vt* to stipulate
stipulazione (stē·pū·lâ·tsyō'nā) *f* stipulation
stirare (stē·râ'rā) *vt* to iron; to stretch
stirarsi (stē·râr'sē) *vr* to stretch out; to stretch one's limbs
stiratrice (stē·râ·trē'chā) *f* laundress
stireria (stē·rā·rē'â) *f* laundry
stiro (stē'rō) *m* ironing; **ferro da** — flatiron
stirpe (stēr'pā) *f* lineage, origin
stitichezza (stē·tē·kā'tsâ) *f* constipation
stitico (stē'tē·kō) *a* constipated; *(fig)* stingy
stiva (stē'vâ) *f (naut)* hold
stivale (stē·vâ'lā) *m* boot
stizza (stē'tsâ) *f* anger, ire
stizzire (stē·tsē'rā) *vt* to vex, irritate
stizzirsi (stē·tsēr'sē) *vr* to become angry
stoffa (stōf'fâ) *f* cloth; material
stoino (stō·ē'nō) *m* door mat
stolto (stōl'tō) *a* foolish
stomachevole (stō·mâ·ke'vō·lā) *a* disgusting
stomaco (stô'mâ·kō) *m* stomach; **dolor di** — stomach ache
stomatico (stō·mâ'tē·kō) *m* tonic
stonare (stō·nâ'rā) *vi* to sing off key; to be out of tune; to be out of place; to jar; *(fig)* to be at loggerheads
stonatura (stō·nâ·tū'râ) *f* blunder; disonant note; dissonance; *(fig)* disagreement
stoppa (stōp'pâ) *f* oakum
stoppino (stōp·pē'nō) *m* wick
storcere * (stôr'chā·rā) *vt* to twist; to sprain
stordimento (stōr·dē·mān'tō) *m* daze, bewilderment; dulling of one's senses
stordire (stōr·dē'rā) *vt* to deafen; to bewilder, confuse; to dull *(senses)*
stordirsi (stōr·dēr'sē) *vr* to have one's senses dulled; to become dazed
stordito (stōr·dē'tō) *a* dizzy; dulled; confused, bewildered
storia (stô'ryā) *f* story; history
storicamente (stō·rē·kâ·mān'tā) *adv* historically
storico (stô'rē·kō) *a* historical; — *m* historian
storione (stō·ryō'nā) *m* sturgeon

stormo (stōr'mō) *m* swarm, flock; *(avi)* flight, wing; **suonare a —** to sound the alarm, sound the alert
storpio (stôr'pyō) *m* cripple; — *a* maimed
storta (stōr'tâ) *f (med)* sprain; *(chem)* retort
storto (stōr'tō) *a* twisted; distorted; **avere gli occhi storti** to be squint-eyed
stoviglie (stō·vē'lyā) *fpl* pottery; china, dishes
strabene (strâ·bā'nā) *adv* extremely well
strabico (strâ'bē·kō) *a* squint-eyed, squinting
strabiliante (strâ·bē·lyân'tā) *a* surprising, astonishing
stracciare (strâ·châ'rā) *vt* to tear, rip; to lacerate
stracciato (strâ·châ'tō) *a* in rags; torn to shreds
straccio (strâ'chō) *m* rag; **–ne** (strâ·chō'nā) *m* ragamuffin
stracco (strâk'kō) *a* very tired, worn-out
strada (strâ'dâ) *f* street; road; **— interrotta** road closed; **— in costruzione** road repairs; **— secondaria** by-pass; **— maestra** highway
stradale (strâ·dâ'lā) *m* avenue: — *a* street, road; **polizia —** traffic patrol; **carta —** road map
strafalcione (strâ·fâl·chō'nā) *m* blunder
strafare * (strâ·fâ'rā) *vi* to work too hard; to overdo
strage (strâ'jā) *f* massacre, butchering; *(fig)* plenty
stramazzare (strâ·mâ·tsâ'rā) *vi* to fall in, collapse; — *vt* to knock over, knock down
strame (strâ'mā) *m* fodder, litter
strampalato (strâm·pâ·lâ'tō) *a* absurd; odd; bizarre
stranezza (strâ·nā'tsâ) *f* whimsy; singularity; oddity
strangolare (strân·gō·lâ'rā) *vt* to choke
straniero (strâ·nyā'rō) *a* foreign: — *m* foreigner; stranger
strano (strâ'nō) *a* stranger, peculiar
straordinario (strâ·ōr·dē·nâ'ryō) *a* extraordinary; — *m* overtime
strapazzare (strâ·pâ·tsâ'rā) *vt* to scold; to mistreat; to scramble *(eggs)*
strapazzarsi (strâ·pâ·tsâr'sē) *vr* to overdo oneself; to act carelessly about one's health
strapazzo (strâ·pâ'tsō) *m* excess; strain; **vestito da —** working cloths; **pittore da —** inferior painter
strapiombo (strâ·pyōm'bō) *m* **a —** jutting out; sheer
strappare (strâp·pâ'rā) *vt* to tear apart; to pull; to snatch; **— il cuore a qualcuno** *(fig)* to break someone's heart
strapparsi (strâp·pâr'sē) *vr* to tear oneself away; **— i capelli** to tear one's hair
strappo (strâp'pō) *m* tear, rent; jerk, start; **— muscolare** muscle strain
strapuntino (strâ·pūn'tē·nō) *m (auto)* bucket seat
straripare (strâ·rē·pâ'ra) *vi* to overflow; to flood its banks *(river)*
strascico (strâ'shē·kō) *m* train *(dress)*; results, aftermath
stratagemma (strâ·tâ·jām'mâ) *m* stratagem, policy, device
stratega (strâ·tā'gâ) *m* strategist
strato (strâ'tō) *m* layer, coat; **–sfera** (strâ·tō·sfā'râ) *f* stratosphere
stravagante (strâ·vâ·gân'tā) *a* eccentric, odd
stravolto (strâ·vōl'tō) *a* agitated, upset
strazio (strâ'tsyō) *m* anguish, torture
strega (strā'gâ) *f* witch
stregone (strā·gō'nā) *m* wizard, warlock
strenna (strān'nâ) *f* gift; tip, gratuity
strenuamente (strā·nwâ·mān'tā) *adv* strenuously, vigorously
strenuo (stre'nwō) active, vigorous
strepito (stre'pē·tō) *m* noise; **–so** (strā·pē·tō'zō) *a* resounding; sensational; noisy
stretta (strāt'tâ) *f* grip, grasp, squeeze; **— al cuore** tug at the heart; **— di mano** handshake; **— di spalle** shrug of one's shoulders
strettezza (strāt·tā'tsâ) *f* difficulty; strictness; narrowness; **— economica** economic difficulties, money worries
stretto (strāt'tō) *a* narrow; — *m (geog)* straits
strillare (strēl·lâ'rā) *vi* to scream
strillo (strēl'lō) *m* scream, shriek; **–ne** (strēl·lō'nā) *m* newsboy
stringa (strēn'gâ) *f* shoelace
stringere * (strēn'jā·rā) *vt&i* to squeeze; to press; to make tighter; **— la mano** to shake hands
stringersi * (strēn'jār·sē) *vr* to narrow; to come close; to draw near; **— nelle spalle** to shrug one's shoulders
striscia (strē'shâ) *f* strip; **–re** (strē·shâ'rā) *vt* to creep; to graze, touch lightly
stritolare (strē·tō·lâ'rā) *vt* to smash; to crush
strizzalimoni (strē·tsâ·lē·mō'nē) *m* lemon squeezer
strizzare (strē·tsâ'rā) *vt* to wring; to squeeze
strofinaccio (strō·fē·nâ'chō) *m* rag; duster
strozzare (stro·tsâ'ra) *vt* to strangle
strozzino (strō·tsē'nō) *m* loan shark *(coll)*
strumento (strū·mān'tō) *m* instrument
strutto (strūt'tō) *m* lard
struzzo (strū'tsō) *m* ostrich
studente (stū·dān'tā) *m*, **studentessa** (stū·dān·tas'sâ) *f* student
studiare (stū·dyâ'rā) *vt* to study
studio (stū'dyō) *m* study; studio
stufa (stū'fâ) *f* stove
stufato (stū·fâ'tō) *m* stew
stufo (stū'fō) *a* fed up, tired, bored
stuoia (stwô'yâ) *f* doormat; matting
stuolo (stwō'lō) *m* crowd, group
stupefacente (stū·pā·fâ·chān'tā) *a* astounding; awe-inspiring; bewildering; — *m* narcotic
stupendo (stū·pān'dō) *a* stupendous, magnificent, wonderful
stupidaggine (stū·pē·dâj'jē·nā) *f* absurdness; foolishness

stupido (stū'pē·dō) *a* dull, stupid, foolish, mentally slow
stupire (stū·pē'rā) *vt* to amaze, astound
stupirsi (stū·pēr'sē) *vr* to be astonished; to wonder at
stupore (stū·pō'rā) *m* stupefaction; wonderment; *(med)* stupor
stupro (stū'prō) *m* rape
sturare (stū·râ'rā) to uncork
stuzzicadenti (stū·tsē·kâ·dān'tē) *m* toothpick
stuzzicante (stū·tsē·kân'tā) *a* provocative, stimulating; vexing
stuzzicare (stū·tsē·kâ'rā) *vt* to whet; to stimulate; to tease, needle
stuzzicarsi (stū·tsē·kâr'sē) *vr* to pick one's teeth
su (sū) *adv&prep* on; over; above; about
subacqueo (sū·bâk'kwā·ō) *a* underwater; **pescatore —** skin diver
subaffittare (sū·bâf·fēt·tâ'rā) *vt* to sublet
subbuglio (sūb·bū'lyō) *m* uproar, bustle, hubbub
subcoscienza (sūb·kō·shān'tsâ) *f* subconscious
subdolo (sūb'dō·lō) *a* shifty, insidious, crafty
subire (sū'·bē'rā) *vt* to suffer, undergo
subito (sū'bē·tō) *adv* at once; — *a* sudden; rapid
sublimato (sū·blē·mâ'tō) *m* sublimate; — **corrosivo** mercuric chloride
sublimazione (sū·blē·mâ·tsyō'nā) *f* sublimation
subodorare (sū·bō·dō·râ'rā) *vt* to suspect; to get an inkling of; to know intuitively
succedere * (sū·che'dā·rā) *vi* to happen; to follow
successivamente (sū·chās·sē·vâ·mān'tā) *adv* consecutively; in succession; thereafter, afterward
successivo (sū·chās·sē'vō) *a* following, next
successo (sū·chās'sō) *m* success; — *a* succeeded; followed
succhiare (sūk·kyâ'rā) *vt* to suck
succhiello (sūk·kyāl'lō) *m* gimlet
succo (sūk'kō) *m* juice; **–so** (sūk·kō'zō) *a* juicy; *(fig)* meaty, substantial
succursale (sūk·kūr·sâ'lā) *f* branch office; agency
sud (sūd) *m* south; **–africano** (sū·dâ·frē·kâ'nō) *a&m* South African; **–americano** (sū·dâ·mā·rē·kâ'nō) *m&a* South American
sudare (sū·dâ'rā) *vi* to perspire; — *vt* to ooze
sudario (sū·dâ'ryō) *m* shroud
suddetto (sūd·dāt'tō) *a* aforementioned
suddito (sūd'dē·tō) *m* citizen, subject
sudicio (sū'dē·chō) *a* filthy, dirty; lewd, smutty
sudiciume (sū·dē·chū'mā) *m* smut; dirt
sudore (sū·dō'rā) *m* perspiration, sweat
sufficiente (sūf·fē·chān'tā) *a* sufficient; **–mente** (sūf·fē·chān·tā·mān'tā) *adv* sufficiently, adequately
sufficienza (sūf·fē·chān'tsâ) *f* sufficiency; abundance
suffragare (sūf·frâ·gâ'rā) *vt* to support, aid, back
suggellare (sūj·jāl·lâ'rā) *vt* to seal
suggerimento (sūj·jā·rē·mān'tō) *m* proposal, advice; suggestion
suggerire (sūj·jā·rē'rā) *vt* to prompt; to suggest
suggeritore (sūj·jā·rē·tō'rā) *m* prompter
suggestione (sūj·jā·styō'nā) *f* suggestion
suggestivo (sūj·jā·stē'vō) *a* interesting; enchanting
sughero (sū'gā·rō) *m* cork
sugna (sū'nyâ) *f* grease; lard
sugo (sū'gō) *m* juice; gravy; *(fig)* main point; pièce de résistance
suicida (swē·chē'dâ) *m&f* suicide *(person)*; **–rsi** (swē·chē·dâr'sē) *vr* to commit suicide
suicidio (swē·chē'dyō) *m* suicide *(act)*
suino (swē'nō) *m* swine; — *a* swinish
sunto (sūn'tō) *m* summary, résumé
suo (sū'ō) *a&pron* his, hers, its, your
suocera (swô'chā·râ) *f* mother-in-law
suocero (swô'chā·rō) *m* father-in-law
suola (swō'lâ) *f* sole *(shoe)*
suolo (swō'lō) *m* soil, earth; ground
suonare (swō·nâ'rā) *vt (mus)* to play; to ring
suonatore (swō·nâ·tō'rā) *m* player, musician
suono (swō'nō) *m* sound; chime, ringing *(bell)*
suora (swō'râ) *f* nun
superare (sū·pā·râ'rā) *vt* to exceed; to do better than
superbia (sū·per'byâ) *f* pride, conceit
superbo (sū·pār'bō) *a* conceited; splendid; haughty
superficiale (sū·pār·fē·châ'lā) *a* superficial
superficie (sū·pār·fē'chā) *f* surface; area
superiore (sū·pā·ryō'rā) *a* superior; higher, upper
superfluo (sū·per'flūō) *a* superflous; — *m* surplus
supermercato (sū·pār·mār·kâ'tō) *m* supermarket
superstite (sū·per'stē·tā) *m* survivor; — *a* surviving
superstizione (sū·pār·stē·tsyō'nā) *f* superstition
superstizioso (sū·pār·stē·tsyō'zō) *a* superstitious
superuomo (sū·pā·rūō'mō) *m* superman
supino (sū·pē'nō) *a* on one's back; supine
supplementare (sūp·plā·mān·tâ'rā) *a* auxiliary, supplementary
supplemento (sūp·plā·mān'tō) *m* supplement; extra fare; additional fee
supplente (sūp·plān'tā) *m* substitute, alternate
supplenza (sūp·plān'tsâ) *f* temporary position; position of an alternate
supplica (sūp'plē·kâ) *f* request; entreaty; **–re** (sūp·plē·kâ'rā) *vt* to implore
supplizio (sūp·plē'tsyō) *m* torment; torture; intense suffering
supporre * (sūp·pōr'rā) *vt&i* to suppose; to conjecture

supposizione (sūp·pō·zē·tsyṓ'nā) *f* supposition
supposta (sūp·pō'stâ) *f* suppository
suppurare (sūp·pū·râ'rā) *vi* to discharge pus, suppurate
suppurazione (sūp·pū·râ·tsyō'nā) *f* discharge of pus, suppuration
supremo (sū·prā'mō) *a* ultimate, last; supreme, absolute
surrealista (sūr·rā·â·lē'stâ) *a&m* surrealist
surrogato (sūr·rō·gâ'tō) *m* substitute, replacement
susina (sū·zē'nâ) *f* plum
sussidiare (sūs·sē·dyâ'rā) *vt* to subsidize, bolster
sussidiario (sūs·sē·dyâ'ryō) *a* additional, subsidiary
sussidio (sūs·sē'dyō) *m* subsidy; contribution
sussiego (sūs·syā'gō) *m* primness, stiffness
sussultare (sūs·sūl·tâ'rā) *vi* to quake; to start, be startled; to throb
sussulto (sūs·sūl'tō) *m* tremble, jump, jerk
sussurrare (sūs·sūr·râ'rā) *vt&i* to sigh, sough *(wind)*; to whisper
sussurro (sūs·sūr'rō) *m* whisper; soughing
svagarsi (zvâ·gâr'sē) *vr* to distract one's mind; to amuse oneself
svago (zvâ'gō) *m* entertainment, recreation
svaligiare (zvâ·lē·jâ'rā) *vt* to burglarize, rob; to strip bare, plunder
svaligiatore (zvâ·lē·jâ·tō'rā) *m* burglar, robber
svalutare (zvâ·lū·tâ'rā) *vt* to depreciate; to devaluate
svalutazione (zvâ·lū·tâ·tsyō'nā) *f* depreciation; devaluating
svanire (zvâ·nē'rā) *vi* to vanish; to evaporate; to fade out; to weaken, lose its force
svantaggiosamente (zvân·tâj·jō·zâ·mān'tā) *adv* unfavorably; prejudicially
svantaggio (zvân·tâj'jō) *m* disadvantage
svariato (zvâ·ryâ'tō) *a* assorted, sundry, divers; not a few
svedese (zvā·dā'zā) *a* Swedish; — *m* Swede
svegliare (zvā·lyâ'rā) *vt* to awake, wake up, awaken; *(fig)* to stimulate
svegliarsi (zvā·lyâr'sē) *vr* to wake up; to be awakened; to be aroused
svelare (zvā·lâ'rā) *vt* to reveal
svelarsi (zvā·lâr'sē) *vr* to show one's true colors; to disclose one's real motives
sveltezza (zvāl·tā'tsâ) *f* slenderness; promptness, rapidity; alertness
svelto (zvāl'tō) *a* alert; slender; quick
svendere (zven'dā·rā) *vt* to sell below cost
svenimento (zvā·nē·mān'tō) *m* faint
svenire * (zvā·nē'rā) *vi* to faint
sventato (zvān·tâ'tō) *a* heedless, careless; — *m* scatterbrain
sventura (zvān·tū'râ) *f* misfortune, mischance
svenuto (zvā·nū'tō) *a* fainted; unconscious
svergognare (zvār·gō·nyâ'rā) *vt* to put to shame; to discountenance
svergognato (zvār·gō·nyâ'tō) *a* shameless, brazen
svestirsi (zvā·stēr'sē) *vr* to undress
Svezia (zve'tsyâ) *f* Sweden
svezzare (zvā·tsâ'rā) *vt* to wean
sviare (zvyâ'rā) *vt* to mislead; to deviate; *(rail)* to switch
sviarsi (zvyâr'sē) *vr* to become lost; to go astray
svignarsela (zvē·nyâr'sā·lâ) *vr* to decamp, abscond; to slip away
sviluppare (zvē·lūp·pâ'rā) *vt* to develop
svilupparsi (zvē·lūp·pâr'sē) *vr* to enlarge; to develop; to grow
sviluppo (zvē·lūp'pō) *m* development; **età dello** — puberty
svincolare (zvēn·kō·lâ'rā) *vt* to redeem; to clear through customs
svincolarsi (zvēn·kō·lâr'sē) *vr* to disengage oneself; to free oneself; to escape
svista (zvē'stâ) *f* oversight
svitare (zvē·tâ'rā) *vt* to unscrew
Svizzera (zvē'tsā·râ) *f* Switzerland
svizzero (zvē'tsā·rō) *a&m* Swiss
svogliatamente (zvō·lyâ·tâ·mān'tā) *adv* unwillingly; grudgingly
svogliato (zvō·lyâ'tō) *a* inattentive; averse, grudging; lackadaisical
svolgere * (zvôl'jā·rā) *vt* to unroll; to display; to carry out; to elaborate on, develop
svolgersi * (zvôl'jār·sē) *vr* to take place; to unfold; to develop
svolgimento (zvōl·jē·mān'tō) *m* handling; solution *(problem)*; development, event
svolta (zvōl'tâ) *f* turn; bend; curve; **–re** (zvōl·tâ'rā) *vt&i* to turn
svotare (zvō·tâ'rā) *vt* to discharge, empty

T

tabaccaio (tâ·bâk·kâ'yō) *m* tobacco dealer, tobacconist
tabaccheria (tâ·bâk·kā·rē'â) *f* cigar store, tobacco shop
tabacco (tâ·bâk'kō) *m* tobacco
tabella (tâ·bāl'lâ) *f* table, chart; bulletin board
tabellone (tâ·bāl·lō'nā) *m* poster
tabernacolo (tâ·bār·nâ'kō·lō) *m* tabernacle
taccagno (tâk·kâ'nyō) *a* stingy, tight-fisted
taccheggiatore (tâk·kāj·jâ·tō'rā) *m* shoplifter
tacchino (tâk·kē'nō) *m* turkey
tacciare (tâ·châ'rā) *vt* to accuse; to blame for
tacco (tâk'kō) *m* heel
taccuino (tâk·kwē'nō) *m* notebook
tacere * (tâ·chā'rā) *vi* to keep quiet; — *vt* to omit; not to mention
taciturno (tâ·chē·tūr'nō) *a* taciturn, uncommunicative; sullen

tachimetro (tâ·kē'mā·trō) *m* speedometer
tafferuglio (tâf·fā·rū'lyō) *m* scuffle
taffetà (tâf·fā·tâ') *m* adhesive tape; taffeta
taglia (tâ'lyâ) *f* reward; size; **–carte** (tâ·lyâ·kâr'tā) *m* paper knife; **–legna** (tâ·lyâ·lā'nyâ) *m* lumberjack; **–ndo** (tâ·lyân'dō) *m* coupon; **–re** (tâ·lyâ'rā) *vt* to cut; **–rsi** (tâ·lyâr'sē) *vr* to cut oneself; **–telle** (tâ·lyâ·tāl'lā) *fpl* noodles; **–tore** (tâ·lyâ·tō'rā) *m* cutter; tailor
tagliente (tâ·lyān'tā) *a* sharp; *(fig)* sarcastic, trenchant
tagliere (tâ·lyā'rā) *m* platter
taglierina (tâ·lyā·rē'nâ) *f* paper cutter
taglio (tâ'lyō) *m* cut; edge, cut side; blade, cutting edge; denomination *(money)*
tagliuola (tâ·lywō'lâ) *f* trap
talco (tâl'kō) *m* talcum powder
tale (tâ'lā) *a* such, so; like, similar; certain, particular
talento (tâ·lān'tō) *m* talent, skill, great ability
talloncino (tâl·lōn·chē'nō) *m* coupon; check stub; voucher
tallone (tâl·lō'nā) *m* heel; *(com)* stub
talmente (tâl·mān'tā) *adv* so very; so much; in that way; so, in such a way
talpa (tâl'pâ) *f* mole
taluno (tâ·lū'nō) *pron* someone, somebody
talvolta (tâl·vōl'tâ) *adv* on occasion, sometimes
tamburello (tâm·bū·rāl'lō) *m* tambourine
tamburino (tâm·bū·rē'nō) *m* drummer
tamburo (tâm·bū'rō) *m* drum
tamponare (tâm·pō·nâ'rā) *vt* to stop up, plug up
tampone (tâm·pō'nā) *m* stamp pad; stopper
tana (tâ'nâ) *f* lair, cave
tanaglie (tâ·nâ'lyā) *fpl* pincers; tongs
tanè (tâ·nā') *a* chestnut color
tanfo (tân'fō) *m* stench; bad odor
tangente (tân·jān'tā) *f&a* tangent
tanghero (tân'gā·rō) *m* boor, yokel
tanti (tân'tē) *a* so many, a great many
tantino (tân·tē'nō) *m* little bit
tanto (tân'tō) *a&adv* so much; so; — **quanto** as much as
tappa (tâp'pâ) *f* stop; lap *(race)*; **–re** (tâp·pâ'rā) *vt* to plug up, plug
tappeto (tâp·pā'tō) *m* rug, carpet
tappezzare (tâp·pā·tsâ'rā) *vt* to upholster; to wallpaper
tappezzeria (tâp·pā·tsā·rē'â) *f* upholstery; wallpaper; **fare** — to be a wallflower *(coll)*
tappezziere (tâp·pā·tsyā'rā) *m* upholsterer; decorator
tappo (tâp'pō) *m* plug, cork; cap, cover
tarantola (tâ·rân'tō·lâ) *f* tarantula
tarchiato (târ·kyâ'tō) *a* stocky
tardare (târ·dâ'rā) *vi* to be late; to be long
tardi (târ'dē) *adv* late
targa (târ'gâ) *f* license plate; — **stradale** street sign
tariffa (tâ·rēf'fâ) *f* scale, rate; price list; tariff, duty
tarlato (târ·lâ'tō) *a* moth-eaten; worm-eaten
tarlo (târ'lō) *m* woodworm, clothes moth
tarma (târ'mâ) *f* moth
tartagliare (târ·tâ·lyâ'rā) *vi* to stammer
tartaruga (târ·tâ·rū'gâ) *f* tortoise, turtle
tartassare (târ·tâs·sâ'rā) *vt* to manhandle, mistreat
tartina (târ·tē'nâ) *f* sandwich
tartufo (târ·tū'fō) *m* truffle
tasca (tâ'skâ) *f* pocket; **–bile** (tâ·skâ'bē·lā) *a* pocket; portable; **–pane** (tâ·skâ·pâ'nā) *m* haversack, shoulder sack
taschino (tâ·skē'nō) *m* vest pocket
tassa (tâs'sâ) *f* tax; duty; **–metro** (tâs·sâ'·mā·trō) *m* taximeter; **–re** (tâs·sâ'rā) *vt* to tax; **–tivamente** (tâs·sâ·tē·vâ·mān'·tā) *adv* exactly; explicitly; positively; **–tivo** (tâs·sâ·tē'vō) *a* exact; compulsory
tassello (tâs·sāl'lō) *m* dowel
tassì (tâs·sē') *m* taxi, cab
tassista (tâs·sē'stâ) *m* taxi driver, cab driver
tasso (tâs'sō) *m* rate of interest
tasso (tâs'sō) *m* badger
tastare (tâ·stâ'rā) *vt* to feel, finger; *(med)* to palpate
tastiera (tâ·styā'râ) *f* keyboard
tasto (tâ'stō) *m (mus, mech)* key; subject
tastoni (tâ·stō'nē) *adv* by groping, gropingly
tattica (tât'tē·kâ) *f* tactics
tatto (tât'tō) *m* sense of touch; tact
tatuaggio (tâ·twâj'jō) *m* tattoo
tatuare (tâ·twâ'rā) *vt* to tattoo
taumaturgo (tâū·mâ·tūr'gō) *m* miracle worker
taurino (tâū·rē'nō) *a* bullish; bull, bull-like
tauromachia (tâū·rō·mâ·kē'â) *f* bull-fighting
taverna (tâ·vār'nâ) *f* tavern
taverniere (tâ·vār·nyā'rā) *m* tavern owner
tavola (tâ'vō·lâ) *f* board; table; plank
tavoletta (tâ·vō·lāt'tâ) *f* tablet
tavolino (tâ·vō·lē'nō) *m* worktable; small table
tavolozza (tâ·vō·lō'tsâ) *f* palette
tazza (tâ'tsâ) *f* cup
te (tā) *pron* you; to you
tè (tā) *m* tea
teatro (tā·â'trō) *m* theater; — **lirico** opera; — **di prosa** legitimate theater; drama
teca (tā'kâ) *f* reliquary; jewel case
tecnica (tek'nē·kâ) *f* technique
tecnicamente (tāk·nē·kâ·mān'tā) *adv* technically
tecnico (tek'nē·kō) *a* technical; — *m* technician; expert
tedesco (tā·dā'skō) *a&m* German
tedio (te'dyō) *m* boredom, ennui; **–so** (tā·dyō'zō) *a* boring
tegame (tā·gâ'mā) *m* pan
teglia (te'lyâ) *f* casserole, baking dish
tegola (te'gō·lâ) *f* roofing tile
teiera (tā·yā'râ) *f* teapot
tela (tā'lâ) *f* cloth; linen; canvas; painting; *(theat)* curtain; — **incerata** oil cloth; — **di ragno** cobweb; **–io** (tâ·lâ'·yō) *m (auto)* chassis; framework; loom

telearma (tā·lā·âr'mâ) *f* guided missile
telecamera (tā·lā·kâ'mā·râ) *f* television camera
telecomandato (tā·lā·kō·mân·dâ'tō) *a* remote-controlled
telecomando (tā·lā·kō·mân'dō) *m* remote control
teleferica (tā·lā·fe'rē·kâ) *f* overhead cable railway, funicular
telefonare (tā·lā·fō·nâ'rā) *vt* to telephone
telefonico (tā·lā·fô'nē·kō) *a* telephone; **elenco** — telephone directory
telefonista (tā·lā·fō·nē'stâ) *m&f* telephone operator
telefono (tā·le'fō·nō) *m* telephone
telefoto (tā·lā·fō'tō) *f* telephotograph
telegenico (tā·lā·je'nē·kō) *a* telegenic
telegiornale (tā·lā·jōr·nâ'lā) *m* television news
telegrafare (tā·lā·grâ·fâ'rā) *vt* to wire, cable
telegrafista (tā·lā·grâ·fē'stâ) *m&f* telegraph operator
telegrafo (tā·le'grâ·fō) *m* telegraph
telegramma (tā·lā·grâm'mâ) *m* telegram
telemetro (tā·le'mā·trō) *m* range finder
teleobiettivo (tā·lā·ō·byāt·tē'vō) *m* telephoto lens
telepatia (tā·lā·pâ·tē'â) *f* telepathy
teleromanzo (tā·lā·rō·mân'dzō) *m* play for television
teleschermo (tā·lā·skār'mō) *m* television screen
telescopio (tā·lā·skô'pyō) *m* telescope
telescrivente (tā·lā·skrē·vān'tā) *m* teleprinter
telespettatore (tā·lā·spāt·tâ·tō'rā) *m* televiewer
telespresso (tā·lā·sprās'sō) *m* telephone message; telegraph message
teletrasmettere (tā·lā·trâ·zmet'tā·rā) *vt* to telecast
teletrasmissione (tā·lā·trâ·zmēs·syō'nā) *f* telecast
televisionare (tā·lā·vē·zyō·nâ'rā) *vt* to telecast, televise
televisione (tā·lā·vē·zyō'nā) *f* television
televisivo (tā·lā·vē·zē'vō) *a* television
televisore (tā·lā·vē·zō'rā) *m* television set
telone (tā·lō'nā) *m* (*theat*) curtain
tema (tā'mâ) *m* subject, theme; problem
temerario (tā·mā·râ'ryō) *a* foolhardy
temere (tā·mā'rā) *vi* to be afraid; — *vt* to fear, be afraid of
temibile (tā·mē'bē·lā) *a* formidable, frightful
temperalapis (tām·pā·râ·lâ'pēs) *m* pencil sharpener
temperamento (tām·pā·râ·mān'tō) *m* temperament
temperanza (tām·pā·rân'tsâ) *f* temperance
temperare (tām·pā·râ'rā) *vt* to temper, lessen; to sharpen; to moderate
temperato (tām·pā·râ'tō) *a* temperate; restrained, reserved
temperatura (tām·pā·râ·tū'râ) *f* temperature
temperino (tām·pā·rē'nō) *m* penknife
tempesta (tām·pā'stâ) *f* storm
tempestivamente (tām·pā·stē·vâ·mān'tā) *adv* promptly; at the right time
tempestoso (tām·pā·stō'zō) *a* stormy
tempia (tem'pyâ) *f* (*anat*) temple
tempio (tem'pyō) *m* temple (*building*)
tempo (tām'pō) *m* time; weather; (*gram*) tense; **–rale** (tām·pō·râ'lā) *m* storm; **–rale** *a* temporal; **–raneo** (tām·pō·râ'nā·ō) *a* temporary, transitory; **–reggiamento** (tām·pō·rāj·jâ·mān'tō) *m* procrastination; **–reggiare** (tām·pō·rāj·jâ'rā) *vi* to procrastinate; **–reggiatore** (tām·pō·rāj·jâ·tō'rā) *m* procrastinator
tempra (tām'prâ) *f* vigor; moral tone, character; attitude; **–re** (tām·prâ'rā) *vt* to harden; to temper
tenace (tā·nâ'chā) *a* tenacious, constant
tenacità (tā·nâ·chē·tâ') *f* stick-to-itiveness (*coll*); tenacity
tenaglia (tā·nâ'lyâ) *f* pincers
tenda (tān'dâ) *f* curtain; tent; awning
tendenza (tān·dān'tsâ) *f* bent, propensity
tendenzioso (tān·dān·tsyō'zō) *a* biased, prejudiced
tendere * (ten'dā·rā) *vt* to stretch out; to hand over; — *vi* to tend, lean
tendina (tān·dē'nâ) *f* window curtain; blind
tenebre (te'nā·brā) *fpl* darkness; gloominess
tenebroso (tā·nā·brō'zō) *a* dark; somber
tenente (tā·nān'tā) *m* lieutenant
tenere * (tā·nā'rā) *vt&i* to hold, hold onto; to maintain, keep; to care for, have an interest in; — **la destra** to keep to the right; — **a mente** to bear in mind; — **conto di** to consider, take into consideration; **non c'è motivo che tenga** there is no reason for it; **non ci tiene affatto** he doesn't care at all; — **al proprio nome** to care about one's reputation
tenerezza (tā·nā·rā'tsâ) *f* tenderness; fondness
tenersi * (tā·nār'sē) *vr* to keep from; to hold oneself; — **per intelligente** to deem oneself clever; — **al corrent dei fatti** to keep abreast of the news; — **in piedi** to remain standing
tenero (te'nā·rō) *a* tender; affectionate; — *m* soft part; weakness, foible
tenia (te'nyâ) *f* tapeworm
tennista (tān·nē'stâ) *m* tennis player
tenore (tā·nō'rā) *m* tenor; text; (*mus*) tenor; tendency; meaning; — **di vita** standard of living
tensione (tān·syō'nā) *f* tension
tentacolo (tān·tâ'kō·lō) *m* tentacle
tentare (tān·tâ'rā) *vt* to try, attempt; to tempt; to touch
tentativo (tān·tâ·tē'vō) *m* attempt
tentatore (tān·tâ·tō'rā) *m* tempter
tentatrice (tān·tâ·trē'chā) *f* temptress
tentazione (tān·tâ·tsyō'nā) *f* temptation
tentennare (tān·tān·nâ'rā) *vi* to waver; to be indecisive; — *vt* to shake
tenue (te'nwā) *a* thin, slight
tenuta (tā·nū'tâ) *f* uniform; estate; landed holdings
teologo (tā·ô'lō·gō) *m* theologian

teoria (tā·ō·rē'â) *f* theory
teorico (tā·ô'rē·kō) *a* theoretical
teorizzare (tā·ō·rē·dzâ'rā) *vi* to theorize
tepido (te'pē·dō) *a* lukewarm, tepid
tepore (tā·pō'rā) *m* warmth
teppa (tāp'pâ) *f* underworld, gangland
teppista (tāp·pē'stâ) *m* gangster
terapia (tā·râ·pē'â) *f* therapy; therapeutics
tergere * (ter'jā·rā) *vt* to wipe, polish
tergicristallo (tār·jē·krē·stâl'lō) *m* windshield wiper
tergiversare (tār·jē·vār·sâ'rā) *vi* to be evasive; to quibble
tergo (tār'gō) *m* back
termale (tār·mâ'lā) *a* thermal; **stazione —** spa, health resort
terme (tār'mā) *fpl* hot springs
terminatamente (tār·mē·nâ·tâ·mān'tā) *adv* exactly; definitively; once and for all
terminare (tār·mē·nâ'rā) *vt&i* to finish, conclude
termine (ter'mē·nā) *m* end; termination; term; stipulation; **a rigor di —** strictly speaking; **in altri termini** in other words
terminologia (tār·mē·nō·lō·jē'â) *f* terminology
termodinamica (tār·mō·dē·nâ'mē·kâ) *f* thermodynamics
termoelettrico (tār·mō·ā·let'trē·kō) *a* thermoelectric
termogeno (tār·mô'jā·nō) *a* thermogenic, heat-producing
termomagnetico (tār·mō·mâ·nye'tē·kō) *a* thermomagnetic
termometro (tār·mô'mā·trō) *m* thermometer
termosifone (tār·mō·sē·fō'nā) *m* radiator
termostato (tār·mō·stâ'tō) *m* thermostat
terra (tār'râ) *f* soil, ground; earth; (*naut*) land; (*elec*) ground; **scendere a —** to land, go ashore; **via —** by land
terraglia (tār·râ'lyâ) *f* earthenware
terrazza (tār·râ'tsâ) *f*, **terrazzo** (tār·râ'tsō) *m* terrace; balcony
terremoto (tār·rā·mō'tō) *m* earthquake
terreno (tār·rā'nō) *m* soil; plot of land; — *a* worldly, temporal
terrestre (tār·rā'strā) *a* terrestrial
terribile (tār·rē'bē·lā) *a* awful, terrible
terrificante (tār·rē·fē·kân'tā) *a* appalling; frightening, horrifying
terrificare (tār·rē·fē·kâ'rā) *vt* to appall; to terrify, horrify
terrifico (tār·rē'fē·kō) *a* dreadful, horrible
territoriale (tār·rē·tō·ryâ'lā) *a* territorial
territorio (tār·rē·tô'ryō) *m* territory, region
terrore (tār·rō'rā) *m* terror, fear
terrorizzare (tār·rō·rē·dzâ'rā) *vt* to terrorize
terzetto (tār·tsāt'tō) *m* trio; group of three
terzino (tār·tsē'nō) *m* fullback (*football*)
terzo (tār'tsō) *a* third
tesa (tā'zâ) *f* hat brim
teschio (te'skyō) *m* skull
tesi (tā'zē) *f* thesis
teso (tā'zō) *a* taut, tightly stretched; strained
tesoreria (tā·zō·rā·rē'â) *f* treasury
tesoriere (tā·zō·ryā'rā) *m* treasurer
tesoro (tā·zō'rō) *m* treasure; sweetheart
tessera (tes'sā·râ) *f* card; identification card
tessere (tes'sā·rā) *vt* to weave
tessile (tes'sē·lā) *a* textile
tessilsacco (tās·sēl·sâk'kō) *m* garment bag
tessuto (tās·sū'tō) *m* fabric, material; (*anat*) tissue
testa (tā'stâ) *f* head; top; **dolor di —** headache; **in testa alla pagina** at the top of the page
testamento (tā·stâ·mān'tō) *m* will
testardaggine (tā·stâr·dâj'jē·nā) *f* stubbornness
testardo (tā·stâr'dō) *a* stubborn
testata (tā·stâ'tâ) *f* headline; heading; (*mil*) warhead
testicolo (tā·stē'kō·lō) *m* testicle
testimone (tā·stē·mō'nā) *m* witness
testimonianza (tā·stē·mō·nyân'tsâ) *f* testimony, evidence
testimoniare (tā·stē·mō·nyâ'rā) *vt* to testify to, give evidence to, attest to
testo (tā'stō) *m* text; copy
testuale (tā·stwâ'lā) *a* verbatim; word-for-word
testualmente (tā·stwâl·mān'tā) *adv* verbatim
tetano (te'tâ·nō) *m* tetanus, lockjaw
tetraedro (tā·trâ·ā'drō) *m* tetrahedron
tetragono (tā·trâ'gō·nō) *m* tetragon; — *a* (*fig*) steadfast, constant, stable
tetro (tā'trō) *a* gloomy, dark
tetto (tāt'tō) *m* roof; **–ia** (tāt·tô'yâ) *f* shed; marquee
ti (tē) *pron* you; to you
tiara (tyâ'râ) *f* tiara
tibia (tē'byâ) *f* shinbone, tibia
ticchio (tēk'kyō) *m* caprice, whim; (*med*) tic
tiepido (tye'pē·dō) *a* lukewarm
tifo (tē'fō) *m* typhus; **–ide** (tē·fô'ē·dā) *f* typhoid fever; **–so** (tē·fō'zō) *m* typhus patient; (*fig*) sports enthusiast, fan
tifone (tē·fō'nā) *m* hurricane; typhoon
tiglio (tē'lyō) *m* linden tree
tigna (tē'nyâ) *f* ringworm
tignola (tē·nyō'lâ) *f* moth
tigre (tē'grā) *f* tiger
tigrotto (tē·grōt'tō) *m* tiger cub
timballo (tēm·bâl'lō) *m* (*cooking*) timbale; kettle drum
timbrare (tēm·brâ'rā) *vt* to postmark; to affix a stamp to, stamp
timbro (tēm'brō) *m* stamp; timbre
timidamente (tē·mē·dâ·mān'tā) *adv* with shyness, timidly
timidezza (tē·mē·dā'tsâ) *f* shyness; timidity
timido (tē'mē·dō) *a* shy; diffident
timone (tē·mō'nā) *m* helm; rudder
timoniere (tē·mō·nyā'rā) *m* helmsman
timore (tē·mō'rā) *m* fear
timoroso (tē·mō·rō'zō) *a* timid, afraid
timpano (tēm'pâ·nō) *m* eardrum; kettledrum
tina (tē'nâ) *f* tub

tinello (tē·nāl'lō) *m* dinette, small dining room
tingere * (tēn'jā·rā) *vt* to dye
tingersi * (tēn'jār·sē) *vr* to dye; — **le labbra** to put on lipstick
tino (tē'nō) *m* tub, vat; **–zza** (tē·nō'tsâ) *f* tub; bathtub
tinta (tēn'tâ) *f* shade; color; **–rella** (tēn·tâ·rāl'lâ) *f* (*coll*) suntan
tintinnare (tēn·tēn·nâ'rā) *vi* to clink; to jingle; to tinkle
tintinnio (tēn·tēn·nē'ō) *m* clinking; jingling; tinkling
tintore (tēn·tō'rā) *m* dry cleaner; dyer
tintoria (tēn·tō·rē'â) *f* dry cleaning shop
tintura (tēn·tū'râ) *f* tincture
tipicamente (tē·pē·kâ·mān'tā) *adv* typically
tipico (tē'pē·kō) *a* typical
tipo (tē'pō) *m* type; pattern, standard; **bel — originale** oddball (*coll*); **–grafia** (tē·pō·grâ·fē'â) *f* printing office; **–grafo** (tē·pô'grâ·fō) *m* printer
tiraggio (tē·râj'jō) *m* draft (*drawing*)
tiralinee (tē·râ·lē'nā·ā) *m* ruling pen
tiranneggiare (tē·rân·nāj·jâ'rā) *vt* to tyrannize, oppress; to lord it over
tirannia (tē·rân·nē'â) *f* tyranny
tiranno (tē·rân'nō) *m* tyrant
tirapiedi (tē·râ·pyā'dē) *m* henchman, collaborator
tiraprazi (tē·râ·prân'dzē) *m* dumbwaiter
tirare (tē·râ'rā) *vt* to pull; to throw; to shoot at; to print, run off an impression of; — *vi* to tend; to blow (*wind*); — **la somma** to find the sum; — **sul prezzo** to bargain; — **le conclusioni** to draw the conclusion; — **avanti** to get ahead; — **diritto** to go straight ahead
tirarsi (tē·râr'sē) *vr* to draw to oneself, pull in; — **indietro** to draw back; (*fig*) to retract one's statement; — **su** to stand up; (*fig*) to pull oneself together; — **dai pasticci** to get out of trouble
tirato (tē·râ'tō) *a* taut, pulled tight; stingy
tiratore (tē·râ·tō'rā) *m* marksman; — **scelto** sharpshooter; **franco** — sniper; — **d'arco** archer; — **di scherma** fencer
tiratura (tē·râ·tū'râ) *f* run, number run (*printing*); circulation; attraction
tirchio (tēr'kyō) *a* stingy
tiretto (tē·rāt'tō) *m* drawer
tiritera (tē·rē·tā'râ) *f* rigmarole; nonsense tale; wordy speech
tiro (tē'rō) *m* pull; extent; throw; shot; stroke (*billiards*); — **a segno** shooting gallery; **venire a** — (*coll*) to get one's hands on; **–cinio** (tē·rō·chē'nyō) *m* apprenticeship, training period
tiroide (tē·rô'ē·dā) *f* (*anat*) thyroid
tisana (tē·zâ'nâ) *f* herb tea
tisi (tē'zē) *f* tuberculosis; **–co** (tē'zē·kō) *a* tuberculous, tubercular
titolare (tē·tō·lâ'rā) *m* owner of a firm; company president; — *a* titular
titolo (tē'tō·lō) *m* title; right; headline, heading; qualification, requisite; — **di studio** degree; **a — di** by way of; in one's capacity as
titubante (tē·tū·bân'tā) *a* hesitant, reluctant
tizio (tē'tsyō) *m* a certain individual, some person, so-and-so
tizzone (tē·tsō'nā) *m* firebrand
toccare (tōk·kâ'rā) *vt&i* to touch; to affect; to be one's turn; — **sul vivo** to hurt deeply, cut to the quick; — **con mano** to make sure of
toccarsi (tōk·kâr'sē) *vr* to meet, reach
toccasana (tōk·kâ·sâ'nâ) *m* panacea, cure-all
tocco (tōk'kō) *m* touch; (*med*) stroke; hint, indication; — *a* touched; crack-brained; **al** — at one o'clock
toga (tō'gâ) *f* official garb; toga
togliere * (tô'lyā·rā) *vt* to take away; to lift off
togliersi * (tô'lyār·sē) *vr* to get away; to extricate oneself; to deprive oneself; — **la vita** to commit suicide; — **di mezzo** to get out of the way; — **le scarpe** to take off one's shoes
tolda (tōl'dâ) *f* (*naut*) deck
toletta (tō·lāt'tâ) *f* dressing table, vanity; toilette, grooming
tollerante (tōl·lā·rân'tā) *a* tolerant, liberal; understanding
tolleranza (tōl·lā·rân'tsâ) *f* leeway, tolerance; understanding; **casa di** — brothel
tollerare (tōl·lā·râ'rā) *vt* to tolerate, bear; to allow, sanction
tomaia (tō·mâ'yâ) *f* vamp; upper (*shoe*)
tomba (tōm'bâ) *f* tomb; grave
tombino (tōm·bē'nō) *m* manhole
tombola (tôm'bō·lâ) *f* lotto; bingo
tomo (tō'mō) *m* volume, tome
tondo (tōn'dō) *a* round; obvious, patent
tonfo (tōn'fō) *m* splash; thud; flop
tonnellaggio (tōn·nāl·lâj'jō) *m* tonnage
tonnellata (tōn·nāl·lâ'tâ) *f* ton
tonno (tōn'nō) *m* tuna, tuna fish
tono (tō'nō) *m* tone; tune; pitch; style, fashion
tonsilla (tōn·sēl'lâ) *f* tonsil
topazio (tō·pâ'tsyō) *m* topaz
topica (tô'pē·kâ) *f* blunder; **fare una** — to put one's foot in it
topo (tō'pō) *m* mouse; — **d'auto** automobile thief; — **di biblioteca** bookworm (*fig*)
topografia (tō·pō·grâ·fē'â) *f* topography
toppa (tōp'pâ) *f* patch; lock
torace (tō·râ'chā) *m* thorax
torbido (tôr'bē·dō) *a* muddy, roiled
torcere * (tôr'chā·rā) *vt* to twist; to wrench
torcersi * (tôr'chār·sē) *vr* to squirm, wriggle
torchio (tôr'kyō) *m* press
torcia (tôr'châ) *f* candle, torch
torcicollo (tōr·chē·kōl'lō) *m* stiff neck; torticollis
torinese (tō·rē·nā'zā) *a&m* Turinese
Torino (tō·rē'nō) *f* Turin
torlo (tōr'lō) *m* yolk
tormenta (tōr·mān'tâ) *f* blizzard; **–re** (tōr·mān·tâ'rā) *vt* to torment, plague; **–rsi**

(tōr·mān·târ'sē) *vr* to worry oneself, be uneasy; to hound oneself
tormento (tōr·mān'tō) *m* torture; anguish, suffering
tornaconto (tōr·nâ·kōn'tō) *m* advantage, account
tornare (tōr·nâ'rā) *vi* to return; to recur
torneo (tōr·nā'ō) *m* competition; jousting
tornio (tôr'nyō) *m* lathe
tornitore (tōr·nē·tō'rā) *m* turner
toro (tō'rō) *m* bull
torpedine (tōr·pe'dē·nā) *f* torpedo
torpediniera (tōr·pā·dē·nyā'râ) *f* torpedo boat
torpedone (tōr·pā·dō'nā) *m* sightseeing bus; motor coach
torpore (tōr·pō'rā) *m* lethargy, drowsiness
torre (tōr'rā) *f* tower
torrente (tōr·rān'tā) *m* torrent, rapids
torrone (tōr·rō'nā) *m* nougat
torsione (tōr·syō'nā) *f* twist, torsion
torso (tōr'sō) *m* (*anat*) trunk, torso
torsolo (tôr'sō·lō) *m* core, pit, stone (*fruit*)
torta (tōr'tâ) *f* cake; pie
torto (tōr'tō) *m* wrong; condemnation; injustice; — *a* twisted, out of shape; **aver** — to be wrong, be in error
tortora (tôr'tō·râ) *f* turtledove
tortuosamente (tōr·twō·zâ·mān'tā) *adv* tortuously; laboriously
tortuoso (tōr·twō'zō) *a* winding; crooked; laborious
tortura (tōr·tū'rā) *f* torture; **–re** (tōr·tū·râ'rā) *vt* to torture; **–rsi** (tōr·tū·râr'sē) *vr* to plague oneself, torture oneself; to hound oneself; — **il cervello** to cudgel one's brains
torvo (tōr'vō) *a* surly, grim
tosare (tō·zâ'rā) *vt* to clip, cut; to shear
Toscana (tō·skâ'nâ) *f* Tuscany
toscano (tō·skâ'nō) *m&a* Tuscan
tosse (tōs'sā) *f* cough
tossico (tôs'sē·kō) *m* poison; — *a* toxic; **–mane** (tōs·sē·kô'mâ·nā) *m* drug addict
tostapane (tō·stâ·pâ'nā) *m* toaster
tostare (tō·stâ'rā) *vt* to roast; to toast
tosto (tō'stō) *adv* immediately; soon; — **che** just as soon as, when
tosto (tō'stō) *a* brazen, impudent; toasted
totale (tō·tâ'lā) *m&a* total
totalizzatore (tō·tâ·lē·dzâ·tō'rā) *m* totalizator; pari-mutuel
totocalcio (tō·tō·kâl'chō) *m* football pool
tovaglia (tō·vâ'lyâ) *f* tablecloth
tovagliolo (tō·vâ·lyō'lō) *m* napkin
tozzo (tō'tsō) *a* stocky; chunky; — *m* piece, chunk
tra (trâ) *prep* among; between
traballare (trâ·bâl·lâ'rā) *vi* to totter; to reel
trabeazione (trâ·bā·â·tsyō'nā) *f* entablature
traboccare (trâ·bōk·kâ'rā) *vi* to overflow
trabocchetto (trâ·bōk·kāt'tō) *m* trap, pitfall
traccia (trâ'châ) *f* trace; **–re** (trâ·châ'rā) *vt* to sketch; to trail; to lay out; **–to** (trâ·châ'tō) *m* tracing; layout
tracolla (trâ·kōl'lâ) *f* shoulder belt; **a** — across the shoulders
tracollo (trâ·kōl'lō) *m* downfall, collapse; (*mech*) breakdown, failure; (*com*) decline, recession
tradimento (trâ·dē·mān'tō) *m* betrayal; deception
tradire (trâ·dē'rā) *vt* to betray; to cheat
tradirsi (trâ·dēr'sē) *vr* to give away one's motives; to defeat one's own purpose
traditore (trâ·dē·tō'rā) *m* traitor; deceiver
tradizione (trâ·dē·tsyō'nā) *f* tradition, custom
tradotta (trâ·dōt'tâ) *f* troop train
tradurre * (trâ·dūr'rā) *vt* to translate
traduttore (trâ·dūt·tō'rā) *m* translator
traduzione (trâ·dū·tsyō'nā) *f* translation
trafelato (trâ·fā·lâ'tō) *a* breathless, out of breath, breathing hard
traffichino (trâf·fē·kē'nō) *m* schemer, meddler
traffico (trâf'fē·kō) *m* traffic; business, trade
trafiletto (trâ·fē·lāt'tō) *m* brief article
traforare (trâ·fō·râ'rā) *vt* to drill through; to pierce
traforo (trâ·fō'rō) *m* tunnel; openwork embroidery
tragedia (trâ·je'dyâ) *f* tragedy
traghetto (trâ·gāt'tō) *m* ferryboat
tragico (trâ'jē·kō) *a* tragic
tragitto (trâ·jēt'tō) *m* run, trip; route
traguardo (trâ·gwâr'dō) *m* (*sport*) finish line; aim, purpose
tralasciare (trâ·lâ·shâ'rā) *vt* to interrupt; to omit; to give up
tram (trâm) *m* streetcar
trama (trâ'mâ) *f* plot; intrigue
trambusto (trâm·bū'stō) *m* confusion; hustle and bustle
tramezza (trâ·mā'dzâ) *f* partition; division
tramezzino (trâ·mā·dzē'nō) *m* sandwich man
tramite (trâ'mē·tā) *m* procedure, course, channel; **per — di** by means of, by way of
tramontana (trâ·mōn·tâ'nâ) *f* north wind
tramontare (trâ·mōn·târ'ā) *vi* to go down, set (*sun*)
tramonto (trâ·mōn'tō) *m* sunset; setting
trampolino (trâm·pō·lē'nō) *m* springboard; trampoline
tranello (trâ·nāl'lō) *m* trap
tranne (trân'nā) *prep* except, with the exception of
tranquillità (trân·kwēl·lē·tâ') *f* tranquillity, peace
tranquillizzare (trân·kwēl·lē·dzâ'rā) *vt* to calm; to pacify
tranquillizzarsi (trân·kwēl·lē·dzâr'sē) *vr* to become quiet, calm down
tranquillo (trân·kwēl'lō) *a* calm, peaceful; restful
transatlantico (trân·zât·lân'tē·kō) *m* ocean liner; — *a* transatlantic
transazione (trân·zâ·tsyō'nā) *f* compromise, agreement to terms; dealing, transaction
transigere * (trân·zē'jā·rā) *vi* to compro-

mise; to agree on terms; to transact business
transito (trân'sē·tō) *m* transit; **vietato il —** no entrance, no admittance; **–rio** (trân·sē·tô'ryō) *a* fleeting, transitory
tranvia (trân·vē'â) *f* streetcar
tranviere (trân·vyā'rā) *m* streetcar conductor
trapano (trâ'pâ·nō) *m* drill
trapelare (trâ·pā·lâ'rā) *vi* to ooze out; to leak through
trapezio (trâ·pe'tsyō) *m* trapeze; (*math*) trapezoid
trapianto (trâ·pyân'tō) *m* transplant, graft; transfer
trappola (trâp'pō·lâ) *f* trap
trapunta (trâ·pūn'tâ) *f* quilt; **–re** (trâ·pūn·tâ'rā) *vt* to quilt
trarre * (trâr'rā) *vt* to draw in, take in, haul in; **— in inganno** to deceive; **— un sospiro** to heave a sigh
trarsi * (trâr'sē) *vr* to extricate oneself, free oneself; **— d'impaccio** to get out of a difficult situation
trasalire (trâ·sâ·lē'rā) *vi* to jump, start; to be startled, taken unaware
trasandato (trâ·zân·dâ'tō) *a* careless, slovenly; abandoned, neglected
trascendere * (trâ·shen'dā·rā) *vt* to transcend; to overstep; to exaggerate; to lose one's composure
trascinare (trâ·shē·nâ'rā) *vt* to drag along; to shuffle (*feet*); to pull along
trascinarsi (trâ·shē·nâr'sē) *vr* to pull oneself along with effort
trascorrere * (trâ·scôr'rā·rā) *vt* to spend (*time*); **—** *vi* to elapse, go by
trascorso (trâ·skōr'sō) *m* lapse (*time*); slight error; **—** *a* travelled, traversed
trascurare (trâ·skū·râ'rā) *vt* to neglect; to be careless about
trascurato (trâ·skū·râ'tō) *a* careless, neglectful
trasferire (trâ·sfā·rē'rā) *vt* to transfer; to make over
trasferirsi (trâ·sfā·rēr'sē) *vr* to move to a new address
trasferta (trâ·sfār'tâ) *f* travel allowance
trasfigurazione (trâ·sfē·gū·râ·tsyō'nā) *f* transfiguration
trasformare (trâ·sfōr·mâ'rā) *vt* to transform
trasformatore (trâ·sfōr·mâ·tō'rā) *m* transformer, converter; changer
trasformazione (trâ·sfōr·mâ·tsyō'nā) *f* transformation; changeover
trasfusione (trâ·sfū·zyō'nā) *f* transfusion
trasgredire (trâ·zgrā·dē'rā) *vt&i* to infringe upon; to violate; to sin against
trasgressione (trâ·zgrās·syō'nā) *f* violation; encroachment
traslocare (trâ·zlō·kâ'rā) *vt&i* to move; to change one's address; to relocate
trasloco (trâ·zlō'kō) *m* moving, change of residence; relocation
trasmettere * (trâ·zmet'tā·rā) *vt (rad)* to broadcast; to forward, transmit
trasmigrazione (trâ·zmē·grâ·tsyō'nā) *f* transmigration
trasmissione (trâ·zmēs·syō'nā) *f* broadcast; transmission
trasmissore (trâ·zmēs·sō'rā) *m* transmitter, forwarder
transmittente (trân·zmēt·tān'tā) *m* sending set, transmitter; **—** *a* transmitting
trasognato (trâ·sō·nyâ'tō) *a* visionary, impractical; dreamy, woolgathering
trasparente (trâ·spâ·rān'tā) *a* transparent; obvious; (*fig*) sincere, straightforward
trasparenza (trâ·spâ·rān'tsâ) *f* transparency; obviousness; (*fig*) sincerity
trasportare (trâ·spōr·tâ'rā) *vt* to transport; to transpose; to draw; to inspire
trasporto (trâ·spōr'tō) *m* transportation; ecstasy, inspiration
trasvolare (trâ·zvō·lâ'rā) *vt* to fly over, fly above
tratta (trât'tâ) *f* bank draft; run, stretch, section; **— delle bianche** white slavery; **–mento** (trât·tâ·mān'tō) *m* treatment, use; **–re** (trât·tâ'rā) *vt* to treat; to make use of; **–rsi** (trât·târ'sē) *vr* to be a matter of; to concern; to fare, live, do; **–rsi di vita o di morte** to be a question of life or death; **si tratta di ciò** that's the question, that's just the point; **–tiva** (trât·tâ·tē'vâ) *f* negotiation; **–to** (trât·tâ'tō) *m* treaty
trattenere * (trât·tā·nā'rā) *vt* to withhold; to check; to hold in, restrain
trattenersi * (trât·tā·nār'sē) *vr* to stay, prolong one's stay; to control oneself, keep one's emotions under control
trattenimento (trât·tā·nē·mān'tō) *m* party; entertainment
trattenuta (trât·tā·nū'tâ) *f* (*com*) deduction
tratto (trât'tō) *m* stroke; jerk; distance; way, manner; time period; **— d'unione** hyphen; **tutto ad un —** without warning, suddenly; **di — in —** occasionally, periodically
trattoria (trât·tō·rē'â) *m* restaurant
trattore (trât·tō'rā) *m* restaurateur; (*mech*) tractor
trattrice (trât·trē'chā) *f* tractor
trave (trâ'vā) *f* rafter, beam
traversare (trâ·vār·sâ'rā) *vt* to cross, go across
traversata (trâ·vār·sâ'tâ) *f* crossing, trip across, trip over
travestito (trâ·vā·stē'tō) *a* disguised; misrepresented
traviare (trâ·vyâ'rā) *vt* to lead astray; to corrupt
travolgente (trâ·vōl·jān'tā) *a* overwhelming, decisive
travolgere * (trâ·vôl'jā·rā) *vt* to overcome; to sweep away; to upset
trazione (trâ·tsyō'nā) *f* drayage, cartage; traction
tre (trā) *a* three
trebbiare (trāb·byâ'rā) *vt&i* to thresh
trebbiatrice (trāb·byâ·trē'chā) *f* threshing machine
treccia (tre'châ) *f* braid
trecento (trā·chān'tō) *a* three hundred; **il T–** the fourteenth century

tredicenne (trā·dē·chān′nā) *a* thirteen years old
tredicesimo (trā·dē·che′zē·mō) *a* thirteenth
tredici (tre′dē·chē) *a* thirteen; **–mila** (trā·dē·chē·mē′lâ) *a* thirteen thousand
tregua (tre′gwâ) *f* truce; rest, peace (*fig*)
tremare (trā·mâ′rā) *vi* to shake, tremble
tremendo (trā·mān′dō) *a* dire; tremendous; dreadful
trementina (trā·mān·tē′nâ) *f* turpentine
tremila (trā·mē′lâ) *a* three thousand
treno (trā′nō) *m* train; **— letto** sleeping car
trenta (trān′tâ) *a* thirty; **–mila** (trān·tâ·mē′lâ) *a* thirty thousand
trentesimo (trān·te′zē·mō) *a&m* thirtieth
tresca (trā′skâ) *f* love affair
triangolare (tryân·gō·lâ′rā) *a* triangular
triangolo (tryân′gō·lō) *m* triangle
tribolazione (trē·bō·lâ·tsyō′nā) *f* tribulation, ordeal
tribù (trē·bū′) *f* tribe
tribuna (trē·bū′nâ) *f* stand; gallery; **–le** (trē·bū·nâ′lā) *m* court, tribunal
triciclo (trē·chē′klō) *m* tricycle
triennale (tryān·nâ′lā) *a* triennial
trienne (tryān′nā) *a* three years old
Trieste (tryā′stā) *f* Trieste
triestino (tryā·stē′nō) *a* Triestine
trifase (trē·fâ′zā) *a* (*elec*) three-phase
trifoglio (trē·fô′lyō) *m* clover
trimestre (trē·mā′strā) *m* quarter (*year*); period of three months
trimotore (trē·mō·tō′rā) *m* (*avi*) trimotor
trincea (trēn·chā′â) *f* trench
trinciare (trēn·châ′rā) *vt* to carve; to slice, cut
trionfo (tryōn′fō) *m* triumph
triplo (trē′plō) *a&m* triple
trippa (trēp′pâ) *f* tripe
triste (trē′stā) *a* unhappy; sad; **–zza** (trē·stā′tsâ) *f* sorrow, sadness
tristo (trē′stō) *a* evil, wicked
tritacarne (trē·tâ·kâr′nā) *vt* meat grinder
tritare (trē·tâ′rā) *vt* to grind; to chop fine, mince
tritolo (trē·tō′lō) *m* trinitrotoluene, TNT
trivellare (trē·vāl·lâ′rā) *vt* to drill, perforate
triviale (trē·vyâ′lā) *a* uncultured, vulgar, common
trofeo (trō·fā′ō) *m* trophy
troia (trô′yâ) *f* sow
Troia (trô′yâ) *f* Troy
troiano (trō·yâ′nō) *m&a* Trojan
tromba (trōm′bâ) *f* horn
trombaio (trōm·bâ′yō) *m* plumber
trombato (trōm·bâ′tō) *a* rejected; defeated at the polls
trombettiere (trōm·bāt·tyā′rā) *m* bugler; trumpeter
trombone (trōm·bō′nā) *m* trombone
troncare (trōn·kâ′rā) *vt* to cut off; to reduce sharply
tronco (trōn′kō) *m* trunk, log; (*rail*) siding; — *a* cut off; curtailed; truncated
trono (trō′nō) *m* throne
tropico (trô′pē·kō) *m* tropic
troppi (trōp′pē) *a* too many
troppo (trōp′pō) *adv* too; too much; — *a&pron* too much
trota (trō′tâ) *f* trout
trotto (trōt′tō) *m* trot
trottola (trôt′tō·lâ) *f* top (*toy*)
trovare (trō·vâ′rā) *vt* to find; to believe, be of the opinion
trovarsi (trō·vâr′sē) *vr* to meet; to feel, be; to be by chance
trovata (trō·vâ′tâ) *f* makeshift; invention
truccare (trūk·kâ′rā) *vt* to trick, deceive
truccarsi (trūk·kâr′sē) *vr* to make up, put on one's makeup
truccatore (trūk·kâ·tō′rā) *m* (*theat*) makeup man
trucco (trūk′kō) *m* trick; cosmetics
truce (trū′chā) *a* savage; merciless, grim; horrifying
truciolo (trū′chō·lō) *m* wood shaving; chip of wood
truffa (trūf′fâ) *f* fraud; **— all'americana** confidence game; **–re** (trūf·fâ′rā) *vt* to swindle; to dupe; **–tore** (trūf·fâ·tō′rā) *m* swindler; confidence man; crook
truppa (trūp′pâ) *f* troop
tu (tū) *pron* you (*fam*)
tubatura (tū·bâ·tū′râ) *f* plumbing system, plumbing
tubercolosario (tū·bār·kō·lō·zâ′ryō) *m* tuberculosis sanatorium
tubercolosi (tū·bār·kō·lō′zē) *f* tuberculosis, consumption
tubercoloso (tū·bār·kō·lō′zō) *a* tubercular; **—** *m&a* consumptive
tubo (tū′bō) *m* pipe, tube
tuffare (tūf·fâ′rā) vt to plunge
tuffarsi (tūf·fâr′sē) *vr* to plunge, dive
tuffo (tūf′fō) *m* dive
tumulto (tū·mūl′tō) *m* din, uproar
tumultuoso (tū·mūl·twō′zō) *a* tumultuous
tuo (tū′ō) *a* your, yours; — *pron* yours
tuono (twō′nō) *m* thundering, thunder
tuorlo (twōr′lō) *m* yolk
turacciolo (tū·râ′chō·lō) *m* stopper, cork
turare (tū·râ′rā) *vt* to cork, plug up; to obstruct, block
turarsi (tū·râr′sē) *vr* to be stopped up
turba (tūr′bâ) *f* disorderly crowd; mob; **–mento** (tūr·bâ·mān′tō) *m* excitement; disturbance; anxiety
turbante (tūr·bân′tā) *m* turban
turbare (tūr·bâ′rā) *vt* to disturb, bother
turbarsi (tūr·bâr′sē) *vr* to become upset; to become perturbed; to grow overcast (*sky*)
turbina (tūr·bē′nâ) *f* turbine
turbine (tūr′bē·nā) *m* whirlwind
turbinosamente (tūr·bē·nō·zâ·mān′tā) *adv* stormily
turbogeneratore (tūr·bō·jā·nā·râ·tō′rā) *m* turbogenerator
turbogetto (tūr·bō·jāt′tō) *m* turbojet
turboreattore (tūr·bō·rā·ât·tō′rā) *m* turbojet
turchese (tūr·kā′zā) *f* turquoise
turchino (tūr·kē′nō) *a* deep blue
turco (tūr′kō) *m* Turk; — *a* Turkish
turista (tū·rē′stâ) *m&f* tourist

turlupinare (tūr·lū·pē·nâ'rā) *vt* to swindle; to hoodwink; to defraud
turlupinatura (tūr·lū·pē·nâ·tū'râ) *f* fraud; trickery; deceit
turno (tūr'nō) *m* shift; turn
turpiloquio (tūr·pē·lô'kwēō) *m* obscene speech, foul language
tuta (tū'tâ) *f* overalls
tutela (tū·tā'lâ) *f* protection; sponsorship, safeguard
tutore (tū·tō'rā) *m* guardian; protector; sponsor
tuttavia (tūt·tâ·vē'â) *adv* notwithstanding, nonetheless; — *conj* in spite of, notwithstanding
tutto (tūt'tō) *a* all; — *m* everything; overall effect; **–ra** (tūt·tō'râ) *adv* still; as yet

U

ubbidiente (ūb·bē·dyān'tā) *a* obedient; meek
ubbidienza (ūb·bē·dyān'tsâ) *f* obedience; meekness
ubbidire (ūb·bē·dē'rā) *vt* to obey; to comply with, fulfill
ubicazione (ū·bē·kâ·tsyō'nā) *f* whereabouts; site, situation
ubriacarsi (ū·bryâ·kâr'sē) *vr* to become drunk; to drink to excess
ubriachezza (ū·bryâ·kā'tsâ) *f* inebriation, drunkenness
ubriaco (ū·bryâ'kō) *a&m* drunk; **–ne** (ū·bryâ'kō·nā) *m* drunk, drunkard
uccello (ū·chāl'lō) *m* bird
uccidere * (ū·chē'dā·rā) *vt* to kill, do away with
uccidersi * (ū·chē'dār·sē) *vr* to kill oneself, do away with oneself
uccisione (ū·chē·zyō'nā) *f* killing
udienza (ū·dyān'tsâ) *f* (*law*) hearing; audience; consideration
udire * (ū·dē'rā) *vt* to hear
udito (ū·dē'tō) *m* sense of hearing; **–rio** (ū·dē·tô'ryō) *m* audience, spectators
ufficiale (ūf·fē·châ'lā) *m* officer; — *a* official; — **pagatore** paymaster
ufficialmente (ūf·fē·châl·mān'tā) *adv* officially; through official channels
ufficio (ūf·fē'chō) *m* office; **–so** (ūf·fē·chō'zō) *a* informal; semiofficial
uggioso (ūj·jō'zō) *a* boring; uninteresting; distasteful
uguaglianza (ū·gwâ·lyân'tsâ) *f* likeness; equality
uguale (ū·gwâ'lā) *a* equal; — *m* peer, equal
ugualmente (ū·gwâl·mān'tā) *adv* just the same; equally
ultimare (ūl·tē·mâ'rā) *vt* to complete, terminate
ultimo (ūl'tē·mō) *a* last, final; recent.
umanità (ū·mâ·nē·tâ') *f* humanity
umanitario (ū·mâ·nē·tâ'ryō) *a&m* humanitarian
umano (ū·mâ'nō) *a* human
umbro (ūm'brō) *m&a* Umbrian
umidità (ū·mē·dē·tâ') *f* humidity
umido (ū'mē·dō) *a* humid, damp; — *m* dampness; stew
umile (ū'mē·lā) *a* humble; lacking in pretention
umiliante (ū·mē·lyân'tā) *a* degrading, humiliating
umiliare (ū·mē·lyâ'rā) *vt* to mortify, humiliate; to degrade
umiliarsi (ū·mē·lyâr'sē) *vr* to humble oneself, degrade oneself
umiliazione (ū·mē·lyâ·tsyô'nā) *f* degradation, humiliation
umiltà (ū·mēl·tâ') *f* humility; unpretentiousness, modesty
umore (ū·mō'rā) *m* mood, humor; **di cattivo** — in a bad mood, out of sorts
umorista (ū·mō·rē'stâ) *m* humorist; wit
umoristico (ū·mō·rē'stē·kō) *a* witty; funny
un (ūn) *art m* the
una (ū'nâ) *art f* the
uncinetto (ūn·chē·nāt'tō) *m* crocheting needle
uncino (ūn·chē'nō) *m* hook
undicesimo (ūn·dē·che'zē·mō) *a&m* eleventh
undici (ūn'dē·chē) *a* eleven
ungere * (ūn'jā·rā) *vt* to grease; to smear grease on
ungherese (ūn·gā·rā'zā) *a&m* Hungarian
Ungheria (ūn·gā·rē'â) *f* Hungary
unghia (ūn'gyâ) *f* fingernail; toenail; claw
unguento (ūn·gwān'tō) *m* salve, ointment
unicamente (ū·nē·kâ·mān'tā) *adv* only, specifically
unificare (ū·nē·fē·kâ'rā) *vt* to unify, join, bring together
unificarsi (ū·nē·fē·kâr'sē) *vr* to be unified, be joined, unite
unificazione (ū·nē·fē·kâ·tsyō'nā) *f* unification, joining
unico (ū'nē·kō) *a* unique; only; specific
uniforme (ū·nē·fōr'mā) *f* uniform; — *a* even, standard, uniform
unione (ū·nyō'nā) *f* union; fusion, blending
unire (ū·nē'rā) *vt* to unite; to attach
unirsi (ū·nēr'sē) *vr* to fuse together; to join, become united
universale (ū·nē·vār·sâ'lā) *a* general; universal; blanket, all-inclusive; **Giudizio** — Last Judgment; **Diluvio** — Deluge, Flood (*eccl*)
università (ū·nē·vār·sē·tâ') *f* university
universitario (ū·nē·vār·sē·tâ'ryō) *a* university; — *m* university student
universo (ū·nē·vār'sō) *m* universe
uno (ū'nō) *art m* the; — *a* one, a, an, any; — *pron* one, a certain one
unto (ūn'tō) *m* fat; grease; — *a* greasy; (*fig*) unclean, dirty
untuoso (ūn·twō'zō) *a* greasy, oily
unzione (ūn·tsyō'nā) *f* ointment; **estrema** — (*eccl*) extreme unction

uomini (wô'mē·nē) *mpl* men
uomo (wō'mō) *m* man; fellow, individual; **come un sol** — with one accord
uova (wō'vâ) *fpl* eggs; — **sode** hard boiled eggs; — **strapazzate** scrambled eggs; — **sbattute** beaten eggs; **caminare sulle** — (*fig*) to walk with mincing steps
uovo (wō'vō) *m* egg; — **fresco** fresh egg; **tuorlo d'** — egg yolk; **cercare il pelo nell'** — to make trivial distinctions; to be petty
uragano (ū·râ·gâ'nō) *m* hurricane
uranio (ū·râ'nyō) *m* uranium
urbanesimo (ūr·bâ·ne'zē·mō) *m* urbanism
urbanistica (ūr·bâ·nē'stē·kâ) *f* city planning
urbanità (ūr·bâ·nē·tâ') *f* politeness, gentility; savoir faire
urbano (ūr·bâ'nō) *a* urban; genteel; — *m* local telephone call
urgente (ūr·jān'tā) *a* urgent; **–mente** (ūr·jān·tā·mān'tā) *adv* urgently
urgenza (ūr·jān'tsâ) *f* urgency, emergency
urina (ū·rē'nâ) *f* urine
urlare (ūr·lâ'rā) *vi* to scream, yell; to holler; to cry out
urlo (ūr'lō) *m* scream, shout; outcry
urna (ūr'nâ) *f* urn; (*pol*) ballot box
urtante (ūr·tân'tā) *a* (*fig*) annoying, exasperating
urtare (ūr·tâ'rā) *vt* to bump into; to shove; to run into, collide with
urtarsi (ūr·târ'sē) *vr* to shove one another; to collide; (*fig*) to become annoyed; to dispute
urto (ūr'tō) *m* shove, push; impact; **essere in** — **con** (*fig*) to be angry with; not to be on speaking terms with; **mettersi in** — **con** to quarrel with, have a misunderstanding with
usanza (ū·zân'tsâ) *f* custom; usage
usare (ū·zâ'rā) *vt* to use; — *vi* to be accustomed to, have the habit of
usarsi (ū·zâr'sē) *vr* to be the fashion; to be in use
usato (ū·zâ'tō) *a* used; usual; secondhand; **più dell'** — unusual, more than usual
usciere (ū·shā'rā) *m* usher; process server
uscio (ū'shō) *m* door; exit
uscire * (ū·shē'rā) *vi* to go out; to exit
uscita (ū·shē'tâ) *f* exit; (*fig*) witty remark; (*com*) expenditure; **entrata e** — (*com*) assets and liabilities
usignuolo (ū·zē·nywō'lō) *m* nightingale
uso (ū'zō) *m* custom; usage; — *a* used, accustomed; **essere in** — to be customary, be in use, be considered fashionable; **secondo l'**— in keeping with tradition; **fuori d'**— obsolete; out of working order
usuale (ū·zwâ'lā) *a* customary; traditional
usualmente (ū·zwâl·mān'tā) *adv* ordinarily, usually; traditionally
usufruire (ū·zū·frūē'rā) *vi* to benefit by, derive advantage from
usura (ū·zū'râ) *f* wear and tear, use; usury; **–io** (ū·zū·râ'yō) *m* usurer, loan shark; (*coll*) money lender
usurpare (ū·zūr·pâ'rā) *vt* to usurp, take over
utensile (ū·tān·sē'lā) *m* utensil; **macchina** — machine tool
utente (ū·tān'tā) *m* user; subscriber
utenza (ū·tān'tsâ) *f* consumers
utero (ū'tā·rō) *m* uterus
utile (ū'tē·lā) *a* useful; — *m* profit; (*com*) dividend
utilità (ū·tē·lē·tâ') *f* utility, service
utilitaria (ū·tē·lē·tâ'ryâ) *f* compact car
utilizzare (ū·tē·lē·dzâ'rā) *vt* to utilize, make use of; to derive profit from
utilizzazione (ū·tē·lē·dzâ·tsyō'nā) *f* utilization, utilizing
utilmente (ū·tēl·mān'tā) *adv* usefully
uva (ū'vâ) *f* grape; — **passa** raisin
uzzolo (ū'dzō·lō) *m* caprice, whim; secret desire

V

vacante (vâ·kân'tā) *a* empty; not in use
vacanza (vâ·kân'tsâ) *f* vacation
vacca (vâk'kâ) *f* cow
vacchetta (vâk·kāt'tâ) *f* cowhide
vaccinare (vâ·chē·nâ'rā) *vt* to vaccinate
vaccino (vâ·chē'nō) *m* vaccine
vacillare (vâ·chēl·lâ'rā) *vt* to waver, be undecided
vacillazione (vâ·chēl·lâ·tsyō'nā) *f* vacillation, indecision; flickering
vacuo (vâ'kwō) *a* empty, meaningless
vagabondo (vâ·gâ·bōn'dō) *m* idler; vagabond
vagamente (vâ·gâ·mān'tā) *adv* vaguely; in a charming way
vaglia (vâ'lyâ) *m* money order; — *f* capability; mettle; worth; **–re** (vâ·lyâ'rā) *vt* to test the merit of, evaluate; to pick out
vago (vâ'gō) *a* vague; lovely, desirable
vagone (vâ·gō'nā) *m* railroad car; — **da letto** sleeping car; — **ristorante** dining car
vaiolo (vâ·yō'lō) *m* smallpox
valanga (vâ·lân'gâ) *f* avalanche
valente (vâ·lān'tā) *a* able; skillful; apt
valere * (vâ·lā'rā) *vi* to be worth; to be valid; to be worthwhile; to be of use, worth the effort; **quanto vale ciò?** what is the price of this? **non** — (*sport*) not to count; **farsi** — to make oneself a name; **vale a dire** in other words, that is to say
valersi * (vâ·lār'sē) *vr* to utilize, make use of; — **di ogni mezzo per raggiungere la meta** to use any means to gain an end
valevole (vâ·le'vō·lā) *a* valid; of help, of use
valico (vâ'lē·kō) *m* pass, gap; break in a mountain range
validità (vâ·lē·dē·tâ') *f* effect, validness; effectiveness
valido (vâ'lē·dō) *a* valid, good; worthwhile

valigia (vâ·lē′jâ) *f* suitcase
valle (vâl′lā) *f* valley
valore (vâ·lō′rā) *m* value; valor
valoroso (vâ·lō·rō′zō) *a* brave, stout-hearted
valuta (vâ·lū′tâ) *f* currency; worth, value; **–re** (vâ·lū·tâ′rā) *vt* to value; to evaluate; **–zione** (vâ·lū·tâ·tsyō′nā) *f* estimate; evaluation
valvola (vâl′vō·lâ) *f* valve; radio tube
vaneggiare (vâ·nāj·jâ′rā) *vi* to rant wildly, rave; to talk deliriously
vanga (vân′gâ) *f* spade
vangelo (vân·jā′lō) *m* Gospel; (*fig*) absolute truth
vaniglia (vâ·nē′lyâ) *f* vanilla
vanità (vâ·nē·tâ′) *f* conceitedness, vainness; shallowness
vanitoso (vâ·nē·tō′zō) *a* vain, conceited; shallow
vano (vâ′nō) *m* room; open space; — *a* vain, empty; conceited
vantaggio (vân·tâj′jō) *m* advantage; **–so** (vân·tâj·jō′zō) *a* advantageous
vantare (vân·tâ′rā) *vt&i* to boast of; to pride oneself on
vantarsi (vân·târ′sē) *vr* to boast, show off
vanto (vân′tō) *m* boast; pride
vanvera (vân′vā·râ) *f* heedlessness; **a —** thoughtlessly, carelessly
vapore (vâ·pō′rā) *m* steam; steamship; **–tto** (vâ·pō·rāt′tō) *m* steamboat
vaporizzatore (vâ·pō·rē·dzâ·tō′rā) *m* atomizer
vaporoso (vâ·pō·rō′zō) *a* diaphanous, filmy; vaporous
varare (vâ·râ′rā) *vt* to launch; **— un affare** (*com*) to set up a business; **— una legge** (*pol*) to pass a bill
varcare (vâr·kâ′rā) *vt* to cross; to overcome; to go beyond
varechina (vâ·rā·kē′nâ) *f* bleach
variazione (vâ·ryâ·tsyō′nā) *f* diversity, variety; modifying
varicella (vâ·rē·chāl′lâ) *f* chicken pox
varietà (vâ·ryā·tâ′) *f* variety; vaudeville; **spettacolo di —** variety show; **teatro di —** music hall
vario (vâ′ryō) *a* different; changing; various, several
varo (vâ′rō) *m* launching; introduction, debut
vasca (vâ′skâ) *f* tub
vasellame (vâ·zāl·lâ′mā) *m* pottery; set of dishes
vaso (vâ′zō) *m* vase; pot
vassoio (vâs·sō′yō) *m* tray
vastità (vâ·stē·tâ′) *f* expanse, width, vastness, extension
vasto (vâ′stō) *a* vast, broad; immense
Vaticano (vâ·tē·kâ′nō) *m* Vatican
vaticinio (vâ·tē·chē′nyō) *m* prophecy
ve (vā) *pron* to you, you; — *adv* there
ve'! (vā) *interj* Look! See!
vecchia (vek′kyâ) *f* old woman
vecchiaia (vāk·kyâ′yâ) *f* old age
vecchio (vek′kyō) *a* old; — *m* old man
vece (vā′chā) *f* place, stead; **fare la — di** to substitute for, replace; **in — di** instead of
vedere * (vā·dā′rā) *vt* to see; to understand; to make note of; **— la luce** to be born; **non — l'ora di** to long for; to look forward to
vedersi * (vā·dār′sē) *vr* to get together, meet
vedova (ve′dō·vâ) *f* widow
vedovo (ve′dō·vō) *m* widower
veduta (vā·dū′tâ) *f* scene, view
vegetale (vā·jā·tâ′lā) *a* vegetable
vegetariano (vā·jā·tâ·ryâ′nō) *a&m* vegetarian
vegetazione (vā·jā·tâ·tsyō′nā) *f* vegetation
vegeto (ve′jā·tō) *a* hardy, thriving
veglia (ve′lyâ) *f* vigil, wake, watch; **–re** (vā·lyâ′rā) *vt* to watch over; to guard
veglione (vā·lyō′nā) *m* costume party, masked ball
veicolo (vā·ē′kō·lō) *m* vehicle
vela (vā′lâ) *f* sail; **–re** (vā·lâ′rā) *vt* to cover up, disguise; **–rsi** (vā·lâr′sē) *vr* to become thick *(voice)*; to wear a veil; **–to** (vā·lâ′tō) *a* veiled
veleno (vā·lā′nō) *m* poison; **–so** (vā·lā·nō′zō) *a* poisonous
veliero (vā·lyā′rō) *m* sailing ship
velivolo (vā·lē′vō·lō) *m (avi)* glider
vellicare (vāl·lē·kâ′rā) *vt* to tickle; to give a pleasant feeling; to please
vello (vāl′lō) *m* fleece; **–so** (vāl·lō′zō) *a* shaggy
velluto (vāl·lū′tō) *m* velvet, velours
velo (vā′lō) *m* gauze; veil
veloce (vā·lō′chā) *a* fast, speedy; **–mente** (vā·lō·chā·mān′tā) *adv* rapidly, quickly
velocipede (vā·lō·chē′pā·dā) *m* tricycle
velocista (vā·lō·chē′stâ) *m* sprinter
velocità (vā·lō·chē·tâ′) *f* speed; **eccesso di —** speeding, exceeding the speed limit
velodromo (vā·lô′drō·mō) *m* bicycle track
vena (vā′nâ) *f* vein; lode *(mining)*; **essere in buona —** to be in the mood
venale (vā·nâ′lā) *a* corruptible; marketable; **prezzo —** sales price
venalità (vā·nâ·lē·tâ′) *f* venality, susceptibility to bribes
vendemmia (vān·dem′myâ) *f* grape harvest; vintage season
vendere (ven′dā·rā) *vt* to sell; **— fumo** *(fig)* to bluff; to dupe; **aver ragione da —** *(coll)* to be completely justified; to be absolutely right
vendetta (vān·dāt′tâ) *f* revenge
vendicare (vān·dē·kâ′rā) *vt* to avenge
vendicarsi (vān·dē·kâr′sē) *vr* to take revenge; to wreak vengeance
vendicativo (vān·dē·kâ·tē′vō) *a* vengeful, vindictive
vendita (ven′dē·tâ) *f* sale
venditore (vān·dē·tō′rā) *m* salesman; dealer
venduto (vān·dū′tō) *a* sold; *(fig)* corrupted, bribed
venerazione (vā·nā·râ·tsyō′nā) *f* deep respect, veneration; worship
venerdì (vā·nār·dē′) *m* Friday
venereo (vā·ne′rā·ō) *a* venereal

Venezia (vā·ne'tsyâ) *f* Venice
veneziano (vā·nā·tsyâ'nō) *a&m* Venetian
venire * (vā·nē'rā) *vi* to come; to occur, take place; — **in mente** to get into one's head; to come to one; to come back to one; — **a galla** to float; to come to the surface; *(fig)* to be revealed, show up
ventaglio (vān·tâ'lyō) *m* fan
ventennio (vān·ten'nyō) *m* twenty-year period
ventesimo (vān·te'zē·mō) *a* twentieth
venti (vān'tē) *a* twenty
ventilatore (vān·tē·lâ·tō'rā) *m* electric fan; ventilator, vent
ventilazione (vān·tē·lâ·tsyō'nā) *f* ventilation
ventina (vān·tē'nâ) *f* score; roughly twenty
vento (vān'tō) *m* wind
ventre (vān'trā) *m* womb; stomach, belly
ventriera (vān·tryā'râ) *f* belt; bellyband
ventriloquo (vān·trē'lō·kwō) *m* ventriloquist
ventura (vān·tū'râ) *f* destiny, fortune
venturo (vān·tū'rō) *a* future; next *(in order)*; coming; **l'anno** — next year
venuta (vā·nū'tâ) *f* arrival; advent
venuto (vā·nū'tō) *a* arrived; **ben** — welcome
veramente (vā·râ·mān'tā) *adv* actually, in fact; really
veranda (vā·rân'dâ) *f* veranda
verbale (vār·bâ'lā) *a* verbal; — *m* minutes of a meeting; declaration
verbo (vār'bō) *m* verb
verdastro (vār·dâ'strō) *a* greenish
verde (vār'dā) *a* green; **ridere** — to laugh out of the wrong side of one's mouth; **essere al** — *(fig)* to be penniless; **età** — tender years, young age
verderame (vār·dā·râ'mā) *m* verdigris
verdetto (vār·dāt'tō) *m* verdict
verdura (vār·dū'râ) *f* vegetables
verecondo (vā·rā·kōn'dō) *a* modest, unassuming
verga (vār'gâ) *f* rod, stick
vergine (ver'jē·nā) *f&a* virgin
vergogna (vār·gō'nyâ) *f* shame, disgrace; modestness
vergognarsi (vār·gō·nyâr'sē) *vr* to feel ashamed, be covered with shame
vergognosamente (vār·gō·nyō·zâ·mān'tā) *adv* shamefully; shamelessly
vergognoso (vār·gō·nyō'zō) *a* bashful, shy; shameful; shameless
verifica (vā·rē'fē·kâ) *f* control; verification; **–re** (vā·rē·fē·kâ'rā) *vt* to check, confirm; **–rsi** (vā·rē·fē·kâr'sē) *vr* to come true, actually happen
verità (vā·rē·tâ') *f* veracity, truth
veritiero (vā·rē·tyā'rō) *a* truthful, honest
verme (vār'mā) *m* worm
vermiglio (vār·mē'lyō) *m* vermilion
vermut (vār'mūt) *m* vermouth
vernice (vār·nē'chā) *f* paint; varnish; preview; patent leather; — **fresca** fresh paint
verniciare (vār·nē·châ'rā) *vt* to paint; to varnish
vero (vā'rō) *a* true; absolute, complete; — *m* truth; **dal** — from life; from nature *(arts)*; **–simiglianza** (vā·rō·sē·mē·lyān'tsâ) *f* likelihood; **–simile** (vā·rō·sē'mē·lā) *a* likely
versamento (vār·sâ·mān'tō) *m* payment; pouring in; investment
versare (vār·sâ'rā) *vt* to pour; to pay in; to invest *(money)*
versione (vār·syō'nā) *f* translation; version
verso (vār'sō) *m* verse; — *prep* towards; about
vertenza (vār·tān'tsâ) *f* quarrel, dispute
verticale (vār·tē·kâ'lā) *a* vertical
vertice (ver'tē·chā) *m* top, summit; *(math)* vertex
vertigine (vār·tē'jē·nā) *f* dizziness
vertiginoso (vār·tē·jē·nō'zō) *a* dizzy
verza (vār'dzâ) *f* cabbage
vescica (vā·shē'kâ) *f* blister; bladder
vescovo (ve'skō·vō) *m* bishop
vespa (vā'spâ) *f* wasp
vestaglia (vā·stâ'lyâ) *f* lady's robe; negligee
veste (vā'stā) *m* dress; — **da camera** dressing gown
vestiario (vā·styâ'ryō) *m* clothes
vestire (vā·stē'rā) *vt* to dress
vestirsi (vā·stēr'sē) *vr* to get dressed
vestito (vā·stē'tō) *m* suit; dress; — *a* dressed; clad
veterinario (vā·tā·rē·nâ'ryō) *m&a* veterinary
vetrata (vā·trâ'tâ) *f* glass partition; glass door
vetrina (vā·trē'nâ) *f* showcase; display window; store window
vetrinista (vā·trē·nē'stâ) *m* window trimmer
vetrino (vā·trē'nō) *m* microscopic slide
vetro (vā'trō) *m* glass; sheet of glass
vetta (vāt'tâ) *f* peak; summit; top
vettura (vāt·tū'râ) *f* car, vehicle
vezzeggiare (vā·tsāj·jâ'rā) *vt* to fondle
vezzeggiativo (vā·tsāj·jâ·tē'vō) *m* pet name, term of endearment; *(gram)* diminutive
vi (vē) *pron* you, to you; — *adv* there
via (vē'â) *f* way; street; — *adv* away; —! *interj* Go away!
viaggiare (vyâj·jâ'rā) *vi* to travel
viaggiatore (vyâj·jâ·tō'rā) *m* passenger; traveler; wayfarer
viaggio (vyâj'jō) *m* trip; voyage; **Buon** —! Have a nice trip!
viale (vyâ'lā) *m* boulevard, avenue
vibrazione (vē·brâ·tsyō'nā) *f* vibration
vicenda (vē·chān'dâ) *f* alteration, change; event, development
vicendevole (vē·chān·de'vō·lā) *a* reciprocal; in common
vicendevolmente (vē·chān·dā·vōl·mān'tā) *adv* mutually
vicerè (vē·chā·rā') *m* viceroy
viceversa (vē·chā·vār'sâ) *adv* conversely; vice versa
vicinanza (vē·chē·nân'tsâ) *f* neighborhood, area

vicinato (vē·chē·nâ'tō) *m* neighborhood; collective neighbors
vicino (vē·chē'nō) *m* neighbor; — *a&adv* near, close
vicolo (vē'kō·lō) *m* alley
vidimare (vē·dē·mâ'rā) *vt* to visa
vidimazione (vē·dē·mâ·tsyō'nā) *f* visé; validation
vietare (vyā·tâ'rā) *vt* to forbid
vietato (vyā·tâ'tō) *a* forbidden; — **fumare** no smoking
vigilare (vē·jē·lâ'rā) *vt* to keep watch over; to keep an eye on
vigile (vē'jē·lā) *m* policeman; — **del fuoco** fireman; — *a* watchful, mindful
vigilia (vē·jē'lyâ) *f* eve; vigil
vigliacco (vē·lyâk'kō) *a* cowardly; yellow *(coll)*; — *m* coward
vigna (vē'nyâ) *f* vineyard
vignetta (vē·nyāt'tâ) *f* sketch, vignette
vigogna (vē·gō'nyâ) *f* vicuna
vigore (vē·gō'rā) *m* energy; vigor; effect, influence; **entrare in** — *(law)* to take effect, go into effect.
vigorosamente (vē·gō·rō·zâ·mān'tā) *adv* energetically, with vigor
vigoroso (vē·gō·rō'zō) *a* strong; vigorous
vile (vē'lā) *a* dastardly; contemptible, mean; — *m* coward; low character
villa (vēl'lâ) *f* villa; country home; **–ggio** (vēl·lâj'jō) *m* village
villano (vēl·lâ'nō) *m* peasant; — *a* rude; coarse; — **rifatto** upstart
villeggiare (vēl·lāj·jâ'rā) *vi* to vacation in the country
villeggiatura (vēl·lāj·jâ·tū'râ) *f* summer vacation in the country
villino (vēl·lē'nō) *m* cottage
viltà (vēl·tâ') *f* cowardliness, cowardice; vile nature
vincere * (vēn'chā·rā) *vt&i* to win; to vanquish
vincersi * (vēn'chār·sē) *vr* to control one's emotions, hold in one's feelings
vincita (vēn'chē·tâ) *f* victory; winning
vincitore (vēn·chē·tō'rā) *m* winner
vincolare (vēn·kō·lâ'rā) *vt* to tie together, bind
vincolo (vēn'kō·lō) *m* lien, attachment; bond, fetter, restraint
vino (vē'nō) *m* wine
viola (vyō'lâ) *f* violet; viola
violare (vyō·lâ'rā) *vt* to violate; to break *(law)*; to desecrate; to rape, ravish
violazione (vyō·lâ·tsyō'nā) *f* rape; violation; — **di domicilio** housebreaking
violentare (vyō·lān·tâ'rā) *vt* to do violence to; to rape
violento (vyō·lān'tō) *a* violent; bestial
violenza (vyō·lān'tsâ) *f* violence
violino (vyō·lē'nō) *m* violin
violoncello (vyō·lōn·chāl'lō) *m* cello
viottolo (vyōt'tō·lō) *m* path, trail
vipera (vē'pā·râ) *f* viper
virare (vē·râ'rā) *vi (naut)* to tack; *(avi)* to bank
virgola (vēr'gō·lâ) *f* comma
virgolette (vēr·gō·lāt'tā) *fpl* quotation marks; **fra** — in quotation marks
virile (vē·rē'lā) *a* manful, courageous, virile
virilità (vē·rē·lē·tâ') *f* courage; power; virility; manhood
virtù (vēr·tū') *f* virtue; ability; strength
virtuoso (vēr·twō'zō) *a* honorable, virtuous
viscere (vē'shā·rā) *fpl* viscera
vischio (vē'skyō) *m* mistletoe
visibilio (vē·zē·bē'lyō) *m* abundance; **andare in** — to go into raptures; to be entranced
visibilità (vē·zē·bē·lē·tâ') *f* visibility
visiera (vē·zyā'râ) *f* peak; visor
visione (vē·zyō'nā) *f* apparition; mental image; vision
visita (vē'zē·tâ) *f* visit; examination; — **doganale** customs inspection; — **medica** medical examination; **–re** (vē·zē·tâ'rā) *vt* to visit, call on
viso (vē'zō) *m* face
visone (vē·zō'nā) *m* mink
vissuto (vēs·sū'tō) *a* lived; worldly-wise, blasé
vista (vē'stâ) *f* view; outlook; sight; **–re** (vē·stâ'rā) *vt* to visa
visto (vē'stō) *a* seen; — *m* visa; **–so** (vē·stō'zō) *a* tawdry, cheap; extensive
vita (vē'tâ) *f* life; waist
vitalità (vē·tâ·lē·tâ') *f* vivacity, animation, vitality
vitalizio (vē·tâ·lē'tsyō) *a* for life; — *m (com)* life annuity
vite (vē'tā) *f* screw; vine; *(avi)* tailspin
vitello (vē·tāl'lō) *m* veal; calf; **–ne** (vē·tāl·lō'nā) *m (coll)* playboy, idler
vittima (vēt'tē·mâ) *f* victim
vitto (vēt'tō) *m* food; — **e alloggio** room and board
vittoria (vēt·tō'ryâ) *f* victory
vittorioso (vēt·tō·ryō'zō) *a* victorious
vituperare (vē·tū·pā·râ'rā) *vt* to abuse; to cast aspersions on
vituperio (vē·tū·pe'ryō) *m* vituperation; defamation; outrage; aspersion
vivace (vē·vâ'chā) *a* vivacious, lively
vivacità (vē·vâ·chē·tâ') *f* exhilaration; vivacity; activeness
vivaio (vē·vâ'yō) *m* nursery, greenhouse; hatchery
vivente (vē·vān'tā) *a* living
vivere * (vē'vā·rā) *vt&i* to live
viveri (vē'vā·rē) *mpl* provisions
vivisezione (vē·vē·sā·tsyō'nā) *f* vivisection
vivo (vē'vō) *a* alive; living
viziare (vē·tsyâ'rā) *vt* to ruin, spoil; to corrupt
viziarsi (vē·tsyâr'sē) *vr* to be spoiled; to be corrupted
vizio (vē'tsyō) *m* vice; bad habit; malfunction, defect; **–so** (vē·tsyō'zō) *a* dissolute; corrupt, vicious
vocabolario (vō·kâ·bō·lâ'ryō) *m* vocabulary
vocabolo (vō·kâ'bō·lō) *m* word; term
vocale (vō·kâ'lā) *a* vocal; — *f* vowel
voce (vō'chā) *f* voice; rumor; word; — **pubblica** public opinion

vogare (vō·gâ'rā) *vi* to row
voglia (vô'lyâ) *f* wish; desire; birthmark
voi (vō'ē) *pron* you; **–altri** (vōē·âl'trē) *pron* you, you others
volante (vō·lân'tā) *m* steering wheel; — *a* flying
volantino (vō·lân·tē'nō) *m* handbill
volare (vō·lâ'rā) *vi* to fly
volatile (vō·lâ'tē·lā) *m* bird; — *a* winged; volatile
volenteroso (vō·lān·tā·rō'zō) *a* willing, pleased; zealous
volentieri (vō·lān·tyā'rē) *adv* willingly
volere * (vō·lā'ra) *vt&i* to wish, want; to feel like; — **bene** to love, be fond of — **dire** to mean; to signify
volgare (vōl·gâ'rā) *a* vulgar; — *m* dialect, vernacular
volgere * (vôl'jā·rā) *vt&i* to turn
volgersi * (vôl'jār·sē) *vr* to turn around, turn about
volgo (vōl'gō) *m* rabble, mob; masses
volitivo (vō·lē·tē'vō) *a* strong-willed, impetuous
volo (vō'lō) *m* flight
volontà (vō·lōn·tâ') *f* will
volontario (vō·lōn·tâ'ryō) *a* voluntary; — *m* volunteer
volpe (vōl'pā) *f* fox; — **argentata** silver fox
volta (vōl'tâ) *f* turn; time; **di — in —** once in a while; **altre volte** in the past, previously
volta (vōl'tâ) *m (elec)* volt
voltaggio (vōl·tâj'jō) *m (elec)* voltage
voltare (vōl·tâ'rā) *vt&i* to turn
voltarsi (vōl·târ'sē) *vr* to turn around
volto (vōl'tō) *m* face
volubile (vō·lū'bē·lā) *a* inconstant; garrulous
volume (vō·lū'mā) *m* mass, volume; book, tome
voluminoso (vō·lū·mē·nō'zō) *a* roomy; voluminous
voluttà (vō·lūt·tâ') *f* lasciviousness, lust
vomitare (vō·mē·tâ'rā) *vt&i* to vomit; to spew forth
vongola (vôn'gō·lâ) *f* clam, mussel
vorace (vō·râ'chā) *a* voracious
voracità (vō·râ·chē·tâ') *f* greed; voracity, hunger
voragine (vō·râ'jē·nā) *f* gulf; abyss
vortice (vôr'tē·chā) *m* whirlwind; whirlpool
vostro (vō'strō) *a* your; — *pron* yours
votare (vō·tâ'rā) *vt&i* to vote
votazione (vō·tâ·tsyō'nā) *f* voting
voto (vō'tō) *m* vote; vow; prayer; desire
vulcanizzare (vūl·kâ·nē·dzâ'rā) *vt* to vulcanize
vulcano (vūl·kâ'nō) *m* volcano
vuotare (vwō·tâ'rā) *vt* to empty; — **il sacco** to speak one's piece; to get something off one's chest
vuotarsi (vwō·târ'sē) *vr* to empty out, become empty
vuoto (vwō'tō) *a* empty; — *m* void; *(phys)* vacuum; emptiness; **a —** to no avail, without result

X

xenofobia (ksā·nō·fō·bē'â) *f* fear of foreigners, xenophobia
Xeres (ksā'rās) *m* Sherry wine
xilofonista (ksē·lō·fō·nē'stâ) *m* xylophone player
xilofono (ksē·lô'fô·nô) *m* xylophone
xilografia (ksē·lō·grâ·fē'â) *m* wood carving; printing with woodcuts
xilografo (ksē·lô'grâ·fō) *m* wood-carver, xylographer

Z

zabaione (dzâ·bâ·yō'nā) *m* eggnog
zafferano (dzâf·fā·râ'nō) *m* saffron
zaffiro (dzâf'fē·rō) *m* sapphire
zaino (dzâ'ē·nō) *m* knapsack
zampa (dzâm'pâ) *f* claw; paw
zampillare (dzâm·pēl·lâ'rā) *vi* to gush forth, pour out
zampillo (dzâm·pēl'lō) *m* squirt, stream; jet, gush
zampino (dzâm·pē'nō) *m* little paw; **mettere lo — dappertutto** *(fig)* to have a finger in every pie; to have many irons in the fire
zampogna (dzâm·pō'nyâ) *f* bagpipe; **–ro** (dzâm·pō·nyâ'rō) *m* bagpipe player
zanna (dzân'nâ) *f* fang; tusk
zanzara (dzân·dzâ'râ) *f* mosquito
zanzariera (dzân·zâ·ryā'râ) *f* mosquito netting
zappa (dzâp'pâ) *f* hoe; **–re** (dzâp·pâ'rā) *vt* to dig in, work *(soil)*
zar (dzâr) *m* czar, **–ina** (dzâ·rē'nā) *f* czarina
zattera (dzât'tā·râ) *f* raft
zavorra (dzâ·vōr'râ) *f* weight, ballast
zebra (dzā'brâ) *f* zebra
zecca (dzāk'kâ) *f* mint; **nuovo di —** brand-new
zelante (dzā·lân'tā) *a* zealous; ambitious
zeppo (dzāp'pō) *a* chock-full, stuffed
zerbino (zār·bē'nō) *m* doormat
zerbinotto (dzār·bē·nōt'tō) *m* dandy; ladies' man
zero (dzā'rō) *m* zero
zia (dzē'â) *f* aunt
zibellino (dzē·bāl·lē'nō) *m* sable
zigomo (dzē'gō·mō) *m* cheekbone
zimbello (dzēm·bāl'lō) *m* laughingstock, butt of humor
zinco (dzēn'kō) *m* zinc
zingaro (dzēn'gâ·rō) *m* gypsy
zio (dzē'ō) *m* uncle
zitella (dzē·tāl'lâ) *f* spinster
zitto (dzēt'tō) *a* silent

zizzania (dzē·dzâ'nyâ) *f* disagreement, discord
zoccolo (dzôk'kō·lō) *m* wooden shoe; wainscotting
zolfanello (dzōl·fâ·nāl'lō) *m* kitchen match
zolfo (dzōl'fō) *m* sulphur
zolla (dzōl'lâ) *f* lump of sod; clod of earth
zolletta (dzōl·lāt'tâ) *f* lump of sugar
zona (dzō'nâ) *f* zone
zoologia (dzō·ō·lō·jē'â) *f* zoology
zoologico (dzō·ō·lô'jē·kō) *a* zoological
zoppicare (dzōp·pē·kâ'rā) *vi* to limp; to be lopsided
zoppo (dzōp'pō) *a* lame; lopsided, uneven
zotico (dzô'tē·kō) *a* rustic, boorish
zucca (dzūk'kâ) *f* squash; pumpkin; *(coll)* ignoramus, dunce
zuccheriera (dzūk·kā·ryā'râ) *f* sugar bowl
zuccherino (dzūk·kā·rē'nō) *m* candy
zucchero (dzūk'kā·rō) *m* sugar
zucchino (dzūk·kē'nō) *m* zucchini
zuffa (dzūf'fâ) *f* scuffle, tussle; quarrel, argument
zuppa (dzūp'pâ) *f* soup
zuppiera (dzūp·pyā'râ) *f* tureen

ITALIAN-ENGLISH FIRST NAMES

A

Abramo (â·brâ'mō) Abraham
Ada (â'dâ) Ada
Adamo (â·dâ'mō) Adam
Adelina (â·dā·lē'nâ) Adeline
Adriano (â·dryâ'nō) Adrian
Agata (â'gâ·tâ) Agatha
Agnese (â·nyā'zā) Agnes
Agnesina (â·nyā·zē'nâ) Aggie
Agostino (â·gō·stē'nō) Austin
Alberto (âl·bār'tō) Albert
Alessandrino (â·lās·sân·drē'nō) Alex, Alec
Alessandro (â·lās·sân'drō) Alexander
Alessio (â·les'syō) Alexis
Alfonso (âl·fōn'sō) Alphonse
Alfredo (âl·frā'dō) Alfred
Alice (â·lē'chā) Alice
Aloisio (â·lō·ē'zyō) Aloysius
Ambrogio (âm·brô'jō) Ambrose
Andrea (ân·drā'â) Andrew
Andreuccio (ân·drā·ū'chō) Andy
Angela (ân'jā·lâ) Angela
Angelica (ân·je'lē·kâ) Angelica
Angelina (ân·jā·lē'nâ) Angeline
Angelo (ân'jā·lō) Angelus
Anna (ân'nâ) Ann
Annetta (ân·nāt'tâ) Annette, Nancy, Annie
Annina (ân·nē'nâ) Nancy, Annie
Anselmo (ân·sāl'mō) Anselm
Antonia (ân·tô'nyâ) Antonia
Antonietta (ân·tō·nyāt'tâ) Antoinette
Antonio (ân·tô'nyō) Anthony, Antoine
Apollodoro (â·pōl·lō·dō'rō) Apollodorus
Arianna (â·ryân'nâ) Ariadne
Arnaldo (âr·nâl'dō) Arnold
Aroldo (â·rōl'dō) Harold
Aronne (â·rōn'nā) Aaron
Arrigo (âr·rē'gō) Henry
Arturo (âr·tū'rō) Arthur
Augusto (âū·gū'stō) August
Aurelia (âū·re'lyâ) Aurelia

B

Baldassarre (bâl·dâs·sâr'rā) Balthazar
Baldovino (bâl·dō·vē'nō) Baldwin
Barbara (bâr'bâ·râ) Barbara
Barnaba (bâr'nâ·bâ) Barnaby
Bartolomeo (bâr·tō·lō·mā'ō) Bartholomew
Basilio (bâ·zē'lyō) Basil
Beatrice (bā·â·trē'chā) Beatrice
Benedetto (bā·nā·dāt'tō) Benedict
Beniamino (bā·nyâ·mē'nō) Benjamin
Berenice (bā·rā·nē'chā) Bernice
Bernardina (bār·nâr·dē'nâ) Bernadine
Bernardino (bār·nâr·dē'nō) Barney
Bernardo (bār·nâr'dō) Bernard
Berta (bār'tâ) Bertha
Bertrando (bār·trân'dō) Bertram, Bertrand
Bianca (byân'kâ) Blanche
Brigida (brē'jē·dâ) Bridget

C

Calvino (kâl·vē'nō) Calvin
Camilla (kâ·mēl'lâ) Camille
Carlo (kâr'lō) Charles
Carlotta (kâr·lōt'tâ) Charlotte
Carlotto (kâr·lōt'tō) Charlie
Carolina (kâ·rō·lē'nâ) Caroline
Caterina (kâ·tā·rē'nâ) Catherine, Katherine, Kathie
Cecilia (chā·chē'lyâ) Cecilia, Cecily
Cecilio (chā·chē'lyō) Cecil
Cesare (che'zâ·rā) Caesar
Chiara (kyâ'râ) Clare, Clara
Clarice (klâ'rē·chā) Clarissa
Clarissa (klâ·rēs'sâ) Clarissa
Claudia (klâ'ū·dyâ) Claudia
Claudiano (klâū·dyâ'nō) Claudian
Claudio (klâ'ū·dyō) Claude
Clemente (klā·mān'tā) Clement
Clemenza (klā·mān'tsâ) Clemence
Clio (klē'ō) Clio
Cloe (klō'ā) Chloe
Cordelia (kōr·de'lyâ) Cordelia
Corinna (kō·rēn'nâ) Corinne
Cornelia (kōr·ne'lyâ) Cornelia
Cornelio (kōr·ne'lyō) Cornelius
Corradino (kōr·râ·dē'nō) Conrad
Corrado (kōr·râ'dō) Conrad
Costanza (kō·stân'tså) Constance
Cristiano (krē·styâ'nō) Christian
Cristina (krē·stē'nâ) Christine
Cristoforo (krē·stô'fō·rō) Christopher

D

Dafne (dâf'nā) Daphne
Damiano (dâ·myâ'nō) Damian
Damone (dâ·mō'nā) Damon
Daniele (dâ·nyā'lā) Daniel
Dante (dân'tā) Dante
Dario (dâ'ryō) Darien
Davide (dâ'vē·dā) David
Davidino (dâ·vē·dē'nō) Davy
Delia (de'lyâ) Delia
Demetrio (dā·me'tryō) Demetrius
Diana (dyâ'nâ) Diane, Diana
Dionigi (dyō·nē'jē) Dennis
Domenico (dō·me'nē·kō) Dominic
Donato (dō·nâ'tō) Donatus
Dora (dō'râ) Dora
Doride (dô'rē·dā) Doris
Dorotea (dō·rō·tā'â) Dorothy
Durante (dū·rân'tā) Durand

E

Edgardo (ād·gâr'dō) Edgar
Editta (ā·dēt'tâ) Edith
Edmondo (ād·mōn'dō) Edmund
Edoardo (ā·dō·âr'dō) Edward
Egidio (ā·jē'dyō) Giles
Elena (e'lā·nâ) Helen, Ellen, Helena
Eleonora (ā·lā·ō·nō'râ) Eleanor
Elia (ā·lē'â) Elias
Elisa (ā·lē'zâ) Eliza
Elisabetta (ā·lē·zâ·bāt'tâ) Elizabeth
Eloisa (ā·lō·ē'zä) Eloise
Elvira (āl·vē'râ) Elvira
Emilia (ā·mē'lyâ) Emily, Emilia
Emilio (ā·mē'lyō) Emile
Emma (ām'mâ) Emma
Enrichetta (ān·rē·kāt'tâ) Harriet, Hatty, Hetty
Enrico (ān·rē'kō) Henry
Erberto (ār·bār'tō) Herbert

Erico (ā·rē'kō) Eric
Ermione (ār·myō'nā) Hermione
Ernestina (ār·nā·stē'nâ) Ernestine
Ernesto (ār·nā'stō) Ernest
Esmondo (ā·zmōn'dō) Esmund
Ester (ā'stār) Esther
Ettore (et'tō·rā) Hector
Eugenia (āū·je'nyâ) Eugenia
Eugenio (āū·je'nyō) Eugene
Eva (ā'vâ) Eve
Evelina (ā·vā·lē'nâ) Evelyn
Ezechiele (ā·dzā·kyā'lā) Ezekiel

F

Fabiano (fâ·byâ'nō) Fabian
Fabrizio (fâ·brē'tsyō) Fabricius
Federica (fā·dā·rē'kâ) Frederica
Federico (fā·dā·rē'kō) Frederick, Fred
Felice (fā·lē'chā) Felix
Felicia (fā·lē'châ) Felicia
Feliciano (fā·lē·châ'nō) Felician
Felicita (fā·lē'chē·tâ) Felicity
Ferdinando (fār·dē·nân'dō) Ferdinand
Fernando (fār·nân'dō) Ferdinand
Filemone (fē·le'mō·nā) Philemon
Filippo (fē·lēp'pō) Philip
Fiorenza (fyō·rān'tsâ) Florence
Flaviano (flâ·vyâ'nō) Flavian
Flavio (flâ'vyō) Flavius
Fortunata (fōr·tū·nâ'tâ) Fortune
Fortunato (fōr·tū·nâ'tō) Fortunatus
Francesca (frân·chā'skâ) Frances
Francesco (frân·chā'skō) Francis, Frank
Fulvia (fūl'vyâ) Fulvia
Fulvio (fūl'vyō) Fulvius

G

Gabriele (gâ·bryā'lā) Gabriel
Gabriella (gâ·bryāl'lâ) Gabriella
Galileo (gâ·lē·lā'ō) Galileo
Geltrude (jāl·trū'dā) Gertrude
Genoveffa (jā·nō·vāf'fâ) Genevieve
Geraldina (jā·râl·dē'nâ) Geraldine
Geraldo (jā·râl'dō) Gerald
Gerardo (jā·râr'dō) Gerard
Geronimo (jā·rô'nē·mō) Jerome
Gervasio (jār·vâ'zyō) Gervase
Giacinta (jâ·chēn'tâ) Hyacinth
Giacobbe (jâ·kōb'bā) Jacob
Giacomina (jâ·kō·mē'nâ) Jenny
Giacomo (jâ'kō·mō) James, Jacques
Giampietro (jâm·pyā'trō) John Peter
Gian Andrea (jân ân·drā'â) John Andrew
Gian Carlo (jân kâr'lō) John Charles
Gian Lorenzo (jân lō·rān'dzō) John Lawrence
Gianmaria (jân·mâ·rē'â) John Marion
Giannetta (jân·nāt'tâ) Jeanette, Jenny
Giannetto (jân·nāt'tō) Jack
Giano (jâ'nō) Ian
Giasone (jâ·zō'nā) Jason
Gilberto (jēl·bār'tō) Gilbert
Gina (jē'nâ) Jean
Gino (jē'nō) Gene
Gioconda (jō·kōn'dâ) Jocunda
Gionata (jô'nâ·tâ) Jonathan
Giordano (jōr·dâ'nō) Jordan
Giorgetto (jōr·jāt'tō) Georgie
Giorgiana (jōr·jâ'nâ) Georgiane

Giorgio (jôr′jō) George
Giovanna (jō·vân′nâ) Jane, Joan, Johanna
Giovanni (jō·vân′nē) John
Giovannina (jō·vân·nē′nâ) Jean
Giuditta (jū·dēt′tâ) Judith
Giulia (jū′lyâ) Julia, Julie
Giuliana (jū·lyâ′nâ) Juliana
Giuliano (jū·lyâ′nō) Julian
Giulietta (jū·lyāt′tâ) Juliet
Giulio (jū′lyō) Julius, Jules
Giuseppe (jū·zāp′pā) Joseph
Giuseppina (jū·zāp·pē′nâ) Josephine
Giustina (jū·stē′nâ) Justina
Giustiniano (jū·stē·nyâ′nō) Justinian
Giustino (jū·stē′nō) Justin
Giusto (jū′stō) Justus
Goffredo (gōf·frā′dō) Godfrey
Gregorio (grā·gô′ryō) Gregory
Gualtiero (gwâl·tyā′rō) Walter
Guglielmino (gū·lyāl·mē′nō) Bill
Guglielmo (gū·lyāl′mō) William
Guido (gwē′dō) Guy
Guntero (gūn·tā′rō) Gunther
Gustavo (gū·stâ′vō) Gustav

I

Ida (ē′dâ) Ida
Ilario (ē·lâ′ryō) Hilary
Irene (ē·rā′na) Irene
Isabella (ē·zâ·bāl′lâ) Isabel
Isacco (ē·zâk′kō) Isaac
Ivone (ē·vō′nā) Yves

L

Lamberto (lâm·bār′tō) Lambert
Laura (lâ′ū·râ) Laura
Lavinia (lâ·vē′nyâ) Lavinia
Leandro (lā·ân′drō) Leander
Leonardo (lā·ō·nâr′dō) Leonard
Leone (lā·ō′nā) Leo
Leonia (lā·ô′nyâ) Leonia
Leonora (lā·ō·nō′râ) Leonore
Leopoldo (lā·ō·pōl′dō) Leopold
Lea (lā′â) Leah
Lidia (lē′dyâ) Lydia
Lionello (lyō·nāl′lō) Lionel
Lisa (lē′zâ) Betty
Lisetta (lē·zāt′tâ) Betsy
Livia (lē′vyâ) Livia
Lodovico (lō·dǫ·vē′kō) Lewis
Lorena (lō·rā′nâ) Lorraine
Lorenzo (lō·rān′dzō) Lawrence
Luca (lū′kâ) Luke, Lucas
Lucano (lū·kâ′nō) Lucan
Lucia (lū·chē′â) Lucy, Lucia
Luciano (lū·châ′nō) Lucian
Lucio (lū′chō) Lucius
Lucrezio (lū·krē′tsyō) Lucretius
Luigi (lwē′jē) Louis
Luisa (lwē′zâ) Louisa

M

Maddalena (mâd·dâ·lā′nâ) Madeleine, Madeline
Magda (mâg′dâ) Maud
Manfredo (mân·frā′dō) Manfred
Manlio (mân′lyō) Manlius
Manuele (mâ·nwā′lā) Manuel
Marcantonio (mâr·kân·tô′nyō) Mark Anthony
Marcellina (mâr·chāl·lē′nâ) Marcelline
Marcellino (mâr·chāl·lē′nō) Marcellinus
Marcello (mâr·chāl′lō) Marcel
Marco (mâr′kō) Mark
Margherita (mâr·gā·rē′tâ) Margaret, Margery, Margot, Madge

Maria (mâ·rē′â) Mary, Marie
Marianna (mâ·ryân′nâ) Marianne
Marietta (mâ·ryāt′tâ) Peggy, Marion, May
Mario (mâ′ryō) Marius
Marta (mâr′tâ) Martha
Martino (mâr·tē′nō) Martin
Massimiliano (mâs·sē·mē·lyâ′nō) Maximilian
Matilde (mâ·tēl′dā) Mathilda
Matteo (mât·tā′ō) Matthew
Maurizio (mâū·rē′tsyō) Maurice
Melissa (mā·lēs′sâ) Melissa
Mercede (mār·chā′dā) Mercedes
Michelangelo (mē·kā·lân′jā·lō) Michaelangelo
Michele (mē·kā′lā) Michael
Michelino (mē·kā·lē′nō) Mike
Minerva (mē·nār′vâ) Minerva
Miranda (mē·rân′dâ) Miranda
Modesto (mō·dā′stō) Modestus
Monica (mô′nē·ka) Monica, Monique

N

Nannetta (nân·nāt′tâ) Nannette
Natale (nâ·tâ′lā) Noel
Natalia (nâ·tâ·lē′â) Natalie
Nataniele (nâ·tâ·nyā′lā) Nathaniel
Nicola (nē·kō′lâ) Nicholas
Nicoletta (nē·kō·lāt′tâ) Nicolette
Nicolò (nē·kō·lō′) Nicholas
Nicoluccio (nē·kō·lū′chō) Nick
Nina (nē′nâ) Nina, Nan
Nino (nē′nō) Nino

O

Ofelia (ō·fe′lyâ) Ophelia
Olivia (ō·lē′vyâ) Olive, Olivia
Oliviero (ō·lē·vyā′rō) Oliver
Omero (ō·mā′rō) Homer
Onofredo (ō·nō·frā′dō) Humphrey
Onorato (ō·nō·râ′tō) Honore
Orazio (ō·râ′tsyō) Horace, Horatio
Orlando (ōr·lân′dō) Orlando
Orsola (ôr′sō·lâ) Ursula
Ortensia (ōr·ten′syâ) Hortense, Hortensia
Oscar (ō′skâr) Oscar
Osvaldo (ō·zvâl′dō) Oswald
Ottavia (ōt·tâ′vyâ) Octavia
Ottaviano (ōt·tâ·vyâ′nō) Octavian
Ottavio (ōt·tâ′vyō) Octavius
Ovidio (ō·vē′dyō) Ovid

P

Panfilo (pân′fē·lō) Pamphilus
Paola (pâ′ō·lâ) Paula
Paolina (pâ·ō·lē′nâ) Paulina
Paolino (pâ·ō·lē′nō) Paulinus
Paolo (pâ′ō·lō) Paul
Pasquale (pâ·skwâ′lā) Pascal
Patrizia (pâ·trē′tsyâ) Patricia
Patrizio (pā·trē′tsyō) Patrick
Penelope (pā·ne′lō·pā) Penelope
Petronilla (pā·trō·nēl′lâ) Petronella
Petronio (pā·trô′nyō) Petronius
Piero (pyā′rō) Peter
Pietro (pyā′trō) Peter
Pietruccio (pyā·trū′chō) Pete
Pindaro (pēn′dâ·rō) Pindar
Placidia (plâ·chē′dyâ) Placidia
Platone (plâ·tō′nā) Plato
Plauto (plâ′ū·tō) Plautus
Plinio (plē′nyō) Pliny
Pompeo (pōm·pā′ō) Pompey

Porfirio (pōr·fē′ryō) Porphyry
Porzia (pôr′tsyâ) Portia
Priscilla (prē·shēl′lâ) Priscilla
Prospero (prô′spā·rō) Prosper
Proteo (prô′tā·ō) Proteus
Prudenza (prū·dān′tsâ) Prudence

Q

Quintiliano (kwēn·tē·lyâ′nō) Quintilian
Quintino (kwēn tē′nō) Quentin

R

Rachele (râ·kā′lā) Rachel
Raffaele (râf·fâ·ā′lā) Raphael
Raimondo (râē·mōn′dō) Raymond
Rainero (râē·nā′rō) Rainerd
Randolfo (rân·dōl′fō) Randolph
Raulo (râ′ū·lō) Ralph
Rea (rā′â) Rhea
Rebecca (rā·bāk′kâ) Rebecca
Reginaldo (rā·jē·nâl′dō) Reginald
Reinardo (rāē·nâr′dō) Reinhard
Renato (rā·nâ′tō) Renatus
Riccardino (rēk·kâr·dē′nō) Dick
Riccardo (rēk·kâr′dō) Richard
Rinaldo (rē·nâl′dō) Reynold, Reggie, Ronald
Roberto (rō·bār′tō) Robert
Rodolfo (rō·dōl′fō) Rudolph, Ralph
Rodrigo (rō·drē′gō) Roderick
Rolando (rō·lân′dō) Roland
Romolo (rô′mō·lō) Romulus
Rosa (rō′zâ) Rose
Rosalia (rō·zâ·lē′â) Rosalie
Rosalinda (rō·zâ·lēn′dâ) Rosalind
Rosamonda (rō·zâ·mōn′dâ) Rosamund
Rosetta (rō·zāt′tâ) Rosette
Rosina (rō·zē′nâ) Rosalie
Rossana (rōs·sâ′nâ) Roxanne
Rufo (rū′fō) Rufus
Ruggero (rūj·jā′rō) Roger
Ruth (rūt) Ruth

S

Salomone (sâ·lō·mō′nā) Solomon
Samuele (sâ·mwā′lā) Samuel
Sandro (sân′drō) Andrew
Sansone (sân·sō′nā) Samson
Sara (sâ′râ) Sarah, Sally
Saul (sâ′ūl) Saul
Saverio (sâ·ve′ryō) Xavier
Sebastiana (sā·bâ·styâ′nâ) Sebastiana
Sebastiano (sā·bâ·styâ′nō) Sebastian
Sempronia (sām·prô′nyâ) Sempronia
Sempronio (sām·prô′nyō) Sempronius
Severo (sā·vā′rō) Severus
Sibilla (sē·bēl′lâ) Sibyl
Sigfrido (sēg·frē′dō) Siegfried
Sigismondo (sē·jē·zmōn′dō) Sigmund
Silvestro (sēl·vā′strō) Silvester
Silvia (sēl′vyâ) Sylvia
Silvio (sēl′vyō) Sylvius
Simeone (sē·mā·ō′nā) Simeon
Simone (sē·mō′nā) Simon
Sofia (sō·fē′â) Sophie
Stefania (stā·fâ′nyâ) Stephanie
Stefano (ste′fâ·nō) Stephen
Stella (stāl′lâ) Estelle, Stella
Stentore (stān·tō′rā) Stentor
Susanna (sū·zân′nâ) Susan, Sue, Susannah
Susetta (sū·zāt′tâ) Susie

T

Tacito (tâ′chē·tō) Tacitus
Taddeo(tâd·dā′ō) Thaddeus
Teobaldo (tā·ō·bâl′dō) Theobald
Teodato (tā·ō·dâ′tō) Theodatus
Teodora (tā·ō·dō′râ) Theodora
Teodorico (tā·ō·dō·rē′kō) Theodoric
Teodoro (tā·ō·dō′rō) Theodore
Teodosia (tā·ō·dô′zyâ) Theodosia
Teodosio (tā·ō·dô′zyō) Theodosius
Terenzio (tā·ren′tsyō) Terence
Teresa (tā·rā′zā) Therese, Teresa
Tibaldo (tē·bâl′dō) Tybald
Timeo (tē·mā′ō) Timaeus
Timoteo (tē·mô′tā·ō) Timothy
Tirone (tē·rō′nā) Tyrone
Tito (tē′tō) Titus
Tommasina(tōm·mâ·zē′nâ)Thomasina
Tommasino (tōm·mâ·zē′nō) Tom
Tommaso (tōm·mâ′zō) Thomas
Tonio (tô′nyō) Tony

U

Ubaldo (ū·bâl′dō) Hubaldus
Uberto (ū·bār′tō) Hubert
Ugo (ū′gō) Hugh
Ulisse (ū·lēs′sā) Ulysses
Ulrico (ūl·rē′kō) Ulric
Umberto (ūm·bār′tō) Humbert
Urania (ū·râ′nyâ) Urania
Urbano (ūr·bâ′nō) Urban

V

Valentina (vâ·lān·tē′nâ) Valentina
Valentino (vâ·lān·tē′nō) Valentine
Valeria (vâ·le′ryâ) Valerie
Valeriano (vâ·lā·ryâ′nō) Valerian
Venere (ve′nā·rā) Venus
Veronica (vā·rô′nē·kâ) Veronica
Vincenza (vēn·chān′dzâ) Vincentia
Vincenzina (vēn·chān·dzē′nâ) Vinny
Vincenzo (vēn·chān′dzō) Vincent
Vilfrido (vēl·frē′dō) Wilfred
Vinfrido (vēn·frē′dō) Winfred
Viola (vyō′lâ) Violet
Virgilio (vēr·jē′lyō) Virgil
Virginia (vēr·jē′nyâ) Virginia
Vitale (vē·tâ′lā) Vitellius
Vito (vē′tō) Vitus
Vittore (vēt·tō′rā) Vic
Vittoria (vēt·tô′ryâ) Victoria
Vittoriano (vēt·tō·ryâ′nō) Victorian
Vittorio (vēt·tô′ryō) Victor
Viviana (vē·vyâ′nâ) Vivian

Z

Zaccaria (dzâk·kâ·rē′â) Zachary
Zaccheo (dzâk·kā′ō) Zaccheus
Zenobia (dzā·nô′byâ) Zenobia
Zenone (dzā·nō′nā) Zeno

ABBREVIATIONS

a adjective
adv adverb
aesp aerospace
agr agriculture
anat anatomy
arch architecture
art article
ast astronomy
auto automobile
avi aviation
biol biology
bot botany
chem chemistry
coll colloquial
com commerce
comp compound
conj conjunction
dent dentistry
eccl ecclesiastic
elec electricity
f feminine
fam familiar
fig figuratively
for formal
geog geography
geol geology
gram grammar

interj interjection
lit literature
m masculine
math mathematics
mech mechanics
med medicine
mil military
min mineralogy
mus music
n noun
naut nautical
phot photography
phys physics
pl plural
pol politics
prep preposition
print printing
pron pronoun
rad radio
rail railway
sl slang
theat theatre
TV television
vi verb intransitive
vt verb transitive
vt&i verb transitive and intransitive
zool zoology

English-Italian

A

a *art* un, uno, una, un'
aback *adv* indietro; **be taken —** rimanere di sasso
abacus *n* abbaco
abandon *vt* abbandonare; **–ment** *n* abbandono
abase *vt* umiliare; **–ment** *n* degradazione, umiliazione
abash *vt* intimidare, svergognare, umiliare
abate *vi* diminuire; **–ment** *n* diminuzione, indebolimento, sconto
abbey *n* abbazia
abbot *n* abate *m*
abbreviate *vt* abbreviare
abbreviation *n* abbreviazione
abdicate *vt&i* abdicare, rinunciare
abdication *n* abdicazione
abdomen *n* addome *m*, ventre *m*
abdominal *a* addominale
abduct *vt* rapire; **–ion** *n* ratto; **–or** *n* rapitore *m*
abed *adv* a letto, infermo
aberration *n* aberrazione
abet *vt* favoreggiare
abeyance *n* giacenza; **in —** giacente, pendente, sospeso
abhor *vt* aborrire; **–rence** *n* aborrimento; **–rent** *a* aborrevole, odioso
abide *vt* sopportare; resistere; **—** *vi* dimorare, continuare; **— by** sostenere, mantenere
abiding *a* dimorante, costante
ability *n* capacità, facoltà
abject *a* abietto, basso, vile
abjure *vt* abiurare
ablative *a* ablativo
ablaze *adv* in fiamme; splendente
able *a* abile, capace; **be — to** potere, essere in grado di, sapere
able-bodied *a* robusto, vigoroso
ablution *n* abluzione
ably *adv* abilmente
abnegate *vt* rinunziare
abnegation *n* rinunzia
abnormal *a* anormale; **—ity** *n* anormalità
aboard *adv&prep* a bordo; **All —!** *interj* Tutti a bordo!; **go —** imbarcarsi
abode *n* dimora
abolish *vt* abolire
abolition *n* abolizione
A-bomb *n* bomba atomica
abominable *a* abominevole, infame
abominate *vt* detestare
abomination *n* abominazione, infamia
aboriginal *a* aborigeno, primitivo
abort *n (aesp)* fallimento
abortion *n* aborto
abortive *a* abortivo; senza esito
abound *vi* abbondare; **–ing** *a* abbondante
about *prep* intorno, intorno a; *(time)* verso, circa; **be — to** essere sul punto di, stare per
above *adv&prep* sopra, su; **— all** soprattutto
above-mentioned *a* sopraccitato
aboveboard *a* sincero; **—** *adv* lealmente
abrasion *n* abrasione, logoramento
abrasive *a* abrasivo; **—** *n* abrasivo
abreast *adv* in linea; **— of the times** conforme ai tempi
abridge *vt* accorciare
abroad *adv* all'estero
abrogate *vt* abrogare; *(abolish)* abolire; *(annul)* annullare
abrupt *a* brusco, improvviso
abscess *n* ascesso
abscond *vi* nascondersi, rendersi latitante
absence *n* assenza; **leave of —** licenza, congedo
absent *a* assente; **–ee** *n* assenteista *m*
absent-minded *a* distratto
absolute *a* assoluto; **–ly** *adv* assolutamente
absolution *n* assoluzione
absolve *vt* assolvere
absorb *vt* assorbire
absorbent *a* assorbente; **— cotton** cotone idrofilo
absorption *n* assorbimento
abstain *v* astenersi
abstemious *a* astemio
abstinence *n* astinenza
abstract *vt* sottrarre; **—** *n&a* astratto, estratto; **—** *n (com)* riassunto; **in the —** in astratto; **–ly** *adv* astrattamente
abstracted *a* distratto; **–ly** *adv* distrattamente

abstraction *n* astrazione
abstruse *a* astruso
absurd *a* assurdo; **–ity** *n* assurdità
abundance *n* abbondanza
abundant *a* abbondante
abuse *vt* maltrattare; — *vi* abusare; — *n* abuso, insulto
abusive *a* abusivo
abut *vi* sfociare, confinare
abyss *n* abisso, profondità
Abyssinia *n* Abissinia
Abyssinian *n&a* abissino
academic *a* accademico, classico
academy *n* accademia, scuola
accede *vi* accedere, consentire, assentire
accelerate *vt* accelerare; — *vi* affrettarsi
acceleration *n* accelerazione
accelerator *n* acceleratore *m*
accent *n* accento, tono; — *vt* accentare, accentuare; **–uate** *vt* accentuare
accept *vt* accettare, accogliere; *(approve)* approvare; **–able** *a* accettabile, ammissibile; **–ance** *n* accettazione; approvazione; *(com)* cambiale *f*
access *n* accesso, entrata
accessory *a* accessorio; — *n* accessorio; *(partner)* complice *m*
accident *n* incidente *m;* **–al** *a* accidentale, fortuito; **–ally** *adv* accidentalmente, per caso
acclaim *vt* acclamare; — *n* acclamazione
acclamation *n* acclamazione
acclimate *vt* acclimatare
accomodate *vt* accomodare, favorire; *(house)* alloggiare; — *vi* accomodarsi, prestarsi, conformarsi; — **oneself** adattarsi
accommodating *a* cortese, accomodante
accommodation *n* accomodamento; **–s** *npl* *(hotel)* alloggiamento
accompaniment *n* accompagnamento
accompanist *n* accompagnatore *m*, accompagnatrice *f*
accompany *vt* accompagnare
accomplice *n* complice *m*
accomplish *vt* realizzare; **–ed** *a* adempiuto, compiuto; **–ment** *n* complimento, effettuazione
accord *vt* accordare; *(grant)* concedere; — *vi* accordarsi; — *n* accordo, concordia; **of one's own** — spontaneamente; **with one** — simultaneamente, di comune accordo; **–ance** *n* conformità
according *a* concedente; — *adv* secondo, conforme a; **–ly** *adv* così, pertanto
accordion *n* fisarmonica; — **player** fisarmonicista *m&f*
accost *vt* accostare, abbordare
account *n (com)* conto; *(report)* resoconto; *(story)* racconto, versione; **of no** — di nessuna importanza; **on** — *(com)* per conto; **on — of** per causa di; **on my** — per conto mio, a causa mia; **on no** — in nessun modo
account *vt (com)* contare; — **for** render conto di
accountant *n* ragioniere *m*, contabile *m*
accounting *n* contabilità
accredit *vt* accreditare; **–ed** *a* accreditato
accrual *a* crescente, montante
accrue *vi* accumularsi; **–d** *a* accumulato
accumulate *vt* accumulare, ammucchiare; — *vi* accumularsi
accumulation *n* accumulazione
accuracy *n* precisione, esattezza
accurate *a* esatto, giusto, preciso
accursed *a* maledetto
accusation *n* accusa
accusative *a&n* accusativo
accuse *vt* accusare; **–d** *a* accusato
accuser *n* accusatore *m*
accustom *vt* abituare; **become –ed** abituarsi
ace *n* asso
acetate *n* acetato
acetic *a* acetico
acetone *n* acetone *m*
acetylene *n* acetilene *m*
ache *n* dolore *m;* — *vi* sentir male, dolere; far male
achieve *vt* raggiungere, conseguire, pervenire; **–ment** *n* raggiungimento; *(goal)* meta; *(result)* esito
acid *n&a* acido; — **test** analisi finale
acid-forming *a* acidico
acidity *n* acidità
acidosis *n* acidosi *f*
acknowledge *vt* riconoscere; — **receipt** accusare ricevuta
acknowledgment *n* riconoscimento, confessione
acme *n* acme *m*, crisi *f*, apogeo
acorn *n* ghianda
acoustic *a* acustico; **–s** *npl* acustica
acquaint *vt* informare; **be –ed** conoscere; **be –ed with** essere edotto di; — **oneself with** fare la conoscenza di
acquaintance *n* conoscenza
acquiesce *vi* consentire a
acquiescence *n* acquiescenza
acquiescent *a* acquiescente, accomodante
acquire *vt* acquistare
acquisition *n* acquisizione, acquisto
acquit *vt* assolvere; — **oneself well** fare buona figura
acquittal *n* assoluzione
acre *n* acro; **–age** *n* superficie *f*
acrid *a* agro
acrobat *n* acrobata *m&f*; **–ics** *npl* acrobazie *fpl*; **–ic** *a* acrobatico
across *adv* dirimpetto; **come** — imbattersi in; — *prep* attraverso
act *n* atto, azione; *(law)* legge *f*; *(of a play)* atto; *(theat)* recitazione, rappresentazione; — *vt* fare; *(behavior)* agire; rappresentare; funzionare; — **as** fungere da
acting *n* azione, recitazione
action *n* azione, fatto; **legal** — azione legale; **–s** condotta
activate *v* attivare
active *a* attivo; **–ly** *adv* attivamente
activity *n* attività
actor *n* attore, interprete *m*
actress *n* attrice, interprete *f*
actual *a* effettivo, reale; **–ly** *adv* effettivamente
actuality *n* attualità
acumen *n* acume *m*
acute *a* acuto; **–ly** *adv* acutamente
adage *n* adagio, proverbio

adamant *a* inflessibile
adapt *v* adattare; **–able** *a* adattabile; **–ability** *n* adattabilità; **–ation** *n* adattamento; **–er** *n (theat)* adattatore *m*
add *vt* aggiungere; *(math)* addizionare, sommare
addendum *n* aggiunta; addendo
addict *vt* assuefare; **drug —** tossicomane *m*
addiction *n* inclinazione; propensione
adding machine *n* addizionatrice *f*
addition *n* aggiunta; *(math)* addizione; **in — to** oltre a; **–al** *a* supplementare, addizionale
addle *vt* confondere; — *vi* confondersi
addle-brained *a* stupido
address *n* indirizzo; — *vt* indirizzare; — *vi* indirizzarsi; **–ee** *n* destinatario
address *n* discorso; — *vt* rivolgere la parola a; — *vi* rivolgersi
adduce *vt* addurre, aggiungere
adenoids *npl* adenoidi *fpl*
adept *n&a* esperto, adepto
adequate *a* sufficiente, adeguato; **–ly** *adv* sufficientemente; **–ness** *n* adeguamento
adhere *vi* aderire
adherent *a&n* aderente *m&f;* **–ly** *adv* aderentemente
adhesion *n* adesione *f*
adhesive *a* adesivo; — **tape** nastro adesivo; — *n* cerotto; **–ness** *n* vischiosità
adipose *a* adiposo, grasso
adit *n* entrata
adjacent *a* contiguo, adiacente
adjective *n* aggettivo
adjoin *vt* aggiungere; — *vi* confinare, essere contiguo; **–ing** *a* contiguo
adjourn *vt* rinviare; — *vi* fare rinvio; *(discussion)* aggiornare; *(meeting)* sciogliere l'adunanza; **–ment** *n* rinvio
adjudication *n* aggiudicazione; condanna, sentenza
adjunct *n* aggiunto
adjust *vt* aggiustare; — **oneself** adattarsi; **–able** *a* aggiustabile; **–ment** *n* accomodamento
adjutant *n* aiutante *m*
ad-lib *vt* improvvisare
administer *vt* amministrare; — *vi* contribuire, somministrare
administrator *n* amministratore *m*
administration *n* amministrazione, governo
admirable *a* ammirevole
admirably *adv* mirabilmente
admiral *n* ammiraglio
admiration *n* ammirazione
admire *vt* ammirare; **–r** *n* ammiratore *m*, ammiratrice *f*
admissible *a* ammissibile
admission *n (acknowledgment)* ammissione, *(entrancé)* ingresso, entrata
admit *vt* ammettere; *(acknowledge)* confessare, riconoscere
admittance *n* entrata, ingresso; **no —** vietato l'ingresso
admittedly *adv* ammissibilmente
admix *vt* mischiare; — *vi* mescolarsi con; **–ture** *n* miscela
admonish *vt* ammonire, riprendere
admonition *n* ammonizione
ado *n* rumore *m*, confusione
adobe *n&a* mattone crudo
adolescence *n* adolescenza
adolescent *a* adolescente
adopt *vt* adottare; **–ed** *a* adottato, adottivo
adoption *n* adozione
adorable *a* adorabile
adoration *a* adorazione
adore *vt* adorare; — *vi* fare atto di adorazione
adorn *vt* adornare, fregiare; — **one's self** adornarsi, abbellirsi
adrenal *a* adrenale; **–in** *n* adrenalina
adrift *a&adv* alla deriva
adroit *a* destro, abile
adsorb *vt* raccogliere, riunire, assorbire
adulation *n* adulazione
adult *a&n* adulto
adulterant *n&a* adulterante
adulterer *n* adultero; adultera
adulterate *vt* adulterare, falsificare
adultery *n* adulterio
advance *vt* avanzare; *(money)* prestare; **pay in —** anticipare; — *vi* andare avanti; **–d** *a* avanzato; — *n* anticipo; *(price, wage)* aumento; — **allowance** anticipio di trasferta; **in —** in anticipo; anticipatamente; **–ment** *n* promozione; anticipo; **make –s** fare approcci, tentar di amicarsi
advantage *n* vantaggio; **take — of** approfittarsi di; **–ous** *a* vantaggioso, conveniente
advent *n* avvenimento
Advent *n* Avvento
adventure *n* avventura; **–some** *a* ardito, corraggioso; **–r** *n* avventuriero; — *vt* avventurare; — *vi* avventurarsi
adventurous *a* avventuroso, corraggioso
adverb *n* avverbio; **–ial** *a* avverbiale
adversary *n* avversario
adverse *a* avverso, contrario
adversity *n* avversità
advertise *vt&i* annunziare; inserire un annunzio; *(publicize)* fare pubblicità; **–ment** *n* pubblicitario
advertiser *n* inserzionista *m*
advertising *n* pubblicità
advice *n* consiglio
advisability *n* prudenza, sagacità
advisable *a* consigliabile; *(suitable)* conveniente; *(wise)* prudente
advise *vt* consigliare; — **with** consultare
advisor *n* consigliere *m*
advisory *a* consultivo
advocate *n (law)* avvocato; *(of cause)* sostenitore *m*, difensore *m*; *(promoter)* propugnatore *m;* — *vt* avvocare, difendere
aerate *vt* aerare, arieggiare
aerial *a* aereo; — *n (rad&TV)* antenna; **–ist** *n* ginnasta *m*, funambulo
aerodynamics *npl* aerodinamica
aeroembolism *n* aeroembolismo
aeromedicine *n* aeromedicina
aeronautics *n* aeronautica
aerosol *n* particola dell'aria; — **bomb** spruzzatore
aerospace *a* aerospazio

aerostat *n* aerostato; **–ic** *a* aerostatico
aerothermodynamics *npl* aerotermodinamica
aesthetic *a* estetico; **–s** *n* estetica
afar *adv* lontano; **from —** da lontano
affability *n* affabilità
affable *a* affabile
affair *n* affare *m*; (*love*) relazione amorosa; (*party*) festa
affect *vt* affettare; (*emotions*) commuovere; **–ed** *a* (*emotions*) commoso; (*manners*) affettato; **–edly** *adv* affetosamente; **–ing** *a* influente
affection *n* affezione; **–ate** *a* affettuoso; **–ately** *adv* affezionatamente
affidavit *n* affidavit *m*; dichiarazione giurata, certificato legale
affiliate *vt* affiliare, associarsi
affiliation *n* affiliazione, associazione
affirm *vt* affermare; **–ation** *n* affermazione, ratifica
affirmative *n* affermativa; **—** *a* affermativo
affix *vt* affiggere
afflict *vt* affliggere
affliction *n* afflizione
affluence *n* affluenza
affluent *a* affluente
afflux *n* afflusso
afford *vt* fornire
affray *n* rissa
affront *n* affronto; **—** *vt* affrontare
afield *adv* lontano; in campo
afire *a* in fiamme
afloat *a* a galla, galleggiante
afoot *a&adv* a piedi, camminando
aforesaid *a* sopraddetto
afoul *a&adv* in collisione
afraid *a* pauroso; **be —** aver paura, temere
African *a&n* africano
aft *adv* (*naut*) a poppa; posteriore
after *prep&adv* dopo; **day — tomorrow** dopodomani; **—** *conj* dopo che; **–ward** *adv* dopo, più tardi
afterburner *n* (*avi*) tubo di scappamento di aviogetto
aftereffect *n* conseguenza, risultato
aftermath *n* postumo; conseguenza
afternoon *n* pomeriggio
afterthought *n* cambiamento d' idea
again *adv* ancora, di nuovo, nuovamente, un'altra volta; **— and —** ripetutamente
against *prep* contro
agape *a&adv* spalancato; con la bocca aperta
age *n* età, era; **–less** *a* sempre giovane; **of —** maggiorenne; **—** *vt&i* invecchiare; **–d** *a* vecchio, invecchiato
agency *n* agenzia; **government —** ente governativo
agent *n* agente, rappresentante *m&f*; sostanza
agglomerate *vt* agglomerare
agglomeration *n* agglomerazione
agglutinin *n* anticorpo agglutinante
aggrandize *vt* ingrandire; **–ment** *n* ingrandimento
aggravate *vt* aggravare, irritare.
aggravation *n* aggravazione, provocazione
aggregate *a* totale; **—** *n* aggregato, totale; **—** *vt* aggregare
aggregation *n* aggregato, riunione
aggression *n* aggressione
aggressive *a* aggressivo, invadente
aggressor *n* aggressore *m*
aghast *a* terrorizzato
agile *a* agile
agility *n* agilità
agitate *vt* agitare
agitation *n* agitazione
agitator *n* agitatore *m*
aglow *a* infuocato, ardente
agnostic *n&a* agnostico
ago *adv* passato, fa; **long —** molto tempo fa
agog *a* eccitato, agitato; **—** *adv* agitatamente; **be all —** essere emozionato
agonize *vi* agonizzare
agonizing *a* agonizzante
agony *n* agonia
agrarian *a* agrario
agree *vi* acconsentire; andare d'accordo, essere d'accordo, mettersi d'accordo; **–able** *a* piacevole
agreement *n* accordo, patto; (*gram*) concordanza; **— with** accordo con; **general —** unanimità; **reach an —** pervenire ad un accordo
agricultural *a* agricolo
agriculture *n* agricoltura
agronomy *n* agronomia
aground *a&adv* incagliato, arenato; **run —** arenare
ahead *adv* avanti, d'avanti; **get —** oltrepassare; **go —** avanzare, andare avanti; **— of time** in anticipo
aid *vt* aiutare; **—** *n* aiuto, assistenza; **first —** pronto soccorso
aide *n* aiutante *m*
ail *vt* addolorare; **—** *vi* soffrire; **What —s you?** Che cosa ti fa soffrire?; **–ment** *n* indisposizione; **–ing** *a* sofferente
aileron *n* alerone *m*
aim *vt* aspirare; (*gun*) mirare; **—** *n* mira; (*purpose*) scopo; **–less** *a* senza scopo
air *n* atmosfera, aria; (*manner*) aspetto, maniera; **— brush** aerografo; **— chamber** camera d'aria; **— gun** fucile ad aria compressa; **— lift** ponte aereo; **— mail** posta aerea; **— pocket** (*avi*) vuoto d'aria; **— pump** pompa pneumatica; **— shaft** (*mine*) pozzo d'aerazione; **up in the —** in aria
air *n* (*avi*) aria; **— base** base aerea; **by —** per via aerea; **— freight** trasporto aereo; **— line** aviolinea; **— terminal** aerostazione; **–way** rotta aerea
air– (*in comp*) **—borne** *a* aerotrasportato; **— condition** *vt* applicare l'aria condizionata; **—mail** *a* per via aerea
air *vt* (*opinion*) esprimere; (*ventilation*) aerare, ventilare
airily *a* leggermente, delicatamente
airless *a* senz'aria
airing *n* passeggiata; (*things*) esposizione all'aria
airplane *n* aeroplano; **— carrier** nave portaerei
airport *n* aeroporto
airtight *a* ermetico

airy *a* arioso
aisle *n* corridoio; *(church)* navata
ajar *a* socchiuso
akin *a* imparentato
alacrity *n* alacrità
a la mode alla moda, di moda
alarm *n* allarme *m; (fright)* spavento; — **clock** sveglia; — **signal** segnale d'allarme; — *vt* allarmare
alarming *a* allarmante
alas *interj* ahimè
albeit *adv* benchè
album *n* album *m*
albumen *n* albume *m*, albumina
alcohol *n* alcool *m*, spirito
alcoholic *n* alcolizzato; — *a* alcoolico
alcove *n* alcova, nicchia
alderman *n* consigliere municipale
ale *n* birra forte
alert *n* allarme *m;* — *a* sveglio, svelto, vigilante
alertness *n* vigilanza
algae *npl* alghe *fpl*
algebra *n* algebra
alias *adv* alias, altrimenti detto
alibi *n* alibi *m; (excuse)* scusa
alien *a&n* straniero, forestiero
alienate *vt* alienare
alight *vi (get off)* scendere, uscire
align *vt* allineare
alignment *n* allineamento
alike *a* simile
alimentary *a* alimentare
alimony *n* alimenti *mpl*
alive *a* vivo, vivente
alkali *n* alcali *m*
alkaline *a* alcalino
all *a&adv* tutto; — **around** tutt'intorno; — **at once** improvvisamente; *(immediately)* subito; — **right** bene, molto bene; — **the better** tanto meglio; **be — in** *(coll)* essere esausto; **by — means** in assoluto; **not at —** nient'affatto; **with — my heart** di tutto cuore
all– *(in comp)* **—out** *a (coll)* massimo; totale; **—over** *a* dalla testa ai piedi *(fig); (coll)* completo; **—round** *a* perfetto
allay *vt* calmare, mitigare
allegation *n* allegazione
allege *vt* dichiarare, pretendere, allegare; **–d** *a* presunto
allegiance *n* lealtà, fedeltà
allegorical *a* allegorico
allegory *n* allegoria
allegro *a* allegro
allergic *a* allergico
allergy *n* allergia
alleviate *vt* alleviare, lenire
alley *n* vicolo; **blind** — vicolo cieco
alliance *n* alleanza
allied *a* alleato
alligator *n* alligatore *m*
alliteration *n* allitterazione
allocate *vt* assegnare, ripartire
allocation *n* collocamento, distribuzione
allot *vt* ripartire; *(assign)* assegnare; *(award)* accordare; **–ment** *n* divisione, porzione
allow *vt* permettere, ammettere, lasciare; — **for** prevedere; **–able** *a* permissibile; **–ance** *n* assegno
alloy *n* lega; — *vt* fondere
allspice *n* pepe di Giamaica
allude *vt* alludere
allure *vt* lusingare, sedurre
allurement *n* simpatia, attrazione
alluring *a* seducente
allusion *n* allusione
alluvial *a* alluviale, alluvionale
ally *n* alleato; — *vt* alleare, collegare
almanac *n* almanacco
almighty *a* onnipotente
Almighty (The) *n* Dio , l'Onnipotente
almond *n* mandorla; — **tree** mandorlo
almost *adv* quasi
alms *npl* limosina, elemosina
aloft *adv* in alto
alone *a* solo; — *adv* solamente, solo, soltanto; **let** — lasciare in pace, lasciare tranquillo
along *adv* avanti; — *prep* per, lungo; — **with** assieme a; **go — with** andare con; **get — with** (*sl, agree*) andare d'accordo con
alongside *adv* lungo il bordo
aloof *adv* in disparte; — *a* riservato
aloud *adv* ad alta voce
alphabet *n* alfabeto; **–ical** *a* alfabetico; **–ize** *vt* disporre in ordine alfabetico
Alps *npl* Alpi *fpl*
already *adv* già
also *adv* anche, pure
altar *n* altare *m;* **high** — altare maggiore
alter *vt* modificare, cambiare; **–ation** *n* modificazione
altercation *n* alterco
alternate *vt* alternare; — *n* supplente *m&f*, sostituto
alternating *a* alternante; — **current** corrente alternata
alternative *n* alternativa
although *conj* benchè, quantunque, sebbene
altimeter *n* altimetro
altitude *n* altitudine *f*, altezza
alto *n* contralto; — *a (mus)* alto
altogether *adv* tutto, completamente; nell'insieme
altruism *n* altruismo
alum *n* allume *m*
aluminum *n* alluminio
always *adv* sempre
A.M., ante meridiem antimeridiano, del mattino
amalgamate *vi* amalgamare, fondere; — *vi* amalgamarsi, fondersi
amass *vt* ammassare
amateur *n&a* dilettante *m&f;* **–ish** *a* dilettante, dilettantesco, da dilettante
amaze *vt* stupire, meravigliare; **–ment** *n* stupore *m*, meraviglia
amazing *a* meraviglioso, stupefacente
amazon *n* amazzone *f*
Amazon River Rio delle Amazzoni
ambassador *n* ambasciatore *m;* — **at large** Ministro senza portafoglio
amber *n* ambra
ambidextrous *a* ambidestro: versatile *(fig)*

ambiguity *n* ambiguità
ambiguous *a* ambiguo
ambition *n* ambizione
ambitious *a* ambizioso
amble *vi* incedere tranquillamente; *(horse)* ambiare; — *n* ambio; andatura tranquilla
ambulance *n* ambulanza
ambulatory *n&a* ambulatorio, ambulante
ambuscade *n* imboscata
ambush *n* imboscata; — *vt* imboscare
ameliorate *vt* migliorare
amen *interj* così sia; amen
amenable *a* sottomesso, arrendevole
amelioration *n* miglioramento
amend *vt* emendare, riformare; **–ed** *a* in compenso; **–ment** *n* emendamento; **–s** *npl* ammenda; **make –s** dar in compenso
amenity *n* amenità
American *n&a* americano; americana
amiable *a* affabile
amiableness *n* amabilità, cordialità
amicable *a* amichevole
amid *prep* fra, nel mezzo di
amiss *adv* male; di traverso, in senso contrario; **take —** prendere in mala parte
amity *n* amicizia, intesa
ammeter *n* amperometro
ammonia *n* ammoniaca
ammunition *n* munizioni *fpl*
amnesia *n* amnesia
amnesty *n* amnistia
amoeba *n* ameba
among *prep* fra, in mezzo di; in mezzo a
amoral *a* amorale
amorous *a* amoroso
amorphous *a* amorfo
amortization *n* amortizzamento
amortize *vt* ammortizzare
amount *n* quantità, somma; *(large)* somma considerevole; *(small)* piccola somma; — *vi* ammontare; **— to something** arrivare a qualcosa *(fig)*
ampere *n* ampere *m*
amperage *n* amperaggio
amphibian *n* anfibio
amphitheater *n* anfiteatro
ample *a* ampio, vasto
amplification *n* ampliazione, amplificazione
amplifier *n* amplificatore *m*
amplify *vt* amplificare, ampliare, *(enlarge)* ingrandire
amplitude *n* ampiezza
amplitude modulation, (AM) *(rad)* ampia modulazione
amply *adv* ampiamente
amputate *vt* amputare
amputation *n* amputazione
amputee *n* amputato, invalido
amulet *n* amuleto
amuse *vt* divertire
amusement *n* divertimento; **— park** parco di divertimenti
amusing *a* divertente; *(funny)* buffo
an *art* un, uno, una, un'
anachronism *n* anacronismo
anagram *n* anagramma *m*
analgesic *n* analgesico; — *a* analgesico
analogous *a* analogo
analogy *n* analogia
analysis *n* analisi *f*
analytical *a* analitico
analyze *vt* analizzare
anarchy *n* anarchia
anathema *n* anatema *m*
anatomical *a* anatomico
anatomy *n* anatomia
ancestor *n* antenato; **–s** *npl* antenati *mpl*
ancestral *a* atavico
ancestry *n* discendenza, origine *f*
anchor *n* ancora; **lie (ride) at —** stare all'ancora; **–age** *n* ancoraggio; — *vt* ancorare; — *vi* ancorarsi
anchorite *n* anacoreta *m*
anchovy *n* acciuga
ancient *a* antico; **very —** antichissimo
and *conj* e, ed; **— so on** e così via
andiron *n* alare *m*
anecdote *n* aneddoto
anemia *n* anemia
anemic *a* anemico
anemometer *n* anemometro
anesthesia *n* anestesia
anesthetic *n&a* anestetico
anew *adv* di nuovo, da capo
angel *n* angelo; *(sl)* finanziatore *m*;
angelic *a* angelico
anger *n* collera, rabbia, stizza
angle *n* angolo; *(corner)* canto; *(opinion)* punto di vista; — *vi* pescare
angler *n* pescatore
Anglo-Saxon *n&a* anglo-sassone *m&f*
angry *a* arrabbiato; **get —** andare in collera; *(med)* infiammato
anguish *n* angoscia
angular *a* angolare
animal *n&a* animale *m*
animate *vt* animare; — *a* animato; **–d** *a* animato, vivace
animation *n* animazione
animosity *n* animosità
anise *n* anice *m*
ankle *n* caviglia
anklets *npl* calzini *mpl*
annals *npl* annali *mpl*
annex *vt* annettere; — *n (building)* annesso; *(com)* succursale; **–ation** *n* annessione
annihilate *vt* annichilire, annichilare, annientare
annihilation *n* annientamento, annichilazione
anniversary *n&a* anniversario
annotate *vt* annotare
annotation *n* annotazione
announce *vt* annunziare, far noto, proclamare; **–ment** *n* annunzio, proclama *m*, partecipazione
announcer *n (rad)* annunciatore *m*
annoy *vt* annoiare, seccare, incomodare; **–ance** *n* noia, molestia, disturbo; **–ing** *a* noioso, fastidioso, seccante
annual *a* annuo; — *n* annuale *m*
annuity *n* annualità, pensione annuale; **life —** rendita vitalizia
annul *vt* annullare
annulment *n* annullamento
annunciation *n* annunciazione
anode *n* anodo

anoint *vt* ungere, consacrare
anomaly *n* anomalia
anon *adv* subito
anonym *n* anonimo
anonymous *a* anonimo, sconosciuto
another *a* un altro, un'altra
answer *n* risposta; **–able** *a* corrispondente; — *vi* rispondere; — **back** *(coll)* ribattere (*fig*); — **for** essere responsabile; — **the description** corrispondere alla descrizione; — **the purpose** servire allo scopo
ant *n* formica
antacid *a&n* antiacido
antagonism *n* antagonismo
antagonist *n* antagonista *m;* **–ic** *a* antagonistico
antagonize *vt* affrontare, mettersi contro
antarctic *a&n* antartico
ante *n* piatto *(coll)*
antecedent *a&n* antecedente, anteriore *m*
antedate *vt* antidatare, prevenire
antelope *n* antilope *m*
antenna *n* antenna
anterior *a* anteriore
anteroom *n* anticamera
anthem *n* inno
anthology *n* antologia
anthracite *n* antracite *f*
anthropoid *a&n* antropoide *m*
anthropology *n* antropologia
antiaircraft *n&a* antiaereo
antibiotic *n&a* antibiotico
antibody *n* anticorpo
antics *npl* buffoni *mpl*; farse *fpl*
anticipate *vt* prevedere, precedere, prevenire
anticipation *n* anticipo, anticipazione; *(qualm)* presentimento
antidote *n* antidoto
antifreeze *n* anticongelante *m*
antihistamine *n* antistamina
antimycin *n* antimicina
antipathy *n* antipatia
antipodes *npl* antipodi *mpl*
antiquated *a* antiquato
antique *a* antico; — *n* oggetto antico
antiquity *n* antichità
antiseptic *a&n* antisettico
antisocial *a* antisociale
antithesis *n* antitesi *f*
antitoxin *n* antitossina
antitrust *a* contro i monopoli
antler *n* corno del cervo
antonym *n* antinomia
anvil *n* incudine *f*
anxiety *n* ansia; *(eagerness)* premura
anxious *a* desideroso; *(worry)* preoccupato; impaziente
any *a&pron* alcuno; — **at all** qualsiasi; qualunque; — **mail** della posta; — **money** del danaro; — **more** di più; — **old thing** *(sl)* qualunque cosa; **not** — nessuno; **not on — account** per niente al mondo
anybody, anyone *pron* uno; — **at all** chiunque, chichessia; — **who** chi; **not** — nessuno
anyhow *adv* in qualsiasi modo, in ogni caso, comunque
anyone *pron* chi, chiunque
anything *pron* qualsiasi cosa
anyway *adv* insomma, in ogni caso, comunque
anywhere *adv* dovunque, in qualsiasi parte
apart *adv* separatamente, in disparte
apartment *n* appartamento; — **house** casa d'appartamenti
apathetic *a* apatico
apathy *n* apatia
ape *n* scimmia; — *vt* imitare
aperture *n* apertura
apex *n* apice *m*, cima, apogeo
aphorism *n* aforisma *m*
apiary *n* apiario, luogo delle api
apiece *adv* ciascuno, ognuno, l'uno
apocryphal *a* apocrifo
apogee *n* apogeo
apologetic *a* apologetico
apologize *vi* scusarsi, chiedere perdono; fare le scuse
apology *n* scusa, apologia
apoplexy *n* apoplessia
apostle *n* apostolo
apostolic *a* apostolico
apostrophe *n* apostrofo
appall *vi* impallidire; **–ing** *a* spaventevole
apparatus *n* apparecchio
apparel *n* vestiario, indumenti *mpl*, abbigliamento
apparent *a* apparente, chiaro; **–ly** *adv* apparentemente
apparition *n* apparizione
appeal *vi* fare appello, ricorrere in appello; *(attract)* attrarre, fare simpatia; — *vt* sottomettere a; — *n* attrazione, atrattiva; *(law)* appello; **–ing** *a* supplichevole
appear *vi* apparire; *(seem)* parere, sembrare; *(show oneself)* esibirsi; presentarsi; **–ance** *n* apparenza; apparizione; *(aspect)* aspetto, aria
appease *vt* calmare, ammansire; **–ment** *n* pacificazione
append *vt* appendere; **–age** *n* appendice *f*
appendectomy *n* appenditomia
appendicitis *n* appendicite *f*
appendix *n* appendice *f*; *(book)* aggiunta
appertain *vi* appartenere
appetite *n* appetito
appetizer *n* *(drink)* aperitivo; *(food)* antipasto
appetizing *a* aperitivo, stimolante d'appetito
applaud *vt* applaudire; — *vi* felicitarsi
applause *n* applauso
apple *n* mela, pomo; — **of one's eye** pupilla dell'occhio; — **orchard** pometo; — **polisher** *(sl)* cortigiano *(fig)*; leccapiedi *m* *(sl)*; — **tree** melo
apple-pie order *(coll)* ordine perfetto
applesauce *n* salsa di mela; *(sl)* storie *fpl* *(fig)*; un sacco di sciocchezze *(fig)*
appliance *n* apparecchio, attrezzo; *(elec)* elettrodomestico
applicable *a* applicabile
applicant *n* candidato
application *n* domanda, applicazione
applied *a* applicato

apply *vt* applicare; — *vi* applicarsi; — **for** sollecitare, chiedere; — **to** rivolgersi a
appoint *vt* nominare; **–ment** *n* appuntamento; nomina
apportion *vt* distribuire; **–ment** *n* distribuzione
apposition *n* apposizione
appraisal *n* stima, valutazione
appraise *vt* valutare
appreciable *a* apprezzabile
appreciate *vt* apprezzare, stimare, gradire; *(realize)* rendersi conto di; — *vi* aumentare di prezzo
appreciation *n* apprezzamento
appreciative *a* apprezzativo
apprehend *vt* comprendere; *(dread)* temere; — *vi* comprendere, supporre
apprenhension *n* apprensione, timore *m*
apprehensive *a* apprensivo, timoroso
apprentice *n* apprendista *m&f*
approach *vt* accostarsi, avvicinarsi; — *vi* avvicinarsi, appressarsi; — *n* accesso, approccio
approbation *n* approvazione
appropriate *a* acconcio, adatto, appropriato; — *vt* stanziare; *(sl)* appropriarsi di
appropriation *n* appropriazione; *(money)* stanziamento
approval *n* approvazione, conferma
approve *vt* approvare, confermare
approving *a* favorevole
approximate *a* approssimativo; **–ly** *adv* approssimativamente, presso a poco, verso; — *vt* approssimare
approximation *n* approssimazione
apricot *n* albicocca; — **tree** albicocco
April *n* aprile *m;* — **Fools' Day** Primo d'aprile
apron *n* grembiule *m*
apropos *adv* a proposito
apt *a* (*proper*) adatto, atto; (*inclined*) disposto, inclinato; **–ness** *n* attitudine *f*
aptitude *n* abilità, attitudine *f*, disposizione
aqualung *n* serbatoio dell'aria
aquaplane *n* acquaplano
aquarium *n* acquario
aquatic *a* acquatico
aqueduct *n* acquedotto
aquiline *a* aquilino
Arabia Arabia
Arab, Arabian *n&a* arabo
arable *a* arabile
arbiter *n* arbitro
arbitrary *a* arbitrario
arbitrate *vt* arbitrare — *vi* arbitrarsi, fare da arbitro
arbitrator *n* arbitro
arbor *n* pergola; **–eal** *a* arboreo; **–etum** *n* arboreto
arc *n* arco; — **lamp** lampada ad arco voltaico; — **light** luce d'arco voltaico; — **welding** arco voltaico
arcade *n* arcata
arch *n* arco, volta; **–way** *n* arcale *m*; passaggio a volta; — *a* principale; *(crafty)* furbo; **–ed** *a* arcato; **–ly** *adv* accortamente; — *vt* arcuare; — *vi* formare arco
archaic *a* arcaico
archbishop *n* arcivescovo
archdiocese *n* arcidiocesi *f*
archeology *n* archeologia
archer *n* arciere *m*; **–y** *n* tiro all'arco
architect *n* architetto; **–ural** *a* architettonico; **–ure** *n* architettura
archives *npl* archivio
arctic *n&a* artico
ardent *a* ardente
ardor *n* ardore *m*
arduous *a* arduo
area *n* zona, regione *f; (surface)* superficie *f*
arena *n* anfiteatro, arena, stadio
argot *n* gergo
argue *vt* discutere, disputare, litigare; — *vi* argomentare, fare discussione
argument *n* discussione, diverbio
arid *a* arido; sterile
arise *vi* alzarzi, levarsi
aristrocracy *n* aristocrazia
aristrocrat *n* aristrocratico; **–ic** *a* aristocratico
arithmetic *n* aritmetica
arm *n* braccio; *(mil)* arma; — **in** — a braccetto; **at –s length** a distanza; **–chair** *n* poltrona; **–ful** *n* bracciata; **–hole** *n* giro; **–pit** *n* ascella; — *vt* armare; — *vi* armarsi
armament *n* armamento
armistice *n* armistizio
armor *n* corazza, blinda; **–y** *n* armeria
armored *a* corazzato, blindato; — **car** autoblinda
army *n* esercito
aroma *n* profumo, fragranza; **–tic** *a* aromatico
around *prep* attorno; — *adv* intorno; all'intorno; (*turning*) in giro
arouse *vt (wake)* svegliare; *(foment)* suscitare; — *vi* svegliarsi
arraign *vt* tradurre; **–ment** *n* traduzione
arrange *vt* ordinare, disporre; **–ment** *n (order)* disposizione, ordine *m; (agreement)* accordo
arrant *a* insigne
array *n* schiera; *(dress)* abbigliamento; — *vt* parare, disporre
arrears *n* arretrati; **be in** — essere in arretrati
arrest *n* arresto; — *vt* arrestare; fermare; — **attention** chiamare l'attenzione
arresting *a* che arresta
arrival *n* arrivo
arrive *vi* arrivare, giungere
arrogance *n* arroganza
arrogant *a* arrogante, prepotente
arrow *n* freccia; **–head** *n* punta di freccia
arsenal *n* arsenale *m*
arsenic *n* arsenico
arson *n* incendio doloso
art *n* arte *f*; **–less** *a* semplice, senz'arte; **the fine –s** le belle arti
artery *n* arteria
artful *a* artificiale; **–ness** *n* artificialità; **–ly** *adv* artificialmente
arthritis *n* artrite *f*
artichoke *n* carciofo
article *n* articolo, oggetto
articulate *vt* articolare, pronunziare;

— *vi* pronunziarsi
articulation *n* articolazione
artifact *n* artefatto
artifice *n* artefice *m*
artificial *a* artificiale; — **insemination** fecondazione artificiale
artillery *n* artiglieria
artisan *n* artigiano
artist *n* artista *m&f;* **–ic** *a* artistico
as *conj&adv* come; — **far** — fino a; — **for** quanto a; — **if** come se; — **it were** generalmente parlando *(coll)*; — **large** — grande come; — **much** — tanto quanto; — **soon** — **possible** il più presto possible; — **to** quanto a; — **well** *(also)* anche, pure; **just** — così; **the same** — come, lo stesso che
asbestos *n* amianto
ascend *vi* montare, salire; — *vt* ascendere, salire; **–ancy** *n* ascendente *m*
ascendant *n* ascendente *m*; — *a* ascendente
ascension *n* ascesa, asçensione
Ascension *n* Ascensione
ascent *n* ascesa, salita, erta
ascertain *vt* accertarsi, constatare, appurare
ascetic *n* asceta *m*; — *a* ascetico
ascribe *vt* ascrivere, attribuire
ash *n* cenere *f; (bot)* frassino; **–can** *n* pattumiera; **–tray** *n* portacenere *m*; **A- Wednesday** Giorno delle Ceneri
ashamed *a* vergognoso; **be** — vergognarsi
ashen *a* di frassino
ashore *adv* a terra; **go** — sbarcare, scendere a terra
Asian, Asiatic *n&a* asiatico
aside *adv* a parte; — **from** eccetto, a parte
asinine *a* asinino
ask *vt* domandare, chiedere; *(invite)* invitare; — *vi* informarsi di; — **about** domandare circa
askance *adv*, lateralmente, di traverso
askew *adv* obliquamente; — *a* obliquo
asleep *a* addormentato; **be** — dormire; **fall** — addormentarsi
asparagus *n* asparago
aspect *n* aspetto
asperity *n* asprezza, rudezza
aspersion *n* aspersione, denigrazione
asphalt *n* asfalto; — *vt* asfaltare
asphyxiate *vt* asfissiare; — *vi* asfissiarsi
asphyxiation *n* asfissia
aspirant *n* aspirante *m*; — *a* aspirante
aspiration *n* aspirazione
aspire *vi* aspirare, bramare
aspirin *n* aspirina
ass *n* asino
assail *vt* assalire, attaccare; **–ant** *n* assalitore *m*, assalitrice *f*
assassin *n* assassino; **–ate** *vt* assassinare, ammazzare
assassination *n* assassinio
assault *n* assalto; — *vt* assalire, attaccare
assay *vt* saggiare; — *n* assaggio, saggio
assemblage *n* raccolta; assemblea
assemble *vt* riunire; — *vi* riunirsi, adunarsi
assembly *n (people)* assemblea, riunione; *(mech)* montaggio; — **line** linea di montaggio; — **line production** produzione in serie
assent *vi* assentire; — *n* consenso
assert *vt* asserire, affermare
assertion *n* asserzione
assess *vt* tassare; **–ment** *n* tassazione, imposta; **–or** *n* assessore *m*; agente delle tasse
asset *n* assetto; **–s** *npl (com)* attività
assiduous *a* assiduo; **–ly** *adv* assiduamente
assign *vt* assegnare, attribuire; **–ment** *n (school)* compito; *(task)* incarico; missione
assimilate *vt* assimilare; — *vi* assimilarsi
assimilation *n* assimilazione
assist *vt* aiutare, assistere; — *vi* aiutare, contribuire a; **–ance** *n* assistenza, aiuto, soccorso, sussidio; **–ant** *n* assistente *m*, aiutante *m*; aggiunto
associate *vt* associare, unire; — *vi* associarsi con; — **with** frequentare; **–d** *a* associato, relazionato
associate *n* compagno di lavoro, collega; — *a* associato
association *n* associazione, società
assort *vt* assortire; — *vi* essere d'accordo; **–ed** *a* assortito; **–ment** *n* scelta; assortimento
assuage *vt* calmare; — *vi* calmarsi
assume *vt* assumere, supporre, usurpare; — *vi* arrogarsi; **–d** *a* assunto; preso; pervenuto a
assuming *a* presuntuoso, altero; — **that** supponendo che
assumption *n* supposizione; arroganza
Assumption *n* Assunzione
assurance *n* certezza, sicurezza, conferma
assure *vt* assicurare, rassicurare; — *vi* assicurarsi di
assured *a* assicurato, sicuro; **–ly** *adv* certamente, sicuramente
aster *n* astero
asterisk *n* asterisco
astern *adv* a poppa
asthma *n* asma; **–tic** *a* asmatico
astigmatism *n* astigmatismo
astir *a&adv* in movimento
astonish *vt* stupire, meravigliare; **–ing** *a* stupefacente, stupendo, straordinario; **–ment** *n* stupore *m*, maraviglia
astound *vt* sbalordire, stupefare
astray *a* sviato; *(lost)* smarrito; — *adv* fuori strada; **go** — fuorviarsi, perdersi; **lead** — sviare, traviare, fuorviare
astride *a* a cavalcioni
astringent *a&n* astringente *m*
astrobiology *n (aesp)* astrobiologia
astronaut *n* astronauta *m*
astronavigation *n* astronavigazione
astronomy *n* astronomia
astrophysics *n* astrofisica
astute *a* astuto, furbo
asunder *adv* separatamente; **put** — collocare separatamente; **tear** – stracciare; —*a* separato
asylum *n* asilo; **insane** — manicomio
at *prep* a, in, da; — **all events** in ogni modo; — **large** in libertà; — **last** finalmente; — **once** subito

atheism *n* ateismo
atheist *n* ateo; **–ic** *a* ateistico
Athens Atene *f*
athlete *n* atleta *m&f;* **—'s foot** *(med)* piede d'atleta
athletic *a* atletico; **— field** campo sportivo; **–s** *npl* atletica
Atlantic *n&a* atlantico
atlas *n* atlante *m*
atmosphere *n* atmosfera; *(surroundings)* ambiente *m*
atmospheric *a* atmosferico
atom *n* atomo; **— bomb** bomba atomica
atomic *a* atomico; **— blast** esplosione atomica; **— energy** energia atomica; **— pile** pila atomica, reattore *m*
atomize *vt* atomizzare, polverizzare; **–r** *n* polverizzatore *m*
atone *vt* riparare, fare ammenda, espiare; **—** *vi* riparare a; **–ment** *n* espiazione
atrocious *a* atroce
atrocity *n* atrocità
atrophy *n* atrofia; **—** *vt* atrofizzare; **—** *vi* atrofizzarsi
attach *vt* attaccare, unire; *(importance)* attribuire; *(law)* sequestrare, requisire; **–ment** *n* attaccamento; *(fondness)* affetto; *(law)* sequestro
attack *vt* attaccare; **—** *n* attacco, aggressione, assalto
attain *vt* raggiungere; **–able** *a* attaccabile; **–ment** *n* attaccamento
attempt *vt* tentare; **–ed** *a* tentato; **—** *n* tentativo; *(crime)* attentato; *(effort)* sforzo
attend *vt (to)* attendere; *(be present)* assistere; *(escort)* scortare; **—** *vi* essere presente, presenziare; **— to** incaricarsi di; **–ance** *n* presenza; *(care)* servizio; *(audience)* pubblico; frequenza; **–ant** *n* attendente, inserviente *m&f*
attention *n* attenzione; **at —** *(mil)* sull'attenti; **attract —** attirare l'attenzione; **call —** richiamare l'attenzione; **give — to** prestare attenzione a; **pay —** stare attento, fare attenzione; **to the — of** attenzione personale
attentive *a* attento; **–ly** *adv* attentamente
attenuate *vt* attenuare, far dimagrire
attest *vt* attestare, legalizzare; **—** *vi* *(law)* testimoniare
attic *n* soffitta; **—** *a* attico, dell'Attica
attire *n* vestito; **—** *vt* vestire, abbigliare
attitude *n* attitudine *f*, posizione; *(behavior)* contegno, atteggiamento
attorney *n* avvocato, procuratore *m*
attract *vt* attrarre, attirare; **—** *vi* esercitare attrazione; **–ive** *a* attraente, bello, gradevole, simpatico
attraction *n* attrazione, simpatia, attrattiva
attribute *vt* attribuire
attribute *n* attributo, qualità; *(trait)* tratto
attributive *a* attributivo
attrition *n* attrito
attune *vt* accordare, mettere a tono
auburn *a* castagno rossiccio
auction *n* asta pubblica; **–eer** *n* imbonitore *m*
audacious *a* audace, ardito
audacity *n* audacia
audible *a* udibile, percettibile
audience *n* pubblico; *(interview)* udienza
audiophile *n* audiofilo, audio-amatore *m*
audio-visual *a* audio-visuale
audit *n* controllo; **–or** *n (com)* revisore dei conti; **—** *vt* controllare, verificare; **–ing** *n* verifica
audition *n* audizione
auditorium *n* auditorio, sala
auditory *a* uditivo
auger *n* succhiello, trivella
augment *vt&i* aumentare
augur *vt&i* augurare
August *n* agosto
august *a* augusto
aunt *n* zia
aura *n* aura, esalazione
aureomycin *n* aureomicina
auricle *n* auricola
aurora *n* aurora
auspices *npl* auspici *mpl;* **under the — of** sotto l'egida di
auspicious *a* auspice, propizio; **–ly** *adv* propiziamente
austere *a* austero
austerity *n* austerità
Australia Australia
Australian *n&a* australiano
Austrian *n&a* austriaco
authentic *a* autentico; **–ity** *n* autenticità
author *a* autore *m*
authoritative *a* autoritario
authority *n* autenticità
authorization *n* autorizzazione
authorize *vt* autorizzare
autobiography *n* autobiografia
autocade *n* treno (*or* fila) di automezzi
autocracy *n* autocrazia
autocrat *n* autocrate *m*; **–ic** *a* autocratico
autogiro *n* autogiro
autograph *n* autografo; **—** *vt* autografare
automatic *a* automatico; **—** *n (mech)* distributore automatico
automation *n* automazione
automaton *n* automa *m*
automobile, auto *n* automobile *f*; **— show** autosalone *m*
automotive *a* automobilistico
autonomous *a* autonomo
autonomy *n* autonomia
autopilot *n* autopilota *m*, pilota automatico
autopsy *n* autopsia
autumn *n* autunno; **–al** *a* autunnale
auxiliary *a* ausiliario; **—** *n* ausiliare *m*
avail *vt&i* valere, servire, giovare; **— oneself of** servirsi di; **—** *n* vantaggio, effetto; **of no —** vano, inutile; **–able** *a* disponibile, trovabile; **–ability** *n* disponibilità
avalanche *n* valanga
avarice *n* avarizia
avaricious *a* avaro; **–ly** *adv* avidamente
avenge *vt* vendicare; vendicarsi di
avenger *n* vendicatore *m*

avenue *n* corso, viale *m*
aver *vt* affermare, certificare
average *n* media; — *a* medio; — *vt* fare una media; — *vi* mostrare la media
averse *a* avverso, contrario
aversion *n* antipatia, avversione; **pet** — antipatia cordiale
avert *vt* allontanare, distogliere
aviary *n* uccelliera
aviation *n* aviazione
aviator *n* aviatore *m*, aviatrice *f*
avid *a* avido; **–ity** *n* avidità
avocation *n* passatempo
avoid *vt* evitare, schivare, scansare, fuggire; **–able** *a* evitabile; **–ance** *n* l'evitare; *(law)* annullamento
avow *vt* confessare; **–al** *n* confessione
await *vt* attendere, aspettare; — *vi* aspettarsi
awake *vt* svegliare; — *vi* svegliarsi; — *a* desto, sveglio
awaken *vt* destare
awakening *n* risveglio; — *a* eccitante
award *n* premio; — *vt* aggiudicare, conferire
aware *a* informato, consapevole; **become** — accorgersi
away *a* assente; — *adv* via; **be** — distare; **go** — andarsene; **keep** — **(from)** tener lontano
awe *n* soggezione
awe-inspiring *a* imponente
awe-struck *a* atterrito, impaurito
awful *a* terribile, spaventoso
awhile *adv* un poco, un momento
awkward *a* goffo, maldestro; **–ly** *adv* goffamente, maldestramente
awl *n* lesina
awning *n* tenda
awry *a&adv* di traverso, di sghembo
ax *(axe)* *n* scure *f*
axiom *n* assioma *m*
axis *n* asse *m*
axle *n* assale *m*
azalea *n* azalea
azon bomb *n* proiettile radiocomandato, bomba radiocomandata
azure *a* azzurro, blu

B

B.A., Bachelor of Arts diplomato in lettere
babble *n* balbettio; — *vt* balbettare; — *vi* dire e ridire, ripetersi
babbling *a* balbettante
babel *n* confusione, parapiglia *m*
baboon *n* babbuino
baby *n* bambino, bambina; *(in affection)* bimbo, bimba; — *a* bambinesco; — **carriage** carrozzino; — **grand piano** pianoforte a mezzacoda
baby *vt* vezzeggiare
baby– *(in comp)* **—sit** *vi* fare da bambinaia; **—sitter** *n* bambinaia
babyhood *n* prima fanciullezza, infanzia
babyish *a* infantile
bachelor *n* scapolo
back *n* dorso; *(chair)* schienale *m; (human)* schiena; *(shoulders)* spalle *fpl;* **turn one's — on** dare la schiena; — *a* di dietro; — **seat** posto di dietro; — **stairs** scala di servizio; — *adv* addietro, dietro; **call** — richiamare; **come** — ritornare; — *vt&i* appoggiare, indietreggiare; *(com)* finanziare; munire di indietro; *(auto)* far marcia indietro; — **down, out** ritirarsi; — **up** indietreggiare
backbite *vt&i* diffamare
backbone *n* spina dorsale; *(fig)* energia *(fig)*
backer *n* protettore *m*; *(sport)* secondo
backfielder *n* *(sport)* giocatore di retrolinea
backfire *n* contraccolpo; *(auto)* ritorno di fiamma
background *n* sfondo; *(environment)* ambiente *m*; *(past)* precedenti *mpl*
backing *n* appoggio, *(com)* sostegno
backlog *n* ceppo
backnumber *n (fig)* parruccone *m*; *(print)* numero arretrato
backstage *n* dietro le quinte
backstitch *n* punto indietro; — *vt&i* cucire a punto indietro
backstop *n (sport)* ostacolo per la palla
backward *a* tardivo; — *adv* di dietro, indietro
backwash *n* risacca
bacon *n* pancetta affumicata
bacteria *npl* batteri *mpl*
bacterial *a* batterico
bacteriology *n* batteriologia
bad *a* cattivo; *(evil)* malo; *(spoiled)* guasto; — **blood** cattivo sangue; — **humor** malumore *m;* — **look** cattivo aspetto; **–ly** *adv* male, malamente; gravemente
badge *n* distintivo, placca
badger *n* tasso; — *vt* seccare, tormentare, stuzzicare
badinage *n* scherzo
baffle *vt* lasciare perplesso, confondere
baffling *a* frustrante, sconcertante
bag *n* sacco; *(luggage)* valigia; *(paper)* sacchetto; *(purse)* borsa; — *vt* insaccare; — *vi* gonfiarsi
baggage *n* bagaglio; — **car** carro-bagagli; — **check** scontrino del bagaglio; — **master** bagagliere *m*; — **room** deposito bagagli
baggy *a* come un sacco; *(hanging)* pendente; *(swollen)* gonfio
bail *n* cauzione; **on** — sotto cauzione; — *vt* rilasciare sotto cauzione; — **out** *(avi)* lanciarsi col paracadute
bailiff *n* ufficiale giudiziario
bailiwick *n* giurisdizione
bait *vt* adescare; — *n* esca
bake *vt* cuocere al forno; — *vi* essere cotto, dissecarsi; **–d** *a* al forno; infornato
baker *n* fornaio; **—y** *n (bread)* panificio, panetteria; *(sweet goods)* pasticceria

baking *n* infornata; — **powder** lievito; — **soda** bicarbonato di soda
balance *n (com)* saldo; *(remainder)* resto; *(scales)* bilancia, bilancio; equilibrio; — **of power** equilibrio politico; — **of trade** bilancia del commercio; — **sheet** bilancio; **lose one's** — perdere l'equilibrio
balance *vt (com)* saldare; *(equalize)* pareggiare, equilibrare; — *vi* equilibrarsi, pareggiarsi; — **an account** chiudere un conto, accertare il saldo
balcony *n* loggia; *(theat)* galleria; *(window)* balcone *m*
bald *a* calvo; **–ness** *n* calvizie *f*
bale *n* balla; **–ful** *a* calamitoso, maligno
balk *vt (hinder)* intralciare; — *vi* impuntarsi, arrestarsi; — *n (coll)* puntiglio; *(obstacle)* ostacolo; **–y** *a* puntiglioso
ball *n* palla, pallone *m*; *(dance)* ballo; — **bearing** cuscinetto a sfere
ballpoint pen *n* penna a sfera
ballad *n* canzone popolare
ballast *n* zavorra
ballet *n* balletto; — **dancer** ballerino, ballerina
ballistic missile *n* missile balistico
ballistics *n* balistica
balloon *n* pallone *m*, palloncino; — **tire** gomma ballon
ballot *n* voto; scheda di votazione; — **box** urna; — **count** scrutinio; — *vt&i* votare a scrutino segreto
ballplayer *n* giocatore di baseball
ballyhoo *n (sl)* baccano, montatura, propaganda sensazionale
balm *n* unguento; **–y** *a* imbalsamato
balsam *n* balsamo
balustrade *n* balaustrata
bamboo *n* bambù *m*; — **curtain** tendina di bambù
bamboozle *vt (coll)* turlupinare; — *vi* turlupinarsi
ban *n* bando; — *vt* interdire, proibire, vietare
banal *a* banale; **–ity** *n* banalità
banana *n* banana
band *n* banda; *(cloth)* striscia, nastro, fascia; *(group)* gruppo; *(mus)* orchestra; — *vt* unire, unirsi; — *vi* associarsi; legarsi con
bandage *n* benda, fascia; — *vt* fasciare, bendare
bandanna *n* fazzoletto
bandit *n* bandito
bandstand *n* piattaforma per orchestra
bane *n* flagello
bang *n* colpo; *(explosion)* detonazione; **–s** *npl (hair)* frangetta; — *vt* colpire, sbattere; — *vi* rumoreggiare, saltare
bangle *n* braccialetto
banish *vt* esiliare, bandire; **–ment** *n* bando, proscrizione, esilio
banister *n* ringhiera
banjo *n* banjo *m*
bank *n (com)* banca, banco; *(river)* riva; *(savings)* cassa di risparmio; **–book** *n* libretto di banca; — *vt* arginare; coprire; depositare in banca; — *vi (embank)* fare banchi; fare il banchiere; *(avi)* virare
banker *n* banchiere *m*
banking *n* servizio bancario
bankrupt *a* fallito; **–cy** *n* bancarotta, fallimento; — *vt* fallire
banner *n* stendardo, bandiera; *(standard)* gonfalone *m*, vessillo
banns *npl* bandi *mpl*, pubblicazione
banquet *n* banchetto
bantamweight *n* peso bantam *(fig)*
banter *n* burla, scherno; — *vt* burlare, schernire; — *vi* burlarsi di
baptism *n* battesimo; **–al** *a* battesimale
baptize *vt* battezzare; *(eccl)* amministrare il battesimo
bar *n (barricade)* sbarra; *(candy)* tavoletta; *(inn)* bar *m*, taverna; *(law)* avvocatura; *(line)* verga; *(mus)* battuta; *(obstacle)* ostacolo; **–keeper, –maid** *n* barista *m&f;* — *prep* eccettuato; — *vt* sbarrare; *(exclude)* escludere
barb *n* punta, spina; **–ed** *a* spinato
barbarian *n&a* barbaro
barbarism *n* barbarie *f*; *(language)* barbarismo
barbarity *n* barbarie *f*, crudeltà
barbarous *a* barbaro
barbecue *n* carne arrostita; — *vt* arrostire
barber *n* barbiere, parrucchiere *m*; **–shop** *n* bottega di barbiere
barbiturate *n* barbiturico
bare *a* nudo; **–faced** *a* sfacciato; col viso scoperto; **–foot** *a* scalzo; **–headed** *a* a testa scoperta; **lay** — svelare; — *vt* scoprire; **–ly** *adv* appena, nudamente
bareness *n* nudità, nudezza
bargain *n* occasione; — *vt* decidere, regolare; — *vi* mercanteggiare
barge *n* chiatta, zattera; — *vt* trasportare con chiatta; — *vi* muoversi lentamente
baritone *n* baritono
bark *n (dog)* abbaiamento; *(tree)* scorza; — *vt* scorticare; — *vi* abbaiare, latrare
barley *n* orzo
barn *n* stalla; granaio; **–yard** *n* aia
barometer *n* barometro
baron *n* barone *m; –***ess** *n* baronessa
baronet *n* baronetto
barracks *npl* caserma
barrage *n* sbarramento
barrel *n* barile *m*, botte *f*; — *vt* imbarilare
barren *a* sterile, arido
barrette *n* fermaglio per i capelli
barricade *n* barricata; — *vt* barricare
barrier *n* barriera
barring *prep* eccettuato, salvo
barrister *n* avvocato
barroom *n* bar *m;* taverna
bartender *n* barista *m*
barter *vt* barattare; — *vi* fare baratto, — *n* baratto, permuta
basal *a* fondamentale, basico; — **metabolism** metabolismo basale
base *n* base *f*; fondamento; — *a* basso; vile; **–less** *a* infondato, senza base; **–ness** *n* bassezza; — *vt* basare
baseball *n* palla a basi, baseball *m*

baseboard *n* zoccolo
basement *n* cantina, sottosuolo
bashful *a* timido; **–ness** *n* timidezza
basic *a* basilare, fondamentale
basil *n* basilico
basin *n (hand)* catinella, lavabo; *(river)* bacino di un fiume
basis *n* base *f*
bask *vt* scaldare; — *vi* scaldarsi
basket *n* paniere *m*, sporta, cesta; *(waste)* cestino; **–ball** *n* pallacanestro; **–ry** *n* mestiere del panieraio
bass *n (fish)* pesce persico; *(mus)* basso; — **horn** corno di bassetto; — **viol** violoncello
bassinet *n* culla
bassoon *n* fagotto
bastard *n&a* bastardo; **–ly** *a* bastardamente
baste *vt (abuse)* bastonare, frustare; *(cooking)* umettare; *(sewing)* imbastire
bastion *n* bastione *m*
bat *n (animal)* pipistrello; *(club)* mazza, bastone *m*; **go on a** — *(sl)* bighellonare; — *vt* battere; — **an eye** batter ciglio
batch *n (bread)* infornata; *(lot)* partita
batch *n* infornata; partita
bated *a* turbato; **with — breath** con voce turbata
bath *n* bagno; **–ometer** *n* batometro; **–robe** *n* accappatoio; **–room** *n* stanza da bagno; **–tub** *n* vasca da bagno
bathe *vt* lavare, bagnare; farsi il bagno; — *vi* fare il bagno
bathing *n* bagno; — **cap** cuffia da bagno; — **suit** costume da bagno
bathyscaphe *n* batiscafo
bathysphere *n* batisfera
baton *n* bacchetta; bastone di comando
battalion *n* battaglione *m*
batter *n (baseball)* battitore *m*; *(cookery)* pastetta; — *vt* battere; *(wreck)* guastare
battery *n* batteria; — **charge** carica della batteria
battle *n* battaglia; **–field** *n* campo di battaglia; — **royal** battaglia strenua; **pitched** — battaglia campale; **sham** — battaglia finta; **–ship** *n* nave da guerra; — *vt* combattere qualcuno; — *vi* battagliare; battersi
bauble *n* bagatella
Bavaria Baviera
Bavarian *n&a* bavarese *m&f*
bawl *vt* sgridare; — **out** *(coll)* dare una lavata di testa *(coll)*; — *n* sgridata, lavata di testa
bay *n (arch)* alcova; *(bot)* lauro, alloro; *(color)* baio; *(geog)* baia; — *a* baio; — **leaf** foglia d'alloro; — **window** finestra sporgente; **hold at** — tenere in iscacco; **keep at** — tenere a bada; **stand at** — essere in iscacco; essere appressato
bay *vt (arch)* arginare; — *vi (animal)* abbaiare
baying *n (animal)* abbaiamento
bayonet *n* baionetta
bayou *n* canaletta
bazaar *n* bazar *m*, emporio; **charity** — pesca di beneficenza
B.C., Before Christ *adv* avanti Cristo
be *vi* essere, esistere, stare; — **ill** star male; — **in a hurry** avere fretta; — **right** aver ragione; — **that as it may** comunque; — **well** star bene
beach *n* spiaggia; **–comber** *n* vagabondo di spiaggia; **–head** *n (mil)* spiaggia di sbarco
beach *vt* tirare in secco
bead *n* grano, chicco; *(pearl)* perla; **tell one's –s** sgranare il rosario
beading *n* inserto per nastrino
beaded *a* perliforme
beady *a* rotondo come perla; *(eyes)* lucente
beak *n* becco
beaker *n* bicchierone *m*, provino
beam *n (arch)* trave *f*; sorriso; *(light)* raggio; *(scale)* asta; **fly on the** — seguire la rotta del radar; — *vt* raggiare, irradiare; — *vi* sorridere
bean *n* fagiolo; *(broad)* fava; *(coffee)* chicco di caffè; *(navy)* fagiolo; *(string)* fagiolino; **spill the –s** *(fig)* divulgare un segreto
beanpole *n* sostegno per piante; **thin as a** — *(sl)* stecchito
bear *n* orso; **–ish** *a* d'orso, rozzo
bear *vt (carry)* portare; *(endure)* sopportare; — **in mind** ricordarsi; — **out** *(prove)* convalidare; — **up** sostenersi, mantenersi
bearable *a* tollerabile, sopportabile
bearer *n* portatore *m*
bearing *n (manner)* comportamento, contegno; *(mech)* cuscinetto; *(naut)* rilevamento; *(reference to)* riferimento; — **on** *prep* relativo; **get one's –s** orientarsi
beard *n* barba; **–ed** *a* barbuto; **–less** *a* imberbe, senza barba
beard *vt (dare)* sfidare; *(defy)* bravare
beast *n* bestia, animale *m*, bruto; — **of burden** bestia da soma; **–ly** *a* bestiale
beat *n* battito; — *vt* battere, picchiare; *(coll)* vincere; *(whip up)* frullare; — *vi* battere, bussare
beaten *a* abbattuto, vinto *(fig)*; battuto; *(defeated)* sconfitto
beater *n* battitore; *(egg)* frullino
beating *n* battito; *(defeat)* sconfitta
beatitude *n* beatitudine *f*
beatific *a* beatifico
beatnik *n (sl)* anticonformista, bohemian
beau *n* fidanzato, innamorato
beautician *n* imbellitore *m*; addetto all'imbellimento
beautiful *a* bello
beautify *vi* abbellire
beauty *n* bellezza; — **contest** concorso di bellezza; — **parlor** salone di bellezza, istituto di bellezza
beaver *n* castoro
becalm *vt* calmare
because *conj* perchè; — **of** per, a causa di, per motivo di
beck *n* **at the — and call of** agli ordini di
beckon *vi* far cenno; — *vt* far cenno a
become *vi* diventare, divenire; *(befit)* convenire; — *vt* addirsi a; — **worthy** essere degno di
becoming *a* conveniente, grazioso

bed *n* letto; *(garden)* aiuola; *(river)* greto; **–clothes, –ding** *npl* biancheria da letto; **–fellow** *n* compagno di letto; **–ridden** *a* degente; **–room** *n* camera da letto; **–sheet** *n* lenzuolo; **–spread** *n* coperta; **–spring** *n* elastico; **–stead** *n* telaio del letto; letto; **–time** *n* ora di andare a letto
bedbug *n* cimice *f*
bedevil *vt* violentare, tormentare
bedlam *n* caos *m*, pandemonio
bedraggle *vt* infangare
bedrock *n* fondamento solido
bedside *n* bordo del letto; — *a* da letto; di capezzale
bee *n* ape *f;* **have a — in one's bonnet** avere un'idea fissa, aver qualcosa nella manica; **make a –line** *(fig)* andare in linea retta
beech *n* faggio
beef *n* manzo; *(meat)* carne bovina; *(ox)* bue *m;* **–steak** *n* bistecca; **–y** *a* grasso, grosso
beehive *n* alveare *m*
beer *n* birra; — **garden** birreria, barristorante *m*; **draft** — birra alla pompa
beeswax *n* cera d'api
beet *n* barbabietola; — **sugar** zucchero di barbabietola
beetle *n* scarafaggio
befall *vi* accadere, capitare, succedere
befit *vt* convenire a; *(adapt)* adattarsi a
befitting *a* conveniente
before *adv* prima; — *prep* prima di; davanti a — *conj* prima che
beforehand *adv* in anticipo
befriend *vt* aiutare; trattare da amico
befuddle *vt* confondere con sofisma
beg *vt* mendicare; pregare, implorare, chiedere; — *vi* domandare, chiedere l'elemosina; — **the question** dare per ammesso
beggar *n* mendicante *m;* **–ly** *a* povero
beget *vt* causare, generare
begin *vt&i* cominciare, principiare; **to — with** prima di tutto
beginner *n* principiante *m*
beginning *n* principio; **in the —** al principio
begrudge *vt* invidiare
beguile *vt* *(cheat)* ingannare; *(distract)* distrarre; *(entice)* sedurre
behalf *n* beneficio, difesa; **in — of** a favore di; **on — of** a nome di
behave, — oneself *vi* comportarsi
behavior *n* comportamento; **–ism** *n* comportismo
behead *vt* decapitare
behest *n* ingiunzione, mandato
behind *prep* dietro, dietro di; — *adv* dietro, indietro; in ritardo
behold *vt* vedere, contemplare, scorgere; —! *interj* ecco! guarda!
behoove *vt* convenire, essere utile *(or* conveniente); — *vi* essere conveniente
being *n* essere *m*, esistenza; creatura; *(human)* essere umano
belabor *vt* lavorare, colpire
belated *a* ritardato
belch *vt&i* eruttare
belfry *n* torre *f*, campanile *m*
Belgian *a&n* belga
Belgium Belgio
belie *vt* diffamare, travisare
belief *n* fede *f*; opinione *f*
believable *a* credibile
believe *vt* credere, pensare; — *vi* credere in
believer *n* credente *m&f*
bell *n* campana; *(door)* campanello; **ring the —** suonare; **–boy** *n* ragazzo, groom d'albergo
belle *n* bella donna
bellicose *a* bellicoso
belligerency *n* aggressività, belligeranza
belligerent *n&a* belligerante *m*
bellow *vt&i* muggire, mugghiare; **–s** *n* mantice *m*
belly *n* pancia, ventre *m*
belong *vi (membership)* far parte; *(ownership)* spettare, appartenere; **–ings** *npl* proprietà, beni *mpl*
beloved *a* benamato, caro, amato, diletto, adorato
below *adv* sotto, giù; — *prep* sotto, al disotto di
belt *n* cintura; *(geog)* zona; *(girdle)* cinghia; — **conveyor** trasportatore a nastro; **hit below the —** fare un tiro mancino; **tighten one's —** stringere la cinghia di un buco; — *vt* cingere; *(coll)* battere
bemoan *vt* deplorare, lamentare, piangere
bench *n* banco; *(garden)* panchina; *(law)* tribunale *m*; — **warrant** mandato di cattura; — *vt* esibire
bend *n* piega, curva; — *vt* piegare; — *vi* piegarsi
beneath *adv* sotto, giù; — *prep* sotto, al disotto di
benediction *n* benedizione
benefactor *n* benefattore *m*
beneficence *n* beneficenza
beneficent *a* caritatevole
beneficial *a* buono, benefico, utile, salutare, vantaggioso
beneficiary *n* beneficiario
benefit *n* beneficio, vantaggio; *(subsidy)* sussidio; **for the — of** a beneficio di; — *vt* beneficare
benevolence *n* benevolenza
benevolent *a* buono, benevolo; *(charitable)* caritatevole
benighted *a* ignorante, oscurato
benign *a* benigno
bent *n* attitudine *f;* disposizione; *(tendency)* tendenza; — *a (crooked)* curvo; *(twisted)* torto
benumb *vt* intorpidire, intirizzire
benzine *n* benzolo
bequeath *vt* fare testamento, testare
bequest *n* lascito
berate *vt* rimproverare
bereave *vt* privare; **–ment** *n* perdita; lutto
bereft *a* privato, spogliato
beret *n* berretto, basco
berkelium *n (chem)* berchelio
berry *n* bacca
berserk *a* vandalico, distruttivo
berth *n* cuccetta, letto; **give a wide —**

to evitare
beseech *vt* supplicare, pregare
beset *vt* circondare, assediare
besetting *a* circondante
beside *prep* accanto a; — **oneself** fuori di sè; — *adv* d'altronde, inoltre
besides *adv* inoltre, per giunta; — *prep* inoltre a
besiege *vt* assediare
bespeak *vt* ordinare, prenotare, sollecitare
best *a* migliore; ottimo; — **man** testimone *m;* — *adv* meglio; **do one's** — fare il possible; **for the** — per il meglio; **get the** — **of** aver il meglio di; **make the** — **of** trar vantaggio di
bestial *a* bestiale; **–ity** *n* bestialità
bestir *vt* eccitare
bestow *vt* elargire, conferire
bet *n* scommessa; **You** —! *interj (coll)* Per certo!; — *vt* scommettere; — *vi* fare una scommessa
beta ray raggio beta
betake *vt* — **oneself** andarsene per conto proprio
betatron *n* betatrone *m*
betide *vt&i* accadere
betray *vt* tradire; — **oneself** tradirsi; **–al** *n* tradimento
betroth *vt* fidanzare; **–al** *n* fidanzamento; **–ed** *n&a* fidanzato
better *n* meglio, vantaggio; **for the** — per il meglio; **so much the** — tanto meglio; — *adv* meglio; — **and** — di bene in meglio; — *a* meglio, migliore; **think** — **of** pensarci meglio; — *vt* migliorare; — **oneself** migliorarsi; **get** — migliorare
between *prep* fra, tra; **betwixt and** — nè l'uno nè l'altro, fra i due; — *adv* nel mezzo, fra i due
bevel *n* angolo; — *vt&i* smussare
bevelled *a* smussato
beverage *n* bevanda, bibita
bevatron *n* bevatrone *m*
bevy *n* gruppo; *(swarm)* sciame *m*
bewail *vt* lamentare; *(regret)* rimpiangere; — *vi* lamentarsi
beware *vt&i* guardarsi da, stare in guardia
bewilder *vt* sgomentare, confondere, turbare; **–ing** *a* sgomentevole; **–ment** *n* sgomento; estasi *f*
bewitch *vt* ammaliare, stregare, incantare: **–ing** *a* affascinante
beyond *prep* al di là di; — *adv&n* al di là; **go** — andare più lontano di
biannual *a* biennale
bias *n* inclinazione; *(prejudice)* pregiudizio; **on the** — di sbieco; **–ed** *a* prevenuto; — *vt* influenzare
bib *n* bavaglino
Bible *n* Bibbia
biblical *a* biblico
bibliography *n* bibliografia
bicarbonate *n* bicarbonato
bicentennial *a* bicentennale
biceps *npl* bicipiti *mpl*
bicker *vi* far questione, litigare, bisticciare
bicycle *n* bicicletta; **ride a** — andare in bicicletta
bid *vt (command)* ordinare; *(offer)* offrire; — *vi* offrire un prezzo; — **adieu** dire addio; — **fair** promettere di; — *n* offerta, licitazione
bidder *n* offerente *m*
bidding *n* invito, offerta, ordine *m*
bide *vt* attendere, aspettare, sopportare; — **one's time** attendere l'occasione
biennial *a&n* biennale
bier *n* bara
bifocal *a* bifocale
big *a* grosso, grande; importante; — **shot** *(sl)* pezzo grosso; **look** — darsi delle arie; **talk** — darsi importanza; **B–Dipper** Orsa Maggiore
bigamist *n* bigamo
bigamous *a* bigamo
bigamy *n* bigamia
big-hearted *a* di buon cuore, generoso
bigot *n* bigotto; **–ry** *n* bigottismo, fanatismo
bigotted *a* bigotto, fanatico
bigwig *n (coll)* pezzo grosso
bilateral *a* bilaterale
bile *n* bile *f*
bilingual *a* bilingue
bilious *a* bilioso
bill *n* conto; *(bird)* becco; *(com)* fattura; — **of fare** lista delle vivande; — **of health** certificato di salute; — **of lading** polizza di carico; — **of sale** atto di vendita; **dollar** — biglietto da un dollaro; **–fold** *n* portafogli *m*, portafoglio; **–ing** *n* carezze *fpl*; — *vt* affigere; *(com)* fatturare; — **and coo** coccolare
billboard *n* albo di avvisi
billet *n (lodging)* accantonamento, alloggio; *(note)* lettera; — *vt* assengnare, collocare
billiards *npl* biliardo
billion *n* miliardo
billionnaire *n* miliardario
billow *n* maroso; — *vi* mareggiare, beccheggiare, rollare; **–y** *a* ondoso, agitato
bimonthly *a&n* bimestrale *m*; *(fortnight)* quindicinale *m;* — *adv* bimestralmente; quindicinalmente
bin *n* madia
bind *vt* legare; *(again)* rilegare; — **oneself** impegnarsi; **–er** *n* legatore *m*
binding *n* legatura; — *a* obbligatorio
bingo *n* tombola
biochemistry *n* biochimica
binoculars *npl* binoccolo
biographer *n* biografo
biographical *a* biografico
biography *n* biografia
biological *a* biologico; — **warfare** *n* guerra biologica
biologist *n* biologo
biology *n* biologia
bionics *npl* bionica
biophysics *n* biofisica
biopsy *n* biopsia
biotin *n (growth factor)* biotina
bipartisan *a* che fa doppio gioco
biped *n* bipede *m&f*
birch *n* betulla
bird *n* uccello; **–'s–eye** *a* a vista d'uc-

cello
birdseed *n* becchime *m*
biretta *n* berretta
birth *n* nascita; **–day** *n* compleanno; **–mark** *n* voglia; **–place** *n* luogo di nascita; **–right** *n* diritto di nascita, primogenitura; **give — to** partorire; dare alla luce
biscuit *n* panino
bisect *vt* bisecare; — *vi* tagliare in due
bishop *n* vescovo; **–ric** *n* vescovato
bit *n (amount)* pezzetto; *(horse)* morso; *(restraint)* freno; *(tool)* punta da trapano; **two –s** *(sl)* un quarto di dollaro
bitch *n* cagna; — *vi (sl)* lagnarsi
bite *vt&i* mordere; *(sting)* pungere; — *vi (fish)* abboccare; — *n* morso; *(mouthful)* boccone *m*
biting *a* mordente, aspro, sarcastico
bitter *a* amaro; **fight to the — end** lottare fino alla fine; **–ly** *adv* amaramente
bitterness *n* amarezza
bituminous *a* bituminoso
bivouac *n* bivacco; — *vi* bivaccare
biweekly *a&adv* ogni due settimane; bisettimanale; due volte la settimana; — *n* bisettimanale *m*
bizarre *a* bizzarro
blab *vi* chiacchierare; — *vt* raccontare
black *a* nero, scuro; — **eye** occhio pesto; — **list** lista nera; — **market** mercato nero, borsa nera; — **sheep** pecora nera; **–smith** *n* fabbro
blackball *vt* votare contro, bocciare, rigettare
blackberry *n* mora selvatica; *(bush)* moro
blackbird *n* merlo
blackboard *n* lavagna
blacken *vt* annerire, infamare; — *vi* annerirsi
blackguard *n* briccone *m*, mascalzone *m*
blackhead *n* punto nero
blackmail *n* ricatto; — *vt* ricattare; **–er** *n* ricattatore *m*
blackout *n* oscuramento; *(med)* amnesia; — *vt* oscurare, obliare
bladder *n* vescica
blade *n* lama; *(grass)* filo; **propeller —** pala d'elica
blame *n* colpa; **–less** *a* innocente; — *vt* dare la colpa
blameworthy *a* biasimevole
blanche *vt* imbiancare; evitare; — *vi* impallidire; tergiversare
bland *a* blando, soave; **–ness** *n* affabilità; **–ly** *adv* blandamente
blandishment *n* blandizia
blank *n&a* bianco; *(void)* vuoto; — **cartridge** cartuccia; — **check** assegno a vuoto; — **verse** verso libero; **–ly** *adv* vagamente
blanket *n (cover)* coperta; — **instructions** ordini generali *mpl;* **–ing** *(rad)* interferenza; — *a* generale; — *vt* coprire con coperta
blare *vi* risuonare, muggire; — *vt* proclamare a suon di tromba; — *n* suono, muggito
blarney *n* adulazione
blasé *a* scettico, blasé, abulico, indifferente
blaspheme *vi* bestemmiare
blasphemous *a* blasfematorio, sacrilego
blasphemy *n* bestemmia
blast *n* colpo di vento; esplosione; *(loud noise)* squillo; **–off** *n (aesp)* lancio; — *vt* far saltare; fare appassire; — **off** *(coll)* esplodere da impazienza; **–ed** *a* appassito, rovinato; **–ing** *n* distruzione, rovina
blatant *a* risuonante; **–ly** *adv* risuonatamente, sonoramente
blaze *n* incendio, fiamma; — *vi* divampare; *(glitter)* brillare; — *vt* far brillare; — **a trail** marchiare una pista
blazing *a* sfolgorante
bleach *vt&i* imbiancare; — *n* varecchina
bleachers *npl (stadium)* scalinate *fpl*
bleak *a* pallido
blear *vt* offuscare; *(vision)* velare; **–ed** offuscato
bleary *a* offuscato; *(of eyes)* infiammato; *(teary)* lagrimoso
bleat *n* belato; — *vi* belare
bleed *vi* sanguinare; — *vt* salassare; **–er** *n (med)* emofiliaco
bleeding *n* emorragia; — *a* sanguinante
blemish *vt* macchiare; — *n* macchia
blend *vt (mingle)* mischiare; *(mix)* mescolare; — *n* miscela; **–er** *n* frullatore *m*
bless *vt* benedire, consacrare; **–ed** *a* felice; **–ing** *n* benedizione
blight *n* ruggine *f*; *(bot)* golpe *f*; — *vt* danneggiare, riardere; *(fig)* guastare
blind *a* cieco; — **alley** vicolo cieco; — **flying** volo cieco; — *vt* accecare; — *n* sotterfugio, pretesto; persiana; *(fig)* finta; **Venetian –s** tende alla veneziana, persiane avvolgibili *fpl*
blinder *n (horse)* paraocchi *m*
blindfold *vt* bendare gli occhi, — *n* benda
blindly *adv* alla cieca
blink *vi (eyes)* sbattere gli occhi; **–er** *n (auto)* segnale di svolta
bliss *n* felicità; **–ful** *a* felice; **–fully** *adv* felicemente
blister *n* vescica, bollicina; — *vi* produrre vesciche
blithe *a* gaio, giocondo
blitz *n* attacco a sorpresa
blizzard *n* tormenta; bufera
bloat *vt* gonfiare; — *vi* gonfiarsi; **–ed** *a* gonfio, gonfiato
blob *n* goccia, macchia
bloc *n (pol)* blocco, gruppo
block *n* blocco; *(of houses)* isolato di case; — **and tackle** paranco; **stumbling** — intoppo; — *vt* bloccare
blockade *n* blocco; *(war)* assedio; **run a —** rompere il blocco; — *vt* bloccare; assediare
blockhead *n* testardo
blonde *a&n* biondo
blood *n* sangue *m;* — **plasma** plasma sanguigno
bloodcurdling *a* atterrito
bloodhound *n* segugio
bloodless *a* esangue
bloodshed *n* spargimento di sangue
bloodshot *a* congestionato

bloodstain *n* macchia di sangue
bloodthirsty *a* assetato di sangue
bloody *a* sanguinario
bloom *n* fiore *m*; — *vi* fiorire; **–ing** *a* in fiore, fiorente
blossom *n* fiore *m*; — *vi* fiorire, sbocciare
blot *vt* disonorare; *(hide)* oscurare; *(spot)* macchiare; — **out** cancellare; — *vi* macchiarsi; — *n* macchia
blotch *n* pustola, grossa macchia
blotter *n* carta sugante, brogliaccio
blotting paper carta asciugante
blouse *n* camicetta; blusa
blow *n* colpo; **–gun, –pipe** *n* cerbottana; **–torch** *n* cannello ossidrico; **come to –s** azzuffarsi; — *vi* soffiare, sbuffare; *(wind)* tirare; — **away** dissipare; — **out** *(fuse)* fulminare; *(light)* spegnere; — **over** soffiar via, rovesciare; — **up** gonfiare; *(photo)* ingrandire
blowout *n (tire)* scoppio
blubber *n* pianto; — *vi* piangere a dirotto; **–ing** *n* singhiozzo
bludgeon *n* randello, mazza; — *vt* colpire con mazza
blue *n* blu; *(azure)* azzurro; *(dark)* turchino; *(light)* celeste; *(sky)* azzurrocielo; **be** — essere depresso; **–berry** *n* mirtillo blu; **–bird** *n* beccafico; **–jay** *n* ghiandaia blu; **–print** *n* cianotipia; **once in a — moon** ad ogni morte di papa; **turn the air** — bestemmiare
blueing *n* indaco
blues *n pl* melanconia; **have the** — essere giù di spirito; *(mus)* musica nostalgica
bluff *n (geog)* scogliera; *(sham)* bluff *m*, smargiassata; — *vt* ingannare, bluffare; — *vi* vantarsi di
bluffer *n* vanaglorioso
bluish *a* bluastro
blunder *n* topica; sbaglio grossolano; — *vi* fare una topica, commettere un errore, equivocarsi
blunt *a* smussato; *(abrupt)* brusco; *(dull)* ottuso; — *vt* ottundere, rintuzzare
bluntly *adv* rudemente
blur *n* disonore *m*; *(mark)* macchia, segno indistinto; — *vt* offuscare, rendere indistinto; — *vi* confondersi
blurb *n* encomio
blurry *a* macchiato
blurt *vt* soffiare, singhiozzare
blush *n* rossore *m;* — *vi* arrossire
bluster *n* fanfaronata; — *vi* fare chiasso; *(weather)* infuriare.
blustering *a* rumoroso
blustery *a* tempestoso
boar *n* verro; **wild** — cinghiale
board *n (com)* consiglio; *(food)* tavola; *(wood)* asse *m;* — **of directors** consiglio di amministrazione; — **of health** ufficio d'igiene; — **of trade** camera di commercio; **on** — a bordo
board *vt* impalcare; prendere a pensione; — *vi (boat)* imbarcarsi; stare a pensione; *(train)* salire in treno
boarder *n* pensionato; *(school)* convittore *m*
boardinghouse *n* pensione
boarding school pensionato, collegio, convitto
boardwalk *n* passeggio, lungomare *m*
boast *n* vanto; — *vt* vantare; — *vi* vantarsi, gloriarsi; **–er** *n* spaccone *m*
boastful *a* millantatore; **–ness** *n* millantaria
boat *n* barca, battello; *(steam)* piroscafo; **in the same** — *(coll)* nella stessa situazione
boating *n* canottaggio
boatman *n* battelliere *m*
boatswain *n* nostromo
bob *n (hair)* orecchino
bob *vt* battere, scuotere; — *vi* dondolare; — **up** *(appear)* apparire improvvisamente
bobby pin molletta per i capelli
bobby socks *(coll)* braccialetti *mpl*
bobby soxer *(coll)* ragazzina, adolescente *f*
bobcat *n* gatto selvatico
bobsled *n* slitta
bode *vt&i* presagire; — **well, (ill)** promettere bene, (male)
bodice *n* busto
bodiless *a* incorporeo
bodily *a* corporeo; — *adv* di peso
body *n* corpo; *(airplane)* fusoliera; *(auto)* carrozzeria; *(corpse)* cadavere *m*; — **politic** corpo governativo; **in a** — tutti insieme
bodyguard *n* guardia del corpo *(or* personale)
bog *n* pantano; — *vt&i* impantanare; — **down** affondare nel pantano
boil *n* bollitura; *(med)* foruncolo; — *vi* bollire; — *vt* lessare, fare bollire; **–ed** *a* bollito
boiler *n* bollitore *m*, caldaia
boiling *a* bollente; — **point** punto d'ebollizione
boisterous *a* turbolento, chiassoso
bold *a* temerario; **–ly** *adv* temerariamente
boldness *n* ardimento, coraggio
boldface *n (type)* grassetto
bold-faced *a* sfrontato, sfacciato
bolero *n* bolero
boll *n* capsula; — **weevil** acaro del cotone
bolster *n* cuscino, cuscinetto; — *vt* accomodare con cuscini; *(fig)* rafforzare
bolt *n* bullone *m*; *(thunder)* fulmine *m*; — **upright** tutto dritto
bolt *vt* scattare; *(food)* trangugiare
bomb *n* bomba; — **bay** *(avi)* forma di sgancio; — **shelter** rifugio aereo; **–proof** *a* a prova di bomba; **–shell** *n* bossolo; **–sight** *n* strumento di sgancio
bombard *vt* bombardare; **–ment** *n* bombardamento
bombast *n* ampollosità; **–ic** *a* ampolloso
bomber *n* bombardiere *m*
bonanza *n* prosperità, fortuna; *(mine)* miniera ricca
bonbon *n* bombone *m*
bond *n* legame *m*, vincolo; *(com)* obbligazione, titolo; — *vt* depositare, immagazzinare; **–ed** *a* depositato; **–holder** *n* portatore *m*
bondage *n* servitù *f*
bondsman *n* avallo, garante *m*; schiavo

bone *n* osso; *(fish)* lisca; **feel in one's –s**; intuire; **have a — to pick** avere un punto da chiarire; **make no –s about** non avere scrupoli per; — *vt* disossare; — **up on** riassumere; **–less** *a* disossato, senz' osso
bone-dry *a* secco come un osso
boner *n (sl)* sproposito
bonehead *n (sl)* testa dura, stupido
bonfire *n* falò
bonnet *n* cuffia
bonus *n* gratifica
bony *a* ossuto
boo *interj* bu! — *vt* burlare, fischiare
booby *n* stupido; — **prize** premio per l'ultimo arrivato; — **trap** tranello, trappola esplosiva
book *n* libro; — **end** appoggialibri *m*; — **jacket** coprilibro; **memorandum** — libretto d'appunti; **–binder** *n* rilegatore *m*; **–case** *n* libreria, scaffale *m*; **–let** *n* libretto; **–mark** *n* segnalibro; **–plate** *n* etichetta di un libro; **–seller** *n* libraio; **–shelf** *n* scaffale *m*; **–store** *n* libreria, negozio di libri
book *vt* registrare; *(reserve)* prenotare, riservare; *(theat)* scritturare; — *vi (travel)* prendere il biglietto; **–ing** *n* registrazione
bookkeeper *n* contabile *m&f*
bookkeeping *n* contabilità
bookmaker *n (sport)* allibratore *m*
bookworm *n* tarlo, tignola; *(fig)* topo di biblioteca
boom *n* rimbombo; *(com)* prosperità improvvisa; *(naut)* boma, asta; — *vi* progredire, prosperare; — *vt* promuovere
boomerang *n* boomerang; — *vi* ritorcersi contro l'autore
boon *n* favore *m*, beneficio; — *a* gaio; buono
boondoggle *n (sl)* lavoro di poco profitto; — *vi (sl)* lavorare per poco
boor *n* zotico; **–ish** *a* rozzo, grossolano, volgare
boost *n (help)* aiuto; *(rise)* rialzo; — *vt (praise)* esaltare; *(increase)* aumentare
booster *n* connessione elettrica a combinazione; — **rocket** *(aesp)* razzo comandato
boot *n* stivale *m*; **to** — in più, in aggiunta; **–less** *a* inutile
bootblack *n* lustrascarpe *m*
booth *n* baracca
bootleg *a* contrabbandato; — *vt&i* contrabbandare
bootlegger *n* contrabbandiere *m*
booty *n* bottino
borax *n* borace *m*
border *n (edge)* orlo; *(geog)* frontiera; — *vt* orlare, confinare; — *vi* essere limitrofo; — **on** confinare con
borderland *n* paese limitrofo
borderline *n* confine *m*; — *a* incerto, dubbioso; — **case** caso incerto
bore *n* buco; *(gun)* calibro; *(mech)* alesaggio; *(person)* noia, seccatore *m*, seccatrice *f*; impiastro *(fig)*; — *vt (pierce)* bucare, forare; *(weary)* annoiare, seccare
boredom *n* noia
boring *a* noioso, seccante
born *a* nato; **be** — *(birth)* nascere
borrow *vt* prendere a prestito; — *vi* fare un prestito; **–er** *n* mutuatario; colui che chiede prestito
bosh *n (coll)* assurdità, stupidaggine *f*
bosom *n* seno; — **friend** amico amato
boss *n (coll)* principale, padrone *m*
botanical *a* botanico
botany *n* botanica
botch *vt* rammendare; — *n* rappezzo, rattoppo
both *a&pron* ambedue, tutt'e due; — *conj* così come, tanto quanto; — **hands** ambe le mani
bother *n* fastidio; — *vt* molestare, dar fastidio, seccare; — *vi* infastidirsi di
bothersome *a* fastidioso, noioso
bottle *n* bottiglia; *(flask)* fiasco; *(vial)* fiala
bottle *vt* imbottigliare; — **up one's feeling** nascondere l'emozione
bottleneck *n* intoppo, congestione di traffico
bottom *n* fondo; **at the** — in fondo; — *a* del fondo, inferiore; infimo, ultimo; **–less** *a* senza fondo
bottom *vt* fondare; *(naut)* sondare
botulism *n* botulismo
boudoir *n* spogliatoio, salottino da signora
bough *n* ramo
bouillon *n* brodo
boulder *n* ciottolo, sasso
boulevard *n* corso, viale *m*
bounce *vi* rimbalzare; — *vt* battere, far saltare; — *n* balzo, rimbalzo
bouncing *a* robusto; pieno di salute
bound *n* rimbalzo; **out of –s** fuori limite; — *a* obbligato, impegnato, rilegato; — **for** diretto a; — **to happen** inevitabile; **–less** *a* illimitato
bound *vi (jump)* balzare; — *vt (limit)* limitare
boundary *n* confine *m*
bountiful *a* generoso, benifico
bounty *n* generosità, bontà
bouquet *n* mazzolino; *(smell)* profumo; *(wine)* aroma *m*
bout *n* partita, turno
bow *n* inchino; *(naut)* prora; — *vi* inchinarsi; *(yield)* cedere; — *vt* inclinare; *(head)* abbassare la testa
bow *n* arco; *(mus)* archetto; *(ribbon)* nodo; *(tie)* cravatta; **draw a long** — esagerare; — *vt* piegare, curvare
bowels *npl* intestini *mpl*, budella *fpl*
bower *n* capanna
bowl *n* scodella, boccia; — *vi* giuocare ai birilli; giocare alle bocce; — **over** stravolgere
bowlegged *a* gambistorto
bowling *n* le bocce; — **alley** pista (*or* salone) di bocce; — **ball** boccia; — **pin** birillo
box *n* scatola; *(case)* cassa; *(slap)* ceffone *m*; *(theat)* palco; — **office** botteghino
box *vt* incassare; *(ears)* schiaffeggiare; *(sport)* fare del pugilato
boxcar *n* furgone, vagone *m*

boxer *n (packer)* imballatore *m; (sport)* pugile *m*
boxing *n* pugilato; — **glove** guanto da pugilato; — **match** partita di pugilato
boy *n* ragazzo; — **scout** Giovane Esploratore
boycott *n* boicottaggio; — *vt* boicottare
boyhood *n* puerizia, adolescenza
boyish *a* fanciullesco
brace *n* sopporto, sostegno; — *vt (bind)* legare; *(support)* sostenere; — **up** rianimarsi
bracelet *n* braccialetto
bracing *a* corroborante, tonico
bracket *n* mensola; *(print)* parentesi quadra
brad *n* chiodino
brag *n* vanteria; — *vi* vantarsi; — *vt* vantarsi di
braggart *n* millantatore *m*
braid *n* cordoncino, spighetta; *(hair)* treccia; — *vt* intrecciare
braille *n* Braille *m*, sistema braille
brain *n* cervello; — **fever** meningite cerebro-spinale; — **storm** *(coll)* confusione mentale; **electronic** — cervello elettronico; **beat one's –s out** *(sl)* spremere il cervello; **rack one's –s** scervellarsi; **–less** *a* poco intelligente, stupido; **–y** *a (coll)* intelligente; — *vt* far saltare le cervella
brainwash *n* psico-inquisizione, lavaggio mentale
braise *vt* brasare; **–d** *a* brasato
brake *n* freno; — **band** freno a nastro; — **lining** tessuto per freni; **apply the** — usare il freno; **release the** — rilasciare il freno; — *vt* frenare
brakeman *n* frenatore *m*
bramble *n* pruno, rovo
bran *n* crusca
branch *n (com)* succursale *f; (rail)* biforcazione; *(tree)* ramo; — *vt* suddividere, ramificare; — *vi* ramificarsi; — **off** diramarsi, biforcarsi; — **out** espandersi
brand *n* marca; — *vt* bollare, marchiare
brandish *vt* brandire
brand-new *a* fiammante
brandy *n* acquavite *f*
brash *a* arrogante
brass *n* ottone *m*; — **band** fanfara; **bold as** — *(coll)* spudorato
brassiere *n* reggiseno, reggipetto
brat *n* moccioso
bravado *n* spacconata
brave *a* coraggioso; — *vt* sfidare; — *n (American Indian)* bravo
bravery *n* coraggio, eroismo
brawl *n* zuffa, rissa; — *vi* sbraitare, gridare
brawn *n* polpa di carne; **–y** *a* muscoloso, forte
bray *n* raglio; — *vi* ragliare
brazen *a* sfrontato, impudente, sfacciato; — *vt* trattare con disprezzo
brazier *n* ottonaio
Brazil Brasile *m*
Brazilian *a&n* brasiliano
breach *n* breccia, rottura, violazione; — **of promise** violazione di promessa; — **of trust, faith** abuso di fiducia; — *vt* aprire una breccia, infrangere
bread *n* pane *m; (graham, wholewheat)* pane integrale; *(rye)* pane di segala; **earn one's** — guadagnarsi il pane; **fresh** — pane fresco; **know which side one's** — **is buttered on** sapere barcarmenarsi; **–board** *n* tagliere per pane; **–line** *n* fila di persone per ricevere alimento gratis; **–winner** *n* lavoratore *m*
bread *vt* impanare; **–ed** *a* impanato
breadth *n* larghezza, estensione
break *vt* rompere, spezzare; *(news)* comunicare; — *vi* rompersi; — **away** farla finita; — **down** *(health)* ammalarsi; *(mech)* avere una panna; — **in on** irrompere su, interrompere; — **into** invadere; — **one's word** mancare alla promessa; — **off** cessare di, smettere; — **out** scoppiare; *(flare)* divampare; *(rise up)* sorgere; — **up** distruggere, abbattere; cessare
break *n* rottura; *(bone)* frattura; *(pause)* interruzione; *(weather)* cambiamento; — **of day** alba; **bad** — sfortuna, scalogna; **give a** — concedere una occasione
breakable *a* fragile
breakage *n* rottura
breakdown *n (auto)* panna; *(damage)* guasto; *(med)* crollo; *(separation)* classificazione
breakfast *n* prima colazione
breakneck *a* sfrenato; *(foolhardy)* azzardato; — *adv* a rompicollo
breakwater *n* frangiflutti *m*
breast *n (anat)* petto, seno; *(woman's)* mammella; — **stroke** nuoto a rana; **make a clean — of it** confessare tutto
breast *vt* affrontare
breath *n* fiato, respiro; **be out of** — essere senza fiato; **gasp for** — ansare; **take one's — away** sconcertare
breathless *a* senza fiato
breathe *vi* respirare, fiatare; — *vt* infondere
breathing *n* respiro; — **space** tempo di tirare il fiato *(fig)*
breath-taking *a* emozianante, sfiatante
breech *n* posteriore *m; (gun)* culatta
breed *vt* generare; allevare; — *vi* moltiplicare; — *n* razza, stirpe *f;* **–er** *n* allevatore *m*
breeding *n* educazione, modi garbati, allevamento
breeze *n* brezza
breezy *a* arieggiato, brioso, vivace
breve *n* breve *m*
breviary *n* breviario
brevity *n* brevità, concisione
brew *n* miscela, fermentazione; — *vt (beer)* fare la birra; *(ferment)* fermentare; *(infuse)* fare un infuso di; *(mix)* miscelare; *(plot)* tramare; **something –ing** gatta ci cova *(fig)*
brewery *n* fabbrica di birra
briar *n* rovo
bribe *n* subornazione, corruzione, seduzione; — *vt* corrompere, subornare
bribery *n* subornazione, corruzione
brick *n* mattone *m*; **–layer** *n* muratore *m*;

–yard *n* fabbrica di mattoni
bridal *a* nuziale; — **gown** abito da sposa
bride *n* sposa, sposina; — **and groom** gli sposi
bridegroom *m* sposo
bridesmaid *n* damigella d'onore
bridge *n* ponte *m; (dent)* ponte dentale; *(game)* bridge *m; (suspension)* ponte sospeso; **–head** *n* testa di ponte; — *vt* costruire un ponte su, fare ponte su
bridle *n* briglia; — **path** galoppatoio; — *vt* frenare; — *vi* raddrizzarsi
brief *a* breve; **in** — in breve; — *n* memoriale *m*, riassunto; *(law)* esposto, citazione; **hold no — for** non essere d'accordo con; **–ly** *adv* in modo conciso; — *vt* dare istruzioni precise; **–ing** *(avi) n* istruzione di volo
brig *n (naut)* brigantino
brigade *n* brigata
bright *a* vivace, brillante, chiaro, intelligente; **–ness** *n* splendore *m; (light)* chiarore *m*; *(mirth)* allegria
brighten *vt* rischiarare; — *vi* rischiararsi
brilliance, brilliancy *n* splendore *m*
brilliant *a* brillante; — *n* brillante *m*, diamante *m*
brim *n* orlo; — **over** traboccare
brimful *a* ricolmo
brine *n* salamoia
bring *vt (carry)* portare; *(lead)* condurre; — **about** effettuare, causare; — **around** convincere; — **forth** produrre; — **oneself to** persuadersi; — **out** emettere; — **to** *(revive)* ravvivare; — **to one's mind** chiamare l'attenzione; — **up** *(child)* educare, allevare; *(subject)* tirare su
brink *n* orlo
brisk *a* attivo, vivace
bristle *n* setola; — *vi* arricciare, rizzare; — *vt* rizzarsi, arricciarsi
bristly *a* setoloso
British *a* britannico
brittle *a* fragile, friabile
broach *vt* introdurre, intavolare, abbordarsi
broad *a* largo; **–jump** *(sport)* salto in lungo; **–side** *n (naut)* bordo; bordato
broadcast *n* radiotrasmissione; — *vt* divulgare; *(rad&TV)* radiotrasmettere
broadcasting *n* radiodiffusione; — *a* trasmittente, radiotrasmittente; — **station** stazione radiotrasmittente
broaden *vi* allargare; — *vt* allargarsi
broad-minded *a* tollerante, liberale, di larghe vedute
brocade *n* broccato
broccoli *n* broccolo
brochure *n* opuscolo
broil *vt* arrostire in graticola; **–ed** *a* ai ferri; **–er** *n* arrostitrice *f*
broke *a (sl)* al verde, senza quattrini
broken *a* rotto; — **English** cattivo inglese
broken– *(in comp)* **—down** *a* scoraggiato; **—hearted** *a* disperato
broker *n (com)* sensale *m*, mediatore *m;* agente *m*
brokerage *n* mediazione
bromide *n* bromuro
bronchial *a* bronchiale; — **tube** bronco
bronchitis *n* bronchite *f*
bronchoscope *n* bronchiscopio
bronze *n* bronzo; — *a* bronzeo; di bronzo
brooch *n* spilla, fermaglio
brood *n* nidiata, covata; *vt&i* covare, meditare; — **over** angosciarsi
brook *n* ruscello; — *vt* sopportare; — **no interference** non tollerare intrusione
broom *n* scopa; *(bot)* ginestra; **–stick** *n* manico di scopa
broth *n* brodo
brothel *n* postribolo
brother *n* fratello; frate *m*; **–hood** *n* fratellanza; **–ly** *a* fraterno
brother-in-law *n* cognato
brow *n* fronte *f;* **knit one's –s** accigliarsi
browbeat *vt* imporre, intimidire
brown *a* bruno; *(hair)* castagno; *(skin)* abbronzato; — **paper** carta straccia; — **sugar** zucchero greggio; — *vt* abbrunire; *(cooking)* dorare, rosolare
browse *vt* pascolare, brucare; — *vi (in books)* scartabellare
bruise *vt* ammaccare; — *n* livido, contusione
bruiser *n* pugile *m*
brunch *n (coll)* combinazione di colazione e pranzo
brunette *a&n* brunetta, bruna
brunt *n* attacco, urto
brush *n* pennello; *(carbon)* elettrodi di carbonio; *(shoe)* spazzola per le scarpe; *(tooth)* spazzolino da denti; — *vt* spazzolare; — **past** sfiorare
brush-off *n (sl)* scoraggiamento
brushwood *n* macchia
brusque *a* brusco, rude
Brussels Brusselle; — **sprouts** *npl* cavoli di Brusselle
brutal *a* brutale; **–ity** *n* brutalità
brute *n* bruto, bestia; — *a* bruto
B.S., Bachelor of Science diploma in scienze; diplomato in scienze
bubble *n* bolla, bollicina; — *vt* far bollire; — *vi* bollire; — **over** traboccare
buccaneer *n* bucaniere, pirata *m*
buck *n* daino; *(sl)* dollaro; **pass the** — *(sl)* scaricare la responsabilità; — *vi* sgroppare; *(auto)* andare a strappi *(fig);* *(horse)* imbizzarrirsi; — *vt* opporsi a *(coll);* — **up** *(coll)* rallegrare
bucket *n* secchia, secchio; — **seat** *(auto)* strapuntino
buckle *n* fibbia; — *vt* affibbiare; — *vi* piegarsi; torcersi
buckshot *n* pallini da caccia
buckwheat *n* grano saraceno
bucolic *a* bucolico
bud *n* bottone *m;* gemma; **nip in the** — prevenire; — *vi* germogliare; — *vt* innestare
buddy *n (coll)* compare *m*, amicone *m;* camerata *m*
budge *vi* muoversi, indietreggiare; — *vt* spostare
budget *n* bilancio; — *vt* fare il bilancio
buff *n* colpo; — *a* marrone chiaro, fulvo; — *vt* lisciare, lucidare
buffalo *n* buffalo

buffer *n* paraurti *m*; *(rail)* respingente *m*
buffet *n (furniture)* credenza; *(meal)* tavola calda; *(service)* servizio di buffet
buffet *vt* colpire, schiaffeggiare; — *vi* fare a pugni
buffoon *n* buffone *m*
bug *n* insetto; *(coll)* microbo
bugbear *n* spauracchio
buggy *n* calesse *m;* **baby** — carrozzina
bugle *n* tromba
bugler *n* trombettiere *m*
build *n (stature)* struttura fisica; **-up** *n* opinione precostruita, propaganda; **-er** *n* costruttore *m;* **-ing** *n* edifizio, fabbricato; — *vt&i* costruire
bulb *n* bulbo, globo; *(elec)* lampadina elettrica; **-ous** *a* bulboso
Bulgarian *n&a* bulgaro
bulge *vt&i* gonfiarsi; — *n* protuberanza
bulk *n* massa, volume *m;* **in** — sciolto; **-head** *n* paratia; **-y** *a* voluminoso
bull *n* toro; — **market** mercato in aumento; **papal** — bolla papale
bulldog *n* mastino
bulldoze *vt (coll)* intimidire
bulldozer *n* apripista *m;* livellatrice *f*
bullet *n* pallottola; **-proof** *a* a prova di pallottole
bulletin *n* bollettino; — **board** albo, tabella per gli avvisi pubblici
bullfight *n* tauromachia, toreo, corrida
bullfighter *n* toreadore *m*, torero
bullfrog *n* rana toro
bullion *n* lingotto d'oro (*or* d'argento)
bully *n* prepotente *m*, gradasso; — *vi* fare il prepotente; — *vt* maltrattare, tiranneggiare
bulwark *n* baluardo; — *vt* fortificare
bum *n (coll)* lazzarone, straccione *m*
bumblebee *n* calabrone *m*
bump *n* colpo, urto, collisione; *(head)* bernoccolo; **-y** *a* pieno di bozze; — *vt* urtare; — *vi* sbattere contro
bumper *n (auto)* paraurti *m*, respingente *m;* — **crop** raccolta eccezionale
bumpkin *n* rusticone, cafone *m*
bumptious *a* presuntuoso
bun *n* panino, focaccia; *(hair)* boccolo
bunch *n* mazzetto; *(grapes)* grappolo; **in -es** a grappoli; — *vt* riunire in fascio; raccogliere; — *vi* gonfiarsi, raccogliersi in
bundle *n* involto, pacco, collo, fascio; *(sticks)* fagotto; — *vt* impaccare, avvolgere; — **off, out** svignarsela
bungalow *n* villino, casetta
bungle *vi* lavorare alla carlona; — *vt* storpiare
bungler *n* incapace *m*
bunion *n* grosso callo al piede
bunk *n* cuccetta; *(sl)* stupidaggine *f*
bunt *vt&i* spingere, cozzare; — *n (baseball)* spintone *m*
bunting *n* bandiere *fpl*
buoy *n* boa; — *vt* sostenere a galla; — *vi* galleggiare
buoyancy *n* leggerezza, elasticità, vivacità
buoyant *a* leggero, galleggiante; *(gay)* allegro
burden *n* fardello, carico; **-some** *a* pesante, opprimente; — *vt* gravare, caricare
bureau *n (furniture)* comò, cassettone *m; (office)* ufficio, ente governativo; **travel** — agenzia di viaggio
bureaucracy *n* burocrazia
burglar *n* svaligiatore, scassinatore *m;* **-y** *n* furto con scasso
burial *n* sepoltura, interramento; — **ground** cimitero
burlap *n* tela da sacco
burlesque *a* burlesco; — *n* burletta; — *vt&i* parodiare, imitare mettendo in ridicolo
burly *a* corpulento
Burma Birmania
burn *n* scottatura, ustione *f;* **-er** *n* bruciatore *m;* — *vt* bruciare
burning *n* incendio; — *a* ardente
burnish *vt* brunire
burnt *a* bruciato
burr *n (accent)* pronuncia forte dell'erre; *(bot)* involucro della castagna; *(mech)* limatura, bava, scoria; *(sound)* suono confuso; *(tool)* trapano; — *vt&i* parlare in erre
burrow *n* tana; — *vt&i* rintanarsi, fare un buco
bursitis *n* borsite *f*
burst *vi* scoppiare; — **into tears** scoppiare in pianto; — *vt* far esplodere; — *n* scoppio, esplosione; accesso; — **of applause** ovazione; esplosione di applausi
bury *vt* seppellire, sotterrare
bus *n* autobus *m*, pullman *m*
busboy *n* garzone, fattorino
bush *n* cespuglio, macchia; **beat around the** — menar il can per l'aia
bushel *n* staio
bushing *n (mech)* boccola
bushy *a* folto
busily *adv* attivamente
business *n* azienda, commercio, affare *m; (kind of work)* faccenda, occupazione; — **cycle** giro d'affari; — **house** casa di commercio; — **office** amministrazione; **make it one's** — prendere per proprio conto; **-man** *n* uomo d'affari
businesslike *a* commerciale, pratico
bust *n* busto; — *vi (sl)* andare in rovina
bustle *n* trambusto, chiasso; **hustle and** — andirivieni *m;* — *vi* affaccendarsi
busy *a* occupato, affaccendato, impegnato; — **oneself** occuparsi
busybody *n* ficcanaso, intrigante *m*
but *prep, conj&adv* ma, però, salvo, eccetto; — **for** senza; **no one** — nessuno eccetto; **all** — quasi
butane *n* butano
butcher *n* macellaio, — **shop** macelleria; — *vt* massacrare
butchery *n* massacro
butler *n* maggiordomo
butt *n (humor)* zimbello; *(cigar)* mozzicone *m*, cicca *(coll)*; *(gun)* calcio; *(target)* bersaglio; — *vt&i* cozzare; — **in** *(coll)* intromettersi
butter *n* burro; — **dish** burriera; — **knife** coltello del burro; — *vt* imburrare; — **up** *(coll)* lusingare; **-ed** *a* imburrato

butterfly *n* farfalla
buttermilk *n* siero del latte
butterscotch *n* caramella al burro
buttocks *npl* natiche *fpl*
button *n* bottone *m*; — *vt* abbottonare; abbottonarsi
buttonhole *n* occhiello; — *vt* attaccare un bottone *(fig)*
buttress *n* pilastro
buxom *a* procace, grassoccio
buy *n* compra; **a good** — un buon acquisto
buyer *n* compratore *m*, compratrice *f*
buy *vt* comprare, acquistare; — **off** corrompere; — **up** accaparrare; — *vi* fare compere
buzz *n* ronzio; — *vi* ronzare; — *vt* sussurrare; *(avi)* ronzare
buzzard *n* bozzagro
buzzer *n* cicalino
by *prep (according to)* secondo; *(near)* presso, vicino a; *(per)* da, per; *(time)* non più tardi di, entro; — *adv* vicino, accanto, in disparte; — **air** per via aerea; — **all means** a tutti i costi; — **and** — prossimamente, fra poco, — **and large** comunque; — **your leave** a tuo beneplacito; — **the way** a proposito; — **train** col treno
bygone *a* passato; — *n* cosa passata
bylaw *n* statuto, regolamento
bypass *n* circonvallazione, strada di deviazione; — *vt* deviare
by-product *n* sottoprodotto
bystander *n* astante, spettatore *m*
byway *n* disvio
byword *n* proverbio; *(ridicule)* oggetto di derisione

C

cab *n* tassì *m*; **–stand** *n* stazione di vetture
cabal *n* cabala; — *vi* intrigare, complottare
cabaret *n* ritrovo notturno, tabarin *m*
cabbage *n* cavolo
cabin *n* cabina; — **steward** cameriere di bordo
cabinet *n (cupboard)* armadio; *(curio)* stipo; *(pol)* consiglio dei ministri; **–maker** *n* ebanista *m*; **–work** *n* ebanisteria
cable *n* cablogramma *m*; *(elec)* filo elettrico, cavo; *(rope)* corda; *(wire)* cavo metallico; — **railway** funivia, funicolare; — *vt* telegrafare; *(rope)* legare con corda; — *vi* mandare un cablogramma
cabman *n* vetturino, fiaccheraio
caboose *n (naut)* cucina, cambusa
cackle *n* chiacchierio; *(hen)* chioccolio; — *vt&i* chiacchierare, chioccolare, chiocciare
cacophony *n* cacofonia
cactus *n* agave *f*, cacto
cad *n* mascalzone *m*
cadaver *n* cadavere *m*; **–ous** *a* cadaverico
caddy *n (golf)* portabastoni *m*; *(tea)* scatola da tè
cadence *n* cadenza
cadenza *n* cadenza
cadet *n* cadetto
café *n* caffè, bar *m*; — **keeper** barista *m*
cafeteria *n* tavola calda, caffè, pasticceria
cage *n* gabbia; — *vt* mettere in gabbia
cagey *a (sl)* astuto
caisson *n (arch)* cassone *m*
cajole *vt* accarezzare, adulare; — *vi* fare carezze, fare adulazioni
cake *n* dolce *m*; *(little)* pasticcino; *(many-layered)* torta; *(soap)* saponetta; — *vt (coagulate)* far quagliare; *(harden)* fare indurire; — *vi* quagliarsi; indurirsi
calamity *n* calamità
calcification *n* calcificazione
calcify *vt* calcificare; — *vi* calcificarsi
calcimine *n* tinta a calce
calcium *n* calcio
calculable *a* calcolabile
calculate *vt* calcolare; — *vi* fare calcoli; *(rely on)* contare su
calculating *a* calcolatore; — **machine** macchina calcolatrice
calculation *n* calcolo, previsione
calculus *n* calcolo
calendar *n* calendario
calf *n* vitello; *(leg)* polpaccio
caliber *n* calibro
calibrate *vt* calibrare
calibration *n* calibrazione
californium *n (chem)* californio
calipers *npl* compassi *mpl*
call *n (appeal)* appello; *(request)* invito; *(social)* visita; *(sound)* voce; *(summons)* chiamata; **make a — on** visitare; **within** — a portata di voce; **–er** *n* visitatore *m*, visitatrice *f*; chiamatore *m*, chiamatrice *f*; **–ing** *n* chiamata, appello; *(work)* professione, vocazione
call *vt&i* chiamare; — **away** attirare; — **back** richiamare; — **down** *(sl)* rimarcare; — **for** esigere; — **forth** designare; — **names** vituperare; — **off** distrarre; — **to mind** ricordarsi; — **to order** richiamare all'ordine; — **the roll** fare l'appello; — **together** riunire; — **up** evocare; *(phone)* telefonare
callous *a* duro, calloso, insensibile; — *vt* incallire; — *vi* incallirsi
callow *a* implume
callus, callous *n* callo
calm *n* calma, tranquillità; — *a* calmo; — *vi* calmarsi; — **down** ammansire, tranquillizzarsi; **become** — calmarsi
calorie *n* caloria
calumny *n* calunnia
calypso *a* calipso
calyx *n* calice *m*
cam *n (mech)* camma
camel *n* cammello; **—'s hair** *(cloth)* pelo di cammello
cameo *n* cammeo
camera *n* macchina fotografica; *(movie)* macchina cinematografica da presa
camerman *n* cineoperatore *m*
camouflage *n* mimetizzazione; — *vt* ma-

scherare, camuffare
camp *n* campo, accampamento; **break —** levare il campo; **–ground** area per campeggio; **—** *vi* campeggiare, far campeggio; accamparsi
campaign *n* campagna; **—** *vi* fare una campagna
camphor *n* canfora
campus *n* area scolastica
can *n* latta; *(tiny)* barattolo; **— opener** apriscatole *m;* **—** *vt* inscatolare, inlattare, mettere in conserva; *(com)* mettere in latta; *(dismiss, sl)* dimettere; **—** *vi (able)* potere, sapere
Canadian *a&n* canadese
canal *n* canale *m*
canary *n* canarino
cancel *vt* annullare, cancellare; **–ed** *a* cancellato, annullato
cancellation *n* annullamento, cancellazione
cancer *n* cancro; **–ous** *a* canceroso, cancrenoso
candid *a* sincero, franco; **–ly** *adv* candidamente
candidate *n* candidato, aspirante *m*
candied *a* candito
candle *n* candela; *(church)* cero; **–light** *n* luce di candela; **–stick** *n* candeliere *m;* **–wick** *n* lucignolo per candele
candor *n* candore, ingenuità
candy *n* dolci, dolciumi, zuccherini *mpl;* **— store** negozio di dolci, pasticceria; **—** *vt* candire
cane *n* canna; bastone *m;* **— (*or* caned) furniture** mobili di vimini (*or* di canna); **sugar —** canna da zucchero
canine *a* canino
canister *n* scatola di latta
canker *n* cancro
canned *a* inscatolato, inlattato; *(mus)* inciso in dischi; (*sl*) dimesso
cannery *n* fabbrica di conserve
cannibal *n* cannibale *m;* **–ism** *n* cannibalismo
cannon *n* cannone *m*
canny *a* abile, prudente
canoe *n* canoa, canotto, sandalino; **—** *vi* remare in canoa
canon *n* canone *m; (mus)* fuga; **— law** diritto canonico
canonize *vt* canonizzare
canopy *n* baldacchino, tenda
cant *n* ipocrisia, affettazione
cantaloupe *n* melone *m*
cantankerous *a* sgradevole, litigioso
cantata *n* cantata
canteen *n (container)* borraccia; *(mil)* casa del soldato, spaccio
canter *n* piccolo galoppo; **—** *vt&i* andare al piccolo galoppo
cantor *n* cantore *m*
canvas *n* canovaccio; *(cloth)* tela
canvass *vt* sollecitare; *(examine)* vagliare; **—** *vi* sollecitare voti; **–er** *n* propagandista; *(com)* piazzista; *(solicitation)* sollecitatore *m; (pol)* agente elettorale
canyon *n* vallone profondo, burrone *m*
cap *n* berretto; *(lid)* coperchio; *(mech)* tappo; **—** *vt (cover)* coprire, *(finish)* completare; **to — it all** per rendere la cosa completa
capability *n* capacità
capable *a* capace, abile; in gamba *(coll)*
capacity *n* abilità, capacità, qualità; **seating —** capacità di luogo
cape *n* mantellina, mantella; *(geog)* capo
caper *n* capriola, salto; *(bot)* cappero; **—** *vi* far capriole
capillary *n* vaso capillare; **—** *a* capillare; **— action** forza capillare
capital *a* capitale, importante, principale, maiuscolo; **— punishment** pena di morte, pena capitale; **—** *n (arch)* capitello; *(com)* capitale *m*; *(geog)* capitale *f*; *(print)* maiuscola; **provincial —** capoluogo di provincia
capitalist *n* capitalista *m&f*
capitalization *n* capitalizzazione
capitalize *vt* capitalizzare
capitol *n* Capitolio
capitulate *vi* capitolare
capitulation *n* capitolazione
capon *n* cappone *m*
caprice *n* capriccio
capricious *a* capriccioso
capsize *vt* capovolgere; **—** *vi* capovolgersi
capsule *n* capsula; *(aesp)* capsula, calotta
captain *n* capitano
caption *n* sottotitolo, didascalia
captivate *vt (charm)* sedurre; *(win)* conquistare, cattivare
captivating *a* seducente
captive *n&a* prigioniero, schiavo
captivity *n* cattività, schiavitù *f,* prigionia
capture *n* cattura, arresto; **—** *vt* catturare, impadronirsi di
car *n* automobile *f,* macchina *(coll);* veicolo; *(rail)* vagone ferroviario; **— pool** intercambio di guida; **armored —** autoblinda; **baggage —** vagone bagagli; **dining —** vagone ristorante; **freight —** vagone merci; **sleeping —** vagone letto; **smoking —** scompartimento fumatori; **side–** *n* motocarrozzino, sidecar *m*
carafe *n* caraffa
caramel *n* caramella; **–ize** *vt&i* candire, caramellare
carat *n* carato
caravan *n* carovana
caraway *n* carvi *m,* comino
carbolic acid *n* acido fenico
carbon *n* carbone *m;* **— paper** carta carbone
carbuncle *n* carbonchio; *(med)* foruncolo
carburetor *n* carburatore *m*
carcass *n* carcassa, carcame *m*
card *n* cartolina, carta; *(catalog, index)* schedario; *(greeting)* cartolina di auguri; **— game** giuoco di carte
cardboard *n* cartone *m*
cardiac *a&n* cardiaco
cardinal *a* cardinale, principale; *(color)* rosso vivo; **—** *n* cardinale *m*
cardiogram *n* cardiogramma
cardiograph *n* cardiografia
cardsharp *n* baro
care *n* attenzione; *(nursing)* cura; *(worry)*

preoccupazione; **take — of** occuparsi di; *(med)* curare; — *vi* curarsi di, badare; — **about** interessarsi di; — **for** *(like, love)* voler bene a; **I don't —** Non m'importa; **What do I —?** Che m'importa?
careen *vt* carenare
career *n* carriera
carefree *a* spensierato
careful *a* accurato, attento; **Be —!** Attenzione!
careless *a* imprudente, negligente; **–ness** *n* negligenza, noncuranza
caress *n* carezza; — *vt* accarezzare
caret *n* segno di richiamo
caretaker *n* custode *m*, portinaio
careworn *a* preoccupato
carfare *n* prezzo della corsa
cargo *n* carico
caricature *n* caricatura; — *vt* mettere in caricatura, caricaturare
caries *npl* carie *f*
carillon *n* cariglione *m*, carillon *m*
carload *n* carico, limite di carico; — **lot** *(com)* lotto di carico, unità di carico
carnage *n* strage *f*, carneficina
carnal *a* carnale
carnation *n* garofano
carnival *n* carnevale *m*, fiera
carnivorous *a* carnivoro
carol *n* canto, canzone *f*
carouse *vi* gozzovigliare
carousel *n* carosello
carp *n (fish)* carpio; — *vi (blame)* censurare; *(quibble)* cavillare
carpenter *n* falegname *m*, carpentiere *m*
carpentry *n* falegnameria
carpet *n* tappeto; — **sweeper** scopa automatica, macchina spazzatrice; **on the —** *(sl)* sul tappeto; **–ing** *n* materiale per tappeti; — *vt* tappetare, coprire con tappeto
carport *n* cappotta
carriage *n* carrozza, carrozzella; *(behavior)* portamento
carrier *n* portatore, vettore *m; (aircraft)* nave portaerei; *(luggage)* portabagaglio; *(pigeon)* piccione viaggiatore
carrion *n* carogna
carrot *n* carota
carry *vi* portare, trasportare; — **away** portar via; — **forward** riportare; — **off** portar via, asportare; — **on** continuare; spingere; — **out** *(accomplish)* realizzare; *(complete)* portare a termine; *(execute)* eseguire; *(move)* portare fuori; — **over** trasportare
cart *n* carretto; **–load** *n* carrettata; — *vt* trasportare
cartage *n* carreggio, trasporto
cartel *n* cartello
cartilage *n* cartilagine *f*
cartographer *n* cartografo
cartography *n* cartografia
carton *n* scatola di cartone; — **of cigarettes** stecca di sigarette
cartoon *n* caricatura; vignetta; **–ist** *n* caricaturista; **animated —** cartone animato
cartridge *n* cartuccia; — **belt** cartucciera; *(mil)* giberna; — **clip** bossolo di cartuccia
cartwheel *n* salto obliquo
carve *vt* scolpire, intagliare; *(food)* trinciare; decorare con figure intagliate
carver *n* intagliatore *m*, *(food)* trinciante *m*
carving *n* intaglio, scultura; — **knife** trinciante *m*
casaba *n* melone d'inverno
cascade *n* cascata; — *vi* cadere in cascata
case *n* cassetta; *(chance)* caso; *(container)* astuccio; *(gram)* caso; **just in —** nel caso che; **–ment** *n* finestra a battenti
cash *n* contante *m;* — **on delivery, C.O.D.** pagamento alla consegna; — **register** registratore di cassa; **hard —** contanti; **pay —** pagare in contanti; — *vt* pagare; incassare
cashbook *n* libro di cassa
cashbox *n* scrigno
cashew (nut) *n* anacardo
cashier *n* cassiere *m*; — *vt* destituire
cashmere *n* casimiro
casing *n (cover)* copertura; *(frame)* telaio; *(packing)* incassamento
cask *n* botte *f*, fusto, barile *m*
casket *n* bara; cofanetto, scrigno
casserole *n* casseruola
cassock *n* tonaca, sottana
cast *vt (metal)* fondere; *(show)* dare le parti; *(throw)* gettare; — **about for** considerare; cercare; — **off** *(discard)* scartare, rigettare; *(naut)* mollare gli ormeggi; — **a ballot** votare; — *n (eye)* leggero strabismo; *(plaster)* calco; *(theat)* complesso
castanets *npl* nacchere *fpl*
castaway *n* naufrago
caste *n* casta
caster *n* gettatore *m*; *(foundry)* fonditore *m*; *(furniture)* rotella
castigate *vt* castigare, punire, correggere
casting *n (sport)* lancio
cast iron ghisa
castle *n* castello, palazzo; fortezza
castoff *n (discard)* scarto; *(jettison)* gettito
castor oil olio di ricino
castrate *vt* castrare
casual *a* accidentale, casuale, fortuito; *(nonchalant)* indifferente, disinvolto; — **clothes** vestito da casa; **–ty** *n (mishap)* accidente; *(victim)* vittima
cat *n* gatto; — **nap** pisolino; **let the — out of the bag** *(fig)* svelare un segreto; **be a –'s paw** fare la testa di ferro *(fig)*
catabolism *n* catabolismo
cataclysm *n* cataclisma; **–ic** *a* disastroso
catafalque *n* catafalco
catalog *n* catalogo; — *vt* catalogare
catalyst *n* catalizzatore *m*
catapult *n* catapulta; — *vt* catapultare
cataract *n* cascata; *(med)* cataratta
catarrh *n* catarro
catastrophe *n* catastrofe *f*
catastrophic *a* catastrofico
catcall *n* miagolio
catch *vt (grab)* afferrare, prendere; *(nab)*

acchiappare; — *vi* afferrarsi; — **a glimpse of** intravedere; — **cold** prendere un raffreddore; — **fire** incendiarsi; — **the train** prendere il treno
catch *n (arrest)* cattura; *(door)* anelli di porta; *(fish)* pesca; *(jewelry)* fermaglio; *(window)* gancio; — **basin** marginatore *m*; **–word** *n* grido popolare, slogan *m*
catching *a* contagioso
catchy *a (attractive)* attraente; *(deceitful)* ingannevole; *(mus)* orecchiabile
catechism *n* catechismo
categorical *a* categorico
category *n* categoria
cater *vt* provvedere; **–er** *n* provveditore, fornitore *m*
caterpillar *n* bruco; *(mech)* trattore a cingoli
caterwaul *vi* miagolare; — *n* miagolio
catfish *n* pesce gatto
catgut *n* minugia
cathartic *a&n* catartico
cathedral *n* cattedrale *f*
catheter *n* catetere *m*
cathode *n* catodo; **–ray tube** lampada a raggi catodici
catholic *a* cattolico
Catholicism *n* Cattolicismo, Cattolicesimo
catnip *n* erba dei gatti
catsup *n* salsa di pomodori
cattiness *n* felinità
cattle *n* bestiame *m*; — **ranch** fattoria di allevamento bovino; **–man** *n* allevatore di bovini
catty *a* dispettoso
Caucasian *n&a* caucasico
caucus *n* comitato elettorale
caudal *a* caudale
cauliflower *n* cavolfiore *m*
causative *a* causativo
cause *n* causa, motivo; **make common — with** far causa comune con; — *vt* causare
causeway *n* marciapiedi *m*
caustic *a* caustico; — *n (chem)* caustico
cauterize *vt* cauterizzare
caution *n* prudenza; cautela; — *vt* prevenire
cautious *a* cauto, prudente
cavalcade *n* cavalcata
cavalier *n* cavaliere *m*
cavalry *n* cavalleria
cave *n* grotta, caverna; — **man** uomo delle caverne, troglodita *m*; — *vt* scavare; — *vi (fail)* fallire; *(sag)* afflosciarsi; — **in** scassare; *(coll)* cedere
cavern *n* caverna
caviar *n* caviale *m*
cavil *n* cavillo; — *vi* cavillare
cavity *n* buco; *(tooth)* carie *f*
caw *n* gracchiamento; — *vi* gracchiare
cayenne *n* pepe di Caienna
cease *vt&i* cessare; *(give up)* smettere; *(interrupt)* interrompere; **–less** *a* incessante
cease-fire *n* tregua
cedar *n* cedro
cede *vt* cedere
cedilla *n* cediglia
ceiling *n* soffitto; *(avi)* massima altitudine
celebrant *n (eccl)* celebrante *m*
celebrate *vt&i* festeggiare, celebrare, commemorare
celebrated *a* celebre, famoso
celebration *n* celebrazione, festa
celebrity *n* celebrità, persona celebre
celery *n* sedano
celestial *a* celeste, divino
celestial mechanics meccanica celeste
celibacy *n* celibato
celibate *n&a* celibe *m*
cell *n* cella; *(anat)* cellula; *(elec)* pila; *(prison)* cella; **–ular** *a* cellulare
cellar *n* cantina
cellist *n* violoncellista *m&f*
cello *n* violoncello
cellophane *n* cellofane *f*
celluloid *n* celluloide *f*
cellulose *n* cellulosa
cement *n* cemento, mastice *m*; *(adhesive)* adesivo; *(dent)* resina indiana; — *vt* cementare, collegare con cemento; attacare; *(dent)* otturare; *(stick)* incollare; — *vi* cementarsi
cemetery *n* cimitero, camposanto
censer *n* incensiere *m*, turibolo
censor *n* censore *m*; — *vt* censurare; **–ship** *n* censura
censure *n* censura; *(reproof)* rimprovero; — *vt* censurare
census *n* censimento
cent *n* centesimo, cento
centenary *n&a* centenario
centennial *a* secolare; — *n* centenario
center *n* centro; — **of attraction** centro d'attrazione; — *vt* centrare; — *vi* essere in centro
centigrade *a* centigrado
centigram *n* centigrammo
centimeter *n* centimetro
centipede *n* millepiedi *m*
central *a* centrale; **–ize** *vt* centralizzare
Central America America Centrale
centralization *n* centralizazzione
centrifugal *a* centrifugo
centripetal *a* centripeto
century *n* secolo
ceramic *a* ceramico; **–s** *npl* ceramica
cereal *n* cereale *m*
cerebellum *n* cervelletto
cerebral *a* cerebrale; — **palsy** paralisi cerebrale
cerebrum *n* cervello, cerebro
ceremonial *a&n* rituale, cerimoniale *m*
ceremonious *a* cerimonioso; **–ly** *adv* cerimoniosamente
ceremony *n* rito, cerimonia, solennità; **without** — senza complimenti
cerise *n* color ciliegia; — *a* di color ciliegia
certain *a* certo, sicuro; — **man** un tale; **for** — di sicuro, in forma certa
certainly *adv* sicuro, certo, certamente; senz'altro, senza dubbio
certainty *n* certezza, sicurezza; **with** — con sicurezza
certificate *n* certificato; *(com)* titolo
certified *a* certificato; — **check** assegno garantito dalla banca; — **milk**

latte certificato; — **public accountant, C.P.A.** ragioniere abilitato
certify *vt* certificare, legalizzare; — **to** garantire
certitude *n* certezza
cervical *a* cervicale
cessation *n* cessazione
cesspool *n* pozzo nero
chafe *vt* irritare; scaldare *(fig)*
chaff *n (husk)* loglio; *(ridicule)* beffa; — *vt&i* beffare
chafing dish scaldavivande *m*
chagrin *n* cruccio, mortificazione
chain *n* catena; — **reaction** reazione a catena; — **store** succursale *f*; — **of events** serie d'eventi
chair *n* sedia; *(deck)* sedia a sdraio; *(folding)* sedia pieghevole; *(professorial)* cattedra; *(wheel)* sedia con rotelle; **take the** — insediarsi; assumere la presidenza
chairman *n* presidente *m;* **–ship** *n* presidenza
chalice *n* calice *m*
chalk *n* gesso; — *vt* scrivere col gesso; — **up** sommare a conto di qualcuno; **–y** *a* calcareo, gessoso
challenge *n* sfida; *(mil)* chi va là; *(law)* ricusazione; — *vt* sfidare, provocare; — **attention** chiamare l'attenzione
challenger *n* sfidante *m*, provocatore *m*, aggressore *m*
chamber *n* camera; *(hall)* aula; *(room)* stanza, sala; **air** — camera d'aria; — **music** musica da camera
chambermaid *n (hotel)* cameriera
Chamber of Comerce Camera di Commercio
chamois *n* camoscio
champ *vt* mordere, masticare; — *n (sl)* campione *m*
champagne *n* spumante *m*, sciampagna *m*
champion *n* campione *m;* **–ship** *n* campionato
chance *n* combinazione, imprevisto; ventura; caso; **by** — per caso, per combinazione; — *a* fortuito, accidentale; — *vi* accadere per caso; — *vt (coll)* tentare, avventurare; — **on** imbattersi con
chancellor *n* cancelliere
chancery *n* cancelleria
chandelier *n* lampadario
change *vt* cambiare, scambiare; cambiarsi; — **hands** cambiare di proprietario; — **one's mind** cambiare idea
change *n* cambio; *(money)* piccolo cambio; — **of heart** conversione; — **of life** cambio di vita; — **of venue** cambio di giurisdizione; **make a** — cambiare, fare un cambiamento
changeable *a* cambiabile, variabile, mutabile
changeless *a* immutabile, costante
changeover *n* cambio
channel *n* canale *m*, stretto; *(rad, TV)* stazione; *(river)* canale *m*; **The English C-** La Manica; — *vt* scannellare, scavare un canale
chant *n* canto; — *vt&i* cantare; **–er** *n* cantore *m*
chaos *n* caos *m*
chaotic *a* caotico
chap *vt&i* crepare; — *n* uomo, giovanotto
chapel *n* cappella
chaperon *n* istitutrice *f*, aia; — *vt* accompagnare
chaplain *n* cappellano
chapter *n* capitolo
char *vt* carbonizzare; — *vi* carbonizzarsi
character *n* carattere *m*, temperamento; *(print)* carattere *m; (theat)* personaggio
characteristic *a* caratteristico; — *n* caratteristica
characterization *n* caratterizzazione
characterize *vt* caratterizzare
charcoal *n* carbone di legna, carbonella; — **burner** carbonaio
charge *n* carica; *(care)* custodia; *(cost)* prezzo, costo; *(law)* accusa; — **account** conto; **be in** — essere in carico di; **free of** — gratis; **in** — **of** in custodia di; — *vt* caricare, accusare; — *vi (mil)* caricare, andare alla carica; — **to account** mettere in conto
chargeable *a* accusabile, imponible, imputable
charger *n (horse)* destriero da carica; *(elec)* carica-batterie
chariot *n* carro; **–eer** *n* carrista *m*, cocchiere *m*
charitable *a* caritatevole
charity *n* carità, bontà; **out of** — a beneficienza
charlatan *n* ciarlatano
charm *n* fascino; *(luck)* portafortuna *m*, amuleto; — *vt* incantare, affascinare; **–ing** *a* affascinante, grazioso, delizioso
chart *n* carta; *(med)* storia clinica; — *vt* fare un piano, tracciare
charter *n* carta, brevetto; — **member** socio fondatore; — *vt (com)* concedere una licenza; *(hire)* noleggiare
chase *vt* cacciare, dare la caccia; — *n* caccia, inseguimento; **give** — dare la caccia a
chasm *n* baratro, abisso, voragine *f*
chassis *n* telaio
chaste *a* casto, puro
chasten *vt* castigare, punire
chastise *vt* castigare, punire
chastisement *n* castigo
chastity *n* castità
chasuble *n* pianeta
chat *vi* chiacchierare, far due chiacchiere; — *n* chiacchiera
chattel *n* mobile *m;* — **mortgage** ipoteca mobiliare
chatter *n* chiacchiera; **–box** *n* chiacchierone *m;* — *vi* chiacchierare, ciarlare
chattering *n* ciarla, chiacchiera; — *a* ciarliero
chatty *a* ciarliero, loquace
cheap *a* economico; a buon mercato; **feel** — essere imbarazzato
cheapen *vt* deprezzare, svilire; *(price)* diminuire di prezzo; — *vi* scemare il valore di
cheapness *n (cost)* buon mercato; *(person)* spregevolezza
check *vt* verificare, controllare; *(stop)*

fermare, arrestare; *(store)* lasciare in deposito; — *vi* provare di aver ragione, — **in** *(register)* registrarsi; — **out** dimettersi

check *n (baggage)* scontrino bagagli; *(bank)* assegno; *(blank)* assegno in bianco; *(cashier's)* assegno di cassa; *(mark)* segno; *(obstacle)* ostacolo; *(traveler's)* assegno per viaggiatore; — **list** lista di verifica; **–book** *n* libretto d'assegni; **–er** *n* controllore *m;* **–up** *n* esame generale, controllo, verifica; **–ed** *a* a quadretti

checkered *a* quadrettato; — **career** vita avventurosa

checkerboard *n* scacchiera

checkers *npl (game)* scacchi *mpl*

checkmate *n* scacco matto; — *vt* dare scacco matto

checkroom *n* vestiario, guardaroba; *(rail)* deposito bagagli

cheek *n* guancia; **–y** *a (coll)* sfacciato

cheekbone *n* zigomo

cheep *n* pigolio; — *vi* pigolare

cheer *n* allegria, gioia; *(hurrah)* grido di gioia; **–less** *a* triste, malinconico; **–y** *a* gioioso, contento; — *vt* rallegrare, consolare, incoraggiare; — **up** gioire, animarsi

cheerful *a* allegro; **–ly** *adv* graziosamente, gaiamente; **–ness** *n* vivacità

cheese *n* cacio, formaggio

chef *n* capo cuoco

chemical *a* chimico; — **engineering** ingegneria chimica; — *n* prodotto chimico

chemist *n* chimico; **–ry** *n* chimica

cherish *vt* accarezzare, nutrire

cherry *n&a* ciliegia; — **tree** ciliegio

cherub *n* cherubino, cherubo; **–ic** *a* cherubico

chess *n* scacchi; **–board** *n* scacchiera; **–men** *npl* pedine degli scacchi

chest *n (anat)* petto, torace *m*; *(container)* cassa, cassone *m*; *(furniture)* comò, cassetone *m*

chestnut *n* marrone *m*, castagna; — **tree** castagno; — *a (color)* castano, marrone, castagno

chevalier *n* cavaliere *m*

chevron *n (mil)* gallone *m*

chew *vt* masticare

chewing gum gomma da masticare, cicla

chiaroscuro *n (arts)* chiaroscuro

chic *a* scic

chicanery *n* intrigo; *(cavil)* sofisticheria

chicken *n* pollo; **–pox** *n* varicella, morbiglione *m*

chicken-hearted *a* timido, pauroso

chicory *n* cicoria

chide *vi* sgridare, rimproverare

chief *n* capo; — *a* principale; — **justice** giudice supremo; — **of staff** capo reparto; **–ly** *adv* sopratutto

chieftain *n* capo, capobanda; condottiero

chiffon *n* sciffon *m*

chilblains *npl* geloni *mpl*

child *n* bambino, bambina, fanciulla, fanciullo; bimbo, bimba; creatura; **with** — incinta; **–birth** *n* parto; **–hood** *n* fanciullezza; *(infancy)* infanzia; **–ish** *a* puerile, infantile; **–less** *a* senza figli; **–like** *a* bambinesco

children *npl* bambini, fanciulli, figli *mpl*

Chile Cile; **–an** *n&a* cileno

chili *n* peperone, peperosso; — **sauce** salsa pepata

chill *n* brividio, raffreddore *m;* — *a* freddo, glaciale; **–y** *a* freddo; *(people)* freddoloso

chill *vt* raffreddare; — *vi* raffreddarsi

chime *n (bell)* cariglione *m; (harmony)* concerto; *(mus)* accordo; — *vt* far risuonare; — *vi* scampanare; risuonare; — **in with** prender parte al concerto; accordarsi con

chimerical *a* chimerico

chimney *n* camino, fumaiolo

chiming *a* scampanante; — *n* scampanio

chimpanzee *n* scimpanzè

chin *n* mento

china *n* porcellana; **–ware** *n* porcellana

chinchilla *n* cinciglia

Chinese *n&a* cinese *m&f*

chink *n* screziatura, fessura

chip *n* frammento, scheggia; — *vt* scheggiare, tagliuzzare; — *vi* scheggiarsi, — **in** *(coll)* pagare la propria quota; **have a — on one's shoulder** *(coll)* essere aggressivo

chipmunk *n* scoiattolo striato

chipper *a (coll)* vivace

chiropractor *n* ortopedico

chirp *vi* cinguettare, trillare; — *n* cinguettio

chisel *n* scalpello, cesello; — *vt* cesellare; *(coll)* turlupinare; **–ed** *a* cesellato

chivalrous *a* cavalleresco, cortese

chivalry *n* cavalleria

chives *npl* cipollina verde

chloremia *n* clorimia

chloride *n* cloruro

chlorinate *vt* clorurare

chlorination *n* clorurazione

chlorine *n* cloro

chloroform *n* cloroformio

chlorophyll *n* clorofilla

chock-full *a* colmo, completamente pieno

chocolate *n* cioccolata, cioccolatino; — *a* di cioccolata

choice *n* scelta; — *a* scelto, raro, squisito

choir *n* coro

choke *vt* strangolare, soffocare; — *vi* *(block)* ingombrarsi, ostruirsi; — **back** ricacciar dentro; — **down** ringoiare; — **off** soffocare; — **up** ingorgare; — *n* *(auto)* diffusore *m*, valvola dell'aria; *(mech)* regolatore *m*

choler *n* collera; **–ic** *a* collerico

cholera *n* colera

cholesterol *n* colesterina

choose *vt (desire)* preferire, decidere *(select)* scegliere; — *vi* preferirsi, volere, decidersi a

choosy *a (coll)* sofistico *(coll)*

chop *vt* tritare, tagliuzzare; *(meat)* sminuzzare; — *n* taglio; *(meat)* costoletta, cotoletta; **–s** *npl (jaws)* mascelle *fpl;* **lick one's –s** leccarsi le labbra

chopped *a* tagliato, tritato

choppy *a* screpolato, increspato

choral *a* corale
chord *n* corda; *(mus)* accordo
chore *n* lavoro, faccenda
choreography *n* coreografia
chorister *n* corista *m&f*
chortle *n* sogghigno; — *vt&i* ridacchiare
chorus *n* *(people)* coro; *(song)* ritornello; — **girl** ballerina; — *vt* far coro a
chosen *a* scelto, preferito
Christ *n* Cristo
christen *vt* battezzare; *(coll)* usare per la prima volta; **-ing** *n* battesimo
Christian *n&a* cristiano; — **name** nome di battesimo
Christianity *n* cristianità
Christmas *n* Natale *m*; **Merry** — Buon Natale
chrome *n* cromo
chrome-plated *a* cromato
chromium *n* cromio
chromogen *n* cromogeno
chromosome *n* cromosomo
chromosphere *n* (ast) cromosfera
chronic *a* cronico
chronicle *n* cronaca
chronological *a* cronologico
chronology *n* cronologia
chrysalis *n* crisalide *f*
chrysanthemum *n* crisantemo
chubby *a* paffuto, grassoccio
chuck *vt* *(throw)* buttare, gettare; — **under the chin** dare un colpetto sotto il mento; — **out** buttare fuori; — *n* *(mech)* mandrino
chuckle *vi* ridacchiare; ridere sotto i baffi; — *n* sogghigno, riso represso
chug *n* *(motor)* rumore d'esplosione; — *vi* fare rumore di esplosione; — **along** guidare provocando esplosioni
chum *n* *(coll)* amico intimo, compagno; — *vi* *(coll)* amicarsi
chump *n* *(coll)* scemo
chunk *n* ceppo; **-y** *a* tozzo
church *n* chiesa, tempio; — **music** musica sacra; — **service** ufficio divino
churlish *a* grossolano
churn *n* zangola; — *vt&i* zangolare; *(froth)* spumeggiare
chute *n* canale di scolo
cider *n* sidro
cigar *n* sigaro; — **store** rivendita di tabacchi; tabaccheria; — **holder** bocchino
cigarette *n* sigaretta; — **butt** cicca, mozzicone; — **case** portasigarette *m*; — **holder** bocchino; — **lighter** accendisigari *m*; **filter** — sigaretta con filtro
cilia *npl* ciglia *fpl*
cinch *n* sottopancia, cigna; *(coll)* certezza; — *vt* assicurare con cigna
cincture *n* cintura
cinder *n* cenere, carbon fossile
cinemascope *n* cinemascopio
cinnamon *n* cannella
cipher *n* cifra *m*, zero
circle *n* circolo; *(astr)* orbita; **dress** — prima galleria; — *vt* circondare, accerchiare; — *vi* formare circolo
circuit *n* circuito; **short** — corto circuito
circuitous *a* tortuoso, indiretto
circular *a&n* circolare *m*
circulate *vt* mettere in circolazione
circulating *a* circolante; — **library** biblioteca circolante
circulation *n* circolazione; *(newspaper)* tiratura
circumcise *vt* circoncidere
circumference *n* circonferenza
circumflex *a* circonflesso
circumlocution *n* circonlocuzione
circumnavigate *vt* circumnavigare
circumscribe *vt* circoscrivere
circumspect *a* circospetto; **-ive** *a* circospettivo
circumspection *n* circospezione
circumstance *n* circostanza, condizione; stato, incidente *m*
circumstances *npl* circostanze *fpl*; **under no** — sotto nessun concetto; in nessun caso; **under the** — nelle circostanze
circumstantial *a* circostanziale; — **evidence** evidenza circostanziale
circumstantiate *vt* dettagliare
circumvent *vt* circonvenire, circuire
circus *n* circo equestre
cirrhosis *n* cirrosi *f*
cirrus *a* *(ast)* cirro; — **cloud** cirro
cistern *n* cisterna
citadel *n* cittadella
citation *n* citazione
cite *vt* citare; allegare testimonianze
citified *a* cittadinizzato
citizen *n* cittadino; **-ship** *n* cittadinanza
citric acid acido citrico
citron *n* cedro
citrus *a* citro; — **fruit** agrume *m*; — **grove** agrumeto
city *n* città; —**hall** municipio; — **planning** piano regolatore; — **editor** redattore del notiziario locale
civic *a* civico; **-s** *npl* diritto civile
civil *a* civile; *(manner)* cortese, urbano; — **engineer** ingegnere civile; — **service** amministrazione civile
civilian *n* borghese *m*
civilization *n* civiltà, civilizzazione
civility *n* cortesia, gentilezza
civilize *vt* civilizzare
civilized *a* civile
clabber *n* quaglio; — *vi* quagliare
clack *vi* scoppiettare, scoccare; — *n* scoppiettamento
clad *a* vestito; *(covered)* coperto
claim *vt* pretendere, reclamare; — *n* pretesa, reclamo
claimant *n* reclamante *m*, pretendente *m*
clairvoyance *n* chiaroveggenza
clairvoyant *a&n* chiaroveggente *m*
clam *n* pettine *m*, vongola; *(person, coll)* chiuso in sè *(fig)*; — **up** *(coll)* rinchiudersi in sè
clamber *vi* arrampicarsi
clammy *a* viscido, colloso, *(humid)* umidiccio
clamor *n* clamore *m*; **-ous** *a* chiassoso
clamp *n* rampone *m*, grappa; *(vise)* morsa; — *vt* stringere con la morsa; — **down** *(coll)* irrigidirsi
clan *n* clan *m*; tribù *f*; *(faction)* fazione
clandestine *a* clandestino
clang, clank *vt&i* risuonare; — *n* clan-

gore *m*
clannish *a* tradizionalista; strettamente unito alla famiglia
clap *vi* applaudire, battere le mani; — *vt* battere; *(fling)* gettare, lanciare; — *n (blow)* colpo; *(hands)* battimano; *(thunder)* scoppio
clapboard *n* assicella per rivestimento; — *a* di assicella per rivestimento
clapping *n* applauso, battimano
claptrap *n* sciocchezza, — *a* sciocco
claque *n* clac *f*; gente pagata per applaudire
claret *n* vino di Borgogna; chiaretto
clarify *vt&i* chiarire, chiarificare
clarinet *n* clarinetto
clarity *n* splendore *m*, chiarezza
clash *vi (collide)* urtarsi, cozzare; *(oppose)* opporsi, contrastare; — *vt* far produrre rumore
clash *n* urto, scontro, contrasto
clasp *n* fermaglio; — *vt* affibbiare, stringere, allacciare
class *n* classe *f*; lezione *f*; **–mate** *n* compagno di scuola; **–room** *n* aula; — **consciousness** coscienza di classe; — *vt* classificare
classic, –al *n&a* classico
classification *n* classificazione
classified *a* classificato; *(confidential)* riservato, segreto
classify *vt* classificare
clatter *n* rumore *m*; fracasso; — *vi* far rumore; — *vt* far fare rumore
clause *n* articolo; *(gram)* clausola; *(law)* proposizione
claustrophobia *n* claustrofobia
clavicle *n* clavicola
claw *n* artiglio; *(hammer)* taglio; *(shellfish)* pinza; — *vt* graffiare, lacerare
clay *n* creta, argilla; — **pigeon** piattello per tiro
clean *a* pulito, **–liness** *n* pulizia, nitidezza; **–ly** *adv* pulitamente
clean *vt* pulire, nettare; — **up** far pulizia; **–ing** *n* pulizia, pulitura
clean-cut *a* delineato, ben delineato
cleaner *n* nettatore, pulitore *m*
cleanse *vt* nettare, pulire
cleanser *n* nettatore, pulitore *m*
clean-shaven *a* rapato a zero
clear *a* chiaro, netto; — **complexion** bella carnagione; **be in the** — essere in regola; **keep** — **of** tenersi lontano da; **–ly** *adv* chiaramente; **–ness** *n* chiarezza
clear *vt* chiarire, chiarificare; — *vi* rischiararsi, schiarirsi; *(weather)* rasserenarsi, rimettersi; — **away** dissipare, svanire; — **the table** sgombrare; — **up** rischiararsi
clear– *(in comp)* **—cut** *a* tagliato nettamente, positivo; **—headed** *a* dalla mente chiara; **—sighted** *a* chiaroveggente
clearance *n (sale)* liquidazione; *(space)* spazio libero
clearing *n* chiarimento; *(debt)* regolamento dei conti; *(explanation)* schiarimento; *(land)* sgombero, dissodamento; *(woods)* radura; — **house** *(com)* stanza di compensazione
clearness *n* chiarezza
cleat *n* gattello
cleavage *n* taglio, fessura
cleave *vi* aderire a, attaccarsi a; — *vt* fendere, spaccare
cleaver *n* scure *f*
clef *n* chiave *f*
cleft *n* fessura; — **palate** labbro leporino
clemency *n* clemenza, mitezza
clement *a* clemente
clench *vt* impugnare; *(teeth, fist)* stringere
clergy *n* clero; **–man** *n* ecclesiastico, pastore *m*; *(priest)* sacerdote *m*, prete *m*
cleric *n* chierico; **–al** *a* clericale **–al work** lavoro d'ufficio
clerk *n* impiegato d'ufficio, commesso di negozio; — *vi* fare l'impiegato d'ufficio
clever *a* abile, capace, scaltro; ingegnoso; **–ly** *adv* abilmente
cleverness *n* abilità, intelligenza, merito
click *n* tintinnio; — *vi* tintinnare; *(sl)* accordarsi
client *n* cliente *m*; **–ele** *n* clientela
cliff *n* scogliera
climactic *a* climatico
climate *n* clima *m*
climax *n* culmine *m*, punto culminante; — *vi* ascendere, culminare
climb *vt&i* montare; *(clamber)* arrampicarsi; *(scale)* scalare; — *n* ascensione; scalata; — **indicator** *(avi)* ascensimetro; **–er** *n* ascensionista *m*
clinch *n* stretta; *(boxing)* abbraccio; — *vt* impugnare, *(boxing)* stringere in pugno; — **a bargain** concludere un affare
clincher *n* rampone *m*, gancio
cling *vi* aderire, aggrapparsi; **–ing** *a* agganciato
clingy *a* tenace
clinic *n* clinica; — *a* clinico; **–al** *a* clinico
clink *vt&i* tintinnare; — **glasses** toccare; *(toast)* fare un brindisi a; — *n* tintinnio; *(sl)* carcere *f*
clinker *n (coal)* scoria
clip *vt* tagliare; *(cut out)* ritagliare; *(cut short)* tagliar corto; *(shear)* tosare; *(words)* storpiare le parole; — *n* gancio; *(coll)* colpo; *(hair)* tosatura, taglio di capelli; *(paper)* fermaglio; **go at a good** — camminare speditamente
clipper *n* macchinetta per tosure; *(naut)* veliero rapido
clippers *npl (hair)* tosatrice *f*
clipping *n* ritaglio di giornale
clique *n* cricca
cloak *n* cappotto; *(mask)* maschera; *(pretext)* pretesto; — *vt (hide)* celare; coprire con mantello
cloakroom *n* guardaroba
clobber *vt (sl)* bastonare
clock *n* pendola, orologio; *(alarm)* sveglia; *(sock)* ricamo; **–maker** n orologiaio; **–wise** *a* destrorso, da sinistra
clockwork *n* orologeria; **go like** — andare come un orologio
clod *n* massa; *(sod)* gleba
clodhopper *n* tanghero; **–s** *npl* scarponi *mpl*
clog *n* intoppo; *(shoe)* zoccolo; — *vt* im-

pacciare, ostruire; — *vi* incagliarsi
cloister *n* chiostro; **–ed** *a* solitario; ritirato dal mondo
close *vt* chiudere; *(end)* finire; — **quarters** corpo a corpo; — **the ranks** serrare le file; — *vi* chiudersi; — *a (airless)* senz'aria; *(compact)* stretto, serrato; *(nearby)* vicino; *(reserved)* riservato; — **call** *(coll)* stretta scappatoia; — **friendship** amicizia stretta; — **shave** scampato liscio; — *adv* vicino; strettamente; — **by** vicino a
close- *(in comp)* **—mouthed** *a* reticente, incomunicativo; **—up** *n* fotografia di primo piano
closed *a* chiuso; — **circuit** circuito chiuso
closefisted *a* misero, avaro
closer *a* più vicino
closet *n* ripostiglio, armadio a muro; — *vt* chiudere nell'armadio
closing *n* chiusura, conclusione; — **of accounts** *(com)* chiusura dei conti
clot *n* coagulo; — *vi* coagularsi; — *vt* coagulare
cloth *n* stoffa, tessuto; — **binding** rilegatura in tela
clothe *vt* vestire, rivestire
clothes *npl* abiti *mpl;* **suit of** — abito completo; — **closet** guardaroba; armadio, guardaroba a muro; **–line** *n* corda per biancheria; **–pin** *n* moletta per la biancheria
clothier *n (maker)* fabbricante di tessuti; *(seller)* commerciante in tessuti
clothing *n* abiti *mpl*, vestiario
cloud *n* nuvola; **–burst** *n* acquazzone *m;* **be in the –s** essere fra le nuvole *(coll);* **–less** *a* sereno; **–y** *a* nuvoloso
cloud *vt* annuvolare; — *vi* rannuvolarsi
clove *n* chiodo di garofano
clover *n* trifoglio; **in** — nella bambagia *(coll)*; **be in** — vivere agiatamente
cloverleaf *n* quadrifoglio
clown *n* pagliaccio, buffone *m*; *(harlequin)* arlecchino; — *vi* fare il pagliaccio
cloy *vt* saziare; — *vi* saziarsi
club *n* circolo; *(card)* fiore *m*; *(weapon)* mazza; — **car** vagone bar; — **sandwich** panino imbottito; — **steak** lombo di manzo
club *vt* bastonare; — *vi* riunirsi
clubfoot *n* piede storto
clubhouse circolo
cluck *vi* chiocciare
clue *n* gomitolo, filo
clump *n* blocco, massa; — *vi* camminare pesantemente; — *vt* ammassare
clumsiness *n* grossolanità; *(weight)* pesantezza
clumsy *a* goffo, maldestro
cluster *n* grappolo; mazzetto; — *vt* riunire, aggrappolare; — *vi* riunirsi, aggrappolarsi
clutch *n* presa; *(auto)* frizione; *(mech)* innesto; — **pedal** pedale di frizione; — *vt* stringere, afferrare; **throw in the** — *(mech)* ingranare
clutches *npl* grinfie *fpl;* **in the** — nelle grinfie
clutter *n* disordine *m*, confusione; — *vt* ingombrare
coach *n (pupil's)* ripetitore *m; (sport)* allenatore *m; (teacher)* istruttore *m; (vehicle)* vettura, carrozza; — *vt* addestrare, preparare, dar lezione di ripetizione; — *vi* scarrozzare; andare in carrozza
coachman *n* cocchiere *m*
coagulant *n* coagulante *m*
coagulate *vt* coagulare; — *vi* coagularsi
coagulation *n* coagulazione
coal *n* carbone *m;* — **mine** miniera di carbone; — **oil** petrolio, kerosina; — **pit** pozzo di carbone; — **tar** catrame di carbone; **bituminous** — carbone bituminoso; **hard** — carbone duro; **soft** — carbone dolce; **rake over the –s** rimproverare, ridicolizzare
coalesce *vi* unirsi, fondersi, coalizzarsi
coalition *n* coalizione
coarse *a* grossolano, volgare, ruvido; **–ly** *adv* grossolanamente; **–ness** *n* grossolanità
coarsen *vt* rendere grossolano; — *vi* arrozzire, diventare grossolano
coast *n* costa, litorale *m;* — **line** litorale; — **guard** guardacosta; **have a clear** — essere fuori pericolo; **–al** *a* costiero; — *vi* costeggiare
coaster *n (glass)* sottobicchiere *m; (naut)* nave costiera; — **brake** freno contro pedale
coat *n* soprabito, pastrano; *(jacket)* giacca; *(paint, varnish)* strato; **–ing** *n (cloth)* stoffa; *(film)* strato; *(paint)* mano *f*; — **of arms** cotta d'arme; scudo nobiliare; **–ed** *a* vestito, coperto; — *vt* rivestire
coatroom *n* guardaroba
coax *vt* pregare con lusinghe; persuadere con moine; — *vi* usare persuasione
coaxing *n* adulazione; **–ingly** *adv* carezzevolmente, adulatamente
coaxial *a* coassiale; — **cable** cavo coassiale
cob *n (corn)* pannocchia; *(swan)* cigno
cobalt *n* cobalto
cobble *vt* rammendare; *(shoes)* rattoppare
cobbler *n* ciabattino
cobra *n* cobra
cobweb *n* ragnatela
cocaine *n* cocaina
cock *n* gallo; *(gun)* cane *m*; *(mech)* ago; — **and bull story** fandonia; **–ade** *n* coccarda; **–roach** *n* scarafaggio; **–sure** *a* sicurissimo; **–y** *a (coll)* vanitoso; arrogante; — *vt* drizzare; — *vi* drizzarsi
cocked *a* drizzato; — **hat** cappello a due punte; **knock into a** — **hat** sconfiggere completamente
cockeyed *a* strabico; *(sl)* a sghembo; alla ventitrè *(coll)*
cockpit *n (avi)* carlinga, abitacolo
cocksure *a* sicurissimo
cocktail *n* cocktail *m;* — **shaker** shaker *m*, bottiglia da cocktail
cocoa *n* cacao; — **butter** burro di cacao
coconut *n* noce di cocco
cocoon *n* bozzolo
C.O.D. contro assegno, pagamento alla consegna
cod, –fish *n* merluzzo; **dried** — baccalà *m*

coda *n* codetta
coddle *vt* vezzeggiare; *(cooking)* cuocere lentamente
code *n* codice *m;* **secret** — cifrario; — *vt* cifrare
codex *n* manoscritto antico
codicil *n* codicillo
cod-liver oil olio di fegato di merluzzo
coeducation *n* coeducazione
coeducational *a* coeducazionale; — **school** scuola mista
coefficient *n* coefficiente *m*
coequal *a* eguale, coéguale
coerce *vt* forzare, costringere, obbligare
coexist *vi* coesistere; **-ence** *n* coesistenza
coffee *n* caffè *m;* — **bean** chicco di caffè; — **mill** macinino da caffè; — **plantation** piantagione di caffè; — **pot** caffettiera; — **shop** caffè, ristorante *m*
coffer *n* cofano, scrigno
coffin *n* bara, cassa da morto
cog *n* dente di ruota; — **railway** ferrovia a cremagliera; **-wheel** *n* ruota dentata, ingranaggio
cogent *a* evidente; urgente; *(strong)* forte, potente
cogitate *vi* cogitare, meditare
cognac *n* cognac *m*
cognate *a* parente, consanguineo
cognizance *n* cognizione
cognizant *a* competente, istruito
cognomen *n* cognome *m*
cohabit *vi* coabitare; **-ation** *n* coabitazione
cohere *vi* aderire a; *(agree)* concordare
coherence *n* coerenza
coherent *a* coerente
cohesion *n* aderenza, coesione
cohesive *a* coesivo
cohort *n* coorte *f*
coiffure *n* pettinatura
coil *vt* avvolgere, arrotolare; — *vi* piegarsi, avvolgersi; — *n* rotolo; *(elec)* bobina
coin *n* moneta; **-age** *n* conio; invenzione; — *vt* coniare, battere moneta; — **a word** inventare una parola
coincide *vi* coincidere
coincidence *n* combinazione, coincidenza, concordanza
coincident *a* coincidente; **-al** *a* coincidentale
coke *n (fuel)* coke *m*
colander *n* colatoio, colabrodo
cold *n* freddo, *(med)* raffreddore *m*; **take** — pigliare un raffreddore, raffreddarsi; — *a* freddo; **be** — *(person)* aver freddo; — **cream** *(cosmetic)* crema di bellezza; — **storage** conservazione a freddo; — **weather** tempo freddo; **-ness** *n* freddezza, freddo; **-ly** *adv* freddamente
cold- *(in comp)* **—blooded** *a* di sangue freddo, insensibile; **—wave** *n (weather)* ondata di freddo
colic *n* colica
coliseum *n* colosseo
colitis *n* colite *f*
collaborate *vt&i* collaborare
collaboration *n* collaborazione
collaborator *n* collaboratore *m*
collapse *vi* crollare, avere un collasso; — *vt* provocare collasso; — *n* crollo; sfacelo; *(med)* collasso, prostrazione; **nervous** — esaurimento nervoso
collapsible *a* pieghevole, ribaltabile
collar *vt* prendere per il collo; *(fig)* catturare
collar *n* collare *m; (coat)* bavero; *(shirt)* colletto; **-bone** *n* clavicola
collate *vt* collazionare
collateral *n&a* collaterale *m*
colleague *n* collega *m&f*
collect *vi* raccogliere, collezionare, riscuotere; *(money)* incassare; **-or** *n* collezionista *m*; *(com)* controllore *m*; *(tax)* esattore *m*
collective *a* collettivo; — **bargaining** contratto collettivo
collection *n* raccolta, collezione
collectivism *n* collettivismo
college *n* collegio; scuola superiore; università; facoltà di università; **electoral** — collegio elettorale
collegiate *a* collegiato
collide *vi* scontrarsi, urtarsi
collie *n* cane da pastore scozzese
collision *n* collisione, scontro, investimento, urto
collocate *vt* collocare
collocation *n* collocamento, collocazione
colloid *n&a* colloide *m*
colloquial *a* familiare; della lingua parlata; **-ism** *n* parola familiare; espressione familiare
colloquy *n* colloquio
collusion *n* collusione, connivenza, complicità
cologne *n* colonia *(coll);* **C-** Colonia
colon *n (anat)* colon *m; (gram)* due punti
colonel *n* colonnello
colonial *a* coloniale
colonist *n* colono
colonize *vt* colonizzare; — *vi* formare una colonia
colony *n* colonia
color *n* colore *m*, colorito; **change** — cambiar colore; **-less** *a* incolore, insulso; — *vt* colorare
coloration *n* colorazione
colorblindness *n* daltonismo
colored *a* colorato; — **people** *npl* gente di colore
coloring *n* colore *m*; colorito; *(skin)* carnagione *f*
colossal *a* colossale
colt *n* puledro
columbine *n* aquilegia
column *n* colonna; *(newspaper)* rubrica, colonna di giornale
coma *n* coma *m*
comatose *a* comatoso
comb *n* pettine *m*; *(cock)* cresta; *(hair)* pettine per capelli; *(honey)* favo; — *vt* pettinare; — **out** *(fig)* eliminare; — *vi* pettinarsi
combat *n* combattimento; — **fatigue** psicopatia di guerra
combat *vt* combattere; — *vi* contendere con; **-ive** *a* combattivo, litigioso
combatant *n&a* combattente *m*

combination *n* combinazione; — **lock** serratura a combinazione
combine *vt* combinare; — *vi* combinarsi, allearsi; — *n (coll)* consorzio, combriccola; *(com)* società; *(mech)* macchina trebbiatrice
combined *a* combinato; — **efforts** sforzi combinati
combustible *a&n* combustibile *m*
combustion *n* combustione; — **chamber** camera di scoppio
come *vi* venire; — **about** accadere; — **after** *(follow)* seguire; *(get)* venire a prendere; — **again** ritornare; — **apart** separàrsi, — **away** venire via; — **back** tornare; — **between** intervenire; — **by** *(get)* ottenare, acquistare; *(pass)* passare; — **down** scendere; — **for** venire per; — **forward** avanzarsi; — **home** tornare a casa; — **in** entrare; **C– in!** Avanti!; **May I (we)** — **in?** Si può?; — **near** avvicinarsi; — **of age** diventare maggiorenne; **off** staccarsi; **C– on!** Andiamo!; — **out** uscire; *(stain)* scomparire; — **through** riuscire; — **to** *(amount to)* ammontare; *(revive)* riaversi; — **to terms** mettersi d'accordo; — **undone** sfarsi; — **up** venire su; venire a galla *(fig)*; — **what may** qualunque cosa avvenga *(fig)*; — **up with** raggiungere
comeback *n* ritorno
comedian *n* comico, buffone *m*; *(theat)* commediante *m*
comedown *n (coll)* caduta
comedy *n* commedia; **musical** — burletta, opera comica, operetta
comeliness *n* bellezza, avvenenza
comely *a* avvenente, grazioso, bello
comet *n* cometa
comfort *n* consolazione, conforto; *(body)* comodità; **–er** *n* confortatore *m*; *(bedding)* imbottita, coltrone *m*; **–able** *a* confortevole; comodo; **–ably** *adv* comodamente; — *vt* confortare, consolare; **–ing** *a* confortante
comic *n* comico; — **book** giornalino per i piccoli; — **opera** opera buffa; — **strip** fumetto; vignetta
comical *a* comico
coming *n* venuta, arrivo; — *a* prossimo
comma *n* virgola
command *vt* comandare, ordinare; — *vi* essere al comando; — *n* comando, ordine *m*, padronanza; **–er** *n* comandante *m*, capo; **–ment** *n* comandamento
commanding *a* autoritario
commando *n* reparto di truppe d'assalto
commandeer *vt* requisire
commemorate *vt* commemorare
commemoration *n* commemorazione
commemorative *a* commemorativo
commence *vt&i* cominciare, incominciare, iniziare, mettersi a
commencement *n (beginning)* inizio; *(graduation)* cerimonia della consegna del diploma
commend *vt (praise)* lodare, elogiare; *(recommend)* raccomandare; **–able** *a* raccomandabile; **–ation** *n* raccomandazione; **–atory** *a* raccomandatorio
commensurate *a* commisurato
comment *n* commento, osservazione; — *vt* commentare, criticare; — *vi* fare commento
commentary *n* commento, annotazioni *fpl*
commentator *n* commentatore *m*
commerce *n* commercio
commercial *a* commerciale; — **art** arte commerciale; — **college** scuola commerciale; — *n (rad, TV)* annunzio pubblicitario, **–ize** *vt* commercializzare
commiserate *vt* commiserare
commiseration *n* commiserazione
commissar *n* commissario; **–iat** *n* commissariato
commissary *n* commissario
commission *n* commissione; provvigione *f*; — **house** ditta per commissioni; — **merchant** commissionario; **out of** — fuori uso; — *vt* commissionare; incaricare con una missione
commissioned *a* inviato in missione, commissionato
commit *vt* fare, affidare, commettere; — **to memory** imparare a memoria
commitment *n* consegna
committee *n* comitato, commissione
commodious *a* comodo
commodity *n* prodotto, derrata
commodore *n* commodoro
common *a* comune; *(usual)* ordinario; *(vulgar)* triviale; — **carrier** vettore *m*; — **sense** buon senso; — **stock** *(com)* titolo in comune; **in** — in comune
commonplace *n* banalità; — *a* banale; volgare
commonwealth *n* stato; repubblica
commotion *n* agitazione, tumulto, chiasso
communal *a* comunale
commune *vi* conferire, discorrere; — **with oneself** meditare
commune *n* comune *m*
communicable *a* comunicabile
communicant *n* comunicando
communicate *vt* comunicare, trasmettere; — *vi* comunicarsi, fare la comunione
communication *n* comunicazione
communicative *a* comunicativo
communion *n* comunione; **take** — comunicarsi
communiqué *n* comunicato ufficiale
communism *n* comunismo
communist *n* comunista *m&f*; **–ic** *a* comunista, comunistico
community *n* comunità, collettività; *(locality)* vicinato; *(village)* paese *m*; — **chest** fondo di comunità; — **center** luogo di riunione di una comunità
communize *vt* socializzare, accomunare
commutation *n* commutazione; — **ticket** abbonamento combinato
commutator *n* commutatore *m*
commute *vt* commutare; sostituire; — *vi* fare sostituzione di; viaggiare giornalmente con abbonamento combinato
commuter *n* colui che viaggia al lavoro
compact *a* compatto; **–ly** *adv* concisamente
compact *n (agreement)* patto, contratto; *(auto)* piccola automobile; *(powder)* portacipria *m*
companion *n* compagno, compagna; **–ship** *n* compagnia, cameratismo, amicizia

companionable *a* socievole
companionway *n* scaletta
company *n* compagnia, società; **part —** separarsi
comparable *a* paragonabile
comparative *a* comparativo, relativo; **–ly** *adv* comparativamente, relativamente
compare *vt* paragonare, confrontare; **— notes** fare uno scambio di idee
comparison *n* paragone *m*, confronto; **beyond —** senza confronto, senza paragone; **in — with** in confronto a
compartment *n* compartimento, scompartimento
compass *n (naut)* bussola; *(range)* limite *m*, portata; **—** *vt* circondare, andare attorno; *(achieve)* compiere
compassion *n* compassione, pietà; **–ate** *a* compassivo, compassionevole
compatible *a* compatibile
compatriot *n* compatriota *m&f*
compel *vt* costringere, obbligare, forzare
compellation *n* appello
compensate *vt* compensare, risarcire; **—** *vi* compensarsi
compensation *n* compenso, ricompensa, indennità
compensator *n* compensatore *m*, compensatrice *f*
compensatory *a* compensativo
compete *vi* concorrere, gareggiare
competence *n* competenza
competent *a* competente, capace, abile
competition *n* competizione, gara, concorso
competitive *a* competitivo
competitor *n* competitore, concorrente *m*
compilation *n* compilazione, raccolta
compile *vt* compilare
compiler *n* compilatore *m*
complain *vi* lamentarsi
complainant *n* accusatore, querelante *m*
complaint *n* lamento; *(protest)* protesta, reclamo, accusa; *(law)* querela; *(med)* malattia, disturbo; **lodge a —** dar querela
complaisance *n* compiacenza
complaisant *a* compiacente
complement *n* complemento; **—** *vt* completare, riempiere; **–ary** *a* complementare
complete *a* finito, completo; **—** *vt* completare, terminare, finire; **–ly** *adv* completamente
completion *n* complemento, fine *f*, termine *m*
complex *a&n* complesso; **inferiority —** *n* complesso di inferiorità
complexion *n* carnagione *f*, colorito
complexity *n* complessità; complicazione
compliance *n* obbedienza, acquiescenza; **in — with** in conformità con
compliant *a* condiscendente
complicate *vt* complicare; **–d** *a* complicato
complication *n* complicazione
complicity *n* complicità
compliment *n* complimento; *(eulogy)* elogio; *(homage)* omaggio; **—** *vt* felicitare, lodare
complimentary *a* laudativo, complimentoso; *(gratis)* gratuito, in omaggio, di favore; **— ticket** biglietto-omaggio
component *a&n* componente
compose *vt* comporre; **—** *vi* fare composizioni, creare; **–d** *a* disinvolto, calmo, tranquillo; **be –d of** consistere di
composer *n* compositore *m*
composite *a* composto
composition *n* composizione, natura, componimento
compositor *n* compositore *m*
compost *n* composto
composure *n* disinvoltura, calma; sangue freddo
compote *n* composta, conserva
compound *vt* comporre, combinare; **—** *vi* venire a una transazione; **— a felony** comporre (*or* sospendere) un'accusa di delitto; **—** *n* composto; **—** *a* composto, composito
comprehend *vt* comprendere, concepire, capire, includere
comprehensible *a* comprensibile
comprehension *n* comprensione
comprehensive *a* comprensivo, spazioso, vasto
compress *n* compressa
compress *vt* comprimere, condensare; **–ed** *a* compresso
compressor *n (mech)* compressore *m*
compression *n* compressione
comprise *vt* comprendere, includere; **–d** *a* compreso, incluso
compromise *n* compromesso, transazione; **—** *vt* compromettere, transigere; **—** *vi* compromettersi
comptometer *n* comptometro
comptroller *n* controllore *m*; **–ship** *n* controlleria
compulsion *n* compulsione, costrizione
compulsive *a* obbligatorio, forzato; **–ly** *adv* forzosamente
compulsory *a* obbligatorio
compunction *n* compunzione
computation *n* computo
compute *vt* calcolare
computer *n* computatore *m*, computatrice *f*
comrade *n* camerata *m*, compagno; **–ship** *n* cameratismo
concave *a* concavo
conceal *vt* celare, nascondere; **–ed** *a* celato, nascosto
concealment *n (deception)* dissimulazione; *(hiding)* celamento
concede *vt* concedere, ammettere
conceit *n* vanità, amor proprio, presunzione, boria; **–ed** *a* presuntuoso, vanitoso, vanesio; **–edly** *adv* vanamente; infatuatamente
conceivable *a* concepibile
conceive *vt&i* concepire, immaginare
concentrate *vt* concentrare; **—** *vi* concentrarsi, raccogliersi; **— on** convergere; **–d** *a* concentrato
concentrate *n* concentrato, essenza
concentration *n* concentrazione
concentric *a* concentrico
concept *n* concetto, idea
conception *n* concezione; *(idea)* concetto
concern *vt* riguardare, concernere, inte-

ressare; — **oneself** interessarsi, occuparsi

concern *n (com)* ditta, azienda; *(interest)* cura, interesse *m*, faccenda, affare *m*; *(worry)* preoccupazione

concerned *a* preoccupato; interessato; **as far as . . . is** — per ciò che riguarda

concerning *prep* di; quanto a, relativo a, riguardante a

concert *n* concerto; **–ed** *a* concertato

concert *vt* concertare; — *vi* concertarsi

concession *n* concessione

conciliate *vt* conciliare

conciliation *n* conciliazione

conciliatory *a* conciliatorio

concise *a* conciso

conclave *n* conclave *m*

conclude *vt&i* concludere, terminare, finire; *(deduce)* dedurre

conclusion *n* conclusione

conclusive *a* conclusivo; **–ly** *adv* conclusivamente

concoct *vt (develop)* elaborare; *(plot)* complottare; *(prepare)* preparare

concoction *n* elaborazione; complottazione; *(mixture)* miscela

concomitant *a* concomitante, accessorio; — *n* compagno, accessorio

concord *n* concordia, armonia; — **grape** uva concordia; — *vi* concordare

concourse *n* concorso, affluenza

concrete *n* cemento, *(arch)* calcestruzzo; — **mixer** betoniera: — *a* concreto; di calcestruzzo

concubine *n* concubina

concupescence *n* concupiscenza

concur *vi* convenire con, concordare con, accordarsi

concurrence *n* concorrenza

concurrent *a* concorrente, simultaneo; **–ly** *adv* simultaneamente

concussion *n* scossa, concussione; *(brain)* trauma, commozione cerebrale

condemn *vt* condannare, biasimare

condemnation *n* condanna

condensation *n* condensazione

condense *vt* condensare, abbreviare

condenser *n* condensatore *m*

condescend *vi* accondiscendere; *(deign)* degnarsi; **–ing** *a* condiscendente

condescension *n* condiscendenza

condiment *n* condimento

condition *n* condizione; **–al** *a* condizionale; — *vt* imporre condizioni; — *vi* stipulare

condole *vi* fare le condoglianze, condolersi

condolence *n* condoglianza

condone *vt* condonare, perdonare, scusare

conduce *vi* contribuire, tendere

conducive *a* tendente, favorevole

conduct *n* condotta, contegno, procedimento

conduct *vt* guidare, dirigere; condurre a; — **oneself** *(behave)* comportarsi; — *vi (phy)* condurre

conductivity *n (elec)* conduttività

conduction *n* conduzione

conductor *n* capotreno; *(streetcar)* conduttore *m*; *(elec)* conduttore *m*; *(mus)* direttore *m*, direttrice *f*

conduit *n* condotto, condotta

cone *n* cono; *(bot)* pigna, pina; *(ice cream)* cono gelato; *(paper)* cartoccio

confection *n* confetto, conserva

confectionery *n* confettureria; — **store** confetteria

confederacy *n* confederazione; lega

confederate *a&n* confederato; — *vt* federare, confederare; — *vi* federarsi, confederarsi

confederation *n* confederazione

confer *vt&i* conferire; — **with** conferire con; avere una conferenza con

conference *n* conferenza, colloquio; *(meeting)* riunione *f*

confess *vt* confessare; — *vi* confessarsi; — **to** ammettere di

confession *n* confessione; **–al** *n* confessionale *m*

confessor *n* confessore *m*

confetti *npl* coriandoli *mpl*

confidant *n* confidente *m*

confide *vt&i* confidare; aver fiducia

confidence *n* fiducia; **in strict** — in stretta confidenza; — **game** abuso di fiducia; — **man** abusatore di fiducia

confident *a* confidente; **–ly** *adv* fiduciosamente

confidential *a* confidenziale

confiding *a* confidente, fiducioso

configuration *n* configurazione

confine *vt* confinare; — **oneself** limitarsi; **–d to bed** obbligato a letto

confinement *n* confino, ritiro; *(law)* reclusione; **solitary** — segregazione cellulare

confirm *vt* confermare; *(eccl)* cresimare; **–ation** *n* conferma; cresima; **–atory** *a* confermatorio; **–ative** *a* confermativo; **–ed** *a* inveterato; **–ing** *a* confermante

confiscate *vt* confiscare

confiscation *n* confisca

conflagration *n* conflagrazione, accensione

conflict *n* conflitto, contrasto

conflict *vi* contrastare, essere in conflitto; **–ing** *a* in conflitto, contrastante

conform *vt* conformare, adattare; — *vi* adattarsi, conformarsi; **–able** *a* conforme a; sottomesso a; **–ation** *n* conformazione; **–ist** *n* conformista *m*; **–ity** *n* conformità

confound *vt* confondere; **–ed** *a* confuso

confront *vt* confrontare, affrontare

confuse *vt* confondere, turbare, sconcertare; **–ed** *a* confuso, disordinato

confusedly *adv* confusamente

confusion *n* confusione; **be covered with** — essere imbarazzato

confute *vt* confutare

congeal *vt* congelare, gelare; coagulare; — *vi* congelarsi; coagularsi; **–ed** *a* congelato

congenial *a* simpatico, gradevole

congenital *a* congenito

congest *vt&i* riunire, ammassare, congestionare

congested *a* riunito, congestionato; — **district** settore superpopolato

congestion *n* congestione *f*

conglomerate *a* conglomerato
conglomeration *n* conglomerazione, conglomerato
congratulate *vt* felicitare
congratulation *n* congratulazione; **–s** *npl* congratulazioni, complimenti
congregate *vt* radunare, riunire; — *vi* adunarsi, riunirsi
congregation *n* congregazione; **–al** *a* congregazionale
congress *n* congresso; **–man** *n* congressista *m*
congressional *a* congressionale, del congresso
congruent *a* congruente
congruity *n* congruismo, congruità
congruous *a* congruo
conical *a* conico
conifer *n* conifera
conjecture *n* congettura, supposizione; — *vt&i* congetturare
conjugal *a* coniugale
conjugate *vt* coniugare
conjugation *n* coniugazione
conjunction *n* congiunzione
conjunctive *a* congiuntivo
conjunctivitis *n* congiuntivite *f*
conjure *vt&i* scongiurare
conjurer *n* prestigiatore *m*
connect *vt* connettere, unire; — *vi* far coincidenza, connettersi, unirsi; **–ing** *a* d'unione, di comunicazione; **–ed** *a* connesso, unito, imparentato
connection *n* rapporto, relazione; *(elec)* connessione, contatto
connivance *n* connivenza
connive *vi* avere connivenza con
conniving *a* connivente
connoisseur *n* intenditore *m*, intenditrice *f*; buongustaio
connotation *n* senso, significato
connote *vt* implicare; significare indirettamente
connubial *a* coniugale, connubiale
conquer *vt&i* vincere, conquistare; **–or** *n* vincitore *m*
conquest *n* conquista
consanguinity *n* consanguinità
conscience *n* coscienza; **in all** — in tutta coscienza
conscience-stricken *a* con peso di coscienza *(fig)*
conscientious *a* coscienzioso; **–ly** *adv* coscienziosamente
conscious *a* conscio, consapevole; **–ly** *adv* consciamente; **–ness** *n* conoscenza, coscienza
conscript *vt* coscrivere, reclutare
conscription *n* coscrizione, reclutamento
consecrate *vt* consacrare, benedire; **–d** *a* consacrato
consecration *n* consacrazione
consecutive *a* consecutivo
consensus *n* consenso
consent *vi* acconsentire; approvare, accettare; — *n* consenso, accordo
consequence *n* conseguenza; **take the –s** pagare le conseguenze
consequent *a* conseguente; **–ly** *adv* in conseguenza, conseguentemente
consequential *a* conseguenziale, logico
conservation *n* conservazione
conservative *a* conservativo; — *n* conservatore *m*, conservatrice *f*
conservatory *n* conservatorio musicale; *(hothouse)* serra; — *a* conservativo
conserve *vt* conservare; *(in syrup)* mettere in conserva
conserve *n* conserva
consider *vt&i* considerare, riflettere sopra; **–ed** *a* considerato; **–able** *a* considerabile; **–ate** *a* considerato, di considerazione
consideration *n* considerazione; **in — of** in considerazione di; **under no —** sotto nessuna circostanza; **take into —** prendere in considerazione; **under —** in esame, allo studio
considering that in considerazione di; considerando che
consign *vt&i* consegnare; **—ee** *n* consegnatario; **–or** *n* depositante *m*; *(sender)* mittente *m*
consignment *n* consegna; deposito; **on —** in deposito
consist *vi* consistere; **–ency** *n* consistenza; **–ent** *a* consistente
consistory *n* concistoro
consolation *n* consolazione
console *vt* consolare
console *n* mensola
consolidate *vt* consolidare; — *vi* consolidarsi
consolidation *n* consolidamento
consommé *n* brodo ristretto
consonant *a&n* consonante *f*
consort *n* consorte *m*
consort *vt* associare, unire; — *vi* associarsi, unirsi; — **with** associarsi con
conspicuous *a* cospicuo; **–ly** *adv* cospicuamente
conspiracy *n* congiura, complotto, cospirazione
conspirator *n* cospiratore *m*, cospiratrice *f*
conspire *vt&i* complottare, congiurare
constabulary *npl* corpo di polizia
constancy *n* costanza
constant *a* costante, ininterrotto; — *n* *(math)* costante *f*; **–ly** *adv* costantemente
constellation *n* costellazione
consternate *vt* costernare; **–d** *a* costernato
consternation *n* costernazione, sgomento
constipate *vt* costipare; **–d** *a* costipato
constipation *n* costipazione
constituency *n* circoscrizione elettorale
constituent *a* costituente
constitute *vt* costituire
constitution *n* costituzione
constitutional *a* costituzionale; — *n* passeggiata igienica
constitutionality *n* costituzionalità
constrain *vt* costringere; **–ed** *a* costretto
constraint *n* costrizione
constrict *vt* costringere
constriction *n* costrizione
constrictor *n* costrittore *m*; **boa —** *n* serpente boa
construct *vt* costruire; **–or** *n* costruttore *m*

construction *n* costruzione; **give a wrong —** mal interpretare; **–al** *a* strutturale; di costruzione
constructive *a* costruttivo
construe *vt* interpretare
consubstantiate *vt* consustanziare
consul *n* console *m*; **–ar** *a* consolare
consulate *n* consolato
consult *vt* consultare; — *vi* consultarsi con; **–ing** *a* consultante; **–ation** *n* consulto; **–ant** *n* consultante *m*
consume *vt* consumare; — *vi* consumarsi; **–d** *a* consumato
consumer *n* consumatore *m*
consummate *a* consumato
consummate *vt* consumare, finire
consummation *n* consumazione
consumption *n* consumazione; *(med)* consunzione
contact *n* contatto; **— lenses** *npl* lenti di contatto
contact *vt&i* fare contatto, mettersi a contatto
contagion *n* contagio
contagious *a* contagioso
contain *vt* contenere; **— oneself** contenersi
contaminate *vt* contaminare
contamination *n* contaminazione
contemplate *vt&i* contemplare, meditare
contemplation *n* contemplazione, meditazione
contemporaneous *a* contemporaneo; **–ly** *adv* contemporaneamente
contemporary *n&a* contemporaneo
contempt *n* disprezzo; **–ible** *a* spregevole
contemptuous *a* sprezzante
contend *vt* contendere, contestare; — *vi* pretendere
content *n* contentezza; **to one's heart's —** a volontà; — *a* contento; **–ed** *a* contento, contentato; — *vt* accontentare
contention *n* controversia; **bone of —** seme di discordia
contentment *n* contentamento
contents *npl* contenuto; **table of —** indice *m*
contest *vt* contestare; — *vi* lottare, concorrere; **–ant** *n* contestante *m*
contest *n* contestazione, concorso; **beauty —** concorso di bellezza
context *n* contesto, senso
contextual *a* contestuale
contiguity *n* contiguità
continguous *a* contiguo
continence *n* continenza
continent *n* continente *m;* **–al** *a* continentale
contingency *n* contingenza
contingent *a* contingente; — *n* contingente *m*
continual *a* continuo; **–ly** *adv* continuamente
continuance *n* continuazione, continuità
continuation *n* continuazione
continue *vt&i* continuare; **–d** *a* continuo
continuity *n* continuità; *(movies)* copione cinematografico; *(radio)* copione per radio
continuous *a* continuo
contort *vt* contorcere, attorcigliare
contortion *n* contorsione; **–ist** *n* contorsionista *m&f*
contour *n* contorno; **— plowing** rilievo topografico
contraband *n* contrabbando
contraception *n* contracconcezione, antifecondazione
contract *n* contratto; **party to a —** contraente *m;* **–ing** *a* contrattante; **–or** *n* contraente *m,* imprenditore *m*; — *vt* *(com)* contrarre
contract *vt (med)* contrarre; **–ed** *a* contrattato; **–ible** *a* contrattile; **–ibility** *n* contrattilità
contraction *n* contrazione
contradict *vt&i* contraddire; **–ory** *a* contradditorio
contradiction *n* contraddizione
contrail *n (avi)* fumeggio, scia
contralto *n* contralto
contrariness *n* contrarietà
contrary *a&n* contrario; **on the —** al contrario
contrast *vi* contrastare; — *vt* mettere in contrasto; — *n* contrasto; **–ing** *a* contrastante
contravene *vt* contravvenire
contribute *vt&i* contribuire
contribution *n* contributo
contributor *n* contributore *m*, contributrice *f*
contributory *a* contributivo
contrite *a* contrito
contrition *n* contrizione
contrivance *n* escogitazione, invenzione
contrive *vt* escogitare; — *vi* ingegnarsi
control *vt* controllare; **— oneself** controllarsi; — *n* controllo; **— stick** *(avi)* cloche *f*, leva di comando; **— tower** *(avi)* torre di controllo
controller *n* controllore *m*
controversial *a* di controversia, controverso
controversy *n* controversia
contusion *n* contusione
conundrum *n* indovinello
convalesce *vi* essere convalescente
convalescence *n* convalescenza
convalescent *a&n* convalescente *m&f;* **— home** convalescenziaro
convection *n* convezione
convene *vt* convenire; — *vi* adunarsi
convenience *n* convenienza, **at one's —** con comodità; a bell'agio
convenient *a* conveniente; **–ly** *adv* convenientemente
convent *n* convento
convention *n* convenzione; **–al** *a* convenzionale
converge *vt&i* convergere
convergence *n* convergenza
convergent *a* convergente
converging *a* convergente
conversant *a* versato in
conversation *n* conversazione, **— piece** *(arts)* gruppo; **–al** *a* di conversazione; **–alist** *n* parlatore *m*, parlatrice *f*
converse *vi* conversare
converse *a* reciproco; **–ly** *adv* reciprocamente, per converso
conversion *n* conversione

convert *vt* convertire; — *vi* convertirsi; **-er** *(elec)* convertitore *m*
convert *n* convertito
convertibility *n* convertibilità
convertible *a* convertibile; — *n (auto)* convertibile, decapottabile *m*
convex *a* convesso
convey *vt* portare, trasmettere, trasferire; — **thanks** inviare ringraziamenti
conveyance *n* trasporto
conveyor *n* trasportatore *m*, trasportatrice *f*
convict *vt* condannare
convict *n* condannato, detenuto, forzato
conviction *n* convinzione
convince *vt* convincere
convincible *a* convincibile
convincing *a* convincente; **-ly** *adv* in modo convincente
convivial *a* conviviale; **-ity** *n* convivialità
convocation *n* convocazione; **-al** *a* convocazionale
convolution *n* convoluzione
convoy *n* convoglio, scorta; — *vt* convogliare, scortare
convulse *vt* agitare, mettere in convulsione; **-d** *a* convulso
convulsion *n* convulsione
convulsive *a* convulsivo
coo *vi* tubare, gemere; **-ing** *n* il tubare
cook *n* cuoco; — *vt&i* cuocere; — **one's goose** *(fig)* dare il colpo di grazia; — **up** *(coll)* arrangiare; **-ed** *a* cotto; *(coll)* falsificato; **-ing** *n* cucina
cookie *n* pasticcino
cool *a* fresco; — *vt&i* raffreddare, rinfrescare; — **down** calmarsi; **-ly** *adv* indifferentemente; **-ing** *a* rinfrescante
cooler *n* rinfrescatoio
cooling-off period periodo di assestamento
coolness *n* fresco; *(manner)* indifferenza
coop *n* stia; — *vt* rinchiudere
co-operate *vi* cooperare
co-operation *n* cooperazione
co-operative *a* cooperativo; — *n* cooperativa
co-ordinate *vt* coordinare; — *vi* coordinarsi
co-ordination *n* coordinazione
co-ordinator *n* coordinatore *m*
coot *n* folaga
cop *n (sl)* poliziotto; — *vt (sl)* acchiappare, afferrare
copartner *n* socio
cope *n* cappa; — *vt* coprire; — **with** lottare contro
coping *n* comignolo
copious *a* copioso
copper *n* rame *m*; **-y** *a* di rame
copra *n* copra *m*
copse *n* bosco ceduo
copy *n* copia; — *vt&i* copiare, imitare; **-book** *n* quaderno; **-cat** *n* scimmia *(fig)*
copyright *n* diritto d'autore; — *vt* patentare; assicurare (*or* comprare) la esclusiva artistica
coquette *n* civetta *(fig)*
coquettish *a* civettuolo, vezzoso
coral *n* corallo; — *a* corallino; di corallo; — **reef** banco di corallo
cord *n* corda, cordone *m*; *(elec)* filo; cavo elettrico; **spinal** — spina dorsale; — *vt* legare con corda; *(wood)* misurare
cordage *n* cordame *m*
corded *a* fatto a corda, di corda
cordial *a* cordiale; — *n* cordiale *m;* **-ly** *adv* cordialmente; **-ity** *n* cordialità
cording *n* legamento; *(wood)* misura
cordon *n* cordone *m*
corduroy *n* corderoy *m*, fustagno; — *a* di corderoy
core *n* cuore *m*; nocciolo; — *vt* vuotare, estrarre il torsolo
co-respondent *n* coimputato
cork *n* sughero, turacciolo; — *a* di sughero; — *vt* turare, tappare; **-screw** *n* cavaturaccioli *m*
corn *vt* salare
corn *n* grano, cereale *m*, granturco; *(foot)* callo; — **borer** *n* parassita del granturco
corncob *n* pannocchia
corner *vt* rincantucciare; — *vi* essere in angolo; trovarsi all'angolo; — *n* angolo; **turn the** — girare l'angolo; **cut -s** *(fig)* accorciare; **-ed** *a* ad angolo, angoloso
cornerstone *n* pietra angolare
cornet *n (mus)* cornetta; *(paper)* cartoccio
cornice *n* cornice *f*
cornstarch *n* amido di grano, fecola di grano
corollary *n* corollario
corona *n* corona
coronary *a* coronario; — **thrombosis** *n* trombosi coronaria
coronation *n* incoronazione
coroner *n* giudice istruttore
coronet *n* corona, diadema
corporal *n (mil)* caporale *m*; *(eccl)* corporale *m*; — *a* corporeo; corporale; — **punishment** punizione corporale
corporate *a* corporativo
corporation *n* corporazione
corporeal *a* corporeo
corps *n* corpo; *(avi)* aviazione, corpo areonautico
corpse *n* corpo, cadavere *m*
corpulence *n* corpulenza
corpulent *a* corpulento
corpuscle *n* corpuscolo
corral *n* recinto; — *vt* raccogliere
correct *vt* correggere; — *a* corretto; **-ive** *a* correttivo, di correzione; **-ness** *n* correttezza; **-ional** *a* correzionale; **-ly** *adv* correttamente
correction *n* correzione
correlate *a* correlazionato, correlativo; — *vt* correlazionare; — *vi* essere in relazione
correlation *n* correlazione
correlative *a&n* correlativo
correspond *vi* corrispondere; **-ent** *n* corrispondente *m;* **-ing** *a* corrispondente
correspondence *n* corrispondenza, — **school** scuola per corrispondenza
corridor *n* corridore *m*
corrigible *a* correggibile
corroborate *vt* corroborare

corroboration *n* corroboramento, corroborazione
corroborator *n* corroboratore; **–y** *a* corroborante
corrode *vt* corrodere, rodere; — *vi* corrodersi, rodersi
corrosion *n* corrosione
corrosive *a* corrosivo
corrugate *vt* corrugare, ondulare; — *vi* corrugarsi, ondularsi, **–d** *a* corrugato, ondulato
corrupt *vt* corrompere; — *vi* corrompersi; **–ibility** *n* corruttibilità; **–ible** *a* corruttibile; **–ive** *a* corruttivo
corruption *n* corruzione
corsage *n* mazzolino
corset *n* corsetto
cortege *n* corteo
cortex *n (anat)* cortice *m*; *(bot)* corteccia
cortisone *n* cortisona
coseismal *a* cosismico
cosine *n* coseno
cosmetic *a&n* cosmetico; **–ian** *n* cosmetico
cosmic *a* cosmico, — **dust** particella cosmica, pulviscolo cosmico; — **rays** raggi cosmici
cosmonaut *n (aesp)* cosmonauta *m&f*
cosmopolitan *a&n* cosmopolita *m*
cosmotron *n* cosmotrone *m*
Cossack *n* Cosacco
cost *n* costo; — **of living** costo della vita; — **price** prezzo di costo; **whatever the** — a qualunque costo; **at all –s** ad ogni costo; **–liness** *n* costosità; **–ly** *a* costoso, caro; — *vt* stimare; — *vi* costare
costume *n* costume *m;* — *vt* vestire in costume
costumer *n* costumista *m&f,* costumiere *m*
cot *n* lettino; culla
cote *n* stabbio; *(dove)* piccionaia; colombaia
coterie *n* combriccola
cottage *n* capanna, villetta
cotton *n* cotone *m;* — *a* di cotone, cotoniero; **absorbent** — cotone idrofilo; — **gin** macchina cardatrice del cotone; **–seed oil** olio di cotone; **–y** *a* cotonato
couch *n* divano, sofà; — *vt* coricare; — *vi* coricarsi, stendersi
cough *n* tosse *f;* — **drop** pastiglia per la tosse; — **syrup** sciroppo per la tosse; **whooping** — tosse asinina; — *vt* espettorare; — *vi* tossire
coughing *n* tosse *f*
council *n* consiglio, concilio; **city** — consiglio comunale; **–or** *n* membro del consiglio, consigliere *m*
counsel *n* consiglio, opinione; **keep one's own** — tenere per sè le proprie opinioni; **take** — consultare; — *vt* consigliare
counselor *n* consigliere *m*
count *vt* contare; *(mus)* solfeggiare; — **me in** conta con me; — **on** contare su; fare affidamento; — *n* conto, calcolo; *(title)* conte *m*; **–down** *n (aesp)* conteggio
countenance *n* viso, sembiante *m;* — *vt&i* appoggiare, favorire, secondare, sostenere; **put out of** — fare confusione; sconcertare
counter *n (calculator)* calcolatore *m,* calcolatrice *f; (game)* gettone *m*; *(person)* contante *m&f*; contatore *m*, contatrice *f*; *(store)* banco; **Geiger** — contatore Geiger; — *a* oppositore, controcorrente *(fig);* — *adv* contro, contrariamente; — *vt* opporre; — *vi* rispondere; *(sport)* controbattere
counteract *vt* contrariare
counterattack *n* contrattacco; — *vt&i* contrattaccare
counterbalance *vt* contrappesare; — *n* contrappeso
counterclaim *n* controreclamo; — *vi* controreclamare
counterclockwise *a* opposto all'orologio
counterfeit *a* contraffatto; — *n* contraffazione; — *vt* contraffare; — *vi* fingere; **–er** *n* contraffattore *m*, contraffatrice *f*
counterirritant *n* contrirritante
countermand *vt* contromandare, annullare
countermarch *n* contromarcia
countermove *n* contromossa; — *vt&i* contromuovere
counteroffensive *n* controffensiva
counterpane *n* contrappunta, coltre *f*
counterpart *n* controparte *f*
counterpoint *n* contrappunto
counterpoise *n* contrappeso; — *vt* controbilanciare
counterrevolution *n* controrivoluzione
countersign *vt* contrassegnare
countersink *vt* fresare, accecare, incassare
counterweight *n* contrappeso
countess *n* contessa
countless *a* innumerevole
countrified *a* rustico
country *n* paese *m*, regione *f*, patria; campagna; *(native)* paese natio; — **club** circolo campestre; *(golf)* campo di golf; **–man** *n* compatriotta *m&f*, contadino, paesano; **–side** *n* campagna, paese; **–wide** *a* in tutto il paese *(fig);* — *a* rurale, di campagna
county *n* contea; — **poor farm** campo di ritiro per i poveri; — **seat** *(privincial)* capoluogo
coup *n* colpo
coupé *n* cupè *m*
couple *n* coppia, paio; — *vt* accoppiare, appaiare; — *vi* accoppiarsi, appaiarsi
coupling *n (mech)* accoppiamento, attacco
coupon *n* cupone *m*, cedola; *(com)* cupone
courage *n* coraggio; — **of one's convictions** coraggio delle proprie opinioni; **–ous** *a* coraggioso
courier *n* corriere *m*
course *n* corso, corsa, carriera; *(meal)* portata; *(river)* corso; *(study)* corso di studi; **a matter of** — cosa naturale; **in due** — regolarmente; **in the** — **of** durante, **of** — naturalmente; **run its** — seguire il suo corso; — *vt&i* correre
court *n* corte *f*, assemblea; **out of** — extra legale; **–house** *n* tribunale *m*, corte *f*, palazzo di giustizia; — *a* di corte, della corte; **–room** *n* sala di corte

court *vt* corteggiare, fare la corte; **–ship** *n* corte *f*, assiduità
courteous *a* cortese
courtesan *n* cortigiana
courtesy *n* cortesia
courtliness *n* cortesia
courtly *a* cortese
court-martial *n* corte marziale
court plaster *n* taffettà inglese
cousin *n* cugino, cugina; **first** — cugino germano
covalence *n (phys)* covalenza
cove *n (arch)* arco; *(geog)* seno
covenant *n* covenzione
cover *vt* coprire; celare, nascondere; — **oneself** coprirsi; — **up** dissimulare, ricoprire interamante; — *n* copertura, coperta; — **charge** prezzo di coperto; **book** — copertina; **take** — proteggersi; **under separate** — separatamente; **–ed** *a* coperto, ricoperto
coverall *n* spolverina
covering *n* copertura
coverlet *n* copriletto
covert *a* coperto, nascosto
covet *vt&i* desiderare; — *vt* bramare, agognare; avere un cattivo desiderio; **–ous** *a* avido, cupido
covey *n* covata, branco
cow *n* vacca; **–boy** *n* vaccaro; **–catcher** *n (engine)* paraurti; **–hand** *n* vaccaro; **–hide** *n* pelle di vacca; — *vt* intimidire; scoraggiare
coward *n* codardo, vile *m;* **–ice** *n* codardia, viltà; **–ly** *a* codardo, vigliacco
cower *vi* accoccolarsi, accovacciarsi
cowl *n* cappuccio
cowlick *n* ciuffo
co-worker *n* compagno di lavore, collaboratore *m*
coy *a* modesto, timido
coyote *n* sciacallo americano
cozily *adv* gradevolmente, comodamente
coziness *n* comodità
cozy *a* accogliente
C.P.A., certified public accountant *n* ragioniere abilitato
crab *n* granchio; — **apple** mela selvatica; **–grass** *n* gramigna; — *vt&i (coll)* avvilire
crack *vt* spaccare, fendere; — *vi* spaccarsi, fendersi; — **a joke** fare scherzi; — **down** *(coll)* costringere con severità; — **up** *(coll)* crollare; *(praise)* vantare
crack *n* fessura, crepa; — **of dawn** *n* prime ore del mattino; **–brained** *a* matto, pazzo; **–ed** *a* spaccato; *(coll)* balzano
cracker *n* biscotto; *(fireworks)* galletta
crackle *vt&i* screpolare; *(sound)* crepitare
cracking *n* scoppiettio, crepito
crack-up *n* collisione; *(med)* collasso
cradle *n* culla; — *vt* mettere nella culla
craft *n* arte *f; (naut)* battello; *(slyness)* astuzia; *(trade)* mestiere *m*; **–ily** *adv* abilmente; *(slyly)* con inganno; **–iness** *n* astuzia **–y** *a (able)* astuto, capace; *(sly)* furbo
craftsman *n* artigiano; **–ship** *n* artefice *m*
crag *n* rupe *f*, picco
craggy *a* roccioso, scosceso
cram *vt* riempire; — *vi* riempirsi; *(coll)* rimpinzare
cramp *n* crampo; — *vt* dare crampi; **–ed** *a* indolenzito, con i crampi
cranberry *n* mortella; — **sauce** salsa di mortella
crane *n* gru *f;* — *vt&i* sollevare con la gru; — **one's neck** allungare il collo
cranial *a* cranico
crank *n* gomito; *(coll)* eccentrico; **–case** *n (auto)* carter *m*; **–shaft** *n* albero a gomito; **–y** *a* debole, capriccioso
cranny *n* fessura, incrinatura; **in nook and** — in ogni dove *(coll)*
crash *vt* fracassare; — *vi* far rumore; — *n* fracasso; *(com)* fallimento; — **landing** *(avi)* atterraggio irregolare
crash-dive *vt (avi)* picchiare
crass *a* crasso, grossolano
crate *n* gabbia per imballaggio; — *vt* ingabbiare
crater *n* cratere *m*
cravat *n* cravatta
crave *vt&i* supplicare, chiedere insistentemente
craven *a* codardo
craving *n* aspirazione, desiderio
craw *n (bird)* gozzo; **stick in one's** — *(coll)* stare nello stomaco *(coll)*
crawfish *n* gameto; — *vi (coll)* indietreggiare
crawl *vi* strisciare; — **with** formicolare; — *n* strisciamento, *(swimming)* stile libero, crawl *m*
crayon *n* matita, lapis *m*
craze *vt* squilibrare, fare impazzire; **–d** *a* folle; ammatassato *(fig)*; — *n* mania
crazy *a* matto, pazzo; illogico; — **bone** gomito
cream *n* crema, panna; *(best)* il meglio; — **cheese** formaggio grasso; — **pitcher** vaso per la crema; — **puff** bignola; — **sauce** salsa bianca; **whipped** — panna montana; **–y** *a* cremoso; **–ery** *n* crimeria; — *vt (sauce)* aggiungere la salsa bianca; *(whip)* frullare
crease *n* piega; — *vt&i* piegare, fare pieghe, sgualcire
crease-resistant *a* antipiega
create *vt* creare
creation *n* creazione
creative *a* creativo
creator *n* creatore *m*
creature *n* creatura; — **comforts** provviste *fpl*
credence *n* credito; *(eccl)* credenza
credential *n* credenziale *f*; **–s** *npl* credenziali *fpl*
credenza *n* credenza
credibility *n* credibilità
credible *a* credibile
credit *n* credito; *(school)* attestato scolastico; — **card** lettera di credito; — **rating** credito commerciale; — **union** cooperativa di credito; **–able** *a* degno di credito; **–or** *n* creditore *m;* — *vt* credere a, fare (*or* dare) credito
credulity *n* credulità
credulous *a* credulo; **–ly** *adv* credulamente
creed *n* credo, fede *f*, simbolo
creek *n* seno, caletta
creel *n* paniere da pesca, nassa

creep *vt&i* strisciare; *(bot)* arrampicarsi; — *n (sl)* rettile *m (fig)*; **–er** *n* rettile *m*; *(bot)* rampicante *m*; **–ing** *a* strisciante; *(bot)* rampicante; **–s** *npl* brividi *mpl*; **–y** *a* strisciante
cremate *vt* cremare, incenerire
cremation *n* cremazione
crematory *n* crematorio
creosote *n* creosoto
crêpe *n* crespo; — **paper** carta increspata
crepitation *n* crepitio, crepitazione
crescendo *n&adv* crescendo
crescent *n* crescente *m*; — *adj* crescente; — **moon** luna crescente
crest *n* cresta; *(bird)* cresta, ciuffo; *(wave)* cresta dell'onda; **–ed** *a* crestato, con la cresta
crestfallen *a* depresso
Crete Creta
cretinism *n* cretinismo
cretonne *n* creton *m*, cotonina
crevice *n* fessura, incrinatura; **–d** *a* fesso, incrinato
crew *n* ciurma, equipaggio; — **cut** capelli a spazzola
crib *n (bed)* culla; *(eccl)* presepe *m*; *(food)* mangiatoia; — *vt* copiare, sottrarre, plagiare
cribbing *n (coll)* plagio
crick *n* crampo, spasimo; — *vt* dare crampi
cricket *n* grillo
crier *n* banditore *m*
crime *n* delitto, crimine *m*; — **wave** onda di delitti
criminal *n&a* criminale
criminologist *n* criminalista *m*, criminologo
criminology *n* criminologia
crimp *vt* arricciare, arruolare; — *n* arruolatore *m*; **put a — in** *(coll)* mettere il bastone fra le ruote *(coll)*; **–y** *a* riccio, ricciuto; arricciato
crimson *n* cremisi *m*; — *a* cremisino, cremisi; — *vt&i* arrossire
cringe *vt* contrarre; — *vi* inchinarsi, fare riverenza
cringing *a* servile; — *n* servilità
crinkle *n* crespa, grinza; ondulazione; — *vt* aggrinzare; — *vi* increspare, incresparsi
cripple *n&a* storpio, zoppo; — *vt* storpiare
crisis *n* crisi *f*
crisp *a* crespo, riccio; *(air)* crespo; *(manner)* insinuante; *(repartee)* vivace; — *vt* ondulare, arricciare, increspare; — *vi* ondularsi, arricciarsi, incresparsi; **–ly** *adv* acutamente; **–ness** *n* l'esser crespo; **–y** *a* crespo
crisscross *a* crociato, incrociato; — *adv* a croce; — *vt&i* incrociare; *(sign)* firmare con la croce; — *n (signature)* segno di croce
criterion *n* criterio
critic *n* critico; **–al** *a* critico; **–ism** *n* critica; **–ize** *vt&i* criticare
croak *vt&i* gracchiare; — n gracchiamento; **–y** *a* rauco
crochet *n* uncinetto; — *vt&i* lavorare all'uncinetto; — **hook** uncinetto
crock *n* pignatta; **–ery** *n* maiolica
crocodile *n* coccodrillo; — **tears** *(fig)* lagrime di coccodrillo
crocus *n* croco, zafferano
crony *n* compagno, amico
crook *n* curvatura; *(coll)* truffatore; **–ed** *a* curvo, piegato; *(person)* perverso; **–edness** *n* curvatura; perversità; — *vt* curvare, piegare; — *vi* curvarsi, piegarsi
croon *vt&i* gemere, canticchiare; **–er** *n* canticchiatore *m*
crop *n* raccolto; *(zool)* gozzo; — *vt (grass)* pascolare; *(hair)* tosare; *(reap)* cogliere; — **off** tagliare; — **up** affiorare, sopravvenire
cropper *n* collasso; *(coll)* caduta; **come a —** stramazzare; fare un capitombolo
cross *n* croce *f*; — **reference** rimando, richiamo; — *a* incrociato, traversale; *(humor)* di malumore; — **as a bear** di pessimo umore; **–bow** *n* balestra; **–walk** *n* passaggio pedonale; — *vt* incrociare, attraversare; — *vi* incrociarsi, attraversarsi; — **out** cancellare
crossbreed *n* incrocio, ibrido; — *vt&i* incrociare razze
cross- *(in comp)* **—country** *a&adv* attraverso i campi; — **examine** *vt* fare controinterrogatorio; **—eyed** *a* strabico; **—grained** *a* a fibre irregolari; *(peevish)* bisbetico; **—hatch** *vt (print)* tratteggiare; **—legged** *a&adv* a gambe incrociate; **—patch** *n* bisbetico; **—piece** *n* traversa; **—road** *n* crocevia; **—section** *n* sezione trasversale; **—town** *a* transurbano
crosscut saw *n* sega a due mani
crossing *n* incrocio; *(rail)* intersezione; **level —** passaggio a livello
cross-purpose *n* equivoco, contradizione, malinteso; **work at —s** contrastare
crosswise *adv&a* di traverso
crossword puzzle *n* cruciverba *m*
crotch *n* forca; *(anat, pants)* inforcatura
crouch *vi* accovacciarsi; essere servile
croup *n* groppa; *(med)* crup *m*; **–y** *a (med)* crupale
crouton *n* crostino
crow *n* corvo, cornacchia; **as the — flies** a volo d'uccello; **eat —** umiliarsi; — *vi (cock)* cantare; *(fig)* cantar vittoria
crowbar *n* leva
crowd *n* folla, ressa; — *vt* affollare, ingombrare; — *vi* affollarsi, affluire; **–ed** *a* affollato, sovraccaricato
crown *n* corona, cima; *(head)* sommità; — *vt* incoronare; — **prince** principe ereditario; **–ing** *a* finale, supremo, ultimo
crow's feet *npl* rughe *fpl*, zampe di gallina *(coll)*
crow's-nest *n (naut)* coffa
crucial *a* cruciale, decisivo
crucible *n* crogiuolo
crucifix *n* crocifisso
crucify *vt* crocifiggere
crude *a* crudo; — **oil** olio grezzo; **–ly** *adv* crudamente; **–ness** *n* crudezza
cruel *a* crudele; **–ty** *n* crudeltà
cruet *n* ampolla
cruise *vi* incrociare, andare in crociera; — *n* crociera
cruiser *n* incrociatore *m*

crumb *n* mollica, briciola; — *vt* sbriciolare, impanare; **–ed** *a* sbriciolato, grattugiato; **–y** *a* pieno di briciole; *(sl)* schifoso
crumble *vt* grattugiare, sbriciolare; — *vi* sbriciolarsi
crumbling *n* sbriciolamento; crollo
crumbly *a* midolloso, friabile
crumple *vt* raggrinzare; — *vi* raggrinzarsi
crunch *vt&i* scricchiolare, sgranocchiare, sgretolare; — *n* scricchiolio; **–ing** *a* scricchiolante
crusade *n* crociata; — *vi* fare una crociata
crusader *n* crociato
crush *vt* schiacciare; — *vi* schiacciarsi; — *n (coll)* infatuazione; *(crowd)* affollamento; **–ing** *a* schiacciante
crust *n* crosta; *(sediment)* deposito; — *vt* incrostare; — *vi* incrostarsi; **–y** *a* incrostato
crustacean *n&a* crostaceo
crutch *n* gruccia, stampella
crux *n* difficoltà; *(puzzle)* indovinello, rebus *m*; — **of the matter** punto cruciale
cry *vt&i* piangere; *(yell)* gridare; **–baby** *n* piagnucolone *(coll)*; — *n* pianto; grido; **–ing** *n* pianti *mpl*; grida *fpl*
cryogenics *npl* criogenica
crypt *n* cripta; **–ic** *a* segreto, nascosto
cryptography *n* criptografia, crittografia
crystal *n* cristallo; — *a* cristallino; di cristallo
crystalline *a* cristallino
crystallize *vt&i* cristallizzare
cub *n* cucciolo; **bear** — orsacchiotto; — **reporter** *(coll)* giornalista inesperto
cubbyhole *n* sgabuzzino
cube *n* cubo; — *vt* cubare; — **root** *n* radice cubica
cubic *a* cubico; — **measure** volume *m*
cubicle *n* cubicolo
cuckoo *n* cuculo; — **clock** orologio a cuculo, pendola
cucumber *n* cetriolo
cud *n* bolo alimentare; **chew the** — ruminare
cuddle *vt* serrare, stringere; — *vi* serrarsi, stringersi, rannicchiarsi; **–some** *a* vezzoso, coccolone
cudgel *n* bastone *m*, randello; **take up the –s for** difendere; — *vt* bastonare
cue *n (billiard)* stecca; *(hair)* codino; *(line)* coda, fila, linea; *(theat)* parola, suggerimento; **give a** — dare lo spunto
cuff *n (blow)* schiaffo, ceffone *m*; *(shirt)* polsino; *(trouser)* risvolto dei pantaloni; — **button** bottone da polsino; — **links** *npl* gemelli *mpl*; **off the** — *(sl)* ufficioso; **on the** — *(sl)* sulla parola; — *vt* schiaffeggiare; prendere a pugni
cuirass *n* corazza
cuisine *n* cucina
culinary *a* culinario
cull *vt* cogliere, scegliere
culminate *vi* culminare
culmination *n* culminazione
culpability *n* colpevolezza, colpabilità
culpable *a* colpabile
culprit *n* colpevole *m*; *(law)* imputato
cult *n* culto
cultivate *vt* coltivare
cultivation *n* coltivazione
cultivator *n* aratro; *(mech)* coltivatore *m*
cultural *a* culturale
culture *n* cultura; — *vt* coltivare
culvert *n* sottopassaggio
cumber *vt* ingombrare, oberare; **–some** *a* ingombrante
cumulative *a* cumulativo
cumulous *a* cumuloso *m*
cumulus (cloud) *n* cumulo
cunning *a* abile; — *n* abilità
cup *n* tazza; — *vt* applicare la ventosa; **–ful** *n* tazza piena; contenuto della tazza
cupboard *n* armadio, credenza
Cupid *n* Cupido
cupidity *n* cupidigia
cupola *n* cupola
cur *n* degenerato; *(dog)* cane bastardo
curable *a* curabile, guaribile
curate *n* curato
curative *a* curativo
curator *n* curatore *m*
curb *n (check)* giogo, freno, barbazzale *m*; *(street)* ciglio di strada; **–ing** *n (fig)* freno; — *vt* frenare, reprimere, mettere il freno
curd *n* latte quagliato
curdle *vt* coagulare, quagliare; — *vi* coagularsi; — **one's blood** agghiacciare il sangue
cure *n* cura; — *vt* curare, guarire; *(by salting)* salare; *(by smoking)* affumicare; *(pelt)* conciare
cure-all *n* toccasana, curatutto, panacea
curfew *n* coprifuoco
curia *n (eccl)* curia
curio *n* anticaglia
curiosity *n* curiosità
curious *a* curioso
curl *vt* arricciare, inanellare; — *vi* arricciarsi, inanellarsi; — **up** aggrovigliarsi; — *n* ricciolo, boccolo; **–y** *a* ricciuto
curlicue *n* ghirigoro
currant *n* ribes *m*
currency *n* circolazione; **foreign** — valuta straniera
current *a* corrente; **–ly** *adv* correntemente; — **events** attualità *fpl*; — **expenses** spese correnti
current *n* corrente *f*; — **density** densità di corrente; **alternating** — corrente alternata; **direct** — corrente diretta
curricular *a* curriculare
curriculum *n* curricolo
curry *vt* condire; — **favor** entrare in grazia
curse *n* maledizione, afflizione; — *vt* maledire; — *vi* bestemmiare; **be –d with** essere afflitto da; **–d** *a* maledetto, afflitto
cursing *n* maledizione
cursive *a* corsivo
cursory *a* rapido, affrettato
curt *a* corto, breve
curtail *vt* accorciare, abbreviare; **–ment** *n* abbreviazione
curtain *n* cortina, tenda; — **call** presentazione agli applausi; — **lecture** rimprovero coniugale; — **raiser** avan-

spettacolo; **iron —** cortina di ferro; — *vt* applicare le cortine; *(hide)* velare
curtsy *n* cortesia, inchino; — *vi* fare cortesia
curvature *n* curvatura
curve *n* curva; — *vt* curvare; — *vi* curvarsi; **–d** *a* curvo
cushion *n* cuscino; — *vt* collocare sopra cuscini; *(pad)* imbottire
cusp *n* cuspide *f;* **–id** *n* dente canino; — *a* cuspidato, acuto
cuspidor *n* sputacchiera
custard *n* crostata
custodial *a* di custodia
custodian *n* custode *m*
custody *n* custodia; **in —** in custodia, arrestato; **take into —** prendere in custodia, arrestare; **have — of** avere custodia di
custom *n* costume *m,* usanza; **–ary** *a* consuetudinario; **–arily** *adv* consuetudinariamente; **–er** *n* cliente *m*; **–house** *n* dogana
custom-built, –made *a* fatto a richiesta
customs *npl* dogana; **— declaration** dichiarazione doganale; **— inspection** ispezione doganale; **— inspector** ispettore doganale
cut *n* taglio; *(blow)* colpo; *(wound)* incisione; *(fig)* affronto; **— and dried** preelaborato, preparato; **— glass** cristallo intagliato
cut *vt&i* tagliare; *(cards)* alzare; *(class) (sl)* marinare la scuola; *(omit)* omettere; *(a person, sl)* far finta di non vedere; *(prices)* ribassare; *(teeth)* mettere i denti; **— and run** *(sl)* svignarsela; tagliare la corda *(coll)*; **— down to size** *(sl)* mettere a posto *(coll)*; **— off** ritagliare, *(detach)* staccare; *(interrupt)* interrompere; **— short** tagliar corto *(coll);* **C– it out!** Smettila!; — *n (print)* cliché *m*
cutaneous *a* cutaneo
cutback *n* riduzione
cute *a (coll)* grazioso
cut-glass *a* di vetro intagliato
cuticle *n* cuticola, pellicola
cutlery *n* coltelleria
cutlet *n* cotoletta, braciola
cutoff *n* scorciatoia
cutout *n* interruttore *m*; *(auto)* valvola; *(picture)* disegno (*or* figura) da ritagliare
cut-rate *a&adv* a buon mercato
cutthroat *n* assassino, sicario; — *a* omicida
cutting *n* taglio; — *a* tagliente
cyanide *n* cianuro
cyclamen *n* ciclamino
cycle *n* ciclo
cyclic, cyclical *a* ciclico
cyclist *n* ciclista *m&f*
cyclone *n* ciclone *m*
cyclotron *n* ciclotrone *m*
cylinder *n* cilindro; **— head** camera di combustione
cylindrical *a* cilindrico
cymbal *n* cembalo; **–ist** *n* suonatore di piatti
cynic *n* cinico; **–ism** *n* cinismo
cynical *a* cinico
cynosure *n* cinosura, *(ast)* Orsa Minore
cypress *n* cipresso
Cyprus Cipro
cyst *n* ciste *f*
Czech *n&a* czeco, ceco
Czechoslovakia Cecoslovacchia

D

dab *vt&i* comprimere; *(pat)* battere leggermente; **— at** macchiare; *(food)* piluccare; — *n* colpetto; *(mud)* zacchera; *(paint)* schizzo; *(small bit)* pizzicotto
dabber *n* tampone *m*
dabble *vt* immergere, bagnare; — *vi* guazzare, immischiarsi
dactyl *n* dattilo
dad, daddy *n* papà *m,* babbo
dadaism *n* dadaismo
dado *n (arch)* dado
daffodil *n* narciso prataiolo
dagger *n* daga, pugnale *m*
dahlia *n* dalia
daily *a* quotidiano, giornaliero; **— newspaper** giornale quotidiano; — *adv* quotidianamente, giornalmente
daintily *adv* delicatamente, gustosamente
daintiness *n* delicatezza, leccornia
dainty *a* delicato, ghiotto
dairy *n* latteria; **— farm** vaccheria; **— products** latticini *mpl*
dais *n* palco
daisy *n* margherita
dale *n* valle *f*
dalliance *n* indugio, ritardo
dally *vi* indugiare, ritardare, dimorarsi
dam *n* diga; *(animal)* madre; **give a tinker's —** non dare nessun valore; — *vt* fornire di diga, frenare, arginare
damage *n* danno; — *vt* danneggiare, nuocere; — *vi* subire danno; **–able** *a* danneggiabile; **–d** *a* danneggiato
damaging *a* danneggiante, dannoso
damask *n* damasco
dame *n* dama, signora
damn *vt* maledire, dannare; — *a* dannato; **–able** *a* maledetto, odioso; **–ation** *n* dannazione; **–ed** *a* dannato
damp *n* umidità, *(mine)* vapore *m*; — *a* umido, umidiccio; **–er** *n (fig)* guastafeste *m; (flue)* regolatore *m; (mus)* sordina; **–ness** *n* umidità
dampen *vt* inumidire, abbattere; — *vi* inumidirsi; abbattersi
dance *vi* danzare, ballare; **make — another tune** far cambiare di tono *(coll)*; **— attendance on** servire con attenzione; — *n* ballo, danza
dancer *n* ballerino, danzatore *m*
dandelion *n* radicchiella
dander *n (coll)* collera; **get one's — up** montare in collera
dandle *vt* dondolare, cullare, accarezzare
dandruff *n* forfora
dandy *n* damerino; — *a (sl)* elegante, ri-

cercato
Dane, Danish *n&a* danese
danger *n* pericolo
dangerous *a* pericoloso; **–ously** *adv* pericolosamente
dangle *vt* far penzolare; — *vi* penzolare; penzolarsi
dank *a* umido, madido
dapper *a* gentile, grazioso
dapple *a* screziato; — *vt* macchiettare, screziare; — *vi* screziarsi, macchiettarsi; **–d** *a* macchiettato, screziato
dare *vt* sfidare; — **say** osare di dire; **–devil** *n* audace *m&f*, temerario
daring *a* ardito, audace; — *n* ardimento, audacia
dark *a* oscuro, nero; — **horse** *(pol)* candidato insignificante; — **secret** segreto profondo; **in the** — all'oscuro; **keep** — lasciare all'oscuro; — *n* oscurità; **–ness** *n* oscurità; **–room** *n* camera oscura
darken *vt* oscurare; — *vi* oscurarsi, imbrunire
darling *n* favorito, diletto; — *a* caro, prediletto
darn *vt* rammendare; — *n* rammendo; **–ed** *a* rammendato; **–ing needle** ago da rammendo
dart *n* dardo; — *vt* dardeggiare; — *vi* slanciarsi, balzare
dash *vt* colpire, rompere; — *vi* rompersi; — **hopes** togliere la speranza; — **off** *(do)* fare frettolosamente; *(go)* precipitarsi *(coll)*
dash *n* impeto, slancio; *(print)* lineeta; *(small amount)* goccia; pizzico
dashing *a* vivace, impetuoso
dashboard *n* cruscotto; *(mudguard)* parafango
dastard *n* vile *m*, codardo; — *a* codardo; **–liness** *n* codardia; **–ly** *adv* codardamente
data *npl* dati *mpl*; — **processing** progressione di date (*or* datistà)
date *n* data; *(bot)* dattero; *(coll)* appuntamento; **out of** — passato, fuori moda; **until now, this** — fino ad oggi, alla data; **up to** — moderno; di moda; — *vt* datare; — *vi* datare da
daub *vt&i (blob)* sgorbiare; *(plaster)* intonacare; *(stain)* imbrattare; — *n* imbratto, sgorbio; *(plaster)* intonaco; **–er** imbrattatore *m*
daughter *n* figlia
daughter-in-law *n* nuora
daunt *vt* intimidire; **–less** *a* intrepido
dauphin *n* delfino
davenport *n* sofà *m*
davit *n (naut)* gru *f*
dawdle *vi* bighellonare
dawdler *n* perdigiorno
dawdling *a* bighellone, fannullone; — *n* bighellonamento
dawn *n* alba, aurora; — *vi* albeggiare; — **on** balenare *(fig)*
day *n* giorno; — **after** — ogni giorno; — **after tomorrow** dopodomani; — **before yesterday** avantieri; — **by** — giorno per giorno; — **in,** — **out** un giorno dopo l'altro; **by the** — alla giornata; **call it a** — averne abbastanza; **every other** — ogni due giorni; **from** — **to** — da un giorno all'altro
daybreak *n* alba
daydream *n* sogno ad occhi aperti; — *vi* sognare ad occhi aperti
day-laborer *n* giornaliere *m*
daylight *n* giorno; **by** — di giorno; — **saving time** ora estiva
day nursery asilo infantile
daytime *n* il giorno; — *a* di giorno
day school scuola diurna
daze *vt* stupefare, sbalordire; — *n* stupore *m*
dazedly *adv* sbalorditamente
dazzle *vt* abbagliare; — *vi* brillare; — *n* abbagliamento
dazzling *a* abbagliante
deacon *n* diacono; **–ess** *n* diaconessa
deactivate *vt* annullare, neutralizzare
dead *a* morto; *(color)* smorto; *(elec)* senza corrente; *(exhaustion, fire)* spento; *(sound)* sordo; — **center** punto morto; **—drunk** ubriaco fradicio; — **end** vicolo cieco; **in a — heat** alla stessa distanza del traguardo; — **letter** giacente *f*; — **loss** perdita totale; — **sleep** sonno profondo; — **sure** sicurissimo; — **weight** peso morto; **the** — i morti
deadliness *n* letalità, natura mortale
deadlock *n* paralisi *f*, ostruzione; — *vt* paralizzare, ostruire
deadly *a* mortale, letale; — *adv* mortalmente, a morte
deaf *a* sordo; **–ness** *n* sordità
deafen *vt* assordare; **–ing** *a* assordante
deaf-mute *n* sordomuto
deal *vt* distribuire; — *vi* agire, comportarsi; *(com)* commerciare, trattare
deal *n (amount)* quantità, parte *f*; *(cards)* mano *f*; *(com)* affare *m*; *(pol)* arrangiamento politico; — **in** *(com)* commerciare in; — **with** aver a che fare, *(concern)* concernere; **a good** — un buon affare; molto; **a great** — moltissimo; **give a square** — trattare giustamente; **make a** — fare un affare; — *a (wood)* di legno di pino
dealer *n (card)* chi distribuisce le carte; *(com)* esercente, distributore *m*
dealing *n* azione, condotta; *(manner of)* modo d'agire; **–s** *npl* pratiche *fpl*
dean *n* decano
dear *n* diletto, caro; — *a* caro, prezioso; *(costly)* costoso; **–ly** *adv* caramente, teneramente; *(amount)* molto; **–ness** *n* carezza; alto prezzo; — **friend** caro amico, cara amica
dearth *n* carestia, scarsità
death *n* morte *f*; — **rate** mortalità; — **rattle** rantolo mortale; — **warrant** ordine d'esecuzione; **–bed** *n* letto di morte; **–less** *a* immortale; **–ly** *a* mortale
debacle *n* sfacelo, disfatta
debar *vt* escludere; *(law)* prescrivere
debark *vt* sbarcare; **–ation** *n* sbarco
debase *vt* avvilire; **–ment** *n* avvilimento
debasing *a* degradante
debatable *a* discutibile
debate *vt* dibattere, discutere; — *n* dibattito, discussione
debater *n* dibattente *m*, oratore *m*, parla-

mentare *m*
debauch *vt* pervertire; — *vi* pervertirsi; **–edly** *adv* perversamente; **–ery** *n* pervertimento
debenture *n* obbligazione
debilitate *vt* debilitare
debilitation *n* debilitazione
debility *n* debolezza
debit *n* debito; — *vt* addebitare
debonaire *a* bonario
debris *n* frammenti *mpl*
debt *n* debito, obbligo; **get into** — andare in deficit; **–or** *n* debitore *m*
debunk *vt (coll)* sgonfiare
debut *n* debutto, esordio; **–ante** *n* debuttante, esordiente *m&f*
decade *n* decade *f*
decadence *n* decadenza
decadent *a* decadente
decalcify *vt* decalcificare
decamp *vi (escape)* svignarsela, scappare; levare il campo (*or* le tende)
decant *vt* decantare; **–er** *n* caraffa
decapitate *vt* decapitare
decapitation *n* decapitazione
decay *vi* decadere, deperire; — *n* decadenza, decadimento; *(putrifaction)* marciume *m*; *(tooth)* carie *f*
decease *vi* decedere; **–d** *a* deceduto
decedent *n* defunto
deceit *n* inganno, frode *f;* **–ful** *a* falso, ingannevole
deceive *vt* ingannare; **–r** *n* ingannatore *m*
December *n* dicembre *m*
decency *n* decenza, modestia
decent *a* decente, modesto
decentralize *vt* decentrare
deception *n* decezione; frode *f*; delusione; inganno
deceptive *a* ingannevole
decibel *n (elec)* decibel *m*
decide *vt* decidere; — *vi* decidersi
decidedly *adv* decisamente
decimal *a&n* decimale *m*
decimate *vt* decimare
decipher *vt* decifrare; **–able** *a* decifrabile
decision *n* decisione; **come to a** — giungere a una decisione
decisive *a* decisivo, deciso
deck *n* ponte *m*, tolda; *(sl)* terra; *(cards)* mazzo di carte; — **chair** sedia a sdraio; **–hand** *n* marinaio di ponte
declaim *vt&i* declamare
declamation *n* declamazione
declamatory *a* declamatorio
declaration *n* dichiarazione
declare *vt* dichiarare; — **oneself** dichiararsi, rivelarsi
declension *n* declino; *(gram)* declinazione
decline *vt&i* declinare; — *n* declino; consunzione
decoction *n* decotto, decozione
decode *vt* decifrare
decompose *vt* decomporre, scomporre; — *vi* decomporsi, scomporsi
decomposition *n* decomposizione
decontaminate *vt* decontaminare
decontrol *vt* liberare dal controllo; — *n* cessazione di controllo
décor *n* decorazione
decorate *vt* decorare
decoration *n* decorazione
decorative *a* decorativo, ornamentale
decorator *n* decoratore *m*
decorous *a* decoroso
decorum *n* decoro
decoy *n (bait)* esca; *(snare)* trappola; — *vt* allettare
decrease *vt&i* diminuire, decrescere
decreasing *a* descrescente; **–ly** *adv* in diminuzione
decree *n* decreto, sentenza; — *vt* decretare
decrepit *a* decrepito
decry *vt* screditare; *(censure)* biasimare; *(disparage)* deprezzare
dedicate *vt* dedicare; *(coll)* inaugurare
dedication *n* dedica
deduce *vt* dedurre, derivare, desumere
deduct *vt* dedurre; **–ible** *a* deducibile
deduction *n* deduzione *f*
deed *n* atto, fatto; **in** — in realtà
deem *vt&i* giudicare, pensare, credere
deep *a* profondo, grave; **–freeze** *vt* congelare; — **seated** profondo; intimo; **go off the** — **end** *(coll)* passare i limiti; **in** — **water** *(fig)* in difficoltà, in cattive acque *(coll);* **–ly** *adv* profondamente
deepness *n* profondità
deepen *vt* approfondire; — *vi* approfondirsi
deep-rooted *a* inveterato
deer *n* cervo
deface *vt* sfigurare; *(discredit)* screditare
defalcation *n* diffalco
defamation *n* diffamazione
defamatory *a* diffamatorio
defame *vt* diffamare
default *n* difetto; *(lack)* mancanza; — *vt* condannare in contumacia; — *vi* essere contumace; **–er** *n* imputato, contumace *m;* **in** — **of** in mancanza di
defeat *vt* sconfiggere; — *n* sconfitta, disfatta; **–ist** *n* disfattista *m*
defect *n* difetto; **–ive** *a* difettoso
defection *n* defezione *f*
defend *vt* difendere; **–ant** *n (law)* accusato; **–er** *n* difensore *m*
defense *n* difesa; **–less** *a* indifeso
defensive *a* difensivo; — *n* difensiva
defer *vt* differire; — *vi* deferire; **–ence** *n* deferenza
deferential *a* deferente
deferment *n* differimento
deferred *a* differito, deferito
defiance *n* sfida, disfida; **in** — **of** a dispetto di
defiant *a* provocante
deficiency *n* deficienza, difetto
deficient *a* deficiente
deficit *n (com)* deficit *m*, ammanco
defile *vt* disonorare; *(sully)* macchiare; — *vi* sfilare; **–ment** *n* profanazione, macchia
definable *a* definibile
define *vt* definire
definite *a* definito; — **article** articolo determinativo; **–ly** *adv* definitamente; certamente; **–ness** *n* determinatezza
definition *n* definizione
deflate *vt* sgonfiare

deflation *n* sgonfiamento; *(economics)* deflazione
deflect *vt&i* deflettere
deflection *n* deviazione
deform *vt* deformare; — *vi* deformarsi; **–ation** *n* deformazione; **–ed** *a* deforme
deformity *n* deformità
defraud *vt* defraudare
defray *vt* pagare
defrock *vt* svestire; *(eccl)* spretare
defrost *vt* sgelare; rimuovere il ghiaccio; **–er** *n* disgelatore *m; (windshield)* visiera termica; **–ing** *n* disgelo
deft *a* destro, abile
defunct *a&n* defunto
defy *vt* sfidare, scartare, resistere a
degeneracy *n* degenerazione
degenerate *a&n* degenerato; — *vi* degenerare
degeneration *n* degenerazione
deglutinate *vt* deglutinare
degradation *n* degradazione
degrade *vt* degradare; **–d** *a* degradato
degrading *a* digradante
degree *n* grado; diploma; **in some** — fino a un certo punto; **to a** — all'estremo; **by –s** gradatamente; a poco a poco
degression *n* degressione, regressione, diminuzione
dehumidify *vt* deumidificare; diminuire l'umidità
dehydrate *vt* disidratare
dehydration *n* disidratazione
deice *vt* prevenire la formazione di ghiaccio; **–r** *n* scioglighiaccio
deification *n* deificazione
deify *vt* deificare
deign *vt* concedere; — *vi* degnarsi
deity *n* deità
deject *vt* abbattere; **–ed** *a* abbattuto
dejection *n* abbattimento; *(med)* deiezione
delay *vt* differire, ritardare; — *vi* indugiare; — *n* indugio; *(deferment)* rinvio
delaying *a* ritardante
delectable *a* dilettevole
delegate *n* delegato; — *vt* delegare
delegation *n* delegazione
delete *vt* cancellare
deletion *n* cancellazione
deliberate *vt&i* deliberare
deliberate *a* deliberato; *(cautious)* cauto
deliberation *n* deliberazione, riflessione
delicacy *n* delicatezza
delicate *a* delicato
delicatessen *n* negozio di cibi prelibati
delicious *a* delizioso, squisito
delight *vt* dilettare; — *vi* dilettarsi; — *n* diletto; **–ed** a deliziato
delightful *a* dilettevole
delineate *vt* delineare
delineation *n* delineazione
delineator *n* disegnatore *m*, delineatore *m*
delinquency *n* delinquenza
delinquent *a&n* delinquente *m&f*; **juvenile** — delinquente giovanile
delirious *a* delirante
delirium *n* delirio
deliver *vt* liberare; *(blow)* lanciare; *(goods)* consegnare; *(med)* far sgravare; *(save)* salvare; *(speech)* enunciare; **be –ed of** partorire; **–ance** *n* rilascio, liberazione
delivery *n* liberazione; *(goods)* consegna; *(mail)* distribuzione; *(med)* parto; *(speech)* dizione; *(sport)* lancio; **general** — fermo in posta; **special** — lettera espresso
delude *vt* deludere
deluge *n* diluvio; — *vt* inondare
delusion *n* delusione, illusione
delve *vt* vangare, sondare
demagogue *n* demagogo; **–ry** *n* pratica demagogica
demand *vt* domandare; *(require)* esigere; — *n* domanda; *(complaint)* reclamo; **in** — ricercato; **on** — *(com)* su domanda
demanding *a* esigente
demarcation *n* demarcazione
demean *vt* degradare, abbassare; — **one's self** avvilirsi
demeanor *n* condotta
demented *a* demente
demerit *n* demerito
demigod *n* semidio
demijohn *n* damigiana
demilitarize *vt* smilitarizzare; sostituire la legge civile a quella marziale
demise *n* morte *m*, decesso; *(law)* cessione, trapasso
demitasse *n* tazzina
demobilization *n* smobilitazione
demobilize *vt* smobilitare
democracy *n* democrazia
democrat *n* democrata *m&f;* **–ic** *a* democratico; **–ically** *adv* democraticamente
demolish *vt* demolire
demolition *n* demolizione
demon *n* demone *m*, demonio; **–iacal** *a* demoniaco, diabolico
demonstrable *a* dimostrabile
demonstrate *vt* dimostrare; — *vi* fare (*or* participare a) dimostrazione
demonstration *n* dimostrazione
demonstrative *a* dimostrativo
demonstrator *n* dimostratore *m*; dimostratrice *f;* dimostrante *m&f*
demoralization *n* demoralizzazione
demoralize *vt* demoralizzare
demote *vt* retrocedere
demotion *n* retrocessione
demount *vt* smontare
demur *vi* esitare, temporeggiare; — *n* esitazione, temporeggiamento
demure *a* sobrio; *(modest)* pudico
demurrage *n* sosta, controstallie *fpl*; *(charges)* magazzinaggio
den *n* covo, tana; *(private room)* studio intimo
denatured *a* denaturato
deniable *a* negabile
deniably *adv* negabilmente
denial *n* diniego, rinnegazione
denizen *n* abitante *m*; *(citizen)* cittadino
Denmark Danimarca
denomination *n* denominazione; *(coin)* taglio, conio; **–al** *a* particolare, settario
denominator *n* denominatore *m*
denote *vt* denotare
denounce *vt* denunciare; **–ment** *n* denuncia

dense *a* denso; *(stupid)* sciocco
density *n* densità
dent *n* incavo, intaccatura; — *vt* incavare, intaccare, dentellare; **–ed** *a* dentellato, intaccato
dental *a* dentale; — **floss** filo per pulire i denti
dentate *a* dentato, dentellato
dentation *n* *(bot)* dentellatura; *(med)* dentizione
dentifrice *n* dentifricio
dentist *n* dentista *m;* **–ry** *n* odontoiatria
denture *n* dentiera, dentatura
denude *vt* denudare
denunciation *n* denuncia
deny *vt* negare, rifiutare; — **oneself** negarsi, privarsi
deodorant *a&n* disodorante, deodorante *m*
deodorize *vt* deodorare
deodorizer *n* deodorante *m&f*
deontology *n* deontologia
depart *(deviate from)* deviare, derogare; *(go)* partire; **–ed** *a* morto, passato; **–ure** *n* partenza, dipartita; morte *f*
department *n* dipartimento; — **store** grande magazzino, bazar *m*, emporio; **–al** *a* dipartimentale
depend *vi* dipendere; — **on** dipendere da; **–ability** *n* affidamento; **–able** *a* fidato; **–ably** *adv* fidatamente; **–ence** *n* dipendenza, fiducia; **–ency** *n* dipendenza; **–ent** *a* dipendente
depict *vt* dipingere
depilatory *n&a* depilatorio
deplete *vt* *(empty)* vuotare; *(exhaust)* esaurire
depletion *n* deplezione, diminuzione, esaurimento
deplorable *a* deplorabile
deplore *vt* deplorare
deploy *vt* dispiegare
depopulate *vt* spopolare; — *vi* spopolarsi
deport *vt* deportare; **–ation** *n* deportazione; **–ment** *n* condotta, comportamento
depose *vt* deporre
deposit *vt* depositare; — *n* deposito; **–or** *n* depositante *m&f;* **–ory** *n* deposito, depositario
deposition *n* deposizione; *(law)* testimonianza, deposizione
depot *n* deposito; *(rail)* stazione
deprave *vt* depravare; **–d** *a* depravato
depravity *n* depravazione
deprecate *vt* deprecare
deprecating *a* screditante
depreciate *vt* deprezzare; — *vi* deprezzarsi
depreciation *n* deprezzamento
depredation *n* depredamento
depress *vt* deprimere; **–ed** *a* depresso; **–ant** *n&a* *(med)* deprimente *m*; **–ing** *a* deprimente, depressivo
depression *n* depressione
deprivation *n* privazione; *(dismissal from office)* deposizione
deprive *vt* privare; *(dismiss)* deporre
depth *n* profondità, abisso *(fig)*; colmo *(fig)*; **beyond one's** — senza fondo *(coll)*
deputation *n* deputazione
deputize *vt* delegare
deputy *n* deputato, delegato
derail *vt* far deragliare; — *vi* deragliare; **–ment** *n* deragliamento
derange *vt* disordinare; **–d** *a* disordinato; *(insane)* pazzo; **–ment** *n* disordine *m*; pazzia
derby *n* *(hat)* bombetta; *(race)* derby *m*
derelict *a* derelitto; — *n* relitto
dereliction *n* abbandono; *(law)* delinquenza
deride *vt* deridere
derision *n* derisione
derisive *a* derisivo
derivation *n* derivazione
derivative *a* derivato, derivativo; — *n* derivato
derive *vt&i* derivare
dermatitis *n* dermatite *f*
dermatologist *n* dermatologo
derogate *vi* derogare
derogation *n* calunnia
derogatory *a* derogatorio
derrick *n* gru meccanica
dervish *n* dervis *m*, dervigio
descant *n* *(mus)* melodia
descend *vt&i* discendere; **be –ed from** discendere da
descendant *n* discendente *m&f*; **–s** *npl* discendenti *mpl*
descent *n* discesa
describe *vt* descrivere
description *n* descrizione; **of all –s** di tutti i generi
descriptive *a* descrittivo
desecrate *vt* profanare, sconsacrare
desecration *n* profanazione
desegregate *vt* integrare, contro-discriminare
desegregation *n* integrazione, antidiscriminazione
desensitize *vt* insensibilizzare
desert *vt&i* disertare; **–er** *n* disertore *m*
desert *n* *(geog)* deserto
desertion *n* diserzione
deserts *npl* *(just reward)* ricompensa secondo il merito
deserve *vt&i* meritare; **–d** *a* meritato
deserving *a* meritevole, degno
desiccate *vt* essicare; — *vi* essicarsi, seccare
design *vt* disegnare; *(plan)* progettare; — *n* disegno; **–s** *npl* piani *mpl*
designer *n* disegnatore *m;* modellista *f*
designing *a* astuto, intrigante
designate *vt* designare
desirability *n* desiderabilità
desirable *a* desiderabile
desire *vt* desiderare; — *n* desiderio
desirous *a* desideroso
desist *vi* desistere
desk *n* scrivania
desolate *a* desolato
desolation *n* desolazione
despair *vi* disperare, disperarsi; — *n* disperazione; **–ing** *a* disperante, disperato
desperate *a* disperato
desperation *n* disperazione
despicable *a* vile, spregevole
despise *vt* disprezzare
despite *prep* nonostante

despoil *vt* spogliare *(fig)*
despondency *n* scoraggiamento
despondent *a* scoraggiato
despot *n* despota *m;* **–ic** *a* dispotico; **–ism** *n* dispotismo
dessert *n* dolci e frutta
destination *n* destinazione
destine *vt* destinare; **–d** *a* destinato
destiny *n* destino
destitute *a* destituito, bisognoso
destitution *n* destituzione, bisogno
destroy *vt* distruggere; **–er** *n (naut)* cacciatorpediniere *m*
destructible *a* distruttibile
destruction *n* distruzione
destructive *a* distruttivo; **–ness** *n* distruttività
desultory *a* saltuario
detach *vt* staccare; **–able** *a* staccabile; **–ed** *a* staccato; **–ment** *n* distacco; *(mil)* distaccamento
detail *n* dettaglio; *(mil)* distaccamento; **go into —** entrare in particolari; **in —** in dettaglio; **–ed** *a* particolareggiato; **—** *vt* dettagliare
detain *vt* detenere
detect *vt* svelare
detective *a&n* rivelatore *m*, investigatore *m*
detection *n* scoperta, rivelazione
detector *n* scopritore, rivelatore *m*; *(elec)* coesore *m; (rad)* detettore *m*
detention *n* detenzione, arresto; *(delay)* ritardo
deter *vt* scoraggiare, dissuadere; *(detain)* trattenare; **–rent** *a&n* preventivo, dissuadente *m*
detergent *a&n* detergente, detersivo
deteriorate *vt* deteriorare; **—** *vi* deteriorarsi
deterioration *n* deterioramento
determinable *a* determinabile
determinate *a* definito, determinato
determination *n* determinazione, risoluzione
determinative *a* determinativo, definitivo
determine *vt* determinare, decidere; **—** *vi* determinarsi, decidersi; **–d** *a* risoluto, determinato, deciso
detest *vt* detestare; **–able** *a* detestabile; **–ation** *n* detestazione
dethrone *vt* detronizzare; **–ment** *n* detronizzazione
detonate *vi* detonare; **—** *vt* far detonare
detonation *n* detonazione
detonator *n* detonatore *m*
detour *n* deviazione, giravolta; **—** *vt&i* deviare
detract *vt&i* detrarre, denigrare; **— from** sparlare di; **–or** *n* detrattore, denigratore *m*
detraction *n* detrazione, diffamazione
detriment *n* detrimento; **–al** *a* dannoso
deuce *n (cards, dice)* due; *(tennis)* 40 pari
devaluate *vt* svalutare
devaluation *n* svalutazione
devalue *vt* svalutare
devastate *vt* devastare; **–d** *a* devastato
devastating *a* devastante, devastatore
devastation *n* devastazione
develop *vt* sviluppare; **—** *vi* svilupparsi; **–ment** *n* sviluppo
developer *n (photo)* sviluppatore *m*
deviate *vi* deviare
deviation *n* deviazione
device *n* disegno; *(plan)* progetto, stratagemma *m*; **leave to one's own –s** lasciare in balia della propria volontà
devil *n* diavolo; **between the — and the deep blue sea** fra l'incudine e il martello *(coll)*; **give the — his due** render giustizia all'avversario; **play the — with** *(coll)* mandare in rovina completa; **–ish** *a* diabolico; **–ment** *n* diavoleria; **–try** *n* diavoleria, azione diabolica
devil-may-care *a (careless)* trascurato; *(dissolute)* scapestrato
devious *a* indiretto, deviato
devise *vt* escogitare; *(law)* legare per testamento
devitalize *vt* privare della vitalità; indebolire
devoid *a* destituito; privo di
devolve *vt* devolvere, passare a, trasferire
devote *vt* dedicare; **— oneself to** dedicarsi a; **–d** *a* devoto
devotee *n* devoto, fanatico; persona dedita
devotion *n* devozione; **–al** *a* devozionale; religioso; **–s** *npl* devozioni *fpl*, preghiere *fpl*
devour *vt* divorare
devout *a* devoto, pio; **–ness** *n* devozione, religiosità
dew *n* rugiada; **— claw** sprone *m*
dewy *a* rugiadoso
dexterity *n* destrezza
dexterous *a* abile, destro
dextrin *n* destrina
dextrose *n* destrosio
diabetes *n* diabete *m*
diabetic *a* diabetico
diabolic, –al *a* diabolico
diacritical *a* diacritico; **— mark** segno diacritico
diadem *n* diadema *m*
diaeresis *n* dieresi *f*
diagnose *vt* diagnosticare
diagnosis *n* diagnosi *f*
diagonal *a&n* diagonale; **–ly** *adv* diagonalmente
diagram *n* diagramma *m;* **–matic** *a* diagrammatico
dial *n* quadrante *m*; *(sun)* meridiana; *(telephone)* disco; **—** *vt* misurare, indicare sul quadrante; **—** *vi (telephone)* discare; fare il numero
dialect *n* dialetto; **–ic, –ical** *a* dialettale, dialettico; **–ics** *npl* dialettica
dialogue *n* dialogo
diameter *n* diametro
diametric, diametrical *a* diametrale
diametrically *adv* diametralmente; **— opposed** diametralmente opposto
diamond *n* rombo; *(baseball)* campo di giuoco; *(cards)* quadri *mpl; (gem)* diamante *m*; **— in the rough** *(fig)* diamante grezzo
diapason *n* diapason *m*
diaper *n (baby's)* pannolino
diaphanous *a* diafano
diaphragm *n* diaframma *m*
diarrhea *n* diarrea

diary *n* diario
diastase *n* diastasi *f*
diathermy *n* diatermia
diatonic *a* diatonico
diatribe *n* diatriba
dice *npl* dadi *mpl*; — *vi* giuocare ai dadi, — *vt (food)* tagliare in dadi
dicker *vi (sl)* contrattare; — *vt* barattare; — *n* buon affare
dictaphone *n* dittafono
dictate *vt&i* dettare; — *n* dettame *m*
dictation *n* dettatura; *(order)* comando
dictator *n* dittatore *m;* **–ship** *n* dittatura
dicatatorial *a* dittatorio, dittatoriale
diction *n* dizione
dictionary *n* dizionario
dictograph *n* dittografo
dictum *n* detto, massima
didactic *a* didattico; **–s** *npl* didattica
die *vi* morire; — **away** morire lentamente, languire; — **off** estinguersi; *(wither)* appassire, svanire; — **out** perire; estinguersi; **–hard** *n* intransigente *m*
die *n (coin)* conio; *(dice)* dado; *(mech)* stampo, marchio; — **casting** pressa, fusione; **the — is cast** il dado è tratto; **–maker** *n* tecnico formista
diesel engine motore Diesel
diet *n (pol)* dieta, assemblea
diet *n* dieta, regime *m*; **be on a —** essere a dieta; **put on a —** mettere a dieta
dietetic *a* dietetico; **–s** *n* dietetica
dietitian *n* dietista *m&f*; *(med)* medico dietista
differ *vi* differire; *(disagree)* dissentire
difference *n* differenza; **split the —** dividere la differenza
different *a* differente, diverso
differential *n&a* differenziale *m*
differentiate *vt* differenziare; — *vi* differenziarsi
differentiation *n* differenziazione
difficult *a* difficile; **–y** *n* difficoltà
difficulties *npl* difficoltà *fpl*; **be in —** essere in difficoltà
diffidence *n* diffidenza, timidezza
diffident *a* diffidente, timido
diffract *vt* diffrangere
diffraction *n* diffrazione
diffuse *a* diffuso; **–r** *n* diffusore *m*
diffusion *n* diffusione
dig *vt&i* scavare; *(hoe)* zappare; — **in** rintanarsi; *(coll)* indagare; — **up** dissotterrare; *(find out)* scoprire; — *n* *(coll)* sarcasmo; *(push)* spinta; *(sl)* sgobbone *m*
digest *n* digesto, compendio
digest *vt* considerare; *(summarize)* riassumere; — *vt&i (food)* digerire
digestible *a* digeribile
digestive *a* digestivo
digger *n (mech)* scavatrice *f*
diggings *npl (coll)* alloggio
digit *n* dito; *(number)* cifra; **–al** *a* digitale
dignified *a* austero, nobile, dignitoso
dignify *vt* dignificare, nobilitare
dignitary *n* dignitario
dignity *n* dignità
digraph *n* digramma *m*
digress *vi* digredire
digression *n* digressione
dike *n* diga
dilapidate *vt* dilapidare; — *vi* dilapidarsi; **–d** *a* dilapidato
dilapidation *n* dilapidazione
dilate *vt* dilatare; — *vi* dilatarsi, espandersi
dilation *n* dilazione, dilatazione
dilatory *a* dilatorio
dilemma *n* dilemma *m*; **the horns of a —** i corni di un dilemma
diligence *n* perserveranza
diligent *a* diligente
dill *n* aneto
dillydally *vi* tentennare, nicchiare
dilute *vt* diluire
diluted *a* diluito; **be —** diluirsi
dilution *n* diluzione
dim *a* oscuro, confuso; — *vt* oscurare, offuscare; **–ly** *adv* oscuramente, confusamente
dime *n* moneta da 10 cents
dimension *n* dimensione; **–al** *a* dimensionale; di dimensione
diminish *vt&i* diminuire
diminutive *a&n* diminutivo
dimmer *n* reostato
dimness *n* oscurità
dimout *n* oscuramento
dimple *n* fossetta, affossamento; — *vi* formare fossette; **–d** *a* increspato
din *n* fracasso; — *vt* stordire
dine *vi* pranzare, desinare; — **out** pranzare fuori
diner *n* chi pranza; *(rail)* vagone ristorante
dinghy *n (naut)* dingo
dinginess *n* oscurità; sporcizia
dingy *a (dark)* oscuro; *(dirty)* sporco
dining *n* pranzo; — **room** sala da pranzo
dinner *n* pranzo, desinare *m*; — **jacket** abito da sera; smoking *m*
dinosaur *n* dinosauro
dint *n* forza; **by — of** a forza di
diocese *n* diocesi *f*
diorama *n* diorama *m*
dioxide *n* biossido
dip *vt* immergere; *(plunge into)* tuffare; — *vi* immergersi; tuffarsi; — **into** attingere a; — **the flag** abbassare la bandiera; — *n* immersione, tuffo
diphtheria *n* difterite *f*
diphthong *n* dittongo
diploma *n* diploma *m*
diplomacy *n* diplomazia
diplomat *n* diplomatico; **–ic** *a* diplomatico
dipper *n (person)* immersionista; *(spoon)* cucchiaione *m*; **Big D–** Orsa Maggiore; **Little D–** Orsa Minore
direct *a* diretto, diritto; — **current** corrente continua; — **object** *(gram)* accusativo; **–ly** *adv (direction)* direttamente; *(time)* immediatamente; **–ive** *n* direttiva
direction *n* direzione; *(address)* indirizzo; — **finder** *(rad)* ondascopio
directions *npl* direzioni *fpl*; *(instructions)* istruzioni, indicazioni *fpl*
director *n* direttore *m*; *(actors)* regista *m*; *(mus)* direttore d'orchestra; **board of –s** consiglio di amministrazione
directory *n* direttorio, guida; *(phone)* guida telefonica

dirge *n* canto funebre
dirt *n* sudiciume *m*
dirtiness *n* sporcizia; *(baseness)* bassezza
dirty *a* sporco, sudicio; — *vt* sporcare, imbrattare
disability *n* incapacità, invalidità; — **insurance** assicurazione per l'invalidità
disable *vt* inabilitare; **–d** *a* invalido
disablement *n* incapacità
disabuse *vt* disingannare
disadvantage *n* svantaggio, perdita, inconveniente *m*
disagree *vi* dissentire, non essere d'accordo
disagreeable *a* antipatico, spiacevole, sgradevole
disagreement *n* disaccordo, divergenza
disallow *vt* disapprovare
disappear *vi* sparire; **–ance** *n* scomparsa
disappoint *vt* ingannare, deludere
disappointment *n* delusione, disappunto
disapproval *n* disapprovazione
disapprove *vt* disapprovare; — *vi* avere cattiva opinione
disarm *vt&i* disarmare
disarming *a* ingenuo
disarmament *n* disarmo; — **conference** conferenza del disarmo
disarrange *vt* scompigliare
disarray *n* confusione
disaster *n* disastro, sciagura
disastrous *a* disastroso, catastrofico
disavow *vt* negare
disband *vt* sbandare, congedare; — *vi* sbandarsi; essere licenziato
disbar *vt (law)* cancellare dall'albo degli avvocati
disbelieve *vt* diffidare, discredere
disburse *vt* sborsare; **–ment** *n* sborso, spese *fpl*
discard *n* rifiuto; *(card)* scarto
discard *vt&i* scartare
discern *vt* discernere, distinguere; — *vi* discriminare; **–ible** *a* percettibile; **–ing** *a* perspicace, giudizioso; **–ment** *n* discernimento
discharge *n (elec)* scarico; *(med)* spurgo; *(mil)* congedo, rilascio
discharge *vt&i (dismiss)* licenziare; *(a duty)* compiere; *(elec)* scaricare; *(gun)* sparare; *(mil)* congedare; *(release)* rilasciare; *(unload)* scaricare; — **an obligation** adempiere un dovere
disciple *n* discepolo
disciplinarian *a* disciplinare
discipline *n* disciplina; — *vt* punire; castigare
disclaim *vt* rinunciare
disclose *vt* svelare, manifestare
disclosure *n* rivelazione
discolor *vt* scolorare, scolorire, cambiar colore; **–ation** *n* scoloramento
discomfort *n* disagio, incomodo
disconcert *vt* sconcertare
disconnect *vt* staccare, tagliare; *(part)* separare; *(elec)* interrompere
discontent *n* malcontento, scontento
discontinue *vt* sospendere, prosciogliere; — *vi* desistere
discontinued *a* sospeso, soppresso, esaurito
discord *n* discordia; **–ant** *a* discordante
discount *n* sconto, ribasso; — **rate** tasso di sconto; — *vt* scontare
discountenance *vt* turbare, sconcertare
discourage *vt* scoraggiare; *(deter)* dissuadere; **—ment** *n* scoraggiamento, scoramento
discouraging *a* scoraggiante
discourse *n* discorso, trattato
discourtesy *n* scortesia
discourteous *a* scortese, sgarbato
discover *vt* scoprire, trovare; **–er** *n* scopritore *m*; **–y** *n* scoperta
discredit *vt* screditare
discreet *a* discreto, prudente
discrepancy *n* discrepanza, divergenza, contraddizione
discretion *n* discrezione, prudenza
discriminate *vt&i* discriminare, distinguere; far distinzione; — **against** far distinzioni nocive contro
discriminating *a* discretivo, da intenditore
discrimination *n* discriminazione, distinzione
discus *n (sport)* disco
discuss *vt* dibattere, parlare di, discutere, ragionare di
discussion *n* discussione
disdain *n* disdegno, disprezzo; — *vt* disdegnare; **–ful** *a* sdegnoso
disease *n* malattia; **–d** *a* malato
disembark *vt* sbarcare; **–ation** *n* sbarco
disenchant *vt* disincantare; **–ment** *n* disincanto, disillusione
disencumber *vt* sgombrare
disengage *vt* liberare; *(mech)* sganciare; — *vi* separarsi da
disfavor *n* disgrazia, sfavore *m*
disfigure *vt* sfigurare, sfregiare
disfranchise *vt* privare della franchigia
disgorge *vt* vomitare, recere
disgrace *n* vergogna, disonore *m*; — *vt* disonorare; **–ful** *a* vergognoso, disonorevole
disgruntled *a* malcontento, di malumore, imbronciato
disguise *vt* travestire, mascherare; — *n* travestimento, finzione, maschera; **in** — camuffato
disgust *n* schifo, disgusto; — *vt* disgustare; **–ing** *a* disgustoso, schifoso
dish *n* piatto, pietanza; — *vt* servire, scodellare; **–water** *n* lavatura di piatti; **–cloth** *n* strofinaccio da piatti; **–pan** *n* recipiente per lavare i piatti; **–towel** *n* strofinaccio per asciugare i piatti
dishearten *vt* scoraggiare
dishevel *vt* scapigliare, scarmigliare; **–ed** *a* scapigliato
dishonest *a* disonesto
dishonor *n* disonore *m*, infamia; — *vt* disonorare, svergognare; **–able** *a* disonorevole; **–ably** *adv* disonorevolmente
dishwarmer *n* scaldavivande *m*
dishwasher *n* lavapiatti *m*; *(person)* sguattero
disillusion *n* disillusione; **–ment** *n* liberazione d'una illusione; — *vt* disilludere
disinclined *a* contrario
disinfect *vt* disinfettare; **–ant** *n&a* disinfettante *m*; **–ion** *n* disinfezione
disinherit *vt* diseredare

disintegrate *vt* disintegrare
disintegration *n* disintegrazione
disinter *vt* disseppellire; **–ment** *n* dissotterramento
disinterested *a* disinteressato
disjoin *vt* disgiungere; — *vi* disgiungersi
disjoint *vt* slogare, disgiungere; **–ed** *a* slogato
disk *n* disco; — **jockey** presentatore di dischi
dislike *n* antipatia, avversione; — *vt* avere in antipatia
dislocate *vt* slogare
dislocation *n (med)* slogatura
dislodge *vt&i* sloggiare, scacciare
disloyal *a* sleale; **–ty** *n* infedeltà, slealtà
dismal *a* triste, misero, funesto
dismantle *vt* smantellare
dismay *vt* costernare; — *n* costernazione
dismember *vt* smembrare
dismiss *vt* licenziare, destituire, congedare; **—a meeting** togliere una seduta; *(oust)* scacciare; **–al** *n* licenziamento, destituzione, congedo
dismount *vi* smontare, scavalcare
disobedience *n* disobbedienza
disobedient *a* disobbediente
disobey *vt* disobbedire a
disobliging *a* senza gentilezza
disorder *n* disordine *m;* **–ed mind** psicopatico; **–ly** *a* disordinato
disorganization *n* disorganizzazione
disorganize *vt* disorganizzare
disown *vt* negare, non confessare, rinunciare
disparage *vt* menomare
disparaging *a* offensivo
dispassionate *a* spassionato; **–ly** *adv* spassionatamente
dispatch *n* prontezza, urgenza, fretta; *(com)* dispaccio, spedizione; — *vt* inviare, spacciare, spedire; *(kill)* uccidere
dispel *vt* dissipare; — *vi* dissiparsi
dispensable *a* non indispensabile
dispensary *n* dispensario
dispensation *n* distribuzione; *(excuse from)* dispensa
dispense *vt* distribuire; *(administer)* amministrare; *(exempt)* dispensare, esentare
dispersal *n* dispersione
disperse *vt* disperdere, spargere; — *vi* disperdersi
dispirit *vt* scoraggiare; **–ed** *a* abbattuto; scoraggiato; (*dismayed*) sgomento
displaced *a* spostato **— person** profugo
displacement *n* spostamento; *(naut)* stazzo; **cylinder** — cilindrata
display *n* mostra, esibizione; — *vt* esporre, mostrare
displease *vt* offendere, dispiacere a
displeasure *n* dispiacere *m*, disapprovazione
disposable *a* disponibile
disposal *n* disposizione
dispose *vt* disporre; — **of** disporre di; *(sell)* vendere
disposed *a* disposto; **ill** — maldisposto, malintenzionato; **be** — **to** avere dispozione per; essere incline per
disposition *n* inclinazione, carattere *m*; *(disposal of)* disposizione; *(temper)* indole *f*
dispossess *vt* espropriare; **–ed** *a* espropriato
disproportionate *a* sproporzionato
disprove *vt* confutare, invalidare
disputable *a* disputabile
dispute *n* disputa, dibattito
disqualification *n* inabilitazione; squalifica
disqualify *vt* squalificare
disquiet *n* inquietudine *f;* travaglio; — *vt* inquietare, tribolare; **–ing** *a* inquietante
disregard *vt* non dare importanza a, trascurare; — *n* negligenza, indifferenza
disreputable *a* vergognoso; screditato, malfamato
disrepute *n* disonore *m*, discredito
disrespect *n* insolenza; mancanza di rispetto; **–ful** *a* irriverente, incivile; **–fully** *adv* irrispettosamente
disrobe *vt* svestire, spogliare; — *vi* spogliarsi
disrupt *vt* rompere
dissatisfaction *n* malcontento
dissatisfied *a* malcontento
dissatisfy *vt* scontentare, dispiacere
dissect *vt* notomizzare, sezionare; **–ion** *n* dissezione
dissemble *vt&i* simulare
dissemblingly *adv* dissimulatamente
disseminate *vt* disseminare, diffondere
dissemination *n* disseminazione
dissension *n* discordia
dissent *vi* dissentire; — *n* dissenso
dissertation *n* dissertazione; *(school)* tesi di laurea
disservice *n* disservizio
dissimilar *a* dissimile; **–ity** *n* dissimilitudine *f*
dissimulate *vt* dissimulare
dissimulation *n* dissimulazione
dissipate *vt* dissipare; — *vi* dissiparsi
dissipation *n* dispersione, dissipazione
dissolute *a* dissoluto, licenzioso; **–ly** *adv* dissolutamente
dissolution *n* dissoluzione, licenza
dissolve *vt* sciogliere, dissolvere; — *vi* disciogliersi
dissonance *n* dissonanza
dissonant *a* dissonante, differente
dissuade *vt* dissuadere
dissuasion *n* dissuasione
distaff *n* rocca, conocchia
distance *n* distanza; **at a — of** alla distanza di
distant *a* distante, lontano; *(reticent)* riservato
distantly *adv (far)* lontanamente; *(coldly)* con distanza
distaste *n* disgusto, dispiacere *m*; *(dislike)* avversione, idiosincrasia
distasteful *a* fastidioso, sgradevole, antipatico
distemper *n* indisposizione; *(med)* malattia; — *vt (disturb)* turbare; fare male, fare ammalare
distend *vt* stendere, allargare; — *vi* distendersi, allargarsi
distill *vt* distillare; **–ed** *a* distillato; **–ation** *n* distillazione

distillery *n* distilleria
distinct *a* distinto; **–ive** *a* distintivo
distinction *n* distinzione
distinguish *vt* distinguere; **–ed** *a* distinto
distinguishing *a* distintivo
distort *vt* contorcere, distorcere; *(alter)* travisare *(fig)*
distortion *n* distorsione
distract *vt* distrarre, svagare; turbare
distracted *a* distratto; divertito; *(upset)* sconvolto; **–ly** *adv* distrattamente
distraction *n* distrazione
distress *n* sfortuna, guaio, miseria, pena, angoscia; — **signal** segnalazione di soccorso; **–ed** *a* spiacente; — *vt* inquietare, affliggere
distribute *vt* distribuire
distribution *n* distribuzione
distributor *n* distributore *m*
district *n* distretto; — **attorney** procuratore di stato
distrust *vt* sospettare; diffidare di; non aver fiducia in; — *n* diffidenza, sfiducia; **–ful** *a* sospettoso
disturb *vt* disturbare; **–ance** *n* disturbo
disuse *n* disuso
ditch *n* fosso, fossato; **fight to the last —** resistere ad oltranza
ditto *n* idem *m*, lo stesso
diuretic *a* diuretico
divan *n* divano, sofà
dive *vi* tuffarsi; *(naut)* immergersi; — *n* immersione, tuffo; *(coll)* bettola; *(avi)* scesa in picchiata
dive– *(in comp)* **—bomber** *n* aereo da picchiata; — **bombing** *n* bombardamento in picchiata
diver *n* tuffatore *m; (deep-sea)* palombaro; *(skin)* sommozzatore *m*
diverge *vi* divergere, deviare, differire
divergence *n* divergenza
diverging *a* divergente
divers *a* assortito
diverse *a* diverso, differente, vario
diversion *n* diversione, divertimento, passatempo; *(turning from)* deviazione; **–ary** *a* ricreativo
diversity *n* diversità
divert *vt* divertire; *(amuse)* svagare; **–ing** *a* divertente
divest *vt* svestire, spogliare; — **oneself** svestirsi, spogliarsi
divide *vt* dividere; — *vi* dividersi, scindersi; **–d** *a* diviso; — *n (geog)* spartiacque *m*
dividend *n* dividendo
divider *n* divisore *m;* **–s** *npl (compass)* compasso a molla
divination *n* divinazione
divine *a* divino; — *vi* profetizzare, fare profezia
diving *n* immersione, tuffo; — **bell** campana da palombaro; — **suit** scafandro
divinity *n* divinità
division *n* divisione; **–al** *a* divisorio, divisionale
divisor *n* divisore *m*
divorce *n* divorzio; — *vt* divorziare, divorziarsi; — **court** tribunale dei divorzi; **sue for a —** chiedere un divorzio
divorcé *n* divorziato, **–e** *n* divorziata
divot *n (golf)* zolla erbosa strappata dal bastone
divulge *vt* rivelare, divulgare
dizziness *n* vertigini *fpl*, stordimento
dizzy *a* vertiginoso; *(coll)* stordito; **feel —** avere le vertigini; **make one —** stordire, dare le vertigini.a
D.N.A., deoxyribonucleic acid *n* D.N.A., acido diossigenucleico
do *vt&i* fare; — **away with** sopprimere; distruggere; — **dishes** lavare i piatti; — **in** *(coll)* rovinare; *(kill)* uccidere; — **one's best** fare del proprio meglio; — **out of** frodare; — **up** rifare, riparare, involgere, abbottonare; — **without** fare senza; **have to — with** aver che fare con; **make —** aggiustarsi con; **this will —** ciò basta
docile *a* docile
dock *n* molo, imbarcadero; **dry —** bacino di carenaggio; — *vt* abbreviare; *(ship)* far entrare in bacino; *(tail)* tagliare la coda; *(wages)* far dedurre dalla paga
docket *n* registro; *(law)* attergato
dockyard *n* cantiere navale
doctor *n* dottore *m*; **–ate** *n* dottorato; — *vt* adulterare; — **oneself** curarsi da sè; **be under a –'s care** essere assisito dal dottore
doctrine *n* dottrina
document *n* documento; **–ary** *a* documentario
documentation *n* documentazione
dodder *vi* tremare; **–ing** *a* tremante
dodge *n* balzo; *(coll)* trucco *(fig)*; — *vt* evitare, schivare, eludere; — *vi* cambiare di posto; sfuggire con sotterfugi
doe *n* daina
doff *vt* cavarsi, togliersi; sbarazzarsi di
dog *n* cane *m*; — **days** canicola; — **one's footsteps** pedinare qualcuno; **let sleeping –s lie** lasciare dormire il cane che dorme; — *vt (follow)* pedinare; *(spy on)* spiare, seguire le orme
dog– *(in comp)* **—eared** *a* sfogliato, spiegazzato; **—eared page** pagina con gli angoli sfogliati; **—tired** *a* stanco morto
dogged *a* ostinato, accanito; **–ly** *adv* risolutamente; *(firmly)* tenacemente; *(stubbornly)* ostinatamente
doghouse *n* canile *m*; **be in the —** *(sl)* essere nei pasticci *(coll)*
dogma *n* dogma *m*; **–tic** *a* dogmatico
dolly *n* tovagliolino, sottocoppa *m*; *(coaster)* sottobicchiere *m*
doing *n* fatto, evento; **be worth —** valere la pena; **–s** *npl* faccende *fpl*, fatti *mpl*
doldrums *npl (naut)* calme equatoriali *fpl*; **be in the —** essere malinconico
dole *n* elemosina, piccola quantità; **–ful** *a* doloroso, lamentevole; — *vt* fare la carità; — **out** distribuire
doll *n* bambola
dollar *n* dollaro
dolly *n (toy)* bambolina; *(truck)* carrello
dolor *n* dolore *m*
dolorous *a* doloroso
dolt *n* balordo, stupido
domain *n* dominio, proprietà
dome *n* cupola

domestic *a* domestico, di famiglia; nazionale; locale; — *n (servant)* domestico
domesticate *vt* addomesticare
domicile *n* domicilio
dominance *n* dominio
dominant *a* dominante
dominate *vt* dominare, predominare
domination *n* dominazione
domineer *vt&i* tiranneggiare, signoreggiare; **-ing** *a* tirannico, prepotente
Dominican Republic *n* Republica domenicana
dominion *n* dominio; colonia autonoma
domino *n* domino
don *vt* indossare; — *n* signore *m*
donate *vt* donare, dare
donation *n* offerta, dono
donkey *n* asino; **make a — of** far passare per stupido *(coll)*
donor *n* donatore *m*, donatrice *f*
doodle *n* allocco, ingenuo; — *vt&i* disegnare (*or* scrivere) distrattamente
doom *n* condanna; **voice of —** la voce della Giustizia Divina; — *vt* condannare; **-ed** *a* predestinato; *(condemned)* condannato
doomsday *n* la fine del mondo
door *n* porta, uscio; **-bell** *n* campanello; **-knob** *n* maniglia della porta; **-man** *n* portiere *m*; **-mat** *n* nettapiedi *m*; **-step** *n* soglia; **-way** *n* vano della porta; **back —** porta di servizio
dope *n* stupefacente *m*; *(sl)* narcotico; *(low-down, sl)* informazione *(fig)*; — *vt (sl)* affettare con stupefacenti
dormant *a* dormiente
dormer window abbaino
dormitory *n* dormitorio
dose *n* dose *f*; — *vt* dosare, somministrare dosi
dossier *n* incartamento
dot *n* punto; **on the —** a punto
dotage *n* rimbambimento
dote *vi* rimbambire; — **on** amare pazzamente
double *n&a* duplicato, doppio; — **feature** due film d'un programma; **one's —** l'altro sè stesso; — *vt* doppiare, raddoppiare; — **back** *(fold)* piegare indietro; *(retrace)* ritornare sui propri passi; — *vi* ripiegare; tornare indietro, girarsi
double- *(in comp)* **—breasted** *a* a due petti; **—cross** *n (sl)* tradimento; doppio giuoco; — *vt* tradire; fare il doppio giuoco; **—edged** *a* a due tagli; **—faced** *a (cloth)* a doppia faccia; *(person)* ipocrita, falso; di faccia doppia *(coll)*
doubt *n* dubbio; **no —** senza dubbio; **put in —** mettere in dubbio; **-ful** *a* dubbioso; **-less** *adv* certamente; senza dubbio; — *vt* dubitare
douche *n* doccia
dough *n* pasta; *(sl)* denaro, soldi *mpl*
doughnut *n* frittella
dove *n* colomba
dovetail *n* coda di rondine; — *vt* unire a coda di rondine
dowager *n (coll)* matrona di prestigio
dowdy *a* malvestito, trasandato
down *n (feather)* piuma; *(hair)* lanugine *f*; — *adv* giù abasso; in basso; — **to** fino a; — **the street** *(be)* giù per la strada; *(go)* per la strada; **go —** scendere; **pay —** pagare la prima quota
down *vt (debase)* umiliare; (lower) abbassare; *(pull)* abbattere; *(swallow)* buttar giù
downcast *a* abbattuto
downfall *n* rovina, caduta
downgrade *n* discesa; — *vt* degradare
downhearted *a* abbattuto, scoraggiato
downhill *a* scendente; — *adv* in discesa
downpour *n* acquazzone *m;* pioggia a catinelle
downright *a* diretto, assoluto, completo; — *adv* assolutamente
downstairs *adv* giù, abbasso, di sotto, in basso, al piano di sotto; — *n* pianterreno
downtown *n* centro della città; — *adv* in città
downwards *adv* abbasso
dowry *n* dote *f*
doze *vi* sonnecchiare
dozen *n* dozzina
drab *a* grigiobruno, monotono; *(color)* nocciuola
draft *n* tiro; *(air)* corrente d'aria; *(com)* tratta; *(drink)* sorsata; *(mil)* leva, coscrizione; *(plan)* disegno; *(sketch)* schizzo; — **beer** birra spillata; **rough —** minuta, brutta copia
draft *vt* disegnare; *(compose)* redigere; *(sketch)* tracciare
draftsman *n* disegnatore *m*
drag *n* draga; *(sl)* influenza, favore *m*; — *vt* trascinare; — *vi* trascinarsi
drag chute *(avi)* paracaduta che frena l'atterraggio
dragnet *n* rete *f*; *(police)* retata
dragon *n* drago
drain *vt* scolare, prosciugare; *(empty)* vuotare; **-pipe** *n* tubo di scarico, tubo di drenaggio
drain *n* canale *m*; *(med)* drenaggio; **-age** *n* drenaggio
drama *n* dramma *m*
dramatic *a* drammatico
dramatist *n* drammaturgo; autore drammatico
dramatize *vt* drammatizzare
drape *n* drappo; — *vt* drappeggiare; — *vi* pendere flosciamente
drapery *n* drappeggio, tendaggio, drapperia
drastic *a* drastico
draw *vt* disegnare; *(attract)* attrarre; *(pull)* tirare; *(sword)* sguainare; *(water)* attingere; — **a sigh** sospirare; — **away** sorpassare; — **back** indietreggiare; — **lots** sorteggiare; — **near** avvicinarsi; — **oneself up** mettersi ritto; — **out** tirar fuori
draw *n* attrazione; *(score)* parte indecisa
drawback *n* svantaggio, inconveniente *m*
drawbridge *n* ponte levatoio
drawer *n* cassetto
drawers *npl (clothing)* mutande *f*
drawing *n* disegno; *(lottery)* lotteria; *(pulling)* tiraggio; *(raffle)* sorteggio; — **card** specchio per le allodole *(fig)*; — **pen** tiralinee *m*; — **room** sala da

ricevimento, salone *m*
drawl *n* voce affettata; — *vi* strascicare le parole
drawn *a* indeciso; *(face)* emaciato; *(sword)* sguainato
dread *n* paura, terrore *m;* — *vt* avere orrore di
dreadful *a* terribile, spaventevole
dream *n* sogno; — *vt* avere una visione di; — *vi* sognare; — **up** inventare; **–er** *n* sognatore *m*
dreamy *a* sognante; *(fantastic)* chimerico
dreary *a* lugubre, cupo, desolato, monotono
dregs *npl* feccia, sedimento
drench *vt* inzuppare, bagnare
dress *n* abbigliamento; vestito da donna; — *vt* vestire; *(med)* medicare; *(wrap)* fasciare; — *vi* vestirsi; **–y** *a (coll)* elegante, vistoso
dresser *n (furniture)* comò, cassettone *m*; *(theat)* guardarobiere *m*; **a good** — persona ben vestita
dressing *n (meat, fowl)* ripieno; *(med)* medicazione; *(salad)* condimento per l'insalata; — **table** toletta
dressmaker *n* sarta; sarto
dribble *vi* gocciolare; — *vt* far gocciolare
dried *a* secco
drift *n (avi)* deriva; deviazione a causa del vento; *(meaning)* significato; *(naut)* deriva, direzione; *(snow)* cumulo di neve; **get the** — *(sl)* comprendere; — *vi* andare alla deriva; — *vt* accumulare
drill *n (mech)* trapano, perforatrice *f*; *(mil)* esercitazione; *(training)* addestramento; — *vt* forare, perforare, *(train)* addestrare
drink *n* bibita, bevanda; **–able** *a* potabile; — *vt* bere; — **a toast** fare un brindisi; — **in** assimilare
drip *vi* sgocciolare; — *vt* far sgocciolare; — *n* sgocciolamento
drive *n* energia, sforzo; *(mech)* trasmissione; *(pressure)* pressione; *(ride)* passeggiata in carrozza; — *vt* guidare; — **away** allontanare; — **back** respingere; — **mad** far ammattire; — *vi* guidare; essere sospinto; andare in veicolo; *(rush)* precipitarsi; — **a bargain** condurre un affare; — **at** tendere a
drive-in *n (restaurant)* autoristorante *m*, autoristoratore *m*; *(theat)* autocinema *m*, cineparco
driver *n (auto)* automobilista, autista *m*; *(bus)* conduttore *m*; *(coachman)* cocchiere *m*
driver's license patente *f*
driveway *n* vialetto d'entrata; passo carreggiabile
driving *a* movente; di guida; — **power** forza di propulsione
drizzle *vt&i* piovigginare; — *n* pioggerella
droll *a* bizzarro, scherzoso, burlone
drone *n* fuco, pecchione *m*; *(avi)* aereo a controllo remoto; — *vt* dire come ronzando; — *vi* ronzare
drool *vi* sbavare, far bava
droop *vi* curvarsi; *(hang)* pendere; — *vt* abbassare
drop *n* goccia; *(descent)* caduta; *(ear)* pendente *m*; *(globule)* globulo
drop *vi* gocciolare; *(prices)* ribassare; — *vt* lasciar cadere; abbandonare, negligere; — **behind** rimanere indietro; — **in** capitare per caso; — **out** mettersi fuori
drop– *(in comp)* **—kick** *(football) n* calcio di rimbalzo; — *vt&i* dare un calcio di rimbalzo; **—leaf** *n* asse accessoria per allungare un tavolo
dropper *n (med)* contagocce *m*
dropsy *n* idropisia, edema *m*
drought *n* siccità
drove *n* gregge *m*, mandra; *(crowd)* folla
drown *vt&i* annegare
drowse *vt* assopire; — *vi* assopirsi
drowsiness *n* sonnolenza, assopimento
drowsy *a* sonnacchioso, sonnolento
drudge *n* sgobbone *m;* uomo di fatica; — *vi* sfacchinare
drudgery *n* facchinata, lavoraccio
drug *n* droga, stupefacente *m*; *(med)* medicinale *m;* — **addict** tossicomane *m;* **be a — on the market** *(com)* essere in troppa concorrenza; — *vt* narcotizzare
druggist *n* farmacista *m*
drugstore *n* farmacia
drum *n (ear)* timpano; *(mus)* tamburo; — *vi (fingers)* tamburellare; *(mus)* tambureggiare; — **into** *(fig)* inculcare; — *vt* tamburellare; — **up** *(get)* sollecitare, ottenere ostentando
drummer *n (com)* commesso viaggiatore; *(mus)* tamburino
drumstick *n (fowl)* coscia; *(mus)* bacchetta di tamburo
drunk *n&a* ubriaco, ebbro; bevuto *(coll)*; **–ard** *n* ubriacone, beone *m;* **–en** *a* ubriaco, ebbro; **–enly** *adv* ebbramente, ubriacamente; da ubriaco
drunkenness *n* ubriachezza
dry *a* secco; — **cell** cellula elettrica secca; — **cleaner** tintore *m*; — **cleaning** pulitura a secco; — **dock** bacino di carenaggio; — **goods** mercerie *fpl;* — *vt* seccare; — **up** seccarsi
dryness *n* aridità
dual *a* doppio, duplice, — **control** doppio controllo
dub *vt* investire; armare cavaliere; *(name)* soprannominare; — **in** *(movies)* doppiare
dubious *a* dubbio, incerto, equivoco
duchess *n* duchessa
duchy *n* ducato
duck *n* anitra; — *vt (avoid)* schivare; *(dip)* immergere; *(plunge)* tuffare; — **the head** chinare la testa; — *vi* immergersi; tuffarsi; schivarsi
duct *n* condotto, tubo
ductless *a* senza condotti; — **gland** ghiandola endocrina
dud *n (failure)* cosa che fa cilecca; *(rag)* cencio; — *a* inutile
dude *n* bellimbusto, zerbinotto
duds *npl (sl, clothes)* abiti *mpl; (things)* roba
due *n&a* debito, dovuto; — **bill** *(com)* cambiale *f*, tratta; **fall —, be —** scadere; **in — time** a tempo debito; — *adv* direttamente

dues *npl* quota, diritti *mpl*, ammontare dovuto
duet *n* duetto
duel *n* duello
duke *n* duca *m*
dull *a* ottuso, noioso; *(color)* oscuro; *(edge)* smussato; — **pain** dolore sordo; **–ness** *n* povertà di spirito; *(surface)* opacità
duly *adv* regolarmente, debitamente
dumb *a* muto; *(coll)* stupido, cretino
dumbly *a* mutamente
dumbbell *n* manubrio
dumbwaiter *n* calapranzi *m*
dumbfound *vt* confondere; far tacere
dummy *n* prestanome *m*; *(cards)* morto; *(manikin)* manichino; *(print)* menabò; *(sl)* stupido; *(straw)* uomo di paglia; — *a* falso, finto
dump *n* mondezzaio; *(sl)* luogo malandato; — *vt* scaricare; svendere in quantità; — *vi* cadere improvvisamente; scaricarsi; **–y** *a* tozzo; *(thickset)* tarchiato
dumps *npl (sl)* malinconia; **be in the —** essere malinconico
dumping ground posto dei rifiuti
dumpling *n* gnocco
dun *vt&i* importunare; *(for money)* insistere nella riscossione
dunce *n* stupido, ignorante *m*, balordo, asino
dune *n* duna
dungeon *n* carcere sotterraneo
dupe *n* gonzo; — *vt* gabbare, truffare, imbrogliare
duplex *a* doppio, duplice
duplicate *n* copia; — *n&a* duplicato; — *vt* riprodurre, duplicare
duplicity *n* doppiezza, duplicità
durable *a* durevole
durability *n* durabilità
duration *n* durata
duress *n* coercizione; **under —** per forza, dietro minaccia
during *prep* durante
dusk *n* crepuscolo, imbrunire *m*
dusky *a* scuro, nerastro, bruno
dust *n* polvere *f*; — **storm** tormenta di sabbia; **throw — in the eyes** *(fig)* gettare polvere negli occhi *(fig)*; **–y** *a* polveroso
dust *vt* spolverare, spazzolare; — *vi* impolverarsi; levare la polvere dai mobili
duster *n* stroffinaccio
Dutch *n&a* olandese *m&f*; — **treat** pagamento alla romana *(coll)*; **go —** *(coll)* fare alla romana
duties *npl* funzioni *fpl*; doveri *mpl*; *(tax)* diritti di dogana
dutiful *a* obbediente
duty *n* dovere *m*; *(mil)* servizio; **on —** di servizio
duty-free *a* franco di dazio; in franchigia
dwarf *n&a* nano; — *vt* rimpicciolire
dwell *vi* abitare, risiedere; — **on** *(a subject)* insistere su
dwelling *n* dimora
dwindle *vt* ridurre; — *vi* diminuire, deperire, ridursi
dye *vt* tingere, colorire; — *vi* tingersi, colorarsi; — *n* tinta, tintura, colore *m*
dyed-in-the-wool *a* tinto prima della confezione
dyer *n* tintore *m*
dying *a* moribondo, morente
dynamic *a* dinamico; **–s** *n* dinamica
dynamite *n* dinamite *f*
dynamo *n* dinamo *f*
dynasty *n* dinastia
dysentery *n* dissenteria
dyspepsia *n* dispepsia
dyspeptic *a* dispeptico

E

each *a* ciascuno, ogni; — *pron* ognuno, ciascheduno; — **other** l'un l'altro
eager *a* desideroso, avido, volenteroso, impaziente; **–ness** *n* ardore *m*, impazienza
eagle *n* aquila
eagle-eyed *a* dalla vista d'aquila
ear *n* orecchio; *(corn)* pannocchia; **in one — and out the other** entrato in un orecchio e uscito dall'altro *(coll)*; **–ache** *n* dolore all'orecchio; mal d'orecchi; **–drum** *n* timpano
earl *n* conte *m*
early *a* mattutino, mattiniero; — **bird** la prima rondine *(fig)*; l'uccello mattiniero; — *adv* di buon'ora, in anticipo
earmark *vt* destinare, serbare, designare
earmuffs *npl* copriorecchi *mpl*
earn *vt&i* guadagnare; *(deserve)* meritare
earnest *a* serio, sincero; — **money** caparra
earnings *npl* salario, guadagni *mpl*
earphone *n* cuffia telefonica
earring *n* orecchino
earth *n* terra; **–ly** *a* terrestre
earthen *a* terreo, di terra; **–ware** *n* terraglie *fpl*
earthquake *n* terremoto
earthworm *n* verme di terra, verme anellide
earwax *n* cerume *m*
ease *n* agio, facilità, disinvoltura; **at —** a proprio agio; **ill at —** in imbarazzo; — *vt* calmare, sollevare
easel *n* cavalletto
easily *adv* facilmente, senza difficoltà
east *n* est, oriente *m*; **the E–** Oriente; **the Far E–** l'estrem'Oriente
Easter *n* Pasqua; — **Sunday** Pasqua; — *a* pasquale
easterly *a&adv* orientale, dell'est
eastern *a* orientale, dell'oriente
easy *a* facile, disinvolto, comodo; — **money** *(coll)* danaro guadagnato facilmente; — **chair** poltrona; **–going** *a* tranquillo, sereno, bonario
eat *vt* mangiare; *(breakfast)* far colazione; *(dinner)* pranzare; — **one's words** ricredersi; **–en** *a* mangiato
eatable *n* commestibile *m*, alimento; —, **edible** *a* commestibile, mangiabile; **–s** *npl* commestibili *mpl*
eavesdrop *vi* origliare

ebb *n* riflusso; — **tide** bassa marea; — *vi* rifluire, abbassarsi; *(decline)* decadere
ebony *n* ebano; — *a* d'ebano
ebullition *n* ebollizione, bollore *m*; *(fig)* agitazione
eccentric *a&n* eccentrico; **–ity** *n* eccentricità
ecclesiastic, –al *n&a* ecclesiastico
echelon *n* scaglione *m*
echo *n* eco *m&f*; — *vt* far eco a; — *vi* echeggiare
eclair *n* pasta di crema
éclat *n* successo, applauso, effetto
eclipse *n* eclisse *m&f*; — *vt* eclissare, superare; — *vi* ecclissarsi
ecliptic *a (ast)* eclittico
economics *n* scienza economica
economist *n* economista *m*
economize *vt&i* economizzare
economy *n* economia
ecru *a* color seta crudo
ecstasy *n* estasi *f*
ecstatic *a* estatico
ecumenical *a* ecumenico
eddy *n* turbine *m*, vortice *m*; — *vt&i* turbinare
edema *n* edema, gonfiore *m*
edge *n* bordo, margine *m*; *(knife)* filo; **have the — on** *(coll)* aver vantaggio; **on —** sul filo; sull'orlo; *(nervous)* irritabile; **–wise** *adv* di taglio; di profilo; — *vi* avanzare gradatamente; camminare di traverso *(fig)*; *(border)* orlare; — *vt* bordare, orlare; *(whet)* affilare
edging *n* bordo, orlo
edible *a* commestibile, mangereccio
edict *n* editto
edifice *n* edificio
edify *vt* edificare
edit *vt* curare, redigere, rivedere
edition *n* edizione
editor *n (book, magazine)* redattore, curatore *m*; *(newspaper)* direttore *m*
editorial *n* editoriale *m*; articolo di fondo
educate *vt* istruire; *(rear)* allevare; **–d** *a* istruito, colto
education *n* istruzione, insegnamento; **physical —** educazione fisica
educational *a* educativo, pedagogico, scolastico
educator *n* educatore *m*, insegnante *m*, maestro
educe *vt* estrarre; *(infer)* dedurre
eel *n* anguilla
eerie *a* lugubre, tetro, irreale, magico
effable *a* esprimibile, pronunciabile
efface *vt* cancellare
effect *n* effetto; — *vt* effettuare, produrre; **–ual** *a* efficace
effective *a* efficace, effettivo
effervescent *a* spumante
efficacious *a* efficace
efficiency *n* efficienza, efficacia
efficient *a* efficiente, capace
effort *n* sforzo
effusive *a* espansivo, esuberante
egg *n* uovo; *(fried)* uovo fritto; *(hard-boiled)* uovo sodo; *(poached)* uovo affogato; *(scrambled)* uovo strapazzato; *(soft-boiled)* uovo da bere, uovo appena bollito; *(sunny side up)* uovo ad occhio di bue; — **white** chiara d'uovo, albume *m*; — **yolk** tuorlo d'uovo; — *vt* lanciare uova contro; — **on** incitare
eggnog *n* zabaione *m*
eggplant *n* melanzana
ego *n* ego
egocentric *a* egocentrico
egoism, egotism *n* egoismo, egotismo
egotist *n* egotista *m*
egress *n* egresso
egret *n* ciuffetto
Egypt Egitto; **–ian** *n&a* egiziano
eider down peluria, lanugine *f*
eight *a* otto; **–ieth** *a* ottantesimo; **–y** *a* ottanta
eighteen *a* diciotto; **–th** *a* diciottesimo; **–th century** il Settecento
eighth *a* ottavo
either *pron&a* ambi; l'uno e l'altro; uno dei due; **in — case** i ambo i casi; **not —** nemmeno; **— . . . or** o . . . o
ejaculation *n* eiaculazione, emissione
eject *vt* espellere, scacciare
ejection *n* espulsione; — *(law)* sfratto
eke *vt* allungare, prolungare; — **out** complementare
elaborate *vt* elaborare; — *a* elaborato, accurato
elan *n* slancio
elapse *vi* decorrere, passare, trascorrere
elastic *n&a* elastico
elated *a* allegro, esultante
elbow *n* gomito; **out at the –s** malconcio; **–room** *n* libertà d'azione; — *vt* dare gomitata a; — *vi* fare gomito; avanzare a gomitate
elder *a* maggiore, anziano
elderly *a* d'una certa età
eldest *a* il maggiore, il più anziano, il più vecchio
elect *a* eletto, nominato; — *vt* eleggere; **the —** gli eletti
election *n* elezione
electioneer *vt* sollecitare voti
electoral *a* elettorale
electric, –al *a* elettrico
electrician *n* elettricista *m*, elettrotecnico
electricity *n* elettricità
electrify *vt* elettrizzare
electrocardiogram *n* elettrocardiogramma *m*
electrocute *vt* folgorare, fulminare
electrocution *n* elettrocuzione
electrode *n* elettrodo
electrodynamics *n* elettrodinamica
electromagnet *n* elettromagnete *m*
electron *n* elettrone *m*
electronic *a* elettronico; — **brain** cervello elettronico; **–s** *n* elettronica
electroplate *vt* placcare con galvanoplastica
elegance *n* eleganza, buon gusto
elegant *a* elegante, di buon gusto
element *n* elemento; **–al** *a* elementare
elements *npl* rudimenti *mpl*
elementary *a* elementare; — **school** scuola elementare
elephant *n* elefante *m*
elevate *vt* elevare, innalzare
elevated *a* elevato; — **railway** ferrovia

soprelevata
elevation *n* elevazione
elevator *n* ascensore *m*; **freight** — montacarichi *m*; — **boy** ragazzo
eleven *a* undici
eleventh *a* undicesimo; — **hour** l'undicesima ora, l'ultima ora per fare qualcosa
elf *n* folletto, fata; **-in** *a* di folletto, incantato
elicit *vt* incitare, educere
elide *vt* elidere
eliminate *vt* eliminare
elimination *n* eliminazione
elision *n* elisione
elite *a* seletto, alto; — *n* il meglio, elite *m*
elk *n* alce *f*
ell *n (building)* ala
eligible *a* eleggibile, desiderabile
ellipse *n* ellisse *f*
ellipsis *n* ellissi *f*
elm *n* olmo
elongate *vt* allungare, estendere; — *vi* aumentare la lunghezza
elope *vi* fuggire per sposarsi
elopement *n* fuga con l'amante
eloquence *n* eloquenza
eloquent *a* eloquente
else *a* altro; **anybody** — chiunque altro; **anything** —? qualche cosa d'altro? **anywhere** — ogni altro luogo; **everything** — tutto il resto; **nobody** — nessun altro; **nothing** — nient'altro; **nowhere** — nessun altro luogo
elsewhere *adv* altrove, in altro luogo
elucidate *vt* chiarire, delucidare
elusive *a* evasivo, elusivo
em *n (print)* unità di spazio
emaciate *vt* emaciare; — *vi* emaciarsi
emaciated *a* magro, smunto, scarno
emancipate *vt* emancipare
emasculation *n* evirazione, sterilizzazione
embalm *vt* imbalsamare
embankment *n* argine *m*, diga; terrapieno
embargo *n* embargo
embark *vt* imbarcare; — *vi* imbarcarsi
embarkation *n* imbarco
embarrass *vt* imbarazzare, mettere in imbarazzo; **-ing** *a* imbarazzante; **-ment** *n* imbarazzo
embassy *n* ambasciata
embellish *vt* abbellire
ember *n* tizzone *m*, brace *f*; **E– Day** Quattro Tempora
embezzle *vt* appropriarsi fraudolentemente
embezzler *n* prevaricatore *m*
emblem *n* emblema *m*
embolism *n* embolia
emboss *vt* lavorare d'incavo, damaschinare
embossed *a* in rilievo
embrace *vt* stringere, abbracciare; — *vi* abbracciarsi; — *n* stretta, abbraccio
embroider *vt* ricamare; **-y** *n* ricamo
embroil *vt* imbrogliare
embryo *n* embrione *m*; **-nic** *a* embrionale
emcee, M.C. *n* cerimoniere *m*; — *vt&i* fare il maestro di cerimonie
emerald *n* smeraldo
emerge *vi* emergere
emergency *n* emergenza; — **exist** uscita di sicurezza; — **landing** atterraggio di fortuna
emery *n* smeriglio
emetic *n&a* emetico
emigrant *n* emigrante *m&f*
emigrate *vi* emigrare
emigration *n* emigrazione
eminence *n* eminenza
eminent *a* eminente
emissary *n* emissario
emit *vt* emettere
emollient *a&n* emolliente *m*
emolument *n* emolumento
emotion *n* emozione; **-al** *a* emotivo
empanel *vt* formare la lista dei giurati
emperor *n* imperatore *m*
emphasis *n* enfasi *f*
emphasize *vt* mettere in rilievo; *(insist on)* insistere su; *(underline)* sottolineare
emphatic *a* enfatico, energico, deciso
emphatically *adv* decisamente
empire *n* impero
employ *vt* impiegare, usare; — *n* impiego
employee *n* impiegato
employer *n* principale *m*; datore di lavoro
employment *n* impiego, occupazione
empower *vt* autorizzare; conferire potere
empress *n* imperatrice *f*
emptiness *n* vuoto, vanità; *(frivolity)* frivolità
empty *a* vuoto; — *vt* vuotare; *(remove)* sgombrare
empty- *(in comp)* **—handed** *a* a mani vuote; **—headed** *a* senza cervello
empyema *n* empiema *m*
emulate *vt* emulare
emulsify *vt* emulsionare
en *n (print)* mezza unità di spazio
enable *vt* consentire; abilitare
enact *vt* decretare, promulgare; **-ment** *n* decreto, promulgazione
enamel *n* smalto; — *vt* smaltare
enamor *vt* innamorare
encamp *vt* accampare; — *vi* accamparsi; **-ment** *n* accampamento
encase, incase *vt* incassare, incassonare; *(cover)* coprire
enchant *vt* incantare; **-ing** *a* incantevole
enchantment *n* incanto, incantesimo
encircle *vt* accerchiare, cingere, circondare
enclose *vt* allegare; *(include)* accludere; *(shut in)* racchiudere
enclosure *n* allegato; *(pen)* recinto
encompass *vt* circondare, abbracciare, racchiudere
encore *n* bis *m*; ripetizione; — *vt (ask for)* chiedere il bis; *(give)* ripetere, bissare
encounter *n* incontro, scontro; *(battle)* combattimento; — *vt* affrontare; *(meet)* incontrare; — *vi* ingaggiare battaglia; incontrarsi
encourage *vt* incoraggiare
encouragement *n* incoraggiamento
encouraging *a* incoraggiante
encroach *vt&i* usurpare, invadere; abusarsi di
encumber *vt* ingombrare, imbarazzare;

(*burden*) opprimere
encyclopedia *n* enciclopedia
end *n* fine *m&f*, estremità: (*purpose*) scopo; **by the — of** prima della fine di; **make both –s meet** sbarcare il lunario; **odds and –s** cianfrusaglie *fpl*; **on —** ritto; **put an — to** mettere fine a
end *vt* terminare, finire; — *vi* finire, cessare
endanger *vt* mettere in pericolo
endear *vt* rendere caro a; fare amare da
endearment *n* amabilità; (*tenderness*) tenerezza
endeavor *vt&i* cercare, tentare; (*strive*) sforzarsi; — *n* tentativo; sforzo
ending *n* fine *f*, conclusione; (*gram*) desinenza
endive *n* indivia
endless *a* interminabile
endocarditis *n* endocardite *f*
endocrine *n&a* endocrina; **–ology** *n* endocrinologia
endorse *vt* approvare (*fig*); (*check*) indorsare, girare; (*guaranty*) garantire, avallare; (*law*) girare
endorsement n avallo, girata, approvazione (*fig*)
endow *vt* dotare; **–ment** *n* dotazione, dono
endurable *a* tollerabile, sopportabile
endurance *n* resistenza, pazienza; **beyond —** intolerabile
endure *vt&i* soffrire, sopportare, (*last*) durare, continuare
enema *n* clistere *m*, enteroclisma *m*, lavativo
enemy *n* nemico
energetic *a* energico, dinamico
energy *n* energia; **atomic —** energia atomica
enervate *vt* scoraggiare
enforce *vt* imporre; (*law*) far rispettare la legge; **–ment** *n* esecuzione; (*law*) applicazione della legge
enfranchise *vt* affrancare
engage *vt* riservare; (*hire*) impegnare; (*reserve*) prenotare; **— in conversation** entrare in conversazione
engaged *a* fidanzato; (*busy*) occupato; (*employed*) impegnato
engagement *n* (*marital*) fidanzamento; (*mil*) scontro; (*promise*) impegno; **keep an —** andare a un appuntamento
engaging *a* attraente
engender *vt* ingenerare, produrre; (*cause*) causare, far nascere
engine *n* motore *m*; macchina; (*rail*) locomotiva
engineer *n* ingegnere *m*; (*avi*) motorista *m*; (*mil*) geniere *m*; (*rail*) macchinista *m*; — *vt* combinare; (*scheme*) macchinare
engineering *n* ingegneria
England Inghilterra
English *n&a* inglese *m&f*; **in plain —** per essere chiaro; in parole povere
Englishman, –woman *n* inglese *m&f*
engrave *vt* incidere, scolpire
engraver *n* incisore *m*
engraving *n* incisione
engross *vt* occupare, assorbire; **be –ed** essere assorto; **–ing** *a* interessante; avvincente
engulf *vt* inghiottire; gettare nel gorgo (*fig*)
enhance *vt* intensificare, aumentare, elevare
enhancement *n* aumento
enigma *n* enigma *m* **–tic** *a* enigmatico
enjoy *vt* godere, gustare; aver piacere di; **–able** *a* piacevole, divertente
enjoyment *n* godimento, piacere *m*
enlarge *vt* ingrandire; — *vi* ingrandirsi
enlargement *n* ingrandimento
enlighten *vt* illuminare, dare schiarimenti; **–ment** *n* schiarimento
enlist *vt* arruolare; — *vi* arruolarsi
enlistment *n* arruolamento
enliven *vt* animare, ravvivare
enmity *n* inimicizia
enormous *a* enorme
enough *a&adv* abbastanza; **be —** bastare; essere sufficiente; **That's —!** Basta!
enrage *vt* irritare, arrabbiare
enrapture *vt* mandare in estasi, estasiare
enrich *vt* arricchire
enrichment *n* arricchimento
enroll *vt* iscrivere; — *vi* iscriversi
ensconce *vt* accomodare; (*hide*) nascondere; (*protect*) proteggere
ensemble *n* insieme *m*; complesso
ensign *n* (*banner*) bandiera; (*insignia*) insegna; (*officer*) guardiamarina *m*
enslave *vt* schiavizzare, cautivare
ensnare *vt* sedurre, allettare; prendere in trappola (*fig*)
ensue *vi* seguire, risultare, derivare
ensuing *a* seguente, successivo, prossimo
entail *vt* importare, occasionare; (*law*) assegnare
entangle *vt* imbrogliare, arruffare, coinvolgere
entente *n* intesa, patto
enter *vt* entrare, penetrare; (*accounting*) portare; (*law*) intentare; (*record*) iscrivere
enterprise *n* impresa
enterprising *a* intraprendente
entertain *vt* divertire; dare un ricevimento; **–ing** *a* divertente
entertainment *n* divertimento, spettacolo
enthrall *vt* incantare, cattivare; (*enslave*) soggiogare
enthrone *vt* incoronare; (*eccl*) investire, intronizzare
enthusiasm *n* entusiasmo
enthusiast *n* entusiasta *m*; **–ic** *a* entusiastico
entice *vt* incitare, adescare, sedurre
enticement *n* fascino, seduzione
enticing *a* seducente, tentatore
entire *a* intero; **–ly** *adv* interamente
entirety *n* tutto, intero, totalità; **in its —** nella sua pienezza; nella sua totalità
entitle *vt* intitolare, nominare; dare un diritto
entity *n* entità
entomologist *n* entomologo
entrails *npl* interiora *fpl*, intestini *mpl*, viscere *fpl*
entrance *n* ingresso, entrata
entrance *vt* estasiare
entrant *n* inscritto, participante *m*; (*be-*

ginner) novizio
entreat *vt* implorare, supplicare
entreaty *n* supplica, sollecitazione, insistenza
entrench *vt* trincerare; — *vi* trasgredire
entrust *vt* affidare a
entry *n* entrata; *(com)* iscrizione, registrazione; — **blank** domanda; **double —** *(bookkeeping)* partita doppia
enumerate *vt* enumerare
enumeration *n* enumerazione
enunciate *vt* pronunziare, enunciare
enunciation *n* enunciazione
envelop *vt* avviluppare, involgere
envelope busta; **window —** busta con finestrina
enviable *a* invidiabile
envious *a* invidioso
environment *n* ambiente *m*
environs *npl* dintorni *mpl*
envoy *n* messo; inviato diplomatico
envy *n* invidia; **be green with —** essere verde d'invidia; — *vt* invidiare
enzyme *n* enzimo
eon *n* era, età
ephedrine *n* efedrina
ephemeral *a* effimero
epic *a* epico; — *n* epopea; **— poem** epico
epicure *n* epicureo; **-an** *a* epicureo
epidemic *n* epidemia; — *a* epidemico
epidermis *n* epidermide *f*
epiglottis *n* epiglotide *f*
epigram *n* epigramma *m*
epigrammatic *a* epigrammatico
epigraph *n* epigrafe *f*
epilepsy *n* epilessia
epileptic *a* epilettico
epilogue *n* epilogo
Epiphany *n* Epifania
episode *n* episodio
epitaph *n* epitaffio
epitome *n* epitome *f*, compendio
epithet *n* epiteto
epoch *n* epoca
Epsom salts sale inglese, solfato di magnesia
equadistant *a* equidistante
equal *n&a* eguale; — *vt* eguagliare; **-ly** *adv* egualmente
equalization *n* equalizzazione
equality *n* eguaglianza
equalize *vt* egualizzare
equanimity *n* equanimità
equation *n* equazione
equator *n* equatore *m*
equatorial *a* equatoriale
equilibrium *n* equilibrio
equinox *n* equinozio
equip *vt* dotare, attrezzare, equipaggiare
equipment *n* macchinario, dotazione, attrezzatura
equitable *a* equo, giusto
equity *n* equità
equivalent *a&n* equivalente *m*
equivocation *n* equivoco
era *n* era, epoca
eradicate *vt* estirpare, sradicare
erase *vt* cancellare
eraser *n* gomma da cancellare
erasure *n* cancellatura
erect *vt* erigere; — *a* eretto, diritto
erg *n* ergon *m*
ergo *adv* ergo, dunque
ergot *n* granosprone *m*, malattia di cereali
ermine *n* ermellino
erode *vt* rodere, consumare
erosion *n* erosione
erotic *a* erotico
err *vi* sbagliarsi; **-ing** *a* errante
errand *n* commissione; — **boy** commesso, fattorino
erratic *a* irregolare, eccentrico
erroneous *a* erroneo
error *n* errore *m*, sbaglio; **typographical —** errore di stampa
erudite *a* erudito
erupt *vi* eruttare
eruption *n* eruzione
erysipelas *n* risipola
escalator *n* scala mobile
escapade *n* scappata, follia
escape *vt* fuggire, evadere; *(evade)* evitare, scansare; — *vi* scappare
escape *n* evasione, fuga; — **valve** *(mech)* valvola di scappamento; **fire —** uscita d'emergenza, uscita d'incendio; **have a narrow —** scampare per miracolo; **make one's —** evadere
escort *n* scorta, compagno; — *vt* scortare, accompagnare
escrow *n* contratto in deposito presso un terzo; deposito di caparra
Eskimo *n&a* esquimese
esophagus *n* esofago
esoteric *a* esoterico
especially *adv* particolarmente, specialmente
espionage *n* spionaggio
essay *n* saggio; — *vt* provare
essence *n* essenza, profumo
essential *a* essenziale; **-ly** *adv* essenzialmente
establish *vt* stabilire, fondare
establishment *n* stabilimento, organizzazione; complesso; *(company)* ditta
estate *n* proprietà; **real —** beni immobili *mpl*
esteem *vt* stimare, rispettare; — *n* stima, considerazione
ester *n* estere *m*
esthete *n* esteta *m&f*
esthetic *a* estetico
estimate *vt* stimare, valutare; *(calculate)* calcolare; — *n* valutazione, perizia, preventivo; *(com)* stima
estimation *n* giudizio, opinone *f*, stima
Estonia Estonia
et cetera (etc.) *n* eccetera *m* (ecc.)
etch *vt* disegnare *(fig)*; incidere all'acquaforte
etching *n* incisione, acquaforte *f*
eternal *a* eterno
eternity *n* eternità
ether *n* etere *m*
ethical *a* etico
ethics *npl* etica
ethnology *n* etnologia
ethyl *n* etile *m*
etiquette *n* etichetta, cerimoniale *m*, convenienza
etude *n (arts)* studio
etymology *n* etimologia

Eucharist *n* Eucaristia
eugenics *npl* eugenetica
eulogy *n* elogio
eunuch *n* eunuco
euphonious *a* eufonico, armonioso
European *n&a* europeo
eurythmics *npl* euritmica, euritmia
euthanasia *n* eutanasia
evacuate *vt* evacuare; *(people)* sfollare
evacuee *n* sfollato
evade *vt* scansare, eludere, schivare
evaluate *vt* valutare
evangelist *n* evangelista *m&f*
evaporate *vt* far evaporare; — *vi* evaporare, svaporare
evaporated *a* evaporato
evaporation *n* evaporazione
evasion *n* evasione, pretesto, sotterfugio
evasive *a* evasivo
eve *n* vigilia
even *a* pari, eguale; — **number** numero pari; — **temper** carattere pacifico; **be — with** essere alla pari; **get — with** sdebitarsi con; — *adv* persino, anche; — **as** nel momento in cui; — **if** anche se; — **so** anche così; — **then** anche allora, di già, a quel tempo; — **though** benchè; **not —** neppure; — *vt* rendere equale, eguagliare; *(com, scale)* bilanciare
evening *n* sera, serata; **during the —** di sera, durante la sera; **every —** ogni sera; **in the —** alla sera; **the — before** la sera precedente; — *a* di sera, serale; — **clothes** abiti da sera
evenly *adv* uniformemente
event *n* evento, avvenimento, caso; *(contest)* gara; **in the — that** in caso che
eventful *a* movimentato, avventuroso; importante
eventual *a* eventuale, finale; **–ly** *adv* finalmente, alla fine, eventualmente
eventuality *n* eventualità
ever *adv* sempre, mai; — **since** dopo, a decorrere da; **for — and —** per sempre; **more than —** più che mai; **scarcely —** quasi mai
evergreen *n* sempreverde *m*
everlasting *a* eterno; *(ceaseless)* incessante; — *n* eternità
every *a* ogni, ciascuno; — **now and then** di tanto in tanto; — **other** uno sì uno no; — **time** ogni volta; — **day** giornalmente; ogni giorno; **–one, –body** *pron* ognuno, ciascuno; *(all)* tutti
everyday *a* quotidiano, comune, per ogni giorno
everything *n* tutto, ogni cosa
everywhere *adv* dovunque
evict *vt* sfrattare; *(dispossess)* espellere, spossessare
eviction *n* sfratto, espulsione
evidence *n* prova, testimonianza; **give —** testimoniare
evident *a* evidente, ovvio
evil *a* cattivo; — *n* male *m*, danno
evildoer *n* malfattore *m*, malfattrice *f*
evil-minded *a* malevolo, perverso, malintenzionato
eviscerate *vt* sviscerare, sventrare
evocation *n* evocazione
evoke *vt* evocare
evolution *n* evoluzione
evolve *vt* evolvere; — *vi* evolversi
ewe *n* pecora
ewer *n* brocca, boccale *m*
exact *a* esatto, preciso; **–ing** *a* esigente; **–ly** *adv* esattamente, precisamente; **–ness** *n* esattezza; — *vt* esigere, pretendere
exaggerate *vt* esagerare
exaggeration *n* esagerazione
exalt *vt* esaltare; **–ed** *a* esaltato, sommo, altolocato; **–ation** *n* esaltazione
examination *n* esame *m*; *(med)* visita; **competitive —** esame di concorso
examine *vt* esaminare
examiner *n* esaminatore *m*, esaminatrice *f*
example *n* esempio
exasperate *vt* esasperare
exasperation *n* esasperazione
excavate *vt* scavare
excavation *n* scavo
exceed *vt* superare, eccedere
exceedingly *adv* eccessivamente
excel *vt* eccellere, superare
excellence, excellency *n* eccellenza
Excellency *n (eccl)* Eccellenza
excellent *a* eccellente, ottimo
excelsior *n* l'eccelso, il migliore
except *vt* escludere, eccettuare; — *prep* fuori di, salvo, eccetto, tranne
exception *n* obiezione, eccezione; **take —** *(object)* obiettare; *(offense)* risentirsi di
exceptional *a* eccezionale
excerpt *vt* estrarre; — *n* estratto, brano, passo
excess *n* eccesso, soverchio; *(exaggeration)* esagerazione; — **baggage** bagaglio in eccedenza; **–ive** *a* troppo, eccessivo
exchange *vt* scambiare; — **greetings** scambiare auguri
exchange *n* cambio; *(com)* borsa; **rate of —** prezzo di cambio
excise *n* dazio, imposta; tributi indiretti *mpl*; — *vt* tassare, daziare; *(cut out)* tagliare
excitable *a* eccitabile, emotivo
excite *vt* eccitare, provocare, suscitare
excited *a* eccitato; **get —** eccitarsi, esaltarsi
excitement *n* agitazione, emozione; *(confusion)* trambusto
exciting *a* emozionante, vivificativo
exclaim *vt* esclamare
exclamation *n* esclamazione; — **point** punto esclamativo
exclude *vt* escludere
exclusion *n* esclusione
exclusive *a* esclusivo, scelto, aristocratico; di classe; — **of** a prescindere da
excommunicate *vt* scomunicare
excommunication *n* scomunica
excresence *n* escrescenza
excrete *vt* escretare
excretion *n* escrezione
excruciating *a* atroce, terribile
excursion *n* escursione, gita
excuse *n* scusa, pretesto; — *vt* scusare; — **oneself** scusarsi
execration *n* esecrazione

execute *vt* eseguire; *(penal)* giustiziare
execution *n* adempimento; esecuzione
executive *a* esecutivo; — *n* dirigente *m*
exemplary *a* esemplare
exemplify *vt* servire d'esempio
exempt *a* esente; — *vt* esentare, dispensare
exemption *n* esenzione
exercise *n* esercizio; — *vt* esercitare, far esercizi, addestrare; — *vi* esercitarsi, addestrarsi
exert *vt* esercitare, compiere; — **oneself** sforzarsi
exertion *n* sforzo
exhale *vt* esalare
exhaust *n* scappamento; *(auto)* tubo di scappamento; — *vt* esaurire
exhausted *a* esaurito, sfinito
exhausting *a* spossante
exhaustion *n* esaurimento
exhaustive *a* esauriente
exhibit *vt* esporre, mostrare; — *n* mostra; *(object)* oggetto esposto; **–or** *n* espositore *m*, esibitore *m*
exhibition *n* mostra, esposizione
exhibitionism *n* esibizionismo
exhilarate *vt* rallegrare, esilarare
exhilarating *a* esilarante
exhilaration *n* ilarità, allegrezza
exhort *vt* esortare; **–ation** *n* esortazione
exhume *vt* esumare
exigencies *npl* esigenze, necessità *fpl*; bisogni *mpl*
exigent *a* urgente, esigente
exile *n* esilio, bando; *(person)* esule *m*; — *vt* esiliare, proscrivere
exist *vi* vivere, esistere; **–ence** *n* esistenza, vita; **–ing** *a* esistente, attuale
existent *a* esistente
existential *a* esistenziale
existentialism *n* esistenzialismo
existentialist *n* esistenzialista *m&f*
exit *n* uscita
exodontist *n* chirurgo odontoiatra
exodus *n* esodo
exonerate *vt* discolpare, prosciogliere
exoneration *n* esonero
exorbitant *a* esorbitante
exorcize *vt* esorcizzare
exotic *a* esotico
expand *vt* espandere, stendere; — *vi* espandersi, dilatarsi
expanse *n* espansione, distesa
expansion *n* espansione
expansive *a* espansivo
expatriate *vt* espatriare
expect *vt* *(anticipate)* prevedere; *(await)* attendere; *(require)* pretendere; **–ancy** *n* attesa, aspettativa
expectant *a* aspettante
expectation *n* aspettativa, speranza
expedient *a* utile, pratico, vantaggioso; — *n* espediente *m*, mezzo, ripiego
expedite *vt* affrettare, sbrigare
expedition *n* spedizione; *(speed)* prontezza
expel *vt* scacciare, espellere
expend *vt* spendere, consumare; **–able** *a* spendibile, consumabile
expenditure *n* spesa
expense *n* spesa, costo
expensive *a* caro, costoso; **be** — essere dispendioso; essere caro
experience *n* pratica, esperienza; — *vt* provare
experienced *a* pratico, esperto
experiment *n* esperimento, prova, esperienza; **–al** *a* sperimentale
expert *a* pratico, esperto; — *n* intenditore *m*, specialista *m*; perito
expertly *adv* destramente
expertness *n* abilità, capacità, destrezza
expiration *n* scadenza, termine *m*
expire *vt* *(die)* spirare; *(end)* scadere
explain *vt* spiegare
explainable *a* spiegabile
explanation *n* spiegazione
explanatory *a* spiegativo, esplicativo, espositivo
explicate *vt* spiegare
explicit *a* esplicito
explode *vi* scoppiare, esplodere; — *vt* far scoppiare; *(theory)* demolire
exploit *n* prodezza, impresa; — *vt* utilizzare, sfruttare
exploration *n* esplorazione
explore *vt* esplorare; *(investigate)* indagare
explorer *n* esploratore *m*
explosion *n* scoppio, esplosione
explosive *a* esplosivo
exponent *n* esponente *m*, rappresentante *m*
export *n* esportazione; — **house** casa d'esportazione
export *vt* esportare; **–er** *n* esportatore *m*
expose *vt* esporre; *(uncover)* smascherare; **–d** *a* esposto, scoperto
exposé *n* esposto, esposizione
exposition *n* mostra, esposizione
expository *a* espositivo
expostulate *vi* lagnarsi, fare rimostranze
expostulation *n* disputa, protesta
exposure *n* esposto, esposizione; *(frostbite)* assideramento; *(photo)* posa; — **meter** *(photo)* esposimetro
express *vt* *(speech)* esprimere, espressare; *(transport)* spedire per espresso; — *a* *(exact)* formale, esplicito; *(speed)* espresso; **–ed** *a* espresso; — *n* espresso
expression *n* espressione
expressive *a* espressivo
expressway *n* autostrada
expropriation *n* espropriazione
expurgate *vt* espurgare
exquisite *a* squisito
extant *a* esistente
extemporaneous *a* estemporaneo, improvviso
extend *vt* estendere, prolungare, allargare; *(put out)* porgere; — *vi* stendersi, prolungarsi, estendersi
extended *a* esteso, prolungato; *(taut)* teso
extension *n* estensione; prolungamento; — **of time** proroga
extensive *a* diffuso, vasto, esteso
extensively *adv* estesamente, considerevolmente
extent *n* grado, punto, limite *m*; **to a certain** — fino ad un certo punto
extenuating *a* estenuante; *(law)* attenuante; — **circumstances** circostanze attenuanti

exterior *n&a* esterno
exterminate *vt* estirpare, sterminare
extermination *n* sterminio
exterminator *n* sterminatore *m*, distruttore *m*
external *a* esterno
extinct *a* estinto; **–ion** *n* estinzione
extinguish *vt* spegnere
extinguisher *n* estintore *m*; spegnitoio; **fire —** estintore d'incendio
extirpate *vt* estirpare, sradicare
extol *vt* estollere, esaltare, vantare
extort *vt* estorcere
extortion *n* estorsione; **–ist** *n* estorsionista *m&f*, strozzino
extra *a* supplementare; **— charges** spese supplementari *fpl*; **— edition** edizione straordinaria; **— pay** supplemento di paga; **—** *adv* in più
extra *n* supplemento; *(theat)* comparsa *m&f*
extract *vt* estrarre; **—** *n* estratto
extraction *n* estrazione; *(lineage)* discendenza, origine *f*
extracurricular *a* fuori dell'ordinario, extracurricolare
extradite *vt* estradare
extradition *n* estradizione
extraneous *a* estraneo
extraordinary *a* straordinario; *(wonderful)* stupendo
extrasensory *a* estrasensoriale; **— perception** percezione estrasensoriale
extravagance *n* prodigalità, spreco
extravagant *a* esagerato; *(price)* esorbitante; *(wasteful)* prodigo
extreme *a&n* estremo; **—** *a* ultimo
extremity *n* estremità
extricate *vt* districare
extrovert *n* estroverso
extrude *vt* espellere; **—** *vi* uscire
exuberance *n* esuberanza
exuberant *a* esuberante
exude *vt* traspirare, trasudare; *(display)* manifestare
exult *vt* esultare; **–ant** *a* esultante
exultation *n* esultazione; *(joy)* giubilo; *(triumph)* trionfo
exultingly *adv* esultando
eye *n* occhio; **— to —** in accordo assoluto; **in the twinkling of an —** in un batter d'occhi; **keep an — on** tenere d'occhio; **cry one's –s out** disfarsi in pianto; **–ball** *n* globo dell'occhio; **–cup** *n* bacinella per gli occhi; **–lid** *n* palpebra; **–sight** *n* vista; **–strain** *n* fatica degli occhi; **–wash** *n* lozione per gli occhi; **—** *vt* sbirciare
eyebrow *n* sopracciglio; **— pencil** matita per le sopracciglia
eyeful *n* occhiata
eyeglasses *npl* occhiali *mpl*, lenti *fpl*
eyelash *n* ciglio; **–es** *npl* ciglia *fpl*
eyelet *n* occhiello
eyetooth *n* dente canino
eyewitness *n* testimone oculare *m&f*

F

fable *n* favola
fabric *n* tessuto, stoffa
fabricate *vt (construct)* costruire; *(create)* creare; *(lie)* inventare, mentire
fabrication *n* fabbricazione; *(invention)* invenzione; *(untruth)* bugia
face *n* faccia, viso; **— card** figura; **— down** a faccia in giù; al rovescio; **— to —** faccia a faccia; **— powder** cipria; **— value** valore nominale; valore apparente; **about —** fare volta faccia; **fall on one's —** cadere con la faccia in giù; **lose —** far cattiva figura; perdere prestigio; **make a —** far boccacce; **on the — of it** sulla faccia; secondo l'apparenza; **save —** salvare la faccia *(fig)*; **—** *vt* confrontare; fronteggiare; **— the issue** confrontare la situazione
facet *n* faccetta; **—** *vt* sfaccettare
facial *a* facciale
facilitate *vt* facilitare
facilities *npl* agevolazioni, facilità, installazioni *fpl*; *(services)* servizi *mpl*; **toilet —** bagno di decenza
facility *n* facilità
facing *n* risvolta; *(building)* rivestimento; *(cloth)* guarnizione
facsimile *n* facsimile *m*
fact *n* fatto; **as a matter of —** in linea di fatto; **in —** effettivamente, infatti; **matter of —** effettivo, positivo; **the — is** il fatto è
faction *n* fazione; *(discord)* discordia *(fig)*; dissenso *(fig)*
factor *n* fattore *m*; *(math)* coefficiente *m*
factory *n* fabbrica
factual *a* effettivo, fattivo
faculty *n (ability)* facoltà, talento; *(school)* corpo degli insegnanti; il personale insegnante
fad *n* capriccio del gusto; moda del momento
fade *vt* far appassire; far sbiadire; **—** *vi (color)* sbiadire; *(wither)* appassire; **— away** appassire; **— out** svanire gradualmente
fade-out *n* sparizione; *(movies, TV, rad)* sparizione graduale
fag *vt* stancare, affaticare; **—** *vi* affaticarsi, sfinirsi di lavoro
fagged out sfinito
fail *vt* mancare, abbandonare; **— to pass** *(examination)* essere bocciato; **— to do** mancare di fare; **—** *vi* venir meno; non riuscrire; *(decline)* deperire; **without —** senza fallo, senz'altro
failing *n* difetto, fallo; **—** *prep* in mancanza di, in difetto di; **— for** debolezza per
failure *n* insuccesso, fallimento, fiasco; *(person)* fallito, caduto
faint *n* svenimento, deliquio; **—** *a* debole, lieve; *(pale)* pallido; **—** *vi* svenire; **— away** svenire
fainthearted *a* timido; *(cowardly)* pusillanime
fainting *n* svenimento
faintly *adv* debolmente
faintness *n* languore *m*

fair *a* leale, equo giusto; *(beautiful)* bello; (*hair*) biondo; (*skin*) bianco; — **chance** buona occasione; — **deal** lealtà; — **name** buona reputazione; — **play** lealtà, giustizia; — **possibility** alta probabilità; — **sex** sesso debole; — **weather** buon tempo
fair *n* fiera, esposizione; **–ground** *n* campo della fiera
fair-minded *a* imparziale, senza pregiudizi
fairness *n* giustizia; **in all** — per essere giusto
fairy *n* fata; — **tale** racconto delle fate, fiaba
faith *n* fede *f*, fiducia; **breach of** — slealtà; mancanza di parola
faithful *a* fedele, leale; **–ness** *n* fedeltà, costanza
faithfully *adv* fedelmente; con fedeltà
faithless *a* infedele, miscredente, sleale
fake *a (coll)* falso; — *vt (coll)* far finta di, simulare; — *n (coll)* contraffazione
faker *n (coll)* imbroglione *m*
fakir *n* fachiro
fall *n* caduta, cascata; *(season)* autunno
fall *vt* cascare, cadere; — **asleep** addormentarsi; — **back** indietreggiare, rinculare; — **behind** rimanere indietro; — — **by the wayside** perdere la giusta via *(fig)*; — **due** scadere; — **for** *(coll)* accettare *(fig)*; essere attratto; — **headlong** cadere a testa giù; — **in love** innamorarsi; — **into a trap** cadere in trappola *(fig)*; — **off** cadere, staccarsi, diminuire; — **on deaf ears** essere ignorato; — **out** rompere, litigare; — **through** fallire; fare fiasco
fallacy *n* fallacia, errore *m*
fallible *a* fallibile
falling *n* caduta; — *a* cadente
fall-out *n* polvere radioattiva
false *a* falso, fallace; *(unfaithful)* infedele; — **alarm** falso allarme; — **bottom** doppio fondo; — **face** maschera; — **teeth** denti finti; **make a** — **step** mettere un passo in falso *(fig)*; fare un passo falso *(fig)*
falsehood *n* menzogna, bugia
falsely *adv* falsamente, fintamente
falsetto *n* falsetto
falsify *vt* falsificare
falsity *n* falsità
falter *vt&i (move)* esitare; *(stammer)* balbettare
fame *n* fama, celebrità
famed *a* rinomato, celebre, conosciuto, famoso
familiar *a* familiare, conosciuto, intimo; **be** — **with** essere familiare con; essere in confidenza con
familiarity *n* familiarità; confidenza; *(knowledge)* conoscenza
family *n* famiglia; — **name** cognome *m*; — **tree** albero genealogico; **be in the** — essere familiare; **be in the** — **way** essere incinta; — *a* di famiglia
famine *n* carestia
famish *vt* affamare; — *vi* soffrire la fame; aver fame
famished *a* affamato
famous *a* famoso, celebre
fan *n* ventaglio; *(elec)* ventilatore *m*; *(coll)* tifoso, entusiasta di uno sport; — *vt* ventilare; far vento; stimolare *(fig)*; — *vi (spread out)* aprirsi a ventaglio
fanatic *a&n* fanatico
fanatical *a* fanatico
fanaticism *n* fanatismo
fanciful *a* fantastico, fantasioso
fancy *a* di fantasia; — *n* fantasia, capriccio; **take a** — **to** simpatizzare per; — *vt* immaginare; — **oneself to be** presumere di sè stesso
fancy– *(in comp)* **—dress party** festa in costume; ballo in maschera; **—free** *a* col cuore libero
fang *n* zanna
fantastic *a* fantastico, bizzarro
fantasy *n* fantasia
far *a&adv* lontano, distante; — **and away** oltremodo; — **and wide** da tutti i lati; — **be it from me** lungi da mè; — **better** molto meglio; — **between** a lunghi intervalli; — **from it** tutt'al contrario; **as** — **as** *(distance)* lontano quanto; **by** — oltremodo; **go** — andar lontano; **just so** — fino a; **so** — finora, talmente
far– *(in comp)* **—fetched** *a* improbabile; forzato; remotamente connesso; **—off** *a* lontano; **—reaching** *a* esteso, di lunga portata
farad *n (elec)* farad *m*
faraway *a* lontano; *(absent)* assente
farce *n* farsa
farcical *a* burlesco
fare *n (food)* cibo; *(transportation)* prezzo di un biglietto; passeggero; **half** — metà prezzo; **full** — prezzo intero
fare *vi* barcamenarsi; — **badly** essere in cattivo stato; — **well** prosperare
farewell *n* addio, commiato; — *a* d'addio
farinaceous *a* farinaceo
farm *n* podere *m*, fattoria; — **hand** bracciante agricolo; **–house** *n* cascina; casa colonica **–yard** *n* aia; — *vt&i* coltivare; *(rent)* affittare
farmer *n* agricoltore *m*
farming *n* agricoltura; — *a* agricolo
farseeing *a* sagace, lungimirante
farsighted *a* previdente; *(sight)* presbite
farther *a* più lontano; — **back** più indietro; — *adv* più lontano, al di là; ancora di più
farthest *a* il più lontano; — *adv* più lontano
fascinate *vt* affascinare, ammaliare, incantare
fascination *n* fascino
fascinating *a* affascinante
Fascism *n* fascismo
fashion *n* moda; *(way)* maniera; — **show** sfilata di moda; **after a** — in certo modo; **in** — di moda
fashion *vt* adattare, foggiare, formare
fashionable *a* elegante, di moda, alla moda
fast *vt* digiunare; — *n* digiuno; — **day** giorno di digiuno; — *a* rapido, veloce; *(color)* solido; *(dissolute)* dissoluto;

(*faithful*) fedele; (*secure*) fermo, stabile; **make** — (*secure*) fissare, assicurare; **sleep** — (*soundly*) dormire profondamente
fasten *vt* attaccare
fastener, fastening *n* fermaglio, legame *m*; (*bolt, latch*) chiavistello
fastidious *a* delicato, schizzinoso; (*exacting*) esigente
fat *n&a* grasso; **get** — diventar grasso, ingrassare
fatal *a* mortale, fatale; decisivo, importante; **–ity** *n* fatalità
fate *n* fato, destino, fatalità; sorte *f*
father *n* padre *m;* **–land** patria; **–ly** *a* paterno; **–less** *a* orfano di padre
father-in-law *n* suocero
fathom *n* (*measure*) braccio; — *vt* sondare scandagliare; (*understand*) profondizzare, capir bene
fatten *vt* ingrassare
fatuous *a* fatuo, vano
faucet *n* rubinetto
fault *n* colpa, mancanza; **at** — in difetto; **find** — criticare, trovare a ridire; **to a** — fino alla meticolosità; **–less** *a* perfetto, irreprensibile; **–y** *a* difettoso
faultfinder *n* critico, censore *m*
faultfinding *n* biasimo, rimprovero
favor *n* favore *m*; **be in** — **of** essere in favore di; **do a** — fare un favore; **find** — **with** essere ben accetto; **show** — mostrare preferenza (*fig*); — *vt* favorire
favorable *a* favorevole
favorite *a&n* prediletto, favorito
fawn *n* daino, cerbiatto; — *a* (*color*) fulvo; — *vi* adulare
fawning *a* servile
fear *n* timore *m*, paura; **–ful** *a* terribile; timoroso; **–less** *a* intrepido, senza paura
feasibility *n* possibilità, praticabilità
feasible *a* praticabile, fattibile, probabile
feast *n* banchetto, festa, festino; — *vt* banchettare, far festa a
feat *n* impresa, prodezza
feather *n* piuma, penna; — **in one's cap** distinzione, vanto; **birds of a** — persone di una sola risma; — *vt* piumare; **–ed** *a* piumato, pennuto
featherbedding *n* obbligazione sindacale di pagare i lavoranti per lavoro non eseguito
featherweight *n* peso piuma
feature *n* tratto, caratteristica; **double** — due film principali; — **story** articolo di fondo; — *vt* ritrarre, rappresentare
features *npl* fattezze *fpl*, fisionomia; (*face*) viso
February *n* febbraio
fecundity *n* fecondità
federal *a* federale
federation *n* federazione
fee *n* onorario; (*law*) diritti *mpl*; (*tax*) tassa; **admission** — (*school*) quota d'iscrizione; (*theat*) prezzo d'entrata
feeble *a* debole, fiacco; **–ness** *n* debolezza
feebly *adv* debolmente
feed *n* foraggio, mangime *m;* — *vt* alimentare, dar da mangiare; — *vi* mangiare; — **on** nutrirsi di
feedback *a* (*elec*) controcircuitico, controgenerante; — *n* sistema controgenerante
feeding *n* alimentazione, mangiata, pascolo; (*animal*) alimento, foraggio; (*meal*) pasto
feel *n* (*sense*) tatto; **–ing** *n* senso, sensazione
feel *vt&i* sentire, sentirsi; (*believe*) credere, ritenere; (*touch*) toccare, tastare; — **better** sentirsi meglio; — **like** aver voglia di; sentirsi come; — **one's way** procedere con prudenza; — **strongly about** avere una opinione positiva
feeler *n* antenna; (*insect*) tentacolo
feeling *n* sensazione, sentimento
feelings *npl* (*emotions*) sensibilità
feet *npl* piedi *mpl*
feign *vt* simulare, fingere; — *vi* fingersi
felicitation *n* felicitazione
felicitous *a* felice, appropriato
feline *a* felino
fell *vt* atterrare, abbattere, ribattere
fellow *n* compagno, collega *m*; (*coll*) persona; — *a* dello stesso gruppo; **–ship** *n* cameratismo; (*scholarship*) borsa di studi
felon *n* malfattore *m*, traditore *m*; (*med*) patereccio
felony *n* fellonia, reato grave
felt *n* feltro
female *n* femmina; — *a* femminile
feminine *a* femminile
femur *n* femore *m*
fence *n* steccato, recinto; (*stolen goods*) ricettatore *m*; **be on the** — essere indeciso; — *vt* cingere; — *vi* (*sport*) tirare di scherma
fencing *n* (*sport*) scherma
fend *vt* parare; — **for oneself** difendersi, arrangiarsi; — **off** parare, sviare
fender *n* parafanghi *m*; (*fireplace*) parafuoco
ferment *n* fermento; agitazione; — *vt* fermentare
fermentation *n* fermentazione; (*yeast*) lievito
fern *n* felce *f*
ferocious *a* feroce
ferret *n* furetto; — *vt&i* cacciare col furetto; — **out** snidare
ferric *a* ferrico
ferry *n* traghetto; — *vt&i* traghettare
fertile *a* fertile
fertility a fertilità
fertilize *vt* fertilizzare
fertilizer *n* fertilizzante *m*; (*manure*) concime *m*
fervency *n* calore, fervore, ardore *m*
fervent *a* fervente; **–ly** *adv* con fervore; fervorosamente
fervid *a* fervido, ardente, caloroso
fester *vi* suppurare; **–ing** *a* ulcerante, suppurante, infezioso
festival *n* festivale *m*, festa
festive *a* festivo, gaio
festivity *n* festività
festoon *n* festone *m*; — *vt* festonare; ornare con festoni
fetching *a* seducente, attraente
fete *n* festa; — *vt* far festa a

fetish *n* feticcio
fetters *npl* ceppi *mpl*, catene *fpl*; schiavitù *f* *(fig)*
fettle *n* stato, ordine *m*, condizione; **in fine** — in ottimo stato
fetlock *n* garretto
fetus *n* feto
feud *n* vendetta, ostilità; inimicizia di famiglie, fra due famiglie; **–al** *a* feudale
fever *n* febbre *f*; **get into a** — eccitarsi
feverish *a* febbricitante, febbrile
few *a&pron* pochi, poche; **a** — alcuni, alcune; **–er** *a* meno; di meno
fiancé *n* fidanzato
fiancée *n* fidanzata
fiasco *n* fiasco
fiat *n* decreto, comando, ordine *m*
fib *n* menzognetta, frottola; — *vt* dire una piccola bugia
fibber *n* bugiardo
fiber *n* fibra
fibrous *a* fibroso
fickle *a* volubile, inconstante, capriccioso
fiction *n* invenzione; *(lit)* romanzo, narrativa
fictitious *a* fittizio, immaginario
fidelity *n* fedeltà; **high** — alta fedeltà
fiddle *n* violino ordinario; **play second** — essere di second'ordine; — *vi (coll)* suonare il violino; — **around** *(coll)* gironzolare
fidget *vi* agitarsi, essere irrequieto
fiduciary *n&a* fiduciario
field *n* campo; *(subject)* settore *m*, soggetto; — **day** giornata campale; — **glasses** binoccolo da campo; — **mouse** arvicola; — *a* campale; di campo; **–er** *n* *(baseball)* ribattitore *m*
fiend *n* diavolo, demonio; **–ish** *a* cattivo, diabolico, perfido
fierce *a* feroce, accanito; **–ness** *n* ferocia, fierezza
fiery *a* focoso, ardente, infocato
fifteen *a* quindici
fifteenth *a* quindicesimo, decimoquinto
fifth *a* quinto; *(mus)* quinta
fiftieth *a* cinquantesimo
fifty *a* cinquanta
fifty-fifty *a&adv* mezzo e mezzo; *(so-so)* così così, nè bene nè male
fig *n* fico; — **tree** fico; **not be worth a** — non valere niente
fight *vt* combattere, lottare; — **a way through** aprirsi un cammino; — **it out** combattere ad oltranza
fight *n* lotta, combattimento, disputa, rissa; **pick a** — **with** provocare
fighter *n* lottatore *m*, combattente *m*
fighting *n* combattimento, battaglia; — *a* combattente, battagliero
figment *n* finzione, invenzione; — **of the imagination** opera della immaginazione
figurative *a* traslato, figurato, allegorico, metaforico
figure *n* taglia, statura; *(math)* cifra; *(mus)* figura; — **of speech** modo di dire; **cut a poor** — fare brutta figura; **–head** *n (naut)* polena; figura di prua; *(fig)* prestanome *m*; — *vt* calcolare; esprimere in figure; *(coll)* supporre; — **out** *(coll)* comprendere, calcolare; — *vi* calcolare; lavorare con figure numeriche; — **on** *(coll)* contare su
figurine *n* statuetta, figurina
filament *n* filamento
filbert *n* nocciuola, avellana
filch *vt* rubacchiare
file *n (folder)* cartella; *(tool)* lima; — **card** cartellino di agendario; — **clerk** impiegato; **in single** — in fila indiana; — *vt* limare; archiviare; classificare; — **by** sfilare
filial *a* filiale
filibuster *n* filibustiere *m*; — *vi* fare il filibustiere
filigree *n* filigrana
filing *n* limatura; collezione; — **cabinet** schedario
fill *vt* riempire; — *vi* riempirsi; — **in** inserire; riempire; — **out** riempire; — *n* sufficienza; **–er** *n* riempitore *m*
fillet *n* benda; *(meat)* filetto
filling *n* ripieno; — **station** stazione di servizio; **tooth** — otturazione, impiombatura; — *a* sazievole
filly *n* cavallina
film *n* film *m*, pellicola; — **library** cineteca; **–y** *a* trasparente
filmstrip *n* film a proiezione fissa
filter *n* filtro; *(photo)* filtro luce; — **tipped** con filtro; — *vt* filtrare
filth *n* sudiciume *m*, sporcizia; **–y** *a* sporco, sudicio; *(obscene)* osceno
filtrate *n* liquido filtrato; — *vt&i* filtrare
filtration *n* filtrazione
fin *n* pinna; natatoia
final *a* finale; **–s** *npl* esami finali
finally *adv* finalmente
finality *a* finalità
finance *n* finanza, **–s** *npl* finanze *fpl*; — *vt* sovvenzionare, finanziare
financier *n* finanziere *m*
financial *a* finanziario
financing *n* finanziamento
find *vi* trovare; *(law)* dichiarare; — **out** indovinare, scoprire; — **fault** trovare a ridire; — **for oneself** trovare per proprio conto; — *n* trovata, scoperta
findings *npl* utensili *mpl*, arnesi *mpl*
fine *a* fino; *(beauty)* bello; — *n* multa, ammenda; — **arts** belle arti *fpl*; — *vt* multare; fare una contravvenzione; **F–!** *interj* Bene!, Molto bene!
Finland Finlandia
finesse *n* finezza, delicatezza
finger *n* dito; — **bowl** lavadita *m*; — **mark** ditata; **ring** — anulare *m*; **–nail** *n* unghia; **–print** *n* impronta digitale; — *vt* tastare, maneggiare
fingering *n* tocco, il tastare; *(mus)* diteggio, tocco
finicky *a* meticoloso; di gusti difficili
finish *vt* terminare, finire; — *n* fine *f*
Finnish *a* finlandese
fir tree abete *m*
fire *n* fuoco, incendio; — **department** servizio di pompieri; — **engine** pompa d'incendio; — **escape** uscita di sicurezza; — **extinguisher** estintore *m*; — **screen** parafuoco; — **station** stazione dei pompieri; **–man** *n* vigile del fuoco; **–plug** *n* idrante *m*, bocca d'incendio

fire *vt* incendiare; *(ceramics)* cuocere; *(coll)* licenziare, congedare; *(weapon)* sparare; — **with enthusiasm** infiammare d'entusiasmo
firearms *npl* armi da fuoco *fpl*
firebrand *n* tizzone *m*, testa calda *(fig)*
firecracker *n* castagnuola, petardo
fireplace *n* focolare *m*, camino
fireproof *a* incombustibile, resistente al fuoco
firewood *n* legna da ardere
fireworks *npl* fuochi d'artificio
firing *n* *(furnace)* alimentazione del fuoco; — **line** linea di tiro; — **pin** percussore *m*; — **squad** plotone d'esecuzione
firm *a* solido, fermo; — *n (com)* ditta, azienda, società
firmament *n* cielo, firmamento
first *a* primo; — **aid** pronto soccorso; — **base** *(sport)* prima base; — **night** *(theat)* première *m*; notte di debutto; — *adv* prima, dapprima; in primo luogo; — **and last time** per prima ed ultima volta; **get to — base** *(sl)* giungere all'oggettivo *(fig)*; raggiungere il proposito
first- *(in comp)* — **born** *n* primogenito; primo nato; —**class** *a* di prima classe; di prima qualità; —**rate** *a* di primo ordine
firsthand *a&adv* di prima mano
fiscal *a* fiscale
fish *n* pesce *m*; — **bone** lisca; **a queer —** *(coll)* un eccentrico; **-hook** *n* amo; **-line** lenza; — *vt&i* pescare; — **for information** sondare, indagare, cercare informazioni
fishing *n* pesca; — **rod** canna da pesca; — **tackle** aggeggi da pesca
fisherman *n* pescatore *m*
fishy *a* pescoso; di pesce; *(coll)* ambiguo, equivoco
fission *n* scissione, fissione; **nuclear —** scissione dell'atomo
fissure *n* fessura, crepatura
fist *n* pugno; **shake a — at** mostrare i pugni a *(fig)*; **-ful** *n* pugnata
fit *n (clothes)* taglio; *(med)* attacco, accesso; **by -s and starts** saltuariamente; — *a* adatto, conveniente, idoneo; *(health)* sano; — **to be tied** *(coll)* furioso; — **to drink** buono da bere; **see — to** considerare appropriato; — *vi* adattarsi; star bene; — **in with** accordarsi con
fitful *a* saltuario, irregolare; **-ly** *adv* a salti
fitness *n* convenienza, attitudine *f*
fix *n* difficoltà; **in a bad —** nei pasticci; — *vt* fissare, stabilire; *(adjust, repair)* aggiustare, riparare
fixation *n* fissazione
fixative *n* fissativo
fixed *a* fisso, stabilito, convenuto; — **charge** spesa di manutenzione
fixings *npl (coll)* accessori *mpl*
fixture *n* infisso; *(elec)* impianto elettrico
fizz *n* spuma; sciampagna *(coll)*; — *vi* spumare, spumeggiare; **-y** *a* gassoso
fizzle *n (coll)* fiasco, fallimento; — *vi (froth)* spumeggiare; *(hiss)* fischiare
flabbiness *n* flaccidità, languidezza
flabby *a* fiacco
flag *n* bandiera; **-pole** *n* asta di bandiera; **-ship** *n* nave ammiraglia
flag *vt (signal)* segnalare con bandiera; — *vi* languire; *(droop)* pendere
flagging *a* diminuente
flagrant *a* flagrante, palese
flair *n* fiuto, attitudine *f*, acume *m*
flake *n* fiocco, falda; —, — **off** *vt* sfaldare; — *vi* sfioccarsi, sfaldarsi
flaky *a* a falde, scaglioso
flamboyant *a* fiammeggiante, sfavillante
flame *n* fiamma; — *vi* fiammeggiare
flaming *a* fiammeggiante; *(emotion)* ardente
flange *n* fiangia
flank *n* lato, fianco; — *vt* fiancheggiare
flannel *n* flanella
flap *n* lembo, tesa; *(noise)* battuta; *(avi)* ipersostentatore *m*, deflettore *m*; — *vt* sbattere, agitare
flare *n* fuoco, fiamma; *(flash)* bagliore *m*; *(gift)* talento; *(rocket)* razzo; — *vi* divampare; — **up** sfuriare, perdere le staffe *(fig)*
flare-up *n* sfuriata
flaring *a* sfolgorante, fiammante
flash *n* flash *m*, lampo, splendore; **in a —** in un lampo; **lightning —** lampo
flash *vi* sfolgorare, lampeggiare; *(lightning)* balenare; — **by** passare come una freccia
flashing *n* lampo, bagliore *m*; — *a* scintillante, lampeggiante
flashlight *n* lampadina tascabile
flashy *a* sgargiante, vistoso
flask *n* fiasco; *(hip)* fiaschetta
flat *n* apartamento; *(mus)* bemolle *m*
flat *a* piano, piatto; — **broke** *(sl)* in bolletta, al verde; — **denial** deciso rifiuto; — **rate** cifra esatta; — **refusal** rifiuto categorico; **fall —** far fiasco
flat *vt (mus)* fare un bemolle
flat- *(in comp)* —**bottomed** *a* a fondo piatto; —**footed** *a* dai piedi piatti
flatiron *n* ferro da stiro
flatten *vt* livellare, appiattire
flatter *vt* lusingare, adulare
flattery *n* lusinga, adulazione
flatware *n* coperti *mpl*, argenteria
flatulent *a* flatulento; vuoto
flaunt *vt* ostentare; — *vi* pavoneggiarsi
flavor *n* gusto, sapore *m*, aroma *m*
flavoring *n* condimento; ciò che dà sapore
flaw *n* difetto, pecca; **-less** *a* perfetto, senza difetti
flax *n* lino; **-en** *a* di lino; *(hair)* biondo
flea *n* pulce *f*
fleck *n* macchia
fledgling *n* novellino; *(bird)* uccelletto
flee *vi* scappare, fuggire
fleecy *a* lanoso
fleet *n* flotta, marina; *(trucks)* equipaggiamento di veicoli; **merchant —** flotta mercantile; — *a* veloce
fleet-footed *a* veloce, svelto
fleeting *a* fugace, effimero
flesh *n* carne *f*; — **color** color carne; — **wound** ferita superficiale
fleshy *a* pingue, carnoso

flex *vt* flettere, piegare
flexible *a* flessibile
flexibility *n* flessibilità
flick *n* buffetto, colpettino; *(whip)* frustatina; — *vt* dare un colpetto a
flicker *vi* tremolare, guizzare, vacillare; — *n* guizzo, tremolio; — **of an eyelash** batter d'occhio
flier *n* aviatore *m*; *(advertisement)* volantino
flight *n* volo; *(escape)* fuga; *(stairs)* rampa di scale; — **pattern** *(avi)* formazione; **put to** — mettere in fuga; **–iness** *n* leggerezza, volubilità; **–y** *a* leggero, volubile, frivolo
flimsiness *n* leggerezza, inconsistenza, frivolità
flimsy *a* sottile, fragile
flinch *vi* ritirarsi, esitare, titubare, indietreggiare
fling *vt* scagliare, lanciare; — *vi* precipitarsi, scagliarsi
fling *n* getto, colpo, lancio; *(attempt)* tentativo
flint *n* pietra focaia
flip *n* ditata, buffetto; — *a* impertinente
flippant *a* impertinente, frivolo
flipper *n* natatoia, pinna
flirt *vi* flirtare; — *n* civetta, fraschetta
flirtation *n* flirt *m*; amoreggiamento
flit *vi* svolazzare
float *vi* galleggiare, fluttuare; — *n* carro allegorico; **–er** *n* spostato
floating *a* galleggiante; — **dock** bacino galleggiante
flock *n* gregge *m*; — *vi* affollarsi, adunarsi
floe *n* banco di ghiaccio
flog *vt* sferzare, staffilare
flood *n* inondazione; — **tide** alta marea; **–gate** *n* chiusa; **–light** *n* proiettore *m*; — *vt* inondare
floor *n* pavimento, suolo; *(building story)* piano; — **polish** lucido per pavimento; **ground** — pianterreno; **tiled** — pavimento a mattonelle; **have the** — avere turno per parlare; — *vt* pavimentare; *(coll)* ridurre in silenzio
flooring *n* pavimentazione
floorwalker *n* capo reparto
flop *n* caduta; *(coll)* insuccesso; — *vt&i* cadere; *(fish)* dibattersi; *(coll)* far fiasco
floral *a* floreale
Florence Firenze *f*
Florentine *a&n* fiorentino
florid *a* florido
florist *n* fioraio, fiorista *m&f*
floss *n* piumino, cascame di seta; **–y** *a* lanuginoso
flounce *n* balza; — *vt* ornare di gale; — **about** dimenarsi; — **out** precipitarsi fuori
flounder *vi* dibattersi; *(speech)* impappinarsi
flour *n* farina; — *vt* infarinare; **–y** *a* farinoso, infarinato
flourish *vt&i* prosperare, fiorire; *(brandish)* brandire; — *n* svolazzo; *(mus)* fioritura, fanfara; *(sword)* mulinello
flourishing *a* fiorente, prosperoso
flout *vt&i* schernire, beffarsi
flow *vi* scorrere; — **into** affluire, influire; **ebb and** — flusso e riflusso; — *n* corso, flusso, corrente *f*; **–ing** *a* fluente, scorrevole; *(tide)* montante
flower *n* fiore *m*; — **shop** negozio di fioraio; — **stand** portafiori *m*, giardiniera; — *vt&i* fiorire; **–ed** *a* fiorito, a fiori
flowering *a* fiorito; — *n* fioritura
flowery *a* infiorato; in fiore; *(language)* fiorito
flu *n (med)* influenza
fluctuate *vi* oscillare, fluttuare
flue *n* tubo, condotto, gola
fluency *n* scorrevolezza, facilità
fluent *a* fluente, scorrevole; **–ly** *adv* correntemente, speditamente
fluff *n* borra; *(hair)* lanugine *f*, peluria; — *vt* rendere soffice; *(bird)* scuotere le penne; — *vi (fig)* scuotersi le penne; **–y** *a* lanuginoso
fluid *a&n* fluido; — **drive** *(auto)* giunto idraulico
fluke *n* colpo di fortuna; caso inaspettato; — *vi (coll)* avere un colpo di fortuna
flunk *vt (coll)* bocciare; — *vi* essere bocciato agli esami; far fiasco
fluorescent *a* fluorescente
fluoridation *n* fluoridazione, fluorazione
fluoride *n* fluorite *f*
fluoroscope *n* fluoroscopio
flurry *n* trambusto, agitazione; *(snow)* mulinello di neve
flush *n* rossore *m*, accesso *(fig)*; *(cards)* flusso; — *vt* snidare *(fig)*; *(level)* livellare; *(rinse)* sciacquare; — *vi* arrossire; — *a* ripieno; *(coll)* a livello; *(print)* allineato
fluster *vt* agitare; — *vi* agitarsi, turbarsi; — *n* agitazione, trambusto
flustered *a* sconcertato
flute *n* flauto
fluting *n* scanalatura
flutter *vt* svolazzare, agitare; — *vi* agitarsi
fly *vi* volare; *(flee)* fuggire; — *vt* sventolare, far volare; *(avi)* pilotare; — **away** scappare; volar via; — **into a rage** perdere il freno *(fig)*; — **off the handle** uscire dai gangheri *(fig)*; — **on the beam** *(avi)* volare radio-guidato; — **over** sorvolare; volare sopra
fly *n* mosca; **–leaf** *n* foglio di guardia; **–paper** *n* carta moschicida; **–weight** *n (sport)* peso mosca; **–wheel** *n (mech)* volante *m*; **on the** — al volo
flying *n* volo, aviazione; — **saucer** disco volante; **blind** — volo cieco; — *a* volante
F.M., frequency modulation modulazione di frequenza
foal *n* puledro, asinello
foam *n* schiuma; — **rubber** gomma piuma
F.O.B., free on board F.O.B., consegna a bordo
focus *n* fuoco, centro; — *vt* mettere a fuoco; **in** — a fuoco; **out of** — sfocato
fodder *n* foraggio
foe *n* avversario, nemico
fog *n* nebbia; **–horn** *n* sirena
foggy *a* nebbioso; **It's** — C'è nebbia
fogy *n* persona antiquata; **–ish** *a* antiquato

foible *n* debole *m*
foil *vt* sventare; *(block)* impedire, — *n* lamina metallica; *(person)* contrasto
foist *vt* imporre, affibbiare
fold *vt* piegare; — *n* piega, piegatura; *(sheep)* ovile *m*; **–er** *n (file)* cartella; **–ing** *a* pieghevole
foliage *n* fogliame *m*
folio *n* folio; — *vt* numerare le pagine
folk *n* gente *f*, popolo; — *a* popolare; del popolo; **–lore** *n* folclore *m*; — **song** canto popolare
follicle *n* follicolo
follow *vt* seguire; — *vi* risultare
following *n* seguito; — *a* seguente
folly *n* follia, assurdità
foment *vt* fomentare
fond *a* affezionato, affettuoso, tenero; amante di; **be — of** voler bene a
fondle *vt* carezzare
fondly *adv* teneramente
fondness *n* affetto, amore *m*
food *n* cibo
fool *n* cretino; **make a — of oneself** mostrarsi sciocco; **–hardy** *a* pericoloso; — *vt* ingannare; — **away** sperperare
foolish *a* sciocco, stupido
foolishness *n* scemenza
foolproof *a* semplicissimo, sicurissimo
foolscap *n (paper)* carta protocollo *f*
foot *n* piede *m*; *(animal)* zampa; *(measure)* piede; *(stand)* base *f*; — **brake** freno a pedale; **have one — in the grave** avere un piede nella fossa *(fig)*; **on —** in piedi; **put one's — down** puntare i piedi; **put one's — in it** mettere lo zampino; **–bridge** *n* passerella; **–hill** *n* collinetta, rialzo di terreno; **–lights** *npl* luci della ribalta; **–print** *n* pedata, traccia, orma; **–sore** *a* con mal di piedi; **–step** *n* passo; **–stool** *n* sgabello; **–wear** *n* calzatura
foot *vt (math)* fare la somma; — *vi* camminare; andare a piedi; — **the bill** pagare il conto
football *n* pallone *m*, palla; *(game)* giuoco del calcio
footing *n* piede *m*, sostegno, base *f*; **lose one's —** perdere l'equilibrio
fop *n* bellimbusto, zerbinotto
for *prep* per; — *conj* perchè; **What —?** A che scopo?
forage *vi* foraggiare
foray *n* scorreria
forbear *vt&i* evitare, pazientare; astenersi da, fare a meno di
forbearance *n* indulgenza, pazienza
forbid *vt* proibire
forbidden *a* proibito, vietato
force *n* forza; **air —** aereonautica; **in —** in vigore; **–s** *npl* forze *fpl*; — *vt* costringere, sforzare, obbligare; — **back** respingere; — **one's way in** aprirsi il cammino con la forza; **–d** *a* costretto, forzato
forceful *a* potente, vigoroso
forceps *npl* forcipi *mpl*
forcibly *adv* energicamente; con forza
ford *n* guado; — *vt* guadare
forearm *n* avambraccio; — *vt* premunire
forebear *n* avo, antenato
foreboding *n* presagio, presentimento
forecast *n* previsione; *(weather)* previsione del tempo, bollettino meteorologico; — *vt* prevedere
foreclose *vt* precludere
foreclosure *n* preclusione
forefather *n* avo, antenato
forefinger *n* dito indice
forefront *n* la parte anteriore, l'anteriore *m*, il davanti *m*
forego *vt&i* precedere
foregoing *a* precedente, summenzionato
foregone *a* predeterminato, preconcetto; — **conclusion** deduzione ovvia
foreground *n* primo piano
forehead *n* fronte *f*
foreign *a* estero, forestiero; — **affairs** affari esteri; — **legion** legione straniera; — **trade** commercio estero
foreigner *n* straniero, straniera
Foreign Office *n* Ministero degli Affari Esteri
foreman *n* caposquadra, capotecnico, capomastro, capo operaio; *(jury)* capo della giuria
foremost *a* primo, principale; il migliore; il più grande
forenoon *n* mattino
forerunner *n* precursore *m*
foresee *vt* prevedere
foreshadow *vt* adombrare, prefigurare; far presentire
foresight *n* previdenza
forest *n* foresta, bosco; — **ranger** guardia forestale, guardaboschi *m*
forestall *vt* prevenire, anticipare, accaparrare
foretell *vt* predire
forethought *n* previdenza, previsione, premeditazione
forever *adv* sempre
forewarn *vt* preavvisare
foreword *n* proemio, prefazione
forfeit *n* multa, ammenda; — *vt* demeritare; perdere il diritto di
forge *n* fucina, forgia; — *vt* fucinare, forgiare, fabbricare; contraffare, falsificare
forgery *n* falsificazione, contraffazione
forget *vt* dimenticare; non ricordarsi
forgetful *a* dimentico, smemorato, negligente; **–ness** *n* dimenticanza; negligenza, smemoratezza
forget-me-not *n* nontiscordardimè *m*
forgive *vt* perdonare; **–ness** *n* perdono
forgiving *a* clemente, indulgente
forgotten *a* dimenticato, rimesso; fatto grazia
fork *n (road)* biforcazione; *(table)* forchetta; *(tool)* forca; *(tree)* forcella; *(trousers)* inforcatura; **tuning —** diapason *m*; — *vt* rimuovere con forca; — *vi* biforcarsi
forlorn *a* infelice, sconsolato, abbandonato
form *n* forma, modulo; — **letter** lettera circolare; **matter of —** questione di forma; **proper —** forma appropriata; **–ation** *n* formazione; **–less** *a* informe, amorfo; — *vt* formare, foggiare; — *vi* formarsi

formal *a* formale, d'etichetta, ufficiale; **— dress** abito da cerimonia
formality *n* cerimonia, formalità
former *a* precedente, passato; **the —** qello, questo; il primo; **–ly** *adv* altre volte, anteriormente, già, precedentemente; tempo fa
formidable *a* formidabile, minaccioso
formula *n* formula
formulate *vt* formulare
fornicate *vi* fornicare
forsake *vt* lasciare, abbandonare; *(renounce)* rinunziare
forsaken *a* abbandonato
fort *n* forte *m*, fortezza
forte *n&adv* forte *m*
forth *adv* avanti; *(outward)* fuori; **and so —** e così via; **–coming** *a* prossimo, futuro, imminente; **–right** *a* franco, esplicito, sincero; **–with** *adv* subito, immediatamente
fortieth *a* quarantesimo
fortification *n* fortificazione
fortify *vt* fortificare
fortitude *n* fortezza, fermezza, coraggio
fortnight *n* due settimane; quindici giorni; una quindicina; **–ly** *a* quindicinale, bisettimanale
fortuitous *a* accidentale, fortuito; **–ly** *adv* fortuitamente, accidentalmente
fortunate *a* fortunato; **–ly** *adv* per fortuna
fortune *n* fortuna; *(fate)* sorte *f*; **— hunter** cacciatore di dote
fortuneteller *n* indovino, indovina
forty *a* quaranta
forum *n* foro, tribunale *m*; dibattito pubblico
forward *a* *(ahead)* avanzato, inoltrato; *(brash)* audace, impertinente, sfacciato; *(daring)* spinto; **—** *adv* avanti; **—** *vt* inoltrare; far seguire
forwardness *n* progresso; *(manner)* impertinenza; precocità
forwards *adv* avanti
fossil *n* fossile *m*; **–ize** *vt* fossilizzare; **–ize** *vi* fossilizzarsi
foster *vt* *(encourage)* incoraggiare, secondare; *(shelter)* allevare, incrementare
foster child figlio adottato, affiliato
foster father padre adottivo
foster mother balia, nutrice, madre adottiva
foster parents genitori adottivi
foul *a* sporco; *(improper)* scorretto; **— ball** palla fuori campo; **— play** giuoco scorretto; condotta disonesta
foul-mouthed *a* osceno, sboccato
found *vt* fondare
foundation *n* fondazione; fondamento, base *f*; *(arch)* fondamenta *fpl*; **— garment** reggicalze *m*
founder *n* fondatore *m*; **—** *vt* affondare; **—** *vi* sprofondare
foundling *n* trovatello
foundry *n* fonderia
fountain *n* fontana; **— pen** penna stilografica
four *a* quattro
four-footed *a* a quattro piedi, a quattro gambe
foursome *n* gruppo di quattro persone; *(golf, cards)* partita a quattro
fourteen *a* quattordici; **–th** *a* quattordicesimo
fourth *a* quarto
fowl *n* pollame *m*
fox *n* volpe *f*; **–hole** *n* trincea; **–y** *a* astuto, furbo
fracas *n* chiasso, fracasso
fraction *n* frazione
fracture *n* frattura; **—** *vt* rompere, fratturare
fragile *a* fragile
fragility *n* fragilità
fragment *n* frammento; **–ary** *a* frammentario
fragrance *n* odore *m*, fragranza, profumo
fragrant *a* fragrante, profumato, odoroso
frail *a* fragile, delicato; **–ty** *n* fragilità, debolezza
frame *n* forma, struttura; *(mech)* telaio; *(picture)* cornice *f*; **— house** casa con struttura di legno; **— of mind** stato d'animo; **–work** *n* struttura, armatura
frame *vt* formare, incorniciare; *(coll)* incriminare con intrigo
framed *a* composto, escogitato, forgiato, incorniciato
France Francia
franchise *n* franchigia; *(com)* esclusiva, privativa
frank *a* sincero, franco
frankly *adv* francamente
frankfurter *n* salsicciotto
frantic *a* frenetico, furioso
frantically *adv* pazzamente, freneticamente
fraternal *a* fraterno
fraternity *n* fratellanza, confraternità
fraternize *vt* fraternizzare
fraud *n* frode *f*; **–ulent** *a* fraudolento
fray *n* lotta, cambattimento; *(scuffle)* zuffa; **—** *vt* consumare; *(ravel)* sfilacciare; *(wear)* logorare; **—** *vi* consumarsi, logorarsi, sfilacciarsi; **–ed** *a* consumato, logoro, sfilacciato
freak *n* ghiribizzo; *(monster)* mostro; *(whim)* capriccio; **–ish** *a* capriccioso; *(abnormal)* strano, anormale
freckle *n* lentiggine *f*; **—** *vi* divenire lentigginoso; **–d** *a* lentigginoso
free *a* libero, gratuito; **— and easy** senza complimenti; **— enterprise** impresa privata; **— hand** mano libera; **— of charge** gratis; **— speech** libertà di parola; **— will** libero arbitrio; **make — with** stralimitarsi; **of one's own — will** di spontanea volontà
free *vt* svincolare; *(exempt)* esimere; *(liberate)* liberare
freedom *n* libertà
free-for-all *n* *(coll)* giuoco (*or* concorso) aperto a chiunque
free fall *n* *(aesp)* mozione nello spazio
freehand *a* a mano libera
freemason *n* framassone *m*
freeway *n* autostrada
freeze *vt* gelare, congelare; **—** *n* gelo, congelamento
freezer *n* congelatore *m*; **deep —** frigorifero a temperatura bassa

freezing *a* gelido, glaciale; — **cold** freddo glaciale
freight *n* carico mercantile; — **train** treno merci
freightage *n* nolo
French *a&n* francese *m;* — **dressing** condimento francese; — **door** porta a due battenti; — **horn** corno inglese; — **leave** uscita alla chetichella; — **seam** orlo francese; — **window** finestra a due battenti
Frenchman, -woman *n* francese *m&f*
frenzied *a* frenetico
frenzy *n* pazzia, frenesia
frequency *n* frequenza; — **modulation** modulazione di frequenza
frequent *a* frequente; **-ly** *adv* frequentemente
fresh *a* fresco; *(sl)* presuntuoso, impertinente; **-ness** *n* freschezza; *(strength)* vigore *m*; **-ly** *adv* di fresco; di recente; **-en** *vt&i* rinfrescare
freshman *n* matricolino, matricola
fresh-water *a* d'acqua dolce
fret *n* agitazione; *(stringed instrument)* tasto; — *vi* agitarsi, irritarsi
fretful *a* irritato, impaziente, inquieto; *(peevish)* stizzoso, scontroso
fretfulness *n* irritabilità
friable *a* friabile
friar *n* frate *m*
friction *n* frizione
Friday *n* venerdì; **Good** — Venerdì Santo
fried *a* fritto
friend *n* amico, amica; **make a** — farsi un amico; **-less** *a* senza amici; **-ly** *a* amichevole; **-ship** *n* amicizia
frieze *n (arch)* fregio
fright *n* spavento; **-en** *vt* spaventare; **-ened** *a* spaventato, impaurito, intimidito; **-ful** *a* spaventoso, spaventevole
frigid *a* freddo, frigido, glaciale
frigidity *n* freddezza, frigidezza, frigidità
frill *n* trina, gala, fronzolo; — *vt* guarnire, orlare; ornare di trine
fringe *n* frangia; — **benefit** introito extrasalariale; — *vt* orlare, ornare con frangia
frisk *vi* sgambettare, saltellare, folleggiare; — *vt (coll)* perquisire addosso; **-y** *a* vispo, vivace
fritter *n* frittella; — *vt* gingillare; — **away** disperdere; *(time)* sprecare il tempo
frivolity *n* frivolità, frivolezza
frivolous *a* frivolo
frizzle *vt* arrostire alla griglia; — *vi* far rumore di friggere
frizzy *a* arricciato
fro *adv* indietro; **to and** — avanti e indietro
frock *n* veste *f*; costume *m;* vestito; *(eccl)* tonaca; sottana
frog *n* rana, ranocchio; *(rail)* incrocio, raccordo; *(trimming)* alamaro; — **in the throat** raucedine *f*
frolic *n* trastullo; — *vi* trastullarsi; **-some** *a* allegro, giocoso, festevole
from *prep* da; da parte di; — **now on** da ora in poi; **take** — *(accept)* accettare; *(deprive of)* privare di
front *n* davanti *m*, facciata; — *a* di avanti; del davanti; **in — of** in faccia, dirimpetto; — *vt&i* affrontare
frontier *n* frontiera, confine *m*
frontispiece *n* frontespizio
frost *n* gelo; **hoar** — brina; **-bite** *n* congelamento; **-bitten** *a* congelato, gelato
frosted *a (food)* candito; *(hoary)* brinato; — **glass** vetro smerigliato
frosting *n* ghiacciata; *(cake)* crosta di zucchero
froth *n* schiuma; — *vt* far spumare; — *vi* spumeggiare, schiumare, spumare
frown *n* cipiglio; sguardo corrucciato; — *vi* accigliarsi; — **on** disapprovare
frowning *a* corrucciato
frowsy *a* sporco, scalcinato
frozen *a* gelato, congelato
frugal *a* parco, frugale
fruit *n* frutto, frutta; — **dealer** fruttivendolo; — **stand** banco di fruttivendolo
fruitful *a* fruttifero; *(profitable)* proficuo
fruition *n* soddisfazione, adempimento
fruitless *a* improduttivo; *(useless)* vano
frustrate *vt* deludere, frustrare
frustration *n* insuccesso, delusione
fry *vt* friggere; — *vi* friggersi
frying pan padella
fuel *n* combustibile *m;* — **oil** petrolio da ardere; — **tank** cisterna per carburanti; — *vt* alimentare con combustibile; — *vi* rifornirsi di carburante
fugitive *a* fuggiasco, evaso; — *n* disertore *m*
fugue *n* fuga
fulcrum *n* fulcro
fulfil *vt* compiere, eseguire, esaudire
fulfilment *n* realizzazione
full *a* pieno; **at — blast** al massimo; — **dress** abito da cerimonie; — **house** *(poker)* un tris e una coppia; *(theat)* teatro esaurito; — **moon** luna piena; — **stop** fermata completa; **at — speed** a tutta velocità; **in** — per esteso; in pieno; **-back** *n (football)* terzino
full- *(in comp)* **—blooded** *a* pieno di vitalità; *(breeding)* puro sangue, di razza; **—blown** *a* in piena fioritura; **—bodied** *a* grasso, pingue; **—faced** *a* dalla faccia piena; **—fledged** *a* completo; **—grown** *a* adulto, maturo; **—length** *a* dalla testa ai piedi; **—term** *a* di periodo completo
fullness *n* pienezza
fully *adv* tutto, interamente, perfettamente
fume *n* emanazione, esalazione; — *vt* affumicare, offuscare; — *vi (anger)* arrabbiarsi, smaniare
fumigate *vt* disinfettare, soffumicare
fumigation *n* fumigazione
fuming *a* collerico, adirato
fun *n* divertimento; **full of** — molto divertente; **have** — divertirsi; **in** — per scherzo; **make — of** burlarsi di
function *n* funzione; — *vi* funzionare
fund *n* capitale liquido, fondo monetario; **sinking** — fondo di ammortamento
fundamental *a* fondamentale
funeral *n* funerale *m;* — **director** assistente funebre; — **home** ditta di pom-

pe funebri
funereal *a* funebre, lugubre
fungicide *n* funghicida *m*
fungus *n* fungo
funnel *n* imbuto
funny *a* buffo, comico, divertente; *(odd)* strano, curioso; — **bone** nervo del gomito
fur *n* pelliccia; — **store** pellicceria
furbish *vt* forbire, lucidare
furious *a* furioso; **-ly** *adv* furiosamente
furlough *n* licenza, congedo
furnace *n* fornace *f*
furnish *vt* ammobiliare; *(supply)* fornire
furnished *a* ammobiliato; — **room** camera ammobiliata
furnishings *npl* arredamenti *mpl*
furniture *n* mobili *mpl*, mobilia
furor *n* furore *m*
furrier *n* pellicciaio
furrow *n* solco
furry *a* peloso; *(tongue)* patinoso
further *a* ulteriore; — *adv* oltre, più in là, oltre a ciò; — *vt* assecondare, agevolare; **without — ado** senza ulteriori difficoltà
furtherance *a* promozione, avanzamento
furthermore *adv* inoltre, d'altronde
furthest *a* il più lontano; — *adv* alla massima distanza
furtive *a* furtivo, occulto; **-ly** *adv* furtivamente
fury *n* furore *m*
fuse *n* valvola, fusibile *m*
fuselage *n (avi)* fusoliera
fuss *n* chiasso, trambusto; — **over nothing** trambusto per un nonnulla; — *vi* inquietarsi, affannarsi
fussy *a* meticoloso, schifiltoso
futile *a* inutile, futile, frivolo, vano
futility *n* futilità
future *a* futuro; — *n* futuro, avvenire *m*; **in the —** nel futuro
futurist *n* futurista *m&f*
futurity *n* avvenire *m*, futuro
fuzz *n* materia volatile (*or* impalpabile)

G

G- *(in comp)* **—force** *n* forza di gravità; **—man** *n* agente federale; **—suit** *n (avi)* scafandro spaziale
gab *n* loquacità, cicaleccio; **gift of —** lingua sciolta; — *vi* cicalare
gabardine *n* gabardina
gabby *a* loquace
gable *n* frontone *m*; — **roof** tetto spiovente
gad *vi* gironzare, girellare; — **about** vagare, andare qua e là
gadabout *n* giramondo
gadget *n* aggeggio, congegno; *(mech)* meccanismo
gaff *n* rampone *m*, uncino; *(naut)* picco di randa
gag *n* bavaglio; *(coll)* scherzo, battuta, trovata; — *vt* imbavagliare; — *vi (theat)* improvvisare
gaiety *n* allegria, gaiezza
gaily *a* gaiamente
gain *n* guadagno; — *vt&i* guadagnare; — **on** diminuire la distanza; — **weight** ingrossare
gainful *a* vantaggioso, lucrativo
gainsay *vt* contraddire; dire di no
gait *n* andatura, portamento, passo
gala *a* di gala
galaxy *n* galassia; *(ast)* Via Lattea
gale *n* tormenta, bufera; — **of laughter** scroscio di risa
gall *n* bile *f*; *(coll)* impudenza, sfacciataggine *f*; — *vt* irritare
gallant *a* galante; *(brave)* coraggioso; *(gay)* gaio; *(imposing)* imponente
gallantry *n* galanteria, coraggio
gallbladder *n* cistifellea
gallery *n* galleria; *(theat)* loggione *m*
galley *n* cucina di bordo; *(naut)* galera; *(print)* bozza di stampa
gallivant *vi* bighellonare, andare a zonzo
gallon *n* gallone *m*
gallop *n* galoppo; — *vi* galoppare
gallows *npl* forca, patibolo
gallstone *n* calcolo biliare, mal della pietra
galore *adv* a iosa, in abbondanza
galoshes *npl* galosce *fpl*
galvanize *vt* galvanizzare
galvanometer *n* galvanometro
gamble *n* giuoco d'azzardo; — *n (coll)* rischio, azzardo; — *vi* giuocare d'azzardo; — *vt* fare scommessa
gambler *n* giocatore *m*
gambling *n* giuoco d'azzardo; — **house** bisca
game *n* giuoco; *(food)* cacciagione *f*; *(coll)* sotterfugio; *(sport)* partita; **make a — of** giocarsi di; **play the — right** essere onesto; — *a* coraggioso; *(lame)* zoppo; **die —** resistere fino in fondo
gamekeeper *n* guardacaccia *m*
gamma *n* gamma; — **globulin** emoglobina; — **ray** raggio gamma
gander *n* maschio dell'oca
gang *n* banda, combriccola; *(work)* squadra; **-plank** *n* passerella; plancia di sbarco
ganglion *n* ganglio
gangrene *n* cancrena
gangrenous *a* cancrenoso
gangster *n* gangster *m*, bandito, delinquente *m*
gangway *n* passaggio, corridoio; *(naut)* pontile *m*; *(mine)* tunnel di miniera
gantlet *n (fig)* sfida; **run the —** superare gli ostacoli
gantry tower *n (aesp)* torre di lancio
gap *n (blank)* lacuna; *(breach)* breccia; *(mountain)* gola, valico
gape *vi (open)* spalancarsi; *(yawn)* sbadigliare; restare a bocca aperta; — **at** guardare attonito
gaping *a* sbadigliante; *(agape)* stordito
garage *n* autorimessa, garage *m*
garb *n* abbligliamento
garbage *n* immondizie *fpl*
garble *vt* mutilare; *(falsify)* falsificare
garden *n* giardino

gardener *n* giardiniere *m*
gardenia *n* gardenia
gargle *vt* gargarizzare; — *n* gargarismo
gargoyle *n* garguglia
garish *a* vistoso, sfarzoso, abbagliante
garland *n* ghirlanda
garlic *n* aglio; — **clove** capo d'aglio
garment *n* indumento; — **industry** industria dell'abbigliamento
garnish *n* guarnizione; *(food)* contorno; — *vt* abbellire, guarnire
garnishee *vt* imporre trattenute sul salario
garrison *n* guarnigione *f*
garret *n* soffitta
garrote *n* cappio; — *vt* strangolare
garter *n* giarrettiera; — **belt** reggicalze *m*; — **snake** biscia
gas *n* gas *m*; *(coll)* benzina; — **heater** stufa a gas; — **meter** contatore del gas; — **stove** cucina a gas; — **tank** *(auto)* serbatoio; **-light** *n* luce di gas
gaseous *a* gassoso
gash *n* taglio, sfregio; — *vt* sguarciare
gasoline *n* benzina
gasp *vi* ansare, boccheggiare; — *n* sospiro, anelito; **last** — ultimo respiro
gasping *n* ansito, affanno; — *a* ansimante, affannoso
gastrectomy *n* rettogastrotomia, gastrorettotomia
gate *n* cancello; porta del cancello
gateway *n* portone *m*
gather *vt* raccogliere; *(infer)* dedurre; *(sewing)* increspare, pieghettare; — *vi* *(meet)* adunarsi
gathering *n* adunata, riunione *f*; *(harvest)* raccolta; *(med)* ascesso, suppurazione; *(people)* adunanza
gaudy *a* sgargiante, vistoso
gauge *n* misura; *(mech)* indicatore *m*; — *vt* misurare; stimare
gaunt *a* sparuto
gauntlet *n* guanto da moschettiere; **take up the** — accettare la sfida; **throw down the** — tirare il guanto di sfida *(fig)*
gauze *n* garza
gavel *n* tributo, gabella
gawk *vi* guardare attorno stupidamente; **-y** *a* balordo, sguaiato
gay *a* allegro, gaio
gaze *vi* guardare; — **at** fissare; — *n* sguardo fisso
gazeteer *n* gazzettiere *m;* dizionario geografico
gear *n* arnesi *mpl*, arredo; *(auto)* meccanismo, ingranaggio; *(equipment)* corredo; *(mech)* congegno; *(tools)* arnesi *mpl*; — **shift** cambio di velocità; **in** — funzionante; **throw out of** — arrestare; *(disable)* mettere fuori posto; — *vt* abbigliare; *(mech)* ingranare
gearing *n* ingranaggio
geiger counter contatore Geiger
gelatin *n* gelatina
gem *n* gemma, gioiello
gender *n* genere *m*
gene *n* tipo genetico
genealogy *n* genealogia
general *a&n* generale *m*; — **delivery** fermo in posta; **in** — in generale
generality *n* generalità
generalization *n* generalizzazione
generally *adv* generalmente; — **speaking** generalmente parlando
generate *vt* generare, produrre
generation *n* generazione
generator *n* generatore *m*
generic *a* generico
generosity *n* generosità
generous *a* generoso
genesis *n* genesi *f*, origine *f*
genetics *n* genetica
Geneva Ginevra
genial *a* cordiale, cortese
geniality *n* genialità
genitals *npl* genitali *mpl*
genitive *a* genitivo
genius *n* genio
Genoa Genova
Genoese *a&n* genovese *m&f*
genteel *a* ammanierato, affettato, ricercato
gentility *n* gentilezza; *(breeding)* nascita aristocratica
gentle *a* *(mild)* dolce, moderato; *(genteel)* raffinato, cortese
gentleman *n* signore *m*; gentiluomo
gentlemen *ipl* gentiluomini *mpl*; signori *mpl*
gentleness *n* dolcezza, tenerezza
gently *adv* dolcemente
gentry *n* gente per bene; benestanti di campagna
genuflection *n* genuflessione
genuine *a* autentico, genuino
genus *n* genere *m*
geochemistry *n* geochimica
geographic, -al *a* geografico
geography *n* geografia
geologist *n* geologo
geology *n* geologia
geometric, -al *a* geometrico
geometry *n* geometria; **solid** — geometria solida; **plane** — geometria piana
geophysics *n* geofisica
geopolitics *n* geopolitica
geranium *n* geranio
geriatrics *n* geriatria
germ *n* germe *m*, microbo
German *a&n* tedesco, tedesca; — **measles** rosolia
germane *a* relativo, pertinente; *(akin)* germano
Germany Germania
germicide *n* germicida
germinate *vi* germinare
gerund *n* gerundio
gestation *n* gestazione
gesticulate *vi* gesticolare
gesture *n* atto, gesto; — *vi* gestire, gesticolare
get *vt* avere, ottenere; *(fetch)* portare; *(receive)* ricevere; — *vi* *(become)* diventare, farsi; *(come)* arrivare; — **about** andare attorno; — **along** avanzare, andare avanti; *(agree with)* andare d'accordo con; — **around** *(avoid)* girare; — **at** raggiungere il segno *(fig)*; — **away** allontanarsi; — **down** scendere; — **even with** vendicarsi, far da pagare;

— **into** entrare, mettersi in; — **rid of** sbarazzarsi di; — **up** alzarsi; — **wind of** avere sentore di
get– *(in comp)* **—together** *n* adunata; **—up** *n (arrangement)* formata; *(coll, dress)* costume *m*; **—up-and-go** *n* energia
getaway *n* fuga
geyser *n* geyser, soffione *m*; *(mech)* stufa a gas
ghastliness *n* orrore, squallore *m*; *(paleness)* pallidezza
ghastly *a* orribile, macabro, cadaverico
ghost *n* spettro, fantasma *m*; — **town** città abbandonata; — **writer** chi scrive in nome altrui; **give up the** — perdersi d'animo; **Holy G–** Spirito Santo
G.I. *(mil)* soldato americano
giant *n* gigante *m*
gibberish *n* ciancia
gibe, (jibe) *n* scherno, beffa; — *vt&i* schernire, beffarsi di
giblets *npl* frattaglie, rigaglie *fpl*
giddiness *n* vertigine *f*, capogiro; *(frivolity)* frivolità
giddy *a* vertiginoso; spensierato *(fig)*; *(scatterbrained)* scervellato; **feel** — avere le vertigini
gift *n* regalo, dono; **–ed** *a* valente, d'ingegno
gigantic *a* enorme, gigantesco
giggle *vi* fare risatine sciocche; — *n* riso sciocco
giggling *a* che ride scioccamente
gild *vt&i* dorare
gills *npl* branchie *fpl*
gilt *n* indoratura, doratura: — *a* dorato
gilt-edged *a* di prim'ordine; dorato sul taglio; — **securities** azioni solide
gimlet *n* succhiello
gimmick *n (sl)* trucco, espediente *m*
gin *n* gin *m*
ginger *n* zenzero; — **ale** gassosa allo zenzero
gingerly *adv* cautamente, delicatamente: — *a* cauto
gingham *n* rigatino
gingivitis *n* gengivite *f*
gird *vt* cingere: *(invest with)* investire: — *vi* schernire
girder *n* trave *f*: **steel** — putrella
girdle *n (belt)* cintura: *(garment)* ventriera elastica: — *vt* cingere: *(circle)* circondare
girl *n* ragazza, fanciulla: *(miss)* signorina: *(coll)* innamorata: **hired** — donna di servizio: **–ish** *a* fanciullesco, femminile. **–hood** *n* fanciullezza
girth *n* circonferenza
gist *n* essenza, sostanza, sunto, punto principale
give *vt* dare: — **account** rendere conto: — **away** presentare; dar via: — **back** restituire: — **birth to** dare alla luce: — **evidence** offrire evidenza: *(show)* dare indicazione: — **off** emettere: — **out** *(emit)* emettere: *(fail)* esaurirsi: — **rise to** dare origine a: — **up** *(renounce)* rinunciare: *(yield)* cedere; — **way** cedere, ritirarsi
given *a* dato, stabilito; disposto: — **name** nome di battesimo; — **time** tempo dato
give-and-take *n* compromesso
giver *n* donatore *m*
gizzard *n* ventriglio
glacial *a* glaciale
glacier *n* ghiacciaio
glad *a* contento, lieto, felice; **–ly** *adv* con piacere, volentieri; **–ness** *n* contentezza, gioia, piacere *m*
gladden *vt* rallegrare, allietare
gladiolus *n* gladiolo
glamour *n* fascino; **–ous** *a* affascinante
glance *n* occhiata, sguardo; **at first** — a prima vista; — *vi* dare un'occhiata; dare uno sguardo
gland *n* glandola; **–ular** *a* glandolare, ghiandolare
glare *n* bagliore *m*, sfolgorio; *(eye)* occhiataccia; — *vi* sfolgorare: gettare sguardi sfologoranti
glaring *a* abbagliante, evidente, lampante
glass *n* vetro, cristallo; — **blower** soffiatore di vetro; — **making** fabbricazione del vetro; **cut** — cristallo tagliato; **drinking** — bicchiere *m*: **magnifying** — lente d'ingrandimento: **stained** — vetrata colorata: **–ful** *n* bicchiere pieno; **–ware** *n* cristalleria; vetrame *m*
glasses *npl (drinking)* bicchieri *mpl*: *(eye)* occhiali *mpl*, lenti *fpl*
glassy *a* vitreo, trasparente, cristallino
glaucoma *n* glaucoma *m*
glaze *n* smalto; — *vt* smaltare
glazier *n* vetraio
gleam *n* raggio; — *vi* luccicare, raggiare
gleaming *a* lucente
glee *n (hilarity)* ilarità: *(joy)* gioia: — **club** circolo di coristi
glib *a* loquace, scorrevole
glide *vi* scivolare; — *n* scivolata
glider *n (avi)* aliante *m*
glimmer *n* barlume *m*
glimpse *n* occhiata, sguardo di sfuggita: — *vt&i* intravedere
glint *n* scintillio, sprazzo di luce: — *vi* scintillare, brillare
glisten *vi* brillare, luccicare
glitter *vi* scintillare; — *n* scintillio
gloat *vi* gongolare; divorare con gli occhi *(fig)*
global *a* globale
globe *n* sfera, globo
globular *a* sferico, globulare
gloom *n (darkness)* tenebre *fpl*, oscurità: *(sorrow)* tristezza: **–y** *a (dark)* tetro, oscuro; *(sad)* melanconico, cupo
glorify *vt* glorificare, magnificare, esaltare
glorious *a* glorioso, splendido
glory *n* gloria, onore *m*; — *vi* gloriarsi
gloss *n* lucidezza: **give a** — lustrare: — *vt* lustrare; lucidare: — **over** adonestare: **–y** *a* lucido
glove *n* guanto, — **shop** guanteria, guantificio; negozio di guanti
glow *vi (flush)* arrossire; *(shine)* brillare: — *n (warmth)* calore *m*; ardore *m*: *(reflection)* riflesso
glower *vi* guardare torvamente
glowing *a* brillante, animato: *(hot)* acceso
glucose *n* glucosio

glue *n* colla; — *vt* incollare
gluey *a* attaccaticcio
glum *a* cupo, arcigno
glut *vt* saziare; *(obstruct)* ingombrare
glutten *n* glutine *m*
glutton *n* ghiottone *m*
gluttonous *a* ghiotto
gluttony *n* ghiottoneria, gola
gnarl *n* nodo
gnarled *a* nodoso
gnarly *a* nodoso
gnat *n* moscerino
gnaw *vt* rosicchiare, rodere
gnawing *n* rodimento; corrosione; — *a* rosicante
go *vi* andare; — **against** andar contro; — **astray** perdersi; — **away** partire; — **back** tornare indietro; — **back on** *(fig)* rinnegare; — **backward** camminare all'indietro; — **beyond** oltrepassare; — **for** *(coll)* andare in cerca di; — **forward** avanzare; — **out** uscire; — **out of one's way** *(detour)* deviarsi, sviarsi; *(favor)* disturbarsi per qualcuno; — **over** *(pass over)* dare una scorsa; *(repeat)* ripetere; *(to)* andare da; — **to sleep** addormentarsi; — **through with** condurre a termine; — **to it** *(coll)* sbrigarsi; — **under** affondare; *(fail)* soccombere; — **with** *(agree)* andare d'accordo; stare con; — **without** fare a meno; **let** — **of** lasciare
go *n (coll)* energia *(fig)*; **all the** — di moda; **have a** — **at it** trattare di fare; **It's a** —! Accettato!; **make a** — **of it** aver esito; **on the** — in movimento; *(busy)* attivo; **no** — *(sl)* impossibile; di nessun profitto
goad *n* pungolo; — *vt* stimolare
goal *n* meta, mira, scopo
goat *n* capro, capra
goatee *n* barbetta, pizzo
gobble *vt* trangugiare
gobbler *n* ghiottone *m*; **turkey** — tacchino
go-between *n* mediatore *m*, intermediario
goblet *n* coppa
God *n* Dio; — **willing** se piace a Dio; **–speed** *n* buon viaggio
god *n* dio; **–child** *n* figlioccio; **–father** *n* padrino; **–mother** *n* madrina; **–send** *n* bazza *(coll)*; fortuna inaspettata; **–less** *a* ateo, empio; **–like** *a* divino; **–liness** *n* santità
goddess *n* dea
goggle-eyed *a* con gli occhi stralunati
goggles *npl* occhialoni *mpl*
goiter *n* gozzo
gold *n* oro
golden *a* dorato, aureo
gold-filled *a* aurifero
golf *n* golf *m*; — **clubs** bastoni *mpl*; — **course** campo di golf; **–bag** *n* borsa dei bastoni; — *vi* giocare al golf
gonad *n* gonade *f*; tessuto generativo
gondola *n* gondola
gone *a* andato, partito; *(finished)* finito; *(used up)* esaurito
gonorrhea *n* gonorrea
good *n* bene *m*; *(usefulness)* utilità; — **breeding** buona educazione; **G– for you!** *interj* Molto bene!; **do** — far bene; **make** — riuscir bene; — *a* buono; — **afternoon, day** buon giorno; — **evening** buona sera; — **nature** indole buona, buona qualità; — **night** buona notte; — **sense** buon senso; — **turn** buon'azione, favore *m*; — *adv* bene; **be** — essere buono; **for** — **and all** per sempre
good– *(in comp)* **—by** *n* addio, arrivederci, arrivederla; **—for-nothing** *n&a* buonanulla *m&f*; **—hearted** *a* di buon cuore; — **humored** *a* di buon umore; **—looking** *a* attraente; **—natured** *a* di buona indole; **—night** *a* di buonanotte; **—sized** *a* grande
Good Friday Venerdì Santo
goodness *n* bontà; **thank** — *interj* grazie a Dio!
goods *npl* merci *fpl*, beni *mpl*; **catch with the** — *(coll)* prendere in flagrante; **deliver the** — *(coll)* consegnare la merce; **household** — masserizie *fpl*; *(utensils)* utensileria
goose *n* oca; — **flesh,** — **pimples** pelle d'oca *(fig)* **wild** — **chase** la luna nel pozzo *(fig)*
gooseberry *n* ribes *m*, uva spina
gore *n (blood)* grumo di sangue; *(sewing)* taglio di stoffa che compone la gonna; — *vt* incornare
gorge *n* burrone *m*; — *vt&i* gozzovigliare
gorgeous *a* splendido, brillante; *(sumptuous)* fastoso; **–ly** *adv* sontuosamente; con gran fastosità
gorilla *n* gorilla *m*
gory *a* insanguinato
gosling *n* papero
gospel *n* vangelo; — **truth** verità sacrosanta; verità di Vangelo
gossamer *n (gauze)* garza; *(web)* ragnatela; **–y** *a* sottilissimo, tenue
gossip *n* pettegolezzo; — *vi* spettegolare
Gothic *a* gotico
gouge *n* sgorbio; — *vt* sgorbiare
gourd *n* zucca
gourmand *n* ghiottone *m*
gourmet *n* buongustaio
gout *n* gotta
govern *vt* governare
governess *n* governante, istitutrice *f*
government *n* governo, controllo; **–al** *a* governativo
governor *n* governatore *m*
gown *n (coverall)* camice *m*; *(dress)* vestito; **dressing** — veste da camera
grab *vt* afferrare, agguantare; — *n* presa, stretta; — **bag** *(coll)* sacco di regali-sopresa
grace *n* grazia; *(pardon)* perdono; — **note** *(mus)* fioritura; **say** — recitare il benedicite; — *vt* adornare
graceful *a* leggiadro, grazioso
gradation *n* gradazione
grade *n* grado, punto; *(school)* voto; — **crossing** *(rail)* passaggio a livello; — **school** scuola elementare; — *vt* classificare; *(score)* dare i punti; *(surface)* livellare
gradual *a* graduale; **–ly** *adv* man mano, via via
graduate *vt* graduare; conferire un di-

ploma; — *vi* diplomarsi, laurearsi; — *a* diplomato; graduato; — *n* laureato; *(measure)* bicchiere graduato
graduation *n* graduazione
graft *n (bot)* innesto; *(med)* trapianto; *(pol, coll)* corruzione; — *vt (bot)* innestare; *(med)* trapiantare
grain *n (cereal)* grano; *(seed)* chicco; *(texture)* filo; *(weight)* grano; *(wood)* filo, venatura; — **alcohol** alcool di grano; **against the** — di malavoglia; controvoglia
gram *n* grammo
grammar *n* grammatica; — **school** scuola elementare
grammarian *n* grammatico
grammatical *a* grammaticale
grand *a* grande, grandioso, magnifico; — **opera** opera; — **piano** pianoforte a coda; **–stand** *n* tribuna
grandchild *n* nipotino, nipotina
granddaughter, grandson *n* nipote *m&f*
grandfather *n* nonno
grandmother *n* nonna
grandparent *n* nonno, nonna
grandeur *n* grandezza, fasto, grandiosità, magnificenza
grandiloquent *a* magniloquente
grandiose *a* grandioso
granite *n* granito
grant *n* dono, concessione; *(school)* borsa di studio; — *vt* accordare; *(acknowledge)* ammettere, riconoscere; **–ing that** dato che; **take for –ed** accettare come vero
granulate *vt* granulare; — *vi* granularsi
granulated *a* granulato; — **sugar** zucchero cristallizzato
grape *n* uva; — **seed** acino; **bunch of –s** grappolo d'uva
grapefruit *n* pompelmo
grapevine *n* vigna coltivata; *(coll)* confidenza di notizie non ufficiali
graph *n* grafico, diagramma *m;* **–ic** *a* grafico
graphite *n* grafite *f*
grapple *n* rampone *m*; — *vt (wrestling)* aggrappare; — *vi* afferrarsi; — **with** *(fig)* lottare contro; *(problems)* trattare
grasp *vt* afferrare; *(understand)* capire; — *n* stretta; *(scope)* portata
grasping *a* avaro, tirchio, spilorcio
grass *n* erba; **blade of** — filo d'erba; **–hopper** *n* cavalletta; **–land** *n* prateria; **–y** a erboso
grate *n (framework)* inferriata; *(grid)* griglia; *(grill)* graticola; — *vt* grattuggiare; *(sound)* raspare; — *vi* stridere
grateful *a* riconoscente, grato; *(pleasing)* gradito; **–ness** *n* gradevolezza, gratitudine *f*
gratification *n (granting of)* appagamento, raggiungimento della meta; *(pleasure)* soddisfazione
gratified *a* gratificato, soddisfatto
gratify *vt* soddisfare; *(please)* accontentare; **–ing** *a* gradevole
grating *n* griglia, inferriata; *(sound)* stridore *m*
gratis *a* gratuito; — *adv* gratis, gratuitamente
gratitude *n* riconoscenza
gratuity *n* mancia
grave *n* tomba, fossa; **–digger** *n* becchino; **–yard** *n* cimitero; — *a* grave, austero
gravel *n* ghiaia
gravitate *vi* propendere, gravitare
gravity *n* gravità
gravy *n* sugo di carne; **–boat** *n* salsiera
gray *a&n* grigio
gray-haired *a* dai capelli grigi
grayness *n* grigiore *m*
graze *vt* rasentare, sfiorare; — *vi* pascolare
grease *n* unto, grasso; — **paint** cerone *m*; **remove** — sgrassare; *(spots)* smacchiare
greasing *n (auto)* ingrassaggio
greasy *a* untuoso, oleoso
great *a* grande, illustre; **a** — **deal** molto; **a** — **many** molti, gran numero; **to a** — **extent** estesamente
great-grandchild *n* pronipote *m&f*
great-grandparents *npl* bisnonni *mpl*
greatly *adv* molto
greatness *n* grandezza
Grecian, Greek *a&n* greco
Greece Grecia
greed, greediness *n* avidità
greedy *a* avido, ingordo
green *a&n* verde *m*; — *n (grassy field)* prato; — **light** *(coll)* luce verde *(fig)*; **–ish** *a* verdastro; **–ness** *n* verdezza, freschezza; *(untrained)* inesperienza
green-eyed *a* dagli occhi verdi; *(fig)* geloso
greenhouse *n* serra
greens *npl* verdura, ortaggio; *(herbs)* erbe *fpl*
greet *vt* salutare
greeting *n* saluto
gregarious *a* socievole, gregario
grenadier *n* granatiere *m*
grenadine *n (pomegranite juice)* granatina
grid *n* grata; *(elec)* sistema di elettrificazione; *(rad, TV)* griglia di valvola
griddle *n* tegamino; plancia per cuocere dolci
gridiron *n* griglia; *(football)* campo di calcio demarcato
grief *n* dolore *m*, pena; **come to** — finire male
grief-stricken *a* afflitto, angosciato
grievance *n* rancore *m*; *(complaint)* gravame *m*, reclamo; *(grudge)* ruggine *f (fig)*; *(wrong)* torto
grieve *vt* addolorare, affliggere, rattristare; — *vi* affliggersi, crucciarsi, addolorarsi
grievous *a* penoso
grill *vt* cuocere sulla graticola; — *n* graticola
grim *a* sinistro; *(cruel)* implacabile; *(stern)* austero
grimace *n* boccaccia, smorfia
grime *n* sudiciume *m*
grimy *a* sudicio
grin *vi* sogghignare; — *n* gran sorriso, smorfia
grind *vt (glass)* smerigliare; *(mill)* macinare; *(teeth)* digrignare; — *n* sgobbamento; *(coll)* fatica; **daily** — *(sl)* fatica quotidiana

grinder *n* macinatore *m*; **knife** — arrotino; **meat** — tritacarne *m*; **organ** — suonatore d'organetto
grinding *n* macinatura; *(sharpening)* affilatura; — *a (sound)* stridente
grindstone *n* mola
grip *vt* stringere, afferrare; — *n* presa, stretta; *(luggage)* valigetta; **come to –s with** essere nel punto critico di una decisione; venire alle mani
gripe *n* crampo, colica; *(sl)* lamentela; — *vt* afferrare, dare crampi di ventre; — *vi (sl)* lamentarsi
gripping *a* impressionante, eccitante
gristle *n* cartilagine *f*
grit *n* sabbia, arenaria; *(coll)* fermezza, coraggio; — *vt (teeth)* digrignare
gritty *a* sabbioso; *(brave)* coraggioso
groan *vi* gemere; — *n* lamento, gemito
grocer *n* rivenditore di generi alimentari
groceries *npl* alimenti *mpl*
grocery *n* negozio di generi alimentari
groggy *a (drunk)* ubbriaco; *(unsteady)* malfermo
groin *n* inguine *m*
groom *n* stalliere *m*; mozzo di stalla; *(wedding)* sposo; — *vt (horse)* strigliare; addestrare; — *vi* addestrarsi
groove *n* incastro, scanalatura; — *vt* scanalare
grope *vi* andare a tastoni; brancolare; — **for** cercare a tastoni
groping *a* brancolante; **–ly** *adv* a tastoni, brancolando
gross *n* grossa; — *a* grosso, volgare, grossolano; *(com)* lordo; — **ignorance** ignoranza crassa
grotesque *a* grottesco
grouch *n* malinconico, tetro; **have a** — essere di malumore; — *vi* lamentarsi, essere di malumore
grouchy *a (coll)* burbero, di cattivo umore
ground *n* suolo, terra; *(basis)* fondamento, fondo; — **floor** pianterreno; **break** — dare inizio a, cominciare; **forbidden** — terreno proibito; **give** — *(retreat)* retrocedere; **hold one's** — star saldo; **–less** *a* infondato, senza base
ground *vt* fondare; *(avi)* proibire il volo; *(elec)* mettere a terra; **–ed** *a* fondato, basato; *(naut)* arenato
ground-control *n (avi)* controllo da terra
grounds *npl (basis)* fondamento; *(coffee)* fondo di caffè, feccia di caffè; *(land)* parco, giardini *mpl*; — **for divorce** movente per il divorzio
groundwork *n* fondamenta, basi *fpl*
group *n* gruppo; — *vt* raggruppare, adunare; — *vi* raggrupparsi
grove *n* boschetto; *(plantation)* piantagione *f*
grovel *vi (flatter)* strisciare; *(stoop)* abbassarsi, umiliarsi
grow *vt* coltivare; — *vi* ingrandire, crescere; *(progress)* progredire; — **better** *(improve)* migliorare; — **dark** oscurare; — **from** provenire; — **into** *(become)* diventare; — **old** invecchiare; — **soft** diventare indulgente; — **up** *(age)* crescere, ingrandire; — **worse** peggiorare
growl *v* ringhiare; — *n* ringhio, brontolio
grown *a* adulto, cresciuto, fatto
grown-up *a&n* adulto, adulta
growth *n* vegetazione; *(increase)* crescita; *(med)* escrescenza
grub *n* verme *m*, bruco; *(coll)* cibo; — *vt* sradicare, estirpare; — *vi* zappare; *(coll)* mangiare
grubby *a* sudicio, sporco, bacato
grudge *n* rancore *m*; **bear a** — aver rancore contro; **have a — against** aver malanimo contro
grudgingly *adv* malvolentieri
gruel *n* farina d'avena cotta in acqua
grueling *a* estenuante, faticoso
gruesome *a* orrendo, macabro, raccapricciante
gruff *a* brusco; **–ness** *n* asprezza, rozzezza
grumble *vt* borbottare; — *vi* lamentarsi
grumpy *a* irritabile, bisbetico; di cattivo umore
grunt *vi* grugnire; — *n* grugnito
guarantee *vt* garantire; — *n* garanzia, garante *m*
guarantor *n* garante *m*, mallevadore *m*
guaranty *n* garanzia
guard *n* protettore *m*; *(person)* guardia *m*; *(rail)* capotreno; **under** — sotto vigilanza; **–rail** *n* controrotaia; — *vt* sorvegliare, proteggere; — **against** premunirsi contro
guardian *n* tutore *m*, tutrice *f*; *(custodian)* custode *m*
guerilla *n* partigiano, guerrigliero; — **warfare** guerriglia
guess *vt&i* indovinare; *(surmise)* credere, supporre; — *n* supposizione, congettura; **rough** — occhio e croce; **–work** *n* congettura
guest *n* invitato
guffaw *n* risata; scoppio di risa
Guiana Guiana
guidance *n* guida, norma; — **beam** luceguida
guide *n* guida; — **rope** *(avi)* stabilizzatore *m*; **–book** *n* guida; **–post** *n* cartello indicatore; — *vt* guidare
guided missile missile guidato
guiding *a* dirigente
guild *n* associazione, corporazione
guile *n* astuzia, frode *f*; **–less** *a* ingenuo
guillotine *n* ghigliottina; — *vt* ghigliottinare
guilt *n* colpa; **–less** *a* innocente; **–y** *a* colpevole
guinea pig porcellino d'India
guise *n* forma, guisa, sembianza
guitar *n* chitarra; **–ist** *n* chitarrista *m*
gulch *n* burrone profondo, baratro
gulf *n* golfo
gull *n* gabbiano; **sea** — gabbiano di mare
gullible *a* credulone
gully *n* burrone *m*, condotto, cunicolo
gulp *n* sorsata, boccone *m*; — *vt* ingoiare
gum *n* gomma; *(anat)* gengiva; *(bot)* resina; — **tree** albero da gomma
bubble — cicla bomba; **chewing** — gomma da masticare
gumdrop *n* pasticca di gomma
gummed *a* gommato, ingommato; — **tape**

nastro adesivo
gummy *a (adherent)* aderente; *(rubber)* gommoso; *(sticky)* attaccaticcio
gumption *n (coll)* spirito d'iniziativa
gun *n* cannone, fucile *m*, pistola; — **barrel** canna di fucile; — **butt** calcio di fucile; — **permit** porto d'armi; **–fire** *n* sparo di cannone; **–man** *n* assassino; **–powder** *n* polvere da sparo; **–shot** *n* tiro di arma da fuoco; **–smith** *n* armaiolo
gunner *n* artigliere *m*; **–y** *n* artiglieria, balistica
gun-shy *a* pauroso delle armi da fuoco
gurgle *vi* gorgogliare; — *n* gorgoglio
gush *vi* zampillare; sgorgare; *(coll)* entusiasmarsi eccessivamente; — *n* zampillo; **–er** *n (oil)* getto di petrolio; **–ing** *a* sgorgante; *(person)* espansivo; **–y** *a* meloso, affettatamente sentimentale
gust *n* raffica; *(rush)* impeto
gusto *n* trasporto, entusiasmo
gusty *a* burrascoso, tempestoso, ventoso
gut *n* budello; — *vt* sventare
guts *npl* intestini *mpl;* budella *fpl*; *(sl)* coraggio, fegato *(fig)*; **have** — *(sl)* aver coraggio
gutter *n (curb)* cunetta; *(roof)* gronda
guttersnipe *n* monello
guttural *a* gutturale
guy *n (sl)* tipo, individuo
gymnasium *n* palestra
gymnastics *npl* ginnastica
gypsy *n* zingaro
gypsum *n* gesso
gyrate *vi* girare
gyration *n* rotazione
gyroscope *n* giroscopio

H

haberdashery *n* merceria
habit *n* abitudine *f*
habitable *a* abitabile
habitation *n* dimora, abitazione
hack *vt* mutilare; tagliare all'azzardo; — *vi* tossicchiare; — *n* lacerazione, taglio; *(cab)* carrozza; — **writer** scrittorello *(fig)*
hackneyed *a* trito, banale
haddock *n* merluzzo; **dried** — baccalà *m*
hag *n* vecchia strega
haggard *a* sparuto, allampanato; *(wild)* selvatico
haggle *vi* mercanteggiare
Hague, The L'Aia
hail *n* grandine *f; (greeting)* saluto; **–stone** *n* chicco di grandine; **–storm** *n* grandinata; — *vi* grandinare; — *vt* salutare, acclamare
hair *n (animal)* peli *mpl*; *(human)* capelli *mpl*; **split –s** cercare il pelo nell'uovo *(fig)*; **–brush** *n* spazzola; **–cut** *n* taglio di capelli; **–dresser** *n* parrucchiere *m*, pettinatrice *f*; **–pin** *n* forcina; **–spring** *n (mech)* molla del bilanciere
hair– *(in comp)* **—do** *n* pettinatura; **—raising** *a (coll)* raccapricciante
hairy *a* capelluto, peloso
hale *a* sano, vigoroso
half *n* metà; — **a dozen** mezza dozzina; — **as much** la metà di; — *a* mezzo; — **brother** fratellastro; fratello uterino; — **sister** sorellastra; sorella uterina; — *adv* a metà; in mezzo
half– *(in comp)* **—and-half** *a* mezzo e mezzo; sì e no; così; **—baked** *a (food)* cotto a metà; *(person)* inesperto; **—breed, —caste** *n* meticcio, mezzosangue *m*; **—holiday** *n* mezza festa; **—hour** *n* mezz'ora; — **life** *n* semisviluppo di una reazione nucleare; **—light** *n* mezza luce; **—slip** *n* sottogonna, sottoveste a vita; **—truth** *n* verità detta a metà; **—turn** *n* mezza volta; **—wit** *n* mezzo stupido
halfhearted *a* indifferente, apatico; senza entusiasmo
half sole mezza suola
halfway *a* equidistante, mezzo; — *adv* a metà, a metà strada
halibut *n* rombo
halitosis *n* alito pesante
hall *n* sala, aula, **–way** *n* corridoio
hallmark *n* marchio ufficiale per garantire il grado di purezza
hallow *vt* consacrare
hallucination *n* allucinazione
halo *n* alone *m*
halt *vi* fermarsi; — *n* fermata, pausa
halter *n* cavezza
halve *vt* dimezzare
halves *npl* **by** — a metà; **go** — dividere la spesa
ham *n* prosciutto; *(coll, rad)* radioamatore *m*, *(coll, theat)* cattivo attore; — **and eggs** uova e prosciutto
hamburger *n* carne macinata *f*; — **on a bun** panino ripieno di polpetta
hammer *n* martello; — *vt* martellare
hamper *n* canestro; — *vt* ostacolare
hamstring *vt* sgarrettare, tagliare i garretti
hand *n* mano *f*; *(measure)* spanna; *(watch)* lancetta; — **and glove** strettamente confidenziale; come pane e cacio; — **in** — strettamente confidenziale *(fig)*; con la mano in mano; — **over** — una mano dopo l'altra; — **to** — di mano in mano; **at** — a portata di mano; **by** — a mano; **by the** — per mano; **out of** — fuori controllo; **have the upper** — aver controllo; **lend a** — dare una mano *(fig)*; **old** — esperto; **on** — fra le mani, alla mano; **on the other** — dall'altro lato, d'altra parte; **show one's** — rivelare le proprie intenzioni; **upper** — sopravvento
hand *vt* porgere; — **down** trasmettere per successione; — **over** *(com)* consegnare
hand– *(in comp)* **—made** *a* fatto a mano; **live —to-mouth** vivere alla giornata
handbag *n* borsa; *(luggage)* valigetta
handbill *n* annunzio, avviso
handbook *n* manuale *m*
handcuff *n* manetta; — *vt* ammanettare
handful *n* pugno, manata; — **of** mano

piena di
handicap *n* ostacolo; *(disadvantage)* svantaggio; — *vt* ostacolare
handicraft *n* artigianato
handkerchief *n* fazzoletto
handle *n* manico; — *vt* maneggiare, toccare
handling *n* manipolazione, maneggio, trattamento
handout *n (sl)* elemosina
hands *npl* mani *fpl;* — **down** *adv* facilmente; — **off** *interj* giù le mani; — **up** *interj* mani in alto; **change** — cambiar mani; **shake** — **with** stringere la mano; **wash one's** — **of** lavarsi le mani *(fig)*
handshake *n* stretta di mano
handsome *a* bello, simpatico, generoso
handspring *n* salto acrobatico
handwork *n* lavoro manuale
handwriting *n* scrittura
handwritten *a* manoscritto; scritto a mano
handy *a* comodo, abile; a portata di mano
handyman *n* fasservizi *m*
hang *vi* pendere, penzolare; *(execute)* impiccare; — **around** indugiare; — **back** esitare; — **in the balance** stare in bilico; — **on** tenersi attaccato a; — **one's head** chinare la testa; — **together** accordarsi; essere attaccato l'un l'altro (fig); — **up** appendere, sospendere
hangar *n* hangar *m*, aviorimessa
hangdog *a* abbattuto
hanger *n* gancio; **coat** — attaccapanni *m*
hanger–on *n* parassita, scroccone *m*, seguace *m*
hanging *n* sospensione; — *a* pensile, pendente; **–s** *npl* tappezzerie *fpl*, tendine *fpl*
hangman *n* boia, carnefice *m*
hangnail *n* pipita
hangover *n* mal di testa dopo una bevuta
hank *n* matassa
hanker *vi* bramare
hankering *n* desiderio ardente
haphazard *a* fortuito, accidentale
happen *vi* accadere, avvenire, capitare; — **on** capitare, imbattersi
happening *n* avvenimento
happily *adv* felicemente
happiness *n* felicità, contentezza
happy *a* felice, contento, lieto
happy-go-lucky *a* spensierato
harangue *n* arringa; — *vt&i* arringare
harass *vt* molestare, tormentare
harbor *n* porto; — *vt&i* albergare
hard *a* duro; difficile, severo; — **and fast** saldo; — **cash** contanti *mpl;* — **coal** antracite *f;* — **luck** scalogna, iella; — **of hearing** duro d'orecchio; — **put** *(coll)* ostacolato; — **to please** difficile d'accontentare; — **up** *(coll)* al verde, nei guai
hard *adv* fortemente; **try** — sforzarsi arduamente
hard– *(in comp)* **—boiled** *a* duro; *(coll)* molto sofisticato; **—earned** *a* guadagnato con fatica; **—working** *a* laborioso, lavoratore
harden *vt* indurare; *(steel)* temprare; **–ed** *a* indurito
hardhearted *a* inumano, duro
hardihood *n* resistenza
hardiness *n* vigore *m*, robustezza
hardly *adv* appena, difficilmente, quasi, duramente
hardness *n* durezza, difficoltà
hardship *n* avversità, pena
hardware *n* ferramenta *fpl*, utensileria; — **store** negozio di ferramenta
hardwood *n* legno duro
hardy *a* robusto, vigoroso; *(daring)* audace
harebrained *a* temerario, imprudente
harlot *n* prostituta
harm *n* male *m*, danno; **–ful** *a* nocivo, dannoso; **–less** *a* innocuo; — *vt* nuocere, fare del male
harmonica *n* armonica
harmonious *a* armonioso, armonico
harmonize *vt&i* armonizzare; *(agree)* concordare; — **with** andar bene con
harmony *n* armonia
harness *n* bardatura, finimenti *mpl*; armatura; *(fig)* restrizione; — *vt* bardare; *(connect)* attaccare
harp *n* arpa; — *vi* suonare l'arpa; — **on** *(fig)* insistere, ripetere
harpoon *n* rampone *m*, fiocina
harridan *n* vecchiaccia
harrow *n* erpice *m*; — *vt* straziare; *(agri)* erpicare; **–ing** *a* straziante, atroce
harry *vt* devastare, saccheggiare
harsh *a* rude, brusco
harshness *n* asprezza; *(sound)* discordanza
harum-scarum *a* scervellato, sventato
harvest *n* raccolto, messe *f*; — **moon** luna della mietitura; — *vt* mietere, fare il raccolto; **–er** *n* mietitore *m*; *(mech)* mietitrice *f*
has-been *n (coll)* decaduto
hash *n* carne macinata; carne tritata con patate
hasp *n* serramento, fermaglio
hassock *n* cuscino
haste *n* furia, fretta; — **makes waste** chi va piano va sano
hasten *vt* affrettare, accelerare; — *vi* affrettarsi
hastily *adv* in fretta, affrettatamente, presto
hasty *a* frettoloso
hat *n* cappello; — **rack** poggia-cappello; **pass the** — fare una colletta; **top** — cappello a cilindro; **–band** *n* nastro del cappello; **–box** *n* cappelliera; **–less** *a* scappellato; senza cappello
hatch *n* covata; *(naut)* boccaporto; — *vt* *(eggs)* covare; *(idea)* tramare; *(print)* tratteggiare; — *vi* uscire dall'uovo
hatchet *n* accetta; **bury the** — riconciliarsi
hate *n* odio; **–ful** *a* odioso; — *vt* detestare, odiare, abominare
hatred *n* odio
haughtily *adv* arrogantemente
haughtiness *n* superbia, alterigia
haughty *a* altezzoso
haul *vt* trasportare, rimorchiare, tirare
haunch *n* anca; *(meat)* coscia
haunt *vt* frequentare; *(follow)* perseguitare; — *n* ricovero, covo, ritiro; **–s**

npl locali preferiti
haunted *a* visitato dagli spiriti
have *vt* possedere, avere; — **a look at** dare una guardata a; — **on** *(wear)* indossare; — **something done** far fare qualche cosa
haven *n* rifugio, porto
havoc *n* strage *f*, rovina; **play — with** devastare
hawk *n* falcone *m*; — *vi* fare il venditore ambulante
hawser *n* gomena
hawthorn *n* biancospino
hay *n* fieno; — **fever** febbre del fieno; **–loft** *n* fienile *m*; **–maker** *n* fienatore *m*; *(boxing)* pugno decisivo; **–rack** *n* covone di fieno; **–stack** *n* mucchio di fieno
hazard *m* rischio, azzardo; — *vt&i* arrischiare; **–ous** *a* azzardato
haze *n* bruma, caligine *f*; — *vt* annebbiare
hazel *n* nocciuolo; — **nut** nocciuola; — *a* di nocciuola
hazy *a* confuso, indistinto; *(misty)* caliginoso
he *pron* egli, lui; — **who** colui che
head *n* testa, capo; *(river)* sorgente *f*; — **of hair** capigliatura; — **over heels** a gambe levate, capovolto; **–s or tails** testa o croce; **at the** — in capo a; alla testa di; **come to a** — raggiungere il colmo; *(med)* suppurare; **from — to foot** da capo a piedi; **go to one's** — montare alla testa; **keep one's** — tenere la testa a posto; **lose one's** — perdere la testa; **out of one's** — fuori di mente
head *vt* capeggiare, dirigere; — **off** stornare, deviare
headache *n* dolor di testa; mal di capo
headdress *n* pettinatura
headfirst *adv* a capofitto
headgear *n* copricapo; *(cap)* cuffia; *(hat)* cappello
heading *n* titolo
headland *n* promontorio, capo
headlight *n* faro, fanale *m*
headline *n* titolo, intestazione *f*
headlong *adv* a capofitto, precipitatamente; — *a* violento, impetuoso
head-on *a&adv* testa-testa
headphone *n* cuffia telefonica
headquarters *npl* sede *f*; quartier generale; ufficio centrale
headrest *n* poggiatesta
headstone *n* lapide *f*
headstrong *a* testardo
headway *n* progresso, cammino; **make** — progredire, far strada
heady *a* che da alla testa
heal *vt* guarire, sanare
healing *n* guarigione *f*; — *a* curativo
health *n* salute *f*, sanità; — **officer** ufficiale sanitario; — **resort** stazione climatica; **bill of** — certificato di salute; **–y** *a* sano; in buona salute
healthful *a* sano; **–ness** *n* salute, salubrità
heap *n* mucchio, cumulo; — *vt* ammassare, ammucchiare
hear *vt* sentire, udire; — **about** sentire riguardo a; — **from** aver notizie di; — **of** essere informato circa
hearing *n (audience)* udienza; *(sense)* udito; — **aid** apparecchio acustico; **hard of** — duro d'orecchio
hearsay *n* diceria, voce *f*
hearse *n* carro funebre
heart *n* cuore *m*; **to one's –'s content** a piacimento, con gioia di cuore; — **trouble** disturbo cardiaco; **by** — a memoria; **with all my** — con tutto il mio cuore; — *a* cardiaco
heartbreaking *a* straziante
heartbroken *a* angosciato, straziato, affranto
heartburn *n* bruciore di stomaco
heartfelt *a* sincero, caldo, profondo, intenso
hearten *vt* incoraggiare
heartiness *n* cordialità
hearth *n* focolare *m*
heartless *a* spietato, senza cuore
heart-rending *a* straziante
heartsick *a* afflitto, abbattuto; con la morte nel cuore *(fig)*
heart-to-heart *a* cuore a cuore
hearty *a* cordiale, vigoroso; *(abundant)* abbondante
heat *n* calore *m*, caldo; *(sport)* eliminatoria, preliminare *m*; **dead** — *(sport)* corsa alla pari; **prickly** — eruzione della pelle per il caldo; **–stroke** *n* insolazione; colpo di caldo; — **wave** ondata di caldo; — *vt* scaldare, riscaldare, infiammare; — *vi* scaldarsi, infiammarsi
heated *a* riscaldato; *(excited)* agitato; *(inflammed)* infiammato
heater *n* riscaldatore *m*; **electric** — stufettina elettrica; **water** — scaldabagno
heathen *n&a* pagano
heating *n* riscaldamento; — **pad** cuscino termico
heat-resistant *a* refrattario al calore; resistente al calore
heave *vt* gettare, sollevare; — *vi* (bulge) gonfiarsi; *(emit)* vomitare; *(lift)* sollevarsi; — **a sigh** emettere un sospiro; — **in sight** apparire; — *n* sollevamento, sussulto
heaven *n* paradiso; *(sky)* cielo; **–ly** *a* celeste, divino
heavily *adv* pesantemente; *(much)* molto, assai; *(seriously)* gravemente
heaviness *n* pesantezza
heavy *a* pesante; **–weight** *n (sport)* peso massimo
heavy-handed *a* severo, oppressivo
Hebrew *n&a* ebreo, ebrea
heckle *vt* cardare, pettinare; interrompere importunamente; **–r** *n* interruttore importuno
hectic *a* agitato, movimentato; *(feverish)* febbrile
hectogram *n* ettogrammo, etto *(coll)*
hedge *n* siepe *f*; barriera; *(defense)* protezione; — *vt* assiepare, circondare di siepe; — **in** *(restrict)* restringere; — *vi* fare siepi; evadere una domanda
hedgehop *vi (avi)* volare a bassa quota; — *n* volo a bassa quota
hedonist *n* edonista *m&f*

heed *vt* badare; dar retta; — *n* attenzione
heel *n* *(foot)* tallone *m*; *(shoe)* tacco; *(coll)* carogna *(fig)* — *vt* rattacconare; — *vi* *(naut)* sbandarsi
heels *npl* tacchi *mpl*; **fall head over** — cadere a gambe levate; **take to one's** — svignarsela; battere i tacchi
hefty *a* vigoroso, robusto, gagliardo
heifer *n* giovenca
height *n* *(altitude)* elevatezza; *(avi)* quota; *(loftiness)* altezza, *(people)* statura; **–en** *vt* aumentare, intensificare
heir *n* erede *m&f;* — **apparant** erede diretto; — **presumptive** erede presunto
heiress *n* ereditiera
heirloom *n* ereditato; mobile di famiglia
hegemony *n* egemonia
helicopter *n* elicottero
heliotherapy *n* elioterapia
heliport *n* eliporto
hell *n* inferno; **–ish** *a* infernale
hellcat *n* megera
hello *interj* salve, ciao; *(phone)* pronto
helm *n* timone *m*; *(control)* comando
helmet *n* casco, elmo
help *vt* aiutare; — **down** aiutare a scendere; — **oneself** aiutarsi; — **out** aiutare; **H– yourself!** Si serva!; **I can't — it** Non è colpa mia
help *n* aiuto, soccorso; *(assistant)* aiutante *m*; *(remedy)* rimedio; **no — for it** è fatale; **–ful** *a* utile; **–less** *a* impotente, debole, indifeso
helping *n* porzione *f*; — *a* utile, soccorrevole
helpmate *n* consorte *m&f*, marito, moglie *f*
helter-skelter *adv* alla rinfusa
hem *n* orlo; — *vt* orlare; — **in** cingere, circondare
hemisphere *n* emisfero
hemoglobin *n* emoglobina
hemolysin *n* *(immunology)* emolisina, anticorpo del sangue
hemophilia *n* emofilia
hemophyliac *n* emofiliaco
hemorrhage *n* emorragia
hemorrhoids *npl* emorroidi *fpl*
hemp *n* canapa
hemstitch *n* orlo a giorno; — *vt* orlare a giorno
hen *n* gallina; *(birds)* femmina; — **tracks** *(writing)* zampa di gallina *(fig)*; **–coop** *n* gallinaio; piccolo pollaio
hence *adv* di qui, da ora; *(therefore)* perciò
henceforth *adv* da ora in poi
henna *n* ennè *f*
hepatic *a* epatico
her *pron* la; lei; — *a* il suo, la sua; **–self** *pron* sè; lei stessa, sè stessa
herald *n* araldo; — *vt* annunziare, proclamare; **–ry** *n* araldica
herb *n* erba; **–ivorous** *a* erbivoro
herd *n* gregge *m*, folla; **the common** — gente ordinaria; — *vi* far gregge
here *adv* qui; qua; — **is,** — **are** ecco; **that's neither — nor there** è di poca importanza; **–abouts** *adv* da queste parti; qui vicino; **–by** *adv* per questo mezzo; per mezzo della presente; **–in** *adv* qui, in questo; qui accluso; **–with** *adv* unitamente
hereafter *adv* da ora in poi; in avvenire; — *n* l'altro mondo
hereditary *a* ereditario
heredity *n* eredità
heresy *n* eresia
heretic *n* eretico
heretofore *adv* fin qui
heritage *n* retaggio
hermaphrodite *n* ermafrodite *m&f*
hermetic *a* ermetico; **–ally** *a* ermeticamente
hermit *n* eremita *m*
hernia *n* ernia
hero *n* eroe *m*; *(theat)* protagonista *m*; **–ic** *a* eroico; **–ics** *npl* eroica; linguaggio letterario; **–ism** *n* eroismo
heroin *n* eroina
heroine *n* eroina, protagonista
herring *n* aringa
hers *pron* il suo, la sua
hesitancy *n* esitazione
hesitate *vi* esitare
hesitation *n* esitazione *f*
heterodox *a* eterodosso
hew *vt* fendere; — **down** abbattere; — **to the line** rimanere negli stretti limiti
hexameter *n* esametro
hiatus *n* iato; lacuna *(fig)*
hibernate *vi* svernare; svernare in letargo
hibernation *n* ibernazione
hiccough *n* singhiozzo; — *vi* avere il singhiozzo
hidden *a* celato, nascosto; segreto, occulto
hide *vt* nascondere, celare; — *vi* nascondersi; — *n* pelle *f*
hide– *(in comp)* **—and-seek** *n* rimpiattino; **—out** *n* nascondiglio
hidebound *a* testardo; di corte vedute *(fig)*
hideous *a* bruttissimo, orribile
hiding *a* che nasconde, che si nasconde
hierarchy *n* gerarchia
hieroglyphics *npl* geroglifici *mpl*
hi-fi *n* *(rad, coll)* alta fedeltà
high *a* alto, elevato; *(drunk, sl)* brillo, ubbriaco; — **and low** ovunque; — **and mighty** arrogante; — **jump** salto in alto; — **noon** pieno mezzogiorno; — **seas** alto mare; — **school** scuola media; — **spirits** coraggio, animo; — **tide** punto culminante; — **time** ultimo momento
high- *(in comp)* **—class** *a* d'alta classe; di qualità superiore; **—grade** *a* di qualità superiore; d'alto grado; **—handed** *a* arbitrario; **—minded** *a* magnanimo; **—necked** *a* dal colletto alto; **—pitched** *a* stridulo, acuto; **—priced** *a* caro, costoso; **—sounding** *a* sonoro, altisonante; **—spirited** *a* audace, vivo, pieno di coraggio (*or* d'energia); **—strung** *a* nervoso, emotivo; **—tension** ad alta tensione; **—test** *a* d'alta prova, con basso grado d'ebollizione
highball *n* whisky con soda e ghiaccio
highbrow *n* sapientone, intellettuale
higher *a* più elevato, superiore
highest *a* il più alto, massimo
highhanded *a* arrogante, prepotente
High Mass *n* Messa Alta
highness *n* elevatezza, altezza; **Your H–**

Sua Altezza
highway *n* camionale *f*; strada maestra; **–man** *n* grassatore *m*, bandito, ladrone di strada
hijack *vt* (*coll*) contrabbandare; rubare; **–ing** *n* contrabbando; furto
hike *n* marcia; gita a piedi; — *vi* vagabondare
hiking *n* escursione, marcia; — *a* d'escursione, di marcia
hilarious *a* ilare, molto allegro
hilarity *n* ilarità
hill *n* collina, colle *m*; **–side** *n* fianco di collina
hilly *a* collinoso, montuoso
hilt *n* elsa, impugnatura
him *pron* lo, lui; **–self** *pron* sè, egli stesso; lui stesso, sè stesso
hind *n* (*zool*) cerva, daina; — *a* posteriore, dietro, di dietro; — **legs** gambe posteriori; **–quarters** *n* quarti di dietro; **–sight** *n* retrospezione
hinder *vt* impedire, ostacolare
hindrance *n* ostacolo, inciampo
hinge *n* cardine *m*; — *vt* incardinare; — **on** dipendere da
hint *n* cenno, traccia; **drop a** — fare una insinuazione; **take a** — capire a volo (*fig*); — *vt&i* insinuare; — **at** alludere
hip *n* anca, fianco
hippodrome *n* ippodromo
hire *vt* noleggiare, prendere in affitto; — *n* noleggio, salario; **for** — da nolo
hireling *n* prezzolato, mercenario
hirsute *a* ispido, irsuto
his *pron* il suo, la sua
hiss *vt&i* fischiare; — *n* sibilo
histamine *n* istamina
historian *n* storico
historic, historical *a* storico
history *n* storia
histrionics *npl* drammaturgia
hit *vt* colpire, battere; — **the ceiling** (*coll*) perdere le staffe (*fig*); — **the jackpot** (*coll*) avere una fortuna sfacciata; — **the mark** dare nel segno; — **the spot** dare giusto nel punto; — *n* colpo, successo; (*coll*) battuta; — **or miss** trascuratamente, a casaccio
hitch *n* impedimento; (*naut*) nodo; — *vt&i* attaccare; **–hike** viaggiare con l'autostop
hitherto *adv* finora; fin qui
hit-or-miss *a* negligente
hive *n* alveare *m*; **–s** *n* (*med*) orticaria
hoard *n* cumulo, mucchio; — *vt* accumulare, ammassare
hoarse *a* rauco
hoary *a* canuto, bianco; (*old*) vecchio
hoax *n* beffa, inganno; (*joke*) scherzo; — *vt* fare uno scherzo; corbellare
hobble *n* imbarazzo, pastoia; (*limp*) zoppicamento; — *vi* zoppicare; — *vt* (*horse*) impastoiare
hobby *n* passatempo, distrazione; — **horse** cavallino a dondolo
hobnob *vi* bere insieme, dare del tu, prendersi confidenza
hobo *n* vagabondo
hock *n* garretto; **in** — (*coll*) in pegno; al Monte di Pietà (*coll*); — *vt* sgarrettare
hocus-pocus *n* giuoco di prestigio
hodgepodge *n* guazzabuglio
hoe *n* zappa; — *vt&i* zappare
hog *n* maiale *m*, porco; **–gish** *a* porcino, suino; (*fig*) bestiale, sporco; **–wash** *n* beverone del porco
hoist *vt* alzare, innalzare; (*naut*) issare; — *n* montacarichi *m*
hold *n* presa; sostegno, appoggio; (*naut*) stiva; — *vt* occupare; (*keep*) tenere; (*sustain*) sopportare; — **back** frenare, impedire; — **forth** offrire, promettere; — **on** star fermo; — **one's tongue** tener la lingua a freno; — **out** resistere a; — **over** aggiornare, posporre, detenere; — **up** sostenere; **get** — **of** impugnare; aver in pugno; **have a** — **on** far presa su; **take** — **of** afferrare; dar di piglio a
holdup *n* furto a mano armata; (*delay*) ritardo
hole *n* foro, buco; **in the** — (*coll*) in debito; **put in a** — (*coll*) imbarrazzare
holiday *n* festa
holiness *n* santità
Holland Olanda
hollow *n* vuoto; — *a* cavo, concavo; (*empty*) vuoto; (*deep*) cupo; (*fig*) falso, vano; (*sound*) sordo; — *vt* scavare
hollow- (*in comp*) **—cheeked** *a* dalle guance infossate; **—eyed** *a* dagli occhi infossati
holly *n* agrifoglio
hollyhock *n* malvarosa, alcea
holster *n* fondina
holy *a* santo; — **water;** acqua santa; **H— Week** settimana santa
homage *n* omaggio, rispetto
home *n* casa, focolare *m*; — **stretch** (*race*) retta finale; — **town** paese natio; **–land** *n* patria; **–less** *a* senza tetto; **–like** *a* comodo, intimo; **–made** *a* casalingo; fatto in casa; **–maker** *n* massaia; padrona di casa; — *a* casalingo, nostrano; di casa
home-coming *n* ritorno a casa
homely *a* brutto, sgraziato
homesick *a* nostalgico; **–ness** *n* nostalgia
homeward *adv&a* verso casa
homicidal *a* omicida
homicide *n* omicidio
homogenized *a* omogeneizzato
homogenous *a* omogeneo
homonym *n* omonimo
homosexual *n* omosessuale
hone *vt* affilare con cote; — *n* cote *f*
honest *a* onesto; (*frank*) veritiero, sincero, leale; **–y** *n* onestà, probità, (*morals*) correttezza
honey *n* miele *m*; (*fig*) tesoro (*fig*), carino; **–comb** *n* favo; **–dew melon** melone melato
honeymoon *n* luna di miele
honor *n* onore *m*; (*glory*) onorificenza; **on my** — sul mio onore; **point of** — punto d'onore; **word of** — parola d'onore; — *vt* onorare; — **a draft** accet-

tare una cambiale; **–ed** *a* onorato, rispettato; **–s** *npl* onori *mpl*
honorable *a* onorevole
honorary *a* onorario, onorifico
hood *n* cappuccio; *(auto)* cofano; *(sl)* mascalzone *m;* camorrista *m (coll)*; **—ed** *a* incappucciato
hoodlum *n (coll* malvivente *m*, teppista *m*
hoodoo *(coll)* iettatore *m*
hoodwink *vt* ingannare
hoof *n* zoccolo, unghia
hook *n* uncino; **— and eye** gancio ad occhio; **by — or crook** con le buone o con le cattive *(coll)*; **on one's own —** indipendente; **–up** *n (rad, TV)* connessione; **–worm** *n* verme intestinale; **—** *vt* agganciare, uncinare
hooky *n* **play —** marinare la scuola
hoop *n* cerchione *m*, cerchio, anello
hop *vi* saltellare; **—** *n* salto, salto su piede; **–s** *npl (bot)* luppoli *mpl*
hope *n* speranza; **—** *vt&i* sperare, aver fiducia, confidare; **–ful** *a* promettente; pieno di speranza; **–less** *a* disperato
hopper *n* tramoggia
hopscotch *n* giuoco fanciullesco dove si saltella
horde *n* orda
horizon *n* orizzonte *m*
hormone *n* ormone *m*
horn *n* tromba; *(animal)* corno; *(auto)* clacson *m*; **— in** *(sl, intrude)* intromettersi; **blow one's own —** lodarsi; **blow the —** strombettare; **–ed** *a* cornuto, cornifero; **–y** *a* corneo, calloso
horns *npl* corna *fpl*; **pull in one's —** mordere il freno *(fig)*
hornet *n* calabrone *m*; **—'s nest** vespaio
horoscope *n* oroscopo
horrible *a* orribile
horrid *a* orrendo, brutto
horrify *vt* atterrire
horror *n* orrore *m*
hors d'œuvres *npl* antipasto
horse *n* cavallo; **— sense** buon senso; **— trainer** cavallerizzo; allenatore di cavalli; **race —** cavallo da corsa; **get on one's high —** *(fig)* darsi delle arie *(coll)*; **work like a —** lavorare come un cavallo; **–man** *n* cavaliere *m*; **–play** *n* giuochi di mano *(fig)*; **–power** *n* cavalli vapore; **–shoe** *n* ferro di cavallo
horseback *n* groppa; **—** *adv* in groppa
horseradish *n* rafano
horticulture *n* orticultura
hose *n* manichetta, tubo flessibile; **—** *npl* calze *fpl*
hosiery *n* calze *fpl;* **— store** negozio di calze
hospitable *a* ospitale
hospital *n* ospedale *m*; clinica; **— insurance** assicurazione ospitaliera; **maternity —** casa di maternità
hospitality *n* ospitalità
hospitalize *vt* ricoverare in ospedale, ospitalizzare
host *n* ospite *m*, padrone di casa *(coll)*; *(inn)* oste *m*; *(crowd)* moltitudine *f*
Host *n (eccl)* Ostia, Particola
hostage *n* ostaggio
hostel *n* locanda; **youth —** albergo per la gioventù
hostess *n* ospite *f*; padrona di casa *(coll)*; *(inn)* ostessa; *(avi)* hostess *f*
hostile *a* ostile
hostility *n* ostilità
hot *a* caldo; *(food)* piccante; **be in — water** *(coll)* essere nei guai; **make it — for** *(coll)* dare filo da torcere; **–bed** *n* concimaia; **–foot** *adv* in fretta e furia; **–house** n serra; **–water bag** borsa dell'acqua calda
hot– *(in comp)* **—blooded** *a* ardente, impetuoso; **—headed** *a* impetuoso; **—rod** *(sl)* vecchia automobile con motore sovralimentato; **—tempered** *a* collerico
hotel *n* albergo, hotel *m*
hotly *adv* caldamente; *(passionately)* veementemente
hound *n* bracco; **—** *vt (fig)* perseguitare
hour *n* ora; **half an —** mezz'ora; **—hand** lancetta delle ore; **per —** per ora; **work by the —** lavorare a ore
hourly *adv* ogni ora, tutte le ore; **—** *a* frequente, che accade ogni ora
house *n* casa; *(com)* ditta; *(legislative)* camera; **full —** *(theat)* sala al completo; **–fly** *n* mosca domestica; **–keeper** *n* governante *f*; **–wife** *n* massaia; **–work** *n* lavoro di casa, faccenda di casa; **—** *vt* alloggiare
housedog *n* cane da guardia
household *n* famiglia, focolare domestico *(fig)*; **— management** gestione della casa
house physician medico residente
housing *n* alloggio; *(mech)* carter *m*
hovel *n* bicocca, capanna, tugurio
hover *vi* gravitare, esitare, attardarsi; **— over** librarsi su
how *adv* come; **— many** quanti *mpl*, quante *fpl*; **— much** quanto; **— often** quante volte
however *conj* però; per quanto; **—** *adv* ciononostante, comunque
howl *vi* urlare; **—** *n* urlo, lamento
hub *n* centro; *(auto)* mozzo; **–cap** *n* piatto della ruota
hubbub *n* tumulto
huckster *n* merciaiolo, trafficante *m*
huddle *n* calca, folla, confusione; **—** *vt* mettere insieme; **—** *vi* accalcarsi, affollarsi
hue *n* tinta; **— and cry** clamore di grida
huff *n* sfuriata; **–y** *a* stizzito
hug *vt* stringere, abbracciare; **—** *n* abbraccio
huge *a* enorme; **–ly** *adv* enormemente; **–ness** *n* enormità
hulk *n (naut)* carcassa di nave; **–ing** *a* grosso, goffo, pesante
hull *n* guscio, baccello; *(bot)* guscio, mallo; **—** *vt* sgusciare
hullabaloo *n* baccano
hum *vt&i (buzz)* ronzare; *(murmur)* mormorare; *(tune)* canticchiare; **—** *vi (tune)* cantarellare; **—** *n* mormorio
human *a* umano; **—** *n* esser umano; **–ly** *adv* umanamente
humane *a* umano, compassionevole
humanitarian *a* umanitario

humanity *n* umanità
humankind *n* umanità; genere umano
humble *a* umile; — *vt* umiliare; — **oneself** umiliarsi
humbly *a* umilmente
humbug *n* inganno, imbroglio; *(quack)* ciarlatano, impostore *m*; — *vt* ingannare, imbrogliare
humdrum *a* banale, monotono
humid *a* umido; **–ity** *n* umidità
humiliate *vt* umiliare
humiliation *n* umiliazione
humility *n* umiltà
humor *n* umore *m*, spirito; **bad** — malumore; **good** — buonumore; — *vt* compiacere; lasciar fare; **–ous** *a* comico, spiritoso, bizzarro, fantastico; *(whimsical)* capriccioso
humorist *n* umorista *m*
hump *n* gobba
hunch *n* gobba; *(coll)* presentimento, intuizione *f*; **–back** *n* gobbo
hundred *a&n* cento; **about a** — un centinaio; **–th** *a* centesimo
Hungarian *a&n* ungherese *m&f*
Hungary Ungheria
hunger *n* fame *f*; — *vi* aver fame, affamarsi, patir fame; — *vt* affamare; — **for** bramare
hungrily *adv* famelicamente
hungry *a* affamato; **be** — aver fame
hunk *n* massa
hunt *n* caccia, inseguimento; — *vt* inseguire, perseguitare, cacciare; — **down** perseguire; — *vi* andare a caccia; — **for** cercare; **–er** *n* cacciatore *m*; **–ing** *n* caccia
hurdle *n* ostacolo; — *vt* superare
hurdy-gurdy *n* organetto di Barberia
hurl *vt* scagliare, lanciare; — **back** rilanciare; *(reply)* ribattere *(fig)*
Hurrah! *interj* Bravo!; Evviva!
hurricane *n* uragano
hurried *a* affrettato; **–ly** *adv* affrettatamente
hurry *n* fretta; **be in a** — aver fretta; **in a** — in fretta; — *vt* affrettare, sollecitare; — *vi* affrettarsi, far presto; — **away** svignarsela, andarsene in fretta, — **back** tornare in fretta; — **on** affrettare, affrettarsi; — **over** fare in fretta, affrettare; — **up** affrettarsi, spicciarsi
hurt *vt* far male a; *(feelings)* offendere; — *vi* dolere; — *n* ferita, male *m*, danno; — *a* danneggiato; ferito; offeso
hurtle *vi (dash)* precipitarsi; — *vt* lanciare
husband *n* marito
husbandry *n* agricoltura
hush *n* silenzio; — *vt&i* azzittire, far tacere, tacere; **H–!** *interj* Stai zitto!
husk *n* guscio, baccello; — *vt* sgusciare; **–iness** *n* raucedine *f*; **–y** *a* robusto; rauco
hussy *n* donna impertinente, sfacciata
hustle *n (coll)* energia; — *vt&i (hurry)* sbrigarsi; *(push)* spingere, dare spintoni; — **and bustle** andirivieni *m*
hustler *n (coll)* persona energica
hut *n* capanna
hutch *n* capanna; **rabbit—** conigliera
hyacinth *n* giacinto
hybrid *n* ibrido
hydrant *n* idrante *m*
hydraulic *a* idraulico; **–s** *npl* idraulica
hydrocarbon *n* idrocarburo
hydrocephalus *n* idrocefalo
hydrochloric *a* idroclorico
hydrofoil *n* aliscafo
hydrogen *n* idrogeno; — **bomb** bomba all'idrogeno; — **peroxide** *n* perossido d'idrogeno, *(chem)* acqua ossigenata
hydrolysis *n* idrolisi *f*
hydrophobia *n* idrofobia
hydroplane *n* idroplano
hydroponics *npl* idrocultura, idroponia
hydrostatics *npl* idrostatica
hydrotherapy *n* idroterapia
hyena *n* iena
hygiene *n* igiene *f*
hygienic *a* igienico
hymn *n* inno
hyperacidity *n* iperacidità
hyperbole *n* iperbole *f*
hypersonic *a* ipersonico, supersonico
hypertension *n* ipertensione
hypertrophy *n* ipertrofia
hyphen *n* trattino, lineetta
hypnotic *a* ipnotico
hypnotism *n* ipnotismo
hypnotize *vt* ipnotizzare
hypochondriac *n&a* ipocondriaco, ipocondriaca
hypocrisy *n* ipocrisia
hypocrite *n* ipocrita *m*
hypocritical *a* ipocrito
hypodermic *a* ipodermico
hypothesis *n* ipotesi *f*
hypothetical *a* ipotetico
hysterectomy *n* isterettomia
hysteria *n* isteria, isterismo
hysterical *a* isterico
hysterics *npl* accesso d'isterismo

I

I *pron* io
ice *n* ghiaccio; — **age** era glaciale; — **bag** *(med)* borsa da ghiaccio; — **cream** gelato; — **pack** lastrone di ghiaccio; — **skates** pattini da ghiaccio; — **water** acqua ghiacciata; **–berg** *n* borgognone *m*; iceberg *m*; **–box** *n* ghiacciaia; **–d** *a* ghiacciato, gelato; *(frosted)* candito; — **a cake** candire un dolce
ice-cream cone cono di gelato
ice-skate *vi* pattinare sul ghiaccio
icicle *n* ghiacciuolo
icily *adv* frigidamente, glacialmente
iciness *n* gelidità; freddo glaciale
icing *n* ghiacciata; *(cake)* canditura
iconoclast *n* iconoclasta *m*
iconoscope *n (TV)* iconoscopio
icy *a* glaciale; gelido
idea *n* idea
ideal *n&a* ideale *m*; **–ist** *n* idealista *m&f*; **–ly** *adv* idealmente; **–ism** *n* idealismo; **–istic** *a* idealista

identical *a* identico
identification *n* identità, identificazione; **— card** carta d'identità
identify *vt (recognize)* riconoscere; **— oneself** farsi riconoscere
identity *n* identità
ideological *a* ideologico
ideology *n* ideologia
idiocy *n* idiozia
idiom *n (language)* idioma *m*; *(phrase)* idiotismo; **–atic** *a* idiomatico
idiosyncracy *n* peculiarità
idiot *n* idiota *m*; **–ic** *a* stupido
idle *a* ozioso; **— capital** capitale congelato; **—** *vt&i* oziare, impigrire; *(motor)* funzionare al minimo; *(time)* perder tempo; **— away** sprecare; **–ness** *n* ozio
idler *n* fannullone *m*; perditempo
idol *n* idolo; **–ize** *vt* indolatrare
idolater *n* idolatra *m&f*
idyllic *a* idillico
i.e., that is ciò è
if *conj* se; **— ever** se mai; **— not** senò; **— so** se è così
ignite *vt* accendere
ignition *n* accensione; **— switch** chiave d'accensione
ignoble *a* ignobile
ignominious *a* infamante, ignominioso
ignominy *n* ignominia
ignoramous *n* ignorante *m*, asino *(fig)*; *(boor)* zotico
ignorance *n* ignoranza
ignorant *a* ignorante
ignore *vt* ignorare; *(inattention)* non dare importanza
ill *a* ammalato; **—** *adv* male; **— will** malvolere *m*; malanimo; mala voglia; **— at ease** inquieto, incomodo; **–ness** *n* malattia, male *m*
ill– *(in comp)* **—advised** *a* malaccorto; **—bred** *a* maleducato; **—disposed** *a* maldisposto; **—humored** *a* di cattivo umore; **—mannered** *a* maleducato, scortese, sgarbato; **—natured** *a* malvagio, cattivo, bisbetico; **—tempered** *a* collerico, irritabile; **—timed** *a* inopportuno, intempestivo
ill-gotten *a* mal acquisto; **— gains** guadagni illeciti
illegal *a* illegale; **–ly** *adv* illegalmente
illegible *a* illeggibile
illegitimate *a* illegittimo
illicit *a* illecito
illiteracy *n* analfabetismo
illiterate *a&n* analfabeta *m&f*
illogical *a* illogico
illuminate *vt* illuminare
illumination *n* illuminazione
illusion *n* illusione
illusive *a* fallace, illusorio
illustrate *vt* illustrare
illustration *n (example)* esempio; *(picture)* illustrazione, figura
illustrious *a* illustre
illustrative *a* illustrativo
image *n* immagine *f*
imaginary *a* immaginario
imagination *n* immaginazione
imaginative *a* immaginativo, fantastico
imagine *vt&i* immaginare, fantasticare; suppore
imbecile *a&n* imbecille *m*
imbecility *n* imbecillaggine *f*, imbecillità; *(foolishness)* sciocchezza; *(stupidity)* ebetismo
imbibe *vt* imbevere, assimilare, assorbire
imbroglio *n* imbroglio
imbue *vt* inculcare, infondere; *(fig)* imbevere
imitate *vt* imitare
imitation *n* imitazione; **—** *a* falso, artificiale
imitator *n* imitatore *m*
immaculate *a* immacolato
immanent *a* immanente
immaterial *a* indifferente; incorporeo
immature *a* immaturo
immaturity *n* immaturità
immeasurable *a* immisurabile, smisurato
immediate *a* immediato; **–ly** *adv* subito
immemorial *a* immemorabile
immense *a* immenso
immensity *n* immensità
immerse *vt* tuffare, immergere
immersion *n* immersione
immigrant *n&a* immigrante *m*
immigrate *vi* immigrare
immigration *n* immigrazione
imminent *a* imminente
immobile *a* immobile, fermo
immobility *n* immobilità
immobilize *vt* immobilizzare
immoderate *a* smodato, immoderato, eccessivo
immodest *a* immodesto, sfacciato, presuntuoso
immoral *a* immorale
immorality *n* immoralità
immortal *a* immortale
immortality *n* immortalità
immovable *a* fermo, irremovibile; *(law)* inamovibile
immune *a* esente, immune
immunology *n* immunologia
immunity *n* immunità; *(exemption)* esenzione
immunization *n* immunizzazione
immunize *vt* immunizzare
imp *n* diavoletto; *(child)* birichino; *(goblin)* folletto; **–ish** *a* birichino, sbarazzino; **–ishly** *adv (malice)* maliziosamente; *(mischief)* birichinamente
impact *n* urto; **—** *vt* ficcare
impair *vt* danneggiare, pregiudicare; nuocere a
impalpable *a* impalpabile
impart *vt* impartire, comunicare, riferire
impartial *a* imparziale; **–ity** *n* imparzialità
impass *n* difficoltà insormontabile; vicolo cieco *(fig)*; **–able, –ive** *a* impassibile
impatience *n* impazienza
impatient *a* impaziente; **get —** impazientirsi
impeach *vt* incriminare; **–able** *a* incriminabile; **–ment** *n* incriminazione, accusa
impeccable *a* impeccabile
impedance *n (elec)* reattanza; *(phy)* trasmittività relativa acustica

impede *vt* ritardare, impedire, ostacolare
impediment *n* ostacolo
impel *vt* costringere, spingere
impend *vi* incombere, soprastare; *(threaten)* minacciare; essere imminente; **–ing** *a* imminente; minaccioso
impenetrable *a* impenetrabile
imperative *a* imperativo, indispensabile
imperfect *a&n* imperfetto
imperfection *n* imperfezione
imperial *a* imperiale, supremo; **–istic** *a* imperialistico; **–ism** *n* imperialismo
imperil *vt* arrischiare, mettere in pericolo
imperishable *a* indistruttibile, imperituro
impermeable *a* impermeabile
impersonal *a* impersonale
impersonate *vt* impersonare, personificare, imitare
impersonation *n* personificazione; *(law)* supposizione di persona
impertinence *n* impertinenza
impertinent *a* impertinente, insolente
imperturbable *a* imperturbabile
impervious *a* impervio
impetuous *a* impetuoso
impetus *n* impulso, impeto, slancio
impiety *n* empietà
impinge *vi* sbattere; — **on** sbattere contro
impious *a* empio
implant *vt* piantare; *(fig)* imprimere, inculcare
implement *n* utensile *m*; implemento; — *vt* effettuare
implicate *vt* implicare
implication *n* implicazione
implicit *a* implicito, assoluto; *(implied)* sottinteso
implied *a* implicito
implore *vt* implorare
imploring *a* supplichevole, implorante; — *n* supplica
imply *vt* implicare, insinuare, suggerire
impolite *a* sgarbato; **–ness** *n* scortesia, villania; maleducazione
imponderable *a* imponderabile
import *vt* importare; — *n* importanza; *(meaning)* senso, significato; **–ation** *n* importazione; — **duties** *npl* diritti doganali; **–er** *n* importatore *m*
importance *n* importanza
important *a* importante; **–ly** *adv* con importanza
impose *vt* imporre; — **on** praticare inganno
imposing *a* imponente
imposition *n* imposizione; *(outrage)* sopruso; *(swindle)* frode *f*
impossibility *n* impossibiltà
impossible *a* impossibile
impost *n* tassa, imposta
impostor *n* impostore *m*
imposture *n* frode *f*, impostura, inganno
impotence *n* impotenza
impotent *a* impotente
impound *vt* sequestrare, confiscare; *(animals)* rinchiudere
impoverish *vt* impoverire
impracticability *n* impraticabilità
impractical *a* non pratico, impraticabile
imprecate *vt* imprecare
imprecation *n* imprecazione
impregnable *a* imprendibile, inespugnabile
impregnate *vt* fecondare, impregnare, imbevere
impress *vt* imprimere; impressionare
impression *n* impressione, idea
impressive *a* imponente, impressionante
imprint *vt* stampare, imprimere; *(fix)* fissare; — *n* stampa
imprison *vt* imprigionare; **–ment** *n* imprigionamento
improbability *n* improbabilità
impromptu *a* improvvisato
improper *a* scorretto, indecente
impropriety *n* sconvenienza; *(gram)* improprietà; *(wrong)* erroneità
improve *vt* migliorare; — *vi* migliorarsi; far progressi; **–ment** *n* miglioramento, perfezionamento
improvident *a* imprudente, imprevidente
improvise *vt* improvvisare
imprudence *n* imprudenza
imprudent *a* imprudente
impudence *n* impudenza
impudent *a* impudente
impugn *vt* impugnare, accusare; contraddire
impunity *n* impunità
impulse *n* impeto, impulso, slancio; **act on** — agire d'impulso
impulsive *a* impulsivo; **–ly** *adv* impulsivamente
impure *a* impuro; *(filthy)* immondo; *(immodest)* impudico
impurity *n* impudicizia, impurità
imputation *n* accusa, imputazione, addebito
impute *vt* imputare
in *prep* in, a, entro; — **spite of** nonostante; — **writing** per iscritto; **be all** — essere sfinito; **have it** — **for** aver rancore per; **know the –s and outs** sapere dell'a alla zeta; **take** — *(absorb)* assorbire; *(attend)* assistere a; *(deceive)* ingannare; — *adv* dentro; **be** — *(at home)* essere a casa
inability *n* incapacità
inaccessible *a* inaccessibile
inaccuracy *n* inesattezza
inaccurate *a* inesatto
inaction *n* inerzia, inazione
inactive *a* inattivo
inactivity *n* inoperosità, inattività
inadvertent *a* incauto, disattento; *(unplanned)* impremeditato; **–ly** *adv* inavvertitamente
inadequacy *n* inettitudine *f*; insufficienza
inadequate *a* inadeguato, *(inexperienced)* inesperto; *(worthless)* inetto
inalienable *a* inalienabile
inane *a* inane, vano, vuoto
inanimate *a* inanimato
inappropriate *a* disadatto; improprio
inaptitude *n* incapacità, inettitudine *f*
inarticulate *a* inarticolato
inasmuch as *conj* poichè, dacchè; in quanto che
inattention *n* disattenzione; *(carelessness)* trascuratezza
inattentive *a* distratto, disattento, trascurato

inaudible *a* inaudibile
inaugurate *vt* inaugurare
inauguration *n* inaugurazione
inauspicious *a (ominous)* infausto; *(unfortunate)* infelice; malaugurato
inborn *a* innato
inbound *a* entrante
incalculable *a* incalcolabile
incapability *n* inettitudine *f*, incapacità
incapable *a* incapace
incapacitate *vt* inabilitare, incapacitare
incapacity *n* inabilità, incapacità
incarcerate *vt* incarcerare
incarnation *n* incarnazione
incase *vt* incassare; chiudere; *(cover)* coprire
incendiary *n&a* incendiario
incense *n* incenso; — *vt* incensare; *(anger)* fare arrabbiare
incentive *n* stimolo, incentivo
incessant *a* incessante
incest *n* incesto
inch *n* dito, pollice *m*; — **by** — gradualmente; **every** — del tutto, completamente; **within an** — **of** per un pelo; — *vt* far avanzare gradualmente; — *vi* avanzare gradualmente
incident *n* incidente *m*; **–al** *a* incidentale; **–ally** *adv* a proposito
incinerate *vt* incenerire
incinerator *n* inceneritore *m*
incipient *a* iniziale, incipiente
incision *n* incisione
incite *vt* incitare
incivility *n* scortesia, villania
inclement *a* duro, inclemente
inclination *n* inclinazione, voglia
incline *n* pendio, pendenza; — *vt&i* inclinare; essere disposto a
inclose, enclose *vt* accludere; *(encircle)* circondare
include *vt* includere, comprendere
including *a* compreso
inclusion *n* inclusione
inclusive *a* inclusivo, incluso
incognito *a* incognito; — *adv* in incognito
incoherence *n* incoerenza
incoherent *a* sconnesso, incoerente
incombustible *a* incombustibile
income *n* stipendio; — **tax** tassa sul reddito
incoming *a* prossimo; *(arriving)* in arrivo
incommode *vt* scomodare, incomodare
incommunicado *a* incommunicato
incommutable *a* incommutabile
incomparable *a* impareggiabile, incomparabile
incompatibility *n* incompatibilità
incompatible *a* incompatibile
incompetence *n* incompetenza
incompetent *a* incompetente
incomplete *a* incompleto, imperfetto
incomprehensible *a* incomprensibile
inconceivable *a* inconcepibile
inconclusive *a* inconclusivo, inconcludente
incongruity *n* assurdità, incongruenza
incongruous *a* assurdo, incongruente
inconsequential *a* illogico, inconsequente
inconsiderable *a* trascurabile, inconsiderabile
inconsiderate *a* sconsiderato, senza riguardi
inconsistency *n* inconsistenza, incongruenza
inconsistent *a* inconsistente, incongruente, incompatibile
incontinent *a* incontinente
incontestable *a* incontrastabile, incontestibile
inconvenience *n* incomodo, disturbo; — *vt* incomodare
inconvenient *a* scomodo
incorporate *vi* fondersi, unirsi; — *vt* incorporare; *(com)* costituire in società anonima; **–d** *a* incorporato, associato
incorporation *n* incorporazione
incorrect *a* sbagliato, scorretto; *(etiquette)* sconveniente
incorrigible *a* incorregibile
incorruptible *a* incorruttibile
increase *vt&i* crescere; aumentare; — *n* aumento
increasing *a* crescente; **–ly** *adv* in aumento
incredible *a* incredibile
incredulity *n* incredulità
incredulous *a* incredulo
increment *n* incremento
incriminate *vt* incriminare, incolpare, imputare
incubate *vt&i* incubare, covare
incubation *n* incubazione
incumbent *n* incaricato, responsabile *m*; — *a* incombente
incur *vt* contrarre; incorrere
incurable *a* inguaribile
indebted *a* obbligato, tenuto, indebitato; **–ness** *n* debito, obbligazione
indecency *n* indecenza; *(immodesty)* scorrettezza
indecent *a* scorretto, indecente
indecision *n* indecisione, perplessità, forse *m*
indecisive *a* non decisivo
indeed *adv* veramente, infatti, davvero
indefatigable *a* instancabile, infaticabile
indefensible *a* indifendibile, insostenibile
indefinable *a* indefinibile
indefinite *a* indeterminato, indefinito
indelicate *a* indelicato, sconveniente
indemnity *n* indennità
indent *vt* frastagliare, intaccare; *(print)* spaziare; **—ation** *n* incavo, intacco
independence *n* indipendenza
independent *a* indipendente
indescribable *a* indescrivibile
indestructible *a* indistruttibile
indeterminate *a* vago, indeterminato
index *n* indice *m*; — **finger** indice; — *vt* fornire di un indice
India India; — **ink** inchiostro di Cina
Indian *a&n* indiano; *(American)* pellirossa *m*; — **summer** estate di San Martino
indicate *vt* indicare
indication *n* indicazione; *(sign)* segno
Indies Indie *fpl*; **East** — Indie orientali; **West** — Indie occidentali
indicative *n&a* indicativo
indicator *n* indicatore *m*
indict *vt* accusare; *(law)* processare; **–ment** *n* atto di accusa
indifference *n* indifferenza

indifferent *a* indifferente
indigenous *a* indigeno
indigent *a* indigente
indigestible *a* indigesto, indigeribile
indigestion *n* indigestione
indignant *a* adirato, sdegnato; **–ly** *adv* indignatamente
indignity *n* indegnità
indirect *a* indiretto
indiscernible *a* impercettibile, indiscernibile
indiscreet *a* indiscreto
indiscretion *n* indiscrezione
indiscriminate *a* indiscriminato, confuso
indispensable *a* indispensabile
indisposed *a* ammalato, indisposto
indisposition *n* indisposizione
indisputable *a* incontestabile, indiscutibile
indistinct *a* indistinto
indistinguishable *a* indiscernibile, indistinguibile
individual *n* individuo; — *a* individuale; **–ism** *n* individualismo; **–ist** *n* individualista *m&f*
indivisible *a* indivisibile
indoctrinate *vt* addottrinare
indolence *n* indolenza
indolent *a* indolente
indomitable *a* indomabile
Indonesia Indonesia
indoor *a* interno; **–s** *adv* dentro, in casa
induce *vt* persuadere, indurre
inducement *n* allettamento, persuasione; *(flattery)* lusinga; *(stimulus)* stimolo
induct *vt* insediare
induction *n* induzione; *(mil)* arruolamento; *(to office)* insediamento; — **coil** rocchetto d'induzione
indulge *vt* contentare, soddisfare, accarezzare *(fig)*; — *vi* indulgere in; abbandonarsi a; — **in** permettersi il lusso di
indulgence *n* indulgenza, privilegio; *(kindness)* favore *m*
indulgent *a* indulgente
industrial *a* industriale; **–ist** *n* industrialista *m&f*; **–ize** *vt* industrializzare; **–ization** *n* industrializzazione
industrious *a* laborioso, industrioso
industry *n* industria, lavoro; *(activity)* attività
inebriate *n* ubbriaco; — *vt* inebriare, ubbriacare; **–d** *a* ubbriacato, inebriato
inedible *a* immangiabile
ineffable *a* ineffabile
ineffective, ineffectual *a* ineffettivo, inefficace, inutile; **–ness** *n* inefficacia, inutilità
inefficacy *n* inefficacia
inefficiency *n* incapacità, inefficienza
inefficient *a* incapace, inefficiente
ineligible *a* ineleggibile
inept *a* incapace, inetto
inert *a* inerte
inertia *n* inerzia
inequality *n* disuguaglianza, ineguaglianza
inequitable *a* ingiusto
ineradicable *a* inestirpabile
inescapable *a* inevitabile
inestimable *a* incalcolabile; *(invaluable)* preziosissimo
inevitable *a* inevitabile
inexcusable *a* imperdonabile, ingiustificabile
inexhaustible *a* inesauribile
inexpedient *a* inefficace
inexpensive *a* economico; poco costoso
inexperience *n* inesperienza
inexperienced *a* inesperto
inexplicable *a* incomprensibile
inexpressible *a* inesprimibile
inexpressive *a* inespressivo
inextricable *a* inestricabile
infallible *a* infallibile
infallibility *n* infallibilità
infamous *a* infame
infancy *n* infanzia; *(law)* minorità
infant *n* infante *m*
infantile *a* bambinesco, puerile; — **paralysis** poliomielite *f*
infantry *n* fanteria
infatuate *vt* infatuare; **become –d** infatuarsi
infatuation *n* infatuazione; *(craze)* pazzia
infect *vt* infettare
infection *n* infezione
infectious *a* infettivo
infer *vt* dedurre, inferire
inference *n* illazione, inferenza
inferior *a* inferiore
inferiority *n* inferiorità; — **complex** complesso d'inferiorità
infernal *a* infernale
inferno *n* inferno
infest *vt* infestare; molestare *(fig)*; **–ation** *n* infestazione, infestamento
infidel *n&a* miscredente *m*
infidelity *n* infedeltà
infiltrate *vt&i* infiltrare, infiltrarsi
infinite *n&a* infinito; **–ly** *adv* infinitamente
infinitive *n* infinito
infinity *n* infinità
infirm *a* debole, infermo, malfermo; **–ity** *n* infermità
infirmary *n* infermeria
inflame *vt* infiammare, irritare; *(fig)* infervorare
inflammable *a* infiammabile
inflammation *n* infiammazione
inflate *vt* dilatare, gonfiare
inflation *n* *(com)* inflazione; *(gas)* gonfiamento; *(of an idea)* esagerazione
inflection *n* inflessione; *(gram)* flessione
inflexible *a* inflessibile
inflict *vt* infliggere
influence *n* influsso; ascendente *m*; — *vt* influenzare, influire
influential *a* influente
influenza *n* influenza
influx *n* affluenza
inform *vt* informare, avvisare; far sapere; — **against** denunciare, accusare **–ant** *n* informatore *m*, informatrice *f*; **–er** *n* delatore *m*, delatrice *f*; **–ed** *a* informato
informal *a* senza cerimonie, intimo; alla mano *(fig)*; **–ity** *n* semplicità; mancanza di cerimonie
information *n* informazione; *(notice)* notizia, avviso; — **bureau** ufficio

informazioni
infraction *n* infrazione, contravvenzione, violazione
infrared *a* infrarosso
infrequent *a* infrequente, raro
infringe *vt* contravvenire, trasgredire, violare, infrangere; **–ment** *n* infrazione, contravvenzione, violazione
infuriate *vt* infuriare; **–d** *a* infuriato, furioso, furibondo, furente
infuse *vt* infondere; *(inspire)* ispirare
infusion *n* infusione; ispirazione
ingenious *a* ingegnoso
ingenuity *n* ingegnosità
ingenuous *a* ingenuo, sincero, semplice
inglorious *a* inglorioso; oscuro *(fig)*
ingrained *a* inerente, inveterato, radicato
ingratiate *vt* ingraziare; **— oneself** ingraziarsi; entrare nelle grazie di
ingratitude *n* ingratitudine *f*
inhabit *vt* abitare; **–able** *a* abitabile **–ant** *n* abitante *m*
inhalant *n* inalatore *m*
inhale *vt* aspirare
inharmonious *a* inarmonioso
inherent *a* inerente
inherit *vt* ereditare; **–ance** *n* eredità
inhibit *vt* proibire, inibire
inhibition *n* inibizione, repressione
inhospitable *a* inospitale
inhuman *a* crudele, inumano; **–ity** *n* crudeltà, inumanità
inimical *a* contrario, ostile, avverso, nemico
inimitable *a* inimitabile
iniquitous *a* iniquo
iniquity *n* iniquità
initial *n&a* iniziale *f*; **–ly** *adv* da principio, inizialmente
initiate *vt* iniziare, cominciare; **—** *n* iniziato
initiation *n* iniziazione
initiative *n* iniziativa
initiator *n* iniziatore *m*
inject *vt* iniettare; **–or** *n (mech)* iniettore *m*
injection *n* iniezione; **— pump** pompa ad iniezione
injudicious *a* sventato, insensato; poco giudizioso
injunction *n* ingiunzione
injure *vt* danneggiare, nuocere; *(wound)* ferire; far male a
injurious *a* dannoso, nocivo
injury *n* ferita, danno; *(wrong)* torto
injustice *n* ingiustizia
ink *n* inchiostro; **— pad** cuscinetto per timbri; **–y** *a (dirty with)* sporco d'inchiostro; color inchiostro; **—** *vt* inchiostrare
inkling *n* sospetto, sentore *m*, indizio
inkstand, inkwell *n* calamaio
inlaid *a* intarsiato
inland *n&a* interno, entroterra; **—** *adv* all'interno
in-laws *npl* parenti acquisiti
inlay *n* intarsio; **—** *vt* intarsiare
inlet *n (geog)* baia, insenatura; braccio di mare; *(mech)* immissione
inmate *n* ricoverato
inn *n* locanda, taverna, osteria
innate *a* ingenito, innato
inner *a* interiore; **— tube** camera d'aria; **–most** *a* il più segreto; il più intimo
inning *n* volta, turno
innocence *n* innocenza
innocent *n&a* innocente *m*
innocuous *a* innocuo
innovate *vi* innovare
innovation *n* innovazione
innuendo *n* malignazione, insinuazione
innumerable *a* innumerevole
inoculate *vt* inoculare
inoculation *n* inoculazione
inoffensive *a* innocuo
inopportune *a* intempestivo, inopportuno
inordinate *a* smoderato, disordinato
inorganic *a* inorganico
inquest *n* inchiesta giudiziaria
inquire *vt&i* chiedere, domandare, investigare; **— after** informarsi di
inquiry *n* domanda, inchiesta
inquisitive *a* curioso
inroad *n* irruzione, incursione, invasione; **make –s on** *(supply)* togliere dalla riserva
insane *a* pazzo, demente; **— asylum** manicomio
insanity *n* pazzia
insatiable *a* ingordo, insaziabile
inscribe *vt* inscrivere, iscrivere
inscription *n* iscrizione
insect *n* insetto; **–icide** *n* insetticida *m*
insecure *a* malfermo, insicuro
insecurity *n* precarietà, instabilità, incertezza
inseminate *vt* inseminare, seminare
insensible *a* insensibile, insensato
insensitive *a* insensitivo
inseparable *a* inseparabile
insert *n* allegato, inserto; **—** *vt* inserire
insertion *n* inserzione
inset *n* inserto, inserzione, riquadro
inside *a&n* interno; **— of** dentro di; *(time, coll)* entro; **— out** a rovescio; **–s** *npl (anat, coll)* intestini *mpl*
insidious *a* insidioso
insight *n* discernimento, perspicacia
insignia *npl* insegne *fpl*
insignificance *n* insignificanza, futilità
insignificant *a* insignificante
insincere *a* insincero, ipocrita
insincerity *n* ipocrisia
insinuate *vt* insinuare; dare ad intendere
insinuation *n* insinuazione
insipid *a* insipido, scipito, sciocco, uggioso
insist *vi* insistere
insistence *n* insistenza
insistent *a* insistente
insolation *n* insolazione
insole *n* soletta
insolence *n* insolenza
insolent *a* insolente
insoluble *a* insolubile
insolvent *a* insolvente
insomnia *n* insonnia
insomuch (as) *conj* a tal punto, talmente che
inspect *vt* visitare, ispezionare
inspection *n* ispezione, visita
inspector *n* ispettore *m*
inspiration *n* ispirazione; **–al** *a* ispirato
inspire *vt* ispirare

inspiring *a* ispirante, suggestivo
install *vt* collocare, installare; **–ation** *n* impianto, installazione; *(to office)* insediamento
installment *n* rata; *(serial)* puntata; **monthly** — rata mensile
instance *n* caso; *(example)* esempio; **for** — per esempio; **in the first** — in primo luogo
instant *n* attimo; **this** — subito; — *a* urgente; **—ly** *adv* immediatamente
instantaneous *a* istantaneo
instead *adv* invece; — **of** in luogo di
instep *n* collo del piede
instigate *vt* incitare, istigare; promuovere
instigation *n* istigazione
instigator *n* incitatore *m*, istigatore *m*
instill *vt* istillare, inculcare
instinct *n* istinto; **–ive** *a* istintivo
institute *n* istituto, — *vt* istituire
institution *n* istituzione
instruct *vt* istruire; **–or** *n* insegnante *m*
instruction *n* istruzione
instrument *n* strumento; — **flying** volo strumentale
instrumental *a* strumentale, utile; — **in** che contribuisce a; **–ist** *n* strumentista *m*
insubordination *n* insubordinazione
insubstantial *a* inconsistente
insufferable *a* insopportabile, insoffribile
insufficiency *n* insufficienza
insufficient *a* insufficiente; **–ly** *adv* insufficientemente
insulate *vt* isolare, separare
insulating *a* isolante
insulation *n* isolamento
insulin *n* insulina
insult *n* insulto, offesa, ingiuria; — *vt* insultare
insuperable *a* insuperabile
insupportable *a* insopportabile
insurable *a* assicurabile
insurance *n* assicurazione; — **broker** agente di assicurazione; **life** — assicurazione sulla vita
insure *vt* assicurare
insurgent *n&a* insorgente *m&f*, insorto, ribelle *m&f*
insurrection *n* sommossa, insurrezione
insurmountable *a* insormontabile
intact *a* intatto; *(safe)* illeso
intake *n* immissione, presa; *(mech)* energia assorbita
intangible *a* intangibile
integral *n* totalità; — *a* integrale
integrate *vt* integrare
integration *n* integrazione
integrity *n* integrità
intellect *n* intelletto
intellectual *a&n* intellettuale *m&f*
intelligence *n* sagacia
intelligent *a* intelligente
intelligible *a* intelligibile
intemperance *n* alcoolismo, intemperanza
intemperate *a* immoderato, intemperato
intend *vt* intendere, *(plan)* progettare
intense *a* intenso, forte
intensify *vt* intensificare, rafforzare
intent *n* intenzione; — *a* intento, attento
intention *n* intenzione; **–al** *a* premeditato
interact *vi* reagire reciprocamente
interaction *n* azione reciproca
intercede *vi* intercedere
intercellular *a* intercellulare
intercept *vt* arrestare, intercettare
interception *n* intercettazione
interceptor *n* intercettatore *m*, intercettatrice *f*
intercession *n* intercessione
interchange *n* intercambio, scambio, contraccambio; — *vt* contraccambiare, scambiare, alternare; **–able** *a* intercambiabile
intercollegiate *a* intercollegiato
intercolonial *a* intercoloniale
intercommunication *n* intercomunicazione
intercostal *a* intercostale
intercourse *n* comunicazioni *fpl*, relazioni *fpl*; *(com)* commercio, traffico; *(sex)* coito
interdenominational *a* interdenominazionale
interdepartmental *a* interdipartimentale
interdependence *n* interdipendenza
interest *n* interesse *m*; — **rate** saggio d'interesse; **–ed** *a* interessato; **–ing** *a* interessante
interfere *vi* interferire; *(meddle)* immischiarsi
interference *n* ingerenza, intervento
interim *n* intervallo; *(meantime)* frattempo; *(tenure)* interinato; — *a* temporaneo; interinale; *(temporary)* provvisorio
interior *a* interno
interject *vt* intercalare, interporre
interjection *n* interiezione
interlace *vt* allacciare, intrecciare
interline *vt* interlineare
interlining *n* ultrafodera
interlock *vt* collegare; — *vi* collegarsi
interloper *n* intruso; *(stranger)* estraneo
interlude *n* intermezzo
intermarriage *n* matrimonio fra parenti; matrimonio fra diverse razze
intermarry *vi* sposarsi fra parenti; sposarsi fra diverse razze
intermediate *a* frapposto, intermedio
intermediary *a&n* intermediario
interminable *a* interminabile
interminably *adv* interminabilmente
intermingle *vt* mescolare, intramezzare; — *vi* mescolarsi, intramezzarsi
intermission *n* intervallo, pausa
intermittent *a* intermittente
intern *vi* internare; — *vt* confinare; — *n (med)* interno; **–al** *a* interno; **–ment** *n* confino, internamento; **–ist** *n* specialista delle malattie interne; **–ship** *n* internato
international *a* internazionale; — **law** diritto internazionale
interplanetary *a* interplanetario
interpolate *vt* inserire, interpolare, intercalare
interpolation *n* interpolazione
interpret *vt* interpretare; **–er** *n* interprete *m&f*; **–ation** *n* interpretazione
interpretative *a* interpretativo
interracial *a* interrazziale
interrelationship *n* correlazione

interrogate *vt* interrogare
interrogation *n* interrogazione; — **mark** punto interrogativo
interrupt *vt* interrompere; **–er** *n (elec)* interruttore *m*
interruption *n* interruzione
intersect *vt* incrociare, intersecare
intersection *n* intersezione; *(street)* incrocio stradale
intersperse *vt* seminare, cospargere, alternare
interstate *a* interstatale
interurban *a* interurbano
interval *n* intervallo
intervene *vi* intervenire
intervention *n* intervento, interposizione
interview *n* colloquio, intervista; — *vt* intervistare
interweave *vt* intrecciare, intessere
interwoven *a* intrecciato, intessuto
intestate *a* intestato
intestinal *a* intestinale
intestines *npl* intestini *mpl*
intimacy *n* intimità
intimate *a* intimo
intimate *vt* accennare, notificare
intimation *n* intimazione, notifica
intimidate *vt* intimidire
intimidation *n* minaccia
into *prep* in
intolerable *a* intollerabile
intolerance *n* intolleranza
intolerant *a* intollerante
intone *vt* intonare
intoxicated *a* ebbro, ubriaco
intoxicating *a* inebriante
intoxication *n* intossicazione; *(alcohol)* ubriachezza
intractable *a* intrattabile
intransitive *a* intransitivo
intravenous *a* endovenoso
intrepid *a* intrepido
intricate *a* complicato, difficile
intrigue *n* intrigo; — *vt* stuzzicare; — *vi* intrigare
intriguing *a* intrigante
intrinsic *a* intrinseco
introduce *vt* introdurre; *(people)* presentare
introduction *n* introduzione; *(people)* presentazione
introductory *a* introduttivo, preliminare
introspection *n* introspezione
introspective *a* introspettivo
introvert *n* introverso
intrude *vt* intrudere; — *vi* ingerirsi, immischiarsi; — **on** disturbare, importunare
intrusion *n* intrusione
intuition *n* intuizione
intuitive *a* intuitivo
inundate *vt* inondare
inundation *n* inondazione
inure *vt* abituare
invade *vt* invadere, violare, assalire; **–r** *n* invasore *m*
invalid *n&a* ammalato, infermo
invalid *a* invalido, non valido
invaluable *a* incalcolabile, inestimabile
invariable *a* invariabile
invariably *adv* sempre, invariabilmente
invasion *n* invasione
inveigle *vt* allettare, sedurre; *(allure)* persuadere; *(deceive)* ingannare
invent *vt* inventare; **–ive** *a* inventivo; **–or** *n* inventore *m*, inventrice *f*
inventory *n* inventario; — *vt* inventariare
inverse *a* inverso
inversion *n* inversione
invert *vt* invertire
invest *vt* impiegare; *(com)* investire; **–or** *n* azionista *m&f*, inversionista *m&f*; **–ment** *n* investimento, impiego
investigate *vt* investigare, esaminare, indagare
investigation *n* inchiesta, investigazione, indagine *f*
investigator *n* investigatore *m*
inveterate *a* inveterato
invigorate *vt* rinvigorire, rinforzare
invigorating *a* corroborante, fortificante
invincible *a* invincibile
inviolable *a* inviolabile
invisibility *n* invisibilità
invisible *a* invisibile
invitation *n* invito
invite *vt* invitare
inviting *a* invitante, attraente, seducente
invocation *n* invocazione
invoice *n* fattura; — *vt* fatturare
invoke *vt* implorare, invocare
involuntary *a* involontario
involve *vt* coinvolgere, implicare; comprendere
involved *a* coinvolto, implicato; **become** — essere coinvolto
invulnerable *a* invulnerabile
inward *a* interno; — **self** fra sè; **–ly** *adv* dentro
iodine *n* iodio
ion *n* ione *m*, iono
iota *n* iota *m*
I.O.U, I owe you cambiale *f*
Iran Iran *m*
Iraq Irac, Irak *m*
irascible *a* irascibile
irate *a* incollerito, irato
IRBM, intermediate range ballistic missile MBMP; missile balistico di media portata
ire *n* collera, ira, rabbia
Ireland Irlanda
iridescent *a* iridescente
iris *n* iris *m*, iride *f*
Irish *a* irlandese
irk *vt* turbare, affligere, annoiare
irksome *a* noioso, seccante
iron *n* ferro; — **curtain** cortina di ferro; — **lung** polmone d'acciaio; **cast** — ghisa; **sheet** — lamiera; **wrought** — ferro battuto; **–clad** *a* irrevocabile, — *vt* stirare; **–ing** *n* stiratura
ironic, –al *a* ironico
irony *n* ironia
irradiate *vt* illuminare, irradiare; *(med)* trattare con radioterapia
irrational *a* irrazionale, illogico
irreconcilable *a* inconciliabile, irreconciliabile
irredeemable *a* irredimibile
irreducible *a* irreducibile
irrefutable *a* irrefutabile

irregular *a* irregolare; **–ity** *n* irregolarità
irrelevance *n* irrilevanza
irrelevant *a* irrilevante
irreligious *a* irreligioso
irremovable *a* irremovibile
irreparable *a* irreparabile
irreproachable *a* irreprensibile, impeccabile
irresolute *a* irresoluto
irresistible *a* irresistibile
irrespective *a* indipendente; — *adv* indipendentemente; — **of** a prescindere da
irresponsibility *n* irresponsabilità
irresponsible *a* irresponsabile
irreverence *n* irriverenza
irreverent *a* irriverente
irreversible *a* irreversibile, irrevocabile
irrigate *vt* irrigare
irrigation *n* irrigazione
irritability *n* irritabilità
irritable *a* irritabile
irritant *n&a* irritante *m*
irritate *vt* irritare
irritating *a* irritante
irritation *n* provocazione, irritazione
Islamism *n* islamismo
island *n* isola; **–er** *n* isolano
isobar *n* isobara
isolate *vt* isolare
isolation *n* isolazione, isolamento **–ism** *n* isolazionismo; **–ist** *n* isolazionista *m&f*
isomer *n* isomero
isothermal *a* isotermico
isotope *n* isotopo
Israel Israele *m*; **–ite** *n* israelita *m&f*
Israeli *a&n* israeliano
issue *n (periodical)* fascicolo; *(problem)* soggetto; *(progeny)* prole *f*; *(result)* esito; **take — with** non essere d'accordo
isthmus *n* istmo
it *pron* esso, essa; lo, la
Italian *a&n* italiano, italiana
italics *npl* corsivi *mpl*
Italy Italia
itch *n* prurito, scabbia; — *vi* prudere, pizzicare; **–ing** *n* prurito, pizzicore *m*; **–y** *a* rognoso
item *n* articolo; **–ize** *vt* specificare; fare la distinta
iterate *vt* ripetere, iterare
itinerant *a* girovago, ambulante
intinerary *n* itinerario
its *pron&a* il suo; la sua
itself *pron* si; sè; esso stesso, sè stesso; essa stessa, sè stessa; **by** — da solo
ivory *n* avorio; — *a* d'avorio
ivy *n* edera

J

jab *n* punzecchiatura; *(stab)* pugnalata; — *vt* punzecchiare, pugnalare
jabber *vi* ciarlare; *(grumble)* borbottare
jabbering *n* chiacchierio, cicaleccio; — *a* ciarlante
jack *vt* levare; — *n (cards)* fante *m*; *(mech)* martinetto, cricco; — **rabbit** lepre *m*
jack– *(in comp)* **—in-the-box** *n* saltamartino; **—of-all-trades** *n* factotum *m*; tuttofare *m&f*
jackass *n* asino
jacket *n* giacchetta, giacca; *(book)* sopraccopertina, coprilibro
jackknife *n* coltello a serramanico
jackpot *n (cards)* monte *m*; *(coll)* successo; *(poker)* piatto; **hit the** — *(sl)* aver fortuna
jade *n (horse)* ronzino; *(min)* giada; *(woman)* donnaccia; — *vt* affaticare, spossare; **–d** *a* spossato
jag *n* tacca, intaccatura; dente di sega; — *vt* frastagliare, dentellare
jagged *a* dentellato, intaccato
jail *n* prigione *f*; carcere *m*; — *vt* incarcerare
jalopy *n (coll)* carcassa
jam *n (cooking)* conserva, marmellata
jam *n* inceppamento, blocco; *(traffic)* ingorgo stradale; **in a** — *(coll)* nelle difficoltà; — *vt* bloccare, intasare; *(mech)* grippare; *(rad)* disturbare; — **on the brakes** frenare di colpo; — **the fingers** schiacciarsi le dita
jangle *vt* far tintinnare; *(bells)* scampanellare; — *vi* stonare, altercare
jangling *a* stonato; — *n (fig)* contesa, alterco
janitor *n* portinaio, custode *m*
January *n* gennaio
Japan Giappone *m*
Japanese *a&n* giapponese *m&f*
jar *vt&i (clash)* urtarsi; *(shake)* vibrare, scuotere; — **one's nerves** dare ai nervi *(fig)*; — *n* scossa, vibrazione; *(clash)* urto, dissonanza; *(container)* giara, boccale *m*
jargon *n* gergo
jaundice *n* itterizia; **–d** *a* geloso
jaunt *n* escursione, gita; **–y** *a* gaio; *(wearing apparel)* azzimato; — *vi* andare a spasso
jaw *n* mascella; **–bone** *n* mandibola; — *vi* *(sl)* ciarlare; rimbrottare
jealous *a* invidioso, geloso
jealousy *n* gelosia, invidia
jeans *npl* tuta di lavoro
jeep *n* camionetta, gip *m*
jeer *n* scherno; — *vt&i* burlare, schernire; — **at** beffarsi di
jeering *n* scherno; — *a* derisorio, beffardo
jellied *a* gelatinato, gelatinoso
jelly *n* gelatina
jeopardize *vt* compromettere, mettere a repentaglio
jeopardy *n* pericolo, rischio, repentaglio
jerk *n* strappo, stratta, scatto; *(sl)* puzzone *m (sl)*; — *vt* strappare; — *vi* scattare; **–y** *a* a sbalzi, spasmodico
jersey *n* maglia
jest *n* scherzo, facezia; **–er** *n* burlone *m*, buffone *m*; — *vi* scherzare
Jesus Christ *n* Gesù Cristo
jet *n (avi)* aerogetto; *(flame)* getto; vampa; *(gas)* becco a gas; *(min)* giavazzo, ambra nera; — **plane** aeroplano a reazione,

aviogetto; — **propulsion** spinta a getto; — *vt* emettere, buttar fuori; — *vi* sgorgare
jet-black *a* nero lucente
jettison *vt* gettare fuori bordo
Jew *n* israelita *m&f*
jewel *n* gioiello; **watch** — rubino; **–er** *n* gioielliere *m*; **–ry** *n* gioielleria
Jewish *a* ebreo
jib *n (naut)* fiocco, vela di bompresso
jibe *vi* accordarsi
jiffy *n (coll)* momento
jig *n (dance)* giga; — *vi* ballare la giga; — *vt* balzellare; **the — is up** *(sl)* è finita la cuccagna *(fig)*; **–saw** *n* sega verticale
jigger *n (measure)* un'oncia e mezzo
jiggle *vt&i* scuotere, agitarsi
jilt *vt* abbandonare; piantare *(coll)*
jingle *n (metal)* tintinnio; *(rhyme)* filastrocca; — *vt* far tintinnare; — *vi* tintinnare
jitters *npl (sl)* nervosità eccessiva; **have the** — essere sulle spine
job *n* lavoro, faccenda; — **lot** *(com)* merce di liquidazione; **–less** *a* disoccupato; — *vi* lavorare a cottimo
jobber *n (com)* cottimista *m*; *(middleman)* grossista *m*, distributore *m*
jockey *n* fantino; — *vt&i (deceive)* ingannare; *(defraud)* imbrogliare; *(racing)* fare il fantino; — **for position** brigare, intrigare
jocular *a* allegro, piacevole, vivace
jog *n* scossa leggera; *(nudge)* spinta; *(road, line)* rientranza; — **trot** trotto regolare; — *vt* scuotere, spingere; — *vi (along)* trotterellare
joggle *vt* scuotere; — *vi* scuotersi
join *vt* congiungere; — *vi* unirsi a; associarsi con; — **in** partecipare
joint *n (anat)* articolazione; *(bot)* nodo; *(geol)* fessura; *(junction)* giuntura; **out of** — *(med)* slogato; in disordine; — **account** conto corrente in comune; — **heir** coerede *m*
joist *n* trave *f*
joke *n* scherzo, barzelletta; **practical** — un tiro birbone; — *vi* scherzare, celiare
joker *n* burlone *m*; *(card)* matta
joking *a* scherzoso, faceto; **–ly** *adv* scherzosamente
jolly *a* gioviale, allegro, divertente
jolt *n* scossa; — *vt&i* scuotere
jostle *vt* pigiare, spingere; — *vi* spingersi, urtarsi, pigiarsi
jot *n* quisquilia; — *vt (down)* prender nota
jounce *vt* scuotere; far sobbalzare; — *vi* scuotersi, sobbalzare
journal *n (bookkeeping)* giornale *m*; *(diary)* diario; *(magazine)* rivista; *(newspaper)* giornale *m*
journalism *n* giornalismo
journalist *n* giornalista *m*
journey *n* viaggio; — *vi* viaggiare
jovial *a* gioviale
joy *n* gioia
joyful *a* allegro, gioioso, festivo; **–ly** *adv* allegramente
joyous *a* gioioso
jubilant *a* giubilante
jubilation *n* giubilo
jubilee *n* giubileo
judge *n* giudice *m*, arbitro; — *vt&i* giudicare; *(think)* credere, intendere, reputare
judgment *n* giudizio; **pass — on** giudicare in materia
judicial *a* giudiziario
judicious *a* giudizioso, assennato
jug *n* boccale *m*, brocca
juggle *vi* giocolare
juggler *n* giocoliere *m*
jugular *a* giugulare
juice *n* succo, sugo
juiciness *n* sugosità
juicy *a* succoso
jukebox *n* fonografo automatico a gettone
July *n* luglio
jumble *n* guazzabuglio; — *vt* confondere, gettare alla rinfusa
jumbo *a* colossale, gigantesco, enorme; — *n* colosso, gigante *m*; *(mammoth)* mastodonte *m (fig)*
jump *vt&i* saltare; — **around** darsi d'attorno; — **to conclusions** arrivare a giudizi precipitati; — *n* salto; **be on the** — essere in agitazione; **–y** *a* agitato
jumping *n* salto; — *a* saltatore, saltante; — **jack** saltamartino
junction *n* incrocio, bivio; *(forking)* biforcazione
June *n* giugno
jungle *n* giungla
junior *a* iuniore, cadetto; — *n* giovane *m&f*; figlio minore; *(student)* studente di terzo anno
junk *n* rottami *mpl*; *(rags)* stracci *mpl*; **–man** *n* rigattiere *m*
junta *n* giunta
jurisdiction *n* giurisdizione
jurisprudence *n* giurisprudenza
jurist *n* giurista *m*
juror *n* giurato
jury *n* giuria; — **box** banco della giuria; **grand** — gran giurì
just *a* giusto; — *adv* appena, soltanto; — **as** nello stesso momente che; — **gone** appena uscito; — **now** or ora; **–ly** *adv* giustamente; a buon diritto
justice *n* giustizia; *(judge)* giudice *m*
justifiable *a* giustificabile, lecito
justification *n* scusa, giustificazione
justify *vt* giustificare
jut *vi* protendersi, sporgere
jute *n* iuta
juvenile *a* giovanile; — *n* giovane *m&f*; — **delinquency** delinquenza minorile; — **delinquent** delinquente giovanile, giovane delinquente
juxtaposition *n* giustapposizione

K

kale *n* cavolo riccio
kaleidoscope *n* caleidoscopio
kaleidoscopic *a* caleidoscopico
kangaroo *n* canguro
kaolin *n* caolino
kapok *n* capoc, kapok *m*
keel *n (naut)* chiglia; — *vi* rollare; capovolgersi; — *vt (naut)* capovolgere; — **over** *(naut)* capovolgersi; *(person)* svenire
keen *a* acuto, affilato, perspicace; *(desirous)* desideroso; **–ly** *adv* acutamente; **–ness** *n* acutezza, vivacità
keep *n* mantenimento; — *vt* tenere, mantenere; — *vi* tenersi; mantenersi; — **aloof** tenersi in disparte; — **an eye on** tener d'occhio; — **back** *(conceal)* nascondere *(fig)*; *(restrain)* trattenere; — **books** tenere la contabilità; — **from** astenersi; — **house** mantenere casa; — **mum** tacere; — **on** continuare
keeping *n* cura, mantenimento; *(care)* custodia; **in** — **with** d'accordo con, in armonia con
keepsake *n* ricordo
ken *n* conoscenza, comprensione
kennel *n* covo, canile *m*
kernel *n* essenza; *(center)* nucleo; *(grain)* chicco; *(nut)* nocciolo
kerosene *n* petrolio; — **lamp** lampada a petrolio
kettle *n* pentola, bollitore *m*; **–drum** *n* timpano
key *n (door, mus)* chiave *f*; *(elec)* chiavetta; *(piano)* tasto; **master** — chiave generale; **–board** *n* tastiera; **–hole** *n* buco della serratura; **–note** *n* tonica, nota dominante; **–stone** *n (arch)* chiave di volta; — *a* principale; — *vt* chiudere a chiave; *(mus)* intonare, accordare
kick *vt&i* prendere a calci; dare un calcio; *(coll)* lamentarsi; — *n* calcio, pedata; *(coll)* lamento; **–off** *n (sport)* calcio d'inizio
kid *n* capretto; *(coll)* bimbo; **handle with** — **gloves** trattare con guanti di velluto; **–skin** *n* pelle di capretto; — *a* di capretto; — *vt (coll)* burlare
kidnap *vt* rapire
kidney *n* rene *m*; — **bean** fagiuolo
kill *vt* ammazzare, uccidere; — *n* uccisione; **–er** *n* assassino
killing *n* assassinio, uccisione; **make a** — *(coll)* fare man bassa *(fig)*; — *a (coll)* schiacciante; *(funny)* esilarante; *(weather)* micidiale
kill-joy *n* guastafeste *m*
kiln *n* fornace *m*, forno
kilo *n* chilo; **–cycle** *n* chilociclo; **–gram** *n* chilogramma *m*, chilo; **–meter** *n* chilometro; **–watt** *n* chilowatt *m*
kin *n* famiglia, parentela; **next of** — il parente più prossimo; **–ship** *n* parentela
kind *a* gentile, buono; — *n* maniera, genere *m*, specie *f*; **nothing of the** — niente del genere; **–hearted** *a* buono, benevolo; **–ly** *adv* gentilmente; **–ness** *n* gentilezza, bontà
kindergarten *n* giardino d'infanzia
kindle *vt* provocare, accendere; dar fuoco a; *(excite)* eccitare; — *vi* accendersi; prender fuoco
kindliness *n* amabilità
kindling wood legna minuta per accendere
kindred *n* parentela, parenti *mpl*; — *a* affine; imparentato
kinetic *a* cinetico; **–s** *npl* cinetica
king *n* re *m*
kingdom *n* regno
kingpin *n (bowling)* birillo centrale; *(coll)* principale *m*, pezzo grosso
king-size *a* di formato gigante
kink *n (knot)* arricciatura; *(muscle)* crampo; **–y** *a* ricciuto
kiss *n* bacio; — *vt* baciare
kit *n* armamentario, corredo; cassetta di arnesi
kitchen *n* cucina; — **stove** fornello, cucina
kite *n (com)* cambiale di favore; *(toy)* aquilone *m*; *(zool)* nibbio; — *vi (com)* aver denaro con cambiale di favore; *(hurry)* volare *(fig)*
kitten *n* gattino; **–ish** *a* come un gattino
kitty *n (cat)* gattino, micino; *(money pool)* piatto, monte *m*
kleptomaniac *n* cleptomane *m&f*
knack *n* abilità
knave *n* briccone *m*, mariuolo; *(cards)* fante *m*
knead *vt* impastare
knee *n* ginocchio; **on one's –s** ginocchioni, in ginocchio; **–cap** *n* rotula
knee– *(in comp)* **—deep** *a* fino alle ginocchia; **—high** *a* all'altezza del ginocchio
kneel *vi* inginocchiarsi
knell *n* rintocco a morto, suono a morto
knickknack *n* ninnolo, gingillo, bagatella
knife *n* coltello; — **grinder** arrotino; — *vt* pugnalare, accoltellare
knight *n* cavaliere *m*; *(chess)* cavallo; **–hood** *n* cavalleria; **–ly** *a* cavalleresco; — *vt* fare cavaliere, creare cavaliere
knight-errant *n* cavaliere errante
knit *vt&i* unire; lavorare a maglia; *(bone)* saldarsi; — **one's brows** aggrottare le ciglia
knitting *n* lavoro a maglia; — **needle** ferro da calza
knob *n* bozza, protuberanza, pomo; **–by** *a* nodoso
knock *vt&i* bussare, picchiare; *(against)* urtare, — **around** *(coll)* sballottare; — **down** atterrare; — **off** *(price)* ribassare; *(work)* smettere il lavoro; — **out** vincere, sopraffare; *(boxing)* mettere fuori combattimento
knocker *n (door)* battente *m*
knocking *n* colpi *mpl*
knock-kneed *a* con le gambe storte
knockout *n* successone; *(boxing)* fuori combattimento
knot *n* nodo; **–hole** *n* foro rimasto nel le-

gno allo staccarsi di un nodo; **–ted** *a* annodato, nodoso; **–ty** *a* nodoso; difficile
knottiness *n (fig)* difficoltà; complicazione; complessità
know *n* conoscenza; **be in the —** saperla lunga
know *vt* sapere; *(acquaint)* conoscere
knowingly *adv* accortamente
known *a* noto, conosciuto
know– *(in comp)* **—how** *n (coll)* conoscenza pratica; il saper fare; **—nothing** *n* ignorante
knowledge *n* sapere *m*; conoscenza, erudizione *f*; *(science)* scienza
knuckle *n (anat)* articolazione; *(finger)* nocca; *(meat)* ossobuco; *(mech)* giunto; **— under** sottomettersi, cedere; **rap over the –s** battere sulle nocche
kowtow *vi (bow)* salutare, toccando il suolo con la fronte, *(submit)* mostrare devozione

L

label *n* etichetta; **—** *vt* classificare; *(mark)* marcare
labial *a* labiale
labor *n* lavoro; **— market** offerta e domanda di lavoro; **— union** sindicato operaio; **hard —** lavori forzati; **–er** *n* bracciante, lavoratore *m*; **—** *vt&i* lavorare; *(distress)* angosciare, soffrire; **be in —** *(birth)* avere le doglie; **–ed** *a* stentato, elaborato
labor-saving *a* che evita fatica
laboratory *n* laboratorio
labyrinth *n* labirinto
lace *n* merletto, trina; *(shoe)* laccio, stringa; **—** *vt (beat)* battere; *(berate)* strigliare *(fig)*; *(connect)* allacciare; *(trim)* gallonare
laceration *n* strappo, lacerazione
lachrymose *a* lagrimoso
lacing *n* allacciamento; *(beating)* battuta; *(diatribe)* strigliata *(fig)*
lack *n* mancanza, difetto; **for — of** in mancanza di; **—** *vt&i* mancare, scarseggiare
lackadaisical *a* lezioso, languido, svenevole
lacking *a* mancante, difettante; **— in** privo di
lackluster *a* opaco
laconic *a* laconico
lacquer *n* lacca
lacrimose *a* lagrimoso
lactation *n* allattamento
lactic *a* lattico; **— acid** acido lattico
lactose *n* lattosio
lacy *a* traforato, calato; di pizzo
lad *n* ragazzo
ladder *n* scala a piuoli
lade *vt* imbarcare, caricare
lading *n* carico, caricamento; **bill of —** polizza di carico
ladle *n* mestolo; **—** *vt* scodellare; **— out** distribuire
lady *n* signora; *(nobility)* nobildonna; **–like** *a* distinto, fine, signorile; **–love** innamorata
lag *vi* attardarsi; restare indietro; **—** *n* ritardo
laggard *n* infingardo
lagoon *n* laguna
laid up *(sick)* ammalato; *(stored)* accumulato
lair *n* tana, covo, nascondiglio
laity *n* laicato; laici *mpl*
lake *n* lago
lamb *n* agnello; **–skin** *n* pelle d'agnello
lame *a* storpio, zoppo; **— excuse** scusa magra; **–ness** *n* difetto; *(med)* zoppicamento; **—** *vt* storpiare; **–ly** *adv* zoppicando, imperfettamente
lament *vt&i* lamentare, lamentarsi; **—** *n* lamento; **–ation** *n* lamentela, lamentazione; **–able** *a* lamentabile
laminate *vt* laminare; **–d plastic** laminati plastici
lamp *n* lampada; **–black** *n* nerofumo; **–post** *n* lampione *m*; **–shade** *n* paralume *m*
lampoon *n* libello, satira; **—** *vt* satireggiare
lance *n* lancia; *(med)* lancetta; **—** *vt (med)* incidere con la lancetta
land *n* terra; *(country)* paese *m*; *(soil)* terreno; **—** *vi (naut)* sbarcare, approdare; *(avi)* atterrare, arrivare; **—** *vt* tirare a terra; **— on one's feet** cadere in piedi
landholder *n* proprietario terriero
landing *n (avi)* atterraggio; *(naut)* approdo, sbarco; *(arch)* pianerottolo; **blind —** atterraggio cieco *or* radiocomandato; **— place** sbarcatoio; **— gear** carrello; **— strip** pista di atterraggio
landlady *n* affittacamere *f*; padrona di casa
landlord *n* locatore *m*
landmark *n* segno di confine; punto di riferimento
land office catasto
landowner *n* proprietario terriero
landscape *n* paesaggio; **— painter** paesista *m*
landslide *n* frana; *(pol)* elezione per maggioranza schiacciante
lane *n (auto)* corsia stradale; *(path)* sentiero; *(street)* vicolo
language *n* lingua, linguaggio; **bad —** turpiloquio
languid *a* languido
languish *vi* languire; **–ing** *a* languido, languente
languor *n* languore *m*; **–ous** *a* languido
lanky *a* allampanato
lanolin *n* lanolina
lantern *n* lanterna
lantern-jawed *a* macilento
Laos Laos
lap *n (anat)* grembo; *(cloth)* falda; *(sport)* giro; **—** *vt* piegare; *(animal)* lappare; *(water)* lambire
lapel *n* risvolto
lapping *a* lambente
lapse *n* dimenticanza; intervallo; *(gap)* lacuna; *(expiration)* decadenza; **—** *vi*

trascorrere; decadere, ricadere
larceny *n* furto
lard *n* strutto, sugna; — *vt* lardellare
larder *n* dispensa
large *a* grosso, ampio; — **as life** in bella vista; **at** — in libertà; al largo (*coll*); in generale; nell'insieme; **-ly** *adv* ampiamente
large-scale *a* in larga scala
largess *n* liberalità, regalo, dono
lariat *n* laccio
lark *n* allodola; *(fun)* divertimento; **go on a** — divertirsi
laryngitis *n* laringite *f*
larynx *n* laringe *f*
laser *n* amplificazione di luce per mezzo d'emissione stimolata di radiazione
lash *n (scourge)* sferza, frusta, flagello; *(eye)* ciglio; — *vt* frustare, sferzare; *(tie)* legare **-ing** *n* battitura; *(punishment)* castigo, flagellazione; *(cable)* gomena
lassitude *n* sfinimento, lassitudine
last *n* fine *f*; *(shoe)* forma da scarpe; — *a* ultimo; — **night** la notte scorsa; — **time** ultima volta; — **week** la settimana scorsa; **at** — finalmente; **next to** — penultimo; **-ly** *adv* finalmente, ultimamente, infine; — *vi* durare; **-ing** *a* duraturo, durevole, durabile
latch *n (door)* serratura, chiavistello; *(gate)* spranga; **-key** *n* chiave di casa; — *vt* chiudere con chiavistello
late *adv* tardi, in ritardo; **of** — recentemente; — *a* tardivo, recente; *(deceased)* fu, defunto, buonanima; **-ly** *adv* recentemente; — **in the night** a notte tarda; — **in the week** verso la fine della settimana
latent *a* latente
later *a* posteriore; *(following)* seguente; — *adv* più tardi
lateral *a* laterale
latest *a* ultimo, più recente; **at the** — al più tardi
lath *n* listello; — *vt* coprire di assicelle; **-ing** *n* listellatura
lathe *n* tornio
lather *n* schiuma, saponata; — *vt* insaponare, schiumare; *(coll)* bastonare; — *vi* spumeggiare
Latin *a&n* latino; — **America** America latina
latitude *n* latitudine *f*; *(of action)* ampiezza; libertà d'azione; carta bianca *(fig)*
latter *a* ultimo; **the** — quest'ultimo, questi
lattice *n* traliccio, graticcio, grata; **-work** *n* graticolato, graticcio, traliccio
laud *vt* esaltare; **-able** *a* lodevole
laugh *vi* ridere; — **at** farsi beffe di; — *n* riso; **-ter** *n* risata, ilarità; — **up one's sleeve** ridere sotto i baffi; **-able** *a* risibile, ridicolo
laughing *a* allegro, ridente; **no — matter** niente da ridere; **-stock** *n* zimbello; **-ly** *adv* ridendo
launch *vt* lanciare, varare; — *vi* imbarcarsi *(fig)*; — *n* varo; *(boat)* lancia
launching *n* lancio, varo; — **pad** *(aesp)* piattaforma di lancio
launder *vi* fare il bucato; — *vt* lavare
laundress *n* lavandaia, stiratrice *f*
laundry *n* bucato; *(place)* lavanderia
lavatory *n* lavabo; *(restroom)* gabinetto di decenza
lavender *n* lavanda; — *a* color lavanda
lavish *a* abbondante, prodigo; — *vt* prodigare, largire; **-ness** *n* prodigalità, profusione, sciupio *(coll)*
law *n* legge *f*, diritto; **according to** — secondo la legge; **lay down the** — dettar legge; **civil** — diritto civile; **-breaker** *n* violatore delle legge; **-maker** *n* legislatore *m*; **-suit** *n* causa, querela
law-abiding *a* rispettoso della legge
lawful *a* legale, legittimo; **-ly** *adv* legittimamente
lawless *a* sfrenato; senza legge; **-ness** *n* licenza, sfrenatezza
lawn *n* praticello, tappeto erboso
lawnmower *n* falciatrice meccanica
lawyer *n* avvocato
lax *a* negligente, trascurato; *(morally)* immorale; **-ity** *n* negligenza; immoralità
laxative *n* lassativo, purgante *m*; — *a* purgativo
lay *vt* collocare, mettere, posare; *(paint)* coprire di pittura; *(spread)* stendere; — **aside** mettere da parte; — **a bet** fare una scommessa; — **bare** scoprire; — **a hand on** mettere le mani su; — **low** abbattere; *(hide)* appiattarsi; — **open** esporre; — **out** preparare, esporre, *(money)* spendere; — **up** conservare; mettere da parte; — *vi (bet)* scommettere; far scommessa; *(egg)* deporre uova
lay *n (position)* situazione, posizione; — **of the land** sistemazione del terreno; **-off** *n* sospensione di lavoro
lay *a* laico, secolare; **-man** *n* laico, secolare *m*
layer *n* strato
layette *n* corredo di neonato
layout *n* progetto, disegno; *(print)* menabò
laze *vi* oziare; esser pigro; vivere nell'inerzia
laziness *n* indolenza, pigrizia
lazy *a* pigro, indolente; **-bones** *n (coll)* indolente *m*
lead *vt (guide)* condurre, guidare; *(head)* capeggiare; *(cause)* indurre; — **away, off** condurre via; — **the way** mostrare il cammino; andare avanti; — *n* direzione, comando; *(elec)* cavo maestro; *(theat)* primo attore, **take the** — prendere il comando
lead *n (min)* piombo; — *a* plumbeo, di piombo; **-en** *a* pesante, plumbeo, di piombo; — **poisoning** saturnismo, colica saturnina; — *vt* impiombare
leader *n* capo, guida, persona autorevole; **-ship** *n* direzione, direttiva
leading *a* principale, primario, primo; — **question** domanda capziosa *or* suggestiva
leaf *n (book)* pagina, foglio; *(bot)* foglia; *(table)* aggiunta; **-let** *n (print)* foglietto, fasciolo; **-less** *a* senza foglie; **-y** *a* frondoso, carico di foglie;

— *vi (bot)* frondeggiare: *(book)* sfogliare le pagine di
league *n (measure)* lega; *(organization)* lega, associazione: **in — with** in lega con
leak *n* fuga, perdita; *(gas)* fuga di gas; **spring a —** *(gas)* fare fuga: *(liquid)* fare acqua; **-age** *n* falla, scolo, filtrazione; — *vt&i* perdere, colare; **— out** *(secret)* trapelare
leaky *a* fesso: che ha una falla
lean *n&a* magro: **-ness** *n* magrezza: — *vt&i* inclinare, appoggiare; **— back one's head** piegare la testa indietro: **— on** appoggiarsi a: **— out** sporgersi
leaning *n* inclinazione, tendenza, pendenza; — *a* tendente, inclinato, pendente
lean-to *n* tettoia, baracchino
leap *vt&i* saltare: — *n* salto: **— year** anno bisestile
leapfrog *n* saltamontone *m*, cavallina
learn *vt* imparare, apprendere: **-er** *n* allievo, scolaro: **-ing** *n* sapere *m*, conoscenza, scienza
learned *a* dotto, erudito, sapiente
lease *n* contratto d'affitto: — *vt* dare (*or* prendere) in affitto
leash *n* laccio, guinzaglio: — *vt* tenere al guinzaglio
least *a&n* minimo: — *adv* minimamente; meno possible; **at —** almeno: **not in the —** in nessun modo, per nulla
leather *n* pelle *f*, cuoio
leathery *a* coriaceo
leave *n* licenza, congedo: permesso: **take — of** accomiatarsi da: — *vt&i* lasciare: *(depart)* partire, andarsene: **— alone** lasciare in pace: **— behind** lasciare indietro: **on —** in licenza: **— out** omettere, tralasciare; **sick —** licenza di convalescenza
leaven *n* lievito; — *vt* lievitare
leavening *n* lievitazione, fermentazione, lievito: — *a* in fermentazione
leavings *npl* avanzi, resti *mpl*
Lebanon Libano
lecher *n* libertino
lecherous *a* lascivo, osceno
lechery *n* libertinaggio, lascivia
lecture *n* conferenza, discorso: *(scolding)* ramanzina: — *vi* far conferenze: — *vt* rimproverare, ammonire
lecturer *n* conferenziere *m*
ledge *n* sporgenza, bordo; *(geol)* strato; *(mountain)* cornice *f*; *(window)* davanzale *m*
ledger *n* libro mastro
leech *n* sanguisuga: **stick like a —** attaccarsi come una sanguisuga
leek *n* porro
leer *n* sbirciata: — *vi* sbirciare: **— at** sogguardare
lees *npl* sedimento
leeward *a&n* sottovento
leeway *n* deriva
left *a&n* sinistra: *(neglected)* trascurato: **— behind** sorpassato, lasciato indietro: **on the —** a sinistra: **-over** *n* rimasuglio: **-ward** *adv* verso sinistra:
left- *(in comp)* **—hand** *a* sinistro: **—handed** *a* mancino; ambiguo; **-wing** *a (pol)* di sinistra; **—winger** *n (pol)* appartenente alla sinistra
leftist *n* persona di sinistra
leg *n* gamba; *(animal)* zampa: *(fowl)* coscia; *(trip)* tappa: **pull someone's —** fare un tiro scherzoso a qualcuno, prendere in giro qualcuno: **shake a —** *(sl)* sbrigarsi: **stand on one's own two legs** essere indipendente: **without a — to stand on** senza nessuna ragione: **on one's last -s** essere alle ultime risorse
legacy *n* eredità
legal *a* giuridico, legale; **-ity** *n* legalità; **-ize** *vt* legalizzare
legate *n* nunzio, legato
legation *n* legazione *f*
legend *n* leggenda: **-ary** *a* leggendario
legerdemain *n* gioco di prestigio
leggings *npl* uose *fpl*
legible *a* leggibile
legion *n* legione *f*
legislate *vi* legiferare
legislation *n* legislazione
legislator *n* legislatore *m*
legislature *n* legislatura
legitimacy *n* legittimità
legitimate *a* legittimo
legume *n* legume *m*
leisure *n* comodo, agio: **at —** a proprio agio; **-ly** *a* deliberato, calmo: **-ly** *adv* comodamente, con comodo: **in a -ly way** senza fretta
lemon *n* limone *m*: **— squeezer** spremilimoni *m*; **— tree** limone *m*: **-ade** *n* limonata
lend *vt* dare in prestito, prestare, imprestare: fornire: **-er** *n* prestatore *m*, prestante *m*; **— a hand** prestar man forte
lending *a* di prestito; — *n* prestito: **— library** biblioteca circolante
lend-lease *n* prestito di guerra
length *n* lunghezza: *(time)* durata: **at —** finalmente; per esteso, diffusamente: **-wise** *a* per il lungo: **-y** *a* lungo: **-en** *vt* allungare
leniency *n* benevolenza, indulgenza
lenient *a* indulgente
lens *n* lente *f*: *(eye)* cristallino: *(magnifying)* lente d'ingrandimento: **— shutter** *(photo)* otturatore *m*
Lent *n* quaresima; **-en** *a* quaresimale, magro
lentil *n* lenticchia, lente *f*
leopard *n* leopardo
leper *n* lebbroso
leprosy *n* lebbra
leprous *a* lebbroso
lesion *n* lesione
less *a* meno, minore, inferiore: — *adv & prep* meno: **-er** *a* minore: più piccolo: **-en** *vt&i* diminuire: **for —than** per meno di; **in — than no time** in men che non si dica: **— and —** sempre meno: **none the —** nondimeno
lessee *n* locatario, affittuario
lesson *n* lezione
lessor *n* locatore *m*
lest *conj* per tema che, affinchè non
let *vt* lasciare, permettere: **— alone** lasciare in pace: **— down** deludere; **— go**

(of) lasciare andare *(coll)*; — **in** lasciar entrare; — **know** far sapere; — **off** perdonare; lasciar passare *(fig)*; — **out** far uscire; *(dress)* allargare; *(secret)* divulgare; — **up** *(coll)* diventar meno rigido; *(slacken)* mollare; **-down** *n* *(coll)* disappunto; **-up** *n* rallentamento
lethargy *n* letargo
letter *n* *(alphabet, mail)* lettera; — **box** *n* cassetta postale; — **carrier** postino; **-head** intestazione; — **of attorney** mandato di procura; — **of credit** lettera di credito; — **opener** aprilettere *m*; **capital** — maiuscola; **dead** — lettera morta; **form** — lettera circolare; **lower-case** — *(print)* minuscola; **registered** — lettera raccomandata; **small** — minuscola; — *vt* scrivere con caratteri alfabetici
lettering *n* caratteri alfabetici; iscrizione
lettuce *n* lattuga
leucocyte *n* leucocite *m*
leukemia *n* leucemia
levee *n* argine *m*; diga
level *a* piano; — **with** a livello con; **do one's — best** fare del proprio meglio; — *n* livello; piano; **be on the** — avere intenzioni oneste; — *vt* livellare; *(aim)* puntare; *(avi)* volare raso terra; — **to the ground** radere al suolo
level-headed *a* equilibrato, di buon senso
lever *n* leva; **control** — *(avi)* asta di comando; **-age** *n* punto d'appoggio, fulcro; influenza, vantaggio
levity *n* leggerezza, frivolità
levulose *n* levulosio
levy *n* imposizione, esazione; — *vt* requisire, esigere; — **a tax** imporre un tributo
lewd *a* libidinoso, dissoluto
lewdness *n* oscenità, libidine *f*
lexicographer *n* lessicografo
lexicon *n* lessico
liabilities *npl* *(com)* passività; *(debts)* impegni *mpl*
liability *n* obbligo
liable *a* responsabile; *(likely)* suscettibile di
liar *n* bugiardo
libel *n* diffamazione *f*; — *vt* diffamare
liberal *a* generoso, liberale; **-ism** *n* liberalismo; **-ity** *n* liberalità; **-ly** *adv* liberalmente; **-ize** *vt* rendere liberale
liberate *vt* liberare
liberation *n* liberazione
liberator *n* liberatore *m*
libertine *n* libertino; — *a* licenzioso
liberty *n* libertà; **take the** — prendersi la libertà
libidinous *a* libidinoso
libido *n* libidine *f*
librarian *n* bibliotecario
library *n* biblioteca
librettist *n* librettista *m&f*
libretto *n* libretto
Libya Libia
license *n* licenza, permesso; — **plate** targa di circolazione; **driver's** — patente di guida; **hunting** — porto d'armi; — *vt* autorizzare
licentious *a* licenzioso, libertino
licentiousness *n* licenziosità
licit *a* lecito
lick *vt* leccare; *(coll)* battere, sconfiggere; — **one's chops** *(fig)* leccarsi i baffi *(fig)*; — **someone's boots** leccare i piedi a qualcuno; — *n* leccata; **give a — and a promise** *(fig)* fare qualche cosa superficialmente
licorice *n* liquirizia
lid *n* coperchio; *(eye)* palpebra
lie *n* menzogna, bugia; — *vi* mentire
lie *vi* trovarsi, stare; giacere; — **down** sdraiarsi, stendersi, coricarsi; — **still** star fermo
lien *n* diritto di rivalsa
lieu *n* luogo; **in — of** in vece di, in luogo di
lieutenant *n* tenente *m*; **second** — sottotenente *m*
life *n* vita; — **annuity** vitalizio; — **belt** salvagente *m*; — **buoy** gavitello di salvataggio; — **expectancy** probabilità di vivere; — **insurance** assicurazione sulla vita; — **preserver** apparecchio di salvataggio, sfollagente *m*; **come to** — ritornare in vita; **for** — a vita; **high** — alta società; **matter of — and death** questione di vita o morte; **-blood** *n* anima *(fig)*; **-boat** *n* battello di salvataggio; **-guard** *n* bagnino; **-long** *a* perpetuo; **-saver** *n* salvavita; **-time** *a* a vita, per la vita; **-work** *n* lavoro di una vita; **still** — natura morta
lifeless *a* inanimato
likelike *a* verosimile, dal vero
life-size *a* al vero, al naturale
lift *vt* sollevare, alzare; — *vi* disiparsi; alzarsi; — *n* sollevamento; *(air)* ponte aereo; *(auto)* passaggio
ligament *n* legamento
ligature *n* legatura
light *n* luce *f*; — **beam** raggio di luce; — **bulb** lampadina; — **meter** *(phot)* fotometro; — **wave** onda luminosa; **bring to** — mettere in luce; **come to** — venire in luce, manifestarsi; **throw — on** gettar luce su *(fig)*; **-hearted** *a* allegro, gaio; **-house** *n* faro; **-weight** *n* *(sport)* peso leggero
light *a* chiaro; *(weight)* leggero
light *vt* accendere; illuminare; — *vi* accendersi; illuminarsi; — **on** *(encounter)* imbattersi in
lighten *vt* illuminare; *(weight)* alleggerire; — *vi* illuminarsi; balenare; alleggerirsi
light- *(in comp)* **—fingered** *a* lesto di mano; **—footed** *a* agile, veloce; **—headed** *a* svenato, leggero; **—year** *n* *(ast)* anno luce
lighting *n* illuminazione
lightning *n* baleno; — **rod** parafulmine *m*; **flash of** — un lampo; **fork** — saetta; **sheet** — lampeggio
ligneous a ligneo
likable *a* simpatico, piacevole
like *a* simile, somigliante; — *prep* simile a, come; — *vt* piacere a; voler bene a, aver simpatia per; — *adv* come, da, nella maniera di; **-ly** *a* probabile; **-ness** *n* rassomiglianza; **-wise** *adv* così, ugualmente; **-lihood** *n* probabilità, verosimiglianza; **feel** — aver voglia di;

look — somigliare a
liken *vt* confrontare, paragonare
liking *n (affection)* affetto, simpatia; *(desire)* inclinazione; *(taste)* gusto; **take a — to** prendere in simpatia
lilac *n* lilla
lily *n* giglio
limb *n* membro; *(tree)* ramo
limber *a* flessibile, agile; — *vt* rendere flessibile
lime *n* calce *f*; *(fruit)* limetta; **–stone** *n* calcare *m*; pietra calcarea
limelight *n* evidenza *(fig)*; **be in the —** essere prominente
limit *n* limite *m*; — *vt* limitare; **–ed** *a* ristretto, limitato; **–less** *a* illimitato
limitation *n* limitazione, limite *m*, riserva
limp *n* zoppicamento; — *vi* zoppicare; **–ing** *a* zoppicante
limp *a* floscio, fiacco, molle; **–ly** *adv* flosciamente
limpid *a* chiaro, limpido, terso
line *n* linea, riga; *(com)* linea d'affari; *(poet)* verso; **draw the —** *(fig)* segnare il limite; — *vt* rigare, segnare; *(articles)* rivestire, ricoprire, foderare; *(rule)* allineare; — **up** allinearsi
lineage *n* lignaggio, stirpe *f*, razza
lined *a (inside)* rivestito, ricoperto, foderato; *(ruled)* lineato
lineal *a* lineale
linear *n* lineare
lineman *n (rail)* guardalinea *m*
linen *n* tela di lino; **bed —** biancheria; — *a* di lino
liner *n (boat)* transatlantico
linesman *n (sport)* arbitro
line-up *n* sfilata
linger *vi* attardarsi; **–ing** *a* ritardato, lungo, lento; *(lasting)* persistente
lingual *a* linguale
linguist *n* linguista *m&f*; **–ics** *npl* linguistica; **–ic** *a* linguistico
liniment *n* linimento
lining *n* fodera, rivestimento
link *n* vincolo; anello di congiunzione; — *vt* concatenare, unire
linoleum *n* linoleum *m*
linotype *n* macchina linotipo
linseed *n* seme di lino; — **oil** olio di lino
lint *n* peluria, cascame *m*
lion *n* leone *m*
lion-hearted *a* dal cuor di leone
lip *n* labbro; — **reading** il capire dal moto delle labbra; — **service** fedeltà a parole
lipstick *n* rossetto per le labbra
liquefaction *n* liquefazione
liquefy *vt* liquefare; — *vi* liquefarsi
liqueur *n* liquore *m*
liquid *a&n* liquido
liquidate *vt* liquidare
liquidation *n* liquidazione
liquor *n* liquore *m*; — **store** negozio di liquori; **hard —** bevanda di alto grado alcoolico
Lisbon Lisbona
lisp *vt&i* parlare bleso; — *n* pronunzia blesa
list *n* elenco, lista; *(naut)* sbandamento; — **price** prezzo marcato; — *vt* elencare; — *vi (naut)* sbandare
listen *vi* ascoltare; **–er** *n* ascoltatore *m*; **–ing** *a* ascoltante
listless *a* indifferente; svogliato; **–ness** svogliatezza
litany *n* litania
liter *n* litro
literacy *n* il saper leggere e scrivere
literal *a* letterale; **–ly** *adv* letteralmente
literary *a* letterario
literate *a* letterato; che sa leggere e scrivere; — *n* letterato, erudito in lettere
literature *n* letteratura
lithe *a* snello, pieghevole
lithograph *n* litografia; **–er** *n* litografo
lithography *n* litografia
litigant *n* litigante *m&f*; parte in causa
litigate *vt (law)* discutere; — *vi* avere una causa in corso; litigare
litigation *n* lite legale
litmus *n* tornasole *m*; — **paper** carta di tornasole
litter *n (animal)* figliata; *(mess)* disordine, sossopra *m*; — *vt* disordinare; — *vi (animal)* partorire; **–ed** *a* disordinato, sossopra
little *a* piccolo; — *n&adv* poco; — **by —** a poco a poco; **a — while** un po' di tempo; **L- Bear** Orsa Minore
liturgy *n* liturgia
live *vt&i* vivere; *(reside)* abitare; — **down** *(past)* far dimenticare; — **from hand to mouth** vivere alla giornata; — *a* vivo, vivente; ardente; — **show** *(TV)* scena dal vero; — **steam** vapore compresso; **–liness** *n* vivacità
livelihood *n* sussistenza, mantenimento
lively *a* vivo, vivace
liven *vt* animare; — *vi* ravvivarsi
liver *n* fegato
livery *n* livrea; — **stable** stalla dove si noleggiano cavalli
livestock *n* bestiame *m*
livid *a* livido
living *n* esistenza, vita, pane quotidiano; — **room** salotto; — **wage** salario livellato alle esigenze vitali; **earn a —** guadagnarsi il pane; **standard of —** tenore di vita; — *a* vivente
lizard *n* lucertola; — *a* di lucertola
llama *n* lama
load *vt* caricare; — *n* carico, peso; **–s of** *(coll)* mucchi di
loaded *a* caricato; — **dice** dadi truccati
loaf *n* pane *m*, forma di pane; — *vi* bighellonare; **–er** *n* bighellone *m*, ozioso; **–ing** *n* ozio
loan *n* prestito; — **shark** strozzino; — *vt* prestare
loathe *vt* detestare; avere a schifo
loathing *n* ripugnanza
loathsome *a* schifoso, disgustoso
lobby *n* vestibolo, atrio; — *vi (pol)* sollecitare voti con manovre influenzabili
lobe *n* lobo
lobster *n* aragosta
local *a* locale; **–ity** *n* località; **–ize** *vt* localizzare; **–ly** *a* localmente

locale *n* scena
locate *vt* collocare; individuare, reperire; **be –d** essere situato
location *n* posto, posizione
lock *n (canal)* chiusa; *(gun)* percussore *m*; *(hair)* ricciolo, ciocca, bioccolo; *(latch)* serratura, toppa; **air —** camera di pressione intermedia; **pick a —** aprire con grimaldello; **under — and key** sotto chiave; **–smith** *n* magnano, chiavaio; **–out** *n (labor)* serrata; **–ed** *a* chiuso a chiave
lock *vt* chiudere a chiave; — *vi* chiudersi; **— in** rinserrare; **— out** chiuder fuori; **— up** rinchiudere
locker *n* ripostiglio; armadietto; baule *m*; tiretto; **— room** spogliatoio
locket *n* ciondolo reliquiario
lockjaw *n* tetano
lockup *n* prigione *f*
locomotion *n* locomozione
locomotive *n* locomotiva; — *a* locomotivo, mobile
locomotor ataxia atassia locomotrice
locus *n (geom)* luogo
locust *n* locusta; **— tree** carrubo
lode *n (geol)* filone metallifero
lodge *n* villetta; locale notturno; — *vt&i* alloggiare; **— a complaint** sporgere querela
lodger *n* inquilino
lodging *n* alloggio
loft *n (attic)* solaio, soffitta; *(dove)* piccionaia; — *vt* mettere in soffitta
lofty *a* elevato, alto; *(noble)* nobile
log *n* ceppo, tronco; *(naut)* libro di bordo; **— cabin** capanna di tronchi d'albero; — *vt&i* tagliare in ceppi
logarithm *n* logaritmo
logger *n* boscaiolo
loggerhead *n* stupido; **be at –s** essere alle prese
logic *n* logica; **–al** *a* logico
logistics *npl* logistica
loin *n* lombo; *(meat)* lombata; **–s** *npl* lombi *mpl*, reni *fpl*
loiter *vi* indugiarsi; gironzolare; **–er** *n* bighellone *m*, ozioso, sfaccendato; **–ing** *n* l'andare a zonzo
loll *vi* penzolare; afflosciarsi — *vt* lasciar penzolare
lollipop *n* caramella
London Londra
lone *a* solo, solitario; **–liness** *n* solitudine *f*; **–ly** *a* solitario, isolato, desolato; **–some** *a* solitario, solo
long *a* lungo; — *adv* per molto tempo, a lungo; **in the — run** nell'insieme; **a — time** molto tempo; **as — as** fin tanto che; **before —** fra poco; **— for** desiderare vivamente, agognare; **–ing** *n* desiderio, brama
long– *(in comp)* **—distance** *a* di lunga distanza; *(phone)* interurbano; **—faced** *a* malinconico, triste; **—legged** *a* dalle gambe lunghe; **—lived** *a* longevo, dalla vita lunga; **—lost** *a* perduto da lungo tempo; **—playing record, LP** disco microsolco; **—standing** *a* esistente da lungo tempo; **—suffering** *a* paziente; **—winded** *a* che ha grande resistenza per correre; *(fig)* tedioso, parolaio
longevity *n* longevità
longhand *n* scrittura ordinaria
longitude *n* longitudine *f*
longshoreman *n* scaricatore del porto
look *vt&i* guardare; *(appear)* sembrare; **— after** aver cura di; **— as if** sembrare che; **— at** guardare, esaminare; *(consider)* considerare; **— away** girar gli occhi; **— back (on)** ricordarsi (di); **— bad** aver cattivo aspetto; **— down on** *(fig)* disprezzare; **— for** cercare; *(expect)* aspettare; **— into** esaminare; **— like** somigliare; **— on** *(face)* dare su; **L– out!** Bada!, Guarda!, Attento! Attenzione!; **— over** esaminare, sorvegliare; **— up** *(word)* cercare; *(glance)* alzare lo sguardo; **— up to** *(admire)* ammirare, respettare; **as it –s to me** come mi sembra, secondo me; **by the –s of it** secondo le apparenze
look *n* aria, sguardo, cera
looking glass specchio
lookout *n* guardia; **be on the —** stare all'erta (*or* in guardia); **That's my —** Ciò spetta a me, É affar mio
loom *n* telaio; — *vi* apparire, profilarsi
loop *n* cappio, nodo scorsoio; *(avi)* cerchio della morte; **–hole** *n* scappatoia
loose *a* sciolto, libero; sfrenato, dissoluto; **at — ends** trascurato, disordinato; indeciso; **— change** spiccioli *mpl*; **–ly** *a* scioltamente; vagamente; **–n** *vt* sciogliere, slegare; — *vi* sciogliersi, allentarsi
loose– *(in comp)* **—jointed** *a* dinoccolato; **—leaf** *a* dai fogli sciolti
looseness *n* scioltezza; *(moral)* immoralità
loot *n* bottino; — *vt* predare
lop *vt* potare; recidere; mozzare; **–sided** *a* mal equilibrato; pendente; asimetrico; **— off** mozzare
lope *vi* correre a lunghi passi; — *n (gait)* passo lungo
lop-eared *a* con gli orecchi penzoloni
loquacious *a* loquace; **–ness** *n* loquacità
Lord *n* Signore *m*, Dio
lord *n* signore, padrone *m*
Lord's Prayer Paternostro
lore *n* sapienza, erudizione
lose *vt&i* perdere; **— one's temper** andare in collera; **— one's way** smarrirsi; **— sight of** perdere di vista; **–r** *n* perditore *m*, perdente *m&f*
losing *a* in perdita, perdente
loss *n* perdita; **be at a —** non sapere cosa fare, essere confuso; **sell at a —** vendere in perdita
lost *a* perduto, perso; *(ruin)* rovinato
lot *n* sorte *f*, destino; *(land)* lotto; *(goods)* partita; **draw –s** tirare a sorte
lotion *n* lozione *f*
lots *npl (coll)* grande quantità, un mucchio
lottery *n* lotteria
loud *a* forte; sgargiante; **–ness** *n* forza, rumorosità; *(of dress)* vistosità
loudspeaker *n* altoparlante *m*
loudmouthed *a* volgare, grossolano
lounge *n* atrio, vestibolo; divano, sofà *m*; — *vi* andare a zonzo, oziare
louse *n* pidocchio

lousy *a* pidocchioso; *(sl)* schifoso
lout *n* villanzone *m*
lovable *a* caro, amabile
love *n* amore *m*, affetto; — **affair** amoruccio, passioncella; **be in** — essere innamorato; **fall in — with** innamorarsi di; **make** — corteggiare; **–less** *a* senza amore; **–liness** *a* bellezza, grazia, incanto; **–lorn** *a* infelice in amore; **–ly** *a* bello, grazioso, piacevole; **–r** *n* amante *m&f*; innamorato; **–sick** *a* innamorato
love *vt* amare, voler bene a
love-making *n* corte, flirteo
loving *a* amoroso; affettuoso; devoto
low *a* basso; vile; depresso; — *adv* basso; — *vi* muggire; — *n (cow)* muggito; **–ly** *a* umile
low– *(in comp)* **—cut** *a* scollato, decoltè; **—down** *a (coll)* vile, meschino; **—pitched** *a (tone)* di tono basso; *(roof)* di bassa inclinazione; **—pressure** *a* di bassa pressione; **—spirited** *a* triste, scoraggiato, abbattuto
lowdown *n (sl)* il nocciolo della questione *(fig)*
lower *a* più basso; — **berth** cuccetta bassa; — *vt* abbassare; *(shame)* avvilire; — *vi* abbassarsi; avvilirsi; *(sink)* affondarsi
lower-case *a* minuscolo
lowland *n* pianura, bassopiano; **–s** pianura del sudest scozzese
lowliness *n* umiltà
lox *n (chem)* ossigeno liquido; salmone affumicato
loyal *a* fedele: **–ist** *n* monarchico; **–ty** *n* fedeltà
lozenge *n* pasticca, pastiglia; *(geom)* losanga
lube *n* olio lubrificante
lubricant *n* lubrificante *m*
lubricate *vt* lubrificare
lubricating lubrificante; — **oil** olio lubrificante
lubrication *n* lubrificazione
lucid *a* lucido: brillante; **–ity** *n* lucidità
luck *n* fortuna; **bad** — disdetta; **good** — buona fortuna; **–ily** *adv* fortunatamente
lucky *a* felice, fortunato; — **charm** amuleto
lucrative *a* lucrativo
ludicrous *a* ridicolo, comico; assurdo, ludicro
lug *n (pull)* strappone *m*; *(mech)* aletta, aggetto; *(projection)* sporgenza; — *vt* spingere; trascinare
luggage *n* bagaglio
lugubrious *a* lugubre
lukewarm *a* tiepido; *(fig)* indifferente
lull *n* sosta, bonaccia, intervallo di calma; — *vt* cullare, calmare; — *vi* calmarsi
lullaby *n* ninnananna
lumber *n* legname *m*; — **dealer** commerciante di legname; **–jack** *n* boscaiolo; **–man** *n* taglialegna *m*; commerciante in legname; **–yard** *n* deposito di legname; — *vi* tagliar legna; **–ing** *a* pesante, ingombrante, goffo
lumen *n* lumen *m*
luminary *n* luminare *m*
lump *n* pezzo; bernoccolo; — **in the throat** nodo alla gola; — **sum** somma globale; — *vt* ammucchiare; prendere all'ingrosso, ammassare; — *vi* muoversi pesantemente; fare mucchio
lunacy *n* demenza, follia, alienazione mentale
lunar *a* lunare
lunatic *a&n* pazzo, matto
lunch, luncheon *n* colazione *f*; — *vi* far colazione
lung *n* polmone *m*; **iron** — *(med)* polmone d'acciaio
lunge *n* slancio; *(fencing)* a fondo; — *vi* slanciarsi; *(fencing)* fare un a fondo
lurch *n* scarto; *(naut)* bordata; *(auto)* sbandata; **leave in the** — lasciare nei guai; — *vi* rollare, sbandare, traballare
lure *n (fishing)* esca; *(fig)* lusinga, allettamento; — **away** sviare; — *vt* adescare, allettare
lurid *a* lurido; scandaloso
lurk *vi* nascondersi; stare in agguato
luscious *a* succolento
lush *a* lussureggiante
lust *n* concupiscenza, lussuria; incontinenza; — *vi* agognare, bramare; **–y** *a* vigoroso, forte
luster *n* splendore *m*, lustro
lustiness *n* vigore *m*
lustrous *a* lucido, brillante, splendente, lustro
lute *n* liuto
luxuriant *a* rigoglioso, lussureggiante
luxurious *a* lussuoso, suntuoso
luxury *n* lusso
lye *n* liscivia; soda caustica
lying *n* mendacia, falsità; — *a* giacente; *(false)* mendace
lying-in hospital casa di maternità
lymph *n* linfa; — **gland** *n* glandola linfatica; **–atic** *a* linfatico
Lyons Lione
lyric *n* lirica; — *a* lirico
lyrical *a* lirico

M

M. A., Master of Arts *n* diplomato in lettere
macabre *a* macabro
macadam *n* macadam *m*, massicciata; — *a* macadamizzato, massicciato
macaroni *n* maccheroni *mpl*
macaroon *n* amaretto
mace *n (spice)* macis *m*; *(club)* mazza
macerate *vt* macerare
machination *n* macchinazione, complotto
machine *n* macchina; — **gun** mitragliatrice *f*; — **shop** officina meccanica; — **tool** macchina utensile
machine-gun *vt* mitragliare
machine-made *a* fatto a macchina
machinery *n* macchine *fpl*; meccanismo; congegno
machinist *n* macchinista *m*, meccanico

mackerel *n* sgombro; — **sky** cielo a pecorelle
macrocosm *n* macrocosmo
macron *n (gram)* lunga
mad *a* pazzo; *(coll)* arrabbiato; **stark** — matto del tutto; **drive** — far impazzire; **get** — *(coll)* adirarsi; **go** — impazzire; **–cap** *n* scervellato, impulsivo; **–man** *n* pazzo, matto, folle *m*
madam *n* madama, signora
madden *vt* far diventar matto, far ammattire; **–ing** *a* da far impazzire
made *a* fatto
Madeira Madera
made-to-order *a* fatto su misura
made-up *a* artificiale, falso; *(cosmetics)* truccato
madly *adv* pazzamente
madness *n* pazzia, follia
Madonna *n* Madonna
madrigal *n* madrigale *m*
magazine *n* rivista; *(mil)* arsenale *m*; **powder** — polveriera
magenta *n&a* cremisi
maggot *n* verme *m*, baco; *(fig)* capriccio, ubbia
magic *n* magia; — *a* magico; **–al** *a* magico; **–ian** *n* mago; illusionista *m*
magistrate *n* magistrato
magnanimity *n* magnanimità
magnanimous *a* magnanimo
magnate *n* magnate *m*; *(coll)* pezzo grosso *(coll)*
magnesia *n* magnesia
magnesium *n* magnesio; — **light** luce al magnesio
magnet *n* calamita; **–ic** *a* magnetico; **–ic recorder** magnetofono; **–ism** *n* magnetismo; **–ize** calamitare, magnetizzare
magneto *n* magnete *m*
magnetohydrodynamics *npl (phy)* magnetoidrodinamica
magnetron *n* tubo catodico regolato con campo magnetico
magnification *n* amplificazione, ingrandimento
magnificence *n* magnificenza
magnificent *a* magnifico
magnify *vt* ingrandire, esagerare
magnifying *a* ingranditore; — *n* ingrandimento; — **glass** lente d'ingrandimento
magnitude *n* grandezza; **of the first** — di somma importanza
magpie *n* gazza
mahogany *n* mogano
maid *n* cameriera, donna di servizio; — **of honor** damigella d'onore; **old** — vecchia zitella
maiden *n* zitella; ragazza; vergine *f*; — **voyage** viaggio inaugurale; — *a* verginale, nubile; — **name** nome da signorina
mail *n (armor)* maglia di ferro
mail *n* posta, corriere *m*; **by return** — a giro di posta; — **delivery** distribuzione della posta; **registered** — posta raccomandata; **–box** *n* cassetta delle lettere; **–man** *n* portalettere *m*; — *vt* imbucare, impostare
mail-order house casa di commercio per corrispondenza
maim *vt* mutilare
main *n (utility)* conduttura principale; — *a* principale; — **office** ufficio principale, sede centrale; — **thing** l'essenziale, il principale; **–land** *n* continente *m*, terraferma; **–ly** *adv* principalmente; **–spring** *n* molla principale di meccanismo; *(fig)* causa basica; **–stay** *(naut)* straglio di maestra; *(fig)* appoggio principale
maintain *vt* sostenere; mantenere
maintenance *n* mantenimento, manutenzione
maize *n* granturco
majestic *a* maestoso; **–ally** *adv* maestosamente
majesty *n* maestà
majolica *n* maiolica
major *a* maggiore; — **general** *(mil)* maggiore generale; — *n (mil)* maggiore *m*; *(law)* maggiorenne *m*; **–domo** *n* maggiordomo; — *vi (study)* specializzarsi
majority *n* maggioranza
make *vt* fare; fabbricare; obbligare; costringere; — **a fool of** prendere per stupido; — **a living** guadagnarsi la vita; — **headway** progredire; — **a point** raggiungere lo scopo; — **believe** far finta di; dar ad intendere; — **no difference** non avere importanza; — **out** *(list, check)* compilare; *(document)* stendere; *(succeed)* riuscire; — **over** *(remake)* rifare; *(transfer)* trasmettere; — **ready** preparare, approntare; — **room** far posto; — **up** *(compose)* comporre; *(complete)* completare; *(reconcile)* fare la pace; — *n* fattura, fabbricazione; marca
make-believe *n* finzione, sembianza; — *a* finto
maker *n* fattore *m*
Maker *n* Creatore *m*
makeshift *n* espediente *m*; — *a* improvvisato
make-up *n (print)* impaginazione *f*; *(cosmetics)* truccatura; *(composition)* composizione, costituzione, struttura; *(theat)* trucco
making *n* fattura, creazione; struttura; **have the –s of** avere la stoffa di
maladjusted *a* inadatto
maladjustment *n* cattivo accomodamento, aggiustatura malfatta
maladroit *a* malaccorto
malady *n* malattia
malar *a* zigomatico; — *n* zigomo
malaria *n* malaria
malcontent *n&a* malcontento
male *a* maschile; — *n* maschio
malefactor *n* malfattore *m*
malevolent *a* malevolo
malfeasance *n* cattiva condotta, misfatto
malformation *n* malformazione, deformazione
malformed *a* deforme
malfunction *n* cattivo funzionamento; — *vi* funzionare male
malice *n* malizia, cattiveria; **with — aforethought** con premeditazione
malicious *a* malevolo, maligno; **–ness** *n* maliziosità
malign *vt* diffamare, calunniare

malignancy *n* malignità
malignant *a* maligno, nocivo
malinger *vi* fingersi ammalato
malleability *n* malleabilità
malleable *a* malleabile
mallet *n* mazzuola; martello di legno
malnutrition *n* denutrizione
malodorous *a* puzzolente
malpractice *n* negligenza professionale
malt *n* malto; **–ed** *a* di malto
Malta Malta
maltreat *vt* maltrattare; **–ment** *n* maltrattamento
mamma *n* mamma, madre *f*
mammal *n* mammifero
mammary *a* mammario
mammoth *n* mammut *m*; — *a (coll)* grande, enorme
man *n* uomo; **old** — vecchio; **young** — giovane *m*, giovanotto; **–hole** *n* chiusino; **–hood** *n* virilità, umanità; **–kind** *n* genere umano; umanità; **–liness** *n* virilità, mascolinità; fermezza virile; — *vt* equipaggiare; **–ly** *a* virile, mascolino, **–ly** *adv* virilmente
manacle *n* manetta; — *vt* ammanettare
manage *vt* dirigere, amministrare, manipolare; — *vi* arrangiarsi, cavarsela *(coll)*; **–able** *a* maneggevole, trattabile; **–ment** *n* direzione *f*; gestione *f*
manager *n* direttore *m*; **–ial** *a* direttivo
managing *a* gerente, amministratore
mandate *n* mandato
mandatory *a* impositorio, obbligatorio
mandible *n* mandibola
mandolin *n* mandolino
mane *n* criniera
man-eating *a* antropofago
maneuver *n* manovra; — *vt* manovrare
manganese *n* manganese *m*
mange *n* rogna, scabbia
manger *n* greppia; *(eccl)* presepio
mangle *n* mangano; — *vt (iron)* manganare; lacerare, sfigurare
mangy *a* scabbioso
manhandle *vt* malmenare
mania *n* mania, pazzia
maniac *n&a* maniaco
manicure *n* manicura; — *vt* far la manicura
manicurist *n* manicure *f*
manifest *n* manifesto; — *a* evidente; — *vt* manifestare; — *vi* manifestarsi; **–ation** *n* manifestazione
manifesto *n* proclama, manifesto
manifold *a* molteplice; multiforme; — *n (mech)* tubo collettore
manikin *n* manichino
manipulate *vt* manipolare
manipulation *n* manipolazione
manipulator *n* manipolatore *m*
manna *n* manna
manner *n* maniera; modo; aria; **in a — of speaking** per modo di dire; **in this** — in questo modo; **–ly** *a* cortese, educato; **–ism** *n* manierismo; **–s** *npl* modo di comportarsi; educazione
man-of-war *n* nave da guerra
manor *n* maniero; feudo, castello
mansion *n* casa signorile
manslaughter *n* omicidio preterintenzionale
mantel *n* mensola di camino
mantilla *n* mantiglia
mantle *n (cape)* mantello; manto; *(fireplace)* cappa
manual *a&n* manuale *m*; — **training** pratica apprendista
manufacture *n* fabbrica, manifattura; — *vt* manifatturare, fabbricare; **–r** *n* manifatturiere, fabbricante *m*
manufacturing *n* fabbricazione; — *a* manifatturante
manumit *vt* emancipare
manure *n* letame, concime *m*
manuscript *n* manoscritto
many *n&a* molti, tanti; **how —, so —** quanti; **as — as** tanti quanti; **too —** troppi
many-sided *a* con molti lati (*or* aspetti)
map *n* carta geografica; — **maker** *n* cartografo; — *vt* fare una carta di; — **out** tracciare; progettare in dettaglio
maple *n* acero
mar *vt (ruin)* guastare; *(spoil)* avariare; *(disfigure)* sfigurare; — *n* guasto, rovina, danno
maraschino *n* maraschino
marathon *n* maratona
marauder *n* predone, predatore *m*
marble *n* marmo; — *a* di marmo; **–d** *a* marmoreo, marmorizzato; — *vt* marmorare, marmorizzare
March *n* marzo
march *n* marcia; — *vi* marciare; — *vt* far marciare; — **by** sfilare
mare *n* giumenta
margarine *n* margarina
margin *n* margine *m*, orlo; — *(com)* deposito di garanzia marginale; **–al** *a* marginale
marginate *vt* marginare
marigold *n* fiorrancio
marimba *n* silofono
marinate *vt* marinare
marine *n* marinaio; **M– Corps** marina; — *a* marino, marittimo
mariner *n* marinaio
marionette *n* marionetta
marital *a* maritale
maritime *a* marittimo
marjoram *n* maggiorana
mark *n* segno; *(school)* voto, punto; *(target)* bersaglio; — **of distinction** segno di distinzione; **question** — punto interrogativo; — *vt* marcare; — **down** *(com)* diminuire il prezzo; — **time** segnare il passo; marcare il tempo; — **up** aumentare il prezzo; **–ed** *a* marcato, distinto, noto; **–er** *n* segnatore *m*; marcatore *m*; **–ing** *n* marchio; segno; **trade–** *n* marca di fabbrica
marked– *(as comp)* **—down** *a* a prezzo ribassato; **—up** *a* a prezzo aumentato
market *n* mercato; — **place** piazza del mercato; — **price** *(com)* prezzo di mercato; **–able** *a* mercantile, commerciabile; **on the** — sul mercato; — *vt* vendere
marketing *n* commercio; — **research** indagine di mercato
marksman *n* tiratore esperto

markup *n (com)* margine di rivendita
marmalade *n* marmellata
maroon *n&a (color)* marrone; — *vt* abbandonare su un'isola
marquee *n* pensilina
marquis *n* marchese *m*
marriage *n* matrimonio; **-able** *a* maritabile, in età da marito; — **license** dispensa di matrimonio
married *a* sposato; *(conjugal)* matrimoniale, coniugale; *(man)* ammogliato; *(woman)* maritata; **get** — sposarsi; — **couple** coniugi *mpl*
marrow *n* midollo
marry *vt* sposare; — *vi* sposarsi
Mars *n* Marte *m*
Marseilles Marsiglia
marsh *n* palude *f*; **-y** *a* paludoso
marshal *n* maresciallo; — **law** legge marziale; — *vt* ordinare; mettere in ordine; — **one's forces** riunire le forze
marshmallow *n (bot)* altea
marsupial *n&a* marsupiale *m*
mart *n* mercato, centro commerciale
marten *n* martora
martial *a* marziale
Martian *a&n* marziano
martinet *n* rigorista *m*
martyr *n* martire *m&f*; **-dom** *n* martirio; — *vt* martirizzare
marvel *n* meraviglia; — *vt* meravigliare; — *vi* meravigliarsi; **-ous** *a* meraviglioso; **-ously** *adv* meravigliosamente
marzipan *n* marzapane *m*
mascara *n* rimmel *m*
mascot *n* mascotte *f*; *(charm)* talismano, portafortuna *m*
masculine *a* maschile
masculinity *n* maschilità, mascolinità
mash *vt* ridurre in polpa, pestare; **-ed** *a* ridotto in poltiglia, schiacciato; passato
mask *n* maschera; — *vt* mascherare
masochism *n* masochismo
mason *n* muratore *m*
masquerade *n* mascherata; *(dance)* ballo in maschera; — *vi* mascherarsi
mass *n* massa, mucchio; — **meeting** comizio; — **production** produzione in massa; **-es** *npl (people)* masse popolari; — *vt* ammassare; — *vi* ammassarsi
Mass *n* Santa Messa
massacre *n* massacro; — *vt* massacrare
massage *n* massaggio; — *vt* massaggiare
masseur *n* massaggiatore *m*
massive *a* massivo
mast *n (naut)* albero
master *n* padrone; maestro *m*; — **hand** mano maestra; — **key** chiave maestra; — **of ceremonies** maestro di cerimonie; — **stroke** colpo maestro; **-ly** *a* magistrale; abile; **-ful** prepotente; **-piece** *n* capolavoro; **-y** *n* possesso; padronanza; maestria; — *vt* dominare
mastermind *n* genio, mente superiore; — *vt* organizzare, dirigere
masticate *vt* masticare
mastication *n* masticazione
mastiff *n* mastino
mastoid *n* mastoide *f*; — *a* mastoideo
mat *n* stuoia; **door** — zerbino; **table** — sottopiatto; **-ted** *a* arruffato; intrecciato
mat *a* opaco
match *n* simile *m*; *(matrimonial)* partito; *(sport)* partita, gara; — *vt (marry)* maritare; *(couple)* accoppiare; *(agree)* accordare; — *vi* maritarsi; **-less** *a* incomparabile
match *n (flame)* fiammifero; **book -es** fiammiferi Minerva *(coll)*
matchbox *n* scatola di fiammiferi
matchmaker *n* combinatore di matrimoni
mate *n* sposo; compagno; *(naut)* secondo di bordo; — *vt&i* accoppiare; accoppiarsi, unirsi
material *a* materiale; — *n* materia, stoffa; materiali *mpl*; **raw —s** materie prime *fpl*; **-ism** materialismo; **-ist** materialista *m*; **-ize** *vi* realizzarsi; **-ly** *adv* materialmente
maternal *a* materno
maternity *n* maternità
mathematical *a* matematico
mathematician *n* matematico
mathematics *npl* matematica
matinee *n* mattinata; rappresentazione diurna
matriarch *n* materfamilias *f*
matriculate *vt* immatricolare; — *vi* immatricolarsi
matriculation *n* immatricolazione
matrimonial *a* matrimoniale
matrimony *n* matrimonio
matrix *n* matrice *f*
matron *n* matrona; *(caretaker)* sorvegliante *f*
matter *n* materia; soggetto; *(med)* pus *m*; **it does not** — non importa; **What is the —?** Cosa c'è?, Che succede?; **as a — of fact** in verità, in realtà; **no — what** non importa che; — *vi* importare; *(med)* produrre pus
matter-of-fact *a* prosaico; effettivo
matting *n (floor covering)* stuoia
mattress *n* materasso; **innerspring** — materasso a molle
mature *a* maturo; — *vt&i* maturare; *(com)* scadere
maturity *n* maturità; *(com)* scadenza
maudlin *a* piagnucoloso, sentimentalone
maul *n* mazza; — *vt* malmenare, stracciare
mausoleum *n* mausoleo
maverick *n* vitello *(or* puledro) non marcato; *(fig)* individuo indipendente
mawkish *a* sdolcinato
maxim *n* massima, principio
maximum *a&n* massimo
May *n* maggio
may *vi* potere, esser possibile; **it — be** può darsi; forse; può essere
maybe *adv* forse
mayhem *n* sfregio
mayonnaise *n* maionese *f*
mayor *n* sindaco
maze *n* labirinto
M.C., Master of Ceremonies presentatore *m*; maestro di cerimonie
M.D., Doctor of Medicine dottore in medicina
me *pron* me, mi
meadow *n* prato
meager *a* scarso
meal *n* pasto; *(grain)* farina; **-time** *n*

ora del pasto; **–y** *a* farinoso
mean *a* cattivo, vile; meschino; avaro; *(average)* mediocre, medio; — *n* medio, mezzo; *(math)* media; — *vt&i* significare, voler dire; **–ness** *n* inferiorità; spregevolezza; avarizia
meander *vi* vagare; serpeggiare; — *n* meandro
meaning *n* significato; **–ful** *a* pieno di significato; **–fulness** *n* significanza; **–less** *a* senza significato
means *npl* mezzi; **by all** — senz'altro, certamente; **by — of** per mezzo di; **by no** — niente affatto
meantime *n* frattempo; — *adv* nel frattempo, frattanto
meanwhile *adv* intanto
measles *npl* morbillo
measly *a (coll)* insignificante
measurable *a* misurabile
measurably *adv* misurabilmente
measure *n* misura; **in some** — in parte; **–ment** *n* misura, dimensione; — *vt* misurare
meat *n* carne *f*; *(fig)* il punto più importante; **–ball** *n* polpetta; **–less** *a* senza carne; **–man** *n* macellaio; **–market** *n* macelleria; **–y** *a* carnoso
mechanic *n* meccanico, macchinista *m*; **–s** *npl* meccanica
mechanical *a* meccanico; — **engineer** ingegnere meccanico; — **engineering** ingegneria meccanica
mechanism *n* meccanismo
mechanize *vt* meccanizzare
medal *n* medaglia
medallion *n* medaglione *m*
meddle *vi* ingerirsi, immischiarsi; ficcare il naso *(fig)*
meddlesome *a* intrigante; intromettente; — **person** ficcanaso
media *npl* mezzi *mpl*; **advertising** — veicoli pubblicitari
median *a&n* medio; mediano
mediate *vt* intercedere; arbitrare; far da moderatore
mediation *n* mediazione
mediator *n* mediatore *m*, intermediario
medical *a* medico; — **examination** visita medica; — **school** facoltà di medicina
medicate *vt* medicare
medication *n* medicatura
medicinal *a* medicinale
medicine *n* medicina; — **chest** cassetta di medicinali; — **dropper** contagocce *m*; — **man** stregone *m*
medieval *a* medioevale
mediocre *a* mediocre
mediocrity *n* mediocrità
meditate *vt&i* contemplare, meditare; *(plan)* tramare
meditation *n* meditazione
meditative *a* meditativo
Mediterranean *a* mediterraneo; — **Sea** mare mediterraneo
medium *n* mezzo; *(spiritualist)* medium *m*; — *a* medio, mediano
medium-sized *a* di media dimensione *or* grandezza
medley *n* mescolanza, miscuglio; farragine *f*
medulla *n (anat)* midollo
meek *a* mite, docile; **–ness** *n* mansuetudine, mitezza
meerschaum *n* schiuma di mare
meet *n* raduno; — *a* appropriato; convenevole; — *vt* incontrare; *(acquaintance)* far la conoscenza di; soddisfare; — *vi* riunirsi; incontrarsi; — **with** incontrarsi con; **go to** — andare incontro a; **make both ends** — *(fig)* sbarcare il lunario
meeting *n (reunion)* riunione *f*; assemblea; *(encounter)* incontro; — **place** ritrovo
megaphone *n* megafono
megaton *n* megatonnellata
melancholy *a* melanconico; — *n* melanconia
meld *n (card)* dichiarazione; — *vt* unire; — *vi* fondersi; *(cards)* dichiararsi
mellow *a* tenero; succoso; maturo; — *vt* maturare; *(soften)* ammorbidire; — *vi* maturarsi; ammorbidirsi
mellowing *n* maturazione; — *a* maturante
mellowness *n* maturità
melodious *a* melodioso
melodrama *n* melodramma *m*
melodramatic *a* melodrammatico
melody *n* melodia
melon *n* melone, popone *m*
melt *vt* fondere, sciogliere; — *vi* fondersi, sciogliersi
melting *n* fusione; liquefazione; *(fig)* intenerimento; — *a* fondente; — **point** punto di fusione; — **pot** crogiuolo
member *n* membro; socio; **–ship** *n* insieme di soci
membrane *n* membrana
memento *n* memento, ricordo, nota
memorable *a* memorabile
memorandum, memo *n* memorandum *m*, appunto
memorial *n* monumento; commemorazione; — *a* commemorativo
memorize *vt* imparare a memoria
memory *n* memoria, ricordo; **commit to** — imparare a memoria
menace *n* minaccia; — *vt* minacciare
menacing *a* minacciante; **–ly** minacciosamente
menagerie *n* serraglio
mend *vt* riparare; raccomodare; — *vi* migliorare
mendable *a* riparabile
mendicant *n&a* mendicante *m*
mending *n* accomodamento, rammendo, riparazione
menial *a* servile, basso
meningitis *n* meningite *f*
meniscus *n* menisco
menopause *n* menopausa
menstruate *vi* aver mestrui
menstruation *n* mestruazione
mental *a* mentale; — **hospital** *n* manicomio
mentality *n* mentalità
mention *n* menzione; — *vt* menzionare; **don't — it** prego; si figuri; niente
mentor *n* mentore *m*
menu *n* carta, lista delle vivande
mercantile *a* mercantile
mercantilism *n* mercantilismo

mercenary *n&a* mercenario
mercerize *vt* mercerizzare
merchandise *n* mercanzia; — *vt&i* commerciare
merchant *n* commerciante *m*; **–man** *n* nave mercantile; — **marine** marina mercantile
merciful *a* pio; misericordioso
merciless *a* spietato
mercurial *a* mercuriale
mercury *n* mercurio
mercy *n* misericordia; clemenza; **at the — of** alla mercè di; **have — on** aver pietà di; aver misericordia di; — **killing** eutanasia
mere *a* solo; semplice; **–ly** *adv* puramente; solamente
merge *vt&i* unire, fondere, fondersi, unirsi; **–r** *n* assorbimento; incorporamento
meridian *n&a* meridiano
meringue *n* meringa
merit *n* merito; — *vt* meritare; **–orious** *a* meritorio; *(person)* meritevole
mermaid *n* sirena
merman *n* tritone *m*
merrily *adv* allegramente
merriment *n* allegria, festevolezza
merry *a* gaio, allegro; **–making** *n* festa; divertimento
merry-go-round *n* carosello, giostra
mesa *n* altipiano
mesh *n* maglia; — *vt&i* ingranare; **in —** in ingranaggio
mesmerize *vt* ipnotizzare
mess *n (mil, naut)* mensa, rancio; — **hall** mensa; — **kit** gavetta e stoviglie da campo
mess *n (dirt)* sporcizia; *(muss)* impiccio; guazzabuglio; *(trouble)* imbroglio; pasticcio *(fig)*; — *vt* sporcare; imbrogliare; **–y** *a* confuso, in disordine
message *n* messaggio
messenger *n* messaggero, fattorino
Messiah *n* Messia *m*
metabolic *a* metabolico
metabolism *n* metabolismo
metal *n* metallo; **—, –lic** *a* metallico
metallurgist *n* metallurgico
metallurgy *n* metallurgia
metamorphose *vt* metamorfosare; — *vi* metamorfosarsi
metamorphosis *a* metamorfosi *f*
metaphor *n* metafora
metaphysical *a* metafisico
metaphysics *npl* metafisica
metatarsal *a* metatarsico
mete *vt* distribuire
meteor *n* meteora; **–ic** *a* meteorico; **–ite** meteorite *f*; **–ological** *a* meteorologico; **–ologist** *n* meteorologo; **–ology** *n* meteorologia
meter *n (distance)* metro; *(device)* contatore, misuratore *m*
method *n* metodo; **–ical** *a* metodico
methyl *n (chem)* metile *m*
meticulous *a* meticoloso
metric *a* metrico; — **system** sistema decimale
metronome *n* metronomo
metropolis *n* metropoli *f*
metropolitan *a* metropolitano
mettle *n* ardore *m*, coraggio, foga
mew *n* miagolio; — *vi* miagolare
Mexican *a&n* messicano
Mexico Messico
mezzanine *n* mezzanino
microbe *n* microbo
microbiology *n* microbiologia
microcosm *n* microcosmo
microfilm *n* microfilm *m*; — *vt* microfilmare
microgroove *n* microsolco
micrometer *n* micrometro
microorganism *n* microrganismo
microphone *n* microfono
microscope *n* microscopio
microscopic, –al *a* microscopico
microwave *n* micro-onda
mid *a* di mezzo, medio; **–day** *n* mezzodì *m*; **–night** *n* mezzanotte *f*
middle *n* mezzo; — **class** borghesia; **–man** *n* intermediario; **–weight** *n (sport)* peso medio
middle-aged *a* di mezz'età
Middle Ages *npl* medioevo
middle-class *a* borghese
middling *a* mediocre; benino
midget *n&a* nano
midriff *n* diaframma *m*
midshipman *n* guardiamarina *m*
midst *n* mezzo; **in the — of** nel mezzo di
midsummer *n* mezza estate
midway *a* a metà strada; intermedio; — *adv* a mezza strada
midwife *n* levatrice *f*
midwinter *n* cuore dell'inverno
mien *n* aria, aspetto, cera
might *n* potere *m*; — **and main** tutte le forze; **–y** *a* potente
migraine *n* emicrania
migrant *n* emigrante, migratore *m*; — *a* migratore
migrate *vi* migrare, emigrare
migration *n* migrazione, emigrazione
migratory *a* migratorio
Milan Milano
milch *a* lattifero
mild *a* mite; **–ly** *adv* mitemente; **–ness** *n* mitezza, dolcezza
mildew *n* muffa; — *vt* macchiare; far ammuffire; — *vi* ammuffirsi
mile *n* miglio; **–stone** *n* pietra miliare
mileage *n* chilometraggio; distanza in miglia
militant *a* militante
militarism *n* militarismo
military *a* militare
militate *vi* militare; combattere
militia *n* milizia
milk *n* latte *m*; — **sugar** lattosio; **–man** *n* lattaio; — *vt* mungere
milky *a* latteo; **the M– Way** la Via Lattea
milksop *n* uomo effeminato
mill *n* mulino; **–stone** *n* mola, macina; — *vt* macinare; *(money)* zigrinare; *(wood)* modellare
millennium *n* millennio
millepede *n* millepiedi *m*
miller *n* mugnaio
milligram *n* milligrammo
millimeter *n* millimetro

milliner *n* modista; **–y** *n* modisteria
million *n* milione *m*; **–aire** *n* milionario; **–th** *a* milionesimo
mime *n* mima; *(person)* mimo; — *vt* mimare
mimeograph *n* mimeografo; ciclostile *m*; — *vt* mimeografare
mimic *n* mimo; — *a* mimico; — *vt* imitare, fare la mimica di; **–ry** *n* mimica
minaret *n* minareto
mince *vt* tritare, tagliuzzare; *(weaken)* indebolire; — *vi* camminare affettatamente — **words** mangiarsi le parole; **–d meat** carne tritata
mind *n* mente *f*; spirito; intenzione; — **reader** che legge il pensiero altrui; **bear in** — tener presente; **be of one** — essere d'accordo; **change one's** — cambiar di parere *or* d'opinione; **have in** — aver in mente, ricordarsi; **make up one's** — decidersi; **peace of** — tranquillità d'animo; **state of** — stato d'animo; **of no** — di nessuna importanza; **–ful** *a* attento; memore; — *vt (heed)* badare a; *(dislike)* dispiacersi; *(look after)* curare
mine *pron* il mio, la mia, i miei, le mie
mine *n* miniera; — **field** campo minato; — **sweeper** dragamine *m*; **–r** *n* minatore *m*; — *vt* minare; *(minerals)* scavare
mineral *a&n* minerale *m*; **–ogist** *n* mineralogo; **–ogy** *n* mineralogia
mingle *vt&i* mischiare; mischiarsi
miniature *n* miniatura; — *a* in miniatura, in piccolo
minimize *vt* sottovalutare, diminuire; dar poca importanza a
minimum *a&n* minimo
mining *n* industria mineraria; — *a* minerario
minion *n* favorito
minister *n* ministro; pastore evangelico; — *vi* soddisfare le necessità
ministry *n (eccl)* sacerdozio; *(pol)* ministero
mink *n* visone *m*
minor *a&n* minorenne *m&f*
minority *n* minoranza
minstrel *n* menestrello
mint *n (bot)* menta; *(fig)* tesoro; *(money)* zecca; — *vt* coniare
minuet *n* minuetto
minus *prep* meno; *(coll)* senza; *n (quantity)* quantità negativa; *(sign)* segno di sottrazione
minute *n* minuto; istante *m*; **any** — da un momento all'altro; — **hand** lancetta dei minuti; **this** — immediatamente
minute *a* minuto, piccolo
minx *n* birichina, sbarazzina
miracle *n* miracolo; — **worker** taumaturgo
miraculous *a* miracoloso
mirage *n* miraggio
mire *n* fango, pantano; — *vt* infangare; — *vi* impantanarsi
mirror *n* specchio; **rear-view** — specchio retrovisivo; — *vt* riflettere; rispecchiare
mirth *n* allegria; ilarità; **–ful** *a* gaio
misadventure *n* disavventura
misalliance *n* cattiva alleanza; matrimonio mal riuscito
misanthrope *n* misantropo
misanthropic *a* misantropico
misapplied *a* mal applicato
misapplication *n* cattiva applicazione
misapprenhension *n* malinteso; equivoco
misappropriate *vt* usare abusivamente
misappropriation *n* appropriazione indebita
misbehave *vi* comportarsi male
misbehavior *n* cattiva condotta
miscalculate *vt* calcolare male; — *vi* sbagliarsi nel calcolo
miscalculation *n* errore di calcolo
miscarriage *n* errore *m*; fiasco; *(med)* aborto; — **of justice** errore giudiziario
miscarry *vi* fallire; *(med)* abortire
miscellaneous *a* miscellaneo
mischance *n* sfortuna
mischief *n* danno; cattiveria; male *m*; *(person)* birichino; *(prank)* birichinata
mischievous *a* dannoso, nocivo; birichino
misconception *n* malinteso; idea sbagliata
misconduct *n* cattiva condotta *or* gestione
misconstruction *n* errata interpretazione
misconstrue *vt* mal interpretare, fraintendere
miscount *n* conto sbagliato
miscreant *n&a* scellerato
misdeal *n* cattiva distribuzione; — *vt&i* distribuire male
misdeed *n* misfatto
misdemeanor *n* reato non grave
misdirect *vt* indirizzare (*or* dirigere) male
miser *n* avaro
miserly *a* avaro
miserable *a* infelice; pietoso; sciagurato
misery *n* angoscia; miseria
misfire *vi* far cilecca
misfit *n* fuori-luogo *m*; pesce fuor d'acqua *(fig)*
misfortune *n* sfortuna; disgrazia
misgiving *n* presentimento, timore *m*, sospetto
misguide *vt* fuorviare, sviare; dirigere male; **–d** *a* maldiretto
mishap *n* incidente *m*
misinform *vt* informare male
misinterpret *vt* interpretare male
misinterpretation *n* malinteso
misjudge *vt* mal giudicare
mislay *vt* mal collocare; *(lose)* smarrire
mislead *vt* fuorviare; **–ing** *a* ingannevole
mismanage *vt* amministrar male
mismanagement *n* cattiva gestione *or* amministrazione
mismatch *vt* assortire male
misnomer *n* uso errato di un titolo *or* nome
misogamist *n* misogamo
misprint *n* errore di stampa; — *vt* stampare erroneamente
mispronounce *vt* pronunziare male
misquote *vt* citare erroneamente
misrepresent *vt* mal rappresentare; **–ation** alterazione
misrule *n* malgoverno; — *vt* governare male
Miss *n* signorina
miss *n* colpo mancato; — *vt* mancare;

(person) rimpiangere; *(train)* perdere
misshapen *a* mal fatto
missile *n* missile *m*, razzo; **guided** — missile telecomandato; — **base** *n* base per missili
missing *a* mancante, disperso
mission *n* missione; **–ary** *n* missionario
missive *n* missiva
misspell *vt&i* compitar male; fare errori d'ortografia
misstate *vt* travisare, esporre erroneamente
misstatement *n* affermazione sbagliata
misstep *n* passo falso
mist *n* bruma; nebbia; **–y** *a* nebbioso; *(fig)* oscuro
mistake *n* errore *m*; sbaglio; — *vt* sbagliare, confondere; **make a** — commetter uno sbaglio
mistaken *a* erroneo; sbagliato
mistimed *a* intempestivo
mistranslate *vt* tradurre male
mistranslation *n* traduzione errata
mistreat *vt* maltrattare; **–ment** *n* maltrattamento
mistress *n* direttrice *f*; *(paramour)* amante *f*
mistrust *n* diffidenza; — *vt* diffidare di; **–ful** *a* diffidente
misunderstand *vt* fraintendere, capir male; **–ing** *n* malinteso
misunderstood *a* malinteso, frainteso
misuse *n* cattivo uso; abuso
misuse *vt* abusare; usar male
mite *n* pochettino; cosa piccolissima
miter *n (eccl)* mitra; *(joint)* ugna; — **box** ugnatura; — *vt* commettere a triangolo
mitigate *vt* mitigare
mitigating *a* mitigante
mitigation *n* mitigamento, mitigazione
mitten *n* mezzo guanto
mix *n* miscela; — *vt* mischiare, confondere; — *vi* mischiarsi; **–ed** *a* mischiato, mescolato; misto
mixed-up *a* confuso
mixture *n* mescolanza, miscuglio
mix-up *n* confusione, guazzabuglio
mizzenmast *n* albero di mezzana
moan *n* lamento; — *vi* lamentarsi, gemere; — *vt* piangere, lamentare
moat *n* fossato
mob *n* folla, canaglia; — *vt* assalire in tumulto; — *vi* tumultuare
mobile *a* mobile
mobility *n* mobilità
mobilization *n* mobilitazione
moccasin *n* mocassino
mock *a* falso, finto; — *vt* canzonare, deridere; **–ery** *n* canzonatura, beffa; **–ing** *a* canzonatorio
modal *a* modale
mode *n* modo, maniera; *(fashion)* moda
model *n* modello, campione *m*; *(artist)* modella; *(mannequin)* indossatrice *f*; — *vt* modellare, plasmare; — *vi* posare, fare la modella; — *a* esemplare
moderate *a* moderato
moderate *vt* moderare; — *vi* moderarsi
moderation *n* moderazione
modern *n* moderno; **–ize** *vt* modernizzare; **–istic** *a* modernista, modernistico
modest *a* modesto; **–y** *n* modestia
modicum *n* quantità modica
modification *n* modifica, modificazione
modify *vt* modificare
modulate *vt* modulare
modulation *n* modulazione
Mohammedan *n&a* maomettano; **–ism** *n* islamismo
moist *a* umido; **–ness** *n* umidità; **–ure** *n* umidità; **–en** *vt* umettare
molar *a&n* molare *m*
molasses *n* melassa
mold *n* stampo; modello; *(bot)* muffa; — *vt* modellare; — *vi* ammuffire; **–y** *a* ammuffito, muffoso; **–iness** *n* muffa
molding *n* formatura, getto, modellazione; *(trim)* modanatura
mole *n* neo; *(zool)* talpa
molecular *a* molecolare; — **biology** biologia molecolare
molecule *n* molecola
molehill *n* tana di talpa; **make a mountain out of a** — fare di una paglia un trave *(fig)*
moleskin *n* pelle di talpa
molest *vt* molestare
mollify *vt* ammollire
mollusk *n* mollusco
molt *vi* mudare, rimpiumarsi; **–en** *a* fuso
mollycoddle *n* vezzeggiato
moment *n* momento; **–ary** *a* momentaneo; **–arily** *adv* momentaneamente; **–ous** *a* critico, decisivo
momentum *n* impulso
monarch *n* monarca *m;* **–y** *n* monarchia
monastery *n* monastero, convento
monastic *a* monastico
Monday *n* lunedì *m*
monetary *a* monetario
money *n* danaro, moneta; *(paper)* banconota; *(counterfeit)* moneta falsa; — **box** salvadanaio; — **order** vaglia; **ready** — danaro contante; **–ed** *a* ricco
money-making *a* redditizio
mongrel *n* meticcio; — *a* meticcio, ibrido
monitor *n (class)* capoclasse *m*; *(rad)* monitore *m*
monk *n* monaco, frate *m*
monkey *n* scimmia; — **wrench** chiave inglese; — *vi (coll)* gingillarsi; — **with** toccare, manomettere
monochromatic *a* monocromatico
monocle *n* monocolo
monogamist *n* monogamo
monogamous *a* monogamo
monogamy *n* monogamia
monogram *n* monogramma *m*
monograph *n* monografia
monologue *n* monologo
monomania *n* monomania
monoplane *n* monoplano
monopolistic *a* monopolista
monopolize *vt* monopolizzare
monopoly *n* monopolio
monorail *n* monovia
monosyllabic *a* monosillabico
monosyllable *n* monosillabo
monotonous *a* monotono
monotony *n* monotonia
monotype *n (print)* monotipo *f*
monoxide *n* monossido; **carbon** — ossido

carbonico
monsoon *n* monsone *m*
monster *n* mostro; — *a* enorme
monstrance *n (eccl)* ostensorio
monstrosity *n* mostruosità
monstrous *a* mostruoso
montage *n* fotomontaggio
month *n* mese *m*; **–'s allowance** quota mensile; **once a —** una volta al mese; **–ly** *a* mensile; **–ly** *adv* mensilmente
monument *n* monumento; **–al** *a* monumentale
moo *vi* muggire
mood *n* umore *m*; disposizione, stato d'animo; *(gram)* modo; **–y** *a* scontroso, mutevole, di cattivo umore; **be in the — to** essere in vena di
moodiness *n* scontrosità, mutevolezza
moon *n* luna; — *vi* bighellonare; **–light** *n* chiaro di luna
moonbeam *n* raggio di luna
moonstruck *a* lunatico
moor *n* moro; **–ish** *a* moresco
moor *n* brughiera, landa; — *vt (naut)* ormeggiare, amarrare; — *vi* ormeggiarsi; **–ing** *n* ormeggio
moose *n* alce *m*
moot *a* discutibile
mop *n* radazza; *(hair)* zazzera; — *vt* radazzare
mope *vi* essere malinconico, avere la luna *(fig)*
moral *a&n* morale *f*; **–s** costumi *mpl*; **–ist** *n* moralista *m*; **–ly** *adv* moralmente **–ize** *vt&i* moralizzare; **–ity** *n* moralità
morale *n* morale *m*, stato d'anima
morass *n* palude *f*
moratorium *n* moratoria
morbid *a* malsano; morboso
more *a* più, maggiore; — *adv* più, ancora; **all the —** al massimo; **not any —** non più; **once —** ancora una volta; **— and —** più e più; **— or less** più o meno **–over** *adv* inoltre, per giunta, di più
mores *npl* usanze *fpl*
morgue *n* camera mortuaria
moribund *a* moribondo
Mormon *n&a* mormone *m*
morning *n* mattina, mattino; — *a* del mattino
moron *n* idiota *m&f*; **–ic** *a* idiota
morose *a* burbero; orso *(fig)*; **–ness** *n* scontrosità
morphine *n* morfina
morsel *n* pezzetto
mortal *a&n* mortale *m*; **–ly** *adv* mortalmente, a morte; **–ity** *n* mortalità
mortar *n* mortaio; *(arch)* malta
mortgage *n* ipoteca; — *vt* ipotecare
mortician *n* impresario di pompe funebri
mortification *n* mortificazione; *(med)* cancrena
mortify *vt* mortificare
mortuary *n* camera mortuaria; — *a* mortuario
mosaic *n&a* mosaico
Moscow Mosca
Moslem *n&a* mussulmano, maomettano
mosque *n* moschea
mosquito *n* zanzara; **— netting** zanzariera
moss *n* musco; **–y** *a* muschioso
most *a* il più, la maggior parte di; — *adv* molto, il più; **at the —** tutt'al più; **for the — part** nella maggior parte; **— likely** probabilmente; **— of all** sopratutto; **–ly** *adv* principalmente
motel *n* autostello
moth *n* falena; *(clothes)* tarma; **— ball** naftalina in palline
mother *n* madre *f*; **–hood** *n* maternità; **–less** *a* orfano di madre; **–ly** *a* materno; **— tongue** lingua materna; — *vt* dar vita a; fare da madre a
mother-in-law *n* suocera
mother-of-pearl *n* madreperla
motif *n* motivo
motion *n* moto, movimento; *(parliamentary)* mozione; **— picture** pellicola cinematografica, film *m*; — *vt* fare segno; far cenno a; **–less** *a* immobile
motivate *vt* motivare, cagionare
motive *n* motivo
motley *a* multicolore; screziato, eterogeneo
motor *n* motore *m*; **–boat** *n* motoscafo; **–bus** *n* autobus *m*; **–cade** *n* sfilata di automezzi; **–car** *n* automobile *f*; **–cycle** *n* motocicletta; **–ist** *n* automobilista *m*; **–man** *n* manovratore *m*; **–scooter** *n* motoretta
motorize *vt* motorizzare
mottle *vt* screziare; macchiare; **–d** *a* screziato; chiazzato
motto *n* divisa, motto
mound *n (pile)* tumulo; *(small hill)* poggio, collinetta
mount *n* monte *m*; *(horse)* cavalcatura; — *vt* ascendere, salire; *(horse)* montare; *(gem)* incastonare; — *vi* salire, innalzarsi; **–ed** *a* montato
mountain *n* montagna; monte *m*; **— climber** alpinista *m*; **— climbing** alpinismo; **— range** catena di montagne; **–eer** *n* montanaro; **–ous** *a* montuoso
mountebank *n* saltimbanco
mounting *n* montaggio; ascensione; *(gem)* incastonatura; — *a* montante; ascendente
mourn *vt&i* piangere, rimpiangere; **–ful** *a* lugubre, triste; **–er** *n* dolente *m&f*; infelice *m&f*
mourning *n* lutto; — *a* dolente, afflitto; **go into —** prendere il lutto
mouse *n* topo; **–trap** *n* trappola per topi; **–y** *a* come un topo
moustache *n* baffi *mpl*
mouth *n (anat)* bocca; *(river)* foce *f*; **by word of —** a viva voce; **make the — water** far venire l'acquolina in bocca; **— organ** armonica; **–piece** *n* imboccatura; — *vt* declamare; mettere in bocca; — *vi* parlare gonfio; **–ful** *n* boccone *m*
movable *a* mobile
move *n* movimento; *(household)* trasloco; *(game)* mossa; **–r** *n* motore *m*; *(household)* traslocatore *m*; **–ment** *n* movimento; — *vt* muovere, far muovere; *(emotions)* commuovere; — *vi* muoversi; progredire; traslocare; **— away** allontanare; **— off** togliere, rimuovere; **— out** portar fuori
movie *n (coll)* pellicola cinematografica;

–s *npl (coll)* cinema *m*
moving *n* movimento; trasloco; — **van** carro-trasporti (*or* traslochi) *m*; — *a* mobile; *(emotional)* commovente
mow *vt* falciare; — **the grass** tagliare l'erba
Mr., Mister *n* signor, signore *m*
Mrs., Missis *n* signora
much *a&adv* molto; **as — as** tanto quanto; **how —** quanto; **so —** tanto; **too —** troppo; **very —** moltissimo; **make — of** dare molta importanza a
mucilage *n* mucillagine *f*
muck *n* letame *m*, fango
mucous *n* mucoso
mucus *n* muco
mud *n* fango
muddle *vt* confondere, far pasticci; — *n* imbroglio, confusione
muddy *a* fangoso; — *vt* intorbidare, infangare
mudguard *n* parafango
muff *n* manicotto; — *vt* impasticciare
muffin *n* panino
muffle *vt* avviluppare, coprire; *(sound)* soffocare
muffler *n* sciarpa da collo; *(auto)* silenziatore *m*
mug *n* boccale *m*
muggy *a* umido
mule *n* mulo
muleteer *n* mulattiere *m*
mulish *a* di mulo; testardo
mull *n* mussola; — *vt (wine)* aromatizzare; — *vt&i (coll)* meditare, ruminare *(fig)*
multicolored *a* multicolore
multigraph *n* ciclostile *m*
multiple *a&n* multiplo
multiplex *a* molteplice, multiplo
multiplication *n* moltiplicazione; — **table** tavola pitagorica
multiplicity *n* molteplicità
multiply *vt* moltiplicare; — *vi* moltiplicarsi
multistage rocket *(aesp)* razzo plurifasico
multitude *n* moltitudine *f*
mumble *vt&i* borbottare
mummify *vt* mummificare
mummy *n* mummia
mumps *npl* orecchioni *mpl*
munch *vt&i* masticare
mundane *a* mondano
municipal *a* municipale
municipality *n* comune *m*, municipio
munificence *n* munificenza
munificent *a* munificente
munitions *npl* munizioni *fpl*
mural *n* pittura murale; — *a* murale
murder *n* omicidio premeditato; — *vt* assassinare; **–er** *n* assassino; **–ess** *n* assassina; **–ous** *a* micidiale
murky *a* nero, oscuro, tenebroso
murmur *n* mormorio; — *vt&i* mormorare
muscatel *n* moscato
muscle *n* muscolo
muscle-bound *a* dai muscoli induriti
muscular *a* muscolare; — **dystrophy** distrofia muscolare
muscularity *n* muscolosità
musculature *n* muscolatura
muse *n* musa; — *vt&i* riflettere, meditare
museum *n* museo
mush *n* polenta, poltiglia; **–y** *a (coll)* sentimentale; — *vi* viaggiare con slitta tirata da cani
mushroom *n* fungo
music *n* musica; — **hall** sala-concerti *f*; **–al** *a* musicale; **–ally** *adv* musicalmente
musicale *n* programma musicale in una riunione
musing *n* meditazione; fantasticheria
musk *n* muschio
musket *n* moschetto; **–eer** *n* moschettiere *m*
muskrat *n* ondatra
muss *n (coll)* disordine *m*; — *vt (coll)* mettere in disordine; **–y** *a (coll)* in disordine; sciatto
mussel *n* dattero di mare
must *n (wine)* mosto; *(bot)* muffa; **–iness** *n* muffa; **–y** *a* ammuffitto; — *vi* ammuffire, ammuffirsi; *(obligation)* dovere
mustard *n* mostarda, senape *f*; — **plaster** senapismo
muster *n* appello; — *vt (mil)* adunare; **to — courage** farsi coraggio
mutability *n* mutabilità
mutable *a* mutabile, mutevole
mutation *n* cambiamento, mutazione
mute *n* muto; *(mus)* sordina; — *a* muto; — *vt* mettere la sordina; **–d** *a* silenziato; *(mus)* in sordina
mutilate *vt* mutilare
mutilation *n* mutilazione
mutinous *a* ammutinato, sedizioso
mutiny *n* ammutinamento; — *vi* ammutinarsi
mutter *vt&i* mormorare
mutton *n* montone *m*, castrato
mutual *a* mutuo
muzzle *n (animal nose)* muso; *(device)* museruola; *(gun)* bocca; — *vt* imbavagliare; far tacere
my *a* il mio, la mia, i miei, le mie
myopia *n* miopia
myopic *a* miope
myosin *n* miosina
myriad *n* miriade *f*; — *a* innumerabile
myrrh *n* mirra
myrtle *n* mirto
myself *pron* me, mi, me stesso
mysterious *a* misterioso
mystery *n* mistero
mystic *n&a* mistico; **–al** *a* mistico; **–ism** *n* misticismo
mystification *n* mistificazione
mystified *a* mistificato
mystify *vt* mistificare
myth *n* mito; **–ical** *a* mitico; **–ological** *a* mitologico; **–ology** *n* mitologia

N

nab *vt (coll)* acchiappare
nacelle *n (avi)* navicella
nag *n* ronzino; — *vt* rimbrottare
nagging *n* rimbrotto; — *a* rimbrottante

nail *n* chiodo; *(finger)* unghia; — **file** lima per le unghie; — **polish** smalto per le unghie; **hit the — on the head** *(fig)* colpire giusto; mettere un dito sulla piaga *(fig)*; — *vt* inchiodare
naive *a* ingenuo
naked *a* nudo; **–ness** *n* nudità
namby-pamby *a* insulso
name *n* nome *m*, rappresentazione; **–sake** *n* omonimo; **–plate** *n* placca per il nome; **–less** *a* senza nome; **–ly** *adv* cioè, ossia; — *vt* menzionare; nominare
nap *n* sonnellino; *(cloth)* pelo
naphtha *n* nafta
napkin *n* tovagliuolo
Naples Napoli
narcissus *n* narciso
narcosis *n* narcosi *f*
narcotic *a&n* narcotico
narcotize *vt* narcotizzare
narrate *vt* narrare
narration *n* narrazione
narrative *n* narrativa
narrator *n* narratore *m*
narrow *a&n* stretto; — **escape** scappatoia miracolosa *(coll)*; — *vt* restringere; — *vi* restringersi
narrow– *(in comp)* **—gauge** *a* a scartamento ridotto; **—minded** *a* gretto
narrowly *adv (almost)* pressochè; strettamente
narrowness *n* grettezza; strettezza
nasal *a* nasale; **–ize** *vt* nasalizzare
nascent *a* nascente
nastiness *n* malvagità; sporcizia
nasty *a* sporco; schifoso, brutto
natal *a* natale
nation *n* nazione
national *a* nazionale; **–ism** *n* nazionalismo; **–ist** *n&a* nazionalista *m&f*; **–ization** *n* nazionalizzazione; **–ize** *vt* nazionalizzare
nationality *n* nazionalità
nationwide *a* attraverso l'intero paese
native *a&n* indigeno, nativo; — **land** paese natio
native-born *a* nato in un luogo indicato
nativity *n* natività
natty *a* ordinato, netto, elegante
natural *a* naturale; — *n (mus)* bequadro; — **history** storia naturale; **–ism** *n* naturalismo; **–ist** *n* naturalista *m&f*; **–ization** *n* naturalizzazione; **–ize** *vt* naturalizzare; **–ly** *adv* naturalmente; **–ness** *n* naturalezza; — **resources** ricchezze naturali
nature *n* natura; **by** — per natura; **from** — dal naturale; **good** — bontà
naught *n* niente *m*, zero
naughtiness *n* cattiveria
naughty *a* cattivello
nausea *n* nausea
nauseate *vt* nauseare; — *vi* sentir nausea
nauseating *a* nauseante
nauseous *a* nauseabondo
nautical *a* nautico; — **mile** miglio marino *or* nautico
nautilus *n* nautilo
naval *a* navale; — **academy** accademia navale; — **officer** ufficiale di marina
nave *n* navata; *(wheel)* mozzo di ruota
navel *n* ombelico
navigable *a* navigabile
navigate *vt&i* navigare
navigation *n* navigazione
navigator *n* navigatore *m*
navy *n* marina; — **bean** fagiuolo bianco; — **blue** blu marino; — **yard** arsenale *m*
nay *n* voto negativo
Nazi *n* nazista *m&f*
neap *a* basso; — **tide** bassa marea
Neapolitan *n&a* napoletano
near *prep* vicino a, presso di; — *a&adv* vicino; **–by** *a&adv* vicino; **–ly** *adv* quasi, pressappoco; **–sighted** *a* miope; — *vt&i* avvicinarsi
neat *a* pulito, lindo; **–ly** *adv* nettamente, pulitamente; **–ness** *n* lindezza, nettezza
nebula *n (ast)* nebulosa
nebulous *a* nebuloso, nuvoloso
necessarily *adv* necessariamente
necessary *a* necessario; **be** — occorrere, bisognare, essere necessario
necessitate *vt* costringere, rendere necessario
necesity *n* necessità
neck *n* collo; *(bottle)* collo; *(dress)* colletto; *(geog)* lingua di terra; **–lace** *n* collana; **–tie** *n* cravatta; **–wear** *n* cravatte e colletti
necromancer *n* negromante *m&f*
necromancy *n* negromanzia
nectar *n* nettare *m*; **–ine** *n* pesca-noce *f*
née *a* nata
need *n* bisogno; — *vt&i* aver bisogno di; **–iness** *n* indigenza; **–less** *a* superfluo; **–lessly** *adv* inutilmente, innecessariamente; **–y** *a* bisognoso
needle *n* ago; — *vt* cucire con l'ago; — *vi* lavorare all'ago; **–work** *n* lavoro all'ago
ne'er-do-well *n* fannullone *m*, buono a nulla
nefarious *a* nefario, ribaldo
negate *vt* negare
negation *n* negazione
negative *n* negazione; *(photo)* negativa; — *a* negativo
neglect *vt* trascurare; — *n* negligenza; **–ful** *a* trascurato
negligee *n* vestaglia
negligence *n* negligenza
negligent *a* negligente
negligible *a* trascurabile
negotiable *a* negoziabile
negotiate *vt&i* negoziare; *(coll)* superare
negotiation *n* negoziato
negotiator *n* negoziatore *m*
Negro *n&a* negro
neigh *n* nitrito; — *vi* nitrire
neighbor *n* vicino; **–hood** *n* vicinato; quartiere *m*; **–ing** *a* vicino; *(country)* limitrofo; **–ly** *a* amichevole
neither *conj* nè; neppure, neanche; — . . . **nor** nè . . . nè; — **of the two** nessuno dei due
nemesis *n* nemesi *f*
neon *n* neon *m*; — **sign** insegna al neon
neophyte *n* neofito
nephew *n* nipote *m*
nepotism *n* nepotismo
nerve *n* nervo; coraggio; *(coll)* audacia
nerve-racking *a* snervante

nervous *a* nervoso; — **system** sistema nervoso; **–ness** *n* nervosità
nervy *a* coraggioso; *(coll)* audace
nest *n* nido; — *vi* annidarsi; — **egg** gruzzolo
nestle *vi* coccolarsi
net *n* rete *f*; *(police)* retata; — *vt* irretire
net *(com) n* guadagno netto; — *a* netto; — **profit** utile netto; — *vt* ricavare, guadagnarsi
nether *a* basso
Netherlands Paesi Bassi, Olanda
netting *n* reticolato
nettle *n* ortica; — *vt* irritare; pungere
network *n* rete *f*; *(rad)* rete radiofonica
neuralgia *n* nevralgia
neurasthenia *n* nevrastenia
neuritis *n* nevrite *f*
neurologist *n* neurologo
neurology *n* neurologia
neurosis *n* neurosi *f*
neurotic *a* nevrotico
neuter *n&a* neutro, neutrale
neutral *a&n* neutrale; neutro; **–ity** *n* neutralità; **–ize** *vt* neutralizzare
neutron *n* neutrone *m*
never *adv* mai; — **ending** infinito; — **mind** non importa, pazienza
nevermore *adv* mai più
nevertheless *adv* però, pure; tuttavia
new *a* nuovo; **–born** *a* neonato, nato da poco; rigenerato; **–comer** *n* nuovo venuto; **–ly** *adv* recentemente; **–ness** *n* novità
newfangled *a* di nuova invenzione
newlywed *n* sposino
New Orleans Nuova Orlean
news *npl* notizia; notizie *fpl*; novità; **–boy** *n* strillone *m*, giornalaio; **–cast** *n* giornale radio; **–man** *n* giornalista *m*; **–paper** *n* giornale *m*; **–print** *n* carta per la stampa di giornale; **–reel** *n* notiziario cinematografico; **–stand** *n* edicola di giornali
New Year anno nuovo; **—'s Day** primo dell'anno, capodanno
New World Nuovo Mondo
New York Nuova York
next *a* prossimo, contiguo; — **day** il giorno successivo, il giorno dopo; — *adv* dopo, poi; — **of kin** il parente più prossimo — **to** accanto a
niacin *n* acido nicotinico
nib *n* punta, pennino
nibble *n* rosicchiamento; bocconcino; — *vt&i* rosicchiare; beccare
nice *a* bello, grazioso, gentile, simpatico; **–ly** *adv* scrupulosamente, esattamente; **–ty** *n* finezza
niche *n* nicchia
nick *n* tacca, incisione *f*; **in the — of time** nel momento più propizio; — *vt* incidere tacche
nickel *n (min)* nichelio, nichel *m*; — *vt* nichelare
nickel-plated *a* nichelato
nicknack *n* gingillo
nickname *n* nomignolo
nicotine *n* nicotina
niece *n* nipote *f*
niggardliness *n* avarizia
niggardly *a* avaro, taccagno
night *n* notte *f*; — **blindness** emeralopia; — **club** ritrovo notturno; — **letter** lettera notturna; — **owl** *(coll)* nottambulo; **at —** di notte; **by —** di notte; **–cap** *n* berretto da notte; **–dress, –gown** *n* indumento da notte; **–fall** *n* il cader della notte; **–mare** *n* incubo; **–shirt** *n* camicia da notte
nightingale *n* usignolo
nightlong *a* di tutta la notte; — *adv* nottetempo; durante tutta la notte
nightly *adv* di notte, nottetempo; — *a* notturno, di ogni notte
nihilism *n* nichilismo
nihilist *n* nichilista *m&f*
nil *n* niente, nulla *m*; — *a* nullo
Nile Nilo
nimble *a* agile
nimbus *n* nimbo; *(cloud)* nembo
nincompoop *n* semplicione *m*
nine *a* nove; **–teen** *a* diciannove; **–teenth** *a* diciannovesimo; **–ty** *a* novanta
ninny *n* imbecille *m*
ninth *a* nono
nip *n (pinch)* pizzicotto; *(bite)* morsicotto; — *vt* pizzicare; mordere; *(squeeze)* spremere; — **in the bud** tagliare il male alla radice *(fig)*
nippers *npl* pinze
nipple *n* capezzolo
nippy *a* piccante; *(cold)* pungente
nit *n* lendine *m*
nitric *a* nitrico
niter *n* nitrato di potassio *or* di sodio
nitrate *n* nitrato
nitrogen *n* azoto; **–ous** *a* di nitrogeno, d'azoto; azotato
nitroglycerin *n* nitroglicerina
nitrous *a* nitroso
nitwit *n* persona poco intelligente
no *adv* no; — *a* nessuno; **by — means** in nessun modo; **in — way** di nessun modo; — **doubt** senza dubbio; — **end** infine *m*; — **less** nientemeno; — **longer** non più; basta; — **such thing** impossible; — **smoking** proibito fumare; — *n* no, voto negativo
nobility *n* nobilità
noble *a* nobile; **–man** *n* nobiluomo; **–ness** *n* nobiltà
nobly *adv* nobilmente
nobody *pron* nessuno; — **else** nessun altro
nocturnal *a* notturno
nocturne *n* notturno
nod *n* cenno della testa; — *vt* accennare col capo; — *vi (doze)* sonnecchiare
node *n* nodo; *(bot)* nocchio
nodule *n* nodulo
noise *n* rumore *m*, chiasso; **make —** far rumore; — *vt* divulgare; — *vi* far rumore
noiseless *a* silenzioso; **–ly** *adv* silenziosamente
noisily *adv* rumorosamente
noisome *a* nocivo
noisiness *n* rumorosità
noisy *a* chiassoso
nomad *n* nomade *m&f*; **–ic** *a* nomade
nomenclature *n* nomenclatura

nominal *a* nominale; **–ly** *adv* nominalmente
nominate *vt* nominare, designare come candidato
nomination *n* nomina, designazione
nominative *a&n* nominativo
nominee *n* designato, candidato
nonacceptance *n* rifiuto di accettazione
nonaggression *n* mancata aggressione
nonaggressive *a* inaggressivo
nonallergic *a* inallergico, non-allergico
nonattendance *n* assenza
nonchalance *n* disinvoltura
nonchalant *a* disinvolto
noncombattant *n* non-combattente
noncombattive *a* non-combattivo
noncommissioned *a (mil)* senza brevetto; **— officer** sottufficiale *m*
noncommittal *a* evasivo, che non vuole impegnarsi
noncompliance *n* inadempienza; opposizione
nonconductor *n* cattivo conduttore, nonconduttore
nonconformist *n* anticonformista, dissidente *m&f*
nondescript *a* indefinibile, inclassificabile
none *pron* nessuno, niente, nulla *m*; — *adv* non; **I have —** non ne ho; **— the less** nondimeno
nonentity *n* nullità, inesistenza
nonessential *n* inessenzialità; — *a* inessenziale
nonexistent *a* inesistente
nonintervention *n* non-intervento, neutralità
nonpareil *a* ineguagliato
nonpayment *n* mancato pagamento
nonplussed *a* imbarazzato
nonprofit *a* senza profitto
nonresistance *n* ubbidienza passiva
nonresident *a&n* non-residente *m*
nonresistant *a* irresistente, passivo
nonrestrictive *a* non-restrittivo
nonsectarian *a* non-settario
nonsense *n* assurdità; **N–!** *(interj)* Macchè!
nonsensical *a* assurdo
nonskid *a* antisdrucciolevole
nonstop *a&adv (avi)* senza scalo; senza fermate
nonsupport *n (law)* mancato sostentamento
nonunion *a* indipendente dai sindacati
noodles *npl* tagliatelle *fpl*
nook *n* angolo
noon *n* mezzogiorno; — *a* meridiano
noose *n* nodo scorsoio; *(fig)* trappola
nor *conj* nè; neppure, neanche; **neither . . . —** nè . . . nè
Nordic *n&a* nordico
norm *n* modello, norma, tipo
normal *a&n* normale *m*; **–cy** *n* normalità; **–ly** *adv* normalmente
Norman *n&a* normanno
north *n* nord *m*; — a settentrionale; **–east** *n* nord-est *m*; **–erly, –ern** *a* settentrionale; **–ward** *adv* verso il nord; **–west** *n* nord-ovest *m*; **N– America** America del Nord; **N– Pole** Polo Nord; **N– Star** stella polare
Norway Norvegia
Norwegian *a&n* norvegese *m&f*
nose *n* naso; *(animal)* muso; *(scent)* fiuto; **— dive** *(avi)* picchiata; **blow one's —** soffiarsi il naso; **lead by the —** menar per il naso; **— bag** *(horse)* sacchetto mangiatoia; **–bleed** *n* sangue del naso, epistassi *f*; **–y** *a (coll)* inquisitivo, ficcanaso; — *vt&i (sniff)* fiutare, annusare; *(pry)* curiosare
nose-dive *vi (avi)* calarsi in picchiata
nostalgia *n* nostalgia
nostril *n* narice *f*; *(horse)* frogia
nostrum *n* toccasana *m*, panacea, sanatoria
not *adv* non; **— even** neppure; **— at all** niente affatto
notability *n* notabilità
notable *a* notabile, notevole; — *n* notabile *m*
notably *adv* notabilmente
notary *n* notaio
notation *n* notazione
notch *n* incisione, intaglio; — *vt* incidere, intagliare
note *n (memo)* nota; *(letter)* biglietto; distinzione; *(mus)* nota musicale; **bank —** banconota; **make — of, take — of** prendere nota di; **sour —** stonatura; **take –s** prendere appunti; — *vt* annotare
notebook *n* taccuino; **loose-leaf —** quaderno d'appunti a fogli staccabili; **— filler** fogli di ricambio
noted *a* noto, famoso
noteworthy *a* degno di nota
nothing *n* niente, nulla *m*; **— but** nient'altro che; **— else** nient'altro; **good for —** buono a nulla
nothingness *n* nulla *m*, oblio
notice *n* avviso; **at short —** con breve dilazione; **give —** licenziare; **take — of** rilevare, osservare; **until further —** fino a nuovo avviso; — *vt* notare, osservare; **–able** *a* apparente
notification *n* notificazione
notify *vt* notificare
notion *n* nozione, idea, opinione *f*
notions *npl* idee *fpl*; *(articles)* piccolezze *fpl*
notoriety *n* notorietà, cattiva fama
notorious *a* famigerato
notwithstanding *prep* malgrado; — *conj* nonostante, malgrado, quantunque, tuttavia
nougat *n* torrone *m*
nought *n* nulla *m*
noun *n* sostantivo
nourish *vt* nutrire; **–ment** *n* nutrimento; **–ing** *a* nutriente
novel *n* romanzo; — *a* nuovo
novelette *n* novella
novelist *n* romanziere *m&f*
novelty *n* novità
November *n* novembre
novena *n* novena
novice *n* novizio
novitiate *n* tirocinio, noviziato
now *adv* ora, adesso; **N–!** *interj* Via! Dunque!; **— and again** di tempo in tempo; qua e là; **— and then** di quando in quando; **till —** finora
nowadays *adv* oggigiorno
nowhere *adv* in nessun luogo

nowise *adv* in nessun modo
noxious *a* nocivo
nozzle *n* ugello, beccuccio
nuance *n* sfumatura
nubile *a* nubile
nuclear *a* nucleare; — **physics** fisica nucleare
nucleus *n* nucleo
nude *n&a* nudo
nudge *n* leggera gomitata; — *vt* attirare l'attenzione con leggera gomitata
nudism *n* nudismo
nudist *n* nudista *m&f*
nudity *n* nudità
nugget *n* pepita
nuisance *n* seccatura
null *a* nullo; — **and void** annullato
nullification *n* annullamento
nullify *vt* annullare
numb *a* intorpidito; — *vt* intorpidire; **–ness** *n* torpore *m*
number *n* numero; — *vt* numerare; **–ed** *a* numerato
numbering *n* numerazione; — *a* numerante; — **machine** numeratrice *f*
numeral *n* numero; — *a* numerale
numerator *n (math)* numeratore *m*
numerical *a* numerico
numerous *a* numeroso
numerousness *n* numerosità
numismatics *npl* numismatica
numismatist *n* numismatico
numskull *n* babbeo, semplicione *m*
nun *n* monaca, suora
nuncio *n (eccl)* nunzio
nunnery *n* convento
nuptial *a* nuziale; **–s** *npl* nozze *fpl*
nurse *n* infermiera; **wet** — balia; — *vt* curare; allattare; **–maid** *n* bambinaia
nursery *n* stanza dei bambini; — **school** asilo infantile
nursing *n* allattamento; — *a* allattante; — **home** casa di salute
nurture *vt* nutrire, alimentare; allevare; — *n* nutrimento
nut *n* noce *f*; *(mech)* dado; **–cracker** *n* schiaccianoci *m*; *(zool)* nocciolaia; **–ty** *a* di nocciola; *(sl)* pazzoide
nutmeg *n* noce moscata
nutrient *n* nutritivo, nutriente *m*
nutriment *n* alimento, nutrimento
nutrition *n* nutrimento
nutritious *a* nutritivo
nutshell *n* guscio di noce; **in a** — in breve
nuzzle *vt&i* fregare col muso, accarezzare col muso
nylon *n* nailon *m*
nymph *n* ninfa

O

oaf *n* semplicione *m*, zotico
oak *n* quercia; **–en** *a* di quercia
oakum *n* stoppa
oar *n* remo
oarlock *n* scalmiera
oarsman *n* rematore *m*
oasis *n* oasi *f*
oath *n* giuramento; bestemmia
oatmeal *n* farinata d'avena
oats *npl* avena; **sow wild** — far vita dissipata
obduracy *n* ostinazione, durezza
obdurate *a* ostinato, duro
obedience *n* ubbidienza
obedient *a* ubbidiente
obeisance *n* deferenza; *(bow)* riverenza
obelisk *n* obelisco
obese *a* obeso
obesity *n* obesità
obey *vt&i* ubbidire
obfuscate *vt* offuscare
obituary *n* necrologia
object *n* oggetto; *(gram)* complemento oggetto; — **lesson** esempio pratico
object *vt&i* fare obiezione, opporsi
objection *n* obiezione; **raise an** — sollevare un'obiezione; **–able** *a* biasimevole
objective *n&a* obbiettivo; **–ly** *adv* obbiettivamente; oggettivamente
objectivity *n* obbiettività
objector *n* oppositore *m*; **consciencious** — obiettore di coscienza
oblation *n* oblazione
obligate *vt* obbligare
obligation *n* obbligo; impegno
obligatory *a* obbligatorio
oblige *vt (require)* obbligare; *(please)* fare un piacere a
obliged *a* riconoscente, obbligato; **be** — *(indebted)* essere obbligato a qualcuno; *(required)* esser costretto a fare qualcosa
obliging *a* compiacente
oblique *a* obliquo
obliterate *vt* cancellare
obliteration *n* obliterazione, cancellazione
oblivion *n* oblio
oblivious *a* immemore, dimentico
oblong *a* oblungo; — *n* rettangolo
obnoxious *a* offensivo, odioso
oboe *n (mus)* oboe *m*
oboist *n* oboista *m&f*
obscene *a* osceno
obscenity *n* oscenità
obscure *a* oscuro; — *vt* offuscare
obscurity *n* oscurità
obsequies *npl* esequie *fpl*
obsequious *a* ossequioso; **–ness** *n* ossequiosità
observable *a* notevole
observance *n* osservanza
observant *a* osservante
observation *n* osservazione; — **car** vagone belvedere
observatory *n* osservatorio
observe *vt&i* osservare; **–r** *n* osservatore *m*
observing *a* osservante
obsess *vt* ossessionare
obsession *n* ossessione
obsessive *a* ossessionante
obsidian *n* ossidiana
obsolescence *n* disuso
obsolete *a* antiquato, fuori uso; **become**

— cadere in disuso
obstacle *n* ostacolo
obstetrician *n* ostetrico
obstetrics *npl* ostetricia
obstinacy *n* ostinazione
obstinate *a* ostinato
obstreperous *a* clamoroso
obstruct *vt* ostruire; impedire; **–ive** *a* ostruttivo
obstruction *n* ostruzione, ostacolo; **–ist** *n* ostruzionista *m&f*
obtain *vt* ottenere; — *vi* prevalere; essere in voga; **–able** *a* ottenibile
obtrusive *a* importuno
obtuse *a* ottuso
obverse *a* obverso; — *n* diritto
obviate *vt* ovviare
obvious *a* evidente, ovvio; **–ly** *adv* ovviamente
occasion *n* occasione; **–al** *a* occasionale, casuale; **–ally** *adv* sporadicamente; a volte; — *vt* causare
occident *n* occidente *m*; **–al** *a&n* occidentale
occiput *n* occipite *m*
occult *a* occulto; **–ism** *n* occultismo
occupancy *n* occupazione
occupant *n* occupante *m&f*; *(tenant)* locatario, inquilino
occupation *n* occupazione, impiego
occupy *vt* occupare
occur *vi* accadere, succedere; venire in mente, **–ing** *a* occorrente
occurrence *n* occorrenza, contingenza, incidente *m*, avvenimento
ocean *n* oceano; **–ic** *a* oceanico; **–ography** *n* oceanografia
ocher *n* ocra
o'clock *adv* **one** — l'una; **two** — le due
octad *n* gruppo di otto
octagon *n* ottagono; **–al** *a* ottagonale
octane *n (chem)* ottano
octave *n* ottavo
octet *n (mus)* ottetto
October *n* ottobre *m*
octopus *n* polpo
ocular *a* oculare
oculist *n* oculista *m*
odd *a (uneven)* dispari, ineguale; *(queer)* originale; **–ity, –ness** *n* bizzarria; **–ly** *adv* bizzarramente
odds *npl* probabilità, vantaggio; — **and ends** ritagli *mpl*, cianfrusaglie *fpl*; **be at — with** essere in lotta con
ode *n* ode *f*
odious *a* odioso
odium *n* odio
odor *n* odore *m*; **–ous** *a* odoroso, fragrante; **–less** *a* inodoro
of *prep* di
off *adv* lontano, distante; — *prep* da, fuori di; — **and on** di quando in quando; — **the record** ufficioso; — **limits** extralimite; **come** — *(loosen)* staccarsi; **far** — remoto; **put** — rinviare **right** — *(coll)* subito; **set** — mettere in rilievo; partire; **take** — *(avi)* decollare; *(remove)* togliere, staccare; **turn** — *(lights, motor)* spegnere; *(road)* cambiare di direzione; **Hands** —! Non toccare!
offal *n* avanzi, rifiuti *mpl*
offbeat *a* originale, strano
off-color *a* difettoso di colore; improprio
offend *vt* offendere; **–er** *n* offensore *m*; **–ing** *a* offensivo
offense *n* offesa; delitto; attacco
offensive *n* offensiva; — *a* offensivo, ingiurioso; **–ly** *adv* offensivamente
offer *vt* offrire; — *n* offerta; proposta; **–ing** *n* offerta; sacrificio
offertory *n (eccl)* offertorio
offhand *a* estemporaneo, impensato, sul momento, impreparato
office *n (business)* ufficio; *(position)* carica; — **boy** fattorino; **–holder** *n* impiegato statale; — **hours** orario d'ufficio
officer *n* ufficiale *m*; poliziotto
official *a* ufficiale; — *n* funzionario; **–ly** *a* ufficialmente
officiate *vi* esercitare le funzioni; *(eccl)* officiare
officious *a* inframmettente
offing *n (naut)* largo; **in the** — in vista
offset *vt* compensare; — *n (print)* rotocalcografia
offshoot *n* germoglio
offshore *a&adv* vicino alla costa
offside *a* fuori giuoco
offspring *n* prole *f*
often *adv* spesso, frequentemente; **how** —? quante volte?
ogle *vt* adocchiare, sbirciare, occhieggiare
ogre *n* orco
ohm *n* ohm *m*
oil *n* olio; **crude** — petrolio grezzo; **mineral** — olio minerale; — **field** campo petrolifero; — **painting** pittura ad olio; — **paints** pitture ad olio; — **well** pozzo petrolifero; — *vt* lubrificare; **–y** *a* untuoso, oleoso
oilcloth *n* tela cerata
ointment *n* unguento
OK, okay *a* buono; — *adv* molto bene; — *n* approvazione; — *vt (coll)* approvare
okra *n* ambretta commestibile
old *a* vecchio; — **age** vecchiaia; — **maid** zitellona; **–ish** *a* vecchiotto; **–ness** *n* vecchiaia, antichità
old– *(in comp)* **—fashioned** *a* antiquato, fuori moda; **—time** *a* antico; **—timer** *n (coll)* persona all'antica; **—world** *a* del Vecchio Mondo
Old World Vecchio Mondo
oleomargarine *n* oleomargarina
olfactory *a* olfattivo
oligarchy *n* oligarchia
olive *n* oliva; — **branch** ramo d'olivo; — **oil** olio d'oliva; — **tree** olivo; — *a* verde oliva
Olympic Games giuochi olimpici
omelet *n* frittata
omen *n* presagio, augurio
ominous *a* infausto, di malaugurio
omission *n* omissione
omit *vt* omettere
omnibus *n* omnibus, autobus *m*
omnipotence *n* onnipotenza
omnipotent *a* onnipotente
omnipresence *n* onnipresenza

omnipresent *a* onnipresente
omniscience *n* onniscienza
omniscient *a* onnisciente
omniverous *a* onnivoro
on *prep* su, sopra; — *adv* avanti; **and so —** e così via
once *adv* una volta; **all at —** ad un tratto; **at —** subito; immediatamente; **— for all** una volta per tutte; **— more** ancora una volta
oncoming *n* l'approssimarsi; — *a* prossimo, che si avvicina
one *n&a* uno, una; **— by —** uno a uno; **at — stroke** d'un colpo; **–ness** *n* unicità, unità; — *pron* l'uno, l'una; qualcuno, qualcuna; **— another** l'un l'altro
one– *(in comp)* **— armed** *a* monco; **— eyed** *a* guercio, che manca d'un occhio; **— horse** *a* con un solo cavallo; *(fig)* povero; insignificante; **—legged** *a* mutilato d'una gamba; **—sided** *a* unilaterale, parziale; **—time** *a* d'una volta; **—track** *a* *(coll)* limitato
onerous *a* oneroso
oneself *pron* sè, se stesso, si
one-way *a* a senso unico; **— ticket** biglietto di sola andata
onion *n* cipolla
onlooker *n* spettatore *m*; spettatrice *f*
only *a* unico, solo; — *adv* solamente, soltanto
onomatopoeia *n* onomatopeia
onrush *n* irruzione
onset *n* assalto, carica, attacco
onslaught *n* assalto, aggressione
onto *prep* sulla cima di, sopra
onus *n* onere, gravame *m*
onward *adv* in avanti
ooze *vi* filtrare; trapelare; — *n* fango; essudazione
oozing *n* gocciolamento; filtrazione; — *a* gocciolante; filtrante
opal *n* opale *f*; **–escent** *a* opalescente
opaque *a* opaco
open *a* aperto; franco; **–handed** *a* generoso; **–hearted** *a* franco, sincero; **— house** ricevimento informale; **— letter** lettera aperta; **–ly** *adv* apertamente; **–ness** *n* franchezza; **— question** questione indecisa; **— secret** segreto di Pulcinella *(coll)*; **— shop** officina indipendente dai sindacati
open– *(in comp)* **—air** *a* d'aria libera; **—eyed** *a* attento, sveglio; **—faced** *a* a viso aperto *(fig)*; **—minded** *a* spregiudicato; **—mouthed** *a* a bocca aperta
opener *n* apritore *m*, apritrice *f*; **eye —** rivelazione; **can —** apriscatole *m*
opening *n* apertura
opera *n* opera; **comic —** opera comica; **light —** operetta; **— glasses** binocolo da teatro; **— hat** gibus *m*; **–tic** *a* lirico; operistico
operate *vt&i* operare, agire, gestire, funzionare
operation *n* operazione; **–al** *a* operazionale *(mil)*
operator *n* operatore, monovratore *m*; *(com)* speculatore *m*; **telegraph —** telegrafista *m&f*; **telephone —** centralinista
opiate *n* oppiato
opine *vt&i* opinare
opinion *n* opinione *f*, parere *m*; **–ated** *a* ostinato, dogmatico; **in my —** a mio parere, secondo il mio avviso
opium *n* oppio
opossum *n* opossum *m*
opponent *n* avversario
opportune *a* opportuno; **–ness** *n* convenienza; **–ly** *adv* a proposito
opportunism *n* opportunismo
opportunist *n* opportunista *m&f*
opportunity *n* occasione
oppose *vt* opporre, avversare
opposing *a* avverso, opposto
opposite *a* opposto; — *prep* in faccia a; — *n* contrario
opposition *n* opposizione
oppress *vt* opprimere; **–ion** *n* oppressione; **–ive** *a* oppressivo; **–or** *n* oppressore *m*
opprobrious *a* obbrobrioso
opprobrium *n* obbrobrio
optic, –al *a* ottico
optician *n* ottico
optics *npl* ottica
optimism *n* ottimismo
optimist *n* ottimista *m&f*; **–ic** *a* ottimistico
optimum *n&a* ottimo
option *n* opzione; **–al** *a* facoltativo
optometry *n* optometria
opulence *n* opulenza
opulent *a* opulento
or *conj* o, ovvero, ossia; **either . . . —** o . . . o, sia . . . sia; **— else** altrimenti, oppure
oracle *n* oracolo
oral *a* orale; **–ly** *adv* oralmente
orange *n* arancia; **— tree** arancio; — *a* *(color)* arancione; **–ade** *n* aranciata
orangutan *n* orango
orate *vt&i* arringare, declamare
oration *n* orazione
orator *n* oratore *m*; **–y** *n* oratorio; **–ical** *a* oratorio
orb *n* orbe *m*
orbit *n* orbita; — *vt* mettere in orbita
orchard *n* frutteto
orchestra *n* orchestra; **–l** *a* orchestrale; **— seat** poltrona
orchestrate *vt* orchestrare
orchestration *n* orchestrazione
orchid *n* orchidea
ordain *vt* ordinare, decretare
ordeal *n* cimento, prova
order *n* ordine *m*; *(com)* ordinazione; **call to —** richiamare all'ordine; **in — that** affinchè, acciocchè; **in — to** allo scopo di; **make to —** fare su ordinazione; **on —** su ordinazione; **out of —** guasto; — *vt* ordinare
orderly *n* *(mil)* ordinanza, attendente *m*; *(hospital)* inserviente *m*; — *a* ordinato; — *adv* ordinatamente
ordinal *a* ordinale
ordinance *n* ordinanza
ordinary *a* ordinario; **out of the —** straordinario
ordination *n* ordinazione
ordnance *n* artiglieria
ore *n* minerale *m*
organ *n* organo; **–ic** *a* organico; **–ism** *n*

organismo; **-ist** *n* organista *m&f*; **— grinder** suonatore d'organetto; **— stop** registro d'organo
organdy *n* organdis *m*
organization *n* organizzazione, complesso
organize *vt* organizzare
organizer *n* organizzatore *m*
orgy *n* orgia
orient *vt* orientare; — *vi* orientarsi
Orient *n* oriente *m*; **-al** *n&a* orientale *m&f*
orientation *n* orientamento
orifice *n* orifizio
origin *n* origine *f*
original *a* originale; **-ity** *n* originalità; **-ly** *adv* originalmente, originariamente
originate *vt&i* creare; derivare, originare
originator *n* originatore *m*
ornament *n* ornamento; **-al** ornamentale; **-ation** ornamentazione; — *vt* ornare, adornare
ornate *a* adorno, ornato
ornithologist *n* ornitologo
ornithology *n* ornitologia
orphan *n* orfano; **-age** *n* orfanotrofio
orthodontia *n* ortodontoiatria
orthodox *a* ortodosso
orthography *n* ortografia
orthopedics *npl* ortopedia
orthopedist *n* ortopedico, ortopedista *m&f*
oscillate *vi* oscillare
oscillation *n* oscillazione
osmosis *n* osmosi *f*
ossification *n* ossificazione
ossify *vt* ossificare; — *vi* ossificarsi
ostensible *a* ostensibile, apparente
ostensibly *adv* apparentemente
ostentation *n* ostentazione
ostentatious *a* ostentativo
osteomyelitis *n* osteomelite *f*
ostracism *n* ostracismo
ostracize *vt* ostracizzare
ostrich *n* struzzo
other *adv* altrimenti; — *a&pron* altro; **each —** l'un l'altro; **every — day** un giorno sì e uno no; **the —s** gli altri *mpl*, le altre *fpl*; **the — world** l'altro mondo
otherworldiness *n* spiritualità
otherworldly *a* spirituale
otherwise *adv* altrimenti
ottoman *n* divano
ought *n* nulla, niente *m*
ought *vi* dovere
ounce *n* oncia
our *a* nostro, nostra; *(pl)* nostri, nostre
ours *pron* il nostro, la nostra; *(pl)* i nostri, le nostre
ourselves *pron* ci, noi stessi
oust *vt* espellere, scacciare
out *adv* fuori; — *a* di fuori; — *n (sport)* fuori *m*, fallo; **— of** fuori di, fuori da; da, di; *(lacking)* senza; **in and —** a zig zag; **way —** uscita
out- *(in comp)* **—and-out** *a* da cima a fondo; **—of-date** *a* sorpassato, fuori moda; **—of-doors** *a&adv* all'aperto, fuori casa; **—of-the-way** *a* remoto, appartato; insolito
outbalance *vt* sbilanciare
outboard *a&adv* fuoribordo; **— motor** motore fuoribordo
outbid *vt (price)* superare l'offerta di
outbound *a* partente
outbreak *n* scoppio; sommossa
outbuilding *n* dipendenza, annesso
outburst *n (anger)* trasporto; esplosione
outcast *n* proscritto
outclass *vt* superare in qualità
outcome *n* risultato, esito
outcry *n* grido
outdated *a* fuori modo, sorpassato
outdistance *vt* lasciar indietro
outdo *vt* sorpassare, superare
outdoor *a* all'aperto; **— exercise** esercizi all'aria libera *or* all'aperto
outdoors *adv* all'aria aperta
outer *a* esterno
outfit *n* equipaggiamento; corredo; gruppo; — *vt* equipaggiare, corredare
outflank *vt* aggirare
outgoing *a* uscente; *(rail)* in partenza
outgrow *vt* superare le misure; **-th** *n* escrecenza; prodotto
outing *n* escursione, gita
outlandish *a* bizzarro, strano
outlast *vt* durare più di, durare oltre
outlaw *n* fuorilegge *m*, bandito; — *vt* proscrivere, bandire
outlay *n (com)* uscita, sborso
outlet *n* sbocco; *(com)* smercio; *(elec)* presa
outline *n* schizzo, abbozzo, — *vt* abbozzare; disegnare
outlive *vt* sopravvivere a
outlook *n* prospettiva
outlying *a* remoto, lontano; *(external)* esterno
outmaneuver *vt* sventare
outmoded *a* messo fuori moda *or* stile
outnumber *vt* sorpassare in numero
outpatient *n (not hospitalized)* malato esterno
outpost *n* avamposto
outpouring *n* spargimento
output *n* produzione
outrage *n* scandalo, oltraggio; — *vt* oltraggiare; **-ous** *a* vergognoso, intollerabile, infame
outrank *vt* superare in rango *or* grado
outright *adv* subito; completamente; — *a* matricolato, completo
outrun *vt* superare in corsa
outs *npl* politici non più in carica; **ins and —** il pro e il contro; **on the —** in discordia
outset *n* principio
outside *a&n* esterno; — *adv* fuori, di fuori; **-r** *n* estraneo
outshine *vi* scintillare, brillare; — *vt* ecclissare
outskirts *npl* dintorni *mpl*
outspoken *a* franco
outspread *a* steso, spiegato; cosparso
outstanding *a* eminente; in sospeso; *(debt)* insoluto, non pagato
outstay *vt* trattenersi più a lungo di; **— one's welcome** restare più del necessario
outstretched *a* steso; allungato
outward *a* esterno; **-ly** *adv* esternamente; all'esterno
outwear *vt* consumare; *(last longer)* du-

rare di più
outweigh *vt* superare in importanza; superare in peso
outwit *vt* superare in intelligenza
outworn *a* consumato; *(obsolete)* superato; *(trite)* banale
oval *a&n* ovale
ovary *n* ovaia
ovate *a* ovato
ovation *n* ovazione
oven *n* forno; **Dutch** — forno olandese
over *prep* sopra; — **again** una volta ancora; — **and** — ripetutamente
overabundance *n* sovrabbondanza
overabundant *a* sovrabbondante
overact *vt&i* esagerare, eccedere; **–ive** *a* eccessivamente attivo
overage *a* troppo vecchio
over-all *a* complessivo
overalls *npl* tuta
overawe *vt* intimidire; **–d** *a* intimidito
overbearing *a* altezzoso
overboard *adv* in mare
overburden *vt* sovraccaricare
overcast *a* offuscato, oscuro; — *vt (sewing)* cucire a punto rasato; *(sky)* offuscare, oscurare; **–ing** *n (sewing)* ricucitura; *(weather)* offuscamento
overcharge *n* sovraccarico; — *vt* sovraccaricare
overcoat *n* soprabito
overcome *vt&i* sormontare, vincere, superare
overconfidence *n* eccesso di fiducia
overconfident *a* troppo fiducioso
overcooked *a* stracotto
overcrowd *vt* affollare in eccesso; **–ing** *n* ingombro
overdeveloped *a* eccessivamente sviluppato
overdo *vt* fare troppo; esagare; — *vi* strafare
overdone *a* esagerato; *(food)* stracotto
overdose *n* dose eccessiva
overdraft *n (com)* assegno eccedente il deposito; *(mech)* corrente d'aria sul fuoco
overdraw *vt* eccedere
overdrawn *a* esagerato; troppo teso
overdrive *n (auto)* marcia sovramoltiplicata
overdue *a* scaduto, moroso
overeat *vt* mangiare troppo
overestimate *vt* sovrastimare, sopravalutare
overexcite *vt* sovreccitare; **–ment** *n* sovreccitazione
overexertion *n* sforzo eccessivo
overexpose *vt* esporre troppo
overexposure *n* sovresposizione
overfatigue *n* fatica eccessiva
overfeed *vt* rimpinzare; — *vi* rimpinzarsi
overfill *vt* sovraccaricare; — *vi* sovraccaricarsi
overflow *n* inondazione, eccedenza; — *vi* traboccare; — *vt* inondare; **–ing** *a* inondante
overgrown *a* cresciuto eccessivamente; coperto completamente
overgrowth *n* cresciuta eccessiva
overhang *vt* soprastare a; — *vi* soprastare; pendere; **–ing** *a* soprasospeso; *(menacing)* minacciante
overhaul *vt* ispezionare, esaminare
overhead *a* di sopra; — *adv* in alto; — *n (com)* spese generali
overhear *vt* sorprendere, udire involontariamente
overheat *vt* surriscaldare
overindulgence *n* intemperanza
overindulgent *a* intemperante; troppo indulgente
overjoyed *a* pieno d'allegria, colmo di gioia
overland *a* terrestre; — *a&adv* per terra, via terra
overlap *vt* sovrappore; — *vi* sovrapporsi; **–ing** *a* sovrapponente
overload *n* sovraccarico; — *vt* sovraccaricare
overlook *vt* passar sopra a, non far caso di; *(position)* dare su
overnight *adv* durante la notte; dall'oggi al domani; — *a* notturno, di una notte
overpass *n* soprappassaggio
overpay *vt* pagare troppo; **–ment** *n* pagamento eccessivo
overpopulated *a* sovrapopolato
overpower *vt* sopraffare; **–ing** *a* prepotente, soggiogante
overproduction *n* sovraproduzione
overrate *vt* sopravvalutare
overreach *vt* oltrepassare; — *vi* andar troppo oltre; — **oneself** strafare
overripe *a* troppo maturo
overrule *vt&i* dominare; *(prevail)* prevalere
overruling *n* prevalenza, dominazione; — *a* prevalente, dominante
overrun *vt* infestare, invadere
overseas *adv* oltremare; — *a* d'oltremare
oversee *vt* sopraintendere; **–r** *n* sopraintendente *m*
overshadow *vt* ombreggiare; *(eclipse)* eclissare
overshoes *npl* soprascarpe, galosce *fpl*
overshoot *vt* oltrepassare
oversight *n* svista, errore *m*
oversleep *vi* dormire fino a tardi
overstatement *n* esagerazione
overstep *vt* oltrepassare
oversupply *n* sovrabbondanza
overt *a* visibile, pubblico, manifesto
overtake *vt* raggiungere
overtax *vt* soprattassare
overthrow *n* disfatta; — *vt* rovesciare
overtime *n* ore straordinarie
overtire *vt* sopraffaticare, strapazzare
overtone *n* superfrequenza sonica
overture *n* proposta; *(mus)* preludio
overturn *vt* capovolgere; — *vi* capovolgersi
overvalue *vt* sopravvalutare
overweight *n* eccesso di peso; — *a* troppo pesante
overwhelm *vt* sopraffare, opprimere; **–ing** *a* schiacciante
overwork *vt* far lavorare troppo; — *vi* lavorare troppo; — *n* eccesso di lavoro
overwrought *a* sovreccitato
overzealous *a* troppo zelante
oviparous *a* oviparo

ovum *n* uovo
owe *vt* dovere; — *vi* essere in debito
owing *a* dovuto; — **to** a causa di
own *a* proprio; — *vt* possedere; — **up to** confessare
owner *n* proprietario; **-ship** *n* possidenza
ox *n* bue *m*; **-en** *npl* buoi *mpl*
oxalic *a* ossalico
oxidation *n* ossidazione
oxide *n* ossido
oxidize *vt* ossidare; — *vi* ossidarsi
oxiacetylene *a* ossiacetilenico
oxygen *n* ossigeno; — **tent** campana d'ossigeno
oyster *n* ostrica
ozone *n* ozono

P

pace *n* passo; — *vt* misurare a passi; percorrere; — *vi* camminare; **keep — with** mantenersi al passo con
pachyderm *n* pachiderma *m*
pacific *a* pacifico
pacifier *n* pacificatore *m*
pacifism *n* pacifismo
pacifist *n* pacifista *m&f*
pacify *vt* placare, calmare
pacifying *n* pacificazione; — *a* pacificatore
pack *n* pacchetto; pacco; *(cards)* mazzo di carte; — **animal** animale da soma; — **horse** cavallo da basto *or* da soma; **-er** *n* imballatore *m*, imballatrice *f*
pack *vt* impaccare; — **one's bags** far le valigie; — **off** scacciare, licenziare; — **up** impaccare, imballare; far fagotto *(fig)*
package *n* involto, pacco; — *vt* impacchettare; mettere in cassa (*or* involucro)
packing *n* imballaggio; *(mech)* guarnizione
packsaddle *n* basto
pact *n* patto
pad *n* cuscinetto; tampone *m*; *(paper)* blocco; — *vt* imbottire; — *vi* viaggiare a piedi
padding *n* imbottitura; materiale per imbottire
paddle *vi* pagaiare; — *vt (coll)* sculacciare; — *n* pagaia; — **steamer** nave a ruote; — **wheel** ruota a pale
paddock *n* passeggiatoio
padlock *n* lucchetto; — *vt* allucchettare
pagan *n&a* pagano; **-ism** *n* paganismo
page *n (book)* pagina; *(lefthand)* verso; *(righthand)* recto; *(boy)* paggio; *(messenger)* fattorino *(coll)*; — *vt (print)* numerare le pagine, impaginare; *(call)* chiamare a voce alta
pageant *n* corteo storico, spettacolo; **-ry** *n* corteo, parata, spettacolo fastoso
pagination *n* impaginazione
pail *n* secchio, secchia
pain *n* dolore *m*; pena; **be in** — soffrire; **take -s** affannarsi, darsi da fare; — *vt* far male a, affliggere, far soffrire; **-ful** *a* penoso, doloroso
painstaking *a* accurato, diligente
paint *n* pittura; colore *m*; vernice *f*; — *vt* dipingere; **-er** *n* pittore *m*; *(house)* verniciatore *m*; imbianchino; **-ing** *n* pittura, quadro
paintbrush *n* pennello
pair *n* paio, coppia; — *vt* accoppiare; — **off** accoppiarsi, mettersi per due
pajamas *npl* pigiama *m*
pal *n (coll)* compagno, amicone *m*
palace *n* palazzo
paladin *n* paladino
palatable *a* saporito
palate *n* palato
palatial *a* grandioso
palatinate *n* palatinato
palatine *n&a* palatino
pale *a* pallido; — *vt* far impallidire; — *vi* impallidire; — *n* palo; confine *m*; **beyond the** — impossible; smoderato; **-ness** *n* pallore *m*
paleography *n* paleografia
paleolithic *a* paleolitico
paleontologist *n* paleontologo
paleontology *n* paleontologia
Palestine Palestina
palette *n* tavolozza; — **knife** spatoletta di pittore
palisade *n* palizzata
pall *n* drappo funebre; coltre *f*; — *vi* diventare insipido; — *vt* rendere insipido; *(fig)* deprimere; **-bearer** *n* chi regge i cordoni in un funerale
pallet *n* giaciglio
palliate *vt* palliare
palliative *n&a* palliativo
pallid *a* pallido
pallor *n* pallore *m*
palm *n (anat)* palmo; *(bot)* palma; **-ist** *n* chiromante *m&f*; — **off** imporre con la frode
Palm Sunday Domenica delle Palme
palpitate *vi* palpitare
palpitation *n* palpitazione
palsied *a* paralizzato
palsy *n* paralisi *f*; — *vt* paralizzare
paltry *a* piccolo; vile, meschino
pamper *vt* viziare, vezzeggiare
pamphlet *n* opuscolo; **-eer** *n* scrittore di opuscoli
pan *n* padella; — **out** aver successo; — **someone** *(coll)* criticare qualcuno
panacea *n* panacea
Pan-American *a* panamericano
pancake *n* frittella
pancreas *n* pancreas *m*
pancreatic *a* pancreatico
pandemonium *n* pandemonio
pander *n* mezzano, ruffiano; — *vi* fare il mezzano
pane *n* vetro; pannello
panegyric *n* panegirico
panel *n* pannello; *(law)* giuria; **jury** — lista dei giurati; — *vt* decorare con pannelli; **-ing** *n* lavoro a pannelli; pannelli *mpl*
pang *n* trafitta; dolore *m*
panic *n* panico; — *vt* procurare panico; — *vi* essere preso da panico; **-ky** *a* timido, pauroso, atterrito

panoply *n* panoplia
panorama *n* panorama
panoramic *a* panoramico
pansy *n* viola del pensiero
pant *vi* ansare, palpitare; — *n* anelito, palpito
panties *npl* mutandine *fpl*
pantheism *n* panteismo
pantheist *n* panteista *m*
pantheistic *a* panteistico
Pantheon *n* Panteon *m*
panther *n* pantera
pantograph *n* pantografo
pantomime *n* pantomima
pantomimist *n* pantomimo
pantry *n* dispensa
pants *npl* calzoni *mpl*
papacy *n* papato
papal *a* papale
paper *n* carta; documento; **blotting** — carta assorbente; **carbon** — carta carbone; — **clip** fermacarte *m*; — **hanger** tappezziere in carta; — **knife** tagliacarte *m*; **-weight** fermacarte *m*; — *a* cartaceo; — *vt (walls)* tappezzare con carta
paperboy *n* strillone *m*
papier-mâché *n* cartapesta
papist *n* papista *m&f*
paprika *n* paprica
papyrus *n* papiro
par *n* pari *f*; **at** — alla pari
parable *n* parabola
parabola *n (math)* parabola
parabolic *a* parabolico
parachute *n* paracadute *m*; — *vt* paracadutare; — *vi* lanciarsi con il paracadute
parachutist *n* paracadutista *m&f*
parade *n* sfilata; *(mil)* parata; — *vt* ostentare; — *vi* sfilare in parata
paradise *n* paradiso
paradox *n* paradosso
paradoxical *a* paradossale
paraffin *n* paraffina
paragon *n* esempio, modello
paragraph *n* paragrafo; — *vt* paragrafare
parallel *a&n* parallelo; — *vt* parallelizzare; **be — with** essere in parallelo con
parallelogram *n* parallelogramma *m*
paralogism *n* paralogismo
paralysis *n* paralisi *f*
paralytic *a&n* paralitico
paralyze *vt* paralizzare
paramount *a* supremo
paramour *n* amante *m&f*
paranoia *n* paranoia
paranoiac *n* paranoico
parapet *n* parapetto
paraphernalia *npl* accessori *mpl*
paraphrase *n* parafrasi *f*; — *vt* parafrasare; — *vi* fare una parafrasi
paraplegia *n (med)* paraplegia
parasite *n* parassita *m*
parasitic *a* parassitico
parasol *n* parasole *m*
parataxis *n* paratassi *f*
paratrooper *n (mil)* paracadutista *m*
paratroops *npl* corpo di paracadutisti
parboil *vt* far bollire a mezzo
parcel *n* pacchetto; — **post** pacco postale; — *vt* dividere in parti, spartire; impacchettare
parch *vt* arrostire; *(dry)* inaridire; — *vi* arrostirsi; inaridirsi
parchment *n* pergamena
pardon *n* perdono; — *vt* perdonare; **-able** *a* perdonabile
pare *vt* pelare; sbucciare
paregoric *n&a (med)* paregorico
parent *n* genitore *m*, genitrice *f*; — *a* madre; natale; nativo; **-age** *n* discendenza, origine *f*, generazione; **-hood** *n* paternità, maternità; genitura; **-s** *npl* genitori *mpl*
parental *a* dei genitori
parenthesis *n* parentesi *f*
parenthetical *a* fra parentisi, parentetico
pariah *n* paria *m&f*
paring *n (peeling)* buccia; sbucciatura; — **knife** trincetto, spacchino
Paris Parigi
parish *n* parrocchia; — *a* parrocchiale; **-ioner** *n* parrocchiano
parity *n* parità
park *n* giardino pubblico, parco; — *vt* parcheggiare
parking *n* parcheggio, posteggio; — **meter** parchimetro; **no** — vietata la sosta (*or* il parcheggio)
parlance *n* linguaggio; il parlare; **in common** — nel linguaggio corrente
parley *n* trattattiva parlamentare; — *vi* parlamentare
parliament *n* parlamento; **-arian** *n* parlamentare *m*
parliamentary *a* parlamentare
parlor *n* salotto; **beauty** — salone di bellezza
Parnassian *a&n* parnassiano
parochial *a* parrocchiale
parody *n* parodia; — *vt* parodiare, imitare
parole *n (law)* condizionale *f*, libertà provvisoria; — *vt* concedere la libertà provvisoria
paroxysm *n* parossismo
parquet *n* parchetto, parchè *m*; — *vt* pavimentare a parchè
parrot *n* pappagallo
parry *vt* evitare, parare
parse *vt (gram)* analizzare
parsley *n* prezzemolo
parsnip *n* pastinaca
parson *n* parroco; **-age** *n* canonica
part *n* parte *f*; *(hair)* riga, scriminatura; *(spare)* pezzo di ricambio; *(speech)* parte del discorso; *(theat)* parte *f*; — *a* parziale; — *adv* in parte; **for my** — per parte mia; **for the most** — per la maggior parte; **from all -s** da ogni lato; **in** — in parte, **take — in** participare a; **take someone's** — prender la parte di qualcuno; **-s** *npl* parti *fpl*; regione; abilità
part *vt* separare; — *vi* separarsi; — **from, with** separarsi da
partake *vi* partecipare, condividere
partial *a* parziale; **-ity** *n* parzialità
participant *n* partecipante *m&f*
participate *vt&i* partecipare

participation *n* partecipazione
participator *n* partecipante *m&f*
participial *a (gram)* participiale
participle *n (gram)* participio
particle *n* particella; granello
particular *n&a* particolare *m*; **–ity** *n* particolarità; **–ization** *n* particolarizzazione; **–ize** *vt* particolareggiare; **–ly** *adv* particolarmente
parting *n* separazione
partisan *n&a* partigiano
partition *n* partizione; tramezzo; divisorio; — *vt* dividere in parti
partitive *a (gram)* partitivo
partly *adv* in parte
partner *n* socio; **–ship** *n* società
party *n* festa; partito; **be a — to** essere complice in; **— line** *(pol)* partito di linea; *(telephone)* ramificazione telefonica
parvenu *n* nuovo ricco, villano rifatto
pass *vi* passare; — *vt* sorpassare; **— away** morire; **— by** passar presso; *(omit)* omettere; **— on** passar oltre; **— out** *(exit)* uscire; *(distribute)* distribuire; *(faint sl)* perdere i sensi; **— over** omettere, tralasciare
pass *n* passo, valico; *(mountain)* gola; *(permit)* permesso; **–able** *a* passabile; attraversabile; **–ive** *a* passivo
passage, –way *n* passaggio
passbook *n* libretto di banca
passenger *n* passeggero
passer-by *n* passante *m*
passing *a* passeggero; — *n (death)* decesso; **in —** fra parentesi
passion *n* passione; **–ate** *a* ardente
passkey *n* chiave comune
Passover *n* Pasqua ebrea
passport *n* passaporto
password *n* parola d'ordine
past *n&a* passato; **— master** maestro, esperto; **— participle** *(gram)* participio passato; **— perfect** *(gram)* passato anteriore; — *prep* dopo, oltre
paste *n* colla; *(food)* pasta; — *vt* incollare
pasteboard *n* cartone *m*
pasteurization *n* pastorizzazione
pasteurize *vt* pastorizzare
pastime *n* passatempo
pastor *n* pastore *m*; **–al** *n&a* pastorale
pastry *n* pasticceria; **— cook** pasticciere *m*; **— shop** pasticceria
pasture *n* pascolo; — *vt&i* pascolare
pasty *a* pastoso
pat *n* colpetto; *(butter)* pezzo; — *a* apposito; opportuno; — *vt* dare un colpetto; accarezzare; **stand —** impuntarsi *(fig)*
patch *n* toppa, pezza; — *vt* rattoppare
patchwork *n* raffazzonatura, rappezzatura
pate *n* testa
patella *n (zool)* patella; rotula
paten *n* disco; *(eccl)* patena
patent *n* brevetto; **— leather** coppale *m*; — *vt* brevettare
patent *a* patente, evidente, ovvio
paternal *a* paterno; **–ism** *n* paternalismo; **–istic** *a* paternalistico
paternity *n* paternità
path *n* sentiero; *(track)* corso, traiettoria
pathetic *a* patetico
pathfinder *n* esploratore *m*
pathological *a* patologico
pathology *n* patologia
pathos *n* patos *m*
pathway *n* sentiero, via
patience *n* pazienza; **loose —** impazientirsi
patient *n&a* paziente *m&f*
patina *n* patina
patriarch *n* patriarca *m*
patrician *n&a* patrizio
patricide *n* parricida *m&f*; *(crime)* parricidio
patrimony *n* patrimonio
patriot *n* patriotta *m*; **–ic** *a* patriottico
patriotism *n* patriottismo
patrol *n* pattuglia; ronda; — *vt* perlustrare
patron *n* patrono, mecenate *m*; *(customer)* cliente *m*
patronize *vt* frequentare; patrocinare; trattare con fare condiscendente
patter *n* picchiettio; — *vt (rain)* picchiettare
pattern *n* disegno; modello; — *vt* modellare
paunch *n* pancia; **–y** *a* panciuto
pauper *n* indigente *m&f*
pause *n* pausa; — *vi* far pausa
pave *vt* pavimentare; **— the way** *(fig)* preparare il cammino *(fig)*
pavement *n* lastricato
pavilion *n* padiglione *m*
paving *n* pavimento; pavimentazione
paw *n* zampa; — *vt* colpire, raspare con le zampe, maneggiare
pawl *n (mech)* dente d'arresto
pawn *n* pegno; *(chess)* pedina; **–broker** *n* prestatore su pegno; **–shop** *n* Monte di Pietà, casa di pegno; **— ticket** polizza di pegno; — *vt* impegnare, dare in pegno
pay *n* paga, salario; **–able** *a* pagabile; **–day** *n* giorno di paga; **–ee** *n* beneficiario; **–er** *n* pagatore *m*, pagatrice *f*; **–ment** *n* pagamento; **— roll** foglio-paga; — *vt* pagare; **— back** restituire; rimborsare; **— no attention** non prestare attenzione; **— off** ammortizzare; liquidare; **— up** pagare completamente, saldare
pay-off *n (coll)* resa dei conti; cosa inaspettata
pea *n* pisello; **–shooter** *n* cerbottana; **— soup** passata di piselli
peace pace *f*; **— offering** sacrifizio propiziatorio; **make — with** rappacificarsi con; **–ably** *adv* pacificamente; **–ful** *a* pacifico, calmo; **–maker** *n* pacificatore *m*
peach *n* pesca; *(tree)* pesco
peacock *n* pavone *m*
peak *n* picco, cima, vetta; *(zenith)* apogeo; **–ed** *a* a punta, appuntito; *(drawn)* scarno
peal *n* scampanio; *(laughter)* risata squillante; *(thunder)* scoppio; — *vi* sonare; scampanare; — *vt* far risonare
peanut *n* arachide *f*
pear *n* pera; *(tree)* pero
pearl *n* perla; **— diver** pescatore di perle;

— **oyster** ostrica perlifera
peasant *n* contadino
peasantry *n* contadini *mpl*
peat *n* torba
pebble *n* ciottolo
pebbly *a* ciottoloso
peccadillo *n* peccatuccio
pecan *n* noce americana; *(tree)* noce americano
peck *n* beccata; *(measure)* quantità di due galloni; — *vt&i* beccare; *(food)* sbocconcellare; — **at** *(criticize)* biasimare; mangiare delicatamente
pectoral *a* pettorale
peculiar *a* strano; **-ity** *n* peculiarità; caratteristica
pedagogical *a* pedagogico
pedagogue *n* pedagogo
pedagogy *n* pedagogia
pedal *n* pedale *m*; — *vt* pedelare
pedant *n* pedante *m*
pedantic *a* pedante
pedantry *n* pedanteria
peddle *vt* vendere in piccole quantità; — *vi* fare il venditore ambulante; **-r** *n* venditore ambulante
pedestal *n* piedestallo
pedestrian *n* pedone *m*
pediatrician *n* pediatra *m*
pedicure *n* callista *m&f*
pedigree *n* genealogia
pediment *n* frontone *m*
pedometer *n* pedometro; passimetro
peek *n* sguardo fugace; — *vi* far capolino
peel *vt* pelare, sbucciare; — *n* buccia
peep *vi (sound)* pigolare; *(look at)* sbirciare, spiare; — *n (sound)* pigolio; occhiata; **-hole** *n* buco; *(opening)* spiraglio; *(slit)* fessura
peer *n* pari *m*; — *vi* spuntare; scuriosare; **-age** *n (pol)* Pari *mpl*; aristocrazia; almanacco nobiliare; **-less** *a* incomparabile
peevish *a* irritabile; stizzoso; **-ness** *n* irritabilità
peg *n* caviglia; — *vt (fasten)* incavicchiare, incavigliare; *(com)* stabilizzare
pell-mell *adv* alla rinfusa; — *a* disordinato
pelt *n* colpo; velocità; *(animal)* pelliccia; *(rain)* scroscio; — *vt* lanciare, scagliare
pelting *n (of objects)* assalto; — *a (rain)* furioso
pelvic *a* pelvico
pelvis *n* pelvi *f*
pen *n* recinto; *(writing)* penna; — **name** pseudonimo d'arte; **ballpoint** — penna a sfera; **-holder** *n* portapenna *m*; — *vt* scrivere a penna; *(enclose)* rinchiudere
penal *a* penale; **-ty** *n* penalità; pena, punizione; **-ize** *vt* penalizzare
penance *n* penitenza
pencil *n* matita, lapis *m*
pendant *n&a* pendente *m*
pending *a* pendente; — *prep* durante; in attesa di
pendulum *n* pendolo
penetrate *vt* penetrare
penetrating *a* penetrante
penetration *n* penetrazione; intuizione
penicillin *n* penicillina
peninsula *n* penisola
peninsular *a* peninsulare
penis *n* pene *m*
penitence *n* penitenza
penitent *a&n* penitente *m*
penitentiary *n* penitenziario
penknife *n* temperino
penmanship *n* calligrafia
pennant *n* fiamma, stendardo, gagliardetto
penniless *a* senza un soldo
penny *n* centesimo di dollaro; soldo
pension *n* pensione *f*; — *vt* pensionare
pensioner *n* pensionato
pensive *a* pensoso
pentagon *n* pentagono; **-al** *a* pentagonale
pentameter *n* pentametro
penthouse *n* tettoia
pent-up *a* confinato
penumbra *n* penombra
penurious *a* povero, bisognoso; avaro
penury *n* penuria
people *n* popolo; gente *f*; — *vt* popolare
pep *n (sl)* energia, vigore *m*
pepper *n* pepe *m*; peperone *m*; — *vt* pepare; **-corn** *n* granello di pepe; **-mint** *n* menta peperina; **-y** *a* pepato
pepsin *n* pepsina
peptic *a* peptico
per *prep* per; — **capita** a testa
perambulate *vi* passeggiare, vagare
perambulatory *a* vagante, perambulatorio
perceivable *a* percettibile
perceive *vt* osservare, accorgersi, percepire
percent *n* per cento; **-age** *n* percentuale *f*
perceptibility *n* percettibilità
perception *n* percezione
perceptive *a* percettivo
perch *n* posatoio; *(fish)* pesce persico; — *vi* posarsi
perchance *adv* per caso
percolate *vt&i* filtrare
percolator *n* filtro, colino
percussion *n* percussione; — **cap** capsula di percussione
perdition *n* perdizione
peremptory *a* perentorio
perennial *a* perenne; — *n* pianta perenne
perfect *a* perfetto
perfect *vt* perfezionare
perfectibility *n* perfezionabilità
perfectible *a* perfettibile
perfection *n* perfezione
perfidious *a* perfido
perfidy *n* perfidia
perforate *vt* perforare
perforation *n* perforazione
perforce *adv* per forza
perform *vt* fare, eseguire; *(theat)* rappresentare, recitare
performance *n* esecuzione; rappresentazione
performer *n* artista *m&f*; esecutore *m*; *(theat)* attore *m*, attrice *f*
perfume *n* profumo; — *vt* profumare
perfumery *n* profumeria
perfunctory *a* negligente, superficiale, formale
perhaps *adv* forse
pericardium *n* pericardio

perigee *n* perigeo
peril *n* pericolo; **–ous** *a* rischioso, pericoloso; — *vt* esporre a pericolo; **be in** — pericolare
perimeter *n* perimetro
period *n* periodo; epoca; *(gram)* punto
periodic *a* periodico
periodical *n* periodico
peripatetic *n&a* peripatetico
peripheral *a* periferico
periphery *n* periferia
periphrasis *n* perifrasi *f*
periscope *n* periscopio
perish *vi* perire; **–able** *a* deperibile
peristalsis *n* peristalsi *f*
peristaltic *a* peristaltico
peritoneum *n* peritoneo
peritonitis *n* peritonite *f*
perjure *vt* spergiurare
perjurer *n* spergiuratore *m*
perjury *n* giuramento falso
perky *a* vivace
permanence *n* permanenza
permanent *a* permanente; — **wave** ondulazione permanente, permanente *f*; **–ly** *adv* permanentemente
permanganate *n* permanganato
permeability *n* permeabilità
permeable *a* permeabile
permeate *vt* permeare
permeation *n* permeazione
permissible *a* permissibile
permission *n* permesso
permissive *a* permissivo, indulgente
permit *n* permesso
permit *vt&i* permettere; lasciare
permutation *n* permuta
pernicious *a* pernicioso
peroration *n* perorazione
peroxide *n* acqua ossigenata
perpendicular *n&a* perpendicolare *f*
perpetrate *vt* perpetrare
perpetration *n* perpetrazione
perpetrator *n* perpetratore *m*
perpetual *a* perpetuo
perpetuate *vt* perpetuare
perpetuation *n* perpetuazione
perplex *vt* imbarazzare, rendere perplesso; **–ing** *a* imbarazzante; **–ity** *n* perplessità
perquisite *n* incerto, mancia; *(right)* requisito
persecute *vt* perseguitare
persecution *n* persecuzione
persecutor *n* persecutore *m*
perseverance *n* perseveranza
persevere *vi* perseverare
persevering *a* perseverante
Persian *a&n* persiano
persiflage *n* frivolezza
persist *vi* persistere; **–ence** *n* persistenza; **–ent** *a* persistente
person *n* persona; **–able** *a* ben fatto, bello; **–age** *n* personaggio; **–al** *a* personale; **–ality** *n* personalità; **–ification** *n* personificazione; **–ify** *vt* personificare
personnel *n* personale *m*
perspective *n* prospettiva
perspicacity *n* perspicacia
perspiration *n* sudore *m*
perspire *vi* traspirare, sudare
persuade *vt* persuadere
persuasion *n* persuasione
persuasive *a* persuasivo
pert *a* impertinente
pertain *vi* riguardare, appartenere; riferirsi a
pertinacious *a* pertinace
pertinacity *n* pertinacia
pertinence *n* pertinenza
pertinent *a* pertinente
perturb *vt* turbare, perturbare; **–ation** *n* perturbazione, perturbamento
Peru Perù
perusal *n* lettura accurata
peruse *vt* leggere attentamente
pervade *vt* pervadere, penetrare
pervasion *n* penetrazione
pervasive *a* penetrante
perverse *a* perverso
perversion *n* perversione
perversity *n* perversità
pervert *vt* depravare, pervertire; — *n* pervertito; **–er** *n* pervertitore *m*
pervious *a* permeabile
pessimism *n* pessimismo
pessimist *n* pessimista *m&f*; **–ic** *a* pessimistico
pest *n* parassita *m*; *(nuisance)* seccatura; **–er** *vt* infastidire
pestilence *n* pestilenza
pestilent *a* pestilente; noioso
pestle *n* pestello
pet *n* favorito, beniamino; — *vt* vezzeggiare; — **name** vezzeggiativo
petal *n* petalo
petition *n* petizione, preghiera; — *vt* rivolgere un'istanza; **–er** *n* richiedente *m*
petrel *n* procellaria
petrify *vt* pietrificare; — *vi* pietrificarsi
petroleum *n* petrolio; — *a* a petrolio, di petrolio
petticoat *n* sottana
pettifog *vi* fare l'azzeccagarbugli; **–ger** *n* azzeccagarbugli *m*; **–ging** *n* cavilli *mpl*
pettiness *n* piccolezza
petty *a* meschino; — **cash** piccola cassa; — **larceny** furterello, piccolo furto; — **officer** sottufficiale di marina
petulance *n* petulanza
petulant *a* petulante
pew *n* panca di chiesa
pewter *a* di peltro; — *n* peltro
phagocyte *n* fagocito
phalanx *n* falange *f*
phallic *a* fallico
phallus *n* fallo
phantom *n* fantasma *m*
Pharaoh *n* Faraone *m*
pharisaic *a* farisaico
Pharisee *n* Fariseo *m*
pharmaceutical *a* farmaceutico
pharmaceutics *npl* farmaceutica
pharmacist *n* farmacista *m*
pharmacologist *n* farmacologo
pharmacology *n* farmacologia
pharmacopoeia *n* farmacopea
pharmacy *n* farmacia
pharynx *n* faringe *f*
phase *n* aspetto, fase *f*
pheasant *n* fagiano
phenol *n* fenolo

phenomenal *a* fenomenale
phenomenon *n* fenomeno
Philadelphia Filadelfia
philander *vi* amoreggiare; **–er** *n* donnaiuolo
philanthropic *a* filantropico
philanthropist *n* filantropo
philanthropy *n* filantropia
philatelic *a* filatelico
philatelist *n* filatelico
philately *n* filatelia
philharmonic *a* filarmonico
Philippines Filippine
philological *a* filologico
philologist *n* filologo
philology *n* filologia
philosopher *n* filosofo
philosophize *vi* filosofare
philosophy *n* filosofia
phlegm *n* flemma; muco
phlegmatic *a* flemmatico
phobia *n* fobia
phoenix *n* fenice *f*
phone *n (coll)* telefono; — *vt&i* telefonare
phonetic *a* fonetico; **–s** *npl* fonetica
phonic *a* fonico
phonograph *n* grammofono, fonografo
phosphate *n* fosfato
phosphite *n* fosfito
phosphorescence *n* fosforescenza
phosphorescent *a* fosforescente
phosphoric *a* fosforico
phosphorous *a* fosforoso
phosphorus *n* fosforo
photodynamics *npl* fotodinamica
photoelectric *a* fotoelettrico; — **cell** cellula fotoelettrica
photoengrave *vt* fotoincidere
photoengraving *n* fotoincisione
photogenic *a* fotogenico
photograph *n* fotografia; **–er** *n* fotografo; **–ic** *a* fotografico; **–y** *n* fotografia; — *vt* fotografare
photogravure *n* fotoincisione
photometer *n* fotometro
photomicrograph *n* microfoto *f*
photostat *n* fotostato; macchina fotostatica; — *vt* fare una copia fotostatica di
photosynthesis *n* fotosintesi *f*
phrase *n* frase *f*; — *vt* formulare; *(mus)* fraseggiare
phraseology *n* fraseologia
phrenetic *a* frenetico
phrenology *n* frenologia
physic *n* purgante *m*
physical *a* fisico
physician *n* medico
physicist *n* fisico
physics *npl* fisica; **solid state** — elettrofisica degli stati solidi
physiognomy *n* fisonomia
physiological *a* fisiologico
physiologist *n* fisiologo
physiology *n* fisiologia
physiotherapy *n* fisioterapia
physique *n* fisico
pianist *n* pianista *m&f*
piano *n* pianoforte *m*; **baby grand** — pianino; **grand** — pianoforte a coda; **upright** — pianoforte verticale; — *a&adv* piano
pica *n (print)* pica
picayune *a* meschino
piccolo *n* ottavino
pick *n* piccone *m*; scelta; — *vt* scegliere; cogliere; — **out** scegliere; — **up** *(tidy)* raccogliere, rassetare
pickax *n* piccone *m*
picket *n (stake)* stacca, picchetto; — **fence** palizzata; — *vt* picchettare
pickle *n* sottaceto; *(coll)* imbarazzo; **in a** — nei pasticci; — *vt* mettere sotto aceto
picklock *n* grimaldello
pickpocket *n* borsaiuolo
pickup *n (auto)* furgoncino; *(speed)* accelerazione; *(phonograph)* pickup, diaframma *m*; *(coll)* conoscenza casuale
picnic *n* merenda in campagna
pictorial *a* pittorico, illustrato; — *n* giornale illustrato
picture *n* quadro; ritratto; — *vt* dipingere; descrivere
picturesque *a* pittoresco
piddling *a* insignificante
pie *n* torta
piebald *a* pezzato; *(fig)* misto, eterogeneo
piece *n* pezzo; — **of one's mind** rimprovero; — **rate** *(com)* compenso a cottimo; — *vt* congiungere; rappezzare
piecemeal *a* separato; a pezzi; — *adv* gradatamente; separatamente; pezzo a pezzo
piecework *n* lavoro a cottimo
pied *a* pezzato; variopinto
Piedmont Piemonte; **—ese** *a&n* piemontese *m&f*
pier *n* molo
pierce *vt&i* perforare
piercing *a* pungente, penetrante
piety *n* pietà, devozione
pig *n* porco, maiale *m*; — **iron** ghisa; **–headed** *a (fig)* ostinato
pigeon *n* piccione *m*, colombo; **clay** — piccione artificiale; **homing** — piccione viaggiatore
pigeon– *(in comp)* **—breasted** *a* di petto a sterno convesso; dal petto di gallina *(fig)*; **—toed** *a* con gli alluci in dentro
pigeonhole *n* nicchia; casella; — *vt* depositare in casellario; *(delay)* posporre
piggish *a* porcino; ghiottone; sporco
piggyback *adv* addosso; a spalle
pigment *n* pigmento; **–ation** *n* pigmentazione
pigpen *n* porcile *m*
pigtail *n* codino; **–s** *npl (hair)* trecce *fpl*
pike *n* picca; *(fish)* luccio; **–r** *n* giocatore timido
pilaster *n (arch)* pilastro
pile *n* mucchio; *(elec)* pila; *(cloth)* pelo; — *vt* ammucchiare
piles *npl (med)* emorroidi *mpl*
pilfer *vt&i* rubacchiare; **–er** *n* ladruncolo; **–ing** *n* rubacchiamento
pilgrim *n* pellegrino; **–age** *n* pellegrinaggio
pill *n* pillola; **–box** scatoletta per le pillole; *(mil)* fortino di cemento
pillar *n* pilastro, colonna
pillory *n* gogna; — *vt* mettere alla gogna
pillow *n* cuscino; **–case** *n* federa; — *vt* adagiare su cuscini
pilot *n* pilota *m*; — **light** fiammella

d'alimentazione; lampada pilota; — *vt* pilotare, guidare
pimiento *n* pimento di Giamaica
pimple *n* pustoletta
pimply *a* foruncoloso, pustoloso
pin *n* spilla, spillo; — **money** denaro dato alla moglie per le spese personali; **on -s and needles** sulle spine, impacciato; — *vt* fissare, attaccare con uno spillo
pinafore *n* grembiulino
pincers *npl* pinze *fpl*, tenaglie *fpl*
pinch *vt* pizzicare; — *n (nip)* pizzicotto; *(quantity)* presa; *(need)* bisogno
pinch-hit *vi (baseball)* sostituire un giuocatore; — **for** sostituire in emergenza
pinch-hitter *n* sostituto; *(baseball)* giuocatore sostituto
pincushion *n* portaspilli *m*
pine *n* pino; — *vi* languire; **to — for** spasimare per
pineapple *n* ananasso *m*; — *a* d'ananasso
ping-pong *n* tennis da tavola
pink *a* color rosa; — **of condition** condizione ideale
pinnacle *n* pinnacolo; apogeo
pinion, *vt* immobilizzare, inceppare
pinpoint *vt* precisare; localizzare; — *n* punta di spillo
pinprick *n* puntata di spillo
pint *n* pinta
pinwheel *n* girandola
pioneer *n* pioniere *m*; — *vt* preparare, aprire; — *vi* fare il pioniere
pious *a* devoto, pio
pipe *n* pipa; tubo; *(mus)* flauto; **-line** *n* tubatura; **-r** *n* flautista *m*
piping *n* tubazione; suono di zampogna (*or* cornamusa); *(food)* decorazione; *(clothing)* orlo ricamato; — **hot** *(liquid)* bollente, caldo caldo
piquancy *n* piccante *m*
piquant *a* piccante
pique *n* picca; — *vt* piccare; — **oneself on** piccarsi di
piracy *n* pirateria; *(lit)* plagio
pirate *n* pirata *m*; — *vi* pirateggiare, corseggiare; — *vt* plagiare; saccheggiare
pirouette *n* piroetta; — *vi* piroettare
pistachio *n* pistacchio
pistol *n* pistola
piston *n* pistone *m*; — **rod** stelo di stantuffo
pit *n* buca, fossa; cava; *(nut)* nocciolo; — *vt (into ground)* interrare; *(mark)* marcare; *(competition)* mettere in gara
pitch *n* punto, grado; *(mus)* tono; *(min)* pece *f*; — **pipe** diapason da fiato; — *vt* buttare, gettare; — *vi (naut)* beccheggiare; **to — in** lavorare alacremente
pitch- *(in comp)* **—black** *a* nerissimo; **—dark** *a* oscuro, nero come la pece
pitchblende *n* pechblenda
pitcher *n* brocca; **baseball** — lanciatore *m*
pitchfork *n* forca; forcone *m*
piteous *a* pietoso; commovente
pitfall *n* trappola; inganno
pith *n* forza; essenza; *(anat, bot)* midollo; **-y** *a (marrow)* midolloso; *(essence)* essenziale, vigoroso
pitiable *a* compassionevole; pietoso; degno di pietà
pitiful *a* pietoso
pitiless *a* spietato, crudele; incompassionevole
pittance *n (portion)* porzioncina; *(charity)* elemosina
pitted *a* butterato
pitter-patter *n* scalpiccio, picchiettio; — *vi* scalpicciare, picchiettare
pituitary *a* pituitario
pity *n* pietà, compassione; — *vt* compiangere
pivot *n* perno; — *vt* imperniare; — *vi* imperniarsi
pixie *n* fata
placard *n* cartellone *m*
placate *vt* placare
place *n* posto, luogo; **in — of** in luogo di; al posto di; invece; **out of —** inopportuno; fuori luogo; fuori posto; — *vi (racing)* piazzare; — *vt* collocare; **take —** succedere; aver luogo; **-ment** *n* collocamento
placenta *n* placenta
plagiarism *n* plagio
plagiarist *n* plagiario
plagiarize *vt* plagiare
plague *n* peste *f*; — *vt* tormentare; appestare
plaid *n* mantello scozzese; — *a (design)* scozzese
plain *n* pianura; — *a* semplice; ovvio; evidente; **-ly** *adv* semplicemente; **-ness** *n* evidenza; semplicità; assenza di bellezza
plainsman *n* abitante della pianura
plain-spoken *a* schietto, franco
plaintiff *n* attore *m*, parte civile
plaintive *a* lamentoso, triste
plan *n* piano; progetto; — *vt* progettare; pianificare
plane *n* pialla; *(avi)* aeroplano; *(level)* piano; — *vt* piallare; spianare
planet *n* pianeta *m*; **-ary** *a* planetario, di pianeta; **-arium** *n* planetario
plank *n* tavola; *(pol)* caposaldo; — *vt* intavolare; *(coll)* pagare; **-ing** *n* impalcatura, intavolatura
plant *n* pianta; *(com)* stabilimento; — *vt* piantare, impiantare; fissare; **-er** *n* piantatore *m*
plantation *n* piantagione *f*
plaque *n* placca
plasma *n* plasma *m*; — **physics** *(phys)* fisica dei plasmi
plaster *n* intonaco; gesso; **adhesive —** sparadrappo; **corn —** cerotto callicida; — **cast** riproduzione in gesso; — **of Paris** gesso da scultore, stucco; **-er** *n* gessaio; intonachista *m&f*; **-ing** *n* ingessatura; intonaco
plasterboard *n* tavola di gesso compensato
plastic *a* plastico; — *n* materia plastica
plasticity *n* plasticità
plat *n* pezzo di terra; — *vt (map or chart)* progettare
plate *n* piatto; placca; *(metal)* lamiera, *(dental)* dentiera, protesi dentale; *(print)* incisione; — **glass** lastra di cristallo (*or* vetro); **-ful** *n* piatto pieno; contenuto di un piatto; — *vt* placcare,

laminare
platen *n* rullo dattilografico; *(print)* pirrone *m*
plateau *n* altipiano
platform *n* piattaforma; *(pol)* programma *m*
plating *n* placcatura
platinum *n* platino; — *a* di platino
platitude *n* banalità; insulsaggine *f*
platitudinous *a* banale
platonic *a* platonico
platter *n* piatto
plaudit *n* applauso
plausibility *n* plausibilità
plausible *a* plausibile
play *n* giuoco; *(theat)* spettacolo; — **on words** giuoco di parole; — *vt&i* giuocare; *(instrument)* suonare; **-ful** *a* scherzevole; **-ground** *n* luogo di ricreazione; campo di giuoco; **-mate** *n* compagno di giuoco; **-off** *n (sports)* partita decisiva; **-thing** *n* trastullo, balocco
playback *n* collaudo di dischi (*or* nastri)
player *n (game)* giocatore; *(mus)* suonatore m; *(theat)* attore *m*
playhouse *n* teatro
playing *n* giuoco; — **cards** carte da giuoco; — **field** campo sportivo
playwright *n* drammaturgo
plea *n* supplica
plead *vi* sollecitare; — *vt* perorare
pleasant *a* ameno, gradevole; **-ness** *n* amenità
please *vt&i* accontentare; —! *interj* per favore!; **as you** — come ti piace
pleased *a* soddisfatto, contento; — **to meet you** *(coll)* lieto di conoscerti
pleasing *a* piacevole
pleasurable *a* piacevole
pleasure *n* piacere *m*
pleat *vt* pieghettare; intrecciare; — *n* piega
plebeian *a* plebeo, volgare; — *n* plebeo
plebiscite *n* plebiscito
plectrum *n* plettro
pledge *n* pegno; brindisi; — *vt* impegnare; brindare a
plenary *a* plenario
plenipotentiary *n&a* plenipotenziario
plentiful *a* copioso, abbondante
plenty *n* abbondanza
plethora *n* pletora
pleurisy *n* pleurite *f*
plexus *n* plesso
pliability *n* pieghevolezza, arrendevolezza
pliable *a* cedevole, arrendevole
pliant *a* pieghevole, flessibile, arrendevole
pliers *npl* pinze *fpl*
plight *n* situazione critica
plod *vi* andare a stento; sgobbare
plodder *n* sgobbone *m*; chi va avanti a stento
plodding *n* stento, sgobbo; — *a* laborioso, sgobbone
plop *n* tonfo; — *vi* fare un tonfo
plot *n* trama; *(intrigue)* complotto; — *vt* complottare, tramare
plotting *n* complotto
plow *n* aratro; **gang** — aratro multiplo; **rotary** — aratro rotativo; — *vt* arare; — **through** profondizzare, sprofondarsi *(fig)*
plowshare *n* vomere *m*
plu-k *n* coraggio, fegato *(fig)*; — *vt* cogliere, togliere; *(pull up)* strappare; **-y** *a* corraggioso
plug *n* tappo; *(elec)* spina; *(advertising, sl)* intromissione reclamistica; **spark** — candela; — *vt* tappare; — **in** inserire la spina; — *vi (coll)* sgobbare
plum *n* susina
plumb *n* piombo; — **line** filo a piombo; — *a* verticale, a piombo; — *adv* a piombo, verticalmente; — *vt* sondare, scandagliare; **-er** *n* idraulico; **-ing** *n* piombatura; lavoro d'idraulico
plume *n* piuma, penna
plummet *n* piombino; *(naut)* scandaglio; — *vi* cadere a piombo
plump *a* paffuto, grassoccio; — *vt* gettare giù; — *vi* piombare; **-ness** *n* grassezza
plunder *n* bottino; — *vt* saccheggiare; rubare
plunge *vt* tuffare; immergere; — *vi* tuffarsi; immergersi; — *n* tuffo, immersione
pluperfect *n (gram)* passato anteriore
plural *a&n* plurale *m*; **-ity** *n* pluralità; *(pol)* maggioranza relativa
plus *prep* più
plush *n* felpa
plutocracy *n* plutocrazia
plutocrat *n* plutocrate *m&f*; **-ic** *a* plutocratico
plutonium *n* plutonio
ply *n (fold)* piega; *(thickness)* spessore *m*; — *vi (work)* applicarsi; viaggiare rutinariamente; — *vt (trade)* esercitare; adoperare; — **with questions** investire con domande
plywood *n* legno compensato
P.M. post meridiem dopo mezzogiorno, del pomeriggio, pomeridiano
pneumatic *a* pneumatico
pneumonia *n* polmonite *f*
poach *vi* sconfinare; — *vt (cooking)* bollire uova in camicia; **-er** *n* bracconiere *m*
pock *n* pustola; **-mark** *n* buttero
pocket *n* tasca; — **book** libro tascabile; **line one's -s** riempirsi le tasche *(fig)*; **-book** *n* portafogli *m*; borsetta da donna; **-knife** *n* temperino; — *a* tascabile; — *vt* intascare; *(feelings)* contenere
pock-marked *a* butterato
pod *n* baccello; *(flock)* branco
poem *n* poesia; poema *m*
poet *n* poeta *m*; **-ic, -ical** *a* poetico; **-ry** *n* poesia
poetics *npl* poetica
poignancy *n* acutezza
poignant *a* piccante
point *n* punto; punta; grado; mira; — **of view** punto di vista; **get to the** — andare al fatto; **make a** — **of** farsi un dovere di; **on the** — **of** sul punto di; **stretch a** — fare un'eccezione; — *vt* indicare; *(sharpen)* appuntare; **to** — **out** segnalare, notare; **to the** — in proposito
point-blank *a* a bruciapelo
pointer *n (dog)* cane da punta; bacchetta

pointless *a* inutile
poise *n* equilibrio; portamento; dignità; — *vt* equilibrare; — *vi* equilibrarsi; esser sospeso
poised *a* disinvolto, imperturbabile
poison *n* veleno; — *vt* avvelenare; **–ing** *n* avvelenamento; **–ous** *a* velenoso
poke *n* colpo, spinta; — *vi* dar colpi; — *vt* cacciare, spingere; — **along** poltrire; — **fun at** scherzare; **buy a pig in a** — comprare alla cieca *(fig)*
poker *n* attizzatoio; *(game)* poker *m*
Poland Polonia
polar *a* polare; — **bear** orso bianco
polarity *n* polarità
polarize *vt* polarizzare
Pole *n* polacco
pole *n* palo; *(geog)* polo; — **vault** salto all'asta
polecat *n* puzzola
police *n* polizia; — **station** commissariato, questura; — *vt* mantenere l'ordine con la polizia; **–man** *n* guardia, poliziotto, vigile urbano
policy *n* politica; — **holder** assicurato; **insurance** — polizza d'assicurazione
poliomyelitis *n* poliomelite *f*
Polish *a* polacco
polish *vt* pulire, levigare; — *n* lucido, vernice *f*; **–ed** *a* raffinato
polite *a* cortese, garbato; **–ness** *n* cortesia
politic, –al *a* politico
politics *npl* politica
politician *n* politico, politicante *m*
polka *n* polka, polca
poll *n* *(pol)* votazione; *(opinion)* referendum *m*; — **tax** testatico; **–s** *npl* urne *fpl*; — *vt* tosare, potare, cimare; ottenere
pollen *n* polline *m*
pollinate *vt* coprire di polline
polling *n* votazione; — **booth** cabina elettorale
pollute *vt* contaminare; violare; **–d** *a* impuro, sudicio; corrotto
pollution *n* polluzione; profanazione
polo *n* *(sport)* polo
polychrome *a* policromo
polyclinic *n* policlinico
polygamist *n* poligamo
polygamous *a* poligamo
polygamy *n* poligamia
polyglot *n* poliglotta *m&f*
polygon *n* poligono; **–al** *a* poligonale
polymer *n* polimero; — **chemistry** polimerologia, chimica dei polimeri
polymerization *n* polimerizzazione
polymorphism *n* polimorfismo
polymorphous *a* polimorfo
Polynesia Polinesia
polyp *n* polipo
polyphonic *a* polifonico
polyphony *n* polifonia
polysyllabic *a* polisillabo
polysyllable *n* polisillabo
polytechnic *a* politecnico
polytheism *n* politeismo
polytheist *n* politeista *m&f*
polytheistic *a* politeistico
pomade *n* pomata
pomegranate *n* melagrana
pommel *n* pomo; — *vt* battere
pomp *n* pompa, fasto; **–ous** *a* pomposo; **–ousness** *n* pomposità
ponder *vt&i* ponderare; riflettere; meditare; **–ous** *a* ponderoso
poniard *n* pugnale *m*; — *vt* pugnalare
pontiff *n* pontefice *m*
pontifical *a* pontificale
pontificate *n* pontificato
pontoon *n* pontone *m*
pony *n* cavallino
poodle *n* cane barbone
pool *n* stagno; *(betting)* piatto di scommesse; *(money)* fondo comune; *(swimming)* piscina; — *vt* mettere in comune
poop *n* *(naut)* poppa
poor *a* povero, cattivo, scadente; — *npl* i poveri *mpl*; **–house** *n* ricovero di mendicità; **–ly** *adv* malamente, male, scarsamente
pop *n* sparo; *(beverage)* gasosa; **–corn** *n* granturco arrostito; **–gun** *n* pistola ad aria compressa; — *vt&i* esplodere, sparare
Pope *n* Papa *m*
poplar *n* pioppo
poplin *n* poplina
poppy *n* papavero
populace *n* plebaglia, popolino
popular *a* popolare; **–ity** *n* popolarità; **–ize** *vt* popolarizzare
populate *vt* popolare
population *n* popolazione
populous *a* popoloso
porcelain *n* porcellana
porch *n* veranda; portico
porcupine *n* porcospino
pore *n* poro
pore *(over)* *vi* ponderare; studiare attentamente
pork *n* carne di porco; — **chop** costoletta di porco
pornographic *a* pornografico
pornography *n* pornografia
porosity *n* porosità
porous *a* poroso
porphyry *n* porfirio
porpoise *n* focena
port *n* porto; *(naut)* babordo; *(wine)* vino d'Oporto; **–folio** *n* cartella; *(pol)* portafoglio; **–hole** *n* portello; oblò; **–able** *a* portabile, portatile
portend *vt* presagire
portent *n* portento; presagio
portentous *a* portentoso, prodigioso
porter *n* facchino, portatore *m*
portion *n* porzione; — *vt* ripartire; dotare
portly *a* corpulento
portrait *n* ritratto; — **painter** ritrattista *m&f*
portray *vt* ritrarre; descrivere; **–al** *n* pittura, descrizione
Portugal Portogallo
Portuguese *a&n* portoghese *m*
pose *n* posa, atteggiamento; — *vt* far posare; — *vi* posare; atteggiarsi; — **as** atteggiarsi; — **questions** porre domande
position *n* posizione; posto; *(job)* impiego; **be in a — to** essere in grado di; — *vt* collocare
positive *a* positivo, assoluto; **–ly** *adv*

positivamente
positivism *n* positivismo
positron *n* positrone *m*; elletrone positivo
posse *n* pattuglia
possess *vt* possedere; **–ed** *a* posseduto; invasato; **–ive** *a* possessivo; **–or** *n* possessore *m*
possibility *n* possibilità
possible *a* possibile
possibly *adv* possibilmente; forse
post *n* posto; palo; — *vt* affiggere; impostare; — **no bills** proibita l'affissione; — **office** ufficio postale
postage *n* affrancatura; — **stamp** francobollo
postal *a* postale
postcard *n* cartolina postale
postdate *vt* posdatare
poster *n* cartellone *m*
posterior *a&n* posteriore *m*
posterity *n* i posteri *mpl*
postgraduate *n&a* universitario
posthaste *adv* subito, immediatamente
posthumous *a* postumo
postman *n* portalettere *m*
postmark *n* timbro postale
postmaster *n* direttore postale
postpaid *a* porto pagato
postpone *vt* rimandare; **–ment** *n* rinvio
postscript *n* poscritto
posture *n* atteggiamento; *(manner)* attitudine *f*
postwar *a* del dopoguerra
pot *n* pentola; vaso; — **roast** arrosto in tegame; — **shot** sparo a caso; — *vt* invasare; — *vi (coll)* sparare; **–hook** *n* gancio del focolare
potable *a* potabile
potash *n* potassa
potassium *n* potassio
potato *n* patata; **sweet** — patata americana
potbellied *a* panciuto
potency *n* potenza, potere *m*
potent *a* potente
potentate *n* potentato
potential *n* potenzialità; — *a* potenziale; **–ity** *n* potenzialità
potion *n* pozione
potluck *n* pasto quotidiano; — *a* alla buona; **take** — desinare alla buona
potter *n* vasaio; **–'s field** cimitero dei poveri; **–'s wheel** ruota del vasaio
pottery *n* ceramica; terraglie, stoviglie *fpl*
pouch *n* borsa
poultice *n* cataplasma
poultry *n* pollame *m*
pounce *(on) vi* balzare su, gettarsi sopra
pound *n* libbra; — *vt* battere, colpire; camminare pesantemente; pulsare
pound *n (animal)* rinchiuso
pour *vt* versare; — *vi* diluviare, piovere a dirotto; — **off** colare, drenare; **–ing** *a* torrenziale
pout *vi* fare il broncio; — *n* broncio
poverty *n* povertà, miseria
poverty-stricken *a* caduto in miseria, impoverito
powder *n* polvere *f*; cipria; — **magazine** polveriera; — **puff** piumino; — **room** toletta per signore; — *vt* impolverare; incipriare; — *vi* incipriarsi; impolverarsi; **–y** *a* polveroso
powdered *a* in polvere; incipriato, impolverato; — **sugar** zucchero al velo
power *n* forza; energia; facoltà; autorità; **–ful** *a* potente; **–less** *a* impotente; **–lessness** *n* impotenza; — **plant** apparato motore; central elettrica
practicability *n* praticabilità
practicable *a* praticabile
practical *a* pratico; — **joke** beffa, burla; **–ly** *adv* praticamente; quasi
practice *n* pratica; *(exercise)* esercizio, uso; *(professional)* clientela; — *vt* praticare, esercitare
practiced *a* abile, esperto
practitioner *n* professionista *m&f*
pragmatic *a* pragmatico
pragmatism *n* pragmatismo
pragmatist *n* pragmatista *m*
prairie *n* prateria
praise *n* lode *f*, elogio; — *vt* lodare; **–worthy** *a* lodevole
prance *vi* impennarsi; pavoneggiarsi
prancing *n* impennata; — *a* rampante
prank *n* burla, tiro birbone
prate *vi* ciarlare, cicalare
prattle *n* ciarla; — *vi* chiacchierare, ciarlare
pray *vt&i* pregare; **–er** *n* preghiera
prayerful *a* devoto, pio
preach *vt&i* predicare; **–er** *n* predicatore *m*; *(minister)* pastore *m*; **–ing** *n* sermone *m*, predica
preamble *n* preambolo
prearrange *vt* predisporre; **–ment** *n* preordinamento
prebend *n (eccl)* prebenda
precarious *a* precario; **–ly** *adv* precariamente; **–ness** *n* precarietà
precaution *n* precauzione; **–ary** *a* precauzionale
precede *vt&i* precedere
precedence *n* precedenza
precedent *n* precedente *m*
precedent *a* precedente
preceding *a* precedente
precept *n* precetto; **–or** *n* precettore *m*
precinct *n* distretto; **–s** *npl* dintorni *mpl*
precious *a* prezioso, caro
precipice *n* precipizio
precipitant *n&a* precipitante *m*
precipitate *n (chem)* precipitato; — *vt&i* precipitare
precipitation *n* precipitazione
precipitous *a* precipitoso
précis *n* sunto
precise *a* preciso; **–ly** *adv* precisamente; **–ness** *n* precisione
precision *n* precisione
preclude *vt* precludere
preclusion *n* preclusione
preclusive *a* preclusivo
precocious *a* precoce; **–ness** *n* precocità
precocity *n* precocità
preconceive *vt* preconcepire; **–d** *a* preconcepito
preconception *n* preconcetto
precursor *n* precursore *m*; **–y** *a* introduttivo
predate *vt* antidatare; predatare; **–d** *a* predatato

predatory *a* rapace; predatorio
predecessor *n* predecessore *m*
predestinate *vt* predestinare; — *a* predestinato
predestination *n* predestinazione
predestine *vt* predestinare
predetermine *vt* predeterminare; **–d** *a* predeterminato
predicament *n* imbarazzo, situazione difficile
predicate *vt* affermare; — *n* predicato
predication *n* predicazione
predict *vt* predire; **–ion** *n* predizione, presagio
predilection *n* predilezione
predispose *vt* predisporre; **–d** *a* predisposto
predisposition *n* predisposizione
predominance *n* predominanza
predominant *a* predominante
predominate *vt&i* predominare, prevalere
preeminence *n* preminenza
preeminent *a* preminente
preempt *vt* acquistare in precedenza
preen *vt&i* lisciarsi le penne; leccarsi *(fig)*
preestablish *vt* prestabilire; **–d** *a* prestabilito
preexist *vt&i* preesistere; **–ence** *n* preesistenza; **–ent** *a* preesistente
prefabricate *vt* prefabbricare; **–d** *a* prefabbricato
preface *n* prefazione; — *vt (book)* fare una prefazione a
prefatory *a* preliminare
prefer *vt* preferire: **–able** *a* preferibile; **–ence** *n* preferenza; **–ential** *a* preferenziale
preferred *a* preferito; *(stock)* privilegiato
prefix *n* prefisso; — *vt* prefiggere, premettere
pregnable *a* prendibile
pregnancy *n* gravidanza, gestazione
pregnant *a* incinta; gravido
preheat *vt* prescaldare; **–ed** *a* prescaldato
prehensile *a* prensile
prehistoric *a* preistorico
prehistory *n* preistoria
prejudge *vt* pregiudicare
prejudgment *n* giudizio prematuro
prejudice *n* pregiudizio; — *vt* pregiudicare; danneggiare
prejudicial *a* pregiudiziale
prelate *n* prelato
preliminary *a&n* preliminare
prelude *n* preludio
premature *a* prematuro; **–ly** *adv* prematuramente; **–ness** *n* prematurità
premeditate *vt* premeditare; **–d** *a* premeditato
premeditation *n* premeditazione
premier *n (pol)* primo ministro
première *n (theat)* prima
premise *n* premessa; **–s** *npl* locali *mpl*; *(logic)* premesse *fpl*; — *vt* premettere
premium *n* premio
premonition *n* presentimento
prenatal *a* prenatale
preoccupation *n* preoccupazione
preoccupy *vt* preoccupare
preordain *vt* preordinare; **–ed** *a* preordinato
prepaid *a* franco di porto
preparation *n* preparazione, preparativo
preparatory *a* preparatorio; — **school** scuola preparatoria
prepare *vt* preparare; — *vi* prepararsi
prepay *vt* pagare in anticipo; **–ment** *n* pagamento anticipato
preponderance *n* preponderanza
preponderant *a* preponderante
preposition *n (gram)* preposizione
prepossessing *a* attraente
prepossession *n* pregiudizio; preoccupazione; prevenzione
preposterous *a* assurdo
prerequisite *a* indispensabile; — *n* requisito
prerogative *n* prerogativa
presage *vt* presagire
prescience *n* prescienza
prescient *a* presciente
prescribe *vt&i* prescrivere
prescription *n* ricetta; prescrizione *f*
presence *n* presenza; — **of mind** prontezza d'animo; **in the — of** alla presenza di
present *n (gift)* regalo, dono; *(time)* presente *m*; — *a* attuale, presente; **at —** ora, adesso
present *vt* presentare, offrire; — **oneself** presentarsi, comparire; **–ation** *n* offerta, presentazione; *(theat)* rappresentazione
presentable *a* presentabile
presentably *adv* presentabilmente
presentiment *n* presentimento
preservation *n* preservazione
preservative *n* preservativo, preservatore *m*
preserve *vt* preservare, conservare
preserve *n* marmellata, conserva
preside *vi* presiedere
presidency *n* presidenza
president *n* presidente *m*
press *vt&i* premere; stringere; stirare; — *n* pressa; torchio; *(print)* stampa, stamperia; *(mech)* pressa; **the —** *(news)* la stampa
pressing *a* urgente, pressante, insistente; — *n* urgenza; pressione; stiratura
pressure *n* pressione; — **cooker** pentola a pressione; **blood —** pressione sanguigna
pressurize *vt (avi&naut)* mantenere la pressione di, pressurizzare
pressurized *a* a pressione; pressurizzato
prestige *n* prestigio
presumable *a* presumibile
presumably *adv* presumibilmente
presume *vt&i* presumere, supporre
presuming *a* presuntuoso
presumption *n* presunzione
presumptive *a* presunto
presumptuous *a* presuntuoso
presuppose *vt* presupporre
presupposition *n* presupposizione
pretend *vt&i* fingere, far finta di
pretender *n* pretendente *m&f*
pretense *n* finzione, pretesto; pretesa
pretention *n* pretesa
pretentious *a* pretenzioso; **–ness** *n* pretenziosità
preterit *n (gram)* preterito

pretext *n* pretesto; **on the — of** col pretesto di
prettiness *n* grazia, leggiadria; eleganza
prettily *adv* graziosamente
pretty *a* carino, grazioso, bello; — *adv* discretamente
prevail *vi* prevalere; **–ing** *a* prevalente; comune
prevalence *n* prevalenza
prevalent *a* generale, comune; prevalente
prevaricate *vi* prevaricare; tergiversare
prevarication *n* tergiversazione; prevaricazione
prevaricator *n* prevaricatore *m*
prevent *vt* impedire, prevenire, evitare; **–able** *a* prevenible; **–ion** *n* prevenzione; **–ative** *n* preventivo
preventive *n* misura preventiva; — *a* preventivo
preview *n* anteprima
previous *a* precedente; **–ly** *adv* prima, anteriormente
prewar *a* d'anteguerra
prey *n* preda; — *vi* predare
price *n* prezzo; **at any —** ad ogni costo; **— cutting** ribasso; **–less** *a* senza prezzo, inestimabile; — *vt* valutare; *(coll)* chiedere il prezzo di
prick *n* puntura; **–ly** *a* spinoso; — *vt* pungere
pride *n* orgoglio, fierezza; **take — in** essere fiero (*or* orgoglioso) di; **— oneself on** vantarsi di; gloriarsi di
priest *n* prete, sacerdote *m*; **–hood** *n* sacerdozio; **–ly** *a* sacerdotale
prig *n* meticoloso, sofistico, presuntuoso
prim *a* meticoloso, cerimonioso; affettato; **–ness** *n* formalità
primacy *n* supremazia
primarily *adv* principalmente; prima di tutto
primary *a* primario
prime *a* primo, principale; — *n* colmo, perfezione; fiore *m*; **in its —** nel suo fiore; — *vt (person)* preparare, istruire; *(gun)* caricare; *(mech)* adescare
primer *n* primo libro
primeval *a* primitivo; **— forests** foreste vergini
priming *n* innesco
primitive *a* primitivo; **–ness** *n* primitività
primogeniture *n* primogenitura
primordial *a* primordiale
primp *vi* prepararsi meticolosamente
primrose *n* primula
prince *n* principe *m*; **–ly** *a* principesco
princess *n* principessa
principal *a* principale; — *n (com)* capitale *m*
principle *n* principio
print *vt&i* stampare; *(letter)* scrivere a stampatello; **out of —** esaurito; — *n* stampa, impressione; *(photo)* positiva; *(type)* caratteri *mpl*; **–er** *n* tipografo
printed *a* stampato; **— matter** stampe *fpl*
printing *n* stampa, tiratura; — *a* tipografico, da stampa; **— press** torchio tipografico
prior *a* precedente, antecedente; **— to** prima di; **–ity** *n* priorità
prior *(eccl)* priore *m*
prism *n* prisma; **–atic** *a* prismatico
prison *n* prigione *f*; **–er** *n* prigioniero
pristine *a* pristino
privacy *n* intimità; segreto
private *a* privato; — *n (mil)* soldato semplice; **–ly** *adv* privatamente, in privato; personalmente
privation *n* privazione
privilege *n* privilegio; — *vt* privilegiare
prize *n* premio; — *a* pregiato
prizefight *n* partita di pugilato; **–er** *n* pugile *m*
pro *n (coll)* professionista *m&f*; — *a* favorevole; **the –s and cons** il pro ed il contro; — *adv* pro, in favore
probability *n* probabilità
probable *a* probabile
probate *vt* provare l'autenticità di
probation *n* periodo di prova; libertà condizionale
probe *n* sonda; investigazione; — *vt* sondare
probity *n* integrità
problem *n* problema *m*; **–atical** *a* problematico
proboscis *n* proboscide *f*
procedure *n* procedimento, procedura
proceed *vi* procedere, continuare; derivare
proceedings *npl* procedimenti *mpl*; *(law)* procedura
proceeds *npl* ricavo; incasso
process *n* corso; procedimento; processo
procession *n* processione; **funeral —** corteo funebre; **–al** *a&n* processionale *m*
proclivity *n* proclività, inclinazione
procrastinate *vt&i* procrastinare, posporre
procrastination *n* procrastinazione
procreate *vt&i* procreare
procreative *a* procreatore, generativo
procreator *n* procreatore *m*
procurable *a* procurabile
procure *vt* procurare, ottenere; **–ment** *n* ottenimento
prod *n* pungolo; — *vt* pungere; *(push)* spingere
prodigal *a* prodigo
prodigious *a* prodigioso; **–ness** *n* prodigiosità
prodigy *n* prodigio
produce *n* frutto; profitto; prodotto
produce *vt* produrre, fabbricare; **–r** *n* produttore *m*
producible *a* producibile
product *n* prodotto
production *n* produzione
productive *a* produttivo; **–ness** produttività
profane *a* profano; — *vt* violare, profanare
profaner *n* profanatore *m*
profanity *n* profanità
profess *vt* professare; pretendere, dichiarare
professed *a* dichiarato; **–ly** *adv* dichiaratamente
profession *n* professione
professional *a* professionale; — *n* professionista *m&f*
professor *n* professore *m*; **–ial** *a* professorale; **–ship** *n* cattedra
proffer *vt* proferire
proficiency *n* abilità

proficient *a* abile, provetto, esperto; **–ly** *adv* espertamente
profile *n* profilo; — *vt* profilare
profit *n* profitto; guadagno; — *vi* profittare, trarre vantaggio; **–able** *a* utile, vantaggioso; **–less** *a* senza profitto, inutile; — **by** trarre profitto da
profiteer *n* profittatore *m*; **–ing** *n* sfruttamento
profligate *a* dissoluto
profound *a* profondo; **–ly** *adv* profondamente; **–ness** *n* profondità
profundity *n* profondità
profuse *a* profuso; prodigo; **–ly** *adv* profusamente; prodigalmente; **–ness** *n* profusione
profusion *n* profusione
progenitor *n* progenitore *m*
progeny *n* progenie *f*
prognosis *n* prognosi *f*
prognosticate *vt* pronosticare
prognostication *n* pronosticazione
program *n* programma *m*; — *vt* progettare, fare programma per
programming *n* *(for computers)* programmazione
progress *n* progresso
progress *vi* progredire, far progressi; **–ive** *a* progressivo
progression *n* progressione
prohibit *vt* proibire
prohibition *n* proibizione
prohibitive *a* proibitivo
project *n* progetto; **–ile** *n* proiettile *m*; **–ion** *(action)* proiezione; sporgenza; **–or** *n* proiettore *m*
project *vt* progettare; — *vi* sporgersi
proletarian *a* proletario
proletariat *n* proletariato
prolific *a* prolifico
prologue *n* prologo
prolong *vt* prolungare; **–ation** *n* prolungazione
promenade *n* passeggiata; — *vi* passeggiare
prominence *n* eminenza, importanza; risalto
prominent *a* eminente; saliente; **–ly** *adv* prominentemente
promiscuous *a* promiscuo
promise *n* promessa; — *vt&i* promettere
promising *a* promettente
promissory *a* promettente; — **note** cambiale *f*
promontory *n* promontorio
promote *vt* promuovere
promoter *n* fautore *m*
promotion *n* avanzamento, promozione
prompt *a* pronto, immediato; puntuale; **–ly** *adv* subito, prontamente; **–ness** *n* prontezza; **–er** *n* suggeritore *m*; — *vt* incitare; *(theat)* suggerire
promulgate *vt* promulgare
promulgation *n* promulgazione
prone *a* prono; — **to** inclinato a *(fig)*
prong *n* rebbio; **–ed** *a* con rebbi
pronominal *a* pronominale
pronoun *n* pronome *m*
pronounce *vt&i* pronunziare; **–able** *a* pronunziabile; **–d** *a* pronunziato; **–ment** *n* dichiarazione
pronunciation *n* pronunzia
proof *n* prova; *(print)* bozza di stampa; **galley** — bozza di composizione; **–reader** *n* corretore di bozze; **–reading** *n* correzione di bozze; — *vt* tirare una bozza
prop *n* puntello; *(theat)* attrezzatura; — *vt* puntellare
propaganda *n* propaganda
propagandist *n* propagandista *m&f*
propagandize *vt* propagandare; — *vi* fare propaganda
propagate *vt* propagare; — *vi* propagarsi
propagation *n* propagazione
propel *vt* spingere avanti
propellant *n* propulsore *m*
propellent *a* motore, propulsore
propeller *n* elica
propensity *n* propensione
proper *a* proprio, corretto; **–ly** *adv* propriamente, appropriatamente; **–ness** *n* convenienza
property *n* proprietà; beni *mpl*
prophecy *n* profezia
prophesy *vt&i* profetizzare
prophet *n* profeta *m*
prophylactic *a* profilattico
prophylaxis *n* profilassi *f*
propinquity *n* propinquità
propitiate *vt* propiziare
propitiation *n* propiziazione
propitious *a* propizio
proponent *n* proponente *m*
proportion *n* proporzione; **–al** *a* proporzionale; **–ate** *a* proporzionato; — *vt* proporzionare
proposal *n* proposta
propose *vt* proporre; — *vi* fare una proposta di matrimonio
proposition *n* proposta, proposizione
propound *vt* proporre
proprietary *a* di proprietà
proprietor *n* proprietario
propriety *n* proprietà
propulsion *n* propulsione; **jet** — propulsione a reazione
prorate *vt* ripartire proporzionalmente; dividere proporzionalmente
prosaic *a* prosaico
proscenium *n* proscenio
proscribe *vt* proscrivere
proscription *n* proscrizione
prose *n* prosa
prosecute *vt* *(law)* processare
prosecution *n* *(law)* processo, querela
prosecutor *n* accusatore *m*; pubblico ministero; *(plaintiff)* parte civile
proselyte *n* proselito
proselytize *vt* convertire
prospect *n* prospetto; *(view)* vista; **–ive** *a* previsto, futuro; — *vt&i* esplorare; cercare
prospector *n* prospettore *m*
prospectus *n* prospetto
prosper *vi* prosperare; — *vt* far prosperare; **–ous** *a* prospero
prosperity *n* prosperità
prostate *n* prostata
prostitute *n* prostituta; — *vt* prostituire
prostitution *n* prostituzione
prostrate *a* abbattuto; prosternato; — *vt*

prostrare
prostration *n* prostrazione
protagonist *n* protagonista *m&f*
protect *vt* proteggere; **–ion** *n* protezione; **–ive** *a* protettivo; **–or** *n* protettore *m*; **–orate** *m* protettorato
protein *n* proteina
protest *n* protesta
protest *vt&i* protestare
Protestant *a&n* protestante *m&f*; **–ism** *n* protestantesimo
protestation *n* protestazione
protocol *n* protocollo
proton *n* protone *m*
protoplasm *n* protoplasma *m*; **–ic** *a* di protoplasma
prototype *n* prototipo
Protozoa *npl* protozoi *mpl*
protozoan *n* protozoo
protract *vt* protrarre; **–or** *n* protrattore *m*; *(anat)* muscolo estensore; *(geometry)* goniometro
protrude *vt* spingere avanti; far uscire; — *vi* sporgersi; proiettarsi
protruding *a* sporgente; spingente avanti
protrusion *n* sporgenza, prominenza
protuberance *n* protuberanza
protuberant *a* protuberante
proud *a* fiero, orgoglioso
provable *a* provabile
prove *vt* provare; — *vi* provarsi
proverb *n* proverbio; **–ial** *a* proverbiale
provide *vt&i* fornire; **–r** *n* provveditore *m*
provided *conj* purchè; — **that** a condizione che
providence *n* provvidenza
provident *a* provvido, previdente; **–ial** *a* provvidenziale
province *n* provincia
provincial *a* provinciale
provision *n* stipulazione *f*; **–al** *a* provvisorio, **–s** *npl* viveri *mpl*; provviste *fpl*
proviso *n* condizione; clausola
provisory *a* provvisorio
provocation *n* provocazione
provocative *a* provocativo
provoke *vt* provocare
provoking *a* provocante
prow *n* prua, prora; **–ess** *n* valore *m*, prodezza
prowl *vi* vagare, gironzolare; **–er** *n* vagabondo
proximity *n* prossimità
proxy *n* procura; **by** — per procura
prudence *n* prudenza
prude *n* schizzinoso; **–ry** *n* schifiltà
prudent *a* prudente; **–ly** *adv* prudentemente
prudish *a* schifiltoso
prune *n* prugna secca; — *vt* potare
pruning *n* potatura
prurience *n* sensualità
prurient *a* lascivo
pry *vi* spiare; ficcare il naso; — *vt* sollevare con una leva; — *n (tool)* leva, palanca
prying *n* curiosità; — *a* curioso, ficcanaso
psalm *n* salmo; **–ist** *n* salmista *m*
psalter *n* salterio
pseudonym *n* pseudonimo
psyche *n* psiche *f*
psychiatric *a* psichiatrico
psychiatrist *n* psichiatra *m&f*
psychiatry *n* psichiatria
psychic *a* psichico
psychoanalist *n* psicoanalista *m&f*
psychoanalysis *n* psicoanalisi *f*
psychological *a* psicologico
psychologist *n* psicologo
psychology *n* psicologia
psychopath *n* psicopatico
psychopathic *a* psicopatico
psychopathology *n* psicopatologia
psychopathy *n* psicopatia
psychosis *n* psicosi *f*
psychosomatic *a* psicosomatico
psychotherapy *n* psicoterapia
puberty *n* pubertà
public *n&a* pubblico; — **works** lavori pubblici *mpl*; **make** — pubblicare
public-spirited *a* con senso civico
publication *n* pubblicazione
publicity *n* pubblicità
publicize *vt* pubblicare
publish *vt* pubblicare; **–er** *n* editore *m*
publishing *n* pubblicazione; — *a* editoriale; — **house** *n* casa editrice
pucker *n* grinza; piega; — *vt* increspare; — *vi* raggrinzarsi
pudding *n* budino
puddle *n* pozzanghera
pudgy *a* tozzo
puerile *a* puerile
Puerto Rico Portorico
puff *n* soffio; — **pastry** pasta sfoglia
puff *vi* soffiare; gonfiarsi; — *vt* gonfiare
puffiness *n* gonfiore *m*; gonfiatura
puffy *a* gonfio
pug *n* cane bolognese; — **nose** naso camuso
pugilism *n* pugilato
pugilist *n* pugilista *m*
pugilistic *a* pugilistico
pugnacious *a* pugnace
pugnacity *n* pugnacità
pug-nosed *a* dal naso camuso
pull *vt* tirare; — **apart** staccare; — **off** cavare, tirar via; — **out** estrarre, strappare; — **oneself together** ricomporsi; — **through** *(recover)* guarire, rimettersi
pull *n* strappo, tiro; *(sl)* influenza, vantaggio
pullet *n* pollastrella
pulley *n* puleggia
pullover *n* pullover *m*
pulmonary *a* polmonare
pulp *n* polpa
pulpit *n* pulpito
pulpy *a* polposo
pulsate *vi* pulsare
pulsation *n* pulsazione
pulse *n* polso
pulverization *n* polverizzazione
pulverize *vt* polverizzare; — *vi* polverizzarsi
pumice *n* pomice *f*
pump *n* pompa; *(shoe)* scarpetta; — *vt&i* pompare; *(inflate)* gonfiare
pumpkin *n* zucca
pun *n* giuoco di parole
punch *n* cazzotto, pugno; *(mech)* punzone *m*; *(drink)* ponce *m*; — *vt* punzonare;

perforare; dare un pugno a
punctilious *a* scrupoloso, puntiglioso, meticoloso
punctual *a* puntuale; **–ity** *n* puntualità
punctuate *vt* punteggiare
punctuation *n* punteggiatura
puncture *n* puntura; *(tire)* foratura; — *vt* pungere, bucare, forare
punctureproof *a* antiperforante
pungency *n* agrezza, natura piccante
pungent *a* pungente
puniness *n* debolezza
punish *vt* castigare, punire; **–able** *a* punibile
punishment *n* punizione; **capital —** pena capitale
punitive *a* punitivo
puny *a* floscio, debole
pup, puppy *n* cucciolo; cagnolino
pupa *n* crisalide *f*
pupil *n* *(eye)* pupilla; *(school)* allievo; alunno, alunna; scolaro, scolara
puppet *n* burattino; **— show** recita di marionette
purchase *n* acquisto, compera; — *vt* acquistare, comperare
purchaser *n* acquirente *m&f*
pure *a* puro; **–ly** *adv* puramente
purgative *n&a* purgante *m*; purgativo
purgatory *n* purgatorio
purge *n* purga, purgante *m*; — vt purgare; — *vi* purgarsi
purification *n* purificazione
purifier *n* purificatore *m*
purify *vt* purificare
purism *n* purismo
purist *n* purista *m*
puritan *n* puritano; **–ical** *a* puritanico
purity *n* purezza
purl *vt* *(knitting)* smerlare; **–ing** *n* smerlo
purloin *vt&i* rubare
purple *n&a* *(color)* viola; **born to the —** *(fig)* di origine regale — *vt* imporporare; — *vi* imporporarsi
purport *n* significato; tenore *m*
purport *vt* significare; presumere, pretendere
purpose *n* scopo; **for the — of** allo scopo di; **on —** intenzionalmente; apposta; **to no —** invano; inutilmente; **–ful** *a* intenzionale; *(resolute)* risoluto; **–ly** *adv* intenzionalmente
purr *n* fusa *fpl*; — *vi* far le fusa; **–ing** *n* fusa *fpl*
purse *n* borsa; *(prize)* denaro; — *vt* increspare; **— the lips** contrarre le labbra; **–r** *n* *(naut)* commissario di bordo
pursuance *n* esecuzione, effettuazione
pursuant *a* inseguente
pursue *vt* perseguire
persuer *n* inseguitore *m*
pursuit *n* inseguimento; **in — of** alla ricerca di
purvey *vt* fornire
purveyor *n* fornitore *m*
pus *n* pus *m*, marcia; **–tule** *n* pustola
push *vt&i* spingere; **— ahead** progressare; **— back** respingere; **— one's way** farsi largo; — *n* spinta; **— button** pulsante *m*
pushover *n* *(sl)* cosa facile
puss *n* micino
put *vt* mettere; collocare; **— down** deporre, metter giù; **— off** posporre; **— on** indossare, mettersi; **— on airs** darsi arie; **— oneself out** disturbarsi *(coll)*; **— out** insoddisfatto; scontento; **— up** *(house)* soggiornare; *(can)* conservare; **— up with** tollerare, soffrire, sopportare
put-up *a* macchinato; **— job** intrigo, truffa
putrefaction *n* putrefazione
putrefy *vt* putrefare; — *vi* putrefarsi
putrid *a* putrido
putty *n* stucco; **— knife** spatola da stucco; — *vt* stuccare
puzzle *n* enigma *m*, rompicapo; **crossword —** cruciverba *m;* — *vt* rendere perplesso; — *vi* scervellarsi; **–ment** *n* sbalordimento, perplessità; **–r** *n* enigma *m*; *(person)* sfinge *f* *(fig)*
puzzling *a* problematico
pygmy, pigmy *n&a* pigmeo
pylon *n* pilone *m*
pyorrhea *n* piorrea
pyramid *n* piramide *f*
pyre *n* pira
pyromaniac *n* piromane *m&f*
pyrometer *n* pirometro
pyrotechnics *npl* pirotecnica
python *n* pitone *m*

Q

quack *n* ciarlatano, impostore *m*; *(duck)* gracidio; — *vi* schiamazzare, gracidare
quackery *n* ciarlataneria
quad *n* *(print)* quadratino
quadrangle *n* quadrangolo
quadrangular *a* quadrangolare
quadrant *n* quadrante *m*
quadratic *n&a* quadratico; **— equation** equazione quadratica
quadrilateral *a* quadrilatero
quadruped *n&a* quadrupede *m*
quadruple *n* *(math)* quadruplo; — *vt* quadruplicare
quadruplets *npl* quartetto di gemelli
quaff *vt&i* tracannare
quagmire *n* acquitrino
quail *n* quaglia; — *vi* scoraggiarsi
quaint *a* strano, pittoresco, originale; **–ness** *n* il pittoresco, originalità
quake *vi* tremare; — *n* tremore *m*, scossa; terremoto
quaking *n* tremolio; — *a* tremolante
qualification *n* qualifica; capacità; limitazione
qualified *a* idoneo; limitato
qualifier *n* qualificatore *m*; *(gram)* qualificativo
qualify *vt* abilitare, qualificare; limitare; — *vi* rendersi idoneo; qualificarsi
qualifying *a* qualificativo; **— heat** *(sport)* eliminatoria

qualitative *a* qualitativo
quality *n* qualità
qualm *n* apprensione; nausea; — **of conscience** scrupolo
quandary *n* dilemma *m*, imbarazzo
quantitative *a* quantitativo
quantity *n* quantità
quantum *n* quanto
quarantine *n* quarantena; — *vt* mettere in quarantena
quarrel *n* lite *f*, disputa; — *vi* litigare; bisticciare; **–some** *a* litigioso
quarry *n (mine)* cava; *(prey)* preda; *(hunting)* selvaggina
quart *n* quarto di gallone
quarter *n (math)* quarta parte, quarto; *(money)* un quarto di dollaro; **–back** *n (football)* terzino; centro attacco; **–master** *n (naut)* secondo capo timoniere; **–s** *(living)* quartiere *m*; alloggio; — *vt (mil)* alloggiare; squartare
quarter *n (time)* un quarto d'ora; **a — past** e un quarto; **a — to** meno un quarto
quarter– *(as comp)* **—deck** *n (naut)* cassero di poppa; **—hour** *n* quarto d'ora
quarterly *n* pubblicazione trimestrale; — *a* trimestrale; — *adv* trimestralmente
quartet *n* quartetto
quartz *n* quarzo
quash *vt* schiacciare
quasi *a&adv* quasi
quatrain *n* quartina
quaver *n* tremolo; *(mus)* croma; — *vi* vibrare; trillare
quay *n* molo
queasy *a* nauseato
queen *n* regina; — *vt (chess)* fare regina; — *vi* fare la regina; **–ly** *a* regale
queer *a* strano, bizzarro; — *vt (sl)* rovinare; **–ness** *n* stranezza, bizzarria
quell *vt* reprimere
quench *vt (thirst)* dissetare; spegnere; — **a fire** estinguere un incendio
querulous *a* querulo
query *n* domanda; — *vt* domandare
quest *n* ricerca; richiesta; **in — of** in cerca di
question *n* domanda; questione *f*; — **mark** punto interrogativo; **ask a —** fare una domanda; **in —** in questione; **out of the —** impossibile; **without —** senza dubbio; **a — of** una questione di; **–able** *a* discutibile; — *vt* interrogare; *(doubt)* discutere, mettere in dubbio
questioner *n* interrogatore *m*
questioning *n* inchiesta; — *a* interrogante, *(dubious)* dubbioso; **–ly** *adv* interrogativamente
questionnaire *n* questionario
queue *n (hair)* codino; *(line)* coda, fila
quibble *vi* sofisticare, cavillare
quibbler *n* cavillatore *m*
quibbling *n* sofisma *m*, cavillo
quick *n* vivo; **the — and the dead** i vivi e i morti; — *a* lesto, pronto, rapido; **–ness** *n* rapidità, vivacità; **–ly** *adv* presto, rapidamente; **–en** *vt* animare; stimolare; — *vi* animarsi; affrettarsi
quickening *n* accelerazione; — *a* eccitante; accelerato
quicklime *n* calce viva
quicksand *n* sabbia mobile
quicksilver *n* mercurio
quick-tempered *a* irascibile
quick-witted *a* di pronto ingegno
quiescence *n* quiescenza
quiescent *a* quiescente; silente
quiet *a* quieto, tranquillo; modesto; calmo; **Keep —!** *interj* Sta zitto!; **be —** stare tranquillo (*or* in silenzio); — *n* calma, quiete *f*; **–ness** *n* quiete *f*; silenzio; **–ly** *adv* silenziosamente; quietamente; — *vt* calmare; quietare; — *vi* calmarsi, quietarsi
quill *n* penna
quilt *n* trapunta; — *vt* trapuntare; **–ed** *a* imbottito
quince *n* cotogna
quinine *n* chinino
quinsy *n* squinanzia
quintal *n* quintale *m*
quintessence *n* quintessenza
quintet *n* quintetto
quintuple *n&a* quintuplo; — *vt* quintuplicare
quip *n* bottata; frizzo
quire *n* quinterno, quaderno
quirk *n* sotterfugio; *(peculiarity)* singolarità; — **of fate** capriccio del destino
quisling *n* disfattista *m&f*; quintacolonnista *m&f*
quit *vt* abbandonare, lasciare
quitclaim *n (law)* remissione, rinunzia
quits *a* pari; **be —** essere pari; **call it —** dichiarare la fine
quitter *n (coward)* codardo; rinunciatario
quite *adv* completamente; realmente; *(coll)* abbastanza
quiver *vi* tremolare; — *n (archery)* faretra; tremito
quivering *n* fremito, tremito
quixotic *a* donchisciottesco
quiz *vt* interrogare, esaminare; — *n* esame superficiale
quizzical *a* interrogante; *(bantering)* beffardo
quondam *a* già, antico
quorum *n* numero legale
quota *n* quota, porzione
quotable *a* citabile
quotation *n* citazione; *(com)* quotazione di borsa; — **marks** virgolette *fpl*
quote *vt* citare; *(com)* quotare
quotient *n* quoziente *m*

R

rabbi *n* rabbino
rabbit *n* coniglio
rabble *n* plebaglia; ressa
rabid *a* rabbioso; *(rabies)* idrofobo
rabies *npl* rabbia, idrofobia
raccoon *n* procione *m*
race *n (people)* razza, stirpe *f*
race *n* corsa; **arms —** corsa agli arma-

menti; **boat** — regata; **foot** — corsa a piedi; **horse** — corsa di cavalli; — **horse** cavallo da corsa; — **track** pista; — *vi* correre; *(compete)* gareggiare; — *vt* far correre; *(motor)* imballare; **–r** *n* corridore *m*
racial *a* razziale
raciness *n* brio
racing *n* corsa, corse *fpl*; — *a* di corsa; dedicato alle corse
racism *n* razzismo
rack *n (clouds)* nembo; rastrelliera; *(coat)* attaccapanni *m*; *(luggage)* reticella; — *vt* torturare; — **and ruin** rovina totale; — **one's brains** *(fig)* torturarsi il cervello; — **up** *(score)* accumulare
racket *n* gazzarra; *(sl)* traffico delittuoso; **tennis** — racchetta; **–eer** *n (sl)* camorrista *m (sl)*
racking *a* terribile, atroce
racy *a* caratteristico; piccante
radar *n* radar *m*
radial *a* radiale
radiance *n* splendore *m*
radiant *a* radiante
radiate *vi* raggiare, irradiarsi; — *vt* irradiare
radiation *n* radiazione
radiator *n* radiatore *m*
radical *a&n* radicale *m*; — **sign** segno di radice; **–ism** *n* radicalismo
radicle *n* radice *f*
radio *n* radio *f*; — **beacon** radiofaro; — **frequency** radiofrequenza; — **set** apparecchio; — **station** stazione radio; — *vt* trasmettere per radio
radioactive *a* radioattivo
radioactivity *n* radioattività
radiobroadcast *n* radiotrasmissione
radiocarbon *n* carbonio radiaoattivo; — **dating** determinazione dell'età di sostanze organiche per mezzo del contenuto di carbonio radioattivo
radiogram *n* radiogramma *m*
radiograph *n* radiografo
radiography *n* radiografia
radiolocation *n* radiolocalizzazione
radiologist *n* radiologo
radiology *n* radiologia
radiometer *n* radiometro
radioscopy *n* radioscopia
radiosensitive *a* radiosensibile
radiotelegraphy *n* radiotelegrafia
radiotherapy *n* radioterapia
radish *n* ravanello
radium *n* radio
radius *n* raggio; **within a — of** entro un raggio di
raffle *n* riffa, tombola; — *vt&i* sorteggiare
raft *n* zattera; *(coll)* quantità di
rafter *n* trave *f*
rag *n* straccio, cencio; **–man** *n* cenciaiolo
ragamuffin *n* straccione *m*
rage *n* furore *m*; **fly into a** — montare in furia; — *vi* arrabbiarsi; infuriare
ragged *a* cencioso
raging *a* furioso, violento
ragout *n* ragù *m*
rags *npl* stracci *mpl*; **be in** — *(fig)* essere in cenci (*or* stracciato)
raid *n* incursione; — *vt* invadere; predare
rail *n* sbarra; ringhiera; **by** — per ferrovia, con il treno; — *vi* rimbrottare; — **at, against** ingiuriare; proferire ingiurie; **–ing** *n* ringhiera; cancellata
raillery *n* derisione
railroad *n* ferrovia; — **station** stazione ferroviaria; — **tracks** rotaie *fpl*, binari *mpl*; — **train** treno; **narrow-gauge** — ferrovia a scartamento ridotto; — *vt (coll)* affrettare
rain *n* pioggia; — **water** acqua piovana; **in the** — alla pioggia; **–bow** *n* arcobaleno; — **check** biglietto per spettacolo all'aperto riusabile in caso di pioggia; **–coat** *n* impermeabile *m*; **–fall** *n* pioggia, precipitazione atmosferica; **–proof** *a* impermeabile; **–storm** *n* uragano di pioggia; **–y** *a* piovoso
raise *vt* alzare, sollevare; *(child)* allevare; *(money)* procurare; — *n* rialzo; aumento
raisin *n* uva passa
rake *n (tool)* rastrello; *(person)* libertino, scapestrato; *(naut)* inclinazione; — *vt* rastrellare, riunire; — **through** frugare; — *vi (naut)* inclinarsi
rakish *a* elegante
rally *n* riunione *f*; *(tennis)* ripresa; — *vt* adunare; *(banter)* beffare; — *vi* adunarsi; riprendersi
ram *n (mech)* stantuffo; *(naut)* sperone *m*; *(animal)* montone *m*; — *vt (beat)* battere; *(cram)* riempire; imbottire; *(naut)* speronare; **–rod** *n* bacchetta di fucile
ramble *vi* vagare; divagare; — *n (stroll)* passeggiata
rambling *a* errante, divagante, — *n* divagazione
ramification *n* ramificazione
ramp *n* rampa
rampage *n* furia, violenza; — *vi* esser violento, sfuriare
rampant *a* violento, aggressivo; *(unchecked)* sfrenato; *(heraldry)* rampante; **be** — imperversare
rampart *n* bastione *m*
ramshackle *a* pericolante, cadente
ranch *n* fattoria per bestiame; **–er** *n* fattore *m*, allevatore di bestiame
rancid *a* rancido; **–ity** *n* rancidezza
rancor *n* rancore *m*
random *a* fortuito; **at** — a casaccio
range *n* catena di montagne; distesa; portata; — **finder** telemetro; **kitchen** — fornello; **in** — a tiro; **out of** — fuori di portata; **–r** *n (forest)* guardia forestale; — *vt* attraversare; — *vi* vagare; variare
rank *n* grado, rango; — *a* rancido, forte; grossolano; *(growth)* esuberante; — *vt* classificare; — *vi* essere classificato; — **with** essere alla pari di
ranking *a* eminente
rankle *vi* infiammarsi
ransack *vt* perquisire; saccheggiare; frugare
ransom *vt* riscattare; — *n* riscatto
rant *vi* smaniare; — *vt* declamare
rap *n* colpetto; *(coll)* condanna, fio; — *vt* battere; — *vi* bussare
rapacious *a* rapace; **–ly** *adv* rapacemente;

–nous *n* rapacità
rape *n* violenza carnale, stupro; — *vt* violare, fare violenza carnale, stuprare; rapire
rapid *a* veloce, rapido; **–ity** *n* rapidità; **–s** *npl* rapida
rapid-fire *a* a tiro rapido
rapier *n* spada
rapport *n* armonia
rapt *a* rapito, estatico
rapture *n* trasporto; estasi *f*
rapturous *a* estatico
rare *a* raro; *(meat)* poco cotto; **–ly** *adv* di rado, raramente
rarefaction *n* rarefazione
rarefied *a* rarefatto
rarefy *vt* rarefare; — *vi* rarefarsi
rarity *n* rarità
rascal *n* briccone *m*
rash *n (med)* eruzione; — *a* temerario; **–ness** *n* imprudenza, avventatezza; **–ly** *adv* imprudentemente; irriflessivamente
rasp *n* raspa; — *vt* raspare; *(fig)* irritare; — *vi (sound)* raschiare
rasping *n* raschiamento; — *a* rauco
raspberry *n* lampone *m*
rat *n* topo, sorcio; **–trap** trappola per topi; **smell a —** subodorare, mangiare la foglia *(fig)*
ratchet *n* rocchetto
rate *n* proporzione; tariffa; velocità; **at the — of** al tasso di; **at any —** (fig) comunque, in ogni modo; **exchange —** quotazione di cambio; **interest —** saggio d'interesse; — *vt* stimare; valutare; — *vi* classificarsi
rather *adv* piuttosto, abbastanza
ratification *n* ratifica
ratify *vt* ratificare
rating *n* classificazione
ratio *n* ragione *f*
ration *n* razione; — *vt* razionare; **–ing** *n* razionamento
rational *a* razionale; **–ize** *vt* razionalizzare
rattle *vi* risonare; sbatacchiare; — *vt* far rumoreggiare; **become –d** *(coll)* confondersi; turbarsi; — *n* rumore *m*; chiacchierio; *(death)* rantolo; *(toy)* sonaglio
rattlebrain *n* chiacchierone *m*
rattlesnake *n* serpente a sonagli
raucous *a* rauco
ravage *vt* devastare; — *n* devastazione
ravaging *a* rovinoso
rave *vi* delirare, vaneggiare; *(coll)* entusiasmarsi
ravel *vt* avviluppare; imbrogliare
ravelling *n* filaccio
raven *n* corvo
ravenous *a* vorace; affamato
ravine *n* burrone *m*, voragine *f*
raving *a* delirante; *(coll)* straordinario; **–s** *npl* deliri *mpl (fig)*
ravish *vt* violare; *(delight)* incantare; **–ing** *a* incantevole
raw *a* crudo; inesperto; — **materials** materie prime; **–ness** *n* crudezza; rozzezza; escoriazione; inesperienza
rawboned *a* scarno
rawhide *n* cuoio greggio
ray *n* raggio; *(zool)* razza; — *vi* raggiare; — *vt* irradiare
rayon *n* raion *m*
raze *vt* radere; *(destroy)* distruggere
razor *n* rasoio; — **blade** lametta da barba; **safety —** rasoio di sicurezza
re *n* **in —** in merito a
reach *vt* raggiungere; arrivare; stendere; — *vi* estendersi; — *n* distesa, portata; **within —** possibile; a portata di mano
react *vi* reagire
reaction *n* reazione; **–ary** *a&n* reazionario
reactor *n* reattore *m*
read *vt* leggere; **–able** *a* leggibile; **–ing** *n* lettura; **–er** *n* lettore *m*; libro di lettura
readily *adv* volentieri; prontamente; facilmente
readiness *n* prontezza; facilità; **in —** pronto, alla mano
readjust *vt* raggiustare; riordinare; **–ment** *n* raggiustamento, riordinamento
readmission *n* riammissione
readmit *vt* riammettere
ready *a* pronto; — **money** contanti *mpl*; — *vt* preparare, predisporre
ready-made *a* confezionato
reaffirm *vt* riaffermare; **–ation** *n* riaffermazione
reagent *n* reagente *m*
real *a* reale; — **estate** beni immobili; **–ism** *n* realismo; **–ist** *n* realista *m&f*; **–istic** *a* realistico; **–istically** *adv* realisticamente; **–ity** *n* realtà
realization *n* realizzazione
realize *vt* accorgersi di; *(com)* realizzare
really *adv* veramente, davvero, effettivamente
realm *n* regno, reame *m*
realtor *n* agente immobiliare
realty *n* beni immobili
ream *vt* alesare; **–er** *n (machine)* alesatrice *f*; *(person)* alesatore *m*
reanimate *vt* rianimare
reanimation *n* rianimazione
reap *vt* mietere; falciare
reaper *n (mech)* mietitrice *f*; *(person)* mietitore *m*, mietitrice *f*
reappear *vi* riapparire; **–ance** *n* riapparizione, ricomparsa
reappoint *vt* rinominare; **–ment** *n* rinomina
reapproach *vt* ravvicinare
rear *n* di dietro, tergo; *(mil)* retroguardia; — *a* posteriore; — **admiral** contrammiraglio; — **guard** retroguardia; — *vt (lift)* erigere; *(young)* allevare; — *vi (horse)* impennarsi
rearm *vt* riarmare; **–ament** *n* riarmo, riarmamento
rearrange *vt* riordinare; **–ment** *n* riordinamento
reascend *vt&i* riascendere
reason *n* motivo, ragione *f*; **by — of** per causa di; **for this —** per questa ragione; **have — to** aver motivo di; **listen to —** ascoltar la ragione; **stand to —** essere innegabile; **–ing** *n* ragionamento; — *vi* ragionare; — *vt* razionalizzare; analizzare
reasonable *a* ragionevole; *(price)* conveniente

reasonably *adv* abbastanza; ragionevolmente
reassemble *vt* riunire ancora; — *vi* riunirsi ancora
reassurance *n* rassicurazione
reassure *vt* rassicurare
reawaken *vt* risvegliare; — *vi* risvegliarsi; **–ing** *n* risveglio
rebate *n* bonifica, sconto, diminuzione; — *vt* dedurre, diminuire
rebel *a&n* ribelle *m*
rebel *vi* ribellarsi
rebellion *n* rivolta
rebellious *a* ribelle
rebind *vt* rilegare, ricostruire
rebirth *n* rinascita
reborn *a* rinato
rebound *n* rimbalzo
rebound *vi* rimbalzare
rebroadcast *n* ritrasmissione; — *vt* ritrasmettere
rebuff *n* *(refusal)* rifiuto; *(repulse)* rigetto
rebuild *vt* ricostruire
rebuke *vt* rimproverare; — *n* rimprovero
recalcitrance *n* ricalcitramento
recalcitrant *a* ricalcitrante
recall *vt* richiamare; *(remember)* rammentare, ricordare; revocare
recall *n* richiamo; revoca
recant *vt* ritrattare; ripudiare; — *vi* ritrattarsi
recap *vt (auto)* ricostruire il battistrada
recapitulate *vt&i* ricapitolare
recapitulation *n* ricapitolazione
recapture *n* ripresa, ricupero; — *vt* ricatturare
recede *vi* recedere, indietreggiare
receding *a* recedente, indietreggiante
receipt *n* quietanza, ricevuta; — *vt* quietanzare
receivable *a* ricevibile; **accounts** — *(com)* conti esigibili
receive *vt* ricevere; **–r** *n* ricevitore *m*, destinatario; *(law)* curatore *m*
receiving *n* ricevimento; *(stolen goods)* ricettazione
recent *a* recente; fresco; **–ly** *adv* recentemente, poco fa
receptacle *n* ricettacolo
reception *n* accoglienza; ricevimento; *(radio)* ricezione
receptionist *n* accoglitrice *f*
receptive *a* ricettivo; **–ness** recettività
recess *n* recesso; nicchia; **school** — ricreazione
recess *vi* aggiornarsi; — *vt* formare rientranza
recession *n* regresso; *(com)* crisi economica; **–al** *a* recessionale
recidivist *n* recidivo
recipe *n* ricetta
recipient *n* recipiente, ricevente *m*
reciprocal *a* reciproco
reciprocate *vt* contraccambiare, reciprocare
reciprocity *n* reciprocità
recital *n* recita; *(telling)* rappresentazione
recitation *n* recitazione
recite *vt* recitare; declamare
reckless *a* temerario
reckon *vi* calcolare; *(coll)* supporre, credere
reckoning *n* computo; **day of** — giorno del giudizio; giorno di retribuzione
reclaim *vt* redimere; *(land)* bonificare
reclamation *n* redenzione; correzione; riforma; *(land)* bonifica
recline *vi* sdraiarsi; adagiarsi; — *vt* reclinare, adagiare
reclining *a* adagiato
recluse *n* eremita *m*
recognition *n* riconoscimento
recognizable *a* riconoscibile
recognizance *n* malleveria
recognize *vt* riconoscere
recoil *vi* ritirarsi, indietreggiare; rimbalzare; *(gun)* rinculare; — *n* indietreggiamento; rimbalzo; *(gun)* rinculo
recollect *vt* ricordare; **–ion** *n* ricordo; memoria
recommence *vt&i* ricominciare
recommend *vt* raccomandare; **–ation** *n* raccomandazione
recompense *n* ricompensa; — *vt* ricompensare
reconcilable *a* riconciliabile
reconcile *vt* riconciliare
reconciliation *n* riconciliazione
reconciliatory *a* riconciliatorio
recondite *a* recondito
recondition *vt* riaccondizionare; **–ing** *n* riaccondizionamento
reconnaisance *n* ricognizione
reconnoiter *vt* perlustrare; — *vi* fare una ricognizione
reconquer *vt* riconquistare
reconsider *vt* riconsiderare; **–ation** *n* riconsiderazione
reconstitute *vt* ricostituire
reconstruct *vt* ricostruire; **–ion** *n* ricostruzione
record *vt* registrare; *(phonograph)* incidere
record *n* registro; *(phonograph)* disco; *(sport)* primato; — **player** giradischi *m*; **off the** — non ufficiale; **–ing** *n* incisione; registrazione; **–s** *npl (law)* precedenti *mpl*
recorder *n* registratore *m*; archivista *m*; **tape** — fonografo (*or* incisore) a nastro
record-breaking *a* primatista
recount *n* ricomputo; riconto; — *vt* ricomputare, ricontare; *(narrate)* raccontare
recountal *n* racconto
recoup *vt* ricuperare, compensare; **–ment** *n* ricupero
recourse *n* rifugio, ricorso; **have — to** ricorrere a
recover *vi* guarire, rimettersi; — *vt* ricuperare; **–y** *n* guarigione *f*, ricupero
re-cover *vt* ricoprire
recreant *a* codardo
recreate *vt* svagare, ristorare; — *vi* ristorarsi, divertirsi
re-create *vt* ricreare
recreation *n* ricreazione, divertimento, svago; **–al** *a* ricreativo
recriminate *vi* recriminare
recrimination *n* recriminazione
recruit *vt* reclutare; — *n* recluta; **–ing** *n* reclutamento

rectal *a* rettale
rectangle *a* rettangolo
rectangular *a* rettangolare
rectifiable *a* corregibile
rectification *n* rettificazione
rectifier *n (elec)* raddrizzatore di corrente
rectify *vt* rettificare; *(elec)* raddrizzare
rectilinear *a* rettilineo
rectitude *n* rettitudine *f*
rector *n (eccl)* parroco, pastore *m*; **-y** *n* casa parrocchiale
rectum *n* retto
recombent *a* giacente
recuperate *vi* guarire, rimettersi; — *vt* ricuperare
recuperation *n* ricuperazione, ricupero
recur *vi* ricorrere; **-rence** *n* ricorrenza; ritorno; **-rent** *a* periodico, ricorrente
red *n&a* rosso; — **light** pericolo; — **pepper** pepe di Caienna; — **tape** *(fig)* burocrazia; **be in the** — *(com)* essere in deficit (*or* passivo); **-cap** *n* facchino; **-head** *n* chi ha i capelli rossi; **-ness** *n* rossore *m*; **-skin** *n (Indian)* pellerossa *m*
red- *(in comp)* **—blooded** *a* energico; — **eyed** cogli occhi infiammati; **—haired** *a* dai capelli rossi; **—handed** *a* con le mani nel sacco; **—hot** *a* rovente; **—letter day** giorno festivo
redden *vi* arrossire; — *vt* colorare di rosso
reddish *a* rossiccio
redecorate *vt* ridecorare
redeem *vt* redimere, riscattare; **-able** *a* redimibile; **-er** *n* chi riscatta
Redeemer *n* Redentore *m*
redemption *n* redenzione, riscatto
rediscover *vt* scoprire di nuovo
redistribute *vt* ridistribuire
redistribution *n* ridistribuzione
redolence *n* fragranza, profumo
redolent *a* fragrante, profumato
redouble *vt* raddoppiare; — *vi* raddoppiarsi
redoubtable *a* formidabile
redound *vi* ridondare
redraft *vt* redigere di nuovo
redress *n* rettifica, riparazione
redress *vt* rettificare
reduce *vt&i* ridurre; *(weight)* dimagrare, dimagrire
reducible *a* riducibile
reduction *n* riduzione
redundancy *n* ridondanza
redundant *a* ridondante
reduplicate *vt* raddoppiare
reduplication *n* raddoppiamento
reecho *vi&t* riecheggiare
reed *n* canna; *(musical instrument)* ancia; — *a* di canna
reeducate *vt* rieducare
reeducation *n* rieducazione
reef *n* scoglio; *(naut)* terzaruolo; — *vt* terzaruolare
reek *vt&i* fumare; esalare; *(stink)* puzzare
reel *n* aspo, bobina; *(spinning)* vacillamento; — **off** snocciolare; **news** — notiziario cinematografico; — *vt* avvolgere; — *vi* girare, vacillare
reeling *n* vacillamento; — *a* vacillante
reelect *vt* rieleggere; **-ion** *n* rielezione
reembark *vi* rimbarcarsi
reembody *vt* rincorporare
reenact *vt* eseguire di nuovo; *(law)* rimettere in vigore
reenlist *vi* riarruolarsi
reenter *vt* rientrare
reentry *n* rientrata
reequip *vt* riequipaggiare
reestablish *vt* ristabilire; **-ment** *n* ristabilimento, restaurazione
reexamination *n* riesame *m*
reexamine *vt* riesaminare
reexport *vt* riesportare; **-ation** *n* riesporto
reface *vt* rifare la facciata di
refashion *vt* rimodernare
refasten *vt* rilegare, riassicurare
refectory *n* refettorio
refer *vi* alludere; — *vt* riferire
referable *a* referibile
reference *n* allusione; referenza; richiamo; **letter of** — lettera di raccomandazione; — **book** libro di consultazione; — **library** biblioteca di consultazione; **with** — **to** rispetto a
referee *n* arbitro; — *vt* arbitrare
referendum *n* referendum *m*
referral *n* riferimento
refill *vt* riempire; — *n* rifornimento, ricambio
refine *vt* raffinare; **-d** *a* colto, raffinato; **-ment** *n* raffinatezza
refinery *n* raffineria
refit *vt* riparare
reflect *vt&i* riflettere, reflettersi, meditare; **-or** *n* riflettore *m*
reflection *n* riflessione; riflesso; critica
reflex *n* riflesso; **-ive** *a* riflessivo
reforest *vt* rimboscare; **-ation** *n* rimboscamento
reform *vt* riformare; — *vi* riformarsi; — *n* riforma; **-atory** *n* riformatorio; **-er** *n* riformatore *m*
reformation *n (moral)* emendamento; riforma
refract *vt* rifrangere; **-ion** *n* rifrazione; **-ive** *a* rifrattivo; **-or** *n* rifrattore *m*; **-ory** *a* rifrangente
refrain *vi* astenersi; — *n* ritornello; aria
refresh *vt* rinfrescare; **-ment** *n* rinfresco; **-ing** *a* rinfrescante
refrigerate *vt* refrigerare
refrigeration *n* refrigerazione
refrigerator *n* frigorifero
refuel *vt&i* rifornire di carburante
refuge *n* ricovero; rifugio; **take** — rifugiarsi
refugee *n* profugo
refulgence *n* splendore *m*
refulgent *a* rifulgente
refund *vt* rimborsare
refund, -ing *n* rimborso
refundable *a* rimborsabile
refurnish *vt* riprovvedere, riammobiliare
refusal *n* rifiuto
refuse *n* rifiuto; immondizie *fpl*
refuse *vt&i* rifiutare
refutation *n* confutazione
refute *vt* refutare
regain *vt* ricuperare, riguadagnare; — **consciousness** riprendersi
regal *a* regale; **-ia** *n* insegne regali

regale *vt (delight)* deliziare; *(fete)* festeggiare
regard *n* riguardo, stima; **have no — for** non aver riguardo per; **in — to** riguardo a; **in this** — sotto questo rispetto; — *vt* riguardare; stimare
regarding *prep* riguardo a
regardless *a* noncurante; — *adv* in ogni modo; — **of** nonostante
regards *npl* saluti *mpl*; **give** — presentare gli omaggi
regatta *n* regata
regency *n* reggenza
regenerate *vt* rigenerare; — *vi* rigenerarsi
regenerate *a* rigenerato
regeneration *n* rigenerazione
regent *n* reggente *m&f*
regime *n* regime *m*
regiment *n* reggimento; — *vt* irreggimentare; **-al** *a* reggimentale; **-ation** *n* reggimentazione
region *n* regione *f*; **-al** *a* regionale
register *n* registro; **cash** — registratore di cassa; — *vt* registrare; *(mail)* raccomandare; — *vi* iscriversi
registrar *n* archivista *m*; segretario
registration *n* registrazione; *(mail)* raccomandazione
registry *n* segretariato
regnant *a* regnante
regress *vi* regredire
regression *n* regressione
regressive *a* regressivo
regret *n* rammarico; **-ful** *a* rincresciuto; **-fully** *adv* con dispiacere; — *vt* rimpiangere; dispiacere di
regrettable *a* increscioso
regroup *vt* raggruppare di nuovo
regular *a* regolare; **-ity** *n* regolarità; **-ly** *adv* regolarmente; **-ize** *vt* regolarizzare
regulate *vt* regolare
regulation *n* regolamento; regola; — *a* regolamentare
regulator *n* regolatore *m*
regurgitate *vt&i* rigurgitare
regurgitation *n* rigurgito
rehabilitate *vt* riabilitare
rehabilitation *n* riabilitazione
rehearsal *n* prova
rehearse *vt* provare, ripetere
reheat *vt* riscaldare
reign *n* regno; — *vi* regnare; **-ing** *a* regnante
reimbursable *a* rimborsabile
reimburse *vt* rimborsare; **-ment** *n* rimborso
rein *n* redine *f*; — *vt* imbrigliare, frenare, controllare
reincarnation *n* reincarnazione
reincorporate *vt* reincorporare
reindeer *n* renna
reinforce *vt* rinforzare; **-d** *a* rinforzato; **-ment** *n* rinforzo
reinsert *vt* inserire di nuovo
reinstate *vt (position)* reintegrare; *(reestablish)* ristabilire; *(replace)* ricollocare; **-ment** *n* ristabilimento; ripristino
reinsurance *n* riassicurazione
reinsure *vt* riassicurare
reinvest *vt* rinvestire; **-ment** *n* rinvestimento
reissue *vt* riemettere; ripubblicare; — *n* riemissione; ripubblicazione
reiterate *vt* reiterare
reiteration *n* reiterazione
reject *n* respinto, rifiuto
reject *vt* scartare
rejection *n* rigetto; reiezione
rejoice *vi* rallegrarsi, gioire; — *vt* rallegrare
rejoicing *n* allegria; gioia
rejoin *vt* riunire di nuovo; *(meet)* raggiungere; *(reply)* replicare; — *vi* riunirsi di nuovo
rejoinder *n* replica
rejuvenate *vt* ringiovanire
rejuvenation *n* ringiovanimento
rekindle *vt* riaccendere; — *vi* riaccendersi
relapse *vi* ricadere; — *n* ricaduta
relate *vt (narrate)* raccontare; mettere in relazione; — *vi* riguardare; **-d** *a* imparentato; *(similar)* affine
relating *a* relativo
relation *n* rapporto, relazione; **in — to** in riferimento a; inerente a; **-ship** *n* rapporto, relazione, parentela
relative *n* parente *m&f*; — *a* relativo
relativity *n* relatività
relax *vt* rilassare; — *vi* rilassarsi, distrarsi; **-ation** *n* distensione, svago; **-ing** *a* calmante
relay *n* cambio, muta; *(elec)* raddrizzatore di corrente; *(rad)* trasmissione; — *vt (mail)* distribuire; *(rebroadcast)* ritrasmettere
release *vt* liberare, rilasciare; — *n* liberazione, rilascio; esonero; *(mech)* scarico
relegate *vt* relegare
relegation *n* relegazione
relent *vi* cedere, attenuarsi; **-less** *a* inflessibile; **-lessness** *n* implacabilità, inflessibilità
relevance *n* applicabilità, rapporto; pertinenza
relevant *a* pertinente, a proposito
reliability *n* fidatezza
reliable *a* degno di fiducia
reliably *adv* fidatamente
reliant *a* fiducioso
reliance *n* fiducia
relic *n* reliquia
relief *n* sollievo; *(help)* sussidio, aiuto; *(replace)* rilievo
relieve *vt* alleviare; esonerare; dare il cambio a
relight *vt* riaccendere
religion *n* religione *f*
religiosity *n* religiosità
religious *a* religioso
reline *vt* rifoderare; *(brakes)* rifasciare
relinquish *vt* abbandonare, rinunciare; **-ment** *n* rinuncia, abbandono
reliquary *n* reliquario
relish *n* gusto; condimento; — *vt (enjoy)* godere; *(taste)* gustare; — *vi* aver sapore di
relive *vt* rivivere
reload *vt* ricaricare
relocate *vt* ricollocare
relocation *n* ricollocazione

reluctance *n* riluttanza
reluctant *a* restio, poco disposto; **–ly** *adv* a malincuore
rely *vi* contare su
remain *vi* restare, rimanere; **–s** *npl* spoglie *fpl*, resti *mpl*
remainder *n* resto
remaining *a* rimanente
remake *vt* rifare
remark *n* osservazione, commento; — *vt* commentare; *(notice)* osservare, notare; **–able** *a* straordinario, notevole
re-mark *vt* marcare di nuovo
remarkably *adv* notevolmente
remarry *vi* risposarsi; — *vt* risposare
remediable *a* rimediabile
remedial *a* curativo, riparatore
remedy *n* rimedio; — *vt* rimediare
remember *vt&i* ricordare, ricordarsi
remembrance *n* memoria, ricordo, rimembranza
remind *vt&i* ricordare; **–er** *n* ricordo, memorandum *m*
reminiscence *n* reminiscenza, ricordo
reminiscent *a* reminiscente, memore
remiss *a* negligente; *(slow)* lento
remissible *a* remissibile
remission *n* remissione, perdono, condono
remit *vt* rimettere; *(decrease)* scemare; **–tal** *n* remissione; **–tance** *n* rimessa; **–ter** *n* mittente *m&f*
remnant *n* resto; scampolo
remodel *vt* ricostruire; rimodellare
remonstrance *n* rimostranza
remonstrate *vt* esprimere protestando; — *vi* rimostrare, protestare
remorse *n* rimorso; **–less** *a* spietato, senza rimorsi; **–ful** *a* pieno di rimorsi, contrito
remote *a* lontano, remoto; — **control** *n* radiotelecomando; **–ly** *adv* remotamente; **–ness** *n* lontananza
remold *vt* rimodellare
remount *vt* rimontare
removable *a* rimovibile
removal *n* trasloco, cambio
remove *vt* togliere, portar via; destituire; **–d** *a* lontano
remunerate *vt* rimunerare
remuneration *n* rimunerazione
remunerative *a* rimunerativo
renaissance *n* rinascimento
renal *a* renale
rename *vt* rinominare
renascence *n* rinascita
renascent *a* rinascente
rend *vt* stracciare, fendere; — *vi* lacerarsi, stracciarsi
render *vt* rendere; *(fat)* sciogliere; *(mus)* eseguire
rendezvous *n* appuntamento; — *vt* radunare; — *vi* riunirsi
rendition *n (mus)* esecuzione
renegade *n* rinnegato; apostata *m*
renege *vi (coll)* rinnegare la parola *(fig)*
renew *vt* rinnovare; ricominciare; — *vi* rinnovarsi; **–al** *n* rinnovo; **–able** *a* rinnovabile
renounce *vt* rinunciare; ripudiare; **–ment** *n* rinuncia
renovate *vt* rinnovare
renovation *n* rinnovazione
renown *n* rinomanza; celebrità, fama; distinzione; **–ed** *a* rinomato
rent *n (cloth)* strappo, spacco; *(income)* reddito; *(property)* affitto; **–al** *n* affitto; *(income)* rendita locativa
rent *vt* affittare, noleggiare; — *vi* venir affittato
renunciation *n* rinuncia
reoccupation *n* rioccupazione
reoccupy *vt* rioccupare
reopen *vt* riaprire; — *vi* riaprirsi; **–ing** *n* riapertura
reorder *vt* riordinare
reorganization *n* riorganizzazione
reorganize *vt&i* riorganizzare
repack *vi* rifare le valige
repaint *vt* ridipingere
repair *vt* riparare, accomodare; — *vi* recarsi; *(withdraw)* ritirarsi; —, **–ing** *n* riparazione; **–able** *a* riparabile; **–man** *n* riparatore *m*
reparable *a* rimediabile, riparabile
reparation *n* riparazione
repartee *n* frizzo, risposta pronta
repast *n* pasto
repatriate *vt&i* rimpatriare
repatriation *n* rimpatrio
repave *vt* rilastricare, ripavimentare
repay *vt* rimborsare, ripagare; valere la pena di, ricompensare; **–able** *a* ricompensabile; rimborsabile; **–ment** *n* restituzione; ricompensa
repeal *n* revoca, abrogazione; — *vt* revocare, abrogare
repeat *vt* ripetere; — *vi* ripetersi; — *n* ripetizione; risuono; **–er** *n* ripetitore *m*; *(law)* recidivo; **–ed** *a* ripetuto; **–edly** *adv* ripetutamente
repeating *a* periodico, ricorrente; — **decimal** decimale periodico
repel *vt* respingere
repellent *a* repellente
repelling *a* repulsivo
repent *vt&i* pentirsi di; **–ance** *n* pentimento; **–ant** *a* penitente; pentito
repercussion *n* ripercussione
repertoire *n* repertorio
repertory *n* deposito; *(theat)* repertorio
repetend *n (math)* decimale periodico
repetition *n* ripetizione
replace *vt* rimettere; sostituire; **–able** *a* rimpiazzabile, sostituibile; **–ment** *n* sostituzione
replant *vt* ripiantare
replate *vt* riplaccare
replay *vt (game)* giocare di nuovo; *(mus)* suonare di nuovo
replenish *vt* empire di nuovo; **–ment** *n* riempimento
replete *a* pieno, sazio
replica *n* copia, replica
reply *vt&i* replicare, rispondere; — *n* replica, risposta
repopulate *vt* ripopolare
repopulation *n* ripopolamento
report *vt* riferire; — *vi* presentarsi, consegnarsi; — *n* rapporto; rendiconto; *(gun)* detonazione; **–ing** *n* cronaca; **–er** *n* cronista *m*; *(newspaper)* giornalista *m&f*

repose *n* riposo; — *vi* riposare; riposarsi
repository *n* deposito, magazzino; *(cemetery)* cripta
repossess *vt* ripossedere, riavere
repossession *n* ripossessione
reprehend *vt* biasimare
reprehensible *a* riprensibile
reprehensibly *adv* reprensibilmente
reprehension *n* riprensione
represent *vt* rappresentare
representation *n* rappresentanza
representative *n* rappresentante *m*; deputato; — *a* rappresentativo; tipico
repress *vt* reprimere; **–ed** *a* represso
repression *n* repressione
repressive *a* repressivo
reprieve *n* sospensione, grazia; — *vt* graziare; *(penal)* rinviare l'esecuzione
reprimand *n* rimprovero; — *vt* rimproverare
reprint *n* ristampa; estratto di stampa; — *vt* ristampare; **–ing** *n* ristampa
reprisal *n* rappresaglia
reproach *n* biasimo, rimprovero; — *vt* rimproverare, sgridare; **–able** *a* riprovevole; **–ful** *a* accusante, criticante; **–less** *a* irreprensibile
reprobate *n&a* reprobo, immorale *m&f*; — *vt* riprovare
reprobation *n* riprovazione
reproduce *vt* riprodurre; — *vi* riprodursi
reproducible *a* riproducibile
reproduction *n* riproduzione
reproductive *a* riproduttivo
reproof *n* rimprovero, biasimo
reprove *vt* rimproverare, riprovare, censurare
reptile *n* rettile *m*
republic *n* repubblica; **–an** *n&a* repubblicano
republish *vt* ripubblicare
repudiate *vt* ripudiare, rigettare
repudiation *n* ripudio, ripulsa; *(law)* interdizione
repugnance *n* ripulsione, ripugnanza
repugnant *a* ripugnante
repulse *vt* respingere, repellere; ricusare; — *n* ripulsa, rifiuto
repulsion *n* repulsione, ripulsa
repulsive *a* schifoso, nauseante, ripulsivo
repurchase *n* ricompera; — *vt* ricomperare
reputable *a* stimabile, rispettabile
reputation *n* riputazione
repute *n* riputazione, stima; **–d** *a* reputato; — *vt* ritenere, reputare
request *n* richiesta; — *vt* chiedere, richiedere; **on** — in base a richiesta
require *vt* esigere; **–ment** *n* requisito, bisogno, necessità
requisite *n* requisito; — *a* richiesto, necessario
requisition *vt* requisire; — *n* requisizione
requital *n* contraccambio; *(retaliation)* rappresaglia
requite *vt* contraccambiare, ricompensare, ripagare
reroute *vt* desviare
resaddle *vt* risellare
resale *n* rivendita
rescind *vt* rescindere, abrogare
rescue *n* liberazione, riscatto; — *vt* liberare, salvare; **–r** *n* liberatore *m*
research *n* ricerca, investigazione; — *vt* investigare; — *vi* fare ricerca
resell *vt* rivendere
resemblance *n* rassomiglianza
resemble *vt* rassomigliare a
resent *vt* risentirsi di; **–ful** *a* rancoroso; **–ment** *n* risentimento
reservation *n* prenotazione; riserva
reserve *n* riserva; — *vt* riservare; *(engage)* prenotare
reserved *a* circospetto, riservato; **–ly** *adv* con riserbo
reservist *n* riservista *m*
reservoir *n* serbatoio, cisterna
reset *vt* rimettere; ricollocare; *(gem)* rincastonare; *(print)* ricomporre
resettle *vt* ristabilire; — *vi* ristabilirsi
reside *vi* risiedere
residence *n* domicilio, residenza
resident *n&a* abitante, residente *m*; **–ial** *a* residenziale
residual *a* residuale
residue *n* residuo
resign *vt* dare le dimissioni; rinunciare; — **oneself** rassegnarsi; **–ed** *a* rassegnato; **–edly** con rassegnazione
resignation *n* rassegnazione; dimissioni *fpl*
resilience *n* elasticità
resilient *a* elastico
resin *n* resina; **–ous** *a* di resina, resinoso
resist *vt&i* resistere; **–ance** *n* resistenza; **–ant** *a* resistente; **–ible** *a* resistibile; **–or** *n (elec)* resistenza
resole *vt* risuolare
resolute *a* risoluto
resolution *n* risoluzione; proponimento
resolve *vt* risolvere, decidere; — *vi* risolversi, decidersi
resonance *n* risonanza
resonant *a* risonante
resonator *n* risonatore *m*
resort *n* ricorso; *(summer)* luogo di villeggiatura; — *vi* ricorrere
resound *vi* risonare; **–ing** *a* risonante
resource *n* risorsa; **–ful** *a* abile, intraprendente, ingegnoso; pieno di risorse; **–fulness** *n* intraprendenza
resources *npl (financial)* mezzi economici; *(natural)* risorse naturali
respect *n* rispetto; **in this** — sotto questo riguardo; **with** — **to** riguardo a; con rispetto a; **–able** *a* rispettabile; **–ability** *n* rispettabilità; **–ful** *a* rispettoso; **–fully** *adv* con rispetto; — *vt* rispettare
respecting *prep* riguardo a, circa
respective *a* rispettivo; **–ly** *adv* rispettivamente
respiration *n* respirazione
respirator *n* respiratore *m*
respiratory *a* respiratorio
respire *vt&i* respirare
respite *n* tregua, respiro
resplendent *a* risplendente
respond *vt&i* rispondere
respondent *n (law)* imputato; — *a* rispondente
response *n* responso, risposta; *(med)* riflesso
responsibility *n* responsabilità

responsible *a* responsabile
responsive *a* accondiscendente, corresponsivo
rest *n* resto; riposo; *(mus)* pausa; *(support)* appoggio, sostegno; **take a —** riposarsi, prendere un riposo; **–ful** *a* calmo; riposante; **–fully** *adv* riposatamente; — *vt&i* riposare; riposarsi
restate *vt* riesporre, ridire
restaurant *n* ristorante *m*
restive *a* restio; ostinato; **–ness** *n* ostinatezza; restio
restless *a* inquieto, irrequieto; **–ness** *n* inquietudine *f*
restock *vt* rifornire
restorable *a* restaurabile
restoration *n* restaurazione, restauro
restorative *n&a* ristorativo
restore *vt* restaurare; restituire
restrain *vt* trattenere
restraint *n* restrizione; detenzione; *(manner)* riservatezza
restrict *vt* restringere; **–ive** *a* restrittivo
restriction *n* restrizione
rest room gabinetto di decenza
result *n* risultato; — *vi* risultare; **as a — of** in seguito a
resultant *a* risultante
résumé *n* riassunto
resume *vt&i* riprendere
resumption *n* ripresa
resurge *vi* risorgere
resurgence *n* risorgimento
resurgent *a* risorgente
resurrect *vt* risuscitare
resurrection *n* risurrezione
resuscitate *vt&i* risuscitare
resuscitation *n* ristabilimento, ravvivamento
ret *vt* macerare
retail *n (com)* dettaglio; vendita al minuto; — *a* al minuto; — *vt* vendere al minuto; dettagliare; **–er** *n* venditore al minuto; dettagliante *m*
retain *vt* ritenere; **–er** *n* servitore *m*; *(law)* onorario
retaining *a* che ritiene; **— wall** muro di sostegno
retake *vt* riprendere
retaliate *vi* render pan per focaccia *(fig)*, rivalersi; — *vt* ritorcere, rendere
retaliation *n* rappresaglia; contraccambio; ritorsione
retaliatory *a* di rappresaglia
retard *vt* ritardare, rallentare; — *vi* tardare; **–ed** *a* ritardato
retch *vi* recere; **–ing** *n* conato di vomito
retell *vt* riraccontare, ridire
retention *n* conservazione; ritenzione
retentive *a* ritentivo; **–ness** *n* ritenitiva, ritentiva
reticence *n* reticenza
reticent *a* reticente
retina *n* retina
retinue *n* corteo, seguito
retire *vt* ritirare; — *vi* ritirarsi; *(to bed)* andare a letto; *(from work)* andare in pensione; **–d** *a* in pensione; a riposo; **–ment** *n* riposo, ritiro
retiring *a* riservato, ritirato
retort *n* ritorsione; *(chem)* storta; — *vt&i* ribattere, rimbeccare, ritorcere
retouch *vt* ritoccare
retrace *vt* riandare, ricalcare
retract *vt* ritirare; ritrattare; — *vi* ritirarsi; ritrattarsi
retractable *a* ritrattabile
retractile *a* retrattile
retraction *n* ritrattazione
retractor *n (anat)* muscolo retrattore
retread *vt (auto)* rifare il battistrada
retreat *n* ritirata; ritiro; — *vi* ritirarsi; recedere; **–ing** *a* ritirante; *(mil)* in ritirata
retrench *vt* ridurre; — *vi* risparmiare; **–ment** *n* risparmio
retribution *n* castigo; ricompensa, retribuzione
retrieve *vt* ricuperare
retroact *vi* retroagire
retroaction *n* retroazione
retroactive *a* retroattivo
retrogradation *n* retrogradazione
retrograde *vi* ritirarsi, retrogradare; — *a* retrogrado
retrogress *vi* retrogredire; **–ion** *n* retrogressione; **–ive** *a* retrogressivo
retrospect, retrospection *n* retrospetto, retrospezione
retroversion *n* retroversione
return *vt* restituire; *(send back)* rinviare; *(reciprocate)* contraccambiare; — *vi* ritornare; — *n* ritorno; — *a* di ritorno; **— match** *(sport)* partita di ritorno; **— ticket** biglietto di andata e ritorno; **in —** per contro; a cambio; **in — for** in cambio di
returnable *a* restituibile
reunion *n* riunione *f*
reunite *vt* riunire; — *vi* riunirsi
revalue *vt* rivalutare
revamp *vt* riorganizzare, rifare
reveal *vt* rivelare
reveille *n (mil)* diana
revel *n* baldoria, festa; — *vi* far baldoria (*or* festa); **–ler** *n* crapulone *m*; **–ry** *n* baldoria
revelation *n* rivelazione *f*
revenge *n* vendetta; **–ful** *a* vendicativo; — *vt* vendicare; **take — on** vendicarsi con
revenue *n* reddito, entrata; fisco
reverberate *vt&i* riverberare, ripercuotere, riflettere
reverberation *n* riverbero
revere *vt* riverire
reverence *n* riverenza; venerazione
reverend *a* reverendo
reverent *a* riverente
reverie *n* fantasticheria; meditazione
reversal *n* inversione; revoca
reverse *n* rovescio; opposto, contrario; — *(auto)* retromarcia; **— side** parte opposta; — *a* opposto; — *vt* invertire
reversion *n* riversione, ritorno
revert *vi* rivolgersi, ritornare
review *n* rivista; *(book)* recensione *f*; — *vt* rivedere; recensire; **–er** *n* recensore *m*, critico
revile *vt* insultare
revise *vt* correggere, rivedere

reviser *n* revisore *m*
revision *n* revisione
revisit *vt* rivisitare
revival *n* risorgimento; risveglio; ravvivamento; *(arts)* riesumazione; *(eccl)* risveglio religioso; **–ist** *n* promotore di risvegli religiosi
revive *vt* ravvivare; — *vi* rianimarsi, rivivere
reviver *n* ravvivatore *m*
revocable *a* revocabile
revocation *n* revoca
revoke *vt* revocare
revolt *vi* ribellarsi; — *vt* nauseare; — *n* rivolta; **–ing** *a* nauseante
revolution *n* rivoluzione; *(mech)* giro; **–ary** *a* rivoluzionario; **–ize** *vt* rivoluzionare
revolve *vt&i* girare
revolver *n* revolver *m*, rivoltella
revolving *a* girevole, giratorio
revue *n (theat)* rivista
revulsion *n* repulsione
revulsive *n&a* revulsivo
reward *n* ricompensa; — *vt* rimunerare, premiare; **–ing** *a* ricompensatore, di ricompensa
rewin *vt* rivincere
rewind *vt* avvolgere di nuovo
reword *vt* ripetere; mettere in altre parole
rewrite *vt* riscrivere; — *n* riscritto
rhapsodical *a* rapsodico
rhapsody *n* rapsodia
Rhenish *a* del Reno
rheometer *n* reometro
rheoscope *n* reoscopo
rheostat *n* reostato
rhetoric *n* rettorica; **–al** *a* rettorico; **–ian** *n* retore *m*
rheumatic *a* reumatico; — **fever** febbre reumatica
rheumatism *n* reumatismo
Rh factor fattore Rh
Rhine Reno; — **wine** vino del Reno
rhinestone *n* strasso
rhinoceros *n* rinoceronte *m*
rhizome *n (bot)* rizoma
rhombus *n (math)* rombo
rhubarb *n* rabarbaro
rhyme *n* rima; — *vt&i* rimare; **no — or reason** senza capo nè coda *(fig)*
rhymester *n* rimatore *m*
rhythm *n* ritmo; **–ic** *a* ritmico
rib *n* costola; — *vt* centinare; *(coll)* beffare, deridere
ribald *a* licenzioso, scurrile; **–ry** *n* scurrilità
ribbing *n* costole *fpl*; centinatura; *(coll)* beffa, presa in giro
ribbon *n* nastro; **tear to —s** fare a brandelli
rice *n* riso; — **field** risaia; — **paper** carta riso (*or* cinese); — **pudding** riso al latte
rich *a* ricco; **–es** *npl* ricchezza; **–ness** *n* ricchezza; **grow —** arricchirsi; **the —** i ricchi
rickets *npl (med)* rachitismo
rickety *a* rachitico
ricochet *vi* rimbalzare; — *n* rimbalzo
rid *vt* sbarazzare, liberare; **get — of** sbarazzarsi di
riddance *n* liberazione
riddle *n* indovinello, enigma *m*; — *vt* risolvere; spiegare; — *vi* parlare per enigmi
riddle *vt (perforate)* crivellare
ride *vt&i* cavalcare; andare in (*or* a); — *n* corsa; cavalcata; passeggiata
rider *n (horseback)* cavaliere *m*; *(jockey)* fantino; *(law)* codicillo, aggiunta
ridge *n* cresta; *(roof)* colmo, comignolo
ridicule *n* ridicolo; — *vt* deridere, mettere in ridicolo
ridiculous *a* ridicolo
riding *n* equitazione; — **boots** stivali per equitazione; — **breeches** calzoni per equitazione; — **habit** abito da amazzone; — **master** maestro d'equitazione; — **school** scuola d'equitazione
rife *a* prevalente, comune; abbondante; — **with** abbondante di
riffraff *n* rifiuti *mpl*; canaglia, marmaglia
rifle *n* fucile *m*; — **range** campo di tiro; portata di fucile; **within — shot** a portata di fucile; — *vt* predare, derubare
rifleman *n* fuciliere *m*
rift *n* crepa, fessura
rig *n* arnese *m*; — *vt (naut)* attrezzare; equipaggiare; *(tamper)* manipolare fraudolentemente
rigging *n (naut)* attrezzatura
right *n* ragione, diritto; — **and wrong** il giusto e l'ingiusto; — **of way** *(law)* diritto di passaggio; — **side** destra; *(material)* dritto; — **side up** a faccia in sù *(fig)*; **have the —** aver il diritto
right *a* giusto, diritto, corretto; — **angle** angolo retto; **all —** benissimo; **be —** aver ragione
right *adv (directly)* dirittamente; *(justly)* giustamente; *(well)* bene; — **and left** destra e sinistra; — **away** subito; **do —** far bene
right *vt* raddrizzare, correggere; — *vi* raddrizzarsi
righteous *a* retto; giusto; virtuoso; **–ly** *adv* rettamente; **–ness** *n* rettitudine *f*
rightful *a* legittimo; giusto; equo; **–ly** *adv* legittimamente; equamente; giustamente
right-handed *a* destro
rightly *adv* rettamente, esattamente
rights *npl* diritti *mpl*; **by —** a rigore, per diritto; **within one's —** nei propri diritti
rigid *a* rigido, severo; **–ity** *n* rigidità, severità; rigidezza; **–ly** *adv* rigidamente
rigmarole *n* tiritera
rigor n rigidità, severità; *(med)* brivido; **–ous** *a* rigoroso; **–ousness** *n* rigorosità; — **mortis** rigidità cadaverica
rile *vt (coll)* irritare
rill *n* ruscello
rim *n (wheel)* cerchione *m*; orlo; *(eyeglass)* montatura; — *vt* orlare, bordare; **–less** *a* senza montatura
rime *vt* brinare; — *n* brina
rind *n* buccia, scorza
rinderpest *n* peste bovina
ring *n* anello; cerchio; — **finger** anulare *m*; **boxing —** ring *m*, quadrato; **wedding —** anello nuziale, fede *f*, vera; —

vt&i suonare; *(surround)* circondare; **-leader** *n* agitatore, capobanda *m*; **-worm** *n* tigna
ringing *n* suono, scampanio; — *a* risuonante, sonoro
rink *n* pista di pattinaggio
rinse *vt* sciacquare; — *n* risciacquata
riot *n* sommossa; **-er** *n* rivoltoso, sedizioso; **-ing** *n* sedizia; libertinaggio; **-ous** *a* sedizioso; libertino
rip *vt* lacerare, scucire; — *vi* lacerarsi; — **open** aprire; — *n* scucitura; strappo; *(coll)* furfante *m*; **-cord** *n* cordella per aprire il paracadute (*or* la valvola del pallone aerostatico)
ripe *a* maturo; **-ness** *n* maturità
ripen *vt&i* maturare; **-ing** *n* maturazione
ripple *n* increspatura; mormorio; — *vt* increspare; — *vi* incresparsi
rippling *n* increspamento; mormorio; — *a* increspato
rise *vi* alzarsi; sorgere; *(increase)* aumentare; — *n* alzata; ascesa; *(ground)* salita, elevazione; **-r** *n* chi si alza; *(stair)* alzata di gradino
risibility *n* risibilità
risible *a* risibile
rising *n* rivolta; levata; *(tide)* flusso; — *a* sorgente, crescente
risk *n* rischio; — *vt* rischiare; **-y** *a* rischioso; **run a** — correre un rischio
riskiness *n* rischiosità
risqué *a* salace
rite *n* rito, cerimonia
ritual *n&a* rituale, cerimoniale *m*; **-ism** *n* ritualismo; **-ist** *n* ritualista *m&f*; **-istic** *a* ritualistico
rival *n&a* rivale; **-ry** *n* rivalità; — *vt* emulare
rive *vt* fendere; — *vi* fendersi
river *n* fiume *m;* **down-** *adv* a valle; **-head** *n* sorgente *f*; **-side** *n* sponda di fiume; **up-** *adv* a monte
rivet *n* bullone *m*, ribattino; — *vt* ribadire, fissare; **-er** ribaditore *m*, ribaditrice *f*
Riviera Riviera
rivulet *n* ruscelletto
roach *n (fish)* lasca; scarafaggio
road *n* strada; — **map** mappa stradale; **main** — strada maestra; **on the** — in cammino; **-bed** *n* fondo stradale; **-block** *n* barricata stradale; **-house** *n* ostello, locanda, albergo; **-side** *n* bordo stradale; **-stead** *n (naut)* rada, ancoraggio; **-way** *n* carreggiata
roadster *n* automobile da sport
roam *vt&i* vagare, percorrere; **-er** *n* vagabondo
roan *a&n* roano
roar *vi* ruggire; — *vt* urlare; — *n* ruggito; *(laughter)* scroscio; **-ing** *a* ruggente; — **with laughter** scoppiare dalle risa
roast *vt* arrostire, torrefare; *(coll)* criticare; — *n* arrosto; — *a* arrostito
roaster *n (coffee)* tostino; *(person)* rosticciere *m*
rob *vt* derubare, rubare
robber *n* ladro; **-y** *n* furto, rapina
robe *n* veste *f*; *(law)* toga; — *vt* vestire; — *vi* vestirsi
robin *n* pettirosso
robot *n* automa *m*
robust *a* vigoroso, robusto; **-ness** *n* robustezza
rock *n* roccia, pietra; — **bottom** il punto più basso; — **crystal** quarzo; — **garden** giardino alpino; — **salt** salgemma *m*; — **wool** *(min)* fibra minerale; — *vt* cullare; — *vi* cullarsi; *(totter)* barcollare; — *vt&i* dondolare; **-y** *a* roccioso
rock-bottom *a* il più basso
rocker *n* dondolo
rocket *n* razzo; — **propulsion** propulsione a razzo
rocking *n* oscillazione; — *a* oscillante; a dondolo; — **chair** sedia a dondolo; — **horse** cavallo a dondolo
rococo *n* rococò
rod *n* verga, pertica; *(curtain)* bacchetta da tenda; *(fishing)* canna; *(measure)* 5 metri circa
rodent *n&a* roditore *m*
roe *n (deer)* capriolo
Roentgen rays raggi Roentgen
rogue *n* furfante *m*
roguish *a* furfante; malizioso; **-ness** *n* furfanteria
roil *vt (turbid)* intorbidire; irritare
roisterer *n* millantatore *m*; schiamazzatore *m*
role *n* parte *f*
roll *n* rotolo; *(bread)* panino; *(film)* bobina di pellicola; *(list)* lista; — **call** appello; — *vt* arrotolare, rotolare; — **over** rovesciarsi; — **up** *(sleeves)* rimboccare; — *vi* rotolarsi; arrotolarsi; rullare; oscillare
roller *n (mech)* cilindro; rullo; — **bearing** cuscinetto a sfere; — **skates** pattini a rotelle
rolling *n* rotolamento; rullio; — **in wealth** ricchissimo; — **mill** laminatoio; — **pin** matterello
roly-poly *a* tozzo
Roman *a&n* romano
Romania Rumania; **-n** *a&n* rumeno
romance *n&a* romanzo; *(mus)* romanza; — *vi* favoleggiare
Romance *a* neolatino, romanzo; — **languages** lingue romanze
Romanesque *n&a* romanico
romantic *a* romantico; **-ism** *n* romanticismo
romp *vi* ruzzare; **-ers** *npl* tuta da bambino
rood *n* crocifisso
roof *n (house)* tetto; *(mouth)* palato; **-ing** *n* tetto; — *vt* ricoprire con tetto; mettere il tetto
rook *n (chess)* torre *f*; *(zool)* cornacchia; — *vt* truffare
room *n* stanza; *(space)* posto, spazio; **make** — **for** far posto per; — **and board** pensione completa; **-er** *n* inquilino; **-ette** *n (rail)* cabina; **-y** *a* spazioso, ampio; — *vt&i* alloggiare
roost *n* pollaio; — *vi* appollaiarsi
rooster *n* gallo
root *n* radice *f*; **square** — radice quadrata; — *vi* radicarsi; — *vt (establish)* radicare; *(plant)* piantare; — **out**

sradicare; **–ed** *a* radicato
rope *n* corda; — *vt* allacciare; — **in** *(sl)* coinvolgere
ropy *a* viscido, viscoso
rosary *n* rosario, corona
rose *a&n* rosa; **–bud** *n* bocciuolo di rosa; **–bush** *n* rosaio; — **water** acqua di rose; — **window** rosone *m*
rose-colored *a* di color rosa; ottimista; **look through — glasses** veder tutto rosa *(fig)*
rosemary *n* rosmarino
rosin *n* resina
roster *n* lista, ruolo
rostrum *n* rostro, tribuna
rosy *a* roseo
rot *vt&i* imputridire; — *n* putrefazione, carie *f*; *(sl)* assurdità
rotary *a* rotatorio; — **press** rotativa
rotate *vt&i* girare, ruotare
rotation *n* rotazione
rote *n* rutina; **by** — a memoria
rotten *a* bacato, putrido, marcio; **–ness** *n* putrefazione
rotund *a* rotondo; **–ity** *n* rotondità
rotunda *n* rotonda
rouge *n* rossetto, belletto; — *vt* imbellettare
rough *a* ruvido; rozzo; *(coll)* difficile; — **draft** abbozzo; **–neck** *n (sl)* grossolano; **–ly** *adv* ruvidamente; aspramente; rozzamente; **–ness** *n* ruvidità
rough vt irruvidire; abbozzare
roughen *vt* irruvidire; arrozzire; — *vi* arrozzarsi; irruvidirsi
roughshod *a* ferrato grossolanamente; **ride — over** trattare duramente
round *a* rotondo; — **number** cifra tonda; — **trip** viaggio di andata e ritorno; **–up** *n (cattle)* raduno, retata *(fig)*; — *n* cerchio; *(gun)* scarica; *(patrol)* ronda; *(series)* serie *f*; *(sport)* ripresa; giro, ciclo; — *adv* intorno; attorno; in giro; — *prep* intorno a; — *vt* arrotondare; completare; circondare; — *vi* arrotondarsi, girarsi; — **up** *(coll)* riunire
roundabout *a* evasivo, indiretto
roundness *n* rotondità
round-shouldered *a* dalle spalle rotonde (*or* curve)
round-the-clock *a&adv* giorno e notte
rouse *vt* svegliare; suscitare; — *vi* svegliarsi
rousing *a* animatore, eccitante
rout *vt* sbaragliare; — *n* sconfitta
route *n* rotta, via
routine *n* rutina, abito; — *a* rutinario, abitudinario; abituale
rove *vi* vagare, errare; **–r** *n* girovago
roving *a* vagabondo
row *n* baruffa, litigio; lite *f*, rissa; — *vi* litigare; bisticciare
row *n* riga, fila; **–boat** *n* barca a remi; — *vi* remare; — *vt* muovere a remi
royal *a* regale, reale, regio; **–ist** *n* monarchico; **–ly** *adv* regalmente
royalty *n* regalità, maestà, monarchia; reali *mpl*; *(book)* diritto d'autore; *(patent)* percentuale sugli utili
rub *n* fregata; ostacolo; frizione; **–down** *n* massaggio; — *vt&i* strofinare, fregare; — **the wrong way** offendere; — **out** cancellare; *(kill, sl)* fare fuori *(sl)*
rubber *n* gomma; *(cards)* partita; — **band** elastico; — **stamp** stampino di gomma; **–ize** *vt* gommare
rubberneck *n (sl)* ficcanaso; — *vi (sl)* ficcare il naso
rubbers *npl* soprascarpe, galosce *fpl*
rubbish *n* immondizie *fpl*; corbellerie *fpl*
rubble *n* pietrisco, breccia
rubric *n* rubrica
ruby *n* rubino
rudder *n* timone *m*
ruddy *a* rubizzo
rude *a* maleducato; rozzo; **–ly** *adv* grossolanamente, rozzamente; **–ness** *n* rozzezza; grossolanità
rudiment *n* rudimento; **–ary** *a* rudimentale
rue *n (bot)* ruta; — *vt* deplorare; pentirsi di; — *vi* pentirsi; addolorarsi; **–ful** *a* malinconico, doloroso
ruff *n* gorgiera
ruffian *n* malfattore *m*, ruffiano
ruffle *vt* arruffare; increspare; turbare; — *vi* arruffarsi; incresparsi; turbarsi; — *n* increspatura; *(drum)* rullio
rug *n* tappeto
rugged *a* ruvido; austero; robusto; **–ness** *n* ruvidezza, inflessibilità
rugose *a* rugoso
rugosity *n* rugosità
ruin *n* rovina; — *vt* rovinare; **–ation** *n* rovina; — *vt* rovinare; **–ed** *a* rovinato; **–ous** *a* rovinoso; in rovina
rule *n* regola; riga; governo; — **of thumb** regola per esperienza; **as a** — di regola; **slide** — regolo calcolatore; — *vi* regnare; — *vt* regolare; governare; *(draw lines)* rigare; **–d** *a* rigato; governato; **–d paper** carta rigata
ruler *n (measure)* regolo; governante *m*
ruling *n* rigatura; governo; *(law)* verdetto; — *a* dominante
rum *n* rum *m*
rumble *n* rimbombo, rintruono; — *vi* rombare, rintronare
rumbling *a* rimbombo, brontolio, rintruono; — *a* rimbombante
ruminant *n (zool)* ruminante *m*
ruminate *vt&i* ruminare; meditare
rumination *n* ruminazione
rummage *vt&i* frugare, rovistare
rumor *n* diceria; — *vt* divulgare; **it is –ed that** corre voce che
rump *n* posteriore *m*, deretano, culo; *(horse)* groppa
rumple *vt* sgualcire, scompigliare
rumpus *n (coll)* strepito, chiasso
run *n* corsa; *(cattle)* recinto; *(cycle)* serie; *(itinerary)* percorso; *(stocking)* smagliatura; **first** — *(movies)* prima visione; **in the long** — a lungo andare; **on the** — in fuga
run *vt&i* correre; *(extend)* stendersi, spandersi; *(machine)* funzionare; *(manage)* dirigere; *(com)* gestire; *(wound)* suppurare; — **away** fuggire; — **across** imbattersi in; — **down** investire; — **for it** darsela a gambe *(fig)*; — **into** cadere in, raggiungere; — **off** fuggire; stam-

pare; versare; — **over** scorrere; *(auto)* investire; ripetere; — **up** accumulare; — **up against** discordare con
runaway *n&a* fuggitivo
rundown *n* ripasso rapido
run-down *a (clock)* scaricato; *(person)* esaurito, debilitato
rung *n* piuolo
run-in *n (coll)* disaccordo
run-of-the-mill *a* comune, ordinario
runner *n (sport)* corridore *m*; *(stocking)* smagliatura
runner-up *n (sport)* secondo arrivato
running *a* corrente; da corsa; *(med)* purulento; — *n* corsa; marcia; funzionamento; — **board** montatoio
runt *n* nano, pigmeo
runway *n* pista
rupture *n* rottura; *(med)* ernia; — *vt* rompere; erniare; — *vi* rompersi; erniarsi
rural *a* rurale
ruse *n* stratagemma *m*
rush *n* furia; — *vi* affrettarsi, sbrigarsi; — *vt* affrettare, sbrigare; — **hour** ora di punta *(coll)*
rush *n (bot)* giunco
rushing *a* precipitoso
russet *n&a* rossetto
Russia Russia
Russian *a&n* russo
rust *n* ruggine *f*; — *vt* arrugginire; — *vi* arrugginirsi; **-y** *a* rugginoso
rustic *a* rustico
rustiness *n* rugginosità
rustle *n* fruscio, mormorio; — *vi* frusciare, stormire
rustler *n* ladro di bestiame
rut *n* solco; trantran *m (coll)*
ruthless *a* spietato; **-ly** *adv* spietatamente
rye *n* segala; *(bread)* pane di segala

S

Sabbath *n (Christian)* domenica; *(Jewish)* sabato
saber *n* sciabola; — *vt* sciabolare
sable *n* zibellino; — *a* di zibellino
sabotage *n* sabotaggio; — *vt* sabotare
saccharin *n* saccarina
sack *n* sacco; **-cloth** *n* tela da sacco; — *vt* insaccare; *(discharge)* licenziare
sack *n (pillage)* saccheggio; — *vt* saccheggiare
sacrament *n* sacramento; **-al** *a* sacramentale
sacred *a* sacro; inviolabile; **-ness** *n* santità
sacrifice *n* sacrifizio; — *vt* sacrificare; *(com)* vendere con perdita
sacrificial *a* sacrificatorio, di sacrifizio
sacrilege *n* sacrilegio
sacrilegious *a* sacrilego
sacristan *n* sagrestano
sacristy *n* sagrestia
sacrosanct *a* sacrosanto
sacrum *n (anat)* osso sacro
sad *a* triste; **-ly** *adv* tristemente; gravemente; dolorosamente; **-ness** *n* tristezza
sadden *vt* rattristare; — *vi* rattristarsi
saddle *n* sella; **-bag** *n* bisaccia; — **horse** cavallo da sella; — *vt* sellare; accollare; gravare; **be -d with** accollarsi di
safe *a* salvo, sicuro; — *n* cassaforte *f*; — **and sound** sano e salvo; **-guard** *n* salvaguardia; **-keeping** *n* custodia; **-ly** *adv* con sicurezza; **-ness** *n* sicurezza
safe-conduct *n* salvacondotto
safety *n* salvezza, sicurezza; impunità; — **belt** cintura di salvataggio; — **glass** vetro compensato, vetro infrangibile; — **match** fiammifero svedese; — **pin** spilla di sicurezza; — **razor** macchinetta da barba; — **valve** valvola di sicurezza
saffron *n* zafferano
sag *vi* cedere; abbassarsi; — *n* cedimento, depressione
sagacious *a* sagace
sagacity *n* sagacità, sagacia
sage *n* savio; *(bot)* salvia; — *a* prudente, saggio
sagging *a* cascante, cedente; spiegazzato; — *n* cedimento
said *a* suddetto, detto, sopradetto
sail *n* vela; — *vt&i* veleggiare; salpare, partire, navigare; **-boat** *n* barca a vela
sailing *n* navigazione; — **ship** nave a vela
sailor *n* marinaio
saint *n* santo; **-ed** *a* sacro, santo, santificato; **-ly** *a* santo, devoto, pio; — *vt* canonizzare
sake *n* amore *m*; ragione *f*; **for the — of** per amor di
salaam *n* salamelecco; — *vt* fare salamelecchi a
salable *a* vendibile
salacious *a* salace
salacity *n* salacità
salad *n* insalata; **fruit** — macedonia di frutta; — **bowl** insalatiera; — **dressing** condimento per insalata
salamander *n* salamandra
salaried *a* salariato
salary *n* stipendio; salario
sale *n* vendita; **auction** — vendita all'asta; **clearance** — liquidazione; **for** — da vendere
sales *npl* vendite *fpl*; — **tax** tassa sulle vendite; **-clerk** *n* venditore in negozio, commesso; **-room** *n* sala di vendita
salesman *n* venditore *m*, commesso; **-ship** *n* arte del vendere; **traveling** — commesso viaggiatore, piazzista *m*
salient *n&a* saliente *m*
saline *a* salino, salso; — *n* salina
saliva *n* saliva
salivary *a* salivare
salivate *vi* salivare
sallow *a* giallastro pallido
sally *n (mil)* sortita; uscita; escursione; — *vi* fare una sortita
salmon *n* salmone *m*
saloon *n* taverna; bar *m*
salt *n* sale *m*; — **water** acqua salata (*or* di mare); **rock** — salgemma; **table** — sale da tavola; **-cellar** *n* saliera; **-peter** *n* salnitro; **-shaker** *n* saliera; — *vt* salare; **-ed** *a* salato; **-y** *a* salato

saltiness *n* salsezza
saltworks *n* salina
salubrious *a* salubre
salutary *a* salutare
salutation *n* saluto
salute *vt* salutare; — *n* saluto; *(cannon)* salva
salvage *n* salvataggio; — *vt* ricuperare, salvare
salvation *n* salvezza, salute *f*
salve *n* unguento, emolliente *m*; — *vt* calmare, lenire
salver *n* vassoio
salvo *n* salva
Samaritan *n* samaritano
same *a* stesso; **all the** — ciò nonostante; lo stesso, tutt'uno; **at the** — **time** con tutto ciò, ciò nonostante, pure; **–ness** *n* uniformità; monotonia
sample *n* campione *m*, esempio; — *vt* saggiare, provare
sampling *n* campionatura
sanatorium *n* casa di cura; stazione climatica
sanctify *vt* santificare
sanctimonious *a* bigotto
sanction *n* sanzione; — *vt* approvare
sanctity *n* santità
sanctuary *n* santuario
sanctum *n* santuario, sacrario; studio riservato; **inner** — sancta sanctorum *(fig)*
sand *n* sabbia, rena; **–s** *npl* spiaggia; **–bag** *n* sacco a terra; — **bar** banco di sabbia; **–box** *n* sabbiera; **–stone** *n* arenaria; **–storm** *n* tempesta di sabbia; — *vt* sabbiare, smerigliare
sandal *n* sandalo; **–wood** *n* legno di sandalo
sandblast *n (mech)* sabbiatrice *f*; — *vt* smerigliare, sabbiare
sandpaper *n* carta vetrata; — *vt* levigare con carta vetrata
sandwich *n* panino ripieno; — *vt* inserire
sandy *a* sabbioso; *(hair)* biondastro
sane *a* equilibrato, savio
sanguinary *a* sanguinario
sanguine *a* sanguigno; ottimista
sanitary *a* igienico; — **napkin** pannolino igienico
sanitarium *n* sanatorio
sanitation igiene *f*
sanity *n* sanità di mente
Sanskrit *n &a* sanscrito
Santa Claus *n* Befana; Babbo Natale, Papà Natale
sap *n* linfa; *(sl)* grullo; — *vt* sottominare, indebolire
sapling *n* arboscello
sarcasm *n* sarcasmo
sarcastic *a* sarcastico
sarcophagus *n* sarcofago
sardine *n* sardina
Sardinia *n* Sardegna; **–n** *a&n* sardo
sardonic *a* sardonico
sash *n* sciarpa; *(window)* telaio
Satan *n* Satana *m*
satanic *a* satanico
satchel *n* borsa, cartella
satellite *n* satellite *m*
satiate *vt* saziare
satiety *n* sazietà
satin *n* raso, satin *m*; **–y** *a* di raso, satinato
satire *n* satira
satirical *a* satirico
satirist *n* satirico
satirize *vt* satireggiare
satisfaction *n* soddisfazione *f*
satisfactory *a* soddisfacente
satisfy *vt&i* soddisfare, contentare
saturate *vt* saturare
saturation *n* saturazione
Saturday *n* sabato
saturnism *n* saturnismo
satyr *n* satiro
sauce *n* salsa; **–box** *n (coll)* sfacciato, insolente *m*; **–pan** *n* casseruola; — *vt* condire
saucer *n* piattino
sauciness *n* sfacciataggine *f*
saucy *a* insolente, sfacciato
Saudi Arabia Arabia Saudita
sauerkraut *n* crauti *mpl*
saunter *vi* bighellonare
sausage *n* salciccia; carne insaccata
savage *a&n* selvaggio; **–ry** *n* barbarie *f*; ferocia
savannah *n* savana
savant *n* dotto
save *vt* salvare; *(keep)* conservare, — *vt&i* risparmiare; — *prep* salvo, tranne, eccetto; **–r** *n* liberatore *m*; *(money)* risparmiatore *m*
saving *a* economico, frugale; — *n* economia
savings *npl* risparmi *mpl*; — **bank** cassa di risparmio; — **account** conto di risparmio
Saviour *n* Salvatore, Redentore *m*
savor *n* sapore *m*, gusto; aroma; — *vt* assaporare; dar sapore; — *vi* aver sapore di, sapere di
savory *a* saporito
saw *n (tool)* sega; *(adage)* proverbio; **–dust** *n* segatura; **–horse** *n* cavalletto per segare; **–mill** *n* segheria
saw-toothed *a* dentato, dentellato
Saxon *n&a* sassone *m&f*
saxaphone *n* sassofono
say *vt&i* dire; **have one's** — dire la sua; **that is to** — vale a dire, cioè
saying *n* detto, massima; **it goes without** — non è neppure il caso di dirlo
scab *n* crosta; *(labor)* crumiro; — *vi* cicatrizzarsi; formar crosta; fare il crumiro
scabbard *n* fodero, guaina
scabby *a* coperto di croste
scabrous *a* osceno; scabroso
scaffold *n* patibolo; impalcatura; **–ing** *n* impalcatura, intelaiatura
scalawag *n* scapestrato, furfante *m*
scald *vt* scottare; — *n* scottata; **–ing** *a* scottante; **–ing** *n* scottatura
scale *n (fish)* squama; *(measurement)* scala; *(weight)* bilancia; — *vt* scalare, assendere; graduare; *(fish)* squamare
scalene *a (math)* scaleno
scales *npl* bilancia; **platform** — basculla
scaling *n* scalata; desquamazione
scallion *n* scalogno
scallop *n (sewing)* smerlo, orlatura;

(zool) mollusco; — vt (cooking) cuocere al gratin; (sewing) festonare, orlare
scalp n cuoio capelluto; — vt scotennare; **–er** n (ticket seller) bagarino, incettatore m
scalpel n bisturi m
scaly a squamoso, scaglioso; (sl) meschino, ladro
scamp n furfante m
scamper n scampo, fuga precipitosa; — vi scampare, fuggire precipitosamente
scan vt (mus) scandire; esaminare; (TV) esplorare
scandal n scandalo; **–ize** vt scandalizzare; **–monger** n maldicente m&f; **–ous** a scandaloso
Scandinavia Scandinavia
Scandinavian a&n scandinavo
scant, scanty a scarso
scantily adv scarsamente
scantiness n scarsezza
scapegoat n capro espiatorio
scapegrace n scapestrato
scapula n scapola
scapular n (eccl) scapolare m
scar n cicatrice f; sfregio; — vi cicatrizzarsi; — vt cicatrizzare, sfregiare
scarab n scarabeo
scarce a scarso; **–ly** adv appena, quasi
scarcity n scarsità
scare n spavento; — vt impaurire, spaventare
scarecrow n spauracchio, spaventapasseri m
scarf n sciarpa, scialle m
scarlet a&n scarlatto; — **fever** scarlattina
scathing a caustico, severo, pungente
scatter vt sparpagliare; — vi disperdersi; **–ed** a sparso; disseminato
scatterbrain n scervellato
scattering n sparpagliamento
scavenger n spazzino
scenario n canovaccio
scene n scena; **–ry** n paesaggio; (view) veduta; (theat) scenario
scenic a scenico
scenography n scenografia
scent n odore m; fiuto; — vt odorare; profumare
scepter n scettro
schedule n programma m; tabella; orario; — vt programmare
schema n schema m
schematic a schematico
scheme n complotto; progetto; — vi macchinare; progettare; — vi far progetti; intrigare; **color** — armonizzazione di colori
schemer n intrigante m&f
scheming n macchinazione; progetti mpl; — a scaltro, intrigante; progettante
scherzo n (mus) scherzo
schism n scisma m; **–atic** n&a scismatico
schist n (geol) schisto
schizophrenia n schizofrenia
schizophrenic n&a schizofrenico
scholar n alunno, studente m, scolaro; (erudite) studioso, erudito; **–ly** a erudito, dotto; **–ship** n erudizione; borsa di studio
scholastic a scolastico; **–ism** n scolasticismo
school n scuola; **high** — scuola media; **–book** n libro scolastico; **–boy** n scolaro; **–girl** n scolara; **–house** n scuola, edificio scolastico; **–room** n aula scolastica; **–teacher** n maestro, maestra; insegnante m&f; — vt disciplinare; istruire
schooling n istruzione; (cost) costo di studi
schooner n (boat) goletta; (glass) bicchierone da birra
sciatica n (med) sciatica
science n scienza; — **fiction** fantascienza
scientific a scientifico
scientist n scienziato
scimitar n scimitarra
scintillate vi scintillare
scintillating a scintillante
scion n discendente m
scissors npl forbici fpl
sclerosis n (med) sclerosi f
scoff vt&i schernire, deridere; **–er** n derisore, schernitore m
scoffing n scherno, derisione; — a derisorio
scold vt&i sgridare, rimproverare; — n megera, bisbetica
scolding n rimprovero, sgridata; **–ly** adv sgridando, con rimprovero
scone n focaccina
scoop n ramaiolo, cucchiaione m; (news) colpo giornalistico; — vt vuotare, scavare
scoot vi (coll) darsela a gambe, scappare; **–er** n monopattino; **motor –er** motonetta
scope n portata
scorbutic a scorbutico
scorch vt bruciare, arrostire; — vi bruciacchiarsi, arrostirsi; **–ed** a bruciato; **–er** n giorno scottante
scorching a bruciante; (remark) sarcastico; — n bruciatura, ustione f
score n (game) punteggio; (mus) spartito, partitura; (number) venti m, ventina; — vt segnare; — vi far punti
scoring n (mus) orchestrazione
scorn n disprezzo; **–ful** a sprezzante, sdegnoso; **–fully** adv sdegnosamente; — vt sdegnare, disprezzare
scorpion n scorpione m
Scot n scozzese m
Scotch n whisky scozzese; — a scozzese
scotch vt sopprimere
scot-free a impune, impunito; (gratis) gratuito
Scotland Scozia
Scotsman n scozzese m
Scottish n&a scozzese m
scoundrel n mascalzone m
scour vt (scout) perlustrare, percorrere; (clean) ripulire; — **the country** battere la campagna (fig); **–ing** n smacchiatura, pulitura
scourge n sferza; — vt sferzare
scout n esploratore m; **–master** n capo esploratore m; **boy** — giovane esploratore; **girl** — giovane esploratrice; — vt&i esplorare

scow *n* chiatta
scowl *n* sguardo torvo, cipiglio; — *vi* accigliarsi
scragginess *n* magrezza
scraggy *a* scarno, magro
scramble *n* mischia, tafferuglio; *(climb)* scalata; — *vt* agitare, mischiare, strapazzare; — *vi (climb)* inerpicarsi; agitarsi; *(struggle)* azzuffarsi; **–d** *a* agitato, strapazzato; **–d eggs** uova strapazzate
scrap *n* pezzo; briciola; **–book** *n* album *m*; — **heap** mucchio di rifiuti; — *vt* rigettare, scartare
scrap *n (sl)* baruffa, zuffa; — *vi (sl)* altercare, bisticciare
scrape *n* imbroglio; *(skin)* spellatura; *(sound)* stridore *m*; — *vt* raschiare; — **together** raggranellare; **–r** *n* raschietto
scratch *n* graffio; *(sport)* linea di partenza; — **pad** blocco di carta per minuta; — **paper** carta per minuta; **from** — dal niente; — *vt* grattare; graffiare; *(sport)* eliminare; **–y** *a* graffiante, aspro; *(writing)* scarabocchiato
scrawl *n* scarabocchio; — *vt&i* scarabocchiare
scrawny *a* magro
scream *n* grido, strillo; **–ing** *n* strilli *mpl*, urla *fpl*; — *vt&i* gridare, urlare
screech *n* grido, urlo; — **owl** barbagianni *m*; — *vt&i* strillare
screen *n* schermo; paravento; — *vt* nascondere; vagliare
screw *n* vite *f*; — **propellor** propulsore a elica; — **thread** impanatura; — *vt* avvitare; *(distort)* torcere; — *vi* avvitarsi; — **up one's courage** farsi coraggio
screwdriver *n* cacciavite *m*
scribble *n* scarabocchio; mala scrittura; — *vt* scribacchiare
scribe *n* scrivano
scrimmage *n* schermaglia
scrimp *vi* economizzare; restringere; **–iness** esiguità; **–y** *a* esiguo
scrip *n* certificato provvisorio
script *n* scrittura, manoscritto; *(print)* corsivo; *(theat)* copione *m*
scriptural *a* scritturale, conforme alla Sacra Scrittura
Scripture *n* Sacra Scrittura
scriptwriter *n* sceneggiatore *m*
scrofula *n (med)* scrofola
scroll *n* rotolo, papiro; *(design)* spirale *m*, voluta; — **saw** sega da traforo; **–work** *n* traforo, arabesco, intarsio
scrotum *(anat)* scroto
scrounge *vt (sl)* scroccare
scrub *vt* strofinare, pulire; — *n* boscaglia, macchia
scrubby *a* stentato
scruff *n* nuca
scruple *n* scrupolo
scrupulous *a* scrupoloso
scrutinize *vt* scrutare
scrutiny *n* indagine *f*, esame *m*
scuba *n* apparato di respirazione per la pesca subacquea
scuff *n (slipper)* ciabatta, pianella; *(shuffle)* scalpiccio; logorio; — *vt&i* logorare; scalpicciare
scuffle *n* rissa, parapiglia; *(shuffling)* scalpiccio; — *vi* azzuffarsi; scalpicciare
sculptor *n* scultore *m*, scultrice *f*
sculpture *n* scultura; — *vt* scolpire
scum *n* schiuma; scoria
scurrilous *a* scurrile; **–ness** *n* scurrilità
scurry *n* sgambettio, fretta; — *vi* sgambettare, affrettarsi
scurvy *n (med)* scorbuto; — *a* meschino, vile
scuttle *n* secchio; *(naut)* boccaporto; — *vi* affrettarsi; — *vt* affondare; — **away** scappare
scythe *n* falce *f*
sea *n* mare *m*; **–board** *n* litorale *m*, spiaggia; **–going** *a* atto al mare; — **breeze** brezza marina; — **gull** gabbiano; — **horse** ippocampo; — **legs** equilibrio da marinaio; — **level** livello del mare; — **lion** otaria; — **of** *(fig)* mare di; — **power** potenza marittima; — **shell** conchiglia marina; — **urchin** echino; — **wall** diga; **at** — in mare; *(confused)* perplesso; **heavy** — mare agitato; **rough** — mare grosso
seacoast *n* costa
seafarer *n* marinaio
seafaring *a* di mare, marino
seal *n* sigillo; *(zool)* foca; — *vt* sigillare; chiudere; **–skin** *n* pelle di foca
sealing *n* sigillazione; — **wax** ceralacca
seam *n* cucitura; **–less** *a* senza cucitura
seaman *n* marinaio; **–like** *a* marinaresco; **–ship** *n* arte marinaresca
seamstress *n* cucitrice *f*
seaplane *n* idrovolante *m*
seaport *n* porto marittimo
sear *vt* cauterizzare; bruciare; insecchire
search *vt&i* cercare, perquisire; far ricerche; — *n* ricerca, perquisizione
searching *n* ricerca, indagine *f*; — *a* penetrante, scrutatore
searchlight *n* riflettore *m*
seashore *n* spiaggia, lido
seasickness *n* mal di mare
seaside *n* marina
season *n* stagione; — **ticket** biglietto d'abbonamento; **out of** — fuori stagione; **–al** *a* stagionale; **–able** *a* di stagione; opportuno
season *vt* condire; *(mature)* stagionare; **–ed** *a (food)* condito; *(aged)* stagionato;
seasoning *n* (wood) stagionatura; *(food)* condimento
seat *n* posto; sedia; sedile *m*; — *vt* far sedere; insediare; provvedere di posti a sedere; **–ed** *a* seduto
seaweed *n* alga marina
seaworthy *a* a tenuta di mare, atto ad affrontare il mare
secede *vi* staccarsi
secession *n* secessione
seclude *vt* secludere, isolare, ritirare; **–d** *a* ritirato, appartato
seclusion *n* ritiro, solitudine *f*
second *a&n* secondo; — **hand** *(watch)* lancetta dei secondi; — **floor** secondo piano; — **nature** seconda natura; — **sight** prescienza; sesto senso, intuizione; **on** — **thought** tutto ben considerato; — *vt* assecondare

secondhand *a* di seconda mano; d'occasione; per sentito dire
second-rate *a* di seconda qualità
secrecy *n* segretezza
secret *n&a* segreto; **keep a —** mantenere il segreto; **–ive** *a* segreto; secretivo; **–ly** *adv* segretamente
secretary *n* segretario; *(desk)* scrittoio
secrete *vt* nascondere; *(exude)* secernere
secretion *n* secrezione
sect *n* setta; **–arian** *a* settario; **–arianism** *n* spirito settario
section *n* sezione; *(city)* quartiere *m*; **–al** *a* sezionale, parziale; — *vt* sezionare
sector *n* settore *m*
secular *a* secolare; *(laic)* laico; *(worldly)* mondano; **–ism** *n* secolarismo; **–ize** *vt* secolarizzare
secure *a* sicuro, al sicuro; — *vt* ottenere, assicurare
security *n* sicurezza; garanzia
securities *npl (com)* titoli *mpl*
sedate *a* posato, calmo, tranquillo; **–ness** *n* posatezza, calma, tranquillità
sedative *n&n* sedativo
sedentary *a* sedentario
sedge *n* giunco
sediment *n* deposito, sedimento; **–ary** *a* sedimentario; **–ation** *n* sedimentazione
sedition *n* sedizione
seditious *a* sedizioso
seduce *vt* sedurre
seducer *n* seduttore *m*
seduction *n* seduzione
seductive *a* seducente, seduttore
sedulity *n* diligenza
sedulous *a* diligente
see *vt&i* vedere; **— about** vedere di; **— through** *(understand)* percepire, intuire; **— to** occuparsi di; **as far as I can —** per quanto io possa vedere; **The Holy S–** La Santa Sede
seed *n* seme *m*, chicco; **–ling** *n* pianticella, piantina; **–y** *a* granoso; pieno di semi; *(fig)* logoro; — *vt (deseed)* sgranare; *(sow)* seminare; — *vi* sgranarsi
seeing *n* vista, visione; — *a* vidente; **— that** visto che
seek *vt&i* ricercare, cercare; **— to** tentare di
seeker *n* cercatore *m*
seem *vi* sembrare, parere; **–ing** *a* apparente; **–ingly** *adv* apparentemente; **–ly** *a* decente, conveniente
seemliness *n* decenza
seep *vi* filtrare; **–age** *n* gocciolamento; trasudamento
seer *n* profeta *m*, veggente *m&f*
seer *n (viewer)* spettatore *m*
seesaw *n* altalena; — *vi* fare l'altalena; dondolare
seethe *vi* agitarsi, fermentare; bollire
segment *n* segmento
segregate *vt* segregare
segregation *n* segregazione
seiche *n* fluttuazione lacustre
seine *n* sciabica
Seine Senna
seismic *a* sismico
seismograph *n* sismografo
seize *vt* afferrare; *(law)* confiscare
seizure *n* cattura; *(law)* confisca; *(med)* attacco, accesso
seldom *adv* raramente
select *vt* scegliere; — *a* scelto; **–ion** *n* scelta, selezione; **–ive** *a* selettivo; **–ivity** selettività
selenite *n* selenite *f*
selenium *n* selenio
self *n* personalità; sè stesso, ego
self- *(in comp)* **—acting** *a* automatico; **—addressed** a indirizzato a sè stesso; **—assurance** *n* sicurezza di sè; **—assured** *a* sicuro di sè; **—centered** *a* egocentrico; **—confidence** *n* fiducia in sè stesso; **—confident** *a* sicuro di sè; **—conscious** *a* imbarazzato; **—contained** riservato; **—control** *n* padronanza di sè; **—defense** *n* legittima difesa; **—denial** *n* astinenza, abnegazione; **—determined** *a* con autodecisione; **—discipline** *n* autodisciplina; **—educated** *a* autodidatta; **—esteem** *n* amor proprio; **—evident** *a* evidente; **—explanatory** *a* ovvio; **—expression** *n* espressione dell'individuo; **—governed** *a* autonomo; **—government** *n* autogoverno, autonomia, indipendenza; **—help** *n* autosufficienza; azione senza l'aiuto altrui; **—importance** *n* boria; **—important** *a* borioso; **—indulgence** *n* indulgenza per sè stesso; **—interest** *n* interesse personale; **—made** *a* fatto da sè; **—possessed** *a* calmo; **—possession** *n* padronanza di sè stesso; **—preservation** *n* istinto di conservazione; **—propelled** *a* automotore; **—regard** *n* rispetto di sè stesso; **—regulating** *a* a regolazione automatica; **—reliance** *n* fiducia in sè; **— reliant** *a* fiducioso di sè stesso; **—respect** *n* dignità; **—restraint** *n* controllo di sè stesso; riservatezza; **—sacrifice** *n* abnegazione; sacrificio di sè stesso; **—satisfied** *a* vanitoso; **—service** *n* autoservizio; **—starter** *n (auto)* avviamento; **—styled** *a* sedicente; **—sufficient** *a* autosufficiente; **—supporting** *a* indipendente; **—taught** *a* autodidatta; **—willed** *a* ostinato
selfish *a* egoistico; egoista; **–ness** *n* egoismo
selfless *a* altruista
selfsame *a* identico; esattamente lo stesso
sell *vt&i* vendere; *(coll)* ingannare; **— out** vender tutto; *(betray)* vendere; **–out** *n* vendita totale, liquidazione; **–er** *n* venditore *m*; negoziante *m*; **–ing** *n* vendita
seltzer *n* acqua di Seltz
selvage *n* cimosa
semantic *a* semantico
semantics *npl* semantica
semaphore *n* semaforo
semblance *n* apparenza, sembianza
semen *n* sperma
semester *n* semestre *m*
semiannual *a* semestrale; **–ly** *adv* semestralmente
semicircle *n* semicerchio
semicolon *n* punto e virgola
semiconscious *a* semicosciente
semifinal *n* semifinale *m*
semimonthly *a* bimensile; quindicinale
seminar *n* seminario

seminary *n* seminario
semination *n* semina
semiofficial *a* semiufficiale
semiprecious *a* semiprezioso
Semitic *a* semitico
semitransparent *a* semitrasparente
semitropical *a* semitropicale
semiweekly *a* bisettimanale
senate *n* senato
senator *n* senatore *m*
send *vt* inviare, mandare, spedire; — **away** mandar via, congedare; — **for** mandar a chiamare; **–er** *n* mittente *m&f*
senile *a* senile
senility *n* senilità
senior *n* anziano, decano; — *a* maggiore; seniore; **–ity** *n* anzianità
sensation *n* sensazione; **–al** *a* sensazionale
sense *n* senso; **common** — buon senso; **make** — aver significato, essere logico; **talk** — parlare con senno; **–less** *a* insensibile; *(silly)* insensato; *(absurd)* assurdo; **–s** *npl* sensi *mpl*; — *vt&i* intuire
sensibility *n* sensibilità
sensible *a* assennato, giudizioso
sensitive *a* sensibile, suscettibile
sensitivity *n* sensibilità
sensitize *vt* sensibilizzare
sensory *a* sensorio
sensual *a* sensuale; **–ism** *n* sensualismo; **–ist** *n* sensualista *m&f*; **–ity** *n* sensualità
sensuous *a* sensuale, sensitivo
sentence *n* sentenza; condanna; *(gram)* frase *f*, periodo; — *vt* condannare
sententious *a* sentenzioso
sentiment *n* sentimento; **–al** *a* sentimentale; **–alism** *n* sentimentalismo; **–alist** *n* sentimentale *m&f*; **–ality** *n* sentimentalità
sentinel *n* sentinella
sentry *n* guardia; — **box** garitta
sepal *n* sepalo
separable *a* separabile
separate *vt* separare; — *vi* separarsi; — *a* diviso, separato; **–ly** *adv* a parte, separatamente
separation *n* separazione
separatism *n* separatismo
sepia *n (color)* seppia
September *n* settembre *m*
septic *a* settico
septicemia *n (med)* setticemia
sepulcher *n* sepolcro
sepulchral *a* sepolcrale
sequel *n* sequela, conseguenza
sequence *n* sequenza, serie *f*, successione
sequester *vt* sequestrare; separare; **–ed** *a* ritirato; sequestrato
sequin *n* lustrino
seraph *n* serafino
seraphic *a* serafico
serenade *n* serenata; — *vt* fare una serenata a
serene *a* sereno; **–ly** *a* serenamente
serenity *n* serenità
serf *n* schiavo, servo; **–dom** *n* servaggio
sergeant *n* sergente *m*
sergeant-at-arms *n* usciere *m*
serial *n* romanzo a puntate; — *a* di serie; periodico; — **number** numero di serie
series *n* serie *f*
serious *a* grave, serio; **–ly** *adv* seriamente, sul serio; **–ness** *n* serietà; **take –ly** prendere sul serio
sermon *n* predica, sermone *m*; **–ize** *vt* sermoneggiare
serous *a* sieroso
serpent *n* serpente *m*; **–ine** *a* serpentino; *(twisting)* tortuoso
serrate *a* dentellato
serried *a* serrato
serum *n* siero
servant *n* domestico; servo; **civil** — impiegato statale
serve *vt&i* servire; — **as** servire da; — **time** *(mil)* prestare servizio; *(law)* scontare una sentenza
service *n* servizio, prestazione; — **station** stazione di servizio; **at your** — ai vostri ordini; **be of** — essere utile; **–s** *npl* prestazioni *fpl*, servizi *mpl*; — *vt* mettere in uso
serviceable *a* durevole; pratico
serviceman *n* militare *m*
servile *a* servile
servility *n* servilità
servitude *n* servitù
sesame *n* sesamo
session *n* sessione, seduta
set *n* servizio, serie *f*, collezione; *(group)* gruppo; *(hair)* messa in piega; *(rad)* apparecchio; *(sport)* partita; *(theat)* scenario
set *vt* mettere, porre, regolare; *(gem)* incastonare; *(table)* apparecchiare; *(type)* comporre; — *vi* mettersi; *(sun)* tramontare; *(congeal)* coagularsi; *(hen)* covare; — **aside** metter da parte; *(law)* annullare; — **forth** mostrare; — **out** *(place)* mettere, posare; *(start)* partire; *(begin)* incominciare; *(plant)* piantare
set *a (firm)* fisso; *(established)* stabilito; *(stubborn)* testardo
setback *n* arresto; *(retreat)* indietreggiamento
settee *n* canapè *m*
setting *n (gem)* incastonatura; *(table)* apparecchiatura, coperto; *(birds)* covata; *(surroundings)* dintorni *mpl*
settle *vt (establish)* stabilire; comporre, aggiustare; *(pay)* saldare; — *vi* stabilirsi; **–ment** *n* accomodamento; pagamento; colonia
settler *n* colono
set-to *n (coll)* abboccamento; *(argument)* discussione
setup *n* organizzazione; *(mech)* montaggio
seven *a* sette; **–teen** *a* diciasette; **–th** *a* settimo; **–ty** *a* settanta
seventeenth *a* diciassettesimo; — **century** secolo diciasettesimo, il seicento
sever *vt* dividere, recidere; — *vi* dividersi; **–ance** *n* separazione, distacco
several *a* parecchi
severe *a* severo; grave
severity *n* severità
sew *vt&i* cucire
sewage *n* acque di scolo
sewer *n* conduttura, fogna, cloaca
sewing *n* cucito; — **machine** macchina da cucire

sex *n* sesso; — **appeal** fascino
sextant *n* sestante *m*
sextet *n* sestetto
sexton *n* sagrestano
sexual *a* sessuale; **–ity** *n* sessualità; **–ly** *adv* sessualmente
shabbiness *n* stato logoro
shabby *a* logoro; mal vestito; — **trick** meschinità
shack *n* baracca
shackle *n* ceppo; — *vt* inceppare
shad *n* alosa; — **roe** uova di alosa
shade *n (color)* tinta; *(shadow)* ombra; *(window)* scuretto; *(lamp)* paralume *m*; **–d** *a* ombreggiato; protetto; all'ombra; — *vt* ombreggiare
shadiness *n* ombrosità
shading *n* sfumatura
shadow *n* ombra; — *vt* oscurare; ombreggiare; *(follow)* pedinare; **–y** *a* ombroso; oscuro; *(ghostly)* spettrale
shady *a* ombroso; sospetto
shaft *n (light)* raggio; *(lightning)* fulmine *m*; *(mech)* albero, asse *m*; *(mine)* pozzo; **crank–** *n* albero a gomito
shaggy *a* irsuto, ispido, scabroso
shah *n* scià *m*
shake *vt* scuotere; — *vi* tremare; — **hands** stringere la mano; **–down** *n* giaciglio improvvisato; *(sl)* estorsione; — **off** disfarsi di
shake-up *n* riorganizzazione energica
shaking *n* scossa, scuotimento; — *a* agitato; debole; *(voice)* tremante
shale *n* schisto
shallop *n* scialuppa
shallow *a* poco profondo; **–ness** *n* poca profondità, superficialità
sham *a* finto, falso; — *n* finzione, finta, impostura; — *vt* simulare, fingere
shambles *npl* macello; strage *f*, carneficina
shame *n* vergogna; pudore *m*; **what a —!** che peccato!; — *vt* disonorare, svergognare; **–faced** *a* timido, vergognoso; **–ful** *a* vergognoso; **–less** *a* svergognato, spudorato
shammy *n* pelle di camoscio
shampoo *n* saponatura; — *vt* lavare
shamrock *n* trifoglio
shank *n* stinco, tibia; gamba
shanty *n* capanna
shape *vt* formare, foggiare; — *vi (coll)* prender forma; — *n* forma; **–less** *a* informe; **–liness** *n* bellezza; simmetria; **–ly** *a* bello; simmetrico
shard *n* coccio
share *n* parte *f*; *(com)* azione *f*; — *vt* dividere, spartire, condividere; — *vi* partecipare; **–cropper** *n* mezzadro; **–holder** *n* azionista *m&f*
sharing *n* spartizione
shark *n* pescecane *m*, squalo; **loan** — strozzino
sharp *a* acuto, tagliente, affilato; *(clever)* astuto, furbo; — **curve** curva stretta; — *n (mus)* diesis *m*; — *adv* preciso; in punto; **two o'clock** — alle due in punto; **–ly** *adv* acutamente; astutamente; **–ness** *n* acume *m*; astuzia; asprezza; **–shooter** *n* tiratore scelto
sharpen *vt* affilare, appuntare; acuire
sharpener *n (mech)* affilatrice *f*; *(grindstone)* arrotino; *(pencil)* temperalapis *m*
sharp-edged *a* affilato
sharp-witted *a* intelligente, acuto
shatter *vt* fracassare; — *vi* fracassarsi
shatterproof *a* infrangibile
shave *vt* fare la barba a; — *vi* radersi, farsi la barba; — *n* sbarbata; **have a close** — *(fig)* cavarsela a malapena; **–r** *n (coll)* imberbe *m*
shaving *n* ritaglio, truciolo; *(beard)* sbarbata; *(hair)* tosatura; — **brush** pennello da barba; — **cream** sapone (*or* crema) da barba
shawl *n* scialle *m*
she *pron* lei, ella, essa
sheaf *n* fascio, covone *m*; — *vt* legare in covoni
shear *n* cesoia; cesoiata; **–ing** *n* tosatura; — *vt* tranciare; *(hair)* tosare; **–s** *npl* cesoie *fpl*
shearer *n* tosatore *m*
sheath *n* fodero, guaina
sheathe *vt* ringuainare
shed *vt (tears)* versare, spargere; *(skin)* spogliarsi di; — **light on** far luce su; — *n* tettoia, capannone *m*
sheen *n* splendore *m*
sheep *n* pecora; **–ish** *a* timido, impacciato; **black** — pecora nera *(fig)*; — **dog** cane da pastore
sheepskin *n (parchment)* pergamena; pelle di pecora
sheer *a* trasparente; *(mere)* mero, semplice, pretto; *(steep)* profondo
sheer *vi (naut)* virare
sheet *n (bed)* lenzuolo; *(glass)* lastra; *(ice)* distesa, lastra; *(metal)* lamiera, lamina; *(paper)* foglio; — *vt* rivestire, foderare; *(laminate)* laminare; **–ing** *n (material)* tela da lenzuola; *(lining)* fodera
sheik *n* sceicco
shelf *n* mensola, scaffale *m*; **put on the** — mettere in disparte
shell *n* conchiglia; guscio; *(mil)* proiettile *m*; — *vt* sbucciare; bombardare; sgranare
shellac *n* gomma-lacca; — *vt* lucidare a spirito
shellfire *n* tiro d'artiglieria
shellfish *n* crostaceo
shellshock *n* psicosi di guerra
shelter *n* rifugio; — *vt* ricoverare, proteggere; nascondere; — *vi* ricoverarsi; mettersi al coperto
shelve *vt* disporre in scaffale; mettere da parte; licenziare; **–s** *npl* scaffali *mpl*
shelving *n* scaffalatura; pendenza
shepherd *n* pastore *m*; **–ess** *n* pastorella; — *vt* guidare, scortare
sherbet *n* sorbetto
sheriff *n* sceriffo
sherry *n* vino di Xeres
shibboleth *n* parola d'ordine
shield *n* scudo, protezione *f*; *(mech)* schermo; — *vt* proteggere, difendere, coprire
shift *vt* cambiare, spostare; — *vi* spostarsi; — **for oneself** indipendenzarsi, cavar-

sela; — *n (auto)* cambiamento; *(squad)* squadra; *(labor)* turno; *(typewriter)* tasto per maiuscole; **–less** *a* pigro, inetto; **–y** *a* scaltro; *(eyes)* sfuggente
shiftiness *n* scaltrezza
shilling *n* scellino
shilly-shally *vi* esitare
shimmer *n* barlume, luccichio; **–y** *a* luccicante; — *vt* luccicare, brillare
shin *n* stinco, tibia; — **up** arrampicarsi
shine *vi* brillare; — *vt* lucidare, lustrare; — *n* splendore *m*; **take a — to** *(coll)* sentir simpatia per
shiner *n (coll)* occhio pesto
shingle *n (roof)* assicella, tegola di legno; *(gravel)* ghiaia; *(hair)* sfumatura di capelli; **hang out one's —** *(coll)* debuttare nella professione; **–s** *(med)* zona, erpete *m*; — *vt (hair)* tagliare corti; *(roof)* coprire di tegole
shining, shiny *a* lucente
ship *n* nave *f*; — *vt* spedire; — *vi* imbarcarsi; **–builder** *n* costruttore navale; **–owner** *n* armatore *m*; **–per** *n* speditore, caricatore *m*; **–shape** *a* ordinato; in ordine; **–wright** *n* impiegato di cantiere navale; **–yard** *n* cantiere navale, arsenale *m*; **on –board** a bordo
shipping *n* imbarco, spedizione; — **room** cantiere di spedizioni; — **clerk** impiegato spedizioniere
shipment *n* spedizione *f*, carico
shipwreck *n* naufragio; — *vt* far naufragare
shire *n* contea
shirk *vt* schivare, scansare
shirker *n* scansafatiche *m*
shirt *n* camicia; **–front** *n* sparato; **–maker** *n* camiciaio, **–waist** *n* blusa; **in — sleeves** in maniche di camicia
shiver *vi* rabbrividire; — *n* brivido, fremito
shoal *n* bassofondo
shock *n* scossa; *(emotion)* emozione; — **absorber** ammortizzatore *m*; — **treatment** *(med)* elettroterapia; — **wave** ripercussione; — *vt* scuotere, *(scandel)* scandalizzare; *(stun)* stordire, colpire; **–ing** *a* ripugnante, scandaloso
shoddy *a* falso; scadente
shoe *n* scarpa; — **polish** lucido da scarpe; — **brush** spazzola da scarpe; **–horn** *n* calzatoio; **–lace** *n* stringa, laccio; **–less** *a* scalzo; **–maker** *n* calzolaio; — **store** calzoleria; — **tree** forma da scarpe; — *vt* calzare; *(horse)* ferrare
shoestring *n* stringa, laccio; piccolo capitale
shoo *vt* spaventare; cacciare via
shoot *vt&i* sparare; scattare; *(kill)* fucilare; *(bot)* germogliare; — **up** balzare, saltare; — *n (bot)* germoglio
shooting *n* tiro; — **gallery** tiro al bersaglio; — **star** stella filante
shop *n* bottega; — *vi* fare delle compere; **–girl** *n* commessa; **–keeper** *n* negoziante *m*; **–lifter** *n* taccheggiatore *m*; **–per** *n* chi va a far spese; **–window** *n* vetrina; **–worn** *a* sciupato
shopping *n* compere *fpl*; — **bag** borsa da spesa; **go —** andare a far spese
shore *n* costa, lido, riva; *(prop)* puntello; — *vt* puntellare
short *a* corto; *(height)* basso; — **circuit** corto circuito; — **cut** scorciatoia; — **story** novella; — **wave** onda corta; **for —** per brevità; **in —** in breve; **make — work of** sbarazzarsi in breve di; **–age** *n* mancanza, deficienza; **–ly** *adv* presto, in breve, tra poco; — *vt (elec)* provocare un corto circuito
short– *(in comp)* **—circuit** *vt (elec)* provocare un corto circuito; **—handed** *a* con personale insufficiente; **—lived** *a* di breve durata, caduco; **—spoken** *a* di poche parole; **—tempered** *a* collerico, irascibile; **—term** *a* a breve scadenza; **—winded** *a* affannoso; *(animals)* bolso
shortcake *n* pasta frolla
shortchange *vt (coll)* imbrogliare nel dare il resto
shortcoming *n* manchevolezza, deficienza
shorten *vt* accorciare, abbreviare, ridurre; — *vi* accorciarsi, ridursi
shortening *n* accorciamento, riduzione, diminuzione; *(cooking)* grasso
shorthand *n* stenografia
shortness *n* piccolezza; scarsità; — **of temper** irascibilità
shorts *npl* mutande *fpl*, calzoni corti, calzoncini *mpl*
shortsighted *a* miope; *(fig)* imprevidente; **–ness** *n* miopia, imprevidenza
shot *n* sparo; *(buckshot)* pallottola, pallini *mpl*; *(drink)* cicchetto *(coll)*; *(person)* tiratore *m*; *(med)* iniezione; *(photo)* scatto; **good —** tiratore scelto
shotgun *n* fucile da caccia; — **shell** cartuccia, bossolo
shoulder *n* spalla; — **blade** scapola — **strap** spallina; — *vt* caricarsi sulle spalle; spingere a spalla; assumere
shout *vt&i* gridare, urlare; — *n* grido; schiamazzo
shove *n* spinta, spintone *m*; — *vt* spingere con forza
shovel *n* pala; — *vt (coal)* scavare; spalare; *(food)* mangiare avidamente, divorare
show *n* spettacolo; *(arts)* mostra, esposizione; — **card** cartello; — **window** vetrata; **–case** *n* vetrina; **–down** *n (coll)* carte in tavola *(fig)*; **–man** *n* espositore *m*; **–manship** *n* abile esposizione; **–room** *n* sala d'esposizione; **–y** *a* vistoso
show *vt* mostrare; — *vi* farsi vedere; — **off** ostentare; — **up** smascherare; smascherarsi
shower *n* acquazzone *m*; doccia; — *vi* fare la doccia; piovere a rovesci; — *vt* riversare, inondare
showiness *n* vistosità
show-off *n* ostentazione; *(person)* millantatore *m*, presuntuoso
shrapnel *n (mil)* granata
shred *n* brandello; — *vt* fare a brandelli, sbrindellare
shrew *n* bisbetica, megera; *(zool)* toporagno; **–ish** *a* bisbetico; **–ishness** *n* temperamento bisbetico
shrewd *a* scaltro, fino; **–ly** *adv* sagacemente; scaltramente; **–ness** *n* sagacia; scaltrezza

shriek *n* grido, urlo; — *vt&i* strillare, gridare
shrill *a* acuto, stridulo; **–ness** *n* acutezza, stridore *m*
shrimp *n* gamberetto di mare
shrine *n* sacrario; reliquario
shrink *vi* restringersi, contrarsi; — *vt* restringere, contrarre; **–age** *n* restringimento, contrazione; — **back** indietreggiare
shrinking *n* diminuzione, contrazione; — *a* restringente
shrivel *vi* contrarsi, raggrinzarsi; — *vt* contrarre, raggrinzare
shroud *n* sudario, velo; *(naut)* sartia; — *vt* avvolgere in sudario, coprire, nascondere
Shrove Tuesday Martedì Grasso
shrub *n* arbusto; **–bery** *n* arbusti *mpl*
shrug *n* scrollata di spalle; — *vi* scrollare le spalle
shrunken *a* accorciato
shuck *vt* sbucciare, sgranare
shudder *vi* rabbrividire; — *n* fremito, brivido
shuffle *n* strascichio; *(deceit)* sotterfugio; *(dance)* passo doppio; *(mus)* scompiglio; — *vt (scuffle)* strascicare; *(confuse)* scompigliare; *(mix)* mischiare; — *vi* strascicarsi; vacillare; *(quibble)* tergiversare; — **off** sbarazzarsi di
shuffleboard *n* giuoco delle piastrelle
shuffling *a* strascicante, evasivo; — *n (feet)* strascichio; *(mixing)* rimescolamento
shun *vt* evitare
shunt *vt&i* derivare; *(discard)* scartare; *(rail)* smistare
shut *vt&i* chiudere, chiudersi; — **down** cessare il lavoro; — **in** rinchiudere; — **off** chiudere; — **out** chiuder fuori; — **up** *(coll)* tacere; far tacere — *a* chiuso; **–down** *n* cessazione del lavoro; **–off** *n* chiusura
shut-in *n* rinchiuso, recluso
shutter *n* scuro, imposta, persiana; *(phot)* otturatore *m*
shuttle *n* spoletta, navetta; — *vi* fare la spola
shuttlecock *n* volano
shy *a* timido; sospettoso; *(lacking)* corto di, mancante di; — *vi* adombrarsi; indietreggiare; **–ly** *adv* timidamente; *(suspiciously)* sospettosamente; **–ness** *n* timidezza, diffidenza
shyster *n* imbroglione, azzeccagarbugli *m*
Siamese *a* siamese; — **twins** fratelli siamesi
sibilant *a* sibilante
sibyl *n* sibilla
Sicilian *a&n* siciliano
Sicily Sicilia
sick *a* ammalato; **–ly** *a* malaticcio; **–bed** letto di dolore; — **leave** licenza di convalescenza
sicken *vt* dar nausea; infastidire; — *vi* ammalarsi; nausearsi; **–ing** *a* nauseante, repulsivo
sickle *n* falce *f*
sickness *n* malattia
side *n* lato; — **by** — fianco a fianco; **–car** *n* motocarrozzella; — **dish** portata secondaria; — **issue** questione secondaria; — **light** fanale laterale; — **line** attività secondaria; supplemento di lavoro; **–long** *a* di lato, obliquo; — **show** baraccone *m*; mostra secondaria; — **street** traversa; **–walk** *n* marciapiede *m*; **–ways** *adv* di lato, a sghembo; **on all –s** da ogni parte; **on one** — da una parte; — *vt* chiudere con pareti; *(coll)* mettere a parte; **–track** *vt&i* sviare; — **with** prendere le parti di; appoggiare; — *a* di fianco, laterale, obliquo
sideboard *n* credenza
side-step *vt* evitare
siding *n (rail)* binario laterale
sidle *vi* camminare di fianco
siege *n* assedio; **lay** — **to** assediare
siesta *n* siesta
sieve *n* staccio, crivello; — *vt* stacciare
sift *vt* stacciare, vagliare; **–er** *n* staccio
sigh *vt&i* sospirare; — *n* sospiro; **–ing** *n* sospiri *mpl*
sight *n* vista; *(gun)* mirino; — **draft** tratta a vista; **at first** — a prima vista; **in** — in vista; **lose** — **of** perdere di vista; **on** — a vista; **out of** — fuori di vista; — *vt* avvistare; prendere di mira; — *vi* mirare; **–less** *a* cieco; invisibile; **–seer** *n* osservatore *m*
sight-see *vi* fare una passeggiata turistica; **–ing** *n* veduta, osservazione, ispezione
sign *n* segno, insegna; — **language** linguaggio a gesti, linguaggio mimico; — **painter** pittore d'insegne; **–post** *n* palo indicatore — *vt&i (signature)* firmare; segnare; — **away** cedere; — **off** *(rad&TV)* finire la trasmissione; — **on** ingaggiarsi; — **up** sottoscriversi
signal *n* segnale *m*; — **light** fanale *m*; — *vt&i* segnalare; far segnali; — *a* notevole; esemplare; **S– Corps** *(mil)* corpo segnalatori
signature *n* firma
signboard *n* insegna
signer *n* firmatario
signet *n* sigillo; — **ring** anello con sigillo
significance *n* significato
significant *a* significante, significativo; importante
signify *vt* significare
silence *n* silenzio; — *vt* far tacere, calmare; *(rebellion)* soffocare *(fig)*
silencer *n* smorzatore *m*
silent *a* silenzioso; — **partner** socio non attivo
silhouette *n* sagoma, profilo; — *vt* delineare, siluettare
silica *n* silice *f*
silicon *n* silicio
silk *n* seta; — *a* di seta; **–en** *a* di seta; serico; dolce; — **screen** stampino di seta; **–iness** *n* setosità; **–worm** *n* baco da seta; **–y** *a* setaceo; di seta, serico; *(fig)* dolce
sill *n (door)* soglia; *(window)* davanzale *m*
silliness *n* sciocchezza, stupidaggine *f*
silly *a* sciocco, scemo
silo *n* silo
silver *n* argento; — *a* d'argento; — **plate** posate e vasellame argentati; **–smith** *n*

argentiere *m*; **–ware** *n* argenteria; **–y** *a* inargentato
silver-plate *vt* argentare
silver-tongued *a* eloquente
similar *a* somigliante, simile; **–ity** *n* analogia; similitudine *f*; somiglianza; **–ly** *adv* similmente
simile *n* paragone *m*; similitudine *f*
similitude *n* somiglianza
simmer *vt&i* bollire; **–ing** *n* bollore *m*, ebollizione
simony *n* simonia
simper *n* smorfia; sorriso affettato; **–ing** *n* affettazione; smorfie *fpl*; — *vi* sorridere con affettazione
simple *a* semplice
simple-minded *a* semplicione, candido; *(med)* deficiente
simpleton *n* semplicione *m*
simplicity *n* semplicità
simplification *n* semplificazione
simplify *vt* semplificare
simply *adv* semplicemente
simulate *vt* simulare
simulation *n* simulazione
simultaneous *a* simultaneo; **–ly** *adv* simultaneamente
sin *n* peccato; — *vi* peccare; **–ful** *a* peccaminoso; **–fulness** *n* colpevolezza; **–ner** *n* peccatore *m*
since *prep* dopo, da; — *conj* dacchè, poichè, giacchè; dopo che; — *adv* dopo, di poi, dopo d'allora
sincere *a* sincero; **–ly** *adv* sinceramente
sincerity *n* sincerità
sine *n (math)* sino
sinecure *n* sinecura
sinew *n* tendine *m*; nervo
sinewy *a* nerboruto, nervoso
sing *vt&i* cantare; **–able** *a* cantabile
singe *vt* bruciacchiare; — *n* bruciacchiata
single *a* singolo; *(man)* celibe; *(woman)* nubile; — **file** fila indiana; **–ness** *n* sincerità; — **out** scegliere, separare, distinguere
single– *(in comp)* **—breasted** *a* a un petto; **—handed** *a* da sè; senza aiuto altrui; **—minded** *a* schietto, sincero
singly *a* uno ad uno, individualmente
singsong *n* cantilena; — *a* monotono
singular *a* singolare; — *n* singolarità; **–ize** *vt* singolarizzare; **–ly** *adv* singolarmente
sinister *a* sinistro
sink *vt&i* affondare; *(money)* investire; *(well)* scavare; — *n* acquaio; **–er** *n (fish line)* piombo; **–age** *n* calo, diminuzione; affondamento
sinking *a* affondante; — **fund** *n* fondo d'ammortamento
sinuosity *n* sinuosità
sinuous *a* sinuoso
sinus *n (anat)* seno nasale, seno frontale
sinusitis *n* sinusite *f*
sip *n* sorso; — *vt&i* sorseggiare
siphon *vt* sifonare; — *n* sifone *m*
sir *n* signore *m*
sire *n* sire, signore *m*; padre; — *vt* procreare, generare
siren *n* sirena
sirloin *n* lombo
sissy *n (coll)* maschio effeminato
sister *n* sorella; *(nun)* suora, monaca, religiosa
sister-in-law *n* cognata
sit *vi* sedere; sedersi; — *vt* far sedere; **–down strike** sciopero bianco; — **up** *(wait up)* vegliare; tenersi dritto
site *n* sito, posizione
sitter *n* modello; *(baby)* bambinaia; *(hen)* chioccia
sitting *n* seduta; riunione; *(arts)* posa; — *a* seduto; posante; — **room** salotto
situate *vt* collocare; **–d** *a* posto, situato; **be –d** trovarsi
situation *n* situazione; impiego
six *a* sei; **–teen** *a* sedici; **–teenth** *a* sedicesimo; **–th** *a* sesto; **–tieth** *a* sessantesimo; **–ty** *a* sessanta
sizable *a* abbastanza grande
size *n* misura, formato, grandezza; — *vt* graduare secondo misura; — **up** giudicare, pesare
sizing *n (fabric)* imbozzimatura
sizzle *vi* sfrigolare; friggere; — *n* sfrigolio
sizzling *a* caldo fumante
skate *n* pattino; **ice** — pattino da ghiaccio; **roller** — pattino a rotelle; — *vi* pattinare; **–r** *n* pattinatore *m*, pattinatrice *f*
skating *n* pattinaggio; — **rink** pista di pattinaggio; **figure** — pattinaggio artistico
skein *n* matassa; gomitolo
skeleton *n* scheletro; — **key** chiave maestra
skeptic *n* scettico *m*; **–al** *a* scettico; **–ism** *n* scetticismo
sketch *vt&i* abbozzare, schizzare; — *n* abozzo, schizzo; **–book** *n* album di schizzi; **–ily** *adv* senza dettagli; **–y** *a* non dettagliato
skew *a* a sghembo, obliquo
skewer *n* spiedo
ski *n* sci *m*; **–er** *n* sciatore *m*, sciatrice *f*; — **lift** sciovia; **–ing** *n* sport dello sci; — *vi* sciare
skid *n (avi)* pattino di coda; *(mech)* freno a scarpa; *(slip)* slittamento, slittata; — *vi* slittare
skiff *n* schifo
skill *n* abilità, destrezza; **–ful** *a* abile, destro, **–fully** *adv* abilmente, accortamente
skilled *a* abile, addestrato; esperto; — **labor** mano d'opera specializzata; — **worker** specialista *m*
skillet *n* padella
skim *vt&i* scremare; scorrere; — **milk** latte scremato
skimp *vt&i (coll)* esser tirchio; economizzare; **–y** *a (coll)* meschino; scarso; tirchio
skin *n* pelle *f*; — **diver** pescatore subacqueo; **–flint** *n* spilorcio; avaro; — *vt* pelare, scorticare; sbucciare
skin-deep *a* superficiale
skinny *a* scarno, magro
skin-tight *a* indossante come un guanto
skip *vi* saltellare; — *vt* omettere; — *n* salto
skipper *n* capitano di mare

skirmish *n* schermaglia; *(mil)* scaramuccia; — *vi* scaramucciare
skirt *n* gonna; — *vt&i* rasentare, orlare, costeggiare
skit *n* parodia, scherzo, farsa
skittish *a* volubile; *(horse)* bizzarro, ombroso
skoal *interj* salute!
skulk *vi* strisciare, accovacciarsi
skull *n* cranio; **–cap** *n* papalina
skunk *n* moffetta; *(coll)* farabutto
sky *n* cielo; **–light** *n* lucernario, abbaino; **–line** *n* orizzonte *m*; **–scraper** *n* grattacielo; **–writing** *n* scrittura con fumi di aeroplano
sky-high *a&adv* fino alle nuvole *(fig)*
skylark *n* allodola
skyrocket *n* razzo; — *vi (coll)* salire con grande velocità
slab *n* lastra
slack *a* lento; fiacco; debole; negligente; — *n (rope)* imbando; — **time** stagione morta; **–er** *n* poltrone *m*; **–ness** *n* incuranza; allentamento; — **off** allentare; allentarsi
slacken *vt* allentare; moderare; — *vi* allentarsi; moderarsi; diminuire
slacks *npl* calzoni *mpl*
slag *n* scoria
slain *n* ucciso; morto
slake *vt* spegnere, placare; *(thirst)* dissetare; — *vi* spegnersi, placarsi
slalom *n (skiing)* slalom *m*
slam *n (door)* sbattuta di porta; *(sl)* critica severa; **grand** — *(cards)* cappotto; — *vt* sbattere; chiudere rumorosamente; *(sl)* criticare severamente; — *vi* sbattersi
slander *n* calunnia; — *vt* calunniare; **–er** calunniatore *m*
slanderous *a* calunnioso
slang *n* gergo populare
slant *n* pendio, declivio; *(viewpoint)* punto di vista; **–ing** *a* inclinato, obliquo; — *vt* far pendere, inclinare; — *vi* pendere, inclinarsi
slap *n* ceffone *m*; *(face)* schiaffo; — *vt* schiaffeggiare
slapstick *n* scena grottesca, farsa; — *a* grottesco
slash *n* taglio; — *vt (cut)* tagliare; *(gash)* squarciare; *(whip)* sferzare; *(reduce)* ridurre
slat *n* striscia; stecca, assicella
slate *n* ardesia; lavagna; tegola d'ardesia; *(pol)* lista di candidati; — *vt* mettere sulla lista dei candidati; *(coll)* stroncare; coprire d'ardesia
slattern *n* sciattona
slaughter *n* strage *f*, carneficina; macellazione; **–house** *n* mattatoio; macello; — *vt* massacrare; *(animals)* macellare
slave *n* schiavo; — **driver** negriero; *(fig)* aguzzino; — *vi* lavorare come schiavo; logorarsi; **–ry** *n* schiavitù *f*
slavish *a* servile; abietto; **–ly** *adv* da schiavo; servilmente; bassamente
slaw *n* insalata di cavoli
slay *vt* uccidere; **–er** *n* assassino; **–ing** *n* uccisione
sleaziness *n* mancanza di consistenza
sleazy *a* senza consistenza
sled *n* slitta
sledge *n* traino; **–hammer** mazza
sleek *a* liscio, levigato; lucido
sleep *vi* dormire; **go to** — addormentarsi
sleep *n* sonno; *(fig)* quiete *f*; **–less** *a* insonne; **–less night** notte bianca; **–ily** *adv* sonnolentemente; **–iness** *n* sonnolenza; **–y** *a* assonnato, sonnacchioso; **be –y** aver sonno
sleeping *n* sonno, riposo; — **car** vagone letto; — **pill** sonnifero; — **sickness** malattia del sonno
sleepwalker *n* sonnambulo
sleepwalking *n* sonnambulismo
sleepyhead *n* dormiglione *m*
sleet *n* nevischio; **–y** *a* nevischioso; — *vi* nevicare e piovere insieme
sleeve *n* manica; **–less** *a* senza maniche; **laugh up one's** — ridere sotto i baffi
sleigh *n* slitta
sleight *n* destrezza; — **of hand** giuoco di prestigio, prestigitazione
slender *a* esile, smilzo, snello; **–ness** *n* snellezza
sleuth *n* segugio
slice *n* fetta; — *vt* affettare
slick destro, abile; scivoloso; — *vt* lisciare, appianare; **–er** *n (coll, person)* imbroglione *m*; *(raincoat)* impermeabile *m*
slide *vi* scivolare; scorrere; — *vt* far scorrere; — *n* scivolata; slitta; *(microscope)* vetrino per microscopio; *(photo)* diapositiva; *(rock)* frana; — **rule** regolo calcolatore; — **valve** valvola a cassetto
slight *a* leggero, minimo; smilzo; — *n* affronto; — *vt* trascurare; disprezzare, denigrare; **–ly** *adv* lievemente, superficialmente; **–ness** *n* snellezza
slim *a* smilzo; **–ness** *n* esiguità, esilità, sottigliezza; — *vi* dimagrire
slime *n* limo, fanghiglia
sliminess *n* viscosità
slimy *a* viscido, viscoso
sling *n* fionda; benda per sostenere un braccio al collo; **–shot** *n* fionda, tirelastico; — *vt* sospendere; *(throw)* lanciare
slink *vi* strisciare; sgusciare; **–y** *a* strisciante
slip *n (error)* sbaglio, svista; *(slide)* scivolata; *(underwear)* sottoveste *f*, combinazione; **–cover** *n* fodera di mobile; **–knot** *n* nodo scorsoio; — *vt&i* sdrucciolare; sgusciare, sfuggire; scorrere, infilare, sbagliarsi
slipper *n* pantofola
slipperiness *n* sdrucciolosità
slippery *a* sdrucciolevole
slipshod *a* trascurato
slipup *n* sbaglio, errore *m*
slipway *n (naut)* scalo
slit *vt* fendere; — *n* fessura
sliver *n* scheggia
slobber *vi* sbavare; — *n* bava; **–y** *a* bavoso
sloe *n* prugnola; — **gin** liquore di prugnola
slog *vi* avanzare a stento
slogan *n* slogan *m*
sloop *n* scialuppa
slop *n* risciacquatura di piatti, pozzan-

ghera; — *vt* versare, spandere; — *vi* traboccare
slope *n* pendio; — *vt&i* inclinare
sloppy *a* fangoso; *(coll)* sciatto, trascurato; viscido
slosh *vi* sguazzare; — *vt* agitare ; — *n* fanghiglia
slot *n* fessura; — **machine** distributore automatico
sloth *n* indolenza; *(zool)* bradipo; **-ful** *a* pigro; **-fulness** *n* pigrizia
slouch *n* scompostura; *(person)* persona goffa, persona curva; negligente *m*; — **hat** cappelo a tesa in giù; **-y** *a* scomposto; — *vi* stare (*or* camminare) scompostamente
slough *n (swamp)* palude *f*
slough *n* spoglia; *(med)* crosta; — *vt&i* spogliarsi di; cambiare la pelle
slovenliness *n* trascuratezza
slovenly *a* trascurato, sudicio
slow *n* lento; ottuso; *(clock)* in ritardo; **-down** *n* rallentamento; **-ly** *adv* adagio, piano, lentamente; **-ness** *n* lentezza; — *vt* ritardare; — *vi* rallentare; — **down** rallentare
slow-motion *a* al rallentatore
sludge *n* melma, fanghiglia
slug *n (metal)* lingotto; *(bullet)* pallottola; *(zool)* lumaca; *(token)* gettone *m*; — *vt (coll)* percuotere
sluggard *n* pigrone *m*
sluggish *a* lento; pigro; **-ness** *n* indolenza; pigrizia
sluice *n* chiusa; canale *m*; cateratta; — *vt&i* inondare, defluire, affluire
slumber *n* sonno; — *vi* dormire; sonnecchiare
slump *n* abbassamento improvviso, tracollo, caduta brusca; — *vi* precipitare; avere un tracollo; affondare
slums *npl* quartieri poveri
slur *n* macchia; diffamazione; *(mus)* legatura; — *vt* pronunciare male; diffamare; *(mus)* legare
slush *n* fanghiglia di neve
slut *n* donnaccia
sly *a* furbo, truffaldino; **on the** — alla chetichella; **-ly** *a* astutamente; furtivamente
smack *n* gusto; aroma; sapore *m*; schiocco; schiaffo; bacione *m*; — *vt* far schioccare, schiaffeggiare; baciare sonoramente; — *vi* sapere di, aver sapore
small *a* piccolo, minuto; — **of the back** *n* le reni *fpl*; — **change** *(money)* spiccioli *mpl*; — **letter** minuscola; — **talk** chiacchiera, banalità
small-minded *a* gretto
smallpox *n* vaiolo
small-town *a* provinciale
smart *n* bruciore, dolore *m*; — *a* intelligente; scaltro; elegante; — **aleck** *(coll)* presuntuoso e antipatico; **-ing** *n* bruciore *m*; **-ing** *a* bruciante; **-ly** *adv* vivacemente; elegantemente; acutamente; dolorosamente; **-ness** *n* acutezza, prontezza di spirito; eleganza
smarten *vt* adornare; abbellire
smash *n* collisione; sconquasso; rovina; — *vt* fracassare; rovinare; — *vi* fallire; fracassarsi; spezzarsi
smashup *n* catastrofe *f*; rovina; crollo; collisione
smattering *n* conoscimento superficiale, infarinatura
smear *n* spalmata; calunnia; — *vt&i* spalmare; calunniare
smell *vt&i* odorare; fiutare; **-y** *a* puzzolente; — *n* odore *m*; *(sense of)* odorato, fiuto, olfatto; **-ing salts** sali *mpl*
smelt *n (fish)* eperlano; — *vt* fondere; **-er** *n* fonditore *m*; **-ing** *n* fusione; **-ing furnace** alto forno
smile *n* sorriso; — *vi* sorridere
smiling *a* sorridente
smirch *vt* insudiciare
smirk *n* sorriso affettato; — *vi* sorridere affettatamente
smite *vt* percuotere, colpire; *(kill)* uccidere
smith *n* fabbro; **-y** fucina
smithereens *npl (coll)* schegge *fpl*; pezzi *mpl*; frantumi *mpl*; frammenti *mpl*; **break to** — andare in frantumi; mandare in frantumi
smock *n* blusa; camice *m*; camiciotto
smoke *n* fumo; — **screen** cortina di fuma; **-stack** *n* fumaiolo; **-less** *a* senza fumo; — *vt&i* fumare; affumicare; **-d** *a* affumicato; **-r** *n* fumatore *m*, fumatrice *f*
smokiness *n* fumosità
smoking *n* fumo, il fumare; — **jacket** giacca da fumo; **no** — proibito fumare
smoky *a* fumoso, fumante
smolder *vt&i* bruciare senza fiamma; covare nelle ceneri; **-ing** *a* covante, che cova
smooth *a* liscio; — *vt* lisciare; piallare; appianare, calmare; **-ly** *adv* agevolmente; **-ness** *n* levigatezza; calma; agevolezza
smooth-shaved *a* imberbe
smooth-tongued *a* adulatore, mellifluo
smother *vt&i* soffocare; nascondere
smudge *n* sgorbio, macchia; — *vt&i* macchiare, sporcare
smudgy *a* macchiato
smug *a* vanitoso, affettato; **-ness** *n* vanità, affettazione
smuggle *vt&i* contrabbandare; **-r** *n* contrabbandiere *m*
smuggling *n* frodo, contrabbando
smut *n* fuligginе *f*; oscenità
smuttiness *n* oscenità
smutty *a* fuligginoso, nero, osceno
snack *n* spuntino; pasto frugale; — *vi* fare uno spuntino
snag *n* nodo; troncone *m*; intoppo; ramo sommerso; — *vt* ostacolare
snail *n* lumaca, chiocciola; **at a —'s pace** a passo di lumaca *(coll)*
snake *n* serpente *m*; — *vi* serpeggiare
snaky *a* tortuoso, serpentino; *(fig)* scaltro
snap *vt&i* spezzare; mordere, azzannare, cercare di mordere; scattare, schioccare; spezzarsi; — *n* scatto, schiocco; morso; *(sl)* cosa facile da farsi; *(coll)* vivacità; **cold** — periodo di freddo; **-shot** *n (photo)* istantanea
snapdragon *n (bot)* bocca di leone
snappish *a* irascibile, bisbetico
snappy *a (coll)* vivo, pungente; elegante; **make it** — *(sl)* fa presto

snare *n* trappola; — *vt* prendere al laccio
snarl *n (animal)* ringhio; *(tangle)* groviglio; — *vi* ringhiare; aggrovigliarsi; — *vt* aggrovigliare
snatch *vt* strappare, ghermire; — *n* presa; strappone *m*
sneak *n* spia; vile *m*; — **thief** ladruncolo; **–y** *a* servile, basso; ficcanaso; — *vt (coll)* rubare, sottrarre; — *vi* strisciare; spiare; — **in** intrufolarsi; — **out** uscire alla chetichella
sneakers *npl* scarpe da ginnastica
sneaking *a* meschino, basso; sospettoso; **–ly** *adv* bassamente; sospettosamente
sneer *n* sogghigno; — *vi* sogghignare; **–ing** *a* derisorio
sneeze *vi* starnutire; — *n* starnuto
snicker *n* risatina celata; — *vi* ridacchiare
sniff *n* fiutata; — *vi* succhiare col naso; frignare
sniffle *n* succhiata di naso; — *vi* succhiare col naso; frignare
snip *n* ritaglio; taglio; brandello; pezzettino; — *vt&i* tagliuzzare
snipe *n (zool)* beccaccino; **–r** *n* cecchino; — *vi* sparare in appostamento
snippy *a* presuntuoso, arioso
snivel *vi* moccicare, piagnucolare, frignare
snob *n* snob *m*
snobbish *a* snobistico; affettato; **–ness** *n* snobismo; affettazione
snoop *vi (coll)* curiosare, ficcare il naso; **–er** *n* ficcanaso
snoot *n (coll)* naso; faccia, smorfia; **–y** *a* arrogante
snooze *n* pisolino; — *vi* sonnecchiare
snore *vi&n* russare *m*
snorer *n* russatore *m*
snoring *n* il russare
snorkel *n* presa d'aria
snort *n* sbuffo; — *vi* sbuffare; **–ing** *n* sbuffamento; **–ing** *a* sbuffante
snout *n* muso; *(pig)* grugno; *(mech)* beccuccio
snow *n* neve *f*; **–bound** *a* bloccato dalla neve; **–drift** *n* ammasso di neve; **–fall** *n* nevicata; **–flake** *n* fiocco di neve; — **line** limite delle nevi perpetue; **–plow** *n* spazzaneve *m*; **–slide** *n* valanga; **–storm** *n* tempesta di neve; **–suit** *n* vestito da neve; — *vi* nevicare; **it is –ing** nevica
snow– *(in comp)* **—blind** *a* accecato dalla neve; **—capped** *a* coronato di neve
snowball *n* palla di neve; — *vt* lanciare palle di neve; — *vi (enlarge)* crescere rapidamente
snowy *a* nevoso
snub *n* rimprovero, affronto; — *vt* trattare freddamente, offendere; — **nose** naso camuso
snuff *n* moccolo; tabacco da fiuto; presa di tabacco; fiutata; — *vt* smoccolare; fiutare
snuffbox *n* tabacchiera
snuffle *vi* fiutare rumorosamente
snug *a* comodo, agevole; ritirato, nascosto, riparato; **–ly** *adv* comodamente, agevolmente; **–ness** *n* comodità
snuggle *vt* vezzeggiare, abbracciare; — *vi* accomodarsi, rannicchiarsi
so *adv&conj* così, tanto, talmente; quindi; di modo che; **and — forth** e così via; eccetera; — **as to** in modo da; — **long!** ciao!, arrivederci!; — **much** tanto; — **then** bene, allora; — **to speak** per così dire
soak *vt* inzuppare; — *vi* inzupparsi, assorbirsi; filtrare
soaking *a* gocciolante, — *n* bagno, immersione
so-and-so *n (coll)* Tal dei Tali
soap *n* sapone *m*; — **bubble** bolla di sapone; **—dish** portasapone *m*; **–stone** *n* steatite *f*; **–suds** *npl* saponata, soluzione saponosa; **bar** — sapone in barre; **toilet** — saponetta; **–y** *a* saponoso; insaponato; — *vt* insaponare
soar *vi* volare; librarsi, acquistare quota; prendere lo slancio
sob *n* singhiozzo; — *vi* singhiozzare
sober *a* sobrio; **–ness** *n* sobrietà; moderazione; — *vt&i* smaltire la sbornia; rinsavire, calmarsi; ritornare in sè
sober-minded *a* serio, sobrio
sobersides *n* musoduro
sobriety *n* sobrietà
sobriquet *n* soprannome *m*
so-called *a* cosiddetto
sociability *n* sociabilità
sociable *a* socievole, affabile
sociably *adv* socievolmente
social *n* trattenimento sociale; — **security** assicurazione sociale; — *a* sociale; socievole, affabile; **–ism** *n* socialismo; **–ist** *n* socialista *m&f*; **–istic** *a* socialista, socialistico; **–ite** *n* persona dell'alta società; **–ize** *vt* socializzare
society *n* società
sociological *a* sociologico
sociologist *n* sociologo
sociology *n* sociologia
sock *n* calzetta, calzino; *(sl)* pugno; — *vt (sl)* colpire, dare un pugno
socket *n (elec)* incavo, portalampada *m*; *(eye)* orbita; *(joint)* manicotto, giunto; *(anat)* articolazione; (tooth) alveolo
sod *n* zolla erbosa
soda *n* soda; **baking** — bicarbonato di soda; — **water** selz *m*, acqua gassosa
sodium *n* sodio; — **chloride** clorato di sodio
sodomy *n* sodomia
sofa *n* sofà, canapè *m*; — **bed** sofà a letto, divano-letto
soft *a* molle; dolce; — **coal** carbone bituminoso; — **drink** bevanda analcoolica; **–ness** *n* morbidezza; tenerezza; debolezza; — **pedal** sordina
soft– *(in comp)* **—boiled** bassotto; — **pedal** *vt (coll)* abbassare il tono; diminuire; **—soap** *vt (coll)* adulare; **—spoken** *a* mellifluo; affabile
soften *vt* ammollire, addolcire, mitigare; — *vi* rammollirsi; addolcirsi; mitigarsi
softhead *n* imbecille *m*
softhearted *a* di buon cuore
soggy *a* inzuppato
soil *n* suolo; terra; sporcizia, macchia; letame; — *vi* sporcarsi
sojourn *n* soggiorno; — *vi* soggiornare
sol *n (mus)* sol *m*

solace *n* consolazione, conforto, — *vt* consolare
solar *a* solare; — **plexus** plesso solare; — **system** sistema solare
sold *a* venduto
solder *vt* saldare; — *vi* saldarsi; — *n* saldatura
soldering *n* saldatura; — **iron** saldatore *m*
soldier *n* soldato; — *vi* fare il soldato
sole *n* *(fish)* sogliola; *(foot)* pianta del piede; *(shoe)* suola; — *a* solo, unico; — *vt* risolare, solare
solecism *n* solecismo
solemn *a* solenne; grave; **–ity** n solennità; **–ization** *n* solennizzamento; **–ize** *vt* solennizzare
solicit *vt&i* sollecitare; fare colletta; pregare; **–ation** *n* sollecitazione, richiesta; **–or** *n* piazzista, propagandista *m*; **–ous** *a* sollecito; **–ude** *n* sollecitudine *f*
solid *a&n* solido; **–arity** solidarietà; — **color** tinta unita; **–ity** *n* solidezza, solidità; **–ify** *vt* solidificare; **–ify** *vi* solidificarsi
solid state physics elettrofisica degli stati solidi
soliloquy *n* soliloquio
solitaire *n* solitario
solitariness *n* solitudine *f*
solitary *a* solitario; — **confinement** segregazione cellulare
solitude *n* solitudine *f*
solo *n&a (mus)* assolo
soloist *n* solista *m&f*
solstice *n* solstizio
solubility *n* solubilità
soluble *a* solubile
solution *n* soluzione
solve *vt* risolvere
solvency *n* solvibilità
solvent *a&n* solvente
somber *a* oscuro, ombroso, fosco; **–ness** *n* foscaggine *f*
some *a* qualche, un po'di; qualcuno; del, della, dei, delle; — *pron* alcuni *mpl*, alcune *fpl*; certi *mpl*; certe *fpl*; ne; — *adv* circa
some *(in comb)* **–body** *pron* qualcuno; **–day** *adv* qualche giorno; **–how** *adv* in qualche modo; **–one** *pron* qualcuno; **–one else** un altro; **–thing** *n* qualcosa; qualche cosa; **–time** *adv* qualche volta, uno di questi giorni; **–times** *adv* qualche volta, talvolta; **–what** *adv* alquanto, un poco; **–where** *adv* in qualche luogo; **–where else** altrove
somersault *n* capitombolo, capriola; — *vi* far salti mortali (or capriole)
somnambulism *n* sonnambulismo
somnambulist *n* sonnambulo
somnolence sonnolenza
somnolent *a* sonnolente
son *n* figlio
sonata *n* sonata
song *n* canzone *f*; **–ster** *n* cantante *m*; **–stress** *n* cantante *f*
sonic *a* di suono, sonico; — **boom** *(avi)* strepito di aviogetto
son-in-law *n* genero
sonnet *n* sonetto
sonneteer *n* sonettista *m&f*
sonority *n* sonorità
sonorous *a* sonoro
soon *adv* presto, subito; **as** — **as** appena che; **How** —? Quando?; **–er** *adv* più presto; piuttosto; prima
soot *n* fuliggine *f*; **–y** *a* fuligginoso, nero
soothe *vt* calmare, lenire
soothing *a* calmante, mite; adulante
soothsayer *n* indovino
soothsaying *n* divinazione
sop *n* zuppa, pappa; —, — **up** *vt* inzuppare, assorbire; — *vi* inzupparsi; **–ing** *a* bagnato, inzuppato
sophist *n* sofista *m&f*
sophisticated *a* sofisticato; ricercato; raffinato
sophistication *n* sofisticazione; adulterazione
sophistry *n* sofisticheria
sophomore *n* studente di secondo anno; fagiolo *(student sl)*
sophomoric *a* inesperto, poco giudizioso
soporific *n&a* soporifero
soprano *n* soprano
sorcerer *n* mago, stregone *m*
sorceress *n* maga, strega
sorcery *n* magia, stregoneria
sordid *a* sordido; **–ly** *adv* sordidamente; **–ness** sordidezza
sore *n* piaga; — *a* doloroso; *(coll)* arrabbiato; **–ness** *n* dolore *m*
sorghum *n* sorgo
sorority *n* associazione fra donne
sorrel *n (bot)* acetosa; — *a&n* sauro
sorrow *n* dolore *m*, pena; **–ful** *a* triste; addolorato; doloroso; — *vi* addolorarsi, affliggersi
sorry *a* spiacente, afflitto, dolente; meschino; **be** — essere spiacente
sort *n* sorta, genere *m*; specie *f*; — *vt* assortire
sortie *n (mil)* sortita
so-so *a&adv* così così
sot *n* ubriacone *m*
sough *vi* stormire, sussurrare
sought *a* cercato, ricercato
soul *n* anima; **–ful** *a* spirituale; **–less** *a* senz'anima
sound *n* suono; rumore *m*; *(geog)* stretto; — **barrier** barriera del suono; — **track** *(movies)* colonna sonora; — **wave** onda sonora; — *a* sano; solido; *(com)* solvente; **–ly** *adv* bene; profondamente; **–ness** *n* sanità; validità; **–less** *a* muto, senza suono
sound *vt* suonare, far suonare; sondare; — *vi* suonare, risuonare; sembrare
sounding *n (naut)* sondaggio; scandaglio; — *a* sonante, risonante, sonoro; — **board** tavola armonica; — **line** *(naut)* sonda, scandaglio
soundproof *a* refrattario al suono, antiacustico
soup *n* minestra; zuppa; — **plate** scodella; **–spoon** *n* cucchiaione *m*; — **tureen** zuppiera; **–y** *a* come zuppa
soupçon *n* pizzico
sour *a* agro; aspro; **–ness** *n* acidità; asprezza; — *vt&i* rendere agro, inacidire; **–ly** *adv* aspramente

source *n* fonte *f*
souse *vt* mettere in salamoia; immergere, inzuppare, tuffare; — *vi* immergersi, inzupparsi, tuffarsi
south *n* sud *m*; **S— America** America del Sud; **S— American** sudamericano
southeast *n* sud-est *m*
southern *a* meridionale
southerner *n* meridionale *m&f*
southpaw *n&a (coll)* mancino
southwest *n* sud-ovest *m*
souvenir *n* ricordo
sovereign *a&n* sovrano
sovereignty *n* sovranità
soviet *n* soviet *m*; — *a* sovietico
sow *n* troia, scrofa
sow *vt&i* seminare; **–er** *n* seminatore *m*; **–ing** *n* semina
soy, soybean *n* soia
spa *n* stazione termale
space *n* spazio; — **capsule** capsula spaziale; — **platform** piattaforma interplanetare; — **suit** tuta spaziale; — **travel** viaggio spaziale; **–man** *n* astronauta *m*; **–ship** *n* astronave *f*; — **station** stazione spaziale; — *vt* spaziare; intervallare
spacing *n* spaziatura
spacious *a* ampio; **–ness** *n* ampiezza
spade *n (cards)* picca; *(tool)* vanga; **call a — a —** dire pane al pane; — *vt* vangare
Spain Spagna
span *n* durata, portata; *(measure)* spanna; — *vt* attraversare, stendersi attraverso; abbracciare; *(measure)* misurare a spanne
spangle *n* paglietta, lustrino; — *vt* adornare con lustrini; — *vi* luccicare
Spaniard *n* spagnolo
spaniel *n* bracco spagnolo
Spanish *n&a* spagnolo
spank *vt* sculacciare; **–ing** *n* sculacciamento
spar *n* antenna; *(avi)* alerone *m*; *(geol)* spato; *(naut)* albero; — *vi* fare un incontro di pugilato, combattere; discutere
spare *vt&i* risparmiare; tralasciare; — *a* di ricambio; smilzo; — **parts** pezzi di ricambio; — **time** tempo libero; — **tire** gomma di ricambio
spareness *n* scarnezza
sparerib *n* costoletta di maiale
sparing *a* frugale; parco, economo
spark *n* scintilla; — **plug** candela
sparkle *vi* scintillare; essere effervescente
sparkling *a* scintillante; effervescente
sparrow *n* passero
sparse *a* rado; **–ly** *adv* radamente; **–ness** *n* radezza
Spartan *n&a* spartano
spasm *n* spasmo, spasimo; **–odic** *a* spasmodico; **–odically** *adv* spasmodicamente
spastic *n&a* spastico
spat *n* battibecco; **–s** *npl (footwear)* ghette *fpl*; — *vi* bisticciare
spatial, spacial *a* spaziale
spatter *vt&i* spruzzare; **–ing** *n* spruzzata
spatula *n* spatola
spawn *n* progenie *f*; *(fish)* uova *fpl*; — *vt&i* generare; deporre uova
spay *vt* sterilizzare
speak *vt&i* parlare; — **out** parlar chiaro; — **up** parlare forte
speaker *n* parlatore, conferenziere, oratore *m*; *(mech)* altoparlante *m*
spear *n (grass)* stelo; fiocina; spiedo; lancia; **–fishing** pesca subacquea; — **gun** fucile subacqueo; **–head** *n* punta di lancia; **–mint** *n* menta; — *vt* trafiggere, fiocinare
special *a* speciale; — **delivery** per espresso; **–ist** *n* specialista *m*; **–ization** *n* specializzazione; **–ize** *vi* specializzarsi; **–ize** *vt* specializzare; **–ty** *n* specialità
specie *n* moneta metallica
species *n* specie *f*
specific *a* specifico; — **gravity** peso specifico; **–ally** *adv* specificamente
specification *n* specificazione
specious *a* specioso
specify *vt* specificare
specimen *n* campione *m*
speck *n (amount)* tantino; macchiolina
speckle *vt* variegare; marcare a puntini; — *n* puntino, macchiolina; **–d** *a* variegato, macchiettato
spectacle *n* spettacolo
spectacles *npl (glasses)* occhiali *mpl*
spectacular *a* spettacoloso, spettacolare, sensazionale
spectator *n* spettatore *m*; spettatrice *f*
specter *n* spettro
spectral *a* spettrale
spectroscope *n* spettroscopio
spectrum *n* spettro
speculate *vi* speculare
speculation *n* speculazione
speculator *n* speculatore *m*
speculative *a* speculativo
speech *n* discorso; linguaggio; **–less** *a* muto; **figure of —** figura rettorica
speed *n* velocità; **–boat** *n* motoscafo; **–ily** *adv* velocemente; **–iness** *n* rapidità; — **limit** velocità massima; **–ometer** *n* contachilometri *m*; **–way** *n* autopista; **–y** *a* rapido; — *vt* affrettare, far accelerare; — *vi* affrettarsi, accelerare, aumentare la velocità
speed-up *n* accelerazione, acceleramento
spell *n* malia; **–bound** *a* affascinato, incantato; **–binder** *n (coll)* oratore che conquista l'auditorio
spell *vt* compitare, sillabare; **–er** *n (book)* sillabario; *(person)* chi compita
spelling *n* ortografia; — **bee** emulazione (*or* gara) in ortografia
spend *vt* spendere; *(time)* trascorrere; esaurire; **–er** *n* consumatore *m*
spendthrift *n* scialacquatore *m*
spent *a* speso; esaurito
sperm *n* sperma *m*; — **whale** capidoglio
spermatozoa *npl* spermatozoi *mpl*
spew *vt&i* vomitare
sphere *n* sfera
spherical *a* sferico
spheroid *n&a* sferoide *m*
sphincter *n (anat)* sfintere *m*
sphinx *n* sfinge *f*
spice *n* spezie *f*; — *vt* condire con spezie

spiciness *n* gusto piccante
spick-and-span *a* pulito alla perfezione
spicy *a* drogato, pepato, piccante
spider *n* ragno; **–y** *a* come un ragno; **— web** ragnatela
spigot *n* turacciolo; zipolo; rubinetto
spike *n* punta; chiodo; *(bot)* aculeo; *(corn)* spiga; — *vt* inchiodare; infilzare
spill *n* caduta; zipolo, legnetto; — *vt* spargere, versare; confessare; — *vi* versarsi, rovesciarsi
spin *vt* filare; girare; — *n* giro; rotazione; *(avi)* vite *f*; avvitamento; corsa
spinach *n* spinaci *mpl*
spinal *a* vertebrale; **— cord** midollo spinale; **— column** colonna vertebrale
spindle *n* fuso, asse *m*
spine *n (anat)* spina dorsale; *(book)* dorso del libro; *(bot)* spina; **–less** *a* invertebrato; slombato
spinet *n (mus)* spinetta
spinning *n* filatura; **— jenny** filatoio; **— mill** filanda; **— wheel** ruota per filare; filatoio; — *a* girante, rollante
spinster *n* zitella
spiny *a* spinoso; difficile
spiral *a&n* spirale *f*
spire *n* cuspide *f*, guglia; *(bot)* stelo
spirit *n* spirito; **— level** livello ad aria; **–less** *a* abbattuto, avvilito; **–ed** *a* vivace, coraggioso; — *vt* animare, ravvivare; **— away** trafugare
spirits *npl* bevande alcooliche; liquori *mpl*; **in high —** di buon umore
spiritual *a* spirituale; **–ism** *n (philosophy)* spiritualismo; spiritismo; **–ist** *n* spiritista *m&f*
spit *n* sputo; *(cooking)* spiedo; *(land)* lingua di terra; — *vt&i* sputare
spite *n* dispetto, rancore *m*, **in — of** malgrado; **–ful** *a* dispettoso; — *vt* vessare; far dispetto a
spitfire *n* stizzoso, irascibile *m*; *(avi)* spitfire *m*
spittle *n* saliva, sputo
spittoon *n* sputacchiera
splash *n* schizzo; — *vt&i* schizzare
spleen *n (organ)* milza; malinconia, malumore *m*; **–ful** *a* bisbetico, imbronciato
splendid *a* splendido, magnifico; **–ly** *adv* splendidamente
splendor *n* splendore *m*
splice *n* calettatura, unione *f*, impiombatura; — *vt* calettare, unire, impiombare
splint *n* stecca
splinter *n* scheggia; — *vt* scheggiare; — *vi* scheggiarsi
split *vt&i* fendere, scindere; spaccarsi; dividere; — *n* fessura, scissione; *(dance)* spaccata
splitting *a* fendente, spaccante; — *n (atom)* scissione; **— headache** mal di testa lancinante
splotch *vt* macchiare, chiazzare; — *n* macchia, chiazza; **–ed** *a* macchiato, chiazzato; **–y** *a* macchiato
splurge *n (coll)* sfoggio, ostentazione; — *vt (coll)* sfoggiare, ostentare
splutter *vi* barbugliare
spoil *vt* guastare, viziare, rovinare; — *vi* guastarsi; infradiciarsi; **–age** *n* deterioramento
spoils *npl* bottino
spoilsport *n* guastafeste *m*
spoke *n* raggio
spokesman *n* portavoce *m&f*
sponge spugna; — *vt&i* usare la spugna; *(coll)* scroccare
sponger *n (coll)* scroccone *m*
sponginess *n* spugnosità
spongy *a* spugnoso
sponsor *n* garante *m*; padrino, madrina; *(rad, TV)* patrocinatore *m*; — *vt* garantire; **–ship** *n* garanzia
spontaneity *n* spontaneità
spontaneous *a* spontaneo; **–ly** *adv* spontaneamente
spool *n* bobina
spoon *n* cucchiaio; **–ful** *n* cucchiaiata
spoor *n* traccia, pista, orma
sporadic *a* sporadico
spore *n* spora
sport *n* sport *m*; *(biol)* anomalia; **–ing** *a* sportivo; **–ive** *a* scherzevole; — *vi* divertirsi; giuocare; — *vt (coll)* ostentare
sportsman *n* sportivo
spot *n* macchia, punto; *(place)* luogo; **be on the —** *(sl)* essere nei guai; **–light** *n* fascio di luce; proiettore *m*; **–less** *a* immacolato; — *vt (place)* collocare; *(blemish)* macchiare; punteggiare
spotted *a* macchiato
spotty *a* macchiato; picchiettato
spouse *n* sposo, sposa
spout *vt* spruzzare; — *vi* sgorgare — *n* sgorgo; becco, tubo
sprain *n* storta; — *vt* storcere
sprawl *vi* sdraiarsi, distendersi; **–ing** *a* sdraiato, disteso
spray *vt* spruzzare, vaporizzare; — *n (flowers)* ramoscello; spruzzo, getto; raffica; *(device)* spruzzatore *m*
spread *n* distesa; *(bed)* coperta da letto; *(bread)* companatico da spalmare; *(coll)* festa, banchetto
spread *vt&i* spargere; *(news)* divulgare, diffondere; stendere, spalmare
spree *n* baldoria
sprig *n* ramoscello; rampollo
sprightliness *n* vivacità
sprightly *a* vivace
spring *n (elasticity)* elasticità; *(leap)* salto, balzo; *(metal)* molla; *(movement)* scatto; *(season)* primavera; *(water)* sorgente *f*; **–board** *n* trampolino; **–lock** *n* serratura a scatto; **— fever** *(fig)* indolenza primaverile; **–y** *a* elastico; — *vt&i* molleggiare; *(water)* scaturire; *(jump)* saltare; *(leak)* aprire; **— from** originare da, provenire da; **— up** balzare su; *(rise)* nascere, sorgere
springlike *a* primaverile
sprinkle *n* aspersione; spruzzata; — *vt* spruzzare; cospargere; — *vi* piovigginare; **–r** *n* spruzzatore *m*
sprinkling *n* spruzzata; spruzzo
sprint *n (sport)* volata; — *vi* fare una volata, correre in volata; **–er** *n* velocista *m*
sprite *n* folletto
sprocket *n* dente di ruota
sprout *n* germoglio; rampollo; — *vi* ger-

mogliare
spruce *a* lindo; — *n (bot)* abete *m*; — *vt* allindare; — *vi* allindarsi
spry *a* agile, lesto; **–ness** agilità
spume *n* schiuma, spuma
spumy *a* spumoso
spun *a* filato
spunk *n (coll)* coraggio
spunky *a (coll)* coraggioso
spur *n* sperone *m*; stimolo; **on the — of the moment** lì per lì, senza riflettere; — *vt* incitare, spronare
spurious *a* spurio
spurn *vt* sdegnare, respingere; **–ing** *n* respingimento
spurt *n* getto, zampillo; *(sport)* scatto, volata; — *vt&i* spruzzare, zampillare, scaturire
sputter *n* spruzzo; balbettio; — *vi* spruzzare; schizzare; balbettare; **–ing** *a* balbettante
sputum *n* sputo
spy *n* spia; — *vt&i* spiare; far la spia
spyglass *n* cannocchiale *m*
squab *n* piccioncino
squabble *n* lite *f*; — *vi* litigare
squad *n* squadra
squadron *n* squadrone *m*; *(avi)* squadriglia
squalid *a* squallido
squall *n (storm)* turbine *m*; strillo; — *vi* strillare, sbraitare; turbinare
squalor *n* squallore *m*
squander *vt* sperperare
square *n* quadrato; piazza; — *a* quadrato; *(com)* saldato; giusto; — *vt* quadrare; — **measure** misura di superficie; — **root** radice quadrata
square-rigged *a (naut)* a vele quadre
squash *n* zucca; schiacciamento; — *vt* schiacciare
squat *vi* accosciarsi; **–ty** *a* tozzo
squawk *n* strido, gracidio; — *vi* gracidare
squeak *vi* squittire; — *n* strido
squeal *n* strillo; *(coll)* delazione; — *vt&i* strillare; *(coll)* delatare
squeamish *a* schifiltoso; **–ness** *n* schizzinosità
squeeze *n* stretta; estorsione; — *vt* spremere; stringere; — *vi* insinuarsi, intromettersi; — **out** spremere; **lemon –r** spremilimone *m*
squelch *n* risposta mordace; — *vt* schiacciare; tacitare, soffocare
squib *n* satira
squid *n* calamaro
squint *n* sguardo strabico; *(med)* strabismo; *(coll)* occhiata di sbieco; — *vi* guardare con gli occhi socchiusi; *(med)* essere strabico
squint-eyed *a* strabico
squinting *n* strabismo; — *a* con gli occhi socchiusi; *(med)* strabico
squire *n* gentiluomo di campagna; scudiere *m*; — *vt* scortare
squirm *vi* contorcersi; **–ing** *n* contorcimento
squirrel *n* scoiattolo
squirt *n (syringe)* siringa; spruzzo; *(coll)* persona meschina, omiciattolo; — *vt&i* spruzzare, zampillare
stab *n* pugnalata, stoccata; — *vt* accoltellare, pugnalare; — **in the back** pugnalare alle spalle; **make a — at** fare un tentativo
stability *n* stabilità
stabilization *n* stabilizzazione
stabilize *vt* stabilizzare; **–r** *n* stabilizzatore *m*
stable *a* fermo, stabile — *n* scuderia, stalla — *vt* mettere nella stalla
staccato *a* staccato
stack *n* mucchio, ammasso; — *vt* ammucchiare; *(cards)* preparare per barare
stadium *n* stadio
staff *n* bastone *m*; *(editorial)* corpo redazionale; *(mus)* pentagramma *m*; *(office)* personale *m*; *(teaching)* corpo degli insegnanti; — **of life** mezzo di prima necessità; il pane quotidiano *(fig)*
stag *n* cervo; — **party** serata per uomini soli
stage *n* scena, palcoscenico, teatro; tappa; — **fright** panico dell'attore; — **manager** direttore di scena; **–coach** *n* diligenza; **–craft** *n* arte scenica; **–hand** *n* macchinista scenico; — *vt* mettere in scena
stagger *vi* vacillare; esitare; — *vt* sconcertare; far barcollare; scuotere; **–ed** *a* a intervalli, d'intervallo, alternato; **–ing** *a* barcollante; titubante
staging *n* messa in scena
stagnancy *n* ristagno
stagnant *a* stagnante
stagnate *vi* ristagnare
stagy *a* teatrale
staid *a* posato, severo, serio; **–ness** *n* gravità, posatezza
stain *n* macchia; — *vt* tingere, macchiare, sporcare; — *vi* sporcarsi, macchiarsi; **–ed** *a* macchiato; sfregiato; **–ed glass** vetro colorato
stainless *a* senza macchia, immacolato; — **steel** acciaio inossidabile
stair *n* gradino, scalino; **–case, –way** *n* scala; **–s** *npl* scale *fpl*; scalinata
stake *n (wager)* posta, scommessa; *(wooden)* palo, stecco; — *vt* scommettere; puntellare; sostenere; — **a claim** dichiararsi proprietario
stalactite *n* stalattite *f*
stalagmite *n* stalagmite *f*
stale *a* raffermo, stantio; — *vt&i* invecchiare; *(baked products)* seccare; **–ness** *n* vecchiezza
stalk *n* stelo; picciuolo; torsolo; — *vi* camminare impettito; — *vt* seguire la pista di
stallion *n* stallone *m*
stalwart *a* robusto; coraggioso
stamen *n* stame *m*
stamina *n* resistenza fisica, vigore *m*
stammer *vt&i* balbettare; **–er** *n* balbuziente *m*; **–ing** *n* balbuzie *f*
stamp *n* impressione; stampa; *(postage)* francobollo; *(revenue)* marca da bollo; *(rubber)* timbro di gomma; — **pad** cuscinetto per timbri; — *vt* battere, pestare, imprimere; *(mail)* affrancare; — *vi* scalpicciare, battere i piedi; — **out** estirpare, sradicare

stampede *n* fuga precipitosa; — *vi* fuggire precipitosamente; — *vt* mettere in fuga precipitosa
stance *n* atteggiamento
stand *n* edicola; fermata; posizione; pausa, sosta; tribuna; **–point** *n* punto di vista; **–still** *n* arresto, fermata; — *vi* stare; fermarsi; star diritto; essere; rimanere; alzarsi; — *vt* mettere; tollerare; — **aside** tenersi da parte; — **back of** rispondere per, garantire per; *(behind)* stare dietro di; — **by** assistere, difendere, sostenere; — **for** tollerare; significare; prendere la parte di; sostituire; — **off** tenersi da parte; **it –s to reason** è ovvio; — **up** tenersi ritto; — **up against** opporsi a; essere contro; — **up for** sostenere, difendere
standard *n* stendardo; criterio, norma; — **of living** tenore di vita; — *a* normale, usuale; standardizzato; **–ization** *n* standardizzazione; **–ize** *vt* standardizzare
standard-bearer *n* portabandiera *m*
stand- *(in comp)* **—by** *n* appoggio; **—in** *n* controfigura
standing *a* permanente, fisso; — *n (duration)* durata; posizione, rango; — **army**; esercito permanente; — **order** ordine permanente; — **room** posto in piedi
standoffish *a* superbo, altero, riservato
stanza *n* strofa
staple *n* prodotto principale; *(metal)* chiodo ad U; — *a* stabilito, principale; **–r** *n (paper)* cucitrice a grappe
star *n* stella, astro; *(print)* asterisco; **evening** — espero; **shooting** — stella filante; **–board** *n* tribordo; **–board** *a* di tribordo; **–gazer** *n* astronomo; **–less** *a* senza stelle; **–light** *n* luce stellare; **–lit** *a* stellato, illuminato di stelle; **–ry** *a* stellato; — *vi* essere un astro cinematografico (*or* teatrale); primeggiare; — *vt* cospargere di stelle; *(mark)* indicare con asterisco
starch *n* amido; — *vt* inamidare; **–iness** *n* inamidatezza; **–y** *a* amidoso
stare *vt&i* guardare fisso; — *n* sguardo fisso
starfish *n* stella di mare
stark *a* inflessibile, rigido; proprio; completo; desolato; — *adv* completamente
starling *n* stornello
starry-eyed *a* dagli occhi scintillanti, dagli occhi sognanti
star-spangled *a* stellato, punteggiato di stelle
start *n* principio; sussulto; vantaggio; partenza; avviamento; — *vt&i* cominciare; trasalire; partire; mettere in moto, fondare; — **again** ricominciare;
starter *n (auto)* avviamento; iniziatore *m*; partente *m*
starting *n* partenza; sussulto; *(begining)* inizio, principio; *(business)* lancio; — **gate, post** palo di partenza; — **point** punto di partenza
startle *vt* far trasalire, sorprendere, spaventare
startling *a* sorprendente; emozionante; allarmante
starvation *n* inedia; fame *f*
starve *vi* morire di fame; — *vt* affamare, far morire di fame
starving *a* famelico
state *n* stato; condizione; **–craft** *n* arte di governo; **–ly** *a* maestoso; **–liness** *n* imponenza, maestà; **–room** *n* cabina; — *a* statale; — *vt* dichiarare
statement *n* dichiarazione, affermazione; *(com)* rendiconto; distinta
statesman *n* uomo di stato; **–ship** *n* arte di governo, politica
static *n* disturbi atmosferici; — *a* statico
station *n* stazione; posto; *(social)* posizione sociale; — **agent, –master** capostazione *m*; — **break** *(rad)* intervallo; — **wagon** giardinetta; — *vt* mettere a posto; collocare
stationary *a* stazionario
stationer *n* cartolaio
stationery *n* articoli di cancelleria; — **store** cartoleria
Stations of the Cross Stazioni della Via Crucis
statistic, –al *a* statistico
statistics *npl* statistica
statistician *n* statistico, esperto in statistica
statuary *n* scultura; statue *fpl*
statue *n* statua; **–sque** *a* scultoreo; statuario
statuette *n* figurina, statuetta
stature *n* statura
status *n* stato, condizione, rango
statute *n* statuto; — **law** legge statutaria
statutory *a* statutario
staunch *a* fermo; leale, fido; — *vt* stagnare
stave *n* doga; *(ladder)* piuola; *(lit)* strofa; — *vt* dogare; — **in** sfondare; — **off** stornare
stay *n* soggiorno; sostegno; *(delay)* proroga; — *vi (remain)* soggiornare, rimanere; *(bear up)* sostenersi; — *vt* prorogare; *(prop)* puntellare; *(stop)* fermare; — **up** *(in place)* stare; *(awake)* vegliare; **–ing power** resistenza
stay-at-home *n* casalingo, persona che ama la propria casa
stead *n* posto; vece *f*; **–fast** *a* risoluto, costante; **–iness** *n* stabilità; **–y** *a* stabile; fisso, fermo
steak *n* bistecca
steal *n (coll)* guadagno senza scrupoli, vantaggio disonesto; — *vt&i* rubare; — **away** allontanarsi furtivamente
stealth *n* segreto; **–ily** *adv* furtivamente; **–y** *a* furtivo, segreto
steam *n* vapore *m*; **–ing** *a* fumante; — **roller** rullo compressore; **–ship** *n* piroscafo; bastimento
steel *n* acciaio; **stainless** — acciaio inossidabile; **tempered** — acciaio temperato; — **engraving** incisione su acciaio; — **mill** acciaieria; — *a* d'acciaio; **–y** *a* acciaioso; duro; — *vt* fortificare, indurire; temprare; — **oneself** indurirsi
steelyard *n* stadera
steep *a* ripido; *(coll)* caro; **–ly** *adv* ripidamente; **–ness** *n* ripidità; — *vt* imbevere, impregnare
steeple *n* campanile *m*, guglia
steeplechase *n* corsa ad ostacoli

steer *n* manzo
steer *vt* guidare; *(naut)* pilotare; — *vi* sterzare; — **clear of** evitare, girar al largo da
steerage *n* pilotaggio, viraggio, guida; terza classe
steering *n* direzione; *(naut)* governo; *(auto)* guida; — **gear** comando; sterzo; — **wheel** volante *m*
steersman *n* timoniere *m*
stein *n* boccale da birra
stellar *a* stellare
stellate *a* stellato
stem *n* gambo; *(bot)* stelo; *(gram)* radice *f*: *(mus)* gamba; *(naut)* prua; *(watch)* caricatore *m*; — *vt* resistere a, arginare; — **from** aver origine da
stench *n* puzza
stencil *n* stampino; — *vt* stampinare
stenographer *n* stenografo, stenografa
stenographic *a* stenagrafico
stenography *n* stenografia
stenotype *n* macchina da stenodattilografia
stentorian *a* stentoreo
step *n* passo; *(stairs)* gradino; *(door)* soglia; — *vi* fare un passo, camminare; — **in** entrare; — **off** misurare a passi; — **on** calpestare; — **out** uscire; **take -s** fare passi *(fig)*
stepbrother *n* fratellastro
stepchild *n* figliastro, figliastra
stepdaughter *n* figliastra
stepfather *n* patrigno
stepladder *n* scala a piuoli
stepmother *n* matrigna
steppe *n* steppa
steppingstone *n* pietra a guado; *(fig)* trampolino *(fig)*
stepsister *n* sorellastra
stepson *n* figliastro
stereographic *a* stereografico
stereophonic *a* stereofonico
stereoscope *n* stereoscopio
stereotype *n* stereotipo; — *vt* stereotipare
sterile *a* sterile
sterility *n* sterilità
sterilization *n* sterilizzazione
sterilize *vt* sterilizzare
sterling *a* genuino, vero; — **silver** argento puro
stern *a* austero, severo; — *n* *(naut)* poppa; **-ly** *adv* severamente; **-ness** *n* severità, austerità
sternum *n* sterno
stethoscope *n* stetoscopio
stevedore *n* stivatore *m*
stew *n* stufatino, ragù *m*; **be in a —** *(coll)* essere in imbarazzo; — *vt* cuocere lentamente; — *vi* cuocersi lentamente
steward *n* economo; *(ship)* cameriere di bordo; **-ess** *(avi)* hostess *f*; **chief —** capo commissario
stick *n* bastone *m*; **-er** *n* *(label)* etichetta; **-ler** *n* pedante *m&f*; rigido; — vt attaccare, fissare, conficcare, appiccicare; *(pierce)* trafiggere; pungere; — *vi* aderire, appiccicarsi; persistere, ostinarsi, preseverare; — **out** sporgersi; — **up** alzarsi; *(rob)* rapinare; — **up for** parlare in difesa di; **-y** *a* appiccicoso
stiff *a* rigido; **-ly** *adv* con difficoltà; rigidamente; — **neck** torcicollo; **-ness** *n* severità, rigidezza; consistenza
stiffen *vt* irrigidire; rassodare; — *vi* irrigidirsi; rassodarsi
stiffening *n* irrigidimento; *(cloth)* rinforzo, imbozzimatura
stifle *vt&i* soffocare
stifling *a* soffocante
stigma *n* stigma
stigmata *npl* stimmate *fpl*
stiletto *n* stiletto
still *vt* calmare; silenziare; — *a* silenzioso; calmo; fermo; — *n* quiete *f*; silenzio; — *adv* ancora, tuttora; **-born** *a* nato morto; — **life** natura morta; **-ness** *n* silenzio, quiete *f*; immobilità
stilted *a* affettato, pomposo
stilts *npl* trampoli *mpl*
stimulant *a&n* stimolante *m*
stimulate *vt* stimolare
stimulation *n* stimolo, incitamento
stimulus *n* stimolo
sting *vt&i* pungere, bruciare, dolere; — *n* puntura d'insetto; bruciore *m*; *(object)* pungiglione *m*; pungolo; **-ing** *a* pungente, mordace
stinginess *n* grettezza
stingy *a* spilorcio; meschino
stink *vi* puzzare; — *n* puzza; **-er** *n* *(sl)* puzzone *(sl)* *m*
stint *n* limite *m*; restrizione; compito; — *vt* limitare; — *vi* economizzare
stipend *n* stipendio
stipple *vt* punteggiare
stippling *n* punteggiatura
stipulate *vt&i* stipulare
stipulation *n* stipulazione
stir *vt* rimescolare; agitare, scuotere; attizzare; — *vi* agitarsi, scuotersi; stormire; — *n* eccitamento; moto; tumulto
stirring *a* emozionante
stirrup *n* staffa
stitch *vt* cucire; — *n* punto; *(knitting)* maglia
stock *n* assortimento; scorta; *(cattle)* bestiame *m*; *(com)* valore *m*, titolo; *(cooking)* brodo; *(gun)* fusto; *(handle)* manico; *(material)* materiale *m*; *(lineage)* schiatta; **-broker** *n* operatore di borsa; — **company** *(theat)* repertorio: compagnia stabile; — **exchange** borsa valori, **-holder** *n* azionista *m*; — **in trade** mercanzia; **take — of** inventariare — *a* disponibile; — *vt* provvedere, fornire; popolare, immettere
stockade *n* stecconata
stocking *n* calza; **in — feet** senza scarpe
stockpile *n* ris..va; — *vt* accumulàre; *(reserve)* immagazzinare
stock-still *a* immobile
stocky *a* tozzo
stockyards *npl* chiusa per il bestiame
stodgy *a* pesante; ingombrante; noioso
stoic *n&a* stoico; **-al** *a* stoico; **-ism** *n* stoicismo
stoke *vt* attizzare; **-er** *n* *(mech)* fochista
stole *n* stola
stolid *a* stolido; impassibile; **-ity** *n* impassibilità, stolidità
stomach *n* stomaco; **-ache** *n* dolore di

stomaco; — *vt* digerire, mangiare; tollerare; **turn one's** — nauseare, stomacare
stone *n* pietra; sasso; *(fruit)* nocciolo; *(med)* calcolo; **–cutter** *n* tagliapietra *m*; **–hearted** *a* dal cuore di pietra; **–less** *a* senza pietre (*or* nocciuolo); **–mason** *n* muratore *m*; **–ware** *n* vasellame di pietra; **–work** *n* muratura; **–y** *a* sassoso; — *a* di pietra; — *vt* lapidare; *(fruit)* togliere il nocciolo a; *(pave)* acciottolare
stone– *(in comp)* **—blind** *a* completamente cieco; **—broke** *a (sl)* in bolletta *(coll)*; **—dead** *a* morto stecchito; **—deaf** *a* sordo come una campana
stoning *n* lapidazione
stooge *n (coll)* tirapiedi *m*
stool *n* sgabello; escremento, feci *mpl*
stoop *vi* chinarsi, abbassarsi; — *vt* inchinare, abbassare; — *n (porch)* portico; curvatura
stop *n* fermata; sosta; interruzione; *(mus)* registro; **–gap** *n* stoppabuchi, turabuchi *m*; sostituto; **–light** *n* semaforo; **–over** *n* sosta, fermata; — **sign** segnale di fermata; — **watch** cronometro; — *vt* fermare; sospendere, cessare; impedire; — *vi* fermarsi; smettere; — **in** visitare; — **off, over** sostare, fermarsi; — **up** otturare
stoppage *n* cessazione
stopper *n* fermante *m*; tappo; chiusura; — *vt* turare, tappare
stopping *n* arresto, fermata; otturazione; — *a* fermante; tappante
storage *n* magazzinaggio; — **battery** accumulatore
store *n* negozio; scorta; magazzino; **in** — in riseva; in deposito; **set — by** dare importanza a; **–house** *n* magazzino; **–keeper** *n* magazziniere; negoziante *m*; **–room** *n* magazzino; — *vt* conservare; immagazzinare; fornire
storied *a* istoriato
stork *n* cicogna
storm *n* tempesta; — **cellar** rifugio per tempesta; — **door** porta antintemperie; — **window** finestra da tempesta; **–bound** *a* bloccato da tempesta; **–proof** *a* a prova di tempesta; **–y** *a* tempestoso; — *vt* assalire; — *vi* imperversare
story *n* favola, racconto; *(building)* piano; **–teller** *n* novelliere *m*; raccontatore *m*; *(liar)* bugiardo
storybook *n* libro di racconti
stout *a* robusto; tarchiato; **–ness** *n* corpulenza; risolutezza
stouthearted *a* intrepido
stove *n (cooking)* fornello; cucina; *(heating)* stufa; **–pipe** *n* tubo della stufa; **–pipe hat** *(coll)* cappello a cilindro
stow *vt* stivare; smettere; — **away** *(naut)* imbarcarsi clandestinamente; **–away** *n* viaggiatore clandestino
straddle *vi* divaricare le gambe; — *vt* sedere a cavalcioni; *(coll)* essere equivoco
straggle *vi* sbandarsi; sperdersi; **–r** *n* disperso; sbandato
straight *a* diritto; retto, onesto; *(drink)* liscio; **–forward** *a* franco, schietto; **–ness** *n* dirittura; rettitudine *f*; **–way** *adv* immediatamente, subito; — *adv* direttamente
straighten *vt* raddrizzare; rassettare; — *vi* raddrizzarsi
strain *n* sforzo, strappo; razza; *(mus)* ritmo, motivo; tono; — *vt* colare, filtrare; sforzare; storcere; — *vi* sforzarsi; storcersi; colarsi
strainer *n* colatoio, colabrodo
strait *n (geog)* stretto; — **jacket** camicia di forza; **–s** *npl* difficoltà *fpl*
straiten *vt* restringere
strait-laced *a* scrupoloso, rigoroso
strand *n* spiaggia, riva, lido; *(thread)* filo; — *vt* far arenare; far incagliare; — *vi* arenarsi; incagliarsi; **be –ed** essere abbandonato
strange *a* strano, singolare; **–ness** *n* singolarità, stranezza; **–ly** *adv* curiosamente, stranamente; **–r** *n* straniero
strangle *vt* strangolare; — *vi* strangolarsi; **–hold** *n* stretta mortale
strangling *n* strangolatura
strangulate *vt* strangolare, strozzare
strangulation *n* strozzatura, strangolatura
strap *n* correggia, cinghia; — *vt* legare, con cinghia; *(punish)* staffilare
strapping *a* robusto
stratagem *n* stratagemma *m*
strategic *a* strategico
strategist *n* stratega *m*
strategy *n* strategia
stratification *n* stratificazione
stratify *vt* stratificare
stratosphere *n* stratosfera
stratum *n* strato
straw *n* paglia; — **vote** votazione preliminare; **last** — *(fig)* colmo
strawberry *n* fragola
stray *vi* fuorviarsi, smarrirsi; — *a* smarrito; sperso; randagio; *(fig)* fortuito; — *n* animale randagio
streak *vt* striare; — *n* striscia; **–y** *a* striato
stream *n* fiume *m*, corso d'aqua, corrente *f*; — *vi* scorrere; fluire; **–er** *n* pennone *m*, banderuola
streamline *vt* sveltire, modernizzare; rendere aerodinamico; **–d** *a* aerodinamico
street *n* strada, via; **–car** *n* tram *m*; **–light** *m* fanale, lampione *m*; — **sweeper** spazzino; *(mech)* spazzatrice meccanica; **–walker** *n* prostituta, donna di marciapiede *(coll)*
strength *n* potenza, forza, energia; resistenza; **at full** — in pieno, al completo
strengthen *vt* rinforzare; consolidare; — *vi* rafforzarsi; consolidarsi
strenuous *a* energico, vigoroso; **–ness** *n* strenuità
streptococcus *n* streptococco
streptomycin *n* streptomicina
stress *n* risalto; sforzo; *(gram)* accento tonico; *(med)* tensione *f*; *(mech)* pressione; — *vt* accentuare, accentare, far risaltare
stretch *n* tensione; stiramento; sforzo; distesa; periodo; **at a** — d'un tratto; — *vt* tendere; stirare; esagerare; sforzare; — *vi* stendersi; stirarsi; allungarsi

stretcher *n (frame)* telaio; *(med)* barella; **–bearer** *n* portabarelle *m*
strew *vt* sparpagliare
striated *a* striato
stricken *a* colpito
strict *a* severo, stretto; **–ly** *adv* strettamente; esattamente; **–ness** *n* esatezza; rigore *m*; **–ure** *n* censura, critica; *(med)* restringimento
stride *n* passo lungo; — *vi* camminare a gran passi
strident *a* stridente
strife *n* conflitto
strike *n* colpo; *(baseball)* battuta; *(labor)* sciopero; *(mine)* scoperta; **be on —** essere in isciopero; **go on —** scioperare; **–breaker** *n* crumiro; **–r** *n (labor)* scioperante *m*; — *vt* colpire; *(mine)* scoprire; *(hour)* scoccare; *(match)* accendere; **— a bargain** concludere un affare; **— out** *(delete)* cancellare; partire; — *vi* scioperare
striking *a* impressionante, notevole, sensazionale; **–ingly** *adv* sensazionalmente
string *n* filo, spago, laccio; *(mus)* corda; **— beans** fagiolini *mpl*; **–y** *a* fibroso
string *vt* legare; **— up** *(hang)* impiccare; **— out** prolungare; **— along** *(coll)* ingannare; **–ed instrument** strumento a corde
stringency *n* severità; limitazione; penuria
stringent *a* stringente; urgente, rigido
strings *npl (mus)* corde; fili; *(coll)* limitazioni *fpl*; **no — attached** senz'obbligazione
strip *n* striscia; — *vt* privare; *(undress)* spogliare; — *vi* spogliarsi; **— tease** spogliarello *(coll)*; **comic —** fumetti *mpl*
stripe *n* striscia, riga; *(mil)* gallone *m*; sferzata; — *vt* rigare
striped *a* rigato
stripling *n* giovanotto
strive *vi* sforzarsi
striving *n* sforzo; — *a* sforzato, forzoso
stroke *n* colpo; tratto; accesso; *(swimming)* bracciata; *(med)* colpo apoplettico; **— of luck** colpo di fortuna; **on the — of** allo scoccare di; — *vt* accarezzare, lisciare
stroll *n* passeggiatina; — *vi* vagare, fare una passeggiata; **–ing** *a* vagabondo, ambulante; **–er** *n (person)* vagabondo, girovago; *(baby's)* carrozzina per neonati, portinfante *m*
strong *a* forte; duro, robusto; **–box** *n* cassaforte *f*; **–hold** *n* fortezza; caposaldo; **–ly** *adv* fortemente
strong-minded *a* ardito, risoluto
strong-willed *a* risoluto
strontium *n* stronzio
strop *n* coramella; — *vt* affilare sulla coramella
strophe *n* strofa
structural *a* strutturale; **— steel** ferro trafilato per strutture
structure *n* struttura, edifizio, costruzione
struggle *n* lotta; — *vi* lottare
strum *vt&i* strimpellare
strumpet *n* prostituta
strut *n* tronfiezza, modo impettito di camminare; *(prop)* puntello; *(avi)* montante *m*; — *vi* pavoneggiarsi
strychnine *n* stricnina
stub *n* ceppo; mozzicone *m*; *(ticket)* matrice *f*; — *vt* estirpare; *(hit)* sbattere; **–by** *a* tozzo; pieno di ceppi
stubble *n* stoppia
stubbly *a* stopposo; *(hair)* ispido
stubborn *a* ostinato, testardo; **–ness** *n* ostinazione
stucco *n* stucco
stuck *a* attaccato; traffitto; incollato
stud *n* borchia; *(stable)* scuderia; *(prop)* pilastrino; **–horse** *n* cavallo da razza; — *vt* guarnire con borchie
student *n* studente *m*, studentessa
studied *a* studiato, affettato
studio *n* studio; **— couch** letto alla turca
studious *a* studioso; **–ness** studiosità
study *n* studio; cura, diligenza; — *vt&i* studiare
stuff *vt (cram)* riempire, imbottire, rimpinzare; *(crowd)* pigiare; *(cooking)* infarcire; imbottire; — *n (things)* stoffa, roba, materia; **— and nonsense** insensatezza; **–ed** *a* imbottito, rimpinzato; **–ing** *n (pillow)* imbottitura; *(food)* ripieno; **–y** *a* soffocante, chiuso; *(coll)* rigido, inflessibile
stultify *vt* rendere ridicolo *(or* insignificante); svalorare
stumble *vi* inciampare; barcollare; — *n (in speech)* papera; inciampata
stumbling *a* inciampante; — *n* inciampamento; *(in speech)* balbettio; **— block** ostacolo; scoglio *(fig)*
stump *n* ceppo, tronco, mozzicone *m*; *(art)* sfumino; — *vt* disorientare, confondere; — *vi* camminare pesantemente; *(pol)* fare tournée di comizi politici
stun *vt* stordire
stunning *a* stupendo, sbalorditivo, meraviglioso; che stordisce
stunt *n (coll)* esibizione, montatura; **— flying** acrobazia aviatoria; — *vt* ostacolare; arrestare lo sviluppo di; — *vi* esibirsi
stupefaction *n* stupefazione
stupefy *vt* istupidire, stupefare; **–ing** *a* stupefacente
stupendous *a* stupendo
stupid *a* stupido, sciocco; **–ity** *n* stupidaggine *f*
stupor *n* stupore, torpore *m*
sturdily *adv* vigorosamente
sturdiness *n* vigore *m*, robustezza
sturdy *a* forte, resistente
stutter *vt&i* tartagliare; — *n* balbuzie *f*; **–er** *n* balbuziente *m&f*; **–ing** *n* balbettamento; **–ing** *a* balbettante
sty *n (med)* orzaiuolo; *(pig)* porcile *m*
style *n* stile *m*, moda; maniera; — *vt* disegnare, stilizzare; chiamare, nominare
stylish *a* elegante
stylist *n* stilista *m&f*
stylistic *a* stilistico
stylize *vt* stilizzare
stylus *n* stilo; puntina di fonografo
stymie *vt* ostacolare
styptic *n&a* astringente; **— pencil** matita emostatica

suable *a* processabile
suave *a* soave, dolce, blando; **–ly** *adv* dolcemente; soavemente; **–ness** *n* soavità
suavity *n* soavità
subagent *n* subagente *m*
subaltern *n&a* subalterno
subcommittee *n* sottocomitato
subconscious *n&a* subcosciente *m*
subconsciousness *n* subcoscienza
subcontract *n* subcontratto, subappalto; — *vt* subappaltare; **–er** *n* subcontrattista, subappaltatore *m*
subcutaneous *a* subcutaneo, sottocutaneo
subdivide *vt* suddividere
subdivision *n* suddivisione
subdue *vt* domare, reprimere; *(light)* attenuare
subheading *n* sottotitolo
subject *n&a* soggetto; suddito; — *vt* sottomettere; **–ive** *a* soggettivo; **–ively** *adv* soggettivamente; **–ivity** *n* soggettività
subjugate *vt* soggiogare
subjugation *n* soggiogamento, soggiogo
subjunctive *a&n* soggiuntivo, congiuntivo
sublease *vt* subaffittare; — *n* subaffitto
sublet *vt* subaffittare
sublimate *vt* sublimare; — *n&a* sublimato
sublimation *n* sublimazione
sublime *n&a* sublime
sublimity *n* sublimità
submarine *n&a* sottomarino
submerge *vt* sommergere; — *vi* sommergersi
submergible *a* sommergibile
submersion *n* sommersione
submission *n* sottomissione
submissive *a* sottomesso; **–ness** *n* sottomissione
submit *vt* presentare; — *vi* sottomettersi
subnormal *a* subnormale
subordinate *a&n* subordinato; — *vt* subordinare
subordination *n* subordinazione
suborn *vt* subornare
subpoena *n* citazione legale di comparizione; — *vt* fare una citazione legale di comparizione
subscribe *vi* abbonarsi; sottoscriversi, aderire; — *vt* sottoscrivere, abbonare
subscriber *n* abbonato; sottoscrittore *m*
subscription *n* abbonamento
subsequent *a* susseguente; **–ly** *adv* susseguentemente
subservience *n* subordinazione, servilismo
subservient *a* subordinato, servile
subside *vi* cedere, sprofondare; diminuire, cessare
subsidiary *n&a* sussidiario
subsidize *vt* sovvenzionare
subsidy *n* sussidio
subsist *vi* sussistere, mantenersi
subsistence *n* sussistenza
subsoil *n* sottosuolo
subspecies *n* sottospecie *f*
substance *n* sostanza, essenza
substantial *a* sostanziale; **–ity** *n* sostanzialità; **–ly** *adv* sostanzialmente
substantive *n&a* sostantivo
substation *n* stazione sussidiaria
substitute *vt* sostituire; — *vi* sostituirsi; — *n* sostituto; surrogato; — *a* sostituto, supplente
substitution *n* sostituzione
substratum *n* sostrato
substructure *n* sostruzione
subterfuge *n* sotterfugio
subterranean *a* sotterraneo
subtitle *n* sottotitolo; didascalia
subtle *a* fino, delicato; subdolo, sottile; **–ty** *n* sottigliezza
subtly *adv* sottilmente
subtract *vt* sottrarre
subtrahend *n* sottraendo
subtraction *n* sottrazione
subtropical *a* quasi tropicale
suburb *n* sobborgo
suburban *a* periferico, suburbano; **–ite** *n* abitante dei sobborghi
subvention *n* sovvenzione
subversive *a* sovversivo
subversion *n* sovversione
subvert *vt* sovvertire
subway *n* ferrovia sotterranea, metropolitana; sottopassaggio
succeed *vi* riuscire, succedere; — *vt* succedere a
succeeding *a* succedente
success *n* successo, riuscita; **–ful** *a* di successo, vittorioso, riuscito; **–ive** *a* successivo
succession *n* successione
successor *n* successore *m*
succinct *a* succinto; **–ly** *adv* succintamente; **–ness** *n* brevità
succor *n* soccorso; — *vt* soccorrere
succumb *vi* soccombere
succulence *n* succolenza
succulent *a* succolento
such *a* tale, simile; — *pron* tale; — **as** come quale
suck *vt* succhiare, poppare; assorbire; — *n* succhiata, poppata; *(coll)* sorsetto; **–er** *n* *(candy)* caramella; *(mech)* stantuffo; *(zool)* succhiatoio; *(bot)* succhione *m*; *(sl)* gonzo
suckle *vt* allattare
suckling *n* lattante *m&f*; — **pig** porcellino di latte
sucrose *n* saccarosio; zucchero di canna
suction *n* aspirazione; — **pump** pompa aspirante
sudden *a* improvviso, inaspettato; **all of a —** tutt'a un tratto; **—ly** *adv* improvvisamente; **–ness** *n* istantaneità, subitaneità
suds *npl* schiuma di sapone; acqua saponata
sue *vt&i* querelare, citare
suede *n* pelle scamosciata
suet *n* sugna
suffer *vi&i* soffrire subire; permettere; **–ing** *a* sofferente; **–ing** *n* sofferenza
suffice *vt&i* bastare
sufficiency *n* sufficienza
sufficient *a* sufficiente; **–ly** *adv* sufficientemente
suffix *n* suffisso
suffocate *vt&i* soffocare
suffocating *a* soffocante
suffocation *n* soffocazione, asfissia
sufferage *n* suffragio

suffuse *vt* aspergere; bagnare; spandere sopra
suffusion *n* suffusione
sugar *n* zucchero; **beet —** zucchero di barbabietola; **brown —** zucchero greggio; **granulated —** zucchero granulato; **lump —** zucchero in zollette; **— bowl** zuccheriera; **— cane** canna da zucchero; **—** *vt* inzuccherare; addolcire; **–y** *a* zuccherino
sugar-coated *a* candito, coperto di zucchero; inzuccherato *(fig, manner)* meloso
suggest *vt* proporre, suggerire, suggestionare; **–ive** *a* suggestivo
suggestion *n* consiglio, proposta, suggerimento
suicide *n* suicida *m&f*; *(act)* suicidio; **commit —** suicidarsi, uccidersi
suit *n (clothing)* abito completo; *(law)* azione; *(courtship)* corte *f*; *(cards)* seme *m*; *(request)* petizione; **—** *vt&i* convenire; piacere a; **follow —** seguire l'esempio; **–able** *a* conveniente; **–ability** *n* accordo, convenienza; adattabilità, opportunità; **–case** *n* valigia; **–ing** *n* stoffa
suite *n* seguito; serie *f*; appartamento; *(furniture)* mobilia
suitor *n* richiedente *m*; pretendente *m*; *(law)* querelante *m*
sulfate *n* solfato
sulfide *n* solfuro
sulfur *n* zolfo
sulk *vi* accigliarsi, essere di malumore; **–iness** *n* malumore *m*; **–y** *a* scontroso
sullen *a* taciturno; imbronciato
sully *vt* sporcare, macchiare
sultan *n* sultano
sultry *a* soffocante, afoso
sum *n* somma, totale *m*; **—** *vt* sommare; **— up** riassumere
sumac *n (bot)* sommacco
summarize *vt* riassumere
summarily *adv* sommariamente
summary *n* sommario
summer *n* estate *f*; **–house** *n* padiglione di giardino; **— resort** stazione estiva; **–time** estate *f*, stagione estiva; **— vacation** vacanze estive; **–y** *a* estivo; **—** *vi (vacation)* villeggiare, passare l'estate
summit *n* vetta, cima; **— conference** conferenza al vertice
summon *vt* convocare; *(law)* citare; **–s** *n (law)* citazione
sumptuous *a* suntuoso; **–ly** *adv* suntuosamente; **–ness** *n* suntuosità
sun *n* sole *m*; **–bath** *n* bagno di sole; **–beam** *n* raggio di sole; **–dial** *n* meridiana; **–down** *n* tramonto; **–glasses** *npl* occhiali da sole; **–lamp** *n* lampada per raggi ultravioletti; **–light, –shine** *n* luce del sole; **–rise** *n* alba, aurora; **–set** *n* tramonto; **–spot** *n* macchia solare; **–stroke** *n* insolazione, colpo di sole; **–lit** *a* soleggiato; **–ny** *a* solatio; allegro
sun *vt* esporre al sole
sunburn *n* abbronzatura, tintarella *(coll)*; scottatura di sole; **—** *vt* abbronzare; bruciare al sole; **—** *vi* abbonzarsi; **–ed** *a* abbronzato; bruciato dal sole
Sunday *n* domenica; **— school** scuola domenicale
sundries *npl* generi diversi
sundry *a* diversi, parecchi
sunken *a* infossato
suntan *n* abbronzatura
sun-tanned *a* abbronzato
sup *vt* sorseggiare; **—** *vi* cenare
superable *a* sormontabile
superabundance *n* sovrabbondanza
superabundant *a* sovrabbondante
superb *a* superbo
supercilious *a* sdegnoso, arrogante; **–ness** *n* arroganza
superficial *a* superficiale; **–ity** *n* superficialità
superfine *a* sopraffino
superfluity *n* superfluità
superfluous *a* superfluo
superhighway *n* autostrada
superhuman *a* sovrumano
superimpose *vt* sovrimporre
superintend *vt* sovrintendere; **–ence** *n* soprintendenza; **–end** *n* sovrintendente, sopraintendente *m*
superior *a&n* superiore *m*; **–ity** *n* superiorità
superlative *a&n* superlativo
superman *n* superuomo
supermarket *n* supermercato
supernatural *a* sovrannaturale
supernumerary *a* in soprannumero; **—** *n* soprannumerario; *(theat)* comparsa
supersaturated *a* soprasaturato
supersede *vt* rimpiazzare, soppiantare
supersensitive *a* ipersensibile
supersonic *a* supersonico, ultrasonoro
superstition *n* superstizione
superstitious *a* superstizioso
superstructure *n* soprastruttura
supervene *vi* sopravvenire
supervise *vt* sorvegliare, sovraintendere
supervision *n* sorveglianza
supervisor *n* sovrintendente, controllore *m*
supine *a* supino
supper *n* cena; **The Last S–** L'Ultima Cena; **–time** *n* ora di cena
supplant *vt* soppiantare
supple *a* flessibile, cedevole, docile, arrendevole; servile; **–ness** *n* flessibilità; arrendevolezza; docilità, servilità
supplement *n* supplemento; **—** *vt* completare; **–ary** *a* supplementare
supplicate *vt&i* supplicare
supplicant *n* supplicante *m&f*
supplication *n* supplica
supplier *n* fornitore *m*
supply *vt* fornire; colmare, soddisfare; **—** *n* rifornimento, provvista; **— and demand** offerta e domanda
support *vt* mantenere; confermare; appoggiare; **—** *n* mantenimento, sostegno; **–er** *n (person)* fautore, sostenitore *m*; *(hosiery)* giarrettiera; *(med)* sospensorio
supposable *a* supponibile
suppose *vt* supporre, credere; **–d** *a* supposto, putativo
supposing *conj* supposto che
supposition *n* supposizione, congettura
suppository *n (med)* supposta
suppress *vt* sopprimere; nascondere
suppression *n* soppressione

suppurate *vi* suppurare
suppuration *n* suppurazione
supremacy *n* supremazia
supreme *a* supremo
surcharge *n* sovraccarico; — *vt* sovraccaricare
sure *a* sicuro, certo; **-ly** *adv* certamente, senz'altro; **make — (that)** accertarsi che; — *adv (coll)* certo, sicuro; **-ly** *adv* certamente; **-ness** *n* sicurezza
sure-footed *a* a piè fermo
surety *n* garanzia; garante *m&f*
surf *n* risacca; **-board** *n* idrosci
surface *n* superficie *f*; **on the —** superficiale; in superficie; — *vt* dare una superficie; lisciare; — *vi* venire alla superficie; — *a* superficiale
surfeit *vt* saziare; — *vi* rimpinzarsi; saziarsi; — *n* sazietà, eccesso
surge *n* ondata; — *vi* sollevarsi
surgeon *n* chirurgo
surgery *n* chirurgia
surgical *a* chirurgico
surging *a* agitato; ondeggiante; — *n* agitazione
surliness *n* arcignezza
surly *a* arcigno
surmise *vt&i* congetturare, supporre; — *n* supposizione; sospetto
surmount *vt* sorpassare, sormontare; **-able** *a* sormontabile
surname *n* cognome *m*
surpass *vt* sorpassare
surplice *n (eccl)* cotta
surplus *n* eccedenza; — *a* in eccedenza
surprise *vt* sorprendere; — *n* sorpresa
surprising *a* sorprendente; **-ly** *adv* sorprendentemente
surrealism *n* surrealismo
surrealist *n* surrealista *m&f*
surrender *n* resa; abbandono; — *vi* arrendersi; — *vt* cedere; rinunziare a
surrepetitious *a* surrettizio; clandestino
surrogate *n* sostituto; surrogato; — *vt* surrogare
surround *vt* circondare; **-ing** *a* circostante
surroundings *npl* dintorni *mpl*; ambiente *m*
surtax *n* sopratassa
surveillance *n* sorveglianza
survey *vt* osservare, stimare; far perizia di, misurare
survey *n* veduta, agrimensura, esame *m*; inchiesta; rilevamento topografico; **-or** *n* agrimensore *m*; geometra *m*
survival *n* sopravvivenza
survive *vi* sopravvivere
surviving *a* sopravvivente
survivor *n* superstite *m&f*
susceptibility *n* suscettibilità
susceptible *a* suscettibile
susceptive *a* suscettivo
suspect *vt&i* sospettare; supporre; — *n* sospetto
suspend *vt* sospendere; **-ers** *npl* bretelle *fpl*
suspense *n* incertezza, ansia, dubbio, **keep in —** tenere con l'animo sospeso
suspension *n* sospensione; **— bridge** ponte sospeso
suspicion *n* sospetto, traccia
suspicious *a* sospettoso, sospetto; **-ness** *n* sospettosità
sustain *vt* sostenere; subire; prolungare; **-ed** *a* sostenuto
sustenance *n* vitto, mantenimento
suture *n* sutura; — *vt* suturare
swab *n* strofinaccio; radazza; tampone *m*; — *vt* lavare, radazzare; tamponare
swaddle *vt* fasciare, involgere
swaddling clothes fasce *fpl*; pannolini per bambini
swagger *n* spacconata; — *vi* darsi arie; camminare pavoneggiandosi; **-er** *n* fanfarone, spaccone *m*
swallow *n* boccone *m*; sorsata; sorso; *(bird)* rondine *f*; — *vt* inghiottire; **— up** assorbire, inghiottire; divorare
swamp *n* palude *f*; — *vt&i* inondare, sommergere; impantanare; rovinare; **-y** *a* paludoso
swan *n* cigno; **-sdown** *n* piuma di cigno
swap *vt (coll)* barattare, scambiare
sward *n* erba
swarm *n* sciame *m*; — *vi* sciamare, brulicare
swarthy *a* bruno, olivastro
swashbuckler *n* rodomonte *m*
swatch *n* campione di stoffa
swath *n* falciata; solco falciato
swathe *n* fascia; — *vt* fasciare
sway *n* oscillazione; dominio; — *vt&i* oscillare; vacillare, dondolare; influenzare; deviare; **-ing** *n* oscillazione
sway-backed *a* insellato; con la schiena curva
swear *vt&i* bestemmiare; giurare; **— by** giurare su; **— in** far fare giuramento; **— to** giurare di; **-ing** *n* giuramento; bestemmia
swearword *n* bestemmia
sweat *n* sudore *m*; fatica; — *vt* sudare; far sudare; *(exploit)* sfruttare; — *vi* trasudare; traspirare
sweater *n* golf *m*, maglia
Swede svedese *m&f*
Sweden Svezia
Swedish *a* svedese
sweep *n* colpo, spazzata, distesa; portata; strascicamento; **chimney —** spazzacamino; **in one —** di un colpo; **make a clean —** far piazza pulita; **— away, off** portar via; **— up, out** spazzare via; **-er** *n* spazzino; *(machine)* spazzatrice *f*; **-ing** *a* rapido, violento; completo, totale; **-ing** *n* spazzatura; lo spazzare; — *vt* spazzare; scopare; sfiorare; percorrere; — *vi* scopare; incedere; stendersi
sweepstakes *npl* lotteria sportiva
sweet *a* dolce; amabile; — *n* dolce *m*; dolcezza; fragranza; **— tooth** *(coll)* goloso; bocca dolce *(fig)*
sweeten *vt* inzuccherare; addolcire; **-ing** *n* inzuccheramento; addolcimento
sweetly *adv* dolcemente
sweetness *n* dolcezza
swell *vt&i* gonfiare; — *n (coll)* elegantone *m (coll)*; elevazione; ondulazione; — *a (coll)* elegante; *(sl)* magnifico
swelling *n* gonfiore *m*
swelter *vi* soffocare dal caldo; — *n* afa
swerve *vi* deviare, sviarsi; — *n* deviazio-

ne; — *vt* sviare, deviare
swift *a* rapido; — *n (bird)* rondone *m*; **–ly** *adv* rapidamente, celermente; **–ness** *n* rapidità, velocità
swill *n* rifiuti *mpl*, risciaquatura
swim *vi* nuotare, bagnarsi; *(head)* girare; — *vt* attraversare a nuoto; — *n* nuotata; **be in the** — essere al corrente; **go for a** — fare il bagno; **–suit** *n* costume da bagno
swimmer *n* nuotatore *m*
swimming *n* nuoto; *(head)* vertigine *f*; — **pool** piscina
swindle *vt* turlupinare, imbrogliare; — *n* truffa
swine *n* maiale *m*; **–herd** *n* porcaio
swing *vi* dondolare; oscillare, rotare; bilanciarsi; — *vt* far girare; far oscillare; — *n* altalena; oscillazione; slancio, dondolio; **in full** — in piena attività
swinging *a* oscillante; ritmico; — **door** porta battente
swipe *n (coll)* colpo; pugno; — *vt (coll)* battere forte; prendere a pugni; *(sl)* rubare
swirl *n* turbine *m*; — *vi* turbinare, vorticare; — *vt* far turbinare
swish *n* sibilo, sferzata; *(water)* sciabordio; *(silk)* fruscio; — *vi* frusciare, sibilare; — *vt* sferzare; far sibilare; **–ing** *a* sferzante, frusciante; **–ing** *n* fruscio
Swiss *a&n* svizzero
switch *n* cambiamento; *(elec)* interruttore *m*; *(rail)* scambio; verga; sferzata; **–board** *n* centralino telefonico; — *vt* sferzare; dimenare; intercambiare; *(rail)* deviare; — *vi* deviarsi; — **off** *(light)* spegnere; chiudere; — **on** *(light)* accendere; aprire
Switzerland Svizzera
swivel *n* perno; mulinello; — **chair** sedia girevole; — *vi* girarsi; imperniarsi; — *vt* rotare
swollen *a* gonfiato
swoon *vi* svenire; — *n* svenimento
swoop *n* colpo, avventata; attacco; — *vi* slanciarsi, avventarsi, piombare su, carlarsi su; — *vt* ghermire
sword *n* spada; **–fish** *n* pesce spada; **–sman** *n* spadaccino
sworn *a* giurato
sycophant *n* sicofante *m&f*
syllabic *a* sillabico
syllable *n* sillaba
syllabus *n* compendio; *(eccl)* sillabo
syllogism *n* sillogismo
sylph *n* silfide *f*
sylvan *a* silvestre
symbiosis *n* simbiosi *f*
symbol *n* simbolo; **–ic** *a* simbolico; **–ism** *n* simbolismo; **–ize** *vt* simbolizzare
symmetrical *a* simmetrico
symmetry *n* simmetria
sympathetic *a* simpatizzante; comprensivo
sympathize *vi* condividere i sentimenti; simpatizzare
sympathy *n* compassione; condoglianza; simpatia
symphonic *a* sinfonico
symphony *n* sinfonia
symposium *n* simposio
symptom *n* sintomo; **–atic** *a* sintomatico
synagogue *n* sinagoga
synchronize *vt&i* sincronizzare
synchronization *n* sincronizzazione
syncopate *vt* sincopare
syncopation *n* sincopatura *f*; musica sincopata
syndicate *n (com)* sindacato, consorzio; associazione
synonym *n* sinonimo
synonymous *a* sinonimo
synopsis *n* sinossi *f*
syntax *n* sintassi *f*
synthesis *n* sintesi *f*
synthesize *vt* sintetizzare
synthetic *a* sintetico
syphilis *n* sifilide *f*
syphilitic *a* sifilitico
Syria Siria; **–c** *a* siriaco; **–n** *n&a* siriano
syringe *n* siringa; — *vt* iniettare, siringare
syrup *n* sciroppo; **–y** *a* sciropposo
system *n* sistema *m*, metodo; *(rail)* rete *f*; **–atic** *a* sistematico; **–atize** *vt* sistematizzare, sistemare

T

tab *n* linguetta; *(label)* etichetta; **keep — on** *(coll)* sorvegliare; *(expenses)* mantenere controllo di; — *vt* fornire di linguetta
tabernacle *n* tabernacolo
table *n* tavola; tabella, indice *m*; **–cloth** *n* tovaglia; **–land** *n* altipiano, acrocoro; **–spoon** *n* cucchiaio da minestra; **turn the –s** capovolgere la situazione; — *vt* posporre
tablet *n* tavoletta; pastiglia; lapide *f*; *(paper)* taccuino
tableware *n* servizio da tavola
taboo *n* tabù *m*; — *a* proibito; — *vt* interdire, proibire
tabular *a* tabellare, tavolare, tabulare
tabulate *vt* catalogare, classificare, disporre in tabelle
tachometer *n* tachimetro
tacit *a* tacito
taciturn *a* taciturno
tack *n* bulletta, chiodino; *(sewing)* imbastitura; *(naut)* virata, bordeggio; — *vt* inchiodare; imbastire; *(naut)* virare
tackle *n (naut)* paranco; carrucola; *(gear)* attrezzatura; *(football)* attacco; — *vt* attaccare; afferrarsi a; intraprendere; *(horse)* bardare
tacky *a* vischioso, attaccaticcio
tact *n* tatto, diplomazia; **–ful** *a* diplomatico; accorto; **–less** *a* senza tatto; **–fully** *adv* con tatto; diplomaticamente
tactical *a* tattico
tactics *npl* tattica
tadpole *n* girino
taffeta *n* taffetà *m*

tag *n* etichetta; — *vt* aggiungere; *(coll)* seguire; mettere l'etichetta a; — **along** *(coll)* accompagnare
tail *n* coda; *(hair)* treccia; — **end** estremità; — **spin** *n* avvitamento; — **wind** vento in poppa; **turn** — darsela a gambe; **–s** *npl (coll)* marsina, frac *m*; — *vt (sl)* pedinare; — *vi* accodarsi
taillight *n* fanale di coda
tailor *n* sarto; — *vi* fare il sarto; — *vt* confezionare; **–ing** *n* sartoria
tailor-made *a* fatto dal sarto, tailleur
taint *n* magagna, infezione; — *vt* contaminare, corrompere, guastare; — *vi* corrompersi, guastarsi
take *n* presa; *(earnings)* guadagno, profitto
take *vt* prendere; portare; accettare, ricevere; — *vi* riuscire; — **after** *(resemble)* rassomigliarsi a; — **away** togliere, levare; — **back** riprendere; — **care of** prendersi cura di; attendere a; — **down** *(lower)* abbassare; *(write)* scrivere, prender nota; — **in** *(comprise)* includere; *(deceive)* ingannare, raggirare; — **off** *(disrobe)* levarsi; *(remove)* levare; *(avi)* decollare; — **on** *(add)* assumere; *(coll)* prendersela; — **on oneself** attribuirsi; — **one's time** non affrettarsi innecessariamente, fare con calma; — **out** togliere, levare, asportare; — **over** *(assume)* succeedere; rilevare; — **place** aver luogo; — **to** *(like)* affezionarsi a; — **up** *(consider)* considerare, trattare
take-off *n (coll)* caricatura; *(avi)* decollo
taking *a* attraente; *(med)* contagioso
talcum *n* talco
tale *n* racconto; *(lie)* fiaba; **–bearer** *n* maldicente *m*
talent *n* talento; **–ed** *a* intelligente, abile, ingegnoso
talk *n* discorso; conversazione, ciarla; *(gossip)* pettegolezzo; — *vi* parlare, conversare; — *vt* dire; esprimere; — **over** discutere su; **–ative** *a* loquace, chiacchierone, ciarliero
talker *n* parlatore *m*; chiacchierone *m*
talking *n* conversazione; chiacchiere *fpl*; — *a* parlante
talking-to *n (coll)* lavata di testa *(fig)*
tall *a* alto, grande; *(coll)* stravagante, straordinario; **–ness** *n* altezza; — **story** panzana
tallow *n* sego
tally *n* targa; tacca; duplicato; conto, verifica; — *vt* registrare; calcolare; far coincidere; — *vi* coincidere
talon *n* artiglio
tambourine *n* tamburino
tame *a* addomesticato; mansueto, docile; **–ness** *n* mansuetudine *f*; **–r** *n* domatore *m*, domatrice *f*; — *vt* addomesticare, domare
tamp *vt (cover)* tamponare; *(beat down)* pestare
tamper *vi* immischiarsi; metterci le mani
tampon *n* tampone *m*
tan *vt (leather)* conciare; abbronzare; *(coll)* percuotere, malmenare; — *a* abbronzato; — *n* abbronzatura; concia
tang *n* aroma forte, sapore *m*
tangent *n&a* tangente *f*; **go (fly) off on a** — filare per la tangente
tangerine *n* mandarino
tangible *a* tangibile
Tangier Tangeri
tangle *vt* ingarbugliare; — *n* groviglio
tank *n* serbatoio; cisterna; *(mil)* carro armato; **gas** — gazometro; **–age** *n* capacità di serbatoio
tankard *n* boccale *m*
tanner *n* conciatore *m*; **–y** conceria
tannic *a* tannico
tannin *n* tannino
tantalize *vt* tormentare; tentare
tantalizing *a* seducente; tormentante, tormentoso; — *n* supplizio di Tantalo, tormento
tantalum *n* tantalio
tantamount *a* equivalente
tantrum *n* escandescenza
tap *vt* colpire leggermente, bussare; *(cask)* spillare; — *n* colpetto; *(water)* rubinetto; *(elec)* presa, spina; — **dance** tiptap *m*
tape *n* nastro; *(adhesive)* sparadrappo, nastro adesivo; *(recording)* nastro fonografico; **red** — pedanteria burocratica; — **measure** metro a nastro; — **recorder** magnetofono; registratore a nastro; — *vt (tie)* legare con nastro; incidere su nastro
taper *n* cero, candela; assottigliamento; — *vi* affusolarsi, assottigliarsi; diminuirsi; — *vt* affusolare, assottigliare; diminuire; **–ing** *a* conico, affusolato
tapestry *n* arazzo
tapeworm *n* tenia
taproot *n* fittone *m*
taps *npl (mil)* silenzio
tar *n* pece *f*, catrame *m*; **–ry** *a* incatramato; — *vt* incatramare
tarantula *n* tarantola
tardiness *n* ritardo
tardy *a* in ritardo
target *n* bersaglio
tariff *n* tariffa
tarnish *n* appannamento; — *vt* macchiare, appannare; — *vi* macchiarsi, appannarsi
tarpaulin *n* tela incatramata; copertone *m*
tarry *vi* fermarsi, arrestarsi, sostare, indugiare, attardarsi, trattenersi
tart *n* crostata; *(woman)* donnaccia; — *a* acido, acerbo; *(fig)* aspro; **–ly** *adv* acidamente, mordacemente; **–ness** *n* acidità, mordacità
tartar *n* tartaro; *(person, fig)* scontroso; **cream of** — cremor di tartaro
task *n* compito; **–master** *n* padrone *m*; **take to** — rimproverare; — *vt* esaurire, affaticare
tassel *n* nappa, fiocco
taste *n* gusto, sapore *m*; — *vt* assaggiare; — *vi* sapere di; **–fully** *adv* elegantemente; **–less** *a* insipido, senza gusto
tastiness *n* squisitezza
tasty *a* saporito
tatter *n* straccio, brandello; — *vt* stracciare; **–ed** *a* cencioso
tatterdemalion *n* straccione *m*
tattle *vi* chiacchierare, pettegolare; **–tale** *n* gazzettino
tatto *n* tatuaggio; *(mil)* ritirata; **beat a** —

battere una ritirata; — *vt* tatuare
taunt *vt* punzecchiare, beffare; — *n* punzecchiatura
taupe *a&n* color talpa
taut *a* teso, rigido; **-ness** *n* tensione, rigidezza
tautology *n* tautologia
tavern *n* osteria; bettola, taverna; **-keeper** *n* oste *m*
tawdriness *n* vistosità
tawdry *a* sfarzoso, chiamativo, vistoso
tawny *a* fulvo, abbronzato
tax *n* imposta, tassa, gravame *m*; — *vt* tassare, gravare; accusare; — **collector** esattore delle imposte; **-payer** *n* contribuente *m&f*; **income** — imposta sul reddito; **-able** *a* tassabile, imponibile; **-ation** *n* tassazione, tasse *fpl*
taxi *n* tassì *m*; — **driver** tassista *m*; — *vi* andare in tassì; *(avi)* rullare
taxidermist *n* impagliatore *m*, tassidermista *m&f*
taxidermy *n* tassidermia
taximeter *n* tassametro
tea *n* tè *m*; **-cup** *n* tazza da tè; **-kettle** *n* bollitore *m*; **-pot** *n* teiera; **-room** *n* sala da tè; **-spoon** *n* cucchiaino
teach *vt* insegnare; **-er** *n* insegnante *m&f*; maestro, maestra; **-ing** *n* insegnamento
team *n* squadra; gruppo; **-mate** *n* compagno di squadra; **-work** *n* sforzo combinato; — *vt* accoppiare, aggruppare
teamster *n* guidatore, carrettiere *m*
tear *n* lagrima; — **gas** gas lacrimogeno; **-ful** *a* lagrimoso, pieno di lagrime; **-fully** *adv* lagrimosamente, piangendo; **-y** *a* lagrimoso; **burst into -s** scoppiare in lagrime; **shed -s** versare lagrime
tear *vt* lacerare, stracciare; — *vi* strapparsi; — **down** precipitarsi, scendere precipiosamente; *(dismantle)* smontare; — **oneself away** andarsene a malincuore; — **up** salire precipitosamente; — *n* strappo; lacerazione; **wear and** — logorio
tease *vt* stuzzicare; importunare; — *n* seccatore *m*
teasing *n* seccatura; — *a* seccante
teat *n* capezzolo, mammella
technical *a* tecnico; **-ity** *n* tecnicismo
technician *n* tecnico
technique *n* tecnica, metodo
technological *a* tecnologico
technology *n* tecnologia
tedious *a* tedioso; **-ly** *adv* tediosamente
tedium *n* tedio, noia
teem *vi* formicolare; abbondare; **-ing** *a* formicolante, abbondante di; fecondo
teen-age *a* adolescente
teen-ager *n* adolescente *m&f*
teeter *vt* dondolare, — *vi* dondolarsi
teeter-totter *n* altalena
teeth *npl* denti *mpl*; **-ing** *n* dentizione
teethe *vi* mettere i denti
teetotaler *n* astemio
telecast *n* teletrasmissione; — *vt&i* teletrasmettere
telegram *n* telegramma *m*
telegraph *n* telegrafo; **-ic** *a* telegrafico; — *vt&i* telegrafare
telegraphy *n* telegrafia
telelens *n* telelente *f*
telemeter *n* telemetro
teleological *a* teleologico
teleology *n* teleologia
telepathic *a* telepatico
telepathy *n* telepatia
telephone *n* telefono; — **book** guida telefonica; — **booth** cabina telefonica; — **dial** disco del telefono; — **exchange** centralino telefonico; — **operator** centralinista, telefonista *m&f*; — *vt&i* telefonare
telephonic *a* telefonico
telephony *n* telefonia
telephoto *a* telefotografico; — **lens** telelente *f*
telephotograph *vt* telefotografare; — *n* telefotografia
telephotography *n* telefotografia
teleprinter *n* telescrivente *m*
telescope *n* telescopio; — *vt* incastrare, introdurre uno dentro l'altro; — *vi* incastrarsi, mettersi uno dentro l'altro
telescopic *a* telescopico
teletypewriter *n* telescrivente *m*, teletipo
televise *vt* trasmettere per televisione
television *n* televisione; — **set** televisore *m*
tell *vt&i* dire, raccontare; — **apart** distinguere; **-er** *n* narratore *m*; **bank -er** *n* cassiere *m*; **-tale** *a* chiacchierone, indiscreto; informatore
telling *n* racconto; — *a* efficace, energico
tellurium *n (chem)* tellurio
temerity *n* temerità
temper *n* umore *m*, indole *f*; collera; tempera; **lose one's** — adirarsi, perdere la calma; — *vt* mitigare, temperare; — *vi* mitigarsi, temperarsi
tempera *n* tempera
temperament *n* temperamento; **-al** *a* temperamentale, impetuoso
temperance *n* temperanza
temperate *a* temperato
temperature *n* temperatura
tempest *n* tempesta
tempestuous *a* tempestoso
temple *n* tempio; *(anat)* tempia
temporal *a* temporale
temporarily *adv* provvisoriamente
temporary *a* temporaneo
temporize *vi* temporeggiare
tempt *vt* tentare, allettare, attrarre; **-ation** *n* tentazione; **-er** *n* tentatore *m*; **-ing** *a* tentatore, seducente; **-ress** *n* tentatrice *f*
ten *a* dieci; **-th** *a* decimo
tenable *a* sostenibile
tenacious *a* adesivo; tenace
tenacity *n* tenacia
tenancy *n* locazione
tenant *n* locatario, inquilino
tend *vt* curare, custodire; — *vi* tendere, piegare
tendency *n* tendenza
tendentious *a* tendenzioso
tender *a* tenero, affettuoso; delicato; **-ness** *n* tenerezza; **-ly** *adv* teneramente
tender *n* offerta; *(money)* valuta; — *vt* porgere, offrire
tenderhearted *a* sensibile, di cuore tenero
tenderloin *n* filetto

tendon *n* tendine *m*
tendril *n* viticcio
tenement *n* casa popolare
tenet *n* dogma *m*; principio; opinione *f*; canone *m*
tennis *n* tennis *m*; — **court** campo da tennis
tenor *n (meaning)* tenore *m*; corso; *(mus)* tenore *m*
tense *a* teso, tenso, rigido; — *n* tempo; — *vt* tendere, rendere teso; — *vi* tendersi; **-ness** *n* tensione
tensile *a* tensile
tension *n* tensione
tent *n* tenda; *(med)* cappa per ossigeno; *(med)* sonda, drenaggio; — *vi* attendarsi
tentacle *n* tentacolo
tentative *a* sperimentale
tenuous *a* tenue
tenure *n* tenuta, possesso, occupazione; gestione *f*
tepid *a* tiepido
term *n* sessione; termine *m*; durata; *(name)* nome; *(office)* periodo uffiale; *(school)* periodo scolastico; — *vt* definire, nominare
terminal *n* terminale *m*; *(elec)* serrafilo; — *a* terminale
terminate *vt&i* finire, concludere, terminare
termination *n* fine *f*; *(gram)* desinenza
terminology *n* terminologia
terminus *n* termine, limite *m*
termite *n* termite *f*
terms *npl* condizioni *fpl*; *(com)* rapporti *mpl*; relazioni *fpl*; patti *mpl*; termini *mpl*; **come to** — venire a condizioni; **on good** — in buoni rapporti
tern *n (zool)* sterna
terrace *n* terrazza; — *vt* terrazzare
terrain *n* terreno
terrestrial *a* terrestre
terrible *a* terribile
terrier *m (zool)* terrier *m*
terrific *a* terrificante; *(coll)* fantastico, fenomenale; **-ally** *adv* spaventevolmente
terrify *vt* spaventare
territorial *a* territoriale
territory *n* territorio
terror *n* terrore *m*; **-ism** *n* terrorismo; **-ist** *n* terrorista *m*
terrorize *vt* terrorizzare
terror-stricken *a* atterrito
terse *a* terso; conciso
tertiary *a* terziario
test *n* esame *m*, prova, collaudo; — **pilot** pilota collaudatore; — **tube** provino; — *vt* provare, analizzare, collaudare; **-er** *n* sperimentatore, collaudatore *m*
testament *n* testamento; **-ary** *a* testamentario
testate *a* testante
testator *n* testatore *m*
testicle *n* testicolo
testify *vt&i* attestare; testimoniare
testimonial *n* attestato
testimony *n* testimonianza
testiness *n* irascibilità
testy *a* permaloso, irascibile
tetanus *n* tetano
tether *n* fune *f*, catena, cavezza; *(abilities)* risorse *fpl*; — *vt* legare, impastoiare
tetrad *n* quaterna; quattro
tetragon *n* tetragono
tetragonal *a* tetragonale, tetragono
tetrahedron *n* tetraedro
tetrameter *n* tetrametro
tetrarch *n* tetrarca *n*
tetrode *n* tetrodo
text *n* testo; **-book** *n* libro di testo; *(manual)* manuale scolastico; **-ual** *a* testuale
textile *a* tessile; — *n* tessuto
texture *n* tessitura; struttura
Thames Tamigi
than *conj* che, che non; di
thank *vt* ringraziare; — **you** grazie
thankful *a* riconoscente; **-fulness** *n* riconoscenza, gratitudine *f*
thankless *a* ingrato
thanks *npl* ringraziamenti *mpl*; grazie *fpl*; **-giving** *n* ringraziamento
that *a&pron* quello, quella; cotesto, cotesta; — *pron* che, ciò, il quale, la quale; — *conj* che; — *adv* tanto, così
thatch *n* paglia; tetto di paglia; stoppia; — *vt* coprire di paglia; **-ed** *a* coperto di paglia; di paglia
thaw *vt&i* disgelare; — *n* disgelo
the *art*, il, lo, la; i, gli *mpl*; le *fpl*
theater *n* teatro
theatrical *a* teatrale
theft *n* furto
their, -s *a&pron* il loro, la loro; i loro *mpl*; le loro *fpl*
theism *n* teismo
theist *n* teista *m&f*
theistic *a* teistico
them *pron* li, loro, essi *mpl*; le, loro, esse *fpl*
theme *n* tema *m*, soggetto
themselves *pron pl* si, sè, sè stessi *mpl*; sè stesse *fpl*
then *adv* allora, in seguito, poi; dunque; anche; **now and** — di tanto in tanto
thence *adv* dunque, quindi
thenceforth *adv* d'allora in poi
theocracy *n* teocrazia
theocratic, -al *a* teocratico
theologian *n* teologo
theological *a* teologico
theology *n* teologia
theorem *n* teorema *m*
theoretical *a* teoretico; **-ly** *adv* teoreticamente
theorist *n* teorico
theorize *vi* teorizzare
theory *n* teoria
theosophy *n* teosofia
therapeutic *a* terapeutico
therapy *n* terapia, terapeutica
there *adv* lì, colà, là; ci, vi; **here and** — qua e là; — **is** c'è, v'è; ecco; — **are** ci sono, vi sono; ecco
thereabouts *adv* nei dintorni; all'incirca
thereafter *adv* d'allora in poi
thereby *adv* con ciò; così
therefore *adv* quindi, perciò
therein *adv* vi, in ciò, in esso
thereon *adv* su ciò, a questo proposito
thereupon *adv* in seguito a ciò, in conseguenza

therewith *adv* con ciò, in seguito a ciò
therm *n* caloria, unità termica; **–ic** termico
thermal *a* termale; — **barrier** *(aesp)* barriera termica
thermodynamics *npl* termodinamica
thermoelectricity *n* termoelettricità
thermometer *n* termometro
thermonuclear *a* termonucleare
thermostat *n* termostato
thermotherapy *n* termoterapia
these *pron & a pl* questi *mpl*; queste *fpl*
thesis *n* tesi *f*
they *pron pl* essi *mpl*, esse *fpl*; loro *m&fpl*; — **say** si dice
thick *a* spesso, folto; *(coll)* intimo; **–ness** *n* spessore *m*; consistenza; densità
thick– *(in comp)* **—skinned** *a* insensibile, dalla pelle dura; **—witted** *a* melenso, stupido
thicken *vt* rendere spesso; — *vi* ispessirsi; **–ing** *n* ispessimento; condensazione
thicket *n* boschetto, macchia
thickheaded *a* babbeo, stupido
thickset *a* denso, folto; robusto, tarchiato
thief *n* ladro
thievery *n* ladrocinio, furto
thievish ladresco
thigh *n* coscia; **–bone** *n* femore *m*
thimble *n* ditale *m*
thin *a* magro; *(hair)* rado; *(line)* sottile; *(voice)* acuto; **–ness** *n* sottigliezza, finezza; *(growth)* radezza; magrezza; **–ly** *adv* sottilmente; — *vt* assottigliare; diradare; — *vi* assottigliarsi; diradarsi
thing *n* cosa; oggetto; affare *m*; **latest** — ultima creazione, ultima moda
think *vt&i* pensare, credere; figurarsi; stimare; — **over** pensarci su; riflettere su; — **so** pensare così; credere di sì; **–able** *a* concepibile, pensabile; **–er** *n* pensatore *m*
thinking *n* pensiero; opinione *f*; — *a* pensante, intelligente, ragionante
thinner *n* solvente *m*
thin-skinned *a* sensibile; dalla pelle delicata
third terzo; **–ly** *adv* in terzo luogo
third-rate *a* di terza categoria, scadente
thirst *n* sete *f*; **–y** *a* assetato; avido; — *vi* aver sete; **be –y** aver sete
thirteen *a* tredici; **–th** *a* tredicesimo
thirtieth *a* trentesimo
thirty *a* trenta
this *a&pron* questo, questa; — *pron* ciò; **like** — così
thistle *n* cardo
thong *n* cinghia, correggia
thorax *n* torace *m*
thorium *n* torio
thorn *n* spina; — **in the flesh** *(fig)* una spada nel fianco *(fig)*, grattacapo; **–y** *a* spinoso
thorough *a* completo, intero, perfetto; meticoloso; **–ness** *n* completezza; perfezione; meticolosità; **–ly** *adv* completamente
thoroughbred *n (horse)* puro-sangue; *(person)* nobile *m&f*
thoroughgoing *a* meticoloso
thoroughfare *n* via pubblica, strada frequentata
those *pron pl* quelli, cotesti *mpl*; quelle, coteste *fpl*; — *a pl* quei, quegli, quelle, cotesti, coteste
though *conj* quantunque, benchè; — *adv* ciononostante; **as** — come se; **even** — anche se
thought *n* pensiero; idea; **–ful** *a* previdente; riguardoso; pensieroso; **–fulness** *n* premura, sollecitudine *f*; previdenza; **–less** *a* sbadato; irriflessivo, spensierato; **–lessness** *n* spensieratezza, sbadataggine *f*
thousand *a* mille; **–th** *a* millesimo
thrash *vt* bastonare; trebbiare; **–ing** *n* battitura, bastonatura
thread *n* filo; *(screw)* filetto, impanatura; — *vt* infilare; — *vi* serpeggiare; — **one's way** passare attraverso, infilarsi; **–bare** *a* logoro; trito
threat *n* minaccia
threaten *vt&i* minacciare; **–ing** *a* minaccioso
three *a* tre; **–fold** *a* triplo, triplice
three– *(in comp)* **—cornered** *a* triangolare; **—dimensional** *a* tridimensionale; **—legged** *a* a tre gambe; a tre piedi; **—ply** *a* di tre fili; **—quarter** *a* di tre quarti; **—speed gear** *(mech)* cambio a tre velocità; **—wheeled** *a* a tre ruote
thresh *vt* trebbiare, battere
thresher *n (mech)* trebbiatrice *f*; *(person)* trebbiatore *m*
threshing *n* trebbiatura; — **machine** trebbiatrice *f*
threshold *n* soglia
thrice *adv* tre volte
thrift *n* economia, risparmio; **–y** *a* frugale, economico
thriftiness *n* frugalità, economia
thrill *vt* commuovere; — *vi* emozionarsi; — *n* emozione
thrilling *a* eccitante, emozionante
thrive *vi* prosperare; aver successo
thriving *a* prospero; vigoroso
throat *n* gola; **sore** — mal di gola; **–y** *a* di gola; gutturale; **clear one's** — schiarirsi la voce
throb *n* pulsazione; battito; — *vi* palpitare
throbbing *n* pulsazione, palpitazione; battito; — *a* pulsante; palpitante
throes *npl* dolori *mpl*; angoscie *fpl*; pene *fpl*; *(childbirth)* doglie *fpl*
thrombosis *n* trombosi *f*
throne *n* trono
throng *n* folla; — *vi* accalcarsi; affollarsi; — *vt* affollare; accalcare
throttle *n* valvola, farfalla; — *vt* strozzare, strangolare; *(mech)* regolare con valvola
through *prep* attraverso; per; durante; a causa di; per mezzo di; — *adv* dal principio alla fine; completamente; — *a* diretto; finito; **–out** *prep* in tutto; da un capo all'altro di; **–out** *adv* dappertutto
throw *n* getto, lancio; **–back** *n* riversione; — *vt* buttare, gettare; — **away** buttar via; *(waste)* scialacquare; — **off** liberarsi di; eludere; — **up** *(hands)* gettare in aria; *(vomit)* rigettare

thrust *n* spinta; *(fencing)* stoccata; *(mech)* propulsione, pressione; — *vt* spingere; imporre; trafiggere, ficcare; — *vi* cacciarsi
thud *n* tonfo, rumore sordo; — *vi* fare un tonfo (*or* un rumore sordo)
thug *n* assassino, strangolatore *m*, sicario
thumb *n* pollice *m*; **–tack** *n* puntina da disegno; — *vt* sporcare con il pollice; — **through** dare uno sguardo a, scartabellare
thump *n* colpo, percossa; tonfo; — *vt* dar pugni a; percuotere; — *vi* fare un tonfo; palpitare
thunder *n* tuono; **–bolt** *n* fulmine *m*; **–cloud, –head** *n* nuvolone *m*; nembo temporalesco; **–storm** *n* temporale *m*; **–struck** *a* stupefatto; — *vi* tuonare
thundering *n* tuono; — *a* tuonante; assordante
Thursday *n* giovedì *m*
thus *adv* così; — **far** fin qui, a questo punto
thwart *vt* impedire
thyme *n* timo
thyroid *n&a* tiroide *f*
tiara *n* tiara
Tiber Tevere
tic *n (med)* ticchio
tick *n (zool)* zecca; *(watch)* tic-tac *m*, battito; — *vi* ticchettare, battere
ticket *n* biglietto; *(label)* etichetta; *(pol)* lista elettorale; *(fine)* contravvenzione, multa; **complimentary** — biglietto di favore; **season** — abbonamento; — **collector** controllore *m*; — **window** sportello
ticking *n* ticchettio; *(cloth)* traliccio; — *a* ticchettante
tickle *n* solletico; — *vt* solleticare; divertire; — *vi* provare solletico
ticklish *a* suscettibile; solleticoso; difficile
tidal *a* di marea; — **wave** maremoto
tidbit *n* bocconcino prelibato
tide *n* marea
tidiness *n* pulizia, nettezza; ordinatezza
tidings *npl* informazioni *fpl*
tidy *a* ordinato, lindo; *(coll)* considerevole; — *n* coprisedia
tie *vt* legare; annodare; pareggiare; — *vi* pareggiarsi; legarsi; — *n* legame *m*; *(neck)* cravatta; *(rail)* traversina; *(sport)* pareggio; *(mus)* legatura
tiepin *n* spillo per la cravatta
tier *n* fila
tie-up *n* interruzione temporaria
tiff *n* bisticcio, stizza
tiger *n* tigre *f*
tight *a* stretto; teso; ermetico; fermo; *(coll)* spilorcio; *(sl)* ubriaco; **–ness** *n* strettezza; **–rope** *n* corda; **–rope walker** funambolo; **–ly** *adv* strettamente; **–en** *vt* stringere; **–en** *vi* stringersi
tightfisted *a* avaro
tight-fitting *a* attillato
tight-lipped *a* impassibile; silenzioso
tights *npl* maglia
tile *n* tegola; mattonella, piastrella; — *vt* coprire con tegole; **–d** *a* coperto di tegole
tiling *n* tegolato
till *prep* fino a; — *conj* finchè; — *n* tiretto di cassa, cassa
till *vt* arare; **–able** *a* coltivabile; **–ing** *n* coltivazione; **–er** *n* coltivatore *m*
tiller *n (naut)* barra del timone
tilt *n* inclinazione; torneo; **full** — a gran velocità; — *vt* inclinare; — *vi* inclinarsi; giostrare; **–ed** *a* inclinato
timber *n* legname *m*; boschi *mpl*
timbre *n* timbro
time *n* tempo; ora; *(era)* epoca; momento; volta; — **after** — tante volte; — **and** (—) **again** ripetutamente; **at the same** — nello stesso tempo; **from** — **to** — di quando in quando; **in, on** — in tempo; **keep** — tenere il tempo; **short** — poco tempo, breve tempo; **a short** — **after** poco dopo; **–less** *a* interminabile; eterno; **–worn** *a* logoro; — *vt* regolare; calcolare il tempo; *(sport)* cronometrare; sincronizzare; cogliere il momento per
time-honored *a* venerabile
timekeeper *n (sport)* cronometrista *m*
timeliness *n* tempestività
timely *a* tempestivo, opportuno, a tempo
timepiece *n* orologio
timetable *n* orario
timid *a* timido
timing *n* sincronizzazione, tempo
tin *n* stagno; latta; — **can** scatola; — **foil** stagnola; — **plate** latta stagnata; **–smith** *n* lattoniere *m*; **–ware** *n* articoli di latta; — *vt* stagnare
tincture *n* tintura
tinder *n* esca
tine *n* rebbio, punta
tinge *n* tintura; pizzico; — *vt* tingere
tingle *n* formicolio, puntura, prurito; — *vi* formicolare
tingling *n* prurito, formicolio
tinker *vi* affaccendarsi
tinkle *vi* tintinnare; — *vt* far tintinnare; — *n* tintinnio
tin-plate *vt* stagnare
tinsel *n* orpello; finzione
tint *n* tinta; — *vt* colorire
tiny *a* minuscolo, piccino
tip *n* punta; *(advice)* consiglio; *(fee)* mancia; *(information)* informazione segreta; — *vt* appuntare; dar la mancia a; inclinare; rivelare una informazione utile; toccare leggermente; — *vi* inclinarsi; — **over** rovesciare; rovesciarsi
tipple *vi* sbevazzare
tippler *n* sbevazzatore *m*
tipsiness *n* ubriachezza
tipsy *a* brillo
tiptoe *vi* camminare in punta di piedi; — *adv* in punta di piedi
tiptop *n (coll)* massimo; colmo; — *a (coll)* eccellente, sommo
tirade *n* sfuriata
tire *n* pneumatico, gomma; — *vt* stancare; annoiare; — *vi* annoiarsi, stancarsi; **–d** *a* stanco; **–dness** *n* stanchezza; **–less** *a* instancabile; **–some** *a* faticoso; noioso, fastidioso
tissue *n* tessuto; — **paper** *n* carta velina
tit *n* — **for tat** colpo per colpo; contrac-

cambio; **give — for tat** rendere pan per focaccia
titanic *a* titanico
titanium *n* titanio
tithe *n* decima
title *n* titolo; diritto; **— page** frontespizio; **—** *vt* intitolare
titlist *n* campione *m*
titrate *vt (chem)* titolare
titration *n (chem)* analisi volumetrica
titter *n* risolino, ridacchiamento; **—** *vi* ridacchiare
titular *a&n* titolare *m*
to *prep* a; verso; per; in; di; **come —** rinvenire; **up —** fino a
toad *n* rospo
toadstool *n* fungo velenoso
toady *n* parassita *m&f*; adulatore *m*; **—** *vt* adulare
toast *vt* abbrustolire; **—** *vi* brindare; **—** *n* pane abbrustolito; brindisi *m*
toaster *n* tostapane *m*
toastmaster *n* direttore dei brindisi
tobacco *n* tabacco
toboggan *n* toboga; **—** *vi* andare in toboga
today *n&adv* oggi *m*; **a week from —** fra una settimana; **a week ago —** una settimana fa
toddle *vi* camminare a passi incerti; **–r** *n* bambino
to-do *n (coll)* daffare *m*
toe *n* dito del piede; *(shoe)* punta; **— the mark (line)** essere ligio al dovere; **—** *vt* toccare con la punta del piede; fornire di punta
toe-dance *vi* ballare sulle punte dei piedi
toenail *n* unghia del piede
toffee *n* caramella
together *adv* insieme
toggle *n (naut)* coccinello; **— switch** *(elec)* interruttore a coltello
togs *npl (coll)* indumenti *mpl*
toil *vi* faticare; **—** *n* fatica, lavoro; **–er** *n* sgobbone *m*; lavoratore *m*; **–some** *a* faticoso, penoso; **–worn** *a* sfinito dalla fatica
toilet *n* toletta; gabinetto; ritirata; **— paper** carta igienica; **— water** acqua di Colonia
token *n* segno; ricordo; prova; *(coin)* gettone; **— payment** pagamento simbolico; **by the same —** per ciò, a conferma di quanto detto; **in — of** in pegno di *(coll)*
tolerable *a* tollerabile
tolerably *adv* tollerabilmente
tolerance *n* tolleranza
tolerant *a* tollerante
tolerate *vt* tollerare
toleration *n* tolleranza
toll *n* pedaggio dazio; *(bells)* rintocco; **— bridge** ponte di pedaggio; **— call** telefonata interurbana; **–house** *n* ufficio daziario; **pay a —** pagare il dazio; **—** *vi* rintoccare; **—** *vt* suonare a rintocchi
tomato *n* pomodoro
tomb *n* tomba; **–stone** *n* lapide *f*, pietra sepolcrale
tomboy *n* maschietta
tomcat *n* gatto
tome *n* tomo, volume *m*
tomfoolery *n* sciocchezza
tomorrow *adv&n* domani *m*; **the day after —** dopodomani; **— morning** domattina; **a week from —** domani a otto
tom-tom *n* tam-tam *m*
ton *n* tonnellata; **–nage** *n* tonnellaggio; *(naut)* stazza
tonal *a* tonale
tonality *n* tonalità
tone *n* tono, intonazione; sfumatura; **— down** attenuare; **–less** senza tono; **—** *vt* intonare
tongs *npl* molle *fpl*, tenaglie *fpl*
tongue *n* lingua; *(shoe)* linguetta; *(bell)* battaglio; *(buckle)* puntale *m*; **on the tip of the —** sulla punta della lingua; **with — in cheek** con ironia, con arguzia
tongue-tied *a* bleso
tonic *a&n* tonico; **—** *n (mus)* tonica
tonight *adv&n* stanotte *f*, stasera
tonsil *n* tonsilla; **–lectomy** *n* tonsillotomia; **–litis** *n* tonsillite *f*
tonsure *vt* tonsurare; **—** *n* tonsura
too *adv* troppo; anche, pure; **— much** troppo
tool *n* utensile *m*; *(person)* agente *m*
toot *n* suono di corno; **—** *vt&i* suonare, fischiettare
tooth *n* dente *m*; **—** *vt* dentellare
toothache *n* mal di denti
toothbrush *n* spazzolino da denti
toothpaste *n* dentifricio
toothpick *n* stuzzicadenti *m*, stecchino
top *n* sommo; colmo; testa; *(bus)* imperiale *m*; *(mountain)* vetta; *(toy)* trottola; **–coat** *n* soprabito; **–flight** *a (coll)* di primissimo ordine; **— hat** cappello a cilindro; **—** *a* massimo, primo; **—** *vt* coronare; raggiungere la vetta; sorpassare; svettare
toper *n* ubriacone *m*
topic *n* tema *m*; argomento; **–al** *a* attuale; topico
topmost *a* più elevato, più in alto
top-notch *a (coll)* eccellente
topographer *n* topografo
topographic *a* topografico
topography *n* topografia
topping *n* cima
topple *vi* capitombolare; **—** *vt* ribaltare
top-secret *a* estremamente segreto
topsy-turvy *a* capovolto
torch *n* fiaccola
torchlight *n* luce di fiaccola; **— parade** fiaccolata
torero *n* torero, toreadore *m*
torment *n* tormento; **—** *vt* tormentare; **–ing** *a* tormentoso; **–or** *n* tormentatore *m*
torn *a* stracciato
tornado *n* tromba d'aria, ciclone *m*, uragano
torpedo *n* siluro; **— boat** torpediniera; **— tube** tubo lanciasiluri; **—** *vt* silurare
torpid *a* tardo; intorpidito
torpor *n* torpore *m*
torrent *n* torrente *m*; **in –s** a torrenti; **–ial** *a* torrenziale
torrid *a* torrido
torsion *n* torsione
torso *n* torso

tort *n (law)* torto
tortoise *n* tartaruga
tortuosity *n* tortuosità
tortuous *a* tortuoso
torture *n* tortura; **-r** *n* torturatore *m*; — *vt* torturare, tormentare
toss *n* scossa, colpo; *(naut)* beccheggio; — **off** tracannare; sbrigare; **-up** *n* testa o croce; **-ing** *n* agitazione, scossa; sballottamento; — *vi* agitarsi; — *vt* gettare, lanciare, sballottare; alzare di colpo
tot *n* bambino, bimbo
total *n* totale *m*, somma; — *a* totale; — *vt* addizionare, sommare; ammontare a; **-ization** *n* totalizzazione; **-ity** *n* totalità
totalitarian *n&a* totalitario; **-ism** *n* totalitarismo
totter *vi* vacillare, **-ing** *a* barcollante
toucan *n* tucano
touch *n* tatto, contatto; *(sl)* stoccata *(fig)*; pizzico; tocco; leggero attacco; **-ing** *a* commovente; **-iness** *n* suscettibilità; **-y** *a* suscettibile; — *vt* toccare; commuovere; concernere, trattare; — *vi* toccarsi; *(naut)* fare scalo
touch-and-go *a* arrischiato; incerto
touchstone *n* pietra di paragone
tough *a* duro; difficile; resistente; violento; ostinato; — *n* tipaccio; **-ly** *adv* difficilmente; ostinatamente; duramente; **-ness** *n* ostinazione; durezza; difficoltà
toughen *vt* indurire; — *vi* indurirsi
tour *n* viaggio, giro; visita; **conducted** — gita in comitiva; — *vi* viaggiare; girare; — *vt* viaggiare attraverso; **-ism** *n* turismo; **-ist** *n* turista *m&f*
tournament *n* torneo; concorso, gara
tousle *vt* scompigliare, disordinare
tow *n* rimorchio; stoppa; **-headed** dai capelli di stoppa *(fig)*; **-line** *n* cavo di rimorchio; — *vt* rimorchiare
toward -s *prep* verso
towel *n* asciugamano; **-ing** *n* stoffa d'asciugamani; — *vt* asciugare
tower *n* torre *f*; *(church)* campanile *m*; — *vi* torreggiare; **-ing** *a* torreggiante
town *n* paese *m*, borgo, città; — **hall** municipio; **-ship** *n* comune *m*
townsman *n* borghese *m*, cittadino
townspeople *npl* cittadinanza
toxic *a* tossico, velenoso
toxicology *n* tossicologia
toxin *n* tossina
toy *n* giocattolo, balocco; — *vi* giocare
trace *n* vestigio, traccia; *(horse)* tirella; — *vt* rintracciare; ricalcare; attribuire; **-able** *a* decalcabile; tracciabile; **-r** *n* ricalcatore, tracciatore *m*; **-ry** *n* intaglio
trachea *n (anat)* trachea
tracheotomy *n* tracheotomia
tracing *n* tracciato, ricalco; — **paper** carta per ricalcare
track *n* orma; sentiero; *(rail)* binario; *(sports)* pista, corsa su pista; — **down** scovare, snidare, catturare; **keep** — **of** seguire il corso di; — *vt* pedinare, seguire la pista di; lasciare le tracce
trackless *a* deserto, senza sentieri
tract *n* tratto, spazio; opuscolo; **-able** *a* trattabile
tractability *n* trattabilità
traction *n* trazione *f*
tractor *n* trattrice *f*
trade *n* commercio; mestiere *m*; — **name** nome commerciale; — **union** sindacato operaio; **-mark** marca di fabbrica; **-r** *n* commerciante, negoziante *m&f*; — *vi* commerciare; — *vt* barattare
tradesman *n* commerciante *m*
tradespeople *npl* gente di commercio, commercianti *mpl*
trading *n* commercio, traffico commerciale; baratto; — *a* commerciale; — **stamps** buoni-regalo
tradition *n* tradizione *f*
traditional *a* tradizionale
traditionalism *n* tradizionalismo
traffic *n* traffico, circolazione *f*; commercio; — **jam** congestione di traffico; — **light** semaforo; — **manager** capo traffico; — **policeman** vigile *m*; — **sign** segnale di traffico; — *vi* commerciare, trafficare
tragedian *n* tragico, attore tragico; *(author)* trageda *m*, dramaturgo
tragedy *n* tragedia
tragic *a* tragico
tragicomedy *n* tragicommedia
trail *n* pista; orme *fpl*; sentiero; strascico; — *vt* trascinare, strascicare; pedinare; seguire a stento; — *vi* trascinarsi
trailer *n* rimorchio; *(movie)* cortometraggio pubblicitario
trailing *a* strisciante
train *n* treno; seguito; *(dress)* strascico; — *vt* addestrare, allenare; *(an animal)* ammaestrare; *(sports)* allenare; istruire; *(gun)* puntare; — *vi* allenarsi; **-ed** *a* ammaestrato, allenato
trainee *n* recluta *m*; novizio
trainer *n* allenatore *m*
training *n* allenamento, addestramento; — *a* allenante; esercitante
trait *n* tratto, caratteristica
traitor *n* traditore *m*; **-ous** *a* traditore
trajectory *n* traiettoria
trammel *vt* impedire, impastoiare; irretire; — *n* pastoia
tramp *n* rumore di passi; camminata; vagabondo; — *vi* camminare pesantemente; vagabondare; — *vt* calpestare; percorrere camminando
trample *vt* calpestare
trance *n* trance *m*
tranquil *a* tranquillo; **-ity** *n* tranquillità; **-ize** *vt* tranquillizzare; **-izer** *n* tranquillante *m*
transact *vt* trattare, negoziare
transaction *n* affare *m*, operazione, transazione
transatlantic *a* transatlantico
transcend *vt* trascendere; **-ency** *n* trascendenza; **-ent** *a* trascendente; **-ental** *a* trascendentale; **-entalism** *n* trascendentalismo
transcontinental *a* transcontinentale
transcribe *vt* trascrivere
transcription *n* trascrizione, copia; *(rad)* registrazione di radiotrasmissione

translation *n* traduzione
translator *n* traduttore *m*
transliterate *vt* trascrivere
translucent *a* translucido
transmigrate *vi* trasmigrare
transmigration *n* trasmigrazione
transmit *vt* trasmettere
transmitter *n* trasmettitore *m*
transmutation *n* trasformazione, trasmutazione
transmute *vt* trasmutare
transoceanic *a* transoceanico
transom *n* lunetta; traversa
transparency *n* trasparenza; *(phot)* diapositiva
transparent *a* trasparente
transpiration *n* traspirazione
transpire *vt&i* traspirare, esalare; *(happen)* accadere
transplant *vt* trapiantare; **–ation** *n* trapianto
transport *vt* trasportare; — *n* trasporto; **–ation** *n* trasporto; mezzo di trasporto; biglietto di viaggio
transpose *vt* trasportare, invertire, trasporre
transposition *n* trasposizione
transship *vt* trasbordare; **–ment** *n* trasbordo
transverse *a* trasversale
trap *n* trappola; inganno; — **door** *n* botola; **set a —** tendere una trappola; — *vt* prendere in trappola; — *vi*
transfer *vt* riportare; cedere; trasferire; — *vi* fare coincidenza; trasferirsi; **–able** *a* trasferibile; — *n* trasferimento; cessione; *(ticket)* biglietto cumulativo
transfiguration *n* trasfigurazione
transfigure *vt* trasfigurare
transfix *vt* trafiggere
transform *vt* trasformare; — *vi* trasformarsi; **–ation** *n* trasformazione
transformer *n (elec)* trasformatore *m*
transfusion *n* trasfusione
transgress *vt* trasgredire; — *vi* peccare, errare
transgression *n* trasgressione
transgressor *n* trasgressore *m*
transience *n* temporaneità
transient *a* transitorio, temporaneo; — *n* transeunte *m&f*
transit *n* transito, trasporto; **in —** di passaggio, di transito, in transito
transition *n* transizione
transitional *a* di transizione
transitive *a* transitivo
transitoriness *n* transitorietà
transitory *a* transitorio
translatable *a* traducibile
translate *vt* tradurre; — *vi* tradursi
stendere trappole
trapeze *n* trapezio
trapezoid *n* trapezoide *m*
trapper *n* cacciatore con trappole
trappings *npl* ornamenti *mpl*
trash *n* immondizie *fpl*; robaccia, **–y** *a* di scarto
trauma *n (med)* trauma *m*; **–tic** *a* traumatico
travail *n* travaglio, doglia; doglia del parto
travel *vi* viaggiare; — *vt* percorrere; — *n* viaggio; *(mech)* corsa, percorso; **–ogue** *n* conferenza su viaggi
traveler *n* viaggiatore *m*, viaggiatrice *f*; **–'s check** *n* assegno per viaggiatori
traveling *a* viaggiante; — *n* il viaggiare; — **salesman** commesso viaggiatore
traversal *n* attraversamento
traverse *vt* attraversare; — *n* traversa; — *a* trasversale
travesty *n* parodia; travisazione; — *vt* travestire
trawl *vt&i* pescare a rete
trawler *n* imbarcazione peschereccia
tray *n* vassoio
treacherous *a* perfido
treachery *n* perfidia
tread *vt* calpestare; percorrere; *(auto)* mettere il battistrada; — *vi* camminare; porre piede; — **water** nuotare diritto; — *n* passo; *(stair)* gradino; *(auto)* battistrada *m*
treadle *n* pedale *m*
treason *n* tradimento; **–able** *a* proditorio; **–ous** *a* sedizioso
treasure *n* tesoro; — *vt* apprezzare, tesaurizzare
treasurer *n* tesoriere *m*
treasury *n* tesoreria
treat *vt&i* trattare; curare; — *vi* negoziare; — *vt* offrire, invitare; — *n* regalo; festa; piacere *m*
treatise *n* trattato
treatment *n* trattamento; cura
treaty *n* trattato
treble *n (math)* triplo; *(mus)* soprano; suono acuto; — *a* triplice; acuto; — *vt* triplicare; — *vi* triplicarsi; — **clef** chiave di sol
tree *n* albero; **–top** *n* cima d'albero; **family —** albero genealogico
trellis *n* graticciata
tremble *n* tremito; — *vi* tremare
trembling *n* tremolio; — *a* tremante
tremendous *a* tremendo; *(coll)* enorme, meraviglioso
tremoló *n* tremolo
tremor *n* tremore *m*, tremito
tremulous *a* tremolante
trench *n* trincea; — **coat** impermeabile *m*
trenchant *a* penetrante, tagliente
trencherman *n* forte mangiatore, buona forchetta
trend *n* tendenza, direzione; — *vi* tendere, dirigersi
trepan *vt (med)* trapanare; — *n* trapano
trepidation *n* trepidazione
trespass *vi* oltrepassare, sconfinare; trasgredire; peccare; **–er** *n* trasgressore *m*
tress *n* treccia
trestle *n* trespolo; cavalletto
trey *n (cards)* tre *m*
triad *n* triade *f*
trial *n* prova; saggio, collaudo; dolore *m*; *(law)* processo
triangle *n* triangolo
triangular *a* triangolare
triangulate *vt* triangolare
triangulation *n* triangolazione
tribal *a* di tribù
tribe *n* tribù *f*
tribesman *n* membro di tribù

tribulation *n* tribolazione
tribunal *n* tribunale *m*
tribune *n* tribuno; *(dais)* tribuna
tributary *n&a* tributario
tribute *n* tributo
triceps *n* tricipite *m*
trick *n* tiro; inganno; destrezza; giuoco di prestigio; **–ery** *n* astuzia, fraudolenza; **–y** *a* scaltro, malizioso, ingannevole; **–iness** *n* furberia, malizia; — *vt* ingannare; **do the** — eliminare il problema
trickle *n* gocciolio; — *vi* gocciolare, stillare
trickling *n* gocciolio
tricolor *n&a* tricolore *m*
tricycle *n* triciclo
tried *a* provato, fido
triennial *a* triennale
trifle *n* inezia, nonnulla *m*; — *vi* gingillarsi; — *vt* sprecare
trifling *a* frivolo; insignificante
trigger *n* grilletto
trigonometry *n* trigonometria
trill *n* trillo; — *vi* trillare; — *vt* far trillare
trillion *n* trilione *m*
trilogy *n* trilogia
trim *a* lindo, attillato; — *vt* decorare, ornare; aggiustare; ordinare; piallare; *(hair)* spuntare; *(sewing)* guarnire; *(trees)* potare; — *n* assetto, ordine *m*; decorazione; **in** — in ordine; **–ness** *n* nettezza; eleganza
trimming *n* ornamento, guarnizione, decorazione
Trinidad La Trinità
trinity *n* trinità
Trinity *n (eccl)* Trinità
trinket *n* gingillo
trio *n* trio
trip *n* viaggio; **take a** — fare un viaggio; **–hammer** *n* maglio a leva, maglio meccanico
trip *vi (stumble)* incespicare; fare uno sbaglio; saltellare; — *vt* far inciampare; cogliere in fallo; *(mech)* sganciare
tripe *n* trippa
triple *a* triplo; **–t** *n* terzina; *(mus)* tripletta; **–ts** *npl* trigemini *mpl*; *vi* triplicare
triplicate *a* triplice; in tre copie; — *n* triplo
tripod *n* tripode *m*
triptych *n* trittico
trite *a* banale; trito
triumph *n* trionfo; vittoria; — *vi* trionfare; **–ant** *a* trionfante
triumvirate *n* triumvirato
triune *a* trino ed uno
trivet *n* treppiede *m*
trivial *a* banale; da nulla
triviality *n* banalità
trochaic *a* trocaico
Trojan *n&a* troiano
troll *vt&i* pescare con esca girante
trolley *n* puleggia; *(bus)* carrello; **–bus** *n* filobus *m*
trollop *n* prostituta, sgualdrina
trombone *n* trombone *m*
troop *n* truppa; **–er** *n* soldato di cavalleria; — *vi* schierarsi, adunarsi; sfilare; affluire; — *vt* raggruppare, radunare
troopship *n* trasporto
trophy *n* trofeo
tropic *n* tropico
tropical *a* tropicale
tropics *npl* i tropici *mpl*
trot *n* trotto; — *vi* trottare; — *vt* far trottare
troubadour *n* trovatore *m*
trouble *n* guaio; disturbo; male *m*; imbarazzo; **–maker** *n* disturbatore, provocatore *m*; **be in** — trovarsi nei pasticci; **take the** — **to** prendersi la pena di; **be worth the** — valer la pena; — *vt* disturbare; turbare; — *vi* disturbarsi; turbarsi; infastidirsi; **–d** *a* turbato, afflitto
troublesome *a* molesto; fastidioso; noioso
trough *n (kneading)* madia; abbeveratoio
trounce *vt* malmenare, battere; *(coll)* sconfiggere
troupe *n* compagnia
trousers *npl* calzoni *mpl*; **short** — *npl* calzoncini *mpl*
trousseau *n* corredo da sposa
trout *n* trota
trowel *n* cazzuola; vanghetta per trapiantare
Troy Troia
truant *a* chi marina la scuola
truce *n* tregua
truck *n* camione *m*; autocarro; — **driver** camionista *m*; — **farm** orto; — **farming** ortofrutticoltura; — **farmer** trafficante d'ortaggi; **have no** — **with** evitare di trattare con; — *vi* scambiare, barattare; carreggiare
truculence *n* trucolenza
truculent *a* trucolento
trudge *vi* camminare faticosamente
true *a* vero; esatto; leale; — *adv* veramente; lealmente; **come** — realizzarsi, avverarsi; — *vt* rettificare, regolare, conformizzare
true-blue *a* costante, fido
truffle *n* tartufo
truism *n* luogo comune, verità banale
truly *adv* veramente
trump *n (card)* briscola; *(coll)* brav'uomo; — *vt* prendere con la briscola; — **up** inventare
trumpery *n* frottole *fpl*
trumpet *n* tromba; — *vi* strombazzare; strombettare; *(elephant)* barrire; **–er** *n* trombettiere *m*
truncate *vt* troncare
truncheon *n* bastone *m*
trundle *vt* far ruzzolare, far rotolare; — *vi* ruzzolare, rotolare
trunk *n* baule *m*; *(auto)* portabagagli *m*; *(body)* torso; *(elephant)* proboscide *f*; *(tree)* tronco
trunks *npl* calzoncini *mpl*, slip *m*, mutandine *fpl*
truss *n* cinto erniario; travata; — *vt* legare; *(prop)* puntellare
trust *n* fiducia, credito; *(com)* trust *m*, consorzio; **–worthy** *a* fidato; **in** — in deposito; — *vt* dar credito a, fidarsi di; — *vi* fidarsi; **–ing** *a* fiducioso; **–ed** *a* fidato
trustee *n* amministratore *m*; **–ship** *n* amministrazione, curatela

truth *n* verità; **to tell the —** a dire il vero; **–ful** *a* sincero, verace
truthfulness *n* veracità
try *vt* provare, tentare; *(law)* giudicare; *(tire)* stancare; **— out** collaudare; mettere a prova; **— on** provare; **—** *n* tentativo, prova
trying *a* difficile, penoso, seccante
tryout *n* prova, saggio
tryst *n* appuntamento
T-shirt *n* maglietta estiva, canottiera
tub *n* tino; **— bath** bagno in vasca; **–by** *a* obeso, grasso, paffuto
tuba *n* tuba
tube *n* tubo, canale *m*; *(rad)* valvola; **inner —** camera d'aria
tuber *n* tubero
tubercle *n* tubercolo
tubercular *a* tubercolare
tuberculosis *n* tubercolosi *f*
tuberous *a* tuberoso
tubing *n* tubatura
tubular *a* tubolare
tuck *n* piegatura; **—** *vt* ripiegare, rimboccare
Tuesday *n* martedì; **Shrove —** Martedì Grasso
tuft *n* ciuffo; *(wool)* fiocco; *(bird)* cresta; **–ed** *a* crestato; fiocchettato; con ciuffi; **—** *vt* trapuntare
tug *vt* tirare con forza; rimorchiare; **—** *n* strappo, tirone *m*; rimorchiatore *m*; **— of war** tiro della fune
tugboat *n* rimorchiatore *m*
tuition *n* tassa scolastica
tulip *n* tulipano
tumble *vi* cadere; agitarsi; capitombolare; **—** *vt* rovesciare, scompigliare **—** *n* caduta; capitombolo
tumbler *n* *(acrobat)* acrobata *m&f*, saltimbanco; *(glass)* bicchiere *m*; *(lock)* nasello
tumble-down *a* caduco, crollante
tumefaction *n* tumefazione
tumor *n* tumore *m*
tumult *n* tumulto; **–ous** *a* tumultuoso
tun *n* barile *m*
tuna, tuna fish *n* tonno
tunable *a* accordabile
tundra *n* tundra
tune *n* melodia, aria; **in —** d'accordo, a tono, intonato; **out of —** fuori tono, in disaccordo, stonato; **–ful** *a* intonato, melodioso; **–r** *n* accordatore *m*; **—***vt* accordare; *(motor)* regolare
tune-up *n* regolazione
tungsten *n* tungsteno
tunic *n* tunica
tuning *n* accordatura; **— fork** diapason *m*
Tunisia Tunisia; **–n** *n&a* tunisino
tunnel *n* galleria, traforo; **—** *vt* traforare
turban *n* turbante *m*
turbid *a* torbido
turbine *n* turbina
turbojet *n* turboreattore *m*, turbogetto
turboprop *n* turbopropulsore *m*, turboelica
turbulence *n* turbolenza
turbulent *a* turbolento
tureen *n* zuppiera
turf *n* zolla erbosa; torba; ippodromo, pista
turgid *a* turgido; **–ity** *n* turgidezza
Turin Torino
Turk *n* turco
Turkey Turchia
turkey *n* tacchino
Turkish *n&a* turco; **— bath** bagno turco
turmoil *n* agitazione
turn *vt* voltare; girare; *(blunt)* smussare; cambiare; **—** *vi* voltarsi; diventare; girare; **— about, around** voltarsi indietro; **— back** tornare indietro; **— off** chiudere; **— on** aprire; dipendere da; **— out** uscire; riuscire; far uscire; *(light)* spegnere; **— over** voltarsi; **— up** presentarsi; scoprire; accadere
turn *n* svolta; turno; giro; cambio; **done to a —** fatto a perfezione; **good —** buona azione; **sharp —** curva stretta; **–coat** *n* opportunista *m*; **–down** *a* rovesciato; **–out** *n* *(com)* produzione; *(audience)* uditorio; **–over** *n* *(com)* giro d'affare; rovesciamento; *(pastry)* focaccia; **–stile** *n* molinello; **–table** *n* *(rail)* piattaforma girevole; *(rad)* piatto giradischi
turpentine *n* trementina
turpitude *n* turpitudine *f*
turquoise *n* turchese *f*
turret *n* torricella
turtle *n* tartaruga; **–dove** tortora; **turn —** capovolgersi
Tuscan *a&n* toscano
Tuscany Toscana
tusk *n* zanna
tussle *n* rissa, zuffa; **—** *vi* azzuffarsi
tutelage *n* tutela
tutelary *a* tutelare
tutor *n* istitutore *m*; **—** *vt* istruire, insegnare
tuxedo *n* smoking *m*
twaddle *n* ciancia; **—** *vi* cianciare
twang *n* tono vibratorio; accento nasale; **speak with a —** parlare col naso
tweak *vt* pizzicare, ritorcere
tweet *vi* cinguettare
tweezers *npl* pinzette *fpl*; *(hair)* mollette *fpl*
twelfth *a* dodicesimo
twelve *a* dodici
twentieth *a* ventesimo
twenty *a* venti
twice *adv* due volte
twiddle *vt* far girare
twig *n* ramoscello
twilight *n* crepuscolo
twin *a&n* gemello
twine *n* spago, corda; **—** *vt* intrecciare; attorcigliare; legare; **—** *vi* attorcigliarsi; serpeggiare
twin-engine *a* bimotore
twinge *n* dolore *m*; spasimo; **—** *vt* pungere **—** *vi* dolere
twinkle *vi* scintillare; ammiccare; **—** *n* scintillio; strizzatina d'occhio, occhiolino
twinkling *n* scintillio, balenio, sfavillio; istante *m*; **in the — of an eye** in un batter d'occhio
twirl *vt&i* rigirare
twist *n* attorcigliamento; torsione; tendenza; treccia; **–er** *n* *(storm)* turbine *m*,

tromba d'aria; — *vt* torcere, contorcere; intrecciare; — *vi* torcersi, contorcersi; **-ed** *a* storto; **-ing** *n* contorcimento
twit *vt* rimproverare, rinfacciare
twitch *n* spasimo; strappo; — *vi* contrarsi, contorcersi; — *vt* strappare
twitter *n* pigolio, cinguettio; agitazione; **all of a** — agitato, nervoso; — *vi* pigolare, cinguettare
two *a* due; **-fold** *a* doppio
two- *(in comp)* **—edged** *a* a doppio taglio; **—faced** *a* a due facce; ipocrito; **—fisted** virile, vigoroso; **—handed** *a* a due mani; **—legged** *a* a due gambe, bipede; **—piece** *a* a due pezzi; **—step** *n* passo doppio; **—way** *a* a doppio senso
tycoon *n* magnate *m*
tympanum *n* timpano
type *n* tipo; *(print)* carattere *m*; — *vt* scrivere a macchina; classificare
typesetter *n* compositore *m*
typewriter *n* macchina da scrivere
typhoid (fever) *n* tifoide *f*
typhoon *n* tifone *m*
typhus *n* tifo
typical *a* tipico; **-ly** *adv* tipicamente
typify *vt* rappresentare, figurare, tipificare
typing *n* dattilografia
typist *n* dattilografo, dattilografa
typographer *n* tipografo
typographical *a* tipografico
typography *n* tipografia
tyrannical *a* tirannico
tyrannize *vt&i* tiranneggiare
tyranny *n* tirannia
tyrant *n* tiranno
Tyrol Tirolo

U

ubiquitous *a* onnipresente
udder *n* poppa
ugliness *n* bruttezza
ugly *a* brutto
ulcer *n* ulcera; **-ate** *vt* ulcerare; **-ate** *vi* ulcerarsi; **-ation** *n* ulcerazione; **-ous** *a* ulceroso
ulterior *a* ulteriore; — **motive** secondo fine
ultimate *a* finale, ultimo
ultimatum *n* ultimatum *m*
ultra *a&n* ultra; **-modern** *a* ultramoderno; **-sonic** *a* ultrasonico; **-violet** *a* ultravioletto
umbilical *a* ombelicale; — **cord** cordone ombelicale
umbilicus *n* ombelico
umbrage *n* ombra, offesa; fogliame *m*; **take** — adombrarsi
umbrella *n* ombrello, parapioggia, paracqua
umpire *n* arbitro; — *vt&i* arbitrare
umpiring *n* arbitraggio
UN, United Nations O.N.U., Organizzazione delle Nazioni Unite
unabashed *a* imperturbato; svergognato
unabated *a* inesausto, non esausto
unabating *a* infaticabile, senza diminuzione di energia
unable *a* incapace; **be** — **to** non potere, essere incapacitato per
unabridged *a* completo, intero
unaccented *a* non accentato, inaccentuato; atono
unacceptable *a* inaccettabile
unaccomodating *a* inadattabile, incondiscendente
unaccompanied *a* solo, non accompagnato; *(mus)* senza accompagnamento
unaccomplished *a* incompiuto
unaccountable *a* inesplicabile; irresponsabile
unaccounted (for) *a* inspiegato; *(missing)* mancante
unaccredited *a* non accreditato
unaccustomed *a* non abituato
unacknowledged *a* non riconosciuto; *(letter)* senza risposta, senza riscontro
unacquainted *a* non informato; — **with** senza familiarità circa
unacquired *a* naturale
unadapted *a* inadatto
unaddressed *a* senza indirizzo
unadorned *a* disadorno
unadulterated *a* genuino, non adulterato, inalterato
unadvisable *a* non consigliabile
unaffected *a* non affettato; *(naive)* semplice
unaffectedness *n* semplicità
unafraid *a* intrepido, senza paura, temerario
unagreeable *a* sgradevole
unaggressive *a* non aggressivo
unaided *a* senz'aiuto
unallowed *a* non permesso
unalloyed *a* puro, senza lega
unalterable *a* inalterabile
unaltered *a* inalterato
unambitious *a* senz'ambizione
unanimity *n* unanimità
unanimous *a* unanime
unannounced *a* non annunziato, inaspettato
unanswerable *a* irrefutabile
unanswered *a* senza risposta
unanticipated *a* non anticipato
unappeased *a* implacato, insoddisfatto
unappetizing *a* poco appetitoso
unappreciated *a* non apprezzato
unappreciative *a* non apprezzativo
unapproachable *a* inaccessibile
unarmed *a* indifeso, inerme
unashamed *a* spudorato, svergognato
unasked *a* non richiesto
unassailable *a* inattaccabile
unassimilated *a* non assimilato
unassisted *a* non assistito
unassuming *a* modesto, senza pretese
unattached *a* libero; non fidanzato; separato
unattainable *a* irraggiungibile
unattended *a* non accompagnato, solo
unattractive *a* poco attraente
unauthentic *a* non autentico
unavailable *a* non disponibile
unavailing *a* inutile, inefficace

unavenged *a* non vendicato
unavoidable *a* inevitabile
unavowed *a* non riconosciuto; inconfessato
unaware *a* inconsapevole; **be — of** ignorare
unawares *adv* all'insaputa; di sorpresa
unbalanced *a* squilibrato
unbandage *vt* sbendare
unbaptized *a* non battezzato
unbar *vt* aprire
unbearable *a* insopportabile
unbearably *adv* insopportabilmente
unbeatable *a* imbattibile
unbeaten *a* imbattuto
unbecoming *a* indecoroso
unbefitting *a* sconvenevole
unbeknown *a* sconosciuto; **— to** all'insaputa di
unbelief *n* incredulità
unbelievable *a* incredibile
unbeliever *n* miscredente *m&f*
unbelieving *a* incredulo
unbend *vt* raddrizzare; allentare; **—** *vi (relax)* rilassarsi; raddrizzarsi; **–ing** *a* inflessibile
unbiased *a* imparziale
unbidden *a* spontaneo; senza invito
unbind *vt* sciogliere
unblamable *a* innocente, irreprensibile
unbleached *a* non candeggiato
unblemished *a* senza macchia, puro
unblock *vt* sbloccare; **–ed** *a* sbloccato
unblushing *a* svergognato
unbolt *vt* aprire, levare il catenaccio; **–ed** *a* aperto, senza catenaccio
unborn *a* non nato, inesistente
unbosom *vt* rivelare, confidare; **— oneself** sfogarsi
unbound *a* sciolto, libero; *(book)* senza rilegare; **–ed** *a* illimitato
unbowed *a* indomito
unbreakable *a* irrompibile, infrangibile
unbred *a* maleducato, grossolano
unbridled *a* sbrigliato, sfrenato
unbroken *a* intatto, non rotto; ininterrotto
unbuckle *vt* sciogliere, sfibbiare
unburden *vt* scaricare
unburied *a* insepolto
unbusinesslike *a* poco commerciale, poco pratico
unbutton *vt* sbottonare; **–ed** *a* sbottonato
uncalled *a* non chiamato
uncalled-for *a* innecessario; impertinente
uncanny *a* irreale, soprannaturale
uncared-for *a* trascurato, negletto
unceasing *a* incessante; **–ly** *adv* continuamente, incessantemente
uncensored *a* incensurato
unceremonious *a* senza cerimonie
uncertain *a* incerto; **–ty** *n* incertezza
uncertified *a* non certificato, non legalizzato
unchain *vt* liberare, sciogliere dalle catene, scatenare
unchallenged *a* non sfidato, senza obbiezione
unchangeable *a* invariabile, immutabile
unchanged *a* inalterato, immutato, invariato
unchanging *a* costante, invariabile
uncharitable *a* non caritatevole, senza carità
uncharted *a* non indicato in una carta marittima
unchaste *a* non casto
unchecked *a* incontrollato, sfrenato
unchivalrous *a* non cavalleresco
unchristian *a* indegno d'un cristiano, poco cristiano
unchristened *a* non battezzato
uncircumspect *a* imprudente
uncircumcised *a* incirconciso
uncivil *a* sgarbato; **–ized** *a* incivile, barbaro
unclaimed *a* non reclamato, non domandato
unclasp *vt* slacciare; **–ed** *a* slacciato, aperto
uncle *n* zio
unclean *a* sporco, sudicio; poco pulito; **–liness** *n* sporcizia; impurità
unclench *vt* aprire
unclothed *a* svestito
unclouded *a* senza nuvole
uncock *vt* disarmare
uncoil *vt* svolgere, srotolare
uncollected *a* non raccolto, non riunito
uncolored *a* non colorato, incoloro
uncombed *a* spettinato
uncomfortable *a* scomodo, a disagio
uncomfortably *adv* scomodamente
uncommitted *a* non commesso; non impegnato, non compromesso
uncommon *a* non comune, raro
uncommunicative *a* riservato, incommunicativo
uncomplaining *a* rassegnato
uncomplete *a* incompleto, incompiuto
uncomplicated *a* semplice
uncomplimentary *a* poco lusinghiero, offensivo
uncompromising *a* intransigente, inflessibile
unconcealed *a* non nascosto, manifesto
unconcern *n* indifferenza; **–ed** *a* indifferente, noncurante
unconditional *a* incondizionale
unconfirmed *a* non confermato
uncongenial *a* incompatibile, antipatico
unconnected *a* sconnesso; staccato, separato; estraneo
unconquerable *a* inconquistabile, invincibile
unconquered *a* invitto, indomito
unconscious *a* inconscio, inconsapevole, privo di sensi; **be — of** ignorare; **–ly** *adv* inconsciamente; **–ness** *n* incoscienza
unconscionable *a* senza scrupoli
unconsecrated *a* non consacrato
unconsidered *a* sconsiderato, inconsiderato
unconstitutional *a* incostituzionale
unconstrained *a* senza costrizione, disinvolto
unconsumed *a* non consumato
uncontaminated *a* incontaminato
uncontested *a* incontestato
uncontradicted *a* non contraddetto
uncontrollable *a* incontrollabile
uncontrolled *a* sfrenato, senza controllo

unconventional *a* non convenzionale
unconverted *a* non convertito
unconvinced *a* non convinto
unconvincing *a* non convincente
uncooked *a* non cotto, non cucinato, crudo
uncork *vt* stappare, sturare, **–ed** *a* sturato, stappato
uncorrected *a* non corretto
uncorroborated *a* non corroborato
uncorrupted *a* incorrotto
uncouple *vt* spaiare, sconnettere
uncouth *n* goffo, grossolano; **–ness** *n* grossolanità, goffaggine *f*
uncover *vt* scoprire; — *vi* scoprirsi
uncrowned *a* senza corona
unction *n* unzione; unguento; **extreme —** *(eccl)* estrema unzione
unctuous *a* untuoso
uncultivated *a* incolto
uncultured *a* incolto
uncurbed *a* indomito
uncured *a* non guarito
uncurtailed *a* non diminuito
uncustomary *a* inusato
uncut *a* intonso, non tagliato
undamaged *a* non danneggiato, indenne
undamped *a* non scoraggiato
undated *a* non datato, senza data
undaunted *a* intrepido
undeceive *vt* disingannare
undecided *a* incerto, indeciso
undecipherable *a* indecifrabile
undefeated *a* invitto, non vinto
undefended *a* indifeso
undefinable *a* indefinibile
undefined *a* indefinito
undelivered *a* non recapitato
undemonstrative *a* non aperto, chiuso, riservato
undeniable *a* innegabile
undeniably *adv* innegabilmente
under *prep* sotto, meno di; **— the circumstances** in tali circostanze, nelle circostanze; — *a* di sotto; inferiore; — *adv* al di sotto, sotto
underage *a* minorenne
underage *n* deficit *m*
underbid *vt* offrire un prezzo inferiore a, fare offerta più bassa di
underbrush *n* cespugli *mpl*, macchie *fpl*
undercarriage *n* carrello d'atterraggio; *(auto)* telaio
undercharge *vt* riscuotere al di sotto del prezzo guisto; caricare insufficientemente
underclothing *n* biancheria personale
undercover *a* segreto, occulto, clandestino
undercurrent *n* corrente subacquea; influenza segreta
undercut *n (tennis)* tiro di taglio; — *vt* vendere (*or* lavorare) a prezzo inferiore a
underdeveloped *a* insufficientemente sviluppato
underdog *n* persona sottomessa
underdone *a* poco cotto; *(meat)* al sangue
underestimate *vt* sottostimare, svalutare
underexpose *vt* dare esposizione insufficiente a
underexposure *n (photo)* esposizione insufficiente
underfed *a* malnutrito
underfoot *adv* sotto i piedi
undergarment *n* sottoveste *f*, indumento personale
undergo *vt* subire
undergraduate studente d'università
underground *a* sotterraneo; — *n (pol)* resistenza clandestina, cospiratori *mpl*; — *adv* sottoterra
undergrowth *n* cespuglio, macchia
underhanded *a* subdolo, furbo; corto di personale; **–ly** *adv* clandestinamente, sottomano, segretamente
underhung *a* sporgente
underlie *vt* costituire la base (*or* fondamenta) di; essere sottoposto a
underline *vt* sottolineare
underling *n* subalterno
underlying *a* fondamentale
undermine *vt* sottominare
undermost *a* infimo
underneath *adv* al di sotto; — *prep* sotto; al di sotto di
undernourished *a* denutrito
undernourishment *n* denutrizione
underpaid *a* mal pagato
underpay *vt* pagare insufficientemente
underpass *n* sottopassaggio
underpinning *n* sottomuro
underprivileged *a* privo del benestare; povero
underproduction *n* produzione insufficiente
underrate *vt* sottovalutare; **–d** *a* sottovalutato
underscore *vt* sottolineare
undersea *a* subacqueo, sottomarino
undersecretary *n* sottosegretario
undersell *vt* svendere, vendere in concorrenza
undershirt *n* maglietta
underside *n* parte inferiore
undersign *vt* sottoscrivere; **–ed** *n&a* sottoscritto
undersized *a* di dimensione al di sotto del normale
underskirt *n* sottogonna
understand *vt&i* capire, comprendere; **–able** *a* comprensibile
understanding *n* comprensione, intesa; intelletto, intelligenza, giudizio; **have an — with** accordarsi con, aver un'intesa con; **on the — that** a condizione che; — *a* intelligente, comprensivo
understate *vt* attenuare; **–ment** *n* affermazione incompleta
understood *a* inteso, sottinteso, capito
understudy *n (theat)* sostituto; — *vt* studiare la parte di
undertake *vt* intraprendere, **–r** *n* imprenditore *m*, imprenditrice *f*; impresario di pompe funebri
undertaking *n* impresa
undertone *n* tono basso (*or* fievole); sfumatura; **in an —** sottovoce
undervalue *vt* sottovalutare, svalutare
underwear *n* biancheria intima
underweight *a* troppo magro
underworld *n* oltretomba; inferno; bas-

sifondi *mpl*; — *a* d'oltretomba; dei bassifondi
underwrite *vt* sottoscrivere, garantire, assicurare; **–r** *n* assicuratore *m*; garante *m*
undeserved *a* immeritato, ingiusto; **–ly** *adv* immeritatamente, ingiustamente
undeserving *a* immeritevole
undesirable *a* sgradito, indesiderabile
undetected *a* nascosto, segreto, non scoperto
undetermined *a* indeterminato, indeciso
undeterred *a* non scoraggiato, non distolto
undeveloped *a* non sviluppato
undeviating *a* diritto, costante, non deviante
undigested *a* indigesto, non digerito
undignified *a* senza dignità
undiluted *a* non diluito
undiminished *a* non diminuito, intero
undiplomatic *a* poco diplomatico
undirected *a* senza direzione
undiscerned *a* inosservato
undiscernible *a* indiscernibile
undiscerning *a* senza discernimento
undisciplined *a* indisciplinato
undiscovered *a* non scoperto
undisclosed *a* nascosto, segreto
undiscriminating *a* senza discernimento, di cattivo gusto
undisguised *a* aperto, non mascherato; **–ly** *adv* apertamente, francamente
undismayed *a* non scoraggiato, senza paura, fermo
undisputed *a* indisputato, indiscusso, incontrastato; fuori discussione
undissolved *a* non disciolto
undistinguishable *a* indistinguibile
undistinguished *a* non distinto; non famoso; volgare, comune
undistorted *a* non distorto
undisturbed *a* indisturbato
undivided *a* indiviso
undo *vt* disfare, sciogliere
undoing *n* rovina; annullamento
undone *a* sciolto, disfatto; rovinato; **come** — sciogliersi
undoubtedly *adv* indubbiamente, senza dubbio
undress *vt* spogliare; — *vi* spogliarsi, svestirsi; **–ed** *a* svestito; non preparato, grezzo
undrinkable *a* imbevibile
undue *a* eccessivo, inconveniente
undulate *vi* ondeggiare; fluttuare; — *vt* far ondeggiare, ondulare
unduly *adv* eccessivamente
undying *a* imperituro, immortale
unearned *a* immeritato, non guadagnato
unearth *vt* dissotterrare scavare; scoprire; **–ed** *a* dissotterrato; scoperto; **–ly** *a* soprannaturale
uneasiness *n* disagio, inquietudine *f*, turbamento
uneasy *a* inquieto, turbato
uneaten *a* non mangiato
unedible immangiabile
uneducated *a* incolto, ignorante
unemotional *a* impassibile, non emotivo
unemployed *a&n* disoccupato
unemployment *n* disoccupazione; — **insurance** assicurazione contro la disoccupazione
unencumbered *a* sgombro; libero di gravami, non ipotecato
unending *a* interminabile
unendurable *a* insopportabile, intollerabile
unenlightened *a* ignorante
unenterprising *a* poco intrapredente
unenviable *a* non invidiabile
unequal *a* ineguale, disuguale; inadatto; **–ed** *a* ineguagliato; **–ly** *adv* inegualmente
unequivocal *a* franco, chiaro; inequivocabile
unerring *a* infallibile
unessential *a* non essenziale, superfluo
uneven *a* ineguale; non piano; dispari; **–ness** *n* ineguaglianza, disuguaglianza; disparità
uneventful *a* senza novità, calmo, monotono
unexampled *a* senza precedenti, inaudito
unexcelled *a* non sorpassato, insuperato
unexceptionable *a* irreprensibile
unexciting *a* non eccitante
unexpected *a* inatteso, inaspettato; **–ly** all'improvviso
unexpired *a* non spirato, non scaduto
unexplained *a* non spiegato, inesplicato
unexplored *a* inesplorato
unexposed *a* non esposto, protetto; nascosto, segreto
unexpressed *a* inespresso
unexpurgated *a* integro, inespurgato
unfaded *a* non appassito, non scolorito
unfailing *a* infallibile
unfair *a* ingiusto; parziale; **–ly** *adv* disonestamente, ingiustamente; **–ness** *n* ingiustizia; parzialità
unfaithful *a* infedele; **–ness** *n* infedeltà
unfaltering *a* deciso, fermo
unfamiliar *a* poco pratico; sconosciuto; **–ity** *n* mancanza di familiarità
unfashionable *a* fuori moda
unfasten *vt* slegare, aprire, sciogliere; — *vi* slegarsi
unfathomable *a* insondabile
unfavorable *a* sfavorevole
unfeasible *a* impraticabile, non fattibile
unfeeling *a* insensibile
unfeigned *a* genuino, non finto
unfertile *a* non fertile, sterile
unfettered *a* senza catene, senza ceppi; libero, illimitato
unfilled *a* vuoto; vacante
unfinished *a* incompleto
unfit *a* incapace; inadatto; **–ness** *n* incapacità; **–ting** *a* sconveniente
unflagging *a* infaticabile
unflattering *a* poco lusinghiero
unflinching *a* risoluto, imperterrito
unfold *vt* spiegare, rivelare; — *vt* spiegarsi
unforced *a* spontaneo
unforeseen *a* inatteso, imprevisto
unforgettable *a* indimenticabile
unforgivable *a* imperdonabile
unforgiven *a* senza perdono, non perdonato

unforgiving *a* implacabile
unforgotten *a* non dimenticato
unformulated *a* non formulato
unfortified *a* debole, non fortificato, indifeso
unfortunate *a* disgraziato, sfortunato, infelice; **–ly** *adv* sfortunatamente, per sfortuna
unfounded *a* infondato
unfrequented *a* infrequentato
unfriendliness *n* inimicizia
unfriendly *a* mal disposto, poco amichevole, sfavorevole; ostile
unfrock *vt (eccl)* spretare
unfruitful *a* infruttuoso; sterile
unfulfilled *a* incompiuto, inadempiuto
unfurl *vt* spiegare, aprire; — *vi* distendersi
unfurnished *a* non ammobiliato
ungainliness *n* goffaggine *f*
ungainly *a* maldestro, goffo; — *adv* maldestramente, goffamente
ungenerous *a* meschino, ingeneroso
ungentlemanly *a* grossolano, rozzo, volgare
ungird *vt* scingere
unglazed *a* senza vetri; non lucidato
ungodliness *a* empietà
ungodly *a* empio; *(coll)* orrendo
ungovernable *a* ingovernabile
ungraceful *a* sgraziato, senza grazia
ungracious *a* scortese; antipatico; **–ly** *adv* scortesemente; **–ness** *n* scortesia, grossolanità
ungrammatical *a* scorretto, non grammaticale
ungrateful *a* ingrato, non riconoscente; **—ness** ingratitudine *f*
ungratified *a* insoddisfatto, non appagato
ungrounded *a* infondato
ungrudging *a* liberale, generoso, di buon cuore; **–ly** *adv* generosamente, di buon cuore, volentieri
unguarded *a* incostudito
unguent *n* unguento
ungulate *n&a* ungulato
unhallowed *a* profano, non consacrato
unhampered *a* non impedito, disimbarazzato
unhand *vt* lasciar andare, lasciare
unhandy *a* maldestro
unhappily *adv* sfortunatamente
unhappiness *n* infelicità, sfortuna
unhappy *a* infelice, scontento, sfortunato
unharmed, unhurt *a* illeso, sano e salvo
unhealthful *a* insalubre
unhealthiness *n* insalubrità
unhealthy *a* malsano, malaticcio
unheard *a* non udito
unheard-of *a* inaudito
unheated *a* non riscaldato
unheeding *a* negligente, disattento
unhesitating *a* risoluto, non esitante; **–ly** *adv* senza esitazione, risolutamente
unhindered *a* disimpacciato, non ostacolato
unhinge *vt* sgangherare; *(mind)* disordinare
unhitch *vt* staccare
unholy *a* empio; *(coll)* terribile
unhoped-for *a* insperato
unhorse *vt* scavalcare
unhook *vt* sganciare
unhurried *a* calmo; **–ly** *adv* senza fretta
unicorn *n* unicorno
unidentified *a* non identificato
unification *n* unificazione
uniform *a&n* uniforme *f*; **–ly** *a* uniformemente
uniformity *n* uniformità
unify *vt* unificare
unilateral *a* unilaterale
unimaginable *a* inimmaginabile
unimaginative *a* senza immaginazione
unimpaired *a* integro, non indebolito
unimpeachable *a* inattaccabile, incontestabile
unimpeded *a* senza ostacoli, non impedito
unimportant *a* poco importante, insignificante
unimposed *a* volontario
unimposing *a* poco imponente
unimpressed *a* non impressionato
unimpressionable *a* non impressionabile
unimpressive *a* poco impressionante
unimproved *a* non migliorato
uninflammable *a* non infiammabile
uninfluenced *a* non influenzato
uninfluential *a* senza influenza
uninformed *a* ignaro, non informato, ignorante
uninhabitable *a* inabitabile
uninhabited *a* disabitato, inabitato
uninitiated *a* non iniziato
uninjured *a* incolume, illeso
uninspired *a* senza ispirazione, non ispirato
unintelligent *a* stupido, poco intelligente
unintelligible *a* incomprensibile
unintentional *a* involontario
uninterested *a* disinteressato
uninteresting *a* poco interessante
uninterrupted *a* ininterrotto
uninvited *a* non invitato
uninviting *a* poco attraente
union *n* unione *f*; **labor** — sindacato; **–ist** *n* unionista *m&f*
unique *a* solo, unico
unison *n* unisono; **in** — all'unisono
unit *n* unità; *(mil)* reparto
Unitarian *n&a* unitario
unite *vt* unire; — *vi* unirsi
united *a* unito
United Arab Republic Repubbliche Arabe Unite
United Kingdom Regno Unito
United Nations Nazioni Unite
United States of America Stati Uniti d'America
unity *n* unità
univalent *a* univalente, monovalente
universal *a* universale; **–ity** *n* universalità; **–ly** *adv* universalmente
universe *n* universo
university *n* università; — *a* universitario
unjust *a* ingiusto; **–ly** *adv* ingiustamente
unjustifiable *a* ingiustificabile
unjustified *a* ingiustificato
unkempt *a* trasandato, spettinato, scarmigliato
unkind *a* sgarbato, poco gentile; **–ness** scortesia

unknot *vt* slegare, snodare
unknowable *a* inconoscibile
unknowingly *adv* inconsapevolmente
unknown *n* sconosciuto; *(math)* incognita; — *a* sconosciuto, ignoto
unlace *vt* slacciare; **–d** *a* slacciato
unladylike *a* non degno d'una signora
unlatch *vt* disserrare
unlawful *a* illegale, illegittimo, illecito; **–ly** *adv* illecitamente; **–ness** *n* illegalità
unlearn *vt* disimparare; **–ed** non imparato; *(person)* ignorante
unleash *vt* sguinzagliare
unleavened *a* senza lievito, non fermentato; — **bread** pane azzimo
unless *conj* a meno che, salvo che, se non
unlettered *a* ignorante, illetterato, analfabeta
unlicensed *a* senza licenza (*or* permesso)
unlifelike *a* inverosimile
unlike *a* dissimile; — *prep* diverso di; **–lihood** *n* improbabilità, inverosimiglianza
unlikely *a* improbabile
unlimited illimitato
unlined *a (paper)* senza righe; *(clothing)* non foderato
unload *vt* scaricare; disfarsi di; **–ing** *n* scarico; **–ed** *a* scaricato, scarico
unlock *vt* disserrare, aprire; **–ed** aperto, dischiuso
unlooked-for inaspettato, inatteso
unloosen *vt* sciogliere, allentare
unlovable *a* antipatico, detestabile
unloving *a* insensibile, non sentimentale, impassivo
unluckiness *n* sfortuna
unlucky *a* sfortunato, disgraziato, sventurato
unman *vt* snervare
unmanageable *a* ribelle, intrattabile
unmanly *a* effeminato, vile, pusillanime
unmannerly *adv* grossolanamente, rozzamente; — *a* scortese, sgarbato
unmarked *a* non marcato, non contrassegnato
unmarketable *a* invendibile
unmarried *a* non sposato
unmask *vt* smascherare; — *vi* smascherasi
unmatched *a* scompagnato, spaiato; incomparato
unmeant *a* involontario
unmeasurable *a* immisurabile
unmelodious *a* stonato, discordante
unmentionable *a* innominabile
unmerciful *a* spietato, senza misericordia
unmerited *a* immeritato
unmindful *a* negligente, smemorato, sventato
unmistakable *a* indubbio, evidente
unmistakably *adv* evidentemente, senza errore, senza dubbio, inequivocabilmente
unmitigated non mitigato; *(complete)* assoluto
unmixed *a* puro, non mischiato, non misto
unmodified *a* non modificato
unmolested *a* indisturbato
unmounted *a (jewel)* non incastonato
unmoor *vt* disormeggiare
unmourned *a* illagrimato
unmoved *a* immobile; impassibile, inesorabile
unmurmering *a* rassegnato
unnamed anonimo, innominato
unnatural *a* innaturale, non naturale; snaturato, contro natura
unnavigable *a* innavigabile
unnecessary *a* superfluo
unneeded *a* innecessario
unnegotiable *a (com)* non negoziabile
unnerve *vt* snervare
unnoticeable *a* inosservabile
unnoticed, unobserved *a* inosservato
unnumbered *a* innumerabile
unobjectionable *a* ineccepible
unobliging *a* scompiacente
unobservant *a* inosservante
unobstructed *a* inostruito, non impedito
unobtainable *a* inottenibile
unobtrusive *a* modesto, discreto, riservato; **–ly** *adv* modestamente, discretamente
unoccupied *a* disoccupato; libero, vacante, non occupato
unofficial *a* non ufficiale, ufficioso
unopened *a* chiuso, non aperto
unopposed *a* incontrastato, senza opposizione
unoriginal *a* non originale
unorthodox *a* eterodosso
unostentatious *a* semplice, senza fasto
unpack *vt* disfare, spacchettare, sballare; — *vi* disfare i bagagli
unpaid *a* non pagato; *(com)* in sospeso; non saldato
unpalatable *a* sgradevole
unparalleled *a* ineguagliabile, incomparato, senza paralleli *(coll)*
unpardonable *a* imperdonabile
unpatriotic *a* non patriottico, poco patriottico
unpaved *a* non pavimentato, senza selciato
unperceivable *a* inosservabile
unperceived *a* inosservato
unperturbed *a* imperturbato
unpin *vt* levare gli spilli da; staccare
unpitying *a* spietato
unpleasant *a* spiacevole; **–ness** *n* spiacevolezza; disaccordo
unpleasing *a* spiacevole
unpolished *a (person)* grossolano, rozzo; *(surface)* grezzo, non lucidato
unpolluted *a* incontaminato
unpopular *a* non popolare, impopolare, non gradito; **–ity** *n* impopolarità
unpracticed *a* inesperto
unprecedented *a* senza precedenti, inaudito
unprejudiced *a* spregiudicato, senza pregiudizi, imparziale
unpremeditated *a* impremeditato
unprepared *a* impreparato
unprepossessing *a* poco attraente
unpresentable *a* impresentabile
unpresuming *a* senza presunzione
unpretentious *a* senza pretese
unpreventable inevitabile
unprincipled *a* immorale, senza principi
unprintable *a* inatto alla stampa, non pubblicabile

unproductive *a* improduttivo
unprofitable *a* inutile, senza profitto, non vantaggioso
unprogressive *a* conservatore, antiprogressivo
unpromising *a* non promettente
unprompted *a* spontaneo, senza suggerimento
unpronounceable *a* impronunziabile
unpropitious *a* impropizio, sfavorevole
unprotected *a* senza protezione, improtetto
unprovable *a* indimostrabile, improvabile
unproved *a* indimostrato, improvato
unprovided *a* sprovvisto
unprovoked *a* non provocato, senza provocazione
unpublished *a* inedito
unpunished *a* impunito
unqualified *a* incompetente; senza riserva; *(law)* senza titoli; *(official)* non autorizzato
unquenchable *a* inestinguibile, insaziabile, indomabile
unquestionable *a* indiscutibile
unquestioned *a* incontestato; non interrogato
unquestioning *a* indiscusso, assoluto
unravel *vt* sbrogliare, dipanare, sfilacciare
unraveled *a* sciolto, dipanato
unread *a (not)* non letto; *(uneducated)* ignorante, incolto; **–able** *a* illeggibile
unreal *a* irreale
unreasonable *a* irragionevole
unreasoning *a* irragionevole
unreciprocated *a* non contraccambiato
unrecognizable *a* irriconoscibile
unrecognized *a* sconosciuto, misconosciuto
unreconcilable *a* inconciliabile
unreconciled *a* inconciliato
unrecorded *a* dimenticato; non registrato
unrectified *a* non rettificato
unredeemed *a* irredento, non riscattato; non ammortizzato; non rimborsato
unredressed *a* non riparato
unreel *vt* svolgere, sgomitolare; — *vi* svolgersi, sgomitolarsi
unreformed *a* non corretto, non riformato
unrefined *a* crudo, grezzo, non raffinato; rozzo
unrefuted *a* irrefutato
unrehearsed *a* improvvisato
unrelated *a* senza rapporti, non imparentato
unrelenting *a* inesorabile, inflessibile
unreliability *n* inattendibilità
unreliable *a* inattendibile; instabile
unremitting *a* assiduo, incessante, senza tregua
unremunerative *a* infruttifero, non rimunerativo
unrepealed *a* non revocato
unrepentant *a* impenitente, incorreggibile
unrepresentative *a* non rappresentativo
unrequited *a* non ricambiato, non corrisposto
unreserved *a* schietto, non riservato; illimitato
unresponsible irresponsabile
unresponsive *a* insensibile, impassibile
unrest *n* inquietudine *f*; sedizione
unrestrained *a* sfrenato, irrepresso
unrestricted *a* illimitato, senza restrizione
unrevenged *a* invendicato
unrewarded *a* irretribuito, senza ricompensa
unrighteous *a* malvagio, iniquo
unripe *a* acerbo, immaturo
unrivaled *a* impareggiabile, senza rivale
unroll *vt* svolgere; — *vi* svolgersi
unromantic *a* non romantico
unruffled *a* calmo, liscio; non increspato
unruled *a* senza righe
unruliness *n* indisciplina
unruly *a* indisciplinato
unsaddle *vt* dissellare, disarcionare
unsafe *a* malsicuro, pericoloso
unsaid *a* non detto
unsalable *a* invendibile
unsalted *a* non salato
unsanctioned *a* non sanzionato
unsanitary *a* insalubre, antigienico
unsatiable *a* insaziabile
unsatisfactory *a* non soddisfacente
unsatisfied *a* insoddisfatto
unsatisfying *a* insoddisfacente
unscathed *a* illeso, incolume
unschooled *a* inesperto, non istruito
unscientific *a* non scientifico
unscrew *vt* svitare
unscrupulous *a* senza scrupoli
unseal *vt* togliere i sigilli da; aprire, dissigillare; **–ed** *a* aperto, non sigillato
unseasonable *a* inopportuno, intempestivo; fuori stagione
unseasoned *a* non stagionato; *(food)* non condito; *(unaccustomed)* non abituato
unseat *vt* deporre; *(horse)* disarcionare; *(pol)* silurare *(fig)*
unseeing *a* non veggente, cieco
unseemliness *a* sconvenienza, indecenza
unseemly *a* sconveniente
unseen *a* invisibile; non visto
unselfish *a* altruista, non egoista; **–ly** *adv* disinteressatamente; **–ness** *n* altruismo, disinteresse *m*
unserviceable *a* inservibile, fuori uso
unsettle *vt* sconvolgere, turbare, disorganizzare
unsettled *a* incerto, disordinato; squilibrato; inabitato; — **accounts** conti pendenti, conti non saldati
unshakeable *a* fermo, irremovibile
unshaken *a* fermo, saldo; imperturbato, imperterrito
unshapely *a* informe, deforme, sgraziato
unshaven *a* non sbarbato
unsheathe *vt* sfoderare, sguainare
unsheltered *a* improtetto, non riparato
unshoe *vt (horse)* togliere i ferri a
unshrinkable *a* irrestringibile
unsightly *a* brutto, sgradevole, deforme
unsigned *a* non firmato, senza firma
unsinkable *a* inaffondabile, non sommergibile
unskillful *a* imperito, inesperto, malaccorto
unskilled *a* inesperto; non specializzato
unsociable *a* insocievole
unsoiled *a* puro, non sporcato, pulito
unsold *a* invenduto

unsolicited *a* non sollecitato, non richiesto
unsolicitous *a* non preoccupato, incurante
unsolved *a* insoluto
unsophisticated *a* semplice
unsought *a* non richiesto
unsound *a* difettoso; errato; malsicuro, debole; **–ness** *n* instabilità; insalubrità; **–ly** *adv* instabilmente, male; non sanamente
unsounded *a* non sondato
unsparing *a* prodigo; inesorabile
unspeakable *a* indicibile; orribile
unspecified *a* non specificato
unspoiled *a* non rovinato, non guasto; *(child)* ben allevato
unspoken *a* non detto, taciuto
unsportsmanlike *a* antisportivo
unstable *a* instabile
unstained *a (character)* immacolato, senza macchia; non dipinto
unstamped *a* non affrancato
unstarched *a* non inamidato
unstated *a* non dichiarato
unsteadiness *n* instabilità
unsteady *a* instabile
unstinted *a* copioso, abbondante
unstrap *vt* sfasciare, slegare
unstressed *a* atono, senza accento
unstring *vt* slegare, sfilare; *(nerves)* snervare
unstrung *a (mus)* senza corde; snervato
unstudied *a* naturale, non sforzato
unsubdued *a* indomato, non sottomesso, indomito
unsubstantial *a* poco sostanziale, poco solido
unsubstantiated *a* non confermato
unsuccessful *a* infruttuoso, senza successo, vano; **–ly** *adv* infruttuosamente, senza successo
unsuitable *a* inadatto, non appropriato, intempestivo
unsuited *a* inadatto, inadeguato
unsullied *a* immacolato, senza macchia, non sporcato
unsung *a* non celebrato
unsupported *a* non sostenuto, non confermato
unsure *a* malsicuro, incerto, pericolante
unsurmountable *a* insormontabile
unsurpassable *a* insorpassabile
unsurpassed *a* insuperato
unsusceptible *a* non suscettibile
unsuspected *a* insospettato
unsuspecting *a* senza sospetto
unsuspicious *a* non sospettoso
unswayed *a* non influenzato
unsweetened *a* non addolcito
unswerving *a* non deviante, fermo, irremovibile
unsymmetrical *a* asimmetrico
unsympathetic *a* non simpatico; ostico; incompassionevole; **–ally** *adv* ostilmente; senza simpatia
unsystematic *a* senza metodo, non sistematico
untainted *a* incorrotto, non guasto
untalented *a* senza talento
untamable *a* indomabile
untamed *a* indomito, non addomesticato
untangle *vt* dipanare, sbrogliare
untapped *a* non utilizzato
untarnished *a* non macchiato, puro; *(moral)* senza macchia
untenable *a* insostenibile
untenanted *a* sfitto, senza inquilini
untended *a* incustodito
untested *a* non collaudato
unthinkable *a* impensabile
unthinking *a* sventato, spensierato
unthought-of impensato
untidiness *n* disordine *m*
untidy *a* disordinato
untie *vt* sciogliere, slegare
until *prep* fino a; — *conj* finchè, finchè non; fino a quando
untillable *a* non coltivabile
untilled *a* non coltivato
untimeliness *n* intempestività
untimely *a* prematuro; inopportuno
untiring *a* indefesso, instancabile
untold *a* non detto; incalcolabile, inesprimibile
untouchable *a* intoccabile, impalpabile
untouched *a* intatto, intoccato
untrained *a* inesperto, non esercitato, non allenato
untrammeled *a* senza impacci, non inceppato
untranslatable *a* intraducibile
untraveled *a (person)* che non ha viaggiato molto; *(road)* non percorso, infrequentato
untried *a* non provato, intentato; non processato
untrimmed *a* disadorno, non guarnito; intonso
untrodden *a* non frequentato
untroubled *a* imperturbato, sereno
untrue *a* mendace, falso; *(faithless)* infedele
untrustworthy *a* mendace, indegno di fede
untruth *n* bugia, menzogna, falsità; **–ful** *a* bugiardo; **–fully** *adv* falsamente; **–fulness** *n* falsità
unturned *a* non girato, non voltato
untutored *a* ignorante, senza istruzione
unusable *a* inusabile, fuori uso
unused *a* non abituato
unusual *a* insolito; **–ness** *n* stranezza, straordinarietà; **–ly** *adv* straordinariamente, insolitamente
unvanquished *a* invitto
unvaried *a* invariato
unvarnished *a* non verniciato; *(fig)* naturale, schietto
unvarying *a* invariabile
unveil *vt* svelare; rivelare; **–ing** *n* scoprimento, inaugurazione
unverifiable *a* non verificabile
unverified *a* non verificato
unversed *a* inabile, inesperto
unvoiced *a* inespresso, non pronunciato; *(gram)* muto
unwanted *a* non richiesto, indesiderato
unwarranted *a* ingiustificato; *(com)* senza garanzia, gratuito
unwary *a* sventato, imprudente
unwavering *a* irremovibile, incrollabile
unweakened *a* non indebolito
unwearing *a* instancabile
unwelcome *a* sgradito

unwell *a* indisposto
unwholesome *a* malsano, nocivo
unwieldy *a* ingombrante, poco maneggevole; *(clumsy)* goffo
unwilling *a* restio, maldisposto, riluttante; **–ly** *adv* malvolentieri
unwind *vt* svolgere, srotolare; — *vi* srotolarsi, svolgersi
unwise *a* imprudente
unwitnessed *n* senza testimoni
unwitting *a* inconsapevole, inconscio; **–ly** *adv* inconsapevolmente
unwonted *a* non abituato
unworkable *a* non lavorabile, inattuabile
unworked *a* non lavorato, incoltivato
unworldly *a* non mondano, spirituale
unworthiness *n* indegnità
unworthy *a* indegno
unwounded *a* illeso
unwrap *vt* aprire, districare, togliere da un involucro
unwrapped *a* sfasciato, non involto
unwrinkled *a* liscio, spianato, senza grinze
unwritten *a* tradizionale, non scritto
unyielding *a* inflessibile, rigido
unyoke *vt* togliere il giogo a
up *n* aumento; **–s and downs** alti e bassi; — *a* in su; montante, salente; scaduto; in piedi; *(sport)* in vantaggio; — *prep* su; su per, verso l'alto di; — **to** fino a
up *vt* mettere su, alzare; — *vi* alzarsi; **be — to** *(coll)* essere capace di, essere in grado di; **bring —** *(child)* educare, allevare; **make —** inventare; *(peace)* rapacificarsi; *(cosmetics)* truccarsi; **speak —** *(openly)* parlare chiaro; *(loudly)* parlare ad alta voce; **walk — and down** camminare su e giù
upbraid *vt* rimproverare
upbringing *n* allevamento, educazione
upheaval *n* sollevamento, tumulto, confusione
uphill *adv* in salita, in su; — *a* montante, difficile
uphold *vt* sostenere, sollevare; **–er** *n* sostenitore *m*
upholster *vt* tappezzare, imbottire; **–y** *n* tappezzeria; **–er** *n* tappezziere *m*
upkeep *n* mantenimento
upland *n* altipiano
uplift *n* edificazione; sollevazione; **–ed** *a* sollevato, elevato, edificato; — *vt* elevare, edificare
uplifting *a* edificante
upon *prep&adv* su, sopra
upper *a* superiore, più in alto; — **case** maiuscole *fpl*; **–cut** *n (boxing)* colpo all' insù; — **hand** superiorità, vantaggio
upper-case *a* maiuscolo
upper-class *a* di classe alta
uppermost *a* superiore, il più alto; — *adv* su, sopra, in alto, al disopra di tutti
upright *a* diritto; onesto
uprising *n* insurrezione
uproar *n* tumulto; **–ious** *a* tumultuoso
uproot *vt* sradicare, estirpare
upset *vt* sconvolgere, rovesciare, agitare; — *vi* capovolgersi; turbarsi; — *a* rovesciato; — *n* sconvolgimento
upshot *n* esito, conclusione
upside-down *a* disordinato
upstairs *adv* sopra, su; — *a* disopra; — *n* piano superiore
upstanding *a* diritto, eretto, onorabile
upstart *n* villano rifatto, nuovo ricco
upstream *adv* a monte
up-to-date *a* aggiornato
upturn *vt* volgere in su; **–ed** *a* volto in su
upward *a&adv* in su, in alto
uranium *n* uranio
urban *a* urbano; **–ity** urbanità
urbane *a* cortese
urchin *n* monello
urea *n* urea
uremia *n* uremia
uremic *a* uremico
ureter *n* uretere *m*
urge *vt* esortare, pregare; — *n* impulso, impeto
urgency *n* urgenza; bisogno
urgent *a* urgente
urging *n* sollecitazione
uric *a* urico
urinal *n* orinale *m*, orinatoio; **–ysis** *n* analisi delle urine
urinate *vi* orinare
urine *n* orina
urn *n* urna; **coffee —** caffettiera
us *pron* noi; ci
usable *a* servibile
usage *n* usanza, uso
use *n* uso, impiego; **–fulness** *n* utilità; **be of —** essere utile; **make — of** far uso di; **What's the —?** A che serve? **–r** *n* utente *m*, chi usa; **–ful** *a* utile; **–less** *a* inutile
use *vt* usare, adoperare, utilizzare; trattare
used *a* usato; abituato; **be — to** essere abituato a; **get — to** abituarsi a; — **up** esaurito, esausto, consumato
usher *n* usciere, portiere *m*; *(theat)* accompagnatore *m*; — *vt* scortare; — **in** annunciare
USSR, Union of Soviet Socialist Republics Unione Repubbliche Sovietiche Socialiste
usual *a* solito, comune; **as —** come al solito; **—ly** *adv* ordinariamente, di solito
usurp *vt* usurpare; **–er** *n* usurpatore *m*, usurpatrice *f*
usurpation *n* usurpazione
usury *n* usura
utensil *n* utensile *m*
uterus *n* utero
utilitarian *a* utilitario
utility *n* utilità; **public —** servizio di pubblica utilità
utilization *n* utilizzazione
utilize *vt* utilizzare
utmost *a* sommo, estremo; — *n* massimo
utter *a* estremo, totale; — *vt* dire, proferire
utterance *n* espressione
utterly *adv* assolutamente, completamente
uvula *n* ugola

V

vacancy *n* posto libero, vacanza, spazio libero; stanza (*or* appartamento) da affittare
vacant *a* vuoto, libero; *(person)* distratto
vacate *vt* sgombrare, lasciar libero
vacation *n* vacanze, ferie *fpl*
vaccinate *vt* vaccinare
vaccination *n* vaccinazione
vaccine *n* vaccino
vacillate *vi* vacillare
vacillation *n* vacillazione
vacuum *n* vuoto; — **cleaner** aspirapolvere *m*; — **tube** *(elec)* valvola termoionica; — *vt* pulire con l'aspirapolvere
vagabond *a&n* vagabondo
vagary *n* capriccio
vagina *n (anat)* vagina
vagrancy *n* vagabondaggio
vagrant *n&a* vagabondo
vague *a* vago, incerto; **-ly** *adv* vagamente; **-ness** *n* vaghezza
vain *a* vano; vanitoso; **in** — invano; **-ness** — *n* vanità; inutilità
vainglorious *a* vanitoso, vanaglorioso
vainglory *n* vanagloria
valedictorian *n (school)* oratore che pronuncia il commiato
valedictory *n* discorso di commiato — *a* di commiato
valence *n (chem)* valenza
valet *n* valletto
valiant *a* prode, valoroso; **-ly** *adv* valorosamente
valid *a* valido; **-ation** *n* convalidazione
validate *vt* convalidare
validity *n* validità
valise *n* valigia
valley *n* valle *f*, vallata
valor *n* valore *m*; **-ous** *a* valoroso; **-ously** *adv* valorosamente
valuable *a* costoso, prezioso, valutabile; **-s** *npl* preziosi *mpl*
valuation *n* stima, valutazione
value *n* valore *m*; **of no** — senza valore; **face** — valore nominale; **-d** *a* stimato, valutato; **-less** *a* senza valore; — *vt* valutare, stimare
valve *n* valvola; **exhaust** — valvola di scappamento; **safety** — valvola di sicurezza
valvular *a* valvolare
vamp *n (shoe)* tomaia; *(flirt)* donna fatale, civetta; *(mus)* improvvisazione; — *vt* mettere la tomaia; *(patch)* rappezzare; *(beguile)* adescare
vampire *n* vampiro
van *n* furgone *m*, carro; **-guard** avanguardia
vanadium *n* vanadio
Van Allen radiation belt zona radioattiva Van Allen
vandal *n* vandalo; **-ism** *n* vandalismo
Vandyke *n* pizzo a punta
vane *n* banderuola
vanilla *n* vaniglia; — **bean** chicco di vaniglia
vanish *vi* svanire, sparire; **-ed** *a* svanito, sparito, scomparso
vanishing *n* sparizione, scomparsa; — *a* che sparisce, evanescente; — **cream** crema evanescente (*or* volatile); — **point** punto all'infinito
vanity *n* vanità; *(furniture)* pettiniera; — **case** portacipria
vanquish *vt* vincere, sopraffare; **-ed** *a* vinto, conquistato; **-er** *n* vincitore *m*
vantage *n* vantaggio; — **point** punto di vantaggio
vapid *a* insipido; **-ity** *n* insipidità; **-ness** *n* insipidezza
vapor *n* vapore *m*; **-ous** *a* vaporoso
vaporization *n* vaporizzazione
vaporize *vt* vaporizzare; — *vi* evaporizzare; **-r** *n* vaporizzatore *m*
variability *n* variabilità
variable *a* variabile
variably *adv* variabilmente
variance *n* disaccordo; divergenza; **at** — **with** in disaccordo con
variant *n* variante *f*; — *a* vario, variante, variabile
variation *n* variazione; modifica
varicose *a* varicoso; — **vein** vena varicosa
varied *a* vario, assortito, variato
variegate *vt* variare
variety *n* varietà
various *a* vario, diverso
varnish *n* vernice *f*; — *vt* verniciare; **-ing** *n* verniciatura
vary *vt&i* variare; **-ing** *a* variante
vascular *a* vascolare
vase *n* vaso
vaseline *n* vaselina
vasomotor *a (anat)* vasomotore
vassal *n* vassallo
vast *a* immenso, vasto; **-ness** *n* vastita, immensità; **-ly** *adv* vastamente
vat *n* tino
Vatican *n* Vaticano; — **City** Città del Vaticano
vaudeville *n* operetta
vault *n* salto; *(arch)* volta; *(bank)* camera blindata; *(burial)* tomba; *(cellar)* sotterraneo, cantina; **-ing** *n* volteggio; — *vi (jump)* volteggiare; — *vt (arch)* costruire a volta
vaunt *vt* vantare; — *n* vanto; **-ing** *n* millanteria
veal *n* vitello; — **cutlet** cotoletta di vitello
vedette *n (mil)* vedetta
veer *n* virata, — *vi* virare, cambiare direzione; — *vt* voltare
vegetable *n* legume *m*, verdura; — *a* vegetale
vegetarian *a&n* vegetariano; **-ism** *n* vegetarianismo
vegetate *vi* vegetare
vegetation *n* vegetazione
vehemence *n* veemenza
vehement *a* veemente; **-ly** *adv* veementemente
vehicle *n* veicolo
vehicular *a* di veicolo
veil *n* velo; **-ed** *a* velato; — *vt* velare; nascondere
vein *n* vena; umore *m*; **-ing** *n* venatura;

–ed *a* venato
veiny *a* venoso
vellum *n* pergamena, cartapecora
velocipede *n* velocipede *m*
velocity *n* velocità
velum *n (anat)* velo
velvet *n* velluto; — *a* di velluto, vellutato
velveteen *n* velluto di cotone
venal *a* venale; **–ity** *n* venalità, **–ly** *adv* venalmente
vend *vt* vendere
vending machine distributore automatico, distributrice a gettone
vendor *n* venditore *m*, venditrice *f*
veneer *n (furniture)* impiallacciatura; — *vt* impiallacciare
venerability *n* venerabilità
venerable *a* venerabile
venerably *adv* venerabilmente
venerate *vt* venerare
veneration *n* venerazione
venereal *a* venereo; — **disease** malattia venerea
Venetian *n&a* veneziano; — **blinds** persiane, gelosie *fpl*
vengeance *n* vendetta; **to wreak** — vendicarsi
vengeful *a* vendicativo; **–ly** *adv* vendicativamente
venial *a* veniale; — **sin** peccato veniale; **–ity** *n* venialità
Venice Venezia
venison *n* carne di cervo
venom *n* veleno; **–ous** *a* velenoso; *(person)* maldicente, malevolo
vent *n* apertura, sfogo; **to give** — **to** dar sfogo a; — *vt* sfogare
ventilate *vt* ventilare
ventilation *n* ventilazione
ventilator *n* ventilatore *m*
ventral *a* ventrale
ventricle *n* ventricolo
ventriloquism *n* ventriloquio
ventriloquist *n* ventriloquo
venture *n* impresa; **–some** *a* avventuroso; — *vt&i* tentare, azzardare, avventurarsi, rischiare
venue *n (law)* sede *f*
veracious *a* verace
veracity *n* veracità
verb *n* verbo
verbal *a* verbale; — **ly** *adv* oralmente
verbatim *a* testuale; — *adv* testualmente
verbose *a* verboso
verbosity *n* verbosità
verdant *a* verdeggiante
verdict *n* verdetto
verdigris *n* verderame *m*
verdure *n* verzura
verge *n* orlo; limite *m*; **on the** — **of** sull'orlo di; — *vi* propendere, tendere; — **on** essere vicino a
verger *n* sagrestano
verifiable *a* verificabile
verification *n* verifica
verify *vt* verificare
verisimilitude *n* verosimiglianza
veritable *a* vero
verity *n* verità
vermiform *a* vermiforme; — **appendix** appendice vermiforme
vermilion *n&a* vermiglione *m*
vermin *npl* insetti e animali nocivi; **–ous** *a* verminoso
vermouth *n* vermut *m*
vernacular *a&n* volgare *m*
vernal *a* primaverile; — **equinox** equinozio di primavera
versatile *a* versatile
versatility *n* versatilità
verse *n* verso, strofa; poesia; **–d** *a* versato
versifier *n* versificatore *m*
versify *vt* versificare
version *n* versione
versus *prep* contro
vertebra *n (anat)* vertebra
vertebral *a* vertebrale
vertebrate *n&a* vertebrato
vertex *n* vertice *m*
vertical *a* verticale
vertiginous *a* vertiginoso
vertigo *n (med)* vertigine *f*
verve *n* entusiasmo, vigore *m*, brio
very *adv* molto; — *a* stesso, vero; **at the** — **last** proprio all'ultimo
vesicle *n* vescichetta, pustola
vespers *npl* vespri *mpl*
vessel *n* nave *f*, vascello; *(anat)* vaso; *(container)* recipiente *m*
vest *n* gilè *m*, panciotto
vest *vt* investire, conferire
vestibule *n* vestibolo
vestige *n* traccia
vestigial *a* rudimentale
vest-pocket *a* tascabile
vestment *n (eccl)* paramento sacerdotale
vestry *n (eccl)* sagrestia
Vesuvius *n* Vesuvio
veteran *n&a* veterano
veterinary *n&a* veterinario
veto *n* veto; — *vt* porre il veto a
vex *vt* irritare; **–ation** *n* vessazione dispiacere *m*; **–atious** *a* fastidioso, irritante; **–ed** *a* vessato, irritato; seccato; contrariato; **–ing** *a* vessante, irritante, contrariante
via *prep* via, per, attraverso
viability *n* viabilità
viable *a* viabile
viaduct *a* viadotto
vial *n* fiala
viand *n* vivanda, cibo
vibrant *a* vibrante
vibrate *vi* vibrare, oscillare; — *vt* far vibrare
vibration *n* vibrazione
vibrator *n* vibratore *m*
vicar *n* vicario; **–age** *n* vicariato, canonica
vicarious *a* indiretto; **–ly** *adv* indirettamente
vice *n* vizio, difetto; depravazione
viceroy *n* vicerè *m*
vice-admiral *n* viceammiraglio
vice-consul *n* viceconsole *m*
vice-president *n* vicepresidente *m*
vicinity *n* vicinanza; **in the** — **of** nei dintorni di
vicious *a* violento; cattivo, maligno, vizioso; **–ness** viziosità; — **circle** circolo vizioso
vicissitude *n* vicenda, vicissitudine *f*
victim *n* vittima; **–ize** *vt* far vittima di

victor *n* vincitore *m*; **–y** *n* vittoria; **–ious** *a* vittorioso
victuals *npl* vettovaglie *fpl*
vicuña *n* vigogna
video *n* televisione; — *a* televisivo
vie *vi* rivaleggiare, gareggiare
Vienna Vienna
Viennese *a&n* Viennese
view *n* veduta, panorama, vista; opinione *f*; **–er** *n* spettatore *m*, spettatrice *f*; **–finder** *n* mirino; **–point** *n* punto di vista; **bird's-eye** — veduta a volo d'uccello; **in** — **of** in vista di; **point of** — punto di vista; — *vt* guardare; considerare
vigil *n* vigilia, veglia; **keep a** — vegliare
vigilance *n* vigilanza; *(med)* insonnia
vigilant *a* vigilante; **–ly** *adv* vigilmente, vigilatamente
vignette *n* vignetta
vigor *n* vigore *m*
vigorous *a* vigoroso; **–ly** *adv* vigorosamente; **–ness** *n* vigorosità
viking *n* vichingo, normanno
vile *a* vile, basso, disgustoso, abbietto; **–ness** *n* bassezza, viltà
vilification *n* vilipendio
vilifier *n* diffamatore *m*
vilify *vt* calunniare, diffamare
villa *n* villa
village *n* villaggio
villager *n* villico
villain *n* farabutto, mascalzone *m*; **–y** *n* infamia, malvagità; **–ous** *a* malvagio, vile, infame
vim *n* vigore *m*, forza
vincible *a* vincibile
vindicable *a* rivendicabile
vindicate *vt* giustificare, rivendicare
vindication *n* rivendicazione
vindicator *n* rivendicatore *m*
vindictive *a* vendicativo; **–ly** *adv* vendicativamente; **–ness** *n* carattere vendicativo
vine *n* pianta rampicante; *(grape)* vite *f*
vinegar *n* aceto
vineyard *n* vigneto, vigna
vintage *n* vendemmia; anno di raccolto di vino; vini *mpl*
vintery *n* vinaio
vinyl *n* vinile *m*; — *a* vinilico
viola *n* viola
violable *a* violabile
violate *vt* violare, violentare, rapire
violation *n* violazione, infrazione
violator *n* violatore, trasgressore *m*
violence *n* violenza
violent *a* violento; **–ly** *adv* violentemente
violet *n* viola mammola, violetta; — *a* violetto
violin *n* violino
violinist *n* violinista *m&f*
viper *n* vipera; **–ous** *a* viperino
virago *n* virago *f*
virgin *a&n* vergine *f*; **–al** *a* verginale; **–ity** *n* verginità
virile *a* maschio, virile
virility *n* virilità
virology *n* virologia
virtual *a* virtuale; **–ly** *adv* virtualmente
virtue *n* virtù *f*; castità; rettitudine *f*; **by** — **of** in virtù di
virtuosity *n* virtuosità
virtuoso *n* virtuoso
virtuous *a* virtuoso
virulence *n* virulenza
virulent *a* virulento
virus *n* virus *m*
visa *n* visto; — *vt* vidimare
visage *n* viso, aspetto
vis-a-vis *adv* a faccia a faccia; — *prep* dirimpetto
viscera *npl (anat)* visceri *mpl*
visceral *a* viscerale
viscid *a* viscido
viscosity *n* viscosità
viscount *n* visconte *m*
viscountess *n* viscontessa
viscous *a* viscoso, vischioso
vise *n* morsetto, morsa
visé *n* visto
visibility *n* visibilità
visible *a* visibile
visibly *adv* visibilmente
vision *n* apparizione, visione; *(sense)* vista; **–ary** *a&n* visionario
visit *vt* visitare; *(inflict)* affliggere, infliggere; — *n* visita; **–ation** *n* visita ufficiale; *(eccl)* visitazione; castigo divino; **–ing** *a* da visita
visitor *n* visitatore *m*, visitatrice *f*
visor *n* visiera
vista *n* vista, prospettiva; visuale *f*
visual *a* visivo
visualize *vt* figurarsi, immaginare
vital *a* vitale, — **statistics** statistiche anagrafiche; **–ly** *adv* vitalmente
vitalism *n* vitalismo
vitality *n* vitalità
vitals *npl* organi vitali
vitamin *n* vitamina
vitiate *vt* corrompere, viziare
vitreous *a* vitreo
vitrify *vt* vetrificare; — *vi* vetrificarsi
vitriol *n* vetriolo; **–ic** *a* vetriolico
vituperation *n* vituperio, vituperazione, insulto
vituperative *a* vituperativo
vivacious *a* vivace, brioso
vivacity *n* vivacità, brio
vivid *a* vivido, vivo; **–ly** *adv* vividamente; **–ness** *n* vividezza
vivify *vt* vivificare
viviparous *a* viviparo
vivisect *vt* vivisezionare; **–ion** *n* vivisezione
vixen *n* volpe femmina; *(woman)* megera; **–ish** *a* bisbetico
viz *adv* cioè, ossia, vale a dire
vocabulary *n* vocabolario
vocal *a* vocale; loquace; **–ist** *n* cantante, vocalista *m&f*; — **cords** corde vocali
vocalization *n* vocalizzazione
vocalize *vt&i* vocalizzare
vocation *n* vocazione, professione; **–al** professionale, di mestiere; **–al school** scuola d'arti e mestieri
vociferous *a* clamoroso, rumoroso; **–ly** *adv* clamorosamente, rumorosamente
vodka *n* vodka
vogue *n* moda, voga; **in** — di moda, in voga
voice *n* voce; **–less** *a* muto, senza voce;

— *vt* esprimere; **–d** *a* espresso, nominato; sonoro
void *n&a* vuoto; — *vt* annullare; — **of** privo di
voidance *n* annullamento
volatile *a* incostante, volatile
volatility *n* volatilità
volatilize *vt* volatilizzare
volcanic *a* vulcanico
volcano *n* vulcano
volition *n* volere *m*, volontà
volley *n* scarica, raffica; **–ball** *n* pallarete, palla a volo; — *vt* lanciare; *(sport)* colpire al volo; *(mil)* sparare a salve
volt *n* volta; **–age** *n* voltaggio; **–ameter** *m* voltametro
volubility *n* volubilità
voluble *a* loquace, volubile
volume *n* volume *m*; massa
volumetric *a* volumetrico
voluminous *a* voluminoso; **–ly** *adv* voluminosamente; **–ness** *n* voluminosità
voluntarily *a* spontaneamente
voluntary *a* volontario
volunteer *n* volontario; — *vt* offrire; — *vi* arruolarsi; offrirsi
voluptuous *a* voluttuoso; **–ness** *n* sensualità
vomit *vt&i* vomitare; **–ing** *n* vomito
voracious *a* vorace; **–ly** *adv* voracemente; **–ness** *n* voracità
voracity *n* voracità
vortex *n* turbine, vortice *m*, gorgo
votary *n* devoto, fedele *m&f*
vote *n* voto; **put to a —** mettere a voto; **–r** *n* elettore *m*, votante *m&f*; — *vt&i* votare
voting *n* votazione, scrutinio; — *a* votante
votive *a* votivo
vouch (for) *vi* rispondere di, garantire per
voucher *n* pezza giustificativa, scontrino
vow *n* voto; — *vt* giurare, far voto di
vowel *n* vocale *f*
voyage *n* viaggio di mare; **–r** *n* viaggiatore *m*; — *vi* navigare
vulcanite *n* vulcanite *f*
vulcanization *n* vulcanizzazione
vulcanize *vt* vulcanizzare
vulgar *a* volgare, triviale, **–ism** *n* volgarità, volgarismo; espressione volgare; **–ity** *n* volgarità; **–ization** *n* volgarizzazione; **–ize** *vt* volgarizzare; **–ly** *adv* volgarmente
Vulgate *n* Vulgata
vulnerability *n* vulnerabilità
vulnerable *a* vulnerabile
vulture *n* avvoltoio
vying *a* in concorrenza

W

wadding *n* ovatta, bambagia
waddle *vi* camminare dondolando, barcollare; — *n* dondolio
wade *vt&i* guadare; — **across** passare a guado
wading *n* guado
wafer cialda; *(eccl)* ostia
waffle *n* cialda; — **iron** *n* ferro per cialde
waft *vt* sollevare, trasportare per aria; spargere; — *vi* levarsi, sollevarsi; fluttuare
wag *n* *(tail)* scorinzolio; scuotimento; *(person)* buontempone *m*; — *vt* scuotere; — *vi* dimenarsi; — **the tail** scodinzolare
wage *n* paga, salario; — **earner** salariato; — *vt* intraprendere; — **war** fare la guerra
wager *n* scommessa; — *vt* scommettere
waggish *a* scherzevole
wagon *n* carro, furgone *m*
waif *n* trovatello
wail *vi* lamentarsi; — *n* lamento, gemito
wainscoting *n* zoccolo di parete
waist *n* cintura; *(blouse)* camicetta; **–line** *n* vita
wait *vt&i* aspettare, attendere; — *n* attesa; **lie in —** stare in agguato, appostarsi
waiter *n* cameriere *m*; **head–** *n* capocameriere *m*
waiting *n* attesa; — **game** temporeggiamento; — **list** prenotazione; — *a* d'aspetto; — **room** anticamera, camera d'aspetto; *(rail)* sala d'aspetto
waitress *n* cameriera
waive *vt* rinunciare a, abbandonare
waiver *n* rinuncia
wake *n* *(death)* veglia funebre; *(naut)* scia; **in the — of** a conseguenza di; — *vi* svegliarsi; — *vt* svegliare
wakeful *a* sveglio; vigile; insonne; **–ness** *n* vigilanza; insonnia
waken *vi* svegliarsi; — *vt* svegliare
Wales Galles
walk *n* passeggiata, camminata; *(path)* sentiero; *(gait)* andatura; **–away** *n* facile vittoria; **–out** *n* *(coll)* sciopero; — *vi* camminare, passeggiare; — *vt* percorrere; **–ing** *a* passeggiante, camminante
walker *n* *(child's)* andarino; camminatore *m*, pedone *m&f*
walkie-talkie *n* trasmittente-ricevente portatile
walk-up *n* *(coll)* casa senza ascensore
wall *n* muro, parete *f*; **–board** *n* *(arch)* paratia, tramezza; **–eyed** *a* strabico; **–paper** *n* carta da parati; — **plug** presa di corrente; **drive to the —** mettere con le spalle al muro *(fig)*; **go to the —** andare contro il muro *(fig)*; — *vt* cingere di mura
wallet *n* portafogli *m*
wallop *vt* *(coll)* colpire violentemente
walloping *a* *(coll)* madornale
wallow *vi* avvoltolarsi
walnut *n* noce *f*
walrus *n* *(zool)* tricheco
waltz *n* valzer *m*; — *vi* ballare il valzer, valzare
wan *a* pallido, smunto
wand *n* verga, bacchetta
wander *vi* errare, vagare; **–er** *n* nomade *m*
wandering *n* vagabondaggio; — *a* errante, nomade

wanderlust *n* istinto nomade
wane *n* declino; — *vi* decrescere, declinare, decadere, calare
waning *a* decadente, declinante; *(moon)* calante
want *vt* volere, desiderare; mancare, aver bisogno di; — *n* desiderio; mancanza, bisogno; **–ing** *a* deficiente, mancante
wanted *a* ricercato
wanton *a* lascivo, immorale; ingiustificato; sfrenato, sconsiderato; **–ness** *n* licenza
war *n* guerra; **cold** — guerra fredda; **–fare** *n* guerra; **–like** *a* bellicoso; **–monger** *n* guerrafondaio; **–path** *n* spedizione militare; **–ship** *n* nave da guerra; **–time** *n* tempo di guerra; — *vi* fare la guerra, guerreggiare
warble *vt&i* gorgheggiare
ward *n* pupillo; *(care)* tutela; *(city)* rione, quartiere *m*; *(hospital)* corsia; — **off** respingere, schivare
warden *n* custode *m*; direttore di prigione
wardrobe *n* guardaroba; *(to wear)* vestiario; — **mistress** *(theat)* vestiarista; — **trunk** baule armadio
wardroom *n (naut)* quadrato degli ufficiali
warehouse *n* magazzino; **–man** *n* magazziniere *m*
wares *npl* mercanzia, merci *fpl*
warhead *n* spoletta esplosiva
warily *a* cautamente
wariness *n* cautela, precauzione
warm *a* caldo; caloroso; **be** — *(person)* aver caldo; *(weather)* fare caldo; **–hearted** *a* di buon cuore, affettuoso; **–ly** calorosamente; — *vt* riscaldare; — *vi* riscaldarsi
warm-blooded *a* dal sangue caldo
warming *n* riscaldamento; — **pan** scaldaletto
warmth *n* calore *m*
warn *vt* ammonire, avvertire
warning *n* avvertimento, preavviso; — *a* avvertente
warp *n (cloth)* ordito, trama; *(wood)* curvatura, inarcamento; *(fig)* deformazione; — *vi* curvarsi; deviarsi; — *vt* ordire; far curvare; *(fig)* stornare, pervertire, influenzare; **–ed** *a* ordito; incurvato; *(fig)* pervertito; influenzato
warrant *vt* giustificare; autorizzare; garantire; — *n* ordine *m*; autorizzazione, giustificazione; *(law)* mandato di cattura; — **officer** sottufficiale; **–ed** *a* certificato, garantito; giustificato
warranty *n* garanzia
warren *n* garenna
warring *a* in conflitto, avverso, ostile
warrior *n* guerriero
Warsaw Varsavia
wart *n* porro, verruca
wary *a* circospetto, cauto; **be** — **of** diffidare di, non fidarsi di
wash *n* lavatura; bucato; *(ship)* sciaquio, risucchio; **–bowl, –stand** *n* lavabo, lavandino; **–room** *n* stanza per lavarsi; gabinetto; **–tub** mastello, tinozza
wash *vt* lavare; — *vi* lavarsi; — **one's hands** lavarsi le mani
washable *a* lavabile
washed-out *a (tired)* sfinito, esausto; *(color)* sbiadito
washer *n (mech)* rosetta, rondella
washerwoman *n* lavandaia
washing *n* lavatura; *(laundry)* lavaggio, bucato; — **machine** macchina lavapanni, lavatrice *f*
washout *n* alluvione *f*, erosione; *(sl)* fiasco; *(school)* bocciato
washy *a* acquoso, bagnato; debole, fiacco
wasp *n* vespa; **–ish** irascibile, stizzoso; **–s' nest** vespaio
wastage *n* sciupio; consumo
waste *n* spreco, perdita; rifiuti *mpl;* sciupio, devastazione; regione incolta; — *a* di scarto, scartato; *(land)* incolto; — *vt* sprecare; sciupare; devastare; dissipare; — *vi* deperire, consumarsi; logorarsi; — **away** sciuparsi; — **of time** perdita di tempo; **–paper** *n* carta straccia; — **pipe** tubo di scarico; **–ed** *a* sciupato, perduto, mancato, sprecato
wastebasket *n* cestino dei rifiuti
wasteful *a* spendereccio, prodigo; **–ness** *n* prodigalità
wasting *n* dissipazione, sperpero
wastrel *n* sprecone *m*
watch *n* veglia; *(naut)* guardia; *(observance)* osservazione; *(care)* sorveglianza; *(timepiece)* orologio da polso; **–er** *n* sorvegliante *m&f*; — *vt&i (care for)* vigilare, sorvegliare; *(observe)* osservare; *(sit up)* vegliare; **–ful** *a* guardingo, cauto, circospetto; **–fulness** *n* vigilanza
watchdog *n* cane da guardia
watchmaker *n* orologiaio
watchman *n* guardiano
watchtower *n* torre d'osservazione
watchword *n* parola d'ordine
water *n* acqua; *(med)* urina; — **bug** insetto acquatico; — **color** acquerello; **–fall** *n* cascata; — **front** settore portuale; **–line** *n* linea d'acqua (*or* d'immersione; **–mark** *n* filigrana di carta; **–melon** *n* cocomero; — **power** energia idraulica; **–proof** *a* impermeabile; **–shed** *n* spartiacque *m*; **–spout** *n* tromba d'acqua; **–tight** *a* impermeabile; **–way** *n* canale navigabile; **–works** *npl* impianto idraulico
water *vt* annacquare; inumidire; *(com)* aumentare il capitale nominale; *(stock)* provvedere d'acqua; *(land)* innaffiare, irrigare; — *vi* rifornirsi d'acqua; *(eyes)* piangere; abbeverarsi; **–ed** *a* annacquato; abbeverato
water– *(in comp)* **—cooled** *a* raffreddato ad acqua; **—logged** *a* inzuppato d'acqua; **—repellent** *a* antiassorbente; **—soaked** *a* inzuppato d'acqua; **—waved** *a* ondulato all'acqua
watering *n (land)* irrigazione; *(stock)* abbeveraggio; rifornimento d'acqua; *(of eyes)* lagrimazione; — **can** innaffiatoio
watery *a* acquoso; annacquato
watt *n* watt *m*
wave *n* onda; *(hair)* ondulazione; *(gesture)* cenno, segno; — **length** *(rad, TV)* lunghezza d'onda; — *vt* ondulare; agitare, brandire; — *vi* ondeggiare; far cenno; **–d** *a* ondulato

wa... vi vacillare, esitare; ondeggiare; -ing a vacillante, esitante, indeciso, irresoluto; -ing n vacillazione
wavy a ondulato, ondeggiante, ondoso; *(line)* serpeggiante
wax n cera; *(ear)* cerume m; — **paper** carta cerata; **sealing** — ceralacca; — vt incerare; — vi divenire, crescere; -y a cereo
way n via, strada; mezzo; maniera, usanza; **all the** — lungo tutto il cammino; in tutti i modi, completamente; **be in the** — ingombrare, impedire; **by the** — a proposito; **by** — **of** via; a titolo di; **give** — cedere, accondiscendere; **give** — **to** lasciare il passo a; **have one's own** — fare a proprio modo; **lose one's** — smarrirsi; **make one's** — farsi largo *(coll)*; **make** — aprire il cammino *(coll)*; **on the** — per istrada, lungo il cammino; **out of the** — fuori strada, fuori mano; **right** — la via giusta; **under** — in marcia, in lavorazione; — **in** entrata; — **out** uscita
wayfarer n viaggiatore m
wayfaring a viaggiante
waylay vt appostare; tendere un agguato
wayside n bordo della strada; **leave by the** — lasciare per strada, lasciare indietro, abbandonare
wayward a ostinato; capriccioso; **-ness** n ostinatezza
we *pron* noi
weak a debole; leggero; fievole, infermo; **-ly** adv debolmente; **-ling** n debole m&f; **-ness** n debolezza, fievolezza, delicatezza
weaken vt indebolire; diluire; attenuare, affievolire; — vi indebolirsi; **-ing** n indebolimento
weak- *(in comp)* **—kneed** a cedevole, timido; debole di ginocchia; **—minded** a poco intelligente; **—sighted** a debole di vista
weakhearted a poco coraggioso
wealth n ricchezza; abbondanza; **-y** a ricco
wean vt slattare, svezzare, disabituare; — vi slattarsi; svezzarsi, disabituarsi
weapon n arma
wear vt portare; stancare; — vi logorarsi; *(last)* durare; **-able** a portabile, indossabile; — **away** consumare; — **out** consumare, logorare; — n uso; logorio; — **and tear** logorio
weariless a instancabile
wearily adv con fatica
weariness n stanchezza
wearing a da indossare; faticoso, esauriente; — **apparel** n indumenti mpl, vestiario
wearisome a faticoso, noioso, fastidioso
weary a stanco, esausto; noioso, pesante; — vt stancare, esaurire; — vi stancarsi
weasel n *(zool)* donnola
weather n tempo; — **bureau** centro meteorologico; **-man** n meteorologo; **-proof** a antintemperie; — **report** previsioni meteorologiche; — **vane** banderola; **-worn** a logorato dalle intemperie, — vi deteriorarsi alle intemperie; — vt esporre alle intemperie; resistere; — **the storm** sormontare gli ostacoli
weather-beaten a battuto dalle intemperie
weave vt tessere; ordire; intrecciare; — n tessitura
weaver n tessitore m
weaving n tessitura
web n tela, tessuto; rete f; *(spider)* ragnatela
webbed a palmato
webbing n trama, tessuto, ordito
web-footed a palmipede
wed vt sposare; — vi sposarsi
wedded a coniugale; sposato
wedding n matrimonio; nozze fpl; — **cake** torta nuziale; — **ring** anello nuziale
wedge n cuneo; — vt incuneare
wedlock n matrimonio, nozze fpl
Wednesday n mercoledì m
wee a minuscolo
weed n erbaccia; **-y** a pieno d'erbacce; — vt&i sarchiare; **—ing** n sarchiatura; **—er** n sarchiatore m; *(mech)* sarchiatrice f
weeds npl *(mourning)* gramaglie fpl
week n settimana; **-day** n giorno feriale; **-end** n fine di settimana; **a** — **from today** oggi a otto
weekly n&a settimanale m; — adv ogni settimana
weep vt&i piangere; **-y** a lagrimoso
weeping vt&i pianto; — a piangente; — **willow** salice piangente
weevil n *(zool)* punteruolo
weft n trama
weigh vt pesare; considerare, valutare; *(naut)* levare; — vi pesare, avere il peso di; aver importanza; — **down** opprimere; — **in** pesarsi; — **one's words** pesare le parole *(fig)*
weigh-in n *(sport)* pesaggio
weight n peso; influenza, importanza; **-iness** n importanza; **-lessness** n *(aesp)* agravitazione; **-y** a pesante, grave; potente; — vt caricare con peso; **gain** — ingrassare; **lose** — dimagrire
weir n chiusa, cateratta
weird a misterioso, strano, bizzarro, fantastico
welcome n accoglienza; — a benvenuto, gradito; — *interj* ben venuto!; **You're** — Non c'è di che, Prego; — vt dare il benvenuto a, fare buon'accoglienza a; gradire
weld vt saldare; **-er** n saldatore m; **-ing** n saldatura
welfare n benessere m; — **state** *(pol)* stato socialista; — **work** lavoro assistenziale
well n pozzo; *(stairs)* tromba di scale; — a buono, bene; sano; fortunato; — adv bene; **-born** a ben nato, di origine altolocata; **be** — star bene
well vi sgorgare
well- *(in comp)* **—advised** a prudente, saggio; **—balanced** a equilibrato; **—behaved** a cortese; **—being** n benessere m; **—bred** a costumato, beneducato; **—done** a benfatto; *(food)* ben cotto; **—earned** a ben meritato; **—educated** a colto; **—founded** a ben fondato; **—informed** a ben informato, istruito;

—**kept** *a* ben tenuto; —**known** *a* ben noto; —**mannered** *a* di buone maniere; —**meaning** *a* ben intenzionato, —**off** *a* agiato, benestante; —**read** *a* erudito; —**spent** *a* ben impiegato; —**suited** *a* adatto; —**timed** *a* opportuno; —**to-do** agiato, ricco
Welsh *n&a* gallese *m*
Welshman *n* gallese *m*
welt *n* bordo, orlo
welter *vi* avvoltolarsi; — *n* confusione
welterweight *n (sport)* peso medio-leggero
wen *n* gozzo
wench *n* popolana
west *n* ovest, occidente *m*; — *a* d'ovest; **–ern** *a* occidentale; **W- Indies** Indie occidentali
wet *a* bagnato, umido; *(paint)* fresco; — **blanket** guastafeste *m (fig)*; **–ness** umidità; — **nurse** balia; — *vt* bagnare
whack *vi (coll)* colpire; — *n (coll)* colpo; legnata, bastonata
whale *n* balena
whaling *n* pesca della balena; — **ship** baleniera
wharf *n* molo, scalo
what *pron* che, cosa, che cosa, ciò; quel che; — *a* che; — *adv* come, che; — *interj* che!? cosa!? **W- did you say?** Come? Che cosa hai detto? **W- is it?** Cos'è? Cosa c'è?
whatever *a* qualsiasi, qualunque; — *pron* qualsiasi cosa, qualunque cosa
whatsoever *pron* checchessia, qualunque cosa; — *a* qualunque, qualsiasi
wheat *n* frumento
wheedle *vt* adulare, vezzeggiare, ottenere con blandizie
wheedling *n* moine *fpl*
wheel *n* ruota; *(naut)* barra; *(auto)* volante *m*; — **chair** sedia a rotelle; — *vi* girare, voltarsi; — *vt* far rotare; trasportare su ruote
wheelbarrow *n* carriola
wheeling *n* rotazione, roteamento; **free-** *n* ruota libera
wheelwright *n* carraio
wheeze *n* respiro ansimante; — *vi* ansimare
wheezing *n* respirazione ansimante; — *a* ansimante, asmatico
wheezy *a* asmatico, ansimante
whelp *m* cucciolo; — *vi* partorire, sgravare
when *conj&adv* quando, qualora; **since** — da quando
whenever *conj* quando, ogni qualvolta che, qualora
where *adv&conj&pron* dove
whereabouts *n* ubicazione; — *adv* dove, in che posto
whereas *conj* stante che, siccome, poichè, mentre
whereat *conj* al che
whereby *adv* per cui, per mezzo del quale
wherefore *adv* perciò, onde, per la qual cosa
wherein *adv* dove
whereupon *conj* al che, dopo di che
wherever *conj* dovunque
wherewithal *n* soldi *mpl*; mezzi *mpl*
whet *vt (knife)* affilare; *(appetite)* stimolare
whether *conj* se, sia, sia che
whetstone *n* cote *f*
whey *n* siero di latte
which *pron* il quale, la quale, che, i quali *mpl*, le quali *fpl*; — *a* quale; — **way** per dove, dove
whichever *a* qualunque, qualsiasi; — *pron* chechessia
whiff *n* sbuffo, soffio
while *n* tempo; momento; — *conj* mentre, intanto che; — **away** trascorrere, passare; **a short — ago** poco fa; **be worth —** valere la pena; **in a little —** tra poco; **once in a —** una volta tanto
whim *n* capriccio
whimper *n* piagnucolio, piagnisteo, lagna; **–er** *n* piagnone, piagnucolone *m*; **–ing** *n* piagnucolio, pianisteo; **–ing** *a* piagnucolante; — *vi* piagnucolare, lagnarsi
whimsical *a* bizzarro, capriccioso
whimsy *n* ubbia, capriccio
whine *vi* piagnucolare; — *n* piagnisteo
whining *n* piagnucolio, piagnisteo, lagna; — *a* piagnucolante, lagnante
whinny *n* nitrito; — *vi* nitrire
whip *n* frusta; sferzata; *(pol)* organizzatore politico; — **hand** vantaggio; — *vt* frustare; frullare; stimolare; *(coll)* sopraffare; — *vi* agitarsi; slanciarsi
whipped *a* frullato; — **cream** panna montata
whipping *n* frustata, battitura
whir *n* fruscio; — *vi* frusciare
whirl — *vi* girare rapidamente; — *vi* far turbinare; — *n* giro rapido, vortice *m*; confusione
whirligig *n* carosello; *(toy)* trottola
whirlpool *n* vortice *m*
whirlwind *n* turbine *m*
whisk *n* spazzata, spazzolata; **–broom** scopetta, scopino; — *vt* spazzare, spazzolare, asportare rapidamente; — *vi* muoversi con leggerezza
whisker *n* pelo di barba
whiskers *npl* barba; *(animal)* baffi *mpl*
whisky *n* whisky *m*
whisper *vt&i* sussurrare; — *n* susurro, bisbiglio; *(rumor)* diceria
whistle *vt&i* fischiare; — *n* fischio; *(instrument)* fischietto
whistler *n* fischiatore *m*
whistling *n* fischiamento
whit *n* iota *m*, inezia
white *a* bianco; pallido; **show the — feather** dar prova di viltà; — **elephant** cosa ingombrante; — **heat** incandescenza; — **lie** bugia innocente; — *n* bianco; *(egg)* albume *m*; **–ness** *n* bianchezza, pallore *m*; purezza, candore *m*
whitecap *n* cresta d'onda
white-faced *a* pallido
whitefish *n* pesce bianco, lavâreto
white-hot *a* incandescente
white-livered *a* vigliacco, codardo
whiten *vt* imbiancare; — *vi* impallidire; imbiancarsi
whitewash *n* calce da imbiancare; — *vi* imbiancare con calce; dare una mano di bianco
whither *adv* dove

whiting *n (fish)* merlano
whitish *a* biancastro
whittle *vt* tagliuzzare, assottigliare
whiz *n* sibilo; *(sl)* esperto, perito; — *vi* fischiare, sibilare; *(hurry)* sfrecciare
who *pron* che; chi; il quale, la quale, i quali, le quali
whoa *interj* ferma!
whole *a* intero, completo; tutto insieme; — **number** numero intero; — **note** semibreve *f*; — **wheat** grano integrale; — **wheat bread** pane integrale; — *n* intero, totale *m*; **in the** — in fin dei conti, in totale
wholeness *n* interezza, totalità
wholesale *n* vendita all'ingrosso; — *a &adv* all'ingrosso; — *a* generale; — *vt &i* vendere all'ingrosso
wholesaler *n* grossista *m*
wholesome *a* salubre, sano; **–ness** salubrità
wholly *adv* del tutto, interamente
whom *pron* chi, che, cui; il quale, la quale, i quali, le quali; **–ever** *pron* chiunque
whoop *n* urlo, grido; **–ing cough** pertosse *f*, tosse canina; — *vi* gridare, urlare
whore *n* prostituta, sgualdrina
whorl *n* spirale *m*, spira
whose *pron* di chi; di cui; il cui, la cui, i cui, le cui
why *adv* perchè
wick *n* lucignolo
wicked *a* cattivo, scellerato; **–ness** *n* malvagità
wicker *n* vimine *m*
wide *a* largo; esteso; lontano; **–spread** *a* diffuso largamente; **far and** — in lungo e in largo; **–ly** *adv* largamente
wide– *(in comp)* **—awake** *a* sveglio; vigile; **—eyed** *a* con gli occhi sbarrati; **—open** *a* spalancato
widen *vt* allargare, ampliare; — *vi* allargarsi, ampliarsi, estendersi
widow *n* vedova; — *vt* vedovare; **–hood** *n* vedovanza
widower *n* vedovo
width *n* larghezza; *(cloth)* altezza
wield *vt* maneggiare; esercitare
wieldy *a* maneggiabile
wife *n* moglie *f*; **–ly** *a* di moglie, coniugale
wig *n* parrucca
wiggle *vt* dimenare; — *vi* dimenarsi; — *n* dimenamento, agitazione; **–r** *n* dimenante *m&f*
wigwag *n* segnalazione con bandierine; — *vi* fare segnalazioni con bandierine
wild *a* selvaggio, selvatico, silvestre, impetuoso; **–s** luoghi inesplorati; **–cat** *n* gatto selvatico; **–cat strike** sciopero non autorizzato; **–ness** *n* selvatichezza; sfrenatezza; **–ly** *adv* selvaticamente, selvaggiamente; sfrenatamente
wilderness *n* luogo selvaggio
wildfire *n* fuoco greco
wild-goose chase tentativo inutile, impresa vana
wile *n* astuzia, raggiro
wiliness *n* malizia, astuzia
will *n* volontà; desiderio; testamento; **free** — libero arbitrio, — *vt&i* ordinare, volere; — *vt* disporre per testamento
willful *a* premeditato, intenzionale; ostinato; **–ness** *n* premeditazione; ostinazione; **–ly** *adv* premeditatamente; ostinatamente
willing *a* pronto, volenteroso; **be** — volere; **–ness** *n* buona volontà; accondiscendenza; **—ly** *adv* volentieri
will-o'-the-wisp *n* fuoco fatuo
willow *n* salice *m*; **–y** *a* pieno di salici; svelto, grazioso
willy-nilly *adv* volente o nolente
wilt *vi* appassire; — *vt* far appassire
wily *a* astuto, malizioso
wimple *n* soggolo
win *vt&i* vincere, guadagnare; — **over** persuadere; — *n* vittoria, vincita
wince *vi* trasalire, indietreggiare
winch *n* argano, manubrio, manovella
wind *n* vento; *(breath)* fiato; **–bag** *n (coll)* chiacchierone *m*, ciarlatano; **–breaker** *n* giacca a vento; **–fall** *n* fortuna inaspettata; **–mill** *n* mulino a vento; **–pipe** *n* trachea; **–storm** *n* bufera da vento; — **tunnel** *(avi)* tunnel per vento artificiale; **get** — **of** aver sentore di; **–less** *a* senza vento; **–y** *a* ventoso; verboso, — *vt* far perdere il fiato; **–ed** *a* ansimante, sfiatato
wind *vt* avvolgere; *(clock)* caricare; — *vi* serpeggiare, avvolgersi; — *n* curva
wind– *(in comp)* **—blown** *a* portato dal vento; scompigliato; **—borne** *a* trasportato dal vento; **—swept** *a* esposto al vento
winding *n* svolta, sinuosità; giro; — *a* serpeggiante, sinuoso; — **sheet** lenzuolo mortuario, sudario
windjammer *n* veliere *m*
windlass *n* argano
window *n* finestra; *(auto, rail)* finestrino; *(store)* vetrina; *(box office)* sportello; — **dresser** *n* vetrinista *m&f*; **–pane** *n* vetro di finestra; **—sill** *n* davanzale *m*; **display** — *n* vetrina
window-shop *vi* guardare vetrine; **–er** *n* chi guarda le vetrine
windshield *n* parabrezza *m*; — **wiper** tergicristallo
windup *n (end)* conclusione
wine *n* vino; — **cellar** *n* cantina; **–glass** *n* bicchiere da vino; **–grower** *n* viticultore *m*; — **growing** viticultura; **–ry** *n* vineria; — **shop** spaccio di vino; — *vt* provvedere di vino
wing *n* ala; **–spread** *n* apertura d'ali; **–less** *a* senz'ali; **–s** *npl (theat)* quinte *fpl*; **take** — prendere il volo; **under the** — **of** sotto la protezione di; — *vt* sorvolare; — *vi* volare
wink *vi* strizzare l'occhio; — *n* ammicco, strizzata d'occhi, occhiolino; istante *m*
winner *n* vincitore *m*, vincitrice *f*
winning *a* vincente, vincitore; seducente; **–s** *npl* guadagni *mpl*, vincita
winnow *vt* vagliare
winsome *a* seducente, affascinante; **–ness** *n* fascino, attrattività
winter *n* inverno; — *vi* svernare; **–ize** *vt* equipaggiare per l'inverno; **–time** *n* stagione invernale

wintriness *n* qualità invernale; freddezza
wintry *a* invernale; freddo; *(fig)* triste, brullo
wipe *vt* asciugare, pulire; — **one's nose** asciugarsi il naso; — **out** cancellare, distruggere
wire *n* filo metallico; *(coll)* telegramma *m*; **barbed** — filo spinato; **–photo** *n* radiofoto *f*; — **tapping** uso di apparecchio speciale per captare conversazioni telefoniche altrui; **–puller** *n* potenza occulta *(fig)*; **–pulling** *n* manovra dei fili *(fig)*; eminenza grigia *(fig)*; — *vt* installare i fili; *(coll)* telegrafare; legare con filo
wire-haired *a* dal pelo rigido; setoloso
wireless *a* senza fili, radiotelegrafico; — *n* radiotelegrafia
wiriness *n* nerbo, nervo; *(hair)* rigidezza
wiring *n* instalazione elettrica
wiry *a* di filo metallico; *(person)* nervoso, nerboruto; *(hair)* rigido
wisdom *n* saggezza; — **tooth** dente del giudizio
wise *a* saggio; — *n* guisa, maniera, modo; **–ly** *adv* saggiamente
wiseacre *n* sapientone *m*, presuntuoso
wish *n* desiderio, voglia, augurio; **–bone** *n* forcella; — *vt&i* desiderare, volere, augurare
wishful *a* desideroso; — **thinking** illusioni *fpl*
wishy-washy *a* insipido
wisp *n* ciuffo, strofinaccio
wisteria *n* glicine *m*
wistful *a* pensoso; nostalgico, sognante; **–ness** *n* nostalgia
wit *n* spirito, arguzia; **to** — cioè, vale a dire; **–less** *a* povero di spirito, senza intelligenza; **–ty** *a* arguto, spiritoso
witch *n* strega; **–craft** *n* stregoneria; — **doctor** stregone *m*; **–ing** *a* incantevole; magico
with *prep* con; **–in** *prep* dentro di; entro; **–in** *adv* dentro; **–out** *prep* senza; fuori di; **–out** *adv* fuori
withdraw *vt* ritirare; — *vi* ritirarsi
withdrawal *n* ritirata, ritiro
wither *vi* appassire; — *vt* far appassire; **–ing** *a* languente; sprezzante
withers *npl* garrese *m*
withhold *vt* trattenere; rifiutare; — *vi* astenersi; **–ing** *n* astensione; rifiuto; detenzione
withstand *vt&i* resistere a, opporsi a
witness *n* testimone *m&f*; testimonianza; **bear** — fare testimonianza; — *vt* testimoniare, presenziare, attestare
witticism *n* frizzo spiritoso, arguzia
wittily *adv* spiritosamente
wittingly *adv* intenzionalmente, apposta
wizard *n* mago, stregone *m*; **–ry** *n* stregoneria, magia
wizen *vt* raggrinzire; — *vi* raggrinzarsi; **–ed** *a* magro, secco, raggrinzito
wobble *vi* vacillare, tremare
wobbling *a* vacillante; — *n* barcollamento
wobbly *a* malfermo, debole
woe *n* guaio, sventura; **–begone** *a* sconsolato; **–ful** *a* triste, doloroso; **–fully** *adv* dolorosamente
wolf *n* lupo; **–ish** *a* lupesco, di lupo, rapace; — *vt* mangiare con voracità
woman *n* donna; **–hood** *n* femminilità; **–ish** *a* effeminato; **–ly** *a* femminino, femminile, muliebre
woman-hater *n* misogino
womb *n* utero; grembo
wonder *n* meraviglia, stupore *m*; **–ful** *a* meraviglioso; **–fully** *adv* mirabilmente, meravigliosamente; **–land** *n* terra delle meraviglie; **–ment** *n* stupore *m*, meraviglia; — *vt&i* meravigliarsi, domandarsi
wondrous *a* meraviglioso, mirabile
wont *n* abitudine *f*
woo *vt* fare la corte a; **–ing** *n* corteggiamento
wood *n* legno; — **alcohol** alcool metilico; **–craft** *n* lavorazione del legno; — **carving** scultura in legno; **–cut** *n* intaglio su legno; **–cutter** *n* boscaiolo, taglialegna; intagliatore in legno; **–land** *n* terreno boscoso; **–pecker** picchio; **–work** *n* lavoro in legno; infissi di legno; intavolato; **–ed** *a* boscoso; **–en** *a* di legno; duro, goffo; inespressivo
wood-carver *n* scultore in legno
woods *npl* bosco, foresta; **–man** *n* boscaiolo; **–y** *a* boscoso, boschivo
woof *n* trama
woofer *n* altoparlante di bassa frequenza
wool *n* lana; **cotton** — ovatta; **steel** — lana d'acciaio; **pull the — over one's eyes** gettar polvere agli occhi *(fig)*; **–en** *a* di lana; **–ly** *a* lanoso, lanuto; *(hair)* crespo
word *n* parola; notizia; **by — of mouth** *adv* oralmente, a voce; **in a** — in una parola; **leave** — lasciar detto; **–less** *a* senza parola, muto; non espresso; **give one's** — dare la propria parola, dare la parola d'onore; **have –s with** aver parole con, litigare; **in other –s** in altre parole; — *vt* esprimere, formulare
wordiness *n* verbosità
wording *n* dicitura; espressione; modo di dire
wordy *a* parolaio, verboso
work *vt* lavorare; far funzionare; far lavorare; causare; — *vi* funzionare; lavorare; fare effetto; — **out** *(succeed)* riuscire, aver esito; — **up** elaborare; *(excite)* eccitare; *(mix)* mischiare; **–able** *a* lavorabile; sfruttabile; **–er** *n* operaio; lavoratore *m*, lavoratrice *f*
work *n* lavoro; opera; **–aday** *a* ordinario; **–bag** *n* borsa degli attrezzi; **–book** *n* manuale *m*; libro di esercizi; diario di lavoro, **–man** *n* artigiano, operaio; **–manship** *n* mano d'opera, esecuzione; abilità artigiana, finitezza; **–out** *n* *(sport)* allenamento; **at** — all'opera; **–s** *npl* opere *fpl*; *(mech)* meccanismo; fabbrica
working *n* funzionamento, operazione; — **capital** capitale d'esercizio; — **class** classe lavoratrice; — **day** giorno di lavoro; — **hours** orario di lavoro
world *n* mondo; — **without end** fino alla fine dei secoli *(fig)*; **for all the** — per tutto l'oro del mondo *(coll)*; **–liness** *n* mondanità; **–ly** *a* mondano, umano, materialista

world-wide *a* mondiale
worm *n* verme *m*; *(screw)* impanatura; — *vt* liberare dai vermi; fare subdolamente; *(secret)* strappare; — *vi* agire subdolamente; serpeggiare; **-s** *npl (med)* parassiti *mpl*; — **one's way into** insinuarsi in
worm-eaten *a* tarlato, bacato; *(out-of-date)* antiquato
wormwood *n (fig)* tribulazione; *(bot)* assenzio
worn *a* consumato, logoro
worn-out *a* esausto; logoro
worried *a* preoccupato, ansioso
worry *n* ansia, preoccupazione; angoscia; — *vi* preoccuparsi, affliggersi; — *vt* preoccupare, annoiare, disturbare
worse *a* peggiore; — *adv* peggio; **be — off** star peggio; **so much the —** tanto peggio
worsen *vt&i* peggiorare
worship *n* adorazione, culto; — *vt&i* adorare, venerare; partecipare a una funzione religiosa
worst *a* il peggiore, il più cattivo; — *adv* alla peggio; — *n* il peggio; — *vt* sopraffare
worsted *n* tessuto di lana pettinata
worth *n* valore *m*, merito; — *a* degno di, del valore di; **be —** valere; **-less** *a* di nessun valore; **-y** *a* degno
worthily *adv* degnamente
worthiness *n* merito
worthwhile *a* che vale la pena
would-be *a* sedicente, preteso; mancato
wound *n* piaga, ferita; — *vt* ferire; offendere
woven *a* tessuto
wraith *n* spettro, fantasma
wrangle *n* bisticcio, alterco, rissa; — *vi* bisticciarsi; altercare
wrap *vt* avvolgere, impaccare, incartare; —*vi* avvolgersi; — *n* mantello
wrapper *n* fascia, involucro
wrapping *n* imballaggio
wrath *n* ira, rabbia
wreak *vt* sfogare; — **vengeance** vendicarsi
wreath *n* corona, ghirlanda; **-e** *vt* inghirlandare, festonare; **-ed** *a* festonato, inghirlandato
wreck *n* naufragio; relitto; rovina; avanzi *mpl*; — *vt* distruggere, rovinare, demolire; **-age** *n* relitto; **-ed** *a* mancato; rovinato; naufragato; **-ing** *a (naut)* di salvataggio
wren *n (zool)* scricciolo
wrench *vt* storcere; — *n* torsione violenta; *(med)* slogatura, distorsione, lussazione; *(mech)* chiave fissa; **monkey —** chiave inglese
wrest *vt* strappare, torcere; — *n* strappo
wrestle *vi* lottare; — *n* lotta; — **with** lottare contro; **-r** *n* lottatore *m*
wrestling *n* lotta; **catch-as-catch-can —** lotta libera
wretch *n* sciagurato, miserabile *m*; **-ed** *a* infelice, meschino, pessimo; **-edness** *n* miseria; meschinità
wrick *n* storta; — *vt* storcersi
wriggle *n* contorsione; dimenamento; — *vi* torcersi, dimenarsi; — *vt* torcere; — **out of** levarsi da
wriggling *n* contorsione
wring *vt* torcere, stringere, spremere; estorcere; — *vi* torcersi; **-er** *n* cilindro da bucato
wringing *n* torsione
wringing-wet *a* inzuppato, gocciolante, bagnato
wrinkle *n* ruga, grinza; **latest —** *(coll)* ultimo grido, ultima moda; — *vt* corrugare; sgualcire; — *vi* raggrinzirsi; **-d** *a* grinzoso, rugoso
wrinkling *n* grinza
wrist *n* polso; **-band** *n* polsino; **-let** *n* braccialetto; — **watch** orologio da polso
writ *n (law)* mandato; **Holy W-** la Sacra Scrittura
write *vt&i* scrivere; — **down** mettere per iscritto; — **off** cancellare; scrivere con facilità
writer *n* scrittore *m*, scrittrice *f*; scrivente *m&f*
write-up *n* resoconto, rapporto
writhe *vi* contorcersi
writhing *n* contorsione
writing *n* scrittura, grafia, scritto; opera; — **desk** scrivania; — **pad** cartella per scrivere; — **paper** carta da scrivere; **in —** per iscritto
written *a* per iscritto, scritto
wrong *n* male *m*; torto; danno; ingiustizia; **-doer** *n* malfattore *m*, malfattrice *f*; peccatore *m*, peccatrice *f*; **-doing** *n* malazione; **be —** aver torto; **do —** far male; peccare; **go —** sbagliar strada *(fig)*; **in the —** dalla parte del torto; in torto; **What's —?** Che c'è di male?
wrong *vt* far male a, danneggiare; offendere; accusare a torto; — *adv* erroneamente, malamente, a torto; **-ly** *adv* male; ingiustamente
wrongful *a* ingiusto; **-ly** *adv* ingiustamente
wroth *a* arrabbiato, stizzito
wrought *a* lavorato; — **iron** ferro battuto
wry *a* storto, torto; **make a — face** fare una smorfia
wryneck *n* torcicollo

X

xenon *n (chem)* xeno
Xmas, Christmas *n* Natale *m*
X ray raggio X
X-ray *vt* fare una radiografia di; — **picture** radiografia
xylography *n* silografia
xylophone *n* silofono
xylophonist *n* silofonista *m*

Y

yacht *n* panfilo
yank *n* strappo; — *vt* strappare; — *vi* dare uno strappone
Yankee *n&a* americano, statunitense *m&f*
yap *n* abbaiamento, latrato, guaito; — *vi* abbaiare; guaire
yard *n* recinto, cortile *m*; *(naut)* antenna; norma; *(measure)* iarda; *(rail)* stazione di smistamento; **–man** *n (rail) n* manovratore *m*; **–stick** stecca d'una iarda
yarn *n* filato; *(coll)* racconto immaginario
yaw *vi (naut)* cambiar rotta, orzare
yawl *n (naut)* iole *f*
yawn *n* sbadiglio; — *vi* sbadigliare; spalancarsi; **–ing** *a* spalancato; sonnolento, sbadigliante; **–ing** *n* sbadiglio
yea *adv* già; sì; — *n* voto affermativo
year *n* anno; **leap** — anno bisestile; **last** — l'anno scorso, l'anno passato; **school** — anno scolastico; **–book** *n* annuario; **–ling** *n* animale d'un anno
yearly *a* annuale; — *adv* ogni anno
yearn *vi* desiderare ardentemente; bramare, agognare; struggersi per
yearning *n* vivo desiderio; — *a* bramoso
yeast *n* lievito
yell *n* strillo, urlo; — *vt&i* urlare, gridare
yellow *a* giallo; *(coll)* vigliacco; — **fever** febbre gialla; — **journalism** giornalismo sensazionale; **–ish** *a* giallastro; **–ness** *n* giallore *m*; — *vt&i* ingiallire
yelp *n* guaito; — *vi* guaire, latrare
yelping *n* guaiti *mpl*; — *a* che guaisce
yen *n (coll)* desiderio vivo; — *vi* agognare, bramare
yes *adv* sì, già
yesterday *adv* ieri; **day before** — ieri l'altro, avant'ieri
yet *conj* però, tuttavia, nondimento; — *adv* ancora, finora; **as** — finora; **not** — non ancora
yew *n (bot)* tasso
yield *vt&i* produrre, rendere, cedere — *n* raccolto, rendita
yodel *n* canto tirolese; — *vi* cantare alla tirolese
yogurt *n* yogurt *m*
yoke *n* giogo; paio; — *vt* accoppiare; aggiogare
yokel *n* zoticone *m*, villano
yolk *n* tuorlo
yonder *adv* laggiù, là
yore *n*; **of** — di un tempo, anticamente
you *pron* tu; Lei, la, Loro; voi
young *a* giovane; — *npl* i nati; *(animal)* cuccioli *mpl*, *(chicks)* pulcini *mpl*; *(people)* i giovani *mpl*; **–ster** *n* fanciullo; — **lady** signorina; — **man** giovanotto
your *a* tuo, vostro; Suo, Loro, tua, vostra, Sua
yours *pron* il tuo, il vostro, il Suo, la tua, la vostra, la Sua, il Loro, la Loro
yourself *pron* tu stesso, voi stesso, Lei stesso, Lei stessa, voi stessa, ti, si, vi
yourselves *pron pl* voi stessi, voi stesse, Loro stessi, Loro stesse, si, vi
youth *n* gioventù *f*, giovinezza; giovane *m*; **–ful** *a* giovanile; **–fulness** *n* giovinezza
yowl *vi* ululare; — *n* ululato
yule *n* Natale *m*; **–tide** *n* feste natalizie

Z

zany *a* comico, buffo; — *n* buffone *m*, semplicione *m*
zeal *n* zelo
zealot *n* zelante *m&f*, zelatore *m*, zelatrice *f*; fanatico
zealous *a* fervente, zelante
zenith *n* zenit, apogeo *m*
zephyr *n* zeffiro
zero *n* zero, nulla *m*; — **hour** ora zero
zest *n* gusto, sapore *m*; interesse, ardore *m*; **–ful** *a* saporito, aromatico; piacevole, gustoso
zigzag *n* zigzag *m*; — *a&adv* a zigzag; — *vi* andare a zigzag, serpeggiare
zinc *n* zinco
zip *n (coll)* energia; sibilo; — *vi* muoversi fulmineamente, scattare, frecciare; sibilare
zipper *n* chiusura lampo
zodiac *n* zodiaco
zone *n* zona; — *vi* dividere in zone; **–d** *a* a zone
zoo *n* giardino zoologico
zoological *a* zoologico
zoologist *n* zoologo
zoology *n* zoologia
zoom *n (avi)* ascesa verticale; rimbombo; — *vi* rimbombare; *(avi)* salire verticalmente
zoonosis *n* zoonosi *f*

ENGLISH-ITALIAN FIRST NAMES

A

Aaron Aronne
Abel Abele
Abraham Abramo
Ada Ada
Adam Adamo
Adelaide Adelaide
Adele Adele
Adeline Adelina
Adolph Adolfo
Adrian Adriano
Agatha Agata
Aggie Agnesina
Agnes Agnese
Albert Alberto
Alec, Alex Alessandrino
Alexander Alessandro
Alexandra Alessandra
Alfred Alfredo
Alice Alice
Althea Altea
Ambrose Ambrogio
Amelia Amelia
Amy Amata
Andrew Andrea, Sandro
Andy Andreuccio
Angela Angela
Ann Anna
Annie Annina, Annetta
Anthony Antonio
Antoine Antonio
Antoinette Antonietta
Antony Antonio
Archibald Arcibaldo
Arnold Arnaldo
Arthur Arturo
August Augusto
Augusta Augusta
Augustine Agostino
Austin Agostino

B

Baldwin Baldovino
Barbara Barbara
Barnaby Barnaba
Barnard Bernardo
Barney Bernardino
Bartholomew Bartolomeo
Basil Basilio
Beatrice Beatrice
Benedict Benedetto
Benjamin Beniamino
Bernadine Bernardina
Bernard Bernardo
Bernice Berenice
Bertha Berta
Bertram Bertrando
Bertrand Bertrando
Betsy Lisetta
Betty Lisa
Bill Guglielmino
Blanche Bianca
Bob Robertuccio
Bridget Brigida

C

Camille Camilla
Caroline Carolina
Catherine Caterina
Cecil Cecilio
Cecilia, Cecily Cecilia
Charles Carlo
Charlie Carlotto
Charlotte Carlotta
Chloe Cloe

Christian Cristiano
Christine Cristina
Christopher Cristoforo
Clara, Clare Chiara
Clarissa Clarissa, Clarice
Claude Claudio
Claudia Claudia
Clement Clemente
Clementine Clementina
Clio Clio
Conrad Corrado, Corradino
Constance Costanza
Cordelia Cordelia
Corinne Corinna
Cornelia Cornelia
Cornelius Cornelio
Cyrus Ciro

D

Daniel Daniele
Daphne Dafne
David Davide
Davy Davidino
Delia Delia
Delilah Dalila
Dennis Diogini
Diana, Diane Diana
Dick Riccardino
Dolores Dolores
Donald Donaldo
Dora Dora
Doris Doride
Dorothy Dorotea

E

Edgar Edgardo
Edith Editta
Edmund Edmondo
Edward Edoardo
Eleanor Eleonora
Elias Elia
Eliza Elisa
Elizabeth Elisabetta
Ellen Elena
Eloise Eloisa
Elvira Elvira
Emanuel Emanuele
Emilia Emilia
Emily Emilia
Emma Emma
Emmie Emmina
Eric Erico
Ernest Ernesto
Ernestine Ernestina
Esmund Esmondo
Estelle Stella
Esther Ester
Eugene Eugenio
Eugenia Eugenia
Eunice Eunice
Evangeline Evangelina
Eve Eva
Evelyn Evelina

F

Fabian Fabiano
Felicia Felicia
Felix Felice
Ferdinand Ferdinando
Flora Flora
Florence Fiorenza
Frances Francesca
Francis Francesco
Frank Francesco
Fred Federico
Frederica Federica
Frederick Federico

G

Gabriel Gabriele
Gabriella Gabriella
Gaylord Gagliardo
Gene Gino
Genevieve Genoveffa
Geoffrey Goffredo
George Giorgio
Georgette Giorgetta
Georgia Giorgia
Georgiane Giorgiana
Georgie Giorgetto
Gerald Geraldo
Geraldine Geraldina
Gerard Gerardo
Gertrude Geltrude
Gilbert Gilberto
Giles Egidio
Godfrey Goffredo
Gregory Gregorio
Gustav Gustavo
Guy Guido

H

Hal Enrico
Hannah Anna
Harold Aroldo
Harriet Enrichetta
Harry Arrigo
Hatty Enrichetta
Hector Ettore
Helen, Helena Elena
Henrietta Enrichetta
Henry Enrico, Arrigo
Herbert Erberto
Hermione Ermione
Hilary Hilario
Homer Omero
Horace Orazio
Horatio Orazio
Hortense Ortensia
Hubert Uberto
Hugh Ugo
Hughie Ugolino
Humbert Umberto
Humphrey Onofredo

I

Ian Giano
Ida Ida
Immanuel Emanuele
Inez Ines
Irene Irene
Iris Iris
Isaac Isacco
Isabel Isabella
Ivan Ivano

J

Jack Giannetto
Jacob Giacobbe
James Giacomo
Jane Giovanna
Jean Giovannina, Gina
Jenny Giannetta, Giacomina
Jeremiah Geremia
Jeremy Geremia
Jerome Geronimo
Jessica Gessica
Jimmy Giacomino
Joan, Joanna Giovanna
Joe Giuseppino
Joey Peppino
Johanna Giovanna
John Giovanni
Johnny Giannino, Giovannino
Jonah Giona
Jonathan Gionata

Jordan Giordano
Joseph Giuseppe
Josephine Giuseppina
Joshua Giosuè
Judith Giuditta
Jules Giulio
Julia Giulia
Julian Giuliano
Juliana Giuliana
Julie Giulia
Juliet Giulietta
Julius Giulio
Justin Giustino
Justina Giustina

K

Katherine Caterina
Kathie Caterina
Kitty Caterina

L

Lambert Lamberto
Larry Lorenzino
Laura Laura
Lavinia Lavinia
Lawrence Lorenzo
Leah Lea
Leda Leda
Lelia Lelia
Leo Leone
Leonard Leonardo
Leonore Leonora
Leopold Leopoldo
Letitia Letizia
Lewie Luigino
Lewis Luigi
Lionel Lionello
Lisa Lisa
Lorraine Lorena
Lou Luigino
Louie Gigi
Louis Luigi
Louisa Luisa
Louise Luigia
Lucas Luca
Lucia Lucia
Lucian Luciano
Lucinda Lucinda
Lucius Lucio
Lucretia Lucrezia
Lucy Lucia
Ludwig Ludovico
Luke Luca
Luther Lutero
Lydia Lidia

M

Madeleine Maddalena
Madeline Maddalena
Malcolm Malcomo
Manfred Manfredo
Manuel Manuele
Margery Margherita
Margot Margherita
Marianne Marianna
Marie Maria
Marion Marietta
Marius Mario
Mark Marco
Martha Marta
Martin Martino
Mary Maria
Mathilda Matilde
Matthew Matteo
Maude Magda
Maurice Maurizio
Maximilian Massimiliano
May Marietta
Melissa Melissa

Mercedes Mercede
Mercia Mercia
Michael Michele
Mike Michelino
Minerva Minerva
Miranda Miranda
Miriam Miriam
Monica Monica
Monique Monica
Morris Maurizio
Moses Mosè

N

Nan Nina
Nancy Annetta, Annina
Nannette Nannetta
Naomi Noemi
Natalie Natalia
Nathaniel Nataniele
Nicholas Nicola, Nicolò
Nick Nicoluccio
Nicolette Nicoletta
Nina Nina
Noah Noè
Noel Natale
Nora Nora

O

Olive Olivia
Oliver Oliviero
Olivia Olivia
Ophelia Ofelia
Orlando Orlando
Oscar Oscar
Oswald Osvaldo
Otto Ottone

P

Patrick Patrizio
Paul Paolo
Paula Paola
Peggy Marietta
Penelope Penelope
Pete Pietruccio
Peter Pietro
Phil Filippuccio
Philip Filippo
Phoebe Feba
Polly Mariuccia
Priscilla Priscilla
Prudence Prudenza

R

Rachel Rachele
Ralph Rodolfo, Raulo
Randall Randolfo
Randolph Randolfo
Raymond Raimondo
Rebecca Rebecca
Reggie Rinaldo
Reginald Reginaldo
Reynold Rinaldo
Richard Riccardo
Robert Roberto
Robin Robertuccio
Roderick Rodrigo
Roger Ruggero
Roland Rolando
Ronald Rinaldo
Rosalie Rosalia, Rosina
Rosalind Rosalinda
Rose Rosa
Rosette Rosetta
Rowland Rolando
Roxanne Rossana
Rudolph Rodolfo
Rufus Rufo
Rupert Ruperto
Ruth Ruth

S

Sally Sara
Samson Sansone
Samuel Samuele
Sarah Sara
Saul Saul
Sebastian Sebastiano
Sibyl Sibilla
Siegfried Sigfrido
Sigmund Sigismondo
Silvester Silvestro
Simon Simone
Solomon Salomone
Sophie Sofia
Stanislas Stanislao
Stella Stella
Stephanie Stefania
Stephen Stefano
Sue Susanna
Susan Susanna
Susannah Susanna
Susie Susetta
Sylvia Silvia

T

Terence Terenzio
Teresa Teresa
Thaddeus Taddeo
Theodora Teodora
Theodore Teodoro
Therese Teresa
Thomas Tommaso
Timothy Timoteo
Titus Tito
Tobias Tobia
Toby Tobia
Tom Tommasino
Tony Tonio
Tyrone Tirone

U

Ulric Ulrico
Ursula Orsola

V

Valentine Valentino
Valerie Veleria
Veronica Veronica
Vic Vittore
Vicky Vittorina
Victor Vittorio
Victoria Vittoria
Virgil Virgilio
Vincent Vincenzo
Vinny Vincenzina
Violet Viola
Virginia Virginia
Vitus Vito
Vivian Viviana
Vladimir Vladimiro

W

Walter Gualtiero
Wilfred Vilfrido
Wilhelm Guglielmo
Wilhelmina Guglielmina
William Guglielmo
Winfred Vinfrido

Y

Yves Ivone
Yvette Ivetta

Z

Zachary Zaccaria

ARRIVAL	**L'ARRIVO**
Where is customs, please?	*La dogana, dov'è, per favore?* (lâ dō·gâ'nâ dō·vā' pār fâ·vō'rā)
My baggage? I think the ones over there are mine.	*I miei bagagli? Credo che siano quelli là.* (ē myā'ē bâ·gâ'lyē krā'dō kā sē'â·nō kwāl'lē lâ)
I have nothing to declare.	*Non ho niente da dichiarare.* (nōn ō nyān'tā dâ dē·kyâ·râ'rā)
There are only personal belongings in that trunk.	*In quel baule ci sono solo effetti personali.* (ēn kwāl bâ·ū'lā chē sō'nō sō'lō āf·fāt'tē pār·sō·nâ'lē)
Excuse me, where can I find a porter?	*Scusi, dove posso trovare un facchino?* (skū'zē dō'vā pōs'sō trō·vâ'rā ūn fâk·kē'nō)
Take everything to a taxi, please.	*Porti tutto in un tassì, per piacere.* (pōr'tē tūt'tō ē·nūn' tâs·sē' pār pyâ·chā'rā)
How much do I owe you?	*Quanto Le devo?* (kwân'tō lā dā'vō)
How much is it?	*Quant'è?* (kwân·tā')
TAXI	**IL TASSÌ**
Will you get a cab for me, please?	*Mi vuol trovare un tassì, per favore.* (mē vwōl trō·vâ'rā ūn tâs·sē' pār fâ·vō'rā)
Take me to Hotel ________.	*Mi porti all'Albergo ________.* (mē pōr'tē âl·lâl·bār'gō)
Is it very far?	*È molto distante?* (ā mōl'tō dē·stân'tā)
Go more slowly, please!	*Vada più piano, La prego!* (vâ'dâ pyū pyâ'nō lâ prā'gō)
Slower!	*Più adagio!* (pyū â·dâ'jō)
Stop here a moment, please.	*Si fermi un momento, per favore.* (sē fār'mē ūn mō·mān'tō pār fâ·vō'rā)
Go ahead.	*Avanti.* (â·vân'tē)
Faster, please.	*Acceleri, per favore.* (â·che'lā·rē pār fâ·vō'rā)
Turn to the left.	*Volti a sinistra.* (vōl'tē â sē·nē'strâ)
Turn to the right.	*Giri a destra.* (jē'rē â dā'strâ)
Keep going straight.	*Vada sempre diritto.* (vâ'dâ sām'prā dē·rēt'tō)
How much is it?	*Quant'è?* (kwân·tā')
Can you change ten thousand lire?	*Può cambiarmi un biglietto da dieci mila?* (pwō kâm·byâr'mē ūn bē·lyāt'tō dâ dyā'chē mē'lâ)
HOTEL	**L'ALBERGO**
Where is the desk?	*Dov'è la direzione?* (dō·vā' lâ dē·rā·tsyō'nā)
Have you reserved a room for me? My name is ________.	*È stata prenotata una camera per me? Mi chiamo ________.* (ā stâ'tâ prā·nō·tâ'tâ ū'nâ kâ'mā·râ pār mā mē kyâ'mō)

Can I pay by the week?

Posso pagare la camera per settimana? (pōs'sō pâ·gâ'rā lâ kâ'mā·râ pār sat·tē·mâ'nâ)

Are meals included?

I pasti sono compresi? (ē pâ'stē sō'nō cōm·prā'zē)

What are your meal times?

A che ore si servono i pasti? (â kā ō'rā sē ser'vō·nō ē pâ'stē)

I'd like a room with two beds, a bath, and air conditioning.

Vorrei una camera a due letti con bagno ed aria condizionata. (vōr·rā'ē ū'nâ kâ'mā·râ â dū'ā lāt'tē kōn bâ'nyō ā·dâ'ryâ kōn·dē·tsyō·nâ'tâ)

I am going to stay a week (two weeks).

Resterò una settimana (due settimane). (rā·stā·rō' ū'nâ sāt·tē·mâ'nâ [dū'ā sāt·tē·mâ'nā])

I want a single room overlooking the square.

Desidero una stanza a un letto che guardi sulla piazza. (dā·zē'dā·rō ū'nâ stân'tsâ â ūn lāt'tō kā gwâr'dē sūl'lâ pyâ'tsâ)

A room on the lake (on the sea) for two nights.

Una camera sul lago (sul mare) per due notti. (ū'nâ kâ'mā·râ sūl lâ'gō [sūl mâ'rā] pār dū'ā nōt'tē)

Will you carry my bag for me?

Mi vuol portare la valigia? (mē vwōl pōr·tâ'rā lâ vâ·lē'jâ)

This room is too expensive. Don't you have something a little cheaper?

Questa camera è troppo cara. Non ha una più a buon mercato? (kwā'stâ kâ'mā·râ ā trōp'pō kâ'râ nōn â ū'nâ pyū â bwōn mār·kâ'tō)

Please bring me some ice.

Mi porti del ghiaccio, per favore. (mē pōr'tē dāl gyâ'chō pār fâ·vō'rā)

Bring me another blanket and another towel, if you please.

Mi dia un'altra coperta e un altro asciugamano, se non Le dispiace. (mē dē'â ū·nâl'trâ kō·pār'tâ ā ū·nâl'trō â·shū·gâ·mâ'nō sā nōn lā dē·spyâ'chā)

Do you have laundry service? I should like to have some things washed.

Avete il servizio per il bucato? Vorrei far lavare della biancheria. (â·vā'tā ēl sār·vē'tsyō pā·rēl' bū·kâ'tō vōr·rā'ē fâr lâ·vâ'rā dāl'lâ byân·kā·rē'â)

Please wake me at eight o'clock.

Mi faccia il piacere di svegliarmi alle otto. (mē fâ'châ ēl pyâ·chā'rā dē zvā·lyâr'mē âl'lā ōt'tō)

I want this suit pressed.

Vorrei far stirare quest'abito. (vōr·rā'ē fâr stē·râ'rā qwā·stâ'bē·tō)

I have a suit to be dry cleaned, a shirt to be ironed, and shoes to be polished.

Ho un vestito da pulire, una camicia da stirare e le scarpe da lucidare. (ō ūn vā·stē'tō dâ pū·lē'rā ū'nâ kâ·mē'châ dâ stē·râ'rā ā lā skâr'pā dâ lū·chē·dâ'rā)

When will they be ready?

Quando saranno pronti? (kwân'do sâ·rân'nō prōn'tē)

Do you have a map of the city?

Ha una pianta della città? (â ū'nâ pyân'tâ dāl'lâ chēt·tâ')

Do you have stamps?

Ha francobolli? (â frân·kō·bōl'lē)

You can buy stamps at the tobacco shop.

I francobolli si comprano al tabaccaio. (ē frân·kō·bōl'lē sē kôm'prâ·nō âl tâ·bâk·kâ'yō)

Are there any letters for me?	*Ci sono lettere per me?* (chē sō'nō let'-tā·rā pār mā)
Please give me my bill.	*Mi dia il conto per favore.* (mē dē'â ēl kōn'tō pār fâ·vō'rā)
Are taxes and service included?	*Il servizio e le tasse sono compresi?* (ēl sār·vē'tsyō ā lā tâs'sā sō'nō kōm·prā'zē)
Will you take a traveler's check?	*Mi può cambiare un assegno per viaggiatori?* (mē pwō kâm·byâ'rā ū·nâs·sā'nyō pār vyâj·jâ·tō'rē)
Have my luggage taken down.	*Mi faccia portar giù le valigie.* (mē fâ'-châ pōr·târ' jū lā vâ·lē'jā)

AT THE RESTAURANT	**AL RISTORANTE**
Waiter, bring me the menu please.	*Cameriere, il menù, per favore.* (kâ·mā·ryā'rā ēl mā·nū' pār fâ·vō'rā)
I'd like an American breakfast.	*Voglio fare colazione all'inglese.* (vô'-lyō fâ'rā kō·lâ·tsyō'nā âl·lēn·glā'-zā)
Bring me two eggs with bacon (with ham), toast, and coffee.	*Mi dia due uova con pancetta (con prosciutto), crostini e caffè.* (mē dē'â dū'ā wō'vâ kōn pân·chāt'tâ [kōn prō·shūt'tō] krō·stē'nē ā kâf·fā')
I'd like the Italian breakfast.	*Vorrei la colazione italiana.* (vōr·rā'ē lâ kō·lâ·tsyō'nā ē·tâ·lyâ'nâ)
Café au lait with rolls, butter, and marmelade.	*Caffelatte con brioche, burro e marmellata.* (kâf·fā·lât'tā kōn brē·ōsh' būr'rō ā mâr·māl·lâ'tâ)
To begin with, a cocktail.	*Per cominciare, un aperitivo.* (pār kō·mēn·châ'rā ū·nâ·pā·rē·tē'vō)
I'll have the table d'hôte.	*Desidero il pasto a prezzo fisso.* (dā·zē'dā·rō ēl pâ'stō â prā'tsō fēs'sō)
Chicken broth, breaded veal cutlet with peas, wine, and fruit.	*Brodo di pollo, cotolette alla milanese con piselli, vino e frutta.* (brō'dō dē pōl'lō kō·tō·lāt'tā âl'lâ mē·lâ·nā'zā kōn pē·zāl'lē vē'nō ā frūt'tâ)
Bring some hors d'oeuvres, tagliatelle Bologna style, roast veal with fried potatoes, and a pint of white wine.	*Porti dell'antipasto, tagliatelle alla bolognese, vitello arrosto con patate fritte e un quartino di bianco.* (pōr'-tē dāl·lân·tē·pâ'stō tâ·lyâ·tāl'lā âl'-lâ bō·lō·nyā'zā vē·tāl'lō âr·rō'stō kōn pâ·tâ'tā frēt'tā ā ūn kwâr·tē'nō dē byân'kō)
Do you have fresh beer?	*Ha della birra fresca?* (â dāl'lâ bēr'râ frā'skâ)
Strong (weak, spiked) coffee and coffee with cream.	*Un caffè ristretto (lungo, macchiato) e un cappuccino.* (ūn kâf·fā' rē·strāt'tō [lūn'gō mâk·kyâ'tō] ā ūn kâp·pū·chē'nō)
Where is the washroom, please?	*Mi dica dov'è la toletta, per favore?* (mē dē'kâ dō·vā' lâ tō·lāt'tâ pār fâ·vō'rā)

Waiter, a fork (spoon, glass, napkin, knife), please.	*Cameriere, una forchetta (un cucchiaio, un bicchiere, un tovagliolo, un coltello) per favore.* (kâ·mā·ryā'rā ū'nâ fōr·kāt'tâ [ūn kūk·kyâ'yō ūn bēk·kyā'rā ūn tō·vâ·lyō'lō ūn kōl·tāl'lō] pār fâ·vō'rā)
Please bring me some butter.	*Mi dia un po' di burro, La prego.* (mē dē'â ūn pō dē būr'rō lâ prā'gō)
Waiter, some more bread, please.	*Cameriere, del pane, per piacere.* (kâ·mā·ryā'rā dāl pâ'nā pār pyâ·chā'rā)
May I please have a glass of milk?	*Mi può dare un bicchiere di latte?* (mē pwō dâ'rā ūn bēk·kyā'rā dē lât'tā)
Cheese	*Formaggio* (fōr·māj'jō)
Grilled steak	*Bistecca ai ferri* (bē·stāk'kâ â'ē fār'rē)
Macaroni and cheese	*Pasta asciuta* (pâ'stâ â·shū'tâ)
Mashed potatoes	*Purè di patate* (pū·rā' dē pâ·tâ'tā)
Mineral water	*Acqua minerale* (âk'kwâ mē·nā·râ'lā)
Seafood soup	*Zuppa di datteri* (dzūp'pâ dē dât'tā·rē)
Steak Florentine style	*Bistecca alla fiorentina* (bē·stāk'kâ âl'lâ fyō·rān·tē'nâ)
Stuffed macaroni in broth	*Tortellini in brodo* (tōr·tāl·lē'nē ēn brō'dō)
Tomato salad	*Insalata di pomodori* (ēn·sâ·lâ'tâ dē pō·mō·dō'rē)
Veal roll in spiced sauce	*Saltimbocca alla romana* (sâl·tēm·bōk'kâ âl'lâ rō·mâ'nâ)
Whipped cream	*Panna montata* (pân'nâ mōn·tâ'tâ)

MONEY — IL DENARO

Can I cash a check here or do I have to go to the bank?	*Posso cambiare qui un assegno o devo andare alla banca?* (pōs'sō kâm·byâ'rā kwē ū·nâs·sā'nyō ō dā'vō ân·dâ'rā âl'lâ bân'kâ)
Is there a bank near here?	*C'è una banca qui vicino?* (chā ū'nâ bân'kâ kwē vē·chē'nō)
Where can I cash a check?	*Dove posso riscuotere un assegno?* (dō'vā pōs'sō rē·skwô'tā·rā ū·nâs·sā'nyō)
What is the rate of exchange?	*Quant'è il cambio?* (kwân·tā' ēl kâm'byō)
Here is my passport.	*Ecco il mio passaporto.* (āk'kō ēl mē'ō pâs·sâ·pōr'tō)
Please give me two 10,000-lire notes and one 5,000.	*Mi dia due biglietti da dieci mila lire ed una da cinque mila, per piacere.* (mē dē'â dū'ā bē·lyāt'tē dâ dyā'chē mē'lâ lē'rā ā·dū'nâ dâ chēn'kwā mē'lâ pār pyâ·chā'rā)

AT THE POST OFFICE — ALLA POSTA

Where is the post office?	*Dov'è la posta?* (dō·vā' lâ pō'stâ)
Is it far from here?	*È lontano?* (ā lōn·tâ'nō)

Is that the telegraph window?	*È quello lo sportello dei telegrammi?* (ā kwāl'lō lō spōr·tāl'lō dā'ē tā·lā·grâm'mē)
I'd like to send a wire to Chicago.	*Vorrei mandare un telegramma a Chicago.* (vōr·rā'ē mân·dâ'rā ūn tā·lā·grâm'mâ â chē·kâ'gō)
Give me two 100-lire stamps.	*Mi dia due francobolli da cento lire.* (mē dē'â dū'ā frân·kō·bōl'lē dâ chān'tō lē'rā)
I'd like this letter sent registered and this package insured.	*Questa lettera me la fa raccomandata e questo pacchetto assicurato.* (kwā'stâ let'tā·râ mā lâ fâ râk·kō·mân·dâ'tâ ā kwā'stō pâk·kāt'tō âs·sē·kū·râ'tō)
Please send it airmail.	*Me la spedisca per via aerea, per piacere.* (mā lâ spā·dē'skâ pār vē'â â·e'rā·â pār pyâ·chā'rā)
Please give me a post card.	*Mi dia una cartolina postale.* (mē dē'â ū'nâ kâr·tō·lē'nâ pō·stâ'lā)
Is this the window for general delivery?	*È qui lo sportello di fermo posta?* (ā kwē lō spōr·tāl'lō dē fār'mō pō'stâ)
Are there any letters for me?	*Ci sono lettere per me?* (chē sō'nō let'tā·rā pār mā)

STORES	**I NEGOZI**
Bakery	*Fornaio, Panetteria* (fōr·nâ'yō pâ·nāt·tā·rē'â)
Barber shop	*Barbiere* (bâr·byā'rā)
Beauty shop	*Salone di bellezza* (sâ·lō'nā dē bāl·lā'tsâ)
Book store	*Libreria* (lē·brā·rē'â)
Dairy store	*Latteria* (lât·tā·rē'â)
Drug store	*Farmacia* (fâr·mâ·chē'â)
Florist	*Fiorista* (fyō·rē'stâ)
Food shop	*Alimentari* (â·lē·mān·tâ'rē)
Butcher shop	*Macelleria* (mâ·chāl·lā·rē'â)
Grocery store	*Salumeria* (sâ·lū·mā·rē'â)
Delicatessen	*Drogheria* (drō·gā·rē'â)
Jewelry shop	*Gioielleria* (jō·yāl·lā·rē'â)
Watchmaker	*Orologeria* (ō·rō·lō·jā·rē'â)
Dress shop	*Casa di mode* (kâ'zâ dē mō'dā)
Dressmaker	*Modisteria* (mō·dē·stā·rē'â)
Tailor shop	*Sartoria* (sâr·tō·rē'â)
Tobacco shop	*Tabacchaio, Tabaccheria, Sali e tabacchi* (tâ·bâk·kâ'yō tâ·bâk·kā·rē'â sâ'lē ā tâ·bâk'kē)
Shoe repair shop	*Ciabattino* (châ·bât·tē'nō)
Shoe store	*Calzoleria* (kâl·tsō·lā·rē'â)
Department store	*Bazar* (bâ·dzâr')
Bar	*Osteria* (ō·stā·rē'â)
Restaurant	*Trattoria* (trât·tō·rē'â)
Liquor store	*Fiaschetteria* (fyâ·skāt·tā·rē'â)

Dry goods store	*Merceria* (mār·chā·rē'â)
Stationery shop	*Cartoleria* (kâr·tō·lā·rē'â)
Perfume shop	*Profumeria* (prō·fū·mā·rē'â)

SHOPPING — GLI ACQUISTI

I am going shopping.	*Vado a fare delle compere.* (vâ'dō â fâ'rā dāl'lā kôm'pā·rā)
I'm going shopping for groceries.	*Vado a far la spesa.* (vâ'dō â fâr lâ spā'zâ)
Is there a grocery store near here?	*C'è un mercato qui vicino?* (chā ūn mār·kâ'tō kwē vē·chē'nō)
Are there any dress shops?	*Ci sono negozi di mode?* (chē sō'nō nā·gō'tsē dē mō'dā)
How much is this hat?	*Quant'è questo cappello?* (kwân·tā' kwā'stō kâp·pāl'lō)
What's the price of a dozen handkerchiefs?	*Quanto costa una dozzina di fazzoletti?* (kwân'tō kō'stâ ū'nâ dō·dzē'nâ dē fâ·tsō·lāt'tē)
Could you show me some blouses?	*Può mostrarmi delle bluse?* (pwō mō·strâr'mē dāl'lā blū'zā)
May I see some stockings (shirts, ties)?	*Mi vuol far vedere delle calze (camicie, cravatte)?* (mē vwōl fâr vā·dā'rā dāl'lā kâl'tsā [kâ·mē'chā krâ·vât'tā])
Show me some leather gloves.	*Mi faccia vedere dei guanti di pelle.* (mē fâ'châ vā·dā'rā dā'ē gwân'tē dē pāl'lā)
What color?	*Di che colore?* (dē kā kō·lō'rā)
What size?	*Di che misura?* (dē kā mē·zū'râ)
May I see something better?	*Mi vuol far vedere una qualità migliore?* (mē vwōl fâr vā·dā'rā ū'nâ kwâ·lē·tâ' mē·lyō'rā)
These shoes go well with the dress.	*Queste scarpe combinano con il vestito.* (kwā'stā skâr'pā kōm·bē'nâ·nō kō·nēl' vā·stē'tō)
I prefer solid colors.	*Preferisco le tinte unite.* (prā·fā·rē'skō lā tēn'tā ū·nē'tā)
Do you have it in white?	*Ce l'ha bianco?* (chā lâ byân'kō)
Do you deliver?	*Fanno servizio a domicilio?* (fân'nō sār·vē'tsyō â dō·mē·chē'lyō)
You can send everything to the hotel.	*Mi può mandare tutto all'albergo.* (mē pwō mân·dâ'rā tūt'tō âl·lâl·bār'gō)
Can you give me a discount?	*Mi può fare uno sconto?* (mē pwō fâ'rā ū'nō skōn'tō)
I'm very sorry, but our prices are fixed.	*Mi dispiace, ma qui si vende a prezzo fisso.* (mē dē·spyâ'chā mâ kwē sē vān'dā â prā'tsō fēs'sō)
We'll give you a ten-percent reduction.	*Le faremo un ribasso del dieci per cento.* (lē fâ·rā'mō ūn rē·bâs'sō dāl dyā'chē pār chān'tō)
Thank you very much! Please take one of these complimentary gifts.	*Molte grazie! La prego, si serva di uno di questi omaggi.* (mōl'tā grā'tsyā lâ prā'gō sē sār'vâ dē ū'nō dē kwā'stē ō·mâj'jē)

I'll take this figurine; it will make a nice souvenir of the Alps.	*Scelgo questa statuetta. È un bel ricordo delle Alpi.* (shāl'gō kwā'stâ stâ·twāt'tâ ā ūn bāl rē·kōr'dō dāl'-lā âl'pē)
We'll send everything out before noon.	*Le manderemo tutto prima di mezzogiorno.* (lē mân·dā·rā'mō tūt'tō prē'mâ dē mā·dzō·jōr'nō)

PHOTOGRAPHY / LA FOTOGRAFIA

May I take pictures?	*È permesso fare fotografie?* (ā pār·mās'sō fâ'rā fō·tō·grâ·fē'ā)
May I take my camera into the museum?	*Posso entrare con la macchina fotografica nel museo?* (pōs'sō ān·trâ'rā kōn lâ mâk'kē·nâ fō·tō·grâ'fē·kâ nāl mū·zā'ō)
How much is the fee for taking pictures?	*Quanto si paga per fare delle fotografie?* (kwân'tō sē pâ'gâ pār fâ'rā dāl'lā fō·tō·grâ·fē'ā)
I need some color film.	*Vorrei delle pellicole per fotografia a colori.* (vōr·rā'ē dāl'lā pāl·lē'kō·lā pār fō·tō·grā·fē'â â kō·lō'rē)
Where can I buy camera supplies?	*Dove posso comprare articoli fotografici?* (dō'vā pōs'sō kōm·prâ'rā âr·tē'kō·lē fō·tō·grâ'fē·chē)
Can you have this roll of films developed?	*Può sviluppare questo rullo?* (pwō zvē·lūp·pâ'rā kwā'stō rūl'lō)
Does the price include development?	*Il costo include anche lo sviluppo?* (ēl kō'stō ēn·klū'dā ân'kā lō zvē·lūp'-pō)
I want three prints of each negative.	*Desidero tre copie di ciascun negativo.* (dā·zē'dā·rō trā kô'pyā dē châ·skūn' nā·gâ·tē'vō)
Do you have movie film?	*Ha pellicole per macchine da presa?* (â pāl·lē'kō·lā pār mâk'kē·nā dâ prā'zâ)
Will you put in the film?	*Vuol caricare la macchina?* (vwōl kâ·rē·kâ'rā lâ mâk'kē·nâ)

EVERYDAY EXPRESSIONS / CONVERSAZIONE GENERALE

Good morning!	*Buon giorno!* (bwōn jōr'nō)
Good evening!	*Buona sera!* (bwō'nâ sā'râ)
Good night!	*Buona notte!* (bwō'nâ nōt'tā)
My name is ____________.	*Mi chiamo ____________.* (mē kyâ'mō)
I understand Italian pretty well, but I don't speak it.	*Capisco l'italiano abbastanza bene, ma non lo parlo.* (kâ·pē'skō lē·tâ·lyâ'-nō âb·bâ·stân'tsâ bā'nā mâ nōn lō pâr'lō)
Do you speak English?	*Parla inglese?* (pâr'lâ ēn·glā'zā)
Where are you going?	*Dove va?* (dō'vā vâ)
Come here, please.	*Venga qua, per piacere.* (vān'gâ kwâ pār pyâ·chā'rā)
I want to show you something.	*Le vorrei far vedere una cosa.* (lā vōr·rā'ē fâr vâ·dā'rā ū'nā kō'zâ)
Speak slowly, please.	*Parli adagio, per favore.* (pâr'lē â·dâ'-jō pār fâ·vō'rā)

I have no time today.	*Oggi non ho tempo.* (ōj'jē nō·nō' tām'-pō)
What can I do for you?	*Desidera?* (dā·zē'dā·râ)
Will you tell me the time?	*Mi vuol dire l'ora?* (mē vwōl dē'rā lō'-râ)
Is there a doctor near here?	*C'è un dottore qui vicino?* (chā ūn dōt·tō'rā kwē vē·chē'nō)
How do you say _____ in Italian?	*Come si dice in italiano _____?* (kō'mā sē dē'chā ē·nē·tâ·lyâ'nō)
What does _____ mean?	*Cosa vuol dire _____?* (kō'zâ vwōl dē'rā)
What is that for?	*A che serve?* (â kā sār'vā)
You know what I mean?	*M'intende?* (mēn·tān'dā)
Do you understand me?	*Mi capisce?* (mē kâ·pē'shā)
I'm sorry, but I don't understand you.	*Mi rincresce, ma non La capisco.* (mē rēn·krā'shā mâ nōn lâ kâ·pē'skō)
I understand you when you speak slowly.	*La capisco quando parla adagio.* (lâ kâ·pē'skō kwân'dō pâr'lâ â·dâ'jō)
Where is the Catholic church?	*Dov'è la chiesa cattolica?* (dō·vā' lâ kyā'zâ kât·tô'lē·kâ)
What time is Mass?	*A que ora c'è messa?* (â kā ō'râ chā mās'sâ)
Thank you very much.	*Mille grazie.* (mēl'lā grâ'tsyā)
You are welcome.	*Prego.* (prā'gō)
How are you?	*Come sta?* (kō'mā stâ)
Fine, thank you, and you?	*Bene, grazie, e Lei?* (bā'nā grâ'tsyâ ā lā'ē)
Please repeat.	*Ripeta, per favore.* (rē·pā'tâ pār fâ·vō'rā)
Excuse me.	*Mi scusi.* (mē skū'zē)
Keep the change.	*Si tenga il resto.* (sē tān'gâ ēl rā'stō)
Think nothing of it!	*S'immagini!* (sēm·mâ'jē·nē)
Of course!	*Senz'altro!* (sān·dzâl'trō)
Please send for a doctor.	*Vorrei un medico, per favore.* (vōr·rā'ē ūn me'dē·kō pār fâ·vō'rā)
Where is the lost-and-found office?	*Da che parte si trova l'ufficio oggetti smarriti?* (dâ kā pâr'tā sē trō'vâ lūf·fē'chō ōj·jāt'tē zmâr·rē'tē)
I'm very happy to hear that.	*Ne sono proprio contento.* (nā sō'nō prô'pryō kōn·tān'tō)
Very glad to meet you!	*Fortunatissimo!* (fōr·tū·nâ·tēs'sē·mō)
It's a real pleasure to make your acquaintance.	*È un vero piacere di fare la Sua conoscenza.* (ā ūn vā'rō pyâ·chā'rā dē fâ'rā lā sū'â kō·nō·shān'tsâ)
Allow me to introduce you to _____.	*Permetta che Le presenti _____.* (pār·māt'tâ kā lā prā·zān'tē)
Good-bye!	*Addio.* (âd·dē'ō)
So long.	*Ciao.* (châ'ō)
Have a pleasant trip!	*Buon viaggio!* (bwōn vyâj'jō)
See you later!	*Arrivederci!* (âr·rē·vā·dār'chē)

Is there someone here who speaks English?	*C'è qui qualcuno che parli inglese?* (chā kwē kwâl·kū'nō kā pâr'lē ēn·glā'zā)
I need an English-speaking guide.	*Ho bisogno d'un cicerone che parli inglese.* (ō bē·zō'nyō dūn chē·chā·rō'nā kā pâr'lē ēn·glā'zā)

WEATHER	**IL TEMPO**
What's the weather like?	*Che tempo fa?* (kā tām'pō fâ)
The weather is nice.	*Fa bel tempo.* (fâ bāl tām'pō)
The weather is bad.	*Fa cattivo tempo.* (fâ kât·tē'vō tām'pō)
It's cold out.	*Fa freddo.* (fâ frād'dō)
It's hot out.	*Fa caldo.* (fâ kâl'dō)
It's cool.	*Fa fresco.* (fâ frā'skō)
It's sunny.	*Fa sole.* (fâ sō'lā)
It's foggy.	*C'è nebbia.* (chā neb'byâ)
It's windy.	*Tira vento.* (tē'râ vān'tō)
It's cloudy.	*È coperto.* (ā kō·pār'tō)
It's snowing.	*Nevica.* (ne'vē·kâ)
It's raining.	*Piove.* (pyō'vā)
It's a beautiful, sunny day.	*C'è un bel sole.* (chā ūn bāl sō'lā)
It's thundering.	*Tuona.* (twō'nâ)
It's lightning.	*Lampeggia.* (lâm·pej'jâ)

TIME	**L'ORA**
What time is it?	*Che ora è?* (kā ō'râ ā)
It is one o'clock.	*E l'una.* (ā lū'nâ)
It is two o'clock.	*Sono le due.* (sō'nō lā dū'ā)
It is eight o'clock.	*Sono le otto.* (sō'nō lā ōt'tō)
It is noon.	*È mezzogiorno.* (ā mā·dzō·jōr'nō)
It is 10:15.	*Sono le dieci e un quarto.* (sō'nō lā dyā'chē ā ūn kwâr'tō)
It is midnight.	*È mezzanotte.* (ā mā·dzâ·nōt'tā)
It is quarter to eleven.	*Sono le undici meno un quarto.* (sō'nō lā ūn'dē·chē mā'nō ūn kwâr'tō)
It is twenty minutes to seven.	*Sono le sette meno venti.* (sō'nō lā sāt'tā mā'nō vān'tē)
The train leaves at 2 P.M.	*Il treno parte alle quattordici.* (ēl trā'nō pâr'tā âl·lā kwât·tôr'dē·chē)
The concert begins at 9 P.M.	*Il concerto comincia alle ventuno.* (ēl kōn·chār'tō kō·mēn'châ âl'lā vān·tū'nō)

(Note that in the last two sentences above the twenty-four hour system of telling time is used, which counts the hours from midnight to midnight. In Italy, the twenty-four hour system is used for all official functions and for train and airline schedules.)

DAYS	**I GIORNI**
Sunday	*domenica* (dō·me'nē·kâ)
Monday	*lunedì* (lū·nā·dē')
Tuesday	*martedì* (mâr·tā·dē')

Wednesday	*mercoledì* (mār·kō·lā·dē')
Thursday	*giovedì* (jō·vā·dē')
Friday	*venerdì* (vā·nār·dē')
Saturday	*sabato* (sâ'bâ·tō)

MONTHS — I MESI

January	*gennaio* (jān·nâ'yō)
February	*febbraio* (fāb·brâ'yō)
March	*marzo* (mâr'tsō)
April	*aprile* (â·prē'lā)
May	*maggio* (mâj'jō)
June	*giugno* (jū'nyō)
July	*luglio* (lū'lyō)
August	*agosto* (â·gō'stō)
September	*settembre* (sāt·tām'brā)
October	*ottobre* (ōt·tō'brā)
November	*novembre* (nō·vām'brā)
December	*dicembre* (dē·chām'brā)

THE SEASONS — LE STAGIONI

Spring	*la primavera* (lâ prē·mâ·vā'râ)
Summer	*l'estate* (lā·stâ'tā)
Fall	*l'autunno* (lâū·tūn'nō)
Winter	*l'inverno* (lēn·vār'nō)

AT THE AIRPORT — ALL'AEROPORTO

What is the flying time to Milan?	*Quante ore di volo ci vorranno per arrivare a Milano?* (kwân'tā ō'rā dē vō'lō chē vōr·rân'nō pā·râr·rē·vâ'rā â mē·lâ'nō)
Will there be many stops?	*Farà molti scali?* (fâ·râ' mōl'tē skâ'lē)
Please give me a one-way ticket only.	*Mi dia solo il biglietto d'andata, per piacere.* (mē dē'â sō'lō ēl bē·lyāt'tō dân·dâ'tâ pār pyâ·chā'rā)
How many pounds of luggage are permitted each passenger?	*Quanti chili di bagaglio sono permessi ad ogni passeggero?* (kwân'tē kē'lē dē bâ·gâ'lyō sō'nō pār·mās'sē â·dō'nyē pâs·sāj·jā'rō)
What is the rate for excess weight?	*Qual'è la tariffa per il peso in eccedenza?* (kwâ·lā' lā tā·rēf'fā pā·rēl' pā'zō ē·nā·chā·dān'tsâ)
What time do we leave?	*A che ora si parte?* (â kā ō'râ sē pâr'tā)
What time do we arrive?	*A que ora si arriva?* (â kā ō'râ sē âr·rē'vâ)
I'd like to reserve a seat, please.	*Vorrei prenotare un posto, per favore.* (vōr·rā'ē prā·nō·tâ'rā ūn pō'stō pār fâ·vō'rā)
Is that the waiting room?	*È quella la sala d'aspetto?* (ā kwāl'lâ lâ sâ'lâ dâ·spāt'tō)
I'll leave my suitcases here.	*Le valigie le lascio qui.* (lā vâ·lē'jā lā lâ'shō kwē)

I'll take this overnight case and my purse with me.	*Questa valigetta e la borsa le porto con me.* (kwā'stâ vâ·lē·jāt'tâ ā lâ bōr'sâ lā pōr'tō kōn mā)
The gate to your plane is number three.	*Il passaggio numero tre è quello del Suo aeroplano.* (ēl pâs·sâj'jō nū'mā·rō trā ā kwāl'lō dāl sū'ō â·ā·rō·plâ'-nō)
At what altitude are we flying?	*A che altitudine stiamo volando?* (â kā âl·tē·tū'dē·nā styâ'mō vō·lân'dō)
We're already a half-hour late.	*Già siamo in ritardo di mezz'ora.* (jâ syâ'mō ēn rē·târ'dō dē mā·dzō'râ)

RAILROAD	**LA FERROVIA**
Where is the ticket window?	*Dov'è la biglietteria?* (dō·vā' lâ bē·lyāt·tā·rē'â)
I want two first class tickets for ______.	*Desidero due biglietti di prima classe per ______.* (dā·zē'dā·rō dū'ā bē·lyāt'tē dē prē'mâ klâs'sā pār)
One way, please.	*Di sola andata, per favore.* (dē sō'lâ ân·dâ'tâ pār fâ·vō'rā)
Round trip.	*Di andata e ritorno.* (dē ân·dâ'tâ ā rē·tōr'nō)
Is the train air-conditioned?	*C'è l'aria condizionata sul treno?* (chā l'â'ryâ kōn·dē·tsyō·nâ'tâ sūl trā'nō)
Is this the train to ______?	*Questo è il treno per ______?* (kwā'stō ā ēl trā'nō pār)
Where is the train to Ravenna?	*Dove si prende il treno per Ravenna?* (dō'vā sē prān'dā ēl trā'nō pār râ·vān'nâ)
I want an upper (lower) berth.	*Vorrei una cuccetta superiore (inferiore).* (vōr rā'ē ū'nâ kū·chāt'tâ sū·pā·ryō'rā [ēn·fā·ryō'rā])
I want a private compartment.	*Vorrei una cabina ad un letto.* (vōr·rā'ē ū'nâ kâ·bē'nâ â·dūn' lāt'tō)
On what track is the train?	*Su che binario è il treno?* (sū kā bē·nâ'-ryō ā ēl trā'nō)
When do we reach ______?	*A che ora arriveremo a ______?* (â kā ō'râ âr·rē·vā·rā'mō â)
Are we on time?	*Siamo in orario?* (syâ'mō ē·nō·râ'ryō)
How late are we?	*Quanto siamo in ritardo?* (kwân'tō syâ'mō ēn rē·târ'dō)
Is there a dining car?	*C'è un vagone ristorante?* (chā ūn vâ·gō'nā rē·stō·rân'tā)
How late do you serve breakfast?	*Fino a che ora si serve la prima colazione?* (fē'nō â kā ō'râ sē sār'vā lâ prē'mâ kō·lâ·tsyō'nā)
When do you start serving lunch?	*A che ora si serve la colazione?* (â kā ō'râ sē sār'vā lâ kō·lâ·tsyō'nā)
Where is the smoking car?	*Da che parte è lo scompartimento per fumatori?* (dâ kā pâr'tā ā lō skōm·pâr·tē·mān'tō pār fū·mâ·tō'rē)
Is the berth made up?	*È fatto il letto?* (ā fât'tō ēl lāt'tō)
Please take down the suitcase.	*Porti giù quella valigia, per favore.* (pōr'tē jū kwāl'lâ vâ·lē'jâ pār fâ·vō'rā)

Is this seat vacant? — *È libero questo posto?* (ā lē'bā·rō kwā'stō pō'stō)

May I open the door? — *Le disturba se apro la porta?* (lā dē·stūr'bâ sā â'prō lâ pōr'tâ)

Do you think we could turn off the fan? — *Non sarebbe bene chiudere il ventilatore?* (nōn sâ·rāb'bā bā'nā kyū'dā·rā ēl vān·tē·lâ·tō'rā)

Have you seen the conductor? — *Ha visto il controllore?* (â vē'stō ēl kōn·trōl·lō'rā)

Can I check this suitcase? — *Posso depositare questa valigia?* (pōs'-sō dā·pō·zē·tâ'rā kwā'stâ vâ·lē'jâ)

AUTOMOBILE — L'AUTOMOBILE

Forty liters of gas, please. — *Quaranta litri di benzina, per favore.* (kwâ·rân'tâ lē'trē dē bān·dzē'nâ pār fâ·vō'rā)

Check the oil. — *Verifichi l'olio.* (vā·rē'fē·kē lô'lyō)

Fill her up. — *Faccia il pieno.* (fâ'châ ēl pyā'nō)

I have a flat tire. — *Ho una gomma a terra.* (ō ū'nâ gōm'-mâ â tār'rā)

Can you fix this puncture? — *Può accomodare la foratura?* (pwō âk·kō·mō·dâ'rā lâ fō·râ·tū'râ)

Where is the next gasoline station? — *Dove si trova il distributore più vicino?* (dō'vā sē trō'vâ ēl dē·strē·bū·tō'rā pyū vē·chē'nō)

My car has developed engine trouble. — *La mia macchina ha un guasto.* (lâ mē'â mâk'kē·nâ â ūn gwā'stō)

Can you tow the car to town? — *Si può rimorchiare la macchina fino in città?* (sē pwō rē·mōr·kyâ'rā lâ mâk'kē·nâ fē'nō ēn chēt'tâ)

Wash it, change the oil, and check the tires. — *La lavi, cambi l'olio, e verifichi le gomme.* (lâ lâ'vē kâm'bē lô'lyō ā vā·rē'fē·kē lā gōm'mā)

What do you charge for a grease job? — *Quanto costa l'ingrassaggio?* (kwân'tō kō'stâ lēn·grâs·sâj'jō)

Is the road in good condition? — *È buona la strada?* (ā bwō'nâ lâ strâ'-dâ)

CONVERTING TEMPERATURES

Fahrenheit to Centigrade

Subtract 32° and multiply by 5/9.
50°F = 10°C   −4°F = −20°C

Centigrade to Fahrenheit

Multiply by 9/5 and add 32°.
40°C = 104°F   20°C = 68°F

CONVERTING MEASUREMENTS

American to Italian

1 gallon = 3.8 liters
1 pound = .45 kilos
1 inch = 2.5 centimeters
1 yard = .9 meter
1 mile = 1.6 kilometers
1 acre = .4 hectares

Italian to American

1 liter = .26 gallons
1 kilo = 2.2 pounds
1 centimeter = .4 inch
1 meter = 1.1 yards
1 kilometer = .6 miles
1 hectare = 2.5 acres

The figures given above are approximate equivalents.

To convert American measurements into their Italian equivalents, or vice versa, multiply as indicated in the examples below.

Examples: To determine the approximate number of liters in ten gallons, multiply 3.8 (liters per gallon) x 10 = 38.1 liters.

To determine the approximate number of miles in 14 kilometers, multiply .6 (miles per kilometer) x 14 = 8.4 miles.

CARDINAL NUMBERS	I NUMERI CARDINALI
1	*uno, una* (ū'nō ū'nâ)
2	*due* (dū'ā)
3	*tre* (trā)
4	*quattro* (kwât'trō)
5	*cinque* (chēn'kwā)
6	*sei* (sā'ē)
7	*sette* (sāt'tā)
8	*otto* (ōt'tō)
9	*nove* (nō'vā)
10	*dieci* (dyā'chē)
11	*undici* (ūn'dē·chē)
12	*dodici* (dô'dē·chē)
13	*tredici* (tre'dē·chē)
14	*quattordici* (kwât·tôr'dē·chē)
15	*quindici* (kwēn'dē·chē)
16	*sedici* (se'dē·chē)
17	*diciassette* (dē·châs·sāt'tā)
18	*diciotto* (dē·chōt'tō)
19	*diciannove* (dē·chân·nō'vā)
20	*venti* (vān'tē)
21	*ventuno* (vān·tū'nō)
22	*ventidue* (vān·tē·dū'ā)
30	*trenta* (trān'tâ)
31	*trentuno* (trān·tū'nō)
40	*quaranta* (kwâ·rân'tâ)
50	*cinquanta* (chēn·kwân'tâ)
60	*sessanta* (sās·sân'tâ)
70	*settanta* (sāt·tân'tâ)
80	*ottanta* (ōt·tân'tâ)
90	*novanta* (nō·vân'tâ)
100	*cento* (chān'tō)
101	*centuno* (chān'tū'nō)
200	*duecento* (dwā·chān'tō)
201	*duecento uno* (dwā·chān'tō ū'nō)
300	*trecento* (trā·chān'tō)
400	*quattrocento* (kwât·trō·chān'tō)
500	*cinquecento* (chēn·kwā·chān'tō)
600	*seicento* (sāē·chān'tō)
700	*settecento* (sāt·tā·chān'tō)

800	*ottocento* (ōt·tō·chān'tō)
900	*novecento* (nō·vā·chān'tō)
1,000	*mille* (mēl'lā)
1,001	*mille e uno* (mēl'lā ā ū'nō)
2,000	*due mila* (dū'ā mē'lâ)
3,000	*tre mila* (trā mē'lâ)
1 million	*un milione* (ūn mē·lyō'nā)
1 billion	*un miliardo* (ūn mē·lyâr'dō)

ORDINAL NUMBERS	**I NUMERI ORDINALI**
First	*primo* (prē'mō)
Second	*secondo* (sā·kōn'dō)
Third	*terzo* (tār'tsō)
Fourth	*quarto* (kwâr'tō)
Fifth	*quinto* (kwēn'tō)
Sixth	*sesto* (sā'stō)
Seventh	*settimo* (set'tē·mō)
Eighth	*ottavo* (ōt·tâ'vō)
Ninth	*nono* (nō'nō)
Tenth	*decimo* (de'chē·mō)
Eleventh	*undicesimo* (ūn·dē·che'zē·mō)
Twelfth	*dodicesimo* (dō·dē·che'zē·mō)
Thirteenth	*tredicesimo* (trā·dē·che'zē·mō)
Fourteenth	*quattordicesimo* (kwât·tōr·dē·che'zē·mō)
Fifteenth	*quindicesimo* (kwēn·dē·che'zē·mō)
Sixteenth	*sedicesimo* (sā·dē·che'zē·mō)
Seventeenth	*diciassettesimo* (dē·châs·sāt·te'zē·mō)
Eighteenth	*diciottesimo* (dē·chōt·te'zē·mō)
Nineteenth	*diciannovesimo* (dē·chân·nō·ve'zē·mō)
Twentieth	*ventesimo* (vān·te'zē·mō)
Twenty-first	*ventesimo primo* (vān·te'zē·mō prē'mō)
Hundredth	*centesimo* (chān·te'zē·mō)
Hundred-and-first	*centesimo primo* (chān·te'zē·mō prē'mō)
Thousandth	*millesimo* (mēl·le'zē·mō)
Millionth	*milionesimo* (mē·lyō·ne'zē·mō)

ITALIAN ROAD SIGNS

Italian road signs, like those in the United States, have typical shapes depending on their function. Many bear worded instructions, but others have only symbols that relay information to the motorist at a glance. The three distinct shapes and their functions are as follows:

a triangular sign indicates danger.

a circular sign gives definite instructions.

a rectangular sign contains special information.

As in the United States, traffic in Italy proceeds on the right-hand side of the street or highway.

SEGNALAZIONI STRADALI	ROAD SIGNS
Curva (kūr'vâ)	*Curve*
Curva pericolosa (kūr'vâ pā·rē·kō·lō'zâ)	*Dangerous curve*
Curva e controcurva (kūr'vâ ā kōn·trō·kūr'vâ)	*S-curve*
Svolta (zvōl'tâ)	*Turn*
Discesa pericolosa (dē·shā'zâ pā·rē·kō·lō'zâ)	*Dangerous descent*
Cunetta (kū·nāt'tâ)	*Dip*
Svolta stretta (zvōl'tâ strāt'tâ)	*Sharp turn*
Dosso (dōs'sō)	*Bump*
Strettoia (strāt·tô'yâ)	*Road narrows*
Incrocio (ēn·krô'chō)	*Intersection*
Arresto all'incrocio (âr·rā'stō âl·lēn·krô'chō)	*Stop at intersection*
Divieto di svolta (dē·vyā'tō dē zvōl'tâ)	*No turns*
Divieto di svolta a destra (dē·vyā'tō dē zvōl'tâ â dā'strâ)	*No right turn*
Divieto di svolta a sinistra (dē·vyā'tō dē zvōl'tâ â sē·nē'strâ)	*No left turn*
Divieto di inversione ad U (dē·vyā'tō dē ēn·vār·syō'nā â·dū')	*No U-turns*
Direzioni consentite (dē·rā·tsyō'nē kōn·sān·tē'tā)	*Right or left turn permitted*
Direzione obbligatoria a destra (dē·rā·tsyō'nā ōb·blē·gâ·tô'ryâ â dā'strâ)	*Right turn only*
Direzione obbligatoria a sinistra (dē·rā·tsyō'nā ōb·blē·gâ·tô'ryâ â sē·nē'strâ)	*Left turn only*
Senso obbligatorio (sān'sō ōb·blē·gâ·tô'ryō)	*One-way traffic (indicated by arrow)*
Senso proibito (sān'sō prōē·bē'tō)	*No entry, one-way traffic*
Senso unico (sān'sō ū'nē·kō)	*One-way traffic (indicated by arrow)*
Tenere la destra (tā·nā'rā lâ dā'strâ)	*Keep to the right*
Divieto di accesso (dē·vyā'tō dē â·chās'sō)	*Do not enter*
Confluenza a destra (kōn·flūān'tsâ â dā'strâ)	*Road entering right*

Preavviso di dare precedenza (prā·âv·vē'zō dē dâ'rā prā·chā·dān'tsâ)	*Priority road ahead*
Dare precedenza (dâ'rā prā·chā·dān'tsâ)	*Yield right-of-way*
Doppio senso di circolazione (dôp'pyō sān'sō dē chēr·kō·lâ·tsyō'nā)	*Two-way traffic*
Fine del doppio senso di circolazione (fē'nā dāl dôp'pyō sān'sō dē chēr·kō·lâ·tsyō'nā)	*End of two-way traffic*
Corsia riservata ai veicoli lenti (kōr·sē'â rē·zār·vâ'tâ â'ē vā·ē'kō·lē lān'tē)	*Lane for slow vehicles*
Semaforo a 150 m. (sā·mâ'fō·rō â chān'tō chēn·kwân'tâ mā'trē)	*Traffic signal, 150 meters*
Semafori sincronizzati 40 km. (sā·mâ'fō·rē sēn·krō·nē·dzâ'tē kwâ·rân'tâ kē·lô'mā·trē)	*Signals set for 40 kilometers per hour*
Rotaia (rō·tâ'yâ)	*Traffic circle*
Divieto di transito ai pedoni (dē·vyā'tō dē trân'sē·tō â'ē pā·dō'nē)	*No pedestrians*
Passaggio per pedoni (pâs·sâj'jō pār pā·dō'nē)	*Pedestrian crosswalk*
Sottopassaggio (sōt·tō·pâs·sâj'jō)	*Underpass*
Parcheggio avanti (pâr·kej'jō â·vân'tē)	*Parking ahead*
Sosta vietata (sō'stâ vyā·tâ'tâ)	*No parking*
Sosta regolamentata (sō'stâ rā·gō·lâ·mān·tâ'tâ)	*Limited parking*
Sosta di emergenza (sō'stâ dē ā·mār·jān'tsâ)	*Emergency parking*
Vicolo cieco (vē'kō·lō chā'kō)	*Dead end*
Rallentare (râl·lān·tâ'rā)	*Slow down*
Strada sdrucciolevole (strâ'dâ zdrū·chō·le'vō·lā)	*Slippery when wet*
Lavori (lâ·vō'rē)	*Men working*
Ponte mobile (pōn'tā mô'bē·lā)	*Drawbridge*
Prudenza (prū·dān'tsâ)	*Caution*
Bambini (bâm·bē'nē)	*Watch for children*
Divieto di sorpasso (dē·vyā'tō dē sōr·pâs'sō)	*No passing*
Fine del divieto di sorpasso (fē'nā dāl dē·vyā'tō dē sōr·pâs'sō)	*End no passing*
Divieto di sorpasso tra autotreni (dē·vyā'tō dē sōr·pâs'sō trâ âū·tō·trā'nē)	*No passing for trailer trucks*
Fine del divieto di sorpasso tra autotreni (fē'nā dāl dē·vyā'tō dē sōr·pâs'sō trâ âū·tō·trā'nē)	*End no passing for trailer trucks*
Riservato alle autovetture (rē·zār·vâ'tō âl'lā âū·tō·vāt·tū'rā)	*Automobile traffic only*
Divieto di transito alle biciclette (dē·vyā'tō dē trân'sē·tō âl'lā bē·chē·klāt'tā)	*No bicycles*
Pista ciclabile (pē'stâ chē·klâ'bē·lā)	*Bicycle path*

Divieto di transito ai motocicli (dē·vyā'tō dē trân'sē·tō â'ē mō·tō·chē'·klē)	*No motorcycles*
Fermata di autobus (fār·mâ'tâ dē â'ū·tō·būs)	*Bus stop*
Via in costruzione (vē'â ēn kō·strū·tsyō'nā)	*Road under construction*
Passaggio a livello con barriere (pâs·sâj'jō â lē·vāl'lō kōn bâr·ryā'rā)	*Guarded railroad crossing*
Passaggio a livello senza barriere (pâs·sâj'jō â lē·vāl'lō sān'tsâ bâr·ryā'rā)	*Unguarded railroad crossing*
Limite massimo di velocità 75 km. (lē'mē·tā mâs'sē·mō dē vā·lō·chē·tâ' sā·tân·tâ·chēn'kwā kē·lô'mā·trē)	*Speed limit 75 kilometers per hour*
Limite minimo di velocità 45 km. (lē'·mē·tā mē'nē·mō dē vā·lō·chē·tâ' kwâ·rân·tâ·chēn'kwā kē·lô'mā·trē)	*Minimum speed 45 kilometers per hour*
Limitazione di velocità (lē·mē·tâ·tsyō'nā dē vā·lō·chē·tâ')	*Speed zone ahead*
Fine della limitazione di velocità (fē'nā dāl'lâ lē·mē·tâ·tsyō'nā dē vā·lō·chē·tâ')	*End speed zone*
Deviazione (dā·vyâ·tsyō'nā)	*Detour*
Autostrada (âū·tō·strâ'dâ)	*Expressway, throughway*
Preavviso di bivio Firenze (prā·âv·vē'·zō dē bē·vē'ō fē·rān'tsā)	*Approaching exit for Florence*
Preavviso di canalizzazione (prā·âv·vē'zō dē kâ·nâ·lē·dzâ·tsyō'nā)	*Enter proper lanes ahead*
Uscita operai (ū·shē'tâ ō·pā·râ'ē)	*Employee exit*
Alt! Dogana (âlt dō·gâ'nâ)	*Stop! Customs*
Assistenza meccanica (âs·sē·stān'tsâ māk·kâ'nē·kâ)	*Garage*
Rifornimento benzina (rē·fōr·nē·mān'·tō bān·dzē'nâ)	*Filling station*
Transito con catene (trân'sē·tō kōn kâ·tā'nā)	*Proceed with chains*
Divieto di segnalazioni acustiche (dē·vyā'tō dē sā·nyâ·lâ·tsyō'nē â·kū'·stē·kā)	*No horns*
Ospedale (ō·spā·dâ'lā)	*Hospital*
Pronto soccorso (prōn'tō sōk·kōr'sō)	*First aid*
Telefono (tā·le'fō·nō)	*Telephone*
Campeggio (kâm·pej'jō)	*Camp site*
Terreno per rimorchi (tār·rā'nō pār rē·mōr'kē)	*Trailer park*
Campeggio e rimorchi (kâm·pej'jō ā rē·mōr'kē)	*Camp site with trailer facilities*
Ostello della gioventù (ō·stāl'lō dāl'lâ jō·vān·tū')	*Youth hostel*
Banchine non transitabili (bân·kē'nā nōn trân·sē·tâ'bē·lē)	*Keep off shoulders*
Caduta di masse (kâ·dū'tâ dē mâs'sā)	*Rock slide*
Frana (frâ'nâ)	*Road washed out*
Strada dissestata (strâ'dâ dēs·sā·stâ'·tâ)	*Road in bad repair*
Spegnere i fari (spe'nyā·rā ē fâ'rē)	*Turn off headlights*

ROAD SYMBOLS

All the following symbols are in use throughout Western Europe except those marked (*ITAL*), which are to be found only in Italy.

1 Danger

Uneven Road

Dangerous Curve

Right Curve

S-curve

Intersection

Traffic Circle

Railroad Crossing, Guarded

Railroad Crossing, Unguarded

Railroad Crossing, Unguarded

Dangerous Hill

Road Narrows

Drawbridge

Men Working

Slippery When Wet

Pedestrian Crosswalk

Watch Out For Children

Cattle Crossing

Side Road

Low-flying Aircraft

Beware of Animals

Caution

Priority Road Ahead

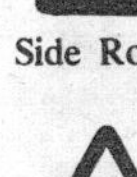
Two-way Traffic

Traffic Signals Ahead

2 Instructions

Road Closed

No Entry

Motor Vehicles Only (*ITAL*)

Motorcycles Only (*ITAL*)

Pedestrians Only (*ITAL*)

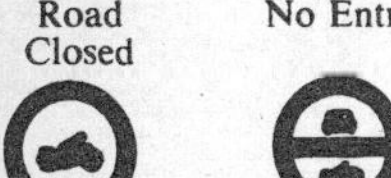

No Motorcycles

No Motor Vehicles

No Bicycles

No Horns

No Left Turn

No Passing

Maximum Width

Maximum Height

Maximum Weight

Speed Limit

Stop at Intersection

Stop Customs

No Parking

No Parking
I Uneven Days
II Even Days

Yield Right-of-way

End Speed Limit

End No Passing

Direction of Traffic

One-way Street (*ITAL*)

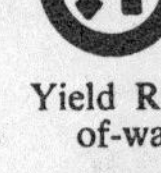

Minimum Speed

3 Information

Priority Road

End of Priority Road

Parking

You Have Right-of-way

Hospital

First Aid

First Aid

Garage

Telephone

Filling Station

Camp Site

Trailer Park

Camp Site with Trailer Facilities

Distance to Camp Site

Expressway (Undivided)

End Expressway (Undivided)

Expressway (Divided)

End Expressway (Undivided)

COUNTRIES OF EUROPE

Country	Capital	Area in Sq. Mi.	Population (latest official estimate)
Austria	Vienna	32,374	7,171,000
Belgium	Brussels	11,779	9,328,000
Bulgaria	Sofia	42,729	8,078,000
Czechoslovakia	Prague	49,370	13,951,000
Denmark	Copenhagen	16,619	4,684,000
Finland	Helsinki	130,120	4,570,000
France	Paris	212,822	48,090,000
Germany—Democratic Rep. (East Germany)	East Berlin	41,646	16,075,000
Federal Rep. (West Germany)	Bonn	95,928	55,678,000
Gr. Britain, see Un. Kingdom			
Greece	Athens	50,548	8,469,000
Hungary	Budapest	35,919	10,110,000
Ireland, Rep. of	Dublin	27,135	2,841,000
Italy	Rome	116,303	50,619,000
Luxembourg	......	998	324,000
Netherlands	Amsterdam & the Hague	12,978	12,079,000
Norway	Oslo	125,065	3,681,000
Poland	Warsaw	120,359	30,940,000
Portugal	Lisbon	35,340	9,112,000
Rumania	Bucharest	91,699	18,813,000
San Marino	......	23	17,000
Spain	Madrid	194,884	31,339,000
Sweden	Stockholm	173,666	7,627,000
Switzerland	Berne	15,941	5,860,000
Turkey	Ankara	301,380	30,256,000
in Asia	......	292,291	26,660,000
in Europe	......	9,089	2,399,000
Union of Soviet Socialist Republics (Soviet Union)	Moscow	8,649,512	224,764,000
in Asia	......	6,619,000	52,946,000
in Europe	......	2,030,512	171,818,000
United Kingdom of Great Britain and North. Ireland		94,198	53,673,000
England and Wales	London	58,348	47,023,000
Scotland	Edinburgh	30,411	5,205,000
Northern Ireland	Belfast	5,439	1,446,000
Vatican City	......	0.17	1,000
Yugoslavia	Belgrade	98,766	19,244,000

SOURCES: *UN Statistical Yearbook, 1963; 1963 Statistical Abstract of the U.S.; UN Statistical Papers,* population report, July, 1964

UNITED STATES OF AMERICA

Area	3,615,211 square miles	(from 1963 *Statistical Abstract of the U.S.*)
Population	1960 official census	179,323,175
	Mid-1963 estimate	189,375,000

(Census Bureau and *UN Population Report*, July, 1964)

EUROPEAN CITIES OVER 1,000,000

(*UN Demographic Yearbook, 1962* Official Estimates)

Name and Country	*Population*	*Name and Country*	*Population*
Moscow, USSR	6,262,000	Milan, Italy	1,581,000*
Berlin, Germany	3,261,000	Barcelona, Spain	1,558,000*
East	1,064,000	Bucharest, Romania	1,229,000
West	2,197,000	Kiev, USSR	1,208,000
London, England	3,195,000	Naples, Italy	1,180,000*
Leningrad, USSR	3,036,000	Warsaw, Poland	1,163,000
Paris, France	2,790,000	Birmingham, England	1,106,000
Madrid, Spain	2,260,000*	Munich, Fed. Rep. of Germany	1,084,000
Rome, Italy	2,161,000*	Glasgow, Scotland	1,055,000
Hamburg, Fed. Rep. of Germany	1,832,000	Gorki, USSR	1,025,000
Budapest, Hungary	1,830,000	Turin, Italy	1,019,000*
Vienna, Austria	1,628,000	Prague, Czechoslovakia	1,005,000

* Metropolitan: includes city and suburban areas

ITALIAN CITIES OVER 250,000

(*UN Demographic Yearbook, 1962*)

English Name	*Italian Name*	*Population**
Rome	Roma (rō′mâ)	2,160,773
Milan	Milano (mē·lâ′nō)	1,580,978
Naples	Napoli (nâ′pō·lē)	1,179,608
Turin	Torino (tō·rē′nō)	1,019,230
Genoa	Genova (je′nō·vâ)	775,106
Palermo	Palermo (pâ·lār′mō)	587,063
Bologna	Bologna (bō·lō′nyâ)	441,143
Florence	Firenze (fē·rān′tsā)	438,138
Catania	Catania (kâ·tâ′nyâ)	361,466
Venice	Venezia (vā·nā′tsyâ)	336,184
Bari	Bari (bâ′rē)	311,268
Trieste	Trieste (tryā′stā)	273,390
Messina	Messina (mās·sē′nâ)	251,423

*Census data for Italy reports metropolitan population only.

U.S. CITIES OVER 250,000

(1960 Official Census)

City and State	Population	City and State	Population
New York, N.Y.	7,781,984	Indianapolis, Ind.	476,258
Chicago, Ill.	3,550,404	Kansas City, Mo.	475,539
Los Angeles, Calif.	2,479,015	Columbus, Ohio	471,316
Philadelphia, Pa.	2,002,512	Phoenix, Ariz.	439,170
Detroit, Mich.	1,670,144	Newark, N.J.	405,220
Baltimore, Md.	939,024	Louisville, Ky.	390,639
Houston, Texas	938,219	Portland, Oreg.	372,676
Cleveland, Ohio	876,050	Oakland, Calif.	367,548
Washington, D.C.	763,956	Fort Worth, Texas	356,268
St. Louis, Mo.	750,026	Long Beach, Calif.	344,168
Milwaukee, Wisc.	741,324	Birmingham, Ala.	340,887
San Francisco, Calif.	740,316	Oklahoma City, Okla.	324,253
Boston, Mass.	697,197	Rochester, N.Y.	318,611
Dallas, Texas	679,684	Toledo, Ohio	318,003
New Orleans, La.	627,525	St. Paul, Minn.	313,411
Pittsburgh, Pa.	604,332	Norfolk, Va.	304,869
San Antonio, Texas	587,718	Omaha, Nebr.	301,598
San Diego, Calif.	573,224	Honolulu, Hawaii	294,194
Seattle, Wash.	557,087	Miami, Fla.	291,688
Buffalo, N.Y.	532,759	Akron, Ohio	290,351
Cincinnati, Ohio	502,550	El Paso, Texas	276,687
Memphis, Tenn.	497,524	Jersey City, N.J.	276,101
Denver, Colo.	493,887	Tampa, Fla.	274,970
Atlanta, Ga.	487,455	Dayton, Ohio	262,332
Minneapolis, Minn.	482,872	Tulsa, Okla.	261,685
Wichita, Kans.	254,698